Sixth Edition

PROFIT WITHOUT HONOR

WHITE-COLLAR CRIME
AND THE LOOTING OF AMERICA

Stephen M. Rosoff
(formerly of the University of Houston-Clear Lake)

Henry N. Pontell
University of California, Irvine

Robert Tillman
St. John's University

Boston   Columbus   Indianapolis   New York   San Francisco   Upper Saddle River
Amsterdam   Cape Town   Dubai   London   Madrid   Milan   Munich   Paris   Montréal   Toronto
Delhi   Mexico City   São Paolo   Sydney   Hong Kong   Seoul   Singapore   Taipei   Tokyo

Editorial Director: Vernon Anthony
Acquisitions Editor: Gary Bauer
Editorial Assistant: Lynda Cramer
Director of Marketing: David Gesell
Senior Marketing Manager: Mary Salzman
Senior Marketing Coordinator: Alicia Wozniak
Senior Marketing Assistant: Les Roberts
Senior Managing Editor: JoEllen Gohr
Production Project Manager: Jessica H. Sykes
Operations Specialist: Holly Shufeldt
Senior Art Director: Jayne Conte
Cover Designer: B. Kenselaar
Cover Art: pogonici/Fotolia
Composition: Jogender Taneja, Aptara®, Inc.
Printer/Binder: Courier
Text Font: Minion 10/12

Library of Congress Cataloging-in-Publication Data

Rosoff, Stephen M.
  Profit without honor: white-collar crime and the looting of America/Stephen M. Rosoff, (formerly of the University of Houston-Clear Lake), Henry N. Pontell, University of California, Irvine, Robert Tillman, St. John's University.—Sixth Edition.
    pages cm
  ISBN-13: 978-0-13-300850-0
  ISBN-10: 0-13-300850-9
  1. White collar crimes—United States.   2. Fraud—United States.   3. Political crimes and offenses—United States.   I. Pontell, Henry N., 1950- II. Tillman, Robert.   III. Title.
  HV6769.R667 2014
  364.16'80973—dc23   2013031111

10 9 8 7 6 5 4 3 2 1

ISBN-10:   0-13-300850-9
ISBN-13: 978-0-13-300850-0

Dedication

In memory of Lillian Rosoff
A woman of resonant kindness and quiet courage
and
In memory of Stephen M. Rosoff
Brilliant teacher, exceptional scholar, and a man of impeccable wit and humor

CONTENTS

PREFACE

NEW TO THIS EDITION

- New introductory case study.
- Updates to older cases throughout the book.
- New insider trading case studies.
- New cases and updates regarding the 2008 financial crisis.
- New cases in computer crime.
- New cases in medical fraud, including a discussion of counterfeit products with a focus on fake medicines.
- A review of the growing problem of the illegal disposal of electronic waste (e-waste).
- A case study of the Deepwater Horizon oil spill in the Gulf of Mexico in 2010 and its criminological implications.
- An expanded discussion on the connection between growing inequality and white-collar crime.
- A discussion of the concept of "organizational culture" and its importance as a cause of white-collar crime.
- A consideration of changing attitudes toward white-collar crime, as exemplified in the Occupy Wall Street movement.

In the short time that has passed since the fifth edition of this book was published, there have been dramatic new developments in the study of white-collar crime. One would surely expect that; for the battle between profit and honor is as old as human commerce. In 2008, the U.S. economy imploded, throwing the nation into the worst financial crisis since the Great Depression. As the country now picks up the pieces and rebuilds its shattered economic infrastructure, politicians, economists, and ordinary citizens point fingers of blame in every direction. But there is at least one thing almost everyone, regardless of class or ideology, can agree on. Whatever market forces or "natural" economic cycles pushed the U.S. economy to the edge of the abyss, it was a lethal concoction of greed, corruption, and criminality that provided the *coup de grace*, the final push over the precipice.

The legendary investor Warren Buffett has a favored aphorism: "After all, you only find out who is swimming naked when the tide goes out." By 2012, the tide had not only gone out, at this writing it is still only starting to come back. And true to Buffett's dictum, a plethora of naked swimmers were revealed.

The subprime mortgage market was exposed as a house of cards, propped up by worthless paper representing worthless loans. Corruption and misrepresentation by giant mortgage lenders like Fannie Mae and Freddie Mac tipped over the first domino. The mortgage collapse quickly metastasized like a deadly cancer. Some of the passengers—and co-conspirators—on the subprime train wreck were among the most hallowed names on Wall Street. Down went Bear Stearns, down went Merrill Lynch, down went Lehman Brothers—all dumped (in Trotsky's famous phrase) into the ash heap of history. From there, the cancer spread to the U.S. stock market and the banks and the insurance companies and the manufacturing sector, and then, because the world is well into the age of the global economy, down went the international financial markets.

It would be simplistic to attribute the entire collapse to white-collar crime. World events and perhaps uncontrollable economic forces played a role, as did an epidemic of stunning, albeit not necessarily criminal, corporate, and political recklessness and incompetence. But it would be even more simplistic to deny that white-collar crimes of unprecedented magnitude have taken place. These crimes are examined and described in this edition.

One of the most conspicuous of the "naked swimmers" was New York investment guru Bernard Madoff, who orchestrated the most costly Ponzi scam in history that flushed away a reported $65 billion from investors—many of them charitable foundations. The Madoff case highlights the shortcomings in financial regulation and oversight that allowed the much larger economic crisis to occur. The events that took Madoff from being a finance superstar to a prisoner in a federal penitentiary where he will almost certainly spend the rest of his life are analyzed in this edition.

Computer crime has continued to emerge as the nation's fastest growing category of crime. This edition continues to highlight the explosion of Internet frauds. Of particular focus are the "pump and dump" swindles that infest the Internet; the nefarious spammers, who flood our e-mail boxes with crooked schemes; so-called "phishing" scams that help cyber-criminals steal our identities; new developments in online international espionage, especially those involving China; activities of those involved in "hactivisim" where the motives for hacking are political, resulting in a form of electronic protest; and those seemingly ubiquitous Nigerian "4-1-9" con games that bait seductive electronic traps for the unwary among us.

Wal-Mart, the world's largest company, remains the symbol of corporate irresponsibility. Allegations of everything from monopolistic practices, to environmental contamination, to violations of labor laws through the exploitation of its own workers and the promotion of slave labor overseas, to illegal union busting, to its callous utilization of "dead peasant insurance," have been leveled against the retailing behemoth. Religious affinity scams also have exploded, costing devout victims hundreds of millions of dollars. Likewise, a shocking new study has revealed a prevalence of embezzlement within the American Roman Catholic Church that is scarcely believable. New and horrifying cases of worker safety violations have been uncovered. Political corruption at all levels of government persists. And even public school education, a social institution never before linked to white-collar crime, has generated stunning and widespread cheating scandals on the parts of teachers and administrators willing to resort to fraud in order to raise state-mandated test scores.

This edition applies particular scrutiny to outrageous and sometimes repulsive abuses of power by the government in the post-9/11 era. Illegal domestic surveillance and the torture of foreign nationals are detailed and exposed as crimes hiding behind a smokescreen of national security.

All of these issues, along with newer cases of many other predatory offenses and rapacious scams, are examined in this updated edition.

So, once again, *Profit Without Honor* seeks to elucidate a very broad subject that only seems to get broader: white-collar crime. How broad? Its domain stretches from the small price-gouging merchant to the huge price-fixing cartel. It can breed in an antiseptic hospital or a toxic dump. It is at home on Main Street, Wall Street, Madison Avenue—even 1600 Pennsylvania Avenue.

Yet, as Americans demonize the Crips and the Bloods, recoil at al-Qaeda, and still obsess over O. J. Simpson, white-collar crime remains the "other" crime problem. The reason for this relative indifference is that the true costs of upperworld misconduct are largely unrecognized.

Compared to murderers, terrorists, and urban gangsters, white-collar criminals do not seem to scare the public very much.

Even the economic expense—by far the most identifiable cost—is typically underestimated by the average citizen. Annual losses from white-collar crime are probably 50 times as great as the losses from ordinary property crime. For example, the price of bailing out a single corrupt savings and loan institution surpassed the total losses of all the bank robberies in American history. The bill for government bailout of the financial services industry, which choked on its own greed, has or soon will exceed a *trillion* dollars. (To put that figure in perspective, consider that a million seconds is about 11 days; a trillion seconds is about 30,000 years.) Indeed, the price tags attached to some white-collar crimes ultimately are so staggering they are difficult to comprehend. They evoke memories of the late Senator Everett McKinley Dirkson's alleged wry quip: "A billion here, a billion there; and pretty soon you're talking about real money!"

But monetary expenditures are only the tip of the topic. The "looting" in the subtitle refers to more than larceny; it implies destruction too. This book argues for an expanded definition of white-collar crime because white-collar crime is not just property crime on a grand scale. It entails higher and more enduring levels of costs—particularly physical and social costs. These less conspicuous effects carry a heavy payment that cannot be measured with a calculator.

White-collar crimes do not leave a chalk outline on the sidewalk or blood spatter on the wall, so the American public, in its understandable preoccupation with street crime, often has overlooked the violent aspects of elite deviance. In his polemic book, *Thinking About Crime*, James Q. Wilson marginalized white-collar crime, lumping it together with "victimless" crimes such as gambling and prostitution. He stated that most citizens (including himself) do not consider white-collar offenses to be very serious compared to street crime. Wilson's intuition about the predominance of such a belief is quite correct, even decades later in the post-Enron era. The belief itself, however, is utterly wrong. *White-Collar criminals cause more pain and death than all "common criminals" combined.*

A likely explanation for the inadequate attention can be derived from a cognitive rule-of-thumb known as the *availability heuristic*, which stipulates that there is a common human tendency to judge the likelihood of occurrences in terms of how readily instances come to mind. Vivid events stick in our memories, and their greater ease of recall misleads us to overrate their frequency relative to less dramatic, but actually more pervasive events. The physical harm wrought by some forms of white-collar crime can be slow and cumulative—like the mythic "death of a thousand cuts." In other words, the human suffering caused by corporate cupidity frequently can take years to materialize, in contrast to the graphic suddenness which usually characterizes street violence. Consequently, it is easy for people to misperceive the extent of the injuries caused. As this book will delineate, environmental crime, hazardous workplaces, medical malfeasance, and unsafe products are lethal manifestations of what Ralph Nader calls "postponed violence."

As for social costs, they are the most insidious and difficult to measure. The victims here are not limited to endangered employees, mistreated patients, or injured consumers, but include all of society—from its component institutions to its transcendent culture. Indeed, a case could be made easily that *every* category of white-collar crime depicted in this book manifests a deleterious effect on some social institution and thereby inflicts damage on society as a whole. To cite just two examples: The insider trading scandals detailed in Chapter 6 and the corporate crimes highlighted in Chapter 7 have eroded public faith in the American economy; likewise the crimes by the government described in Chapter 9 and the political corruption related in Chapter 10 have devalued the democratic process.

It should also be noted that much of the existing white-collar crime literature focuses on offenders—those who commit these crimes, their motives and methods. This is certainly an illuminating perspective, but not the only perspective. This book seeks to shed light on the *victims* of white-collar crime as well. Victimology is a critical element because it helps give the problem the personal relevance it has sometimes lacked. The more predatory white-collar crime is perceived to be, the less likely it will continue to be dismissed as a mere appendix to the crime problem.

One additional preliminary comment seems appropriate—and it concerns the style of the chapters that follow. We have chosen to present our material in an occasionally flippant and hopefully engaging manner. But despite its intermittent irreverence, this is a serious book on an important subject. It is not difficult to write mordantly about con artists charging people $30 for a "solar clothes dryer," then mailing them a piece of rope and some clothespins (Chapter 2), or greedy doctors billing Medicare for pregnancy tests performed on elderly males (Chapter 11), or religious charlatans peddling trashy "holy shower caps" to thousands of faithful proselytes (Chapter 5). It is likewise easy for readers to ridicule those who are duped by such flagrant deceit. So it is worthwhile to bear in mind an old maxim: when you slip on a banana peel it's tragedy; only when *someone else* slips is it comedy. A reiterate lesson of this book is that white-collar crime spares no one. Everybody reading this sentence (or writing it, for that matter) has been somebody's victim. Each of us would do well to remember just how much alike a window and a mirror can be.

To access supplementary materials online, instructors need to request an instructor access code. Go to **www.pearsonhighered.com/irc** to register for an instructor access code. Within 48 hours of registering, you will receive a confirming e-mail including an instructor access code. Once you have received your code, go to the site and log on for full instructions on downloading the materials you wish to use.

Here you will find:

- Test Generator
- PowerPoint Lecture Presentation

ACKNOWLEDGMENTS

Since the publication of the last edition, we have lost a dear friend, dedicated teacher, and noted scholar in Stephen Rosoff, whose major contributions to this book will continue to educate and inform students for generations to come. A professor of criminology at the University of Houston—Clear Lake for many years, Steve passed away in March, 2010, at the age of 64. He had undergone esophageal surgery, followed by a number of additional operations, had shown incredible strength in battling through these maladies, and was recovering at a rehabilitation unit in Houston when his heart failed him. He was a very popular instructor at UH who created a highly successful criminology curriculum with a thriving master's degree program that attracted a large number of Houston police officers.

Steve's family moved from Brooklyn to Boston when he was very young. A lifelong baseball fanatic, he played in Little League, and few persons knew more about the sport, its players, and its statistics. He was a loyal Red Sox fan and attended one of the championship games at Fenway Park when his team won the World Series.

A gifted child and a voracious reader, Steve graduated from English High School in Boston at the age of 15, and entered UMass Amherst where he studied drama. Given his young age, it proved to be a difficult experience and he dropped out after a year. He went to work in his family's pickle business ("Rosoff's Pickles"), was employed as an actor and producer in theatre and film over the next decade and a half, and began taking psychology courses through Harvard extension. In his early thirties he matriculated at Harvard and graduated in three years, number two in his class, with a major in psychology.

Steve arrived at UC, Irvine's Program in Social Ecology in the early 1980s to begin his doctoral work in human development. He had been attracted by the advertised interdisciplinary environment and the "strange name" of the degree. After his first year he worked as a research assistantship on a federally funded study of Medicaid fraud and shifted his scholarly interests to law and psychology, medical sociology, criminology, and white-collar crime. He completed a stellar master's thesis on the social psychology of the sanctioning of high-status defendants (later published in *Law & Human Behavior*, the top-rated journal in law and psychology), and placed articles in medical journals on issues related to miscreant physicians. Missing the East Coast, he applied and was accepted into Harvard's Ph.D. program in psychology, where he spent his third year of graduate work. Not finding a mentor for his interests in the punishment of the well-to-do, he returned to UCI to write his doctoral dissertation the following year.

Steve's wit and wry sense of humor is shown in a short piece that he contributed to the *Sage Handbook of Field Work*. "Interviewing offenders of any hued collar is a tricky business," he started out. "If I were interviewing a convicted burglar I would probably call him Charlie (or whatever his first name is), while he might call me 'Doc.' There is a role reversal when the offender is an elite deviant. I respectfully called the Medicaid fraud subject Dr. So-and-So. And I might well be called Steve in return—or called nothing at all." Then Steve added the punch line: "No problem. When the interview ends, I'm still the one without a parole officer."

He taught enormously popular graduate courses at UH in social deviance, law and society, crime and the media, law and psychology, criminological theory, organized crime, juvenile delinquency, crime in the cinema, and white-collar and corporate crime. He was a brilliant, gifted, and hard-working instructor who still found time to publish articles and book chapters. Steve presented papers at conferences in Australia, Hungary, Thailand, and Italy, and was a regular participant at criminology conferences in the U.S. He was invited to discuss his work at a major conference on control fraud organized by noted economist James Galbraith at the University of

Texas, Austin, and was a delegate and presenter at a U.N. Crime Congress. The Head of the FBI's Behavioral Sciences Unit invited him to a 3-day closed conference on cyber crime at Quantico. Always ahead of the curve, Steve was the first major writer on cyber crime in criminology.

Besides all of these significant academic accomplishments, Steve Rosoff was a first-rate human being whose absolute unpretentiousness belied his enormous intellectual prowess. In addition to baseball, he was also a movie and media expert. His life was teaching. His immense kindness toward animals saw him rescue numerous dogs who became members of his family. He had a keen eye for injustice, an impeccable wit, and an almost non-stop sense of humor. As one colleague astutely observed, "He was probably the funniest smart person I have ever known and the smartest funny person as well." His co-authors recognize and honor his major contributions to all aspects of this text. It stands as his legacy, or as Steve so elegantly described, "His footprints in the sand."

The authors gratefully acknowledge the efforts of an energetic platoon of students who ably served as research assistants as this book was being prepared.

At the University of Houston-Clear Lake, they are (in alphabetical order): (**FIRST EDITION**) Pam Biggs, Chrissie Blevin, Robbie Cartwright, Susan Dinbali, Mykal Le, Monica Madrid-Hall, Tom Mayfield, Bill McCollum, J. J. McKinzie, Becky Richter, Sarah Smith, and Dave Weimer. (**SECOND EDITION**) Brenda Birdow, Shannon Boudreaux, Monica Contreras, Monique Dasant-Crawford, Debra Kalmbach, Tammy Merrimon, Kevin Morgan, Stephen Morrison, Marian Olivarez, Julie Patterson, Emilia Satsky, Antonia Vasquez, Elizabeth Wade, Jamison Wise, and Pearline Williams. (**THIRD EDITION**) Earl Armstrong, Larry Baimbridge, Melinda Biersdorfer, Tracy Cantrell, Rita Cortez, Mark Fougerousse, Marc Holmes, Sharon Hosea, Cynthia Lee, Rob Lovelace, Audra Mitchell, Rogelio Ruiz, Christopher Staggs, Dave Thomas, and Antonia Vasquez. (**FOURTH EDITION**) Joyce Taylor. (**FIFTH EDITION**) Samanda Rubin, Deidre Russell.

At the University of California, Irvine, they are (**FIRST EDITION**) graduate researcher Susan Will (currently a professor at John Jay College) and undergraduates Steven Rennie, Cindy Guttierez, and Shauhin Talesh (currently a professor at UCI). (**SECOND EDITION**) Helena Rene, Pei-San Tsai, Paul Rodriguez, Jennifer Cabatbat, Erin Morgan, Frances Lee, Denise Chang, Linda Shen, and Tai-Ling Tsai. (**SIXTH EDITION**) graduate researcher Adam Ghazi-Tehrani, who made major contributions throughout the text and especially in Chapter 12, and undergraduates Sarah Turk (UCLA) and Megumi Iida.

Thank you all for work well done.

Numerous colleagues generously have contributed their special insights. Notable among them are Steven Egger and Howard Eisner at the University of Houston, Clear Lake, Paul Jesilow, James Diego Vigil, Elliott Currie, John Dombrink Gilverto Conchas, Farghalli Mohamed and Sanjeev Dewan of UC Irvine; Otto Reyer of Western University of Health Sciences; and Bill Black of the University of Missouri, Kansas City.

The authors also appreciate the efforts of several scholars who reviewed the first edition of this book and offered their judicious evaluations. This sixth edition still benefits from their insights and professionalism. They are (in alphabetical order): Curtis Clarke, Athabasca University; Lynn Cooper, California State University, Sacramento; David Shichor, California State University, San Bernadino; and Ernie Thompson, University of La Verne.

In addition, Virginia Randall, Angela Peters, and Marilea Ferguson of UH—Clear Lake and Judy Omiya of UC Irvine provided superb secretarial support for the early editions. Ms. Randall's efforts in particular have risen far above the call of duty. We are deeply indebted.

To Frank Belsky, sincere appreciation for many valuable suggestions. To Barbara Levine, whose sharp eye is a treasure, thanks for giving so graciously of your time.

To Frank Mortimer—thanks, friend.

And to the inimitable Gilbert Geis, who left us in 2012 at the age of 87, our profound and eternal gratitude for your encouragement and inspiration.

ABOUT THE AUTHORS

Stephen M. Rosoff was professor of criminology at the University of Houston—Clear Lake. He received his Ph.D. in social ecology from the University of California, Irvine. He had written extensively on white-collar crime and professional deviance, particularly in the areas of medical fraud and computer crime. His scholarship appeared in numerous journals and books around the world. He is co-author of *Social Deviance* (McGraw Hill, 2011).

Henry N. Pontell is professor of criminology, law and society in the School of Social Ecology at the University of California, Irvine. He received his Ph.D. in sociology from the State University of New York at Stony Brook. His scholarly work has focused on financial and medical fraud and the role of corporate crime in major financial debacles, among other areas in criminology. His books include *Big Money Crime: Fraud and Politics in the Savings and Loan Crisis* (UC Press); *Prescription for Profit: How Doctors Defraud Medicaid* (UC Press) and *International Handbook of White-Collar and Corporate Crime* (Springer).

Robert H. Tillman is professor of sociology at St. John's University in New York City. He received his Ph.D. in sociology from the University of California, Davis. He is the author and co-author of several books on white-collar crime, including *Big Money Crime: Fraud and Politics in the Savings and Loan Crisis* (University of California Press) and *Pump and Dump: The Rancid Rules of the New Economy* (Rutgers University Press).

Introduction

It could have been a classic rags-to-riches, son-of-poor-immigrants-makes-good, American Dream, success story. Instead, it morphed into an American Nightmare. On January 13, 2003, Rod Blagojevich, the son of a Serbian immigrant who grew up in a hardscrabble working-class neighborhood in Chicago, and who worked his way through college delivering pizzas, was sworn in as the fortieth governor of the state of Illinois.[1] Initially Blagojevich was popular with his constituents and the media whom he kept entertained with his carefully coiffed hair, his Elvis impressions, and his frequent quotations of classic literature. But soon the story veered dramatically from this upbeat trajectory when, in the early morning hours of December 9, 2008, FBI agents showed up at the governor's home in Chicago and arrested him on charges of political corruption.[2]

In two federal cases Governor Blagojevich was charged with a wide range of crimes that began *even before he took office.* The U.S. Attorney summarized the allegations against the governor in the following way: "Blagojevich put a 'for sale' sign on the naming of a United States Senator; involved himself personally in pay-to-play schemes with the urgency of a salesman meeting his annual sales target; and corruptly used his office in an effort to trample editorial voices of criticism."[3] The specific charges referred to numerous instances in which Blagojevich sought to obtain campaign contributions in exchange for government contracts and appointments as well as efforts to use financial pressure to force the *Chicago Tribune* to fire an editor who had been critical of the governor.[4]

But the charge that got the media's attention and which brought him national notoriety was his attempt to sell a seat in the U.S. Senate. When then Senator Barrack Obama was elected president, the governor had the authority to appoint a replacement. In this situation Blagojevich saw an opportunity to make some easy money, as revealed in a conversation, secretly recorded by federal agents:

> I mean I, I've got this thing [the Senate seat] and it's (bleeping) . . . golden. . . . And I, I'm just not giving it up for (bleeping) nothing.[5]

From his comments it was clear that Blagojevich saw the Senate seat at his ticket out of his relatively low-paying job as governor and into a lucrative position after he left office and that he was willing to consider various offers, including: Secretary of the U.S. Dept. of Health and

Human Services ("HEW, what's it called? What is that thing?" as Blago referred to it in one taped conversation), various ambassadorships, leadership of a major private foundation, and even the possibility of appointing himself to the Senate ("if . . . they're not going to offer anything of any value, then I might just take it.")[6]

Despite the seriousness of the charges against him, Blagojevich seemed to relish his new-found fame and notoriety. While under indictment he appeared as a contestant on the reality television show *Celebrity Apprentice*, published a memoir, hosted an AM radio talk show in Chicago, and was a guest on the morning talk show, *Today*, where he told the interviewer that all he was guilty of was "political horse trading" and compared himself to the Biblical figure of David in his fight against a Goliath in the form of federal prosecutors.[7] At one point he even had his wife Patti appear on the reality TV show *I'm a Celebrity . . . Get Me Out of Here!* and ate a tarantula.[8] The jurors in his second trial were not swayed by these media antics and convicted him on 18 counts. Blagojevich was sentenced to serve 14 years in federal prison. As of spring, 2012, the former political power broker and media celebrity was a long-term resident at the Federal Correctional Institution Englewood in Littleton, Colorado, where he was washing pots and pans and planning to teach Shakespeare to the other inmates.[9]

In his personal characteristics, his view of the world and his place in it, Blagojevich had much in common with many of the white-collar criminals to be discussed in this book. He was obsessed with money and consumed by a desire to acquire the trappings of great wealth. His naked greed and ambition were vividly displayed in a profanity-laced telephone conversation with his advisors in 2008 in which the governor complained that he and his wife were "struggling financially" and went on to describe his frustrations:

> I don't wanna be governor for the next two years. I wanna get going. I'll, I, this has been two (bleeping) (bleeping) years . . . . It's no good. I gotta get moving. The whole world's passing me by and I'm stuck in this (bleeping) job as governor now. Everybody's passing me by and I'm stuck.[10]

Despite his claim about their financial difficulties, the couple reportedly spent $400,000 on clothes in a six-year period, including $1,300 spent on ties on a single day.[11] Blagojevich also shared with many other white-collar criminals a sense of entitlement that leads them to believe that they deserve whatever they've acquired (legally or illegally), and a conviction that they have done nothing wrong, or at least nothing that other people in their positions do not routinely do.

If history plays a guiding role in understanding such malfeasance, then one could conclude that Blagojevich was nothing more than a product of his immediate environment. He was a politician who was merely following a hallowed tradition in Chicago politics, in which "pay-to-play" and other corrupt practices are just the way government business gets done, and the only reason he ended up in prison was that he bucked the local political machine and started "hustling for cash" on his own.[12] After all, Blagojevich was the fourth Illinois governor to be sentenced to prison since the early 1970s, including his immediate predecessor, George Ryan, who was serving a term of six and one-half years in a federal prison on the day Blagojevich was arrested.[13]

The Blagojevich case is a colorful example of the pervasiveness of white-collar crime in our society. On any given day, one might pick up a newspaper and read stories reporting bribery scandals among politicians at every tier of government, crooked deals involving Wall Street financiers, or the raffish schemes of predatory con artists. And these are only the stories that make it into the press. Behind them are innumerable cases of corruption, fraud, and abuse that are never uncovered or reported. Yet, when most Americans talk about the "crime problem," they have in mind images of the violent murders, rapes, assaults, and robberies relentlessly portrayed in television "docudramas" and in gory detail by the tabloid press. The public's fears are not unwarranted; street crime remains at intolerably high levels in the United States. The problem is that these concerns can eclipse our understanding of other kinds of crime—particularly white-collar offenses that are in many less obvious ways much more harmful to society at large.

This book surveys the forms, causes, and consequences of white-collar crime. In it, the authors strive to give the reader a sense not only of the relevant social scientific theories but also of the mechanics of white-collar crime: how these schemes work, who perpetrates them, and how they are tied to the environments in which they occur. The authors also hope to convey the scope of "upperworld" criminality to demonstrate the degree to which it has become ingrained in our major social institutions and our culture.

THE HISTORY OF A CONCEPT

The term "white-collar crime" is a social science construct that has transcended its academic roots and entered the public lexicon. Its origin can be precisely located. In 1939, Professor Edwin Sutherland of Indiana University delivered the presidential address to the American Sociological Society, in which he argued for the need to expand criminological thinking to include behaviors and persons not generally thought of—either by the public or by most scholars of the time—as crime and criminals. As he later explained in a classic book, most theories of crime focus on those offenses committed in overwhelming disproportion by members of the social underclass. Sutherland contended that such an exclusive perspective ignores the fact that "persons of the upper socioeconomic class engage in much criminal behavior; that this behavior differs from the criminal behavior of the lower socioeconomic classes principally in the administrative proce-dures used in dealing with the offenders."[14] He called these offenses *white-collar crimes,* a meta-phor meant to distinguish the occupational status of those who worked in office buildings from those who worked in factories or practiced other "blue-collar" trades or were unemployed.

Sutherland defined white-collar crime as "crimes committed by a person of respectability and high social status in the course of his occupation."[15] With this definition, he connected two distinct elements: the social status of the offender and the occupational mechanism by which the offense is committed.

In Sutherland's view, prevailing theories about the causes of crime were based on naive assumptions regarding the validity of official statistics gathered from public institutions like courts and prisons, which always have overrepresented the poor and the powerless. Sutherland asserted that those statistics were prone to extreme bias as they failed to reflect two important facts. First, "persons of the upper socioeconomic class are more powerful politically and finan-cially and escape arrest and conviction to a greater extent than persons who lack such power."[16] Second, and more importantly to Sutherland, the justice system is inclined to employ a very dif-ferent procedural apparatus for dealing with white-collar offenders.

> Persons who violate laws regarding restraint of trade, advertising, pure food and drugs, and similar practices are not arrested by uniformed policemen, are not tried in criminal courts, and are not committed to prisons; this illegal behavior receives the attention of administrative commissions and of courts operating under civil or equity jurisdiction. *For this reason such violations of law are not included in the crimi-nal statistics nor are individual cases brought to the attention of scholars who write the theories of criminal behavior* [emphasis added].[17]

Sutherland supported his position with data that revealed substantial numbers of criminal and administrative violations among the biggest corporations in the country. He further concluded that "the financial cost of white-collar crime is probably several times as great as the cost of all the crimes customarily regarded as the 'crime problem'."[18] As an illustration, he noted that "an officer of a chain grocery store in one year embezzled $800,000, which was six times as much as the annual losses from 500 burglaries and robberies of the stores in that chain."[19]

Sutherland's work was groundbreaking, forging a new theoretical path and setting a research agenda for many future scholars. Indeed, his development of the concept of white-collar crime exemplifies what Peter Berger has labeled the "debunking motif" in sociology. The process of debunking involves "looking for levels of reality other than those given in the official interpretations of society."[20] In fundamentally altering the study of crime by focusing attention upon an elite form of lawbreaking previously ignored by criminologists, Sutherland thus "debunked" theories "which blamed such factors as poverty, broken homes, and Freudian fixations for illegal behavior."[21]

It must be noted, however, that Sutherland's ideas were not incubated in a vacuum, but rather reflected the historical context in which they developed. Sutherland was 56 years old when he delivered his influential speech in 1939, so much of his intellectual germination took place in the early part of the 20th century—an era that witnessed an acceleration of the shift of the United States from a rural, agrarian society to an urban, industrial one. A major part of that transformation, of course, was the emergence of modern corporations as the dominant force in the U.S. economy.

The increasing power of a handful of big companies and their seeming immunity to laws designed only to restrict the behavior of deviant individuals had led to the "public's dawning sense of vulnerability, unease, and anger."[22] That outrage eventually inspired a popular social movement to expose the abuses of big business. At the turn of the century, journalists known as "muckrakers" began to write shocking accounts of outrageous corporate conduct. Upton Sinclair, for example, published a scathing critique of the meatpacking industry in 1904, titled *The Jungle,* in which he detailed the horrendous conditions faced by immigrant workers desperate for a weekly wage.[23] Sinclair's exposé of unsanitary practices spurred the establishment of the Food and Drug Administration (FDA), the first federal agency empowered to create and enforce standards in the food processing industry (Chapter 3).

Around the same time, other journalists took aim at the monopolies that were establishing strangleholds on major sectors of the economy. The expanding corporations of the late 19th century had discovered a simple truth: it was more profitable to collude than to compete. The culmination of this assault on the free market was the formation of national trusts, through which various companies would fix prices or pool their operations under a single administration in order to eliminate competition. In an effort to curb such conspiracies, Congress passed the Sherman Antitrust Act of 1890 (Chapter 2). Although very few cases were prosecuted during the early years of the act, corporations were at least forced to rethink their strategies and turn toward a more "legitimate" form of expansion, the merger. Between 1895 and 1908, thousands of companies disappeared as larger firms gobbled them up.[24]

The corporation that came to symbolize the strategic use of mergers and trusts was the Standard Oil Company, headed by John D. Rockefeller. By ruthlessly destroying his competitors, Rockefeller had created an empire that controlled virtually the entire American petroleum industry. Ida Tarbell, a muckraker whose own father had been ruined by Rockefeller, chronicled the gluttony of Standard Oil. Her articles helped ignite public sentiment against Rockefeller and encouraged President Theodore Roosevelt to "bust" the Standard Oil trust. In 1909, the courts finally ordered Standard Oil to dissolve itself into a number of smaller companies.[25]

Still other writers decried the increasing concentration of economic power among rapacious oligopolies. Frank Norris' thinly fictionalized book, *The Octopus,* described how four powerful companies had conspired to control the vast railroad empire of the American West.[26] In *Other People's Money, and How the Bankers Use It,* Louis Brandeis, who would later become a distinguished Supreme Court Justice, warned of a "financial oligarchy" run by a network of interlocking directorates, through which officers of investment banks, life insurance companies, and railroad corporations sat on each other's boards, conducting transactions that benefited the members of what Brandeis called the "Money Trust."[27] The result was an economy run by and for the members of this elite group, who had become, in Brandeis' words, "masters [of] America's business world, so that practically no large enterprise can be undertaken successfully without their participation or approval."[28] Brandeis singled out banker J.P. Morgan for the harshest criticism. Morgan epitomized the 19th century robber baron, and his House of Morgan symbolized "monopolistic and predatory control over the financial resources of the country."[29]

An even more direct influence on Sutherland's work was a 1907 book by sociologist E.A. Ross. The book was titled *Sin and Society,* and in it Ross vividly expressed his dismay about corrupt business practices: "Nationwide is the zone of devastation of the adulterator, the rebater, the commercial freebooter, the fraud promoter, the humbug healer, the law-defying monopolist."[30]

Behind all this corruption was a social type that Ross called the *criminaloid.* Such an individual enjoys a public image as a pillar of the community and a paragon of virtue; but beneath this veneer of respectability could be found a very different persona, one that is committed to personal gain through any means. Ross' criminaloid is clearly the antecedent of Sutherland's white-collar criminal.

The Roaring Twenties were a bonanza for white-collar crime. The feeding frenzy unleashed by an exploding economy attracted bold predators. The flashy (and notoriously unsuccessful) gambler Nicky Arnstein, husband of Broadway star Fannie Brice, went to prison for a bungled $3,000,000 bond swindle in 1920.[31] That same year, "Count" Victor Lustig emigrated to America from Bohemia and became one of the most legendary con men ever. Lustig's string of amazing swindles defies credulity. So brazen was Lustig that he even dared to count among his many victims the vicious Chicago crime boss Al Capone. Victor Lustig is best remembered as *the man who sold the Eiffel Tower*[32]—a feat he somehow managed to accomplish twice. The fast-talking Scotsman Arthur Ferguson also made a profitable career out of peddling famous landmarks to gullible tourists, starting in London, where he collected hefty down payments on Big Ben and Buckingham Palace. When Ferguson moved to the United States in 1925, he soon sold the White House on the installment plan to a wealthy rancher. He later served a prison sentence for attempting to sell the Statue of Liberty.[33]

Ponzis

An especially remarkable figure of this era was a diminutive, glib-tongued immigrant named Charles Ponzi. As a young man Ponzi had been an inept petty thief in his native Italy. His parents reportedly shipped him across the Atlantic just to get rid of him. By the time he settled in Boston in 1911, he had already served two prison terms in the United States and Canada.[34] But in Boston Ponzi found his mendacious Muse. Although his audacious career was relatively brief, he remains one of the most influential white-collar criminals in American history. The ingenious strategy he refined has inspired (and will no doubt continue to inspire) generations of crooks.

In 1919, Ponzi announced that his Financial Exchange Company of Boston would guarantee an incredible 50 percent return to investors within 45 days. The plan ostensibly was to purchase international postage coupons in countries where the exchange rate was low and then resell them in countries with higher rates. It was a primitive form of the technique now known as arbitrage—which was refined so deviously by Ivan Boesky in the 1980s. Within six months,

Ponzi had persuaded 20,000 investors to give him nearly $10 million. The secret of Ponzi's smoke screen was that he paid off early investors with new investors' money, thereby attracting more and more investors. At its height, his company had a *daily* cash flow of $250,000—a phenomenal amount for that time.[35] The mathematics of pyramid scams, however, give them a relatively short lifespan. Soon after the *Boston Globe* published a sensational exposé in 1920,[36] Ponzi was arrested, convicted of fraud, sentenced to four years in federal prison, and later deported. He died a pauper in 1949, in Brazil, where he had run a hot-dog stand.[37] Eighty years later, pyramid investment scams that promise income from the recruitment of others, rather than from the sale of a product, are still commonly known as Ponzis.[38]

If anything, Ponzi schemes are now bigger than ever. According to one prosecutor, "there's a pyramiding frenzy going on in the United States, and hundreds of millions of dollars are exchanging hands."[39] One of the more outrageous recent cases involved R. Allen Stanford, the founder of Antigua-based Stanford International Bank. In a relatively short period of time the bank had grown spectacularly, selling over $8 billion in certificates of deposits to investors from all over the world. The main attraction for those investors was the high yields consistently returned by those CDs. Stanford, a Texas native, cut a wide swath in Antigua where he owned the popular, local cricket team, sponsored an international cricket tournament where the grand prize was $20 million, and was even made a Knight by Queen Elizabeth in recognition for all of his good deeds in the country. Everything was fine until February 16, 2009, when federal agents raided his Houston office and sealed it off, treating it as a crime scene. That same day the Securities and Exchange Commission filed suit against Stanford alleging that he had "executed a massive Ponzi scheme" that resulted in losses of $7 billion to clients. Instead of investing the money, Stanford and his colleagues simply used it to pay off some early investors and diverted much of the rest to themselves in the form of lavish salaries and loans.[40] Stanford was eventually convicted on criminal charges and in June, 2012, was sentenced to 110 years in prison. At his sentencing Stanford accused the government of engaging in "Gestapo tactics" which had "dismembered" his business.[41] A different point of view was offered by a group representing some of Stanford's victims which claimed that the disgraced banker was guilty of "financial terrorism."[42]

Other recent Ponzi cases include the following:

- In October 2011, Nicholas Cosmo, of Long Island, New York, was sentenced to 25 years in prison for operating his firm, Agape Inc., as a Ponzi scheme. Prosecutors claimed that he stole over $400 million from investors from all over the world who believed his promises of double-digit returns on their investment. Cosmo told investors he was using their money to make short-term bridge loans to small companies when in fact he was simply using the classic tactic of paying off early investors with funds from later investors.[43] According to the SEC, "This Ponzi scheme spread like wildfire through Long Island's middle-class communities because this small group of individuals blindly promoted the offerings as particularly safe and profitable . . ."[44]

- Houston police raided a meeting of the Jubilee Celebration Paradigm and seized more than $730,000 from participants. The operation was part of a multimillion dollar nationwide pyramid scheme. To join, one needed to pay $2,000 in cash and recruit two more members.[45] A few months later, police raided another pyramid meeting in Houston. This time it was the Ya-Ya Girls, an operation that persuaded women to invest $5,000 in hopes of getting a return of $40,000.[46]

- In 2003, former Harlem Globetrotters player Clyde "The Glide" Austin and two other men were arraigned on federal charges of fraud, money laundering, and conspiracy. They allegedly promoted a pyramid scheme that bilked investors out of more than $10 million, while promising high-yield "secret and exclusive investment opportunities." According to prosecutors, many of the 200 investors were members of churches associated with the defendants.[47]

- San Francisco attorney Nikolai Tehin was sentenced to 14 years in prison in 2005 for stealing millions of dollars from clients, including struggling immigrants and children born with disabilities. Tehin had stolen $1.3 million owed to dozens of low-income migrant workers from Mexico, whom he had represented in a suit against their landlord for failing to keep his clients' rental units habitable. Tehin also pilfered $1 million from malpractice settlements—including cases involving a baby born with severe brain damage, two children born with cystic fibrosis, and a young girl who died under medical supervision. Tehin used some of the settlement money to pay off other clients, in a typical Ponzi scheme. He spent the rest on a lavish lifestyle that included a 73-foot yacht, an $8 million home, and a fleet of luxury cars.[48]

- In 2007, North Carolina swindler Richard Dompier was convicted of mail fraud, tax fraud, and money laundering and sentenced to 10 years in federal prison for operating an international Ponzi scheme. He also was ordered to pay $2.8 million in restitution to his victims. Utilizing the Internet and direct mail, Dompier's company, New Millennium Group (NMG), told potential investors that if they invested $98, the company would provide them with a one-ounce bar of silver and commission checks totaling $15,853.50 over a 14-month period. In fact, the NMG silver program was a front with no legitimate business activities. Taking a page from the Ponzi handbook, Dompier paid initial investors with funds obtained from later investors. Dompier sold over 75,000 silver bars to more than 5,000 customers in 41 countries, promising them they would collectively receive about $1.2 billion.[49] In an ironic twist, it was revealed that Dompier himself had been swindled out of $200,000 by one of those ubiquitous and clumsy Nigerian e-mail scams[50] (discussed in Chapter 12). Who says you can't con a con man?

- One of Charles Ponzi's most nefarious reincarnations was David Burry, who defrauded relatives and neighbors out of more than $25 million—much of it the retirement savings and children's college funds of lifelong friends. He used their money to buy luxury cars and homes, a 48-foot yacht, a private helicopter, and other conspicuous trappings of wealth.[51] Burry was the owner of CF Foods, a wholesale candy distributor. The company, like Burry, appeared to be very successful; but it too was a classic Ponzi. Burry promised investors returns of 18 to 30 percent, but instead of generating sales and profits, he simply paid off some old investors with money from newer investors and pocketed the rest.[52] The sense of personal betrayal was devastating. David Burry was known in his community as a man who gave generously to charities and went to church regularly every Sunday. He even attended Bible classes—though he evidently missed the one covering the Fifth Commandment: Thou shalt not steal.

- People who recently received e-mails with a subject line that read, "Hotter than anything you've ever seen,"[53] probably thought it was one of those tacky sex ads. But it was worse. It was a pyramid investment offer:

  Follow the simple instructions and in two weeks you will have US$10,000 in your bank account. Because of the LOW INVESTMENT, SPEED and HIGH POTENTIAL, this program has a VERY HIGH RESPONSE RATE![54]

According to the U.S. Postal Inspection Service, 80 percent of the scams involving junk e-mail (known as "spam") are for pyramid schemes.[55] E-mail has provided a perfect new environment for one of the most rudimentary cons—the chain letter. Chain letters can sound so seductive—until one does the math. For example, if you are number 6 in the chain, the letter must go five more rounds before you move to the top of the list. If everyone is expected to send the chain to five other persons, who each in turn must send it to five others, and so on, that means that almost 10 million people have to respond before you collect a dime.[56] Good luck.

The Great Depression

Public skepticism about the morality of big business, which had been fostered by writers like Brandeis and Ross, intensified during the Great Depression of the 1930s. The stock market crash of 1929 had laid bare the reckless speculation and rampant frauds that had fueled the economic boom of the 1920s. One sardonic journalist of that time quipped: "If you steal $25, you're a thief. If you steal $250,000, you're an embezzler. If you steal $2,500,000, you're a financier."[57]

In 1933, the nation was rocked by a monetary crisis that eventually led to the closure of over 500 banks. This was before the establishment of federal deposit insurance, so depositors simply lost their money in one stroke, wiping out the life savings of thousands of working men and women. Quite understandably, there was great public resentment toward banks and bankers—an attitude that was captured in a popular folk song written by Woody Guthrie about the colorful bank robber Pretty Boy Floyd.

As Guthrie's lyrics suggested, the notorious gangsters who captured the public's attention during the 1930s often became unlikely folk heroes because, in a perverse way, they exemplified the populist spirit of defiance of big business and big government. Part of the admiration of "public enemies" was probably based on a few well-publicized acts of community benevolence. Pretty Boy Floyd, for example, was noted for distributing turkey dinners to the poor on Thanksgiving Day. But another aspect of that popularity undoubtedly stemmed from the deep antipathy that many victims of the Depression felt toward big business and their sense, however misguided, that outlaws represented the struggles of the "common man." This, then, was the environment in which Sutherland developed his ideas about white-collar crime—an environment where the battered masses were openly hostile to the economic elite.

Despite its resonance, however, Sutherland's message did not spark an immediate stampede of academic attention. Indeed, it was not until the 1970s that his ideas would be more fully applied to empirical research. This delay was due mainly to historical circumstance. Sutherland's seminal work, *White-Collar Crime*, was not published until 1949. It coincided with the dawn of an era of conformity which spanned nearly 20 years, during which the populist antiauthority spirit was replaced by an atmosphere of public confidence in the ability of corporate America to guide the country to new heights of prosperity. Even within the discipline of sociology, the dominant theoretical position was functionalism, a perspective that focused on societal equilibrium and the maintenance of the status quo, rather than on inequality and flaws in the social system.

Often enough this faith in the good intentions of corporate America proved to be misplaced. The "Great Salad Oil Swindle" of 1963 stands out as such an instance. The Allied Crude Vegetable Oil Refining Corporation devised an elaborate and ingenious way of vastly inflating its inventory of salad oil.

> [The company] filled many of its vats with water, adding only a top layer of oil. Pipes connected the vats underground, so that the layer of oil could be shifted across the vats as needed during the inventory observation procedure.[58]

By the time this massive hoax was uncovered, Allied had sold its financiers $175 million worth of phantom salad oil.[59]

The flamboyant Texas wheeler-dealer Billie Sol Estes perpetrated a similar deception during this same era. Estes had cornered the liquid fertilizer (anhydrous ammonia) market in 1959 by dropping his retail price from $100 a ton to $20, running his competitors out of business. Since his wholesale cost was $80, the price war inevitably drained Estes' capital, and he could not pay his bills. His wily solution was to keep borrowing large amounts of money from his creditors. Billie Sol later explained: "You borrow enough from a banker and you no longer have a creditor. . . . You get into somebody deep enough, and you've got a partner."[60]

As collateral Estes used government contracts he had received to store surplus grain in his warehouses, along with his assurances that he would be receiving many additional contracts—with the help of his friend and political benefactor, then Senator Lyndon Johnson of Texas. Estes later "borrowed" millions more from other lenders, this time using as collateral suspicious mortgages he held on huge metal tanks in which his liquid fertilizer was stored. Unlike the Great Salad Oil Swindle, it was not the contents of the tanks that did not exist—it was the tanks themselves. They had not even been built.

Estes was arrested and later convicted on a bevy of charges related to his invisible assets. He was sentenced in 1963 to 15 years in federal prison.[61] Lyndon Johnson, who had adroitly distanced himself from his former crony, was never formally implicated and remained largely untouched by the scandal. Twenty months later, he was the president of the United States.

Despite such revelations as the oil and fertilizer tank frauds, and the huge electrical equipment price-fixing conspiracy detailed in Chapter 2, most Americans of that time were less inclined to view business as a problem than as a solution. This mood changed abruptly, however, during the late 1960s and early 1970s, when social unrest once again brought into question the legitimacy of those holding power. A number of important events reinforced this renascent skepticism: the Watergate scandal, the unpopular Vietnam War, and stories of unlawful conduct on the part of the CIA and FBI. The complicity of large corporations in these abuses of power served to discredit the integrity of the economic, as well as the political, elite. Surveys conducted during this period found that the public's trust in business and political leaders had diminished significantly. One poll reported, for example, that the proportion of Americans who indicated "a great deal of confidence" in the people running major companies declined from 55 percent in 1966 to just 16 percent in 1976.[62]

A by-product of this revival of mass cynicism was a heightening of interest in white-collar crime. In the 1970s, the Justice Department undertook some unusually vigorous prosecutions of white-collar offenders, including such corrupt politicians as Vice President Spiro Agnew, several state governors, and White House budget director Bert Lance.[63] Even the FBI, which had never before demonstrated much passion in this area, substantially increased its budget for white-collar crime investigations.[64]

The disillusionment with political and business leaders in the 1970s also generated a resurgence of academic work on white-collar crime, as sociologists and criminologists rediscovered many of the notions raised by Sutherland decades earlier. An important study by Clinard and Yeager utilized some of Sutherland's empirical methods to reveal high levels of lawbreaking among major American corporations.[65] A number of other studies documented the dynamics of white-collar criminality in such industries as securities,[66] automobiles,[67] liquor,[68] and prescription drugs.[69]

In addition, criminologists undertook examinations of the justice system's response to white-collar crime, testing the hypothesis that higher-status offenders received preferential treatment.[70] Theorists also began to look for the sources of white-collar criminality in organizational characteristics[71] and to acknowledge the uniqueness of corporate crime.[72]

And then came the 1980s. It was a period that spawned white-collar crimes of such unprecedented magnitude that it was already dubbed the "greed decade" before it was half over. In 1983, the FBI investigated 1,825 cases of white-collar crimes involving losses of $100,000 or more. In 1988, the number had jumped to 3,448—an increase of 89 percent in five years.[73] The excesses of this era were often attributed to a cultural shift in which Americans became dominated by unbridled material ambition. Business schools and BMW dealerships prospered, while public schools decayed and urban streets became war zones. Many observers believed that this change in values was a reflection of a presidential administration whose philosophy stressed 19th century rugged individualism, in which the right of the individual to prosper outweighed the collective welfare of society. The primary role of government became the elimination of any obstacles to profit. The "Greed is good" credo extolled winning by any means. It is now evident that a favorite means was white-collar crime.

Some offenders became household names. On Wall Street, investment broker Ivan Boesky illegally manipulated the stock market and in the process redefined the crime of insider trading. On an even grander scale, junk bond guru Michael Milken started a chain reaction that buried the American economy under massive debt, when he oversold billions of dollars worth of high-risk securities to banks, insurance companies, and other financial institutions. In California, perfidious entrepreneur Charles Keating plundered the Lincoln Savings and Loan (S&L) Association, causing the biggest bank failure in American history and contributing heavily to a numbing bailout of the S&L industry at the expense of innocent taxpayers. The unholy trio of Boesky, Milken, and Keating all went to prison, and their respective stories are chronicled in detail in subsequent chapters. But they were only high-profile representatives of a time when a stunned public witnessed a seemingly endless procession of revelations about misconduct at all levels of business and government.

Consider, for example, the rise and fall of Barry Minkow. This book will relate many case studies of white-collar crime—some notorious, some obscure. But none is more astonishing or more reflective of the anything-for-a-buck mentality that permeated the 1980s than the tale of a young man, barely out of his teens, who created a make-believe company and came within weeks of swindling some of the savviest grown-ups on Wall Street out of $80 million.

CASE STUDY
The $80 Million Kid

In 1981, a 16-year-old Los Angeles high-school student and aspiring bodybuilder named Barry Minkow borrowed $1,500 and formed a carpet cleaning company he named ZZZZ Best (pronounced Zee-Best). The largely unregulated carpet cleaning business has long been riddled with questionable practices—from deceptive advertising to "bait-and-switch" telephone solicitations, through which glib hustlers can double or triple a low-priced contract by talking customers into costly extra services after entering their homes. Minkow, boyishly charming, intensely ambitious, and completely unscrupulous, had been learning the business part-time since he was 14 and was now eager to go out and swindle people on his own.

ZZZZ Best initially was a failure. Minkow ignored the day-to-day cost controls required of any new enterprise in favor of reveling in the flashy role of teenage tycoon. By the time he turned 17, he was heavily in debt. His curious solution was to open a second location—which he financed by stealing his grandmother's jewelry.

As his bills mounted, and Minkow could no longer even meet his payroll, he turned to insurance fraud to raise cash. In 1983, he kicked a hole in his office door and reported that he had been robbed. He contacted his adjuster and claimed the loss by theft of several $1,000 "Corwell Triple-Vac Dual-Pump Water-Heated Steam Cleaners," a nonexistent machine for which he produced fake invoices. His staged break-in netted Minkow about $16,000. He would later repeat this scam a number of times at other ZZZZ Best locations.

In order to secure new loans, bank officers demanded financial statements and tax returns. Since Minkow had never prepared or filed either, he resorted to counterfeiting. He used bogus paperwork, along with his talent for inventing impressive-sounding but fictitious equipment, to entice a $30,000 loan from a private investor—a reputed mobster. In addition, Minkow stole over $10,000 worth of blank money orders, which he used to pay off some of his more pressing debts. He also began resorting to credit card fraud by adding zeroes to customers' bills.

In retrospect, it seems incredible that ZZZZ Best managed to stay afloat; yet somehow it continued to operate. Still too young to buy a drink, Minkow drove a new sports car and purchased an expensive condominium. His parents were now working for him; he insisted that they call him Mr. Minkow.

Had Barry Minkow been arrested at this point—as he clearly should have been—the story of ZZZZ Best would hardly be worth telling. Minkow could be dismissed as a precocious sociopath whose childish greed was hopelessly overmatched in the adult world. But it seemed to be the adult world that was overmatched. In 1985, he found a way to elevate a sleazy little scam to major white-collar crime status. If lenders were willing to believe in a company that barely existed except on forged documents, why not make ZZZZ Best even bigger and more attractive to investors?

Using stolen insurance company stationery, Minkow awarded himself hundreds of thousands of dollars in fictitious fire and water damage restoration contracts. One of his most outrageous claims was that he had successfully bid on a $3 million contract to restore an eight-story building in the small town of Arroyo Garden, California. The tallest building in Arroyo Garden was only three stories high. Asked by lenders for pictures of the job site, Minkow provided photographs shot from shoe level and cropped at the roof of the building, creating the illusion of additional stories. This crude ploy somehow satisfied bank loan officers. Nobody seemed to wonder how these million-dollar contracts were falling into the lap of a 19-year-old kid. A federal prosecutor would later observe that if carpet cleaning were really so profitable, he would have tossed his desk out the window and changed careers.[74]

In 1986, Minkow decided to make ZZZZ Best a public corporation. "If the public could be persuaded to buy large amounts of ZZZZ Best stock—as investors surely would after that stock had been hyped by a salesman as good as Barry had become—it would provide new sources of cash that *would not have to be paid back*."[75] It was the very essence of the "creative financing" that propelled the 1980s. Since his doctored financial statements, however, could never survive scrutiny from the SEC, he utilized a backdoor method, known as a *shell route*. ZZZZ Best merged with Morningstar Industries, an inactive Utah mineral exploration firm, and acquired Morningstar's publicly owned shares in exchange for stock in the newly formed corporation. Minkow personally received 76 percent of the shares. He was now worth *$12 million* on paper. The mayor of Los Angeles declared November 8, 1986, Barry Minkow Day.

(Continued)

ZZZZ Best had never been anything more than a preposterous Ponzi scheme—a pyramid swindle in which money was raised continually from new investors to pay off old investors. Minkow made it look as easy as Ponzi had six decades earlier. By April of 1987, ZZZZ Best stock was selling for $18 a share. The company's book value (total shares multiplied by price per share) was $210 million. Barry Minkow was now worth $109 million on paper.

In 1987, less than a month after Minkow's 21st birthday, he met with the preeminent Wall Street firm Drexel Burnham Lambert, whose junk bond department, led by superstar Michael Milken, had revolutionized the high-yield, high-risk securities industry by fueling a voracious takeover binge driven by massive debt. Drexel agreed to raise $80 million, via junk bonds, for ZZZZ Best to buy out KeyServ, a Philadelphia-based cleaning service that operated in 43 major markets under contract to Sears, Roebuck, & Company. "By buying KeyServ, ZZZZ Best could get off the Ponzi treadmill, take advantage of the revered Sears name, pay off its other debts, do away with the nonexistent damage-restoration business, and (theoretically) live happily ever after."[76]

Drexel also proposed a future deal in which it would raise an astounding $650 million for ZZZZ Best to launch a hostile takeover of Service Master, a multibillion dollar commercial cleaning contractor. Barry Minkow did not even have to ask.

Thanks to a number of television appearances in which he showcased his manic charisma, Minkow became something of a media celebrity. Influential magazines like *Newsweek, Inc.,* and *American Banker* ran features on the emerging legend of an entrepreneurial prodigy. Far less flattering, however, was an investigative report published in the *Los Angeles Times* on May 22, 1987. It would forever puncture the ZZZZ Best myth and collapse Barry Minkow's phony little empire.

It was all laid out in the 1,200-word article.[77] Within a month, ZZZZ Best stock plummeted from $18 to $6. The world had finally seen the real Barry Minkow and his perversion of the American dream.

In July 1987, Minkow resigned from ZZZZ Best at the age of 22, citing ill health. Shares were now selling for just pennies. In 1988, he was indicted by a federal grand jury, and the case of *United States v. Barry J. Minkow* went to trial. In the words of one attorney: "It's astounding that a fellow who's hardly shaving could cause a financial debacle of this kind."[78] Minkow was charged with bank, stock, and mail fraud, money laundering, racketeering, conspiracy, and tax evasion. ZZZZ Best, a company once purported to be worth hundreds of millions of dollars, auctioned off its entire assets for only $62,000—not even enough to cover Minkow's bail. He was convicted on all 57 counts and received a stiff 25-year prison sentence. Some time later, when Assistant U.S. Attorney Maury Leiter was touring the new federal detention center in downtown Los Angeles, he heard one of the prisoners call his name. It was Barry Minkow:

"Hey, Mr. Leiter—how do you like the place?"

"It seems very nice," the prosecutor said.

"It's real nice," Barry agreed. "The carpets are real clean, too. And they're gonna stay that way, for a long, long time."[79]

If the 1980s was the "greed decade," the 1990s might well be dubbed the "betrayal decade." The huge institutionalized corruption that marked the S&L collapse and the insider trading scandals may not have been as manifest, but stories surfaced again and again of persons abusing their positions of trust to deceive and betray. Indeed, the signature phrase of the 1990s may have been uttered by the victim of a multimillion dollar embezzlement: "I'm hurt and angry that our trust was betrayed."[80]

According to a study conducted by the Association of Certified Fraud Examiners, white-collar crime actually appeared to be on the upswing in the 1990s.[81] The group's 1998 survey of 600 fraud auditors reported that eight out of ten believed that white-collar crime had worsened over the previous five years.[82]

Tax Fraud

Perhaps emblematic of the 1990s was the tax fraud imprisonment of Catalina Vasquez Villalpando. Tax evasion is a fairly routine offense; except in this case Ms. Villalpando was the *treasurer of the United States.* All the paper money printed in the United States between 1990 and 1994 thus bore the signature of a convicted felon.[83]

Other major tax frauds of that decade included the case of Stew Leonard, Sr., a Connecticut dairy retailer who once received a Presidential Award for Entrepreneurial Achievement from Ronald Reagan. Leonard's crime (appropriately enough) involved the *skimming* of money from his milk stores, which defrauded the federal government out of more than $17 million in taxes. He pleaded guilty of conspiracy in 1993.[84]

Paul Bekins, majority shareholder of the well-known Bekins Moving and Storage Company, pleaded guilty of filing a false tax return. He was charged with concealing $3.7 million in income to avoid paying $1.3 million in taxes in 1998 and 1999.[85] As part of his plea, Bekins agreed to testify against two Americans who operated a consulting company based in the Caribbean that helped clients hide income offshore to evade taxes.[86]

In 2005, KPMG, the nation's fourth largest accounting firm, admitted to criminal wrongdoing and agreed to pay a $456 million fine[87] for selling fraudulent tax shelters that helped wealthy clients evade $2.5 billion in taxes during the 1990s.[88] "[KPMG's] 'products,' many going by esoteric acronyms such as FLIP, BLIPS and OPIS, allowed wealthy taxpayers, typically those who had recently had a large taxable gain, to create losses that could be written off to reduce or eliminate taxes on the gain."[89] For example, BLIPS (Bond Linked Issue Premium Structure) was an unlawful tax shelter sold by KPMG to 186 wealthy clients.[90] KPMG reportedly earned $124 million from its tax shelters[91] and insisted that the firm had not broken the law but merely exploited the tax code.[92]

Presidio Advisory Services, a "tax shelter mill"[93] formed in the 1990s by two former KPMG executives, reportedly earned $134 million selling BLIPS.[94] In late 2008, the two "creative accountants," former KPMG tax partner Robert Pfaff and former KPMG senior tax manager John Larson, were convicted on 12 counts of tax evasion.[95] In 2009, both men were handed steep sentences. Larson received a 10-year prison term and a $6 million fine,[96] while Pfaff received a 97 months and a $3 million fine.[97]

From the California cell biologist who faked his research findings—supposedly linking electric power to cancer—in order to win a $3.3 million grant from the federal government[98] to the world-famous thoroughbred farm accused of killing a champion stallion to collect on a $35 million insurance policy,[99] the 1990s was a cornucopia of corruption.

Embezzlement

Another sign of the "betrayal decade" was the proliferation of embezzlement—a crime of flagrant betrayal. For example, Donald Bunsis, a once-trusted lawyer and financial adviser, was sentenced to 15 months in federal prison in 1997 after he embezzled more than $2 million from elderly clients—many of them long-time friends.[100]

The decade also witnessed three separate trade groups victimized by trusted insiders. In the early 1990s, the Washington-based Edison Electric Institute discovered that one of its employees had siphoned off more than $600,000 by inventing fake vendors and opening checking accounts in their names.[101] In 1997, the chief financial officer of the California-based American Electronics Association diverted more than $800,000.[102] And two years later, the president of the Washington-based Natural Gas Supply Association pleaded guilty to charges that he had embezzled $2.8 million. He had created a number of fictitious "consultants" and had pocketed their hefty fees.[103] According to the prosecutor, most of the stolen money went to "food, drink, [and] travel."[104]

Also in 1997, the chief financial officer of a California meat exporting company confessed to the "wrongful taking" of between $85 million and $95 million.[105] Although his annual salary was "only" $150,000, his lifestyle was strikingly ostentatious by any standards. He even owned his own nightclub—Club Cha Cha. And his estranged wife, who allegedly had received 70 percent of what he pilfered, was even more conspicuous in her consumption. She reportedly owned 20 thoroughbred horses, an exotic car dealership, and several huge estates in exclusive areas. Each of her homes was decorated with sumptuous furniture and rare antiques. One had a giant aquarium containing sharks; another had precisely landscaped pens filled with llamas, emus, and ostriches.[106] By some accounts, this alleged embezzlement is believed to be the *biggest* ever in the United States.[107]

Perhaps the most memorable embezzlement of the 1990s, however, was not the biggest—only the oddest.

CASE STUDY
Prell for Ponies?

In 1994, *Forbes* magazine ran a glowing feature on a little-known entrepreneur named Roger Dunavant, who had taken over Straight Arrow Products, a small Bethlehem, Pennsylvania, manufacturer of horse-care products. In an act of unaccountable inspiration, Dunavant had begun marketing the company's horse shampoo, *Mane 'n Tail,* for human use.[108] If the concept seems a little silly, it is far sillier that people actually started buying this stuff and washing their hair with it—in droves. Straight Arrow's sales went from $500,000 in 1990 to $44 million in 1994.[109]

Dunavant became a celebrity. People magazine shot him taking a bubble bath with his kids. Ernst & Young named him a 1995 Manufacturing Entrepreneur of the Year. Advertising Age even featured Straight Arrow as one of its 1996 Marketing 100.[110]

Straight Arrow had begun in Phil and Bonnie Katsev's kitchen in 1971. When the equestrian couple divorced, Bonnie Katsev wound up as sole owner. In the early 1990s, tired of running the business, she sold half the firm to her head salesman, Roger Dunavant, and half to her 23-year-old son, Devon.[111] Devon Katsev had little interest in the business. "Although he had idly taken a few courses at a local community college and had attended welding school to learn how to fit pipes, the long-haired dreamer thought mainly of becoming a rock star."[112]

Dunavant's imaginative marketing strategy "transformed Straight Arrow from a steady seller of equine products to a fast-growing cosmetics firm for humans."[113] He took his horse shampoo to drugstores, supermarkets, and department store chains. He also began to hype *Mane 'n Tail* with outrageous lies. He told reporters that *Mane 'n*
(Continued)

Tail made his hair grow so fast that he had to cut it every week. He said that doctors were recommending the shampoo to chemotherapy patients.[114]

By this time, Dunavant was routinely representing himself as the sole owner of Straight Arrow, even though he owned only half the company. He started covering his personal expenses with company funds. As his alleged misappropriation went unnoticed, he began transferring assets from Straight Arrow into firms owned by his family. Straight Arrow also began leasing office space "at four times market value from a company partly owned by his wife."[115] *Forbes,* which once hailed Roger Dunavant, now called him "a classic con man."[116]

"While Dunavant pillaged Straight Arrow, his 'partner' Devon Katzev didn't notice a thing."[117] Between 1990 and 1994, Dunavant granted himself $7.3 million in compensation. During this same period, Devon Katzev, who owned half the firm, happily received $600 a week—plus $300 a month as car allowance.[118] Katzev, sounding a bit like the Jeff Spicoli character in *Fast Times at Ridgemont High,* would later testify in court: "I was kind of, like, my hair's long, I'm in this rock status. I was, like, all right."[119]

But in 1993, young Katzev got serious. He had heard rumors about how his partner was looting the company. He finally took a good look at the books and hit Roger Dunavant with a lawsuit.[120] "In February 1996 Dunavant was ordered to repay Straight Arrow $4.5 million. As court-ordered audits of Straight Arrow's books continue, he may be coughing up a lot more."[121]

Roger Dunavant was booted from his job, and Devon Katzev was named Straight Arrow's president. Katzev vowed to make Straight Arrow what it once was, but it may have been too late. The circus was leaving town. Wal-Mart had already moved *Mane 'n Tail* off its beauty shelves and into its pet department.[122] A Wal-Mart spokesman explained: "The trend didn't last."[123] The national sales manager for a rival firm agrees: "The horse-shampoo fad is over."[124]

Bobby Keith Moser was sentenced to 15 years in prison for bilking his clients' trust funds between 1996 and 2004. Moser had agreed to plead guilty but had failed to show up for his court appearance. He had jumped bail and fled to far-off Madagascar, where he was tracked down by federal agents. Moser, an Arkansas tax lawyer, was also convicted of tax fraud.[125]

In 1999, Rosemary Heinen was hired as a $92,000-a-year applications manager in the information technology department at the corporate headquarters of Starbucks Coffee. Within three weeks, Heinen (who had been fired from her previous job for stealing money) had set up an imaginary business, RAD Consulting Services, and began billing Starbucks for work that was never done. Filing hundreds of fraudulent invoices over a 10-month period, she received 48 checks from Starbucks totaling nearly $4 million.[126]

At her trial, Heinen claimed that a combination of psychiatric disorders, including acute depression, obsessive-compulsive disorder, and impulse control disorder, had left her in a trance-like state and had caused her to embezzle. She claimed to be a "shop-aholic" who could not control her profligate spending. Her home was so cluttered with merchandise stacked nearly to the ceiling that there was barely room for her family to live. "Even after declaring bankruptcy in 1996, Heinen acquired 34 cars, two motorcycles, a yacht, three grand pianos and two homes among an endless list of other items."[127] The judge acknowledged that Heinen was mentally ill—but not legally insane, since she clearly could discern right from wrong. In 2002, Rosemary Heinen was convicted and sentenced.[128] The only thing she would be spending was four years in prison.

The shocking tale of a small-town bank, straddling the edges of the Old and New Millennia, further revealed how the embezzlement epidemic of the betrayal decade of the 1990s flowed right into the 21st century.

CASE STUDY
Breaking the Bank

On September 1, 1999, the Office of the Comptroller of the Currency (OCC) closed the First National Bank of Keystone, declaring that its investigators were unable to account for about $515 million of the bank's $1.1 billion of recorded assets. The 85-year-old mortgage bank had long been the economic pillar of Keystone, West Virginia, a small town in the state's depressed coal mining region. Insider fraud had turned Keystone's only financial institution into one of the costliest bank failures since the Great Depression. So many federal regulators descended on Keystone that their presence swelled the town's population by 10 percent.[129] By 2002, estimated losses to the Federal Deposit Insurance Corporation (FDIC), the government agency that compensates depositors when a bank fails, would exceed $800 million.[130]

Keystone's business had long centered on providing home equity loans for home improvement and debt consolidation. It was considered one of the most profitable small banks in the country.[131] But in 1993, it began to purchase large volumes of low-quality loans from third parties to repackage into asset-backed securities that could be sold to investors in the financial markets. By the time the investigators had swooped in, Keystone had processed $2.6 billion of these risky loans.[132]

Regulators had become suspicious that the dubious loans recorded on the bank's books had, in fact, already been sold. Court testimony later confirmed that senior bank executives had manipulated computer records so that sold assets "miraculously appeared back on the books."[133]

Bank officers attempted to thwart the investigation. "[T]hey altered documents and desperately tried to break a microfilm machine in an effort to stop regulators viewing records."[134] They also buried several dump truck loads of documents and microfilm on a ranch owned by one of the bank officials and her husband. A search of the ranch recovered enough buried bank records to fill 370 file boxes.[135] Terry Church, a former director and vice president of the bank, and Michael Graham, the former executive vice president of Keystone Mortgage (a wholly owned subsidiary), were convicted in 2000 of obstructing bank examiners and were sentenced to more than four years in prison.[136]

Church would later plead guilty to other more serious charges and was given an additional sentence of 27 years.[137] Those charges related to a scheme between Church and Billie Jean Cherry, the 77-year-old former chairman of the bank and former mayor of Keystone, to seize control of millions of dollars of accounts owned by the estate of the deceased president of Keystone Bank, J. Knox McConnell.[138] Billie Jean had shared a 30-year personal relationship with Knox, and she believed the money was rightfully hers. A federal jury disagreed. After a lengthy trial, she was convicted of multiple counts of fraud and conspiracy, and handed a 16-year prison sentence. Cherry, who by then was approaching her 80th birthday, grimly joked to the press that she hoped "to 'cheat' the federal government out of some of those years."[139]

Some other notable recent embezzlement cases include the following:

• In 2004, Jason Herrington, a former investment officer at Civitas Bankgroup in Tennessee, pleaded guilty to embezzling $453,000. A routine review by a company auditor revealed that Herrington, a son of Civitas's president, was depositing bank funds into his personal account and using it for online sports gambling. When he was arrested,

Herrington admitted stealing the money but insisted he intended to pay it back.[140] Herrington thus conforms perfectly to criminologist Donald Cressey's psychological profile of the "typical" embezzler detailed in his classic book *Other People's Money*. Herrington meets all three of Cressey's criteria: (1) a non-sharable financial problem (Herrington's gambling addiction); (2) knowledge of and access to the workings of the target enterprise (Herrington's trusted position at the bank); and, (3) perhaps most important, a rationalization of the act permitting the offender to preserve a noncriminal self-image (Herrington's self-deceptive claim that he would return the money).[141]

- In 2007, accounting manager John Hoeffner pleaded guilty to embezzling from a major New York City contractor in order to finance a lavish lifestyle. Over a two-year period, while working as a project accountant for the Tishman Construction Corp., Hoeffner forged invoices and vendor checks related to a $220 million cancer research center that Tishman was building for Yeshiva University's Albert Einstein School of Medicine in the Bronx. Hoeffner deposited more than $2.7 million into his own accounts. Authorities also learned that, prior to joining Tishman, Hoeffner had served as project consultant for Bovis Lend Lease, a construction firm, working on a project for New York's Riker's Island Prison and had embezzled $372,000. When the missing funds were discovered by his successor at Bovis, Hoeffner had agreed to repay the company and was not prosecuted. This serial embezzler was not so lucky the second time around. As part of his plea bargain, Hoeffner agreed to repay Tishman $1.4 million *and* serve at least seven years in prison.[142]

- Also in 2008, Alberto Vilar, a high-profile money manager and patron of the arts, was convicted by a federal jury in Manhattan of defrauding clients of his firm, Amerindo Investment Advisors. After a two-month trial and reportedly heated deliberations, the jury found him guilty on all 12 counts of fraud and money laundering.[143] At Amerindo's peak, when it managed $10 billion, Vilar gambled with clients' money on the dot-com boom of the late 1990s instead of the safe investments he promised. When the dot-com market crashed in 2000, shriveling Amerindo's holdings, Vilar lost millions of dollars. He turned to fraud to satisfy investors who were demanding their money back.[144] One of the key witnesses was long-time Vilar client and friend Lily Cates (mother of actress Phoebe Cates), who charged that Vilar stole $5 million from her. An Amerindo employee testified that she had been ordered to cut and paste Cates's signature on a money transfer authorization.[145] Vilar's dedication to the arts added an interesting twist to the case. He was one of the all-time top benefactors of New York's Metropolitan Opera, as well as other major opera companies. He even continued to commit millions of dollars to his cultural causes long after his fortune had disappeared.[146] Evidently, Vilar did not hear the Fat Lady sing.

In 2007, the *Houston Chronicle* ran a feature story on accountant and ex-convict Barry Webne. It was one of those uplifting tales of redemption and rehabilitation that newspapers and their readers seem to find so appealing. Webne had joined an Ohio manufacturing company in 1991 and over the next four years had embezzled about $1 million from the firm by systematically overpaying himself. Webne was convicted in 1996 and was sentenced to 30 months in prison but was released early after six months, having learned his lesson. He emerged a changed and repentant man. He set up an antifraud Web site and became a white-collar crime consultant and speaker. He even wrote a book, *The Everyday Guide to Detecting and Preventing Employee Theft*.[147] Webne's warning to business owners was blunt: "Wise up or get fleeced."[148] But he also offered a more optimistic message about embezzlement: "We can control this crime 100 percent if business owners will pay attention."[149]

Less than a year after the *Chronicle* story was published, Barry Webne was arrested again for—what else?—embezzlement. He was charged with bilking his new employer out of more than $1 million between 2001 and 2006.[150] In October 2008, Webne was sentenced to five years and three months in prison—the maximum term recommended under federal sentencing guidelines.[151] In his self-serving and hypocritical interview 15 months earlier, given while he was secretly embezzling money, Barry Webne boasted about how easily he had deflected outside auditors in his "former" life of crime: "Put [me] up against auditors with absolutely no fraud experience and I'll have them for lunch. I'll make their heads spin until they're convinced I'm trustworthy."[152]

As the Keystone bank failure, along with the other embezzlement cases cited and, of course, the massive financial crimes of Enron, WorldCom, et al. and the huge Madoff Ponzi scandal (see Chapter 7) indicate, the first decade of the New Millennium likely dwarfed the 1980s and 1990s in perfidy. The ubiquity of white-collar crime was even revealed beneath the rubble of one of the worst days in American history.

CASE STUDY
Russian Roulette

On September 11, 2001, foreign terrorists destroyed the landmark twin towers of the World Trade Center in New York City. Since then, thousands of pieces of mail a day reportedly are still being sent to businesses formerly housed there. Included among those letters must surely be some addressed to First Equity Enterprises. They will never be answered. This is not because the operators of that firm were among the thousands of victims who lost their lives in the tragedy, but because First Equity—purportedly a clearing house for spot currency trading—was a massive fraud. When anxious investors began checking on the safety of their money, they made a shocking discovery. *There was no money.*

Two months later, it was alleged that traders at First Equity conspired to conceal $105 million in missing funds by claiming the funds were somehow lost in the attack. A lawsuit charged that three executives absconded with the money and were attempting to steal an additional $160 million

from clients of the firm to cover up the original losses.[153]

The president of First Equity, Gary Farberov, pleaded guilty at year's end of conspiring with his boss—Andre Koudachev, a fugitive Russian believed to be hiding in Moscow—to transfer investors' funds to overseas bank accounts. According to the FBI, First Equity had been nothing more than a slick boiler room operation with a famous address, soliciting investors worldwide then stringing them along with gaudy promises and nimble lies.[154]

In June 2003 four more First Equity associates were convicted in federal court of fraud, money laundering, and conspiracy. They had spent their clients' money on "bonuses, salaries, commissions, apartments, cars, expense accounts and well-appointed offices."[155] Prosecutors set the number of bilked investors at 1,400.[156] Both literally *and* figuratively, First Equity Enterprises had collapsed.

MEASURING WHITE-COLLAR CRIME

Since the 1930s, when the FBI first began collecting crime statistics in its Uniform Crime Reports, the federal government has poured billions of dollars into the creation of data bases that measure traditional, or "street," crimes. As a result, American criminologists now have access to an array of sophisticated data sets that allow them to study crime from a number of perspectives: reported versus unreported crimes; consequences to victims; trends over time; and geographical distributions across the national level, or down to individual city blocks. By contrast, government agencies—federal, state, and local—have devoted relatively few resources to gathering data specific to white-collar crime. There are virtually no systematic counts, for instance, of the numbers of white-collar offenses that occur in a given year or the number of individuals arrested for these offenses. Indeed, it is disappointing that we have progressed so little since Sutherland first criticized the class biases in official crime statistics.

At least part of the problem results from the difficulties in arriving at a precise definition of white-collar crime. Deciding which crimes are and which are not white-collar crimes is sometimes not an easy matter to resolve. Even more encumbering is the fact that most white-collar crimes are never reported, constituting a substantial, but unmeasurable, "dark figure." While many street crimes—such as theft, assault, and rape—also go unreported, the numbers are undoubtedly much greater for white-collar crimes, since, in so many cases, victims are not even aware that they have been victimized. When large manufacturers conspire to fix prices, for example, consumers know only that the cost of their purchases has increased, not that it has done so artificially because of illegal, anticompetitive practices.

Another reason why the government has failed to produce better data on white-collar crime is ideological. Until recently, most officials simply did not consider these offenses to be as serious as street crime, believing that data collection should be directed toward the kinds of traditional crimes typically committed by the lower class. From this perspective, systematic efforts to count crimes committed mainly by middle and upper class businessmen are stifled in order to avoid stigmatizing respectable members of the business community.[157]

For all the reasons we have just noted, researchers have been forced to generate their own statistical data on white-collar crime, in order to determine its prevalence—that is, the extent to which it occurs in the population as a whole. These efforts usually have taken one of three forms: cross-sectional studies of large corporations; industry-specific studies; and victimization surveys. The first two types of analysis have relied on the official records of regulatory and law enforcement agencies. Victimization surveys, on the other hand, have sought to measure the public's exposure to white-collar crime.

Cross-Sectional Studies

In his pioneering 1949 study, Sutherland examined the records of criminal and civil courts, as well as administrative agencies, looking for adverse decisions against the 70 biggest manufacturing, mining, and mercantile corporations over the 70-year period up to 1945. "Adverse decisions" consisted of criminal convictions, civil judgments, and actions taken against a company by a regulatory agency or commission.[158] Such a methodology provides an overly conservative measure of corporate criminality, since—as we have noted—most white-collar crimes are never reported or sanctioned, and because many of the infractions that are detected are settled out of court. Nonetheless, these data can provide at least a sense of the extent of crime among the corporate elite.

Sutherland found that every one of the 70 corporations in his sample had incurred one or more adverse decisions, with the two most prolific transgressors incurring a total of 50 violations each. Combined, the firms under consideration recorded 980 violations, and, of these, 158 (16 percent) were criminal offenses. Looked at another way, 41 of the 70 corporations (60 percent) had been convicted on criminal charges, averaging four convictions each. Sutherland remarked that "in many states persons with four convictions are defined by statute to be 'habitual criminals,'" implying that many major corporations would also qualify for that label—customarily applied to "common" criminals.[159]

In the 1970s, Marshall Clinard and Peter Yeager updated and expanded Sutherland's analysis by conducting a similar study of the 477 largest publicly owned manufacturing corporations in the United States. They examined criminal, civil, and administrative actions either initiated or completed by 25 federal agencies against these companies in 1975 and 1976. Offenses included administrative violations, such as failure to report information to authorities; financial violations, such as illegal payments; labor violations, such as occupational safety and health violations; manufacturing violations, such as the marketing of unsafe products; and illegal trade practices, such as price fixing. Clinard and Yeager found that three-fifths of the 477 manufacturers had at least one action initiated against them in the two-year period under consideration. Moreover, they found that crime was highly concentrated among certain firms. Just 38 companies were responsible for 52 percent of all recorded violations, with the heaviest concentration in the oil, pharmaceutical, and automobile industries. The data further indicated that larger corporations were more likely than smaller ones to have committed offenses.[160]

The Clinard and Yeager study was followed by several analyses conducted by journalists, each producing congruent findings. One investigation considered federal criminal cases—limited only to bribery, fraud, illegal political contributions, tax evasion, or antitrust violations—against the 1,043 companies that were on the *Fortune* magazine list of the 800 largest industrial corporations at some point between 1970 and 1990. Even using this restrictive range of offenses, 117 (11 percent) of the companies—or their executives—had been charged with at least one of those crimes during the period in question. Interestingly, only 50 executives from just 15 companies actually were sentenced to jail in connection with these cases.[161] Another investigation reported that among the nation's 500 largest corporations, 23 percent had been the subject of criminal or civil actions for serious misconduct over a 10-year period. Among the 25 biggest companies, 14 had incurred criminal convictions or civil penalties in excess of $50,000.[162]

One area where corporate malfeasance has been well-documented has been financial statement fraud. This occurs when corporations, in essence, "cook their books," giving investors misleading information about the company's performance, often in an attempt to increase the firm's share price. Indicators of this practice are financial restatements, acknowledgements by companies that their past financial statements were inaccurate and need to be corrected. (see Chapter 7) A study by the General Accounting Office found that between 1997 and mid-2002, nearly 10 percent of all firms listed on the three major American stock exchanges were forced to "restate" their financial results.[163] While this may seem like a lot, it pales in comparison to China where, over the last two decades, the economy has shown spectacular growth and foreigners have been eager to invest. One analysis found that between 1990 and 2003, one-sixth of the 1,200 firms listed on the Shanghai and Shenzhen stock exchanges had been accused of securities fraud by Chinese regulators.[164]

Viewed together, all these cross-sectional studies indicate that white-collar crime is relatively commonplace among large corporations—especially if one also considers the "dark figure" of unreported offenses. This does not necessarily mean, of course, that these companies are committing unlawful acts on a daily basis. But the findings do suggest that at some point most major firms, or their executives, will be accused of committing business crimes.

Industry-Specific Studies

Industry-specific studies have confirmed the findings of both Sutherland and Clinard/Yeager that criminal and civil penalties tend to be concentrated in certain industries. We will examine some evidence from several major industries with relatively high rates of criminality.

First, consider defense contractors—firms that are repeatedly awarded lucrative contracts by the federal government for defense-related work. Included in this category are companies such as General Dynamics, Lockheed, and McDonnell Douglas that build the fighter planes, aircraft carriers, and sophisticated weapons for the Army, Navy, and Air Force. A study of the top 100 defense contractors (based on the values of their contracts in 1985), conducted by the General Accounting Office (GAO), found that half of these firms had been the subject of criminal investigations by the Justice Department between 1982 and 1985. These investigations centered on cases of suspected defense procurement fraud, involving allegations of overcharging, defective products, and conflicts of interest. Furthermore, 28 of the 100 contractors had been the targets of multiple investigations.[165]

Next, consider the securities industry. Generally, we think of securities fraud in terms of the high-profile insider trading cases on Wall Street, or the heavily publicized stock swindles of crooks like Barry Minkow,[166] or sensational scandals like that of future trader Nicholas Leeson, who single-handedly caused the failure of Britain's ancient Baring Bank in 1995, when he lost $1.24 billion in unauthorized transactions.[167] It would be shortsighted, however, to exclude other segments of this industry. In the 1980s, rigged trading was also uncovered on the Chicago Mercantile Exchange and the Chicago Board of Trade.[168] Not to be overlooked either are the thousands of brokers around the country who handle accounts for small, individual investors. How honest are they? Little empirical evidence on this subject existed until a 1992 study, conducted by the SEC, probed trading practices at 161 branch offices of nine large brokerage firms. Together, these firms accounted for 49 percent of all customer accounts in the United States. The SEC reported instances of "excessive trading, unsuitable recommendations, unauthorized trading, [and] improper mutual fund switching" at one-quarter of the offices it examined.[169] Investigators selected 14 branch offices of one of the nine firms for closer scrutiny. At eight of those offices, they found evidence of routine broker misconduct in handling the accounts of elderly clients.[170]

In late 1995, criminal charges were filed against 11 securities salesmen in a nationwide Justice Department crackdown on "rogue brokers."[171] Among the charges were allegations that the brokers traded securities in customers' accounts without permission and stole from customers by altering trading statements. Some victims reportedly lost their life savings or their children's college funds. Attorney General Janet Reno called the alleged crimes an "inhumane and serious threat to the investment industry."[172] Even more recently, Merrill Lynch agreed to pay a $750,000 fine to settle state charges in Massachusetts that "it failed to properly oversee one executive who committed fraud and another who mismanaged clients' portfolios."[173]

But the problem is not limited to a handful of major securities dealers. Half the 101 small and midsized brokerages examined by the SEC in 1995 had hired persons with disciplinary histories. The report noted lax supervision by many firms, which pay little attention to the illegal conduct of some unsavory traders in their employ. Many "rogue brokers" dodge from one Wall Street address to another, honing their sleazy sales pitches.[174] In one case, regulators identified a broker with a history of unsavory practices and customer complaints who worked at six firms in one year.[175] The chairman of the SEC put it bluntly: "The industry is not policing its own ranks."[176]

Examples from other industries abound. A study by a global business investigations and intelligence firm reports that nearly 40 percent of senior managers at Internet companies have questionable backgrounds—such as criminal convictions or organized crime connections.[177]

Finally, consider the S&L industry of the 1980s, which became institutionally corrupt on a scale seldom witnessed. Between 1980 and 1992, hundreds of S&Ls were forced to shut down due to insolvency. One major study found suspected fraud at two-thirds of the 686 insolvent S&Ls that were under the supervision of the Resolution Trust Corporation in 1992. Losses due to fraud at each of those institutions averaged over $12 million.[178]

Thus, while white-collar crime is no stranger to the entire corporate world, it is clearly concentrated in specific industries whose structures are conducive to criminality. As we shall see in later chapters, these "criminogenic" industries create both opportunities for crime and conditions that conceal illegal acts from the authorities.

Victimization Surveys

Another way to measure the extent of white-collar crime is to ask members of the public about their exposure to it. Victimization surveys have been used for many years to gain more accurate information about the prevalence of street crime. Only recently, however, has this method been used to collect data on white-collar crime. A survey conducted in 1991, for example, asked respondents about personal fraud, defined as "the misrepresentation of facts and the deliberate intent to deceive with the promise of goods, services, or other financial benefits that in fact do not exist or that were never intended to be provided."[179] Of the more than 1,200 subjects randomly selected for the sample, nearly *one-third* reported that they had been the targets of an attempted or successful fraud in the previous year. The mean loss from those frauds was $216. The most common forms described were scams involving "free prizes," followed by automobile repair rip-offs (Chapter 2).[180]

THE COSTS OF WHITE-COLLAR CRIME

Given the paucity of official data on white-collar crime, it is not surprising that precise estimates of the economic costs of those offenses are also difficult to determine. Nevertheless, a number of government agencies and private organizations have offered estimates that can help ascertain the magnitude of the problem. The victimization survey cited in the previous section, for example, estimated that personal frauds alone—such as repair scams and "free prize" swindles—cost American taxpayers about $40 billion annually. In 1974 the U.S. Chamber of Commerce produced a similar $40 billion estimate for the following aggregated offenses: bribery, fraud, kickbacks, payoffs, computer crime, consumer fraud, illegal competition, deceptive practices, embezzlement, pilferage, receiving stolen property, and securities theft.[181]

In 1976, the Joint Economic Committee of Congress "estimated that the short-term direct dollar costs of certain white-collar crimes—not including product safety, environmental, chemical, and antitrust violations—is roughly $44 billion a year."[182] If we add to that figure the $30–$60 billion lost annually to antitrust violations[183] and the approximate $25 billion cost to taxpayers for fraud committed against federal agencies,[184] we derive a conservative estimate that increases the cost of white-collar crime in the 1970s to at least $100 billion. Taking inflation into account, that cost today would probably be closer to $250 billion—a figure consistent with more recent projections by the Senate Judiciary Committee.[185]

To appreciate just how much $250 billion is, consider that the U.S. Bureau of Justice Statistics estimated in 1992 that the monetary costs to all victims of personal crimes (e.g., robbery, assault, larceny) and household crimes (e.g., burglary, motor vehicle theft) totaled 17.6 billion in that year. This figure includes "losses from property theft or damage, cash losses, medical expenses, and amount of pay lost because of injury or activities related to the crime."[186] Yet even that inclusive total represents only 6 percent of the projected annual losses from white-collar crime.

The overall cost differential between white-collar crime and street crime can be underscored as well by the notorious case of Lincoln Savings and Loan, the fraudulent thrift institution run by Charles Keating. After the bank was seized by federal regulators, the price of paying off Lincoln's debts eventually climbed to $3.4 billion.[187] According to the FBI, the losses from all bank robberies in the United States in 1992 was $35 million[188]—about 1 percent of Keating's misappropriation. It is thus likely that the total costs of all American bank robberies in the last 100 years is less than the cost of bailing out a single corrupt S&L.

The consequences of corporate accounting fraud can also be extremely expensive. One study found that shareholders in corporations accused of securities fraud, following financial restatements, lost a total of $84 billion, one day after the restatement was announced, as the value of those shares dropped.[189] Even this figure probably understates the long-term losses to investors in fraudulent companies. The market capitalization (the total value of all outstanding shares) at Enron, for example, went from a peak of $70 billion to *zero* after the corporation declared bankruptcy, meaning that, at least on paper, shareholders saw the value of their investment decline by $70 billion after the crimes at the company became public.[190]

In addition, some costs of white-collar criminality cannot be measured in dollars and cents. These include the physical consequences of crimes such as industrial pollution, the illegal dumping of toxic wastes, injuries and deaths of workers exposed to illegal hazards on the job, and unsafe products marketed to consumers. There are also social and political costs. When influential business executives, powerful politicians, and respected members of the professions are seen flaunting the system, often suffering little or no punishment for their misdeeds, it weakens the average citizen's respect for the law. One legal scholar has referred to this effect as the "demoralization costs" of the unequal sanctioning of wealthy criminals: "When persons are treated unequally in an area in which they believe equal treatment is a right, both they and their sympathizers (a potentially much larger group) suffer psychic injury that may lead them to reduce their contributions to society, or to take anti-social actions in revenge."[191] Such "anti-social actions" could take the form of property crime committed by members of the underclass, who hear stories about preferential treatment of elite offenders and get a message that "crime pays."

PUBLIC PERCEPTION OF WHITE-COLLAR CRIME

One of the reasons why the government pays so little attention to white-collar crime is that members of the public do not express nearly the same degree of outrage over it as they do over street crime, which has become the overriding social issue of our time. Surveys have found that Americans tend to view white-collar crime as a problem, but not a particularly severe one.[192] A 1979 survey, for instance, reported that residents of a small Midwestern community ranked white-collar offenses as far less serious than street crimes involving the theft of property worth $25 or more.[193] Evidently, despite the billions of dollars lost to white-collar crime each year, most Americans still do not accord it a very high priority on their lists of pressing concerns—even today, beneath the rubble of the "greed decade."

Such relative apathy may in turn be explained by the fact that many business crimes are complex and confusing; they often manifest no clear-cut "villains" and "victims" the way that street crimes and even political scandals do. To illustrate this important point, compare the public responses to two events. In 1992, the media revealed that one of the many "perks" provided to members of the U.S. House of Representatives was check-writing privileges at a quasi-bank run by the federal government. In sharp variance with the rules enforced at "real" banks, congressional depositors were not required to have sufficient funds in their accounts in order for their bank to cover their checks. This peculiar feature permitted many members of Congress to "bounce" large checks routinely and without penalty.[194] Indeed, records reveal that representatives have been bouncing checks at the House bank since as far back as 1830.[195] In a 12-month period between July 1989 and June 1990, there were 8,331 bad checks[196]—an average of 19 per member. When the so-called "Rubbergate" story broke in the press, the popular reaction was one of anger, disgust, and demand for reform. A cry of "throw the bums out" swept the country, causing considerable alarm among incumbent legislators—many of whom lost their seats in 1994.

Contrast this reaction with the public's response to another scandal that had occurred in the preceding year, when it was reported by the media that a major Wall Street investment firm, Salomon Brothers, had "rigged" the U.S. treasury bond market.[197] Salomon was one of a select group of buyers allowed to bid on government securities in what is called the "primary market." Those bonds are then resold on a "secondary market" to the public at large. In order to ensure that the primary market remains competitive, federal regulations prohibit individuals or firms from purchasing more than 35 percent of any bond issue. But on at least three occasions, Salomon traders far exceeded that limit by submitting camouflaged bids in the names of clients. Salomon thus effectively cornered the treasury bond market and, in the process, illegally inflated its profits.[198]

Despite the serious economic ramifications of its violations, there were no widespread cries to ban Salomon Brothers from the government securities market. Radio talk shows did not fill the airwaves with the voices of angry callers demanding more accountability on Wall Street. Officers at big investment firms did not fear that their jobs had been placed in jeopardy by an incensed citizenry. In fact, just a few months after the bond scandal, brokerage executives enjoyed the largest increase in their compensation packages in years.[199]

Clearly, there were substantial differences in the public repercussions generated by the sensational Rubbergate and the not-so-sensational Treasury bid-rigging cases. The former involved behaviors that most people could understand and relate to. Ordinary persons are well aware that if they write checks on accounts holding insufficient funds, they face at the very least a financial penalty from their bank and perhaps even criminal sanctions. The consequences of bond market manipulation, however, are much more difficult to visualize and comprehend.[200]

Yet, the injury caused by Salomon Brothers was substantially greater than a bunch of checks kited by irresponsible politicians. Salomon's unlawful practices increased the interest that the government—that is to say, the taxpayers—had to pay out to investors. Over time, the ensuing losses will run into billions of dollars. Just as it was with the Boesky, Milken, and Keating cases, the treasury bond scandal came with a delayed detonator. It is an insidious feature of many white-collar crimes that, like Carl Sandburg's fog, they creep in on little cat feet,[201] often unnoticed by a distracted public—until the bill comes due.

ABOUT THIS BOOK

The chapters that follow provide detailed descriptions of numerous forms of white-collar crime. This book covers a broad spectrum in order to illustrate the pervasiveness of upper-world criminality across a wide range of institutions, including business, government, the medical profession, and even religious organizations and involving a remarkably diverse set of actors—including executives, doctors, politicians, and computer hackers. The authors have attempted to infuse each chapter with a historical perspective by describing some selected cases from the past in order to illustrate that white-collar crime is not solely a contemporary social problem but has a long and vivid history.

Chapter 2 focuses on some of the deceptive practices that affect many of us directly as consumers. It is a lengthy chapter because consumer fraud is the most prolific of all white-collar crimes. A variety of examples are presented of scams perpetrated by crooked auto repairmen, slick telemarketers, and sleazy merchants. Also emphasized is how some unlawful schemes are carried out at high corporate levels in the form of price fixing, price gouging, and false advertising.

Chapter 3 details the sale of dangerous or defective products to consumers by greedy manufacturers who are fully aware of the potential for harm. Also described are unscrupulous quacks who peddle worthless and sometimes lethal medicines and cures. Many of these practices underscore the fact that some forms of white-collar crime are just as violent as the more dramatic crimes of murder, rape, and robbery.

Chapter 4 explores two other categories of "violent" white-collar crime. The deliberate pollution of the natural environment has become one of the most prevalent of all corporate offenses. We will examine some of the deleterious effects of the tons of deadly chemicals and toxic waste that are dumped illegally in the United States every year. In addition, an amoral trend in this area, as we shall see, is the export of hazardous substances to Third World countries, whose citizens often have no freedom to protest. This chapter also reviews some of the punitive weapons developed by lawmakers, courts, and regulators in recent years in an attempt to combat such virulent attacks on the environment. A related kind of white-collar crime occurs in the workplace environment, when an employer knowingly permits unsafe conditions to exist. This chapter looks at the tragic consequences to workers of on-the-job exposure to asbestos, radiation, poisons, and pesticides. It examines, as well, the reasons why federal and state officials generally have failed to curb habitual violations by permitting employers to exploit legal loopholes that enable them to evade responsibility for the suffering they cause. Here too, we will see how American companies have exported hazardous work conditions overseas, where safety regulations are much more lax.

The social cost of white-collar crime refers to an erosion of the vital trust that people place in their elite institutions. If the public comes to believe that those institutions are corrupt, that the "game is rigged," then it becomes more difficult for society to carry out its basic functions. Chapters 5 through 10 examine social institutions whose legitimacy has been weakened by extensive fraud.

Chapter 5 considers the corruption of two vital cultural institutions: the mass media and religion. **Chapter 6** contains an examination of securities fraud, including a comprehensive overview of the insider trading scandals that shook Wall Street in the 1980s and continue to reappear. Newer developments in computer-driven securities fraud, as well as the invasion of organized crime into the securities markets, are also analyzed. The recent economic crisis and how swindlers like Bernard Madoff and others have cheated investors out of billions of dollars is described. Attention is given to how all those crimes have weakened the confidence of investors and posed a serious threat to the entire American economy.

Chapter 7 explores the chain reaction of multibillion dollar accounting frauds and stunning corporate failures that ushered in the New Millennium. Special consideration is given to the Enron debacle, as well as the shocking crimes uncovered in its wake. The chapter contains tales of "in your face" greed so out of control that it eclipses fiction.

Chapter 8 investigates the S&L scandals of the 1980s, along with related frauds within fiduciary enterprises such as pension funds and insurance companies. It argues how changes in government policies, particularly deregulatory legislation, opened the doors wide to misappropriation in what may well have been the most costly set of white-collar crimes ever committed.

Chapters 9 and **10** focus on the abuses of power that occur within political institutions. Criminologists have become increasingly more interested in lawless activities undertaken on behalf of the government and its leaders. **Chapter 9** chronicles cases of crimes through which government organizations and agencies have sought to achieve covert governmental goals through unethical or illegal means. Subtopics include the use of unknowing or unwilling human "guinea pigs" for officially sponsored medical experimentation, violations of the domestic sovereignty of other nations, and the surveillance and persecution of American citizens by agents of the government. Watergate, the Iran-Contra Affair, and the infamous Tuskegee study of untreated syphilis all serve as jarring examples of offenses in these areas. The recent shocking revelations about the use of torture by agents of the U.S. government is detailed.

Chapter 10 analyzes the proliferation of political corruption in the United States, concentrating on the structural features of certain institutions and organizations that facilitate malfeasance on the part of individual politicians and officials. Corruption is surveyed across all branches of government—executive, legislative, and judicial—and across all levels of authority—federal, state, and local. Separate consideration is given to police corruption, which represents a unique fusion of white-collar and street crime.

In the S&L debacle, as noted earlier, the ultimate victims were taxpayers, because they had to pick up the tab in the form of massive financial bailouts of failed S&Ls. **Chapter 11** explores another form of white-collar crime in which taxpayers ultimately foot the bill: Medicaid fraud. Medicaid is the government-funded health benefit program that provides medical care to low-income Americans, sometimes by high-income crooks. Special attention is given to the structure of Medicaid, as well as Medicare, which seems to encourage abusive practices by physicians, hospital administrators, nursing home operators, home care providers, medical equipment suppliers, and other healthcare professionals.

One of the fascinating aspects of white-collar crime is the way in which new technology creates opportunities for new types of thievery. Nowhere has this been more evident than in the area of computer crime, now the fastest growing form of crime. **Chapter 12** describes a variety of computer-based offenses, including high-tech embezzlement, malicious hacking and denial-of-service attacks, the dissemination of pernicious computer viruses and worms, industrial and international espionage, long-distance telephone toll frauds, and computer piracy operations that undermine the "new economy."

Finally, **Chapter 13** seeks to tie together the sundry topics of the preceding chapters by addressing fundamental issues and questions regarding societal, institutional, and organizational causes of white-collar crime. Major sociological and criminological explanations are considered, along with the distinctive manner in which law enforcement agencies, the mass media, and the general public respond to white-collar crime. This chapter also examines broader economic, environmental, and human consequences, stressing the need for popular recognition that white-collar crime can be enormously destructive in both direct and indirect ways.

This book concludes, however, on a more optimistic note by focusing on some effective strategies for controlling corporate lawlessness. The authors will argue that things may not be as hopeless as they appear. Ordinary citizens have more resources at their disposal than they may realize to combat what too often seems to be the insatiable greed of the white-collar criminal.

Notes

1. Coen, Jeff and Chase, John. *Golden: How Rod Blagojevich Talked Himself Out of the Governor's Office and into Prison.* Chicago: Chicago Review Press. 2012. 1–24.

2. *Ibid.*, 299.

3. United States Attorney, Northern District of Illinois [press release]. "Illinois Gov. Rod R. Blagojevich and His Chief of Staff John Harris Arrested on Federal Corruption Charges." December 9, 2008.

4. *Ibid.*

5. Zorn, Eric. "The Blagojevich Transcripts in Chronological Order." *chicagotribune.com.* July 5, 2011.

6. *Ibid.*

7. *msnbc.com.* "Prosecution Failed, Blagojevich Says." August, 22, 2010.

8. *huffingtonpost.com.* "Blagojevich: Patti Ate Tarantula For Her Family." July 3, 2009.

9. *huffingtonpost.com.* "Rod Blagojevich Washing Dishes In Prison, Will Teach Shakespeare After 90-Day Dish Duty Stint Ends." April 23, 2012.

10. Zorn, *op. cit.*

11. Robinson, Mike and Tarm, Michael. "Blagojevich Trial: Rod And Patti Spent $400,000 On Clothes Over Six Years." *huffingtonpost.com.* July 1, 2010.

12. Kass, John. "Not All of Blagojevich's Missteps were Criminal, Some Were Just Stupid." *chicagotribune. com.* March 15, 2012.

13. NBCNEWS.com. "Illinois Has a Long Legacy of Public Corruption." *nbcnews.com.* December 9, 2008.

14. Sutherland, Edwin H. *White-Collar Crime: The Uncut Version.* New Haven, CT: Yale University Press, 1983; 7.

15. *Ibid.*, 7.

16. *Ibid.*, 6.

17. *Ibid.*, 7.

18. *Ibid.*, 9.

19. *Ibid.*, 9.

20. Berger, Peter. *Invitation to Sociology: A Humanistic Perspective.* New York: Anchor, 1963; 38.

21. Geis, Gilbert and Goff, Colin. "Introduction." In Sutherland, *op. cit.*, ix–x.

22. McCormick, Richard. "The Discovery that Business Corrupts Politics." *American Historical Review* 86, 1981: 256.

23. Sinclair, Upton. *The Jungle.* New York: Harper and Brothers, 1951.

24. Fligstein, Neil. *The Transformation of Corporate Control.* Cambridge, MA: Harvard University Press, 1990.

25. Yergin, Daniel. *The Prize.* NY: Simon and Schuster, 1991.

26. Norris, Frank. *The Octopus: A Story of California.* New York: Penguin, 1986.

27. Brandeis, Louis. *Other People's Money, and How the Bankers Use It.* New York: Kelly, 1971, 4.

28. *Ibid.*, 4.

29. *Ibid.*, 4.

30. Ross, E.A. *Sin and Society: An Analysis of Latter-Day Inequity.* New York: Houghton, Mifflin, 1965; 54.

31. Obermair, Otto G. "A Century of New York's Crimes, Criminals, and Trial Lawyers." *The New York Law Journal* 10, 2000: 19–24. Arnstein was later immortalized in the popular musical play and movie *Funny Girl.*

32. Robinson, James F. *The Man Who Sold the Eiffel Tower.* New York: Pocket Books, 1963.

33. Goebel, Greg. "The Confidence Artists." *vectorsite. net.*

34. *Ibid.*

35. *Crimes of the 20th Century: A Chronology.* New York: Crescent Books, 1991.

36. *Boston Globe.* "Ponzi Secret Dark to French Bankers." August 2, 1920: 1, 3.

37. Russell, James. "Ponzi-Like Schemes Snare Unwary Around the World." *Miami Herald,* August 8, 1994: 1K.

38. As recently as 1995, the Foundation for New Era Philanthropy was accused of operating a massive Ponzi scheme in which charitable organizations were promised they would double their endowments in just 6 months with large matching gifts from anonymous donors. "These donors apparently didn't exist and new contributions are alleged to have been used as the source to 'double' the old contribution" (Johnston, Jeffrey L. "Following the Trail of Financial Statement Fraud." *Business Credit* 97, October 1995: 47).

39. Zuniga, Jo Ann. "3 Arrested in Pyramid Scheme." *Houston Chronicle,* September 9, 2000: 35A.

40. *Securities and Exchange Commission v. Stanford International Bank, Ltd., et al.,* Case No.: 3:09-cv-0298-N (N.D. Tex, 2009) ("Complaint").

41. Hennessy-Fiske, Molly. "R. Allen Stanford Sentenced to 110 Years for Ponzi Scheme." *latimes.com,* June 14, 2012.

42. Gilbert, Daniel and Eaglesham, Jeane. "Stanford Hit With 110 Years." *wsj.com,* June 14, 2012.

43. Weidlich Thomas "Nicholas Cosmo Receives 25 Years in Prison for $413 Million Ponzi Scheme." *bloomberg.com,* October 14, 2011.

44. Securities and Exchange Commission. "SEC Charges 14 Sales Agents In $415 Million Long Island-Based Ponzi Scheme." *sec.gov,* June 12, 2012.

45. Asher, Ed. "Arrests Crack Fraud Scheme, Authorities Say." *Houston Chronicle,* December 13, 1999: 1A, 6A.

46. Zuniga, *op. cit.*

47. *Houston Chronicle.* "Ex-Globetrotter Pleads Innocent in Fraud Case." June 17, 2003: 2A.

48. Kravets, David. "Lawyer Who Stole Settlement Money Sentenced to 14 Years in Prison." *sfgate. com,* April 19, 2005.

49. *irs.gov.* "Promoter of International Pyramid Scheme Sentenced to 10 Years in Prison." August 27, 2007.

50. *crimes-of-persuasion.com.* "Pyramid Investment Scammer Falls Victim to Nigerian Money Scam." January 1, 2007.

51. Raghavan, Sudarsan. "Man's Exemplary Ways Deceive Many." *Houston Chronicle,* January 8, 2000: 23A.

52. *Ibid.*

53. Weise, Elizabeth. "Spam Scam Slams a Chain of Fools." *USA Today,* February 8, 2000: 3D.

54. *Ibid.*

55. Miller, Leslie. "Senders of Junk E-Mail Warned." *USA Today,* February 6, 1998: 1D.

56. Weise, *op. cit.*

57. *The Nation.* "The National City Bank Scandal." March, 1933: 248.

58. Marvin, Mary Jo. "Swindles in the 1990s: Con Artists Are Thriving." *USA Today Magazine,* September 1994: 83.

59. Schilit, *op. cit.*

60. Quoted in Moore, Evan. "Billie Sol Estes: Last One Standing." *Texas* (*Houston Chronicle* Magazine), June 23, 1996: 10.

61. Estes was paroled in 1971 after serving 8 years. He returned to prison in 1979 for tax evasion. He was released again in 1984.

62. Orr, Kelly. "Corporate Crime, the Untold Story." *U.S. News and World Report,* September 6, 1982: 29.

63. Katz, Jack. "The Social Movement Against White-Collar Crime." In Bittner, Egon and Messinger, Sheldon (Eds.), *Criminology Review Yearbook,* Vol. 2. Beverly Hills, CA: Sage, 1980: 161–181.

64. Webster, William. "An Examination of FBI Theory and Methodology Regarding White-Collar Crime Investigations and Prevention." *American Criminal Law Review* 17, 1980; 276.

65. Clinard, Marshall and Yeager, Peter. *Corporate Crime.* New York: The Free Press, 1980.

66. Shapiro, Susan. *Wayward Capitalists.* New Haven, CT: Yale University Press, 1984.

67. Leonard, William and Weber, Marvin. "Automakers and Dealers: A Study of Criminogenic Market Forces." *Law and Society Review* 4, 1970: 407–424.

68. Denzin, Norman. "Notes on the Criminogenic Hypothesis: A Case Study of the American Liquor Industry." *American Sociological Review* 42, 1977: 905–920.

69. Braithwaite, John. *Corporate Crime in the Pharmaceutical Industry.* London: Routledge and Kegan Paul, 1984.

70. See, for examples: Wheeler, Stanton, Weisburd, David, and Bode, Nancy. "Sentencing the White-Collar Offender: Rhetoric and Reality." *American Sociological Review* 47, 1982: 641–649; Hagen, John, Nagel, Ilene, and Albonetti, Celesta. "Differential Sentencing of White-Collar Offenders." *American Sociological Review* 45, 1980: 802–820.

71. Gross, Edward. "Organizational Crime: A Theoretical Perspective." In Denzin, Norman (Ed.). *Studies in Symbolic Interaction,* Vol. I. Greenwich, CT: JAI Press, 1978; 55–85; Schraeger, Laura and Short, James. "Towards a Sociology of Organizational Crime." *Social Problems* 25, 1978: 407–419; Wheeler, Stanton and Rothman, Mitchell. "The Organization as Weapon in White-Collar Crime." *Michigan Law Review* 80, 1982: 1403–1426.

72. Coffee, John. "No Soul to Damn, No Body to Kick: An Unscandalized Inquiry into the Problem of Corporate Punishment." *Michigan Law Review* 79, 1981: 386–457.

73. Sheehy, Sandy. "Super Sleuth—White-Collar Criminals Beware: Ed Pankau Is Looking for You." *Profiles,* July 1992: 38–40.

74. Domanick, Joe. *Faking It in America: Barry Minkow and the Great ZZZZ Best Scam.* Chicago, IL: Contemporary Books, 1989.

75. *Ibid.,* 126.

76. Akst, Daniel. *Wonder Boy: Barry Minkow—The Kid Who Swindled Wall Street.* NY: Charles Scribner's Sons, 1990; 5.

77. Akst, Daniel. "Behind 'Whiz Kid' Is a Trail of False Credit Card Billings." *Los Angeles Times,* May 22, 1987: Sec. IV, 1, 3.

78. Akst, 1990, *op. cit.,* 270.

79. *Ibid.,* 272. Barry Minkow, still not yet 30, was paroled in 1994 after serving five years. While incarcerated, he underwent a self-proclaimed religious conversion and conducted evangelical Bible classes for small groups of inmates. Whether this represented a sincere spiritual transformation or just another scam only God and Minkow know for sure. But many who

remember the "old" Barry (including investors who lost their life savings in the ZZZZ Best collapse) remain skeptical.

80. Quoted in: Ivanovich, David. "How Big Embezzlement Surfaced." *Houston Chronicle.* July 2, 1999: 1C, 8C.

81. *Houston Chronicle.* "Collared." August 15, 1998: 38A.

82. *Ibid.*

83. *Houston Chronicle.* "Former U.S. Treasurer Sentenced to Prison, Fined for Tax Evasion." September 14, 1994: A11.

84. Levy, Clifford. "Store Founder Pleads Guilty in Fraud Case." *nytimes.com,* July 23, 1993.

85. United States Department of Justice (press release). "Seattle Man Pleads Guilty to Filing False Tax Return." September 30, 2004.

86. Torres, Blanca. "Bekins Moving Official Pleads Guilty in Tax Case." *seattletimes.com,* October 1, 2004.

87. *bloomberg.com.* "KPMG Will Pay $456 Mln Fine to Avoid Prosecution, People Say," August 27, 2005. *USAToday.com.* "First Andersen; Now KPMG," August 31, 2005.

88. *webcpa.com.* "Another Guilty Plea in KPMG Tax Shelter Case," December 26, 2006. *bloomberg.com.* "Bush Administration Seeks Settlement in KPMG Tax Case," August 3, 2005.

89. Crenshaw, Albert B. and Johnson, Carrie. "Regretful KPMG Asks For a Break." *Washington Post,* June 17, 2005: D1.

90. *latimes.com.* "8 May Be Charged in Probe of KPMG," August 25, 2005.

91. Weber, Joseph. "How Big a Cloud Is KPMG Under?" *businessweek.com,* June 17, 2005.

92. *USAToday.com.* "Report: Ex-KPMG Partners May Face Charges," August 3, 2005.

93. Glovin, David and Larson, Erik. "Former KPMG Executives Get Mixed Verdicts in Tax Case." *bloomberg.com,* December 17, 2008.

94. Browning, Lynnley. "Advisor to Plead Guilty in KPMG Tax Shelter Case." *nytimes.com,* August 20, 2007.

95. *AccountancyAge.com.* "Ex-KPMG Staff Found Guilty in US Tax Shelter Case," August 18, 2008.

96. *lawyrs.net* "Former KPMG Manager Larson Gets 10 Years for Tax Evasion," April 1, 2009.

97. Kearney, Christine. "Ex-KPMG Executives Sentenced to Steep Prison Terms." *uk.reuters.com.* April 2, 2009.

98. Safire, William. "Bureaucratic Bunglers Going Unpunished." *Houston Chronicle.* July 27, 1999: 18A.

99. Truex, Alyn. "Paradise Lost." *Houston Chronicle.* February 6, 2000: 1B, 13B. Tedford, Deborah. "Calumet Farms Officials Found Guilty of Bribery." *Houston Chronicle.* February 8, 2000: 1A, 8A.

100. Fried, Joseph P. "Financial Advisor Sentenced to 15 Months and Restitution." *New York Times.* March 10, 1997: B3.

101. Ivanovich, *op. cit.*

102. *Ibid.*

103. *Ibid.*

104. Quoted in *ibid,* 8C.

105. Gilmore, Janet. "Embezzler Comes Clean." *New York Daily News.* March 30, 1997: 1, 12.

106. *Ibid.*

107. *Ibid.*

108. Conlin, Michelle. "King Lear?" *Forbes* 158. September 23, 1996: 126–127.

109. *Ibid.*

110. *Ibid,* 126.

111. *Ibid.*

112. *Ibid,* 126.

113. *Ibid,* 126.

114. *Ibid.*

115. *Ibid,* 127.

116. *Ibid,* 127.

117. *Ibid,* 127.

118. *Ibid.*

119. Quoted in *ibid,* 127.

120. *Ibid.*

121. *Ibid,* 127.

122. *Ibid.*

123. Quoted in *ibid.,* 127.

124. Quoted in *ibid,* 127.

125. *irs.gov.* "Tax Attorney Sentenced to Prison for 15 Years." June 5, 2005.

126. Brady, Noel S. "Starbucks Embezzler Sentenced to Four Years." *kingcountyjournal. com,* November 23, 2002.

127. *Ibid.*

128. *Ibid.*

129. Engen, John R. "The Collapse of Keystone." *bankdirector.com,* October 2001.

130. *erisk.com.* "Case Study: First National Bank of Keystone." June 2002.

131. *Ibid.*

132. *Ibid.*

133. *Ibid.*

134. *Ibid.*

135. *Ibid.*

136. *Ibid.*

137. *Ibid.*

138. *Ibid.*

139. Quoted in Corcoran, Sr., David H. "The Corcoran Column: Editor Reminisces About Pittsburgh Bankers & Crime in Keystone." *glenvillenews.com,* August 6, 2004.

140. Ward, Getahn. "Former Bank Executive Faces Fines, Jail Sentence." *The Tennessean,* July 25, 2002: 4.

141. Cressey, Donald R. *Other People's Money: A Study in the Social Psychology of Embezzlement.* Glencoe, IL: Free Press, 1953.

142. *enr.construction.com.* "Ex-Tishman Manager Pleads Guilty to Embezzling $2.8 Million." August 5, 2007.

143. McCool, Grant. "Jury Finds Money Manager Vilar Guilty of Fraud." *reuters.com,* November 19, 2008.

144. Wakin, Daniel. "Music Patron Is Convicted of Fraud." *New York Times,* November 20, 2008: 1A.

145. Barnett, Megan. "Alberto Vilar's Fat Lady Has Sung." *portfolio.com,* November 19, 2008.

146. Stewart, James B. "The Opera Lover." *The New Yorker,* February 13 & 20, 2006: 108–122.

147. Grant, Alison. "Business Owners Never Think They Will Be a Victim." *Houston Chronicle,* August 6, 2007: D1, D4.

148. Quoted in *ibid.,* D1.

149. *Ibid.*

150. *cleveland.com/business.* "Fraud Prevention Expert Accused of Embezzlement . . . again." February 24, 2008.

151. *toledoblade.com.* "Convicted Embezzler Gets More Than Five Years in Prison." October 20, 2008.

152. Quoted in Grant, *op. cit.,* D4.

153. *ctdata.com.* "Currency Traders Allegedly Attempted to Use Attack to Hide Losses." November 8, 2001.

154. *nctimes.net.* "World Trade Center Broker Pleads Guilty to $110 Million Fraud." December 8, 2001.

155. *asia.reuters.com.* "Jury Convicts 4 in Currency Trade Fraud." June 27, 2003.

156. *cnn.com.* "Four Convicted in $100 Million Fraud." June 27, 2003.

157. For an example of this rationale, see the testimony of Richard Sparks before the House Committee on the Judiciary Subcommittee on Crime, in "White-Collar Crime," 95th Congress, 2nd Session, July 19, 1978: 162–165.

158. Sutherland, *op. cit.*

159. *Ibid.*

160. Clinard and Yaeger, *op. cit.*

161. Ross, Irwin. "How Lawless are Big Companies?" *Fortune,* December 1, 1980: 57–64.

162. Orr, Kelly. "Corporate Crime: The Untold Story." *U.S. News and World Report,* September 6, 1982: 25–29.

163. General Accounting Office. "Financial Statement Restatements: Trends, Market Impacts, Regulatory Responses, and Remaining Challenges." GA0-03-138. 2002.

164. Zhang, Yi. "Law, Corporate Governance, and Corporate Scandal in an Emerging Economy: Insights from China." Social Science Research Network. Working Paper. 2006.

165. U.S. General Accounting Office. *Defense Procurement Fraud: Cases Sent to the Department of Justice's Defense Procurement Fraud Unit* (GAO/GGD-86-142FS). Washington, D.C.: SEC, 1994.

166. What young Barry Minkow was to the 1980s, sixty-ish Robert Reed Rogers may be to the 1990s. Rogers, with at least a 20-year history of involvement in suspected scams, from precious metals to health care, was the CEO of Comparator Systems, a tiny Los Angeles company that was accused by the SEC in 1996 of one of the biggest stock swindles of the decade. Rogers' firm supposedly had developed a fingerprint identification device that would let businesses and governments quickly and affordably verify that people are who they claim to be. Not only was this machine slow and inefficient, Comparator did not even own it. Rogers allegedly stole a prototype from a Scottish inventor.

167. Blessed with superb salesmanship, Rogers attracted a throng of investors, including a high-ranking FBI agent, a Harvard astronomer, the former U.S. Ambassador to Italy, the crown prince of Yugoslavia's displaced royal family—who later committed suicide in the Comparator workshop—as well as many retirees and other small investors. The company had been publicly traded since 1979. Its initial offering was underwritten by the Denver-based penny stock specialist Blinder & Robinson—known derisively as "Blind 'em and Rob 'em." The founder of this sleazy (and now defunct) operation, Meyer Blinder, would later be convicted of racketeering and securities fraud. Eventually, Comparator had an incredible 600 million outstanding shares. By comparison, IBM (one of the largest corporations in the world) has 540 million outstanding shares.

168. Beginning in February, 1996, false rumors generated by unknown sources began flooding the Internet claiming that Comparator was negotiating a major deal with MasterCard International. When Comparator stock began to rise, Rogers fueled the fire with press releases that the company was negotiating with other important potential customers, including several foreign governments and large hospital chains wishing to provide technological assurance that mothers went home with the right babies. The result was a trading frenzy never before witnessed on Wall Street.

169. Over just three days in May, Comparator stock soared from 6 cents a share to nearly $2—about a 3,000 percent gain. It was the most active stock ever traded on the Nasdaq exchange, accounting for a quarter of Nasdaq's total volume over the three-day period. Market regulators halted trading of the stock after it discovered that Comparator had no customers and no commercially viable products.

170. On June 11, Comparator was delisted from the Nasdaq market. Some brokers, however, continued to quote the stock over the phone, and the following day a remarkable 2.2 million shares were traded. One dealer was bidding a mill (one-tenth of a penny) for the shares. One best not doubt that hope springs eternal.

171. And if one ever doubts, too, that America is still the land of opportunity, one need only take note that a company with worthless assets, a product it did not own, and a 29-person payroll it had not met in 11 years, became "valued" at $1 billion in 72 hours. (From Henry, David and Schmit, Julie. "The Big Lie." *USA Today,* June 7, 1996: 1B-3B; Miller, Greg and Lee, Don. "Comparator Conundrum: Honest Mistake or Con Job?" *Los Angeles Times,* June 8, 1996: A1, A26–A28; Henry, David. "Nasdaq Takes Comparator off Market." *USA Today,* June 12, 1996: 1B; Henry, David. "Comparator Still Finds Some Takers." *USA Today,* June 13, 1996: 1B.)

172. Day, Jacqueline. "Courting Disaster or Simply Business as Usual." *Bank Systems & Technology* 32, April, 1995: 38–41; Millman, Gregory J. *The Vandal's Crown: How Rebel Currency Traders Overthrew the World's Central Banks.* New York: Free Press, 1995.

173. Langberg, Mike. "White Collar Crime Erodes Faith in Business." *San Jose Mercury News,* February 12, 1989: p: 1E.

174. U.S. Securities Exchange Commission. *The Large Firm Project.* Washington, D.C.: SEC, 1994; ii. A dramatic example of alleged criminal abuses at major firms was a Paine-Webber broker who killed himself after he was accused of swindling three Beverly Hills clients out of a total of $115,000 (Kadetsky, Elizabeth. "A Tale of Two Scandals." *Working Woman* 19, September, 1994: 9–10).

175. *Ibid.*

176. Woodyard, Chris. "Local Stockbrokers Charged with Fraud." *Houston Chronicle,* December 1, 1995: 1C, 3C.

177. *Ibid.,* 1C.

178. *Houston Chronicle.* "Brokerage to Pay Fine over Two Execs' Actions." May 16, 2000: 5C.

179. Baldo, Anthony. "Sweeping the Street." *Financial World* (Special Edition), August 16, 1994: 61–63.

180. Lowry, Tom. "SEC: Half of Brokerages Use 'Rogue' Traders." *USA Today,* March 19, 1996: 1A.

181. Quoted in *ibid.,* 1A.

182. Barnes, Cecily. "Questionable Pasts Follow Internet Executives, Study Finds." *CNET.com,* October 26, 2000.

183. Pontell, Henry, Calavita, Kitty, and Tillman, Robert. *Fraud in the S&L Industry: White-Collar Crime and Government Response.* Final Report to the National Institute of Justice, Washington, D.C., 1994.

184. Titus, Richard, Heinzelmann, Fred, and Boyle, John. "Victimization of Persons by Fraud." *Crime and Delinquency* 41, 1995: 54.

185. *Ibid.*

186. U.S. Chamber of Commerce. *A Handbook on White-Collar Crime: Everyone's Loss.* Washington, D.C.: U.S. Government Printing Office, 1974.

187. Conyers, John. "Corporate and White-Collar Crime: A View by the Chairman of the House Subcommittee on Crime." *American Criminal Law Review* 17, 1980: 288.

188. *Ibid.*

189. Tillman, Robert and Indergaard, Michael. *Control Overrides in Financial Statement Fraud.* Institute for Fraud Prevention. 2007. *http://www.theifp.org/research/grants/recentstudies.html.*

190. Tillman, Robert and Indergaard, Michael. *Pump and Dump: The Rancid Rules of the New Economy.* 2005. New Brunswick, NJ: Rutgers University Press, p. 85.

191. U.S. General Accounting Office. "Federal Agencies Can, and Should, Do More to Combat Fraud in Government Agencies" (GGD-78-62). Washington, D.C.: U.S. Government Printing Office, 1978.

192. U.S. Congress, Senate Committee on the Judiciary. "White-Collar Crime." 99th Congress, 2nd Session, Part 1. February 27, 1986.

193. Titus *et al., op. cit.,* 59.

194. Granelli, James. "Forecast Is for $3.4 billion to Liquidate Lincoln Savings." *Los Angeles Times,* October 31, 1993: D1.

195. Federal Bureau of Investigation. *Uniform Crime Reports for the United States, 1992.* Washington, D.C.: U.S. Government Printing Office, 1993.

196. Coffee, John. Corporate Crime and Punishment: A Non-Chicago View of the Economics of Criminal Sanctions." *American Criminal Law Review* 17, 1980: 448.

197. Rossi, Peter, Waite, Emily, Bose, Christen, and Berk, Richard. "The Seriousness of Crimes: Normative Structure and Individual Differences." *American Sociological Review* 39, 1974: 224–237.

198. Cullen, Francis, Link, Bruce, and Polanzi, Craig. "The Seriousness of Crime Revisited." *Criminology* 20, 1982: 83–102.

199. Schwarzkopf, LeRoy C. "Rubbergate/ Kitegate: The House Bank Scandal." *Government Public Review* 19, 1992: 307–309.

200. Kuntz, Phil. "Check-Kiting at the House Bank: How It Worked, How It Didn't." *Congressional Quarterly Weekly Report,* February 29, 1992: 446–451.

201. This case appears to be yet another of those warped Horatio Alger stories so indigenous to Wall Street. When the accused had started at Kidder in 1991, after being fired by two other investment firms, he was reportedly sleeping on the floor of his one-room Manhattan apartment. Two years later, he had "earned" $9 million in bonuses.

In 1996, the SEC began holding lengthy hearings on the scandal. The targeted suspect denied any wrongdoing, characterizing himself as the victim of an attempt by Kidder to pin huge losses suffered by its highly visible mortgage department on an African-American scapegoat. In light of the evidence, most financial analysts found this defense spurious, although Kidder was roundly condemned for lax supervision and flawed accounting procedures. When the dust settles, it may very well turn out that the accused was both a crook *and* a scapegoat (Bary, Andrew. "Trading Points: Kidder Management's Excuse: Don't Blame Us, We're in Charge." *Barrons* 74, April 25, 1994: MW10-MW11; Queenan, Joe. "A Sure Tip-Off." *Barrons* 74, May 2, 1994: 54; Spiro, Leah N. "Why Didn't Kidder Catch on?" *Business Week* 3369, May 2, 1994: 121; *Economist.* "Kidder Peabody: Curioser." Vol. 331, June 11, 1994: 102–105; Celarier, Michelle. "Computer Fraud on Wall Street." *Global Finance* 8, July, 1994: 44–49; Mack, Gracian. "Another Scandal on Wall Street." *Black Enterprise* 24, July, 1994: 41–42; Spiro, Leah N. "They Said, He Said at Kidder Peabody." *Business Week* 3384, August 8, 1994: 60–62; Zecher, Joshua. "Kidder Fiasco Alarms Wall Street." *Wall Street & Technology* 12, September, 1994: 36–42; Weathers, Dianne. "Street Life." *Essence* 25, November, 1994: 81–82; Kerr, Ian. "The Fall of the House of Kidder." *Euromoney* 309, January, 1995: 30–34; *Jet.* "Wall Street Wiz Says Ex-Bosses Knew About $350 Million in Phony Deals." Vol. 87, March 13, 1995: 38; *Houston Chronicle.* "Ex-Kidder Trader: Bond Profit Strategy Not Wrong." May 26, 1996: 2C).

Gugliotta, Guy. "Congress: Membership Has Its Privileges." *Washington Post National Weekly Edition,* October 7–13, 1991: 15.

2

Crimes Against Consumers

On March 8, 1999, the U.S. Senate Permanent Subcommittee on Investigations convened hearings on the predatory marketing practices of sweepstakes companies. The Chair, Senator Susan M. Collins, characterized that industry's tactics as "increasingly deceptive and increasingly aggressive."[1] She cited scores of vulnerable consumers who had squandered their life savings on magazine subscriptions after being given the false impression that they were "guaranteed winners" of or "finalists" for a multimillion-dollar prize. Sen. Collins noted: "The disclaimer is in very small print and in a shaded background that doesn't show up."[2]

The first day of the hearings featured witnesses describing the experiences of their aging parents or in-laws who depleted their savings pursuing prizes but never winning. One woman testified that her elderly mother had spent about $40,000 on subscriptions in just two years. Another woman told the committee that her 86-year-old father had pleaded with her not to attend the hearings. "He is concerned that I am ruining his chances of winning."[3]

> Patti McElligott of Tyler, Texas said her late father-in-law had more than 158 magazine subscriptions, including 32 subscriptions to U.S. News and World Report. Even after the retired Army officer died, McElligott said she received a sweepstakes promotion declaring that his "estate is a winner."[4]

The most dramatic moment occurred when Eustace Hall, a 65-year-old retired medical technologist, broke down and sobbed while detailing his sweepstakes addiction. He had spent over $15,000 on contests since 1992 trying to help put his daughter through law school. He had been forced to return to work, refinance his house, and tap his pension. He had never won a dime.[5]

He pointed to a letter he had received from Publishers Clearing House—a major sweepstakes firm—in 1997. The letter stated that he was on the firm's "Best Customer List" and informed him of an upcoming contest.

> In the personalized letter, contest manager Dorothy Addeo wrote that she was "in a bit of hot water" because her boss wanted to know why "someone as nice as Eustace Hall doesn't win." Her mission, she said was to "personally guarantee" that Hall be a winner.[6]

Hall took this "personal guarantee" at face value. He believed his loyalty in ordering a multitude of subscriptions from Publishers Clearing House had finally been rewarded. He had no idea that this same "personal guarantee" had been mailed to 9 million other customers.[7]

Computer-generated personalized letters are a standard marketing ploy in the sweepstakes industry. The letters are skillfully constructed to draw the elderly, the retired, and the disabled into a seemingly personal relationship with the contest manager—typically a fictitious individual whose "signature" appears on each letter. Publishers Clearing House admits that it is all made up. But Christopher Irving, the company's director of consumer affairs, argues: "In terms of using a fictitious name, that's standard business practice followed by many, many, many companies."[8] A news release from Publishers Clearing House ridicules its critics: "Shhhhhh! Don't tell, but Betty Crocker, Uncle Sam, and Josephine the Plumber aren't real people either."[9]

True. But Betty Crocker has never promised consumers anything more grandiose than flakier piecrust—not $5 million, as Eustace Hall was "guaranteed."

When Deborah J. Holland, senior vice president of Publishers Clearing House, testified on the second day of the hearings, she dismissed Hall's letter: "This was advertising, a promotion, just like 'ring around the collar.'"[10] Committee member Senator Carl Levin saw it very differently: "You lied to a customer."[11]

CASE STUDY
"Family" Values

In December 1997 an elderly California man got off a plane in Tampa, Florida, for the *second* time in four months.[12] On each occasion he had expected to be greeted by television personality Ed McMahon, who was going to make him a millionaire a dozen times over. The 88-year-old retired steamfitter had received spectacular news: RICHARD LUSK, FINAL RESULTS ARE IN AND THEY'RE OFFICIAL: YOU'RE OUR NEWEST $12 MILLION WINNER.[13]

The man was overjoyed. He would soon be able to care properly for his bedridden wife of 65 years. It seemed too good to be true but it *had* to be true. "After all, the familiar face of Ed McMahon was on the envelope. Lusk trusts Ed McMahon."[14] But where was Ed? Not in Tampa.

And Ed was evidently not in Tampa either when a 53-year-old woman desperately borrowed money in order to fly to Florida with her two daughters from her neighborhood in the slums of Baltimore in order to collect the $11 million Ed told her she had "won." Her letter had been even more urgent:

COME FORWARD IN THE NEXT 5 DAYS—OR LOSE IT ALL. WE ARE WAITING FOR THE $11 MILLION WINNING NUMBER TO ARRIVE AT OUR TAMPA FLORIDA HEADQUARTERS.[15] So highly personalized was the message that it included documents that looked like official government papers, even threatening prosecution if anyone but her tampered with the letter.

A 76-year-old Florida woman, living on Social Security with her disabled husband, thought that the hundreds of precious dollars she had invested in magazine subscriptions had reaped a spectacular dividend when she received a mailing that read: YOU STAND ALONE AT THE TOP—YOU'VE SWEPT PAST 200,000+ OTHER WINNERS WITH OUR FIRST $11,075,000 PRIZE IN HISTORY.[16] She called the nearby American Family prize center to find out when she should come to collect her check. "[She] was told that the office was guarded and closed to the public."[17] Her grand prize turned out to be less than grand. In fact it turned out to be nothing.

(Continued)

These sad stories are hardly unique. Since 1994, more than 20 people, mostly elderly, have arrived in Tampa with stars in their eyes. "The stars soon turned to tears."[18] One sympathetic airport police officer has seen it too many times.

> We take them aside and show them the fine print—and sometimes it takes us quite awhile to find the disclaimer. We say, "See this little fine print? See where it says: Only if you have the winning number?" Then they start crying.[19]

This heartless ruse is the work of American Family Publishers, a New Jersey-based company half-owned by the giant Time Warner conglomerate. Its business is selling magazine subscriptions—millions of magazine subscriptions. For its efforts it receives 90 percent of the price of a subscription.[20] Huge ongoing sweepstakes are its signature marketing tool. It mails out an incredible 200 million promotional letters each year.

American Family employs two high-profile shills to help bait its traps: McMahon and the iconic media mogul Dick Clark, whose earlier brushes with questionable ethics are described in Chapter 6. McMahon resorts to defensive semantics when his role is criticized. He insists: "[T]here is a 'may' and an 'if' qualifying every sentence in American Family's promotions."[21] Clark appears to be less defensive. When he was asked if he had any misgivings about endorsing the sweepstakes, Clark replied: "None whatsoever."[22]

Nineteen percent of American Family's customers are over 65. In fact, the company has offered to sell the names and addresses of about 470,000 senior citizens, classified as "repeat customers," to other contests.[23] The elderly seem to be especially susceptible to American Family's seductive deceit. A Georgia Tech professor, specializing in aging and memory, explains: "Cognitive processes change in the normal course of aging . . . and those changes may leave some elderly people less able than they once were to evaluate sweepstakes pitches."[24] He also speculates that the elderly constitute a genera-

tion that may be misled more easily than younger generations. "They're less cynical about what they read and more trusting about what they see."[25] One retiree—with a fixed monthly income of about $900—took a 26-hour bus trip to Tampa to collect his promised jackpot. He acknowledged that he spends as much as $200 a month on magazines hoping to win the sweepstakes: "I run out of food now and then the fourth week of every month."[26]

The deceptive enticements that the company has perfected are blared at the elderly—and the not-so-elderly—by Clark and McMahon in big bold letters.

- **[Addressee's name], it's down to a 2-person race for the $11,000,000—You and one other person were issued the winning number—whoever returns it first gets it all.**
- **We have reserved an $11,000,000 sum in your name.**
- **Are you willing to risk letting your alternate take it all?[27]**
- **A mammoth fortune is at stake here—more money than you can possibly imagine. Don't risk letting $11.075,000 slip through your hands.[28]**

The "*if* you hold the winning number" disclaimers, however, are "typically in tiny print that is difficult for the elderly to read."[29] As Senator Collins observed, "People should not need a law degree or a magnifying glass to read the rules."[30]

Early in 1998, Florida filed suit against American Family, Ed McMahon, and Dick Clark claiming that their marketing scheme duped millions of Americans into buying unneeded magazines and tricked countless consumers into believing that they were sweepstakes winners. A major allegation was the company's use of deceptive language to mislead customers into thinking that they had no chance of winning without buying magazines. By law, making a purchase cannot elevate a contestant's odds in a legitimate sweepstakes.

American Family denied any wrongdoing, claiming that more than 400 winners have received

(*Continued*)

more than $77 million since the company entered the sweepstakes market in 1978.[31] But it was time for damage control. Barely six weeks later an agreement was announced under which American Family would stop promoting its sweepstakes with the slogan, "You're our next winner." The company further agreed to display prominently a "No Purchase Necessary" statement and offer customers a money-back guarantee. The agreement was the culmination of a coordinated multistate effort.[32] Thirty-two states would each receive $50,000. Florida and three other states, which rejected the agreement, reached a much heftier $4 million settlement with American Family in 1999.[33]

These state settlements, however, did not include lawsuits filed by disgruntled individual consumers, which continued to pile up. American Family repeatedly declared that it would not settle private lawsuits.[34] When a federal court in New Jersey consolidated these cases into dozens of class action suits,[35] American Family filed for Chapter 11 bankruptcy protection.[36]

Finally, in late 1999, American Family Publishers raised the white flag. The company offered to pay out $33 million to settle all outstanding claims.[37] Under the agreement, approved by the federal court, anyone who had spent more than $40 in a single year since 1992 purchasing magazine subscriptions from American Family and who had believed that their purchases had improved their odds of winning could file for a refund.[38] In addition, every American Family customer since 1992 would be entered automatically in a $1 million sweepstakes, with 10 people, chosen at random, receiving $100,000 each.[39] The company also agreed that future mailings would disclose the odds of winning, clearly state that no purchase is necessary, and print the rules in large type. It further agreed to discontinue its use of official-looking "government" documents.[40]

After American Family Publishers filed for bankruptcy, CEO Susan Caughman insisted: "It was not our intention to be deceptive."[41] Many law enforcers strongly disagree. Florida alleged that American Family "defrauded customers by repeatedly billing them for the same subscription and not paying them refunds when subscribers died."[42] The attorney general of Connecticut also rebuts Ms. Caughman's astonishing contention: "This is consumer deception at its worst."[43] This sentiment was echoed succinctly by another one of American Family's "best customers"—a 73-year-old New Jersey widow who subscribed to 20 magazines a year: "We were snookered."[44]

DIAL F FOR FRAUD

In 1990, more than 1.5 million American families found postcards in their mailboxes announcing: **ONE OF THE FOLLOWING PRIZES IS BEING HELD IN YOUR NAME!** The message seemed to guarantee that the addressee would receive a Mercedes automobile, a $10,000 cashier's check, a full-length mink coat, or a Hawaiian vacation for two simply by calling a 900 telephone number—at a cost of only $9.90.[45] A subsequent federal investigation revealed that the chance of someone winning any prize other than the Hawaiian vacation was effectively nonexistent. Moreover, winners of the "free" trip had to pay for their own airfare at greatly inflated prices through participating hotels. "The conditions were so unfair that less than one percent of those winning the vacation claimed their prize."[46] This transparent rip-off generated over $800,000 in telephone charges. According to the U.S. Postal Inspection Service, another 900-number sweepstakes scheme "bilked 170,854 callers out of $1.7 million in six weeks at $9.95 a pop."[47] As one personal finance writer has asserted: "It's not a prize if you pay for it."[48]

The burgeoning 900-number telephone industry illustrates how easily old crimes like consumer fraud can dovetail with new technology. From its benign inception in 1980,[49] when the first 900 number flashed on television screens during the Carter–Reagan presidential debate and invited viewers to vote for the winner by placing a 50-cent call, pay-per-call telephone services have become a billion-dollar key to American pocketbooks. In 1991, there were more than 10,000 "900 programs" in the United States—an increase of over 3,000 percent in just three years.[50] About 17 percent of American households make at least one 900 call each year.[51] One waggish columnist has declared: "I have seen the future, and it costs $2 for the first minute and $1 for each minute thereafter."[52]

This is not to say that all 900-number services are fraudulent. Many legitimate businesses provide useful information or technical support to customers on a pay-per-call basis. There is now even a service called Tele-Lawyer, which dispenses legal advice for $3 per minute.[53] But the opportunities for consumer abuse are rampant—as the following vignettes amply attest:

- A Seattle television advertiser told children to "call Santa Claus" by holding their phone up to the television speaker—which then emitted electronic tones that automatically dialed a 900 number and billed the household.[54]

- The developmentally challenged son of a North Carolina couple ran up over $9,000 in charges in less than a month by dialing a pay-per-minute "chat line." Apparently, the women at that 900 service had persuaded the young man to give them his home number, because, according to his mother, "[W]e're getting collect calls from them in jail asking for bail money!"[55]

- For a $2.99 call to a 900 telephone number, a Houston company offered American citizens the opportunity to win a free ride on the Russian space station. So many calls came in from around the country that the telephone system handling them collapsed.[56]

- An 11-year-old Tennessee boy answered the telephone and was told that he could win a free vacation trip for his parents if he would call a 900 number and answer the question: "What is the name of Batman's car?" He immediately called the number, correctly identified the Batmobile, and was then instructed to call another 900 number. "Eight months later, all his parents had received was a $120.72 phone bill."[57]

- For a $10 phone call, a Cleveland entrepreneur promised to fax a personalized message to Saddam Hussein during Operation Desert Storm. He claimed the proceeds would be used to help clean up the Persian Gulf oil spill and sponsor a welcome-home parade for American troops.[58]

- A Houston firm hired people responding to a help-wanted ad to pose as psychics on a 900 "hot line." Many of those who called these "psychics" reportedly were desperately distraught—in some cases even suicidal—over personal or medical problems. They were offered a free two-minute reading. When their free time elapsed, however, an additional 10 minutes would cost $32; employees were trained to keep callers on the line as long as possible. A spokesman for the company defended the service, arguing that it was "like counseling for poor people, the ones who can't afford $150 an hour for a shrink."[59] The only flaw in that philanthropic defense is that customers placing a 40-minute call to his phony network could be charged the same $150 psychiatrist's fee to hear advice from an out-of-work pool cleaner.

- The 909 long distance prefix for the Caribbean is also a favorite of electronic "junk mail" scams. Victims frequently find 809 messages on their pagers, and, not recognizing the international prefix, return the call, only to find a recording of someone providing worthless information while "talking very slowly."[60] In one case, unwitting callers were connected to a male impotency hotline recording, which produced hefty charges on their next phone bill.[61] An even more reprehensible version of this scam is worked by crooks who leave messages on telephone answering machines—either angry warnings about a nonexistent overdue bill or shocking news that a family member has been killed. In either case, stunned victims are instructed to call an "809" number immediately. One promoter raked in $50,000 in one month by billing "customers" $100 per call.[62]

Live "sex lines" now account for an estimated 5 to 10 percent of all "900" minutes logged.[63] One firm offered recorded sexually explicit "900" messages at "regular long-distance rates." It neglected to mention that the call was to the Netherlands Antilles.[64]

A particularly devious form of predation involves the unauthorized use of these "phone sex" services by minors, which reportedly is now epidemic. Promoters target teenage boys, drowning in their own testosterone. "And though all sex numbers say, 'You must be 18 to call,' who's checking?"[65] A 15-year-old Ohio boy once rang up a *$40,000* bill in one month by incessantly calling the Ultimate Pleasure Connection.[66]

THE MYTH OF THE FREE MARKET

Deceptive sweepstakes and dishonest 900-number[67] practices represent, of course, only two specks in the expansive universe of consumer abuse, for, of all the myriad forms of white-collar crime, crimes against consumers are the most prolific.[68] Only a relatively small number of adult patrons may be inclined to dial "900" sex lines at $10 a minute; but from the humble roll of mints each of us has purchased to the costly new car most of us have or will one day buy, we are all consumers.

Indeed, the modern capitalist state is fueled by the profits generated by the consumption of goods and services. Proponents of a pure free-market economy contend that, left to itself, the economy affords consumers sufficient protection, since unrestrained competition reduces prices and impels producers to improve the quality and safety of their goods and services.[69] These assertions, however, are based on an idealized *laissez-faire* model, which—as even the most libertarian economists would concede—has never existed. As we shall see later in this chapter, true competition has been more illusory than real in many markets.

Opponents of government regulation and legal intervention also argue that, since most businesses are law-abiding, there is no need for state controls. This position seems no more logical than proposing to raze our prisons, since most citizens are law-abiding.

A few hidebound theorists still adhere to the venerable rule of *caveat emptor* (let the buyer beware). "[They] point out that the best interests of consumers are served by giving them goods and services at the lowest possible price, and letting them decide whether or not to take the risk of getting unsatisfactory goods at low prices."[70] The flaw in such reasoning is that modern markets are often too complex for buyers to adequately understand the costs and risks of purchases. The *caveat emptor* doctrine, established by Roman law in the early years of the Empire, was predicated on the notion that purchasers could inspect the quality of goods before agreeing to buy. The problem then, as it still is today, was the risk of latent defects.[71] Furthermore, the assumption that cheapness is all the consumer wants is misguided.[72]

Crimes against consumers carry a heavy social cost. "Breakdowns in dealings between buyers and sellers affect the quality of life, the quantity of life, the reality of justice, and the credibility of government."[73] It is worth recalling that to the tiny Lilliputians of *Gulliver's Travels,* fraud was considered a far more serious crime than theft and was usually punished by death. Common sense and simple precautions, Swift wrote, can deter the thief; "but Honesty hath no Fence against superior Cunning."[74]

It is thus imperative that somewhere between the stifling governmental interference that has failed miserably in noncapitalist economies and the hands-off policy implied by the *caveat emptor* rule, a balance must be struck. American consumers, seeking nothing more than fair value in the marketplace, deserve to be protected. At the very least, a superordinate doctrine of *caveat venditor* (let the *seller* beware) must be institutionalized.

Over this chapter and the next (Chapter 3), we will consider six broad categories of crimes against consumers: (1) consumer fraud, (2) false advertising, (3) price-fixing, (4) adulterated food, (5) dangerous drugs and devices, and (6) quackery. As will be the case in subsequent chapters, such gross classification serves as a way to organize a substantial volume of material in a convenient but necessarily arbitrary format. Quite obviously, there is considerable overlap among the categories. *All* crimes against consumers could be treated as fraud, for example, in that they all involve deceptive practices. For our purposes, however, consumer fraud is operationalized as those relevant crimes that do not fall distinctly within the other five categories.

CONSUMER FRAUD

Consumer fraud has been condemned since Biblical times.[75] In the 13th century, Thomas Aquinas, in his *Summa Theologica,* condemned "a man who sells a lame horse as a fast one."[76] Seven hundred years later, a U.S. senator concluded that nearly a quarter of all the money spent by American consumers was for "nothing of value."[77] Consumer fraud entails the use of deceit, lies, or misrepresentations to entice customers to buy goods or services.[78] Sometimes, we read about instances so preposterous that even the solemn Thomas Aquinas might have struggled to suppress a grin.

- For years, one urban furniture store held a "Going Out of Business" sale every Friday. The owner invariably changed his mind over the weekend and opened for business as usual on Monday.[79]

- A "disabled" young man selling magazine subscriptions house-to-house, purportedly to pay for an operation, was observed by one homemaker literally jumping from his car, running around to the other side, pulling out a pair of crutches, and then hobbling up to her door.[80]

- Some 28,000 people shelled out $80 million to a company called Culture Farms in order to get rich quick by "growing smelly milk cultures on their windowsills."[81]

- A New Jersey jewelry company marketed "Faux Black Culture Pearls." Its ads featured terms like "brilliant," "fiery," and "dazzling." It also promised to include a "certificate of authenticity." Since "faux" is the French word for "false," the firm was actually guaranteeing that this cheap plastic piece of costume jewelry was *authentically false*.[82]

- A Texas mail-order firm ran newspaper ads throughout the country asking bald people to send samples of their remaining hair for an expert "scalp analysis" in order to determine if their locks could be restored. "Apparently they felt they could help everyone who applied . . . including the National Better Business Bureau employee who mailed hair from his cocker spaniel."[83]

- Other mail-order companies have advertised a "solar clothes dryer" and sent customers a small piece of old-fashioned clothesline and some clothespins. For $3.95, customers purchased a "universal coat hanger" and received a 10-cent nail.[84]

- Yet another disreputable mail-order company stated in its ad: "Money returned if not satisfactory." When disgruntled customers sought a refund, they received a notice stating: "Your money is entirely satisfactory and we therefore decline to return it."[85]

- A woman entered one of those familiar "You May Be a Winner" sweepstakes and "won" a mink coat. Unfortunately, it was made from the fur around the animal's genital area. According to a consumer advocate: "It had a unique odor when it rained."[86]
- A Chicago dance studio, which targeted lonely widows, reportedly sewed small Coke bottles into the pants of male instructors in a way designed to make the women think that their teachers had become sexually aroused by dancing with them.[87]

Stories like these conform to the Hollywood image of the roguish con artist. But there is a visceral meanness to many consumer frauds that belies any endearing stereotype. There is surely nothing roguish, for example, about some private adoption agencies that collect advance payments of $20,000 or more with no intention of ever finding babies for desperate infertile couples;[88] or phony finance companies that collect upfront fees from the creditless poor and then disappear without providing the promised loans;[89] or "affinity" swindlers who perpetrate investment frauds against victims who are linked to them by religion or ethnic background;[90] or crooked land promoters who beguile elderly couples into squandering their life savings on retirement property located in barren deserts or uninhabitable swamps.[91]

There is nothing amusing either about post-disaster con artists. When Hurricane Hugo hit the South Carolina coast in 1989, phony contractors canvassed neighborhoods collecting up-front material fees for needed repairs. After they would disappear, complaining victims would not even know their names or the names of their companies. A local consumer advocate recalls: "Some would have no better ID to report than 'He was driving a dark pickup.'"[92] And when hurricanes Katrina and Rita devastated the Gulf Coast in 2005, they spawned a host of bogus charity Web sites, fraudulent investment promotions, and other get-rich-quick schemes, along with the usual home- and roof-repair scams.[93]

The recent collapse of the home mortgage market, leaving millions of homes in foreclosure, has fueled a wave of rescue scams. In the most common version, a crooked rescue company offers to take over legal ownership of the home—temporarily of course. The homeowner then pays "rent" to the company, which is supposed to pay the mortgage, promising to return the home once the owner has regained his or her financial footing. Scammers often hide a deed-transfer clause in refinancing documents so that homeowners do not realize they have signed over title to their house.[94] The con artists then borrow as much as they can against the equity in the house, while collecting rent from the former owner—without ever making any mortgage payments. "In the end, the property still goes into foreclosure, and any equity the homeowner had built up is gone. Their financial ruin is complete."[95]

Another type of foreclosure scam involves phony offers to negotiate on behalf of people about to lose their homes. Legitimate credit counselors, many of them government certified, can help homeowners negotiate foreclosures. But some scammers promise to negotiate with a lender for a fee, then just take the money and run.[96]

A veteran police investigator has observed: "Society has come to view those who fall prey to confidence criminals as either greedy, gullible, or brain dead."[97] But while it is reassuring to believe that only the foolish can be swindled, "it often is the people who think they are too smart to fall for a scam who end up cheated."[98] Even persons whose judgment and business acumen are otherwise beyond reproach have been swindled in misleading franchise deals, worthless "rare" coin investments, fictitious vacation packages from bogus travel agencies, and innumerable other shady schemes. Individuals as sophisticated as filmmaker Woody Allen, author Erica Jong, the late sportscaster Don Drysdale, and even the noted economist Arthur Laffer reportedly have been victimized.[99] The truth is that anyone is vulnerable. Virtually all of us have been ripped off at one time or another—often again and again, sometimes without ever knowing it. A state securities commissioner has warned: "No one is safe—your doctor, the retired couple next door or the man who picks up your garbage."[100]

One of the best ways to understand the extent of consumer fraud is through surveys of victims. The 1991 survey discussed in Chapter 1 provided baseline data showing that nearly one-third of all American adults are the targets of either an attempted or successful "personal fraud"—the great majority of which are consumer frauds—every year.[101] One of the more extensive surveys conducted by the Federal Trade Commission (FTC) in 2004 asked respondents whether, in the past year, they had been victimized by one or more of 10 specific types of consumer fraud, including: credit repair fraud, advance loan schemes, and buyers club membership scams. Based on their results the researchers estimated that 25 million adult Americans, or over 11 percent of the adult population, had been victimized by one or more of these scams in a single year. A study commissioned by the American Association of Retired Persons (AARP) took a broader look at consumer fraud and abuse and found that about three-quarters of respondents reported having a "bad experience" in purchasing an item or a service in the past year, with the most common problem related to purchasing a defective product.[102] When the AARP researchers asked respondents about which professions they felt were most dishonest, at the top of the list was, not surprisingly, used car dealers; 75 percent of those interviewed stated that more than half of all used car dealers misled consumers.[103] In terms of the prevalence of consumer fraud, the FTC estimated that the total number of such offenses perpetrated annually was *35 million*. In comparison, all street crimes numbered about *24 million* in 2004.[104]

Auto-Repair Rip-Offs

In a Harris poll, business managers were asked to choose the industry they believed required the most attention from the consumer movement. The landslide "winner" was auto repairs.[105] A Roper poll reported that 70 percent of respondents believed that they were "quite often" or "almost always" deceived or overcharged by auto mechanics.[106] A former chairman of the Senate Consumer Subcommittee has reported that letters about auto repairs make up the largest category of complaints that the congressional panel receives.[107] The FTC has charged that 30 percent of the billions of dollars Americans spend annually to fix their cars goes for unnecessary work.[108] "By simple arithmetic this means—however incredible it may seem—that every day of the year auto repair shops cheat Americans out of $57 million."[109]

Many of those frauds are committed by greedy mechanics in independent repair shops. An unfortunate Mexican tourist brought his expensive French Citroen to a Dallas shop, which replaced a number of parts at a cost of $850. When a city consumer affairs investigator dismantled that car later, responding to the owner's complaint, it was discovered that several of the "replaced" parts had in fact never been replaced at all. They simply "had been buffed down to their shiny metallic surface in an apparent attempt to make them look new."[110]

In 1987, an investigative reporter drove a three-year-old Oldsmobile Cutlass across the country, stopping at 225 garages in 18 states. The car had been meticulously prepared prior to departure and was in perfect running order—"engine tuned, transmission serviced, new spark plugs, brakes, shock absorbers, struts, fan belts and hoses."[111] Every vital component had been checked and, if there were any doubt, replaced. Before each stop, the reporter pulled a single spark plug wire loose. At 56 percent of the garages, mechanics performed unnecessary work or charged for repairs not done. Estimates ran as high as $495. Some mechanics even deliberately sabotaged the vehicle in order to fatten repair bills.[112]

Far more troubling, however, is that much of the auto repair fraud that has been uncovered implicates major corporate chains, whose stature and public trust are far removed from fly-by-night garages. Criminologist Paul Jesilow had research assistants bring a perfectly functioning car battery to 338 California sites for testing, including such corporate giants as K-Mart, Goodyear, and Firestone. All the confederates employed in the study were female because women are believed to be particular targets of auto repair fraud. The battery was pre- and post-tested by the researchers and was found able to sustain a 200-volt load for 15 seconds—equivalent to starting a car on a very cold day with the heater and radio running. Nevertheless, nearly 10 percent of the sites recommended the purchase of a new battery.[113]

Probably the most well-documented case of auto repair fraud involved Sears, Roebuck & Company, one of the country's biggest retailers. In 1990, prompted by a growing number of complaints, the California Department of Consumer Affairs launched an 18-month undercover investigation of billing practices at 33 Sears automotive repair centers. In its final report, the department described how its agents had been overcharged nearly 90 percent of the time, by an average of $223.[114] Agents had taken 38 cars with worn brakes but no other mechanical defects to Sears centers throughout the state. In 35 cases, they were told that additional and more expensive repairs were required.

> The worst example was in the San Francisco suburb of Concord, where an agent was overcharged $585 to have the front brake pads, front and rear springs, and control-arm bushings replaced. In other instances, cars were returned damaged or even unsafe, with loose brake parts or improperly installed coil springs.[115]

The report blamed Sears' commission-based pay schedule, which rewarded unnecessary work. The company earlier had cut mechanics' hourly wages and put them on piece-work incentives, while simultaneously pressuring service advisers to meet sales quotas.[116] Sears initially denied all allegations, but soon hoisted the white flag and began placing full-page newspaper ads conceding (albeit in the passive voice) that what it termed "mistakes" had occurred. It rescinded commission payments for automotive service advisors.[117] In 1992, in what was believed to be the largest consumer fraud settlement ever reached, Sears agreed to provide refunds for overcharged customers throughout California, reimburse the state $3.5 million to cover the cost of the investigation, and contribute $1.5 million to mechanic training programs. In addition, the company pledged to distribute $46.6 million in coupons to disgruntled consumers nationwide.[118]

Telemarketing Fraud

Another form of consumer fraud becoming increasingly more invasive is the telemarketing swindle. In 1988, aggressive con artists were using telephones to reach out and cheat consumers out of an estimated $10 billion.[119] In 1992, the total was revised upward to $15 billion.[120] By 1995, the figure had swollen to more than $40 billion,[121] and a survey commissioned by the Consumer Protection Network reported that 90 percent of Americans had been targeted at least once.[122] One could argue that heavy selling has supplanted heavy breathing as the defining feature of the modern obscene phone call.

Of course, not all phone sales are made by crooks. Many reputable companies utilize telemarketing to promote their products and services. But the assortment of telephone scams is bewildering. At the lower end of the scale, supplies of "miracle" vitamins are peddled for $100 or more. "Unfortunately, the product is generally worth around $30—if it arrives at all."[123]

Similarly disingenuous was a company which called families with an "exciting" announcement that they had won a power boat. "Predictably, the $200 shipping costs tangibly exceeded the less than $50 value of a rubber inflatable boat with a battery driven eggbeater-like engine."[124]

At the higher end, thousands of dollars are sucked into bogus investments in precious and strategic metals, oil and gas drilling, coins, gems, foreign currencies, penny stocks, and just about anything else with an allure of big profits.[125] A Georgia woman, for example, invested $10,000 in a $2-a-share gold-mining corporation pitched over the phone by a penny stock brokerage firm. A year later, the stock had fallen to 20 cents. When the victim belatedly checked out her investment, she discovered that the company owned some land near a gold mine—but did not own the mine.[126]

In recent years foreign currency frauds have become increasingly lucrative. Telemarketers were quick to jump on this bandwagon. Forex scams tempt customers with sophisticated-sounding offers emphasizing the lure of **leverage**: the right to "control" a large amount of foreign currency with an investment representing only a fraction of the total cost. Coupled with "expert" predictions of rising currency prices, these contracts promise huge returns over a short time with little or no downside risk. In a typical case, investors may be assured of earning tens of thousands of dollars in just a few weeks, with an initial investment of "only" $5,000. The money, of course, is never invested; it is kept by the con artists. For example, David Luger, who operated Worldwide Forex, was sentenced to 13 years in a Florida prison in 2006 for telemarketing fraud.[127] Luger had been bilking victims out of millions of dollars for years.

In 2006, Russell Cline was sentenced to 97 months in prison after pleading guilty to fraud and money laundering. Cline had enticed novice forex investors by promising returns of 60 to 200 percent.[128] Starting in 1998, Cline and his company, Orion International, fraudulently solicited customers to purchase illegal off-exchange forex options and futures contracts by misrepresenting the profits and risks. In 2005, the incarcerated Cline was ordered to pay more than $33 million in one of the largest individual fines ever imposed by the Commodity Futures Trading Commission (CFTC), the federal agency responsible for currency trading.

In 2007, Kenneth Hodgell and Kenneth Kempton were sentenced to 120 and 87 months, respectively, in federal prison for running a telemarketing operation that purported to raise money from investors for a range of purposes, including financing and operating insurance companies, mining and refining gold, issuing consumer rebate cards, operating community centers, financing medical research, and building a religious theme park. None of the money in fact was invested in anything other than the homes and hefty bank accounts of the two Kenneths. In addition to their prison terms, Hodgell and Kempton were ordered to forfeit $2.3 million and to pay over $20 million in restitution to more than 50 victims, many of whom were targeted through churches.[129]

The most ruthless telemarketers are nothing if not opportunistic; they will exploit any misfortune, from natural disaster, to illness, to war, to death. Following natural disasters, con artists often call local residents under the pretext of charity solicitations and pocket the donations.[130] Customers have also been given the ghoulish chance to reap big profits by supposedly investing in life insurance policies on persons with AIDS.[131] Unauthorized telemarketers have solicited contributions for a San Diego summer camp for young burn victims. The camp never received a penny of the proceeds.[132] Global tensions likewise generate a receptive environment for fraud. The conflict in the Persian Gulf in 1991 enabled swindlers pushing domestic energy investments to "play on Americans' fear of dependence on foreign oil."[133] When two Virginia firefighters were killed in a terrible 1996 warehouse fire, telemarketers began calling local residents claiming to be raising funds for the families of the victims. Predictably, neither of the families ever received any money.[134] And when the work of renowned Spanish painter Salvador Dali jumped in value following the artist's death, reams of fake Dali prints were sold to unsuspecting investors. A Virginia chiropractor bought seven counterfeit prints for $8,700.[135] "Salvador Dali fakes are so common now that the Better Business Bureau . . . refers to complaints as 'Hello, Dali' calls."[136]

Perhaps the most cynical opportunism of all involves the targeting of the elderly. According to a congressional subcommittee, senior citizens, who comprise about 12 percent of our population, make up at least 30 percent of fraud victims.[137] The reason for such disproportionate selection is that high-pressure telemarketers know that the elderly often have substantial savings, lump-sum pensions, or home equity. America's over-65 population has a combined personal income of more than $800 billion and accounts for almost 75 percent of the net worth of the nation's households.[138] Also, the elderly tend to be home more often than younger people. Moreover, studies indicate that the longer one remains on the phone, the better the chance a telemarketer has of making a sale. Older people are products of a generation that stressed politeness; so they are less inclined to hang up abruptly.[139]

Many senior citizens not only have cash but are desperately lonely—an enticing combination for telemarketers determined to test the boundaries of sleaze. Elderly Florida residents were willing to pay $20,000 for a lifetime's worth of dance lessons. "Some were too frail to walk."[140] In St. Louis, similarly incongruous long-term dance lesson contracts were sold for between $80,000 and $250,000.[141]

In 1994, an 85-year-old woman was referred to the National Fraud Information Center (NFIC) by a private mail carrier after she had called to have a $20,000 check delivered to some "nice man" in Florida. "When interviewed by the NFIC counselor, the woman was unable to tell what the $20,000 was for. 'They just told me to send it, and that's what I mean to do,' she replied."[142]

An 80-year-old New York woman sent thousands of dollars to a Chattanooga, Tennessee, telemarketing operation because she had become "addicted" to the attention they paid her.

> "I've been a widow for 19 years. It's very lonely. They were nice on the phone. They became my friends."[143]

One older couple lost their entire life savings of $350,000 to a relentless rare coin operation.[144] A 72-year-old former school superintendent was fleeced of $225,000 in a commodities contract scam run by a precious metals firm in Newport Beach, California. Another Newport Beach commodities dealer snatched $10,000 from a Baptist minister in rural upstate New York.[145] Con artists generally favor warmer climates, and Newport Beach, on the coast of upscale Orange County, has become the "Emerald City" of telemarketing fraud. "An office-space glut in swindler-riddled Orange County enables crooks to negotiate several months of free rent, then skip out to a new site when the payments come due."[146] The FBI estimates that there are 5,000 "boiler rooms" in Southern California alone.[147]

At the heart of telemarketing fraud are the infamous "boiler rooms"—spartan offices containing little else but banks of telephones[148] manned by glib hustlers working their way through computerized "sucker lists" with carefully scripted pitches.

> Once they get you on the phone, salesmen quickly activate your greed glands. That is accomplished by asking a simple question, such as "If you could make 30 percent on your savings in the next three months without taking any risks, would you be interested?" Only Mother Teresa would say no.[149]

The classic telephone swindle consists of three calls known as the *front,* the *drive,* and the *close.*[150] The front will introduce the customer to the scheme. The salesman tries to learn how much money the "mark" has—or, more precisely, how much of it he can grab. He promises to send descriptive literature, which usually arrives a few days later and consists of an impressive-looking folder containing a great deal of unspecific material but little concrete information. The drive comes shortly after the folder is received. Now the salesman makes his hard sell, bombarding the target with empty slogans and statistics. The close follows within a short time. The salesman tries to create a sense of urgency, and it is here that many worn-down consumers finally cave in.

Victims are called "marks" because, once fleeced, they are marked as lifelong targets. A recurring form of telemarketing fraud is the "reload" scam, in which swindlers take a second shot at consumers who already have been victimized.[151] Their pitch is brazen but can be psychologically compelling to someone desperate to recoup painful financial losses.

> Hello, Mrs. Luckless? This is John DeRoach with the Guys-Next-Door Brokerage, and I'm calling you today because I understand you lost a lot of money with the Trust-Is-Us Coin Co . . . Yeah, they were real crooks . . . $10,000, huh? Tsk, tsk, tsk. What a shame. Well, I've got a program here with a legitimate company that will allow you to double your money and make up your losses. All we need to get started is $5,000."[152]

A typical reload scam was perpetrated by California crook William Vorburger, Jr. He operated Valley Precision Imaging and Desert Medical Imaging, both supposedly body-scanning clinics, and Multivision, an Internet shopping Web site. Vorburger told investors that he would use their money to expand his businesses, which would result in high rates of return. He admitted in his plea bargain that none of these businesses ever actually started running or made a single dollar in profits. Vorburger later "reloaded," warning his mostly elderly victims that they would lose all the money they had already invested if they did not send in more money. In total, Vorburger's 15 victims sent him over $1 million. He was convicted of fraud and money laundering, sentenced to 108 months in prison, and ordered to repay his investors.[153]

An especially despicable variation on "reload" is the so-called "rip and tear" scam. Here, telemarketers call previous victims, posing as law enforcement agents. They offer to help recover some of the victim's losses if the victim will pay an official fee for the recovery effort.[154]

CASE STUDY
The Attack of the Toner-Phoner

One of the biggest and most incredible telemarketing assaults on an individual target ever reported was a variation of the reload technique, combining elements of traditional business fraud with outright blackmail.[155] The office manager for a small school district in a Philadelphia suburb received a long-distance call from a California office-supplies distributor. She ordered some green felt-tipped pens that teachers had been requesting, and, when the shipment subsequently arrived with an invoice, she wrote out a check for a few hundred dollars and sent it to the company.

After she placed several more legitimate orders, a company representative, calling himself "Mr. Chester," an alias of indicted fugitive Marc Suckman, contacted her and told her that because

(Continued)

she was such a good customer they would like to send her a pocket tape recorder as a token of their appreciation. This gift-giving ploy is a "hook" frequently used by office supplies hustlers, who are sometimes called "toner-phoners," for the copy machine accessories many of them push. She agreed to accept this inexpensive present—a seemingly innocuous decision that ultimately would ruin her life.

A few weeks later, Mr. Chester phoned to say he was shipping the balance of her order. In fact, there was no balance, since she had not placed an order; but Mr. Chester convinced her that she had done so and was thus obligated. Once she acquiesced, Mr. Chester began calling monthly, pressing one order after another on her. When cartons of colored markers began filling the storage closet, leaving little room for other supplies, she informed Mr. Chester that the school district did not need any more pens. She was told that there was an outstanding balance of nearly $4,000, for which he demanded a final check to close out the account. When she balked at this absurd claim, Mr. Chester threatened that if she did not pay that amount, he would inform the school board that she had solicited a personal gift for placing the orders. He had no idea how effective this threat would be.

[S]he was terrified of losing her job. . . . Her two kids were approaching college age and

she and her husband, a mailman and part-time coach at the school, were saving every penny to pay for tuition.[156]

She agreed to settle the fraudulent account, believing that she had heard the last of Mr. Chester. But, as any less naive person could have predicted, he called back a month later, claiming a new outstanding balance of $4,200. When she resisted, Mr. Chester threatened to reveal that she had already sent his company an unauthorized check for goods she never received. She paid that bill and others that followed—sometimes three a month. She covered up her coerced embezzlement by juggling computer records and whiting out names on canceled checks.

Eventually, the deficit grew so gargantuan that she could no longer balance the books, even dishonestly. When a new superintendent discovered the financial discrepancies, she was arrested by the FBI and quickly confessed. Over just a three-year period, she had sent Mr. Chester (Suckman) over 130 checks totaling more than *$2 million*—about a third of the school district's entire budget—in payment for absolutely nothing. And all she had ever personally gained from her illegal efforts was a cheap Taiwanese tape recorder. Batteries not included.

As the staggering costs of telemarketing fraud spiral upward, law enforcers have begun to allocate more attention and resources to this problem. Between 1995 and 1998, an FBI operation dubbed *Double Barrel* produced criminal charges against nearly 1,000 telemarketers. Double Barrel utilized retired FBI agents and postal inspectors, as well as senior citizens recruited by the American Association of Retired Persons (AARP), to pose as previous marks targeted by "reload" scams. They recorded the phone calls for evidence. These volunteers produced over 11,000 recordings of conversations with scammers.[157] In the words of one FBI agent assigned to Double Barrel:

The tapes are the best evidence we've ever had. You've got them saying, "I can guarantee you're going to win that car. What color would you like, Mabel?" You can get all the lies on tape.[158]

One AARP volunteer, who has produced about 3,000 recordings, adds: "When you know you're taping them, it's really kind of comical. They're hanging themselves."[159]

Two of the most notable figures caught in the Double Barrel were John A. Field III and Marcus K. Dalton. Field is a former federal prosecutor and former director of enforcement for the U.S. CFTC, who switched from fighting crime to committing crime. His operation sold units of the imaginary United Currency Exchange Ltd. of London. Field also served as something of a guru to con artists, advising telemarketers on how to structure their offerings to avoid scrutiny from federal regulators.[160] Dalton, considered one of the country's most prolific securities fraud artists, admitted to selling at least $80 million in bogus securities, "including phony wireless cable operations, bridge loans to finance a wireless venture in American Samoa, and fraudulent shares in Treasure Chest Television, a children's programming investment."[161]

Like other white-collar criminals, telemarketing fraudsters tend to view their victims as deserving of their plight. In a study of convicted telemarketers, Shover and his colleagues quoted one whose views of his victims were typical.

> If these people can't read, so be it. Screw them, you know. It [doesn't say] *everybody's* gonna get the diamond and sapphire tennis bracelet. They're dumb enough not to read, dumb enough to send me the money, I really don't care, you know. I'm doing what I have to do to stay out of jail. They're doing what they have to do to fix their fix. They're promo junkies, and we're gonna find them and get them, and we're gonna keep getting them. And they're gonna keep buying, and, you know what I used to say, "They're gonna blow their money in Vegas, they're gonna spend it *somewhere*. I want to be the one to get it.[162]

This "deserving victim" rationalization was just one of many that telemarketers used to justify the fleecing of unsuspecting consumers. Another common "technique of neutralization" (see Chapter 13) was to claim that

> They were involved in sales transactions that were, in fact, not appreciably different from those typically encountered in legitimate commercial settings. Telemarketers did not see themselves as exploiting innocent and undeserving victims. Instead, they were simply engaging in what they defined as routine sales transactions.[163]

. . . And the Poor Get Poorer

People in financial difficulty are often easy prey because of their desperation. Fraudulent loan companies purchase lists of persons experiencing hard times, such as those involved in foreclosure proceedings, and either telephone them or mail them loan applications guaranteeing approval—in exchange for up-front fees. One such company operated in Arizona in the summer of 1991. It received 1,702 loan applications, each accompanied by a $249 "fee." When one does the math, one finds that "this modestly-sized scheme grossed almost $425,000 in just 90 days."[164] In 2003, another Arizona telemarketing company settled federal fraud charges of swindling tens of thousands of people out of at least $20 million in an advance-fee credit card scheme. The firm allegedly employed hundreds of boiler-room operators trained to trick consumers into sharing personal financial information and then charge their credit cards and take money from their bank accounts without permission. Ironically, the company also sold protection services against identity theft and telemarketing fraud.[165] The Better Business Bureau estimates that advance-fee loan scams cost consumers more than $1 million each month.[166]

In late 2006, the co-owners and three office managers of Gecko Communications, a Kansas City, Missouri, telemarketing firm, received federal prison sentences ranging from 24 to

135 months for defrauding an estimated 50,000 victims out of more than $15 million.[167] Gecko bought lists of creditless persons from brokers, and its telemarketers fraudulently offered them preapproved credit cards for an advance fee of about $200. According to the U.S. Attorney's office in Missouri,

> In reality, not a single customer received a credit card; at most, victims only received applications for credit cards. These were low-income and credit-challenged people who couldn't qualify for credit cards, as the defendants knew, so an application was worthless to them.[168]

Unscrupulous players in the burgeoning home equity loan business constitute another example of how financially desperate people can be exploited by so-called "bird dog" salesmen. The market for high-rate second mortgages to disadvantaged consumers is estimated at $35 billion.[169]

> Hundreds of thousands of homeowners have been victimized in the past decade. Tens of thousands have lost their homes; still more have seen their equity sucked out by exorbitant fees and usurious interest rates charged by predatory mortgage companies. . . . Many are targets because they are old or illiterate. Others are vulnerable simply because they are poor.[170]

An elderly Alabama man with a poor credit history was given a home equity loan for $1,353. The interest was so high and bloated with so many fees, charges, and points (a point equals 1 percent of the mortgage principal) that his effective annual rate was 61.4 percent.[171] A Georgia woman took out a $5,000 home improvement loan at such high interest that she had to refinance the loan twice. "By the third loan, she would have been required to repay a total of $63,000 if she had not declared personal bankruptcy."[172] After receiving her loan, a California woman faced monthly payments of $2,000—on an income of $1,000.[173]

As in the preceding case, some second mortgages are structured so that repayment is impossible. The real goal is foreclosure. The firm can then resell the house to another buyer who cannot afford the payments, and the cycle begins again. It is not unusual for a finance company to resell the same home four or five times.[174]

Many of these companies are owned or backed by "respectable" banks, who are lured by the big money in home equity loans but repelled by the dirtiness of the business. Participation by proxy allows mainstream financial institutions to enjoy the best of both worlds—usurious profits and clean hands. Fleet Financial, New England's largest bank, illustrated this symbiosis when it extended a $7.5 million line of credit to one of that region's most notorious lenders—Resource Financial. According to a study, three-quarters of the families who borrow money from Resource lose their homes.[175] When a reporter asked Fleet vice president Robert Lougee, Jr., about his bank's complicity in the mass foreclosure game, he declared: "These people may be poor and illiterate, but no one puts a gun to their head and tells them to sign."[176]

In a Pennsylvania case, Transamerica Financial Services and the prestigious Mellon Bank paid a $6.2 million settlement after the two companies were accused of a kickback scheme involving loans to low-income applicants.[177] Transamerica Financial Services has a history of exploiting the poor. In 1990 the company foreclosed on the home of an impoverished, mentally disabled Arizona widow who was unable to repay a loan at a rate of $499 a month. Her total income was $438 a month. A judge halted the foreclosure, ruling that Transamerica "knew or should have known" that the woman was not competent when she signed the loan paper.[178]

CASE STUDY
Broken by Brokers

Like many seniors, 92-year-old Richard Guthrie of Iowa entered a few sweepstakes hoping to get lucky. Little did he know that as a result his name would be entered in a database owned by InfoUSA, one of the country's largest list brokers. The controversial Nebraska-based company is perhaps best known for paying former president Bill Clinton $2 million in consulting fees and donating heavily to the political campaigns of Senator Hillary Clinton.[179]

List brokers are compilers of consumer information. InfoUSA then sold Guthrie's name—and data on millions of other elderly Americans—to known scammers for 8.5 cents apiece.[180] Many list brokers deal with clients who use the information illegally. This is especially true in the case of "elderly" lists. The brokers vie for the scammers' attention by giving their lists names such as "Elderly Opportunity Seekers," "Suffering Seniors," "Oldies but Goodies," and "4.7 million people with cancer or Alzheimer's disease."[181] One list even proclaimed blatantly: "These people are gullible. They want to believe that their luck can change."[182] As one Canadian law enforcement official has observed, "Only one kind of customer wants to buy lists of seniors interested in lotteries and sweepstakes. If someone advertises a list by saying it contains gullible or elderly people, it's like putting a sign out saying, 'Thieves welcome here.'"[183]

As Mr. Guthrie sat alone at home, surrounded by his Purple Heart medal from World War II, photos of his eight children, and mementos of his late wife, his telephone started to ring day and night. After criminals tricked him into divulging his banking information, they went to Wachovia, then the nation's fourth-largest bank, and raided his account. These swindlers, with the assistance of Wachovia and InfoUSA, were thus able to steal Richard Guthrie's life savings

of more than $100,000.[184] Guthrie later said in an interview:

> I loved getting those calls. Since my wife passed away, I don't have many people to talk with. I didn't even know they were stealing from me until everything was gone.[185]

Banks like Wachovia and list brokers like InfoUSA often confront evidence that their services are used for fraud. But, according to government investigators, neither company stopped working with crooks even after executives were warned that they were aiding continuing crimes. Instead, they collected millions of dollars in fees from scam artists.

Guthrie's name was on a list titled "Astroluck." InfoUSA sold their Astroluck list to dozens of customers, including some that had been sued for deceptive mailing, had been the subject of numerous consumer complaints, had been shut down by the government, and even one that was being prosecuted at the time for running a lottery scam.[186]

Thieves who prey on innocent elders like Mr. Guthrie typically call and pose as government workers or pharmacy employees. They tell their victims that the Social Security Administration's computers had crashed or that their prescription records were incomplete. They warn that unless they provide banking information, their payments or medicine would be delayed. Guthrie nervously complied. He later said, "I was afraid if I didn't give her my bank information, I wouldn't have the money for my heart medicine."[187]

Criminals use the banking data to create unsigned checks that withdraw funds from victims' accounts. Such checks are allowed under a provision of the banking code, but most banks prefer electronic fund transfers, which can serve the same purpose and are less susceptible to fraud.[188]

(Continued)

So, when unsigned checks are printed, the difficult part is finding a bank willing to accept them. In the case of Mr. Guthrie, that bank was Wachovia.

There is little evidence that Wachovia ever screened most of the firms that profited from the withdrawals—as banking laws require. In a lawsuit filed against the company that printed all those unsigned checks, Payment Processing Center (PPC), the U.S. attorney in Philadelphia said Wachovia received *thousands* of warnings that it was processing fraudulent checks, but ignored them. Wachovia continued to accept unsigned checks provided by PPC until the government filed suit in 2006.[189] The suit against PPC ended in early 2007. A court-appointed receiver was ordered to liquidate the firm.

By 2007, just as he feared, Richard Guthrie's financial freedom was gone. He was receiving a $50-a-week allowance to buy food. His children assumed ownership of his home, and his grandson controlled his bank account. He needed to ask permission for additional purchases.[190]

At least the telemarketers stopped calling . . . because he couldn't buy anything. He was off the list.

CASE STUDY
Chased by Chase

In 2007, a nervous young man sat down before a microphone and addressed the U.S. Senate Permanent Subcommittee on Investigations:

> My name is Wes Wannemacher, and I come from Lima, Ohio. I am married and raising a small family. I wish I could come here and tell you that I've always paid my bills on time, but my goal isn't to convince you that I'm the most responsible adult in the United States. Despite these and other faults, I am well liked and respected in my community.
>
> Toward the end of 2001, I had just accepted a higher paying job, and my wedding was approaching. My wife and I wanted to show everyone a good time and have a memorable experience. As a young adult, I really had no idea how much my wedding would cost. I had applied for and received a credit card from Chase with a $3,000 credit limit. This was quickly reached after paying for flowers and a photographer. I charged a total of $3,200 on this card and never charged anything beyond that. I have been trying ever since to pay it off.[191]

Wannemacher then proceeded to tell a horror story about what could be called the "Bill from Hell." Between 2002 and 2004 other financial obligations arose in Wannemacher's life and he began making whatever minimum payment was required on his Chase bill. Since Chase couldn't evict him from his home or turn off his lights, the bill was sometimes relegated to the back burner. In 2005, with the bill mounting and a second child due, Wannemacher offered to settle with Chase for $3,000—his original line of credit. He was turned down, and he went back to making payments and watching the balance rise. By 2006, the balance exceeded $5,300 and Wannemacher was facing bankruptcy. When his stepdaughter accrued medical bills not covered by his insurance, he was quickly overwhelmed and enrolled in a debt-counseling program. His counselor assumed his power of attorney and sent proposals to all his creditors seeking to work out a payment plan. Chase was the only one to refuse. Chase tried to convince Wannemacher not to enroll in debt counseling and to make direct payments. In 2007, Chase finally accepted a payment plan of $147 a month for 47 months, totaling $6,100.[192]

(Continued)

At the time Wannemacher appeared before Congress, he had paid Chase $6,300 over six years—nearly double his initial debt. And he still had a balance of *$4,400*. If he had paid Chase off in full, right then and there, it would have come to $10,700 for a $3,200 loan. Only after he testified and his plight was detailed by the media did Chase suddenly call and forgive his balance.[193] The chief executive of Chase Card Services later publicly apologized to Wannemacher:[194] "We blew it. Our policies and procedures failed, and we regret it."[195]

That's good for Wesley Wannemacher, but what about all the other consumers who have been similarly overcharged? This is an important question because Wesley Wannemacher's story is far from unique. "[M]illions of consumers have been caught in spiraling debt as credit card issuers have flooded them with solicitations, then squeezed them with record-high fees and usurious interest rates for the slightest infractions."[196] Many card issuers hit consumers with penalty rates of over 32 percent for late payments—and apply these outrageous rates to customers' entire balances, not just new charges. Some issuers even impose these rates on cardholders who pay them on time but are late paying another creditor. This practice is known as "universal default."[197] "That's akin to a mortgage holder raising your rate because you paid your phone bill late."[198]

For years, Congress largely ignored public outcries about the byzantine world of credit card rules and penalties, as credit card issuers flooded Washington with campaign cash. But many members are now advocating some tighter measure of control over the credit card industry. For unless Congress is prepared to intervene individually in each case of a consumer ensnared in a web of credit card debt, like Mr. Wannemacher, it needs to establish new regulations that ensure that credit card issuers do not behave like Mafia loan sharks.

Another popular way to fleece the poor is through disreputable vocational schools. Telemarketers plunder the federal student loan programs, which have been described as "a multi-billion-dollar swamp of fraud."[199] At a school for medical assistants in Atlanta, "many poor black single mothers had gone into hock for $4,800 for the promise of a well-paying job in a doctor's office."[200] The entire school consisted of a reference center holding a handful of books and supplies, and a large "boiler" room containing 75 telephones where recruiters solicited students.[201]

These schools are pitched as stepping-stones to a better life. A typical script goes: "Listen, young lady, you have two children and no husband. What are you ever going to do with your life?"[202] The sad truth is that these fraudulent training programs dump sincerely motivated students on a treadmill that leads nowhere, burdened with tuition debts they cannot ever pay. For example, a truck-driving school recruited a Texas woman. She later learned that she could not even qualify for a state commercial license—because she only has one foot.[203]

A Georgia trade school charges over $4,000 to train students to work as aides in nursing homes—a job that pays barely more than minimum wage. "The public vocational school down the street also trains aides—for $20."[204] Another school charges $3,000 to train armed security guards. The state requires only 12 hours of training to obtain a license, but the school's program fills up 300 hours—largely padded with old war movies.[205]

In 2004, the state of Pennsylvania sued a Texas online university after that school sold an MBA degree for $299 to a deputy attorney general's cat. The transcript listed the cat's course work and a 3.5 grade point average.[206]

FALSE ADVERTISING

Closely related to consumer fraud is the practice of false advertising.[207] A renowned British writer has observed: "Advertisements are now so numerous that . . . it [has] therefore become necessary to gain attention by magnificence of promise."[208] The remarkable thing about this comment is that Dr. Samuel Johnson penned it in *1759.*

In theory at least, the multibillion-dollar American advertising industry serves as a conduit between businesses' need to inform and the public's need to know. Many critics contend, however, that in practice advertising provides very little useful information to consumers, whose desire to evaluate products and services in a knowledgeable way remains largely unfulfilled.[209] The reason for this is that advertising has become—or perhaps has always been—more a tool for manipulation than education. Indeed, of the three advertisement categories classified by the FTC, *informative* ads are probably the least visible. Far more ubiquitous is a second category—*puffing* ads, featuring self-serving ballyhoo or irrelevant celebrity endorsements.[210]

The third and most insidious category, *deceptive* ads, is characterized by misleading or untrue claims,[211] sometimes supported by rigged tests and photographic trickery.[212] While the industry as a whole may be fair game for criticism, deceptive practices warrant the most serious attention. Puffery can be used as a shield to avoid accountability for a claim about a product or service[213] and may confuse or even offend the sensibilities of consumers; but false advertising crosses the line between exaggerative license and unmitigated fraud.

The FTC's authority over the advertising industry predates the advent of network television.[214] Thus, every TV commercial ever run has been subject to FTC regulation. Many consumer advocates have given the FTC and other regulatory agencies low overall grades in this area through the years, but the government has displayed occasional flashes of toughness.

In the 1970s, the FTC ruled that the makers of the popular over-the-counter pain reliever, Anacin, had deceptively advertised their product by making a slew of false claims. Consumers were told, for instance, that Anacin (a blend of aspirin and caffeine) could relieve depression, stress, nervousness, and fatigue—which it could not; could bring relief within 22 seconds— which it could not; was recommended more by physicians than aspirin—which it was not; and was the strongest nonprescription analgesic available—which it was not.[215] In a similar, more recent case, Norvartis, the world's second-largest drug maker, was ordered by the FTC in 1999 to run advertisements correcting earlier claims that its Doan's back-pain pills are better than other analgesic medicines.[216]

In the 1980s, the Beech-Nut Nutrition Corporation, a leading manufacturer of baby foods, advertised its apple juice as "100 percent fruit juice." This apple juice was also said to contain no sugar. In fact, it was loaded with sugar. What it did not contain was apple juice. When stories of Beech-Nut's appalling deception began to surface, the company shipped its entire remaining 26,000-case inventory to the Caribbean, where the juiceless juice was sold to unwitting parents. Over a 10-year period, Beech-Nut had been able to "extract as much as $60 million from consumers"[217] for what one of its own scientists later called "a fraudulent chemical cocktail"[218] masquerading as baby food. In 1988, Beech-Nut's president and vice president of operations were convicted of violating federal food and drug laws.[219]

In a similar 1995 case, the owner of Carrington Foods was ordered to pay a $78,000 fine after a felony conviction for misbranding. Packages of Miss Sally's Stuffed Crabs bore bright stickers proclaiming "More Crabmeat Than Ever." Miss Sally's product not only did not contain more crabmeat than ever, it contained no crabmeat whatsoever.[220]

The intensity of state and federal regulation seemed to increase a bit in the 1990s. But whether this reflects tougher enforcement policies or just more willingness by advertisers to test the limits of tolerable hyperbole is not altogether clear.

A survey of recent cases includes the following:

- The Home Shopping Network reached a settlement with the New York attorney general's office, under which it agreed to curb deceptive advertising of jewelry. The network generally flashes a "retail value" on the screen and then cuts its "sale price" far below that figure. The state had alleged that the suggested retail prices were "drastically inflated."[221] Jewelry is the "bread and butter" of electronic shopping, leading in sales volume and profit margin. In an even more recent case, Home Shopping was slapped with a $1.1 million fine by the FTC for airing advertisements making unsubstantiated claims for skin care, weight loss, and PMS/menopause products.[222]

- NordicTrack, a major marketer of indoor exercise equipment, agreed to settle an FTC complaint regarding fatuous claims the company's ads made about how much weight NordicTrack users could expect to lose.[223] The FTC has also obtained a settlement agreement from Jenny Craig, Inc., in response to charges of deceptive advertising in connection with the Jenny Craig diet program's claims about weight loss, price, and safety.[224]

- The FTC settled charges with Schering-Plough Healthcare Products, the marketer of Coppertone Kids sunscreens for children. Ads for 6-Hour Waterproof Sunblock were deemed deceptive in their claims that one application provides six hours of protection from the sun for children engaged in sustained vigorous activity. The FTC charged that such a claim was unsubstantiated and untested by the company. The director of the FTC's Bureau of Consumer Protection said: "You can't use a smokescreen to sell a sunscreen."[225]

- The FTC also settled charges against computer makers Dell and Micron for disseminating misleading ads about computer leases. Both companies had placed important cost information in "inconspicuous or unreadable fine print or omitted such information altogether."[226] Apple Computer was similarly found to have engaged in false advertising in its "Apple Assurance" campaign. Apple Assurance offered consumers free access to live, technical support for as long as they own their Apple product. According to the FTC: "Apple, however, subsequently began charging these consumers $35 for such access."[227]

- R.J. Reynolds Tobacco agreed to modify its advertising for Winston "no additives" cigarettes. The FTC alleged that Reynolds implied, without any reasonable basis, that Winston cigarettes are safer to smoke because they contain no additives. Reynolds agreed to make a prominent disclosure in future Winston ads: **No additives in our tobacco does NOT mean a safer cigarette**. According to the FTC: "[T]here's no such thing as a 'Safe Smoke'."[228]

- Providian Financial, one of the largest credit card issuers in the United States, agreed to pay at least $300 million to consumers to settle claims that it used deceptive advertising practices. Providian's Guaranteed Savings Rate Program promised customers a lower rate than they had been receiving on balances transferred from other cards. But according to the federal Office of the Comptroller of the Currency (OCC), some customers actually ended up with *higher* rates than before.[229]

- The FTC sued SlimAmerica, Inc., for false claims about the company's "Super-Formula" diet pills, as advertised in newspapers, magazines, and the Internet.[230] A 90-day supply of Super Formula sold for $129.95. Ads promised that Super-Formula is "absolutely guaranteed to blast up to 49 pounds off you in only 29 days."[231] Also included was an endorsement by Howard Retzer, M.D. According to the FTC, the company made between $5.3 million and $17.7 million from the sale of Super-Formula. A federal judge ruled that the product was worthless and that the company's claims (and "Dr." Retzer's credentials) were misrepresented.[232] SlimAmerica was ordered to reimburse thousands of defrauded customers $8.3 million.[233]

- Kevin Trudeau, a deft huckster whose Infomercials once flooded late-night television, was fined $1 million by the FTC for false and misleading pitches he made on behalf of six products. The products included the Mega Memory system, which claimed it could teach anyone to have a photographic memory; the Sable Hair Farming System, which claimed it could prevent or reverse baldness; Eden's Secret Nature's Purifying Product, which claimed to cure illnesses and cause weight loss; and the Addiction Breaking System, which claimed that a series of gestures such as tapping the face and rolling the eyes could end addictions to alcohol, tobacco, and drugs.[234] Trudeau is an old hand at lawbreaking, with a record of prior felony convictions for larceny and credit card fraud.[235] More recently, Trudeau has written a controversial book on natural cures and now—without a trace of irony—bills himself as "America's foremost consumer advocate." "Despite no medical training and a record of criminal convictions, Trudeau has managed to sell millions of books on 'natural cures.'"[236] An FTC assistant director commented: "Just because it's on television, doesn't mean that it's true."[237]

One of the fastest growing market segments in the United States is in the area of nutrition. Anyone who doubts how health-conscious many Americans have become need only observe grocery shelves now stocked with such improbably named products as Spam Lite and Lo-Fat Twinkies. But as the demand for healthier foods has increased, so has the use of misrepresentation in advertising and labeling. Even when claims such as "cholesterol free," "high fiber," and "low sodium" are strictly accurate, they may still be confusing. For one thing, such claims do not necessarily mean that a product is good for you.[238] For example, certain brands of peanut butter advertised as "cholesterol free" are nonetheless high in saturated fats, which can raise blood cholesterol levels.[239]

Two cases, both decided in 1994, illustrate typical objections to questionable nutritional claims. In one instance, the FTC ruled that Stouffer Lean Cuisine frozen foods had made deceptive "low sodium" assertions in a $3 million advertising campaign.[240] In the other case, the Hillshire Farms division of the Sara Lee Corporation agreed to pay a $130,000 fine and change the advertising of its "lite" meat products. According to the government's allegations, the company had misleadingly suggested that several products were low in fat, when they were not.[241]

Another deceptive labeling practice involves the term "natural." Some cosmetics companies, for instance, make their products "natural" merely by adding tiny amounts (perhaps 0.1 percent) of herbal extract mixtures that provide no benefit to the consumer.[242]

One of the fastest growing forms of deceptive product claims occurs in ads for weight-loss products. The weight-loss industry—and it is an industry—is huge. More than 68 million Americans are trying to lose weight at any point in time and in 2000 they spent over $34.7 billion on weight-loss products and programs. These millions of consumers are often desperate to do something about their weight and are easy prey for hucksters who are more than willing to sell them false hopes in the form of worthless devices and drugs. As the Federal Trade Commission noted:

> The struggle to shed unwanted pounds usually resolves itself into choosing between responsible products or programs that offer methods for achieving moderate weight loss over time and "miracle" products or services that promise fast and easy weight loss without sacrifice.[243]

All too often overweight Americans choose the latter.

The FTC has focused attention on false claims made in the advertisements for these products. The agency studied 300 ads found in newspapers, magazines, and on late-night television programs and examined them for the veracity of their claims. The study found that: "Nearly 40 percent of the ads . . . made at least one representation that almost certainly is false and 55 percent of the ads made at least one representation that is very likely to be false or, at the very least, lacks adequate substantiation."[244] Many of the ads examined made claims that were scientifically implausible and were simply "too good to be true." Included in this category were claims that:

"the user can lose a pound a day or more over extended periods of time; that substantial weight loss (without surgery) can be achieved without diet or exercise; and that users can lose weight regardless of how much they eat. Also falling into this category are claims that a diet pill can cause weight loss in selective parts of the body or block absorption of all fat in the diet."

Weight-loss product advertisers frequently used testimonials from purported users that grossly exaggerated their weight-loss experience. One boldly claimed:

7 weeks ago I weighed 268 lbs, now I am down to just 148 lbs! During this time I didn't change my eating habits at all: the pounds must have disappeared only due to the new slimming capsule. My appearance is so different that my friends actually believe that I had liposuction.

The FTC report noted that this kind of weight loss is simply impossible:

The product featured in this advertisement claims to work by preventing the absorption of fat in the digestive system. In fact, weight loss of this magnitude would require a net calorie deficit of 8,571 calories per day over the course of seven weeks. Even complete fasting would not produce this kind of result. Nevertheless, this testimonial was disseminated to millions of Americans through *Cosmopolitan*, *Soap Opera Digest*, *National Enquirer*, *Women's Day*, *Let's Live*, *Women's Own*, *McCall's*, *Star*, and *First for Women*. [245]

Advertisements in the FTC sample also frequently displayed before-and-after photos of supposed beneficiaries of their products. In the "before" picture, the user is often photographed in poor lighting, with slumping posture, scraggly hair, pale skin and a scowling face. In the "after" photo, by contrast, the subject is typically photographed with bright lighting (often studio quality), is standing with perfect posture, has a new hairdo, a gleaming sun tan, and a broad smile on his or her face. Often an actual difference in weight is hard to detect.

The FTC concluded that the "1990s saw an explosion in dietary supplement marketing, many of which are of unproven value and/or have been linked to serious health risks."[246] One of the reasons for this dramatic increase was a change in federal law. The Dietary Supplement Health and Education Act of 1994 (DSHEA) placed many of these bogus weight-loss products into a category called "dietary supplements" and treated them essentially as foods. As such, these products do not have to undergo the rigorous, pre-market scrutiny that weight-loss products deemed to be "drugs" do and their claims do not have to be verified before they are advertised to unsuspecting consumers.[247] While they are subject to FTC provisions regarding false advertising, the peddlers of these scientifically dubious products can make millions before federal regulators get around to shutting them down.

No type of deceptive advertising has generated more public outrage than that aimed at children. The United States is one of the few countries in the world that permits advertisers to sell products to children via television. Most nations consider this practice to be immoral. In fact, a recent survey by *Advertising Age* magazine reported that 62 percent of Americans want children's ads taken off the air entirely.[248] The average American child, who spends a staggering amount of time watching television, views about 25,000 commercials a year.[249] The majority are for food products of negligible nutritional value—mainly heavily sugared cereals, soft drinks, and candy. The American Academy of Pediatrics has called for a ban on children's food ads, maintaining that such messages contribute to a national obesity problem.[250]

Many of the remaining ads are for toys. Any parent who has ever cleaned out a closet full of long-abandoned playthings that a young son or daughter had once pleaded for readily understands that most toys are junk. Shoddily constructed and easily broken, they are rarely able to perform as advertised. In an "attitude inoculation" study led by Norma Feshbach, elementary school children were shown commercials for a toy, then immediately were given the same item. Feshbach challenged them to make the toy do what they had just witnessed on television. They seldom could.[251]

Children, so easy to persuade, are "an advertiser's dream."[252] They are hopelessly overmatched against skilled teams of animators, professional writers and juvenile actors, child psychologists, and cinematographers employing a menu of special effects[253]—all working to manipulate them. Peggy Charren, founder of Action for Children's Television (ACT), has written: "The ads feature more children and better animation than the programs they interrupt. Children like commercials, and corporations know how to take advantage of this sad fact of life."[254] In response to criticism, the best the toy companies and television broadcasters can do is argue weakly that commercials help parents teach their children "consumer skills."[255]

Even older children can be highly vulnerable to dishonest media promotions. Consider the sensational scandal surrounding the pop-singing duo, Milli Vanilli. "Milli Vanilli was the stage name for two young performers, Robert 'Rob' Pilatus and Fabrice 'Fab' Morvan, who had come out of nowhere, released their hit album and won the 1990 Grammy Award for best new artist."[256] In their year of stardom, according to one mind-boggling estimate, Milli Vanilli had generated revenues of $200 million.[257] Then it was revealed that Pilatus and Morvan were only nice-looking, lip-synching front men for an unscrupulous music producer. They had not sung a single note on their recordings or videos. Milli Vanilli would have been more aptly named Phoni Baloni.

The primary victims of this fraud were adolescent females, who had lavished their adoration and consumer dollars on Rob and Fab. In an ironic touch, requiring no elaboration, Milli Vanilli's hit album was titled "Girl You Know It's True."

Bait and Switch

Some years back, the *New York Times* reported a story about a woman who had responded to a bedding store's published advertisement offering a full-size Sealy superfirm mattress for $48. When a salesman showed her the item, it was leaning against a storeroom wall, soiled and looking, in the customer's words, "like one of those mattresses on the sidewalk waiting for a sanitation pickup."[258] What the woman had encountered was one of the oldest and most durable forms of false advertising—the bait and switch.

The FTC defines *bait and switch* as "an alluring but insincere offer to sell a product or service which the advertiser does not intend or want to sell."[259] The merchant's objective, of course, is to switch the buyer to another higher-priced, more profitable item. For example, a Virginia dealer reportedly spent many hundreds of dollars each month advertising Singer sewing machines at remarkably low prices, yet never sold one. Customers would be shown a beat-up, obsolete model (the "bait"), which the salesman would immediately disparage. Disappointed shoppers were then pressured to buy a less well-known and more expensive brand (the "switch").[260]

Bait and switch is the mainstay of some sleazy retail stores. In sales parlance, their advertised merchandise is "nailed to the floor."[261] The manager of one such business is said to have pointed to a portable television and warned his sales staff: "Any guy who lets that set go out the door goes with it."[262]

Certain researchers have concluded that bait and switch is ultimately a self-destructive strategy with built-in disincentives.[263] In other words, it is argued that once a store gets a bad reputation resulting from the practice, it will suffer financial losses.[264] This prediction is flawed because the assumption that consumers are "effortlessly rational" is naive.[265] With almost any variety of consumer fraud, pride or cognitive dissonance sometimes thwarts rationality. Cognitive dissonance, a psychological construct, refers to the internal conflict that often results when an individual receives information that contradicts fundamental personal beliefs.[266] Thus, if a person holding a competent and prudent self-image is "ripped off," a state of cognitive dissonance is created. That state may be relieved—that is, returned to cognitive balance—either by modifying one's self-image ("I guess I'm not so smart after all!") or by reinterpreting the event ("I wasn't really ripped off!"). The latter may be the more attractive, though less rational, option, since it is more ego-supporting than the former. Simply put, many people just cannot admit to being duped—not even to themselves.

PRICE-FIXING

Price-fixing is criminalized under the Sherman Antitrust Act of 1890, one of the most important pieces of legislation in American history. The Act came of age in 1911 with the dissolution of the immense Standard Oil and American Tobacco empires. Over time, additional federal regulations were enacted (most notably the Clayton Act, the Federal Trade Commission Act, and the Kefauver-Cellar Act), and states now have their own antitrust statutes as well. The most visible case in recent years was the breakup of the vast AT&T telephone monopoly in 1982. In 1994, the antitrust division of the Justice Department prosecuted 60 criminal cases.[267]

Antitrust laws prohibit practices that unreasonably deprive consumers of the advantages of competition—the *sine qua non* of capitalism.

> When competitors agree to fix prices, rig bids, or allocate customers, consumers lose the benefits of competition. The prices that result when competitors agree in these ways are artificially high; such prices do not accurately reflect cost and therefore distort the allocation of society's resources. The result is a loss not only to U.S. consumers and taxpayers, but also the U.S. economy.[268]

In a truly competitive market, businesses attract consumers by holding prices down and keeping quality up. When competitors conspire to fix prices, however, consumers pay higher prices for inferior goods and services. In other words, collusive arrangements among nominal competitors unlawfully maximize corporate profits at the consumer's expense.

The illegality of price-fixing has not often deterred its practice. A study of 582 large American corporations concluded that "violations of the nation's antitrust laws are common in a wide variety of industries."[269] Recent cases in which price-fixing sanctions were applied by courts or administrative agencies include such diverse industries as steel,[270] lead smelting,[271] glass,[272] oil drilling,[273] natural gas,[274] commercial explosives,[275] chemicals,[276] disability insurance,[277] urology services,[278] vitamins,[279] athletic shoes,[280] residential doors,[281] scouring pads,[282] plastic dinnerware,[283] toys,[284] video games,[285] music CDs,[286] infant formula,[287] white bread,[288] and Passover matzo.[289]

One reason for the failure of deterrent measures is that the government's commitment to price-fixing regulation has been erratic. The intensity of enforcement has depended on the political regime and the prevailing ideology in Washington at a particular time.[290] Studies report that price-fixing is most apt to occur during Republican administrations because of that party's traditional pro-business and antiregulatory philosophy.[291] During the eight Reagan years in the 1980s, for instance, the number of antitrust suits filed by the federal government shrunk from 142 to 19.[292] On the other hand, studies also indicate that Republican judges tend to impose harsher sentences for individual antitrust offenders than Democratic judges, perhaps because Republican judges are less inclined to side with criminal defendants generally.[293]

Regarding antitrust enforcement, the eight Clinton years in the 1990s can perhaps be characterized as schizophrenic. On the one hand, the second half of that decade spawned the reemergence of the merger mania that defined the 1980s. By 1995, proposed mergers that might have been unthinkable just a few years before were flying past the Justice Department—sometimes without even slowing down: Exxon and Mobil;[294] Chevron and Texaco;[295] BP and Amoco;[296] BP Amoco and Atlantic Richfield;[297] Reading & Bates and Falcon Drilling;[298] Dow and Union Carbide;[299] Time Warner and Turner Broadcasting;[300] AOL and Netscape;[301] Time Warner and AOL;[302] IBM and Lotus;[303] Disney and Capital Cities/ABC; Westinghouse and CBS; Unilever and Bestfoods;[304] Kimberly-Clark and Scott Paper; Chemical Banking and Chase Manhattan;[305] American International Group and SunAmerica;[306] AT&T and Teleport; and the Union Pacific and Southern Pacific railroads.[307] On the other hand, the Clinton administration took a more activist approach to antitrust policy—most notably in the Microsoft case.[308]

Even the regional telephone companies formed by the breakup of the AT&T monopoly have high-stepped into re-conglomeration. On April 1, 1996, Southwestern Bell and Pacific Telesis announced a proposed merger.[309] Just three weeks later, Nynex and Bell Atlantic announced merger plans.[310] In 1998, a merger was proposed between SBC Communications (formerly Southwestern Bell) and Ameritech (another former "Baby Bell").[311] And in 2000, the Federal Communications Commission approved the merger of Bell Atlantic and GTE—a union that would create the largest local telephone company in the United States.[312]

On the other hand, the 1990s also witnessed an abundance of stiff sanctions and record-breaking fines for price-fixing and other antitrust violations. For example, in the largest civil antitrust settlement ever, up to that time, 37 brokerages involved in a massive price-rigging conspiracy agreed in 1998 to pay $1.03 billion to investors who were overcharged for Nasdaq-listed stocks. The companies making payouts included the biggest names in the securities world—for example, Merrill Lynch, Goldman Sachs, and Salomon Smith Barney. The case revolved around the practice of quoting stocks for customers to the nearest quarter of a dollar rather than the nearest eighth, thus generating extra profits.[313]

The largest class-action settlement of an antitrust case is the $1.05 billion imposed in 1999 on seven pharmaceutical companies that virtually control the vitamin market in the United States. These firms had conspired for years to raise and fix vitamin prices worldwide. The settlement followed 14 prosecutions by the Justice Department's antitrust division that had led to $875 million in criminal fines.[314]

In 1999, oil-field services companies Smith International and Schlumberger became the first companies in 16 years to be found guilty of criminal contempt in violation of an antitrust decree.[315] The companies had formed a joint fluid drilling venture in violation of a court order. Each firm was fined $750,000 but was allowed to continue operating the joint venture in exchange for payment of a $13.1 million civil penalty.[316]

In 1996, Archer Daniels Midland (ADM), the grain- and soybean-processing conglomerate, whose products are found in everything from shampoo to soft drinks, agreed to pay a then-record $100 million price-fixing fine involving lysene (used in animal feed) and citric acid (used in food and beverages). In exchange, the government agreed to drop potentially far more costly antitrust charges relating to high-fructose corn syrup, ADM's most important product.[317] Despite the size of the fine, financial analysts concluded that ADM—long known as one of the most powerful and politically connected corporations, doling out enormous political contributions to both Democrats and Republicans[318]—had made a "good deal." The company held over $2 billion in cash at the time, so the fine was less than might have been anticipated had the corn syrup investigation continued. In fact, ADM's stock actually *rose* following the settlement.[319]

ADM's corporate culture was perfectly captured in a meeting between an ADM executive and a foreign competitor, secretly taped by the FBI: "We have a saying here in this company that penetrates the whole company. Our competitors are our friends. Our customers are the enemy."[320]

The ADM record for the largest antitrust fine fell in 1998 when UCAR International, the *country's* largest producer of graphite electrodes—which provide the heat source for steel mills—was fined $110 million after it admitted scheming to fix prices.[321] That record fell a year later when SGL Carbon Aktiengesellschaft, the *world's* largest producer of graphite electrodes, became the fourth member of the carbon–graphite cartel fined by the Justice Department for price-fixing. The fine in this case was $135 million. Robert J. Koehler, CEO of the German-based corporation, also agreed to pay a $10 million fine—the largest antitrust fine ever levied against an individual.[322]

Another $135 million fine was imposed on Mylan Laboratories, the country's second-largest maker of generic drugs, after it was found to have fixed prices of two widely prescribed antianxiety medications. The company had conspired to control ingredients for the two drugs, then raised prices by as much as *3,000 percent*. The price of one drug was raised from $7.30 for a bottle of 500 tablets to $190. The other drug rose from $11.36 for a bottle of 500 to $377.[323] Mylan Chairman Milan Puskar agreed to the settlement but continued to dispute the accusations: "We continue to believe we acted properly."[324] One can only ponder how Mr. Puskar defines "improper."

But it was the pharmaceutical industry that shattered the record for antitrust fines in 1999, when the Swiss pharmaceutical giant Hoffman-LaRoche paid a $500 million fine for its part in a global price-fixing conspiracy.[325] That year, the Justice Department's antitrust division raked in an unprecedented $1 billion in fines and penalties.[326]

The administration of President George W. Bush was unambiguous in its stance on antitrust regulation. In his first six months in office, Bush quickly delivered on his election promise to keep big business out of the courtroom by quietly dropping a key case against the airline industry, scaling back another case against tobacco companies, and preparing the groundwork to ease up on the antitrust actions against Microsoft and Visa.[327] During his first presidential campaign, Bush had argued that antitrust laws should apply only to price-fixing. This radical position distanced the government from its longstanding role overseeing corporate mergers, investigating monopolies, and monitoring predatory pricing.[328] And even price-fixing cases became rare under President Bush. One of the notable exceptions occurred in 2004 when chipmaker Infineon Technologies pleaded guilty to fixing prices for dynamic random access memory (DRAM) computer memory chips and agreed to pay a $160 million fine.[329] This was the third-largest antitrust fine ever[330]—and the largest not involving pharmaceuticals.

By the final years of Bush's second term, particularly in the wake of the implosion of the financial service industry in late 2008, some of America's biggest financial institutions began merging and creating huge mega-banks: Bank of America—Merrill Lynch; Wells Fargo—Wachovia; JP Morgan Chase—Washington Mutual; JP Morgan Chase—Bear Stearns; PNC Financial Services—National City Corp.; M&T Bank—Provident. Critics contend that mega-mergers give too few companies too much control of important markets or products. If the Age of the Monopoly is over, the Age of the Oligopoly appears to be alive and well.

CASE STUDY
Microsoft = Macro-Monopoly

No company symbolizes the "new economy" of the late 20th and early 21st centuries like Microsoft. Its meteoric rise to market supremacy is legendary. Founded in 1975 by Bill Gates and Paul Allen, it started with three employees and $16,005 in revenues. By 1991, its Windows operating system was on more than 90 percent of the personal computers in the world. By 1998 the company had a market cap of $263 billion;[331] and Gates, with assets estimated at $58 billion, was hailed as the richest person on the planet—perhaps the wealthiest man who ever lived.

The success of Microsoft, however, quickly became a source of enormous controversy. Admirers of the company pointed to it as the perfect exemplar of successful modern capitalism. One noted economist, writing in defense of Microsoft, maintains: "[R]unning other companies out of business and gaining market share is what capitalistic competition is all about."[332] Other scholars echo this sentiment, characterizing Microsoft's aggressive marketing practices simply as "brutally competitive."[333]

Critics, however, accused the company of ruthlessly squashing competitors like bugs on a windshield. This "bug" metaphor would probably not be lost on Rob Glaser, a former Microsoft executive and CEO of RealNetworks (a company that makes software for sending video over the Internet). Glaser told the Senate Judiciary Committee that Microsoft had placed a "bug" in its rival's Windows program that "broke" RealNetworks' software.[334] According to a Silicon Valley antitrust lawyer, "The only thing the robber barons did that Bill Gates hasn't done is use dynamite against their competitors."[335]

Consumer advocates also accused Microsoft of price-gouging. They point out that at a time when computer prices were falling sharply, Microsoft's prices for its operating systems more than doubled. "In 1990 the operating system represented about 4 percent of the price of a computer; today the system makes up over 12 percent."[336] Former senator Howard Metzenbaum, chairman of the Consumer Federation of America, was one of Microsoft's harshest critics:

> Because of its monopoly, Microsoft can skimp on quality. It ships products with avoidable defects, sells upgrades that are often of marginal value and is not pushed to develop truly innovative products. Microsoft has repeatedly imitated the innovative leaders in the industry and then driven them out of the market.[337]

(Continued)

In 1991 the FTC undertook an investigation of whether Microsoft had monopolized the market for PC operating systems. When it concluded that investigation two years later, the FTC turned the case over to the antitrust division of the Justice Department. The following year, the case was seemingly settled with a consent decree, under which Microsoft agreed to give computer makers more leeway in using software from competitors.[338]

When Microsoft launched Windows 95 in 1995, it did not include an Internet browser. Its fledgling Explorer browser had to be purchased separately. But by the end of the year, Gates had shifted Microsoft's corporate strategy toward the Internet, and the company began distributing Internet Explorer for free. When Explorer 4.0 was launched in 1997, it took dead aim at Netscape Communication, the dominant player in the browser market. The strategy was simple and effective. Microsoft demanded that computer manufacturers install Internet Explorer as a condition of installing Windows 95.[339] Such a practice is known as "bundling."

In its 1994 agreement with the Justice Department, Microsoft had consented not to require computer manufacturers to install "separate" products. Microsoft was only permitted to bundle "integrated" products with Windows. For example, Windows Explorer, which organizes files, was viewed as an "integrated" component of Windows.[340]

In 1997, the Justice Department sued Microsoft. It contended that Internet Explorer was a "separate" product and its bundling thus violated the consent decree. The government argued that Explorer was clearly separate from Windows because: (1) it could be "uninstalled" without compromising the operation of Windows; and (2) Microsoft had given away Internet Explorer for years as a distinct, stand-alone product.[341]

Two months after the suit was filed, a U.S. district court judge issued a preliminary injunction ordering Microsoft to stop forcing PC makers to install its browser. Six months later (June 1998), however, a federal appeals court overturned the injunction.[342] It was a victory for Microsoft, but a short-lived one; for the cork was now out of the bottle, and the case against Microsoft had moved well beyond bundling.

A month before the injunction was lifted, the Justice Department and 20 state attorney generals sued Microsoft, this time charging that the company had illegally used its monopolistic power to hurt competitors and stifle innovation in the software industry.[343] "A steady stream of accusations began appearing in court papers and leaked press accounts depicting Microsoft "not as a tough negotiator but as a back-alley enforcer."[344]

Gates stood accused of masterminding a conspiracy to kill off a rival company, Netscape, levering his monopolistic control over one market to take over another.[345] The government alleged that Microsoft had employed predatory practices against a virtual "Who's Who" of high tech: Netscape, Apple, Intel, AOL, and Compaq, as well as others.[346] The government's chief counsel, David Boies, announced that he intended to ask every witness to stake his or her credibility on whether Windows constitutes a monopoly. He declared: "I doubt even [Microsoft's] witnesses will be able to keep a straight face."[347]

Microsoft, however, strongly rejected the dreaded M word. Although by 1998 its Windows and DOS systems controlled 97 percent of the world market, it asserted that monopoly and market share are not the same.[348] It questioned how the government could possibly be acting in the best interests of consumers by forcing it to stop giving away its product for free.[349] The company further argued that it had integrated its browser into its new Windows 98 operating system so it cannot be separated as a stand-alone product.[350] Microsoft's chief counsel, William Neukom, denounced the government's case as "desperate" and "cynical."[351]

And so, on October 19, 1998, one of the most important antitrust trials in American history began. How important? The *New Republic* put it in perspective: "[T]his is not merely an argument about one company or one very, very rich man. At

(*Continued*)

its heart, the Microsoft monopoly trial will determine who writes the business rules of cyberspace—the government or Microsoft.[352]

Before the trial was an hour old, the packed courtroom got to see and hear that "very, very rich man." Not in person; Gates never attended the trial. The lawyer representing the states who had joined in the suit charged Gates with a "lack of intestinal fortitude" to testify.[353] But he had been deposed on videotape several months earlier. At the time, government lawyers had complained that Gates had been "evasive and non-responsive."[354] Boies now offered a persuasive illustration of the Gates' stonewalling style by showing a brief clip from the deposition. Gates, looking "at once deeply uncomfortable and deeply bored,"[355] was asked by an unseen interrogator: "Have you ever read the complaint in this case?"[356] Gates replied: "No."[357]

Two hours of excerpts, culled from his 20-hour deposition, made Gates (according to *Time*) "look like he was the worst CEO in America."[358] He was asked about a damning piece of evidence: an email he had written about Microsoft's plans to use Apple Computer to "undermine" archrival Sun Microsystems. He responded that he could not remember sending the message and had no idea what he could have meant by it. And although Microsoft had held two well-documented negotiations with Netscape in 1995, Gates claimed he had only learned of these negotiations from an article in the *Wall Street Journal*.[359]

[I]t was a difficult line to swallow. Gates as a fuzzy-headed amnesiac? This is a man revered . . . for his awesome "bandwidth" (geekspeak for intelligence). Gates' memory is so capacious that at age 11, he astounded friends and family by memorizing all 107 verses of the Sermon on the Mount. He's so driven and detail oriented that he favors baths over showers so he can study while he soaks.[360]

Gates was so disingenuous that the presiding judge laughed out loud—along with the rest of the courtroom—at a particularly blatant obfuscation, when Gates asked the meaning of the word "we."

The Gates in the video . . . paused for 20 seconds or more while formulating some answers. When the going got tough, he rocked back and forth in his chair like a toy dog in a car window. He testily parsed fine distinctions (Microsoft's "deal" with Apple vs. their "relationship") and professed to be nonplussed by common Anglo-Saxon words ("I have no idea what you're talking about when you say 'ask'").[361]

Boies' strategy seemed clear. Expose the boss as a liar and thus erode the company's credibility. Time and again, Gates claimed to have been out of the loop during discussions and key meetings. And time and again, his taped testimony was contradicted by memos and emails written by him—each one enlarged on a 10-foot video screen. Regarding the negotiations with Netscape that Gates claimed to have only learned of from the *Wall Street Journal*, Boies presented an internal Microsoft email that Gates had written on the same day as the meeting. "I think there is a very powerful deal of some kind we can do with Netscape."[362]

Netscape turned down Gates' proposal that Microsoft would agree not to develop a rival browser for non-Windows operating systems if Netscape agreed to stay out of the Windows market. Netscape co-founder Marc Andreesen would later compare the unsuccessful meeting to "a visit from Don Corleone. I expected to find a bloody computer monitor in my bed the next day."[363]

Using Microsoft's own paper trail, "the government portrayed a company obsessed with crushing its competitor . . . and willing to use every tool at its disposal, including threats and financial inducements to force or persuade other companies to drop any planned or existing alliances with Netscape."[364] Microsoft's legal team derided such evidence as "snippets." Their repeated use of this term became a running joke. In fact, an anti-Microsoft group had

(Continued)

"Free the Snippets" buttons made up and handed them out to reporters at the courthouse.[365]

But the "snippets" Boies chose were "killers." For example, Gates was quoted in an email that recaps a meeting he held with AOL executives: "How much do we need to pay you to screw Netscape?"[366]

One of the government's most compelling witnesses against Microsoft was Apple vice president Avadis Tevanian. In 1997, the two archrivals had entered into a stunning partnership when Microsoft helped bail Apple out of a financial slump with an infusion of $150 million.[367] Tevanian recounted a series of 1997 meetings in which Microsoft intimidated Apple. Microsoft allegedly had threatened to withhold its business software, Microsoft Office, from Apple's signature Macintosh computer. The price tag for Microsoft's continued cooperation was making Internet Explorer Apple's default browser.[368]

Tevanian also alleged that Microsoft had demanded that Apple stop making its QuickTime multimedia software for Windows-based computers. According to Tevanian, Microsoft used the same threat again: It would pull support for Microsoft Office, which was critical to Apple.[369]

> Tevanian recounted a sinister moment in which an Apple executive, surprised by a Microsoft demand that the company drop [QuickTime], asked, "Do you want us to knife the baby?" Yes, the Microsoft executive reportedly replied, "we're talking about knifing the baby."[370]

He added that when Apple refused to abandon QuickTime, Microsoft sabotaged it so it would have problems running on computers using Internet Explorer.[371] To punctuate Tavanian's testimony, the government introduced a handwritten note from Apple's chief financial officer. It read in part:

> Apple needed to ensure that Microsoft would continue to provide MS Office for

Mac, or we were dead. . . . They were threatening to abandon Mac. [The] trading card was making Internet Explorer [the] default browser.[372]

Conspicuously absent among the roll call of witnesses were the PC manufacturers—"the most obvious victims of alleged Microsoft coercion."[373] Some industry insiders contend that the PC makers were silenced by the very power the government was seeking to curb.[374] According to one former CEO, "Nobody in the PC business wants to be near this."[375] A noted antitrust attorney adds: "They couldn't find anyone brave enough to come forward and risk the wrath of Microsoft."[376] Boies quoted a Hewlett-Packard memo to Microsoft:

> "If we had a choice of another supplier based on your actions in this area," writes an HP exec, "you would not be our supplier of choice." But of course HP has no choice. That's the point.[377]

Compaq, then the number one PC maker, even agreed to testify *for* Microsoft—despite itself being a past victim of Gates' bullying tactics. In 1996, Compaq had entered into a deal with America Online that would have displayed AOL's screen before the familiar Windows screen. According to a Compaq insider, when Microsoft threatened, Compaq backed down.[378] Furthermore, the company attested in Justice Department depositions that Microsoft had applied serious pressure when Compaq attempted to put Netscape's browser on its computers alongside Windows.[379]

Closing arguments from both sides ended in September 1999. On November 5, Judge Thomas Penfield Jackson, a Republican and Reagan appointee, delivered his first finding of fact. In a blistering ruling, Judge Jackson declared that Microsoft *is* a monopoly that stifles competition and hurts consumers. He agreed with nearly all the government's allegations.[380] By this time it had become clear what sanctions the government was seeking. It wanted to impose

(Continued)

the antitrust version of the "death penalty"[381]—the breakup of the company into what were already being dubbed "Baby Bills."[382]

The court's second finding of fact was issued on April 3, 2000. In another stinging rebuke, Judge Jackson ruled that Microsoft "maintained its monopoly power by anticompetitive means and attempted to monopolize the Web browser market."[383] Jackson said that Microsoft had put an "oppressive thumb on the scale of competitive fortune."[384]

The final and most dramatic finding of fact was announced on June 7, 2000. Calling Microsoft "untrustworthy"[385] and an "unrepentant law-breaker,"[386] Judge Jackson ordered the software giant to be split into two companies. Bill Gates called the ruling "an unwarranted and unjustified intrusion."[387] The imposed breakup was of course stayed pending appeal—a process believed likely to take years. Microsoft expressed firm confidence that it would ultimately prevail. Bill Gates seemed especially lifted by the case's shift to the appellate courts: "I'm reminded of the old saying, 'Today is the first day of the rest of your life.'"[388]

In September, 2000, the U.S. Supreme Court declined to "fast track" the Microsoft appeal by hearing it immediately. It handed the case to the federal appeals court in Washington, D.C. This decision was seen as a victory for the company. The D.C. court had already sided with Microsoft in an earlier case, while the Rehnquist Court had an unpredictable record on antitrust cases.[389]

The following summer, the federal appeals court issued two decisions on the fate of Microsoft. It was a classic good news/bad news scenario for the company. The good news was that the court threw out Judge Jackson's ruling splitting Microsoft in two. The bad news was that the court nevertheless agreed *unanimously* with Jackson's decision that Microsoft *was* an illegal monopoly.[390]

It was a remarkable ruling—even more stunning in its unanimity. Microsoft's arrogant "admit-nothing" strategy was already being described as "one of the greatest blunders in American corporate history."[391] Most antitrust experts agree that the case could have been settled early and easily, had Microsoft conceded the obvious, made a few concessions, taken a slap on the wrist, and vowed to sin no more. Instead, it bet on Bill Gates, whose testimony quickly degenerated from haughty invincibility, to Clintonesque nitpicking over the meaning of simple words, to outright prevarication. "Petulant, self-pitying, convinced of his own righteousness, Gates had no intention of admitting his company had done anything wrong. Instead, he decided to stonewall, and in the process he became the prosecution's star witness."[392]

Microsoft filed an appeal to the Supreme Court, but by this time a pro-business Republican administration had taken control of the Justice Department. In this new political environment, it seemed like the perfect time for Microsoft to finally settle the long-running case.

By November 2001, Microsoft and the Justice Department had hammered out a proposed settlement. Under the terms of the agreement, Microsoft would be barred from "exclusive dealing"—that is, it could no longer enter into licensing agreements with PC manufacturers that restrict them from working with other software developers.[393] Microsoft would also be required to provide other software makers access to elements of its application programming interfaces (APIs)—that is, its source code, which is necessary for them to make their applications work under the Windows operating system.[394] The settlement also called for an independent, on-site, three-member panel of computer experts to monitor Microsoft's compliance.

At a press conference, Bill Gates declared: "While this settlement imposes new rules and regulations, we believe that settling the case now is the right thing to do for our customers, for the technology industry, and for the economy."[395] U.S. Attorney General John Ashcroft insisted that the settlement "opens the marketplace to competition by requiring Microsoft to disclose information it previously considered proprietary and by permitting other companies to do business with competitors without fear of retribution."[396]

(Continued)

Exactly one year later, a federal judge approved most of the settlement. Judge Colleen Kollar-Kotelly wrote: "The court is satisfied that the parties have reached a settlement which comports with the public interest."[397] One controversial change in her decision was the elimination of the independent technical committee to assess Microsoft's compliance. In its place there would be a "corporate compliance committee"—consisting solely of Microsoft board members.

Despite the cheerleading from Gates, Ashcroft, and Kollar-Kotelly, not everyone was happy with the settlement. A prominent law professor wrote:

> [T]he settlement agreement was carefully tilted in favor of Microsoft. . . . In all its details, the agreement was tailored to give the appearance of more protection against monopolization than was actually achieved.[398]

One antitrust expert called it an "embarrassment for the Justice Department."[399] Another critic noted that under the agreement, Microsoft's newer Windows XP remains a "closed environment" and that "Microsoft will be able to pursue its Windows XP strategy unimpeded."[400] He further warned:

> Unless you happen to be among the few adventuresome types who insist on finding a different way, you'll be paying Microsoft one way or another, for every digital step you take. It will truly be a Microsoft world, even more so than it is today.[401]

So, was the Microsoft settlement half full or half empty? By 2003, rival companies were again complaining about Microsoft's familiar tactics in its pursuit of control of the $40 billion-a-year market in servers—powerful computers that run office networks.[402] Server software made by Sun Microsystems, IBM, and other competitors need to interact seamlessly with Microsoft Windows in order to perform well. But to do that, these rivals need access to the APIs that run Windows. A blistering editorial stated: "Though the settlement requires Microsoft to grant access to this code under 'reasonable terms,' the company has thrown up unreasonable roadblocks to doing so."[403] Thus far the Justice Department has seemed reluctant to drag Gates back into court. Critics who had earlier characterized the settlement as too lenient, were now saying "I told you so." That editorial concluded:

> [A]ggressive enforcement is what the Justice Department promised when it agreed to the settlement. And it's the best way to ensure that consumers are protected from a repeat of Microsoft's past monopolistic behavior.[404]

Another corporation that has been singled out by critics for allegedly monopolistic practices is the giant retailer Wal-Mart. With its chain of more than 3,000 stores, it has altered the economic (and physical) landscape of the United States and has literally changed the way America shops. Wal-Mart has probably replaced Microsoft as our most controversial corporation; for it arguably represents both the best—and the worst—of capitalism.

CASE STUDY
Wal-Mart: Everyday Low Prices—and Practices

Wal-Mart is capitalism at its best because it offers consumers the lowest possible prices on almost any item, from toys to clothing to small appliances to music CDs to sporting goods to food. Its prices for all these things—and many more—are invariably lower than those of competitors. Indeed, it seems

(Continued)

to be becoming increasingly questionable whether Wal-Mart even has competitors. It does more business than Target, Sears, K-Mart, J.C. Penney, Safeway, and Kroger combined.[405] The company's self-proclaimed "everyday low prices" is not hype. Wal-Mart is well known for squeezing price concessions from its vendors. It is famous as well for forcing suppliers to redesign everything from their packaging to their computer systems to cut down the cost to consumers.[406] But there is a dark side to Wal-Mart beneath the deeply discounted toasters. The company's very size, and the power that goes with it, may also reflect the worst of capitalism.

Wal-Mart is now the biggest corporation in the United States and the largest private employer. Its annual sales exceed $250 billion—greater than the gross domestic product of 161 countries.[407] Its annual profits are nearing $8 billion. It sells in one month what the number two retailer, Home Depot, sells in a year.[408] Obviously, a contract with Wal-Mart is crucial to even the largest consumer-goods manufacturers. "Wal-Mart does not hesitate to use its power, magnifying the Darwinian forces already at work in modern global capitalism."[409] In its eternal quest to offer the lowest prices, Wal-Mart extorts profit-killing concessions from all its suppliers, forcing them to close factories and cut jobs.[410] Domestic manufacturers are now seeing imports sold so cheaply to Wal-Mart that they cannot compete "even if they paid their workers nothing."[411]

Ask a Wal-Mart vendor about the company, and what you get back is either evasive rote or near-hysterical fear:

> "We are one of Wal-Mart's biggest suppliers, and they are our biggest customer, by far. We have a great relationship. That's all I can say. Are we done now?[412]

> "Are you meshuga [crazy]? Why in the world would we talk about Wal-Mart? Ask me about anything else, we'll talk. But not Wal-Mart."[413]

Being a Wal-Mart vendor can be reminiscent of the lady from the familiar limerick, who rode on the back of a tiger. She may not have wanted to be there, but she couldn't jump off for fear of being chewed up and devoured.

Sometimes it's a vendor's management who get sucked into the Wal-Mart vortex. For example, consider the experience of Vlasic, the well-known pickle company. In the late 1990s, Wal-Mart decided to sell Vlasic kosher dill pickles in one-gallon jars.

> Wal-Mart priced it at $2.97—a year's supply of pickles for less than $3! "They were using it as a 'statement item,'" says Pat Hunn, who calls himself the "mad scientist" of Vlasic's gallon jar. "Wal-Mart was putting it before consumers, saying, 'This represents what Wal-Mart's about. You can buy a stinkin' gallon of pickles for $2.97. And it's the nation's top brand."[414]

Clearly, by offering consumers a gallon of kosher dills for less money than most grocers charge for a quart, Wal-Mart was providing a service to its customers. At $2.97, shoppers could afford to throw half the pickles away when they spoil and still save money. But Vlasic was caught in a bind familiar to Wal-Mart suppliers. It had spent millions of dollars in advertising over the years promoting itself as a premium brand. Now Wal-Mart was practically giving the Vlasic name away. Would its customers really buy pickles in a 12-pound jar the size of a small aquarium? The answer is a resounding **yes**. Its stores were soon selling 240,000 oversized jars a week. In the words of a former Vlasic executive, "Whole fields of cucumbers were heading out the door."

Sometimes doing business with Wal-Mart can be the rock and not doing business with Wal-Mart can be the hard place. Vlasic was trapped. Wal-Mart's grocery shelves had become so indispensable to Vlasic's regular product line that the risk of being placed in the "penalty box" (Wal-Mart slang for punishing a balky vendor by taking its products off the shelves) ensured compliance, however reluctant. When the $2.97 pickles started

(*Continued*)

flying out of stores, Wal-Mart's share of Vlasic's sales rose to 30 percent. But Vlasic's profits actually began shrinking, as its business was reshaped by the gallon jar. Vlasic was riding the tiger—right into bankruptcy, which it declared in 2001.[415]

Most times, it's a supplier's workforce that suffers the collateral damage. Consider the experience of one of America's most iconic brands, Levi jeans. In a market where half the jeans now sold are for under $20, the Levi Strauss company and its $30-and-up Levis had seen declining sales for several years. In fact, Wal-Mart's own inexpensive house brand jeans, Faded Glory, was nearly matching Levi Strauss'" annual revenues.[416] In 2002, Levi Strauss finally signed a Wal-Mart contract. In one sense, an ailing company was "rescued" by a benevolent despot. In another sense, however, it was killed, then reincarnated as something different, something less. Because its jeans were too expensive for Wal-Mart (Faded Glory jeans reportedly are made by workers earning 23 cents an hour[417]), it developed a fresh line: The Levi Strauss Signature brand.[418] By the following summer, its sales had nearly doubled. But just as Vlasic Pickle discovered, a glass that is half full is also half empty. Signature jeans reportedly have the look and feel of exactly what they are—cheap. "Cheap and disappointing to find labeled with Levi Strauss's name."[419] There's nothing wrong with inexpensive jeans, *per se,* but Levi Strauss's shift from *its* way to the Wal-Mart Way carried another less conspicuous price tag. It could no longer afford to manufacture its clothing domestically. Shortly after the Signature line was created, Levi Strauss closed its last two American factories and laid off 2,500 workers, 21 percent of its work force.[420] A company, long hailed for its social conscience, that once had 60 clothing plants in the United States had left the manufacturing business forever and become just another importer.

So many of Wal-Mart's wares are manufactured under conditions that are appalling—even by the lax standards of the Third World. Certainly, American companies had been moving jobs offshore for decades before Wal-Mart emerged as the 800-pound gorilla of retailing, "[b]ut there is no question that the chain is helping accelerate the loss of American jobs to low-wage countries like China."[421] Nearly 10 percent of all Chinese exports to the United States are sold to Wal-Mart; and 53 percent of Wal-Mart's imports come from China. For example, Kathie Lee handbags are produced at the Qin Shi Factory in Zhongshan City. This line of merchandise is fronted by entertainer Kathie Lee Gifford, who had earlier been pummeled by the media when it was revealed that her Kathie Lee blouses were made in a Central American sweat shop by child labor.[422]

There are about 1,000 workers at the Qin Shi Factory. Most of them are young men in their mid- to late teens. Almost all are migrants from rural areas. The daily work shift is 12 to 14 hours, seven days a week. Such long hours are illegal even under Chinese law. At the end of the day, the workers are brought to cramped dorm rooms. They sleep on metal bunk beds and are housed 16 to a room. "At most, workers are allowed outside of the factory for just one and one half hours a day. Otherwise they are locked in." The company monitors bathroom breaks. A worker away from his station for more than eight minutes is fined. "Fines for violating any of the strict company rules are severe, a practice made even worse by the fact that armed company security guards can keep 30 percent of any fines they levy against the workers."[423] Workers are charged 80 rmb ($9.64) for a three-year work contract, which includes "two dismal meals a day."[424] They are also charged 560 rmb ($67.47) for their dorm. This is an enormous sum, given that the highest take-home pay a group of researchers found in the factory was just 10 cents an hour.[425] Due to the myriad fines, charges, and deductions, one worker reportedly earned 36 cents for an entire month's labor, toiling 98 hours a week. Indeed, according to a published report, 46 percent of the workers earn nothing at all and are actually in debt to the company.[426] The young men of the Qin Shi Factory are little more than indentured servants, locked inside Kathie Lee's dungeon.

(Continued)

Wal-Mart's stinginess is legendary. When Hurricane Katrina devastated the Louisiana and Mississippi coasts in 2005, Wal-Mart had to shut down 43 stores, leaving 10,000 employees without a place to work. Of course, other big employers in the area faced the same crisis. Harrah's Entertainment, for example, which had to shut down three heavily damaged casinos in the affected areas, announced that the company would continue to pay its more than 6,000 employees for at least 90 days to give its workers time to recover. Wal-Mart announced that it would pay hourly workers in the closed stores for *three days,* then discontinue payments.[427] Another example of the Wal-Mart Way occurred in a Colorado store shortly before Christmas in 2002. A Wal-Mart manager agreed to allow a local charity group to place a big box outside the store for customers to donate toys, bought inside, for needy tots. The woman who had organized the toy drive later said she had been thrilled one day to find the box nearly filled; but when she returned a few hours later, it was empty. When she confronted the manager, he admitted that he had ordered the toys put back on the shelves. He told her he would replace the toys only if she produced receipts proving that they had been purchased—an impossible task.[428] Merry Christmas, kids.

The Wal-Mart Way seems to take Henry Ford's once-revolutionary business model and twist it inside out. Ford paid workers ample wages (for his time) so that they could afford to purchase his automobiles. Wal-Mart pays penurious wages so that its workers can afford to shop only at its stores. In 2001, the average annual wages for Wal-Mart employees fell nearly $800 below the federal poverty line for a family of three.[429] Wal-Mart's salaries are so low that many of its full-time workers qualify for food stamps and other government-funded welfare.[430] Its low wages, high deductibles, and strict eligibility requirements shut tens of thousands of employees out of Wal-Mart's health plan, forcing them to rely on taxpayer-funded health care.[431] In the words of one outraged critic, "Wal-Mart is stealing money from overburdened

health care for the poor to subsidize their low wage practices."[432] A California assemblywoman held a press conference in 2003 aimed at exposing Wal-Mart's "welfare scam." She displayed an official company document labeled *Wal-Mart: Instructions for Associates.* The document explained to employees how to apply for food stamps, Medicaid, and other public assistance.[433] The three congressional sponsors of the Health Care Accountability Act (HCAA), introduced in 2005, termed this practice the "Wal-Mart Health Care Tax"—the price everyone else pays to provide Wal-Mart workers with affordable health care.[434] Wal-Mart is not only the biggest company in the United States, it is also the second most-sued entity in the country, behind only the federal government. Some of the litigation suggests business practices that might have been learned at the Qin Shi Factory.

Because Wal-Mart often builds stores in communities that offer residents few alternative jobs, workers are put in an environment of fear. At the North Salem, Oregon, store, employees were compelled to work off the clock—without pay—to finish assigned tasks.[435] They would clock out, then return to complete their tasks—stocking shelves, shelving returns, and straightening up their areas. A former lawn and garden department manager testified that he had worked off the clock because he was afraid of being fired.[436] A former personnel manager, who was in charge of payroll at two stores, testified that she routinely docked overtime hours from workers' paychecks at the direction of her bosses.[437] One group of customer-service and snack bar "associates" worked without pay beyond the regular 40-hour work week so often that they became known as the "Over 40 Club."[438] In Missouri, where another lawsuit was filed, current and former employees had their own stories to tell. One related how, as soon as she arrived, a manager would often tell her to rush to a cash register and start ringing up purchases, without clocking in. "Sometimes, she said, she worked for three hours before clocking in."[439] Other times, after clocking out from her 10 p.m. to 8 a.m. shift, she

(Continued)

says she was ordered to round up shopping carts in the parking lot.[440] In California, a woman who worked stocking the health and beauty aids department declared: "We worked off the clock pretty much every shift."[441] In Michigan, it was charged that managers demanded that workers clean up the store after punching out at night. "Even if they didn't want to stay late, employees were stuck in the store because the doors were locked. They had to wait for a manager to agree to let them leave."[442] This latter allegation of locked-in workers, if confirmed, evokes the unpleasant image of one of Wal-Mart's Chinese prison camps.

Well over 50 class-action lawsuits have been filed against Wal-Mart by its own "associates" (Wal-Mart's treacle term for its workers) alleging that the company habitually forced employees to work off the clock for no pay. In 2000, Wal-Mart reportedly settled a case involving 69,000 Colorado "associates" for $50 million.[443] It later settled a similar New Mexico case involving 120 employees for a reported sum of $500,000 per plaintiff.[444] The first such case to actually go to court occurred in 2002, when a federal jury ruled that Wal-Mart had, over a 6-year period, forced employees to work overtime without pay.[445] The plaintiffs were "associates" at 18 stores in Oregon. According to the testimony of witnesses, departments that failed to meet the company's quotas were subjected to humiliating reprimands. For example, managers would present a trophy, sculpted in the form of a donkey's rear end, called the "Horse's Ass Award."[446] It was a sharp contrast to the cheerful, family-friendly image of happy customers and smiling employees that Wal-Mart has long cultivated. The employees who testified were not smiling one bit.

In October 2006, a Pennsylvania jury ruled that Wal-Mart had forced hourly employees in that state to work through breaks and beyond their shifts without overtime pay.[447] Almost 187,000 current and former Wal-Mart workers were awarded $62.3 million.[448] In January 2007, Wal-Mart agreed to pay $33.5 million to settle a federal lawsuit that accused the company of violating overtime laws involving more than 86,000 workers. A spokesman for the U.S. Department of Labor said that the settlement was one of the largest ever reached by the department's Fair Labor Practices Division.[449] A spokesman for Wal-Mart said: "I don't think these are particularly unusual violations."[450]

The Supreme Judicial Court of Massachusetts must have defined "unusual" differently, when it reinstated a class-action suit filed on behalf of 67,000 Wal-Mart workers in that state. A 2006 trial court ruling had decertified the lawsuit, but the state Supreme Court vacated that ruling.[451]

And the hits just keep on rolling. In December 2008, Wal-Mart agreed to settle a Minnesota class-action suit involving some 100,000 current and former hourly employees for $54 million.[452] The settlement also included a payment to the state of Minnesota.[453]

The lawsuit was filled with familiar allegations. Workers were not paid for missed rest breaks or missed lunch breaks. Managers altered time sheets to show breaks were taken when they were not and adhered to a "one-minute punch" where workers went unpaid for entire shifts. Furthermore, Wal-Mart regularly had employees work for no pay during "off the clock" periods of time before and after shifts.[454]

With the settlement, Wal-Mart avoided going to trial. Six months earlier, a Minnesota judge had ruled that Wal-Mart had committed more than *two million* violations of that state's Fair Labor Practices Act[455] and could, as a result, face more than $2 billion in fines. The judge threatened a $1,000 penalty for each violation.[456]

In the words of one attorney, "[It] is time for Wal-Mart to face the music."[457] On December 23, 2008, the world's largest retailer threw in the towel (made in China, no doubt). Wal-Mart announced that it would settle 63 pending lawsuits over wage-and-hour violations. Depending on how many claims are submitted by Wal-Mart's 1.4 million employees, the settlement could range

(Continued)

from $352 million to $640 million.[458] Many pundits believed that Wal-Mart, with strong Republican ties, wanted to settle the cases before the new Democratic administration assumed power in 2009.[459]

Wal-Mart holds the all-time record for the most suits filed against an employer by the Equal Employment Opportunity Commission. In an Arizona case, for example, the company was fined $750,000 for flagrant discrimination against the disabled.[460] A lawyer from *Business Week* (a publication not noted for pro-labor advocacy) declared: "I have never seen this kind of blatant disregard for the law."[461]

It has been suggested that Arkansas-based Wal-Mart's original management, including founder Sam Walton, were products of rural Ozark society—a roughly hewn culture considered by many to be extremely sexist. So perhaps it is not surprising that, at this writing, Wal-Mart is the target of what might become the biggest discrimination lawsuit ever. In 2003, six current and former female employees in California filed a sex discrimination suit against the company.[462] The following year, a federal judge turned the case into a class-action. The judge ruled that the six plaintiffs presented "largely uncontested descriptive statistics which show that women working in Wal-Mart stores are paid less than men in every region, that pay disparities exist in most job categories, that the salary gap widens over time even for men and women hired into the same jobs at the same time, that women take longer to enter into management positions, and that the higher one looks in the organization, the lower the percentage of women."[463] Because 72 percent of Wal-Mart's workforce is female, what the company probably perceived as nuisance litigation involving a handful of plaintiffs had become a huge class action with potentially *1.6 million plaintiffs*.[464]

In 2005, Wal-Mart asked a federal appellate court to overturn the class-action certification.[465] On February 6, 2007, the U.S. Court of Appeals for the Ninth Circuit in San Francisco, without commenting on the merits of the case, ruled two to one that the largest sex discrimination lawsuit in American history could proceed as a class action.[466] In response, Wal-Mart said it intended to continue appealing the ruling, all the way to the Supreme Court, if necessary,[467] which could delay any trial for years. However, most experts expect the company to settle, given the risk of astronomical damages. Prior class action discrimination cases against Publix Super Markets ($85 million), Home Depot ($104 million), Texaco ($176 million), and Coca-Cola ($192 million) had all been settled out of court.[468]

The dissenting judge on the Court of Appeals, who considered the suit "unjust," declared: "Not everybody wants to be a Wal-Mart manager. Those women who want to be managers may find better opportunities elsewhere."[469] But even this business-friendly judge acknowledged that given the potentially "stratospheric" class-action damages, "a rational defendant will settle."[470]

The complaints of one of the original plaintiffs is more or less typical of the accusations directed at Wal-Mart in the case.

> After thirty years of retail experience, Deborah Gunter began working at a Riverside, California, Wal-Mart in 1996 as a photo lab clerk. She says she applied for management positions and was passed over for less experienced men. She requested further training and never got it. When she was transferred to the Tire Lube Express department, she did the work of a support manager but never got the title or the pay. Her supervisor sexually harassed her, and when she complained, her hours were reduced, she says. After she trained a man to fill the support manager job, he got the title and salary, and her hours were reduced. When she complained about her reduced hours and discriminatory treatment, she was fired.[471]

Two of the original plaintiffs are African-American and have also filed racial discrimination suits against Wal-Mart.[472]

(Continued)

Among the company's other types of legal troubles are multiple violations of child labor laws. In 2005, Wal-Mart was fined by the U.S. Department of Labor for ignoring the youth employment provisions of the Fair Labor Standards Act.[473] Wal-Mart had employed 85 minors (16 and 17 years old) who performed prohibited activities, including operating fork lifts and unloading dangerous scrap paper balers. In one store, a teenage worker was injured operating a chain saw.[474]

A raid of 61 Wal-Mart stores in 2003 resulted in the arrest of 250 illegal aliens who worked at the stores, mostly on cleaning crews.[475] The undocumented workers were employed by janitor contracting services and hired by Wal-Mart in 21 states. Many of these aliens—from Mexico, Russia, Mongolia, Poland, and a host of other countries—worked seven nights a week without overtime or injury compensation. In yet another creepy emulation of the Kathie Lee model of employee confinement, they were often locked in the store until morning.[476] Wal-Mart agreed to pay an $11 million fine. "Officials said at the time of the raids the investigation involved wiretaps that revealed Wal-Mart executives were aware that the subcontractors used illegal workers."[477]

Wal-Mart has also been a defendant in at least 28 complaints brought by the National Labor Relations Board since 2001, citing proscribed antiunion activities such as intimidating, interrogating, or punishing employees.[478] Although Sam Walton was an impassioned foe of collective bargaining, the company has always maintained that it is "pro-associate" rather than antiunion. Nevertheless, Wal-Mart has been accused repeatedly of intimidating employees who even discuss unionizing, threatening to close stores where unions are making gains, and restricting union access to its employees.[479]

Wal-Mart sought a trespassing injunction in 1999 against the United Food and Commercial Workers Union, after UFCW organizers entered 120 stores to distribute union information to employees. In 2002, a friendly circuit court judge in Benton County, Arkansas—home of Wal-Mart's corporate headquarters—finally granted the injunction. The judge restricted the union's organizing activates not only across Arkansas but across the entire country as well.[480] That decision would later be overturned due to its spectacular overbreadth, but Wal-Mart had made its point: STAY OUT.

In 2000, ten butchers at a Wal-Mart Supercenter in Jacksonville, Texas, voted to join a union. A month later the company closed its butcher departments in Jacksonville and everywhere else, and switched to prepackaged meats. Wal-Mart claimed it was preparing to make the switch all along; but, coincidence or otherwise, a chilling message had been sent. Because ten butchers in rural Texas joined a union, every in-store Wal-Mart butcher's job nationwide was eliminated.[481]

The PBS program *Frontline* aired a report in 2004 on the battle between Wal-Mart and organized labor. During the broadcast, a former Wal-Mart manager told how he had dealt with the union issue:

> I used to stand in front of my workers and lie to them. I used to say the talking points, that the union's a cult. "You don't want to join a union. It's a cult. Why pay someone to speak for you? You can speak for yourself." . . . What I didn't tell the workers was that "If you have a union contract you might get better pay. You might be able to negotiate with your employer to have your healthcare completely paid for."[482]

Wal-Mart's vice president of communications sees things very differently. She insists that most of the company's workers don't want a union: "They've tried to organize us for so long, it's an embarrassment for them."[483] According to a published report, however, at the first sign of union activity, Wal-Mart managers are supposed to call a hotline, prompting a visit from a special team from corporate headquarters.[484]

(Continued)

Finally, one of the most incendiary components of the Wal-Mart Way is its practice of taking out life insurance policies on its lower-level employees, with the company receiving all the benefits when they die. This is known as "dead janitors" insurance[485]—or, more commonly, "dead peasant" insurance.[486] For years, the laws in most states had restricted companies to purchasing life insurance policies only for executives and key employees, whose experience and responsibilities made them integral to the company's management. Allowing employers to insure rank-and-file workers, it was feared, might encourage negligence that could financially benefit companies at the cost of workers' lives.[487] But when laws began to change and restrictions were lifted, Wal-Mart started investing heavily in dead peasant policies, eventually purchasing more than 350,000 of them.[488] The policies were a lucrative tax shelter. Not only are a portion of the premiums deductible, but, more importantly, companies are able to borrow against the policies, then write off the interest paid on the loans.[489] And, of course, Wal-Mart is the beneficiary when the "peasant" dies. *The proceeds of these policies have reportedly been used to fund Wal-Mart's executive retirement plan.*[490]

When an assistant manager of a New Hampshire store died on the job of a fatal heart attack, his widow was shocked to discover that Wal-Mart had purchased life insurance on her husband and named itself the beneficiary. Wal-Mart pocketed at least $300,000 from her husband's death. She and her two children pocketed nothing.[491]

In 2002, Wal-Mart was sued in Texas, where the law still restricts life insurance on low-level workers.[492] Secretly taking out such a policy in Texas is illegal.[493] In such a circumstance, the deceased's family would be entitled to collect the benefits. The widow of a Wal-Mart employee, whose death had brought the company more than $60,000, was successful in her claim. A Texas editorial ripped into Wal-Mart. It accused the company of "collective psychopathy."[494] It wondered rhetorically how concerned the Wal-Mart board of directors would feel if they discovered that Wal-Mart employees were taking out secret life insurance policies on *them*.[495] It added: "The ghoulishness of this practice speaks to the utter disregard—indeed contempt—that Wal-Mart holds for its 'associates'."[496] When a Wal-Mart employee was trampled to death the morning after Thanksgiving in 2008 by 2,000 frenzied Long Island shoppers in frantic pursuit of "Black Friday" bargains, the company issued a statement of support to the man's family: "We take care of our own."[497] It would be easier to believe this reassuring message—if one could somehow ignore all the evidence to the contrary.

Wal-Mart's most recent wave of bad publicity has come from south of the border. In April 2012, the *New York Times* published a lengthy article which detailed the widespread use of bribery by Wal-Mart executives in Mexico to obtain permits to build new stores around the country.[498] In the early 2000s, the country's consumer market was growing rapidly and Wal-Mart hoped to take advantage of the new demand by being one of the first on the ground. But government wheels turn slowly in Mexico unless aided by hired facilitators, or "gestores," who smooth the process with bribes. A former Wal-Mart executive described how he and his associates fanned out across the country delivering envelopes of cash to "mayors and city council members, obscure urban planners, low-level bureaucrats who issued permits—anyone with the power to thwart Wal-Mart's growth." The executive referred to what they were doing as "working 'the dark side of the moon.'" The goal of the campaign, he reported,

> was to build hundreds of new stores so fast that competitors would not have time to react. Bribes, he explained, accelerated growth. They got zoning maps changed. They made environmental objections vanish. Permits that typically took months to process magically materialized in days.

(Continued)

Among other things, Wal-Mart's practices in Mexico appear to have violated American law, particularly, the Foreign Corrupt Practices Act which "makes it unlawful to bribe foreign government officials to obtain or retain business." Individuals convicted under the law can be sentenced to prison for up to five years.[499] As of this writing no one at Wal-Mart has been formally charged with any wrongdoing related to the bribery scheme.

Columnist Neal R. Pierce has criticized Wal-Mart's "low-road" approach: "Wal-Mart has become the poster child for an era of unfettered globalized corporate operations."[500] Leo Hindery, Jr., former telecom carrier CEO turned political activist, has called Wal-Mart "a destabilizing business model, a dangerous detriment to America's middle class."[501] Hindery further notes that as recently as 2002 (the year of Sam Walton's death), the Business Roundtable of top corporate leaders was promoting a "high-road" approach under which corporations had a major responsibility not just to stockholders but to their employees, society at large, and the nation's economy. Today, the Business Roundtable—indeed most of the corporate world—focuses almost exclusively on profits.[502]

Two frequent targets of major antitrust litigation are the oil industry and the airline industry. In response to the oil shortage of 1972–1973, which drove up retail prices to levels consumers could scarcely believe, four states (California, Oregon, Washington, and Arizona) filed class-action suits against seven major oil corporations. The suits alleged that the shortage had resulted from an unlawful conspiracy among Exxon, Shell, Mobil, Texaco, Chevron, Unocal, and ARCO to fix the price of gasoline.

After 17 years of legal maneuvers, the so-called "Seven Sisters" began settling the cases. In January 1992, Exxon agreed to pay the plaintiffs $9.9 million.[503] In April, ARCO, Texaco, and Unocal agreed to pay a total of $63 million.[504] The following year, Chevron, Mobil, and Shell finally settled, just days before a scheduled trial, for a total of $77 million.[505] Although none of the defendants admitted any wrongdoing, and the $150 million combined settlement was far less than the billions sought, the attorney generals of the four states considered the agreements a hard-earned victory for long-suffering consumers.

While the Seven Sisters were dragging their "fourteen feet" through the judicial system, another class-action suit was being filed in federal court—this one aimed at the country's leading airlines. The defendants were charged with using an electronic fare data base to fix prices. Among the specific allegations against American, Continental, Delta, Northwest, PanAm, TWA, United, and USAir was that fares were kept artificially high because airlines sent coded signals to competitors announcing future fare hikes that each would match.[506]

By 1992, all the companies except PanAm (which had gone out of business) agreed to out-of-court settlements releasing them from the case.[507] The terms of the settlements were controversial and very unpopular with the flying public. The $458 million that the airlines had put up in return for passengers dropping price-fixing claims was in the form of discount coupons rather than cash. Instead of getting refunds, the 10 million ticket buyers who had flown with the affected carriers from 1988 through mid-1992 would have to pay the airlines more money in order to recoup past losses. The coupons, moreover, expired just three years after the settlement and were useful for only a small portion of the price of full-fare tickets—at best 10 percent. Some frequent fliers calculated that they would have to buy as many as 60 round-trip, undiscounted tickets in order to get full credit for the coupons that were due.[508] In addition, applications for coupons required filling out a complicated claim form containing four pages of fine print.

> [P]eople who filled out the simplest Form A, which involved no itemization, got a $25 voucher, four $10 vouchers and one for $5, for a total of $73. Those who filled Form B got two $25 vouchers, two for $10 and one $9, for a total of $79. Those who itemized on Form C got $79, plus 0.232 percent (0.00232) of their claims.[509]

Most ordinary travelers expressed a strong sense of frustration with this gibberish. One typical customer received $159 worth of coupons, but after wrestling with all the complex requirements, she concluded: "They are valueless."[510] Analysts estimated that fewer than 10 percent of the coupons would ever be redeemed by individual consumers.

The only major beneficiaries were large corporations. IBM, for example, received $3.3 million in discounts. "Their coupons were delivered in filing cabinets rather than envelopes."[511] The other big winners were the plaintiffs' lawyers, for whom the settlement had provided $14 million in fees. One business magazine suggested puckishly that those attorneys be paid in *coupons*.[512]

Although price-fixing is a crime, it is usually punished (as in the preceding examples) by means of corporate fines and administrative sanctions negotiated out of court. This policy rests on the notion that public exposure serves as a deterrent even when formal sanctions are weak.[513] Given the seemingly never-ending proliferation of price-fixing cases, however, such an assertion seems questionable. Yet, judges have been reluctant to impose criminal sanctions, especially jail sentences, on individual antitrust violators.[514] Consequently, jail sentences may have little deterrent effect because of their infrequent use and relative lightness.[515]

One form of price-fixing that *has* yielded criminal sanctions in a number of cases is the practice of bid-rigging. Perhaps offenses in this area are taken more seriously by the criminal justice system because the government itself is most often the victim, rather than individual consumers. Such was the case in the 1950s when manufacturers of heavy electrical equipment made a mockery of free enterprise.

CASE STUDY
The Great Electrical Conspiracy

Except for Watergate (Chapter 9) and the Enron accounting fraud (Chapter 7), no white-collar crime in American history probably has been analyzed more thoroughly than the so-called "Great Electrical Conspiracy." Although it is often treated as a single crime, it actually consisted, like both Watergate and Enron, of a cluster of interrelated conspiracies. At least twenty distinct product lines were involved, and a network of more than forty manufacturers were implicated.[516]

The collusion that would become a cultural norm within the electrical equipment industry emerged, not from a tradition of cooperation, but out of a climate of ferocious competition. In 1954, the Westinghouse corporation developed an improved transformer, which enabled it to jump into a market that had been long dominated by General Electric (GE). To recapture their position, GE launched an all-out price war, slashing prices on transformers and many other electrical products to

(Continued)

below cost. The ensuing battle cost the bigger companies millions of dollars and devastated smaller manufacturers.[517] When the price wars became incompatible with top management's demands for higher profits,[518] the industry's response was a decision to conspire rather than compete.

Instead of submitting competitive sealed bids for lucrative government contracts, executives began holding secret meetings at which they would agree in advance on prices and divide up the contracts among their respective firms. The customary sealed bids were thus reduced to a charade, since the "low" bid and winning bidder had been predetermined. The companies had effectively formed an illegal cartel—a flagrant violation of the Sherman Antitrust Act.

The scheme became unglued in 1959, when a communication miscue within the cartel resulted in the submission of identical, supposedly competitive bids to the federally controlled Tennessee Valley Authority (TVA). The TVA is the largest generator of electricity in the United States and a purchaser of enormous amounts of electrical power equipment. When this story broke, the press demanded an investigation. The Justice Department examined TVA records and discovered 24 other instances of matching bids over a three-year period. Some of these bids were figured down to one one-hundredth of a cent.[519]

The investigation soon revealed that bid-rigging was by no means peculiar to the TVA. It had become an endemic way of life industry-wide.[520] Over the years, electrical manufacturers had cheated taxpayers out of perhaps as much as a billion dollars by keeping prices at an unnecessarily high level.

> It represents real money, just as would money obtained through a bank robbery (in fact, hundreds or thousands of robberies). Whenever a municipal government was overcharged $250,000 for a turbine, its taxpayers had to make up the difference. Whenever a power and light company

bought a generator for 10 percent more than it was really worth, its customers paid correspondingly more for the energy they consumed.[521]

Ultimately, fines totaling about $2 million were handed out—mostly to GE and Westinghouse. Given the pecuniary magnitude of the crimes, the amount seems insignificant. Criminologist Gilbert Geis, whose work first ignited academic interest in the case, has noted that a $400,000 fine levied at GE would be equivalent to a man earning $175,000 a year receiving a $3 parking ticket.[522]

In 1961, 45 executives from 29 corporations were indicted for criminal conspiracy. All either admitted their guilt or pleaded *nolo contendere* (no contest). Thirty-one were convicted, of whom seven received jail sentences of 30 days.[523] Four were vice presidents, two were division managers, and one was a sales manager.[524] The other 24 convicted defendants were given suspended sentences. Good behavior earned the incongruous convicts a 5-day reduction in their terms. During their brief stay, they were described as "model prisoners." In fact, a warden called them "the most intelligent prisoners" he had housed all year.[525]

One aspect of this case that has long intrigued researchers was the unanimous rejection of any criminal self-identity among those convicted. For example, an officer of the Allis-Chalmers corporation explained that he had participated only because he had believed it had been part of his duty. In a memorable quote, one GE executive described the agreements as "illegal but not criminal." Yet if one examines the dynamics of the conspiracy—the clandestine meetings, the frequent use of public telephones, the fake names and secret codes—one recognizes techniques and behaviors that are strikingly characteristic of organized crime.

Many of the defendants further argued that they had been performing a positive service to the economy by stabilizing prices. In other words, "they shifted blame to the market structure rather than to themselves."[526] Self-serving neutralizations

(Continued)

are, of course, typical of most criminals—of any-colored collar.

Westinghouse stood by its offending executives, calling each a "reputable citizen," a "respected and valued member of the community," who had not acted for personal gain.[527] This denial of individual benefit offers no hint of the likely professional rewards attached to profitable bid-rigging.

In sharp contrast, GE fired all its convicted officers, condemning them for violating the company's purportedly strict ethical policy. Many observers, however, felt that GE was scapegoating its former executives for the sake of public relations. When one of the defendants was asked if he thought he had been "thrown to the wolves" by top management, his answer was yes.[528]

Bid-rigging has remained one of the most irrepressible of all antitrust violations. "Despite repeated waves of federal and state enforcement, it reappears with remarkable consistency."[529] In the 1980s, more than half the criminal cases filed by the Antitrust Division of the Justice Department concerned the rigging of sealed-bid procurement auctions.[530]

Almost all of the companies that supply food to New York City's schoolchildren were charged in 2000 by the Justice Department in a bid-rigging scheme that overcharged the city at least $21 million. Thirteen companies and 22 individuals were accused of conspiring to fix prices on more than $200 million worth of food. As of this writing, six companies and 12 individuals have agreed to plead guilty.[531]

The dairy industry has been the most conspicuous violator in recent cases. Since the early 1980s, companies have conspired to rig the bids to supply milk to schools and other public institutions (including, ironically, prisons) in a number of states. More than 100 people and companies have been convicted of bid-rigging charges related to school milk prices.[532] At least 18 persons have gone to prison.[533] The initial investigation took place in Florida in 1988, where seven dairies "allegedly negotiated with their competitors to determine which would win each school contract and at what price, after which the other firms submitted bids higher than that of the designated winner."[534]

A year later, the scandal crossed into neighboring Georgia, where that state's attorney general declared "there was a 'significant likelihood' that local school districts . . . had been the victims of violations of antitrust laws and that suspected bid-rigging could have cost the districts 'tens of millions of dollars' over the 10-year period being investigated by his office."[535]

By 1993, unmistakable evidence had been uncovered in at least 20 states that executives at some of the biggest national and regional dairy companies had conspired to rig bids on federal and state milk contracts, sometimes for decades.[536] For example, the giant Borden corporation agreed to pay a $5.2 million fine after it admitted to antitrust charges relating to bid-rigging in its contracts with American military installations.[537]

A massive bid-rigging scandal was settled in early 2006 when the American International Group (AIG), the world's largest insurer, agreed to pay out about $1.6 billion to resolve investigations by the Securities and Exchange Commission (SEC) and in response to a class-action suit filed by the ubiquitous New York attorney general Eliot Spitzer.[538] In addition to charges of illegal accounting and sales practices, AIG allegedly had conspired to "fix" the excess casualty insurance market. AIG had misled clients into believing that it had obtained bids for their excess casualty business in an open and competitive process. In fact, the process had been rigged, allowing conspirators to obtain fraudulently millions of dollars in commissions and fees.[539]

Price Gouging

Another practice falling under the general price-fixing rubric is price gouging. In 2005, in response to a case first filed in 1991 alleging damages going back to 1983, a federal judge finally ordered Exxon Mobil to pay damages to more than 10,000 gas station owners who had been overcharged for gasoline for more than a decade by the world's largest oil company. Depending on its appeal, Exxon potentially could owe the class-action plaintiffs over $1 billion. The dealers had filed a class-action suit because the company had charged them a 3 percent credit card transaction processing fee. The dealers had been offered a discount for cash on wholesale fuel prices to offset the credit card fee, but Exxon had never delivered the discounts.

Price gouging refers to "the practice of taking extraordinary advantage of consumers because of the bias of the law, monopoly of the market, or because of contrived or real shortages."[540] A vivid and reprehensible example could be seen immediately following Hurricane Andrew, which devastated Florida in 1992. Prices on urgently needed supplies were raised to outrageously high levels.[541] The same greedy scenario was replayed after the serious earthquake that struck Los Angeles in 1994. Many local merchants immediately doubled and even quintupled prices on essential items such as bottled water and batteries.[542] Price gouging includes spiraling price increases divorced from economic reality. This appears to have been the case when the price of infant formula shot up 155 percent during the 1980s, while the price of milk rose only 36 percent.[543]

Price gouging reflects corporate opportunism at its most ruthless. When a worldwide shortage of sugar caused sharp price increases for American manufacturers several years ago, products using sugar understandably rose in price concomitantly. The cost of soda, for example, went up 15 to 25 cents a can. Less understandably, however, when the sugar shortage ended and prices returned to normal, the cost of soda remained at its higher, shortage-created level. Furthermore, in an illustration of how willing corporations are to exploit consumers by gouging prices whenever possible, diet soda (containing *no* sugar) had also jumped in price. Moreover, *all* the major soft drink companies employed the same strategy—suggesting price-fixing as well.[544]

Cereal manufacturing is an $8 billion-a-year industry with over 200 brands on grocery shelves. It is an enormously profitable business, where the cardboard box sometimes costs producers more than the cereal inside.[545] Since the early 1980s (when the government dropped a lengthy investigation),[546] prices have gone up 90 percent (twice the increase for other foods)[547] with "little apparent relation to true costs."[548] In 1995, a New York Congressman called on the FTC to reinvestigate possible antitrust violations. Speaking from the cereal section of a local supermarket, surrounded by $4 boxes of Rice Krispies, Frosted Flakes, Honey Nut Cheerios, and the like, he declared: "When I come down this aisle, my blood pressure goes up 10 points."[549] One investigative report was titled "Snap, Crackle, and Price-Fixing?"[550] In 1999, both Kellogg's and General Mills announced new price increases for their cereals—at a time when farm prices were falling.[551]

The pricing practices of the American pharmaceutical industry have come under particular scrutiny. The United States is the only Western nation that does not control the cost of prescription drugs. Perhaps as a consequence, accusations of price gouging have been leveled at that industry for decades. In 1978, ABC News reported, for example, that the Mylan Pharmaceutical Company was producing three versions of the drug erythromycin, each a different color but otherwise *identical*. "The pink version is the generic and sells for $6.20; the yellow pills are marketed by Smith-Kline and sell for $9.20; and the orange ones are called Bristamycin and are marketed for $14.00."[552] A 1993 ABC News program reported that an inexpensive drug used to worm sheep was raised in price 10,000 percent when it was discovered that the drug could treat colon cancer in humans.[553]

Since 1980, prices for prescription drugs have risen three times faster than prices for all other products.[554] "The increases have forced millions of Americans of limited means to stop taking the medicines they need."[555] Senior citizens use the most prescription drugs of any age group—about 30 percent of the total annual sales in the United States. According to one U.S. senator, "Over 5 million people over 55 now say they are having to make choices between food and their prescription drugs."[556] A 1986 survey by the AARP reported that 18,400,000 respondents over 65 said that they had trouble paying for their medications.[557]

A scathing congressional report released in 1991 attacked the "excessive and unreasonable profits"[558] generated by pharmaceutical corporations. This report noted that the drug industry's average 15.5 percent profit margin more than triples the 4.6 percent margin of the average Fortune 500 company. It was projected that if prices continued to spiral at the current rate, a prescription that had cost $20 in 1980 would rise to over $120 in the year 2000—a 500 percent increase.[559]

Nineteen pharmaceutical companies agreed in 1999 to pay more than $176 million to settle a class-action lawsuit alleging that they gouged the public by overcharging pharmacies for medicines while cutting prices for HMOs and big volume buyers such as mail-order drug firms. This was the second time in three months that a court had found that major drug makers had conspired to destroy competition between retailers and health maintenance organizations.[560]

Drug manufacturers contend that soaring prices reflect huge research and development expenses, which compel them to plow most of their profits into R&D. According to the Pharmaceutical Manufacturing Association, the average cost to bring a new drug to market in 1990 was $231 million. Critics counter that drug companies lump marketing research costs into their R&D budgets and that promotional and advertising expenditures actually exceed those associated with true research and development.[561]

The alleged excesses within the pharmaceutical industry raise disturbing questions about where the line between profit and profiteering is drawn. In the words of a California Congressman, "Never have so few made such gross amounts of money from so many sick people."[562]

As the pharmaceutical industry's record toward the elderly demonstrates, price gouging is often directed at the easiest targets. Likewise, the poor, especially those who are members of minority groups, have long been singled out for victimization.[563]

When the President's Commission on Civil Disorders[564] issued its report on urban rioting in 1968, one of its most significant (though largely unnoticed) findings was that ghetto residents suffered constant abuses by local merchants. "[M]ost big purchases—furniture, appliances, cars, home improvements—are grossly overpriced."[565]

In the 1990s, racial tensions were attributed to the "systematic exploitation of minorities by banks, insurance companies, department stores, and other businesses."[566] For instance, drivers who happen to live in certain inner-city zip code areas usually pay higher auto insurance rates, regardless of their driving records. Bankers systematically "redline" entire neighborhoods, refusing to lend money to residents, who are then forced into the waiting arms of rapacious finance companies charging sky-high interest rates. Pawnshops, long a traditional symbol of inner-city usury, have staged a remarkable and very profitable comeback—doubling in number since the mid-1980s. At least five national pawnshop chains are now publicly traded on the New York Stock Exchange. One of the largest, Cash America (with over 250 units), charges up to 200 percent annual interest on its loans.[567]

The crude slum gougers described by the President's Commission may be less conspicuous today, but they are still prowling the fringes of the economic mainstream, separating the weak from the herd like practiced predators. Some have found new places to lie in ambush—behind store signs blaring RENT-TO-OWN. The rent-to-own industry developed about 30 years ago as a way to skirt new usury laws designed to limit interest rates that inner-city merchants were charging consumers who bought on credit. "By redefining such transactions as rentals with 'the option to buy,' rent-to-own dealers are free to charge interest rates of 100, 200, even 300 percent."[568] No wonder business reportedly has been booming. How else could one buy a $400 set of children's bunk beds for $16.99 a week for 78 weeks—a total of $1,325?[569]

Rent-to-own dealers defend their business as the only one willing to help low-income people who are shunned by banks and department stores. The leader of the industry's trade association has pledged: "Our customers have as much right to the American Dream as anyone else."[570] Unfortunately, they have to rent it.

Knockoff Rip-Offs

A special type of price gouging involves the covert substitution of low-quality counterfeit versions of brand-name consumer products—known as knockoffs. The MGM-Grand Hotel in Reno, for example, once refilled 16,000 bottles with cheaper liquor over a 14-month period between 1978 and 1979. Worse still, any unmixed liquor left untouched by customers leaving the hotel's Ziegfeld Showroom was "recycled"—that is, poured back into the bottle for the next customer. "Some of the drinks wound up with more mileage on them than the hoofers in the chorus line."[571]

Another practice, known as "economic adulteration," involves the use of cheaper, inferior ingredients to cheat customers and undercut competition.[572] In recent years, the Food and Drug Administration (FDA) has won convictions against companies and individuals engaged in making and selling bogus fruit juice, maple syrup, honey, seafood, and other food products.[573] So-called "fake food" does not generally pose a health problem, but, in the words of the president of an edible oil trade organization, "No one wants to pay for something they're not getting."[574] Olive oil is, in fact, one of the most frequently counterfeited food products. The FDA has uncovered many examples of olive oil labeled "extra virgin" (from the first pressing) that contained up to 90 percent soybean oil.[575] Reports from panels of testers in California reveal that 60 to 70 percent of the olive oil sold as extra virgin in that state is actually a lower-quality oil.[576]

The knockoff business is booming. In 1982, worldwide losses to American manufacturers due to counterfeiting or trademark infringement were $5.5 billion. In 1995, the annual cost had ballooned to $200 billion.[577] For example, in that year, Procter & Gamble (P&G) discovered counterfeit diluted bottles of its popular Head & Shoulders dandruff shampoo on shelves at a large supermarket chain.[578]

Most fakes today are made in China, a good many of them by children as young as eight years old. They are sent there—or sometimes sold—by their families to work in clandestine factories that produce counterfeit luxury goods.[579]

The most flagrant counterfeiting practice is probably the bootlegging of Blu-rays, DVDs, video games, and computer software (Chapter 12). For example, in 2001, U.S. Customs officials seized a shipping container in Los Angeles filled with $100 million in fake Microsoft software, including 31,000 copies of the Windows operating system.[580]

Knockoffs pervade a variety of other markets as well. Shoddy facsimiles of upscale furniture can be purchased at a fraction of the price. Often these pieces are superficially indistinguishable from the real thing until they begin to fall apart in a few years.[581] The garment industry (where the term "knockoff" was coined) has a long tradition of perfectly legal imitation, since copyright laws do not generally protect clothing designs.[582] Usually knockoffs are marketed as such, and consumers knowingly sacrifice quality for style. However, when the designer is counterfeited along with the design, a knockoff becomes a rip-off. For example, consumers have been victimized by bogus labels misrepresenting Levi, Jordache, and Guess jeans and couturiers Gucci, Cartier, and Ralph Lauren,[583] and even by garments misappropriating the official National Football League insignia.[584] A recent study reports that 10 to 20 percent of e-commerce sites that sell luxury items are offering knockoffs—from fake Calvin Klein jeans to ersatz Rolex watches.[585]

Consumers commonly fall prey to illicit knockoff jewelry. A single operation by U.S. Customs seized 500,000 fake designer watches.[586] As a callow teenager years ago, one of the authors of this book purchased a "Bulova" wristwatch at a bargain price from a street vendor. It was not until the watch stopped running a few months later that he realized that the tiny trademark read "**Bolivia**."

Some forms of product counterfeiting have much more serious consequences and in the next chapter we will consider one of them: fake pharmaceuticals. There we will see how consumers, many of them living in underdeveloped countries, may suffer serious medical consequences, and even death, when they unwittingly take "medicines" that lack key ingredients.

Notes

1. Quoted in Mayer, Caroline E. "Senate Panel to Open Sweepstakes Hearings." *Washington Post,* March 8, 1999: A5.
2. Quoted *ibid.,* A5.
3. Quoted in CNN (*cnn.com*). "Senate Probes Magazine Sweepstakes." March 9, 1999: 2.
4. *Ibid.,* 2.
5. Zagorin, Adam. "Sweepstakes under Scrutiny." *Time,* March 22, 1999: 71.
6. Mayer, Caroline E. "Sweepstakes Industry Defends Its Practices." *Washington Post,* March 10, 1999: E4.
7. Mannix, Margaret. "Congratulations, You're a Loser." *U.S. News & World Report,* March 22, 1999: 74.
8. Quoted in *Houston Chronicle,* "OK, but Ed McMahon Is Real—Isn't He?" April 15, 1999, C1.
9. Quoted in *ibid.,* C1.
10. Quoted in Mayer, March 10, 1999, *op. cit.,* E4.
11. Quoted in *ibid.,* E4.
12. *Atlanta Journal and Constitution.* "Dick Clark, Ed McMahon Listed in Fla. Suit against Sweepstakes." February 3, 1998: 4E.
13. McCormick, Darlene and Stidham, Jeff. "Man Believes He Won Prize Again." *Tampa Tribune.* January 31, 1998: 1. Kennedy, Helen. "Sweepstakes Sparks Suits." *New York Daily News.* February 15, 1998: 8.
14. Kennedy, Helen. "You're a Winner!" *Houston Chronicle,* February 22, 1998: 5A.
15. *Ibid.*
16. *New York Times.* "For Sweepstakes 'Winners,' Millions Are a Mirage." March 8, 1998: 30.
17. Wilborn, Paul. "Sweepstakes Player Sues for 'Winnings'." *St. Petersburg Times,* January 21, 1998: 1A.
18. *Ibid.*
19. Quoted in *ibid.,* 4A.
20. Lowry, Tom. "Sweepstakes Giant Agrees to Tone Down Mailings." *USA Today,* March 17, 1998: 1B.
21. Quoted in Kennedy, *op. cit.,* 4A.
22. Quoted in *ibid.,* 4A.
23. *Wall Street Journal.* "Sweepstakes Firm Accused of Preying on the Elderly." November 9, 1998: 13C.
24. Quoted in Biederman, Patricia W. "Elderly Subscribe to Contest Obsession." *Los Angeles Times,* February 7, 1998: A1.
25. Quoted in *ibid.,* A1.
26. Quoted in Wilborn, Paul. "Contest Hopeful Buses from N.Y." *St. Petersburg Times,* August 12, 1998: 1B.
27. Lowry, Tim. "Settlement Won't End American Family Woes." *USA Today,* March 20, 1998: 2B.
28. Mayer, Caroline. "Sweepstakes." *Washington Post,* March 1, 1999: 6D.
29. Lowry, March 20, 1998, *op. cit.,* 2B.
30. Quoted in Mannix, *op. cit.,* 74.
31. Sharp, Deborah and O'Donnell, Jayne. "Lawsuit Calls 'You're a Winner' Mailings a 'Ruse'." *USA Today,* February 3, 1998: 1A.
32. Lowry, March 20, 1998, *op. cit.*

33. *Wall Street Journal.* "American Family Set to Pay Out $4 Million in Settlement Accord." June 2, 1999: B16.

34. Lowry, March 20, 1998, *op. cit.*

35. White, Erin. "Sweepstakes Concern Seeks Creditor Shield." *Wall Street Journal*, November 1, 1999: B1.

36. Johnson, Greg. "Sweepstakes Operator Seeks Court Protection." *Los Angeles Times.* October 30, 1999: C1. Wilborn, Paul. "Sweepstakes Settlement Expected." *St. Petersburg Times.* October 30, 1999: 1A. *New York Times.* Sweepstakes Operator Makes Bankruptcy Filing." October 30, 1999: C1.

37. *Wall Street Journal.* "American Family Will Pay $33 Million in Settlement." December 10, 1999: C14.

38. Nathan, Sara. "American Family Will Pay $33 Million Settlement." *USA Today*, December 10, 1999: 1B.

39. *Ibid.*

40. *Ibid.*

41. Quoted in *ibid.*, 2B.

42. *Ibid*, 1B. The attorney general of Florida has also alleged that American Family has offered to sell nearly 470,000 names of senior citizens to other contests.

43. Quoted in *ibid.*, 2B.

44. Quoted in *ibid.*, 1B.

45. Sutton, Remar. "Dial '900' for Trouble." *Reader's Digest* 139, August, 1991: 39–43.

46. *Ibid.*, 41.

47. Davis, Kristin. "You Have Definitely Not Won." *Kiplinger's Personal Finance Magazine*, July, 1992: 56.

48. *Ibid.*, 56.

49. Pay-per-call telephone services actually predate the 900 area code by several years. As early as 1974, New Yorkers could phone a service called Dial-a-Joke and for a small fee hear comedian Henny Youngman deliver a sampling of his dusty one-liners.

50. Cobb, Nathan. "Dialing for Dollars." *St. Paul Pioneer Press,* July 4, 1991: 1F.

51. Gibson, William E. "Agencies Try to Put Dial-It Abuse on Hold." *Ft. Lauderdale Sun-Sentinel,* April 18, 1990: 1A.

52. Quoted in Cobb, *op. cit.*, 1F.

53. *Ibid.*

54. Mills, Mike. "FCC Proposes Clampdown on 900-Number Services." *Congressional Quarterly,* March 16, 1991: 664–666.

55. Sutton, *op. cit.*, 39.

56. Belkin, Lisa. "Offer of Free Voyage in Space Sends 2 on Trip to Texas Jail." *New York Times,* February 7, 1991: B13.

57. Sutton, *op. cit.*, 39.

58. Mills, *op. cit.*

59. Sallee, Rad. "Workers See no Future as Psychics on Hot Line." *Houston Chronicle,* April 7, 1996: 30A.

60. Stoeltje, Melissa F. "'Electronic Junk Mail'." *Houston Chronicle,* October 23, 1996: 10D.

61. *Ibid.*

62. *Ibid.*

63. Cobb, *op. cit.*

64. Crowe, Rosalie R. "Telemarketing Scams Boom: Few Report Losses." *Phoenix Gazette,* July 7, 1992: B4.

65. Sutton, *op. cit.*, 42.

66. Mills, *op. cit.*

67. In 1994, federal regulators proposed a crackdown on companies—mainly adult entertainment providers—that misleadingly charge customers large sums for services on toll-free *800* numbers. (*New York Times.* "'800' Numbers Revoked." August 11, 1994: D6.)

68. Glick, Rush G. and Newsom, Robert S. *Fraud Investigation: Fundamentals for Police.* Springfield, Illinois: Charles C Thomas, 1974.

69. Goldring, John. *Consumers or Victims?* Sidney, Australia: George Allen & Unwin, 1982.

70. *Ibid.*, 20.

71. Reitz, John C. "A History of Cutoff Rules as a Form of *Caveat Emptor:* Part II—From Roman Law to the Modern Civil and Common Law." *The American Journal of Comparative Law* 37, 1989: 247–299.

72. *Ibid.*

73. Best, Arthur. *When Consumers Complain.* New York: Columbia University Press, 1981; 3.

74. Swift, Jonathan. *Gulliver's Travels* (Second Edition). New York: Norton, 1961; 39. This book was originally published in 1726.

75. "Ye shall not steal, neither deal falsely, neither lie to one another." (*Leviticus* 19:11).

76. Aquinas, Thomas. "On Fraud Committed in Buying and Selling." In Monroe, Arthur E. (Ed.), *Early Economic Thought.* Cambridge, MA: Harvard University Press, 1930; 60.

77. Quoted in: Thio, Alex. *Deviant Behavior* (Third Edition). New York: Harper & Row, 1988; 432.

78. *Ibid.*

79. Cartwright, Joe and Patterson, Jerry. *Been Taken Lately?* New York: Grove Press, 1974.

80. *Ibid.*

81. Linden, Dana W. "Closing In." *Forbes* 15, June 7, 1993: 52.

82. York, Pamela. "'Faux' Fools Victims." *Postal Inspection Service Bulletin,* Spring 1990: 11–14.

83. Cartwright and Patterson, *op. cit.*, 57.

84. Marvin, Mary Jo. "Swindles in the 1990s: Con Artists Are Thriving." *USA Today Magazine,* September 1994: 80–84.

85. Quoted in Cartwright and Patterson, *op. cit.,* 66.

86. Quoted in: Kubiske, Daniel E. "Congratulations! You May Be a Fraud Victim!" *Everyday Law,* May 1989: 24.

87. *Ibid.*

88. Lewin, Tamar. "Undelivered Adoptions Investigated in 3 States." *New York Times,* March 22, 1992: 16.

89. Nieves, Evelyn. "Region's Quick-Cash Frauds Snare Desperate Consumers." *New York Times,* February 7, 1992: A1; *Consumers' Research.* "Protect Yourself Against Advance-Fee Loan Scams." December, 1991: 16–19.

90. Marvin, *op. cit.,* 83. Deepak Gulati, an Indian immigrant in New York City, for example, sold bogus 12 percent promissory notes to his countrymen. Gulati's operation was a run-of-the-mill Ponzi scam, using funds from new investors to pay dividends to earlier ones. There was nothing run-of-the-mill, however, about the $3.2 million Gulati stole from his fellow immigrants.

91. Cartwright and Patterson, *op. cit.*

92. Razzi, Elizabeth. "Scams That Add Insult to Injury: When Big Disasters Strike, Petty Chiselers Are Close Behind." *Kiplinger's Personal Finance Magazine,* May 1994: 88.

93. Farrell, Greg. "Hurricanes Whip Up Shady Investments." *USA Today,* October 10, 2005: 3B.

94. *Ibid.*

95. Knox, Noelle. "Con Artists Circle Over Homeowners on the Edge." *USA Today,* November 9, 2007.

96. Leinwand, Donna. "Foreclosure Rescue Scams Multiply." *USA Today,* August 4, 2008, 3A.

97. Marvin, *op, cit.,* 80.

98. *Ibid.,* 80.

99. Bekey, Michelle. "Dial S-W-I-N-D-L-E." *Modern Maturity,* April, 1991: 31, 32, 36, 37, 40, 44, 88, 89.

100. Harris, Marlys. "You May Already Be a Victim of Fraud." *Money* 118, August, 1989: 74–91.

101. Titus, Richard, Heinzelmann, Fred, and Boyle, John. "Victimization of Persons by Fraud." *Crime and Delinquency* 41, 1995: 54.

102. Princeton Survey Research Associates. "Consumer Behavior, Experience and Attitudes." (1999) Princeton, New Jersey.

103. *Ibid.,* 45.

104. Bureau of Justice Statistics, "Criminal Victimization, 2004." NCJ 210674. (2005). These include property crimes, violent crimes and personal thefts.

105. Seib, Gerald F. "Dallas Ordinance Against Car Repair Frauds." In Johnson, John M. and Douglas, Jack D. (Eds.), *Crime at the Top: Deviance in Business and the Professions.* Philadelphia: J.B. Lippincott, 1978; 319–322.

106. Glickman, Arthur P. *Mr. Badwrench: How You Can Survive the $20-Billion-a-year Auto Repair Ripoff.* New York: Wideview Books, 1981.

107. *Ibid.*

108. *Ibid.*

109. Blumberg, Paul. *The Predatory Society: Deception in the American Marketplace.* New York: Oxford University Press, 1989. A government survey was even more damning. It found that "53 percent of the money spent on car repairs was wasted because of overcharges, work not performed, wrong repairs, and incompetent work" (Thio, *op. cit.,* 432).

110. Seib, *op. cit.,* 320.

111. Sikorsky, Robert. "Highway Robbery: The Scandal of Auto Repair in America." *Reader's Digest,* May 1987: 91.

112. *Ibid.,* 91–99.

113. Jesilow, Paul, Geis, Gilbert, and O'Brien, Mary Jane. "Experimental Evidence that Publicity Has No Effect in Suppressing Auto Repair Fraud." *Sociology and Social Research* 70, 1986: 222–223.

114. *National Petroleum News.* "California Accuses Sears of Bilking Auto Service Customers." Vol. 84, August, 1992: 21–22.

115. Yin, Tung. "Retailing: Sears Is Accused of Billing Fraud at Auto Centers." *Wall Street Journal,* June 12, 1992: B1.

116. Quinn, Judy. "Employee Motivation: Repair Job." *Incentive* 166, October, 1992: 40–46.

117. Fisher, Lawrence M. "Company News: Sears Ousts Chairman of Auto Division." *New York Times,* December 19, 1992: 39.

118. Ringer, Richard. "Company News: A President for Sears Automotive." *New York Times,* April 13, 1993: D15.

119. Miller, Thomas J. "Telemarketing: Reach Out and Cheat Someone." *State Government* 61, 1988: 98–99.

120. Crowe, *op. cit.*

121. Hassell, Greg. "A Hang-Up about Phone Solicitors." *Houston Chronicle,* March 13, 1996: 1C. Block, Sandra. "Scam Victims Get Help from FBI, AARP." *USA Today,* December 5, 1996: B1.

122. Ramirez, Anthony. "A Crackdown on Phone Marketing." *New York Times,* February 10, 1995: D1.

123. Bekey, *op. cit.,* 32.

124. Miller, *op. cit.,* 98.

125. *Ibid.*

126. Harris, *op. cit.*

127. *home.att.net.* "West Palm Beach Florida." May 5, 2006.

128. *forexhelp.com.* "Ex-Currency Trader Ordered to Pay $33M." January 12, 2006.

129. *irs.gov.* "Two Sentenced in Investment Fraud Scheme." August 27, 2007. *nctimes.com.* "Pair Sentenced for Cheating Investors Out of Millions." August 28, 2007.

130. Smith, Marguerite T. "Guard Against Charity Scams." *Money* 23, February, 1994: 19. Also see Goldstein, Linda. "FTC Targeting Charitable Solicitation Fraud." *Telemarketing* 12, June, 1994: 18–19.

131. Marvin, *op. cit.*

132. Hager, Robert. "Charity Frauds Use Real Sob Stories." *MSNBC.com,* December 14, 1998.

133. Bekey, *op. cit.*, 36.

134. Hager, *op. cit.*

135. Harris, *op. cit.*

136. Bekey, *op. cit.*, 40. In 1995, the U.S. Postal Inspection Service outraged the art world when it announced plans to auction off more than 12,000 *fake* Dali prints it had seized from a major art fraud operation. Asked if the forgeries could re-enter the art market after purchase, a spokesman for the Postal Inspection Service replied: "I'm sure anything is possible." (Blumenthal, Ralph. "Government Sale of Fake Dalis Raises Ire." *Houston Chronicle,* November 7, 1995: 4D.)

137. In addition to telemarketing fraud, the elderly have always been the favorite target of classic confidence swindles, such as the "pigeon drop" and the "phony bank examiner." For a description of these and other "con games" run on older victims see: Friedman, Monroe. "Confidence Swindles of Older Consumers." *Journal of Consumer Affairs* 26, 1992: 20–46.

138. Wangrin, Mark. "Addressing the Elderly: Senior Citizens a Popular Target for Mail Marketers." *Austin American Statesman,* June 19, 1994: A1.

139. Kahn, K. Pica. "AARP Warns Older Adults About Scams." *Houston Chronicle 50 Plus Supplement,* September 24, 1999: 1, 9.

140. Seeman, Bruce T. "Swindlers Target Lonely, Unwary Seniors." *Miami Herald,* July 8, 1993: 1BR.

141. Tighe, Theresa. "Swindlers Zero in on Elderly: Older People Have Assets and the Vultures Know It." *St. Louis Post-Dispatch,* January 30, 1994: 1D.

142. Barker, John. "Consumer Fraud." *Credit World* 82, 1994: 32.

143. *New York Times.* "Phone Swindlers Dangle Prizes to Cheat Elderly Out of Millions." June 29, 1997: 17.

144. Tighe, *op, cit.*

145. Harris, *op. cit.*

146. Bekey, *op. cit.*, 32.

147. Leeds, Jeff. "Officials Put Pressure on Telemarketers." *Los Angeles Times,* August 20, 1998: A23.

148. It seems appalling that telephone companies, which often subject individual customers to exhaustive credit checks, require next to nothing in the way of disclosure from businesses requesting "800" numbers.

149. Harris, *op. cit.*, 79.

150. *Ibid.*

151. Crowe, *op. cit.*

152. Harris, *op. cit.*, 77.

153. *irs.gov.* "Fraudulent Investment Operator Sentenced to 108 Months in Prison." April 7, 2008.

154. Huffstutter, P. J. "Dozens in O.C. Held in Telemarketing Fraud Inquiries." *Los Angeles Times,* December 18, 1998: C1, C8.

155. The description of this case is gleaned from Moore, Thomas. "A New Scam: Tele-Blackmail." *U.S. News & World Report,* June 11, 1990: 51–52.

156. Moore, *op. cit.*, 52.

157. *Los Angeles Times.* "Nearly 1,000 Telemarketers Arrested in 2 1/2 Year Probe." December 18, 1998: A41.

158. Quoted in *Houston Chronicle.* "FBI Uses New Wrinkle to 'Scam' Con Artists." June 29, 1998: 3A.

159. Quoted in *ibid.,* 3A.

160. *Los Angeles Times.* "Ex-O.C. Man Pleads Guilty to Telemarketing Fraud." December 18, 1998: C10.

161. *Ibid.,* C10.

162. Shover, Neal, Coffey, Glenn, and Sanders, Clinton. "Dialing for Dollars: Opportunities, Justifications, and Telemarketing Fraud." 2004. *Qualitative Sociology.* 27 (1): 70.

163. *Ibid.,* 71.

164. *Consumers' Research.* "Protect Yourself Against Advance-Fee Loan Scams." December 1991: 17.

165. *Houston Chronicle.* "Telemarketing Company Settles Fraud Charges." February 14, 2003: 25A.

166. *Ibid.*

167. *irs.gov.* Gecko Communications Owners and Managers Sentenced in $15.6 Million Telemarketing Fraud." December 19, 2006.

168. News Release from the Office of the United States Attorney, Western District of Missouri. "Jury Convicts Gecko Communications Owner, Managers in Telemarketing Fraud." March 26, 2006.

169. Hudson, Mike. "Robbin' the Hood." *Mother Jones* 19, July, 1994: 25–29.

170. Hudson, Mike. "Stealing Home." *Washington Monthly,* June 1992: 23.

171. Crosier, Louis. "Home Equity Scams Foreclose on the American Dream." *Public Citizen,* Summer 1994: 10–12.
172. *Ibid.,* 12.
173. *Ibid.*
174. *Ibid.*
175. *Ibid.*
176. Quoted in *ibid.,* 25.
177. Hudson, *op. cit.*
178. Quoted in *ibid.,* 27.
179. Harrop, Froma. "This Is Why the Clintons Still Bother Me so Much." *Houston Chronicle,* June 4, 2007: B7.
180. Koman, Richard. "List Brokers Welcome Thieves Who Target Elderly. *government.zdnet.com,* May 22, 2007.
181. Duhigg, Charles. "Bilking the Elderly, With a Corporate Assist." *New York Times,* May 20, 2007, 1B.
182. Koman, *op. cit.*
183. Quoted in *ibid.*
184. *Ibid.*
185. Quoted in *ibid.*
186. *Ibid.*
187. Quoted in *ibid.*
188. *Ibid.*
189. *Ibid.*
190. *Ibid.*
191. U.S. Senate Permanent Subcommittee on Investigations. Testimony of Wesley Wannemacher. March 7, 2007.
192. *Ibid.*
193. *USA Today.* "When Interest Rates Hit 32 percent, There Ought to Be a Law." March 9, 2007: 11A.
194. Day, Kathleen. "Bank Chief to Apologize for Overcharges." *Washington Post,* March 7, 2007: D1.
195. Singletary, Michelle. "How They Rig the Credit Card Game." *Washington Post,* March 11, 2007: F1.
196. *USA Today, op. cit.*
197. Singletary, *op. cit.*
198. *USA Today, op.cit.*
199. Hardie, Ann. "Bad Trade Schools Rip Off the Poor—and Taxpayers." *Atlanta Journal & Constitution,* January 28, 1990: 1A.
200. *Ibid.*
201. *Ibid.*
202. Quoted in *ibid.*
203. *Ibid.*
204. *Ibid.,* A1.
205. *Ibid.*
206. Scolforo, Mark. "Online School That Gave Cat an MBA Is Sued." *channels.netscape.com,* December 7, 2004.
207. For a more precise legal definition of deceptive advertising, see Preston, Ivan L. "The Definition of Deceptiveness in Advertising and Other Commercial Speech." *Catholic University Law Review* 39, 1990: 1035–1039.
208. Quoted in Clark, Charles S. "Advertising Under Attack, Part Two." *CQ Researcher* 18, 1991: 673.
209. Swagler, Roger M. *Caveat Emptor: An Introductory Analysis of Consumer Problems.* Lexington, MA: D.C. Heath, 1975.
210. Thio, *op. cit.*
211. A recent example would be the Home Shopping Network's commercials for baseballs autographed by Hall-of-Fame catcher Johnny Bench. Viewers were told that the baseballs were worth $129 but were available at the "sensational" price of $49.95. A sports collectible price guide puts the value of a Bench-autographed ball at $35. Both the Home Shopping Network and Bench himself were cited for misrepresentation by the New York City Consumer Affairs Agency (*New York Times.* "And Here's the Pitch." October 8, 1993: B12.).
212. An example of deceptive cinematography would be a 1979 case, in which the nation's largest toymaker was found guilty of running a misleading ad which showed a toy horse standing on its own—by means of special camera techniques and film editing—when the horse, in fact, could not stand (Eitzen, D. Stanley and Timmer, Doug A. *Criminology: Crime and Criminal Justice.* New York: John Wiley & Sons, 1985).
213. Simonson, Alexander and Holbrook, Morris B. "Permissible Puffery Versus Actionable Warranty in Advertising and Salestalk: An Empirical Investigation." *Public Policy & Marketing* 12, 1993: 216–233.
214. Swagler, *op. cit.*
215. Clinard, Marshall B. and Yeager, Peter C. *Corporate Crime.* New York: Free Press, 1980.
216. *Los Angeles Times.* "FTC Orders Novartis to Run Ads Retracting Claims About Doan's." May 28, 1999: C5. *Houston Chronicle.* "Maker of Pills May Appeal Order on Ads." May 30, 1999: 17A.
217. *Consumer Reports.* "Bad Apples: In the Executive Suite." May 1989: 294.
218. Quoted in *ibid.,* 294.
219. Traub, James. "Into the Mouths of Babes." *New York Times Magazine,* July 24, 1988: 18–20, 37–38, 52–53.
220. Henkel, John. "Seafood Maker Fined for Misbranding." *FDA Consumer* 29, November 1995: 33–34.

221. Robichaux, Mark. "Home Shopping Agrees to Revise Policy on Jewelry." *Wall Street Journal,* May 6, 1994: B8.

222. *Los Angeles Times.* "Home Shopping Network to Pay Fine." April 16, 1999: C2.

223. Walsh, Sharon. "FTC Cites NordicTrack for Making False Claims." *Houston Chronicle,* February 16, 1996: 10A.

224. *ftc.gov.* "FTC Reaches Settlement with Jenny Craig to End Diet Program Advertising Litigation." May 29, 1997.

225. Quoted in *ftc.gov.* "Company Settles FTC Charges: Ads for Coppertone Kids Sunblock Were Deceptive." February 18, 1997.

226. *ftc.gov.* "Dell Computer and Micron Electronics Settle FTC Charges that Ads Misled Consumers About the Costs of Leasing Computers." May 13, 1999.

227. *ftc.gov.* "Apple Computer Settles FTC Charges that It's 'Apple Assurance' Program Was Deceptive." January 26, 1999.

228. *ftc.gov.* FTC Accepts Settlement of Charges That Ads for Winston "No Additive" Cigarettes Are Deceptive." March 3, 1999. *Los Angeles Times.* "RJR Agrees to 'No Additive' Explanation on Ads." March 4, 1999: C6.

229. Dugas, Christine. "Providian to Pay $300 M to Settle Deception Charges." *USA Today,* June 29, 2000: 1B.

230. *mealeys.com.* "$8.3 Million Refund Ordered in False Advertising Case." *Mealey's Litigation Report* 2, August 12, 1999.

231. Hladky, Mary. "Federal Judge Weighs in on Fraudulent Diet Drug Program." *The Legal Intelligencer,* July 21, 1999: 4.

232. *mealeys.com, op. cit.*

233. *Baltimore Sun.* "Diet Pill Company ordered to Refund $8 Million." July 20, 1999: 5A. *Atlanta Journal and Constitution.* "Dissatisfied Dieters Can Get Money Back for Pills." July 21, 1999: 6F.

234. Gillis, Michael. "False-Claims Complaints Settled by TV Pitchman." *Chicago Sun-Times,* January 14, 1998: 9. *Houston Chronicle.* "Infomercial Pitchman, Associates Fined $1 Million." January 14, 1998: 3C.

235. Gattuso, Gregg. "DRTV Host Charged in Pyramid Scheme." *Direct Marketing* 59, May 1996: 10–11.

236. *Orange County Register.* "Infomercial Star Trudeau Charged." September 15, 2007: 2.

237. Quoted in Gillis, *op. cit.,* 9.

238. Jouzaitis, Carol. "Read Those Labels Carefully and You Still May Be Misled." *Chicago Tribune,* June 18, 1990: 4.

239. *Ibid.*

240. *New York Times.* "F.T.C. Warning for Stouffer." October 5, 1994: D18.

241. *New York Times.* "Ad Settlement by Sara Lee." August 8, 1994: D8.

242. Goldemberg, Robert L. "Nature's Miracles." *Drug & Cosmetic Industry* 157, November 1995: 46–49.

243. Federal Trade Commission. *Weight-Loss Advertising: An Analysis of Current Trends.* 2002: 1.

244. *Ibid.,* 10.

245. *Ibid.,* 10.

246. *Ibid.,* 1.

247. *Ibid.,* 28.

248. Clark, Charles S. "Advertising under Attack, Part One." *CQ Researcher,* 18, 1991: 659–670.

249. Choate, Robert B. "How Television Grabs Kids for Fun and Profit." In Heilbronner, Robert L. and London, Paul (Eds.), *Corporate Social Policy,* Reading, MA: Addison-Wesley, 1975; 181–186.

250. Clark, Part One, *op. cit.*

251. Myers, David G. *Social Psychology* (Third Edition). New York: McGraw-Hill, 1990.

252. *Ibid.,* 264.

253. Favorite tricks include speeding up the film or tape to make the toy appear faster and more powerful than it is, and utilizing wide-angle lenses and extreme close-ups to make it look much bigger.

254. Quoted in Clark, Part One, *op. cit.,* 666.

255. Myers, *op. cit.*

256. Stevens, Amy. "The Mouthpiece: Class-Action Lawyers Brawl over Big Fees in Milli Vanilli Fraud; They Line up Teen 'Victims' of the Lip-Synching Duo; Judge Notes Strong Odor, Rob and Fab or Fab and Tide?" *Wall Street Journal,* October 24, 1991: A1.

257. *Ibid.*

258. Blumenthal, Ralph. "When Buying a Bed, Beware." *New York Times,* February 22, 1979: C1, C8.

259. Quoted in Howard, 218.

260. Johnson and Douglas, *op. cit.*

261. *Ibid.,* 29.

262. *Ibid.,* 29.

263. Nelson, Phillip. "Advertising as Information." *Journal of Political Economy* 82, 1974: 729–754.

264. Gerstner, Eitan and Hess, James D. "Can Bait and Switch Benefit Consumers?" *Marketing Science* 9, 1990: 114–124.

265. Nagler, Matthew G. "Rather Bait than Switch: Deceptive Advertising with Bounded Consumer Rationality." *Journal of Public Economics* 51, 1993: 360.

266. Akerlof, George A. and Dickens, William T. "The Economic Consequences of Cognitive Dissonance." *American Economic Review* 72, 1982: 307–319.

See also: Festinger, Leon. *A Theory of Cognitive Dissonance.* New York: Harper and Row, 1957.

267. Fix, Janet L. "Justice Dept. Fixated on Price Fixing." *USA Today,* September 8, 1995: 1B.

268. U.S. Department of Justice. "Antitrust Enforcement and the Consumer." 1992: 1.

269. Clinard, Marshall B. *et al., Illegal Corporate Behavior.* Washington, D.C.: Government Printing Office, 1979; 184. It should also be noted that price-fixing is not confined to products; prices for services may be fixed as well. In 1990, three Arizona dentists were convicted of conspiring to fix the price of managed-care contracts. This was the first time in more than 50 years that price-fixing charges had been filed against healthcare providers (*Modern Healthcare.* "Both Sides 'Win' Appeal of Price-Fixing Convictions." September 2, 1992: 96).

270. Bryant, Adam. "USX Must Pay $630 Million in Price-Fixing." *New York Times,* May 29, 1993: 33.

271. *ftc.gov.* "Quexco to Settle FTC Charges." May 14, 1999.

272. *Wall Street Journal.* "Major Glass Makers Convicted by Jury in Price-Fixing Case." December 24, 1991: B4.

273. U.S. Department of Justice. "Antitrust Enforcement and the Consumer." Washington, D.C.: U.S. Government Printing Office, 2001.

274. *New York Times.* "Gas Concerns to Settle Suit." September 26, 1990: D4.

275. Enr. "Price-Fixing Charges Made." Vol. 235, September 18, 1995: 18.

276. Liedtke, Michael. "Former Bayer AG Exec Will Plead Guilty to Price-Fixing Scheme." *Associated Press.* May 16, 2005.

277. *ftc.gov.* "Two Leading Providers of Disability Insurance Agree to Resolve FTC Antitrust Concerns." May 18, 1999.

278. *ftc.gov.* "Chicago-Area Doctors, Firms Settle FCT Charges over Fixing Prices for Kidney Stone Treatment." January 8, 1998.

279. *USA Today.* "Millions Awarded in Vitamin Price Fixing." June 16, 2003: 1B.

280. *New York Times.* "Keds to Pay to Settle Suits." September 28, 1993: D7. *sddt.com.* "New Balance Shoe Agrees to Settle Price-Fixing Complaint." June 13, 1996.

281. *Wall Street Journal.* "Premdor to Pay Fines Totaling $6 Million in Price-Fixing Case." June 15, 1994: A8.

282. *New York Times.* "Company News: U.S. Says Miles Will Pay Fine in Price Fixing." October 29, 1993: D3.

283. *New York Times.* "Plastic Ware Price Fixing." June 10, 1994: D4.

284. *ftc.gov.* "FTC Upholds Charges that Toys "R" Us Induced Toy Makers to Stop Selling Desirable Toys to Warehouse Clubs." October 14, 1998. *ag.ohio.gov.* "Attorney General Montgomery Sues Toys "R" Us and Major Toy Manufacturers for Price-Fixing." November 17, 1997.

285. Tomasson, Robert E. "Nintendo to Pay $25 Million in Rebates in Price Fixing." *New York Times,* April 11, 1991: D1.

286. *CNN.com.* "Judge: Millions of CD Buyers Owed Money." June 16, 2003.

287. Pear, Robert. "Company News: Mead Johnson to Pay $38.76 Million Settlement." *New York Times,* July 3, 1992: D3. Also: Ramsey, Ross. "Makers of Baby Formula Settle with State for $1.5 Million." *Houston Chronicle,* November 18, 1995: 1A, 18A; *Houston Chronicle,* "Abbott to Settle Formula Price-Fixing Claims." May 25, 1996: 3C.

288. *Houston Chronicle.* "Mrs. Baird's Bakeries Guilty of Price-Fixing." February 15, 1996: 1C.

289. *Wall Street Journal.* Kosher Food Firm is Fined $1 Million in Price-Fixing Case." May 20, 1991: B5.

290. Wood, H. Dan and Anderson, James E. "The Politics of U.S. Antitrust Regulation." *American Journal of Political Science* 17, 1993: 1–39.

291. Simpson, Sally S. "Cycles of Illegality: Antitrust Violations in Corporate America." *Social Forces* 65, 1991: 943–963.

292. Hage, David. "Hidden Monopolies." *U.S. News & World Report,* February 3, 1992: 42–48.

293. Cohen, Mark A. "The Role of Criminal Sanctions in Antitrust Enforcement." *Contemporary Policy Issues,* October 1989: 36–46.

294. Owen, Jane D. "Founder Surely Would Be Troubled by Exxon Mobil." *Houston Chronicle,* May 31, 2000: 23A.

295. Ivanovich, David. "Chevron, Texaco Agree to Merge." *Houston Chronicle,* October 16, 2000: 1A.

296. *news.BBC.co.uk.* "BP and Amoco in Oil Mega-Merger." August 11, 1998.

297. Oppel, Richard A., Jr. "BP Amoco, Arco Push for Deal OK." *Houston Chronicle,* January 14, 2000: 1C, 3C. *ABCnews.com.* "Oil Merger Gets OK." April 13, 2000.

298. Davis, Michael. "Reading & Bates, Falcon to Combine." *Houston Chronicle,* July 11, 1997: C1. While neither of these corporations may be a household word, their merger creates the largest offshore drilling company in the world.

299. Moore, Angela. "Chemistry Now Right for Dow, Union Carbide Merger." *biz.yahoo.com,* February 2, 2001.

300. Lieberman, David. "FTC Questions Time Warner CEO." *USA Today,* March 1, 1996: 1B.

301. *msnbc.com.* "Judge Questions Role of AOL Deal." October 14, 1998.

302. Geewax, Marilyn. "AOL-Time Warner Deal Approved." *Houston Chronicle,* January 12, 2001: 1C. Silverman, Dwight. "Mega-Merger to Unite AOL, Time Warner. *Houston Chronicle,* January 11, 2000: 1A.

303. Lundquist, Eric. "Lotus CEO Sees Lots of Growth Ahead." *dailynew.yahoo.com,* January 17, 2001.

304. *Houston Chronicle.* "Unilever Agrees to Buy Bestfoods for $20.3 Billion." June 7, 2000: 1C.

305. Fix, Janet L. "Even Big Mergers Don't Ring Antitrust Alarms." *USA Today,* August 31, 1995: 1B.

306. *Houston Chronicle.* "Insurance Titans Set to Merge in $16.4 Billion Transaction." August 21, 1998: 3C.

307. Henderson, Pam. "Will Rail Mergers Leave You Sidetracked?" *Farm Journal* (Central Edition) 119, December, 1995: Z8–13. See also: Phillips, Don. "Rail Merger: Is too Much Power Being Placed in too Few Hands?" *Houston Chronicle,* October 22, 1995: 15A; *Houston Chronicle,* "Merge with Care: Success of Two Railroads' Union Depends on Safeguards." April 6, 1996: 30A.

308. Bartlett, Bruce. "Bush's Views on Antitrust." National Center for Policy Analysis, 2008.

309. Shiver, Jube, Jr. "Two More Baby Bells Plan to Join." *Houston Chronicle,* April 22, 1996: 1A, 6A.

310. Lynch, David. "2 Phone Giants to Merge." *USA Today,* April 22, 1996: 1A. See also: Henry, David. "Bell-Nynex Deal Receives Static." *USA Today,* April 23, 1996: 1B.

311. Reggie, *op. cit.*

312. *Ibid.*

313. Neumeister, Larry. "$1 Billion Nasdaq Settlement OK'd." *Houston Chronicle,* November 10, 1998: 1C, 12C. *nandotimes.com,* "Judge Approves $1 Billion Nasdaq Price-Fixing Settlement." November 10, 1998.

314. O'Donnell, Jayne. "Vitamin Makers to Settle." *USA Today,* November 3, 1999: 1B.

315. Davis, Michael. "Smith, Schlumberger Hit With Fines." *Houston Chronicle,* December 10, 1999: 1C, 3C. The last company to be cited for contempt of an antitrust decree was the Boston dairy firm H.P. Hood, which was fined $102,000 in 1983, after it acquired control of three other New England dairies in violation of a 1981 consent decree.

316. *Ibid.*

317. Kelley, Matt. "Price-Fixing by Company Brings $100 Million Fine." *Houston Chronicle,* October 15, 1996: 1A, 8A.

318. Eichenwald, Kurt. *The Informant: A True Story.* New York: Broadway Books; 2000.

319. Willette, Anne. "Archer Daniels Midland OKs Record Price-Fix Fine." *USA Today,* October 15, 1996: 1A.

320. Quoted in: Galvin, John. "The New Business Ethics." *Smart Business* 13, June 2000: 88.

321. Sniffen, Michael J. "Steel Supplier Fined $110 Million for Price-Fixing." *detnews.com,* April 8, 1998.

322. Cox, Meki. "$135 Million Fine in Price-Fixing Case." *Orange County Register,* May 5, 1999: C3.

323. Bernstein, Sharon. "Drug Maker to Settle Case for $135 Million." *Orange County Register,* July 13, 2000: C1.

324. Quoted in *ibid.,* C1.

325. Galvin, *op. cit.*

326. *Ibid.*

327. Hughes, Duncan. "Business Set to Score as Bush Goes Soft on Antitrust Cases." *Sunday Business* (London), May 6, 2001.

328. Bartlett, *op. cit.*

329. O'Donnell, Jayne and Kessler, Michelle. "Infineon Accepts $160 Million Fine for Fixing Prices of Chips." *USA Today,* September 16. 2004, 1B.

330. O'Donnell, Jayne and Kessler, Michelle. "Infineon Accepts $160M Fine for Fixing Prices on Chips." *USA Today,* September 16, 2004: 1B.

331. *Time.* "The Tale of the Gates Tapes." November 16, 1998: 74.

332. Thurow, Lester C. "Microsoft Case Is About a Good Capitalist Practice: Running Your Competition Out of Business." *USA Today,* November 3, 1999: 31A.

333. McKenzie, Richard B. and Shughart, William F., II. "Is Microsoft a Monopolist?" *Independent Review* 3, Fall, 1998: 165.

334. Cortese, Amy, Garland, Susan B., and Hamm, Steve. "The Case of the Missing PC Makers." *Business Week.* September 21, 1998: 38, 40.

335. Quoted in McKenzie and Shughart, 166. The statement was probably a reference to a complaint lodged by the American Banana Company early in the 20th century. Archrival United Fruit was accused of using dynamite to blow up American Banana's Central American facilities in order to preserve its domination of the banana export market.

336. Metzenbaum, Howard and Cooper, Mark. "Consumers Ought to Fret About Microsoft Monopoly." *Houston Chronicle,* October 20, 1998: 19A.

337. *Ibid.,* 19A.

338. *USA Today.* "Important Dates in Antitrust Battle." April 3, 2000: 6A.

339. McKenzie and Shughart, *op.cit.*

340. *Ibid.*

341. *Ibid.*

342. Elhauge, Einer. "Microsoft Won Appeal, but Decision Was Incorrect." *Houston Chronicle*, July 2, 1998: 35A.

343. Brinkley, Joel. "States Plan to Sue to Stop Windows 98." *Orange County Register*, April 30, 1998: 1. One of the original 20 plaintiff states, Texas, would later withdraw from the suit.

344. Mitchell, Russ. "Finally, the Trial Is About to Begin." *U.S. News & World Report* 125: October 19, 1998: 48.

345. Wolfe, Richard. "What's at Stake in the Microsoft Trial?" *New Republic* 22. November 16, 1998: 22. Wilson, Dave. "Feds' 1st Blow: Video of Gates." *Orange County Register*. October 20, 1998: C1, C12.

346. Taylor, Chris. "Gates in the Dock." *Time* 152, October 19, 1998: 68, 69.

347. Quoted in *ibid.*, 69.

348. *Ibid.*

349. Miller, Greg and Helm, Leslie. "Microsoft Case Tried in Court of Public Opinion." *Los Angeles Times*, May 20, 1998: D1, D10.

350. *Los Angeles Times*. "U.S. May Seek Wider Actions Against Microsoft." October 8, 1998: C3.

351. *Ibid.*

352. Wolfe, *op. cit.*, 22.

353. Sandberg, Jared. "Storming Gates." *Newsweek*. November 2, 1998: 42.

354. Quoted in: *Los Angeles Times*. "Government Lawyers Grill Bill Gates for a Second Day." August 29, 1998: D2.

355. *Fortune*. "High Noon." November 23, 1998: 162.

356. Quoted in *ibid.*, 162.

357. Quoted in *ibid.*, 162.

358. *Time*. "The Tale of the Gates Tapes." November 16, 1998: 74.

359. *Ibid.*

360. *Ibid.*, 74.

361. *Los Angeles Times*. "Gates' Taped Pretrial Testimony Provokes Laughter From Judge." November 17, 1998: C3.

362. *Fortune, op. cit.*, 163.

363. Quoted in: *Orange County Register*. "Microsoft: Case Turns on Allegation of an Attempt to Split Browser Market." October 20, 1998: C1, C12.

364. Brinkley, Joel and Lohr, Steve. "Strong Evidence Contradicts Gates." *Houston Chronicle*, October 20, 1998: 1C, 10C.

365. *Fortune, op. cit.*

366. Quoted in *Fortune, op. cit.*, 163. Ironically, in the middle of the trial, AOL announced plans to buy Netscape for $10 billion.

367. Eun-Kyng, Kim. "Apple: Microsoft's $150 Million Partnership Had a Sinister Side." *Orange County Register*, November 2, 1998: 12.

368. Shiver, Jube, Jr. "Microsoft Threatened Apple, U.S. Contends." *Los Angeles Times,* October 28, 1998: C3.

369. Eun-Kyng, *op. cit.*

370. *Time*, November 16, 1988, *op. cit.*, 74.

371. Eun-Kyng, *op. cit.*

372. Quoted in *ibid.*, 12.

373. Cortese *et al.*, 38.

374. *Ibid.*

375. Quoted in *ibid.*, 38.

376. Quoted in *ibid.*, 38.

377. *Fortune, op. cit.*, 164.

378. *Ibid.*

379. *Ibid.*

380. Bridis, Ted. "Federal Lawyers Want Microsoft Split Three Ways." *Houston Chronicle,* January 13, 2000: 1C, 8C.

381. *Ibid.*

382. "Baby Bills" is obviously a tongue-in-cheek reference to Gates' name and the regional telephone companies that emerged from the break-up of AT&T in the 1980s. These new companies quickly became known as "Baby Bells."

383. Quoted in Silverman, Dwight. "Federal Judge Says Microsoft Broke the Law." *Houston Chronicle,* April 4, 2000: 1A.

384. Ignatius, David. "There Was a Hero in Microsoft Case— the Judge." *Houston Chronicle*, April 6, 2000: 27A.

385. Davidson, Paul. "Microsoft Split Ordered." *USA Today*, June 8, 2000: 1A.

386. *Ibid.*

387. Quoted in *ibid.*, 1A.

388. Quoted in Davidson, Paul. "Microsoft Awaits a New Hand." *USA Today*, June 8, 2000: 1B.

389. Davidson, Paul and Biskupic, Joan. "Microsoft Case Sent to Appeals Court." *USA Today,* September 27, 2000: 1B.

390. *cnnmoney.com.* "Microsoft Appeals Ruling." August 7, 2001.

391. Bray, Hiawatha. "Microsoft Madness." *Houston Chronicle, Zest Magazine,* February 11, 2001: 23.

392. *Ibid.*, 23.

393. *cnnmoney.com.* "DOJ, Microsoft Settle." November 2, 2001.

394. *Ibid.*

395. Quoted in *ibid.*

396. *Ibid.*

397. Quoted in *cnnmoney.com.* "Judge OKs Microsoft Settlement." November 1, 2002.

398. Moglen, Eben. "Shaking Up the Microsoft Settlement." *emoglen.law.columbia.edu,* January 28, 2002.

399. Quoted in *pff.org.* "Microsoft Settlement 'An Embarrassment'." November 6, 2001.

400. Quoted in *ibid.*

401. *Ibid.*

402. *USA Today.* "Yet Again, Microsoft Flexes Its Mighty Muscles." June 23, 2003: 14A.

403. *Ibid.*

404. *Ibid.*

405. Fishman, Charles. "The Wal-Mart You Don't Know." *Fast Company,* December 2003, 68–73.

406. Willis, Danielle. "Assessing Wal-Mart's Monopoly." *businesstoday.org,* Fall 2004.

407. Lippman, Dave. "Let's Talk about Why I Hate Wal-Mart." *davelippman.com.*

408. Fishman, *op. cit.*

409. Fishman, *op. cit.*

410. Willis, *op. cit.*

411. *Ibid.*

412. Quoted in Fishman, *op. cit.*

413. Quoted in *ibid.*

414. *Ibid.*

415. *Ibid.*

416. *Ibid.*

417. Lippman, Dave. "Let's Talk about Why I Hate Wal-Mart." *davelippman.com.*

418. Fishman, *op. cit.*

419. *Ibid.*

420. Willis, *op. cit.*

421. Fishman, *op. cit.*

422. *lizmichael.com*

423. *Ibid.*

424. *Ibid.*

425. *Ibid.*

426. *Ibid.*

427. Warren, Susan. "Employers Struggle to Pick Up the Pieces After Katrina." *The Wall Street Journal Online,* September 2, 2005.

428. Wheeler, Tim. "Wal-Mart—the Nation's Worst Workplace Bully." *pww.org,* January 24, 2003.

429. *intellectualpoison.com.* "Wal-Mart Is Pure Evil." April 7, 2004.

430. *massteacher.org.* "MTA Tells Wal-Mart to 'Wake up'." August 24, 2005.

431. *ufcw.org.* "Kennedy, Corzine and Weiner Introduce New Health Care Legislation to Hold Companies Like Wal-Mart Accountable." June 22, 2005.

432. Newman, Nathan. "Wal-Mart: Stealing Health Care." *nathannewman.org,* May 12, 2004.

433. Featherstone, Lisa. "Wal-Mart's Benefit Plan—Welfare and Food Stamps." *democraticwings.com,* December 21, 2004.

434. *ufcw.com, op. cit.*

435. *seattletimes.com.* November 27, 2002.

436. Hunsberger, *op. cit.*

437. *Ibid.*

438. *Ibid.*

439. Greenhouse, Steven. "Suits Say Wal-Mart Forces Workers to Toil Off the Clock." *sullivan-county.com.*

440. *Ibid.*

441. Quoted in *ibid.*

442. Wheeler, *op. cit.*

443. Draffan, George. "Multimillion Dollar Fines & Settlements Paid by Corporations." *endgame.org,* September 2, 2005.

444. *Ibid.*

445. Manning, Jeff. "Jury Finds Wal-Mart Broke Laws on Overtime." *The Oregonian,* December 20, 2002.

446. Hunsberger, Brent. "Testimony Conflicts with Wal-Mart's Image." *walmartsurvivor.com,* November 26, 2002.

447. Joynce, Amy. "Wal-Mart Workers Win Wage Suit." *Washington Post,* October 13, 2006: D2.

448. *Houston Chronicle.* "Wal-Mart to Settle 63 Labor Suits." December 24, 2006: D4.

449. Greenhouse, Steven. "Wal-Mart Settles U.S. Suit about Overtime." *nytimes.com,* January 26, 2007.

450. Quoted in *ibid.*

451. Goodison, Donna. "Wal-Mart Suit to Go Forward." *massaflcio.org,* September 24, 2008.

452. Kucera, Barb. "Wal-Mart Workers in Minnesota Win $54 Million." *tcdailyplanet.net,* December 9, 2008.

453. *birmingham.bizjournals.com.* "Wal-Mart Settles Minnesota Class-Action Suit for $54M." December 9, 2008.

454. Kucera, Barb. "Wal-Mart Lawsuit Exposes Widespread Worker Abuse." *tcdailyplanet.net,* September 26, 2007.

455. Kucera, *op. cit.*

456. Greenhouse, Steven. "Wal-Mart to Pay $54 Million to Settle Suit over Wages." *nytimes.com,* December 10, 2008.

457. Quoted in Greenhouse, *op. cit.*

458. *wfsb.com.* "Wal-Mart to Pay $640 Million to Labor Suit." December 24, 2008.

459. *Houston Chronicle.* "Wal-Mart to Settle 63 Labor Suits." December 24, 2008: D4.

460. *intellectualpoison.com, op. cit.*

461. Quoted in *ibid.*

462. Freedman, Michael. "Wal-Mart's Women Trouble." *forbes.com,* July 22, 2003.

463. Quoted in Joyce, Amy. "Wal-Mart to Appeal Status of Class Action Bias Suit." *Washington Post,* August 6, 2005: D1.

464. Freedman, *op.cit.*

465. Joyce, *op. cit.*

466. Joyce, Amy. "Wal-Mart Loses Bid to Block Group Bias Suit." *Washington Post,* February 7, 2007: D1.

467. Egelko, Bob. "Wal-Mart Sex Discrimination Suit Advances." *sfgate.com,* February 7, 2007.

468. Freedman, *op. cit.*

469. Quoted in *cnnmoney.com.* "Wal-Mart to Appeal Discrimination Suit Status." February 6, 2007.

470. Quoted in Egelko, *op. cit.*

471. Featherstone, Liza. "Wal-Mart Values." *The Nation.* December 16, 2002.

472. *Ibid.*

473. ESA News Release. "Wal-Mart Agrees to Pay Fine for Violating Child Labor Laws." *dol.gov,* February 14, 2005.

474. *Ibid.*

475. *talkleft.com.* "250 Undocumented Workers Arrested in Wal-Mart Probe." October 23, 2003.

476. Draffan, *op. cit.*

477. *Ibid.*

478. Armour, *op. cit.*

479. *Frontline.* "Wal-Mart vs. the Unions." *pbs.org,* November 16, 2004.

480. *Ibid.*

481. Armour, *op. cit.*

482. Quoted in *ibid.*

483. Quoted in Pinto, Barbara. "Union Battleground: Do Smiling Faces at Wal-Mart Belie Employee Unhappiness?" *abcnews.go.com,* February 5, 2002.

484. Schweitzer, *op. cit.*

485. Schweitzer, Barry. "A Matter of Policy." *Boston Globe,* December 10, 2002.

486. Meyer, R. H. "Wal-Mart's Dead Peasant Policy." *texassportfishing.com,* January 10, 2003.

487. Schweitzer, *op. cit.*

488. *texassportfishing.com, op. cit.*

489. Schweitzer, *op. cit.*

490. *texassportfishing.com, op. cit.*

491. Schweitzer, *op. cit.*

492. *Ibid.*

493. Sixel, L. M. "Dow Chemical Is Accused of 'Dead Peasant' Insurance." *Houston Chronicle,* June 6, 2002.

494. *texassportfishing.com, op. cit.*

495. *Ibid.*

496. *Ibid.*

497. *USA Today.* "Family of Man Trampled in N.Y. Sues Wal-Mart." December 4, 2008: 3A.

498. Barstow, David. "Wal-Mart Hushed Up a Vast Mexican Bribery Case." *New York Times.* April 12, 2012.

499. U.S. Department of Justice. "Lay-Person's Guide to the FCPA." n.d. http://www.justice.gov/criminal/fraud/fcpa/docs/lay-persons-guide.pdf.

500. Pierce, Neal R. "Confronting Wal-Mart's Low-Road Approach to Profit." *Houston Chronicle,* November 28, 2006: B7.

501. Quoted in *ibid.*

502. *Ibid.*

503. *Wall Street Journal.* "Exxon Corp.: Gasoline Price-Fixing Case Is Settled for $9.9 Million." January 15, 1992: B4. *New York Times.* "Exxon Moves to Settle Suits for $9.9 Million." January 15, 1992: D4.

504. *Wall Street Journal.* "Three Oil Companies to Pay $63 to 4 Western States." April 23, 1992: A4.

505. *New York Times.* "3 Oil Concerns in Settlement." January 12, 1993: B20.

506. *Wall Street Journal.* "Class-Action Status Granted in Airline Price-Fixing Suit." August 8, 1991: A5.

507. *Wall Street Journal.* "NWA, TWA Agree to Alter Pricing Action." June 21, 1991: B1. *New York Times.* "2 Airlines Settle Claims." June 24, 1991: D2. *New York Times.* "Company News: Continental Air in Settlement." June 16, 1992: D5. Pulley, Brett and O'Brian, Bridget. "More Airlines to Settle Suit on Price-Fixing; Delta, United of UAL, AMR and USAir Agree to Pay Cash, Discount Coupons." *Wall Street Journal,* June 23, 1992: A3.

508. McMenamin, Bridgid. "Paper for Us, Money for Them." *Forbes,* October 26, 1992: 272–274.

509. Wade, Betsy. "Practical Traveler; An Unhappy Lot of Plaintiffs." *New York Times,* January 22, 1995: Sec. 5, 4.

510. Quoted in *ibid.*, Sec. 5, 4.

511. *Ibid.*

512. McMenamin, *op. cit.*

513. Scott, Donald W. "Policing Corporate Collusion." *Criminology* 27, 1989: 559–584.

514. Cohen, *op. cit.*

515. Among individual antitrust offenders sentenced to jail between 1975 and 1980, the average time served was about one month in misdemeanor cases and three months in felony cases.

516. Baker, Wayne E. and Faulkner, Robert R. "The Social Organization of Conspiracy: Illegal Networks in the Heavy Electrical Equipment Industry." *American Sociological Review* 58, 1993: 837–860.

517. Herling, John. *The Great Price Conspiracy: The Story of the Antitrust Violations in the Electrical Industry,* Washington, D.C.: Robert B. Luce, 1962.

518. Scherer, Frederick M. *Industrial Market and Economic Performance* (Second Edition), Boston, MA: Houghton Mifflin, 1980.

519. Herling, *op. cit.*

520. Geis, Gilbert. "The Heavy Electrical Equipment Antitrust Case of 1961." In: Geis, Gilbert (Ed.), *White-Collar Criminal: The Offender in Business and the Professions.* New York: Atherton, 1968; 103–118.

521. Pontell, Henry N., Rosoff, Stephen M., and Goode, Erich. "White-Collar Crime." In: Goode, Erich, *Deviant Behavior* (Fourth Edition). Englewood Cliffs, NJ: Prentice Hall, 1994; 345–371.

522. Geis, *op. cit.*

523. Lewis, Anthony. "7 Electrical Officials Get Jail Terms in Trust Case." *New York Times,* February 7, 1961: 1, 26.

524. *Ibid.*

525. Quoted in *ibid.*, 105.

526. Pontell, *et. al.,* 357.

527. Geis, *op. cit.*, 110.

528. *Ibid.*

529. Howard, Jeffrey H. and Kaserman, David. "Proof of Damages in Construction Industry Bid-Rigging Cases." *The Antitrust Bulletin* 34, 1989: 359.

530. Porter, Robert H. and Zona, J. Douglas. "Detection of Bid-Rigging in Procurement Auctions." *Journal of Political Economy* 101, 1993: 518–538.

531. Bacon, John. "Companies Admit NYC School Lunch Ripoffs." *USA Today*, June 2, 2000: 3A.

532. Schmidt, Peter. "Bid Rigging Among School Suppliers Becoming 'Pervasive,' Experts Fear." *Education Week* 13, September 22, 1993: 1, 18.

533. Hage, David, Boroughs, Don L., and Black, Robert F. "Hidden Monopolies." *US News & World Report* 112, February 3, 1992: 42–48.

534. *Education Week.* "Milk Distributor in Florida Pleads Guilty to Conspiracy Charge in Bid-Rigging Case." May 11, 1988: 5.

535. Schmidt, Peter. "Justice Department Probing Milk Bid-Rigging in Georgia." *Education Week* 8, May 24, 1989: 4.

536. Henriques, Diana B. "Evidence Mounts of Rigged Bidding in Milk Industry." *New York Times,* May 23, 1993: 1.

537. *New York Times.* "Borden Fined $5.2 Million." September 15, 1993: D11.

538. Urban, Rob and Stein, George. "AIG's $1.6 Billion Settlement to Include Bid-Rigging." *bloomberg.com*, February 6, 2006.

539. *consumeraffairs.com.* "Insurance Executives Indicated for Bid Rigging, Fraud." September 15, 2005.

540. Eitzen and Timmer, *op. cit.,* 302.

541. Seligman, Daniel. "Hurray for Avarice." *European Economic Review* 36, May, 1992: 146.

542. Razzi, *op. cit.*

543. *Consumer Reports.* "The Sour Tale of Baby-Formula Pricing." Vol. 58, October, 1993: 626.

544. *Ibid.*

545. Hightower, Jim. *Eat Your Heart Out.* New York: Crown, 1975. Hightower points out that two cereals produced by General Mills—*Wheaties* and *Total*–are nearly identical. *Total* is *Wheaties* with 3/4 of a cent worth of sprayed-on vitamins. The only other difference is that *Total* retails for about 40 percent more than *Wheaties.*

546. Baldwin, Deborah. "The Cornflake Cartel." *Common Cause Magazine,* Summer 1993: 32–36. In 1972, the FTC filed a complaint for price-fixing against the country's four largest breakfast cereal companies. Those companies—Kellogg, General Mills, General Foods (Post), and Quaker Oats–controlled 91 percent of the market at that time (Sobel, Lester [Ed.]. *Corruption in Business.* New York: Facts on File, 1977).

547. Schulte, Brigid. "Snap, Crackle and Price-Fixing?" *Miami Herald,* March 8, 1995: 1A.

548. *Wall Street Journal.* "Congressmen Seek Inquiry into Cereal Pricing Method." March 8, 1995: A12.

549. ABC News 20/20. *Transcript #1512.* Denver, CO: Journal Graphics, 1995; 6.

550. Schulte, *op. cit.*

551. *WCVB.com.* "Cereal Prices Rising." April 23, 1999.

552. Eitzen and Timmer, *op. cit.,* 303.

553. ABC News. "Bitter Pill to Swallow." Television Program: *Primetime Live* 290, March 25, 1993.

554. Warden, Chris. "The Prescription for High Drug Prices." *Consumers' Research Magazine* 75, December 1992: 10–14.

555. Rovner, Julie. "Prescription Drug Prices." *CQ Researcher,* July 17, 1992: 599.

556. Quoted in *ibid.*, 600.

557. Pryor, David. "Prescription Drug Industry Must Be Reformed." *USA Today Magazine* 122, March, 1994: 74–75.

558. Quoted in *ibid.*, 600.

559. *Ibid.*, 599–624.

560. Lite, Jordan. "Drug Companies Settle Price-Gouging Suit." *Orange County Register*, February 20, 1999: G2.

561. *Ibid.*

562. Quoted in *ibid.*, 614.

563. Caplovitz, David. *The Poor Pay More: Consumer Practices of Low-Income Families*, New York: Free Press, 1967.

564. The Commission was chaired by Governor Otto Kerner of Illinois, who would later go to prison for bribery (see Chapter 8).

565. Miller, James N. "Slum Swindlers Must Go!" *Reader's Digest,* November, 1969: 169.

566. Green, Mark. "How Minorities Are Sold Short." *New York Times,* June 18, 1990: A21.

567. Hudson, *op. cit.*

568. *Ibid.,* 22.

569. *Ibid.*

570. *Ibid.,* 22.

571. *time.com.* "Used Booze," February 4, 1980.

572. Kurtzweil, Paula. "Fake Food Fight." *FDA Consumer Magazine* (online), March–April 1999.

573. *Ibid.*

574. Quoted in *ibid.*

575. Weise, Elizabeth. "That Label Could Be Costly Lie." *USA Today,* January 20, 2009: 1D. 2D.

576. *Ibid.*

577. Young, Catherine and Light, Larry. "Out! Out! Damned Knockoffs." *Business Week* 3441, September 11, 1995: 6.

578. Gilgoff, Henry. "Rip-offs of Popular Products Victimizes Both Consumers and Manufacturers." *Newsday.* August 27, 1995: 1. Eldridge, Earle. "Bogus Shampoo Scalps Consumers." *USA Today,* August 17, 1995: 1B.

579. Thomas, Dana. "Counterfeits Are Literally Terrorism's Purse Strings." *Houston Chronicle,* September 3, 2007: B7.

580. *Ibid.*

581. Owens, Mitchell. "The Knowable Knack of the Knockoff." *New York Times,* June 17, 1993: 61.

582. Daria, Irene. "Fashion's One-Two Punch: The Knockoff." *Glamour* 41, April, 1993: 199.

583. *Ibid.* Engardio, Pete, Vogel, Todd, and Lee, Dinah. "Companies Are Knocking Off the Knockoff Outfits." *Business Week* 3071, September 26, 1988: 86–88.

584. Weber, Joseph. "Here Comes the Blitz on Knockoff Artists." *Business Week* 3350, December 13, 1993: 8.

585. *Business 2.0.* "Cyberscams." March, 1999: 8.

586. Engardio, *et al., op. cit.*

3

Unsafe Products

During television's "Golden Age," the distinguished broadcaster Edward R. Murrow hosted a celebrity interview program called *Person to Person*. One week in 1954, Murrow's guest was movie star Humphrey Bogart. The two men were chain-smokers, so the image beamed to millions of primitive black-and-white screens became so progressively cloudy that many viewers probably began turning knobs in a frantic effort to fix their sets. Within 10 years, Bogart and Murrow were both dead of smoking-related cancer.[1]

For decades, smoking has been recognized as the primary preventable cause of death in the United States. For much of that time, it was popularly perceived more as a psychologically gratifying habit than a physical addiction. Then, in 1994—exactly 40 years after Bogart and Murrow's exhibition of synchronized puffing—the Food and Drug Administration (FDA) leveled an extraordinary accusation against the tobacco industry. "Simply put, the agency asserted that the reason many cigarette smokers find it close to impossible to break the habit is because the industry *makes* it close to impossible."[2]

It had always been assumed by the majority of the American public that the nicotine in cigarettes was only the residue of the nicotine that occurs naturally in tobacco. Few consumers would have suspected that additional nicotine might actually be sprayed on tobacco as it is processed. The commissioner of the FDA cited "mounting evidence" that nicotine is an addictive drug—five to ten times more potent than cocaine—and that cigarette manufacturers boost its levels to satisfy this addiction. A government pharmacologist has said of nicotine: "It works like a drug, it looks like a drug, it is a drug pure and simple."[3]

While tobacco companies publicly assert that nicotine is merely a flavor molecule, even they privately admit that it is a drug.[4] An internal memorandum from the Philip Morris Capital Corporation acknowledges that cigarettes, in effect, are nothing more than "nicotine-delivery systems."[5]

An RJ Reynolds memorandum states: "Nicotine is known to be a habit-forming alkaloid, hence the confirmed user of tobacco products is primarily seeking the physiological 'satisfaction' derived from nicotine."[6] Another confidential internal memo written in 1963 by the general counsel for the Brown & Williamson tobacco company declares: "We are in the business of selling nicotine."[7] When the press obtained this latter document in 1994, Brown & Williamson's response was, "We continue to maintain the position that cigarettes aren't addictive."[8] However, a former top scientist for Brown & Williamson testified under oath that "the company's lawyers repeatedly hid damaging scientific research."[9] One memo explicitly discussed "burying" unfavorable test results.[10] Another uncovered memo (this one from *1958*) reveals that Philip Morris executives rejected an internal report urging the company to remove benzopyrene, a known carcinogen, from its cigarettes.[11] And in the 1970s, "an industry scientist discovered how to remove harmful carbon monoxide from cigarette smoke but industry lawyers suppressed the research."[12]

Nevertheless, the Tobacco Institute still insists that "smoking . . . has yet to be proven to have a causal role in the development of diseases."[13] However, memos from the 1960s indicate that the industry's own research had concluded by then that smoking causes lung cancer and heart disease—studies never made public until they were "leaked" more than 30 years later.[14] Among other things, corporate documents revealed that "the industry destroyed results of its own product testing when the results showed 'biological activity,' a euphemism for ill-health effects."[15]

When the heads of the seven major American tobacco companies[16] were subpoenaed before a congressional committee in 1994, they were pelted with case histories of people who had died from the effects of smoking. All expressed sorrow over those deaths but denied that any of the deceased had been addicted to cigarettes. William Campbell, then president of Philip Morris, swore under oath: "I really don't accept that smoking is addictive."[17] Later, however, he was forced to concede at the hearing that his company had suppressed publication of a rat study, conducted in 1983 by its own scientists, demonstrating that nicotine *is* addictive.[18] In 1996, three former Philip Morris employees charged that the company routinely manipulated nicotine levels of its cigarettes. One of them, a former plant manager, said that tobacco was monitored for nicotine every hour 24 hours a day. If it fell below desired levels, the tobacco was reblended and the nicotine was boosted.[19] These whistle-blowers' sworn affidavits once again contradicted testimony by the CEO of Philip Morris, who had told Congress under oath that his company "does not manipulate nor independently control the level of nicotine in our cigarettes."[20]

In 1998, the big lie was again exposed when a California company, DNA Plant Technology (DNAP), pleaded guilty to conspiring with Brown & Williamson to boost the nicotine level in tobacco. "DNAP illegally shipped and smuggled genetically altered seeds to Brazil, where Brown & Williamson grew a tobacco plant called Y-1 that contained twice the amount of nicotine in naturally cured tobacco."[21]

Following the congressional hearings, the American Medical Association (AMA), in its sharpest attack ever on the tobacco industry, declared that cigarette makers had "duped" the public by concealing decades of research on the harmful effects of smoking.[22] The AMA concluded: "No right-thinking individual can ignore the evidence of tobacco industry duplicity. We should all be outraged."[23]

The tobacco industry "has used its money to distort the truth, influence politicians and intimidate any who would expose its secrets."[24] And while the industry has complained vociferously of the use of scare tactics by its enemies, it has long resorted to scare tactics of its own. Tobacco companies warn that "health Nazis" are out to bankrupt stockholders and put tens of thousands of employees on welfare.[25]

Once-secret Philip Morris documents reveal that the company has even used the threat of economic reprisals to intimidate drug firms marketing stop-smoking products. For example, when Merrill Dow Pharmaceuticals began marketing Nicorette gum in 1984, Philip Morris retaliated by canceling chemical purchases from Merrill Dow's parent company, Dow Chemical. In order to appease Philip Morris, Dow agreed to tone down its marketing of Nicorette and target only a narrow band of smokers who have been trying to quit, rather than attacking cigarettes directly or imploring all smokers to quit.[26] In a memo, Dow assured Philip Morris that it was "committed to avoid contribution to the anti-cigarette effort."[27] Dow's reward for its capitulation was a resumption of chemical orders from Philip Morris.

Although there have been a number of product liability and wrongful death suits filed against tobacco companies, no plaintiff had ever collected a dime in damages stemming from the use of tobacco until 1996.[28] The industry had won every previous case on the grounds that smokers knowingly accept the risks.[29] Even a 1995 case, in which a plaintiff suing Lorillard Tobacco was awarded $2 million by a California jury after claiming that he had contracted cancer from cigarettes, was an anomaly. California law protects tobacco companies against lawsuits for smoking-related illness or death, but in this case the disease was *not* attributed to tobacco but to the *asbestos* used in filter tips.[30] In 1996, however, a Florida man, suffering from lung cancer, was awarded $750,000 by a circuit court jury in a suit against Brown & Williamson.[31]

Perhaps spurred by the Florida verdict, the first retreat was sounded in the tobacco wars a few weeks later when Liggett Group (one of the smallest of the major tobacco firms) announced it was settling claims in a massive class-action suit filed by a woman on behalf of her 47-year-old husband, who had died of lung cancer, and 50 million other smokers.[32] The widow had declared that she wanted the industry to pay for its "deception" over the addictiveness of nicotine.[33] Liggett agreed to pay 5 percent of its pretax income, up to $50 million a year, to fund programs to help smokers quit the habit. The other companies named in the suit emphatically declined to participate in the proposed settlement.[34] Industry leader Phillip Morris USA thundered: "We intend to fight and win."[35] Two months later, the tobacco industry did indeed win a major victory when a federal appeals court threw out the class-action suit.[36] The plaintiffs vowed to carry their fight to the Supreme Court. They also announced plans to file 50 separate state class actions.

By 1997, 22 states had also filed suit against the tobacco oligopoly seeking to recoup millions of dollars in public funds spent to treat smoking-related health problems. Once again, Liggett broke ranks when it was announced that, as part of a settlement with these states, the company would publicly acknowledge on its packages that cigarettes *are* addictive and cause cancer. This time, Liggett reportedly agreed to pay the states $25 million up front plus 25 percent of its pretax profits for the next 25 years. Liggett further pledged to turn over what was called a "treasure trove of incriminating documents," including marketing memoranda and lawyers' notes from 30 years of meetings with other tobacco companies. Within weeks, the first of such documents was released to the public. A 1960s memorandum revealed how the tobacco industry weighed what it termed "ethnic factors":

> "Spanish and Negro groups like to purchase only the best of everything—they are not looking for bargains . . . [T]here must be a racial slant in the marketing efforts" toward Hispanics and blacks, while "promotion must be smart and sophisticated" for the Jewish market.[37]

A 1981 RJ Reynolds marketing plan stated: "The majority of blacks . . . do not respond well to sophisticated or subtle humor in advertising."[38] A 1973 Reynolds marketing profile included a study of black smokers aged 14 to 20.[39]

The most serious charge raised against the tobacco industry involves its covert campaigns to addict teenagers to nicotine in order to create lifetime smokers. A lawyer who has represented many sick smokers argues that the formula is as simple as it is treacherous: "As smokers get older, as smokers die, as smokers quit because they're sick, or for other reasons, there is only one source of replacement smokers—and that is kids."[40] One Philip Morris memo flatly declared: "Today's teenager is tomorrow's potential regular customer."[41]

The tobacco companies are well aware that 90 percent of adult smokers began smoking as teenagers.[42] Moreover, a 1996 study reports that underage smokers (12 to 17 years old) are three times more likely than adults to be influenced by cigarette advertisements.[43] One of the Liggett documents recommended new packaging concepts for cigarettes to make them more appealing to youngsters.[44] A corporate memo reveals that the RJ Reynolds Tobacco Company "proposed marketing cigarettes to 14 to 18 year old smokers as early as the 1970s."[45] A series of 1972 documents from Brown & Williamson discuss that company's efforts to attract young smokers with honey- and cola-flavored cigarettes.[46] Another Reynolds memo, from 1988, discussed the company's plans "to saturate areas where young people gathered, such as fast-food restaurants, video-game arcades, and outdoor basketball courts, with billboards and posters promoting its products."[47]

Still another Reynolds memo even suggested that teen rebellion might make the risks of smoking more attractive to that underage market:[48]

> We are . . . unfairly constrained from directly promoting cigarettes to the youth market [identified as] the approximately twenty-one year old and under group.
>
> We should simply recognize that most of the "21 and under" group will inevitably become smokers and offer them an opportunity to use our brands.
>
> The beginning smoker and inhaler [called the "learning smoker"] has a low tolerance for smoke irritation, hence the smoke should be as bland as possible.
>
> [Cigarettes] should be marketed as a way to fight "stress" and other pressures of the teen years.[49]

Reynolds has denied that the memo reflects company policy, but it frequently has been singled out for marketing practices that target underage smokers—particularly its Joe Camel cartoon campaign.[50] Since cigarette advertising is banned on television, tobacco companies also pay Hollywood producers to place their lethal products in films—especially action movies popular with teenagers. Philip Morris reportedly paid $350,000 to plug its cigarettes in a James Bond thriller, appropriately titled "License to Kill."[51]

A study by the federal Centers for Disease Control and Prevention (CDC), released in 1996, reports that the percentage of high school students who smoke now exceeds the percentage of smokers in the adult population.[52] A 17-year-old Connecticut girl, whose neighbor happens to be the CEO of Phillip Morris, articulated the plight of the teenage nicotine addict: "I try and try, but I can't quit."[53]

Victor Crawford, a former lobbyist for the Tobacco Institute, whose job it was for many years to protect cigarette makers from restrictions, changed sides in 1991 after developing throat cancer. His new message to young consumers was blunt and personal:

> [H]e said that for about five years in the 1980s, he was part of a well-organized campaign that used "some of the smartest people in America' to figure out 'how to get you to smoke . . . As tobacco kills off people like me, they need kids like you to replace me."[54]

Crawford, once a two-and-a-half-pack-a-day smoker, died of cancer in 1996 at the age of 63. His widow said that he had felt "tremendous remorse" about his role in promoting smoking: "He realized that it was wrong, that you don't market death."[55]

After lengthy negotiations, the tobacco industry agreed, in 1997, to a proposed settlement with the attorney generals of 40 states, which had been seeking compensation for decades of smoking-related health costs.[56] Under the agreement, the tobacco companies would pay damages of $368 billion.[57]

The next time tobacco executives appeared before Congress to discuss the proposed settlement, they conceded for the first time in a public forum that nicotine *is* addictive.[58] A few months later, however, Congress rejected the settlement and the deal was declared "dead" by the chairman of RJR Nabisco (parent company of RJ Reynolds), as his company and four other major tobacco firms withdrew from the deal. The Clinton administration and Congress had tried to raise the settlement to $516 billion and place even tougher restrictions on the industry than those agreed to by the states.[59]

Four states—Minnesota,[60] Texas,[61] Florida,[62] and Mississippi[63]—settled separately with the tobacco industry in 1997 and 1998 for a combined $40 billion.[64] By 1999, the remaining states had signed on to a $206 billion settlement[65]—the largest civil settlement in American history. The companies also agreed to spend $1.7 billion to finance antismoking advertising and study youth smoking, and to eliminate any advertising that appeals to children.[66]

Nothing in the agreement with the states precluded individual lawsuits, however; such cases had seldom proved successful. Up to then, tobacco companies had won all but six of the more than 1,000 lawsuits filed by individuals since the 1950s.[67] Even in Florida, where the $750,000 jury award discussed earlier transpired, two subsequent cases involving similar plaintiffs suffering from smoking-related cancer had failed.[68] But two of tobacco's six losses came back-to-back in 1999. Cases in San Francisco and Portland had resulted in judgments totaling $131 million.[69] It seemed to some observers that momentum was starting to build against the companies.

Big Tobacco faced an even more serious threat from class-action litigation, a largely untested arena. Prior to 1998 only one class-action suit against the industry had been tried— from flight attendants who claimed that second-hand smoke had made them ill. In that case, the companies agreed to a $300 million settlement to establish a research foundation.[70] A 1997 class-action suit filed in Pennsylvania had not been tried; it had been thrown out by a federal judge on technical grounds.[71] It was considered a big win for Big Tobacco. But it may have been its last hurrah. Florida had launched its own class-action suit; and this one *would* go to trial.

CASE STUDY
"Lots of Zeros"

When jury selection began in Florida in 1998 for a $200 billion smoker's class-action suit against the nation's cigarette makers, it was "high noon" for Big Tobacco. The industry had come prepared to fight. There would be no pretrial settlement, such as in the flight attendants case the previous year. "That was a different time," a spokesman for RJ Reynolds declared.[72]

The smokers charged that the tobacco industry had made a defective product and had conspired to deceive the public about smoking-related illnesses.[73] The lawsuit alleged: "Cigarettes are a product that when used as directed will inevitably cause death and disease to a large percentage of its users."[74] Hundreds of the plaintiffs were in the courtroom on the first day—some of them with

(*Continued*)

portable oxygen tanks. "Questioning began amid a steady backdrop of coughing, wheezing, and the sound of electronic voice boxes."[75]

At the center of the suit was the issue of addiction—the same ground on which the earlier Pennsylvania class action had been tossed. Plaintiffs claimed that it was impossible for them to kick the habit. In the words of one of their attorneys, "The essence of the conspiracy and fraud of these defendants has been to get smokers hooked on nicotine as young as possible and make lifelong customers of them."[76]

The attorney for Philip Morris argued: "You can't defraud somebody by hiding something they already knew."[77] He pointed out that health concerns about smoking had been raised as early as 1604 and that cigarettes were already being called "coffin nails" in the 19th century.[78] The industry further maintained that those who want to quit can do so. Industry lawyers challenged the plaintiffs' addiction claim by contending that 46 million people had quit smoking for good in the previous 30 years.[79]

On July 7, 1999—after eight months of testimony—the Florida jury dealt a crushing blow to Big Tobacco, finding that cigarette manufacturers had conspired to "mislead smokers about the addictive and deadly nature of their product."[80] The verdict ruled that cigarette makers had "acted with reckless disregard"[81] and "engaged in extreme and outrageous conduct."[82]

Although there were only nine named plaintiffs, the suit had been brought on behalf of as many as 500,000 sick Florida smokers.[83] Legal experts believed that the case had opened the door for similar class-action suits in other states. The executive director of Citizens for a Tobacco-Free Society proclaimed: "The Marlboro Man just fell off his horse into quicksand."[84]

The second phase of the trial concluded in April 2000, when three plaintiffs, chosen to represent the hundreds of thousands of smokers in the potential class, were awarded $12.7 million in compensatory damages by the same jury.[85] Legal experts predicted that this verdict would be a harbinger of a huge punitive damage award against the tobacco industry when that jury began the third phase of the trial—the determination of damages on behalf of the entire Florida class.[86]

The predictions could not have been more prescient. On July 14, 2000, the tobacco industry was ordered to pay $145 billion to Florida smokers who had become sick or had died as a result of their addiction to cigarettes. It was the largest jury award in U.S. history.[87] To put the size of the award in perspective, it exceeded the entire national budget of Canada.[88] The damages were apportioned against the defendants according to their market share—ranging from $74 billion against Philip Morris down to $790 million against Ligget Group.[89] After reading the breakdown, the judge muttered: "Lots of zeros."[90]

Many judicial authorities, as well as the tobacco attorneys, expected the spectacular award to be overturned or at least trimmed drastically. But four months later, a circuit judge upheld the verdict, rejecting claims that the amount would bankrupt the tobacco industry.[91] The founder of Smokefree Educational Services, a former Wall Street executive, also dismissed the bankruptcy threat:

> Cigarette makers "can raise the price of cigarettes tomorrow and take in as much money as they need to pay," he said. "They have the luxury that smokers are addicted."[92]

Since the verdict, the tobacco industry has tried mightily to reshape its image. As part of its $100 million corporate image campaign, Philip Morris has unveiled a new Web site, on which it unequivocally states for the first time that there is an "overwhelming medical and scientific consensus that cigarette smoking causes diseases including lung cancer, emphysema and heart disease."[93] The company has also finally conceded at tobacco hearings held by the World Health Organization in 2000 that cigarettes are addictive.[94] Most remarkable of all, Philip Morris now

(*Continued*)

refers to nicotine as a "drug" and has even said that the company could accept some regulation of tobacco by the FDA.[95]

But for all the belated admissions, the stunning damages were never paid out. On May 21, 2003, the Florida Third District Court of Appeal reversed the jury's verdict and overturned the mammoth award. The court determined that the award would be bankrupting, in violation of Florida law. More significantly, the appeals court ruled that the case should not have had class-action status since each smoker in the case had "unique and different experiences" that would require separate litigation.[96] Many observers believed that the ruling weakened plaintiffs' arguments in pending class-action cases and might well deter future litigation. Moreover, a strongly pro-business and anti-litigation Congress seemed determined to pass legislation dramatically capping punitive damages on future product liability lawsuits.

Meanwhile, thousands of other tobacco suits, both individual and class action, remain pending in a state of limbo. But whatever finally happens, prolonged future appellate litigation will surely outlive all the original plaintiffs. Before the verdict was overturned, Big Tobacco's timetable for paying off the Florida claims was about 75 years.[97] Now its timetable is never.

The tobacco industry symbolizes the "postponed violence" of white-collar crime. Although it is less obvious, less immediate, less directly traceable to its perpetrators than the violence associated with street crime, to victims it is no less devastating.[98] Even if one excludes tobacco from the equation, the statistics are grim. "According to the National Commission on Product Safety, 20 million Americans have suffered injuries from using unsafe consumer products."[99] Of those victims, 110,000 are permanently disabled—and 30,000 are permanently dead.

Using automobile manufacturing as a model, we can identify two basic elements of corporate disregard for consumer safety: (1) resistance against safety devices and (2) defects in design. The first element may be illustrated by the early refusal of General Motors (GM) to install safety glass in its cars. In 1929, the president of GM dismissed safety glass as too costly. His response to efforts promoting that product's use in windshields: "We are not a charitable institution."[100]

The second element, faulty design, is illustrated only too well by the Ford Pinto debacle of the 1970s. Preproduction crash tests had established that the Pinto's fuel system ruptured easily in rear-end collisions, causing an explosion. Ford, however, had already begun tooling assembly-line machinery for the Pinto, so the management, desperate to compete with Volkswagen for the emerging subcompact market, chose to manufacture the car as it was.[101]

Ford could have replaced the gas tanks with safer ones at a cost of $11 per car but decided that this expense would not be cost-effective.

> This decision was based on the following calculations. The $11 repairs for all Pintos would cost $137 million but 180 burn deaths and 180 serious burn injuries and 21,000 burned vehicles would cost only $49.5 million (each death was figured at $200,000 and each injury at $67,000). Therefore, the company could anticipate a saving or profit of $87.5 million by continuing to make and sell the cars that were expected to kill or injure several hundred people.[102]

Fiery crashes involving Pintos began to occur with alarming regularity. Ford's liability estimates, however, were way off the mark. Liability suits against the Pinto increased, and judgments were routinely found against Ford. "In 1978, a jury in California awarded $127.8 million—including $125 million in punitive damages—to a teenager badly burned when his 1972 Pinto burst into flames after being hit in the rear by a car traveling 35 miles an hour."[103] That same year, the Department of Transportation announced that its tests had proven that the Pinto was unsafe and ordered a recall.

Ford's indifference to human life remains a testimony to the great paradox of white-collar violence: "A human being who would not harm you on an individual face-to-face basis, who is charitable, civic-minded, loving, and devout, will wound or kill you from behind the corporate veil."[104]

The same criminal justice system that unhesitatingly locks up murderers and muggers seems ill-equipped to deal with cases like that of the Pinto. Ford was charged, under the doctrine of corporate criminal liability, with reckless homicide in an Indiana trial. But the company was acquitted after mounting a successful million-dollar defense based on the scary premise that the Pinto was no more dangerous than other comparably sized cars of its time.[105] In 1979, an angry writer observed: "One wonders how long Ford Motor Company would continue to market lethal cars were [chairman] Henry Ford II and [president] Lee Iacocca serving 20-year terms in Leavenworth for consumer homicide."[106]

If anything positive came out of the Pinto tragedies, it is that automakers are probably far more reluctant today to ignore design defects *post facto,* as Ford did. For example, in the face of a problem remarkably reminiscent of the Pinto, Navistar International, the nation's largest manufacturer of school buses, was quick to recall tens of thousands of vehicles in 1992 after government tests showed that the fuel tanks could rupture, producing a fire hazard in a collision.[107]

On the other hand, the continuous occurrence of such recalls still raises serious questions of how willing auto manufacturers are to put consumer safety ahead of bottom-line considerations *pre facto.* In 2000, Ford was in trouble again. A federal judge took the unprecedented step of ordering the recall of 1.7 million Ford cars and trucks sold in California, accusing the automaker of concealing a dangerous design flaw that can cause the vehicles to stall in traffic. Never before had a federal judge ordered an automotive recall.[108] Ford had already settled (without admitting any wrongdoing) dozens of personal injury and wrongful death lawsuits in which one of its vehicles was suspected of stalling.[109]

Ford's woes continued that same year when Bridgestone Corp., the maker of Firestone tires, announced a recall of up to 20 million ATX, ATX II, and Wilderness tires. Although the tires in question were used by various automakers and were popular replacement tires, most were found as original equipment on Ford's best-selling Explorer sport utility vehicle and its Ranger and F-series pickup truck.[110] At the time of the recall, the National Highway Traffic Safety Administration (NHTSA) was investigating the role of these tires—specifically tread separation—in crashes that had caused 46 deaths, making it the deadliest flaw ever to result in a product recall.[111] This was Firestone's second time around the recall block. Several years earlier, its "500" radial tires had a serious defect that caused the steel belt to separate from the tire. This problem led to "thousands of accidents, hundreds of injuries, and 34 known fatalities."[112] In the end, Firestone was fined a token $50,000.

Because of the magnitude of the ATX/Wilderness recall, it proceeded very slowly. Indeed, in the two weeks following the announcement, three more people were killed, in separate accidents, while riding on the recalled tires.[113] Within a month the suspected death toll had risen to 88.[114]

Ford was also rebuked for its failure to notify the government when it had begun replacing Firestone tires on its sport utility vehicles in 10 Middle East countries, Malaysia, Thailand, and Venzuala *a year earlier.* Federal law requires companies to notify NHTSA regulators if they believe they have discovered a product defect.[115] Ford employees in other countries had raised serious questions about the quality of Firestone tires, as well as the tiremaker's integrity, 19 months before the American recall.[116]

But most of the blame was ascribed to Firestone. Company documents revealed that it had received more than 1,500 legal claims, dating back to 1997, for property damage, injuries, and deaths resulting from failures of its ATX and Wilderness tires. Yet in response to numerous inquiries from Ford, Firestone repeatedly blamed abuse by customers, who underinflate their tires or overload their vehicles.[117] "What Firestone appears to have missed is that sport utility vehicles require more reliable tires than cars because they are more likely to roll over when they lose a tire."[118]

Since their problems have been so visible, the automobile and tire industries serve as familiar exemplars of corporate violence; but they are by no means the only businesses that have threatened the health and lives of innocent consumers. Ralph Nader and other consumer advocates have long decried the willingness of manufacturers to risk personal injury in order to trim production costs. For example, a 13-year-old Minnesota boy had both his arms cut off in 1985 while operating a forage blower, a farm machine that throws grain up a silo. This horrifying accident could have been prevented by a safety guard, which would have cost the manufacturer $2. These simple devices that automatically stop a spinning shaft when it is jammed are required in many European countries—but not in the United States.[119]

The list of consumer products known to be dangerous and defective runs on and on. A leather protection spray recently left over 1,000 people in 18 states complaining of respiratory ailments.[120] About the same time, a Chicago manufacturer recalled 10,000 gas furnaces with faulty vent systems, which had been linked to 10 carbon monoxide deaths.[121] J.C. Penney had to recall 1.4 million electric food processors after some of them had started unexpectedly and amputated the fingers of a number of owners.[122]

A product as innocuous as a fisherman's worm shocker may actually have taken more lives than the Pinto. In 1993, the federal government announced the recall of an electronic device used by fishermen to shock worms to bring them to the surface of the ground for use as bait. Over a 20-year period, such devices reportedly had caused the deaths by electrocution of more than 30 people—mostly children.[123]

Children, in fact, are a special concern to those who work in the area of consumer safety.[124] Greenpeace, the environmental watchdog group, has issued a list of 28 vinyl children's products that it says contains dangerous levels of lead and cadmium.[125] The National Highway Safety Administration has recalled nearly a million children's car seats because of tests showing that push-button latch releases could jam in a crash, making it difficult to remove a child.[126] The Consumer Product Safety Commission (CPSC) convinced the Gerber corporation to recall about 10 million of its NUK pacifiers because they could fall apart and choke young children.[127] Fisher-Price recalled 420,000 of its Snuggle Light dolls, after five children choked on the dolls' cloth caps.[128]

A 2000 investigation offered disturbing news. In the previous three years, 75 percent of the most dangerous problems that led to recalls of products used by children were never voluntarily reported to the government.[129] Cosco, for example, did not even recall a defective stroller until a year after the company had received 3,000 complaints of lock failure that resulted in more than 200 reports of injuries to infants.[130] The mother of one of those 200 children states: "It's scary that parents can have children that have been injured after the company knew it was a problem. . . . It's scary that companies can get away with it."[131]

According to the CPSC, Baby's Dream Furniture, a Georgia company, waited until it had received eight reports of children having their fingers amputated or crushed in its cribs before it reported the problem. The cribs were, of course, recalled, and the company agreed to pay $200,000 in civil penalties.[132]

What happens to products after they are found to be safety hazards? Unlike socks in the dryer, they do not simply disappear into some mysterious land of the lost. Sometimes, they are simply sold again. In 2000, a California company was fined $75,000 for selling previously recalled sweaters that were so flammable that "they burned faster than newspaper."[133]

In 1977, the Environmental Defense Fund asked the CPSC to halt the sale of garments treated with TRIS—a flame retardant commonly used in children's sleepwear. TRIS was found to be a potent carcinogenic (cancer-causing) chemical. The group cited tests done by the Cancer Institute, declaring that "the evidence is conclusive that this is as clear a case of a carcinogen as we are going to find."[134] The government agreed and two months later halted the further sale of any TRIS-treated clothing.[135] But this was not the end of the TRIS story. According to a congressional committee report, issued the next year, approximately 2.4 million TRIS-treated garments were shipped overseas to be sold in the Third World following the domestic ban.[136] This practice—known as "dumping"—is a common response by American manufacturers of hazardous products that get banned from the domestic market.[137]

ADULTERATED FOOD

In 1905, Upton Sinclair published *The Jungle*, an electrifying exposé of unsanitary practices inside the American meatpacking industry. Consider just one brief excerpt from the book:

> [T]here was a trap in the pipe, where all the scraps of meat and odds and ends of refuse were caught, and every few days it was the old man's task to clean these out, and shovel their contents into one of the trucks with the rest of the meat![138]

Sinclair further described how spoiled meat was sold, how slaughtered livestock were piled into decaying storerooms overrun with rats, how sausages were stuffed with dung. He reported that workers sometimes would fall into rendering vats and be overlooked for days, until only their bones could be fished out. The rest of their remains would end up in consumers' pantries, mixed into containers of lard.

Although food had been regulated in the United States since the 19th century,[139] early legislation had proven to be ineffectual. *The Jungle* served as a catalyst for the enactment of tougher federal laws—such as the Food and Drug, and the Meat Inspection Acts of 1906.[140] This latter piece of legislation, however, applied only to meat sold in interstate commerce. Meat processed and sold within a single state (roughly 25 percent of all the meat consumed in the United States) was not subject to the law. The consequences of this loophole have been described graphically:

> Surveys of packing houses in Delaware, Virginia, and North Carolina found the following tidbits in the meat: animal hair, sawdust, flies, abscessed pork livers, and snuff spit out by the meat workers . . . Such plants were not all minor operations; some were run by the giants—Armour, Swift, and Wilson.[141]

In response to such disgusting conditions, the Wholesome Meat Act was passed in 1967, requiring that states must at least match federal inspection standards.[142] But the siren song of the cash register continued to entice abuses. The Hormel company, for example, used to repackage and resell stale meat returned by retailers.

> When the original customers returned the meat to Hormel, they used the following terms to describe it: "moldy liverloaf, sour party hams, leaking bologna, discolored bacon, off-conditioned hams, and slick and slimy spareribs." Hormel renewed these

products with cosmetic measures . . . Spareribs returned for sliminess, discoloration, and stickiness were rejuvenated through curing and smoking, renamed Windsor Loins, and sold in ghetto stores for more than fresh pork chops.[143]

In 1970, the General Accounting Office (GAO) investigated 40 meat plants previously cited for sanitation violations by the United States Department of Agriculture (USDA) and found that 30 of them had not been cleaned up. "In these plants, the GAO found cow or pig carcasses contaminated with cockroaches, flies, rodents, livestock stomach contents, mouse droppings, rust or moisture."[144] "The GAO's understated conclusion: 'A serious problem of unsanitary conditions exists in the food-manufacturing industry'."[145]

And while there are 7,000 full-time federal meat inspectors, nonmeat food processing plants are inspected on average only once every 10 years.[146] A panel of experts, in a 1998 report to Congress, called for a major overhaul of the nation's food protection systems.[147]

Currently, about 5,000 American deaths a year[148] and 76 million cases of food poisoning[149] are associated with tainted food. The poultry industry is considered especially pathogenic because of its susceptibility to *salmonella* bacteria—the leading cause of foodborne sickness.[150] *Salmonella* usually produces nonlethal, flu-like symptoms, but in certain cases it can be more deadly—particularly to children and the elderly.[151] According to one estimate, at least half the chickens in retail stores harbor *salmonella*.[152] At processing plants, birds often become contaminated by fecal and urine wastes. Typically, a single individual checks 60 to 70 slaughtered chickens per minute.

For decades, there has been no question that more inspectors, more thorough examinations of carcasses, and improved standards of sanitation were desperately needed.[153] In 1996, a crucial first step was taken when the USDA drafted new meat inspection rules calling for increased microbial testing for *salmonella* in place of the traditional "sniff and poke" method.

But *salmonella* is not the only health problem linked to the poultry industry. Poultry is also highly susceptible to the *campylobacter* bacterium—considered the leading bacterial cause of foodborne illness, with an estimated 2 to 8 million cases of *campylobacter*-linked cases reported each year.[154] In 1997, the federal Centers for Disease Control and Prevention estimated that *campylobacter* infects between 70 and 90 percent of all chickens. Although not considered as deadly as *salmonella*, it can cause illnesses equally as debilitating and has been linked to a serious paralytic disease. *Campylobacter* is responsible for as many as 800 deaths a year.[155]

Having considered the state of meat production then and now, we must not overlook the issue of future health risks. An increasingly popular technique, known as forced molting, prolongs the fertility of older birds. Hens are starved for a week or more in order to make them lose their feathers, after which they lay more eggs. The danger here is that molted birds are *5,000 times* more susceptible to *salmonella* than normally fed birds.[156] The introduction of recombinant DNA-derived growth hormones for use in meat production raises even newer questions about meat safety. Most of these compounds are steroid or sex hormones. Steroids are fat-soluble, implying that residues could be carried through meat into human tissues.[157] Since scientists do not completely agree on how growth hormones even work, their ultimate safety will be determined by a generation of consumers thrown into an expendable role once occupied by medieval food tasters.

In addition to meat and poultry, the Food and Drug Act granted the federal government broad regulatory powers over the entire food industry. For instance, concerns have been raised about the seafood industry, which has generated a number of health and safety problems related to natural viral and bacterial pathogens,[158] as well as toxic and chemical contamination from a marine environment polluted with sewage, pesticides, and industrial chemicals.[159] In 1993, seafood accounted for 20 percent of all reported incidents of food illnesses in the United States.[160] The FDA estimates that 114,000 Americans suffer seafood poisoning each year.[161]

In the biggest documented case of food poisoning ever, 224,000 persons got sick in 1994 from eating bacteria-tainted ice cream made at a Minnesota plant. It took two years for officials to trace the source.[162]

In 2009, the FDA charged that a Georgia peanut butter plant operated by Peanut Corp. of America had knowingly shipped *salmonella*-laced products as far back as 2007, "at times sending out tainted products after tests confirmed contamination." The *salmonella* outbreak was blamed for at least eight deaths and 575 illnesses in 43 states.[163] The House Energy and Commerce Committee released internal company e-mails between the company president and the Georgia plant manager. After being informed that some products had tested positive for *salmonella*, the president told the plant manager to "turn them loose," complaining that the delay in shipping "is costing us huge $$$$$."[164] The committee's investigations panel questioned both executives, but each invoked the Fifth Amendment. Investigators also heard testimony from victims' families. One man, whose mother had died at a cancer rehabilitation clinic in Minnesota after eating tainted peanut butter, angrily told the panel: "Cancer couldn't claim her, but peanut butter did."[165]

State Health Services closed a peanut processing plant in Texas, run by the same company, after dead rodents, rodent excrement, and bird feathers were found in an infected crawl space in the plant's production area.[166] It was later discovered that the plant was unlicensed and had operated for years without an inspection.[167] A full product recall was ordered.

Daily newspapers frequently carry stories about recalls of hazardous food products. Even granola bars—the emblematic snack food of health-conscious "yuppies"—have been adulterated. Sixteen hundred cases were recalled in 1993 because they contained particles of metal.[168]

If there is one grocery product above all in which consumers have a right to expect purity, it is baby food. Yet even this industry has failed to measure up to the public's trust. An analysis conducted by two environmental groups in 1995 found traces of pesticides in 53 percent of the baby food tested. Samples from all the major manufacturers were included in the study. Among the pesticides detected were neurotoxins and "probable human carcinogens."[169] According to the National Academy of Sciences,

> Children are more susceptible than adults to most pesticides . . . [If they] are exposed to compounds that act in the nervous systems during periods of vulnerability, they can be left with lifelong deficits. If they're exposed to carcinogens, it can set the stage for cancer later.[170]

The public-be-damned attitude of food packers is epitomized by the H. J. Heinz Company, which recalled 12,000 cases of baby food from retailers after complaints that the jars contained pieces of rubber. According to a company spokesman, Heinz did not notify consumers about the recall *because tests showed the rubber was not a health hazard.*[171] That may be so, but what are the chances that the chairman of the board would let *his* child eat rubber?

DANGEROUS DRUGS AND DEVICES

The 1906 Food and Drug Act, of course, covered drugs. Unfortunately, effective regulation was even slower to develop in the pharmaceutical area than was the case with food (Chapter 2). Many drugs of dubious safety were sold without prescriptions until well into the 1930s.[172] The event most responsible for galvanizing public sentiment toward more rigorous protection was the deaths in 1937 of 107 children who were poisoned by a "cure-all" tonic known as Elixir Sulfanilamide.[173] After that incident, the law was changed to require the testing of all new drugs to establish their safety. The FDA is empowered to oversee the determination of potential therapeutic benefits and the associated risks of medication.

Pharmaceutical manufacturers are also regulated by common law tort doctrine, making them subject to strict liability[174]—that is, product liability is imposed even in the absence of any purposeful intent to harm. An example of tort liability would be the widely used antiobesity drug treatment fen-phen (a combination of the drugs fenfluramine and phentermine). American Home Products, which marketed the dangerous fenfluramine part of the fen-phen combination under the brand name Pondimin (phentermine has not been associated with health problems and remains on the market), became the target of a class-action lawsuit in 1999 involving thousands of fen-phen users. American Home had pulled Pondimin off the market in 1997 at the request of the FDA, after a Mayo Clinic study linked it to potentially fatal heart valve damage. Dozens of fen-phen cases had been settled quietly out of court, but the same week a large class-action suit was filed in New Jersey, a jury awarded a 35-year-old Texas woman $23 million after she successfully argued that American Home Products had hid evidence that its diet drug caused valvular heart disease. The plaintiff blamed American Home Products for the lifetime of heart problems she now faces, including the inevitable surgery she will require to replace two heart valves as her ailments progress.[175]

Another well-publicized liability case involved the drug Bendectin, which was once commonly prescribed to treat the nausea and vomiting associated with morning sickness in pregnant women. Bendectin became the target of many tort lawsuits alleging that it caused horrible birth defects in the children of some mothers who took the drug.[176] Eventually, the manufacturer withdrew Bendectin from the market and submitted to a $110 million class-action settlement.

The Bendectin controversy revived painful memories of the most tragic case of an inadequately tested drug ever—the nightmarish story of thalidomide. Developed in Europe, thalidomide was a sleeping potion for which the pharmaceutical firm of Richardson-Merrell purchased the American sales rights in 1959. In 1961, Merrell learned that the drug had been withdrawn from the German market because it was suspected of causing terrible birth defects. "Even so, Merrell continued to distribute free pills to doctors who gave them to patients, including pregnant women."[177]

Despite heavy pressure by Merrell,[178] the FDA successfully kept thalidomide off the American market on the basis of unfavorable foreign reports. Merrell, of course, did not realize it at the time, but the FDA had saved the company. Had thalidomide been approved, Merrell unquestionably would later have been sued out of existence.[179] For by 1962, it was conclusively recognized that, in medical parlance, thalidomide was a teratogen (from the Latin word for "monster")—a drug which causes congenital malformation in fetuses.

About 8,000 thalidomide babies were born in 46 countries. Their distinctive range of deformities was described by the *Sunday Times* of London in 1979 in a story about surviving victims who were by then in their teens: "Some have no arms, just flippers from the shoulder; some no legs, just toes from their hips; some have limbless trunks, with just a head and body."[180]

Most of these births occurred outside the United States. The relatively small number of American thalidomide babies was limited to those whose mothers had been given free samples—such as a 16-year-old unwed high school student in Los Angeles[181]—and those whose mothers had taken the drug overseas during pregnancy—such as a New York woman who had given birth at a U.S. Army hospital in Spain.[182]

Obviously, the United States was extraordinarily fortunate that the FDA had refused to approve thalidomide. Nevertheless, Merrell-Richardson's conduct was irresponsible by any conscionable standard. The company had no information about thalidomide's effects in early pregnancy when it had begun testing the drug on humans by distributing it to private physicians for use on their patients. "[B]ut it repeatedly assured doctors that the drug was safe for everyone—*including* pregnant women."[183] It had never bothered to conduct tests on pregnant animals. Some of the toxicity tests it did perform on nonpregnant animals, however, had yielded alarming results. When thalidomide was administered in syrup form to six female rats, they all died. When administered to 30 male rats, 23 died within a day. When given to a healthy dog, it twitched and vomited for nearly three hours and died the next morning. Merrell never revealed these findings to the FDA and continued its clinical trials on humans, eventually distributing 2.5 million thalidomide tablets to 1,267 doctors. At the time, both figures were the highest ever recorded for clinical trials in the United States.[184]

In an incredible postscript, the FDA finally approved thalidomide in 1998—as a treatment for leprosy. Although there are believed to be fewer than 100 lepers in the United States, doctors would also be free to prescribe it for other purposes. And since thalidomide has shown some promise as a possible treatment for cancer and AIDS, it is likely that its use will extend well beyond a handful of leprosy patients. However, the FDA imposed unprecedented restrictions.

> The FDA is requiring doctors who prescribe thalidomide and pharmacies that sell it to register with the agency and undergo specific training on how to warn patients about the drug's dangers. Female patients will not get a prescription without a pregnancy test, and they must undergo regular pregnancy tests throughout the use of the drug. Women will also have to agree to use two reliable forms of contraception . . . All patients will view a disturbing video warning delivered by a thalidomide victim.[185]

Although the FDA stressed its confidence that the safeguards would be effective, the head of its Center for Drug Evaluation and Research added: "No drug is 100 percent safe."[186] In the case of thalidomide, that would seem to be a stunning understatement.

Pharmaceutical manufacturing is the only American industry with a safety record arguably worse than that of the automakers. Richardson-Merrell, the company that sought to bring thalidomide to the United States, had the ignominious distinction of marketing a second disastrous "wonder" drug simultaneously. It was called MER/29, a cholesterol inhibitor intended for use by heart patients. First marketed in 1960, MER/29 had become Merrell's biggest-selling prescription drug within a year. It was used by nearly 400,000 Americans.[187] When a rival firm, conducting comparative tests using MER/29, reported that lab animals had developed cataracts in their eyes, Merrell dismissed those results, claiming its own tests had produced no cataracts whatsoever. Yet at that time Merrell already knew that 25 out of 29 rats in its own laboratories had incurred eye damage after being given the drug.[188] In 1962, a technician employed by Merrell admitted that she had been ordered by a company executive to falsify her report of a study in which MER/29 had apparently caused blindness in laboratory monkeys.[189]

By the time MER/29 was taken off the market in 1962, at least 5,000 users had suffered serious side effects. When a Richardson-Merrell vice president and two laboratory supervisors were charged with fraud, they entered the familiar no contest plea. Defendants could have received up to five years in prison, but a sympathetic judge gave them only six months probation. The company was fined $80,000; it had made an $18 million profit that year.[190]

Twenty years later, another pharmaceutical giant, Eli Lilly, marketed a painkiller called Oraflex, intended for arthritis patients. Evidence later showed that Lilly had known that 26 deaths had been linked to the drug overseas. The company never shared this information with the FDA when it had applied for permission to sell Oraflex in the United States. Within six months of its introduction, Oraflex was withdrawn from the American market after reports of new deaths began circulating. In 1985, Lilly pleaded guilty of attempting to conceal illegally the lethal hazards of Oraflex. "The total punishment handed out for a crime that is believed to have killed 49 people and injured 916 more was a $25,000 fine for Lilly and a $15,000 fine for one executive."[191]

In a recent Southern California case, a physician and two employees of a pharmaceutical laboratory pled guilty to charges that they conspired to falsify test results used by the FDA to determine the safety and effectiveness of a variety of drugs.[192] The falsified results involved almost a dozen human clinical trials on drugs to treat asthma, birth control, diabetes, and sinusitis. The firm was hired by major drug firms to perform the tests. In one study, the lab created dozens of fake patients. In others, the researchers used their own blood and medical data from their own family members to submit bogus test results to the drug companies and the government. The apparent motive was to save money and time when legitimate test subjects were difficult to locate.[193]

CASE STUDY
Halcion Daze

In January 1992, the world watched as President George H. W. Bush vomited and fainted at a state dinner in Japan. Although his aides quickly attributed the president's collapse to the flu, questions persisted about the possible side effects of the controversial sleeping pill Halcion, which Bush acknowledged that he took occasionally. Some Halcion critics openly speculated that the drug could even be connected to Bush's familiar fractured speech patterns that comedians loved to lampoon. Observers were particularly intrigued by a garbled campaign address the president delivered in New Hampshire about a month later, in which he referred to the Nitty Gritty Dirt Band as the "Nitty Ditty Nitty Gritty Great Bird."[194]

The strange tale of Halcion is yet another instance of an alleged cover-up on the part of a major pharmaceutical manufacturer, in this case, Upjohn. "Over the years, at least 100 law suits have been filed by users of the drug or their family members, as psychotic episodes and even homi-

cides were blamed on its use."[195] Once the world's most popular sleeping pill, Halcion has since been banned in a number of countries, including Britain,[196] Norway,[197] and the Netherlands.[198] Halcion is the trade name for triazolam, a member of the benzodiazepine family, which includes other popular sleep hypnotics, as well as tranquilizers such as Valium.[199] Upjohn first synthesized Halcion in 1969 and submitted a new drug application to the FDA the following year.[200] The company believed that Halcion was potentially more profitable than any sleeping pill ever produced. It knocked people out fast but cleared the body so quickly that users did not experience the next-day hangover characteristic of barbiturates or other benzodiazepine hypnotics.[201] Early tests, however, raised plenty of red flags. A researcher at the University of California-Irvine College of Medicine found cases of amnesia among his subjects given Halcion.[202] A renowned medical scientist at the University of Edinburgh in Scotland reported that

(Continued)

Halcion could cause harsh episodes of "rebound anxiety" in patients as the drug wears off.[203] He later described Halcion as "brain poison."[204]

A 1979 corporate memo written by an Upjohn executive tacitly acknowledged that the tests were in trouble: "[T]he FDA will never approve Halcion without tremendous pressure. We have the people willing to exert the pressure but we must orchestrate it."[205] The company was particularly well equipped to exert such pressure. "[A] former deputy commissioner of the FDA who had become a senior vice president at Upjohn had meetings and telephone conversations with FDA personnel who were involved in a review of the drug's approval."[206] In November 1982, the FDA approved Halcion and it became available by prescription in the United States the following spring.

Seldom, however, has such a potent drug been approved under more questionable circumstances. It is now known that the findings of the original domestic research trial in 1972–1973 omitted about a third of the adverse reactions suffered by a group of Michigan prison inmates used as subjects.[207] Upjohn has characterized the omissions as "transcription errors."[208] In another early test, a Houston psychiatrist fudged his results by enrolling himself, his nurse, and at least 14 patients multiple times in the same study under different initials. When he was asked why so many subjects shared the same birth date, he lied, claiming he had utilized sets of twins.[209] An FDA audit has also revealed that a Vicksburg, Mississippi, psychiatrist fabricated a six-month clinical trial. The agency has found no evidence that patients in this study ever actually took Halcion, although the doctor submitted a highly favorable report on the drug.[210]

The debate reached the public agenda when a San Francisco writer questioned the FDA's approval of Halcion in a widely discussed magazine article. She described the intense reaction she had experienced with Halcion. "[After two weeks], my heart pounded and I was on the verge of tears much of the time. The slightest danger, such as having to make a left turn in traffic, put me in a sweat."[211] Her therapist, having heard only good reports about Halcion, never considered taking her off the drug. After six months, she "became convinced that the world was on the brink of nuclear war or invasion from space."[212]

In the face of such negative publicity, a memorandum written by Upjohn's marketing department recommended a "containment" strategy to protect sales. The first suggested tactic was to attribute the mounting criticism to the controversial Church of Scientology—an easy target as a scapegoat because of its campaigns against certain prescription drugs.[213]

In December 1991, an FDA official undertook an investigation of Halcion's safety. He spent three months in Upjohn's Michigan headquarters examining records and interviewing employees. He concluded that Upjohn had "engaged in an ongoing pattern of misconduct."[214] The investigator exhorted his agency to refer the case to the Justice Department so that a grand jury could determine if crimes had been committed. The FDA responded promptly—by reassigning the official, who soon retired. His report was not released until 1994.[215] A prominent specialist in sleep disorders has offered a very critical explanation of why the probe was aborted: "I think that investigation was getting too close to the FDA and eventually they were going to be investigating themselves."[216]

In addition, the physician who managed Upjohn's Drug Experience Unit during the 1980s submitted an alarming report to the company. He warned that Halcion users might "kill somebody without knowing it."[217] His bosses told him that he had to "refine" his management techniques and was demoted. He later resigned.[218] His fears proved to be chillingly prophetic, however; for even more disturbing than the claims of amnesia or anxiety were subsequent reports that Halcion could cause bizarre delusions, hostile paranoia, and delirious behavior in some users. "Upjohn may believe such reactions are flukes, no more likely with one benzodiazepine than another, but the company has never convincingly explained

(*Continued*)

Halcion's remarkable ability to generate weird stories."[219] These include the following eruptions of hallucinations, rage, suicide, and murder:

- In 1986, a retired railroad clerk living in New Orleans was prescribed Halcion after surgery for lymphoma. After taking the drug for several months (Upjohn now recommends administration for no more than seven to ten days), he began to undergo a significant personality change. He regularly screamed at his invalid mother and 92-year-old aunt, then quickly forgot each incident. Only after he saw a television feature on the controversy surrounding Halcion did the confused man decide to stop taking it. It reportedly took his doctor two months to wean him from the drug, after which his former mild-mannered personality returned.[220]
- In 1987, a 65-year-old Texas retiree was prescribed Halcion after complaining of insomnia. During the eight months he took the drug, "he terrorized his wife, attempted suicide, talked of murder and was twice committed to a mental hospital."[221] Although the man admittedly had a history of psychological instability and problems with alcohol, he maintained that he had never been violent, aggressive, or suicidal until taking Halcion.[222] He filed a suit against Upjohn after watching a news story about Halcion. In 1994, however, a federal jury ruled against him in his litigation, believing that he was already unstable before taking Halcion.[223]
- Also in 1987, a partially disabled former Texas police officer placed the barrel of a rifle to the head of a sleeping friend and pulled the trigger, while the two men were away on a hunting trip. After returning home from the cabin a few hours later, the man telephoned the county sheriff's office and reported that he had "had to kill an ol' boy,"[224] whose name he could not even remember. His lawyers later contended that he had been

suffering catastrophic side effects from the extended use of Halcion. At the time of the killing, he had been taking Halcion for about 700 days—"690 days longer than is now recommended."[225] His dosage was also double the current maximum.

The man was convicted of murder and sentenced to life in prison. The Halcion issue was never raised at his trial because the drug's alleged effects were still not widely known. In fact, he had continued to take Halcion while in jail awaiting trial and had attempted suicide there twice.

When he appealed for a new trial, one of his allies was Dallas psychiatrist James Grigson. Known as "Dr. Death," Grigson has testified in over 140 capital murder cases—almost always for the *prosecution*. Yet Grigson said he was "100 percent sure" that the defendant was legally insane when he shot his friend and was equally certain that Halcion was the sole cause of his insanity.[226] Nevertheless, the defendant was denied a new trial because Texas law requires that new trial motions based on newly discovered evidence must be made within 60 days. In a curious twist, a Dallas jury awarded the convicted murderer $2.15 million in a 1992 lawsuit, ruling that Upjohn had been "grossly negligent in marketing a defective product—Halcion."[227] In 1994, however, a Texas appeals court reversed the decision and nullified the award, ruling that Upjohn had caused the plaintiff no injury.[228]

- In 1988, a municipal judge in Orange County, California, who had just won reelection, shot himself to death. Friends and acquaintances initially were baffled, but the victim's family later blamed Upjohn, declaring that his three years of Halcion use after a 1985 automobile accident had caused the erratic mental state which drove him to suicide.[229]
- Also in 1988, a 57-year-old Utah woman pumped eight bullets into the head of her sleeping 83-year-old mother. The woman had been taking Halcion for several months

(Continued)

prior to the shooting and had no memory of the killing. In contrast to the Texas shooting, "[c]ourt-ordered psychiatrists found [she] was 'involuntarily intoxicated' on Halcion at the time of the shooting, and [she] was never prosecuted."[230] The woman later settled a multimillion dollar lawsuit against Upjohn shortly before her civil case came to trial in 1991.[231] To make an already tragic story even worse, however, the woman's memory of what she had done gradually began to return, and she took her own life in 1994.[232]

- In 1990, a police officer in Kalamazoo, Michigan, who had been convicted and imprisoned for stabbing his estranged wife in the heart six years earlier, was acquitted at a retrial. According to new testimony, he had taken a double dose of Halcion three hours before the near-fatal attack and claimed no memory of the crime. After seeing a television magazine program describing Halcion's possible side effects, he became convinced that the drug had fueled his assaultive rage. He appealed his conviction and eventually won his freedom.[233]

- In 1991, a 37-year-old Colorado businessman, who had been taking Halcion for about three weeks, woke up in a psychotic frenzy. He began rolling up the carpets in his home, while babbling incoherently to his wife. Later, he went on a rampage, barging into neighbors' houses, acting out a "Wild West" fantasy. When he tried to grab a police officer's gun, he was restrained and taken to a local hospital. Criminal charges were subsequently dismissed, and the man was sent home after the district attorney became convinced that his irrational conduct had been caused by Halcion.[234]

- In 1992, a 45-year-old New York advertising executive bludgeoned his father into a coma. He had been visiting his parents' home in Laguna Hills, California, just after his mother's death. He and his father had been drinking into the night, and his father gave him some Halcion to help him sleep. He testified that he awoke during the night and mistook his father for a grotesque intruder—with a face that appeared to have "melted." He called 911 and reported the intruder, but when police arrived they found his father lying in a pool of blood—"his skull split from neck to forehead."[235] The victim later died without ever regaining consciousness. A criminal jury acquitted the defendant, blaming the horrifying act on the combination of alcohol and Halcion.[236]

- In 1993, a 56-year-old Houston nurse settled a lawsuit against Upjohn for an undisclosed amount of money. She claimed she had become psychotic after taking the drug for more than two years. The suit alleged that she had grown "paranoid, aggressive, suicidal, and totally irrational."[237] As a result, she had been locked up in a mental institution for two weeks.

- In 1994, two widows from the same small Kentucky town settled separate negligence suits against Upjohn. The women contended that their husbands had each committed suicide while under the influence of Halcion.[238]

- Also in 1994, a lawsuit was filed in federal court in Texas charging that Upjohn, along with the FDA and others, had concealed Halcion's dangerous side effects. This was the first case to go beyond specific adverse reactions and allege a full-blown conspiracy among manufacturer, researchers, regulators, and lawyers.[239] One of the plaintiffs claimed he had experienced "personality changes, paranoia, depression, hostility and aggression" while taking Halcion.[240] The other asserted she had suffered "memory loss, mood swings, temperament changes and violent rages" attributable to the drug.[241] She also said that she had contemplated suicide and threatened her husband with a gun.

(Continued)

It remains to be seen how successful this latter case—or any of the other pending Halcion lawsuits[242]—will be. Thus far, Upjohn has fared quite well in court. It has lost only one jury verdict, and, as noted, that award was overturned on appeal. It has also made out-of-court settlements in a number of other cases for amounts believed to be relatively modest. Upjohn employs the same high-powered law firm that has represented the tobacco industry with so much ferocity in recent years,[243] so the failure of Halcion litigation is no big surprise.

However, a new FDA report issued in 1996 finally acknowledged what critics have alleged for two decades: that Upjohn had "suppressed, minimized and misrepresented" the lethal dangers posed by Halcion.[244] The report urged the Justice Department to investigate whether Upjohn had suppressed early test results. Upjohn denies any legal or ethical transgressions. The company has declared that it "puts nothing ahead of patients' health."[245] Perhaps so, but the head of psychiatry at a major medical school offers a markedly different assessment of Halcion:

This is a very dangerous drug . . . No other benzodiazepine has such a narrow margin of safety. The only justification for keeping it on the market is to ensure the company's profitability. From a public-health standpoint, there is no reason at all.[246]

Medical devices constitute a category of consumer products that has come to be recognized as requiring its own form of government regulation. An example of the types of cases included under this category would be that of an Indiana man who sold *used* heart pacemakers. Some had been dropped on the floor during surgery; others had been determined to be faulty and were removed from patients' chests. The pacemakers were sent to Indiana, sterilized, repackaged, and sold as new.[247] The irresponsible entrepreneur, Michael M. Walton, was convicted of fraud in 1994 and received a six-year sentence.[248] In 1993, a Boston company that made heart catheters agreed in a plea bargain to pay $61 million in fines to settle a case in which they were accused of using patients as "guinea pigs" to test new products. The tests resulted in the death of at least one patient. The company lied to the FDA, and covered up malfunctions in the catheters, which sometimes had failed to deflate in people's arteries and had broken off inside their hearts, necessitating emergency surgeries. The federal prosecutor maintained that the acts were "aimed at enriching the company which made tens of millions of dollars off the sale of adulterated catheters."[249]

The Food, Drug, and Cosmetic Act of 1938 placed medical devices under federal control, and they were first subjected to premarket review under the Medical Device Amendments of 1976.[250] Those amendments were enacted primarily in response to a single case—that of the Dalkon Shield.

The Dalkon Shield was an intrauterine birth control device (IUD) marketed by the A. H. Robins Company, a major pharmaceutical manufacturer. Between 1971 and 1974, 2.2 million American women were fitted with the Dalkon Shield. Robins trumpeted it as "the safest and most satisfying form of contraception."[251] The company had bought the device from a small Connecticut firm owned by its inventor. At a production cost of 35 cents per unit and a wholesale price (to doctors) of around $4, Robins had reason to believe it had struck gold.

The company launched the most aggressive promotional campaign in its history. So eager was Robins to sell the shield that it never took the time to test the device adequately. All its data were based on a single medical study of questionable validity—conducted by the inventor, who obviously had a financial stake in the success of the device.[252] With every bogus claim, Robins added another room to its house of lies. The Dalkon Shield turned out to be one of the most immorally misrepresented products ever exposed.

In addition to being unsafe, the shield was not even very effective. Five percent of its wearers became pregnant—a statistic far removed from the 1.1 percent falsely advertised. Many of the women who conceived with the shield in place suffered a previously rare type of miscarriage known as spontaneous abortion. Still others, in the second trimester, experienced the even rarer infected miscarriage, or septic abortion.[253] The cause of infection was a design defect in the wick used to insert and remove the device. "[I]t served as a pathway for bacteria-laden fluids to travel up into the uterus."[254] Robins became aware of this problem early, but continued fraudulently misrepresenting the shield. When one employee spoke up about his concerns over the safety of the device, he was reprimanded for insubordination and threatened with dismissal.[255]

At least 20 women died as a result of the Dalkon Shield. In addition, hundreds of others who conceived while wearing the shield gave birth prematurely to infants with "grave congenital defects, including blindness, cerebral palsy, and mental retardation."[256] Thousands of women were left with reproductive organs so badly scarred that they would never be able to conceive children.

H. R. Robins declared bankruptcy in 1986, after paying out more than $378 million to settle 9,200 lawsuits. In 1989, a federal judge accepted a plan to reorganize the company that included the creation of a $2.5 billion fund to compensate victims.[257]

In 1985, a Florida woman discovered that she had been chemically poisoned:

> I looked down at my blouse, meaning to straighten it, and gasped. The blouse was becoming soaked with a foul-smelling liquid. Inside the hospital, I could not stand unaided; I could not sign my name, and I could barely speak.[258]

As this harrowing first-person account attests, the successor to the Dalkon Shield as the medical device most likely to cause innocent women agony is the silicone-gel breast implant. For three decades, 150,000 women a year received these implants. Because they had already been in wide use, they had escaped the official scrutiny imposed by the Medical Devices Amendment of 1976. But in 1992, after a review of the industry's safety claims, the FDA called an immediate halt to silicone breast enlargement.

> FDA advisers reviewed evidence submitted by several implant makers and ruled that none really knew whether its product was safe. The devices have been known to leak or rupture, bleeding silicone into the body. But the makers hadn't determined how often that happens or with what possible consequences. Nor could the manufacturers say . . . how often migrating silicone prompts the immune system to attack healthy tissues.[259]

Corporate memos revealed in subsequent litigation have shown that scientists working for Dow Corning, the leading producer of silicone implants, were worried about leaks and ruptures since the 1970s.[260] One of its own engineers had warned the company that it was conducting "experimental surgery on humans."[261] A few months after the moratorium, Dow Corning further disclosed that it had faked the quality control records of some implants it produced.[262] In 1993, a consumer research group accused Dow Corning of withholding data from long-term toxicity studies, in which laboratory animals had allegedly suffered negative effects from silicone, including birth defects, nervous system disorders, and death.[263] A preliminary study conducted at a New York medical center hinted that children breast-fed by mothers with silicone gel implants may develop symptoms of an autoimmune attack.[264] By that point, the silicone implant industry was effectively out of business. The remainder of the story is a tale of high-stakes consumer litigation and corporate accountability.

A federal jury in Georgia awarded $5.4 million (later reduced by the judge to $2.27 million) to a 31-year-old librarian whose implants, manufactured by Baxter Healthcare, ruptured, leaving her with immune system disorders attributed to silicone.[265] A Texas jury recommended a record award of $25 million to a 45-year-old woman who said she developed an autoimmune disease from ruptured silicone-gel breast implants, manufactured by the Medical Engineering Corporation.[266] Another Texas jury awarded three women a total of $27.9 million in damages in a lawsuit charging the 3M Corporation and two smaller companies with the manufacture of leaking implants that caused severe illnesses. A few weeks later, 3M announced that it had agreed to contribute $325 million to a fund to compensate women who had received its implants.[267]

In 1994, Dow Corning agreed to pay $4.25 billion to cover liability claims against its implants.[268] A year later, the company raced into bankruptcy protection after determining that its $4.25 billion settlement fund was inadequate to cover the 300,000 to 400,000 impending claims.[269] In addition to claims of immune system disorders, other victims have charged that their defective implants had caused connective tissue diseases such as rheumatoid arthritis, scleroderma, and lupus.[270]

As a result of the Dow Corning bankruptcy, women alleging that silicone breast implants had caused them serious health problems began suing Dow Chemical, which (along with Corning, Inc.) owned Dow Corning. Dow previously had been insulated from liability. However, a Nevada jury ordered the corporation to pay $10 million to a 46-year-old woman who had developed skin disorders and tremors from her implants.[271]

The first class-action suit regarding silicone implants was filed against Dow in Louisiana on behalf of 1,800 women. In 1997 a jury held Dow liable, finding that the company was negligent and intentionally had withheld information from women and their doctors about implant dangers.[272]

Even the newer saline-filled breast implants, which have replaced the silicone ones, are not without serious risks. A government advisory board reported in 2000 that saline implants "break open at 'alarmingly high' rates and require women to undergo repeated surgeries."[273] About 130,000 women receive saline implants each year, and up to 27 percent are removed within three years following implantation. Most of these removed implants have leaked into patients' bodies. Some are blackened with fungus and blamed for infections and excruciating breast pain. The FDA has never declared saline-filled implants safe.[274]

CASE STUDY
Rely Tampons

Procter & Gamble (P&G) is one of the largest, best known, and successful corporations in the United States. Its products are found in virtually every American home. But beneath the company's "99 44/100% pure" image, lurks an amoral tale of greed, power, and death: the story of the Rely tampon.

In the 1960s, researchers at P&G began working on an ultra-absorbent tampon that was

(*Continued*)

expected to dominate the feminine hygiene industry. Made of superthirsty synthetics like polyester and a derivative of wood pulp, Rely (as the product would be named) was ballyhooed as the most effective sanitary protection item ever developed.[275] Tampons had been made of cotton since their invention in the 1930s by a Denver barber, who called his product Tampax.[276]

Rely tampons were introduced to the general public in early 1980 after five years of test marketing. One of the test sites had been Rochester, New York, where free samples were distributed. A local consumer advocate immediately began getting phone calls from women reporting vomiting and diarrhea after using Rely. She asked P&G for a copy of its safety records but was refused. P&G blamed the adverse reactions on allergies. The company did not mention that it was already receiving more than one hundred complaints per month about a product not yet even widely available.[277]

In 1980, *60 million* sample packages of Rely were sent to 80 percent of U.S. households. By the middle of the year, Rely had captured a quarter of the tampon market and was on the verge of overtaking industry leader Tampax. That same year, however, the CDC began observing a startling phenomenon. It identified 55 fatal cases and 1,066 nonfatal case of toxic shock syndrome. This rare disease was beginning to surface primarily in young menstruating women.[278]

> Symptoms of the disease . . . include high fever, a sunburnlike rash, and low blood pressure. After a while, a victim's skin peels off the hands and feet. Breathing becomes difficult, and the lungs fill with fluid until she suffocates or her heart stops. The name is derived from the severe prolonged shock that accompanies the illness.[279]

The CDC informed P&G that it was preparing to conduct a study of toxic shock and tampon use. P&G's response was the same as it had been over the five years it had known of the danger—say

nothing and do nothing. "The company instructed its sales force not to discuss toxic shock . . . But if asked, the salespeople were given canned answers that denied any link between tampons and toxic shock."[280] The only notable action P&G took was to postpone a major high school promotion it had planned.

Women continued to complain that they became ill after using Rely. In July 1980, the death of an Ohio woman—the mother of a six-month-old infant—was strongly linked to Rely. In September, the CDC concluded its study in which 70 percent of the victims of toxic shock syndrome reportedly had used Rely.

On September 21, 1980, P&G announced it was pulling Rely from the shelves. "Though Procter & Gamble is often lauded for voluntarily withdrawing Rely . . . it seems clear the company didn't act until the FDA threatened to act for them. And the FDA didn't act until women died."[281]

The day after the announcement, P&G met with the FDA.

> P&G spent much of the meeting debating whether the action would be called a withdrawal or a recall. P&G disliked "recall" because it seemed to imply safety violations. Exasperated FDA officials finally said, "If you don't want to call it a recall, we'll call it a *banana*." During the meeting, that's exactly how they referred to it.[282]

P&G signed a court agreement, under which it undertook a massive advertising campaign to notify women to stop using Rely tampons. It also agreed to buy back the product from consumers. P&G, however, adamantly refused to admit that Rely was defective or that the company had done anything wrong.

P&G was sued by a Cedar Rapids, Iowa, man whose 24-year-old wife had died of toxic shock syndrome in 1980, four days after she began using Rely and two weeks before the product was taken off the market. Although the evidence seemed

(Continued)

compelling, suing a giant corporation like P&G is never easy. The plaintiff reportedly was bullied by an army of P&G lawyers in his deposition. He was asked irrelevant questions about his late wife's sexual history—for example, whether she had engaged in oral sex with him, whether she had ever been sexually promiscuous with other men. "The idea was to humiliate and scare him into settling the case before it went to trial."[283]

P&G also mobilized its almost limitless financial resources along with its enormous influence in the scientific community. The plaintiff's attorney found it nearly impossible to enlist physicians as expert witnesses because P&G quickly offered lucrative research grants to any doctors researching toxic shock—with the stipulation that all findings be submitted to the company prior to submission for publication.[284] One scientist, whose findings (critical of Rely) had already been reported in the *Wall Street Journal,* renounced them after he had received several hundred thousand dollars in grant money from P&G.[285] Another researcher testified for the defense that Rely tampons were *not* to blame for toxic shock. "He too had received P&G grants."[286]

P&G conducted several mock trials in Lincoln, Nebraska, a city chosen for its demographic similarity to Cedar Rapids. "Jurors" were questioned about what they liked and disliked in the simulated testimony. "Just as it uses focus groups to determine the best way to market toothpaste and detergent, P&G researched how to sell itself in a courtroom. On the third try, its attorneys got the verdict they wanted."[287] P&G even distributed free samples of its products throughout Cedar Rapids before the trial, as a transparent way to drum up goodwill.[288]

But, despite all its legal and public relations clout, P&G had left a paper trail. One especially damning memo, written well before the victim's death, disclosed the corporation's decision *not* to release warnings about toxic shock.[289] Unlike the mock jury in Lincoln, the real one in Cedar Rapids ruled in favor of the plaintiff and awarded him $300,000.

At least 38 deaths from toxic shock syndrome have been attributed to Rely tampons. Since Rely was taken off the market, the CDC reports that the number of toxic shock cases has dropped dramatically.[290] P&G has long since settled most of the other Rely litigation, including that of a St. Louis girl who became sick after using Rely, two weeks before her 16th birthday.

By the end of the month, she had trouble breathing and tried to free herself from the hospital respirator. Doctors had to tranquilize her to keep her calm. In late September, she suffered cardiac arrest.[291]

The young victim's attorney, a former Republican state senator, remains bitter at P&G to this day: "If this was the socially responsible company that they pretend they are, this little girl would be alive . . . With all the power the bastards had to get out the word, they could've saved her life."[292]

QUACKERY

Quackery refers both to medical products that are worthless and to persons who cannot deliver miraculous cures they promise.[293] There are no swindlers more depraved than those who prey upon the ill. Sadly, the United States has a history of tolerance for medical quackery perhaps unmatched. The roots of this permissiveness may be traced back to the Colonial era, when such questionable remedies as Daffy's Elixer, Turlington's Balsam of Life, and Bateman's Pectoral Drops were sold by merchants of every stripe.[294]

By the eve of the 20th century, patent medicines had become an important American industry. A single vendor, such as the maker of the widely popular Pinkham's Vegetable Compound, could spend about $1,000,000 a year on advertising alone.[295] Competition was keen; whether it was Palmer's Hole in the Wall Capsules or Aunt Fanny's Worm Candy, name recognition was considered crucial. The particular formula might change from time to time, the diseases for which medicines were touted might vary, but the trademark endured.[296]

Then came the Food and Drug Act of 1906. Within two years, the first quackery trial under the new statute took place, pitting the federal government against Robert N. Harper, the manufacturer of a favored remedy named Cuforhedake Brane-Fude (pronounced "cure-for-headache brain food"). Harper was convicted, and President Theodore Roosevelt personally urged the prosecutor to seek a prison term for the defendant in order to make an example of him. The judge, however, did not lock Harper up, but instead fined him $700—perhaps initiating a tradition of wrist slapping that remains a feature of many white-collar crime sentences to this day. Since Harper had made $2 million from Cuforhedake Brane-Fude,[297] it seems safe to deduce that he came out substantially ahead.

Today quackery is big business, robbing consumers of $25 billion each year.[298] In the words of the FDA, "Difficult to curtail, health frauds, like crab grass, sprout up here, there, and everywhere."[299] Quackery flourishes because it appeals to emotion rather than reason. An official of the Consumer Health Information Institute has declared: "Quacks provide simple answers to complex problems. The one cause, one cure solution is very comforting."[300]

Teenagers, impatient with the pace of puberty, are one fertile ground for quackery.[301] But, as is the case with most categories of consumer fraud, the elderly are the primary targets, contributing $10 billion (a full 40 percent) to the total cost.[302] Besides being the fastest-growing segment of the population, the elderly are, understandably, the most ailment prone. The fact that "80 percent of America's elderly have at least one chronic health problem that restricts them one out of every 12 days"[303] leaves the aged especially vulnerable to fraudulent gimmicks and concoctions. Sixty percent of those who resort to untested therapies are over 65.[304]

Quackery can entail more than just fraud; there is also a heavy human and social cost. Quackery can delay timely and appropriate treatment of medical conditions and cause severe illness or death.[305] Some products and services are not only useless, but lethal. One expert has declared, "quackery kills more people than those who die from all crimes of violence put together."[306] And many of these ultimate victims are far from elderly. Consider the example of a 16-year-old diabetic girl in Montana, whose parents were convinced by a mystical quack that her daily insulin injections were unnecessary. "By tapping her chest, he said, he could stimulate their daughter's own insulin-making capacity." The girl died in three days. A short time later, her parents received a $6,325 bill for chest-tapping services rendered.[307]

Quackery at its most venal thrives on persons afflicted with life-threatening illnesses for which there are no known cures. This has never been more apparent than in the promotion of bogus AIDS treatments. Desperate consumers spend an estimated $1 billion annually on fraudulent AIDS remedies.[308] Underground "guerrilla clinics," offering homemade treatments, have sprung up all over the world.[309] Quacks invent scientific-sounding rationales for their therapies.[310] In 1990, for instance, a California doctor began injecting some of his AIDS patients with typhoid vaccine in order to activate the syphilis virus, which he then expected to eradicate, along with the HIV virus. He reportedly had read about this untested and unapproved procedure in a music magazine called *SPIN*.[311] Among other pseudoscientific therapies are herbal tea made from the bark of Brazilian trees,[312] injections of hydrogen peroxide, pills derived from the cells of infected mice, baths in a chlorine bleach solution, and timed exposure of the genitals and rectum to the sun's rays.[313]

The chairman of a health fraud prevention organization observes: "Everything has been converted into an AIDS treatment."[314] Capsules containing poisonous metals are dispensed.

Processed algae (nicknamed "pond scum") sell for $20 a bottle. "One man masquerading as a Ph.D. was injecting his patients with a processed byproduct of their own urine at $100 per injection."[315] A European quack reportedly squeezed big profits from the misery of sick and dying people by selling them a costly and potentially dangerous powder based on extract of human excrement.[316]

Other afflictions also attract their share of quackery. Thalassotherapy, a spa-styled seaweed bath, promises to relieve stress and chronic fatigue.[317] A magnet placed in men's briefs has been sold as a treatment for impotence—as has an exotic nostrum named "Crocodile Penis Pills."[318]

Snake venom has been peddled to arthritics,[319] and shark-cartilage pills promise to prevent cancer.[320] This latter claim was the basis of a popular 1993 book, *Sharks Don't Get Cancer*.[321] Since sharks *do* get cancer, the entire premise of the book was fallacious. Nevertheless, Americans have since spent millions of dollars on shark cartilage supplements in the desperate hope of curing their malignancies.[322]

Gerovital, a Romanian dental anesthetic, was brought to the United States illegally and sold as a cure for angina, hypertension, depression, deafness, diabetes, and Parkinson's disease. No health claims have ever been substantiated for Gerovital, and it has caused respiratory difficulties and convulsions in some users.[323] Germanium, a nonessential element marketed as a dietary supplement, has been promoted as a treatment for Alzheimer's disease. Germanium is worse than ineffective; it has caused irreversible kidney damage and death.[324]

In 1998, A Virginia doctor was indicted on charges of fraud. He had allegedly hastened the death of four cancer patients by treating them with intravenous doses of T-UP, a trade name for an aloe vera solution. The intravenous use of aloe vera is not approved by the FDA and is illegal in the United States. The doctor's assistant, a former automobile mechanic who allegedly administered many of the intravenous treatments, was charged with nursing without a license.[325] Also charged with consumer fraud were the owners of T-UP, Inc., of Maryland. That state's attorney general, Joseph Curran, Jr., called it the most "egregious" fraud he had ever seen: "These men are the 1990's version of snake oil salesmen. They're dealing with a very, very vulnerable group, and the claims they've made to people who are suffering from these terrible diseases border on sinister."[326]

One of the unfortunate patients was a 57-year-old bricklayer suffering from prostate cancer. The Virginia clinic had promised to shrink his grapefruit-sized tumor to the size of a pea.

> Within two days of beginning intravenous aloe vera treatments . . . [his] body turned purple and began to swell. The skin on his toes cracked open. He died a painful death.[327]

Chelation therapy is touted as a cure for arteriosclerosis (hardening of the arteries). Patients are infused intravenously with an amino acid that purportedly flushes plaque from clogged blood vessels. "No one has ever substantiated this claim."[328] Cellular therapy consists of injections of DNA isolated from the fetuses of sheep and cattle. It is promoted for treating heart attacks, as well as such conditions as colitis, Down syndrome, acne, radiation damage, senility, and sterility. Not only is this unapproved treatment worthless, but it can also transmit animal viruses, including the one that causes the deadly type of bovine encephalitis known as "mad cow disease."[329]

For years, metabolic therapy—which allegedly detoxifies the body through the use of unproven drugs and bizarre procedures like *coffee enemas*—has been promoted as an unorthodox cure for cancer. "The American Cancer Society has not been able to trace a single documented cure of cancer by metabolic therapy, yet thousands of Americans continue to try it—typically at a cost of $6,000 (payable in advance) for a three-week session at a clinic."[330] Patients who go to these quack clinics (many of them in Mexico) often abandon legitimate cancer treatments.[331]

Actor Steve McQueen died of lung cancer in 1980 while undergoing "treatment" at a metabolic clinic in Tijuana.[332]

There are three basic forms of quackery:

(1) Nutrition: "Unsound nutrition claims are made on radio, television, in newspapers, books, and magazines, from persons ranging from self-designated 'nutrition experts' to graduates of unaccredited correspondence schools selling nutrition products and services of questionable merit, if any."[333] A 47-year-old Pennsylvania woman, for example, was told she had cervical cancer. With an immediate hysterectomy, her doctors rated her chance of recovery at 90 percent. Instead, she visited a macrobiotic diet center, where she was told that proper foods would cure her disease. She put off the needed surgery and embarked on a diet of brown rice and roots. These foods supposedly could bring her body's opposing forces of "yin" and "yang" into balance. A "nutrition consultant" persuaded the wife of a 67-year-old Pennsylvania man with colon cancer that a special diet would bring remission. He prescribed raw vegetables and the juices of wheat grass and watermelon rind.[334]

In addition to their state of residence and their reliance on peculiar dietary regimens, the unfortunate patients in the preceding illustrations share another thing in common. Within a few months of starting their respective "treatments," they were both dead.

(2) Drugs: The eternal dream of discovering the Fountain of Youth has created a boom market for fake antiaging drugs. Zumba Forte, derived from the bark of the West African yohimbe tree, is billed as a "sexual tonic" and aphrodisiac for older men. It acts as an adrenergic receptor-blocking agent and causes dangerously low blood pressure.[335] Another spurious rejuvenator, methyltestosterone, is a chemical derivative of the male sex hormone. It can cause liver and prostate cancer, as well as hepatitis, jaundice, and testicular atrophy.[336]

In the United States, the quest for a slender body is nearly as universal as the search for immortality. For years, the back pages of many popular magazines and supermarket tabloids have contained advertisements for miraculous over-the-counter diet pills. Promises that overweight customers can lose six to ten pounds a week without exercise, while wolfing down fried chicken, ice cream, and cheeseburgers, are the centerpiece of such ads. The *Healthy Weight Journal* reports that it has never found a single mail order diet pill that could live up to its advertised claims.[337] In the well-chosen words of New York City's commissioner of consumer affairs, those claims are a "fat lie."[338]

One brand of diet pill, known as Cal-Ban 3000, was recalled by the FDA as a health hazard. Cal-Ban contained a vegetable gum that swells when it absorbs moisture. The idea was that the swelling in the user's stomach would make dieters feel more full. The problem was that, when taken with water, the gum could swell up in the throat and cause a dangerous obstruction. In several cases, surgery was required to remove a mass of Cal-Ban. The product was linked to numerous serious injuries and at least one death.[339]

(3) Devices: There is a labyrinthine array of quack devices currently available to consumers. Some of them are merely incredible, such as the use of gemstones to "cure" a multitude of maladies.[340] Some are truly ridiculous, such as "Chinese Magic Weight-Loss Earrings."[341] Some are even spectacular in their absurdity. Four million women have spent $9.95 for a foot-operated breast enlarger. How this device even functions is barely imaginable. It offers users a choice of three cup sizes—"large, larger, and even larger."[342]

Magnetic therapy has become a hot trend of the early 21st century—a trend so lucrative that some professional athletes are adding brand name magnets to their list of endorsements. Americans now spend more than $500 million a year on magnetic mattress pads, back wraps, shoe inserts, seat cushions, and bracelets, although magnetic therapy has never been approved by the FDA.[343] In the interest of full disclosure it should be noted that one of the authors of this book now regularly wears a magnetic bracelet—much to the chagrin of the other authors.

Because of its painful symptoms and high incidence rate, arthritis particularly has long attracted charlatans hawking weird therapeutic contraptions to desperate sufferers. The most famous of these is the copper bracelet, which has sold for as much as $35 or more. In a single year, 50 million of these pieces of junk were peddled.[344] Countless other elaborate devices are also falsely claimed to cure arthritis. "Among these are the Zerret Applicator, the Spectro-Chrome, Neurocalometer, Oscilloclast, Roto-View, Blender Queen, Relaxacisor, Micro-dynameter, Diapulse, E-meter, and the Detoxacolon, many of which are supposed to benefit the arthritic by using various colored lights to cast 'healing' rays."[345]

An especially outlandish device was the Magic Spike—a small brass tube, the inside of which supposedly was radioactive. (It was not.) For arthritis, the tube was to be placed over the affected joint. This strange product was marketed as a cure-all and had many other purported uses just as senseless. For example, persons with high blood pressure were instructed to wear it low on the body, so it could "pull" their blood pressure down. The Magic Spike was sold for $306.[346] When its two promoters were convicted of fraud, they were each sentenced to one year in prison. The trial judge denounced them as "despicable quacks" and stated that he regretted he could not hand them longer terms.[347]

One quack who did receive a longer term was British citizen Basil Wainwright, who was sentenced in 1994 to 37 months in a federal prison for selling unapproved ozone generators as a cure for cancer and AIDS. The scheme swindled investors and desperate patients out of hundreds of thousands of dollars. "At least three patients who bought the 'cure' died."[348] Ozone is a toxic form of oxygen with no accepted medical uses in the United States. Wainwright's devices were sold to individuals who were instructed to administer the ozone gas through the rectum or vagina. Ozone reacts with the body to cause several potentially dangerous effects, including damage to the immune system and irritation of tissues lining the respiratory tract.[349] An FDA official described Wainwright as a "'career criminal' who has spent almost his entire adult life perpetrating frauds and left a trail of human misery in his wake."[350]

CASE STUDY
The King of the Quacks: Dudley LeBlanc

In 1943, a Louisiana politician named Dudley LeBlanc began selling a tonic he had mixed in barrels behind his barn. He named his elixer Hadacol. Legend has it that whenever LeBlanc was asked where he found that name he replied, "Hadacol it something!" Hadacol was a blend of B vitamins, some minerals, honey, diluted hydrochloric acid, and plenty of alcohol. (Some Southern druggists dispensed Hadacol in shot glasses.) LeBlanc claimed that Hadacol could relieve an implausible range of ailments—"anemia, arthritis, asthma, diabetes, epilepsy, heart trouble, high and low blood pressure, gallstones, paralysis, and ulcers."[351] Almost immediately, it generated astonishing profits. LeBlanc would become the most successful quack in American history. One pharmacist recalled: "They came in to buy Hadacol when they didn't have money to buy food. They had holes in their shoes and they paid $3.50 a bottle for Hadacol."[352]

(Continued)

By 1950, LeBlanc was grossing more than $20 million annually, with an advertising budget of a million dollars a month. His spectacular traveling medicine show featured such big-name performers as George Burns and Gracie Allen, Judy Garland, Mickey Rooney, Carmen Miranda, Cesar Romero, Minnie Pearl, and two of the Marx Brothers.

Eventually, LeBlanc caught the attention of the FDA, as well as the Federal Trade Commission and the Bureau of Internal Revenue.[353] Against such formidable opposition, the Hadacol bubble inevitably burst.

Was Hadacol really good for anything? Dudley LeBlanc himself was once asked that question in a television interview. His response: "[I]t was good for five and a half million for me last year."[354]

Counterfeit Medicines

When most of us hear the term "counterfeit products" we tend to think of fake Gucci bags, phony perfumes, and knock-off jeans, items whose only harm seems to be the embarrassment suffered by buyers when the goods' true provenance is discovered. But these items are only part of the worldwide market in counterfeit products. A much more serious problem is found in another part of that market: the global manufacture and sale of counterfeit medicines.

The World Health Organization estimates that 10% of the global medicine supply is counterfeit. This proportion varies tremendously from developed to less developed countries. Although the figure is estimated to be about 1% in the U.S. and Europe,

> "in some developing countries in Africa, Asia and Latin America, the share is much higher, between 10% and 30%. As much as 50% to 60% of anti-infective medications tested in parts of Asia and Africa have been found to have active ingredients outside of acceptable limits."[355]

The problem is particularly acute for critical drugs necessary for survival in many poor countries. One analysis of "counterfeit chloroquine, the traditional anti-malarial, in seven African countries showed not only the high percentage of the sample that failed to meet drug standards, but also how widely spread the counterfeits were, showing up everywhere, from district hospitals to local vendors and households."[356] A study of anti-malarial drugs in seven countries in Southeast Asia found that 35% of the samples examined failed chemical analyses.[357]

The criminals who sell these fake drugs show a remarkably callous disregard for the lives of the desperate individuals who are forced to buy them. Many of those consumers know there is a high likelihood that they are not getting the real thing, but are faced with a choice between fakes or nothing. The consequences of taking substandard or counterfeit medicine range from reducing the drugs' effectiveness to death. Horror stories abound about the effects of phony pharmaceuticals.

One of the more tragic stories took place in Panama. In 2006, officials at a large public hospital there began to notice an increase in the number of patients exhibiting the symptoms of a rare neurological disorder. In many cases the symptoms would rapidly worsen leading to death. Doctors were at first baffled by the upsurge in this deadly illness whose source they could not verify. A significant clue came when a prominent doctor at the hospital noticed that one patient who ultimately died began to develop the symptoms after he had taken cough syrup, given to him by hospital staff. Samples of the medicine was sent to the Centers for Disease Control in the U.S. where analyses revealed that they contained lethal doses of a toxic substance, diethylene glycol. The doctor's relief at discovering the source of the problem was replaced by panic when he learned that "government officials [in Panama] unwittingly mixed diethylene glycol into 260,000 bottles of cold medicine—with devastating results."[358]

A later investigation revealed that this was no accident. The syrup's ingredients had traveled through a "toxic pipeline" that circled the globe, beginning with a chemical manufacturer in China, the Taixing Glycerine Factory. The company's owners had knowingly substituted diethylene glycol, a chemical that is often used in anti-freeze, for the much more expensive pharmaceutical grade syrup that is used in cough medicine. They then sold it to a Chinese distributor who sent it out into the global market along with a phony certificate of analysis which showed the product to be 99.5% pure. The syrup then traveled through a series of middlemen around the world—none of whom checked its authenticity—until it finally ended up in Panama where officials used it in cough syrup that they distributed to the largely poor participants in government health programs. Somewhere between 100 and 365 individuals who took the cough medicine ultimately died.[359]

While Chinese authorities have acknowledged counterfeit medicines are a problem, as of 2007 no one in China had been prosecuted for producing the toxic syrup that claimed so many victims in Panama.[360] Two years after the catastrophe, the Chinese distributor that sold the syrup to the middlemen who eventually sold it to the government of Panama were still very much in business, attending trade shows and marketing their products, apparently unscathed by their involvement in this deadly business.[361]

The problem of counterfeit medicines, while more common in developing countries, is surfacing with increasing frequency in affluent countries, like the United States. In late 2011, for example, the makers of the widely used cancer drug, Avastin, announced that counterfeit versions of the drug had shown up in 19 offices of doctors, mostly in California, who had purchased them at cut-rate prices from what they thought was a legitimate supplier.[362] That supplier turned out to be a defunct business that had been run out of a residence in a small town in Montana that claimed ties to a pharmaceutical supplier in Barbados.[363] The fake drug contained none of the required active ingredient and would therefore have been useless in treating cancer, putting patients at real risk of having their untreated conditions worsen, possibly with fatal consequences.

The potential number of victims was even greater in a Florida case involving fake medications used in the treatment of cancer and HIV/AIDs. In 2001 state investigators there uncovered a scheme in which counterfeiters had "relabeled approximately 110,000 bottles of low strength Epogen® to make the bottles appear to contain a high strength Procrit®, a drug 20 times the strength of the Epogen® in the bottles."[364] They then sold the fake Procrit to wholesalers around the country, earning an illicit profit of $46 million. Investigators discovered 800 boxes of the phony medicine in a warehouse in Texas but in the end were able to recover only 10% of the counterfeit drugs. This meant that "instead of receiving the proper dosage, a large number of seriously ill cancer or HIV/AIDS patients may have received lower dosages than needed. . ." Lab tests revealed that "not only did the vials contain no medicine but the water also carried bacteria, which could set off life-threatening infections in cancer and AIDS patients."[365]

The deadly consequences of counterfeit medicines gives lie to the common assumption that white-collar crimes result only in financial losses. This fact will become even more evident in the next chapter where we consider some of the harms associated with willful efforts to destroy the environment.

Notes

1. This vignette was suggested by the boyhood reminiscences of a former smoker who has become a leading anti-tobacco crusader (White, Larry C. *Merchants of Death: The American Tobacco Industry*. New York: Beech Tree Books, 1988). According to the World Bank, tobacco-related diseases, such as those that took the lives of Bogart and Murrow, kill about 3 million people a year worldwide, and the annual death toll is expected to climb to 10 million by 2025 (*Houston Chronicle*. "Toll From Tobacco." June 4, 1996: 6A).

2. *New York Times*. "Addiction by Design?" March 6, 1994: E14.

3. Vedantam, Shankar. "Tobacco Industry, Government Debate Researchers' Findings." *Houston Chronicle*, March 30, 1996: 6A.

4. Schwartz, John. "Philip Morris Phrase Could Burn the Firm." *Houston Chronicle*, December 9, 1995: 4A.

5. Freedman, Alix M. "Philip Morris Memo Likens Nicotine to Cocaine." *Wall Street Journal*, December 8, 1995: B1, B14.

6. From "Research Planning Memorandum on the Nature of the Tobacco Business and the Crucial Role of Nicotine Therein." 1972. Quoted in *USA Today*. "Tobacco Firm's Documents Note Smoking-Drug Analogy." October 6, 1995: 4D.

7. Quoted in Shapiro, Eben. "Tobacco Firms May Face New Pressure with Disclosure of Executive's Memo." *Wall Street Journal*, May 9, 1994: A4.

8. Quoted in *ibid.*, A4.

9. Stolberg, Sheryl. "Tobacco Exec Lied to Congress about Nicotine, Scientist Charges." *Houston Chronicle*, January 27, 1996: 4A.

10. Schwartz, John. "Tobacco Files Show Firms Discussed Burying Research." *Houston Chronicle*, September 18, 1996: 2A.

11. *USA Today*. "Another Nail in Coffin of Tobacco Firms' Credibility." October 24, 1996: 12A.

12. Mishra, Raja. "More Fuel for the Fire." *Houston Chronicle*, April 23, 1998: 11A.

13. Quoted in *Newsweek*. "Mostly Smoke." July 4, 1994: 45.

14. Shapiro, *op. cit.*

15. Mishra, *op. cit.*, 11A.

16. The tobacco industry is often cited as an example of an oligopoly—a market completely controlled by a handful of companies. Philip Morris USA and RJ Reynolds control about 70 percent of the market, with the remaining share divided among Brown & Williamson, the American Tobacco Company, Liggett Group, Inc., Lorillard Tobacco, and the United States Tobacco Company.

17. Quoted in Wall, James M. "The Market Monster." *Christian Century* 112, August 16, 1995: p. 763.

18. Marwick, Charles. "Tobacco Hearings: Penetrating the Smoke Screen." *JAMA* 271, 1994: 1562.

19. Friend, Tim. "New Heat on Tobacco Firm." *USA Today*, March 19, 1996: 1A. Also: *USA Today*. "Tobacco Industry under Fire." March 19, 1996: 2B.

20. Quoted in *Houston Chronicle*. "Nicotine Manipulated, Ex-Officials Say." March 19, 1996: 6A.

21. Hohler, Bob. "Firm Admits Nicotine Boost in Cigarettes." *Boston Globe*, January 8, 1998: A3.

22. Levy, Doug. "AMA: Public 'Duped' by Tobacco Firms." *USA Today*, July 14, 1995: 1A.

23. Quoted in Schwartz, John. "Battle Cry Is Sounded on Tobacco." *Houston Chronicle*, July 14, 1995: 1A, 14A.

24. *USA Today*. "With Clout Fading, Tobacco Companies Are on the Run." March 15, 1996: 12A.

25. Cox, Patrick. "Cut Companies Some Slack." *USA Today*, March 15, 1996: 12A.

26. Levin, Myron. "Tobacco Industry Targeted Stop-Smoking Products." *Houston Chronicle*, February 14, 1999: 10A, 11A.

27. Quoted in *ibid.*, 11A.

28. An alleged smoking victim was "successful" in a lower court in a 1983 New Jersey case, but the jury verdict was overturned by a federal judge (*Houston Chronicle*. "$2 Million Award in Cigarette Asbestos Case." September 2, 1995: 11A).

29. Levy, Doug. "Partial Deal Expected in Tobacco Suit." *USA Today*, March 13, 1996: 1A. In 1988, the survivors of a New Jersey woman won $400,000 in a lawsuit against a tobacco company. The award was overturned on appeal, however, and the lawsuit was dropped in 1992. In 1990, a Mississippi jury agreed that cigarettes had killed a longtime smoker but awarded no damages because it found American Tobacco and the victim to be equally at fault (Word, Ron. "Lucky Strike for Ex-Smoker." *Boston Herald*, August 10, 1996: 3).

30. *Ibid.*

31. Word, Ron. "Lucky Strike for Ex-Smoker." *Boston Herald*, August 10, 1996: 3.

32. Zegart, Dan. "Breathing Fire on Tobacco." *Nation* 261, August 28, 1995: 193–196.

33. Levy, March 13, 1996, *op. cit.*

34. Henry, David and Levy, Doug. "Big Tobacco Firms Vow to Fight Suits." *USA Today*, March 14, 1996: 1A.

35. Quoted in: Schwartz, John. "Major Tobacco Company Will Settle Claims in Class-Action Lawsuit." *Houston Chronicle*, March 14, 1996: 3A. See also Levy, Doug. "Settlement Breaches Tobacco's Fortress." *USA Today*, March 14, 1996: 1D, 2S.

36. Wells, Melanie. "Court Ruling Gives Tobacco Stocks a Boost." *USA Today*, May 24, 1996: 1B. *Houston Chronicle*. "Appeals Court Tosses Out Class-Action Tobacco Suit." May 24, 1996: 1A, 18A.

37. "Documents Reveal Tobacco Marketing Strategies." *USA Today*, April 2, 1997: 1D. See also "Tobacco Firm Reaches Settlement With States." *Houston Chronicle*, March 20, 1997: 21A.

38. Quoted in Kellman, Laurie. "Cigarette Maker Plotted Sweet Snare for Youths." *Houston Chronicle*, February 6, 1998: 4A.

39. *Ibid.*

40. Quoted in *usatoday.com* "Tobacco Firms: Smoking Risks Well-Known." October 20, 1998.

41. Quoted in Meckler, Laura. "Teen Gets Pitch to Buy Cigarettes." *Houston Chronicle*, February 2, 1998: 3A.

42. *Ibid.*

43. Stolberg, Sheryl. "Underage Smokers Three Times as Likely to Be Influenced by Ads." *Houston Chronicle*, April 4, 1996: 18A.

44. *USA Today*. "Documents Reveal Tobacco Marketing Strategies." April 2, 1997: 1D.

45. From "Planning Assumptions and Forecast for the Period 1977–1986 for R. J. Reynolds Tobacco Company. Quoted in *USA Today*, September 6, 1995, *op. cit.*: 4D.

46. Kellman, *op. cit.*

47. Meier, Barry. "Memos Show Teens Targets for Tobacco." *Houston Chronicle*, January 15, 1998: 2A.

48. Schwartz, John. "Official Made Plan to Draw Teen Smokers." *Houston Chronicle*, October 4, 1995: 2A.

49. Quoted in *ibid.*, 2A.

50. *Ibid*. In 1996, the FDA was empowered by President Clinton to further restrict the promotion and sale of cigarettes to teenagers. The President vowed that his actions would put the Joe Camel advertising icon "out of our children's reach forever" (McDonald, Greg. "New Rules Aimed at Tobacco." *Houston Chronicle*, August 24, 1996: 1A, 16A).

51. *Consumer Reports*. "Selling to Children." August 1990: 518–521.

52. Friend, Tim. "Teen Smoking Rate Highest Since 1970s." *USA Today*, May 24, 1996: 1A.

53. Quoted in Frankel, Bruce. "Just Like That, Teens Smoke." *USA Today*, May 24, 1996: 3A.

54. *Boston Globe*. "Clinton, Ex-Lobbyist Hit Tobacco Industry." August 13, 1995: 29.

55. Moss, Desda. "Ex-Tobacco Lobbyist Tried to 'Undo Damage'." *USA Today*, March 5, 1996: 7A.

56. *cnn.com*. "Tobacco Talks Adjourn: Both Sides Claim Progress Being Made." July 31, 1998.

57. *cnn.com*. "5 Tobacco Firms Withdraw From Deal." April 8, 1998.

58. Lee, Jessica. "Execs Admit Nicotine's Addictive." *USA Today*, January 30, 1998: 4A.

59. *cnn.com*. "Big Tobacco Won't Work Toward Settlement." April 8, 1998.

60. Johnson, Kevin V. "Ad Allegations Open Minn. Tobacco Trial." *USA Today*, January 27, 1998: 1D. *cnn.com*. "Settlement Reached in Minnesota Tobacco Case." May 8, 1998. *cnn.com*. "Tobacco Industry 'Surrenders' to Minnesota." May 8, 1998. *cnn.com*. "Settlement Reached in Tobacco Lawsuit." May 8, 1998.

61. *cnn.com* "Texas Tobacco Settlement Held Up Over Attorney's Fees." May 8, 1998.

62. Levy, Doug. "Florida Settles Tobacco Suit." August 26, 1997: 1A.

63. *cnn.com*, July 31, 1998, *op. cit.*

64. *cnn.com*. "Settlement Reached by States With the Tobacco Industry." May 9, 1998.

65. *usatoday.com*. "Most States Signing on to Tobacco Deal." November 20, 1998.

66. *Ibid.*

67. Willing, Richard. "Damages Could Be Eye-Popping." *USA Today*, July 8, 1999: 3A.

68. Schwartz, John. "Big Tobacco Wins Another Court Victory." *Houston Chronicle*, November 1, 1997, 5A.

69. Willing, *op. cit.*

70. *usatoday.com*. "Tobacco Firms: Smoking Risks Well-Known." October 20, 1998.

71. Schwartz, John and Torry, Saundra. "Judge Snuffs Out Class-Action Case Against Tobacco." *Houston Chronicle*, October 18, 1997: 2A.

72. Quoted in *cnn.com*. "Tobacco Industry Says It Won't Settle $200 Billion Lawsuit." July 6, 1998.

73. *cnn.com*. "Jury Selection Begins in Florida Tobacco Trial." July 6, 1998.

74. Quoted in *ibid.*

75. *Ibid.*

76. Quoted in *usatoday.com*, October 20, 1998, *op. cit.*

77. Quoted in *Houston Chronicle*. "Tobacco Attorney Argues Smokers Knew the Risks." October 21, 1998: 9A.

78. *Ibid.*

79. *Ibid.*

80. Sharp, Deborah. "Jury: Tobacco Industry Liable." *USA Today,* July 8, 1999: 1A.

81. Quoted in Meier, Barry. "Florida Jury Awards Damages to Smokers in Class-Action Suit." *Houston Chronicle,* April 8, 2000: 2A.

82. Quoted in *ibid.*, 2A.

83. Sharp, *op. cit.*

84. Quoted in *ibid.,* 1A.

85. *Ibid.*

86. Morton, Mathew. "Product Liability: Florida Jury Finds that Cigarettes Caused Smoker's Disease." *Journal of Law, Medicine & Ethics* 28, Summer 2000: 197. Lavelle, Marianne. "A Hazy Tobacco Verdict." *U.S. News & World Report* 127: July 19, 1999: 29. Cohen, Adam. "Smoked!" *Time Atlantic* 56, July 24, 2000: 38. *Nation's Health.* "Jury Favors Plaintiffs in Class Action Lawsuit." Vol. 29. August 1999: 1. Daynard, Richard A. "The Engle Verdicts and Tobacco Litigation." *BMJ: British Medical Journal* 321, August 5, 2000: 313.

87. *Houston Chronicle.* "Record Jury Award Stuns Big Tobacco." July 15, 2000: 1A, 14A.

88. Sullivan, Patrick. "A Smoke Signal from Florida." *CMAJ: Canadian Medical Association Journal* 163, August 22, 200: 432.

89. *Ibid.*

90. Quoted in *ibid.,* 17A.

91. *Houston Chronicle.* "Tobacco Verdict in Florida Is Upheld." November 7, 2000: 4A.

92. Quoted in Wilson, Catherine. "Smokers May Never Get Money." *Houston Chronicle,* July 16, 2000: 1A, 17A.

93. Meier, Barry. "Tobacco Firm Admits Smoking Causes Cancer." *Houston Chronicle,* October 14, 1999: 5A.

94. *Houston Chronicle.* "Tobacco Firm Concedes that Cigarettes Are Addictive." October 13, 2000: 7A.

95. *Houston Chronicle.* "Philip Morris Appears to Be Open to Regulation." March 3, 2000: 25A.

96. Choe, Howard. "The Smoke Around Big Tobacco Clears." *Business Week Online,* May 22, 2003. Roman, Monica. "Light One Up for Big Tobacco." *Business Week* 3835, June 2, 2003: 36.

97. *Ibid.*

98. Thio, *op. cit.*

99. *Ibid.*, 424.

100. Quoted in Mintz and Cohen, 260.

101. Dowie, Mark. "Pinto Madness." In Hills, Stuart. *Corporate Violence: Injury and Death for Profit.* Totowa, NJ: Bowman & Littlefield, 1988: 13–29.

102. Thio, *op. cit.*, 425.

103. Eitzen and Timmer, *op. cit.*, 308.

104. Mintz, Morton. "At Any Cost: Corporate Greed, Women, and the Dalkon Shield." In Hills, Stuart (Ed.). *Corporate Violence: Injury and Death for Profit.* Totowa, NJ: Rowman & Littlefield, 1987; 31.

105. Coleman, James W. *The Criminal Elite: The Sociology of White-Collar Crime* (Third Edition). New York: St. Martin's, 1994.

106. Dowie, *op. cit.*, 29. After moving to Chrysler, Iacocca was once quoted as insisting that "Safety doesn't sell!"

107. Meier, Barry. "Large Recall of School Buses Is Ordered to Fix Fuel Tanks." *New York Times,* July 23, 1992: A16.

108. Kravets, David. "Calif. Judge Orders Ford Recall." *schwab-news.excite.com,* October 11, 2000. Ford had actually sold about 23 million of the vehicles in question, but the judge's jurisdiction in the matter did not extend beyond California.

109. *Ibid.*

110. Skrzycki, Cindy. "Firestone to Recall Millions of Tires." *Houston Chronicle,* August 9, 2000: 1A, 14A.

111. Healey, James. R. "Tires to Be Recalled." *USA Today,* August 9, 2000: 1A.

112. Frank and Lynch, *op. cit.*, 66.

113. Nathan, Sara. "More People Die Despite Recall." *USA Today,* August 22, 2000: 1B.

114. Healey, James R. and Woodyard, Chris. "Tire Concerns Go Back 1 1/2 Years Before Recall." *USA Today,* September 11, 2000: 1B.

115. *Houston Chronicle.* "Feds Rebuke Ford Over Lack of Tire Alert." August 25, 2000: 3A.

116. Healey and Woodyard, *op. cit.*

117. *Houston Chronicle.* "Tire Recall Has Trail of Missed Chances." September 11, 2000: 2A.

118. *Ibid.*

119. Nye, Peter. "The Faces of Product Liability: Keeping the Courthouse Door Open." *Public Citizen,* November/December 1992: 16–21.

120. *New York Times.* "Warning on Leather Spray." January 10, 1993: 23.

121. Williams, Lena. "Faulty Furnaces Evade Recall." *New York Times,* March 3, 1994: C9.

122. *Ibid.*

123. Applebome, Peter. "Recall Is Ordered for Worm Probes." *New York Times,* June 10, 1993: A18.

124. Swartz, Edward M. "When Products Injure Children." *Trial,* August 1989: 50–54.

125. Berselli, Beth. "Greenpeace Tackles Toy Industry, Warns of Hazardous Vinyl." *Houston Chronicle,* October 11, 1997: 18A.

126. *New York Times*. "A Million Auto Child-Safety Seats Recalled." October 30, 1992: A21. In 1995, Consumers Union tested 25 brands of child safety seats and reported that three failed to protect. According to the independent testing organization, the three brands in question broke loose in 30-mph test crashes (*Houston Chronicle*. "3 Child Safety Seats Fail to Protect." July 27, 1995: 10A).

127. *New York Times*. "Company Recalls Pacifiers." October 5, 1994: A19.

128. *New York Times*. "420,000 Snuggle Light Dolls Are Recalled by Fisher-Price." August 15, 1994: 18.

129. O'Donnell, Jayne. "Suffering in Silence." *USA Today*, April 3, 2000: 1B, 2B.

130. *Ibid*.

131. Quoted in *ibid*, 2B.

132. *Ibid*.

133. *schwab-news.excite.com*. "Co. Fined for Flammable Sweaters." October 11, 2000.

134. *New York Times*. "Ban Asked on Children's Wear with Flame Retardant." February 9, 1977: A25.

135. Brozan, Nadine. "U.S. Bans a Flame Retardant Used in Children's Sleepwear." *New York Times*, April 6, 1977: A14.

136. *New York Times*. "Supplementary Material from the Associated Press." October 19, 1978: 77.

137. Dowie, Mark and Mother Jones. "The Dumping of Hazardous Products on Foreign Markets." In Hills, Stuart L. *Corporate Violence: Injury and Death for Profit*. Totowa, NJ: Rowman & Littlefield, 1988: 47–58.

138. Sinclair, Upton. *The Jungle*. New York: Harper and Brothers, 1951; 61. This book was originally published in 1905.

139. Okun, Mitchell. *Fair Play in the Marketplace: The First Battle for Pure Food and Drugs*. DeKalb, IL: Northern Illinois University Press, 1980.

140. Frank and Lynch, *op. cit.*

141. McCaghy, E. H. *Deviant Behavior, Crime, Conflict, and Interest Groups*. New York: Macmillan, 1976: 215.

142. Eitzen and Timmer, *op. cit.*

143. Wellford, Harrison. *Sowing the Wind: A Report from Ralph Nader's Center for Study of Responsive Laws on Food Safety and the Chemical Harvest*. New York: Grossman, 1972; 69.

144. Snyder, Jean. "About the Meat You Are Buying." *Today's Health* 49, December, 1971: 39.

145. Quoted in Ross, Irwin. "How Safe Is Our Food?" *Reader's Digest,* September, 1972: 121.

146. McFarling, Usha L. "Improved Food Safety Advised." *Houston Chronicle*, August 21, 1998: 9A.

147. *Ibid*.

148. Monmaney, Terence. "Tainted Food Has Major Impact." *Houston Chronicle*, September 17, 1998: 14A. See also: Coorsh, Richard. "Modern Meat Infection." *Consumer's Research* 78, 1995: 6.

149. *Ibid*. See also: Williams, Carol J. "Russia's Fowl Play Could Backfire." *Houston Chronicle*, March 17, 1996: 32A.

150. *Ibid*. *Salmonella* is, of course, not limited to contaminated poultry. Other meat products, particularly ground beef, are also susceptible to the bacteria. For example, a California meat packer had to recall more than 825,000 lbs. of ground beef products in August, 2009, because they appeared to be contaminated with *Salmonella Newport*—a dangerous strain that is resistant to many commonly prescribed drugs. Illnesses linked to the beef had been reported in 11 states with more than 21 people affected in Colorado alone (Weise, Elizabeth. "Salmonella Beef Recall Hits 11 States." *usatoday.com*, August 8, 2009, *slashfood.com*, "Ground Beef Recalled on Salmonellosis Risk," August 7, 2009).

151. *FDA Consumer*. "Infant Formulas Recalled." Vol. 27, 1993: 3.

152. Cowley, Geoffrey and McCormick, John. "How Safe Is Our Food?" *Newsweek* 121, 1993: 7–10.

153. Hunter, Beatrice T. "Will Beefed up Inspection Assure Food Safety?" *Consumer's Research* 76, 1993: 17–21.

154. Burros, Marian. "Poultry Bacterium Getting Upper Hand, Health Officials Fear." *Houston Chronicle*, October 20, 1997: 2A.

155. *Ibid*.

156. *Houston Chronicle*. "Breeders' Ploy Can Lead to Salmonella." May 21, 1996: 4C.

157. Kuchler, Fred and MacClelland, John. "The Demand for Food Safety: An Historical Perspective on Recombinant DNA-Derived Animal Growth Hormones." *Policy Studies Journal* 17, 1988: 125–135.

158. Hunter, Beatrice T. "Improving the Fish Inspection Program." *Consumers' Research,* August 1989: 10–15.

159. DeWaal, Caroline S. and Obester, Tricia. "Seafood Safety: Consumers and Manufacturers at Risk." *USA Today Magazine,* July, 1994: 24–26.

160. *Ibid*.

161. Schwartz, John. "U.S. Unveils 'Fundamental Shift' in Procedures for Seafood Safety." *Houston Chronicle*, December 6, 1995: 14A.

162. *Houston Chronicle*. "Largest Food Poison Case." May 16, 1996: 10A.

163. Blackledge, Brett J. and Alonso-Zaldivar, Ricardo. "FDA: Ga. Plant Knowingly Shipped Tainted Products." *seattletimes.com*, February 7, 2009.

164. Quoted in Zhang, Jane and Jargon, Julie. "Peanut Corp. Emails Cast Harsh Light on Executive." *wsj.com*, February 12, 2009.

165. Quoted in *ibid.*

166. *cnn.com*. "Dead Rodents, Excrement in Peanut Processor Lead to Recall," February 12, 2009.

167. *woai.com*. "Firm Tied to Peanut Butter Recall Ran Unlicensed Texas Plant," February 3, 2009.

168. *New York Times*. "Maker Recalls Granola Bars." March 16, 1993: A17.

169. Manning, Anita. "Baby Food Has Traces of Pesticide." *USA Today,* July 26, 1995: 1D.

170. Quoted in *ibid.*, 1D.

171. *Wall Street Journal*. "Heinz Recalls Baby Food Containing Bits of Rubber." July 15, 1991: B5.

172. Frank and Lynch, *op. cit.* Lethal problems with non-prescription drugs continue to occur, though with less frequency. Six brands of aerosol cough remedies were recalled after an ingredient was linked to 21 deaths (*Changing Times*. "The Dangers that Come in Spray Cans." August, 1975: 17–19).

173. Janesh, Barbara J. "How Those Little Pills Went to Market." *Everyday Law,* January 1989: 40–44.

174. Stoll, R. Ryan. "A Question of Competence: The Judicial Role in the Regulation of Pharmaceuticals." *Food, Drug, Cosmetic Law Journal* 45, 1990: 279–299.

175. *Houston Chronicle*. "Woman Wins $23 Million in Fen-Phen Case." August 7, 1999: 1A, 18A.

176. Dowie, Mark and Marshall, Carolyn. "The Bendectin Cover-Up." In Ermann, M. David and Lundman, Richard J. (Eds.). *Corporate and Governmental Deviance: Problems of Organizational Behavior in Contemporary Society.* New York: Oxford University Press, 1982; 262–279.

177. Dowie and Marshall, *op. cit.*, 263.

178. A medical researcher, employed by Merrell, wrote an article, defending thalidomide, in the prestigious *American Journal of Obstetrics and Gynecology*. This same scientist was also the inventor of Bendectin—another one of Richardson-Merrell's defective drugs, described earlier in this chapter (Dowie and Marshall, *op. cit.*).

179. Dowie and Marshall, *op. cit.*

180. Knightley, Phillip, Evans, Harold, Potter, Elaine, and Wallace, Marjorie. *Suffer the Children: The Story of Thalidomide.* New York: Viking Press, 1979; 1.

181. *Ibid.*

182. *New York Times*. "3 Babies Born Deformed Here; Thalidomide Taken by Mothers." July 27, 1962: 12.

183. Knightley, *et al.*, 69.

184. *Ibid.*

185. Schwartz, John. "FDA Warily OKs Use of Thalidomide for Leprosy Lesions." *Houston Chronicle,* July 17, 1998: 2A.

186. Quoted in *ibid.*, 2A.

187. *Ibid.*

188. *Ibid.*

189. Frank and Lynch, *op. cit.*

190. Coleman, *op. cit.*

191. *Ibid.*, 86. More recently, a similarly named antiinfection drug, Omniflex, was withdrawn from the market by its manufacturer, Abbott Laboratories, after it was linked to three deaths and fifty cases of adverse side effects, including kidney failure (*New York Times*. "Drug Is Recalled by Maker after Being Tied to 3 Deaths." June 6, 1992: 9).

192. Olmos, David R. "3 Plead Guilty in Lab Test Fraud." *Los Angeles Times,* September 27, 1999: A10.

193. *Ibid.*

194. Quoted in Cobb, Kim. "Bush's Halcion Use Divulged after Falling Ill on Japan Trip." *Houston Chronicle,* September 11, 1994: 21A.

195. Cobb, Kim. "FDA Admits Mistake, Urges Probe of Halcion." *Houston Chronicle,* June 1, 1996: 1A.

196. *Health Letter*. "Dangerous Drug Interactions with the Sleeping Pill Triazolam (Halcion)." Vol. 11, March, 1995: 10; Stephenson, John. "Commercial Confidence: Secrecy or Openness?" *Pharmaceutical Executive* 14, December, 1994: 24–26.

197. Reed, Steven R. "Sleep Merchants/The Halcion Story: FDA Ignored Own Halcion Findings." *Houston Chronicle,* September 13, 1994: 1A.

198. O'Donnell, Peter. "Ghosts from the Past." *Pharmaceutical Executive* 15, June, 1995: 36.

199. Cowley, Geoffrey. "Dreams or Nightmare?" *Newsweek* 118, August 19, 1991: 44–51.

200. *Houston Chronicle*. "Sleep Merchants/Halcion Chronology." September 11, 1994: 22A.

201. Cowley, *op. cit.*

202. *Ibid.*

203. *Ibid.*

204. Quoted in Reed, Steven R. "Sleep Merchants/the Halcion Story: Upjohn Paid Heavily to Discredit Critics." *Houston Chronicle,* September 14, 1994: 1A.

205. Quoted in *Houston Chronicle*. "Sleep Merchants: Upjohn's Paper Trail." September 11, 1994: 20A.

206. Reed, Steven R. "Federal Report Targets Upjohn for 'Misconduct.'" *Houston Chronicle,* May 1, 1994: 1A.

207. Cobb, "FDA Admits Mistake," June 1, 1996, *op. cit.*

208. Quoted in Reed, Steven R. "Sleep Merchants/ The Halcion Story: Hidden Nightmares." *Houston Chronicle,* September 11, 1994: 1A.

209. Reed, Steven R. "Sleep Merchants/The Halcion Story: Halcion Research Called into Question." *Houston Chronicle,* September 12, 1994: 1A.

210. *Ibid.*

211. Quoted in Cowley, *op. cit.,* 49.

212. Quoted in *ibid.,* 47.

213. Reed, "Hidden Nightmares," September 11, 1994, *op. cit.*

214. Quoted in Reed, "FDA Ignored Own Halcion Findings," September 13, 1994, *op. cit.,* 1A.

215. *Ibid.*

216. Quoted in *ibid.,* 1A.

217. Quoted in Reed, Steven R. "Bearer of Bad News." *Houston Chronicle,* September 14, 1994: 7A.

218. *Ibid.*

219. Cowley, *op. cit.,* 49.

220. Cobb, Kim. "Sleep Merchants/Troubled Experiences." *Houston Chronicle,* September 11, 1994: 21A.

221. Tedford, Deborah. "Lawsuit Cites Man's Woes while He Was on Halcion." *Houston Chronicle,* March 9, 1994: 30A.

222. *Ibid.*

223. Urban, Jerry. "Man Loses Lawsuit against Halcion Maker." *Houston Chronicle,* March 31, 1994: 26A.

224. Quoted in Reed, Steven R. "Through a Halcion Haze." *Houston Chronicle,* January 23, 1994: 1A.

225. *Ibid.,* 1A.

226. *Ibid.,* 1A.

227. Reed, Steven R. "Appeals Court Sets Aside Lone Halcion Award." *Houston Chronicle,* August 30, 1994: 9A.

228. *Ibid.*

229. *Ibid.*

230. Cobb, Kim. "FDA Admits Mistake, Urges Probe of Halcion," June 1, 1996, *op. cit.:* 16A

231. Cobb, Kim. "Sleep Merchants/Groundbreaking, Heartbreaking Case." *Houston Chronicle,* September 11, 1994: 20A.

232. Cobb, Kim. "Woman in '88 Halcion Case Takes Own Life." *Houston Chronicle,* July 23, 1994: 1A.

233. Cowley, *op. cit.*

234. Cobb, Kim. "Jim Ayers Believes Halcion Triggered Rampage." *Houston Chronicle,* September 11, 1994: 22A.

235. Cobb, Kim. "Sleep Merchants: Troubled Experiences." *Houston Chronicle,* September 11, 1994: 21A.

236. *Ibid.*

237. Quoted in Cobb, "Troubled Experiences," September 11, 1994, *op. cit.,* 21A.

238. Cobb, Kim and Reed, Steven R. "Sleep Merchants: The Halcion Story." *Houston Chronicle,* September 15, 1994: 1A.

239. Reed, Steven R. "Halcion Lawsuit Alleges FDA, Upjohn Conspiracy." *Houston Chronicle,* January 7, 1994: 29A.

240. *Ibid.,* 29.

241. *Ibid.,* 29.

242. Two shareholder class-action suits against Upjohn have even been filed in federal court, claiming that Upjohn's directors and officers breached their responsibilities to investors by obscuring potential financial losses posed by product liability. The shareholders charge that Upjohn failed to disclose the severe side effects of Halcion and concealed testing problems and adverse results that occurred in clinical trials of the drug—in violation of the Securities Exchange Act of 1934. Fittingly, one of the lead attorneys representing the shareholders is himself a former Halcion user. In his words: "It nearly destroyed my career. I had terrible, terrible, depression" (quoted in Cobb, Kim. "Sleep Merchants: Internal Ills." *Houston Chronicle,* September 15, 1994: 15A).

243. Himelstein, Linda. "Did Big Tobacco's Barrister Set up a Smokescreen?" *Business Week* 3388, September 5, 1994: 68–70.

244. Reed, "Hidden Nightmares," September 11, 1994, *op. cit.,* 1A.

245. Quoted in *ibid.,* 1A.

246. Quoted in Cowley, *op. cit.,* 45.

247. *Kiplinger's Personal Finance Magazine.* "Gyps and Frauds Update." May, 1994: 11.

248. Ropp, Kevin L. "Selling Used Pacemakers Lands Businessman in Jail." *FDA Consumer* 27, December, 1993: 38–40.

249. *Galveston Daily News.* "Heart Catheter Firm Will Pay $61 Million Fine." October 17, 1993: 9B.

250. Hutt, Peter B. "A History of Regulation of Adulteration and Misbranding of Medical Devices." *Food, Drug, Cosmetic Law Journal* 44, 1989: 99–117.

251. Perry, Susan and Dawson, Jim. *Nightmare: Women and the Dalkon Shield.* New York: Macmillan, 1985.

252. *Ibid.*

253. Mintz, *op. cit.*

254. Coleman, *op. cit.,* 86.

255. *Ibid.*

256. Mintz, *op. cit.,* 31.

257. Coleman, *op. cit.*

258. Kendall, Pamela. Torn Illusions: *One Woman's Tragic Experience with the Silicone Conspiracy.* Far Hills, New York: Horizon Press, 1994; 24.

259. Cowley, Geoffrey. "Calling a Halt to the Big Business of Silicone Implants." *Newsweek,* January 20, 1992: 56.

260. *Ibid.*

261. Quoted in Smart, Tim. "This Man Sounded the Silicone Alarm—in 1976." *Business Week,* January 27, 1992: 34.

262. Rensberger, Boyce. "Breast Implant Records Were 'Faked'." *Washington Post,* November 3, 1992: A3.

263. Priest, Dana. "Dow Corning Accused of Withholding Silicone Data." *Washington Post,* January 16, 1993: A5.

264. Fackelmann, K. A. "Implants Linked to Disorders in Children." *Science News* 145, 1993: 70.

265. Lewin, Tamar. "As Silicone Issue Grows, Women Take Agony and Anger to Court." *New York Times,* January 19, 1992: 1.

266. *New York Times.* "Record $25 Million Awarded in Silicone-Gel Implant Case." December 24, 1992: A13.

267. *New York Times.* "3M Will Pay $325 Million to Settle Implant Suits." April 12, 1994, B8.

268. *Houston Chronicle.* "Dow Corning Files for Bankruptcy." May 16, 1995: 1C.

269. *Ibid.*

270. *USA Today.* "Implant Fiasco: A Case of Putting Safety Last." May 17, 1995: 12A.

271. Meier, Barry. "Penalties Rise in Breast Implant Case." *Houston Chronicle,* October 31, 1995: 4A.

272. McConnaughey, Janet. "Dow Liable for Implants, Jury Decides." *Orange County Register.* August 19, 1997: 3. *Houston Chronicle.* "Jury Rules Against Dow Chemical." August 19, 1997: 1A. Alexander, Keith. "Jury: Dow Chemical Negligent." *USA Today,* August 19, 1997: 1A.

273. *Houston Chronicle.* "FDA Advisory Panel Deems One Brand of Breast Implants Safe." March 2, 2000: 5A.

274. *Ibid.*

275. Houpert, Karen and Pushkar, Katherine. "Pulling the Plug on the Sanitary Protection Industry." *Village Voice* 40, February 7, 1995: 33–40.

276. Swasy, Alecia. "Rely Tampons and Toxic Shock Syndrome: Procter & Gamble's Responses." In Ermann, M. David and Lundman, Richard J. (Eds.), *Corporate and Governmental Deviance* (Fifth Edition). New York: Oxford University Press, 1996.

277. *Ibid.*

278. Houppert and Pushkar, *op. cit.*

279. Swasy, 1996, 183–184.

280. *Ibid.,* 283.

281. Houppert and Pushkar, *op. cit.,* 33.

282. Swasy, 1996, *op. cit.,* 287.

283. Swasy, Alecia. *Soap Opera: The Inside Story of Procter & Gamble.* New York: Time Books, 1993.

284. *Ibid.*

285. Riley, Tom. *The Price of a Life: One Woman's Death from Toxic Shock.* Bethesda, MD: Adler & Adler, 1986. Upon publication of this book, Riley received numerous offers to appear on television talk shows. All his bookings were mysteriously canceled at the last minute, however. Apparently no one was willing to risk offending P&G, the country's largest television advertiser. The book also has a suspicious history of disappearing from library shelves.

286. Swasy, 1993, *op. cit.,* 143.

287. *Ibid.,* 144.

288. *Ibid.*

289. Riley, *op. cit.*

290. Swasy, 1993, *op. cit.*

291. *Ibid.,* 151.

292. Quoted in *ibid.,* 151.

293. Schaller, Warren E. and Carroll, Charles R. *Health, Quackery & the Consumer.* Philadelphia: W.B. Saunders, 1976.

294. Young, James H. *The Medical Messiahs: A Social History of Health Quackery in Twentieth-Century America.* Princeton, NJ: Princeton University Press, 1967.

295. Waldron, George B. "What America Spends on Advertising." *Chatauquan* 38, 1903: 156.

296. Young, *op. cit.*

297. *Ibid.*

298. Nishiwaki, Robin and Bouchard, Carla. "Combating Nutrition Quackery: The San Bernadino County Experience." *American Journal of Public Health* 79, 1989: 652–653. The $25 billion figure was derived from a five-year government study headed by former Congressman Claude Pepper.

299. *FDA Consumer.* "Top 10 Health Frauds." October 1989: 29.

300. Quoted in *ibid.,* 82.

301. *Consumers' Research.* "Quackery Targets Teens." Vol. 71, April, 1988: 24–26.

302. Grossman, Ellie. "Curing the Incurable." *Safety and Health,* February 1992: 51.

303. *Ibid.,* 51. The estimate is from the National Center for Health Services Research.

304. Napier, Kristine. "Unproven Medical Treatments Lure Elderly." *FDA Consumer,* March 1994: 32–37.

305. Marvin, *op. cit.*

306. Quoted in Grossman, *op. cit.,* 169.

307. Michelmore, Peter. "Beware the Health Hucksters." *Readers Digest* 134, January, 1989: 114.

308. Hartigan, Neil F. "Health Quackery: Diet Pills to AIDS Cures." *Journal of State Government* 62, 1989: 102.

309. Pogash, Carol. "Miracle Cure or Snake Oil?" *San Francisco Chronicle Magazine,* July 18, 1993: 6–9.

310. Segal, Marian. "Defrauding the Desperate." *FDA Consumer* 21, October, 1987: 16–19.

311. *FDA Consumer,* 1989, *op. cit.*

312. *Ibid.*

313. Segal, Marian. "Defrauding the Desperate: Quackery and AIDS." *FDA Consumer,* October, 1988: 17–19.

314. *Ibid.,* 17.

315. *Ibid.,* 17.

316. Campbell, Duncan and Townson, Nigel. "Let Them Eat Shit." *New Statesman & Society* 2, 1989: 10–12.

317. Goldemberg, *op. cit.*

318. Napier, *op. cit.*

319. *Ibid.*

320. Poppy, John. "Bad-Faith Healers." *Men's Health.* 9, December, 1994: 106–109.

321. Lane, I. William and Comac, Linda. *Sharks Don't Get Cancer.* Garden City Park, New York: Avery, 1992.

322. Rosenfeld, Isadore. "Shark Cartilage to Prevent Cancer? Forget It." *Parade,* January 14, 2001: 16. In 1996, a Connecticut marketing company was fined for advertising pills made from shark parts, which promised "amazing health benefits." *Dubuque Telegraph Herald.* "Ads for Bigger Breasts, etc., Quashed." May 31, 1996: 7.

323. Napier, *op. cit.*

324. *Ibid.*

325. Smith, Leef. "Md. Businessmen Accused of Fraud in Marketing of Aloe Vera as Cure." *Washington Post,* May 8, 1998: B1.

326. Quoted in *ibid.,* B1.

327. Lipton, Eric and Smith, Leef. "Was Cancer 'Cure' a Painful Lie?" *Washington Post,* February 25, 1998: A1.

328. Michelmore, *op. cit.,* 116.

329. Segal, 1992, *op. cit.*

330. *Ibid.,* 116.

331. *FDA Consumer, op. cit.*

332. *Ibid.*

333. Nishiwaki and Bouchard, *op. cit.,* 652.

334. Michelmore, *op. cit.*

335. Segal, Marian. "Family Indicted for Fountain of Youth Fraud." *FDA Consumer* 26, July, 1992: 36–37.

336. *Ibid.*

337. Barrett, Stephen. "Stronger Laws Needed to Stop Mail Fraud." *Healthy Weight Journal* 9, May, 1995: 55.

338. Quoted in *Kiplinger's Personal Finance Magazine, op. cit.,* 11.

339. Meier, Barry. "Consumer's World: Diet-Pill Death Raises Questions on F.D.A. Role." *New York Times,* August 4, 1990: 48.

340. Thompson, Sharon E. "Gems as Medicine—or—Stone Quackery?" *Lapidary Journal* 49, May, 1995: 49–52.

341. *FDA Consumer, op. cit.*

342. Divine, Mary. "The Skeptical Curator." *Minneapolis—St. Paul* 22, May, 1994: 28.

343. Ruibal, Sal. "Ironclad Cures for Pain?" *USA Today,* August 20, 1997: 3C.

344. Schaller and Carroll, *op. cit.*

345. *Ibid.,* 281.

346. *Ibid.*

347. Quoted in *ibid.,* 230.

348. Farley, Dixie. "'Career Criminal' Faces Jail and Possible Deportation." *FDA Consumer* 28, 1994: 30.

349. *Ibid.,* 30–32.

350. *Ibid.,* 30.

351. Young, *op. cit.,* 320.

352. *Ibid.,* 317.

353. *Ibid.*

354. Quoted in *ibid.,* 328.

355. United Nations Office on Drugs and Crime. *The Globalization of Crime.* 2010: 184.

356. *Ibid.,*186

357. Gaurvika M.L. Nayyar, Bremen, Joel G., Newton, Paul N., and Herrington, James, "Poor-quality Antimalarial Drugs in Southeast Asia and Sub-Saharan Africa." *The Lance Infectious Diseases* 12, June 2012: 488–496.

358. Bogdanich, Walt and Hooker, Jake. "From China to Panama, a Trail of Poisoned Medicine." *nytimes.com.* May 6, 2007.

359. *Ibid.*

360. *Ibid.*

361. Bredar, John [Producer] and Naim, Moses[Producer]. "Illicit: The Dark Trade" [DVD] 2008. National Geographic.

362. Rockoff, Jonathan and Weaver, Christopher. "Fake Cancer Drug Found in U.S." *wsj.com.* February 15, 2012.

363. CBS Evening News, "Fake Avastin Tied to Small Montana Distributor." February 16, 2012.

364. Office of Program Policy Analysis and Government Accountability, an office of the Florida Legislature. "Counterfeit and Diverted Drugs Threaten Public Health and Waste State Dollars." Report No. 03-18. February, 2003: 3.

365. Kestin, Sally and LaMendola, Bob. "Three Accused of Selling Fake Drug." *sunsentinel.com.* May 22, 2003.

4

Environmental Crime

The previous chapter, in its consideration of dangerous and defective consumer products, punctured the prevalent myth that white-collar crimes are nonviolent and carry little in the way of physical costs. In fact, the human cost of white-collar crime is nothing less than devastating. Social activist Ralph Nader has written that "[t]he harm done to human health and safety by business crime should dispel the distinguishing characteristic of 'white-collar crime' as being the absence of physical threat."[1] Testifying before Congress in 1978, the noted criminologist Gilbert Geis observed: "It is quite possible that more people have died from corporate conducted or corporate condoned violence . . . than have been victims of more traditional kinds of murder."[2]

This chapter will consider how pollution of the natural environment and the workplace can be especially deadly examples of what Nader calls "postponed violence."[3] The Environmental Protection Agency (EPA) has urged courts to "view environmental crime for what it really is—a crime of violence and an egregious departure from responsible citizenship."[4]

THE NATURAL ENVIRONMENT

Sometimes the human costs of environmental negligence are indirect, though tragic nonetheless. An example of indirect physical costs can be found in the aftermath of the disastrous Alaskan oil spill of 1989,[5] for which the Exxon Corporation received a $900 million civil penalty and a $100 million criminal fine.[6] The lifestyle of the Native American population in Kodiak was devastated. Villagers reportedly suffered a 700 percent increase in emotional problems in the months after the spill. The alcoholism rate soared, and eight suicides occurred in just a six-week period.[7]

All too often, however, the physical costs of corporate recklessness are brutally direct. The EPA estimates that, of the 100 billion tons of hazardous waste produced each year in the United States, 90 percent is disposed of in an environmentally unsafe manner.[8] This certainly was the case at the infamous Love Canal, the upstate New York community that has become the symbol of environmental crime.

CASE STUDY
Love Canal

From 1942 to 1953, the Hooker Chemical Corporation (a subsidiary of Occidental Petroleum) burned more than 20 million pounds of chemical waste in an abandoned waterway near Niagara Falls. The canal was then covered up and sold for one dollar to the local board of education, which built an elementary school on the site. A housing development soon followed.[9]

In 1977, melting snow forced contaminated groundwater into residents' basements, where it oozed up in the form of black sludge. Two hundred chemical compounds were identified, including dioxin ("the most toxic synthetic compound ever made"[10]) and benzene, called "the most powerful carcinogen known."[11] When an unusually high number of miscarriages were observed in the vicinity, the New York health commissioner declared an emergency and advised pregnant women to move away.[12] "[A] survey also revealed that in a neighborhood not far from Love Canal only one of the 16 pregnancies in 1979 ended in the birth of a healthy baby, while four ended in miscarriages, two babies were stillborn, and nine were born deformed."[13]

> [A] 1980 study of more than 900 children from the area produced some chilling results. Seizures, learning problems, eye and skin irritations, incontinence, and severe abdominal pains were much more prevalent among Love Canal children than among children from nearby neighborhoods.[14]

A 1987 follow-up study revealed that children born in the Love Canal area had significantly lower birth weights[15] and impaired growth compared to other children.[16] Although Love Canal eventually was evacuated, it was too late for many prenatal victims. For example, the daughter of one resident was born with bone disease, dental deformities, and learning problems.[17] Another resident, after two miscarriages, gave birth to a daughter whose knee was afflicted with tumors.[18]

Lois Gibbs, the housewife-turned-activist who organized the residents of Love Canal, described the misery of an entire community:

> All around me I saw things happening to my neighbors—multiple miscarriages, birth defects, cancer deaths, epilepsy, central nervous disorders, and more. . . [W]e were never warned. We had no idea we were living on top of a chemical graveyard.[19]

In 1994, in response to a call from environmentalists to ban the use of chlorine in manufacturing, which produces dioxin as a by-product, the EPA issued a report that verified what the residents of Love Canal had long suspected. According to the EPA, "Dioxin can cause cancer and other health problems even at very low levels of exposure."[20]

One of the most disturbing aspects of the Love Canal debacle was that much of the attendant pain and anxiety could have been avoided. Internal memoranda from the files of Hooker Chemical indicate that the company knew of the peril as early as 1958, when it investigated the burning of three school children who had come in contact with leaking drums of benzene hexachloride near their school.[21] Hooker failed to notify any authorities and opted to do nothing in order to avoid a $50 million cleanup bill.[22] One of the confidential memos iterated: "We should not do anything unless requested by the school board."[23]

When the U.S. House subcommittee examined hazardous waste practices in 1979, a young Tennessee Congressman (and future vice president), Albert Gore, condemned Hooker's action—or more precisely—inaction: "The events we have seen take place at Love Canal could have been avoided if you had heeded these early warnings."[24]

(*Continued*)

But the company had not heeded those early warnings—nor, apparently, Gore's. In 1990, Hooker was back in court, this time in connection with its waste site in Hyde Park, New York. The Hyde Park landfill contains 80,000 tons of chemical deposits—including over one ton of dioxin.[25]

In 1995, after a 16-year dispute, Occidental Petroleum, the parent company of Hooker Chemical, finally agreed to reimburse the federal government $129 million for cleaning up Love Canal.[26]

Improbable as it sounds, by 1998—20 years after President Jimmy Carter declared a state of emergency—people had moved back to Love Canal. Although the waterway itself was buried under a plastic liner along with scores of homes, and a fenced area of topsoil and clay was declared permanently off limits, the EPA declared the rest of Love Canal safe. The Love Canal Revitalization Agency reported that it had sold 232 of the 239 homes it renovated. Love Canal was renamed Black Creek Village.[26a] One of the new residents of Black Creek Village confidently insisted: "This is the most tested piece of real estate in the United States."[26b] Less convinced was a former resident, whose seven-year-old son had died of kidney disease likely brought on by exposure to dioxin before the family had escaped. On a visit to her old neighborhood, she lamented: "The children are what bother me when I see them running around this neighborhood. I'm so frightened for them."[26c]

This chapter will examine similar patterns of corporate malfeasance that have contaminated our environment. In such cases, innocent members of the public become the victims of greed, negligence, and irresponsibility.

Water Pollution

To a tourist standing on a wharf, such famous landmarks as Boston Harbor or San Francisco Bay are like scenic three-dimensional postcards. However, beneath the surface (literally), there is nothing beautiful to behold:

> What is happening underwater . . . is not for the squeamish. Scuba divers talk of swimming through clouds of toilet paper and half-dissolved feces, of bay bottoms covered by a foul and toxic combination of sediment, sewage and petrochemical waste appropriately known as "black mayonnaise."[27]

For years, Boston Harbor served as America's largest cesspool, collecting the waste of 3 million metropolitan residents. "Local beaches are littered with grease balls, tampon applicators and the occasional condom—all of which are apparently released by the antiquated and overloaded sewage system."[28] Fish, which once abounded in the harbor, virtually disappeared. Those remaining often suffered from fin rot and tumors.

Moreover, the harbor bottom contained high concentrations of pesticides and industrial waste, suspected of being carcinogenic. Fortunately, changes in environmental laws appear to have turned things around more recently. In 1990, a Massachusetts firm, Borjohn Optical Technology, became the first company convicted under the new "knowing endangerment" amendment to the federal Water Quality Act. Borjohn had discharged toxic concentrations of nickel and nitric acid into Boston Harbor.[29]

The resuscitation of Boston Harbor is unfortunately not typical. Millions of tons of sludge from municipal sewage treatment plants in the Metropolitan New York area are dumped each year at a site off the New Jersey coast. This sludge has already entered the oceanic food chain, and the long-term impact remains to be seen.[30]

Beaches from Maine to Texas have been plagued by toxic debris. In the summer of 1988, for example, large amounts of illegally dumped medical waste washed ashore across public beaches along the New York–New Jersey coast. Among the debris were hypodermic needles, IV tubing, catheter bags, and vials of blood—some of which tested positive for AIDS.[31] Over 9 million people resided in the affected areas.

The culprits in the medical waste debacle are dishonest haulers who contract with hospitals to dispose of their waste at special dump sites around the country, but who avoid costly transportation expenses by simply tossing infected material into the ocean. Some health-care facilities themselves also have been implicated in the surreptitious dumping of their own debris in order to save disposal costs, which usually are 10 times higher for medical waste than for other types of waste.[32]

Our harbors and beaches, however, are not the only source of dangerous pollution. Our drinking water sometimes has been contaminated by the illegal dumping or careless storage of toxic waste. In Massachusetts, 28 public water sources were shut down over an 18-month period in 1979–1980.[33] In California, thousands of underground storage tanks containing fuels and industrial solvents currently are leaking into groundwater.[34] Even the community of Lake Arrowhead, long renowned for its pure drinking water, has been affected. Some local residents developed red lumps on their necks from showering.[35]

Without water, of course, there can be no human life; but water also can be directly related to disease and death. According to the World Health Organization, more than three-quarters of all human disease is waterborne.[36] Because technologically advanced societies, like the United States, employ modern water treatment practices, nonmalignant waterborne diseases, such as cholera, typhoid, and dysentery, are largely nonexistent. It is the category of malignant waterborne diseases that has created serious health problems in the United States. Three major kinds of contamination have been identified: (1) organic contamination, which has been linked to various forms of cancer; (2) inorganic contamination, most notably metals such as lead, which are suspected of causing developmental problems in children;[37] and (3) radioactivity, which is believed to cause prenatal damage.[38]

Some water contamination occurs unintentionally, as through the natural corrosion of old pipes or the inadvertent runoff of agricultural chemicals. In 1985, for example, the town of Woodstock, New York, began finding large quantities of asbestos in its water supply. The problem became so acute that clumps of fibers were falling on people in the shower.[39] The source of the contamination was a network of aging pipes built of asbestos-laced cement. Although the carcinogenic properties of asbestos is an area of medical controversy, a number of scientists have related waterborne asbestos to gastrointestinal cancer.[40]

Some of the water contamination problems, though, are hardly unintentional and can be attributed directly to illegal practices at privately owned dump sites. For example, a disposal firm in Rockland County, New York, whose permit limited it to the handling of construction debris, such as wood, concrete, and plaster, was charging neighboring communities for unlawfully storing their incinerated garbage. As a result of leaching, the water supply in West Nyack, New York, became contaminated by trichloroethylene (TCE), an industrial solvent and degreasing agent "known to have adverse effects on the human nervous system, the cardiovascular system, the liver and the kidney."[41]

Some of the most reckless tales of toxic dumping involve the waste-hauling practices of illicit trucking operations. One week before a federal waste-monitoring system was to take effect in late 1980, thousands of tons of toxic wastes were hurriedly disposed of in a last-minute rush to circumvent the new law. As the deadline drew nearer, some hazardous materials even were dumped from moving trucks onto interstate highways or abandoned in shopping center parking lots around the country.[42] The proper disposal of hazardous waste is costly—"in some parts of the country averaging $2,000 to $4,000 a truckload."[43] Consequently, certain unscrupulous trucking companies and individual drivers choose to dump dangerous waste illegally and pocket the savings. Other offenders simply abandon dilapidated trucks along with their toxic cargo. "In New York City, for example, authorities routinely impound unattended trucks carrying dangerous waste products."[44]

Truckers, known as "sludge runners," actually open the spigots of their storage tanks and release toxic waste as they drive. A popular venue for sludge runners was the Mianus River Bridge in Connecticut. Gallons of corrosive liquid would drain off the span, not only polluting the river below but eventually weakening the metal support joints of the structure. When the rotting joints finally broke apart in 1983, the bridge collapsed.[45]

Much of our poisoned water is not due to illegal hauling, however, but is the result of criminal negligence on the part of industrial corporations themselves. This was the case, for example, when the FBI raided Colorado's Rocky Flats nuclear weapons plant in 1989. "The facility, which was owned by the Department of Energy and operated by Rockwell International, was the nation's only plant making plutonium triggers used to set off nuclear warheads."[46] The plant had become so contaminated that eventual cleanup costs are projected to be $2 billion.[47] It also has been calculated that the radioactive contamination at Rocky Flats will remain for 24,000 years.[48]

Furthermore, it was discovered that Rocky Flats was dumping radioactive matter into local rivers.[49] A criminal grand jury indicted Rockwell, but, in a controversial decision, the Justice Department did not sign the indictments, opting instead for a plea-bargained fine of $18.5 million.[50] Since Rockwell had also received a $22.6 million performance bonus, it actually came out $4.1 million ahead. A report in the *Bulletin of the Atomic Scientists* was titled, "The Wages of Sin? About $4.1 Million."[51] A congressional committee decried this arrangement as a miscarriage of justice. When members of the grand jury publicly protested the lack of an indictment, *they* became the subjects of a government investigation.[52] As *US News and World Report* noted, "The Justice Department is supposed to prosecute companies for environmental crimes, not look the other way."[53]

The EPA has estimated that as many as 30,000 waste sites may pose significant health problems related to water contamination.[54] For example, the town of Yellow Creek, Kentucky, had its water supply poisoned when a tannery began disgorging chromium into the local creek. Chromium is a highly toxic metal that is extremely dangerous to human life.[55] It took seven years of community agitation before the contamination was cleaned up. During that time, children endured chronic diarrhea and vomiting, while adults were stricken with ulcers, kidney problems, and miscarriages. One family, living right along the creek, suffered six cancer deaths in five years.[56]

Illegal dumping by the Velsicol chemical company of Memphis had contaminated the wells at a number of farms in Toone, Tennessee. Several families suffered chronic depression for four years, "until they discovered chloroform in their drinking water at levels equaling a daily sedative."[57] How potent was Velsicol's waste? Consider the following repercussions:

> The truck driver who hauled Velsicol's leaking barrels of chemical wastes from Memphis to Toone lost his sight after continued exposure to the corrosive fumes. His 29-year-old son, who worked alongside him, developed nerve damage. Although formerly a keen athlete, the young man's once-powerful legs began to tremor uncontrollably; one summer, he drowned while swimming.[58]

Of all the waste-site-related health hazards, the contamination of drinking water probably represents the most serious threat because of its potential to affect the greatest number of people.[59] Nearly half the people in America, including about one-third of those residing in our largest cities and most of our rural population, depend on groundwater for their drinking supplies.[60] "When poisonous materials are dumped or seep into the earth, they mix with precipitation, percolate through the soil . . . and then become part of the water supply."[61] Once a water supply is contaminated, it can remain so for decades or even centuries or millennia.

So persistent are the effects of water contamination that, in 1990, families in Ponca City, Oklahoma, were paid $40,000 to abandon their homes and leave their neighborhood. The Conoco oil company, which had contaminated the community's drinking water, had opted to minimize its exposure to litigation by surrounding its refinery with a ring of deserted houses.[62]

Toxic water has been linked to a variety of ailments including kidney disorder, digestive problems, chronic headaches, blurred vision, and peeling skin.[63] In addition, water contamination also has been connected to a virtual catalogue of birth defects. For example, after the Fairchild Camera and Instrument Company of San Jose, California, leaked an industrial solvent into one neighborhood's drinking supply, the number of babies born with congenital heart deformities rose sharply. Although the state health department was equivocal in its conclusions, the company agreed to a financial settlement in a lawsuit filed on behalf of 117 affected children.[64]

The most serious health problem related to water contamination undoubtedly is cancer—especially when it afflicts children. Children seem to be more vulnerable to the effects of chemical exposures than adults.[65] "Their behavior, diet, developing physiology, and growth needs all contribute to children's unique susceptibility to toxic harm."[66]

CASE STUDY
The Woburn Leukemia Cluster

Woburn, Massachusetts, is a lower-middle-class community 12 miles north of Boston. Since the 19th century, Woburn has been an industrial town, first as a leather-tanning center and later as a popular venue for the chemical and plastic industries. The source of Woburn's water supply is Lake Mishawum.

In the 1930s, townspeople began noticing that Lake Mishawum often took on a red coloring and emitted a nauseating odor.[67] Residents continued to complain about discoloration, bad smell, and bad taste in their water through the 1970s. In 1978, Woburn was forced to close two wells because of a high carbon-chloroform extract (CCE) concentration, far in excess of the accepted limits of public safety.[68] The problem was attributed to the town's chlorination method. The real source of the toxic pollution, as well as its full extent and tragic consequences, had not yet been recognized.

There was, however, at least one resident who had become obsessed with the danger of Woburn's contaminated water. Annie Anderson, a housewife whose son Jimmy was diagnosed with acute lymphocytic leukemia in 1972, started hearing of other such cases and meeting families of other victims at stores and at the hospital where Jimmy was being treated. "In 1973, she began to suspect that the growing number of leukemia cases might have been caused by something carried in the water."[69] She asked the state to test Woburn's water supply, but her request was denied. Anderson's suspicions initially were dismissed as the displaced anger of a distraught parent.[70] Her family pastor was asked

(Continued)

by her husband to try to get her mind off what he felt was an erroneous obsession. The pastor would later recall: "I set out to prove her wrong, that cancer and leukemia don't run in neighborhoods, but she was right."[71]

Annie Anderson's claims received a more official measure of validation in June 1979, when scientists from the EPA tested the wetlands surrounding the two closed wells and found "dangerous levels of lead, arsenic, and chromium."[72] She soon produced a map plotted with known cases of childhood leukemia in Woburn. Twelve such cases were identified, with six of them closely clustered within blocks of the Anderson home. On January 18, 1981, 12-year-old Jimmy Anderson died of leukemia.

Five days after the boy's death, the Massachusetts Department of Public Health (DPH) released a report confirming a statistically improbable incidence of childhood leukemia in Woburn, as well as an elevated incidence of kidney cancer. Although the DPH was somewhat vague in its findings, eight families of young leukemia victims, relying on additional data generated by the Harvard School of Public Health, filed a $100 million lawsuit in 1982 against the alleged sources of the carcinogenic water. The main defendant was the Cryovac Division of the giant W. R. Grace Corporation. Grace was accused of negligent waste disposal practices leading to groundwater contamination and its resultant diseases.[73] The suit sought damages for wrongful death, pain and suffering, medical expenses, and mental anguish—including a legally untested claim of anticipatory distress concerning potential future illness.[74] The trial was held in 1986. Expert witnesses presented evidence of a "chemical causeway" from the Grace plant to the victims' water supply. The company denied

that it was the primary source of the contamination. In response to evidence of the presence of TCE on its property, it contended that trespassers had dumped it there—even though a number of eyewitnesses, including workers and executives, testified that they had seen the firm dump toxic wastes.[75] A contractor testified that he had been asked in 1974 by the manager of the Cryovac facility "to build a pit in which to bury chemical wastes."[76] In the face of such compelling evidence, Grace changed its strategy. It argued that even if its chemicals were present in the town's water supply, none had been shown to be carcinogenic.

After 77 days of the trial, the jury ruled that W. R. Grace negligently had dumped chemicals on its property. The judge, whom most observers had perceived as sympathetic to the defense, set aside the verdict on the grounds that the jury had not understood the highly technical data upon which the case had been based. He ordered a new trial, but a few days later, Grace reached an out-of-court settlement with the families for $8 million.

But Grace's troubles were not over. Annie Anderson's long-sought moment of vindication likely came when Grace admitted in U.S. District Court that it had provided false information to the EPA in 1982 in response to questions about its toxic waste disposal practices. A criminal indictment was handed down in 1988.[77] The company entered a plea bargain in which it agreed to plead guilty to one of the 12 charges and pay the maximum fine of $10,000.[78]

As a grim postscript, it can be noted that in the period between the filing of the original lawsuit in 1982 and the termination of the trial in 1986, seven more Woburn children were diagnosed with leukemia—nearly four times the state average.[79]

The Woburn leukemia scandal revealed how far a corporation can be willing to go to cover up lethal environmental contamination. This was further demonstrated in the 2000 case *Anderson v. Pacific Gas and Electric,* a class-action suit later made famous in the movie *Erin Brokovich.* For years, Pacific Gas and Electric (PG&E) had used hexavalent chromium (chromium-6) as an anticorrosion agent in its compressor plant located in Hinkley, California. The leachate from the plant contaminated the area's private groundwater wells. The company's own tests allegedly had revealed the problem, but PG&E hid its findings for years. All the while, Hinkley residents reported many major health problems, from birth defects to cancer. The case ended with an out-of-court settlement of $333 million.[80]

More recently, the second-largest chemical maker in the United States was accused by the government of withholding information linking one of its most popular products, the stick-resistant cookware coating Teflon, to serious health risks.

CASE STUDY
Out of the Frying Pan, Into the Fire

In 2004, more than 50 years after DuPont started producing Teflon near the Ohio River town of Parkersburg, West Virginia, the EPA charged that the company had concealed information that a chemical used to make Teflon may cause cancer, birth defects, and other serious medical problems.[81] According to the EPA, scientists had begun finding perfluorooctanoic acid (PFOA), a waxy, soap-like substance, in the blood of people worldwide—some as far away as rural China. It has been estimated that PFOA is in the blood of more than 90 percent of the U.S. population.[82] It takes years for PFOA to leave the body, and exposure to even low levels could be harmful.[83] Teflon is one of DuPont's most valuable assets, used not only in frying pans but also in carpets, clothing, eyeglasses, electrical wires, and fast-food packaging.[84]

> Now DuPont has to worry that Teflon and the materials used to make it have perhaps become a bit too ubiquitous. Teflon constituents have found their way into rivers, soil, wild animals and humans according to company, government environmental officials, and others. Evidence suggests that some of the materials known to cause cancer and other problems in animals, may be making people sick.[85]

It is now known that in 1981 DuPont's own scientists at the Parkersburg plant had discovered startling evidence that PFOA had contaminated local drinking water supplies and that children of plant workers had PFOA in their blood. Some of these children were born with birth defects of the eyes and nostrils.[86] The *Washington Post* later reported that internal DuPont documents show the company had detected high PFOA levels in the blood of childbearing female workers. The company sent a letter to these women denying a relationship between birth defects and the chemical, but adding that, as a precaution, they should consult with their personal physicians prior to contemplating pregnancy.[87] The studies sent the company scrambling as executives confronted the reality that a key ingredient in their signature Teflon product line was in human fetal cord blood and in every glass of water drawn in two local towns. Female workers were pulled from the production line, outside consultants were hired to find holes in the studies, and clandestine tap-water testing programs were expanded to the next ring of surrounding communities.[88]

Somewhere in the DuPont chain of command, a decision was made to keep the troubling information secret. And over the next two decades, the documents and test results, stashed away in company filing cabinets, may have been forgotten by all but just a small group of company officials and scientists.[89]

The buried documents finally surfaced during the pretrial discovery stage of a local class-action lawsuit over what was initially thought to be recent PFOA contamination in tap water. In 2003, an activist organization that researches connections between health and the environment began scouring the pages and reported a near

(Continued)

20-year cover-up at DuPont.[90] The Environmental Working Group petitioned the EPA to investigate whether DuPont had violated the Toxic Substances Control Act, which requires immediate reporting of any findings that show "a substantial risk of injury to health or the environment."[91]

By the time the EPA filed charges against DuPont the following year, the company had reaped billions of dollars in profits since it had discovered and then concealed the risk of PFOA two decades earlier.[92] In September 2004, just a few months after the incriminating documents were uncovered, DuPont offered to settle the now expanded class-action suit. The company agreed to pay more than $300 million to as many as 60,000 residents of West Virginia and Ohio.[93]

A network television investigative report on the dangers of Teflon featured an interview with a 22-year-old man whose mother had worked at the Parkersburg plant while she was pregnant. He was born with one nostril and a deformed eye, and has endured more than 30 surgeries. He blames his mother's exposure to PFOA for his debilitating birth defects. "I've never ever felt normal," he said. "You can't feel normal when you walk outside and every single person looks at you."[94]

Air Pollution

Many of the same toxic chemicals that have poisoned the water we drink also have contaminated the air we breathe. The term "air pollution" usually brings to mind images of belching smokestacks, noxious smog, and acid rain. Certainly, all these phenomena are serious threats to public health. For example, a 1973 government survey discovered that the Bunker Hill smelting complex was exposing the neighboring community of Kellogg, Idaho, to dangerous levels of arsenic air pollution.[95] Two years later, airborne emissions from the Asarco lead smelting plant in El Paso, Texas, was cited by the United States Centers for Disease Control as a cause of neuropsychological dysfunction in local children.[96] A study of nine major cities conducted by the American Lung Association between 1981 and 1990 attributed 3 percent of all deaths to outdoor air pollution.[97] In New York City, hundreds of deaths have been attributed to huge quantities of particles and gases produced by power and industrial plants and held in place by occasional stagnant air masses.[98] Californians have grown accustomed to periodic smog alerts. In the Rust Belt, urbanites have become almost as aware of their city's air quality index as its daily temperature.

A trio of investigative journalists conducted an eight-month study in 2008, which identified 435 schools (some less than 10 years old) in the United States where the air outside was saturated with carcinogens at levels more than 50 times higher than what is officially deemed acceptable.[99] Moreover, according to the report, about half the nation's schools are located in what the government calls "vulnerable zones"—areas close enough to industrial sites that they could be affected by chemical accidents.[100] Most of these "at-risk" schools have been built on or near toxic chemicals because the land is cheap. "Children are especially susceptible to toxic chemicals, which can cause respiratory illnesses."[101]

Respiratory disease has in fact become the most rapidly increasing form of death in America.[102] Every day massive amounts of toxic particles and gases are emitted into the air. Many citizens literally are choking to death on the "treacherous residues [of a] small-minded, money-blinded, out of control technology."[103]

So the term "air pollution" probably suggests an outdoor risk to most citizens, but this perception is dangerously false. "[A] flurry of reports in the popular and scientific literature call attention to a greater variety of potentially harmful pollutants indoors than had ever been of concern outdoors."[104] The best documented example is asbestos; it is at the center of one of the most egregious of all environmental crimes.

Asbestos is a mineral found in rocks, and it has been used in construction since the time of ancient Rome.[105] It does not occur naturally in homes. It has been added purposely to many types of building materials, including textured paint, pipe wrap, boarded and spray-on insulation, ceiling and floor tiles, roofing shingles, wall plaster, and cement. In many respects, it lives up to its modern nickname—the "magic mineral."[106] "The mineral acts as an insulator and fire retardant; it strengthens concrete and sound-proofs; it allows for high traction and resists chemical breakdown."[107]

Unfortunately, asbestos fibers, particularly in older homes and buildings, can crumble and become airborne. When inhaled, these fibers can cause a potentially lethal illness called asbestosis, which scars the lungs, stifles breathing, and impedes the flow of oxygen to the blood. One writer contends that 25 million Americans could be victims of asbestos-related diseases[108] like asbestosis and mesothelioma, a cancer of the linings of the lungs. Many of the victims are not succumbing to occupational exposure but to the asbestos inside their homes and schools. Approximately 10,000 deaths each year are attributed to asbestos.[109] Little wonder the "magic mineral" also has been called "the most widespread toxic substance in the nation."[110]

Researchers at the University of Texas Medical Branch even have suggested a link between asbestos and the mysterious sudden infant death syndrome (SIDS). They performed autopsies on 17 SIDS victims and found that six had asbestos in their lungs—at levels comparable to adults with lung cancer.[111]

The health dangers of asbestos have been recognized for many decades. The first report directly linking asbestos exposure to disease was published in the *British Medical Journal* in 1924.[1132] Internal memoranda have revealed that Johns-Manville, the giant firm which has dominated the asbestos industry for over a hundred years, has been aware of reported asbestos hazards since at least 1930.[113] In 1965, its own confidential findings reported that 44 percent of its workers exposed to asbestos for 10 to 19 years suffered from asbestosis. The company's public position remained that no scientific proof existed that working with asbestos causes asbestosis.[114] This contention seemed as illogical as denying that food poisoning is caused by food.

In 1992, Johns-Manville, one of the nation's largest corporations and the world's biggest asbestos producer, filed for bankruptcy protection—despite 1991 sales of $2.2 billion. The company's strategy was intended to halt the threat of inevitable asbestosis lawsuits by minimizing its liability. Manville's attorneys promised that the company would conduct "business as usual" during the reorganization.[115]

More recently, as asbestos litigation has proliferated, victims' attorneys have used the legal discovery process to unearth thousands of incriminating corporate documents detailing an escalating cycle of denial and cover-up for nearly a half century. Some of the correspondence reveals a pattern of suppression of information. For example, Johns-Manville and Raybestos-Manhattan conspired to distort the results of a 1935 study of the health effects of asbestos sponsored by the industry.

> In effect, the documents reveal the smoking gun of corporate irresponsibility. . . [They] also allow us a much clearer picture—unique in the annals of industrial health in the U.S.—of how one industry established a corporate policy of covering

up its products' hazards. The result has been needless loss of tens of thousands of lives over several decades with many thousands more expected, as well as profound human suffering by the victims of asbestos diseases and their families.[116]

We will examine more of these documents in the second half of this chapter when we consider the contamination of the work environment. For now, it can be observed that the obvious failure of the asbestos industry to take any meaningful remedial action for over a half century was spurred solely by the profit motive. As one criminologist has lamented, "The priority of profits over human life sometimes leads to corporate actions that look like premeditated murder."[117]

E-Waste

One of the predicted benefits from the computer revolution was the move towards a "paperless office" in which digitized files and email would replace hard copies as the dominant form of communication in the workplace[118] and reduce the threat to the world's forests. In fact, not only has paper use not declined[19] but computers and other electronic devices have created new threats to the environment in the form of what is known as e-waste. Most of us probably never think about what happens to our old computers, televisions, cell phones, and MP3 players—when they become obsolete we just discard them and move on to the next, improved version. But these products don't just disappear; they often end up in someone's community or even backyard where they can wreak enormous environmental destruction.

The problem is that these electronic devices, which might seem to be clean extensions of the cyber world, are in fact filled with toxic chemicals. Among the worst are computer CRT screens that, on average, contain four pounds of lead, exposure to which can cause neurological problems, especially among children.[120] Another toxic substance used in computers and other electronic devices is cadmium, which can cause serious health problems and damage to the environment. But these devices also contain valuable metals, like copper and gold, which can be separated from their original sources and resold on the global precious metals market. There are environmentally sound and safe methods for recycling those metals but they are expensive. In many third world countries, where labor is cheap and workers are often desperate for money, thriving industries have emerged to accomplish this goal through old-fashioned, hands-on techniques. Workers, many of whom are children, in these industries are often exposed to deadly chemicals and toxins without the protection of safety glasses or proper breathing devices, causing them to inhale deadly toxic fumes on a daily basis.

Many countries, particularly in Asia and Africa, have become toxic waste safe havens. According to the U.S. Government Accountability Office, "a thriving international trade has emerged in used electronics, largely from industrialized to developing countries."[121] Countries like India, China, and Cambodia have become the final resting place for the vast quantities of e-waste generated by Western countries and "a substantial quantity. . . ends up in countries where the items are handled and disposed of in a manner that threatens human health and the environment."[122]

What was once a trickle of electronic products ending up in the global waste cycle has become a flood. In 2007, Americans disposed of over 26 million television sets, 205 million computer products, and 140 million cell phones. This totaled to 2.9 million tons of e-waste in 2006 alone.[123] How much of this is illegally shipped abroad is unknown but experts suspect the amount is substantial given the potential profits in the industry; the U.S. Geological Survey reports that 1 metric ton of computer scrap contains more gold than 17 metric tons of ore.[124]

The recycling of electronic products is such a lucrative business that even U.S. prisons have gotten in on the action. Since 1997, Federal Bureau of Prisons (BOP) facilities around the country have been in the business of recycling electronic components and equipment, operating through an organization known as UNICOR, a corporation run by the federal prison system. An investigation by the Department of Justice's Inspector General revealed that inmates involved in the work were exposed to toxic chemicals at dangerously high levels.[125] Moreover, according to the investigators, inmates had loaded e-waste on to shipping containers and that "UNICOR did not seek any information about the fate of its e-waste and whether it was being unlawfully disposed of abroad. . ."[126]

In contrast to other countries around the world, the U.S., whose citizens are the world's largest consumers of electronic products, has relatively weak laws regulating the export of e-waste. Most electronic devices are deemed to be "commodities" rather than "waste" and are not subject to the Resource Conservation and Recovery Act.[127] In 2006, the EPA issued a new regulation covering the export of electronic devices; however, the new rule covered only CRT monitors and no other computer components and no other electronic devices. And, notification is required only when the monitors are being exported for reuse, not metal extraction.[128] The General Accountability Office found that even these minimal restrictions on the export of e-waste were routinely flaunted and "exporters can ship most types of used electronic products, such as computers, printers, and cell phones, without restriction."[129]

CASE STUDY
The Hemlock Horrors

Midland, Michigan, is a company town, and the company is Dow Chemical. Indeed, a sign at the nearest airport reads "Welcome to Dow Country." A few miles from Midland, there is a small community with the chillingly prophetic name of Hemlock. Since the late 1970s, things reportedly have been happening in Hemlock for which the term "strange" would be an understatement.[130]

Local hunters claim to have shot deer whose meat was green. Farmers describe three-legged chickens, epileptic mice, bald cows, and geese born with their wings on backward. "[N]ot a few eyes in Hemlock were turning in search of an answer to that historical benefactor in Midland, the Dow Chemical Company."[131]

Midland's version of Annie Anderson was Diane Herbert, who resided near the mammoth Dow Complex. Like her Woburn counterpart, Mrs. Herbert became obsessed with explaining unusual reports of neighborhood illnesses—

including chloracne (a serious skin condition), beltline hives, and even the development of hard lumps on her own back. Mrs. Herbert worked nearly alone for years, conducting a quiet letter-writing campaign. However by 1983 she was making occasional television appearances and receiving modest financial support from the environmental group Greenpeace. It was becoming evident to her that the sorts of biological anomalies plaguing tiny Hemlock were also present in Midland. Witnesses described hawks that could not fly, squirrels with no tails, even a female peacock born with fancy male feathers. Dogs seemed to be contracting cancer and suffering heart attacks at an accelerated rate; some reportedly developed swollen glands the size of grapefruits. More alarming still, the human population was beset by nosebleeds, headaches, and thyroid problems. Saginaw County, where Hemlock is situated, had an infant mortality rate 67 percent above normal.

(Continued)

When Michael Brown, the journalist who earlier had illuminated the Love Canal story, investigated conditions in Midland, his chief suspect was airborne dioxin—the same chemical compound that (in a waterborne form) had wreaked havoc at Love Canal. Researchers at the EPA have concluded that dioxin affects fetal development and the immune system.[132] Other scientists have linked dioxin to "digestive disorders, effects on some essential enzyme systems, aches and pains of muscles and joints, effects on the nervous system, and psychiatric effects."[133] The effects of dioxin on laboratory animals has been reported to be even more debilitating, including several forms of cancer, liver disease, and birth defects.[134] And, after decades of debate, an EPA report drafted in 2000 finally concluded that dioxin does cause cancer and other health risks in humans.[135] Tiny amounts of dioxin are known to become part of the food chain.[136] Brown had become something of an authority on dioxin. He knew that dioxin had been associated with soft-tissue sarcoma, a rare form of cancer that afflicts muscles, cartilage, nerves, blood vessels, fat, and tendons.

Clearly, if dioxin was causing cancers in Midland, it seemed likely that soft-tissue sarcoma would be among them. When it showed at abnormal levels, it was rather like spotting a ripple in the water that could be the head of the Loch Ness monster.[137]

Brown described a graph depicting birth defects in Midland during the 1970s: "[T]he line during that period had risen to a craggy peak that put one in mind of Mount Everest."[138] Midland's rate of birth defects seemed irrefutably excessive: three times the expected number of cleft palates; nearly five times the expected cases of urogenital defects. Brown also observed a disproportionate incidence of congenital heart defects and mental retardation. In his words, "Something seemed to be very wrong, and it carried the ring of dioxin."[139]

Among Brown's most compelling Midland reports were stories of entire families afflicted with oral pus sacs, of farmers falling off their tractors from seizures, of a young girl born with deformed black teeth shaped like rabbit ears, of people losing chunks of their memories; one woman suddenly forgot how to play the piano after 11 years of lessons.[140]

Dow, one of America's most powerful corporations—whose slogan boasts that "Dow Lets You Do Great Things," and whose diverse menu of products ranges from Styrofoam and Saran Wrap to Napalm and Agent Orange—denied any connection with the bizarre health problems afflicting the Midland-Hemlock vicinity. Dow's own researchers maintained that their own dioxin experiments had yielded no abnormal cancer rates in laboratory rats.

Yet when the EPA tested the soil at the Dow complex for dioxin, it found levels *six times higher* than at Love Canal. "[T]he EPA was finally concluding what so many had guessed and feared all along: 'Air emissions from the Dow Chemical plant are the likely source of contamination in the Midland area'."[141]

REGULATION AND ENFORCEMENT

Uniontown, Ohio, was the site of the aptly named Industrial Excess Landfill—a 30-acre dump containing 750,000 metric tons of toxic waste. Methane gas regularly wafted from the dump, and, one day in 1984, it collected inside a local home. The house promptly exploded.[142]

In 1982, residents of Times Beach, Missouri, discovered that their whole community had been poisoned. A decade earlier, the town had hired a firm to spray a slick coat of oil on 10 miles of unpaved streets to reduce a dust problem. Unfortunately, that firm was also in the business of hauling toxic waste from a downstate chemical factory, and it recognized an opportunity to collect two fees for the same job. Consequently, Times Beach unknowingly became a toxic dump.

> Incredible as it might sound, dioxin had been sprayed, dumped or used as grading fill near a home for the aged, near a Methodist church, at calf farms, and in horse arenas, where birds literally fell from their roosts and horses died in droves.[143]

Because of pervasive dioxin contamination, the government bought all the homes in Times Beach. In a chilling replay of Love Canal, the community was evacuated, and an entire town ceased to exist.[144] Among those forced to abandon their town, an all too familiar roll call of strange illnesses developed. Four sisters, who evacuated as teenagers, all developed serious reproductive problems. The last mayor of Times Beach has reported that one of her daughters has epilepsy and another has thyroid problems, her son is afflicted with Grave's disease, and her ex-husband suffers from immune-system disorders.[145]

A dozen years later, the EPA issued a report that finally verified what former residents of Love Canal and Times Beach long had feared. Dioxin is one of the most toxic substances ever produced and "can cause cancer and other health problems even at very low levels of exposure."[146]

These stories are vivid, but appropriate, representations of the 1980s—surely a golden age of environmental crime. When the Reagan administration assumed power in 1981, it brought to Washington a clear antiregulation agenda. It is difficult to find any evidence of compatibility between deregulation and environmental safety. To a president with no environmentalist constituency, environmental crime simply was not an important priority. Indeed, according to an EPA estimate, about 90 percent of chemical wastes were disposed illegally in the early 1980s.[147]

> If the Carter administration reluctantly implemented the complex and expensive laws meant to guard the public from toxic harm, the Reagan administration robustly set about demolishing them. "Government is not the solution to our problem," the new president declared in his first inaugural address. "Government is the problem." Accordingly, the Reagan administration softened the bite of environmental regulators by extracting crucial staff and funding as though they were impacted wisdom teeth.[148]

Rita Lavelle, the new Assistant Administrator of the EPA, articulated some of the revised goals of the agency:

1. Change perception (local and national) of Love Canal from dangerous to benign.
2. Obtain credible data that 50 of the nation's most dangerous hazardous waste sites have been rendered benign.
3. Provide credible proof that industries operating today are not dangerous to the public health.[149]

Lavelle would later go to prison for perjury, but she was not lying about her objectives. "Her view that the nation's environmental problems could be resolved through the magic of public relations reflected the perverse fantasy life that separated Reagan administration deregulators from the growing number of ordinary citizens who now feared for the health of their communities."[150]

The indifference to environmental crimes, which characterized the 1980s, spawned a number of insidious by-products. Two of the more appalling ones are "environmental racism"[151] and "toxic terrorism."[152]

Environmental Racism

Toxic waste dumps are not randomly distributed across America. They often are located in communities with high percentages of minority residents.[153] In the words of one black newspaper publisher, "these dangerous facilities are put in communities of people considered to be marginal, not as important or valuable as white people."[154]

In 1987, for example, one-third of the total hazardous waste landfills operating in the 48 contiguous states were located in just five Southern states and represented well over 50 percent of the nation's hazardous waste landfill capacity. Four of those nine sites, representing about 60 percent of the landfill total for the Southern region, were in three zip code areas and comprised predominantly African-Americans—although African-Americans make up only about 20 percent of the South's total population.[155]

One of those sites was in the town of Emelle, Alabama, with a 79 percent black population. Emelle was the home of the world's largest toxic waste dump, owned and operated by Chemwaste, a company that "had been repeatedly sued for millions of dollars by the EPA and various state regulatory agencies for numerous violations of standard safety practices at its waste disposal sites throughout the country."[156] Chemwaste dubbed the Emelle dump the "Cadillac of Landfills."[157] The town's residents could not have disagreed more. A local activist charged that Chemwaste was turning his community into "the pay toilet of America."[158]

Another of the most problematic dumps is one in predominantly black Warren County, North Carolina, which was selected in 1982 as the burial site for more than 32,000 cubic yards of soil contaminated with highly toxic polychlorinated biphenyls (PCBs).[159] The residents of Warren County demonstrated in opposition to their unsolicited selection, but were unable to halt the landfill construction. As is generally the case with the disenfranchised, their protests went largely unheard. Public opposition to the siting of noxious facilities has been taken far more seriously in middle- and upper-income localities.

> The NIMBY (not in my backyard) syndrome has been the usual reaction in these communities. As affluent communities became more active in opposing a certain facility, the siting effort shifted toward more powerless communities. Opposition groups often called for the facilities to be sited "somewhere else." The Somewhere, U.S.A., was often in poor, powerless, and minority communities.[160]

In a similar vein, the children of McFarland, California, a small town whose residents are mostly Latino farm workers, are dying from cancer at a rate four times the national average. This harrowing statistic has been attributed to exposure to toxic chemical pesticides. Like the residents of Warren County and Emelle, the people of McFarland have sought help from the federal government, but have yet to receive it.[161]

In 1994, a group of 20 utility companies started negotiations aimed at burying highly radioactive nuclear waste under an Apache reservation in Mescalero, New Mexico.[162] This facility, one of several being proposed for tribal reservations nationwide, is being touted by proponents as a much-needed source of jobs and income. Critics have voiced grave concerns over health and safety issues.

Toxic Terrorism

One of President Carter's *last* official acts was the issuance of an executive order toughening the notification requirements for companies wishing to export products whose use is restricted in the United States. One of President Reagan's *first* official acts was the immediate revocation of the month-old Carter order.[163] America could "now expand its program of poisoning the world"[164] by engaging in what has been termed "toxic terrorism." Toxic terrorism can assume any of three forms.

(1) *The Sale of Dangerous Chemicals:* American companies have developed "a multi-billion dollar toxic chemical trade which includes the global peddling of millions of pounds of pesticides—including some so dangerous that they wouldn't even be allowed to be used in America under the EPA's weak standards."[165] The president of the National Agricultural Chemicals Association defended this practice in 1981: "We should not impose on these countries a standard that we have imposed on ourselves."[166] That same year, the White House deputy adviser for consumer affairs reiterated the new spirit of deregulation: "We can't be the world's nanny."[167]

One such pesticide, for example, has been sold regularly to the Philippines. "Unaware of the chemical's harmful effects, three rural tribesmen once turned hoses on each other as a joke. They all died."[168] Velsicol Chemical Company used to manufacture a nerve-attacking pesticide called leptophos—so lethal that when it was used in Egyptian cotton fields, 2,000-pound water buffalo began dropping dead.[169]

To compound the offense, hundreds of tons of pesticides, too lethal for domestic use, have been included in American foreign aid programs.[170] Many of these lethal pesticides later come back to threaten the health of the American public in the form of imported produce and other food. In 1975, traces of leptophos were found in nearly half the imported Mexican tomatoes sampled by federal food and drug inspectors.[171] This seems frighteningly reminiscent of Rachel Carson's dire prophecies in her famous book, *Silent Spring*, in which she warned of "sinister" pesticides and their power to alter the very nature of life on earth.[172] It was surely not by caprice that Velsicol, the manufacturer of leptophos, had tried to block the publication of *Silent Spring* in 1962.[173] Since *Silent Spring* was published, "at least 136 active ingredients in pesticides have been found to cause cancer in humans or animals."[174]

(2) *The Export of Hazardous Waste:* The 1980s also witnessed the emergence of a "shadow industry" involving the export of toxic waste from the United States to other nations.[175] The search for foreign markets for hazardous residues and contaminated sludge was spurred by the closing of many domestic landfills due to public health problems and the shrinking capacity. In addition, the economics of foreign dumping undoubtedly were attractive. When the cost of legitimately disposing of toxic waste in the United States was about $2,500 per ton, some impoverished countries, burdened by massive foreign debts, were accepting as little as $3.00 per ton to dispose of toxins within their borders.[176] In 1987, for example, it actually was cheaper to ship waste by barge to the Caribbean than to move it overland just 40 miles.[177]

Surprisingly, the majority of the legally exported waste of that period ended up in Canada, where restrictions were far less stringent than in the United States.[178] However, it soon was recognized that the future of foreign dumping rested in the Third World. "Since 1980, thirty-five of the seventy-five approved destinations for these exports have been underdeveloped nations, including the Philippines, Mexico, and many in Central America and the Middle East."[179] A 1988 report also listed the African nations of Zaire, Guinea, Gabon, and Sierra Leone as favorite dumping grounds for exported waste.[180]

Little concern was demonstrated regarding the health and environmental repercussions of toxic exports. A U.S. Commerce Department official summed up the American "hands off" policy: "After [it] gets there, the country can do whatever it wants with it. I assume it gets tossed out."[181] Of course, "tossing out" hazardous waste is precisely the practice that produced Love Canal, Times Beach, and so many other domestic environmental horror stories described in this chapter.

The American government not only permitted the hazardous waste trade, certain agencies encouraged it. Among the contaminated material shipped to such countries as India, South Korea, Nigeria, and Zimbabwe during the 1980s were wastes from the U.S. Army and Navy, the Department of Defense, and the Department of Agriculture. One entrepreneur even attempted to buy lead-tainted paper from the Treasury Department's Bureau of Engraving and ship it to Africa to be resold as toilet paper.[182]

In 1987, an official in the EPA's Office of International Activities defended the Reagan administration's "buyer beware" philosophy: "At EPA, we're not in a position to say, 'That's a bad deal,' or 'They don't know what they're doing.' If the receiving country says yes, there's nothing we can do about the shipments."[183]

(3) *The Construction of Polluting Factories:*   In the Mexican border town of Matamoros, they are called *masquiladores*.[184] They are American-owned factories that have crossed the Rio Grande for two very profitable reasons. First of all, the labor is cheap. Indeed, in the 1980s real wages in Mexico fell by 50 percent. Most *masquila* workers are young—many only 13 or 14 years old. "Some of the proudest names of U.S. business are riding on the backs of Mexican children—from General Electric and Westinghouse to Ford, General Motors, and Chrysler."[185]

Second, environmental regulation is lax. These plants have filled the sky and the water with a staggering amount of chemical pollution. With this contamination have come all the accompanying human miseries. A disturbing pattern of deformities and mental retardation has been observed among the children of the area. Their mothers had all worked in the masquiladores zone and had been exposed to toxic chemicals.[186] "Just over the border in the South Texas Rio Grande Valley, eighty babies were born with fatally underdeveloped brains during a five-year period—more than double the national average."[187] It has been said that the U.S.–Mexico border has become "a two-thousand mile Love Canal."[188]

Among the wastes generated are the known carcinogen TCE, deadly PCPs, copper cyanide (a by-product of electroplating), methylene chloride, and sundry other toxic substances.[189] Many company officials claim they return their wastes to the United States. However, in 1988, a director of the U.S. Customs Service declared that he had never seen a single barrel of chemical waste enter the United States from Mexico.[190] So where does all that toxic waste really go?

Some wastes are put in drums and stored right at the factories. As these containers get old, they often begin to leak. In 1987, dozens of chemical drums were observed outside the Zenith plant in Agua Prieta. They were marked *sucios*—Spanish for "dirty."[191] Some are dumped unscrupulously at regular city dumps in border towns. Numerous clandestine dumps also proliferate in the Mexican desert.[192] For example, in 1988 General Motors (GM) contracted with a Mexican firm to dispose of several hundred barrels of paint sludge at a hazardous waste site near Monterrey. The drums never arrived; they had been dumped instead in the desert. When they were discovered, the Mexican firm claimed that the desert site was actually a temporary open-air dump. Worse yet, GM would not even acknowledge that the sludge was dangerous. A spokeswoman for GM declared: "The paint sludge was nonhazardous material in containers *mistakenly labeled hazardous waste.*"[193]

Because of its proximity—and because *masquila* wages are among the lowest in the world—Mexico has become a haven for American corporate polluters; but it is hardly unique. In December 1984, for example, the Indian slum city of Bhopal suffered the worst industrial accident in history.

A storage tank containing the dangerous chemical methyl isocyanate gas (MIC) began to leak at a pesticide plant owned by the giant American corporation Union Carbide. What followed that night was a virtual kaleidoscope of death.

> People were choking and gasping for breath. Some fell as they ran, and some lay on the roadside vomiting and defecating. Others, too weak to run, tried to clutch onto people passing them in the hope of being carried forward.[194]

Before the week was over, nearly 3,000 people had died, and more than 300,000 had been injured.[195] "Union Carbide's standard reply to all queries that night remained, 'Everything is under control'."[196] Eight years later, an average of five Bhopal victims per week were still dying.[197]

THE SUPERFUND

In 1980, Congress passed the Comprehensive Environmental Response, Compensation, and Liability Act (CERCLA)—better known as "Superfund."[198] The legislation, which provided remedies for uncontrolled and abandoned hazardous waste sites, was a political response to the public outcry over the Love Canal scandal.[199]

Under CERCLA, the parties responsible for the hazardous conditions are supposed to do the cleanup themselves or reimburse the government for doing it. Unfortunately, in the words of the environmental consultant who turned in a blistering report to Congress in 1988, "this is a program that hardly ever gets anything right."[200] Superfund is widely regarded as one of the most ineffective pieces of legislation ever enacted in the United States. It is not supportable through its original scheme of fines and industry fees, and the final cleanup bill almost certainly will be handed to taxpayers. Some experts predict that Superfund's eventual cost may even exceed that of the savings and loan bailout (Chapter 5).[201]

Superfund is the epitome of all the environmental half-measures to emerge from the 1980s. CERCLA was designed ostensibly to please many environmentalists by throwing an unprecedented amount of money ($1.6 billion) at its cleanup task. However, its true beneficiary was the waste disposal industry, delighted at the prospect of enormous future profits.

In effect, all that Superfund generally does is take waste from one landfill and move it to another. In some cases, disposal firms, which are the very targets of Superfund sanctions, receive lucrative contracts to move their own illegally dumped toxins. In 1982, an outspoken EPA official summed up the Superfund fiasco: "[W]hat they're doing is buying more iron lungs instead of investing in the vaccine."[202]

The deficiencies of Superfund may be exemplified by briefly reviewing the story of one contaminated site—Brio, a 50-acre abandoned refinery located 18 miles south of Houston:

1957–1982: The Brio facility was operated as an oil refinery by a succession of owners, until going bankrupt. During that period, waste material was deposited in unlined pits and covered with soil. Between 500,000 and 700,000 cubic yards of soil was contaminated with fuel oil residues, styrene tars, heavy metals, and volatile organic compounds (VOCs). Groundwater under the site also was contaminated with vinyl chloride and benzene.[203]

1984: Brio was designated a federally controlled Superfund site.[204]

January 1988: The EPA finally proposed cleanup plans for Brio. It recommended that contaminated soil and sludge be excavated and destroyed in an on-site mobile incinerator.[205]

September 1988: More than 200 homeowners from the nearby 500-acre South Bend subdivision filed suit against the companies allegedly responsible for the contamination of Brio. Several doctors and scientists insisted that the site posed significant health risks. The EPA maintained that Brio represented no threat to the community.[206]

1989: The residents of South Bend conducted an informal health survey of their community. According to their findings, "10 of 12 mothers who were pregnant at the time chemical pits were disturbed in early 1987 gave birth to children with physical defects."[207] The parents of one pair of siblings who had grown up in South Bend described their children's ongoing medical problems. The daughter suffered from chronic nosebleeds and ovarian cysts; the son suffered upper-respiratory infections that had left him with a speech impediment.[208] Another set of anguished parents reported serious medical conditions in all three of their children. One daughter was born without reproductive organs; another daughter had autoimmune and hearing problems; the son suffered from strabismus, an eye coordination defect.[209] Stories of children stricken with spina bifida, as well as congenital heart, lung, and brain defects were also collected.

March 1992: The elementary school in South Bend closed.[210]

June 1992: The buyout of homes in South Bend began.[211]

September 1993: A Brio investigation in *Time* reported, "Virtually nothing has been done."[212]

October 1993: Brio task force officials acknowledged that chemical emissions from the site were draining into nearby Clear Creek. Levels of TCE were termed "dangerously high."[213] The EPA assured area residents that the fish in the creek were safe to eat. The EPA, however, did issue a stop-work order at the Brio site when inspectors noticed a chemical release problem involving the carcinogens vinyl chloride and methylene chloride.[214] One public health official went as far as to recommend the evacuation of South Bend, but the EPA decided against it. It also was revealed that the site contractor, Chemical Waste Management (the owners of the controversial Emelle, Alabama, landfill, which we examined earlier), had waited almost a month before releasing the toxicity report on Brio's poisoned air.[215]

November 1993: The Texas state health commissioner warned against eating fish from Clear Creek, saying that the Brio facility had contaminated them.[216]

January 1994: Construction of the on-site incinerator was completed at a cost of $18 million.[217]

April 1994: Work was halted at Brio before the incinerator was ever used.[218] Ten years had elapsed since Brio was designated a Superfund site, and the EPA admitted that "the cleanup was still in its infancy."[219] Under orders from the EPA, hazardous material was no longer even being handled at Brio, pending the formulation of a new plan.[220]

May 1994: The EPA acknowledged that it was considering paying for the relocation of South Bend's remaining residents, since the Brio task force has refused to do so.[221]

October 1994: A medical study was released on the health risks of living next to Brio. The report backed away from suggestions that the numerous illnesses found in adjacent neighborhoods were linked to the Superfund dump. Interestingly, however, when the co-author of the report was asked by reporters whether he personally would feel comfortable living next to Brio, he replied, "Ah, well, I'm not going to get into that. I have no comment."[222]

February 5, 1995: The Brio Site Task Force reported to the Friendswood City Council that only nine families remained in the 687 homes in the South Bend subdivision.[223]

August 25, 1995: Only two homes in South Bend were now occupied. The Brio Site Task Force released three new proposals for the much-delayed cleanup effort. Each plan carried a price tag of at least $40 million. A spokesperson for the task force surprised absolutely no one when she declared, "We still have a long road ahead of us."[224]

The torpid tale of Brio underscores the failure of Superfund. For over a decade, bureaucratic red tape and wholesale litigation have combined to thwart any meaningful remediation. It has been said of Superfund that "the only people who have cleaned up have been lawyers."[225] Since the Superfund program began, private companies have spent $4.7 billion on legal fees—more than a third of their total expenditures for toxic cleanups.[226] Indeed, despite numerous financial settlements over the years, at least 18 lawsuits were still pending by 1994 against the chemical companies comprising the Brio task force—including such corporate giants as Monsanto, Arco, and Chevron[227]—and the cleanup remained in limbo. Meanwhile, the city of Pearland, Texas, sitting in the shadow of Brio, is said to have developed the highest cancer rate in the nation.[228]

Regrettably, there is little reason for optimism regarding CERCLA in the years to come. Originally, Superfund listed over 1,200 priority projects—and this represented "only a fraction of the sites anticipated to become future disasters."[229] The actual number of contaminated waste sites eventually could exceed 10,000.[230] A single company—GM—has been linked to 200 Superfund sites.[231] In its first 13 years, Superfund managed to redeem a total of 33 hazardous sites. At that rate, the original 1,200 sites should be cleaned up in about 500 years.

There were, on the other hand, some encouraging indications that the criminal justice system's routinized wrist-slapping of the 1980s appeared to give way to tougher sanctioning policies in the 1990s. One significant change in enforcement policy has an increased determination on the part of prosecutors to pursue convictions of individual managers rather than corporations.[232] Through most of the 1980s, the sanctioning of environmental criminals had been most remarkable for its inconsistency. "The courts had so much discretion that individuals convicted of the same offense could receive widely disparate sentences; one could receive 20 years in prison and another simply be placed on probation."[233] However, in 1987 new federal sentencing guidelines were established, and objective numerical formulas largely replaced judicial subjectivity.[234]

Five categories of sanctions exist for environmental crime. They may be imposed individually or in combination.

FINES Prescribed financial penalties are increased and decreased according to a mathematical weighting of specific aggravating or mitigating factors.[235] Chief among those factors is whether an environmental offense is deemed simple negligence or "willful" negligence. Under the simple negligence standard, "it must be shown that the violation resulted from a lack of due care."[236] Actual knowledge of the violation need not be shown. For example, in 1992, the PureGro pesticide company was fined $100,000 for illegally dumping dirt contaminated with toxic substances in an undeveloped area of California's Imperial County.[237] Willful negligence requires actual knowledge of illegality or a reckless intent to further an illegal objective.[238] An example of willful negligence occurred in 1993, when Bethlehem Steel was fined $6 million for its "willful failure to comply with environmental laws."[239]

Other examples of fines levied against corporate polluters include the following cases:

Texaco was fined $750,000 for failing to conduct important tests on a California offshore oil rig.[240]

Ocean Spray Cranberries was fined $400,000 for discharging acidic wastewater from its Massachusetts plant.[241]

Ashland Oil was fined $2.5 million for a collapsed storage tank in Pennsylvania that discharged more than 700,000 gallons of diesel fuel into the Ohio and Monongahela Rivers.[242]

Chevron agreed in 2000 to pay a $6 million fine for violations of the Clean Air Act at its offshore loading terminal in El Segundo, California.[243]

Also in 2000, Koch Industries, one of the largest privately held companies in the United States, agreed to pay a $30 million fine for spilling an estimated 3 million gallons of oil, over an eight-year period, from its pipeline system in six states.[244]

In 2004, the PQ Corporation, a Pennsylvania-based manufacturer of inorganic chemicals used in detergents and adhesives, pled guilty to violating the Clean Water Act (CWA) by improperly discharging wastewater into public sewers and drinking water in three states. PQ agreed to pay a $450,000 fine.[245]

In a 2005 case, a county judge ordered home retailer Menard, Inc., to pay more than $2 million in fines for illegally discharging pollutants into Wisconsin waters. The company had disposed of solvents, cleaners, and oil by dumping them into the Chippewa River.[246]

Finally, it should be noted that Wal-Mart, the giant retailer whose shameful record of labor law violations was examined in Chapter 2, also has a history of environmental infractions. In 2001, the company paid a civil penalty of $1 million for storm water violations at 17 sites in several states.[247] That fine evidently was an insufficient deterrent. In a federal case brought by the Department of Justice and the EPA three years later, Wal-Mart agreed to pay $3.1 million for more storm water violations at its construction sites nationwide.[248] In 2005, Wal-Mart was in trouble again. The company was fined $1.15 million for allowing garden chemicals from 22 stores in Connecticut to pollute local rivers and streams.[249] The state's attorney general declared: "Wal-Mart's environmental record here seems as low as its prices."[250]

RESTITUTION   Court-ordered restitution involves offenders paying victims for any loss caused by the offense or the performance of remedial measures to eliminate present or future harm associated with the offenses, such as a mandatory cleanup.[251] For example, the government took the large Sherwin-Williams paint company to court in 1993, seeking to force the firm to clean up contamination at its Chicago factory.[252] That same year, Sbicca, a California shoe company, admitted attempting to smuggle toxic waste into Mexico and was ordered to pay all expenses incurred by the California Department of Toxic Substance Control and the U.S. Customs Service in their investigations of the case—in addition to a heavy fine.[253]

PROBATION   Supervised probation entails the imposition of "environmental audits" on offending companies.[254] For example, the Pratt and Whitney jet engine division of United Technologies Corporation was fined $5.3 million in 1993 and then placed on probation for abuses in handling and discharging hazardous wastes. Under the settlement, the company agreed to undergo extensive audits of its environmental practices until the year 2000.[255]

NONTRADITIONAL SANCTIONS   Some judges have ordered offending firms to give money to various state or local environmental programs. "For example, when the Transit Mix Concrete Company pleaded guilty to knowingly discharging pollutants into a tributary of the Arkansas River without a permit, the court . . . ordered the firm to spend $55,000 on a community service project, with the 'suggestion' that the money be spent on improving hiking trails near the river."[256] There also have been cases in which companies were ordered to place advertisements in local newspapers publicly apologizing for their actions. Two such cases were those of Vermont Industries and the General Wood Preserving Company of North Carolina.[257]

In 1996, Dow Chemical was fined $192,000 by Texas environmental officials for 25 different air quality violations. Under a novel arrangement, the company was ordered to pay $100,000 of that fine to help protect and restore the prairie chicken—one of the most critically endangered of all native bird species, with less than 50 remaining in the wild.[258]

INCARCERATION In the 1980s, the government often treated environmental cheaters like minor tax cheaters, assessing fines but seldom locking up offenders. In 1985, federal courts handed out less than two years of total prison terms for environmental crimes. Five years later, the total had jumped to 37 years, and the trend has remained upward.[259] The EPA now recognizes criminal sanctions as its most powerful tool. According to the Department of Justice, more than half of the individuals convicted of environmental crimes since 1990 have gone to prison.[260] For example, in 1993 the two top executives of Allied Applicators, a Texas spray-painting company, were handed three-year sentences for ordering the dumping of 13 barrels of lead solvents at a dead-end street in Houston. The district attorney had asked for probation, "[b]ut the judge apparently wanted to send a message to polluters by sending the president and vice president to prison."[261]

Criminal law is a relatively new tool for enforcing environmental statutes.[262] Advocates of criminal prosecution argue that incarceration provides a greater deterrence effect than civil penalties, because it "discourages corporate willingness to view environmental misconduct as a mere economic risk."[263] Moreover, even stronger criminal enforcement efforts are predicted for future cases of what has been called "toxic turpitude."[264] A recent example would be the 2009 criminal conviction of the president of HPI Products, Inc., a St. Joseph, Missouri, chemical company. William Garvey pleaded guilty to illegally dumping pesticide-contaminated water into the city's sewer system for two years. A civil complaint by the government further alleged that HPI generated and improperly stored and disposed of hundreds of thousands of pounds of hazardous waste for more than 20 years.[265] As of this writing, Garvey is awaiting sentence and could receive up to three years in prison. He and others like him "who disregarded their responsibilities under the environmental laws will find that there truly is nowhere to run and nowhere to hide."[266]

A recent example of this approach occurred in Terrell, Texas, in 2008, when a former employee of Fujicolor Processing pleaded guilty to willfully concealing and covering up material facts in reports required to be filed under the CWA. Gerald Lakota was responsible for environmental compliance at the plant, which included preparing and submitting wastewater Discharge Monitoring Reports. In order to ensure compliance, Lakota "cherry-picked" samples of the facility's wastewater effluent. Samples that were out of compliance were not reported. The film-finishing process at the plant generated a significant amount of wastewater that contained silver. Lakota falsely represented his "good" samples as representative of the facility's discharge, when he knew this was not true, thus creating the impression that the plant was meeting its effluent limits. The Assistant Attorney General for the Justice Department's Environment and Natural Resources Division stated: "Submitting false information in order to mislead authorities is illegal and will not be tolerated."[267] The Special Agent-in-Charge of the Dallas Area Office for the EPA's Criminal Investigation Division adds: "Violators who submit false reports or bogus data undermine our efforts to protect the public and the environment and they will be vigorously prosecuted."[268] At this writing, Lakota has not yet been sentenced; but he faces up to five years in prison. Fujicolor had earlier pleaded guilty and agreed to pay a $200,000 criminal fine for negligence.[269]

THE WORKPLACE ENVIRONMENT

Years ago, coal miners took caged canaries underground with them as a primitive early warning detection system for lethal carbon monoxide gas. If the bird collapsed and died, the miners knew to evacuate. An investigative report on occupational health hazards, written in 1976, offered a morbid analogy: "Today . . . American workers have themselves become canaries."[270]

As many as 20 percent of all cancer cases are believed to stem from carcinogens in the workplace.[271] It has been estimated that at least 5 percent of deaths from heart disease result from occupational causes. Indeed, about one-third of all diagnosed medical conditions are said to be job related.[272] When one factors in the injuries and deaths caused by industrial accidents, the grand total is a sad reflection of institutionalized negligence.

One of the most shocking accidents occurred in 1968 when a coal mine blew up in Farmington, West Virginia, killing 78 men.[273] This was by no means the deadliest mine accident in American history, but it was the first major one of the television era. A horrified nation heard the calamitous roar of incendiary eruptions and saw immense clouds of black smoke drifting across their screens like a funereal pall.

This tragic incident, more than any other event, likely prompted the enactment of the Occupational Safety and Health Act of 1970. The language of the Act contained a clear statement of its purpose and statutory mandate: "[T]o assure as far as possible every working man and woman in the Nation safe and healthful working conditions."[274] In the Act's first decade, the two best-known employee endangerment cases probably were the Kepone debacle in Virginia and the Scotia mine disasters in Kentucky.

CASE STUDY
Kepone

Kepone is a highly toxic pesticide developed by Allied Chemical Corporation in the 1950s. It was sold mainly to banana growers in Latin America, Africa, and Asia. By the early 1960s, several studies, including one by Allied itself, revealed the tendency of Kepone to induce tremors. Other research noted liver abnormalities and possible cancer links. In addition, laboratory tests on rats produced kidney lesions in females and atrophy of the testes and sterility or impaired reproductive performance in males.[275]

None of these findings, however, slowed down the commercial production of Kepone. In 1973, Allied, perhaps concerned about its liability for such a dangerous substance, set up a new corporation, ironically named Life Science Products (LSP), to process Kepone exclusively for them. LSP was housed in an abandoned filling station near the Allied plant in Hopewell, Virginia. The facility was an environmental nightmare come true. Neighbors complained that the plant's airborne emissions sometimes were so thick that traffic in the area was halted.[276] Toxic dust saturated workers' clothing and hair—even the sandwiches they brought from home.[277] Workers at LSP began to develop the "Kepone shakes," sometimes within two weeks of starting work.[278] "One man later recalled that when he stopped off for a beer after work, friends had to help him hold the glass."[279] Local doctors, who allegedly had "informal agreements" with the company, diagnosed workers' problems as hypertension and prescribed tranquilizers and psychotherapy.[280]

In 1975, one worker, who could not stop trembling, saw a specialist, who in turn contacted

(Continued)

the state epidemiologist. When that official began examining workers coming off their shifts at LSP, he quickly realized that a major industrial scandal was unraveling. The first man he saw was "a 23-year-old who was so sick he was unable to stand up due to unsteadiness."[281] Within days, LSP was shut down.

Federal criminal indictments were brought against Allied and LSP, citing 1,096 violations.[282] Two former Allied executives, who had gone to work for LSP when it was created, were tried on charges involving the pollution of a local waterway in the years when Allied had manufactured Kepone. They were acquitted, and, consequently, charges were dropped against a group of their sub-ordinates—even though they had already pleaded guilty. LSP was convicted, however, and fined $3.8 million. This was merely symbolic, since LSP was by that time long defunct and had no assets. Because, technically speaking, LSP was not a subsidiary of Allied Chemical, but an independent contractor, Allied was never sanctioned for its role in the damage done to the Kepone workers, although it was fined for violating federal water pollution control laws when it dumped quantities of Kepone in the James River.[283] Virginia had been forced to prohibit the consumption of fish from the James River,[284] and unacceptable amounts of Kepone had even appeared in some Chesapeake Bay bluefish.[285]

The state epidemiologist who uncovered the so-called "Kepone mob" warned at the time that the disaster could well be repeated elsewhere.[286] His words proved prophetic, for, in 1976, workers at the Bayport, Texas, chemical plant, where Velsicol manufactured leptophos (the pesticide that would kill over 1,200 water buffalo in Egypt), suffered an outbreak of nervous disorders described by one official as "another Kepone case."[287] Employees were stricken with "partial paralysis, failure of muscular coordination, blurred vision, choking sensations, and dizziness."[288] In addition, two workers were diagnosed with multiple sclerosis, and three others contracted encephalitis.[289] One ex-worker, a 33-year-old former Army paratrooper who was exposed to leptophos for only 10 months, became almost completely disabled from nervous system damage. Doctors called his condition "spastic paralysis of the lower extremities," but he offered a less clinically detached description: "My spine is deteriorating. It's dissolving."[290]

When Velsicol finally halted the production of leptophos in 1976, it told the government that it was not motivated by concerns about safety, but by a "softening of the market."[291] Besides, Velsicol had already developed a successor to leptophos—a pesticide called EPN—twice as poisonous as leptophos and, unlike its predecessor, licensed for domestic use. Studies at the Duke University medical school have reported that it takes only half as much EPN as leptophos to kill a laboratory animal.[292]

CASE STUDY
The Scotia Coal Mine Disaster

At the same time the Texas workers were being debilitated by Velsicol, the Scotia case was unfolding at a coal mine in Kentucky. The Scotia mine was owned by the Blue Diamond Coal Company, which, in 1976—the worst economic year since the Great Depression—was generating record profits.[293] Blue

(Continued)

Diamond was typical of many of the nation's coal producers. "No one connected in any way with the management of the company displayed any visible concern for land, air, or water. They regarded environmentalists as nuts."[294]

Scotia's overriding goal was to dig coal and make money. Many of the miners probably agreed. As a nonunionized mine, Scotia was paying relatively high wages in an effort to discourage any interest in the United Mineworkers of America. A man willing to work seven days a week, including holidays, might have earned $30,000 in a good year.[295]

Unfortunately, 1976 was anything but a good year. On March 9, in an explosion at an uninspected section of the mine, 15 miners died. Mechanical equipment had set off accumulated gases, for which no one had bothered to test. Two days later, 11 more men were killed by a second explosion.[296]

Coal mining, of course, is a tough job and, even under the best of conditions, a dangerous one.[297] The shame is that many of America's mines do not approach any semblance of the "best of conditions," as the Scotia explosions graphically demonstrate.

> The gritty work of running the pits [rests with] low-echelon foremen and superintendents of mediocre competence. . . Top management avoids the tipples and tunnels and knows little about the guts of the operation. [It] delegates responsibility ever downward.[298]

Despite lengthy investigative hearings, no indictments, corporative or individual, ever were handed down relating to Scotia. Despite 26 deaths and a long record of serious violations, no sanctions for negligence ever were levied against the owners of the mine.

As the Kepone and Scotia cases illustrate, employees may be victimized either in terms of health (Allied Chemical) or safety (Blue Diamond Coal). Both these areas warrant further exploration.

Employee Health: Hazardous Substances

ASBESTOS   The adverse effects of asbestos, which were discussed earlier in this chapter, have been well documented. In 1978, the U.S. Department of Health, Education and Welfare concluded that "as many as half of the 8 to 11 million Americans who worked with asbestos during and after World War II might die of lung cancer as a result of their exposure."[299] A 20-year follow-up study of former workers at a New Jersey asbestos insulation plant, which had moved to Texas in 1954,[300] reported an excessive incidence of fatal lung cancer—even in men who had been employed there for one month or less.[301] Many Americans said to be at risk worked with asbestos in wartime shipyards. A medical survey of a sample of 360 persons exposed to asbestos at a Northern California shipyard revealed that 59 percent of them had lung abnormalities.[302] A study of over 6,000 former workers at the Long Beach Naval Shipyard in Southern California reported that at least 31 percent of those who had worked there 17 years or longer were suffering from asbestosis.[303]

Numerous victims later sued major companies such as Johns-Manville and Raybestos-Manhattan. Lawyers representing asbestos victims have produced reams of long-suppressed corporate minutes and correspondence indicating that these firms knew of the hazards to their workers many years before they would later claim awareness. For example, minutes of two 1933 Johns-Manville board of directors meetings state that the company voted to settle 11 pending asbestosis cases for $35,000 in exchange for a written agreement that the afflicted employees would drop all present and future claims. According to one federal judge, who has examined some of these documents, they reflect "a conscious effort by the industry in the 1930s to down-play, or arguably suppress, the dissemination of information to employees and the public for fear of the promotion of lawsuits."[304]

Perhaps most disturbing of all is a confidential 1949 report written by the medical director of Johns-Manville, recommending that workers stricken with asbestosis—but who had not yet developed symptoms—should *not* be informed of their illness. According to the report, "As long as the man feels well, is happy at home and at work and his physical condition remains good, he should be permitted to live and work in peace."[305]

In keeping with its policy of suppression, the industry did not warn workers of the dangers of asbestos exposure until 1964. That delay was critical to millions of workers, since asbestos-related diseases generally take at least 15 years to develop.[306] Thus, by the time an entire generation of asbestos workers was informed of the health risks, it was too late to arrest their diseases.

In 1972, Johns-Manville decided against the installation of a dust-control system to protect its workers. The company's executives had calculated that, given the system's $12 million price tag and its $5 million a year operating cost, it was more economical to pay $1 million a year in workmen's compensation for employees disabled or killed by asbestos dust.[307]

It was reported in 1994 that dozens of teachers at a Bronx, New York, high school had contracted cancer since the school opened in 1976. Sixteen had died. The school had been shut down in 1993 for asbestos cleanup.[308]

In 1995, a Texas court found three asbestos makers, Owens Corning, Pittsburgh Corning, and Fuller-Austin Insulation, liable for $42.6 million in damages for causing the disease or deaths of 11 former workers. After the trial, the foreman of the jury declared: "The evidence was over-whelming."[309]

Another Texas jury awarded $115 million in 1998 to 21 steelworkers for asbestosis they contracted while working at an Alabama steel mill. The case was tried in Texas because Alabama law requires that asbestos lawsuits be filed within a year of exposure—a classic "Catch 22," since "[s]ymptoms of asbestosis may not become evident until 15 to 20 years after exposure."[310] Finding that the Carborundum Company acted with "gross negligence and malice,"[311] the jury's award included $100 million in punitive damages. It took the jury only 30 minutes to reach a verdict. Carborundum is the manufacturer of an asbestos-containing grinding wheel that was used to cut pipe at a U.S. Steel plant in Birmingham, Alabama. Testimony revealed that Carborundum had failed to warn workers of health dangers they faced when using the tool. The steelworkers were not even given masks to wear while wielding the tool inches from their faces. The plaintiffs, though appreciative of the verdict, said that the judgment would not compensate them for their failing health. One of them lamented: "This is great, but I've got to walk around with it in my lungs the rest of my life. . . . I feel like justice has been done, but money's no good to a dead man."[312] Indeed, two of the original defendants had already died before the case even made it to court.[313]

A growing number of asbestos victims without any direct or long-term connection to its production are now being identified. At least one litigant contracted asbestosis from exposure to fibers over just three working summers during his college years.[314] Also, there are count-less victims of what is called secondary or nonoccupational exposure.[315] A number of wives are believed to have contracted lung cancer "simply by washing the asbestos-laden clothes of their husbands."[316] A 50-year-old Maine woman attributes her terminal mesothelioma (a cancer of the chest lining) to exposure to her husband's work clothes when he worked at a local iron works and regularly came in contact with asbestos. Her husband adds:

> The whole issue of take-home toxins doesn't get enough education. Workers aren't generally aware of the concerns of bringing it home. . . People need to know.[317]

An investigative report published in 1999 charged that a closed vermiculite mine has killed at least 192 people in Libby, Montana, over the preceding 40 years. The mine had released more than two tons of asbestos per day into the air, six days a week.[318] To put the extent of this tragedy in perspective, 192 deaths represents nearly 8 percent of the population in a town of 2,500 like Libby. That would be the equivalent of over 600,000 deaths in New York City. It is no surprise, then, that Libby is considered one of the nation's worst public health disasters in years.

Mining for vermiculite, a mineral used for insulation and gardening, releases tremolite asbestos—a rare and extremely toxic form of asbestos. In addition to the miners who contracted asbestosis, lung cancer, and mesothelioma, relatives also have been stricken due to exposure to contaminated work clothes.[319] One woman lost her miner husband to asbestosis; now four of her five grown children have the disease. None of her children had ever worked in the mine.[320] Another Libby resident was diagnosed with asbestosis 34 years after he quit working at the mine. His wife and two of his children have also come done with the disease.[321]

Finally, in a case, horrifying in its callousness, three men were indicted by the Justice Department in 1998 for allegedly recruiting 20 homeless workers to remove nearly two miles of asbestos insulation from a manufacturing plant in Marshfield, Wisconsin. According to federal prosecutors, the three defendants recruited the homeless men in a soup kitchen in Chattanooga, Tennessee. They gave them fake identification, promised them work, then put them on a bus bound for Wisconsin.[322] In the words of Attorney General Janet Reno: "Knowingly removing asbestos improperly is criminal. Exploiting the homeless to do this work is cruel."[323]

COTTON DUST   Cotton dust contains certain particulate materials that produce a serious and, in its later stages, irreversible lung disease called byssinosis[324]—or brown lung. The story of brown lung is yet another tale of powerful and greedy corporations willing to sacrifice workers' lives upon the altar of maximum profits.

In 1980, the number of textile workers in North and South Carolina afflicted with byssinosis was estimated to be as high as 35,000. Nevertheless, from their inception until 1980, the workmen's compensation boards of those two states granted only 320 disability awards for brown lung. The average award to these "lucky" recipients was less than $15,000—a sum that was supposed to pay medical bills and then provide for the remaining years of the victim's life. In reality, after deducting medical and legal fees, this compensation for a shortened, more painful life span seldom amounted to a single year's wages.[325]

Such inadequate treatment reflects how ferociously the textile mills have fought workmen's compensation claims over the years. "While only two percent of all other compensation cases are contested by employers in the Carolinas, until 1980, eighty percent of the North Carolina and one hundred percent of the South Carolina brown lung cases were litigated by the textile companies."[326]

Since then, due in large part to the slow but dogged expansion of unionization, the companies have softened their resistance—but only moderately. The Southern textile industry, after all, was built upon a traditional foundation of "authoritarian and often illegal rule in the workplace."[327] For example, J. P. Stevens, the country's second-largest textile manufacturer, has been singled out by the National Labor Relations Board as the greatest labor law violator in America.

Many Stevens workers who have complained of unhealthy conditions or have tried to organize protests on behalf of employee safety have been intimidated or fired.[328]

Often, local doctors are in the employ of the textile companies. Until fairly recently, many of these doctors denied the very existence of byssinosis, although it has been a widely recognized medical condition since the 1940s. Thus, many cases went unreported because they were recorded as bronchitis or emphysema—with no designated occupational cause. One investigator describes a company doctor who once made the "mistake" of properly diagnosing byssinosis in a worker and was summarily dismissed by the textile firm.[329] One can only wonder how many unsophisticated textile workers have grown old before their time and gone to premature graves unaware of their industry's long pattern of criminal negligence.

Over a seven-year period, more than 60 percent of the mills in North Carolina and nearly 80 percent of those in South Carolina which were inspected by the Occupational Safety and Health Administration (OSHA)—the Labor Department agency charged with enforcing the Occupational Safety and Health Act—were found to exceed mandated cotton dust limits. In 75 percent of these cases, the dust levels were three times the permissible standard. Until 1980, the typical fine for noncompliance was $50, and most fines were never paid.[330]

In 1977, OSHA actually lowered its standard in a compromise with President Carter's Council on Wage and Price Stability, which was concerned that increasing the textile industry's dust reduction costs would fuel inflation. OSHA, which had feared being made a scapegoat for the spiraling inflation of that decade, later acknowledged that the price of their "cost effectiveness consideration" was an estimated 5,200 additional cases of brown lung. These 5,200 victims saved the cotton processors about $600 million.[331] It was, to say the least, a very cynical trade. Since 1981, OSHA has improved its record slightly, but major enforcement problems remain.[332]

Richard Guarasci, in his landmark article, *Death by Cotton Dust*, documents the refusal of the textile industry to recognize brown lung and that industry's resolve to fight all byssinosis claims and fiercely resist OSHA regulation.[333] Guarasci quotes one victim's description of his plight: "My bossman . . . said to me: 'You don't have no brown lung. There is no such thing'."[334]

The last word here goes to a man whose 40 years in a South Carolina cotton mill had left him with 57 percent of his breathing capacity and a monthly pension of $22:

> The good Lord gives man the breath to breathe and I don't think the textile mills have the right to take it away. . . I want my lungs back.[335]

RADIOACTIVITY   There is a cluster of shoddy little homes in Cove, Arizona, where uranium once was mined for atomic bombs. These shanties formerly housed Navajo miners. Many of them died young from lung cancer; many others are still dying from the effects of radioactive exposure decades ago. In the 1940s, the U.S. government recruited young Navajos away from their fields and flocks, promising them high wages to dig for uranium ore. The government neglected to warn them, however, of the excessive levels of radiation in the mines and the terrible health dangers posed by radiation.[336] Former Interior Secretary Stewart Udall, who represented the Navajos in their claims against the federal government argued: "The case of the Navajo uranium miners is one of egregious government malfeasance."[337]

In 1990, Congress passed a bill officially acknowledging that the government had exposed about 220,000 military personnel and 150,000 civilians to harmful radiation between 1945 and 1953. Included in the Radiation Exposure Compensation Act was a provision for monetary compensation to victims of radiation sickness.[338] According to an OSHA study, out of a sample of 4,200 uranium miners studied longitudinally, 400 died of lung cancer—five times the national average.[339]

Radiation may be less visible than cotton dust, but it can be no less lethal. For example, a nuclear weapons factory in Fernald, Ohio, for years released radioactive wastes through faulty filters or unfiltered vents.[340] In 1994, the University of Cincinnati released a mortality study of over 1,000 workers at the Fernald plant between 1953 and 1991. Analyses of medical records revealed that those workers "died at a significantly younger age and suffered a higher incidence of lung, intestinal, and blood cancrs than the American population as a whole."[341]

The causal link between radiation and cancer has been acknowledged for over a century. Indeed, as early as the 16th century, miners of pitchblende (a form of uranium ore) in Germany and Czechoslovakia were known to develop fatal lung diseases almost invariably.[342] More recently, dentists' chronic exposure to X-rays is said to contribute to their abnormally high rates of leukemia, Hodgkin's disease, and suicide.[343]

In 1979, an incinerator worker at the controversial Rocky Flats Nuclear Weapons Complex began developing odd-shaped bruises on her upper torso and painful red sores on her skin. She also suffered periods of nausea and diarrhea and debilitating fatigue.[344] She would later learn that these are classic symptoms of radiation sickness. When she complained to the Rockwell Corporation, which managed the facility, she was told that her problems were a common reaction to the caustic solution in which her work clothes were washed. Her union representative interceded on her behalf and was told that "Rockwell does not recognize the skin as an organ."[345]

According to the afflicted employee, when she announced her intention to testify before the grand jury, which had convened in the wake of the FBI raid on Rocky Flats, she was warned that "whistleblowers would be dealt with 'surely and completely'."[346] A short time later, she discovered that a hole had been punched in the work gloves she used to handle plutonium ore. As a result, her hair, face, neck, arms, and mouth became contaminated. Although the monitor alarm that detects airborne radiation sounded immediately, she was left unattended for 15 minutes. She later would describe the steep price of whistle-blowing:

> I was chased on the highway by a private investigator hired by Rockwell. There were incidents of vandalism at my home. My mail was tampered with.[347]

Former Energy Secretary Hazel O'Leary has acknowledged that workers who expose flaws at nuclear weapons plants and laboratories are harassed regularly by their bosses,[348] and their careers are sometimes ruined by their former agencies.[349] In a videotaped deposition on behalf of a whistle-blower, whose lawsuit alleged that he was punished by the Department of Energy for raising safety concerns about the Oak Ridge nuclear weapons site in Tennessee, O'Leary said: "[There] has been a practice of repeated and long-term reprisal."[350]

In 2000, federal nuclear regulators began investigating the burial of as much as 1,600 tons of nuclear weapons hardware on a 3,000 acre Energy Department site near Paducah, Kentucky. The material is under a leased portion of the site, known as the Paducah Gaseous Diffusion Plant, operated by U.S. Enrichment Corp. (USEC). USEC is a private company that processes uranium for use in commercial nuclear power plants. A health and safety specialist, employed by USEC, had asked for the investigation in order to determine if USEC employees were at risk.[351] In a memo to the Nuclear Regulatory Commission he wrote:

> I am deeply concerned for the safety of personnel working at the plant. . . . Some sanity needs to be put back into the system and personal safety needs to have commensurate emphasis with national security.[352]

For years Paducah employees have complained about an increased number of cancers they believe are linked to exposure between the 1950s and 1970s to uranium dust they did not know was laced with plutonium.[353] Plutonium is highly radioactive and "can cause cancer if ingested, even in minute amounts."[354]

BERYLLIUM   In 1999, an investigative report in an Ohio newspaper charged that, since 1950, the U.S. government has risked the lives of thousands of workers by knowingly exposing them to dangerous levels of beryllium, a metal critical to the military.[355] Beryllium is a strong lightweight metal used to encase nuclear weapons. It creates a dust that when breathed can cause berylliosis, an incurable disease marked by lung inflammation and ulceration. Berylliosis can be fatal if not treated, and symptoms may not appear for 15 to 30 years.[356]

Workers at private weapons plants in Ohio and Pennsylvania allegedly were exposed to levels of beryllium dust 100 times federal safety limits. There are an estimated 1,200 cases of berylliosis nationwide, but it is believed that many other cases have been misdiagnosed or not yet detected.[357] "At the nation's largest beryllium plant at Emore, just outside Toledo, at least 39 workers have contracted the disease and six have died."[358] The investigative report also alleged that the plant never consistently met federal safety standards.[359]

The Rocky Flats nuclear weapons plant in Colorado, discussed earlier in this chapter, is another facility that has left a legacy of disease, debilitation, and death. For years, workers who built triggers for nuclear weapons during the Cold War were exposed to beryllium dust while on the job. Many experts believe that this nonradioactive dust will turn out to be more deadly to former Rocky Flats workers than the radioactive plutonium handled there. At least 26 former workers have been diagnosed with berylliosis—a figure expected to grow dramatically.

Workers at Rocky Flats were supposed to be protected against beryllium dust by an elaborate ventilation system. Since Rocky Flats was shut down, serious questions have arisen about the safety of the air filters utilized, as well as the airways that linked buildings.[360] The worker who changed those filters between 1970 and 1977 now suffers from berylliosis. Although he never worked on any weapons, the fine particles trapped in filters destroyed his health. In his words, "I've coughed 'til it feels like my head is going to explode."[361]

Employee Safety: Industrial Accidents

Tyson Foods is the largest poultry processing company in the United States, with 50,000 employees in 59 plants. In 1999, two of those employees, working at an animal feed plant in Kentucky, died in a vat of decomposing chicken parts. One of them had fallen in while trying to retrieve a broken scoop. The other was lowered in to rescue him. Both men were overcome by lethal methane gas. Investigators from the state Labor Commission recommended a fine of $139,500. When several other cases against Tyson were thrown into the mix, the total penalties rose to $184,515.[362] The teenage stepson of the worker who fell into the vat told the local press, "I don't think they paid enough."[363] It's hard to say whether that young man was demanding vengeance or justice, but it is worth noting that Tyson's 2004 profits were $403 million. The fine thus represented .0004 percent of those profits. To put that in perspective, .0004 percent of $100 is four cents.

Indeed, the deterrence effect of such wrist-slapping fines is questionable. Five other Tyson workers were killed on the job that same year. One died from head trauma after a fall in the chiller room at a Maryland poultry plant. There were two fatalities at a Virginia plant. And two workers were electrocuted fatally in chicken houses.[364] Indeed, in 2000 another Tyson complex in Kentucky was slapped by OSHA with $269,000 in fines for 73 serious safety violations.[365] So much for deterrence.

There are more than 6,000 fatal work injuries in the United States each year.[366] Included in the annual toll are the approximately 70 adolescents who die each year from injuries on the job. The worst industrial accident in American history occurred in Texas in 1947. Witnesses compared the scene to the then-recent images of World War II bombing raids.

CASE STUDY
The Texas City Disaster I

On April 16, 1947, the 441-foot French-registered vessel *S.S. Grandcamp* sat in the port of Texas City, Texas. The *Grandcamp* was loaded with 2,300 tons of ammonium nitrate. It had arrived from nearby Houston because port authorities there did not permit the loading of ammonium nitrate. Another ship, the *High Flyer,* loaded with an additional 961 tons of ammonium nitrate, sat 600 feet away from the *Grandcamp.* The ammonium nitrate in both ships and in the nearby warehouse was meant as fertilizer scheduled for delivery to European farmers. But ammonium nitrate is a dangerous cargo also used in high explosives. Indeed, it is the same substance domestic terrorists would use almost 50 years later to blow up the Murrah Federal Building in Oklahoma City.

In mid-morning a fire was discovered deep in the hold of the *Grandcamp.* It attracted a crowd of spectators along the shoreline, no doubt believing they were a safe distance away. No one has ever determined exactly how the fire started. It may have been spontaneous combustion; it may have been the result of a discarded cigarette; or it may even have been sabotage. Whatever the cause, the effect was catastrophic. The captain ordered his men to "steam the hold." This is a nautical firefighting method, using steam instead of water in order to preserve the cargo. It was a disastrous strategy, producing more heat and leading to thermal runaway. In less than 15 minutes, the ammonium nitrate reached its explosive threshold of 850 degrees and detonated.

The tremendous blast sent a tsunami surging over the shoreline and set waterfront refineries on fire. Windows were shattered in Houston 40 miles away. People even felt the shock in Louisiana, 250 miles away. The explosion blew over 6,000 tons of *Grandcamp* in the air; some of the shrapnel flew at supersonic speed. The official casualty estimate was later set at 567; but many victims were incinerated or literally blown to bits, so the official total is believed to be an underestimate. The fire burned for days. More firefighters died that night than in any previous fire in American history. Fifteen hours after the first fire, the *High Flyer* exploded, killing at least two more people. In all, over 5,000 people were injured.

The disaster prompted the first class-action lawsuit against the U.S. government under the then-new Federal Tort Claims Act. In 1950, the federal district court found the United States responsible for a litany of negligent acts, involving standards for the manufacturing, packaging, and labeling of ammonium nitrate. Two years later, a federal appeals court overturned that decision. And the following year, the U.S. Supreme Court affirmed the appeals court ruling, stating that the district court had no jurisdiction to find the U.S. government liable for "negligent planning decisions" which were properly delegated to various departments and agencies. In 1955, Congress decided to grant legislative relief. When the last claim was processed in 1957, nearly $17 million had been paid out to victims and their families.[367]

We already have observed what a dangerous job coal mining is. According to OSHA, two other occupations rank as similarly hazardous: construction and steel making.

Texas recorded 1,436 construction deaths during the 1980s, more than any other state, despite a huge economic decline in the latter part of the decade.[368] On October 31, 1988, for example, a crane operator for the Baytown Construction Company of Texas was electrocuted when his cable came in contact with an overhead power line. The operator, who had been employed by Baytown for only a week, had been unloading pipe with the crane. The electrified cable energized an attached pipe, which in turn transmitted 7,620 volts of electricity into the employee's body.

When Baytown was cited by OSHA for violating the requirement that cranes be operated with a minimum 10 feet of clearance between any crane part and power lines, the company blamed the accident on the deceased operator, calling it "unavoidable employee misconduct."[369] The federal courts, however, ruled that Baytown was responsible, because it had neglected to train its employee properly regarding job safety and had failed to provide adequate protection for him. Similarly, several fatal electrocution cases have been filed in California involving undertrained tree-trimmers.[370]

The 10-feet standard had been affirmed earlier in a 1979 case, when a federal court had ruled that the Georgia Electric Company had permitted employees to erect a steel light pole within 10 feet of an energized power line. "The Court found that the indifference of an employer, who was aware of its duty to conform and had ample opportunity to acquaint itself with the requirements of OSHA but never did, coupled with its disregard for safety of its employees, supported a finding of willful violation."[371]

The number of deaths caused by contact of mechanical equipment with uninsulated power lines appears to be increasing. This trend is particularly disturbing because the technology to avoid most of these fatalities has been commercially available since the 1950s.

Most hoisting equipment can be fitted with a proximity warning device similar to a radar detector. As the boom approaches the energy field, the warning device senses the electro-magnetic signals emitted by power lines and sounds an alarm inside the operating cabin.[372]

Cranes also easily can be equipped with insulated cages that surround the boom and prevent the conduction of electricity into the crane even if power line contact is made.[373] Unfortunately, many construction companies do not provide these safety features, alleging that proximity warning devices and boom cages give operators a false sense of security. Apparently, they believe that the risk of impending death helps keep employees more alert. Some construction companies also question the reliability of the two devices, although, in about 40 years, "there have been no reported deaths or injuries caused by their failure to perform."[374]

Inadequate hoisting equipment poses a threat to more than just the operator. Anyone in the vicinity is at risk. In 1992, a 3,000 pound water tank was being hoisted at the Oak Ridge nuclear plant in Tennessee when one of its two straps snapped. A worker named David Wickes was killed. In a chilling postscript to this tragedy, Wickes' sister found a piece of notebook paper in his wallet, on which he had been scribbling a list of safety problems he was documenting. All the factors that had contributed to her brother's death—incorrect straps, improper forklift, untrained personnel, negligent safety standards—were on his list.[375]

In 1990, a construction worker plunged to his death from a Manhattan building as he stepped backwards to avoid being hit by a steel brace that had suddenly snapped free. A few weeks later, the victim's employer, American Steel, was cited by OSHA for violating safety standards requiring fall prevention devices. OSHA proposed a fine of $720.[376] Congressional testimony in 1992 revealed that a number of other employees of American Steel had died as a result of similar safety violations. "In each case, a single OSHA citation had been issued along with a fine of a few hundred dollars."[377]

The gruesome consequences of corporate negligence regarding the safety—indeed the lives—of innocent workers is further illustrated in the following three case studies. The first involves another fatal industrial accident in Texas City, Texas, the site of the worst industrial accident in American history in 1947, described earlier in this chapter. At the time of this second disaster, Texas City was already known locally as "Toxic City," because it was home to four chemical plants and three oil refineries.

CASE STUDY
The Texas City Disaster II

British Petroleum's (BP) Texas City Refinery is the third largest oil refinery in the United States, turning nearly a half million barrels of raw crude oil into fuel every day. On March 23, 2005, a geyser of vaporizing gasoline spewed from the 113-foot vent stack at the refinery's huge steel isomerization unit into the open air. The escaping fuel almost seemed to be looking for a spark. Tragically, it found one.

The "isom" unit, which boosts the octane level of gasoline, had just returned to operation after two weeks offline. As workers restarted one of the components of the unit, abnormal pressure built up in the production tower. This triggered three relief valves to open, allowing the volatile fuel to escape into a 10 × 20-foot "blowdown" drum. So much fuel flooded the drum that its capacity was rapidly exceeded. Liquid and vapor shot straight up the vent stack. A frantic call was heard over a handheld radio: "Stop all work! Stop all work!" But too much equipment was running to shut it all down. As gasoline vapor was sucked into its engine, a pickup truck idling at the base of the stack began to rev up. A worker ran to turn it off, but he was too late. "Somewhere in the cloud of fumes, perhaps from the truck's engine, a spark touched off the gas and ignited a firestorm."[378] Fifteen workers were killed and 170 others were injured.

OSHA slapped BP with a $21 million fine and cited the company for more than 300 violations related to the blast.[379] BP blamed the accident on workers, citing "a series of failures by BP personnel before and during the startup of the isomerization process unit."[380] But the U.S. Chemical Safety and Hazard Investigation Board (CSB) investigated the accident and issued a scathing report, assigning blame to numerous factors: equipment failure, lax maintenance and inspection, faulty management, and a dangerous working culture at the site. Most damning, the CSB report found that BP had failed to heed or implement safety recommendations made before the blast. The CSB chairman pointed to cost-cutting measures by BP. He charged that BP knew of "significant safety problems" at the refinery months or years before the explosion but that "unsafe and antiquated equipment designs were left in place, and unacceptable deficiencies in preventive maintenance were tolerated."[381]

The report noted that maintenance spending had declined throughout the 1990s when the refinery belonged to Amoco, Corp. After Amoco merged with BP, further cuts were imposed. The chairman concluded: "Every successful corporation must contain its costs. But at an aging facility like Texas City, it is not responsible to cut budgets related to safety and maintenance without thoroughly examining the impact on the risk of a catastrophic accident."[382] BP publicly apologized: "We are deeply sorry for what occurred and for the suffering caused by our mistakes."[383]

In the aftermath of the disaster, BP faced over 3,000 legal claims. The company resolved more than 1,250 of the claims out of court in 2006, including all the death-related ones, but still faced over 1,700 other claims. One of them was a lawsuit filed by Eva Rowe, who had lost both her parents in

(Continued)

the horrifying explosion. She was only 20 years old at the time. Ms. Rowe had turned down a settlement and was determined to go to trial. She said on a *60 Minutes* interview that she wanted the truth to come out in a trial. She declared, "If we settle and all, everything we know has to remain confidential. I don't want that to happen."[384]

When Rowe finally did agree to settle in November 2006, the terms were extraordinary. BP agreed to release 7 million pages of sealed corporate documents that would have been presented during a trial. Many of them revealed lapses in safety and environmental practices.[385] The company also agreed to donate more than $32 million to schools and hospitals—starting with a $12.5 million donation to the Bocker Burn Unit in Galveston, where nearly two dozen of the victims were treated.[386] Eva Rowe was determined to give her parents' deaths some meaning. "I miss them very much, but they would be extremely proud," she said. "They *are* extremely proud."[387]

Within weeks, BP settled two more injury cases.[388] In April 2007, plaintiffs' attorney Brent Coon deposed the former CEO of BP, Lord John Browne, about Browne's role in ordering 26 percent worldwide refinery cost cuts prior to the explosion and his awareness of unsafe plant conditions in Texas City.[389] Two months later, OSHA issued five more citations against BP, including four "serious" violations and one "willful" violation.[390] A week later, the first BP trial began in Galveston. Eight cases had been scheduled originally, but four had been settled, leaving four plaintiffs remaining. That same day, BP agreed to an out-of-court settlement over the suicide of one Texas City worker six weeks after the fire.[391]

The first witness to testify was the refinery's former manager. He described a 2004 report from a consulting firm that warned of safety fears that were almost pandemic among workers. The report stated: "We have never seen a site where the notion 'I could die today' was so real for so many."[392] The former plant manager admitted underestimating the dangers of having portable trailers on site. The

15 fatalities all involved workers in and around a trailer.[393]

As the trial entered its second week, jurors heard about 20 years of safety fears.[394] Yet, when Pat Gower, BP's vice president of North America refining, testified in week three, he still blamed careless workers. "If they'd followed the startup procedures, we wouldn't have had this accident."[395] When it was pointed out to him that Lord Browne had already taken responsibility for "every death," Gower insisted: "With 6,000 people, we can't watch everyone."[396]

The day after Gower's extrapunitive testimony, the trial suddenly ended in a surprise settlement.[397] Neither the four plaintiffs nor BP publicly discussed the financial details.[398] Ten pending suits were also settled, leaving about 1,200 still pending.[399]

On October 26, 2007, BP agreed to pay a $50 million criminal fine and plead guilty to a felony violation of the Clean Air Act. The company also announced additional agreements to pay restitution and criminal fines totaling $373 million. The money was part of a $1.6 billion fund to compensate victims. BP had reported an adjusted net profit of $22 billion in 2006—or about $60 million per day.[400]

When the second BP civil trial began in December 2007, the attorneys for the eight injured plaintiffs, using four-year-old documents about decrepit facilities and past-due maintenance, argued that the company had willfully fostered an unsafe work environment to save money.[401] They contended that BP valued profits over safety and put off upgrades and repairs amid budget cuts in the years leading up to the tragedy.[402]

The son of one of the defendants testified that his father went from being a "great athlete" to a man who could not even physically stand to play catch. "We went to a tailgate at a football game a couple of months ago, and we always used to throw the football around. This time, he threw it once or twice and said, 'Son, I just can't do it anymore'."[403]

Two days later, BP announced that it had already spent the entire $1.6 billion fund it had set aside.[404] Nevertheless, on the ninth day of the second

(Continued)

trial, it ended as the first trial had—in a settlement. As with the first trial, as well, the financial details were unannounced.[405]

The third civil trial began in May 2008.[406] An air pollution expert testified that BP ignored the problem of its outmoded equipment. "It's my opinion that failure was intentional."[407] Once again, the case was settled mid-trial.[408]

Shakespeare's famous dictum that "the past is prologue" underscores the grim coincidence that the BP accident shared the same venue as the 1947 Texas City disaster. And, as some other sage once noted, the more things change the more they stay the same. On February 18, 2008, another Texas oil refinery, this one in the town of Big Spring, was rocked by an explosion.[409] Five workers were injured. Fortunately, only a skeleton crew of 40 people were at the site of the Alon USA refinery because of the Presidents Day holiday. While by no means comparable to the Texas City tragedy, the explosion did shake buildings miles away.[410] In Texas, perhaps it is the *blast* that is prologue.

The second of this pair of case studies also involves British Petroleum and suggests that Edwin Sutherland's argument (discussed in Chapter 1) that many of the corporations of his era could be considered "habitual offenders" remains relevant today.

CASE STUDY
The Deepwater Horizon Oil Spill

One might think that after all the company had been through in the aftermath of the Texas City disaster of 2005—all the millions it had paid out in government fines and legal settlements, the felony conviction, the scathing government reports that were harshly critical of the company's practices—British Petroleum would have learned a lesson, would have changed its ways and altered the deficient "corporate safety culture," which, the Chemical Safety Board concluded, caused the Texas City disaster.[411] Indeed, this is what a BP executive said the company was doing when it agreed to plead guilty to criminal charges: "These agreements are an admission that. . . our operations failed to meet our own standards and the requirements of the law. . .They represent an absolute commitment to work with the government as we continue our efforts to prevent another tragedy like Texas City. . ."[412] But, tragic events just a few years later would prove that nothing had really changed at British Petroleum.

On April 20, 2010, at approximately 9:50 PM, a massive explosion, the first of many, ripped through a drilling rig known as the Deepwater Horizon which was operating in the Gulf of Mexico, 49 miles off the Louisiana coast. A firestorm swept across the rig's derrick as the well experienced a "blow out" that sent hundreds of barrels of oil and gas up the well shaft from three miles below the ocean floor and past the blow out preventer, a device that was supposed to stop the flow and seal the well, but had failed. Within minutes, as flames engulfed the 20-story rig, some of the crew were able to flee in lifeboats but others, without access to the boats, jumped overboard. Fortunately, the water was calm that night and most who got off the rig were able to make it to the Bankston, a supply vessel that was operating nearby. In the end, 110 crew members were able to escape the doomed rig, but 11 died that night.[413] The fire raged on for 18 hours and on the morning of April 22 the rig listed, collapsed and sank to the bottom of the Gulf of Mexico.

After the rig had collapsed, a second, much longer, phase of the Deepwater Horizon disaster

(*Continued*)

began. The well was still uncapped and oil was spewing uncontrollably into the Gulf. Over the next 86 days BP and the government tried to stop the flow, but repeatedly failed. During that time billions of barrels of oil spread across the Gulf of Mexico. Initially, government officials estimated that approximately 5,000 barrels of oil was flowing out of the well every day, but those estimates were soon moved upwards to as much as 25,000 barrels a day.[414] On August 4, 2010, after the well was finally capped the government came out with an estimate that 4.9 billion barrels of oil had been dispersed.[415] What happened to that oil became the subject of some controversy, with government officials initially claiming that as much as 75% was "gone"—it had either evaporated, or burned, or was recovered at the wellhead. But critics argued that these estimates were overly optimistic and much more oil was out there, washing up on beaches and degrading the environment.[416] Whatever the precise fate of the released oil, a later investigation by a national commission empaneled by the President concluded that: "The Deepwater Horizon blowout produced the largest accidental marine oil spill in U.S. history, an acute human and environmental tragedy."[417]

Clearly, the oil spill was unintentional, but was it truly an unforeseeable accident? The oil well was operated by British Petroleum which subcontracted parts of the operation to other companies including Haliburton and Transocean, which actually owned the Deepwater Horizon drilling rig. But it was BP that "had both the overall responsibility for everything that went on and was in the best position to promote a culture of safety on the rig."[418] The presidential commission investigating the causes of the disaster concluded:

> The blowout was not the product of a series of aberrational decisions made by rogue industry or government officials that could not have been anticipated or expected to occur again. Rather, the root causes are systemic and, absent significant reform in both industry practices and government policies, might well recur.[419]

The commission focused specifically on decisions by BP and the contractors to implement policies that favored cost savings over safety. For example, on the day of the blow-out, BP had arranged for a team to test the cement barrier which had recently been poured and which would have normally kept the pressure even, helping to prevent the well from blowing out. But on the morning of the 20th, BP made the decision to send the team home without conducting the test, saving at least $128,000.[420]

The President's commission was relatively restrained in its criticisms of BP, focusing its most critical comments on the industry as a whole rather than BP specifically. Others were more pointed in their criticisms. At a congressional hearing on the oil spill, Rep. Bart Stupak of Michigan told BP's CEO, Tony Hayward: "BP blew it. You cut corners to save money and time." At the same hearing, Rep. John Sullivan of Oklahoma pointed out that over the past five years BP had picked up 370 safety violations and paid $373 million in fines, while competitors Sunoco and ConocoPhillips had eight violations and ExxonMobil had just one.[421] In his testimony before the committee, Hayward disclaimed any responsibility for the Deepwater disaster, telling the committee that he was out of the loop about how the well at the Deepwater site was being drilled, leading to this exchange.

> "But you are the CEO of the company," said Michael Burgess, a normally oil-friendly Republican from Texas.
>
> "With respect, sir, we draw hundreds of wells around the world each year," Hayward told him.
>
> "Yeah, I know," Burgess said. "That's what scares me."[422]

What would change the systematic root causes identified by the Commission? While British Petroleum will ultimately have to pay out more than $30 billion for legal settlements and cleanup costs associated with the oil spill, what

(Continued)

has not happened is the imposition of any kind of formal punishment on those at the top of the organization.[423] As of this writing only one person has faced criminal charges in connection with the Deepwater Horizon disaster. In April, 2012, a BP engineer was charged with destroying evidence when he deleted emails that discussed the amount of oil leaking into the Gulf of Mexico.[424] But no executives at BP, Transocean, or Haliburton have been charged. A number of critics have suggested that without criminal prosecution of high-level executives, the culture of the oil industry will not change and there will be little to prevent future disasters. This view was well-expressed by Joe Nocera, a columnist for the *New York Times*:

> "But there is another reason corporate executives need to be prosecuted when corporate crimes take place. It sends a signal to every other executive about what is—and is not—acceptable behavior. The threat of prison can change a culture faster and more effectively than even the heftiest fine.

CASE STUDY
Combustible Dust

Built in 1916, the Dixie Crystals sugar refinery sits on the bank of the Savannah River. Owned by the giant Texas-based Imperial Sugar, it was the main employer of the small town of Port Wentworth, Georgia. The facility refined 14.5 million hundredweight of mostly imported raw sugar in 2007, making it the second-largest sugar refinery in the United States. It provided 9 percent of the nation's sugar requirements. It was an antiquated factory, with much of the machinery dating back nearly 30 years. But it was kept in operation because it had good access to rail for shipping.[425]

On the morning of February 7, 2008, the refinery was leveled by a huge explosion. Thirteen people were killed and 42 were injured, many critically. In fact, six months later, three of the workers were still in an Augusta burn center 130 miles away.[426] Imperial CEO John Sheptor blamed the accident on volatile sugar dust in a silo where sugar was stored before being packaged. Sugar dust can become combustible and ignite like gun powder if it is too dry and builds up a static electric charge.[427] "The result was as devastating as a bomb. Floors inside the plant collapsed, flames spread throughout the refinery, metal girders buckled into twisted heaps and shredded sheet metal littered the wreckage."[428]

When Imperial's executive vice president, Graham H. Graham, had toured the plant in late 2007, he found the conditions "shocking."

> "The floors were dirty and dangerous," the executive later said. There were puddles of liquid sugar and piles of sugar dust. But this was no Willy Wonka factory. This sugar-coated mess was a "combustible environment," the executive reported to his superiors—a disaster waiting to happen.[429]

Imperial later tried to discredit Graham. Business-friendly Georgia senator Saxby Chambliss helped in the effort. According to an editorial in the *Savannah Morning News*, Chambliss "verbally mugged" Graham at a U.S. Senate hearing.[430] Chambliss suggested that Graham was a liar and cut him off in mid-answer.[431]

In late July 2008, nearly six months after the disaster, the OSHA completed its investigation. The head of OSHA declared: "[T]his catastrophic incident could have been prevented if Imperial

(Continued)

Sugar had complied with existing OSHA safety and health standards."[432] The investigation also determined that officials of the company were well aware of the hazardous conditions but took no reasonable actions to reduce the danger. OSHA issued citations proposing penalties of more than $8.7 million—the third largest fine in the history of OSHA.[433]

The U.S. Chemical Safety and Hazard Investigation Board also undertook an immediate investigation. The CSB had been greatly concerned about dust explosions since at least 2003, when three deadly ones had erupted in the same year. One occurred at the West Pharmaceutical Services plant in Kinston, North Carolina, on January 29. Six workers were killed and 38 others were injured, many gravely. The powerful blast could be felt 25 miles away, and burning debris ignited fires in woods two miles away. The fire at the plant burned for two days.[434] The plant was so severely damaged that it had to be demolished and rebuilt from scratch.

West Pharmaceutical is one of the world's largest manufacturers of rubber components for syringes and drug vials. The CSB determined that the blast was caused by the ignition of a substantial amount of powdery polyethylene dust, which had accumulated out of sight above a suspended ceiling over a production area where slabs of rubber were made. The airborne dust had been drawn above the suspended ceiling by heating and air-conditioning ducts, where it gradually built up to a thickness of one-half inch. The National Fire Code limits combustible dust accumulations to 1/32 of an inch.[435]

In its final report, the CSB ruled that the West explosion could have been prevented if the facility had been designed to take into account the hazards of combustible dust and if the company had followed the safety standards and practices set by the government agencies.[436] The CSB noted that West's own files included documents warning of the explosive properties of polyethylene powder, but the company had failed to attend to these warnings.[437] Sadly, it took six deaths to inspire West Pharmaceutical to read the manual.

The second 2003 dust explosion occurred on February 20 at the CTA Acoustics fiberglass insulation plant in Corbin, Kentucky. Seven workers were killed and more than 30 were injured.[438] The CSB attributed the terrible accident to the ignition of a phenolic resin powder, used as a binder in the production of fiberglass foam for the automotive industry. The resin is similar in consistency to talcum powder and is highly combustible when dispersed in air. The plant's four production lines had a history of small fires erupting near the ovens. The explosion and fire occurred on a production line that was partially shut down and being cleaned. During the cleaning, a thick cloud of dust dispersed around the line and was ignited by a fire from the line's oven, which was still operating, causing a series of explosions. The fire quickly spread.[439]

The final CSB report determined that CTA's management training and maintenance procedures were inadequate.[440] According to the CSB, CTA knew combustible dust in the plant could explode but did not communicate the danger to workers. Many CTA personnel were thus unaware of the catastrophic potential of accumulated resin dust.[441] The report also blamed Borden Chemicals, which supplied phenolic resin powder to CTA.[442] Investigators found that Borden Chemicals' material safety data sheets (MSDSs) for the resin it supplied to CTA did note that resin dust was combustible but did not warn explicitly about the dust's explosive properties. Moreover, it was revealed that Borden did not tell its customers of the explosion hazard even after a catastrophic 1999 fire at the Jahn Foundry in Springfield, Massachusetts, ignited by phenolic resin supplied by Borden. The accident killed three workers and seriously injured nine others.[443] CTA sued Borden and, in 2007, a Kentucky jury found Borden "100 percent liable" for the tragedy.[444]

The third 2003 incident was a series of dust explosions at the Hayes Lemmerz manufacturing plant in Huntington, Indiana. Hayes Lemmerz makes cast aluminum automotive wheels, and the

(Continued)

explosion was fueled by accumulated aluminum dust, a highly flammable by-product of the wheel production process.[445] One worker was killed and another critically burned.[446]

The explosion originated near an aluminum chip melting furnace. The process produced aluminum dust, which is flammable when mixed with air. Dust had accumulated on surfaces in the work area and was ignited by a flash fire that escaped from the hood of the furnace.[447] Even though the facility had a history of small dust fires, the CSB investigation found that plant operators had not addressed the dangers of aluminum dust ignition. The Board also faulted OSHA for not identifying accumulated dust as a potential threat.[448] In its final report, the CSB pointed a stern finger at Hayes Lemmerz's management:

> This accident followed a classic syndrome we call "normalization of deviation," in which organizations come to accept as "normal" fires, leaks or so-called small explosions. The company failed to investigate the smaller fires as abnormal situations needing correction or as warnings of potentially larger

more destructive events. The CSB almost always finds that this behavior precedes a tragedy.[449]

In March 2008, Tammy Miser, who had lost her brother in the Hayes Lemmerz fire, testified before the House Education and Labor Committee in support of the proposed Combustible Dust and Fire Prevention Act of 2008:

> I strongly believe that OSHA is a necessity, but only if it is working. In this case, it has failed and failed miserably. Not only have they failed these families but also the families that lost loved ones in the dust explosions of 2003 that the CSB studied.[450]

The Combustible Dust Act passed the U.S. House the following month, but later stalled in the Senate. The Bush administration had strongly opposed the bill and had issued a veto threat. In early 2009, just before the one-year anniversary of the Imperial Sugar mill explosion, the bill was reintroduced in Congress. At this writing, it has not yet come to either floor for a vote.

Although, as we have seen, there is no shortage of competition, the industry believed to have the highest injury rate in the United States is the manufacture of cast-iron water and sewer pipes. The dominant company in that industry is also the one with the worst safety record: McWane, Inc. It has been called "one of the most dangerous businesses in America."[451]

CASE STUDY
The McWane Way

Based in Birmingham, Alabama, McWane employs about 5,000 workers in a dozen American plants. McWane has been cited for nearly 500 safety violations since 1995—*four times more than its six major competitors combined*.[452] During that same period,

more than 4,600 injuries have been reported in McWane's foundries.[453]

Supervisors routinely run roughshod over safety and environmental laws that inter-
(Continued)

fere with production in the slightest. They dump polluted water under cover of night. They bully injured workers. They intimidate union leaders.[454]

According to current and former McWane employees, the company operates under a financial incentive system that puts the lives of workers at risk every day. Workers who protest dangerous conditions are "bull's-eyed"—marked for termination.[455]

"The people, they're nothing," said Robert S. Rester, a former McWane plant manager who spoke at length about his 24 years with the company. "They're just numbers. You move them in and out. I mean, if they don't do the job, you fire them. If they get hurt, complain about safety, you put a bull's eye on them."[456]

"In plant after plant, year after year, McWane workers have been maimed, burned, sickened and killed by the same safety and health failures."[457] Machines are missing safety guards; flammable materials are mishandled; respirators are not provided; employees are not trained.[458] At least nine workers have been killed in McWane plants since 1995.[459] Most of those deaths received little more than cursory attention from state and local law enforcers. "The police often did little more than photograph the body and call the coroner."[460] OSHA referred only one of the deaths to the Justice Department, and that case ended with a single misdemeanor plea. No McWane executive has ever been charged.[461]

One of the victims was killed at McWane's Kennedy Valve plant in Elmira, New York. He had been ordered to incinerate gallons of paint in an industrial oven, despite specific instructions against this by the paint manufacturer and explicit warnings on the paint labels. He was further instructed to stay there and monitor the controls on the oven door. "When the oven exploded, the heavy steel door flew out and crushed him against a pillar."[462]

Another death occurred in 2000 at Tyler Pipe, a McWane subsidiary located in Tyler, Texas. It has been said that "only the desperate seek work at Tyler Pipe."[463]

Behind a high metal fence lies a workplace that is part Dickens and part Darwin, a dim, dirty, hellishly hot place where men are regularly disfigured by amputations and burns, where turnover is so high that convicts are recruited from local prisons, where some workers urinate in their pants because their bosses refuse to let them step away from the manufacturing line for even a few moments.[464]

The victim was a 48-year-old maintenance man working the aptly named graveyard shift. In his second month on the job, he descended into a deep pit to service an aging conveyer belt that carried sand. Federal regulations require belts to be shut down when maintenance is done on them, but this belt was not shut down. The worker had been trained to adjust the belt while it was still running, so the company could avoid costly downtime. Federal rules also require safety guards on conveyer belts to prevent workers from getting caught and crushed. This belt had no safety guards.

He was found on his knees. His left arm had been crushed first, the skin torn off. His head had been pulled between belt and rollers. His skull had split.[465]

Since 1997, there have been five amputations at Tyler Pipe, resulting from unshielded conveyer belts. One of the victims was missing for more than two and a half hours. His cries for help had been drowned out by the factory's noise. When he was finally heard, he was found standing on top of his hard hat, trying to relieve the pressure on his arm that had been rubbed down to the bone.[466]

EXPORTING OCCUPATIONAL DISEASE

As the Bethlehem Steel, BP, and Imperial Sugar case studies illustrate, many of our most dangerous industries are housed in old plants requiring major renovations to meet state and federal safety standards. "Faced with this reality, some manufacturers find it economically attractive to move hazardous manufacturing plants to less restrictive locales rather than stay where they are and meet tough regulations."[467]

Not surprisingly, one of the industries relying increasingly on "runaway shops" is that pacesetter of environmental crime, asbestos manufacturing. High American wages, combined with federal regulations requiring that workers be informed of the mortal hazards of asbestos and be provided with regular medical examinations and mandatory on-site monitoring to assure that exposure does not exceed the legal standard, have spurred a mass exodus.[468] For example, one American firm, Amatex, closed its asbestos yarn mill in Pennsylvania in 1972 and moved to the small *masquila* towns of Agua Pieta (across the Arizona border) and Ciudad Juarez (across the Texas border). Five years later, a prominent American industrial health specialist visited the Agua Pieta plant and gave a somber account of conditions there. He described machinery caked with asbestos waste and floors covered with asbestos debris. "Asbestos waste clings to the fence that encloses the brick plant and is strewn across the dirt road behind the plant where children walk to school."[469] Likewise, workers at the Juarez plant were not warned by Amatex of the health risks of asbestos, nor were they provided with respiratory protection or even a change of clothes for work.

Asbestos textile plants have been built by American companies in Taiwan, South Korea, Venezuela, and Brazil. Brazil offers an especially hospitable environment because of a perverse policy under which pay increments for certain hazardous industries serve as disincentives for worker health and safety. Small wage premiums are allotted to dangerous occupations, but the pay increases are discontinued if the hazard is eliminated. In effect, by making workers suffer pay cuts in exchange for improved working conditions, Brazil has made unsafe work environments economically attractive and undermined any efforts to improve conditions. "Management has the choice of taking steps to protect workers or paying them extra for losing their health, and presumably does whichever costs less."[470]

Another fugitive industry is the mining and refining of mineral ores. Once again, lax environmental and workplace regulations present an obvious temptation to American firms unwilling to comply with all the domestic air and water pollution standards, worker health and safety laws, and waste disposal requirements. In addition, many cash-poor but mineral-rich foreign nations have been willing, even eager, to "accept or ignore substantial worker health hazards and pollution as the price of economic development."[471] An entry in the *Congressional Record* of June 29, 1978, contains the following indictment of this shameless form of quasi-colonial exploitation:

> A starving man might accept a polluting factory even at great peril to future generations of man and other living things. He could hardly be blamed for that, but can the same be said for those who wish to profit from his misery?[472]

REGULATION AND ENFORCEMENT . . . OR MAYBE NOT

The same commitment to deregulation that undermined the EPA in the 1980s dramatically changed the orientation of OSHA under the Reagan administration. While still a candidate, the president had expressed a general disdain for OSHA and its punitive enforcement policies.

Consequently, he appointed the owner of a construction company that had been cited by OSHA for a number of safety and health violations as OSHA's new chief administrator.[473]

In addition, President Reagan's first Secretary of Labor almost immediately withdrew a series of safety and health standards promulgated near the end of the Carter administration.[474] These rules had been established to address some of the most serious issues regarding the protection of American workers—including imposing more stringent cotton dust[475] and airborne lead[476] standards, as well as the mandatory labeling of all toxic chemicals used in the workplace[477] and the publication of an annual list of suspected industrial carcinogens.[478] The effect of rescinding these "midnight rules" (so-called because of their creation in the waning hours of the Carter presidency) was literally a matter of life and death. The tougher cotton dust standard alone reportedly would have prevented 21,000 cases of brown lung a year.[479]

The biggest change occurred in the relationship between OSHA and industry. OSHA inspectors during the Reagan years were inclined to interpret violations as the result of good faith mistakes—unless there was compelling evidence to the contrary.

> This would explain the dramatic decrease in the number of willful violations after the Reagan administration took office. These declined from 1,009 in 1980 to 269 in 1981, 100 in 1982, and 164 in 1983.[480]

In addition, the number of follow-up inspections conducted to determine if cited conditions had been corrected was substantially reduced. In many cases, a letter from an employer stipulating that the problems had been corrected was considered sufficient verification.[481]

Morale at OSHA became dispirited, especially during the second Reagan term. Following the 1984 election, it was reported that "purges reminiscent of the McCarthy era were being conducted at OSHA."[482] Administrators were quoted as "urging subordinates to get rid of the 'communists' in the agency."[483] One OSHA inspector in the agency's Baltimore area office resigned in disgust over OSHA's failure to listen to its own inspectors. While driving on a family trip, he had observed workers on Maryland's Kent Narrows Bridge standing on 65-foot concrete pier caps and jumping to and from crane-suspended platforms—without any fall protection. When he reported what he had seen to his superiors, his concerns allegedly were ignored. Eleven days later, a worker at the bridge died from a fall under the very circumstances the inspector had described.[484]

More recently, there is little question that worker safety has eroded further under the Bush administration, which assumed power vowing to limit new rules and roll back what it considered cumbersome regulations that imposed unnecessary costs on businesses. Throughout the administration, political appointees—often former executives of the industries they were supposed to oversee—have eased regulation or weakened enforcement.[485] Almost as soon as Bush took office, OSHA felt the effects of his antigovernment philosophy. In its first two years, the Bush administration yanked 22 items off OSHA's regulatory agenda.[486]

Under President Bush, OSHA issued the fewest significant standards in its history. It imposed only one major safety rule. And the only meaningful health standard it issued was ordered by a federal court.[487] And (according to the *New York Times*) even in its waning days, the Bush administration rushed to finalize a "secret" OSHA rule that would make it tougher to protect workers from hazardous substances like combustible dust. The rule increased the amount of scientific analysis necessary to permit the regulation of workers' exposure to certain chemicals. The rule also adds two additional years to what was already an eight-year-long approval process. Moreover, the rule severely limits the options of Bush's successor, Barack Obama, to do anything about it.[488]

The need for an improved OSHA is compelling. One only needs to consider the 132 deaths and 760 injuries resulting from dust explosions in American workplaces since 1980, including the three 2003 cases discussed earlier and the Georgia sugar dust disaster of 2008. Even the near-record penalty levied by OSHA against Imperial Sugar is relatively inconsequential. "Imperial Sugar has denied the most serious charges, and with all the appeals, it may be years before the company pays up, if at all."[489] At this writing, litigation from families of the dead victims and from injured survivors is still pending—and the outcome remains to be seen. Furthermore, many of the injured are likely to have difficulty getting enough workmen's compensation from a state notoriously stingy about such benefits.[490]

Civil/Administrative Sanctions

OSHA, like the EPA, appeared to begin moving in the 1990s from its unaggressive posture of the 1980s back to its more traditional adversarial stance. In the area of administrative sanctions, however, the overall effectiveness of OSHA remained less than exemplary. One reason for this is the continued presence of deregulation advocates. A shocking illustration of residual indifference to health and safety in the workplace is a 1992 letter from the Office of Management and Budget (OMB) to the Labor Department. In this letter, OMB puts forth the curious argument that more lives would be saved if the protection given to workers was *reduced*. OMB argues that the costs of compliance could force employers to lower wages. "[H]igher paid workers tend to take better care of themselves and if they can no longer afford to do so, more may be killed than saved."[491] A Labor Department spokesperson has characterized OMB's logic as "bizarre" and "ridiculous."[492] As the Executive Director of the National Safe Workplace Institute has asserted, "When government is less than tough, it unwittingly encourages marginal actors to take risks they would not take if government sanctions were appropriately severe."[493]

At a 1992 hearing, Congressman (now Senator) Charles Schumer declared that more than 200,000 American workers had died in work-related accidents since the passage of the Occupational Safety and Health Act 22 years earlier. He decried the absence of serious sanctions in the overwhelming majority of these cases. In Schumer's words, "The penalty for removing a tag from a mattress is higher than the penalties for creating worksite conditions that kill."[494] The president of a large labor union has observed dismissively that to a wealthy corporation, civil penalties, even substantial ones, are merely another "cost of doing business."[495] Because most major OSHA cases are settled out of court—usually for less than the penalty originally proposed—trials have been rare.[496] Thus, for administrative sanctions to be a more effective deterrent, the size of allowable fines probably would have to be increased markedly. Presumably, this would generate an echo effect on negotiated settlements and increase the "cost of doing business" to a level where compliance with health and safety regulations would become a more economical alternative to paying out megafines.

To that end, OSHA began utilizing two aggressive enforcement tactics in the 1990s: (1) the "egregious multiplier" policy and (2) the "repeated" policy. The egregious multiplier policy, also known as the instance-by-instance policy, is the "policy under which OSHA proposes a separate penalty for each instance of a violation or, in some cases, for each employee exposed to a particular hazard."[497] This power has been in the OSHA arsenal for some time, but was seldom exercised during the Reagan years. The deterrence value of the egregious multiplier was iterated in 1992 by a federal judge deliberating the case of the Interstate Lead Company, a secondary lead smelter located in Alabama. "A secondary lead smelter typically reclaims lead from used automobile batteries by busting them apart to get the lead plates out, then melting down the lead and removing the impurities. It is usually a dirty, messy job."[498] The toxic effect of lead, of course, "has been well known for a very long time, and it was one of the first substances for which OSHA chose to develop a comprehensive standard."[499] That standard requires protective clothing, exposure monitoring, and regular blood tests for employees. Interstate Lead was a chronic violator, having been cited seven times between 1976 and 1989. The first six citations were settled out of court or through the uncontested payment of OSHA fines. The judge in the seventh case, however, characterized the company's compliance record as "stonewalling." In his view, Interstate Lead willfully had failed to obey almost every relevant section of the lead standard.[500]

Consequently, the judge determined that there was sufficient justification for the egregious multiplier policy and he imposed instance-by-instance penalties totaling over $1.7 million. He explained his actions as an affirmation of competitive fairness:

> If the penalties assessed are substantially less than the money saved by correcting the condition, the economic consideration provides a strong incentive to those employers to ignore the standards. A violator of the standards in such circumstances tends to enjoy an unfair economic benefit over competitors who have complied with the standards. The employer who proceeds to act in good faith should not suffer from unethical competition.[501]

The "repeated" policy was a product of a series of enforcement changes made by OSHA in 1992. Previously, violations had been classified as repeated only when they had occurred at a fixed or permanent facility within a single Area Office's geographical jurisdiction.[502] Under the revised policy, OSHA could cite as repeated any violation evaluated as "high gravity serious" on the basis of previous citations at any facility of the same employer—regardless of location. Later, OSHA went even further and eliminated the gravity requirement, determining that any violations could be cited as repeated.[503]

The "repeated" policy represents a very significant development in administrative enforcement and could increase considerably the protection of workers endangered by chronically negligent employers. However, the strongest deterrent effect in the area of worker health and safety probably rests in the criminal courts.

Criminal Sanctions

OSHA is something of a paper tiger when it comes to criminal prosecution. First of all, the agency has no direct enforcement powers; it must convince the Justice Department to bring charges. Second, for all its renascent vigor regarding administrative sanctions and civil penalties, many of OSHA's teeth were pulled during the deregulatory years (1980–1992), "in the name of getting government off the back of business."[504] Thus, many states have assumed the initiative and have sought to apply their own more stringent criminal laws. They are no longer persuaded by the stale claim that corporate officers are isolated by the bureaucratic layers of complex organizations and therefore seldom know about criminal activity.[505] This clumsy and self-serving argument is nothing more than the corporate version of the long-discredited Nuremberg defense.

Obviously, one cannot incarcerate a corporation nor easily "kill" it, but some states seem to have shown a greater willingness to hold corporate officers and managers criminally liable for decisions that endanger employees.[506] For example, in California, the Los Angeles County District Attorney's Office created a special section in 1985 to investigate workplace accidents and fatalities. This innovation has directly led to the prosecution of more than 50 criminal cases.[507]

The first prosecution resulting from the new section was a 1986 involuntary manslaughter case filed against Michael Maggio, the president of a small company that was drilling an elevator shaft. At about 33 feet, an obstacle was hit. Maggio ordered an employee to descend the shaft and remove the obstacle. The employee was lowered by cable to the bottom of the hole with his foot inserted in a sling.

> The air was not tested, the walls or sides of the hole were not encased or shored, and the victim was not placed in a safety harness. Almost immediately, the victim went into convulsions. . . By the time the victim was removed, he was dead.[508]

Maggio pleaded no contest and was sentenced to 60 days in the county jail, and, as a condition of probation, was required to implement a comprehensive accident prevention plan for his company.[509]

Probably the best known of the Los Angeles cases involving alleged crimes against employees was the 1986–1987 trial of the director of the motion picture *The Twilight Zone* and four of his associates. They were charged with manslaughter in the decapitation of actor Vic Morrow and the deaths of two child actors during the filming of a battle scene involving a crashed helicopter. The defendants were acquitted after a stormy 10-month trial,[510] but Los Angeles County had sent out a strong message that workplace fatalities would not be dismissed lightly—even in its most cherished and glamorous industry. Former district attorney Ira Reiner, who established the occupational safety and health enforcement section, has written: "[T]he program has made a substantial difference in convincing corporate managers and supervisors that safety in the workplace should be given high priority. . . The number of prosecutions may be small, but, like a barking dog, their very presence may deter thousands of violations."[511] Other jurisdictions have since followed Reiner's lead.

In fact, California now has a small team of circuit-riding prosecutors pursuing criminal cases against employers who kill workers by violating workplace safety laws.[512] A particularly gruesome case took place in 2002 in the agricultural town of Gustine, on the edge of the San Joaquin Valley. Two workers at the Aguiar-Faria & Sons dairy, both illegal immigrants from Mexico, drowned in a deep dark sump hole filled with cow manure. "Between them, they had eight pennies in their pockets; their lungs, however, were packed with bovine excrement."[513] The prosecutor assembled enough evidence of criminal negligence to persuade a grand jury to indict the farm's general manager and its herdsman for involuntary manslaughter and other felonies.[514] In the prosecutor's damning words: "Just imagine the incredible despair and anguish as you're drowning in manure."[515]

It is painful to imagine, too, the agony suffered by a 22-year-old plumber's apprentice, who was buried alive under a rush of collapsing mud, while working on a sewer pipe in a 10-foot deep trench. The victim's mother told an investigator from the coroner's office that her son had often spoken about his fear of being buried alive. He had described how he had been sent into deep trenches without safety equipment, such as the large metal boxes placed in excavations to create a sheltered workplace.[516]

> "Was there a trench box?" she asked the investigator. He paused, she recalled. "He says, 'Ma'am, no safety procedures were followed. None'."[517]

For the victim's employer, Moeves Plumbing of Cincinnati, it was the second fatal accident of this type. In 1989, another of the company's workers had been buried alive under nearly identical circumstances.[518]

In a Pulitzer Prize-winning investigative report, the *New York Times* identified 1,242 cases between 1982 and 2002 in which 2,197 workers were killed on the job because their employers "willfully" violated safety laws. "With full knowledge of their responsibilities, they ignored accepted safety precautions, removed safety devices to speed up production or denied workers protective gear."[519] Yet, in 93 percent of those cases, OSHA declined to seek criminal prosecution.

> Every one of their deaths was a potential crime. Workers decapitated on assembly lines, shredded in machinery, burned beyond recognition, electrocuted, buried alive—all of them killed, investigators concluded, because their employers willfully violated workplace safety laws.[520]

Incarcerating corporate officials whose decisions or neglect endanger workers is predicated on the belief that this is a far more effective deterrent than fines[521]—for corporations may "simply pass on the costs of the fines to employees as lower wages, to consumers as higher prices, and to shareholders as lower dividends."[522] If individual corporate officers and managers know that they could face criminal prosecution, they would be more likely to spend money on necessary improvements rather than opt for short-term profit maximization at the expense of health and safety.[523] "The possibility of a jail sentence may significantly alter an individual decision maker's calculus when facing the decision of what resources to expend on worker safety."[524]

Criminologist Gilbert Geis contends that society will not view corporate crime in the same light as other crimes until white-collar criminals are punished in the same way as other criminals. Geis reports that even convicted corporate officers agree that holding them criminally liable is a very effective deterrent.[525] Furthermore, at the organizational level, when one attaches a criminal stigma to a corporation, the corporation's likely response will be to attempt to regain public confidence by repairing its image—presumably by correcting or modifying its behavior.[526]

In addition to its deterrence effect, retribution theorists would argue that criminal prosecution is appropriate because corporate recklessness and irresponsibility regarding health and safety are morally intolerable to the community.[527] So, from a "just deserts" perspective, the incarceration of environmental criminals—with the attendant loss of liberty and employment, as well as the acute embarrassment—has become increasingly attractive.[528]

A number of landmark cases of employee endangerment have been prosecuted as common law offenses, ranging from battery to homicide. Let us examine briefly four of the more striking examples.

COMMONWEALTH V. GODIN (1977) In this case, the president of Pyro Products, a Massachusetts fireworks manufacturer, was convicted of manslaughter following an explosion in which three employees were killed. The structure that blew up was one of 21 buildings in the Pyro complex. Historically, it had been used for the drying of fireworks and the completion of their manufacture by inserting charges. However, at the time of the explosion the building was being used abnormally for the storage of large quantities of fireworks, due to a prolonged labor strike that had backed up production. According to testimony, employees had warned the defendant on a number of occasions about the risk of excess accumulation. According to the jurors, failure to consider the potential dangers constituted reckless behavior and caused the needless loss of three lives.[529]

PEOPLE V. PYMM (1989) In 1981, a worker at the Pymm Thermometer plant in Brooklyn wrote to OSHA asking for an inspector to examine conditions there. His brief letter concluded: "We only make the minimum wage, so at least we will know our health is okay."[530]

What OSHA found at Pymm was deplorable.

No protective gear was being used to reduce workers' exposure to mercury—no respirator masks, no aprons, and no gloves. Work surfaces were covered with mercury, and even the area where workers ate their lunch was contaminated with mercury.[531]

OSHA fined the company and set up a deadline for cleaning up the factory. In true 1980s fashion, however, one deadline after another came and went without any evidence of compliance. Moreover, in 1984, acting on a tip from a former Pymm employee, OSHA discovered a mercury salvage operation hidden in a cellar at the Pymm plant—"a cellar virtually without ventilation, filled with broken thermometers, with pools of mercury on the floor, and noxious vapors in the air, which produced permanent brain damage in one employee."[532] In all, 42 employees were injured by Pymm's appallingly wanton conduct.[533] Pymm, its owners, and managers were indicted for criminal assault and reckless endangerment and were quickly convicted by a New York jury.

NORTH CAROLINA V. ROE (1992)   On September 3, 1992, a fire started near some huge grease-filled vats in the frying room at the Imperial Food Products poultry plant in Hamlet, North Carolina. Twenty-five employees were killed,[534] and 56 more were injured.[535] It was the most deadly industrial fire since the infamous 1911 Triangle Shirtwaist Fire in New York City, in which 145 workers lost their lives.[536] The Imperial plant had no fire alarm or sprinkler system, in violation of occupational safety laws. But the most shocking discovery was that fire exits had been padlocked to prevent employees from stealing chickens.[537] The plant had never had a single safety inspection in its 11 years of operation, however, so this practice was not revealed until after the fire—when charred bodies were found at the sealed doors in poses of escape.[538] A witness later testified: "They were screaming 'Let me out!'. . . They were beating on the door."[539]

One year later, the owner of the plant entered a plea bargain with the state and pleaded guilty to 25 counts of involuntary manslaughter. He was sentenced to nearly 20 years in prison.[540]

ILLINOIS V. O'NEIL (1985)   Film Recovery Systems was a small Chicago-area corporation engaged in the salvage extraction of silver from used X-ray plates. At its peak, the company generated annual revenues of $13–20 million. It used a recycling process that included soaking the plates in a cyanide solution. Pure silver was then recovered by electrolysis. Employees manually added and removed the plates from the plant's 140 cyanide tanks.[541] Most of these employees were illegal aliens from Mexico and Poland who could not speak or read much English. To them, CYANIDE was just another mysterious word on a label.

Cyanide, however, is so highly poisonous if swallowed, inhaled, or absorbed through the skin that "workers must be protected with rubber gloves, boots, aprons, respirators, and effective ventilation."[542] At the Film Recovery plant, none of these normal precautions were taken. On February 10, 1983, one employee, a 59-year-old Polish immigrant named Stefan Golab, staggered from the cyanide tank where he was working and collapsed in an adjacent lunchroom. "His fellow workers dragged him outside and called an ambulance while Golab went into convulsions, frothed at the mouth, and passed out. When the ambulance arrived at the hospital, Golab was dead."[543] An autopsy revealed that Golab had succumbed to a lethal dose of cyanide.

A week after Golab's death, OSHA visited the plant and cited the company for 17 violations. Among other findings, employees were given unapproved cloth gloves and *paper* respirators, both of which were ineffective against cyanide fumes. When the inspector asked the president of the firm why employees were not trained or educated regarding the hazards of cyanide, the president replied that he did not want to scare his workers away.[544]

That same week, the director of the County Department of Environmental Control visited the plant. He reported his findings to the County Prosecutor, who began considering the idea of filing involuntary manslaughter charges. Over the next eight months, the story became increasingly more horrible. The prosecutor would later call Film Recovery "a huge gas chamber."[545]

Investigators encountered a worker who had lost 80 percent of his vision in one eye from a cyanide splash at his tank. They learned of workers who vomited regularly and suffered recurring headaches and dizziness. They heard that when workers would complain, they were told simply to step outside for some fresh air. They saw that the plant had no vents to shunt the deadly fumes from the building. Even the first aid kit was found to be filthy and held only an empty aspirin box.[546]

Slowly, the prosecutor was being drawn to a radical but inescapable conclusion: what happened to Stefan Golab was more than involuntary manslaughter. Accordingly, the president of Film Recovery Systems, along with his plant manager and plant foreman, was indicted for murder. This was an unprecedented charge. There had been occasional manslaughter convictions relating to the death of workers through reckless negligence on the part of employers (such as the Pyro Fireworks case), but never had an employer been charged with murder in such a case. To the prosecutor, however, murder seemed a reasonable charge under the circumstances. In his words:

> People talk about this case extending the law and being so unusual. That's not really so. We were just applying the old, basic law in a different area. Firing a gun into a crowd is murder. We had the crowd—the workers. The cyanide was the gun.[547]

At the close of the trial, the three defendants were convicted, and the judge handed them each a 25-year prison sentence. It was a stunning conclusion to an extraordinary case. Regarding the company president, the judge noted that the defendant had testified that he knew cyanide gas was present in the plant and that it could be fatal if inhaled. Regarding the plant manager, the judge observed that the defendant was sufficiently aware of the dangers of cyanide to wear the appropriate equipment denied to the workers.[548] And regarding the plant foreman, the judge recounted that the defendant had painted over the skull-and-crossbones symbol on the cyanide labels, even though he knew that workers were getting sick.[549]

The Film Recovery convictions were overturned in 1990 on technical grounds—the corporation (found guilty of involuntary manslaughter) and the individual defendants (found guilty of murder) had been convicted of mutually inconsistent offenses.[550] Nevertheless, the case represents a legal landmark, despite its eventual reversal. Although corporate criminal liability has been recognized in the United States for well over a century, courts had hesitated, until Film Recovery Systems, to convict corporations of crimes such as homicide, which require a specific criminal intent (*mens rea*) or a malicious spirit (*malus animus*). This reluctance also rested on the general use of the term "person" in homicide statutes and the impossibility of imposing the legally prescribed punishment of incarceration on a corporation.[551]

Film Recovery Systems, however, marked a new trend in corporate homicide prosecutions. The courts now recognize that criminal prosecution can be a strong deterrent against work-related deaths. The stigma of such a conviction, for example, can make it difficult for a company to hire and maintain an adequate labor force. As the number of corporate homicide prosecutions increases, more and more companies are likely to realize that the effects of criminal stigmatization are potentially far more devastating than civil penalties or administrative sanctions.[552] In addition, corporate homicide prosecutions can have an incapacitation effect, as convicted companies like Film Recovery Systems are forced out of business.[553]

The Film Recovery case undoubtedly inspired prosecutors in later cases; indeed, it is doubtful if there ever would have been a Pymm Thermometer case, for example, if there had not been a Film Recovery case. It also may have sensitized some corporations to the issue of worker safety. The man who prosecuted the case has written: "To save a life is as important as it is to redress a wrong which takes a life."[554] If this is so, then the Film Recovery case was surely not a wasted effort.

COMMON LAW FOR UNCOMMON CRIMES?

Despite some successful common law prosecutions of environmental criminals at the state level, this trend has not been embraced unqualifiedly. The General Counsel of the U.S. Chamber of Commerce has argued that Congress, through the Occupational Safety and Health Act, has given the federal government jurisdiction in this area, and "there is, therefore, no rationale for states to regulate safety through enforcement of their general criminal laws."[555] Such a contention is based on the Supremacy Clause of the Constitution, which invalidates state laws that interfere with or are contrary to federal law—a principle known as the *preemption doctrine*.[556]

Although preemption has been interpreted by its advocates to preclude state prosecutions for crimes by employers, other jurists see no fundamental conflict in concurrent (as opposed to exclusively federal) supervision of workplace safety. In the landmark case, *People v. Chicago Magnet Wire Corporation* (1989), the Illinois Supreme Court ruled that the state was *not* preempted from prosecuting officials of a wire manufacturing company for aggravated battery in the injury of dozens of employees who had been exposed to highly toxic substances, even though such conduct was also regulated by federal health and safety standards.[557] Subsequently, "every other state supreme court which has addressed this issue has followed the Illinois holding."[558]

However, in *Gade v. National Solid Wastes Management Association* (1992), the United States Supreme Court determined that Illinois laws regulating the training and licensing of hazardous waste site workers *were* preempted by federal safety and health standards. While the Court did not directly address whether federal statute also preempts states from criminal prosecution in this area, earlier assumptions clearly have been challenged by the Court's reasoning in the *Gade* decision.[559]

The flaw in applying the preemption doctrine to crimes in the workplace is that preemption would require states to afford less protection to one class of persons—employees—than to others. For example, consider the Pyro Fireworks case. Under the preemption doctrine, the state would not have had the jurisdiction to prosecute the president of the company under common law for the deaths of the three workers; that responsibility would fall to the Department of Justice. Yet, if a neighbor or passerby also had been killed in the same explosion, the state could have prosecuted—for that death only. In other words, all four deaths would have been the result of the same criminal negligence, but only one would not be preempted from state criminal prosecution. This would seem to be an illogical and unjustifiable inequity, at odds with the residual legislative authority ("reserved powers") granted to the states by the Tenth Amendment.

Another argument against common law prosecutions for crimes by employers is offered by a former EPA Counsel. She contends that "criminal poisoning" and workplace poisoning are distinctly different, with only the former involving *mens rea*—that is, an "evil" or criminal state of mind.[560] In other words, incarceration would reduce "decent and respectable employers"[561] to the level of common criminals. One of the defendants in the Pymm Thermometer case employed this rationale before the court after he was sentenced to weekends in the city jail for 6 months: "I've always done my best—if my best wasn't good enough, please do not send me to jail for that."[562] Likewise, the attorney representing one of the convicted defendants in the Film Recovery Systems case told the judge at the sentencing hearing:

> The man who is standing before you about to be sentenced is a classic example of middle class America . . . The story of his background is probably similar to the story of millions of other men and women in this country . . . who have attempted through their labors to provide their families with a decent home.[563]

This familiar "illegal but not criminal" rationale also fails to hold up under scrutiny. It is a long-standing statutory principle that a person who causes the death of another person—however unintentionally—while engaged in the violation of any law is guilty of homicide.[564] The equation is a simple one: "Since the days of the common law . . . certain actions, while not taken with intent to kill, have been deemed equivalent to murder when they caused a death."[565] In recent years, this principle has been applied with a jihad-like ferocity to unintentional deaths caused by drunken drivers. Why not to white-collar criminals? Is an indifferent employer who is aware of safety regulations but chooses not to comply, and thus endangers the lives of employees, any less reckless or negligent than the drunken driver?

"[T]he public, prosecutors, and judges have begun to identify some kinds of risks taken by corporations as intolerable."[566] In the Film Recovery case, for example, the judge found that the defendants were well aware of the substantial risk of cyanide poisoning. When such outrageous risks actually cause death, a charge of homicide is wholly consistent with the moral tradition of American criminal law. In all the aforementioned common law convictions, each defendant violated his "duty of care to another human being."[567] The consequent "accidents" were not really accidents at all. They were crimes.

Common law prosecutions can serve an auxiliary purpose as well, by heightening popular recognition of the violent side of white-collar crime. The common law approach seems an appropriate attempt to raise public consciousness and help achieve the essential societal goal of workplace safety. Until white-collar crime is punished like street crime, it will not be perceived as comparably serious. Many members of the public nevertheless remain uncomfortable with the idea of sending businesspersons, however negligent or callous, to prison—as if they were "real" criminals. The Citizen's Clearinghouse for Hazardous Wastes argues that these offenders *are* real criminals. That organization has campaigned passionately for common law prosecutions: "Rich people's money is not more important than employees' lives, and the laws need to recognize that."[568]

In 2003, Senator Jon Corzine of New Jersey circulated a letter to his colleagues seeking support for his proposed Wrongful Death Accountability Act. This legislation would have increased the maximum federal criminal penalty for employers, who cause the death of a worker by willfully violating safety laws, from 6 months to 10 years.[569] When OSHA's top administrator was asked whether he supported the proposal, he replied tersely: "We have no position."

Notes

1. Nader, Ralph. "Business Crime." *New Republic* 157, July 1, 1967: 7.
2. Quoted in Anderson, George M. "White-Collar Crime." *America* 144, March 30, 1981: 446.
3. Quoted in Thio, Alex. *Deviant Behavior* (Third Edition). New York: Harper & Row, 1988: 424.
4. Quoted in Parker, Patricia. "Crime and Punishment." *Buzzworm: The Environmental Journal*, March/April 1992: 35.
5. Badger, T. A. "Jury: Exxon, Hazelwood Both Reckless." *Houston Post*, June 14, 1994: A1, A8.
6. Parker, *op. cit.*

7. Davidson, Art. *In the Wake of the Exxon Valdez: The Devastating Impact of the Alaska Oil Spill.* San Francisco, CA: Sierra Club Books, 1990.

8. Humphreys, Steven L. "An Enemy of the People: Prosecuting the Corporate Polluter as a Common Law Criminal." *American University Law Review* 39, Winter 1990: 311–354.

9. Griffin, Melanie L. "The Legacy of Love Canal." *Sierra* 73, 1988: 26–30.

10. Tallmer, Matt. "Chemical Dumping as a Corporate Way of Life." In Hills, Stuart L. (Ed.). *Corporate Violence: Injury and Death for Profit.* Totowa, NJ: Rowman & Littlefield, 1988: 114.

11. *Ibid.*

12. Danzo, Andrew. "The Big Sleazy: Love Canal Ten Years Later." *The Washington Monthly* 20, September 1988: 11–17.

13. Thio, *op. cit.*, 434.

14. Griffin, *op. cit.*, 27.

15. Paigen, Beverly and Goldman, Lynn R. "Lessons from Love Canal: The Role of the Public and the Use of Birth Weight, Growth, and Indigenous Wildlife to Evaluate Health Risk." In Andelman, Julian B. and Underhill, Dwight W. (Eds.). *Health Effects from Hazardous Waste Sites.* Chelsea, MI: Lewis, 1987.

16. Paigen, Beverly, Goldman, Lynn R., Magnant, Mary M., Highland, Joseph H., and Steegmann, A. T., Jr. "Growth of Children Living Near the Hazardous Waste Site, Love Canal." *Human Biology* 59, 1987: 489–508.

17. Cunningham, Miles. "The Return to Love Canal: Signs of Life over Stillness." *Insight* 4, October 24, 1988: 20–22.

18. Griffin, *op. cit.*

19. Quoted in Kraus, Celene. "Grass-Root Consumer Protests and Toxic Wastes: Developing a Critical Political View." *Community Development Journal* 23, 1988: 258–265. See also Gibbs, Lois. *Love Canal: My Story.* Albany, NY: State University of New York Press, 1982.

20. Howlett, Debbie and Tyson, Rae. "Toxicity of Times Beach 'No Longer in Doubt'." *USA Today*, September 13, 1994: 10A.

21. Mitchell, Grayson. "Firm Knew of Peril in Love Canal Chemical Waste 20 Years Ago, Investigators Say." *Los Angeles Times*, April 11, 1979: 4, 8.

22. Thio, *op. cit.*

23. Mitchell, *op. cit.*, 4.

24. Quoted in Mitchell, *op. cit.*, 4.

25. Humphreys, *op. cit.*

26. Johnson, Kevin. "Firm to Pay $129 Million for Love Canal Cleanup." *USA Today*, December 22, 1995: 1A.

26a. *cnn.com.* "Despite Toxic History, Residents Return to love Canal," August 7, 1998.

26b. Quoted in *Ibid.*

26c. Quoted in *Ibid.*

27. Morganthau, Tom. "Don't Go Near the Water." *Newsweek* 112, August 1, 1988: 43.

28. *Ibid.*, 44.

29. Schwartz, Jr., Robert G. "Criminalizing Occupational Safety Violations: The Use of 'Knowing Endangerment' Statutes to Punish Employers Who Maintain Toxic Working Conditions." *Harvard Environmental Law Review* 14, 1990: 487–507.

30. Kenworthy, Tom. "Researchers Chart Impact of Dumping Sludge at Sea." *Washington Post*, November 12, 1992: A13.

31. *Ibid.*, 43.

32. *Ibid.*, 44.

33. Knight, *op. cit.*

34. Kelley, Darryl. "Tests of Buried Tanks Lag: Leaks into Water Feared." *Los Angeles Times*, August 28, 1988: A1, A3, A24, A25.

35. Kelley, Darryl. "Lake Arrowhead Community Gets Taste of Underground Pollution: Gas Odor Poisons Faith in Mountain Drinking Water." *Los Angeles Times*, August 28, 1988: A3, A22.

36. Guest, Ian. "The Water Decade 1981–1990." *World Health*, January 1979: 2–5.

37. Landrigan, Philip J., Whitworth, Randolph, H., Baloh, Robert W., Staehling, Norman W., Barthel, William F., and Rosenblum, Bernard F. "Neuropsychological Dysfunction in Children with Chronic Low-Level Lead Absorption." *The Lancet* 1, March 29, 1974: 708–712.

38. Guest, *Ibid.*

39. Prose, Francine. "Woodstock: A Town Afraid to Drink Water." *New York Times Magazine*, April 13, 1986: 42.

40. Gay, Kathlyn. *Silent Killers: Radon and Other Hazards.* New York: Franklin Watts, 1988.

41. Block, Alan A. and Scarpitti, Frank R. *Poisoning for Profit: The Mafia and Toxic Waste in America.* New York: William Morrow, 1985; 29.

42. Knight, Michael. "Toxic Wastes Hurriedly Dumped before New Law Goes into Effect." *New York Times*, 1980: 1, 28.

43. Salzano, Julienne. "Sludge Runners Keep on Trucking." *FBI Law Enforcement Bulletin* 64, May 1995: 23.

44. *Ibid.*, 24.

45. *Ibid.*

46. Sachs, Andrea. "Rebellious Grand Jurors Hire Lawyer." *ABA Journal* 79, February 1993: 31.

47. *Ibid.*

48. Brever, Jacqueline. "Nuclear Whistleblower." *The Progressive* 57, July 1993: 36.

49. *Harper's.* "The Rocky Flats Cover-Up, Continued." Vol. 285, December 1992: 19–23.

50. Schneider, Keith. "U.S. Shares Blame in Abuses at A-Plant." *New York Times*, March 27, 1992: A12. Wald, Mathew. "Rockwell to Plead Guilty and Pay Large Fine for Dumping Waste." *New York Times*, March 26, 1992: A1, A21.

51. Rothstein, Linda. "The Wages of Sin? About $4.1 Million." *Bulletin of the Atomic Scientists* 49, January 1993: 5.

52. Sachs, *op. cit.*

53. *U.S. News & World Report.* "Miscarriage of Justice at Rocky Flats." Vol. 114, January 18, 1993: 14.

54. Department of Health, Education, and Welfare. Report of the Subcommittee on the Potential Health Effects of Toxic Chemical Dumps on the DHEW Committee to Coordinate Environmental and Related Problems. Washington, D.C.: U.S. Department of Health, Education, and Welfare, May 1980.

55. Setterberg, Fred and Shavelson, Lonny. *Toxic Nation: The Fight to Save Our Communities from Chemical Contamination.* New York: Wiley, 1993.

56. *Ibid.*

57. *Ibid.*, 95.

58. *Ibid.*, 95–96.

59. Marsh, Gary M. and Caplan, Richard J. "Evaluating Health Effects of Exposure at Hazardous Waste Sites: A Review of the State-of-the-Art, with Recommendations for Future Research." In Andelman, Julian B. and Underhill, Dwight W. (Eds.). *Health Effects from Hazardous Waste Sites.* Chelsea, MI: Lewis Publishers, 1987; 3–80.

60. Gay, *op. cit.*

61. *Ibid.*, 74.

62. Suro, Robert. "Refinery's Neighbors Count Sorrows as Well as Riches." *New York Times*, April 4, 1990: A14.

63. *Ibid.*

64. Setterberg and Shavelson, *op. cit.*

65. *Ibid.*

66. *Ibid.*, 50.

67. Brown, Phil and Mikkelsen, Edwin J. *No Safe Place: Toxic Waste, Leukemia, and Community Action.* Berkeley, CA: University of California Press, 1990.

68. *Ibid.*

69. *Ibid.*, 11.

70. DiPerna, Paula. *Cluster Mystery: Epidemic and the Children of Woburn.* St. Louis, MO: Mosby, 1985.

71. Knight, Michael. "Pollution Is an Old Neighbor in Massachusetts." *New York Times*, May 16, 1980; A16.

72. Brown, Phil. "Popular Epidemiology: Community Response to Toxic Waste-Induced Disease in Woburn, Massachusetts." *Science, Technology, & Human Values* 12, 1987: 79.

73. Brown, *op. cit.*

74. Brown and Mikkelsen, *op. cit.*

75. Doherty, William F. "Jury: Firm Fouled Wells in Woburn." *Boston Globe*, July 29, 1986: 1.

76. Brown and Mikkelsen, *op. cit.*, 28.

77. Brown and Mikkelsen, *op. cit.*

78. The Federal Code was later amended to increase the maximum fine in future cases like Woburn's to $500,000.

79. Brown and Mikkelsen, *op. cit.*

80. *On Tap Magazine.* "The Villain of Hinkley, California." National Drinking Water Clearinghouse. Spring 2003.

81. Hawthorne, Michael. "U.S. Officials Accuse DuPont of Concealing Teflon Ingredient's Health Risk." *100777.com*, January 18, 2005.

82. *tapeitimes.com.* "DuPont in Deep Water over Teflon's Hidden Danger to Humans and the Environment." August 8, 2004.

83. Hawthorne, *op. cit.*

84. *tapeitimes.com, op. cit.*

85. *Ibid.*

86. *ewg.org.* "EPA Finds DuPont Guilty of Withholding Teflon Blood and Water Pollution Studies." July 15, 2004.

87. Baran, Madeleine. "EPA Holds DuPont's Teflon over Flame; Not Hot Enough, Say Activists." *news-standardnews.net*, July 11, 2004.

88. *Ibid.*

89. *Ibid.*

90. *Ibid.*

91. *Ibid.*

92. *Ibid.*

93. *legalnewswatch.com.* "DuPont Agrees to Pay $300M to Settle Class Action Lawsuit." September 9, 2004. *msnbc.msn.com.* "DuPont to Settle Teflon Lawsuit." September 9, 2004.

94. Quoted in *ibid.*

95. Castleman, Barry I. "The Export of Hazardous Factories to Developing Nations." *International Journal of Health Services* 9, 1979: 569–606.

96. Landrigan, Phillip J. *et al.* "Neuropsychological Dysfunction in Children with Chronic Low-Level Lead Absorption." *Lancet* 1, 1975: 708–712.

97. Levy, Doug. "Dirty Air Kills in Clean Cities." *USA Today*, May 23, 1995: 1A.

98. Glasser, Marvin, Greenberg, Leonard, and Field, Franklyn. "Mortality and Morbidity during a Period of High Levels of Air Pollution." *Archives of Environmental Health* 15, 584–594. Bach, Wilfred. *Atmospheric Pollution.* New York: McGraw-Hill, 1972.

99. Heath, Brad, Morrison, Blake, and Reed, Dan. "When Schools Are Built, Toxic Air Rarely Considered." *USA Today*, December 30, 2008: 1A, 2A.

100. *Ibid.*

101. *Ibid.*, 2A.

102. *Ibid.*

103. *Ibid.*, 5.

104. Ziegenfus, Robert C. "Air Quality and Health." In Greenberg, Michael R. (Ed.) *Public Health and the Environment: The United States Experience.* New York: Guilford Press, 1987: 139–172.

105. Gay, *op. cit.*

106. Kotelchuck, David. "Asbestos: 'The Funeral Dress of Kings'—and Others." In Rosner, David and Markowitz, Gerald (Eds.) *Dying for Work: Workers' Safety and Health in Twentieth-Century America.* Bloomington, IN: Indiana University Press, 1987: 193.

107. Gay, *op. cit.*, 29.

108. Brodeur, Paul. *Outrageous Misconduct: The Asbestos Industry on Trial.* New York: Pantheon Books, 1985.

109. Gay, *op. cit.*

110. *Ibid.*, 29.

111. Gay, *op. cit.*

112. Cooke, W. E. "Fibrosis of the Lungs Due to the Inhalation of Asbestos Dust." *British Medical Journal* 2, 1924: 147.

113. Castleman, Barry T. *Asbestos: Medical and Legal Aspects.* New York: Harcourt Brace Jovanovich, 1984.

114. Lavelle, Michael J. "Business Ethics: Tone Set at the Top." *Richmond Times-Dispatch*, April 16, 1989: F3.

115. Feder, Barnaby J. "Manville Submits Bankruptcy Filing to Halt Lawsuits." *New York Times*, August 27, 1982: A1, D4.

116. Kotelchuck, *op. cit.*, 192.

117. Thio, *op. cit.*, 424.

118. Pake, George. "The Office of the Future." *businessweek.com.* June 30, 1975.

119. Sellen, Abigail and Harper, Richard. *The Myth of the Paperless Office.* Cambridge, MA: MIT Press, 2002.

120. Government Accountability Office. "Electronic Waste." GAO-08-1044. 2008.

121. *Ibid.*, 1.

122. *Ibid.*, 5.

123. Data based on EPA estimates, as reported in Electronics TakeBack Coalition, "Facts and Figures on E-Waste and Recycling." *electronicstakeback.com.* February 21, 2012.

124. "Electronic Waste: Actions Needed to Provide Assurance That Used Federal Electronics Are Disposed of in an Environmentally Responsible Manner." Government Accountability Office, 2012, 10.

125. U.S. Dept. of Justice, Office of the Inspector General. "A Review of Federal Prison Industries' Electronic-Waste Recycling Program." 2010.

126. *Ibid.*, 23.

127. Gibbs, Carole, McGarrell, Edmund and Axelrod, Mark. "Transnational White-Collar Crime and Risk: Lessons from the Global Trade in Electronic Waste." *Criminology and Public Policy* 9(3): 547.

128. "Electronic Waste: Actions Needed to Provide Assurance That Used Federal Electronics Are Disposed of in an Environmentally Responsible Manner." Government Accountability Office, 2012, 22.

129. *Ibid.*

130. The description of the Midland/Hemlock environmental phenomena is taken largely from a vivid—and very frightening—account in Michael Brown's *The Toxic Cloud: The Poisoning of America's Air.*

131. *Ibid.*, 24.

132. *Houston Post.* "Dioxin Threat to Fetuses." May 11, 1994: A16.

133. Tschirley, Fred H. "Dioxin." *Scientific American*, February 1986: 29–35.

134. Gay, *op. cit.*

135. Watson, Traci. "Dioxin Draft Stops Short of Calling for More Cuts." *USA Today*, May 18, 2000: 15A.

136. *Houston Post*, May 11, 1994, A16.

137. Brown, *op. cit.*, 34–35.

138. *Ibid.*, 36.

139. *Ibid.*, 41.

140. *Ibid.*

141. *Ibid.*, 48.

142. Setterberg and Shavelson, *op. cit.*

143. Brown, *op. cit.*, 128.

144. *Reader's Digest.* "Our Toxic-Waste Time Bomb." March 1986: 181–186.

145. Howlett and Tyson, *op. cit.*

146. Howlett, Debbie and Tyson, Rae. "Toxicity of Times Beach 'No Longer in Doubt'." *USA Today*, September 13, 1994: 10A.

147. Cohen, Jessica. "Environmental Crime: Polluters in One Community Are Learning that Crime Doesn't Pay." *Omni* 15, January 1993: 24.

148. *Ibid.*, 121.

149. Lash, Jonathan, Gillman, Katherine, and Sheridan, David. *A Season of Spoils: The Story of the Reagan Administration's Assault on the Environment.* New York: Random House, 1984.

150. Setterberg and Shavelson, *op. cit.*, 122.

151. *Ibid.*, 216.

152. Ruffins, Paul. "'Toxic Terrorism' Invades Third World Nations." *Black Enterprise* 19, November 1988: 31.

153. Bullard, Robert D. and Wright, Beverly H. "Toxic Waste and the African American Community." *Urban League Review 13*, 1989–1990: 67–75.

154. Setterberg and Shavelson. *op. cit.*, 229.

155. Bullard and Wright, *op. cit.*

156. Setterberg and Shavelson, *op. cit.*, 234.

157. *Ibid.*

158. *Ibid.*, 238.

159. Bullard and Wright, *op. cit.*

160. *Ibid.*, 71.

161. Setterberg and Shavelson, *op. cit.*

162. Montes, Eduardo. "Tempers Flare over Tribe's Talks to Store Nuclear Waste." *Houston Chronicle*, July 10; 1994: 25A.

163. Grossman, Karl. *The Poison Conspiracy.* Sag Harbor, NY: Permanent Press, 1983.

164. *Ibid.*, 218.

165. *Ibid.*, 210.

166. Quoted in *ibid.*, 211.

167. Quoted in *ibid.*, 211.

168. *Ibid.*, 211.

169. Castleman, *op. cit.*

170. Milius, Peter and Morgan, Dan. "Hazardous Pesticides Sent as Aid." *Washington Post*, December 8, 1976: A1. Milius, Peter. "Leptophos Handled at 9 Plants in U.S." *Washington Post*, December 4, 1976: A1. Morgan, Dan and Milius, Peter. "U.S. Is Pesticide Arsenal for World." *Washington Post*, December 26, 1976: A1, A6, A7.

171. Milius, Peter and Morgan, Dan. "Leptophos Found on Imported Tomatoes." *Washington Post*, December 9, 1976: A1, A6, A7.

172. Carson, Rachel. *Silent Spring.* Boston, MA: Houghton Mifflin, 1962.

173. Milius, Peter and Morgan, Dan. "EPA Challenging 4 Velsicol Pesticides." *Washington Post*, December 14, 1976: A1, A6.

174. Honey, Martha. "Pesticides: Nowhere to Hide." *Ms.* 6, July 1995: 20.

175. Porterfield, Andrew and Weir, David. "The Export of U.S. Toxic Wastes." *The Nation* 245, October 3, 1987: 325, 341–344.

176. Ruffins, *op. cit.*

177. *Ibid.*

178. *Ibid.*

179. *Ibid.*, 343.

180. *World Press Review.* "The North's Garbage Goes South: The Third World Fears It Will Become the Global Dump." Vol. 35, November 1988: 30–32.

181. Quoted in Porterfield and Weir, *op. cit.*, 343.

182. *Ibid.*

183. Quoted in *ibid.*, 344.

184. Setterberg and Shavelson, *op. cit.*

185. Greider, William. "Across the Border." *Utne Reader* 55, January/February 1993: 84.

186. *Ibid.*

187. Setterberg and Shavelson, *op. cit.*, 98.

188. Greider, William. "How We Export Jobs and Disease." *Rolling Stone*, September 3, 1992: 32–33.

189. Juffer, Jane. "Dump at the Border: U.S. Firms Make a Mexican Wasteland." *The Progressive* 52, October 1988: 24–29.

190. *Ibid.*

191. *Ibid.*

192. *Ibid.*

193. Quoted in *ibid.*, 36.

194. Shrivastava, Paul. *Bhopal: Anatomy of a Crisis.* Cambridge, MA: Ballinger, 1987: 2.

195. Hazarika, Sanjoy. "Bhopal Payments by Union Carbide Set at $470 Million." *New York Times*, February 15, 1989: A1, D3.

196. Nanda, Meera. "Secrecy Was Bhopal's Real Disaster: Why Was Information Hidden from the Public?" *Science for the People*, November/December 1985: 13.

197. Kumar, Sanjay. "India: The Second Bhopal Tragedy." *The Lancet* 341, May 8, 1993: 1205–1206.

198. Greenberg, Michael R. and Anderson, Richard F. *Hazardous Waste Sites: The Credibility Gap.* New Brunswick, NJ: Center for Urban Policy Research, 1984.

199. Landers, Robert K. "Living with Hazardous Wastes." *Editorial Research Reports* 2, 1988: 378–387.

200. Setterberg and Shavelson, *op. cit.*, 123.

201. Viviano, Frank. "Superfund Costs May Top S&L Bailout." *San Francisco Chronicle*, May 29, 1991: A1.

202. Quoted in Grossman, *op. cit.*, 128.

203. United States Environmental Protection Agency—Region 6: "Progress at Superfund Sites in Texas." Dallas: EPA, Winter 1993/1994: 5.

204. Harper, Scott. "Industries Cleaning up Brio Site Balk at Tougher EPA Guidelines." *Houston Post*, April 15, 1994: A15.

205. Dawson, Bill. "EPA Proposes Cleanup Plans for Four Houston-Area 'Superfund' Sites." *Houston Chronicle*, January 22, 1988: A22.

206. Kreps, Mary Ann. "EPA Downplays Brio Health Risks, Some Say." *Houston Chronicle*, September 29, 1988: A25.

207. Harper, Scott. "Brio Site's Remaining Neighbors Feel Trapped." *Houston Post*, May 8, 1994: A1, A21.

208. Deaton, Rebecca. "Neighborhood in Transition." *Houston Chronicle*, July 15, 1992: A31.

209. *Dallas Morning News*. "Driven from Home." October 4, 1992: A45.

210. Rendon, Ruth. "3 Brio Cleanup Proposals Carry $40 Million Tags." *Houston Chronicle*, August 25, 1995: 1A. 8A.

211. *Ibid.*

212. Van Voorst, Bruce. "Toxic Dumps: The Lawyers' Money Pit." *Time*, September 13, 1993: 63.

213. Greene, Andrea D. "Resident Urges Warning Signs Near Toxic Spill." *Houston Chronicle*, October 8, 1993: A25.

214. *Houston Chronicle*. "EPA Halts Work at Brio." October 9, 1993: A36.

215. Rendon, Ruth. "Chemical Release at Brio Cleanup Spurs List of Evacuation Standards." *Houston Chronicle*, October 15, 1993: A29.

216. Rendon, Ruth. "State Warning: Don't Eat Clear Creek Fish." *Houston Chronicle*, November 19, 1993: A33.

217. Rendon, August 25, 1995, *op. cit.*

218. *Ibid.*

219. Harper, April 15, 1994, *op. cit.*, A15.

220. Harper, Scott. "Brio—It's a Dirty Job, and Nobody's Able to Do It." *Houston Post*, April 19, 1994: A1, A24.

221. Harper, May 8, 1994, *op. cit.*

222. Harper, Scott. "'No Comment' on Toxic Dump." *Houston Post*, October 9, 1994: A33.

223. Lutz, Heidi. "10 Percent HL&P Cut Possible." *Galveston Daily News*, February 6, 1995: 14.

224. Rendon, August 25, 1995, *op. cit.*, 8A.

225. Carney, Dan. "Nation's Leaders Having Hard Time Cleaning up Superfund Legislation." *Houston Post*, April 24, 1994: A14.

226. Sablatura, Bob. "With Superfund, Lawyers Clean Up." *Houston Chronicle*, October 23, 1995: 1A, 6A.

227. Harper, May 8, 1994, *op. cit.*

228. Setterberg and Shavelson, *op. cit.*

229. *Ibid.*, 123.

230. *Ibid.*

231. Mother Jones 18. "Toxic Ten: America's Truant Corporations." January 1993: 39–42. *Business & Society Review* 84. "America's Worst Toxic Polluters." Winter 1993: 21–23.

232. Litvan, Laura M. "The Growing Ranks of Enviro-Cops." *Nations Business* 82, June 1994: 129–132.

233. Dreux, Mark S. and Zimmerman, Craig H. "The Proposed Federal Sentencing Guidelines for Environmental Crimes." *Occupational Hazards*, July 1993: 46.

234. Kafin, Robert J. and Port, Gail. "Criminal Sanctions Lead to Higher Fines and Jail." *National Law Journal*, July 23, 1990: 20–23.

235. Dreux and Zimmerman, *op. cit.*

236. Riesel, Daniel. "Criminal Prosecution and Defense of Environmental Wrongs." *Environmental Law Reporter* 15, March 1985: 10071.

237. *Los Angeles Times*. "Firm Pleads Guilty in Toxic Dumping." January 15, 1993: A30.

238. Riesel, *op. cit.*

239. *Wall Street Journal*. "Bethlehem Steel Fined for Waste Violations at Indiana Facility." September 7, 1993: B5.

240. Sanders, Alain L. "Battling Crimes against Nature." *Time* 135, March 12, 1990: 54.

241. *Ibid.*

242. *Ibid.*

243. *Houston Chronicle*. "Chevron to Pay Pollution Fine." August 24, 2000: 2C.

244. Ivanovich, David. "Pipeline Firm Fined by EPA." *Houston Chronicle*. January 14, 2000: 1A, 10A.

245. Bergman, Cynthia. "Pennsylvania Company Pleads Guilty in Multi-State Wastewater Pollution Case." *EPA Newsroom*. May 25, 2004.

246. *wisinfo.com*. "Menard's Fined $2M for Pollution." August 9, 2005.

247. *Memphis Business Journal*. "Wal-Mart to Pay $3.1 Million to Settle Clean Water Violations." *bizjournals.com*, May 12, 2004.

248. *Ibid.*

249. Kalra, Ritu. "Wal-Mart to Pay $1.15 Million Fine for Polluting Connecticut Waterways." *Hartford Courant*, August 16, 2005: 1B.

250. Quoted in *ibid*.

251. Dreux and Zimmerman, *op. cit.*

252. *Wall Street Journal*. "EPA Sues Sherwin-Williams; Pattern of Pollution at Paint Factory Is Alleged." July 19, 1993: B4.

253. Abrahamson, Alan. "Firm Fined for Smuggling Toxic Waste." *Los Angeles Times*, January 15, 1993: A3, A41.

254. Cohen, Mark. "Environmental Crime and Punishment: Legal/Economic Theory and Empirical Evidence on Enforcement of Federal Environmental Statutes." *Environmental Crime* 82, 1992: 1082.

255. Naj, Amal K. "United Technologies Fined $5.3 Million for Series of Environmental Violations." *Wall Street Journal*, August 24, 1993: B6.

256. *Ibid.*, 1083.

257. *Ibid.*

258. Dawson, Bill. "Dow Fine to Benefit Rare Fowl." *Houston Chronicle*, June 13, 1996: 37A, 42A.

259. Stipp, David. "Toxic Turpitude: Environmental Crime Can Land Executives in Prison These Days." *Wall Street Journal*, September 10, 1990: A1.

260. Parker, *op. cit.*

261. Zuniga, Jo Ann. "Pair Convicted of Hazardous Dumping." *Houston Chronicle*, December 8, 1993: 1.

262. Brewer, Wayne. "Traditional Policing and Environmental Enforcement." *FBI Law Enforcement Bulletin* 64, May, 1995: 6–13.

263. Humphreys, *op. cit.*, 325.

264. Stipp, *op. cit.*

265. Morris, Mark. "Chemical Company Official Pleads Guilty in Illegal Dumping." *kansascity.com*, January 27, 2009.

266. Marzulla, Roger J. and Kappel, Brett G. "Nowhere to Run, Nowhere to Hide: Criminal Liability for Violations of Environmental Statutes in the 1990s." *Columbia Journal of Environmental Law* 16, 1991: 203.

267. Quoted in U.S. Department of Justice [press release]. "Former Fujicolor Employee Pleads Guilty to Environmental Crime." *usdoj.gov*, June 18, 2008.

268. Quoted in *ibid.*

269. *Ibid.*

270. Cooper, Richard T. and Steiger, Paul E. "Occupational Health Hazards—A National Crisis." *Los Angeles Times*, June 27, 1976: A1.

271. Clay, Thomas R. *Combating Cancer in the Workplace: Implementation of the California Occupational Carcinogens Control Act*. University of California, Irvine: Unpublished doctoral dissertation, 1984.

272. *Ibid.*

273. Wokutch, Richard E. *Cooperation and Conflict in Occupational Safety and Health*. New York: Praeger, 1990.

274. Ashford, Nicholas A. and Caldart, Charles C. *Technology, Law, and the Working Environment*. New York: Van Nostrand Reinhold, 1991: 88.

275. Stone, Christopher D. "A Slap on the Wrist for the Kepone Mob." *Business and Society Review*, Summer 1977: 4–11.

276. Bray, Thomas. "Health Hazard: Chemical Firm's Story Underscores Problems of Cleaning up Plants." *Wall Street Journal*, December 2, 1975: 1, 38.

277. Stone, *op. cit.*

278. *Ibid.*

279. Cooper, *op. cit.*, A24.

280. Stone, *op. cit.*

281. *Ibid.*, 6.

282. Kiernan, Laura. "Kepone Indictments Cite 1,096 Violations: Manufacturing Firms, Hopewell Face Charges." *Washington Post*, May 8, 1976: A1, A6.

283. *Washington Post*. "Paying the Costs of Kepone." February 4, 1977: A20.

284. Kiernan, Laura. "Key Kepone Case Figure Pleads Guilty." *Washington Post*, August 11, 1976: C1, C4.

285. *Washington Post*. "Coping with Kepone." July 16, 1976: A26.

286. Smith, J. Y. "Kepone Indictments Cite 1,096 Violations: Contamination Problems Still Plague Va. Area." *Washington Post*, May 8, 1976: A1, A6.

287. Milius, Peter. "Kepone-Like Case at Texas Pesticide Plant Probe." *Washington Post*, December 1, 1976: A1, A4.

288. *Ibid.*, A1.

289. *Ibid.*

290. Milius, Peter. "2nd Plant Linked to Pesticide." *Washington Post*, December 3, 1976: A1, A7.

291. Milius, Peter. "Pesticide Sales Halt Laid to Economics, Not Safety." *Washington Post*, December 2, 1976: A13.

292. *Ibid.*

293. Caudill, Harry M. "Manslaughter in a Coal Mine." *The Nation* 224, April 23, 1977: 492–497.

294. *Ibid.*, 494.

295. *Ibid.*

296. *Ibid.*

297. Mullins, Vicki. "A Day in the Life of a Coal Mine Inspector." *Women & Work: News from the United States Department of Labor* 7, November 1992: 1–3.

298. Caudill, *op. cit.*, 496.

299. Weinstein, Henry. "Did Industry Suppress Asbestos Data?" *Los Angeles Times*, October 23, 1978: 3.

300. Brodeur, Paul. *Expendable Americans*. New York: Viking Press, 1974.

301. Castleman, *op. cit.*

302. *Ibid.*

303. *Ibid.*

304. *Ibid.*, 3.

305. *Ibid.*, 27.

306. *Ibid.*

307. Thio, *op. cit.*

308. Stone, Andrea. "String of Teachers' Cancers Sounds Alarm at NYC School." *USA Today*, September 30, 1994: 2A.

309. Flynn, George. "Jurors Award $42 Million in Asbestos Cases." *Houston Chronicle*, November 23, 1995: 1A.

310. Olafson, Steve. "21 Steelworkers Who Contracted Asbestos Disease Win $115 Million." *Houston Chronicle*, February 20, 1998: 1A, 14A.

311. *Ibid*, 1A.

312. Quoted in *ibid*, 1A.

313. *Ibid*.

314. Weinstein, *op. cit.*

315. Ritter, John. "Town Clenched in Suffocating Grip of Asbestos." *USA Today*, February 1, 2000: 8A.

316. *Ibid.*, 3.

317. Armour, Stephanie. "Workers Unwittingly Take Home Toxins." *USA Today*, October 5, 2000: 1A, 4A, 6A.

318. *Houston Chronicle*. "192 Asbestos Deaths in Small Town over Last 40 years, Paper Reports." November 21, 1999: 26A.

319. *Ibid*.

320. Ritter, February 1, 2000, *op. cit.*

321. *Houston Chronicle*. "House Action Is Delayed on Bill to Streamline Asbestos Claims." March 15, 2000: 9A.

322. Cannon, Angie. "Homeless Recruited as Asbestos Workers." *Houston Chronicle*, April 25, 1998: 2A.

323. Quoted in *ibid*, 2A.

324. McCaffrey, *op. cit.*

325. Guarasci, Richard. "Death by Cotton Dust." In Hills, Stuart L. (Ed.) *Corporate Violence: Injury and Death for Profit*, Totowa, NJ: Rowman & Littlefield, 1987; 76–92.

326. *Ibid.*, 79.

327. *Ibid.*, 79.

328. *New York Times*. "Stevens Mill Workers Protest Their Lack of a Contract." August 8, 1979: A13.

329. Guarasci, *op. cit.*

330. *Ibid*.

331. McCaffrey, *op. cit.*, 114–115.

332. Guarasci, *op. cit.*

333. *Ibid*.

334. *Ibid.*, 88.

335. Quoted in *ibid.*, 78, 86.

336. Schneider, Keith. "A Valley of Death for the Navajo Uranium Miners." *New York Times*, May 3, 1993: A1. *New York Times*. "Uranium Miners Tell Panel Radiation Caused Ailments." May 14, 1990: 20.

337. Dumas, Kitty. "House OKs Radiation Payments for Miners and 'Downwinders'." *Congressional Quarterly*, June 9, 1990: 1794.

338. *New York Times*. "House Votes Funds for Western Victims of Radiation Illness." June 6, 1990: A22.

339. Schneider, Keith. "Uranium Miners Inherit Dispute's Sad Legacy." *New York Times*, January 9, 1990: A1.

340. Wald, Mathew. "Court Says Ohio Can Penalize U.S." *New York Times*, June 12, 1990: A17.

341. Schneider, Keith. "Study of Nuclear Workers Finds High Cancer Rates." *New York Times*, April 13, 1994: A16.

342. Phillips, B. J. "The Case of Karen Silkwood." *Ms.*, April 1975: 61.

343. Cooper and Steiger, *op. cit.*

344. Brever, *op. cit.*

345. *Ibid.*, 35.

346. *Ibid*.

347. *Ibid.*, 35.

348. Eisler, Peter. "O'Leary Admits Whistle-Blowers Face Reprisal." *USA Today*, May 21, 1998: 1A.

349. Eisler, Peter. "Whistle-Blowers Finally Getting Back at DOE." *USA Today*, May 21, 1998: 7A.

350. Quoted in *ibid*, 1A.

351. *Houston Chronicle*. "Latest Find at Kentucky Plant." February 16, 2000: 10A.

352. Quoted in *ibid*.

353. *Houston Chronicle*. "Compensation Proposed for Workers Sickened by Plutonium." September 17, 1999: 15A.

354. *Ibid*.

355. *Houston Chronicle*. "U.S. Reportedly Knew about Metal that Put Workers Lives at Risk." March 29, 1999: 2A.

356. Scanlon, Bill. "Beryllium Disease Hits 26th Rocky Flats Worker." *archives.insidedenver.com*, November 7, 1992. *Rocky Mountain News*. "Database Provides Information on Flats Radiation Research." *archives. insidedenver.com*. April, 7, 1994. *Rocky Mountain News*. "Flats Workers Sue over Ailment." *archives. insidedenver.com*. November 10, 1996.

357. *Houston Chronicle*, March 29, 1999, *op. cit.*

358. *Ibid*.

359. *Ibid*.

360. Scanlon, Bill. "Flats Restart Gets Mixed Blessing if Various Panels Vouch for Safety." *archives.insid-edenver.com*. August 26, 1991.

361. Quoted in Morson, Bernie. "Rocky Future: Ex-Workers at Rocky Flats Believe Health Hazards That Lurked There Years Ago Still Linger." *archives.insid-edenver.com*, December 21, 1997.

362. *spewingforth.blogspot.com*. "Tyson 'Slapped on the Wrist' for Killing Two Employees." July 7, 2005.

363. Quoted in *ibid*.

364. *Ibid*.

365. *Ibid*.

366. Bureau of Labor Statistics. "National Census of Fatal Occupational Injuries, 1996." August 7, 1997.

367. *wikipedia.org*. "Texas City Disaster." December 10, 2008.

368. Morris, Jim. "OSHA Drops 'Numbers' Emphasis in Its Work." *Houston Chronicle*, October 23, 1994: 1A, 20A.

369. *Occupational Hazards*. "Contested Cases." June 1993: 57.

370. Reiner, Ira and Chatten-Brown, Jan. "When It Is Not an Accident, but a Crime: Prosecutors Get Tough with OSHA." *Northern Kentucky Law Review* 17, Fall 1989: 83–103.

371. Rabassa, Santiago C. "Employment-Related Crimes." *American Criminal Law Review* 30, Spring 1993: 545–563.

372. Mongeluzzi, Robert J. "Electrocution Accidents on the Job: Heavy-Equipment Workers Put Their Lives on the Line." *Trial* 25, March 1989: 69.

373. *Ibid.*

374. *Ibid.*, 69.

375. Pasternak, Douglas and Cary, Peter. "Department of Horrors: America's Energy Agency and Its Appalling Record of Worker Safety." *U.S. News & World Report*, January 24, 1994: 47–49.

376. Spayd, Liz. "Fines for Work Safety Violations Under Fire." *Washington Post*, May 29, 1992: A21.

377. *Ibid.*, A21.

378. Price, Tom and Aulds, T.J. "What Went Wrong: Oil Refinery Disaster." *popularmechanics.com*, July 2005.

379. Collette, Mark. "OSHA" Fines BP for Safety Violations." *galvnews.com*, July 21, 2007.

380. *printthis.clickability.com*. BP Accepts Blame for Deadly Refinery Explosion." May 18, 2005.

381. Quoted in Mufson, Steven. "Cost-Cutting Led to Blast at BP Plant, Probe Finds." *Washington Post*, October 31, 2006: D1.

382. Quoted in *ibid.*

383. Quoted in *ibid.*

384. Quoted in *cbsnews.com*. "Daughter of BP Victims Fights and Wins." January 9, 2007.

385. *iht.com*. "BP Settles More Claims from a Texas Refinery Fire." February 23, 2007.

386. *cbsnews.com*, *op. cit.*

387. Quoted in *ibid.*

388. *iht.com*, *op. cit.*

389. *texascityexplosion.com*. "Attorney Brent Coon to Depose Former BP CEO Lord Browne in BP Explosion Case Today." April 4, 2007.

390. Collette, *op. cit.*

391. Mortished, Carl. "BP Agrees to Settle Out of Court over Suicide of Texas City Worker." *business.timesonline.co.uk*, September 6, 2007.

392. Williams, Scott E. "Plant's Former Manager Leads Off BP Trial." *galvnews.com*, September 7, 2007.

393. Williams, Scott E. "BP Trial Enters Week 2." *galvnews.com*, September 11, 2007.

394. Williams, Scott E. "Jurors Hear about 20 Years of Safety Fears." *galvnews.com*, September 12, 2007.

395. Quoted in Calkins, Laurel Brubaker and Fisk, Margaret Cronin. "BP Executive Blames Workers for Texas Refinery Blast." *iht.com*, September 17, 2007.

396. Quoted in *ibid.*

397. Rhor, Monica. "Settlement Ends First BP Explosion Trial." *washingtonpost.com*, September 18, 2007.

398. Hays, Kristen. "BP Explosion Trial Ends Early with 4 Settlements." *galvnews.com*, September 18, 2007.

399. *washingtonpost.com*. "BP Blast's First Trial Ends with Payout." September 19, 2007.

400. Collette, Mark. "BP to Pay $50 Million in Fines for Deadly Blast." *galvnews.com*, October 26, 2007.

401. Williams, Scott E. "Attorneys Argue BP Knew Refinery Needed Fixes." *galvnews.com*, December 13, 2007.

402. *Laredo Morning Times*. "Settlement Reached in BP Explosion Civil Trial." September 19, 2007.

403. Quoted in Williams, Scott E. "Workers, Relatives Recount BP Explosions." *galvnews.com*, December 15, 2007.

404. Williams, Scott E. "BP: $1.6 Billion in Blast Money Is Gone." *galvnews.com*, December 17, 2007.

405. Williams, Scott E. "BP Case Settles." *galvnews.com*, December 19, 2007.

406. Williams, Scott E. "Next Round of BP Trials under Way." *galvnews.com*, May 20, 2008.

407. Quoted in Hem, Brad. "Witness Says BP Misled Officials." *texascityexplosion.com*, June 18, 2008.

408. Brent Coon & Associates [press release]. "Remaining Four Cases Settled in BP Trial After Intensive Negotiations." July 22, 2008.

409. *cbsnews.com*. "Refinery Explosion Rocks Texas Town." February 18, 2008.

410. *msnbc.msn.com*. "Blast Big Enough to Be Felt Miles Away, but Few Working Due to Holiday." February 18, 2008.

411. U.S. Chemical Safety and Hazard Investigation Board. "Investigation Report: Refinery Explosion and Fire." Report No. 2005-04-I-TX. 2007.

412. British Petroleum [press release]. "BP America Announces Resolution of Texas City, Alaska, Propane Trading, Law Enforcement Investigations." October 25, 2007.

413. Lustgarten, Abrahm. *Run to Failure: BP and the Making of the Deepwater Horizon Disaster*. 2012. NY: W.W. Norton. Barstow, David, Rhode, David and Saul, Stephanie. "Deepwater Horizon's Final Hours." *nytimes.com*, December 25, 2010. National Commission on the BP Deepwater Horizon Oil Spill and Offshore Drilling. *Deepwater: The Gulf Oil Disaster and the Future of Offshore Drilling Report to the President*. 2011.

414. National Commission on the BP Deepwater Horizon Oil Spill, 146-147.

415. *Ibid.*, 168.

416. *Ibid.*, 168-169.

417. *Ibid.*, 173.

418. *Ibid.*, 223.

419. *Ibid.*, 122.

420. Lustgarten, 2012, 314-315.

421. Associated Press. "BP CEO Tony Hayward Goes To Capitol Hill, Gets Pilloried By Congress." *huffingtonpost.com*. June 17, 2010.

422. Lustgarten, 2012, 335.

423. Lustgarten, Abrahm. "A Stain that Won't Go Away." *nytimes.com*. April 19, 2012.

424. Krauss, Clifford. "Engineer Arrested in BP Oil Spill Case." *nytimes.com*. April 24, 2012.

425. *wikipedia.com*. "2008 Georgia Sugar Refinery Explosion." November 4, 2008.

426. *nytimes.com*. "A Bitter Story about Sugar and Death in Savannah." August 19, 2008.

427. *msnbc.msn.com*. "Dozens Injured in Blast." February 8, 2008.

428. *Ibid.*

429. *Ibid.*

430. Quoted in *nytimes.com*. A Bitter Story about Sugar and Death in Savannah." August 19, 2008.

431. Peterson, Larry. "Chambliss in Sugar Furor." *savannahnow.com*, July 30, 2008.

432. Quoted in Dewan, Shaila. "OSHA Seeks $8.7 Million Fine against Sugar Company." *gsmlaborcouncil.org*, July 26, 2008.

433. *zimbio.com*. "OSHA Issues Third Largest Fine in History Following Sugar Refinery Explosion." July 28, 2008.

434. Smith, Sandy. "Investigation Finds Inadequate Dust Controls Caused West Pharmaceutical Explosion." *EHSToday*, October 13, 2004.

435. *Ibid.*

436. *OSB Investigation Digest*. Dust Explosion at West Pharmaceutical Services. April 2005.

437. *Ibid.*

438. Alford, Roger. "Explosion Injures Workers." Associated Press, February 21, 2003.

439. *labor.state.vt.us*. "Preliminary CBS Findings Indicate Combustible Dust Caused Fatal CTA Explosion."

440. *chemsafety.gov*. "CTA Acoustics Dust Explosion and Fire Corbin, KY, Issued on February 15, 2005."

441. Smith, Sandy. "CSB Investigation Focused on Ignition Source in CTA Acoustics Accident." *EHSToday*, February 25, 2004.

442. CSB [press release]. "Chemical Safety Board Investigation Finds CTA Acoustics Explosion Caused by Dust Hazard That Was Known to Management, Phenolic Resin Supplier." February 15, 2005.

443. Mansdorf, Zack. "Joint Report Released on Foundry Explosion." *EHSToday*, October 15, 1999.

444. Stoll-Keenan-Ogden [press release]. "CTA Acoustics Accepts Jury Verdict." May 22, 2007. OSHA did cite the Jahn Foundry for safety and health violations following the explosion and imposed a $148,500 penalty. But, like CTA, Jahn successfully sued Borden Chemicals. (*osha.gov* [press release]. "Jahn Foundry Corp. to Pay $148,500 Penalty, Correct Hazards and Establish Comprehensive Safety and Health Program at Its Massachusetts Plants Following February Catastrophic Dust Explosion." August 24, 1999).

445. CSB. "Hayes Lemmerz Dust Explosions and Fire" Huntington, Indiana, October 29, 2003. *chemsafety.gov*, October 5, 2005.

446. CSB [press release]. "CSB Team Heading to Site of Explosions at Indiana Automotive Parts Factory." *csb.gov*, October 30, 2003.

447. CSB. "CSB Investigators Find Likely Source of Dust Explosion at Indiana Automotive Plant." *csb.gov*, November 5, 2003.

448. International Code Council. "Investigation Reports on Hayes-Lemmerz International Aluminum Dust Explosion." *iccsafe.org*, June 2005.

449. Quoted in CSB. "CSB Determines Fatal 2003 Incident at Hayes Lemmerz Plant in Indiana Most Likely Caused by Aluminum in Dust Collection System." *csb.gov*, October 5, 2005.

450. Quoted in *free-pree-release.com*. "The Combustible Dust Explosion and Fire Prevention Act of 2008." March 10, 2008.

451. Barstow, David and Bergman, Lowell. "Family's Profits Wrung from Blood and Sweat." *nytimes. com*, January 9, 2003.

452. *Ibid.*

453. Simonson, Ellen. "Bottom Line Should Never Have Priority over Safety." *The Daily Cougar Online*, January 14, 2003.

454. Barstow and Bergman, January 9, 2003, *op. cit.*

455. *Ibid.*

456. Quoted in *ibid.*

457. *Ibid.*

458. *Ibid.*

459. *Ibid.*

460. Barstow, David and Bergman, Lowell. "Deaths on the Job, Slaps on the Wrist." *nytimes.com*, January 10, 2003.

461. *Ibid.*

462. Kotelchuck, David. "McWane, Inc: A Tale from Dickens." *U.S. News Health and Safety,* January 2003.

463. Barstow, David and Bergman, Lowell. "At a Texas Foundry, an Indifference to Life." *nytimes.com,* January 8, 2003.

464. *Ibid.*

465. *Ibid.*

466. *pbs.org.* "Frontline: A Dangerous Business." September 27, 2003.

467. Castleman, *op. cit.*, 569–570.

468. *Ibid.*

469. Quoted in *ibid.*, 576.

470. *Ibid.*, 578.

471. *Ibid.*, 589.

472. Quoted in *ibid.*, 599.

473. Wokutch, *op. cit.*

474. Calavita, Kitty. "The Demise of the Occupational Safety and Health Administration: A Case Study in Symbolic Action." *Social Problems* 30, April 1983: 437–448.

475. Palisano, Peg. "Reagan's OSHA Team—They Hit the Ground Running." *Occupational Hazards* 43, 1981: 67–74.

476. *Occupational Hazards* 44. "OSHA Communique." 1982: 39–40.

477. Engel, Paul. "Close-up on OSHA's Proposed New Chemical Labeling Standard." *Occupational Hazards* 44, 1982: 35–39.

478. *Occupational Hazards* 44. "Showdown Looms over OSHA's Cancer Policy." 1982: 60–63.

479. Verespe, Michael A. "Has OSHA Improved?" *Industry Week*, August 4, 1980: 48–56.

480. Wokutch. *op. cit.*, 45.

481. *Ibid.*

482. *Ibid.*, 41.

483. *Ibid.*

484. Morris, Jim. "Dangerous Bridge Led to OSHA Official's Resignation." *Houston Chronicle*, October 23, 1994: 20A.

485. Labaton, Stephen. "OSHA Leaves Worker Safety in Hands of Industry." *nytimes.com*, April 25, 2007.

486. *lasvegassun.com.* "Worker Safety Eroded during the Bush Years." December 2, 2008.

487. Labaton, *op. cit.*

488. Lewis, Robert and Sapien, Joaquin. "Bush Moves Forward with 'Secret' OSHA Rule." *propublica.org*, December 1, 2008.

489. *nytimes.com*, August 19, 2008, *op. cit.*

490. *Ibid.*

491. Swoboda, Frank. "OMB's Logic: Less Protection Saves Lives." *Washington Post*, March 17, 1992: A15.

492. *Ibid.*

493. Kinney, Joseph A. "Foreword: Justice and the Problem of Unsafe Work." *Northern Kentucky Law Review* 17, Fall 1989: 1–7.

494. Quoted in *ibid.*, A21.

495. Quoted in Rabassa, *op. cit.*, 551.

496. Tyson, Patrick R. "Court Favors Huge OSHA Penalties." *Safety and Health* 146, November 1992: 19–24.

497. *Ibid.*, 19.

498. *Ibid.*, 21.

499. *Ibid.*

500. *Ibid.*

501. *Ibid.*, 23.

502. Gombar, Robert C. and Yohay, Stephen C. "OSHA 'Repeated' Violations—It's Time for Reexamination." *Employee Relations Law Journal* 18, Fall 1992: 315–324.

503. *Ibid.*

504. Jefferson, Jon. "Dying for Work." *ABA Journal*, February 1993: 48.

505. Dunmire, Thea D. "The Problems with Using Common Law Criminal Statutes to Deter Exposure to Chemical Substances in the Workplace. *Northern Kentucky Law Review* 17, Fall 1989: 53–81.

506. Humphreys, *op. cit.*

507. Jefferson, Jon. "L.A. Law: Prosecuting Workplace Killers." *ABA Journal*, January 1993: 48.

508. Reiner and Chatten-Brown, *op. cit.*, 97.

509. *Ibid.*

510. Feldman, Paul. "All 'Twilight Zone' Figures Acquitted." *Los Angeles Times*, May 30, 1987: 1, 28, 29.

511. Reiner and Chatten-Brown, *op. cit.*, 103.

512. Barstow, David. "California Leads in Making Employer Pay for Job Deaths." *nytimes.com,* December 23, 2003.

513. *Ibid.*

514. *Ibid.*

515. Quoted in *ibid.*

516. Barstow, David. "A Trench Caves In; a Young Worker Is Dead. Is It a Crime?" *nytimes.com,* December 21, 2003.

517. Quoted in *ibid.*

518. *Ibid.*

519. *New York Times* (Editorial). "Occupational Hazards." December 23, 2003.

520. Barstow, David. "U.S. Rarely Charges for Deaths in Workplace." *nytimes.com.* December 22, 2003.

521. Dutzman, Joleane. "State Criminal Prosecutions: Putting Teeth in the Occupational Safety and Health Act." *George Mason University Law Review* 12, Summer 1990: 737–755.

522. Uelmen, Amelia J. "Trashing State Criminal Sanctions?: OSHA Preemption Jurisprudence in Light of Gade v. National Solid Wastes Management Association." *American Criminal Law Review* 30, Winter 1993: 373–415.

523. Orland, Leonard. "Reflections on Corporate Crime: Law in Search of Theory and Scholarship." *American Criminal Law Review* 17, 1980: 501–520.

524. Uelmen, *op. cit.*, 379.

525. Geis, Gilbert. "Criminal Penalties for Corporate Criminals." *Criminal Law Bulletin* 8, 1972: 377–380.

526. Koprowicz, Kenneth M. "Corporate Criminal Liability for Workplace Hazards: A Viable Option for Enforcing Workplace Safety?" *Brooklyn Law Review* 52, 1986: 183–227.

527. Bennett, Steven C. "Developments in the Movement against Corporate Crimes." *New York University Law Review* 65, 1990: 871–874.

528. Dutzman, *op. cit.*

529. Koprowicz, *op. cit.*

530. Quoted in Reiner and Chatten-Brown, *op. cit.*, 89.

531. *Ibid.*, 89.

532. *Ibid.*, 89.

533. Uelmen, *op. cit.*

534. Smothers, Ronald. "25 Die, Many Reported Trapped, as Blaze Engulfs Carolina Plant." *New York Times*, September 4, 1991: A1, B7.

535. Miller, Lenore. "Revisiting the 'Jungle.'" *Washington Post*, October 20, 1992: A20.

536. Jefferson, *op. cit.*

537. *Ibid.*

538. Smothers, *op. cit.*

539. Quoted in *ibid.*, A1.

540. *New York Times.* "Meat-Plant Owner Pleads Guilty in a Blaze That Killed 25 People." September 15, 1992: A6.

541. Wang, Charleston C. K. *How to Manage Workplace-Derived Hazards and Avoid Liability.* Park Ridge, NJ: Noyes Publications, 1987.

542. Frank, Nancy K. and Lynch, Michael J. *Corporate Crime: Corporate Violence.* New York: Harrow and Heston, 1992.

543. *Ibid.*, 43.

544. Siegel, Barry. "Murder Case a Corporate Landmark." *Los Angeles Times*, September 15, 1985: 1, 8, 9.

545. Wang, *op. cit.*, 183.

546. Siegel, *op. cit.*

547. *Ibid.*, 8.

548. Frank, *op. cit.*

549. Siegel, *op. cit.*

550. Rabassa, Santiago C. "Employment Related Crimes." *American Criminal Law Review* 30, 1993: 545–563.

551. Koprowicz, *op. cit.*

552. Helverson, Alana L. "Can a Corporation Commit Murder?" *Washington University Law Quarterly* 64, 1986: 967–984.

553. *Ibid.*

554. Magnuson, Jay C. and Leviton, Gareth C. "Policy Considerations in Corporate Criminal Prosecutions after People v. Film Recovery Systems, Inc. *Notre Dame Law Review* 62, 1987: 939.

555. Bokat, Stephen A. "Criminal Enforcement of OSHA: Employers' Rights at Risk." *Northern Kentucky Law Review* 17, Fall 1989: 135–151.

556. Ducat, Craig R. and Chase, Harold W. *Constitutional Interpretation: Powers of Government* (5th Edition). New York: West Publishing, 1992.

557. Uelmen, *op. cit.*

558. *Ibid.*, 387.

559. *Ibid.*

560. Dunmire, *op. cit.*

561. Uelmen, *op. cit.*, 375.

562. Quoted in *ibid.*, 375.

563. Siegel, Barry. "Cyanide Trial in Illinois Makes History, Headlines." *Los Angeles Times*, September 16, 1985: 8.

564. Rodella, Patricia. "Corporate Criminal Liability for Homicide: Has the Fiction Been Extended Too Far?" *Journal of Law and Commerce* 4, 1984: 95–125.

565. Michael, Alan C. "Defining Unintended Murder." *Columbia Law Review* 85, May 1985: 786.

566. Frank, Nancy. "Unintended Murder and Corporate Risk-Taking: Defining the Concept Justiciability." *Journal of Criminal Justice* 16, 1988: 24.

567. Reiner and Chatten-Brown, *op. cit.*, 103.

568. Quoted in Parker, *op. cit.*, 35.

569. Barstow, David and Bergman, Lowell. "OSHA to Address Persistent Violators of Job Safety Rules." *pulitzer.org*, March 11, 2003.

5

Institutional Corruption: Mass Media and Religion

In preceding chapters, we have examined the consequences of white-collar crime in terms of physical or financial costs. There is, however, another type of cost—perhaps less obvious or directly measurable, but far more pervasive. That would be the social cost. Here, the victims are not limited to endangered employees or exploited consumers, but include all of society. As Sutherland observed many years ago: "White-collar crimes violate trust and therefore create distrust; this lowers social morale and produces social disorganization."[1]

To understand the notion of social disorganization in Sutherland's context, one must first consider its opposite—social organization. Social organization usually is seen by sociologists as a synthesis of culture and institutional structure.[2] While both these components are implicated in white-collar crime, culture seems to be more *cause* and institutional structure more *effect*—although there is clearly reciprocity in the relationship.

White-collar crime mirrors American culture, with its strong emphasis on achievement and what has been termed the "fetishism of money."[3] Robert Merton, who has proposed a link between crime and culture since the 1930s, argues that money is the yardstick by which achievement is measured in the United States.[4] In other words, money is how we "keep score" in our materialistic culture. To theorists like Merton, there can be little doubt that the quest for financial success and competitive superiority makes our culture relatively hospitable to white-collar crime. For example, research reports that unethical behavior is often determined by situational competition,[5] and illegal conduct becomes increasingly likely as the corporate environment becomes more competitive.[6]

But it is the other component of social organization, institutional structure, in which the effects—that is, the social costs—of white-collar crime are more visible. Institutions have been called "the lengthened shadows of men."[7] They are defined as "relatively stable sets of norms and values, statuses and roles, and groups and organizations."[8] As such, institutions regulate human conduct and interaction in order to meet society's basic needs.[9] They allow a society to "endure over time despite the constant 'coming and going' of individual members."[10] Another influential social theorist, Talcott Parsons, referred to institutions as "the 'backbone' of the social system."[11] To extend Parsons' metaphor, a weakening of important social institutions is like the progressive degeneration of a backbone; it can incapacitate or even kill a society. And this is the crux of

Sutherland's thesis: that the erosion of the public's confidence in its social institutions can tear apart the fabric of American society by attacking our most fundamental beliefs.

It would be difficult to identify a significant social or cultural institution uncontaminated by white-collar crime. In this chapter, we will consider two important examples: the mass media and religion. It must be acknowledged, however, that a case could be made easily that *every* category of white-collar crime depicted in this book manifests a deleterious effect on some social institution and thereby inflicts damage on society as a whole. To cite two obvious examples, the crimes committed by the government described in Chapter 9 and the political corruption examined in Chapter 10 have significantly devalued the democratic process.

THE MASS MEDIA

The mass media have been identified as among the most influential sources for the "social construction of reality."[12] In other words, each person constructs his or her perception of the world through a socialization process resting heavily on shared knowledge—much of it derived from the mass media. Since almost all Americans have access to the same media, we tend to construct similar social realities[13]—a process that communication theorist George Gerbner has termed *worldview cultivation*.[14] Consequently, corruption of the mass media can change the very way we think about the world.[15]

Television, the most dominant and pervasive of all modern mass media, generated a major corruption scandal in its first decade of preeminence.

A few weeks after the House Commerce Subcommittee had concluded its examination of the quiz shows, it reconvened to investigate another systemic scandal—this one involving the music industry.

CASE STUDY
The Quiz Show Scandal

By 1955, television's most popular and highest-rated entertainment genre was the big money quiz show. Programs like *The $64,000 Question* and *Twenty-One* awarded millions of dollars in prizes to contestants who seemed to demonstrate an encyclopedic range of knowledge. After a sensational Congressional investigation in 1959, however, it was revealed that these "geniuses" were fakes and that the programs had been "fixed." Those contestants, whom the producers, sponsors, and networks had deemed appealing, had been routinely given the correct answers in advance.[16] A major motion picture documenting these events (*Quiz Show*) was released in 1994, right after this case study had been written for the first edition of this book.

Some apologists have characterized the quiz show fraud as a "victimless crime." But was it? The passage of time allows for a less myopic assessment of the social consequences of television's first white-collar crime scandal. Decades have elapsed since contestants were taught by producers to lie and cheat in order to sell sponsors' lipstick and iron tonic. In their hunger for higher ratings, the networks had demonstrated at the very least a willingness to tolerate an endemic fraud and to abet its subsequent cover-up. With the benefit of hindsight, it now could be argued that those who rigged the quiz shows were engaged in a criminal conspiracy to rob the American people of their idealism and promote in its place a dispiriting national

(Continued)

cynicism. It has been said that "[t]he worst part of a scandal is that is actually scandalizes."[17] Perhaps so, but the worst part of the quiz show scandal may have been its *failure* to scandalize. Instead, like so many white-collar crimes, it helped make dishonesty more respectable. After the Congressional hearings had adjourned, a "man on the street" interview asked passers-by, "Would you have any qualms about appearing on a TV quiz show if it were rigged and you knew you would win a large sum of money?" Two-thirds of those queried responded that they would have no qualms and would appear.[18]

National cynicism no doubt also was fueled by the selective nature of the prosecutions resulting from the quiz show fraud. Almost all of those who were indicted, arrested, convicted, and sentenced were former contestants. The privileged few who owned or controlled the quiz programs and who reaped enormous profits from them seemed to be beyond the reach of the criminal justice system. It is reasonable to wonder how much less cynically the public might have reacted if it had been the engine that derailed, rather than the caboose.

The most serious effect of the quiz show scandal, however, was the long-term corruption of our preeminent mass medium. The scandal occurred when the television industry was barely out of its infancy, still forming the moral codes and conduct norms it would carry into its adulthood.[19] If the child truly is the father of the man, then whatever ethical shortcomings television has since displayed—everything from fraudulent advertising practices to dissembled news reports to "dramatized" documentaries to the perfidious televangelists—may be a product of its misspent youth.

CASE STUDY
Payola

As the 1950's wound down, "[t]he U.S. was becoming familiar with a new word, 'payola,' trade jargon for bribes to promote certain records over the air."[20] These bribes came from music publishers or record manufacturers and distributors, and were paid to both disk jockeys and station managers.

What seemed to outside observers to be an insidious new form of corruption really was just an extension of a longstanding tradition of bribery in the music industry. At least as early as the 1890s, "gifts and money were given to performers [by music publishers] as an inducement to sing particular songs."[21] For example, the composer of "After the Ball" originally helped popularize that classic tune by paying the star of a lavish musical review $500 and a percentage of future royalties in exchange for placing the song in the show.[22]

By the 1920s, the surest way to launch a new song successfully was to induce a vaudeville head-liner to use it in his or her act. The most charismatic entertainer of that period was Al Jolson, and it became commonly acknowledged as a show business truism that "to get Jolson to sing a song was to have a big hit on your hands."[23] Jolson often received a percentage of a song's royalties by being given undeserved collaborating credit as the song's lyricist or composer. One publisher even gave Jolson an expensive race horse as a "gift."[24]

Likewise, by the 1930s, dance band leaders routinely were bribed by music publishers to induce them to include certain songs in their radio programs.[25] The most prominent band leaders sometimes were even given a financial interest in the publishing house or in the copyright of a song.[26] It was during this period that the term "payola" was coined by the show business periodical, *Variety*, which reported that payola had become accepted within the music industry as a

(*Continued*)

normal business practice. A writer who chronicled radio's "big band" era observed: "There is little philanthropy in Tin Pan Alley. If you scratch my back, I must scratch yours—or your palm."[27]

By the 1950s, radio was providing an even more hospitable climate for bribery, because many more recordings were produced than could be played on the air, creating a fierce level of competition.[28] By that time, the nature of payola had changed radically. Record companies had replaced music publishers as the primary source of illicit payoffs, and disk jockeys had replaced singers and musicians as the primary recipients. A Detroit disk jockey, in his congressional testimony, described the new mechanics of payola in 1959:

> I was often approached by small companies who were having a tough time getting their stuff on the air. They would say, "Well, how much do you want to ride this record for the next three weeks?" They might offer $100 for a one-week ride, which would have meant playing the record several times a day to make it popular. Many disk jockeys are on the weekly payroll of five to 10 record companies, which can mean a side income of $25,000 to $50,000 a year. The payment is by cash in an envelope.[29]

Congress heard testimony from an array of disk jockeys working in the major radio markets. "[T]he hearings demonstrated the enormous moral confusion which [existed] over payola."[30] Almost all the disk jockeys admitted they had accepted large sums of money, but most denied that the money had bought air time for records; they maintained it was a legitimate fee system for "auditioning" records.[31] A former Boston disk jockey, who had accepted about $10,000 in payola over a three-year period,[32] was an unapologetic exception, offering his own candid analysis: "This seems to be the American way of life . . . I'll do for you. What would you do for me?"[33] The effect of such testimony "was to suggest that payola was

widespread."[34] Furthermore there seemed to be an almost total lack of any serious effort on the part of the broadcasting industry to prevent payola.[35]

Many who testified lost their jobs. Among them was one of the country's best known radio personalities—Alan Freed, the self-proclaimed "King of Rock 'n Roll." Freed denied that he had received payola, but admitted accepting gifts from companies after playing their records. He characterized such payments as "consultant fees."[36] Freed added a trenchant observation: "What they call payola in the disk-jockey business, they call lobbying in Washington."[37]

Other testimony described a disk-jockey convention held in Miami Beach in 1959, at which eighteen record companies reportedly picked up a $118,000 tab for hotel rooms, meals, liquor, and call girls. The hearings further revealed that major figures in the broadcasting industry sometimes were given as much as a 50 percent interest in a singer's contract or a record's profits in exchange for promoting the artist or the song.[38] This complex practice was especially evident when the subcommittee turned its attention to television in May, 1960. A subpoena was issued to one of the most influential figures in the music business—Dick Clark, the host of ABC-TV's *American Bandstand*, a televised "record hop" viewed daily by millions of loyal teenage fans.

Clark told that he never played a record for any type of material consideration, monetary or otherwise.[39] However, he had amassed a personal fortune in the previous three years, and this left many members skeptical. One Congressman coined the term, "Clarkola."[40]

Actually, in a literal sense, Clark's denial probably was true. His stature in the music industry transcended conventional payola. He did not need to rely on crude cash bribes in surreptitious envelopes. Like Jolson forty years earlier, Clark had developed a far more profitable system.

> It hinged on his numerous corporate holdings. . . . The music, the records and the singers

(*Continued*)

involved with these companies gained a special place in Clark's programs, which the committee said gave them systematic preference.[41]

For example, over a two-year period Clark had given far less air time to Elvis Presley, the sovereign "rock 'n roll" star, than to newcomer Duane Eddy. Clark had no financial stake in Presley, but he had stock positions in companies that held rights to Eddy.[42] Clark was accused by one committee member of exploiting his position: "By almost any reasonable test, records you had an interest in were played more than the ones you didn't."[43] Clark's incredible reply: "I did not consciously favor such records. Maybe I did so without realizing it."[44]

In addition, Clark acknowledged owning the copyrights to 160 songs—143 of which had been given to him as "gifts:"

A shining example was a record called *16 Candles*. Before getting the copyright, Clark spun it only four times in 10 weeks, and it got nowhere. Once he owned it, Clark played it 27 times in less than three months and it went up like a rocket. Each time the record was purchased Clark shared in the profits to the merry tune of $12,000.[45]

Clark, of course, deflected the payola scandal and went on to become one of television's wealthiest and most successful producers. Moreover—as Chapter 2 details—he still found the time to shill for a disreputable sweepstakes promotion that at best straddles the cusp between deception and outright fraud.

As a result of the Congressional hearings, the Communications Act of 1934 was amended in 1960 to prohibit cash payments and other favors given to disk jockeys by record producers and distributors. However, more than a decade later, it was reported widely that payola continued to flourish.[46] Payments in cash or in illegal drugs[47] allegedly still were being made. Hearings by the Federal Communications Commission (FCC) "left

little doubt that payola had not been stopped by the change in the law."[48]

In 1973, the Department of Justice and the Internal Revenue Service began a new round of payola investigations,[49] which concluded that payola had been received by radio station employees in at least sixteen American cities. By 1975, sixteen individuals and six corporations had been indicted by grand juries in Newark, Philadelphia, and Los Angeles for violating the amended Communications Act, as well as for bribery, mail fraud, tax evasion, and perjury.[50]

In 1976, a New York grand jury indicted the former president of CBS Records and another CBS executive for engaging in payola.[51] That same year, four executives of the Brunswick Record Company were fined and given prisons terms after radio station music directors (who had been granted immunity) testified that they had received cash payments from Brunswick representatives.[52] "The lawyers for the executives had argued that 'cash payments were a way of life in the record industry and part of the promotion end of the business,' to which the judge replied, 'If this is true, then the record business is a dirty business indeed.'"[53]

In 1999, two company executives of Fonovisa, one of the biggest independent Latin music labels in the world, pleaded not guilty to federal charges related to payola payments.[54] Guillermo Santiso and Jesus Gilberto Moreno were found to have participated in fraudulent activities since 1992, when they reported $1.5 million in promotional expenses that never actually occurred.[55] The payola payments came in 1996, when the company wrote checks worth $425,000 to a promotion company, which in turn kicked the money back to Fonovisa. Fonovisa then used the money to pay different program directors.[56] Investigators also found that in 1997, Moreno had made more than $1 million in fraudulent payments to additional radio program directors.[57] After an initial plea of not guilty, the two executives changed their tune and pleaded guilty on July 22 of 1999.[58] Guillermo became the first senior record company

(Continued)

executive to be convicted under federal payola statutes enacted following the scandal of the fifties.[59] Guillermo was fined $200,000 and was given two years probation, while Jesus Gilberto Moreno was fined $50,000 and sentenced to two years probation.[60] Fonovisa was fined $700,000 for both the fraudulent tax returns and the payola payments.[61]

The broadcasting industry has never seemed willing to acknowledge the inherent corruption of payola, which is why the problem still persists decades after the first scandal. When new allegations surfaced in the press in 1998. The radio journal *M Street Daily* declared: "It's not improper to accept payments for things you put on the air."[62] Some scholars share this assessment. Finance professor Michael Rozeff insists: "Payola is not an extraneous inducement that interferes with music being played for its own merits. . . . The public selects its own bad (and good) music."[63] Likewise, economist Ronald Coase, who conducted the definitive analysis of payola in 1979, argued that payola is a way for record companies to back expected winners, which helps radio stations allocate scarce bandwidth.[64] And journalist James Surowiecki, although critical of payola, notes that the practice does have a certain rationale: "By putting money behind a record, a label signals its belief that the record has a chance to be a hit; no company will spend a lot of money trying to sell something it doesn't have high hopes for. And hits, of course, are the only thing that radio cares about."[65]

One person who disagreed with the *M Street Daily* was then—New York Attorney General Eliot Spitzer. After receiving tips from industry insiders, Spitzer's office began a year-long investigation of payola that culminated in July 2005 with an announced settlement with Sony BMG Music Entertainment, one of the world's leading record companies. Sony agreed to stop making illegal payments and providing expensive gifts to radio stations and their employees in return for airplay. The investigation had revealed that Sony had offered outright bribes to radio programmers, including expensive vacation packages and valuable merchandise. The company had taken steps to conceal many of the bribes by using fictitious "contest winners" to make it appear as though the payments and gifts were going to radio listeners instead of station employees. Sony issued a statement acknowledging its improper conduct and pledged to abide by the law. The company also agreed to donate $10 million to a New York charity aimed at funding music education and appreciation programs.[66] Four months later, a similar settlement was reached with Warner Music Group, the third largest record company in the United States.[67]

Universal Music Group, the world's largest music company, agreed to pay a $12 million fine.[68] Under the terms of the settlement, the company agreed to stop making payments and providing expensive gifts to radio stations and their employees in exchange for "airplay" of particular artists' songs.[69] Spitzer's office had uncovered emails revealing that Universal executives were not only aware of the payoffs but also regularly trained and pressured subordinates to buy airplay.[70]

The focus of investigation later shifted from the recording industry to the radio industry. In February 2006, Spitzer announced he had proof that some of the country's largest radio corporations and networks had taken money and other unlawful forms of compensation to play certain songs on the air. Spitzer added: "The behavior has been unethical, improper, illegal and a sanction of some severity clearly should be imposed."[71]

Seven months later, CBS Radio, the country's third-largest radio conglomerate, agreed to make a $2 million charitable contribution to settle the allegations. According to Spitzer, CBS Radio stations "openly solicited illegal financial benefits, expensive vacation packages," and other valuable items from record labels "in exchange for playing the labels' songs."[72]

The New York investigation went federal in 2007. Under a consent decree with the Federal Communications Commission, four of the biggest radio broadcast companies—CBS, Clear Channel,

(Continued)

Entercom, and Citadel—agreed to pay a combined $12.5 million fine and pledge that their 1,653 stations would not engage in payola practices.[73] A separate deal was also negotiated, under which the broadcasters agreed to provide 8,400 half-hour segments of free airtime for independent record labels and local artists over the following three years. "Independent" was defined as any record label not owned or controlled by the nation's four dominant music labels: Sony BMG, Warner Music, Universal Music Group, and EMI Group.[74]

However in late 2008, 18 months after the signing of the FCC sponsored Rules of Engagement, a survey reported that independent artists and labels were still being shut out of broadcast radio. According to the survey, over 90 percent of independent labels experienced no change in their relationship with commercial radio since the settlement. And over 40 percent reported that payola remains a determining factor in commercial radio airplay.[75] As they say on the radio, stay tuned.

Although the electronic media are clearly the most dominant form of mass communication, the print media have not been without their share of duplicity. In 1981, for example, the Pulitzer Prize for feature writing[76] was awarded to *Washington Post* reporter Janet Cooke for her gut-wrenching account of an 8-year-old heroin addict named Jimmy.[77] Two days later, the prize was withdrawn and Cooke resigned from her job after admitting that her "Jimmy" story was a fabrication.[78] Executive editor Ben Bradlee acknowledged: "The credibility of a newspaper is its most precious asset. When that integrity is questioned and found wanting, the wounds are grievous."[79] In its contrite *apologia*, the *Post* took a hard look at itself and the news media in general: "How could this have happened? What does it say . . . about the reliability of other stories?"[80]

One of the most intriguing American literary frauds of the 20th Century was *The Autobiography of Howard Hughes*. In 1971, publishing giant McGraw-Hill announced the purchase of Hughes' memoirs, as narrated to writer Clifford Irving. Irving had produced a stack of personal correspondence from the legendary billionaire recluse in which Hughes expressed his approval for the project. On that basis, H.R. Hughes was paid an advance of $750,000 for what was considered the publishing coup of the century. Hughes, after all, had built Trans-World Airlines, had himself set many speed records as a pilot, had been awarded a rare Presidential Medal of Honor, had run a major movie studio, had owned virtually every big hotel-casino in Las Vegas, had been linked romantically with some of the most glamorous women in the world, and—if all that were not enough—he was widely believed to be insane. The finished product was a detailed first-person account of Hughes' extraordinary business career, as well as his remarkable personal escapades. The problem was that Hughes had not dictated his life story, had never met Irving, and had not even known of the book until McGraw-Hill's announcement. Irving, a meticulous researcher, had created a fantastic literary hoax. He had endorsed the publisher's checks by forging "H.R. Hughes," and his wife had deposited them in a Swiss bank under the name Helga Renate Hughes. The fraud was exposed dramatically when Hughes, who had not been seen or heard in public in years, held a press conference (via speaker phone) to denounce the mendacious memoirs. Many observers still doubt that the vigorous and rational-sounding voice on the speaker was actually Howard Hughes. They believe it was more likely an imposter hired by Hughes or his business associates to expose Irving's brazen hoax.

Clifford Irving was convicted of grand larceny in federal court and was sentenced to 2 1/2 years' imprisonment.[81] Although Irving became a successful novelist after his parole, his fictional masterpiece, *The Autobiography of Howard Hughes*, has never been published.[82]

In 1999, Lawrence X. Cusack III was sentenced to six to eight years in prison for forging love letters between President John F. Kennedy and movie star Marilyn Monroe. Cusack had cheated investors out of nearly $7 million between 1993 and 1997 by selling documents bearing Kennedy's forged signature. The judge excoriated Cusack for his "nearly sociopathic disregard for the impact his actions would have on others."[83]

The biggest selling book in the United States in 2005 (1.17 million copies) was *A Million Little Pieces*, author James Frey's nonfiction memoir of his grimy past as a drug addict, alcoholic, and career criminal.[84] The book originally had been released in hardcover in 2003 to modest interest; but the paperback edition released two years later skyrocketed to the top of the *New York Times* Best Seller List and remained there for a 15 weeks. Most of its remarkable sales were generated from its selection by media mogul Oprah Winfrey for her powerful book club. Previously, Winfrey had chosen as her featured selections safe "classic" novels by such mainstream literary figures as William Faulkner, John Steinbeck, Pearl Buck, and Leo Tolstoy.[85] In sharp contrast, on her October 26, 2005, television program titled "The Man Who Kept Oprah Awake at Night," Winfrey hailed *A Million Little Pieces* as "like nothing you've ever read before."[86] Her passionate and weepy endorsement turned a vulgar 430-page memoir into a publishing phenomenon almost literally overnight.

But skyrockets have a way of crashing back to earth. In January, 2006, the *Smoking Gun* investigative Website revealed that the juiciest part of Frey's "nonfiction" was fiction—"wholly fabricated or wildly embellished details of his purported criminal career, jail terms, and status as an outlaw 'wanted in three states.'"[87] Frey had taken a book he once reportedly had tried to peddle as fiction, a book that devoted entire repulsive paragraphs to the viscosity of his own vomit, and re-packaged it as a true story. When opportunity came knocking, its name was Oprah.

After the *Smoking Gun* expose', Winfrey initially stood by Frey, then later angrily denounced him on national television. Frey reluctantly added a three-page foreword to his book, in which he acknowledged that he had fabricated important details. Frey appears to have landed on his feet. The editor in chief of *Publishers Weekly* called Frey's admission a "novel approach" to a memoir:

> "He told a fish story, and it got bigger and bigger . . . He's been flogged in the public court of Oprah and he's repented, and he will come back. It's a great scenario that Americans love."[88]

Love and Consequences, the gripping autobiography of Margaret B. Jones, received critical raves in 2008. Jones was a half-white, half-Native American young woman, who grew up in a foster home in gang-infested South Central Los Angeles and once sold drugs for the Bloods street gang. Or did she? The problem was that Margaret B. Jones never existed. She was a figment of the imagination of Margaret Seltzer, a 33-year-old white woman, who grew up with her biological family in California's affluent San Fernando Valley, graduated from an exclusive private school, and never ran drugs for any gang.[89] Seltzer was unmasked when her older sister read a profile of "Jones" in the *New York Times*, accompanied by a photograph. She notified the publisher, Riverhead Books, that the supposed memoir was a fraud. Riverhead recalled *Love and Consequences* and canceled a scheduled book tour.[90]

In late 2008, the publishing industry had yet another "here we go again" moment when Berkley Books announced the cancellation of Herman Rosenblat's World War II memoir *Angel at the Fence* a week before its scheduled publication. Rosenblat, a 79-year-old Holocaust survivor, had written the touching story of how he had met his wife while he was a prisoner in the infamous Buchenwald concentration camp. According to Rosenblat's account, his future wife Roma lived nearby with her family pretending to be Christians. They would meet at opposite sides of a barbed wire fence, and she would sneak him food to help him survive. They lost touch when he was moved to another camp, but, remarkably, they met again on a blind date in New York in the 1950s and later married.[91]

While historical records attest that Rosenblat was confined at Buchenwald, Holocaust scholars, familiar with the physical layout there, insisted that his story made no sense.[92] Rosenblat finally admitted that he had embellished his memoir. Another publisher, Lerner, had to pull a children's book titled *Angel Girl*, based on Rosenblat's discredited story.[93]

Like James Frey's fake memoirs, *Angel at the Fence* had been endorsed unwittingly by Oprah Winfrey.[94] Once again, Oprah's Book Club had become Oprah's Liar's Club.

RELIGION

When Dick Clark became the focus of the payola investigation in 1960, one of his most vigorous defenders was pop singer Bobby Darin, who said of Clark: "He is as innocent of doing harm as any clergyman I know."[95] Although Darin surely did not intend to be facetious, his "clergyman" analogy may not have been the best way to verify Clark's integrity—as we shall see next, when we examine another battered cultural institution: religion.

Religion is one of the most fundamental cultural institutions. It arose from man's perception of a power outside himself, which provides moral constraint, behavioral reinforcement, and attitudinal support. To the great sociologist, Emile Durkheim, religion is society's consciousness of itself.[96] Religion helps to hold a society together, "enabling both the group and the individual to cope with the problems of everyday life."[97] Because faith is, by definition, the very essence of religion, an erosion of public trust probably damages religion more than most other social institutions. Betrayals of faith seem to be occurring with alarming regularity in the United States, which has experienced a series of highly publicized white-collar crimes involving religious figures since the 1980s.

A shocking 2006 survey conducted by researchers at Villanova University reported that *85 percent* of the 60 Roman Catholic dioceses responding had discovered embezzlement of church funds over a five-year period—with 11 percent reporting that more than $500,000 had been stolen.[98]

Recent examples of peculating priests and pilfering parishioners abound:

- Brian Lisowski, the former pastor of a Chicago Roman Catholic Church, pleaded guilty in 2005 to stealing $1.6 million from his parish between 1999 and 2004. He made full restitution and was sentenced to four years in prison. Lisowski had resigned in 2004 after the police found him with a prostitute.[99] Lisowski's embezzlement was discovered when collections went up dramatically after he left.[100] He had secretly installed a safe in a bedroom wall of the church's rectory, separate from the actual church safe, and skimmed $2,500 to $3,000 a week from collections, raffles, and wedding and funeral donations. Lisowski deposited nearly $450,000 into several personal bank accounts and put nearly $400,000 in hundred-dollar bills in a safe deposit box. He also gave $262,000 to what prosecutors called a "close female friend."[101]

- In 2006, Monsignor John Woolsey, one of the pillars of the New York Archdiocese, was sentenced to four years in prison for stealing more than $800,000 from his affluent Upper East Side parish. He had used the money "to finance a lifestyle more in keeping with that of a corporate CEO, including golf outings, the purchase of expensive watches, and cosmetic dental work."[102]

- Also in 2006, Joseph DeRusso, a former buyer for the Archdiocese of New York, admitted in federal court that he embezzled more than $1 million by diverting funds earmarked to buy food for parochial school children to companies he secretly controlled.[103] In another scheme, DeRusso took more than $1.2 million in kickbacks from vendors.[104]

- Two Irish-born priests from a church in Delray Beach, Florida, embezzled $8.6 million from their parishioners over a 42-year period ending in 2006.[105] One of the priests, 79-year-old Father John Skehan, admitted that he had never deposited one cent from the church collection plate into a church bank account. The cash was all pocketed and put into slush funds. The priests spent the money on vacation homes, luxury travel, gambling in Las Vegas casinos (where they were treated as "high rollers"), and on secret girlfriends.[106] Skehan told police that he saw himself as the CEO of a multimillion dollar company who wasn't properly compensated.[107] In March of 2009, Skehan was sentenced to 14 months in prison. After serving 12 months, Skehan was released and put on probation. Though actively barred from serving in the ministry, he will still receive a pension from the diocese.[108]

- When Father Rodney Lee Rodis arrived in Louisa County, Virginia, in 1993 as a substitute priest, the local congregation was divided and attendance was at an all-time low. But Rodis, a native of the Philippines standing barely five feet tall, was a charismatic cleric. He united his parishioners and built the rolls of his two churches up to 360 families. He also raised hundreds of thousands of dollars for improvements.[109] He retired in 2006 at age 50, citing poor health. His grateful congregations held a fundraiser for him and raised $27,000.[110] But in 2007, the retired priest stunned his former flock when he was arrested for bilking his churches out of hundreds of thousands of dollars. Between 2002 and 2006, Father Rodis embezzled between $600,000 and $700,000 by instructing his parishioners to mail contributions to a post office box that he controlled. He would then transfer the money to a personal bank account.[111] Most shocking of all was the revelation that Rodney Rodis had been living a double life. His parishioners naturally assumed that Rodis lived in the rectory next to the church where he counseled them, married them, and heard their confessions. In fact, he was living a secular life in a suburban home in neighboring Spotsylvania County—with his wife and three children![112] One of his former congregants summed up the parish's bitter sense of betrayal in the wake of the scandal: "I still have my faith in God, but it has shaken my faith in humanity."[113] In October 2008, the jury for Rodis' case recommended a sentence of 200 years, which was later reduced to 13 years by the judge.[114] The prison term was to be served consecutively with another 5-year sentence given to Rodis for mail and wire fraud, and money laundering. He was also ordered to pay $432,000 in restitution.[115]

- Father Michael Jude Fay, a 56-year-old Roman Catholic priest with a taste for high living, pleaded guilty in 2007 to federal charges of defrauding his Darien, Connecticut, parishioners out of nearly $1 million between 1999 and 2006, when he was forced to resign.[116] Father Fay had secretly opened two bank accounts, into which he deposited $980,000 in church funds. He used the funds for lavish personal expenses, including trips he took to Europe, the Caribbean, and Las Vegas,[117] accompanied by a man with whom he shared a clandestine romantic relationship.[118] He also misappropriated church money for other luxuries like limousine rides, upscale parties, expensive jewelry—even blond highlights for his hair.[119] Fay was sentenced to 37 months in prison. The judge rejected calls from Fay's supporters for an alternative sentence. She declared sternly: "A sentence of probation would be impunity for a crime of enormity."[120]

- Elizabeth Fields was found guilty in 2007 of stealing over $9,000 from her Bath, Pennsylvania, church's Sunday collections.[121] Fields had been secretly videotaped in the parish rectory as she altered the collection tally sheets so the money she swiped would not appear as a shortfall.[122] At the time, she was the city's mayor.

- Joseph Smith, the former chief financial officer of the Cleveland Diocese, was convicted in 2008 of federal tax fraud and of looting church funds. Smith's assistant, Anton Zgoznick (who was convicted in 2007 in a separate trial), had set up secret accounts to pay Smith kickbacks totaling $785,000 in return for contracts worth $17.5 million.[123] Smith, an attorney and CPA, also embezzled money from the Catholic Cemeteries Association.[124] Joseph Smith was sentenced to a year and a day in prison.[125]

- In the 1960s there were the Singing Nun and the Flying Nun. In 2006, Sister Barbara Markey became the Stealing Nun. Markey was a clinical psychologist with an international reputation, a renowned speaker, and the co-author of a popular marriage preparation program for the Catholic Church.[126] She had served as the director of the Archdiocese of Omaha's Catholic Family Life Office until she was fired after an audit turned up financial irregularities.[127] Archdiocese officials accused Markey of embezzling as much as $800,000.[128] In 2008, Barbara Markey was sentenced to three-to-five years in prison and ordered to pay $125,000 in restitution.[129] The 73-year-old nun admitted to losing most of the money at casinos.[130] She also spent $31,000 on clothing.[131] Evidently, Sister Markey had an expensive gambling "habit."

In 2007 alone, there were more than 20 Roman Catholic churches in 17 states dealing with embezzlement cases.[132] Just as the Catholic Church in the U.S. was beginning to recover from the sordid sexual abuse and molestation scandals of recent years, it appears to have entered a new kind of moral crisis. The increasing number of Catholic clergy getting caught with their hands in the collection baskets has prompted questions about priestly arrogance. The accountant for the afore mentioned Delray Beach, Florida, church, from which nearly $9 million had been embezzled by two older priests, notes that some priests still carry "an Old-World attitude that what's in the collection basket is theirs personally to do with as they wish."[133]

Other analysts have suggested that some priests resent seeing how comparatively well their Episcopal or Jewish counterparts live, in contrast to their own parsimonious and celibate lifestyles.[134]

Whatever the reason for the embezzlement scandals, the solution no doubt rests in better financial controls. Embezzlement is a plague afflicting almost all nonprofit organizations, given their typically lax accounting practices. The operator of a watchdog site, *Churchsecurity. info* notes that America's 19,000 Roman Catholic churches, which gather about $6 billion a year from parishioners, "are still often medieval in the way they secure or don't secure Sunday collections."[135] The executive director of a Roman Catholic church management roundtable insists: "It is true that the church is not a company . . . but it is comprised of people, finances, and facilities. Catholic theology demands that those are managed well—and not just well, but to the highest, exemplary degrees of stewardship."[136]

To thwart embezzlement, parishes and dioceses clearly need to be more vigilant, more transparent in the way they handle money and more accountable for what happens to it.[137] "They need rigorous systems of internal controls—ways to make sure everything is accounted for."[138] The co-author of the Villanova study, mentioned earlier, says that "parish-finance councils—which are required by canon law but are too often as ornamental as stained glass—'have to stop acting like rubber stamps for priests.'"[139]

Clerical enrichment is, however, not an exclusively Catholic problem. As we shall see, Protestant denominations have been victimized as well. And Protestant televangelists and faith healers, who are even less transparent and accountable than their Catholic counterparts, have committed some huge financial crimes.

CASE STUDY
"Lyin'" Henry Lyons

The National Baptist Convention, USA, one of the largest and most influential African-American Protestant denominations, with nearly one million members, was rocked in 1999 by the conviction of its president Henry J. Lyons. Rev. Lyons, once an advisor to President Clinton on racial policies, was found guilty in a Florida criminal court of swindling millions of dollars from companies that sought to do business with his followers and grand theft in the disappearance of almost $250,000 from the Anti-Defamation League of B'nai Brith (a large national Jewish organization)—money donated to help re-build firebombed Black churches in the South.[140]

Lyons stole more than $4 million from corporations that wanted to sell everything from cemetery plots to insurance policies to credit cards to the church's members. He duped these companies by promising them access to nonexistent membership mailing lists. Lyons created his phony lists using a computerized telephone directory. The Loewen Group, the world's second-largest funeral home company, was the biggest victim, shelling out nearly $3 million. Another company, Globe Life Insurance, paid Lyons $1 million for a fabricated list. The company realized it had been duped when it received a complaint from a Grand Dragon of the Ku Klux Klan, who had received a sales letter from Globe with Lyons' endorsement.[141]

Lyons diverted the money to a secret bank account and used it to support an opulent lifestyle for himself and his mistress. He purchased a waterfront home, a 20-carat diamond (said to be "the size of a dime"), two Mercedes automobiles and a Rolls-Royce.[142] Lyons' problems began when his wife, allegedly in a jealous rage, set fire to the $700,000 home he owned with his mistress. The fire led to closer scrutiny of his lavish finances.[143]

Lyons' attorneys argued that "the personal use of church money is the way that black churches in the U.S. 'do business.'"[144] It is difficult to determine how much of this assertion is neutralizing rhetoric and how much is a statement of fact. It is noteworthy, however, that most of the leaders of the National Baptist Convention, USA, as well as many of its rank and file members stood firmly behind Rev. Lyons. The pastor of an affiliated Houston church portrayed Lyons as the *victim*—a victim of having too much power and too little accountability. "What Dr. Lyons did is what many of us would have done if given the same opportunities and the same almost unlimited access to money and power."[145]

A sobbing Henry J. Lyons pleaded for mercy as he was sentenced to 5 1/2 years in prison and was ordered to repay $2.5 million. He belabored the obvious when he told the presiding judge: "I cannot shake the feeling that I have let so many people down."[146] He apologized tearfully for the theft of the B'nai Brith money intended to restore burned churches: "It stinks in God's nostrils and I know it stinks in the law's nostrils and it stinks to me."[147] The judge's reply was terse: "It's time to pay the piper, Dr. Lyons."[148]

Some recent embezzlement cases involving other American churches and synagogues include the following:

- In 2005, the former pastor of the Morning Star Missionary Baptist Church in Queens, New York, admitted to embezzling over $30,000 for his own use. The Rev. Charles Betts, 68, had led the congregation for over three decades. The Queens District Attorney declared: "[His] conduct represents a gross betrayal of trust of his parishioners who looked to him for spiritual guidance and moral leadership."[149]

- The Presbyterian Church USA, based in Louisville, Kentucky, fired its second-ranking finance officer in 2006 after she admitted embezzling more than $130,000.[150] A routine audit revealed that Judy Golliher had diverted most of the funds into her personal bank account. She had stolen the rest of the money through cash advances on the church's credit card.[151] In 2007, Golliher was sentenced to probation after pleading guilty. She avoided prison by making full restitution.[152]

- In 2002, Doina Stanescu, a former bookkeeper at Temple Menorah in Redondo Beach, California, was arrested on charges that she embezzled nearly $100,000 from the synagogue. Stanescu, who was an employee and not a member of the congregation, had been beset by desperate financial problems for years. Not long after she started working at Temple Menorah, she went to the synagogue's computer and began printing checks made out in her name. She forged the signatures of her supervisors.[153] When she finally turned herself in, after first threatening suicide, she claimed she had sent the money to Romania to help pay for her ailing father's medical expenses. While police were unable to verify this story, they did discover that she had been making steady trips to Las Vegas casinos. Stanescu was sentenced to one year in county jail.[154]

- Matthew Beise, the former treasurer for the Cross Evangelical Lutheran Church of Rockford, Minnesota, was sentenced to 14 years in prison in 2008 for stealing $266,000 from the church, which he used to buy luxury items and child pornography. There was nothing high-tech about Beise's embezzlement. He simply deposited church money into his personal bank account.[155]

CASE STUDY
The Devil Made Him Do It

Many of the religious embezzlement cases we've examined have shared fundamental similarities. A few have been more unusual, even surprising. But, occasionally, a case will be so audacious that it is jaw-dropping.[156] This would surely apply to Randall Radic, former pastor of the First Congregational Church in the small city of Ripon, California. Radic did not merely steal *from* his church. He stole his *church*.

Radic had been the local pastor for nearly 10 years, preaching to a congregation comprised mostly of senior citizens in the 80s and 90s—some close to 100.[157] He had a good reputation, and members of his church loved his sermons. They felt lucky to have such a man as their spiritual leader.

Radic's faithful flock even provided him with a house free of charge. Unfortunately, Randall Radic was a complete crook and took advantage of his church's trust and generosity. He prepared fraudulent documents that appeared to give him title to the parsonage. He used church property as collateral to take out $200,000 in personal loans. He followed this up by forging papers that gave him the power to sell the nearly 100-year-old church building—which he did. His buyers, a husband and wife team of real estate investors, paid him $525,000 for the church, which they planned

(*Continued*)

to convert into offices.[158] The first thing he did with the money was run out and buy a brand new BMW for $102,000.[159]

The church's former choir director recalled: "We didn't know anything about it until the bank called us and said he bought a BMW."[160] Actually, all he had to do was look out the window. "Surprisingly, the pastor did not hide the vehicle; rather Radic and his fiancée—his eighth—brazenly drove it around town."[161]

After investigators began making inquiries, Radic fled to Denver. When prosecutors coaxed him back in 2005, he was arrested.[162] About $500,000 of the $700,000 Radic illegally obtained was eventually recovered. The rest is long gone and hard to find.

Randall Radic spent six months in jail awaiting trial. Ever the opportunist and facing serious prison time, he offered a deal with prosecutors. If they would agree to drop all but one charge, he would agree to snitch on a fellow jail inmate in an upcom-

ing death penalty trial.[163] The prosecutors took the deal. Radic was released and would serve no more time. As he awaited sentencing from the comfort of his home, he began blogging on the Internet. In a flippant, almost gleeful, tone, he wrote about his double life as a sinner—and even tried to peddle his story as a tell-all book he titled *Snitch*.[164]

I need an agent, so I can get an advance, so I can eat and finish my book. . . . Can you do anything to succor a former Old Catholic Priest gone wrong? Who simply embezzled, but HAS learned his lesson (the hard way), having been incarcerated with pedophiles, murderers and gangbangers.[165]

Snitch, retitled *A Priest in Hell: Gangs, Murderers and Snitching in a California Jail*, was published in 2009.[166] Randall Radic's first jailhouse memoir, *The Sound of Meat*, was published in 2008. It was billed as a "(fairly) truthful memoir."[167]

PHONY FAITH HEALERS

Another way in which white-collar crime has insinuated itself into the religious arena is through the practice of fraudulent faith healing.[168] Faith healing is probably as old as religion itself. The traditional Christian notion that certain people can heal sickness by means of special divine gifts is derived from the New Testament.[169] The present-day American belief in this practice originated in Indiana in the 1940s with the Reverend William Branham, a former game warden whose fire-and-brimstone tent revivals included "miraculous" cures. "Branham was so convincing a preacher that, when he died in a 1965 automobile accident, he wasn't buried for four months because his flock expected him to rise from the dead at Easter. He didn't."[170]

Branham's success inspired dozens of imitators, and traveling tent revivals began crisscrossing the country, spreading the gospel and passing the collection plate. Some religious entrepreneurs, such as Oral Roberts and Rex Humbard, discovered the enormous potential of radio to enlarge their congregations. Later, the popularization of television in the 1950s made media stars out of some preachers and turned faith healing into a multimillion dollar industry.

One of those early stars was A. A. Allen, who founded his own community of Miracle Valley, Arizona, in 1958. From there Allen broadcast a daily one-hour radio program to 58 stations across the United States and several other countries, and a weekly television program to 43 states. Miracle Valley also contained a private airstrip, a 3,000 seat church, a recording studio, a publishing plant, and a "telephone prayer center." Allen's ministry soon was generating revenues of nearly $4 million a year.[171]

Like many faith healers, Allen had a life history at odds with his pious stage persona:

A. A. Allen began his career as a minister of the Assemblies of God in his twenties. He worked at it successfully until 1955, when he jumped bail on a drunken driving charge and was defrocked . . . In typical fashion, he immediately re-ordained himself and started up his big moneymaker, the Miracle Revival Fellowship. He went "under canvas" and began touring with his big tent show.[172]

When Allen discovered radio and television, he abandoned his tent shows and switched to the electronic media. Allen had a galvanizing stage presence. *Look* magazine praised his "purity" and "nobility."[173] Nevertheless, Allen's ascribed virtues did not prevent him from resorting to the shabbiest sorts of fraud. He peddled jars of water and containers of dirt from Miracle Valley over the airwaves, claiming these products could heal the afflicted. Allen himself eventually joined the ranks of the afflicted and died in 1970 of liver disease brought on by acute alcoholism.[174]

CASE STUDY
Peter Popoff

The most dramatic exposé of fraudulent faith healing occurred in 1986 and involved the Reverend Peter Popoff and his Miracle and Blessing Crusade, which was aired at that time on over fifty television stations in the United States.[175] The Bulgarian-born Popoff[176] and his California-based organization reportedly had a computerized mailing list containing the names of over 100,000 contributors, who were solicited for donations relentlessly every two weeks.[177]

In 1986, he *admitted* to an operating cost of $550,000 a month; his actual grossed income can only be guessed. Because Popoff—like all evangelists—is not required by any government agency to account to anyone for any of the money that is taken in, except whatever he decides to pay himself as personal income, it is difficult to know just how much is collected.[178]

Popoff's written appeals for money were masterfully created to convey a sense of dire urgency. For example, one elderly woman sent Popoff her entire life savings of $21,000 for a bizarre plan to float Russian Bibles into the Soviet Union attached to balloons. Popoff's proposed airlift—which was of course physically impossible (as well as a violation of international law)—reportedly generated a wave of contributions so immense that it arrived daily in 100-pound mail sacks. It also has been reported that these donations yielded only "three-hundred ordinary party balloons and two small tanks of helium."[179]

Another outrageous scheme involved sending out plastic shower caps to Popoff's mailing list. Each of these cheap items was represented as a "Holy Shower Cap." Recipients were instructed to wear the cap once, then wrap it around a check or some cash and send it back to Popoff. Reportedly, a single mailing of "Holy Shower Caps" netted $100,000 in contributions—which, incredibly, was considered a failure by Popoff's usual standards.[180]

Popoff's reputation among his followers was built on his purported healing ability. Faith healers are a prime target of James Randi ("The Amazing Randi"), a veteran magician who has emerged over the years as America's foremost debunker of paranormal claims. By the mid-1980s, Popoff had moved to the top of Randi's "hit list." At a

(Continued)

1986 news conference, Randi issued an angry denouncement:

> He excoriated Popoff for urging people to throw their pills up on stage during crusades. Although Popoff later insisted he wanted only illegal drugs discarded, Randi reported finding diabetes medication, nitroglycerine tablets, and digitalis prescriptions among the litter on Popoff's stage.[181]

The Popoff-Randi showdown occurred in a Detroit auditorium in April, 1986. Randi and a group of allies had prepared a trap for the greedy charlatan. Among those confederates was Don Henvick, who had been following the Popoff crusade around for months. Donning disguises, he already had been "cured" twice by Popoff— of alcoholism in San Francisco and arthritis in Anaheim, California.

This time the 38-year-old, 260 pound mailman posed as a woman suffering from uterine cancer—a notion so absurd that Popoff could not possibly be fooled if he was receiving messages from God.[182]

One of Popoff's most impressive feats was his apparent ability to run around a revival hall and quickly call out the names of afflicted persons, along with their respective afflictions.[183] This was an old mentalist's trick that Randi had recognized at a previous Popoff revival in Houston. Popoff's wife, Elizabeth, toured the audience before the service engaging members in seemingly casual conversation—which was carried backstage to her husband by a radio transmitter hidden in her oversized purse. Popoff would transcribe all the relevant information.

> When the evangelist later made his rounds of the audience, he had in his left ear a hidden miniature receiver that enabled Elizabeth, now backstage, to direct him to those members of the audience she had already pumped for information.[184]

Earlier, Randi had elicited the help of an electronics expert, who identified the frequency of the signal that was broadcast by Elizabeth Popoff to her husband. That evening, Randi placed eavesdropping equipment in a trash bag by some bushes next to the trailer where Mrs. Popoff was seated in front of a microphone and a bank of closed-circuit monitors. She was relaying information to her husband inside the auditorium.[185] Throughout the afternoon, Mrs. Popoff secretly was taped while she transmitted names, addresses, and diseases, mixed with snide comments about audience members, such as, "Oh, look at that butt."[186]

When "Bernice Manicoff," AKA Don Henvick, arrived at the auditorium, "she" was escorted to a wheelchair and placed in it by one of Popoff's employees. As planned, Henvick said he (she) was suffering from uterine cancer. Midway through the revival, Popoff approached Henvick, while receiving a radio message from his wife:

> There's one there, looks like she has a beard. Her name is Bernice Manicoff. The doctors think she has cancer of the uterus.[187]

Popoff placed his hands on "Bernice," and went into his act:

> Dr. Jesus is going to burn all those cancer cells out of your body . . . I tell you, you're going to feel new strength. It's going to surge through you—THERE IT IS![188]

Suddenly, back in the control room, Elizabeth Popoff recognized Henvick and panicked:

> That's not a woman. . . . Hey, isn't that the guy who was in Anaheim? Pete, that's the man who was in Anaheim you said had arthritis. . . . Get rid of him.[189]

A short time later, Randi appeared on the *Tonight Show* television program and played a video taped segment of Popoff's performance

(Continued)

overlaid with an audio track of Mrs. Popoff's transmissions. The studio audience was flabbergasted, and even host Johnny Carson was visibly shocked at such blatant fakery. As a result of this exposure, donations to Popoff's ministry fell so sharply that he soon declared bankruptcy.[190]

Some persons perhaps are persuaded to ridicule Popoff's flock as gullible fools, all but asking to be bilked. This, however, would be an overly harsh and shortsighted judgment. Swindlers, masquerading as respectable clergy, prey on desperate, vulnerable people. Many of their victims no doubt are gravely ill; most are prompted by a devout religious faith. It is difficult to find a suitable word to characterize phony faith healers—"contemptible" hardly seems adequate.

THE TELEVANGELISTS

Another category of religious crime—the one that probably has received the most public attention in recent years—is the misappropriation of funds by televangelists. Religious broadcasting has been part of American culture since the invention of electronic media. For example, radio provided an effective vehicle for the flamboyant revivalist Aimee Semple McPherson in the 1920s[191] and the vituperative priest Charles E. Coughlin in the 1930s.[192] Over the decades, religious broadcasters periodically have generated controversy as they have used the airwaves to transmit unorthodox spiritual and political messages.

When television eclipsed radio, evangelists, perhaps due to their tradition of theatricality, seemed to have little trouble making the transition. The real turning point, however, came with the introduction of satellite broadcasting and cable reception, which spurred an unprecedented growth of religious television. From the late 1960s through the early 1980s, the average number of Americans viewing religious television programs soared from 5 million to 25 million.[193] "The ancillary projects of the televangelists, including cathedrals, colleges and universities, religious theme parks, and total-living communities, also grew at a phenomenal rate."[194]

As the audiences grew, so too did the revenues. By 1986, the most successful televangelists were presiding over financial empires. Pat Robertson, who would run for President of the United States in 1988, was earning a reported $183 million annually from his Virginia-based Christian Broadcasting Network (CBN) and from contributions to his daily *700 Club* program. In fact, Robertson agreed in 1998, after a 10-year legal battle, to pay what was termed a "significant" fine to the Internal Revenue Service for using CBN money to finance his presidential campaign. The network also agreed to accept retroactive loss of tax-exempt status for 1986 and 1987.[195]

In Tulsa, Oklahoma, Oral Roberts was overseeing a $500 million complex, containing Oral Roberts University and the City of Faith Hospital. Roberts' annual budget was about $120 million, most of it raised through donations.

In Garden Grove, California, Robert Schuller was syndicating his weekly *Hour of Power* broadcast from his $20 million Crystal Cathedral. Schuller's contributions were reported at about $42 million a year.

Jerry Falwell's Virginia ministry, including Liberty University and a 22,000-member church, was generating about $84 million annually, mainly from contributions solicited on Falwell's 1.5 million-subscriber cable television system.

And in Baton Rouge, Louisiana, singer-turned-preacher Jimmy Swaggart was raking in an estimated $142 million a year from his daily and weekly television programs, Bible college, and elaborate tours.[196]

Although most of these televangelists were earning salaries that could have been considered modest, relative to the size of their respective operations (e.g., Robertson, $60,000; Schuller, $80,000; Swaggart, $86,000; Falwell, $100,000),[197] their opulent lifestyles seemed far in excess of their reported personal incomes.

One of the most conspicuous salary-lifestyle discrepancies belonged to Jimmy Swaggart. A 1987 *Time* article analyzed Swaggart's personal finances:

> In 1985, the Swaggarts borrowed $2 million from the ministry to build three luxurious homes in a wealthy Baton Rouge subdivision. They have the use of a $250,000 ministry "retreat" in California and say that such luxury items as twin Lincoln Town Cars and handsomely furnished offices come from donors.[198]

Also in 1987, some of his former associates charged that Swaggart had raised $20 million for a children's fund, but had spent less than 10 percent on needy children.

Swaggart, whose spellbinding oratory usually featured harangues against sexual immorality, was disgraced in 1988, when stories of his own moral turpitude were reported by the press. He was forced to admit long-standing obsessions with prostitutes, voyeurism, and pornography. Before millions of riveted television viewers, he verbally fell on his sword with a tearful, histrionic apology, delivered in his inimitable style. Swaggart's flock, however, so conditioned by his intolerant tirades against Catholics, Jews, secular humanists, mental health professionals, intellectuals, liberals, gays, and so many other species of social scapegoats, were ill-disposed to forgive sin—even their shepherd's. Swaggart was dismissed from his Assemblies of God denomination and expelled from the National Religious Broadcasters association.[199] Although he quickly established his own denomination and continued to preach and plead for money, his tempestuous sermons virtually disappeared from the airwaves.

CASE STUDY
The PTL Club—Praise The Lord and Pass The Loot

The most sensational of the televangelist scandals involved the PTL (Praise The Lord) ministry led by the husband-and-wife team of Jim and Tammy Faye Bakker. Like Jimmy Swaggart, the Bakkers were members of the Assemblies of God denomination, a Pentecostal sect holding evangelical or fundamentalist views and stressing miraculous "gifts," such as prophecy and glossolalia (speaking in tongues).[200] Also like Swaggart, the Bakkers would become very rich.

After several years as traveling revivalists, the Bakkers had entered the public spotlight in 1965, when they were invited to join Pat Robertson's Christian Broadcasting Network. Jim Bakker proved to be a gifted preacher, and he was soon doing a morning radio program and hosting the *700 Club* at night.

Jim Bakker reportedly became angered when he was told by CBN management that he would receive no salary while he was recuperating at home from what Tammy Faye called a "nervous breakdown." Bakker became anxious to leave Robertson's organization. In November, 1972, the two charismatics parted after a seven-year association.

A few months later, the Bakkers started the *Praise The Lord* show for Paul Crouch's Trinity Broadcasting Network in southern California.

(Continued)

By 1974, however, they were back on the traveling evangelical circuit. After six more months, they began a new television ministry in Charlotte, North Carolina. "From California, they brought with them the initials 'PTL'."[201] From the very beginning, the PTL ministry was characterized by questionable financial practices. This ignited a ferocious enmity between Bakker and the FCC that would continue for years to come.

By 1976, the PTL show was aired on seventy stations and twenty-eight cable systems in North America. Jim Bakker had built Heritage Village in Charlotte, and, on his 30th birthday in 1978, he broke ground for the new PTL complex in Fort Mill, South Carolina, 20 miles south of Charlotte:[202]

> By then Bakker had developed the habit of speaking less than truthfully about his financial operations. In the summer of 1978 he announced that Tammy and he had given "every penny" of their life savings to PTL. Only days later he made a $6,000 payment on a houseboat.[203]

The first major PTL scandal erupted in 1979, when it was reported that $350,000 raised by PTL for the stated purpose of upgrading its overseas television capacity had been diverted to pay bills at the Bakker home.[204] In 1982, three members of the FCC voted to prosecute Jim Bakker for using the airwaves to solicit funds fraudulently. They were barely overruled by a four-member majority, who opted for administrative sanctions.

For the Bakkers, 1984 would prove to be both the best and worst of times. The year began auspiciously, when Jim Bakker announced the formation of the Lifetime Partnership Plan, which sought to persuade a hundred thousand PTL supporters to donate at least $1,000 apiece in exchange for three free nights at the planned Heritage Grand Hotel every year of their lives.[205] In May, Bakker was commended by President Reagan for his efforts on behalf of a proposed School Prayer Amendment.[206]

At about the same time, however, a 21-year-old church secretary named Jessica Hahn began accusing Bakker and members of his inner circle of sexual misconduct.[207] Ms. Hahn eventually received a payment from PTL—reportedly $115,000.[208] Whether this was "hush money," as the press implied, or an out-of-court settlement for emotional trauma, as Hahn claimed, is a matter of opinion. It has been alleged, however, that Hahn's money was funneled through the building contractor at Heritage Park under the guise of construction invoices.[209] One British journalist offered a tongue-in-cheek suggestion that PTL now stood for "Pay The Lady."[210]

In November, 1985, Bakker was hit by a double-barreled assault. The IRS, which had been examining PTL's tax returns, threatened to revoke the ministry's tax-exempt status, because of the excessive pay and perquisites the Bakkers were receiving.[211] At the same time, the FCC released a 4,500 page report on its five-year investigation of PTL. Both these attacks encouraged closer media scrutiny, and, by the following year, the gaudy extravagance of the Bakkers was widely reported: forty-seven bank accounts,[212] six luxurious homes, complete with gold-plated bathroom fixtures,[213] a $1.9 million annual salary, a Rolls-Royce and a Mercedes-Benz, "and for the lacquered Tammy, a wardrobe worthy of Imelda Marcos."[214] Perhaps the most prodigal symbols of the Bakkers' conspicuous consumption were the $5,900 multistory playhouse constructed for the Bakker children[215] and the huge air-conditioned doghouse built for Tammy's Saint Bernard.[216]

As the negative publicity grew, PTL tried to lower its profile. In December, 1986, PTL withdrew from the Evangelical Council for Financial Responsibility. A few months later, Jim Bakker announced that he had "temporarily" entrusted his ministry to Jerry Falwell. By the end of April, 1987, however, Falwell publicly was vilifying Bakker as a liar, an embezzler, and a sexual deviant, declaring that Bakker would never return to PTL as long as he, Falwell, remained in charge.

(Continued)

To demonstrate his intentions, Falwell fired Bakker's entire inner circle. What may have begun as a rescue mission quickly had become a hostile takeover.[217]

Bakker reportedly was enraged. Falwell, after all, was a former ally. Furthermore, Falwell's ministry, *The Old Time Gospel Hour*, had itself been the target of allegations of misappropriation. A former Falwell employee recently had charged that the ministry had "raised more than $4 million in a 1979 appeal for Cambodian Refugees but had sent a mere $100,000 to aid the victims."[218]

Falwell announced that PTL was $72 million in debt and in imminent danger of shutting down. He emphasized that the greed of the Bakkers had driven PTL to the brink of bankruptcy.[219] When Falwell had taken over PTL, he had promised that one thing he would not do was "beg for money on the air."[220] Within two months, he was begging for money on the air.

In May, 1987, Jim Bakker was defrocked by the Assemblies of God for his self-confessed adultery and for alleged homosexual activity. A few weeks later, Bakker appeared on ABC-TV's *Nightline*, generating the highest ratings in the history of that program. He described Falwell as a thief who had stolen PTL from him. Asked about the large bonuses he and his wife had collected from PTL, Bakker acknowledged, "We should have said no."[221]

On September 21, 1987, a federal grand jury convened in Charlotte to hear testimony in a criminal investigation of Bakker and PTL. Two weeks later, "Falwell and his board of directors abruptly resigned."[222] Falwell's efforts to keep PTL afloat had failed. In a hyperbolic parting shot, Falwell contended that Bakker had created "probably the greatest scab and cancer on the face of Christianity in two thousand years of church history."[223]

Meanwhile, the Bakkers announced plans for a $2 billion religious retreat in California's Mojave Desert. "Nothing came of the plan. As the summer heat descended on the desert, the Bakkers moved back to Charlotte and into a house paid for by the Bring Bakker Back Club."[224]

In April, 1988, the bankruptcy court ordered the 2,300 acre Heritage U.S.A. put up for sale. Jim Bakker made a $172 million offer, but could not raise the $3 million down payment.[225] His proposed 26-city "Farewell for Now" tour had to be canceled because of slow ticket sales.[226] "The IRS told the court PTL could owe as much as $82 million in back taxes, depending on how much of the organization's operations are determined to be tax exempt."[227] In December, PTL's assets were sold to a Toronto real estate developer (ironically, an ordained rabbi) for $65 million.[228]

In December, 1988, the Federal Government handed down a 28-page indictment of Jim Bakker, including 24 counts of fraud and conspiracy. Bakker was charged with taking huge bonuses "out of the PTL trough."[229] He also was accused of vastly overselling his Lifetime Partnership Plan. "[S]ome 9,700 hapless 'partners' were offered the right to stay regularly in what turned out to be a single bunkhouse with 48 beds."[230]

Incredibly, Jim and Tammy Bakker returned to television on January 2, 1989—just three weeks after Jim's indictment—with an hour-long weekday program broadcast from the home of a wealthy Charlotte Amway distributor. The show was carried by only a handful of stations, and was soon taken off the air because of zoning restrictions against the use of a private home for television broadcasting. Time clearly was running out for the Bakkers and the peripatetic remains of their ministry.

In April 1989, they moved to Orlando, Florida. In May, they resumed their broadcast from a little-used shopping center. On June 1, 1989, the Bakkers learned that the IRS had filed a lien claiming the Bakkers owed $666,492 in back taxes for 1981 and $565,434 for 1982.[231]

(*Continued*)

Jim Bakker stood trial in February, 1989, and was convicted in Federal Court of fraudulently raising more than $158 million in contributions. Many observers within the legal community anticipated a short sentence or perhaps even probation. After all, the government had been investigating PTL seemingly forever, but had shown little inclination to press charges. Years earlier, Bakker had denied responsibility for a $13 million accounting discrepancy by suggesting that "the devil got into the computer."[232] Even then, the government had declined to prosecute.

However, the judge in Bakker's case was Robert Potter—known as "Maximum Bob" because of his penchant for stiff sentences. Potter handed Bakker a stunning 45-year prison term, declaring, "Those of us who do have a religion are sick of being saps for money-grubbing preachers and priests."[233] Although Bakker's sentence was later reduced to 18 years, it was still an unexpectedly severe punishment. Jim Bakker, who already had lost PTL and most of his personal wealth,

now had lost his freedom. Moreover, he would soon lose Tammy Faye. In 1992, the Bakkers were divorced,[234] and Tammy remarried while her ex-husband served his sentence. Jim Bakker was paroled in the summer of 1994. He returned to Charlotte—but not to his once-luxurious lifestyle. The preacher whose PTL ministry had collected over $150 million was released to a halfway house operated by the Salvation Army.[235]

Jim Bakker was far from the only loser, however. The final report of the court-appointed bankruptcy trustees overseeing the liquidation of Bakker's religious empire revealed that, while $40 million had been paid to PTL creditors, "the many thousands of small contributors whom Mr. Bakker defrauded got nothing."[236] After his release, Bakker announced that he planned to write inspirational books in order to help people who have suffered great personal losses in their lives. Perhaps he could start with his former contributors—although they would be well-advised to hold their wallets, rather than their breath.

The religious scandals of the 1980s have generated a number of effects. First, and most apparent, has been the decline of the teleministries. Long gone, of course, are the days when the Bakkers could draw 6,000 ardent followers at their Heritage U.S.A. services. In 1991, the remnants of the Praise The Lord Club had been reduced to some leased space in an industrial complex on the outskirts of Fort Mill. On a "good" Sunday, PTL would attract perhaps 150 worshippers. Notably absent were any television cameras. The Jim and Tammy show, which once reached millions of viewers each day, had become a fading memory.

Jimmy Swaggart lost over 80 percent of his former audience of 2.2 million viewers.[237] Oral Roberts, who created a furor in 1987 when he threatened that God would kill him if he did not raise $4.5 million, reportedly lost half his viewers along with half his former revenues.[238] Jerry Falwell's television ministry was downsized substantially as well. By the 1990s, his *Old Time Gospel Hour* was carried on few stations.[239]

A second consequence of the religious scandals is the damage inflicted on those electronic ministries not directly tainted by ecclesiastic crimes. An editorial in *Christianity Today*, an evangelical journal, laments this "bad apple" effect: "[Q]uestions about one minister's morals impute suspicions to others."[240] A time-series study reports that the percentage of people attributing trustworthiness to *all* televangelists as a group "fell from 41 percent in 1980 to 23 percent in 1987 (after the first scandals broke), to 16 percent in 1989 near the end of the disclosures."[241] The major exception appears to be Billy Graham, whose occasional prime-time crusades still garner high television ratings. Graham's viewership remains at record levels, suggesting the continuing presence of "a faithful group of hard-core viewers whose donations are shifting but not declining."[242] Graham's revenues are especially impressive, given that his crusades are "notable in their lack of appeals for money."[243]

A third effect is an overall weakening of organized religion. Another *Christianity Today* editorial decries the legacy of what it terms "religious hucksters" and notes that "when prominent representatives of the faith are discredited . . . all Christians suffer."[244] Indeed, overall church membership declined in 1988, after the PTL scandal.[245] Pharmacists now rate higher than ministers in polls of occupational esteem.[246] A more subtle problem also has been detected. In the wake of the scandals, the core mission of televangelism—the winning of converts—seems to have been lost. Surveys of viewers report that almost all are already believers; studies of recent converts reveal that less than 1 percent became Christians through a televised ministry.[247] This suggests that televangelists—even those with untarnished reputations—may now simply be "preaching to the choir." As the dean of one Baptist seminary observed in 1992:

> "Televangelism is no longer the 'anointed method' it was in the 1970s and early 1980s. People on both sides of the camera have lost confidence in it. Its prime time has passed."[248]

RELIGIOUS AFFINITY SCAMS

Yet another likely effect of the ecclesiastical scandals is that the enormous sums of cash generated by conniving televangelists undoubtedly attracted the attention of more secular crooks. Like jackals drawn by the stench of rotting carrion, con artists are always lured by the smell of money. "The theme in these types of cases is that the perpetrators make faith in God synonymous with faith in their investment plan, and you can't separate the two."[249] The Indiana state security commissioner, Brad Skolnik, underscored this problem when he said: "Cloaking an investment with religion can give it a false aura of safety."[250]

Religious affinity fraud seems especially insidious because it exploits the trust, friendship, and cohesiveness that exists in people sharing a common spiritual identity. A past president of the North American Securities Administrators Association (NASAA) says: "Religious affinity fraud is a huge problem, and it's phenomenal what's been occurring all over the country."[251] Another past NASAA president declares: "I've been a securities regulator for 20 years, and I've seen more money stolen in the name of God than in any other way."[252]

A sensational example occurred in 2004, when the FBI arrested seven people accused of running a large affinity fraud that stretched across several states. Over a period of more than 10 years, the defendants allegedly had bilked more than 100 investors out of somewhere between $20 million and $50 million[253] by claiming to have access to a secret *1.6 trillion* trust fund created by descendants of Mormon Church founder Joseph Smith.[254] Mormons allegedly were the victims. They were told that they were needed to bring Smith's money "home." [255] "Investigators said the suspects used religion to target wealthy investors, including holding prayer meetings and describing plans to build a religious theme park"[256]—a ploy lifted right out of the PTL playbook. The defendants not only were not Joseph Smith's descendants, as they claimed to be, but also reportedly were not even Mormons. They operated their alleged scam out of a San Diego liquor store.[257]

Other recent cases include the following:

- In Florida, a 55-year-old woman named Elizabeth Morgan received a considerable sum of money from her late husband's life insurance policy and from a successful malpractice suit related to his unexpected death. A member of the Jehovah's Witnesses religion, Mrs. Morgan felt comfortable putting the money in the hands of an elder of her congregation to invest in real estate. She bought $764,000 worth of promissory notes from Raymond Knowles, a financial consultant and former missionary she had known from her church for many years. For two years, she received monthly interest checks; but eventually her checks started coming late, and then not at all. When she tried to get her investment back, the money was nowhere to be found. In 2003, a federal jury convicted Knowles of 16 fraud counts. He had ripped off at least $2 million dollars from Elizabeth Morgan and more than 50 other Jehovah's Witnesses. In Mrs. Morgan's words: "I lost everything. That was money I had to live off for the rest of my life. I was forced to sell my house and declare bankruptcy."[258] In January 2003, Reverend Knowles was sentenced to 57 months in prison and ordered to pay $4.7 million restitution.[259]

- In Tennessee, federal regulators shut down Capital Plus Worldwide Financial Services after more than 100 investors, most of them recruited from African-American churches, sunk nearly $4 million into non-existent debentures purportedly issued by European banks. Investors had been promised that their money would be used to rebuild war-torn African nations and would generate an annual return of between 96 and 120 percent.[260] Ricardo Gant, who operated Capital Plus, was sentenced to 10 years in prison in 2005.[261]

- In Michigan, regulators shut down the IRM Corporation after it had raised about $400 million from investors in at least five states through the sale of fraudulent limited partnerships supposedly tied to the California real estate market. Most of the victims had been recruited either in person through church-based organizations or through religious television and radio programs. IRM was described as a classic Ponzi, continually soliciting new investors in order to make interest payments to previous investors.[262]

- In Washington state, regulators shut down a company which had targeted members of the Quaker faith (Society of Friends). Island Mortgage had collected over $26 million in "premiums" for non-existent health insurance. Company founder Philip Harmon was sentenced to 8 years in prison.[263]

- The Baptist Foundation of Arizona raised $590 million from thousands of Baptists across the nation during most of the 1990s. It promised investors high interest rates and pledged to use its funds to build churches. BFA later was revealed to be one of the largest Ponzis in the world. In 2001, three BFA executives pled guilty to fraud—two years after their crooked foundation declared bankruptcy.[264]

- In Florida, General Ministries International (GMI) Church was accused of operating a scam of mammoth proportions. Between 1993 and 1999, GMI took in nearly $580 million, promising tens of thousands of victims that the church would double their money through divinely inspired investments in foreign currency, precious metals, and diamond mines in Africa.[265] In 2001, Gerald Payne, GMI's founder, was sentenced to 27 years in prison on charges ranging from conspiracy, to money laundering, to fraud. His wife Betty Payne was sentenced to nearly 13 years.[266] In its time, the Internal Revenue Service considered it one of the largest Ponzi schemes it had ever investigated.[267]

CASE STUDY
Abraham Kennard—Preying on the Praying

Early in 2004, a federal grand jury returned a 91-count indictment against 45-year-old Abraham Kennard,[268] charging him with scamming more than 1,600 African-American churches and hundreds of individuals out of nearly $9 million.[269] According to prosecutors, Kennard had run a Ponzi that had targeted a tight national network of black preachers.[270] He had launched the alleged scheme in 2001 when he began promising poor black churches a forgivable loan or non-refundable grant of $50,000 for every $3,000 in fees a church paid his company, Network International Investment Corporation.[271] Kennard claimed that Network International had built Christian resorts worldwide and had $346 million available to fund the loans and grants.[272] Kennard gave a series of presentations for his "Church Funding Project" at locations throughout the country. He also solicited investors at his Web site and by telephone, using a commissioned sales force.[273] Within a year, churches in 41 states had invested $8.7 million.[274] Much of money allegedly had been spent on limousines, leased private jets, and luxury cars, used by Kennard and his girlfriend, family, and friends.[275] The government had seized, among other things, 20 cars, including Cadillac Escalades, Cadillac Sevilles, Cadillac Devilles, Mercedes Benzes, plus a Harley Davidson motorcycle and four boats.[276] In his opening statement, Kennard declared: "It's not a law against riding in a Cadillac if you don't want to ride in a Volkswagen."[277]

Abraham Kennard denied all the charges. He declared that the prosecutors had "mistaken a dream for a scheme."[278] The U.S. Attorney countered: "It was a nightmare."[279] When his trial opened in January, 2005, Kennard surprised the courtroom by firing his attorney minutes before jury selection was to begin. Kennard, who claimed to hold three honorary doctorate degrees and a high school diploma, announced that he would defend himself,[280] telling the court, "I believe God is with me."[281] When his former lawyer was asked whether Kennard could put up a good defense, the attorney replied: "What do you think?"[282]

In his opening address to the jury, the federal prosecutor characterized Kennard's operation as a religious affinity scam. He called it "a disturbing scheme that preyed upon the trusting members of the faith community."[283]

Many of the government's witnesses were pastors of poor African-American churches, who claimed that Kennard had lured them into investments he swore would yield fabulous returns for their flocks. A minister from Menassas, Virginia, testified that his church had sent Kennard a check for $18,000 and never recovered a cent.[284]

> "He came in with his entourage and his bodyguard and told us we needed to sign up that night because they were getting ready for a disbursement. . . . He appealed to us, to struggling churches."[285]

The pastor of St. Mark's Primitive Baptist Church in Springfield, Tennessee, testified that he had taken $3,000 out of his personal savings to invest with Kennard. "He believed Kennard would make good on his promise that St. Mark's and its 20 members would receive $200,000 to remodel their building."[286] Like other victims, he had been told by Kennard that the Network International's investors included movie stars using the Church Funding Project as a tax write-off. He had been especially impressed by a videotape featuring Kennard and Bernard Holyfield, brother of former heavyweight boxing champion Evander Holyfield. "He showed the Holyfield tape and said Holyfield was an investor. That influenced me to join."[287] Prosecutors said that Holyfield had been

(Continued)

paid $22,000 to make the tape and had invested nothing.[288]

A minister from the Greater Cathedral Worship Center in Nashville, Tennessee, described how a close-knit network of black preachers had succumbed to a "domino effect."[289] Another minister, from Victory Worship Center in Birmingham, Alabama insisted: "It wasn't about ignorance. It was about trust."[290]

Kennard's brother, who had earlier pleaded guilty to conspiracy to commit money laundering, testified that he had laundered money for Kennard through a shell company he had started. He added that Kennard had gambled away a big chunk of the money at slot machines at the MGM Grand Casino in Las Vegas.[291]

The trial lasted 3 weeks, but the jury needed only a few hours to find Abraham Kennard guilty. On February 7, 2005, he was convicted on all counts, including money laundering, conspiracy, tax evasion, and mail fraud.[292]

At his sentencing hearing three months later, Kennard told the judge that God would have helped him make good on his promises to his financially shattered clients if the FBI hadn't arrested him.[293] U.S. District Judge Harold L. Murphy was unmoved. He sentenced Kennard to 17 years in prison. He saved his sympathy for the victims:

"These people lost everything they had. Some even lost their church. The court cannot ignore that."[294]

TAKING THE LORD'S NAME IN GAIN

The control of all the categories of white-collar crime examined in this book depends largely upon vigorous enforcement on the part government agencies—*except* in the area of religious fraud. Here, the government generally has been reluctant to involve itself in the policing of religious commerce because of the First Amendment's protection regarding the free exercise of religion. Thus, a considerable reliance has been put on self-regulation.

In 1988, when the religious broadcasting industry was shaken by the PTL debacle, the National Religious Broadcasters approved a stronger code of ethics in order to restore credibility in its financial and fundraising activities. Among other things, the code requires members to submit audited reports annually, disclosing all financial information except salaries.[295] In addition, the NRB established restrictive guidelines concerning the placement of family members on payrolls. Nepotism has been a long-standing problem with the electronic churches. Jimmy Swaggart, for example, once kept seventeen relatives on his payroll.[296]

The new code also stressed a tougher stance regarding religious broadcasters whose integrity is compromised. As one writer has observed: "Integrity is at the heart and core of what it means to be a minister."[297] In the past, fallen church leaders had resorted to hand-wringing confessions and teary pleas for forgiveness, followed by aggressive efforts to reclaim their thrones. This strategy had enabled preachers like Swaggart and Bakker to accomplish the improbable feat of appearing to be both arrogant and contrite simultaneously. The NRB code, while acknowledging that forgiveness is a central aspect of Christianity, implied that forgiveness need not necessarily entail restoration to leadership.[298]

Unfortunately, good intentions do not always yield good outcomes. Although the NRB code was approved nearly unanimously, little subsequent progress has been made in the area of enforcement, and compliance has moved at a snail's pace. For example, since enactment of the code, Paul Crouch's Trinity Broadcasting Network, the largest producer of religious programming in the world, has come under fire. The FCC is investigating allegations of financial improprieties. Crouch is being sued by his former personnel director, who claims she was fired for failing to "go along with allegedly illegal and unethical practices."[299] One of the practices in question is Crouch's policy of ordaining the managers of his chain of television stations as ministers, "which allows them to deduct their housing expenses as parsonages."[300] This permits Crouch to pay them less money. Another allegation is that "Crouch and his wife supplement their combined annual salaries of $150,000 by charging almost everything they use—their three homes, living expenses, fleet of cars and a corporate jet—to their not-for-profit ministry."[301]

Moreover, in 1993—five years after approval of the NRB code—a judge fined Dallas evangelist Robert Tilton over $80,000 for "refusing to provide records related to the healing miracles about which he had boasted in his television ministry."[302] This fine occurred in response to a $50 million lawsuit filed against Tilton by a woman accusing him of fraud stemming from the solicitation of donations in exchange for praying for her husband's health. The woman claimed that "The miracles-for-money offers arrived by mail for months after her husband's death."[303] The lawsuit further alleged that Tilton had defrauded at least 500 contributors through false claims that he could heal sick and injured people. A Texas court, however, disallowed most of the woman's claims.

Tilton had earlier been the subject of a 1991 ABC-TV report which charged that prayer requests received by Tilton's ministry were thrown away after the enclosed contributions were removed.[304] "In the wake of the ABC report, Tilton canceled his Success-N-Life television program."[305] Tilton's teleministry, which once appeared on 200 stations and netted $80 million a year, had become mired in a morass of litigation. By 1995, Tilton's church membership had shrunk from 10,000 to less than 1,000.[306] The first case against Tilton to make it to trial was a lawsuit filed by a Florida couple who had donated $3,500 toward a proposed crisis center. According to the couple's attorney, his clients' contribution was "nothing more than fuel for Tilton's lavish lifestyle."[307] A Dallas jury agreed, and, in 1994, the couple was awarded $1.5 million in actual and punitive damages. This verdict prompted the judge who had rejected the earlier fraud suit against Tilton to reinstate the plaintiff's claim.[308]

Tilton's avarice is rivaled by the excesses of evangelist Tony Alamo, who was convicted and jailed in 1994 for understating his large personal income and failing to file tax returns from 1986 to 1988. Alamo's California-based ministry is a multimillion dollar enterprise with business interests in several other states. Alamo also had married *eight* different women from his congregation. Some of his brides were as young as 15 years old; others already had husbands, whom he expelled from his church after claiming their wives.[309]

The conduct of religious entrepreneurs like Crouch, Tilton, and Alamo would seem to cast doubt on the efficacy of any self-regulating code of ethics. Why has self-regulation not been a more successful antidote to religious fraud? For the same basic inadequacy that has caused it to come up short in every other milieu susceptible to white-collar crime—business, banking, investing, politics, health care, and so on. Self-regulation may be a useful control mechanism, but it obviously is not a sufficient one.

A number of critics have contended that the self-regulation of religious broadcasting must be supplemented with some measure of external control. For Constitutional reasons already noted, this is not a comfortable role for the government.[310] Perhaps the solution lies in placing external control over television ministries in the hands of the large evangelical denominations themselves, rather than individual ministers. Although Jim Bakker and Jimmy Swaggart were both members of the Assemblies of God, they were largely independent operators. "Both had their own local churches . . . partly to ensure nonprofit status in the eyes of the Internal Revenue Service."[311] If the televangelists were more accountable to denomination officials and, indeed, to local pastors, the fundraising ethics and personal lifestyles of the electronic preachers would be of day-to-day concern, rather than of concern only when exposed by the news media.

An even more stringent alternative would be to make television ministries accountable to a board of directors composed of respected business leaders from outside the ministry. This has long been the approach favored by the Reverend Billy Graham. In 1987, Graham's salary was $59,000 plus a housing allowance and a limited number of expenses—remarkably modest for a ministry that had collected donations of over $66 million the previous year.[312] Graham allows himself no access to unaudited gifts. Decades ago, he turned over financial control of his ministry to an independent board of directors. This governing board publicly issues audited financial statements regularly. By contrast, Oral Roberts, for example, reportedly *never* issues financial statements. Only a handful of close associates know how much money he collects or how the donations are used.[313] It is understandable that Graham's public standing has remained consistently favorable,[314] even as so many other clerical reputations have crumbled. In 1995, an annual nationwide poll reported that Billy Graham was the "most admired" American for the fourth year in a row.[315] Between 1963 and 1999, Graham also made the Gallup Poll's top ten list of admired Americans an incredible 35 years in a row.[316]

HELPING THE NEEDY . . . OR THE GREEDY?

Finally, there may be another less direct but very troubling consequence of religious fraud warranting consideration. This is the possibility of a contagion effect upon the secular fundraising community. In 1992, the United Way, one of America's foremost charitable organizations, was rocked by a series of revelations strikingly reminiscent of the gross excesses of the televangelists. The United Way president, William Aramony, was forced to resign when stories were reported in the press concerning his annual salary of nearly a half million dollars and his placement of numerous friends and relatives on the United Way payroll. At the local level, flagrant extravagance also was reported. The head of the United Way of New York, for example, reportedly maintained a $4,700-a-month apartment and a membership in an exclusive private club—both paid for by the charity.[317]

In 1994, Aramony was the principal target of a 71-count criminal indictment, alleging that he misappropriated $1.5 million. Among the specific charges were that: (1) he spent $383,000 of United Way money to buy a New York apartment and $72,000 to furnish it; (2) he authorized a $10,000 payment for a European vacation for his girlfriend and himself; (3) he routed a $60,000 bogus "consulting fee" to his girlfriend for renovating her Florida home and paying off her taxes; (4) he diverted $325,000 to a dummy company he had created and used some of the funds to purchase a plush Florida condominium.[318] At the trial, Aramony's girlfriend testified that United Way paid her a salary of $80,000 for working "an hour or so."[319] By the time she left the witness stand, she had spent far longer testifying than she had ever spent earning her "no show" salary.[320]

Aramony was convicted of fraud, conspiracy, and money laundering and was handed a seven-year prison sentence.[321] Like the teleministries, the United Way experienced a public backlash. A third of United Way's local chapters dropped out of the organization;[322] contributions for 1992 were reported to be down significantly—as much as 15 percent in some chapters,[323] more than $100 million overall.[324] Five years later, donations for social service charities were still down 5 percent from pre-Aramony levels.[325] Moreover, a new controversy erupted in 1996 over $292,000 in severance pay promised to Aramony's successor after she resigned.[326] The charity once more appeared to be testing the fragility of the public trust in 1998 when a federal judge ruled that Aramony was owed a $2.38 million pension by the United Way. The president of the United Way reacted angrily:

> "I was stunned. . . . All of us were amazed that he could bring this suit to begin with. How could he, given the damage he's done to this organization?"[327]

The United Way took another stunning hit eight years later in 2003, when the former vice president for finance of the East Lansing, Michigan, chapter was convicted of embezzling nearly $2 million over a seven-year period. Jacquelyn Allen-MacGregor, who had worked for the Capital Area United Way for 20 years, pleaded guilty to federal counts of check forging and engaging in an illegal financial transaction. It was believed to be the biggest embezzlement case in United Way history.[328]

MacGregor had used the money to buy expensive show horses. When she stood before the judge awaiting her sentence, she apologized to the charity. She said, "I do believe that I'm obsessed with horses."[329] Her lawyer characterized her behavior as "an addiction"[330] and asked the court for leniency advancing the preposterous argument that she had spent all the money on horses—not on herself. The judge, however, stayed within federal sentencing guidelines and handed MacGregor a four-year sentence, noting how the crime had badly tarnished the United Way's image.[331]

Indeed, given the vital social services provided by the United Way, any dissipation of confidence among its donors is a disturbing development, with implications clearly more important than Jim Bakker's deserted cathedral or fleet of empty tour buses. The building of fewer day-care centers, job-training facilities, and substance abuse clinics seems far more problematic for society in the long run than the construction of fewer Biblical theme parks.

Of course, the United Way is not the only major charity rocked by financial scandals. In 2000, Daniel Wiant, an executive of the American Cancer Society, pleaded guilty to embezzling nearly $8 million from that charity. Wiant admitted to bank fraud, money laundering, and mail fraud in the thefts that began in 1997.[332] He used some of the money to pay for an addition to his home, plush landscaping, and two all-terrain vehicles. The balance was secretly transferred from the Cancer Society to a bank in Austria.[333]

In 2003, the Federal Trade Commission announced that it had filed charges against five fundraising operations it accused of using deceptive promises to swindle contributors out of millions of dollars. The director of the FTC's Bureau of Consumer Protection lamented:

> "These are particularly heartless scams. . . . By diverting donors' charitable dollars, these scam artists undermine the public's confidence in legitimate charitable fund raising."[334]

One of the accused firms operated six separate "nonprofit" corporations based in Anaheim, California. According to the FTC, the six organizations—American Veterans' Council, Children's AIDS Council, Children's Relief Services, Disabled Children's Charity, Firefighters' Assistance Foundation, and Police and Sheriffs' Support Fund—were all fakes controlled by "unscrupulous fund raisers for their personal profit."[335] These organizations "collected millions of dollars by providing telemarketers with false claims that donations would fund scholarships for veterans and their families and provide children with braces and wheelchairs."[336]

Another organization, based in Pompano Beach, Florida, solicits donations for more than 75 actual charities, including the Virginia Firefighters Foundation and the Texas Fraternal Order of Police. According to the FTC, however, the company's telemarketers falsely claim to be members of law enforcement or firefighting agencies. The company keeps to 90 percent of the donations it collects.[337]

The federal prosecutor's warning in the Aramony case that, "[S]ociety won't tolerate individuals who are charged with protecting the precious assets of charity diverting those assets for their own personal use,"[338] was directed at secular fraud. But it could just as easily have been aimed at all the faithless purveyors of faith, who have turned their ministries into shabby confidence games.

In the General Ministries International case described earlier, swindlers Gerald and Betty Payne often had hooked their devout victims by citing **Luke 6:38**: *Give, and it shall be given unto you.*[339] Investors in GMI—or any other religious affinity scam—would have been better served if they had turned to **Revelation 16:15**: *Behold I come as a thief.*

Notes

1. Sutherland, Edwin H. *White-Collar Crime*. New York: Dryden, 1949: p. 9.
2. Messner, Steven F. and Rosenfeld, Richard. *Crime and the American Dream*. Belmont, California: Wadsworth, 1994.
3. Taylor, Ian, Walton, Paul, and Young, Jock. *The New Criminology: For a Social Theory of Deviance*. New York: Harper and Row, 1973: p. 94.
4. Merton, Robert K. "Social Structure and Anomie." *American Sociological Review* 3, 1938: 672–682.
5. Trevino, Linda K. "Ethical Decision Making in Organizations: A Person-Situation Interactionist Model." *Academy of Management Review* 11, 1986: 601-617.
6. Staw, Barry M. and Szwajkowski, Eugene. "The Scarcity-Munificence Component of Organizational Environments and the Commission of Illegal Acts." *Administrative Science Quarterly* 20, 1975: 345–354.
7. Mann, Arthur. "When Tammany Was Supreme." Introduction to Riordan, William L. *Plunkitt of Tammany Hall*. New York: E. P. Dutton, 1963; p. xv.
8. Bassis, Michael S., Gelles, Richard J., and Levine, Ann. *Sociology: An Introduction* (Fourth Edition). New York: McGraw-Hill, 1991: p. 142.
9. Messner and Rosenfeld, *op. cit.*: p. 72.
10. *Ibid.*, p. 72.
11. Parsons, Talcott. *Essays in Sociological Theory*. New York: Free Press, 1964: p. 239.
12. Quinney, Richard. *The Social Reality of Crime*. Boston: Little, Brown, 1970.
13. Surette, *op. cit.*
14. Gerbner, George. "Television and Its Viewers: What Social Science Sees." Rand Paper Series. Santa Monica, California: Rand Corporation, 1976.
15. Even the venerated oceanographer and television star Jacques Cousteau was accused in 1998 by his own film team of faking scenes in his popular documentaries. In one case it was alleged that an octopus was "encouraged" to scramble out of a tank and hop overboard by having assistants pour bleach into the tank. (*Houston Chronicle*. "Something Fishy?" May 11, 1998: p. 2A.)
16. Anderson, Kent. *Television Fraud: The History and Implications of the Quiz Show Scandals*. Westport, Connecticut: Greenwood Press, 1978. Karp, Walter. "The Quiz-Show Scandal." *American Heritage* 40, May/June 1989: 77-88. Stone, Joseph and Yohn, Tim. *Prime Time and Misdemeanors: Investigating the 1950s TV Quiz Scandal: D.A.'s Account*. New Brunswick, New Jersey: Rutgers University Press, 1992.
17. *America: A Catholic Review, op. cit.*, p. 98.
18. Allen, James E., Jr. "The TV 'Fixes' and Teacher Responsibility." *School and Society*, April 23, 1960: p. 202.
19. After a conspicuous absence of 40 years, big-money quiz shows returned to prime time television in 1999 with the debut of *Who Wants to Be a Millionaire*. This program dwarfed its predecessors with a top prize of one million dollars. It immediately became one of the highest rated programs on network television. (Bauder, David. "Hot Game Show Boosts ABC to Its First Sweeps Victory in Five Years." *Houston Chronicle*, December 1, 1999: p. 5D.)
20. *Life*. "Gimme, Gimme, Gimme on the Old Payola." November 23, 1959: p. 45.
21. Coase, Ronald. "Payola in Radio and Television Broadcasting." *Journal of Law and Economics* 22, 1979: 272.

22. Ewen, David. *The Life and Death of Tin Pan Alley*. New York: Funk and Wagnall's, 1964.

23. Coase, *op. cit.*, p. 273.

24. *Ibid.*

25. *Variety*. "Bribery to Get Song Plugs Rampant, Despite Pledges and Grandstanding." February 9, 1938: p. 1.

26. *Variety*. "Coercion Widely Used on Pubs [publishers]." February 23, 1938: pp. 1, 43.

27. Goldberg, Isaac. *Tin Pan Alley: A Chronicle of the American Popular Music Racket*. New York: The John Day Company, 1930; p. 210.

28. *Ibid.*

29. McKenzie, Ed. "A Deejay's Exposé—and Views of the Trade." *Life* 47, November 23, 1959: p. 46.

30. *Newsweek*. "Good-by, Ookie Dookie." February 22, 1960: p. 60.

31. *Ibid.*

32. Coase, *op. cit.*

33. *Ibid.*, p. 60.

34. Coase, *op. cit.*, p. 293.

35. Denisoff, Serge. *Solid Gold: The Popular Record Industry*. Brunswick, New Jersey: Transaction Books, 1975.

36. *Newsweek*. "Jockeys on a Rough Ride." December 7, 1959: p. 98.

37. *Ibid.*, p. 98.

38. McKenzie, *op. cit.*

39. *Life*. "Music Biz Goes Round and Round: It Comes Out Clarkola." May 16, 1960: p. 118.

40. *Ibid.*, p. 120.

41. *Ibid.*, p. 120.

42. *Ibid.*, p. 120.

43. *Ibid.*, p. 120.

44. *Ibid.*, p. 120.

45. *Ibid.*, p. 120.

46. Passman, Arnold. *The Deejays*. New York: MacMillan, 1971.

47. Anderson, Jack. "Disc Jockey Play-for-Drugs Outlined." *Washington Post*, April 21, 1972: C21.

48. Coase, *op. cot.*: 304.

49. Coase, *op. cit.*

50. *Ibid.*

51. *Ibid.*

52. *Ibid.*

53. *Ibid.*, 305.

54. Philips, Chuck. "Record Label Exec Agrees to Plead Guilty to Payola." *latimes.com*. July 1, 1999.

55. *Ibid.*

56. *Ibid.*

57. Philips, Chuck. "U.S. Widens Probe Into Bribery in Latin Radio." *latimes.com*. November 3, 1999.

58. *Ibid.*

59. *Ibid.*

60. Philips, Chuck. "Record Label Exec Agrees to Plead Guilty to Payola." *latimes.com*. July 1, 1999.

61. Morris, Chris. "Newsline . . ." *Billboard*. October 9, 1999: p. 97.

62. Johnson, Dean. "WXKS Parent Denies Payola." *Boston Herald*. December 18, 1998: p. S16.

63. Rozeff, Michael. "Payola Unbound." *LewRockwell.com*, November 26, 2005.

64. Coase, *op. cit.*

65. Suroweicki, James. "Paying to Play." *The New Yorker* (online), July 12, 2004.

66. Office of New York State Attorney General Eliot Spitzer. Press Release. July 25, 2005.

67. Office of New York State Attorney General Eliot Spitzer. Press Release. November 22, 2005.

68. Leeds, Jeff. "Universal Music Settles Big Payola Case." *nytimes.com*. May 12, 2006.

69. *oag.state.ny.us*. "Universal Music Settles Payola Probe." May 11, 2006.

70. *Ibid.*

71. *news.monsterandcritics.com*. "Payola Probe Turns From Labels to Radio." February 9, 2006.

72. Quoted in Ross, Brian and Walter, Vic. "CBS Radio Pays $2 Million to Settle Payola Allegations." *abcnews.com*, October 18, 2006.

73. *Los Angeles Times*. "FCC Announces Payola Settlement." April 14, 2007: p. C3.

74. *Ibid.*

75. *hypebot.com*. "A2M Study: Payola Still Keeps Indies Music Off Air." October 21, 2008,

76. Peterson, Cass. "Post Writer Wins Pulitzer for Story on Child Addict." April 14, 1981: pp. A1. A5. Although the Pulitzer carries a cash prize of only $1,000, it is considered the most prestigious award in journalism and can "make" a career—particularly for a young reporter like Cooke.

77. Cooke, Janet. "Jimmy's World: 8-Year-Old Heroin Addict Lives for a Fix." *Washington Post*, April 14, 1981 (originally published September 28, 1981): p. C6.

78. Maraniss, David A. "Post Reporter's Pulitzer Prize Is Withdrawn." *Washington Post*, April 16, 1981: pp. A1, A25. It was further revealed that Cooke had also falsified her autobiography to the Pulitzer Advisory Board.

79. Quoted in *Ibid.*, p. A1. In 1996, Janet Cooke resurfaced after 15 years of professional exile, publicly seeking a "second chance." The president of a national association of African-American journalists offered no hope of forgiveness: "Making up the news

has long been considered the worst crime in journalism . . . If she deserves a second chance, let her write fiction" (Quoted in Neuharth, Al. "Why You Deserve a Second Chance." *USA Today*, May 17, 1996: p. 13A).

80. *Washington Post*. "The End of the 'Jimmy' Story." April 16, 1981: p. A18.

81. Irving, Clifford. *The Hoax*. Sagaponack, NY: The Permanent Press, 1981.

82. Dwarfing even the prodigious Hughes deception, the most lucrative literary hoax ever perpetrated was the fake sixty-two volume "Hitler Diaries" for which the West German magazine *Stern* paid $3.75 million to journalist and Nazi aficionado Gerd Heidemann in 1983. In addition to the many factual and stylistic errors in the diaries, the labels on the individual volumes contained polyester threads, and some pages were written with a mechanical pencil. Polyester and mechanical pencils were not even invented until after the war. With eyes apparently tightly shut, *Stern* sold the foreign serialization rights for over $3 million to such major publications as *Newsweek* and *Life*. After the error-riddled forgery was unmasked, Heidemann was convicted of fraud by a German court and given a 4 1/2 year sentence. Most of the payoff money was never recovered. Calling the diaries "the most expensive waste-paper collection in the world," the publisher of *Stern* stated tersely: "We have reason to be ashamed."

83. *Houston Chronicle*. "Judge Won't Write Off JFK Forgeries." September 17, 1999: p. 25A.

84. *thesmokinggun.com*. "The Man Who Conned Oprah." January 8, 2006.

85. *Ibid*.

86. Quoted in *Ibid*.

87. *Ibid*.

88. Quoted in *cbsnews.com*. "Frey Adds Apology to Book." February 1, 2006.

89. Pool, Bob. "Author Admits Gang-Life 'Memoir' Was All Fiction." *Los Angeles Times*. March 4, 2008: p. B4.

90. Rich, Motoko. "Tracking the Fallout of (Another) Literary Fraud." *newyorktimes.com*. March 5, 2008.

91. Italie, Hillel. "Anger, Sadness Over a Holocaust Survivor's Fabricated Story That Led to Cancellation of Book." *baltimore.metromix.com*, December 29, 2008.

92. Whittington, Mark. "Angel at the Fence Pulled From Publication." *associatedcontent.com*, December 28, 2008.

93. *Houston Chronicle*. "Recantation Claims Children's Book." December 31, 2008: p. A2.

94. *huffingtonpost.com*. "Publisher Says It Will Cancel Publication of Disputed Holocaust Memoir." December 27, 2008.

95. *Ibid*., p. 121

96. Durkheim, Emile. *The Elementary Forms of Religious Life*. New York: Free Press, 1965. This book was originally published in 1915.

97. Greeley, Andrew M. *Unsecular Man*. New York: Schocken Books, 1972.

98. Goodstein, Laurie. "Embezzlement Seen in 85% of Catholic Dioceses." *Deseret News* (online), January 9, 2007.

99. Coen, Jeff. "Priest Confesses to Stealing $1.6 Million." *Chicago Tribune* (online), July 27, 2005.

100. Smietana, Bob. "Insiders Steal Big From Unsuspecting Churches." *Christian Century* (online), March 8, 2005.

101. Coen, *op. cit*.

102. Hartocollis, Anemona. "Monsignor Gets 4-Year Sentence for Large Thefts From His East Side Parish." *nytimes.com*, September 23, 2006.

103. Moritz, Owen. "N.J. Man Pleads Guilty to Church Embezzle of 1M." *nydailynews.com*, August 5, 2006.

104. *Ibid*.

105. Gumbel, Andrew. "Florida priests 'embezzled $8.6m from parishioners.'" *independent.co.uk*, September 30, 2006.

106. O'Brien, Jason. "Priest Tells How He Took Millions From the Church Collection Plate." *The Independent* (online). October 12, 2006.

107. *miamiherald.com*. "Priest's Image: Underpaid CEO." October 8, 2006.

108. O'Connor, Lona and Ross, Allison. "Disgraced Delray Beach Priest Rev. John Skehan Released from Prison." *palmbeachpost.com*. April 26, 2010.

109. Rondeaux, Candace. "Va. Priest's Double Life Devastates Parishioners." *Washington Post*, January 30, 2007: p. A1.

110. Neill, Steve. "Parishes Feel Betrayed by Secretly Married Priest Accused of Embezzlement." *catholic.org*, February 1, 2007.

111. Bacon, Lisa A. "Retired Priest Sentenced for Bilking Two Churches." *nytimes.com*, February 22, 2008.

112. Gould, Pamela. "Spotsy 'Family' Had Neighbors Fooled." *fredericksburg.com*, January 15, 2007.

113. Quoted in Rondeaux, *op. cit*.

114. "Rodis Sentenced to 13 Years: Ex-priest Stole from Louisa Parishes." *dailyprogress.com*. January 15, 2009.

115. Lariosa, Joseph. "Pinoy Ex-priest in US Appeals Embezzlement Conviction." *gmanetwork.com*. January 16, 2009.

116. Cowan, Alison Leigh. "Priest Pleads Guilty to Defrauding Parish." *nytimes.com*, September 13, 2007.

117. *Ibid.*

118. *Darien Times* (online). "Father Fay Admits It." September 13, 2007.

119. Cowan, *op. cit.*

120. Quoted in Cowan, Alison Leigh. "37-Month Sentence for Priest Who Defrauded Parish." *nytimes.com*, December 8, 2007.

121. Snyder, Cindy. "Ex-Mayor Guilty of Church Theft." *keystonenews.com*, October 13, 2007.

122. Feuerherd, Joe. "85% of Dioceses Report Embezzlements." *ncrcafe.org*. December 21, 2006.

123. Maag, Christopher. "Cleveland Diocese Accused of Impropriety as Embezzlement Trial Nears." *nytimes.com*, August 20, 2007.

124. *Ibid.*

125. *irs.gov.* "Former Chief Financial Officer of Catholic Diocese of Cleveland Sentenced for Tax Crimes." December 11, 2008.

126. Gallagher, Chuck. "Nun Sense—Sister Barbara Markey Pleads Guilty to Theft." *wordpress.com*, April 1, 2008.

127. *foxnews.com.* "Nun Pleads Guilty to Taking Archdiocese Money, Using it to Gamble." April 1, 2008.

128. *cathnews.com.* "Three Years for Thieving Nun." July 15, 2008.

129. *Ibid.*

130. *huliq.com.* "Sister Barbara Markey Pleads Guilty For Money Stealing."April 1, 2008.

131. *closedcafeteria.com.* "Sister Barbara Markey Pleads Guilty," April 2, 2008.

132. Matheson, Kathy. "Stopping Church Embezzlement." *wsusignpost.com*, February 13, 2008.

133. Padgett, Tim. "When Priests Pilfer." *time.com*, February 15, 2007.

134. *Ibid.*

135. Quoted in *Ibid.*

136. Quoted in Matheson, *op. cit.*

137. Martin, Michelle. "Catholic Church Scandals Reveal Need for Parish Fiscal Transparency." *catholic.org*, December 19, 2006.

138. *Ibid.*

139. Quoted in Padgett, *op. cit.*

140. *Jet.* "Rev. Henry Lyons Found Guilty of Racketeering, Grand Theft." March 15, 1999: pp. 16-18.

141. *Ibid.*

142. *Jet.* "Trial Begins for Rev. Henry Lyons, Head of National Baptist Convention." February 1, 1999: p. 24.

143. Leisner, Pat. "Baptist Leader Sentenced to Prison." *Washington Post* Search Archives. March 31, 1999.

144. *The Christian Century.* "Lyons Found Guilty." March, 1999: p. 302.

145. Quoted in: *Houston Chronicle.* "Lyons Says He's 'Truly Repentant,' Resigns National Baptist Position." March 17, 1999: p. 7A.

146. Quoted in *Ibid.*

147. Quoted in *Ibid.*

148. Quoted in: *Houston Chronicle.* "Minister gets 5 1/2 Year Prison Term in Swindling Case." April 1, 1999: p. 12A. When Henry Lyons went to prison, a number of leaders from the National Baptist Convention, USA had hoped to convince political activist Rev. Jesse Jackson, a member of the denomination, to serve out the balance of Lyons' term. Jackson declined the offer. Ironically, a little over a year later Jackson himself would become embroiled in a controversy involving his own long-time mistress, with whom it was revealed he had a daughter out of wedlock. The Rainbow-PUSH Coalition, headed by Jackson, acknowledged that it had paid the woman a $15,000 advance on a contract to do consulting for the organization and $20,000 in "moving expenses." (*Houston Chronicle.* "Coalition gave 'Severance Pay' to Mother of Jackson's Child." January 20, 2001: p. 17A.)

149. Quoted in *northcountrygazette.org.* "Former Queens Pastor Ordered to Repay Stolen Church Funds." September 16, 2005.

150. Gomez, Alan. "Bishops Look at Fleecing of Flocks." *usatoday.com*, March 2, 2007.

151. *wfn.org.* "Investigation Shows Embezzlement Totaled $132,837." October 3, 2006.

152. *wkyt.com.* "Ex-Presbyterian Treasurer Avoiding Prison With Payments." August 16, 2007.

153. Therolf, Garrett. "Temple Theft Reveals a Gambler's Sad Saga." *Los Angeles Times.* February 3, 2002: p. B6.

154. Meri, Jean. "Synagogue Bookkeeper Sentenced." *Los Angeles Times.* March 29, 2002: p. B5.

155. *startribune.com.* "Treasurer Gets 14-Year Sentence For Embezzling From Rockford Church," October 10, 2008.

156. Heslop, Gordon. "The Audacious Pastor: A Trusted Church Leader Embezzles More than US $700,000 From His Congregation." *bnet.com*, February 16, 2007.

157. *Los Angeles Times.* "Pastor Who Fleeced Flock Avoids a Long Prison Term." February 12, 2007: p. B4.

158. *Ibid.*

159. *shortnews.com*. "Pastor Convicted of Embezzlement—Sells Church to Buy a BMW." January 31, 2006.
160. Quoted in *javno.com*. "Priest Steals From Entire Church in California." February 15, 2007.
161. Heslop, *op. cit.*
162. Burke, Garance. "Pastor Betrays His Flock's Trust." *seattletimes.com*, February 13, 2007.
163. *Los Angeles Times, op. cit.*
164. Lynn, Judi. "Pastor Stole Church From His Congregation." *democraticunderground.com*, February 12, 2007.
165. Gray, Tyler. "'Father Felony' Bilks Flock, Dodges Jail, Scores Book Deal." *radaronline.com*, February 13, 2007.
166. Radic, Randall. *A Priest in Hell: Gangs, Murderers and Snitching in a California Jail.* Toronto, Canada: Ecw Press, 2009.
167. Radic, Randall. *The Sound of Meat.* Ephemera Bound Publishing: 2008.
168. Much of the background and case materials described in this section are derived from James Randi's remarkable exposé of phony faith healers, *The Faith Healers* (Updated Edition). Buffalo, New York: Prometheus Books, 1989.
169. "Now the manifestations of the Spirit is given to everyone for profit. To one through the Spirit is given the utterance of wisdom; and to another the utterance of knowledge, according to the same Spirit; to another the *gift of healing* [italics added], in the one Spirit; to another the working of miracles; to another prophecy; to another the distinguishing of spirits; to another various kinds of tongues; to another interpretation of tongues." *I Corinthians 12: 7-10.*
170. Randi, James. *The Faith Healers* (Revised Edition). Buffalo, New York: Prometheus Books, 1989: p. 31.
171. *Ibid.*
172. *Ibid.*, p. 85.
173. Hedgepeth, William. "Brother A.A. Allen on the Gospel Trail: He Feels, He Heels, & He Turns You on with God." *Look* 33, 1969: p. 31.
174. *Ibid.*
175. Tierney, John. "Fleecing the Flock." *Discover* 11, November, 1987: 50-58.
176. Dart, John. "Skeptics' Revelations." *Los Angeles Times*, May 11, 1986: D1,2.
177. Randi, *op. cit.*
178. *Ibid.*, p. 139.
179. *Ibid.*, p. 175.
180. *Ibid.*
181. Tierney, *op. cit.*, p. 53.
182. *Ibid.*, p. 53.
183. Jaroff, Leon. "Fighting Against Flimflam." *Time* 131, June 13, 1988: 70–72.
184. Jaroff, *op. cit.*, p. 72.
185. Randi, *op. cit.*
186. Tierney, *op. cit.*, p. 56.
187. *Ibid.*, p. 56.
188. *Ibid.*, p. 56.
189. Randi, *op. cit.*, p. 151.
190. *U.S. News & World Report.* "Duping the Faithful: Charlatans in the Church." March 29, 1993: p. 51.
191. Schultze, Quentin J. *Televangelism and American Culture: The Business of Popular Religion.* Grand Rapids, Michigan: Baker Book House, 1991.
192. Bruce, Steve. *Pray TV: Televangelism in America.* New York: Routledge, 1990.
193. Hadden, Jeffrey K. and Shupe, Anson. *Televangelism: Power and Politics on God's Frontier.* New York: Henry Holt, 1988.
194. Hadden, Jeffrey K. "The Rise and Fall of American Televangelism." *Annals of the American Academy of Political and Social Science* 527, 1993: p. 120.
195. Edsall, Thomas B. "Robertson Network Agrees to 'Significant' Fine by IRS." *Houston Chronicle.* March 21, 1998: p. 10A.
196. Income estimates for the Robertson, Roberts, Schuller, Falwell, and Swaggart ministries are derived from: Ostling, Richard "TV's Unholy Row." *Time* 129, April 6, 1987: 60–67.
197. Ostling, *op. cit.*
198. Ostling, Richard N. "Enterprising Evangelism." *Time* 130, August 3, 1987: p. 53.
199. Woodward, Kenneth. "What Profits a Preacher?" *Newsweek* 109, May 4, 1987: p. 68. Steinfels, Peter. "The Swaggart Case: When a Religious Leader Strays, What Path Should Be Followed?" *New York Times*, February 28, 1988: p. E7.
200. Ostling, April 6, 1987, *op. cit.*
201. *Ibid.*, p. 45.
202. Shepard, Charles. *Forgiven: The Rise and Fall of Jim Bakker and the PTL Ministry.* New York: Atlantic Monthly Press, 1989.
203. Barnhart, *op. cit.*, pp. 4-5.
204. Shepard, *op. cit.*
205. *Ibid.*
206. Barnhart, *op. cit.*
207. Hackett, George. "Paying the Wages of Sin: Sexual Mischief and a Payoff Disgrace a Preacher." *Newsweek* 109, March 30, 1987: p. 28.
208. Ostling, Richard N. "A Really Bad Day at Fort Mill." *Time* 129, March 30, 1987: p. 70.

209. Barnhart, *op. cit.*

210. *The Economist.* "Pity the Lot." June 6, 1987: p. 26.

211. Ostling, Richard N. "Taking Command at Fort Mill." *Time* 129, May 11, 1987: p. 60.

212. Barnhart, *op. cit.*

213. Barnhart, *op. cit.*

214. Watson, Russell. "Fresh Out of Miracles." *Newsweek* 109, May 11, 1987: p. 70.

215. Tidwell, Gary L. "The Anatomy of a Fraud." *Fund Raising Management* 24, May, 1993: 58-62.

216. Shepard, *op. cit.*

217. Martz, *op. cit.*

218. Woodward, May 4, 1987, *op. cit.*

219. Ostling, Richard N. "Of God and Greed." *Time* 129, June 8, 1987: 70-74.

220. Gates, David. "Falwell and the PTL: 'Send Money'." *Newsweek* 109, May 25, 1987: p. 6.

221. Shepard, *op. cit.*, p. 70.

222. Shepard, *op. cit.*, p. 548.

223. *Ibid.*, p. 548.

224. *Ibid.*, p. 549.

225. Barnhart, *op. cit.*

226. *Christian Century.* "The Televangelist Fiasco: Top '87 Religion Story." December 23, 1987: 1163-1165.

227. *Christianity Today.* "Rendering Unto Caesar." January 15, 1988: p. 54.

228. Barnhart, *op. cit.*

229. Ostling, Richard N. "Jim Bakker's Crumbling World." *Time* 132, December 19, 1988: p. 72.

230. *Ibid.*, p. 72.

231. Shepard, *op. cit.*, p. 552.

232. Hackett, *op. cit.*, p. 28.

233. Sanders, Alain L. "The Wrath of 'Maximum Bob'." *Time* 134, November 6, 1989: p. 62.

234. Frank, Jeffrey A. "Tammy & Jim, Together no More." *Washington Post*, March 13, 1992: F1, F3.

235. *Houston Post.* "Jim Bakker Arrives at Halfway House." July 2, 1994: p. A4.

236. *New York Times.* "Donors to Bakker Get Nothing." November 15, 1992: p. 31.

237. Shipp, E. R. "Scandals Emptied Pews of Electronic Churches." *New York Times*, March 3, 1991: p. 24.

238. *The Economist.* "To Err Is Human." March 28, 1987: 26-32.

239. *Ibid.*

240. Muck, Terry C. "The Bakker Tragedy." *Christianity Today* 31, May 15, 1987: p. 14.

241. Smith, Tom W. "The Polls: Poll Trends—Religious Beliefs and Behaviors and the Televangelist Scandals of 1987-1988." *Public Opinion Quarterly* 56, 1992: p. 361.

242. *Psychology Today.* "TV Preachers Still Rake It In." November, 1988: p. 6.

243. Sidey, Ken. "Addicted to Broadcasting." *Christianity Today* 36, February 10, 1992: p. 12.

244. *Ibid.*, p. 12.

245. Smith, *op. cit.*

246. Plagenz, George R. "Clergy Mistakenly Steps off Pedestal to Be 'Like the Rest of Us'." *Houston Post*, January 22, 1994: p. E4.

247. Sidey, *op. cit.*

248. *Ibid.*, p. 12.

249. Bergal, Jenni. "Religion-Based Scams Take Lord's Name in Gain." *sun-sentinel.com.* January 26, 2003.

250. National Association of Securities Administrators, *op. cit.*

251. Quoted in *Ibid.*

252. Quoted in North American Securities Administrators Association. "Investment Frauds Using Religion on the Rise, State Regulators Warn." *nasaa.org.* August 7, 2001.

253. *religionnewsblog.com.* "FBI Arrests Suspects Who Targeted Mormons in Alleged Fraud Scheme." August 19, 2004.

254. Soto, Onell R. "Huge Fraud Ring Broken, FBI Says." *signonsandiego.com.* August 19, 2004.

255. *Ibid.*

256. *religionnewsblog.com*, *op. cit.*

257. *Ibid.*

258. Quoted in Bergal, *op. cit.*

259. "Church Elder Ordered to Repay $4.7 Million to Fleeced Flock." *sun-sentinel.com.* March 18, 2003.

260. North American Securities Administrators Association, *op. cit.*

261. Lineberger, Mark. "Man Gets 28 Months for Church Fraud." *kinston.com.* March 12, 2005.

262. North American Securities Administrators Association, *op. cit.*

263. *Ibid.*

264. Farrell, Greg. "Scams Use Name of God to Con Christians." *usatody.com.* August 8, 2001.

265. North American Securities Administrators Association, *op. cit.*

266. *Ibid.*

267. *christianitytoday.com.* "Greater Ministries Defendants Found Guilty." December 20, 2008.

268. *www.religionnewsblog.com.* "Two Men Indicted in Church Scam." January 20, 2004.

269. Arey, Norman. "Alleged Church Bilker on Trial." *Atlanta Journal-Constitution* (online). January 10, 2005.

270. *USA Today*. "Minister Stole From 1,600 Churches." May 6, 2005: 3A.

271. www.religionnewsblog.com 2004, *op. cit.*

272. Arey, January 10, 2005, *op. cit.*

273. *Ibid.*

274. *Ibid.*

275. *Ibid.*

276. *www.religionnewsblog.com*. "Pastors Say Man Swindled Poor Churches." January 20, 2005.

277. Quoted in *www.rickcross.com*. "Preacher 'Stole Millions From Black Churches.'" February 8, 2005.

278. Quoted in *www.religionnewblog.com*, January 20, 2005, *op. cit.*

279. *www.religionnewsblog.com*. "Preacher Accused of Preying on Faithful Awaits Verdict." February 4, 2005.

280. Arey, Norman. "Alleged Defrauder to Defend Himself." *Atlanta Journal-Constitution* (online). January 11, 2005.

281. Quoted in *Ibid.*

282. Quoted in *Ibid.*

283. Quoted in Rankin, Bill. "2 Georgians Accused of Massive Scam of Churches." *Atlanta Journal-Constitution* (online). January 21, 2004.

284. *www.religionnewsblog.com* 2005. *op. cit.*

285. Quoted in *Ibid.*

286. *Ibid.*

287. Quoted in *Ibid.*

288. *Ibid.*

289. Quoted in *Ibid.*

290. Quoted in *Ibid.*

291. *www.religionnewsblog.com*. "Defendant's Brother Tells of Gambling." January 29, 2005.

292. Gregory, Lauren. "Verdict: Kennard Guilty." *Rome News-Tribune* (GA). February 8, 2005.

293. Shirek, Jon. *www.11alive.com*. May 5, 2005.

294. Quoted in Haines, Erin. "Preacher Gets 17 Years After Bilking Churches." *Athens Banner-Herald* (GA/online). May 6, 2005.

295. *nytimes.com.* "Religious Broadcasters Adopt Stiffer Ethics Code," February 4, 1988.

296. Ostling, August 3, 1987, *op. cit.*

297. Stenfels, *op. cit.*, p. E7.

298. *Ibid.*

299. Woodward, Kenneth L. "The T Stands for Trouble." *Newsweek* 119, March 30, 1992: p. 60.

300. *Ibid.*, p. 61.

301. *Ibid.*, p. 61.

302. Reed, Steven R. "Evangelist Tilton Told to Pay $81,742 Fine for Files Delay." *Houston Chronicle*, September 4, 1993: p. 38A.

303. *Ibid..* p. 38A.

304. Brown, Rich. "Trouble in Paradise?" *Broadcasting* 121, December 2, 1991: 28–30.

305. *Houston Post*. "Jury: Tilton Defrauded Fla. Couple." April 22, 1994: p. A22.

306. *Houston Chronicle*. "Lawsuit Thrown Out." December 16, 1995: p. 36A.

307. *Ibid.*, p. A21.

308. *Houston Post*. "Tilton Sees Fraud Suit Reinstated." April 24, 1994: p. A26.

309. *New York Times*. "Jury Convicts an Evangelist of Tax Evasion." June 12, 1994: p. 30.

310. Oden, Thomas C. "Full Disclosure: Broadcast Ministries Can no Longer Have Financial Secrets." *Christianity Today* 32, 1988: 40–41.

311. Schultze, *op. cit.*, p. 228.

312. Ostling, Richard N. "Enterprising Evangelism." *Time* 130, August 3, 1987: 50–53.

313. *Ibid.*

314. *Washington Post*. "Billy Graham's Star on Walk of Fame." October 21, 1989: p. B6.

315. *Houston Chronicle*. "Write-Ins Get Him 2nd." December 14, 1995: p. 2A.

316. *USA Today*. "Billy Graham: 35 Years in a Row." December 15, 1999: p. 8A.

317. Stodghill, Ron II. "United They Stand?" *Business Week* 3288, October 19, 1992: p. 40.

318. *Houston Post*. "Ex-United Way Head Indicted for Misusing Funds." September 14, 1994: p. A11.

319. Quoted in *Galveston Daily News*, *op. cit.*, p. 3A.

320. *Ibid.*

321. *Galveston Daily News*. "United Way Ex-President Guilty." April 4, 1995. p. 3A; *Houston Chronicle*. "United Way Ex-President Gets 7 Years." June 23, 1995: p. 16A.

322. Gartner, Michael. "Aborted United Way Deal Failed Smell Test." *USA Today*, June 18, 1996: p. 13A.

323. Segal, Troy. "They Didn't Even Give at the Office." *Business Week* 3302, January 25, 1993: 68–69.

324. Gartner, *op. cit.*

325. Johnston, David C. "Neediest Suffer as Donations to United Way Dwindle." *Houston Chronicle*. November 9, 1997: p. 16A,

326. *Ibid.*

327. Quoted in: Wee, Eric L. "Judge Upholds $2 Million Pension for Convicted Ex-United Way Leader." *Houston Chronicle*. October 26, 1998: p. 8A.

328. *www.sptimes.com.* "Ex-United Way Officer Guilty of Embezzling." February 7, 2003.

329. Quoted in Prichard, James. "Former United Way Executive Sentenced to 4 Years for Embezzlement." *www.signonsandiego.com*. June 17, 2003.

330. Quoted in *Ibid.*

331. *Ibid.*

332. Gillespie, Charley. "Former Cancer Society Official Pleads Guilty to Embezzlement." *Houston Chronicle.* August 26, 2000: p. 25A.

333. *Ibid.*

334. Quoted in Ho, David. "FTC, State Agencies Target Charity Scams." *Houston Chronicle.* May 21, 2003: 3A.

335. *Ibid.*

336. *Ibid.*

337. *Ibid.*

338. *Ibid.*, p. 3A.

339. *Ibid.*

6

Securities Fraud

As a freckle-faced 13-year-old, Darlene Gillespie, was one of the nine original Mouseketeers on television's *Mickey Mouse Club*. So popular was young Darlene that, while dozens of mouse-eared moppets came and went, she was kept on for the show's entire 1955–1959 run. She was even featured in her own serial: *Corky and White Shadow*.[1] The Disney publicity department proclaimed she had "more bounce to the ounce than a bottle of soda pop."[2] In 1998, she bounced right into federal court.

As an unfreckled 56-year-old, Darlene Gillespie was convicted on 12 counts of conspiracy, securities fraud, mail fraud, obstruction of justice, and perjury.[3] Gillespie and her boyfriend, who was also convicted, operated a scheme to make money in the stock market without paying for any stock.[4] The couple had bought more than 194,000 shares valued at $827,000 by writing checks on closed and overdrawn accounts.[5] They also had created a fictional person to make their transactions; then lied about this nonexistent agent to the Securities and Exchange Commission.[6] In 1999, Gillespie was sentenced to two years in prison.[7]

Darlene Gillespie's stunning fall from *Mouseketeer* to *racketeer* is just a striking example of the relentless attacks on American securities markets by crooks of all flavors. In the preceding chapter, we have seen how white-collar crime inflicts serious damage on vital social institutions such as the mass media and religion. But no institution is damaged more by fraud and other illicit activities than the economy.

Economy refers to activities organized around the production and distribution of goods and services. Simply put, the economy functions to satisfy people's basic material requirements. Many scholars have suggested that in the United States the economy is the most dominant of all social institutions. As such, the importance of the American people maintaining a trust in their economy cannot be overstated. When this trust is betrayed, everyone pays.

Ever since the Industrial Revolution crossed the Atlantic—but especially since the 1980s—white-collar crime has sapped the American economy and undermined the public interest. Specifically, we will look at securities fraud, because the honest trading of securities is the "soul" of a successful capitalist economy.

PAPER ENTREPRENEURISM

If the American economy has weakened as a social institution, one factor may be the emergence of a newer, less productive, brand of capitalism—known pejoratively as "paper entrepreneurism."[8] It has been lamented that the best financial minds in America are now wasted on computer-generated models that produce nothing but enormous paper profits and zero-sum games of dubious value to the overall economy.[9] There has been a growing public perception since the early 1980s that the nucleus of the American economy has shifted from investing to trading, from industrial production to deal making. During the 1980s, a full one-third of the Fortune 500 companies were either taken over or went private.[10]

Indeed, the 1980s have been viewed retrospectively as the decade when greed came out of the closet. The love of money, which once "dared not speak its name," refused to shut up. Nowhere was the new dignification of greed more pronounced or the spiraling decline of public trust more problematic than on Wall Street, which grew more and more estranged from Main Street.

Public confidence in the honesty of its financial markets—without which they hardly could exist—was shaken in the 1980s by a seemingly endless chain of scandals. For example, the former chairman and a former vice-president of Technical Equities Corporation, a California investment advisory firm, pleaded guilty in 1988 to three felony counts of securities fraud. The men were charged with misleading investors and misrepresenting the financial condition of their firm's investments. Technical Equities had failed in 1986 along with numerous limited partnerships that it had sold to about 1,200 mostly affluent clients. The clients' losses were estimated at about $150 million.[11]

Prudential Securities defrauded thousands of customers when its brokers lured them into risky investments by deliberately making false statements about the financial returns investors could expect. After the Securities and Exchange Commission (SEC) sued it, Prudential was forced to repay more than $700 million to its victimized clients.[12]

One of most repercussive cases involved the giant brokerage house, E. F. Hutton. Like many investment firms, Hutton had suffered during the recession of the 1970s and was experiencing financial difficulty. The company began writing huge overdrafts in order to profit from the "float"—that is, the interest that banks can earn on funds they hold while waiting for a check to clear.[13] Con-artists refer to this scheme as "check kiting."

> Hutton would pay its bills with a check that was covered by another check that was written on a different bank, which was covered by a check written on still another bank and so on. While all the banks were waiting for these various checks to clear, Hutton was getting a kind of interest-free loan. In 1980, the first year the scheme got into full swing, Hutton saved about $27 million in interest, which accounted for about a third of its profits.[14]

The scheme unraveled in 1982, and, after lengthy negotiations, Hutton agreed in 1985 to pay a $2 million fine.[15] For a company as wealthy as Hutton, this penalty was little more than a slap on the wrist. Moreover, no individuals were ever prosecuted. But in an industry built on trust and reputation, Hutton was finished as a major player. Not too long after the settlement, Hutton was sold to another firm and lost its corporate identity forever. As we shall see shortly, an even more lethal fate was awaiting the firm of Drexel Burnham Lambert at the end of the decade; for the demise of E. F. Hutton was just a prologue to the immensely scaled crimes that were to follow.

In this chapter, two categories of securities fraud will be considered: *insider trading* and *stock manipulation*. Clearly the distinction between these two crimes is blurred. The former will be detailed as a traditional offense committed, as the term suggests, by corporate and brokerage insiders. The latter will be examined as a more inclusive arena for fraud, incorporating the technology of the so-called "new economy" and creating unprecedented illegal opportunities to market outsiders as well—from teenage cyberpunks to sleazy swindlers to Mafia racketeers.

And finally, this chapter will look at the shocking financial scandal that came to light in late 2008. One of the country's most prominent investment managers confessed to running an almost unimaginable **$65 billion** Ponzi scheme.[16] The stunning economic consequences—and ruined lives—resulting from this alleged crime are still reverberating throughout the world.

INSIDER TRADING

Insider trading was criminalized under the Securities Exchange Act of 1934. As defined by the Securities Exchange Commission (SEC), insider traders are stockholders, directors, officers, or any recipients of information not publicly available who take advantage of such limited disclosure for their own benefit.[17] The SEC has determined that insiders have a "fiduciary duty" to refrain not only from trading on their private information also from disclosing it as well.[18]

In the first half of the decade—before Boesky and Milken became household names—a pair of cases shocked the business world and raised the crime of insider trading to public consciousness. The first case involved Paul Thayer, the former CEO of LTV Corporation, a large steel and aerospace company based in Dallas. Thayer was serving as Deputy Secretary of Defense in 1984—a post to which his friend Ronald Reagan had appointed him—when he was charged by the SEC with being the linchpin of an insider trading ring.[19]

In 1981, LTV was exploring the possibility of making a takeover offer for the Grumman Corporation, another big aerospace contractor. During the pre-takeover negotiations, Thayer allegedly leaked word of LTV's impending bid for Grumman to his Dallas stockbroker and close friend, Billy Bob Harris, who in turn passed the word to a circle of his friends, lovers, and business associates. One of the recipients of this inside information was a stockbroker at the Atlanta office of Bear Stearns, and he relayed it to a New York colleague, who agreed to split the profits earned through the purchase of Grumman stock. Another of Harris' friends made the same deal with two Boston associates. Thayer's leak was barely hours old and already its ripple effects were eddying widely.

When the news of LTV's offer of $45 a share for Grumman stock was announced publicly less than a week later, the Thayer-Harris network had purchased over 100,000 shares at around $25 per share. The stock jumped more than ten points the day of the announcement, generating profits of about $800,000 to Billy Bob and his cronies.

Later that year, Thayer leaked word of an imminent financial turnaround for the slumping LTV to his girlfriend and to Harris. Acting on this inside information, Harris bought LTV stock on margin for his own account and through the accounts of his father and three friends. The following day, LTV announced its earnings had tripled for the year and raised its dividend substantially. The stock of course increased in value almost immediately. Billy Bob and his group cashed in and took their quick profits.

Thayer, who reportedly never conducted insider trading on his own behalf and did not personally profit from his friends' transactions, seemed to relish the role of "Texas-sized sugar daddy,"[20] and soon began leaking inside information from other companies on whose boards he sat—notably Anheuser-Busch and Allied Corporation. When he learned that Busch was considering a takeover bid for a Texas baking company, he again gave this information to his girlfriend and to the ubiquitous Billy Bob Harris. Once more, the "good old boy" network (or more correctly, the "good old person" network, since it included a female flight attendant and a female aerobics instructor) grabbed more than 100,000 shares of the target firm. When the takeover was announced, the group walked away with over $200,000 in profits.

When the Allied Corporation was preparing a takeover offer for the Bendix Corporation, the scenario was repeated on an even grander scale, and the illegal profits exceeded $750,000. This was to be Paul Thayer's final betrayal of trust. The SEC had detected the pre-announcement run-up in price of Bendix shares and charged Thayer with leaking inside information. Thayer and Harris were indicted by the U.S. Department of Justice. Thayer, who initially had denied all charges, pleaded guilty in 1985 and, despite requests for mercy from such illustrious friends as Gerald Ford and Barry Goldwater,[21] he was given a 4-year prison sentence. This punishment stunned many observers, but the government had "hooked a big fish" and apparently was intent on filleting Thayer as an example to others.[22]

The other sensational insider trading scandal of the early 1980s began in 1983, when R. Foster Winans, a journalist who co-authored the daily "Heard on the Street" column for the *Wall Street Journal*, was asked a fateful question by Peter Brant, a prominent stockbroker from the firm of Kidder Peabody: "Wouldn't you like to be a millionaire?" The reply was immediate: "Sure."[23] And with that, a criminal conspiracy was spawned.

That a reporter earning $575 a week could have possessed the potential to greatly enrich an already wealthy man and perhaps generate a personal fortune as well may seem strange; but the "Heard" column exerts a powerful influence upon market professionals, who read it ritually every workday morning. By cultivating a network of market analysts and expert sources, the column serves as an early signal of a company's imminent growth or failure. A positive or negative story can elevate the price of a stock significantly—or sink it. Knowing the contents of a "Heard" column prior to its publication could be an invaluable tool to an investor skilled in the intricacies of buying short or going long on a stock. Such inside information has been compared to "having your own time machine . . . of knowing the winning horse in the fifth race at Belmont before post time."[24] Indeed, insider trading has been termed "the financial equivalent of fixing a race."[25]

This conspiracy lasted little over a year, with Brant regularly receiving advance information about "Heard" columns. Winans never did become a millionaire—his share of the illegal profits came to only about $30,000. When an investigation by the American Stock Exchange revealed a link between "Heard" columns and the trading patterns of one of the Brant's "clients," it all came crashing down in a pile of shattered careers and ruined lives. The conspirators and their accomplices were convicted in 1985, receiving tough sentences and heavy fines. It was, in the words of the man who then headed the SEC Enforcement Division, a "celebrity hanging."[26]

Unfortunately, if the high-profile prosecutions in the Thayer and *Wall Street Journal* cases were meant to deter future violations by unscrupulous insiders, their effects seem to have been minimal. As evidence, consider the career of Dennis Levine, a man so thoroughly dishonest that his biographer calls him "Wall Street's worst nightmare come true."[27]

CASE STUDY
Dennis Levine

In the rarified atmosphere of the investment banking community, where the plushest offices often are reserved for aristocratic scions with Ivy League MBAs, Dennis Levine was an anomaly. Born to a middle-class family in the Bayside section of Queens and educated at a tuition-free public

(*Continued*)

university, he was hardly an obvious candidate for dazzling success in his chosen arena; but dazzle he did. Fueled by the ever-dangerous mixture of ambition and amorality, he elbowed his way up the Wall Street food chain. Dennis Levine was determined to swim with the sharks; it was his own perverse facsimile of the American dream.

By 1980, Levine had taken an entry-level position in the mergers and acquisitions (M & A) department of Smith Barney. Talented and still only 28 years old, he could have proceeded up a linear path toward an honorable and lucrative career; but that was to be the proverbial road not taken. The ink was barely dry on his new business cards when he began testing the mechanics of insider trading. "In June, 1980 he made a profit of about $4000 by buying—and then selling after the price climbed—1500 shares of Dart Industries, Inc., one day before the public announcement of a merger offer by Kraft."[28] The proceeds from this first transaction were deposited in the Bahamian branch of a Swiss bank, where Levine had set up a dummy account earlier that year with the help of two accomplices—a corporate attorney from a prominent New York law firm[29] and an international banker from the investment firm of Lazard Freres.[30] From that point on, it was simply a matter of progressively raising the stakes—which Dennis Levine fully intended to do.

In 1981, Levine became a vice-president in the M & A department of Lehman Brothers. There he continued making illegal insider trades and carrying suitcases filled with money to and from Nassau. He was accumulating a substantial cash reserve in his secret account, which now was controlled by a virtually untraceable Panamanian holding company he had set up for himself. By 1984, he was ready, and eager, for a big score.

Lehman Brothers represented American Stores, a Utah-based retail conglomerate that was secretly planning an attempted acquisition of Jewel Companies, a Chicago-based supermarket and drugstore chain. Levine, of course, was privy to this inside information, and Diamond Holdings (his Panamanian company) purchased 75,000 shares of Jewel for $3.7 million. He even leaked the merger story to the press anonymously to drive up the value of his Jewel stock more quickly. When the two companies eventually merged, Levine sold his shares for a $1.2 million profit.[31]

January 1985: Levine went to work for Drexel Burnham as a managing director of M & A. He was given a base salary of $140,000 and a minimum guaranteed annual bonus of $750,000 along with 1000 shares of Drexel stock worth about $100,000.[32] Obviously, 1985 would be a very good year for the public Dennis Levine. And for the private Dennis Levine, it would be spectacular. Just four illegal trades in a four-month period would generate profits of nearly $6 million.[33]

February 1985: Ten days after starting at Drexel, Levine learned of a confidential plan by Drexel client Coastal Corporation to acquire American Natural Resources (ANR), a gas pipeline company. From a pay phone he called his Swiss broker in Nassau and bought 145,000 shares of ANR for $7 million—almost his entire "Panamanian" holdings. When ANR agreed to accept Coastal's offer two months later, Levine made nearly $1.4 in profits.[34]

March 1985: A confederate at the firm of Goldman Sachs informed Levine that Goldman Sachs had been hired by McGraw-Edison Company in connection with a proposed buy-out by Forstman Little & Company. Levine bought 80,000 shares for $3.4 million. A week later, the buy-out was announced, and Levine sold his stock at a profit of over $900,000.[35]

April 1985: Levine learned from his confederate at Lazard Freres that Houston Natural Gas Corporation (HNG) was in secret merger talks with InterNorth, another energy company. Levine bought 75,000 shares of HNG for $4 million. Two weeks later, the merger

(*Continued*)

was announced, and another $900,000 was added to his Bahamian account.[36]

May 1985: Yet another confederate, this one at Shearson Lehman Brothers, leaked details to Levine of a proposed merger between R.J. Reynolds, the big tobacco firm, and Nabisco Brands, the giant food company. Levine, sensing a huge opportunity, dumped his entire Diamond account into Nabisco stock—over $9 million. A few weeks later, Nabisco went public regarding its merger talks with Reynolds, and its stock took a sizable jump. Levine cashed in at a profit of $2.7 million.[37] This was to be his biggest single coup among the estimated $12.6 million in illegal trades Levine made in his career.[38]

By the autumn of 1985, however, the Enforcement Division of the SEC had become increasingly concerned about the apparent proliferation of insider trading. Every announcement of a proposed merger, acquisition, or leveraged buyout seemed to be preceded by heavier-than-usual sales in the stock of the target company. A major investigation had been undertaken, and the name of a certain Swiss bank in The Bahamas kept cropping up again and again.[39]

Levine's bankers were being pressured to explain twenty-eight suspicious transactions extending from 1983 through 1985. In 1986, "Mr. Diamond" finally was identified as Dennis Levine. He was arrested in May 1986, convicted in February 1987, fined $11.6 million, and sentenced to 2 years in prison—of which he served 17 months. After Levine's arrest, a long-time Wall Street luminary wrote: "The cancer is greed. Too much money is coming together with too many young people who have little or no institutional memory, or sense of tradition."[40]

Following his release, Levine became president of a financial consulting firm in New York.[41] He announced his intention to start a $100 million offshore investment fund.[42] Rumors had abounded since his arrest that he still had a great deal of "Diamond" money left, carefully hidden away.[43] In 1990, the Ethics Club at the Columbia Business School initiated a lecture series by white-collar felons. The first speaker invited was Dennis Levine.[44]

If Levine's punishment seems remarkably light compared to that of Paul Thayer, who was by any standard far less corrupt, it is because Levine was a dealmaker to the very end. He plea-bargained his relatively lenient sentence in exchange for testifying as a government witness against his co-conspirators.[45] He would not be the last convicted insider to cut such a deal.

Dennis Levine's cooperation was considered important because the SEC recognized that he did not commit his crimes in unabated isolation. About thirty of his alleged fifty-four illegal trades involved stocks in companies whose takeover deals were not handled by Levine or the firm for which he worked.[46] In fact, the Levine investigation had already paid a big dividend a few months earlier in the form of one of the richest and most visible figures on Wall Street—Ivan Boesky.

CASE STUDY
Ivan Boesky

Boesky was born in Detroit in 1938. Beyond that, the details of his biography often vary considerably from source to source.[47] Some writers depict his childhood as one of poverty—this is the version favored by Boesky himself. Other sources portray his early life as one of upper-middle class comfort.

(Continued)

Boesky claimed to have graduated from Cranwood, an elite prep school, whose tuition he financed by selling ice cream from a truck. While he apparently did attend Cranwood for a while, he graduated from an inner city Detroit high school. Boesky reportedly liked to give others the impression that he was a Harvard graduate as well, when, in fact, he never attended that university. He did, however, donate a large sum of money, which garnered him an honorary position on the advisory board of the Harvard School of Public Health. This position enabled him to join the prestigious New York branch of the Harvard Club, and he often conducted business there. In sum, depending on what one chooses to believe, Boesky was either a self-made man—or a self-invented one.

Ivan Boesky graduated from the Detroit School of Law, but was unable to land a job with any of that city's big law firms. While in school, however, he had met and married a wealthy woman whose father owned (among other things) the famous Beverly Hills Hotel. His new father-in-law reportedly did not think much of Boesky, nicknaming him "Ivan the Bum."[48]

Boesky moved his family to New York in 1966 to seek his fortune. Although he was at times unemployed, the Boeskys lived in a luxurious Park Avenue apartment, compliments of his father-in-law. Boesky moved through a series of positions with various Wall Street firms. He was fired from one job on the first day, after losing $20,000 on a deal.[49]

Finally, in 1972, Boesky was hired by the small brokerage house of Edwards & Hanly. Surprisingly, given his checkered employment history, he was put in charge of the company's modest arbitrage department and given a free hand to develop it. It was here that the Boesky legend first took root. He had found his niche in the esoteric domain of arbitrage, where he was quickly skirting rules and outmaneuvering peers. On one occasion, he was censured and fined by the New York Stock Exchange. Along the way, "Ivan the Bum" had picked up a new nickname that would endure

for the rest of his Wall Street career—"Ivan the Terrible."[50]

Arbitragers (alternatively known as arbitrageurs) are investment specialists who speculate in so-called "deal stocks," either on behalf of a brokerage house, an investment bank, or a limited partnership. It is not a new concept; arbitrage has existed for well over a hundred years,[51] but for most of that time it occupied a relatively obscure position in the Wall Street milieu.

The basic dynamics of arbitrage are not especially complicated. Boesky himself explained the process in his 1985 book.[52] Company A and Company B are negotiating a merger, which if consummated would result in the exchange of one share of Company A stock (currently valued at $50) for each share of Company B stock (currently valued at $30). It is the task of the arbitrager to assess the likelihood that the proposed deal will be made. If his assessment is positive, he will then offer to buy the outstanding stock of Company B at a price somewhere between the current value of $30 and the potential takeover value of $50—for example, $43. The Company B shareholders would be faced with a choice of waiting several months to reap a potential profit of $20 a share on a deal that may or may not happen, or to accept the arbitrager's offer for an immediate guaranteed profit of $13 a share. Many times, Company B's shareholders opt not to wait and instead choose to settle for the certain (though smaller) profit. The arbitrager then buys the Company B stock and immediately sells Company A stock short at $50, which locks in a sure profit—if the deal goes through. Let us say the merger is completed three months later, as the arbitrager had predicted. He would then exchange his $43 Company B stock for $50 Company A stock, and, after covering his short sales, he would net a three-month profit of 16.3 percent—for an annualized return of over 65 percent.

Eventually, the undercapitalized Edwards & Hanly went bankrupt, and in 1975 Boesky started his own firm. He proved to be a brilliant investor,

(Continued)

and his limited partnership accumulated holdings of $90 million in just five years.

Boesky's investors had trounced the stock market average. Someone who invested $1 with Boesky in April 1975 would have had $7.54 at the end of 1980 compared with $2.19 if the money had been invested in the stock market.[53]

In 1980, Boesky sold his company, but started another one the following year. At its height, his investment fund was returning a "staggering 142 percent."[54] However, by 1984 the wheels seemed to be coming off the Boesky machine. He was now underperforming the market with a yield of only 7.7 percent. More importantly, unlike many of his peers who cultivated a preferred anonymity, Boesky craved personal fame. His reputation and considerable ego clearly were in jeopardy. This made him an ideal candidate for recruitment into Dennis Levine's insider network.[55]

Predictably, those who have chronicled the Boesky-Levine nexus differ as to who first approached whom. It is acknowledged, however, that the money-hungry investment banker had long admired, almost to the point of obsession, the larger-than-life arbitrager. However it was initiated, the relationship began shortly after Levine had moved to Drexel from Lehman in early 1985. Levine began doling out inside information to Boesky on such imminent deals as the ANC-Coastal and HNG-InterNorth mergers.[56] Some accounts speculate that Boesky's initially toll-free hotline to Levine exploited Levine's urge to ingratiate himself with his "idol," but this explanation probably underestimates Levine's cunning. Boesky could serve as a kind of "insurance policy" to Levine. Many traders still followed Boesky's lead, and if he committed his vast financial resources to Levine's "deal stocks," other buyers would pour in—assuring a run-up in price and a profit for Levine.[57] Moreover, by April 1985, the two men had struck a new deal. Levine's

inside information would no longer be toll-free. He was to receive 5 percent of Boesky's profits.[58] For Boesky, too, it was an attractive arrangement. He could use Levine's illegal network to restore his sagging legend.

It was a marriage made in heaven—or, in the terminology Wall Street prefers, a "perfect synergy." Each party brought a rich dowry to the union: Levine airtight information and Boesky enormous capital to put this information to maximum advantage.[59]

Boesky went on to make far more money from Levine's deals, such as the RJR-Nabisco takeover, than Levine himself. Furthermore, he never paid Dennis Levine one nickel of the promised "5 percent commission."[60] Levine, the young man who had wanted to swim with the sharks, was chewed up and spit out by one of the most carnivorous.

But once the SEC had "bought" Levine's services as a friendly witness, Boesky's days were numbered—and he knew it. Although arbitragers as an investor class are the most insulated against charges of insider trading, since rumors and market intelligence are their everyday tools,[61] they are of course forbidden to trade on "tips they know come from a tainted source."[62] Since no source was more tainted than Dennis Levine, Boesky realized he was going to prison. In desperation, he took a page from the Levine playbook and agreed to help apprehend and testify against other insiders in order to avoid a longer sentence. Thus, in September 1986, Ivan Boesky officially was enrolled as a government agent.[63] Two months later he faced a federal judge, who was made aware of his ongoing cooperation. Accordingly, Boesky was fined a "mere" $100 million ($50 million in restitution, $50 million in penalties).[64] Several weeks later he received a sentence of 3 years—not nearly as severe as it could have been had he chosen to protect his associates.

If "mere" seems like a strange description of a $100 million fine, consider that Boesky had been
(*Continued*)

permitted by the prosecution to liquidate his current holdings of an estimated $1 billion in "deal stocks" on the open market *prior* to the announcement of his co-optation by the government.[65] In effect, the SEC allowed Boesky to trade on and profit from inside information about *his own arrest*.[66] This controversial dispensation enabled him to avoid the panic that was sure to ensue when it was revealed that "Agent" Boesky had been recording his conversations with some of the most influential figures in the investment community.[67] As one veteran reporter observed at the time: "It's something like capturing the whorehouse madam: now the cops have her date-book."[68]

As feared, the Dow Jones Industrial Average plummeted the day the Boesky scandal was confirmed.[69] "Deal stocks" were hit especially hard, of course; it was estimated that arbitragers lost somewhere between $1 billion and $2 billion[70] in the week following the Boesky hearing. The arbi-

trage department at a single firm, Merrill Lynch, reportedly "lost $40 million in the trading dip after Boesky's plea."[71] It further has been estimated that Boesky had made at least $203 million in illegal trades—more than four times the SEC's $50 million claim.[72] It is little wonder that *Fortune* magazine dubbed him "Crook of the Year."[73] Despite the magnitude of his fines, Boesky was permitted to walk out of prison a very rich man. Indeed, when he was released at the end of 1989, he left his wife after suing *her* for $50 million in alimony[74], purchased two homes in France, and reportedly lived like a maharajah.

Given all the repercussions, had the SEC made a good bargain with Ivan Boesky? They clearly thought so. By February 1987, Boesky had already helped them build a case against one of the reigning "whiz kids" of Wall Street—Martin Siegel, the talented young investment banker with the firm of Kidder Peabody.

CASE STUDY
Martin Siegel

Siegel was yet another product of a comfortable middle-class urban environment. His father had co-owned three shoe stores in the Boston area, but had gone bankrupt when Siegel was 20 years old. The elder Siegel never recovered financially or emotionally from the failure of his business.[75] The bankruptcy left an indelible impression on the son as well. Martin Siegel became haunted by the fear of failure and reportedly was a compulsive saver even after he became rich.

Since Kidder had no arbitrage department in the early 1980s, Siegel had begun utilizing Ivan Boesky as a source for takeover valuations. Siegel and Boesky soon developed a close professional and later personal relationship. Like so many others, Siegel was awed by Boesky's vast wealth and opulent lifestyle. One evening in 1982, the two

men met by chance at the Harvard Club (Siegel, a Harvard Business School graduate, was also a member). In the course of their impromptu meeting, Siegel complained to Boesky about his personal financial worries. This conversation would prove to be a judgmental error that ultimately would wreck Martin Siegel's life; but Siegel was no innocent dupe. He surely realized that for an M & A insider to cry poverty to an unprincipled arbitrager is "like placing red meat before a lion."[76] By the end of the evening, Siegel had been seduced. He had agreed to provide Boesky with inside information in exchange for a percentage of the profits Boesky would derive from that information.

Siegel went to work on Boesky's behalf almost immediately. One of his clients, the Martin Marietta Corporation, was fighting a takeover bid

(Continued)

by Bendix. Siegel had devised a so-called "Pac-Man" defense, in which the target company, Martin Marietta, would make a counteroffer to buy the suitor company, Bendix—for $1.5 billion. Siegel leaked this top-secret plan to Boesky, who then accumulated Bendix shares and made a handsome profit when those shares jumped in value after Siegel's strategy was made public. Siegel was paid $125,000 by Boesky. The payoff had all the trimmings of a cloak-and-dagger operation—which in a sense it was. The money was delivered in a suitcase to a public location by a courier who exchanged secret passwords with Siegel. Future dealings were to be initiated by Siegel, who would call Boesky from a pay phone and simply say, "Let's have coffee." The two would then meet at a predetermined time and place.[77]

By the end of 1984, Siegel had received a total of something between $575,000[78] and $700,000[79] from Boesky—depending on which source one chooses. However, he was becoming increasingly nervous (and perhaps even guilt-ridden) about his participation in a criminal conspiracy. When Boesky suggested that Siegel should open a foreign bank account to handle the illegal payments, this was the last straw. "Throughout 1985, [Siegel] resisted Boesky's efforts to obtain more information and refused to accept any more money."[80] When Siegel moved to Drexel in 1986 to become the co-head of M & A, this reportedly infuriated Boesky. What did he need another source at Drexel for? He already had Dennis Levine.

In November 1986, the Boesky fine was announced, along with the news that Boesky had been cooperating in an ongoing undercover investigation. Siegel reacted much the same as Boesky had when Levine's conscription had been announced months earlier. He, too, rushed to cut a deal and agreed to become a government witness against his former confederates. By December, a plea bargain had been finalized. The government would seize all of Siegel's assets except his two homes and his pension plan contributions.[81] Martin Siegel's longstanding fear of ruination had become a self-fulfilling prophecy.

He would, however, receive a prison sentence of only 2 months. In exchange, Siegel would point a finger at other insider traders and testify for the government in any cases where his testimony was deemed relevant.

Siegel's first catch would be Robert Freeman, the head of arbitrage at Goldman Sachs and a partner at that powerful investment banking firm. Siegel had entered an arrangement with Freeman to swap inside information.[82] For example, Freeman was accused of giving Siegel confidential information about Unocal, a Goldman Sachs client, concerning Unocal's plans to buy back 50 million shares of its own stock as a defense against a takeover attempt by Mesa Petroleum. At about the same time, a Kidder client, Kohlberg, Kravis, Roberts & Company (KKR) was bidding for Storer Communications. Siegel, in similar fashion, had informed Freeman of KKR's plans.[83] Both men—and their firms—allegedly had profited from this unlawful symbiosis.

Freeman eventually pleaded guilty and ended up serving 4 months in jail in 1990.[84] He also paid two fines totaling $2.1 million.[85] Unlike Levine, Boesky, and Siegel, Freeman generally was viewed with sympathy by his peers.[86] In contrast to his accuser, he was not denounced as a venal "yuppie," recklessly careening along the fast track. He had been with Goldman Sachs for 22 years and was regarded as a member of the establishment.[87] Perhaps even more importantly, he was the *rara avis* of insider traders; he never agreed to testify against former associates to save his own skin. Apparently, even in a corrupted environment, loyalty sometimes begets loyalty. After his release, Freeman was soon back in the market, reportedly running "very big money" for himself out of his suburban New York home.[88]

Fortunately for the government, it had little need for Freeman. It was Ivan Boesky who mattered most. He had agreed to help the SEC stalk the biggest quarry of all—a man who effectively had re-invented the leveraged buyout and almost single-handedly elevated high-yield junk bonds from the ridiculous to the sublime—Michael Milken.

CASE STUDY
Michael Milken

Milken was born in the city of Encino in southern California's San Fernando Valley in 1946. His father was a successful accountant. Milken graduated Phi Beta Kappa from Berkeley and attended the Wharton business school at the University of Pennsylvania. While at Wharton, he worked part-time for two years in the Philadelphia office of what was then called Drexel Harriman Ripley. After leaving Wharton in 1970, he was offered a full-time position in the research department at the Wall Street office of the firm (which had just been renamed Drexel Firestone).[89]

Milken soon gravitated to the company's bond-trading department. Since his undergraduate days, a small, arcane corner of the bond market—high-yield, low-grade bonds, or what one Drexel executive derisively labeled "crap"—had entranced him."[90] These would later be renamed (reportedly by Milken himself, much to his everlasting regret) "junk bonds." The story goes that Milken was meeting with one of his early clients, Meshulam Riklis. Riklis was the force behind a number of major acquisitions such as the liquor distributor Schenley and several well-known department store chains. After studying Riklis's portfolio, Milken reportedly remarked: "Rik, this is 'junk'."[91]

Most of the bonds being traded at the time Milken landed on Wall Street were investment-grade and rated AAA. They were virtually risk-free, but barely yielded more than U.S. Treasury bonds. Milken's specialty, however, became the sub-investment-grade, deep-discount bonds, rated BB+ or lower.[92] One of his professors at Berkeley had published a 20-year study maintaining that a portfolio of low-grade bonds—if sufficiently large and diversified—consistently would outperform a higher-grade portfolio. Even though some of the low-grade bonds inevitably would default, the greater overall yield of the nondefaulting bonds would more than compensate—or so the theory went.

In the mid-1970s, there was little market demand for junk bonds, and not much trading was being conducted. Investors were reluctant to go near unrated debt. In addition to the intrinsic risk, many of the bonds were issued by relatively obscure companies, about whom comprehensive financial research was seldom available. Junk bonds were thus trapped in a spiral, in which light trading would translate into low liquidity, which would then re-translate into light trading, and so on. But Michael Milken, a "workaholic" of seemingly limitless energy, began to find a niche for junk bonds. "Starting with $2 million in capital in 1973, he was generating astounding 100 percent rates of return, earning bonus pools for himself and his people that were approaching $1 million a year."[93]

In 1975, Milken was allowed to set up a semi-autonomous bond-trading unit with a remarkable bonus arrangement giving Milken and his team 35 percent of the profits they generated. By 1977, his organization controlled 25 percent of Wall Street's entire high-yield bond market. Milken promoted his wares with an almost evangelical zeal, and this was to change the very dynamics of capitalism. Junk bonds could enable corporate raiders "to make multibillion-dollar acquisitions, even if they had relatively few assets to begin with."[94] Often, these raiders would soon begin stripping assets from their new acquisitions in order to service the debt.

In addition to his flair for the creative non-use of cash, Milken's success in reshaping the junk bond market can be credited to that market's almost complete lack of regulation. In 1977, Milken convinced his firm (now renamed Drexel Burnham) to underwrite new issues of high-yield bonds from heavily leveraged companies and market them directly to the public. Since few formal rules existed, Drexel took a commission of 3–4 percent for underwriting these issues—an astonishing

(Continued)

figure compared with the customary seven-eighths of 1 percent in the high-grade bond arena. Milken, in turn, was given 30 percent of Drexel's commissions. Milken often would give his salesperson a miserly cut of 1 percent and pocket the remaining 29 percent for himself.[95] Later that year, Milken created the idea for the first junk bond mutual fund.[96] Junk bonds were now being traded with increasing regularity, and with that came the long-missing element of liquidity.

In 1978, Milken decided to move his operation to his native Los Angeles. This would remove him from any day-to-day control by Drexel management and allow him to expand his domain from trading and underwriting into investment banking and mergers and acquisitions. Drexel was not thrilled at the prospect of putting Milken on a 3,000-mile leash, but "[i]t was already obvious that Milken's success had little to do with Drexel, and that Drexel's success had everything to do with Milken."[97] Indeed, by this time Milken was generating almost *100 percent* of Drexel's profits.

Milken's first West Coast client was Steve Wynn. Five years earlier, Wynn had taken control of a seedy downtown Las Vegas casino called the Golden Nugget, spruced it up, added a hotel, and increased annual profits from $1.1 million in 1973 to $7.7 million in 1978. Wynn was yearning to open a Golden Nugget in Atlantic City, which was beginning to dwarf Las Vegas in revenues. Investment bankers long had eschewed the gaming industry because of its unsavory reputation and because it was not considered a growth industry at that time. So how does a company worth $10 million raise $100 million? Steve Wynn's answer was a fellow Wharton alumnus named Michael Milken. Over the next two years, Drexel raised $160 million for Wynn's project. Six years later, Wynn would sell his Atlantic City casino for $440 million.[98] In countless interviews over the years, Wynn has been quick to credit his stunning success to Milken. It was also Wynn who perhaps best described the secret of Milken's operation: "Venture capital masquerading as debt finance."[99]

When the 1980 recession hit, Milken took a characteristically contrarian position; when other investment bankers were bailing out, he was increasing Drexel's hegemony in the junk bond market. Milken had devised creative ways to restructure debt, so that while some underwriters were suffering default rates as high as 17 percent, Drexel's defaults never exceeded 2 percent during that period.[100] Some prophets of doom may have warned that Drexel merely was postponing the day of reckoning, but few were listening—least of all Milken. In fact, by 1983 the junk bond business was bigger than ever. Drexel (now renamed Drexel Burnham Lambert) was entrenched firmly on top, and Michael Milken was hailed as The King.

Let us now jump ahead momentarily to the autumn of 1987. "Agent" Boesky had been enrolled in what some were deriding as the SEC's "Frequent Liars Program"[101] and was preparing to help build prosecutable cases against some of his associates at five major brokerage houses.[102] He was instructed to place phone calls to everyone he had implicated and arrange meetings. The plan was to "wire" him at those meetings and tape-record incriminating evidence. One call, for example, went to Martin Siegel; another to Michael Milken. Milken agreed to meet with Boesky, and in mid-October they dined in Boesky's sumptuous Beverly Hills hotel suite.[103]

The Milken–Boesky relationship had begun in 1981 when Boesky was seeking sufficient capital to become a "merchant broker"—Boesky's preferred term for corporate raider.[104] Drexel seemed the perfect source, so Boesky made a West Coast pilgrimage to see The King. Boesky was after Vanguard, his late father-in-law's company, whose holdings included the Beverly Hills Hotel where Boesky was staying (and where Boesky would secretly tape-record Milken years later). Boesky, so accustomed to mesmerizing others, was himself awed by Milken.

From Boesky's perspective, the meeting had been a glorious success, for in 1983 Milken arranged $100 million for the Vanguard (now known as Northview) deal. Boesky began traveling

(Continued)

regularly to Beverly Hills to oversee his interest in the hotel, so he and Milken became ever closer. It is no quirk that of the six charges of which Milken eventually would be convicted, four involved dealings with Boesky. The two men engaged in a number of reciprocal "parking" arrangements. Parking refers to one investor buying and holding stock for another in order to conceal the true owner's identity. The true owner typically guarantees the titular buyer against loss.[105] For Boesky, parking stock with Milken would allow him to circumvent SEC regulations requiring public notification of the acquisition of a 5 percent or greater stake in a company. In other words, Boesky could buy just under 5 percent himself and then buy more through Milken. For Milken, parking a stock with Boesky would be useful if the purchase involved a Drexel client, restricting Milken (or anyone at Drexel) from buying it.[106] Either way, the practice of parking stock is illegal.

In 1985, plans were drawn up for the largest arbitrage organization in history. Boesky would dissolve his corporation and raise $220 million from a new group of limited partners. Then Milken would raise $660 million with junk bonds. This would provide Boesky with the resources to mount a raid on almost any company. Boesky, as usual, had little trouble attracting partners to put up $220 million. Milken, on the other hand, was hard pressed to sell investors on a $660 million arbitrage fund. Eventually, however, the money was raised. It is worth noting that $100 million of the debt was purchased by Charles Keating's Lincoln Savings,[107] which was to figure so prominently in the S&L debacle a few years later (Chapter 5). In effect, Milken now owned Boesky's soul. One of Boesky's close associates observed: "It is obvious that Boesky wouldn't pee without Milken's consent."[108]

A subsequent example of the parking arrangement involved Wickes Corporation, the Los Angeles-based home building products company, which was emerging from bankruptcy in the Spring of 1986. The Wickes chairman was eager to acquire National Gypsum, so Michael Milken and Drexel raised hundreds of millions of dollars for that purpose by issuing junk bonds and preferred stock. The preferred stock was an expensive proposition, because it paid a walloping 10 percent dividend, which was necessary to attract investors. There was, however, an unusual provision written into the preferred offering: If the price of Wickes stock rose to a certain level, the company could redeem its preferred stock and give investors common stock, which paid no dividends. Milken had Boesky manipulate the price of Wickes stock by purchasing 2.8 million shares over a relatively short period of time. This naturally inflated the price, which allowed Drexel's client to eliminate its preferred dividend and save $15 million a year.[109]

Thus, when Milken and Boesky met in Boesky's hotel suite in 1987, they brought to the dinner table a tangled history of collusion. Prosecutors had coached Boesky on where to direct the conversation, but Milken had heard rumors of Boesky's impending hearing and behaved circumspectly. For instance, when Boesky mentioned an illegal $3.5 million kickback that he owed Milken from the arbitrage fund deal, Milken told him to keep it. At one point Milken even warned Boesky, who was wearing a hidden recording device taped to his body, to be wary of electronic surveillance.[110]

When the news of Boesky's ongoing cooperation was announced a few weeks later, Milken's caution seemed justified. Although Boesky had been involved in enough crooked deals to put dozens of careers at risk, most of Wall Street realized that the primary targets of the Boesky arrangement had to be Milken and Drexel.

By mid-1988, however, Boesky was in prison and the Milken case seemingly had stalled. Milken, moreover, had hired an aggressive public relations firm that had begun packaging him to the American people as a "national treasure."[111] Milken, who had always been a very private man, started giving self-serving interviews to selected journalists. He even took a group of 1,700 underprivileged children to a baseball game. The public was seeing a philanthropic Michael Milken at his carefully orchestrated best.

(Continued)

That same public saw a very different picture when Milken was subpoenaed to testify before a Congressional investigation subcommittee later that year. He immediately invoked the Fifth Amendment and refused to answer a single question. After adjournment, the chairman held an angry press conference in which he excoriated Milken—flatly accusing him of insider trading and market manipulation.

In September 1988, Milken's top salesman defected to the government in exchange for immunity from prosecution.[112] This "triggered a stampede of other 'friendly' witnesses eager to cooperate."[113] That same month, the government filed a lawsuit against Milken and Drexel. In November, federal racketeering (RICO) charges were filed—a clear precursor to a criminal indictment. Drexel had enough. It entered a plea bargain in which it agreed to acknowledge wrongdoing, pay a $650 million fine (an all-time record), and suspend Milken, withholding his enormous annual bonus.[114] On March 29, 1989, Milken was indicted by a federal grand jury on 98 felony counts and RICO charges. Six months later, the junk bond market collapsed.

In February 1990, Drexel filed for bankruptcy. There was a grim symmetry to it all. The "greed" decade had opened with the downfall of E. F. Hutton and had closed with the implosion of Drexel Burnham Lambert. The road between had become strewn with the professional remains of Paul Thayer, Peter Brant, Dennis Levine, Ivan Boesky, Martin Siegel, Robert Freeman, and a cast of supporting players. Only Milken remained. Like a tontine in reverse, the harshest punishment had been saved for the last survivor. Milken agreed to plead guilty to six counts and to pay a fine of *$600 million*. On November 21, 1990, Michael Milken received a 10-year prison sentence.

Milken broke down completely. He began to shriek and wail so loudly that it attracted the attention of people throughout the courthouse. Fearing that he would faint, federal marshals rushed in with an oxygen tank. Milken's hysteria had subsided only slightly by the time he got to the airport for his chartered flight back to Los Angeles: During the entire trip, he lay in his wife's arms sobbing. At 44, Milken had seen his carefully constructed edifice definitively collapse.[115]

Milken's sentence was later reduced to 2 years. After his parole in 1993, he began teaching a business course at UCLA under the oversight of Professor Bradford Cornell. The class consisted mainly of case studies of Milken's deals. One student has described the class and Milken's input:

He had to win every point . . . He would debate Cornell and to make sure he'd won, he'd make some dig like: "Now that kind of thinking is why Bradford is a professor." The implication was, *I made a billion dollars. Who are you going to listen to?*[116]

At the end of the term, Milken held a dinner for his students and presented each of them with a plaque embossed with twelve "Milken Maxims." Number 6 stated: "The 1980s was a time for giving."[117]

"Professor" Milken probably never addressed the issue of motivation in his lectures. Many people still may wonder why persons earning incomes of seven, eight, or even nine figures would cheat and steal. Jaded respondents likely would counter that the question answers itself: cheating and stealing are precisely why these individuals accumulated so much money. Greed no doubt is a reasonable explanation of insider trading. To Milken and his fellow travelers—indeed to so many white-collar criminals—the question of "How much is enough?" is not only unanswerable, it is unworthy of consideration. One might just as well ask, "How high is up?"

Greed, though, may not be the only explanation. Egomania cannot be overlooked. For example, the noted economist Paul Samuelson has written of Ivan Boesky: "His need was not simply to be rich, but to be seen as richer and smarter than anyone else."[118] One writer even has compared the criminogenic Wall Street subculture to a male bonding group—a kind of postgraduate college fraternity. "As in all fraternities, the values that draw praise are male values: bigness, wealth, and, most of all, being on the inside."[119] In such a hyper-masculine environment, insider trading can be a means of demonstrating wealth, connections, and bigness simultaneously.

There is a certain appeal to the masculinity contest hypothesis. However, dismissing insider trading as merely an elaboration of locker-room braggadocio is not nearly adequate. Perhaps the best explanation is also the most parsimonious. Why did insider traders do it? Because they could. Because for years we let them. Because at some level we may even have admired them. A society that is unwilling to equate white-collar crime to street crime, in terms of seriousness and social cost, cannot effectively inhibit insider traders. A culture that extols the often-conflicting values of acquisitiveness and probity creates the sort of ambivalence that can motivate insider trading, then excuse it.

One of Dennis Levine's former professors has defended his protégé: "Dennis wasn't taking money from orphans and widows. His was a victimless crime."[120] This is a careless argument, but not an unexpected one. Because insider trading does not leave a chalk outline on the sidewalk or put bloodstains on the walls, it can be mistaken for a victimless crime. Nevertheless, insider trading is very much a predatory crime. "The victim is the investing public, individually or institutionally."[121]

Some economists, however, have maintained that while the morality of insider trading may be questionable, its effects have been distorted by the mass media. Such critics contend that the financial markets actually would benefit from a more relaxed regulatory attitude regarding insider trading.[122]

> When an insider knows something the stock market doesn't and acts on the strength of that knowledge, he moves share prices closer to where they will be when the news eventually gets out. In this view, insider dealing acts as an "economic lubricant."[123]

This point of view seemingly rejects the "fixed race" and "level playing field" analogies in favor of a pure *laissez-faire* model. Financial markets are not gambling casinos, as it is argued; so the overriding issue is not fairness, but efficiency. This argument would be more compelling if the economy were meant, in fact, to achieve homeostasis within a moral vacuum; but, as we stressed at the beginning of this chapter, the economy is a *social* institution. Efficiency alone will not sustain it. It must be perceived as fair; the public must trust it.

Thus, from a social perspective, insider traders have "tainted the free enterprise system."[124] They did this by subverting the very essence of capitalism—the notion that there ought to be a positive correlation between risk and potential return to investors. "Those willing to accept higher levels of risk should be rewarded with potentially higher levels of return."[125] But the insider trader collects the highest returns with little risk at all, while the ordinary investor, who assumes most of the risk, is exploited like some naive bumpkin lured into a rigged game of chance. The lawyer who prosecuted Ivan Boesky took note of this in his opening statement:

> [I]nvestors' worst fears that they are playing against a stacked deck on Wall Street are true . . . Mr. Boesky has committed very great crimes. He has, in effect, stolen great sums of money from an investing public that believed that everyone started the game with the same chance of winning.[126]

Although many people have reviled Ivan Boesky in similar or even stronger terms, the brunt of public hostility has been reserved for Michael Milken. Milken has become the personification of Wall Street corruption. A sizable percentage of Americans blame Milken and his junk bonds for the rise of paper entrepreneurism and the erosion of traditional industrial productivity. By the mid-1980s, even Fortune 500 companies had become actual or potential targets of leveraged buyouts, financed in large measure by high-yield bonds. Some of these companies were forced to submit to so-called "greenmail," where they would be compelled to buy back a raider's stock at a huge premium to make him go away.[127] This, of course, diverted corporate assets, which could have been used for research and development or job creation.

Moreover, the fraud that accompanied so many leveraged buyouts has been linked to the bankruptcy of a number of corporations.[128] This was particularly the case with smaller businesses that had raised cash through junk bonds. It has been reported that "[o]f the 104 small firms involved in public issues of nonconvertible Drexel junk bonds since 1977, 24 percent had defaulted on their debt or were bankrupt by mid-1990—five times the default rate of comparable firms."[129] And even if the price of a corporate takeover is not outright bankruptcy, it invariably is reduced productivity—and a significant loss of jobs. "Research indicates that firms subjected to protracted takeover battles do very little work, and experience little growth during and immediately after the takeover period."[130]

Corporate restructuring generally means "downsizing," which is essentially a euphemism for large-scale layoffs and firings. An editorial cartoon some years back captures the harsh reality of downsizing. Three anguished-looking men are reading identical newspapers headlined "Dow Jones Hits 5000!" The title of this book is more than a mild play on words. Profit "earned" not as the result of increased productivity but at the expense of discarded employees truly is "profit without honor."

Many employees who lose their jobs as a result of leveraged buyouts cannot find another. Furthermore, displaced workers who find other employment usually do so at a lower salary level.[131] Thus, the merger mania of the 1980s not only expanded the ranks of the unemployed, but contributed to a reduced standard of living among the reemployed. And even among those employees fortunate enough to survive mass layoffs, fear and anger can limit their risk-taking and often hurt productivity.[132] Historian Kevin Starr has analyzed the social effects of restructuring: "Americans never used to be envious of wealth, since rich people also created jobs—but now people don't get rich by putting people to work, but by putting people out of work."[133] It has become an economic fact of life that stock prices generally jump when companies terminate workers.[134] Again, because restructuring usually is necessitated by the heavy debt service created by leveraged deals, some critics have singled out Michael Milken for blame for the woeful human cost of downsizing.

The true extent of Milken's culpability, however, remains a subject of debate. Milken's defenders argue that all he did is popularize a product—the junk bond[135]—that was neither intrinsically good nor bad. The same instrument that helped bankrupt Bloomingdale's and 7-Eleven also helped create MCI and Turner Broadcasting. Milken himself denies that he did anything wrong. Reportedly, he now regrets his decision to plead guilty.[136] "As with so many ex-cons, the vision of himself as a victim is one that Milken still harbors."[137]

The pro-Milken arguments are not entirely devoid of merit. Financial affairs journalist James Glassman has written: "For all their faults, Michael Milken . . . and other wheeler dealers of the 1980s found real money that went into real businesses."[138] But it is difficult to separate Milken from the collapse of the junk bond market and the consequent aftershocks. Indeed, some of Milken's severest critics contend that his "product" was a fraud sustained mainly through Milken's gift for "hype." They point out how he routinely overfunded his issuers, so they, in turn, could buy the bonds of other issuers.[139] This type of fraud, resembling a gigantic chain letter, is a variation of the classic Ponzi swindle. One critic has characterized Milken as the central figure in the "biggest scam ever."[140]

The widely respected financier, Felix Rohatyn, senior partner at Lazard Freres, was an early and outspoken critic of megadeals financed with junk bonds. Testifying before Congress in 1985, he emphasized the social cost of market manipulation: "It completely fails to take into account the fact that a large corporation is an entity with responsibilities to employees, customers, and communities."[141] Years before the collapse, Rohatyn was warning anyone who would listen that junk bonds were not secure and that their high rates of interest would inflict stifling debt upon corporations that could be serviced only through the divestiture of assets.[142] Where others saw The King, Rohatyn saw a naked emperor.

If Milken's ascribed "genius" was genius at all, it was not in recognizing the value of junk bonds, but in recognizing their lack of value—and creating a high demand for them nonetheless. Indeed, one of the indicators of Milken's inflated reputation is the surprisingly mediocre performance of junk bonds. The 10-year return for "high-yield" bond funds in the 1980s was 145 percent. This return was considerably lower than that for A-rated corporate bonds (+202 percent) or even conservative treasury bonds (+177 percent).[143] One is tempted to conclude that the "genius" label bestowed on Michael Milken may have been hyperbolic.

Of all the consequences brought on by the downfall of the junk market, none has received more attention than the ensuing decline of the savings and loan industry (Chapter 5). Some of the most criminally mismanaged of these institutions were clients of Milken—including the now-defunct Columbia Savings & Loan of Beverly Hills[144] and the notorious Lincoln Savings & Loan of Irvine, California. Lincoln became the largest bank failure in American history,[145] and its chairman, Charles Keating, Jr., was handed a 10-year prison sentence in 1992 for defrauding customers by selling them $250 million in unsecured bonds falsely represented as secure.[146]

Milken's defenders have argued that those S&L's that got into trouble by overinvesting in junk were headed for bankruptcy regardless.[147] It could be counter argued that absolving Milken from complicity in the S&L scandal on such questionable grounds is somewhat akin to exonerating the murderer of a 90-year-old invalid because she was sure to die soon anyway.

When Federal Judge Kimba Wood sentenced Michael Milken, she noted how a decade of insider trading, corporate raiding, and market manipulation had hurt the confidence of individual investors, upon whom the American economy ultimately depends.[148] The corrupted image of that economy had led many small investors to abandon the stock market and conclude that "the Wall Street game is best played by the well-connected."[149] Judge Wood acknowledged that Milken's heavy fine and forced removal from the securities industry represented a substantial penalty; but she also felt a responsibility to send a stern warning to the next generation of ambitious MBAs by locking up Milken: "I believe that a prison term is required for the purposes of general deterrence; that is, the need to deter others from violating the law."[150]

At least two basic approaches have been advocated to eliminate or at least reduce the incidence of insider trading: decrease the profit or increase the risk. Diminishing the profit is the aim of a proposal from the legendary investor Warren Buffett, one of the most successful capitalists in history—who, in 1993, was proclaimed the richest man in America.[151] Buffett is a long-term investor, who has always believed that the rewards of capitalism should emanate from business building, not from paper shuffling—or, to paraphrase columnist George Will, from pie producing, not pie dividing.[152] Testifying before a Congressional Subcommittee in 1991, Buffett declared: "I have no trouble with there being very tough penalties administered by very tough people for anybody who messes around with this market."[153]

Buffett's cure for insider trading is to impose a tax of *100 percent* on all profits earned from the sale of any stocks owned for less than one year. In Buffett's words: "The most enticing category of inside information—that relating to takeovers—would become useless."[154] Since radical ideas, especially ones entailing tax increases, seldom come from unradical multibillionaires, Buffett's proposal merits thoughtful assessment—although Buffett may be too wealthy to appreciate the average investor's need for liquidity.

The other approach to controlling insider trading—escalating the risk—is reflected in Judge Wood's deterrence strategy. How successful has that strategy been? Consider the following examples of non-deterrence:

- The very week that Ivan Boesky was paying out his $100 million fine, a young analyst with Morgan Stanley allegedly was conspiring with a Taiwanese investor to generate profits of $19 million from inside information about pending mergers to which the analyst was privy.[155]

- In 1987, a broker with a prestigious regional firm in Florida was fined for leaking confidential information about several corporations to selected clients. He contended that he was just following company policy.[156]

- In 1988, fast-food magnate Carl Karcher and his son were accused by the SEC of passing confidential information to relatives, which allowed the relatives to "dump" their shares of CKE (the Carl's Jr. chain headed by the Karchers) just four days before a public report of seriously declining profits. This information enabled the relatives to avoid $310,000 in losses.[157] The case eventually was settled out of court, and the Karchers were fined.

- Also in 1988, a consultant employed by game-show producer Merv Griffin passed inside information about Griffin's planned buyout offer for the hotel/casino company Resorts International to reputed organized crime figures. These crime figures used it to turn illegal profits when the stock later soared from $22 a share to $35 after Griffin's bid was announced.[158]

- In 1989, an employee at a pharmaceutical firm relayed insider information through her aunt to a pair of Hollywood film producers, who netted profits of over $400,000.[159]

- In 1991, the head of the bond trading desk at Salomon Brothers was accused of manipulating the bidding at government auctions of Treasury securities (Chapter 1), thus allowing his firm—and himself—to reap millions of dollars in illegal profits.[160] Shortly before this new scandal erupted, he sold $1.7 million worth of his personal shares of Salomon stock. When the disclosure came, the value of those shares decreased by about $500,000. It was alleged in the financial press that, like Ivan Boesky before him, the so-called "Salomon cowboy"[161] appeared to profit by inside information concerning his own impending arrest.[162]

- Just weeks before Michael Milken received his prison sentence in 1990, an employee of AT&T illegally traded on sensitive information he possessed regarding AT&T's intentions to acquire the NCR and Teradata Corporations. He later was fined more than $550,000.[163]

- A few weeks after Milken went to prison in 1991, two employees of Vista Chemical, a large Texas company, used confidential information about Vista's impending merger with a German firm to reap profits of nearly $900,000. In 1993, they were convicted in a Houston court, in one of the few insider trading prosecutions ever to take place outside of New York.[164]

- Shortly after Milken was released from prison in 1993, Harvard Business School withheld an MBA degree from a student indicted on insider trading charges which involved alleged profits of $500,000.[165]

- In late 1992, a young financial analyst for a large New York law firm discovered the identity of two companies that were about to be acquired by clients of that firm. According to the SEC, she passed this inside information to her father, who bought stock in the target companies, sold it immediately after the deals were announced, pocketed $60,000 in quick profits, then gave his daughter two gifts totaling $4,000.[166]

- In January 1993, a former director of the Foxboro Company—a Massachusetts-based high-tech manufacturer—was fined $2.1 million for insider trading in connection with the 1990 acquisition of that firm by a British company.[167]

- In March 1993, criminal indictments were filed against an insider trading ring, which allegedly had garnered illegal profits of $4.5 million in 1990 from nonpublic information about a proposed buyout of a French economy hotel chain by Motel 6.[168]

- One of the oddest insider trading cases also occurred in July of 1993. A judge ruled that a New York stockbroker had violated insider trading laws by receiving nonpublic information from the psychiatrist of the wife of a noted financier. The broker was fined more than $160,000 to offset profits he had made.[169]

- Also in 1994, the Grumman corporation, which had figured so prominently in the early Paul Thayer–Billy Bob Harris insider trading case, again became linked to an SEC investigation. On the Friday before a Monday announcement that Grumman would be acquired by Martin Marietta for nearly $2 billion, Grumman stock rose 8.5 percent—a strong sign of possible insider trading. Even more suspicious was that heavy buying had taken place in Grumman call options (contracts giving buyers the right to purchase Grumman shares at fixed prices) just four days before the deal was publicized. "After the announcement, Grumman shares jumped 36 percent, locking in big profits for options buyers."[170] One buyer reportedly made $400,000 on just two trades.[171]

- In February 1995, Oded Aboodi, one of Wall Street's master deal-makers, agreed to pay $1 million in penalties to settle insider trading charges brought by the SEC. Aboodi had helped structure a $2.7 billion stock offering for Time Warner, which was struggling to ease its post-merger debt. Aboodi knew, of course, that the new stock would cause existing stock to fall in value. On the day of the planned stock offering, Aboodi sold 20,000 shares of Time Warner and avoided $413,700 in losses.[172]

- In June 1995, two brothers, Richard and John Woodward, pleaded guilty to charges related to insider trading. Over a four-year period, Richard, a lawyer with a large Wall Street firm, gave his brother information regarding companies targeted for takeover by the firm's clients. John would then purchase stock. The pair netted over $250,000 in profits[173]

- A 62-year-old former broker with Oppenheimer & Company was sentenced to 10 months in jail for insider trading. The presiding judge lectured the defendant in words that echoed those delivered to Michael Milken two years earlier: "When a guy in your position commits a crime that undermines the financial and justice systems, society demands a sentence of general deterrence."[174]

Despite the assertions of the judge in the preceding vignette, it is difficult to measure the deterrent effect of the prison sentences given to Milken, Boesky, or anyone else. The number of potential insider traders dissuaded by the incarceration of others is, by its nature, indeterminable. However, all the aforementioned cases suggest that insider trading continued to occur even as some of Wall Street's biggest stars were being arrested and locked up. And there is plenty of reason to believe that it still proliferates.[175] The 1990s—supposedly the decade for rethinking the excesses of the 1980s—has seen a discouraging continuance of securities fraud. According to a 1994 report by *Business Week*: "[I]nsider trading is alive and well—and growing."[176]

Corporate takeovers totaled $339.4 billion in 1994, easily topping the previous record set in the 1988 heyday of junk-financed mergers. Also setting a record that same year were the 45 insider trading cases brought by the SEC.[177] In its investigation, *Business Week* analyzed the 100 largest stock deals of 1994 and came to a stunning conclusion: "One out of every three of the merger deals or tender offers was proceeded by stock-price run-ups or abnormal volume that couldn't be explained by publicly available information."[178] To cite just one of many suspicious examples, stock in American Cyanamid jumped 60 percent in value the day before American Home Products launched a hostile takeover bid.[179]

Furthermore, fund managers, brokers, and big traders have come under increasing attack since the 1990s for "front running"—a smaller, harder-to-detect, and increasingly pervasive form of insider trading. Front running refers to managers buying stock for themselves *before* buying it for their funds, or one broker tipping off another trader of an impending transaction in return for some kind of kickback. In either case, a quick profit is usually made, since stocks almost always rise following a large institutional purchase.[180] The practice is, of course, unethical and completely illegal.

Describing front running as "just another of the schemes that invariably arise when aggressive young men and lots of money are in close proximity,"[181] *Fortune* magazine has detailed the mechanics of this crime using an unidentified but very real young trader:

> Less than an hour before the closing bell, a wealthy young Manhattan day trader we'll call "Billy" got a call from the trading desk of a major brokerage firm. A big client was buying a million shares of Network Associates. Did Billy want to sell? The caller knew quite well that Billy did not have a million shares of Network Associates lying around. And Billy knew perfectly well that the call was not really about filling the client's order. . . . Billy quickly bought 40,000 [shares of] Network Associates, anticipating that the client's million-share buy order would cause the stock to rise. It did. Billy had unloaded his shares at a profit of around $80,000. Not bad for less than an hour's work—as long as you're willing to ignore that Billy and his pal had just committed a crime.[182]

As always, the insider's (in this case "Billy's") profits came at the expense of the legitimate investor (in this case his confederate's institutional client), "which paid a higher price than it would have had its confidential trading intentions not been betrayed."[183] Anyone who owns shares in a mutual fund or a 401(k) has probably been cheated by a front-runner. "At its basic level, an inside tip on an institution's trading plans amounts to stealing from an institution. While the theft may be small on any given trade, the constant nibbling at the margins of trades can reduce a fund's annual rate of return."[184]

CASE STUDY
The Great "Chat Room" Conspiracy

On March 14, 2000, nineteen people were arrested by federal authorities in the largest criminal insider trading case ever, in terms of the number of people who allegedly made illegal trades and the number of business deals for which inside information was stolen.[185] The case was also notable because it was

(Continued)

the first in which the Internet had been the center of an insider trading scheme. Four broker-dealers were among those charged,[186] but most of those accused were amateur profiteers—including a waiter, a retired schoolteacher, and a dentist.[187] The criminal conspiracy revolved around John Freeman, a 34-year-old ex-waiter, aspiring actor, and part-time computer graphics worker, who was employed as a late night "temp" at two major Wall Street investment bankers—Goldman Sachs and Credit Suisse First Boston. His job entailed creating or revising graphics, flow charts, spreadsheets, and other documents. His "unofficial" duties consisted of pilfering documents before they were shredded, stealing papers from printers, ransacking garbage pails, and rummaging through the desks of employees to uncover confidential information about mergers and acquisitions.[188]

In mid-1997, Freeman was in an AOL chat room where a group of investors was bemoaning money they had lost on a company that manufactures helmets. He connected with two of the chatters—James Cooper, a Kentucky insurance agent, and Benton Erskine, vice president of a West Virginia laser printing company. The three men formed an anonymous online relationship, and a few months later Freeman told the other two that he could get them inside information. They agreed to pay Freeman a percentage of their profits in return.[189]

Cooper passed the material to his brother Benjamin, part-owner of a day-trading Web site, and stockbroker Chad Conner. Conner helped the "tipees" (as prosecutors would later call them) get an unsecured bank loan to finance their trading.[190] The list of co-conspirators grew longer as time went on and included an assortment of friends, relatives, and associates.[191]

Over a three-year period, Freeman passed on stolen information involving Regal Cinemas, Illinois Central Railroad, Baker Hughes, Ciena, and many other corporations involved in sensitive negotiations.[192] The "Chat Room Gang" bought stock in the targeted companies before the merg-

ers and quickly sold it when the stock soared afterward.[193]

The renegade chatters made a total of 23 illegal trades,[194] netting a combined profit of $8.4 million.[195] Some of the "tipees" kicked back fees to Freeman, who had complained over the Internet that he was "too broke to invest."[196] Usually his "commissions" arrived in the form of birthday cards stuffed with cash.[197] Despite his "birthday presents" Freeman never staked any of his own money, believing the stock market to be too risky.[198] His share of the illegal profits came to "only" $110,000. That may be a lot of money in absolute terms. But just one of his beneficiaries, a Manhattan waiter and former co-worker, allegedly made $285,000, and—in a "man bites dog" story of a waiter tipping a customer—a regular patron at the restaurant where that waiter was employed netted a profit of $445,000.[199] The waiter reportedly paid off Freeman with cases of wine.[200]

The plot began to unravel in early 1998 when computers monitoring trades at the American Stock Exchange (Amex) flagged unusual trading in three firms.

Amex analysts checked to see who was doing the trading and found many of the same names popping up for each of the far-flung firms—Oregon Metallurgical, DSC Communications of Plano, Texas, and Coherent Communications of Ashburn, Va. Analysts also noted that several traders were from Bowling Green, Ky. and Tennessee—not exactly the hotbed of investment in the United States. . . . And in each case the trades had taken place before news reports about the firms.[201]

John Coffee, a Columbia Law School professor who specializes in corporate securities law has observed: "This is *The Gang That Couldn't Shoot Straight* of insider trading. . . . [It] is one of the dumber schemes I've encountered, because they left too much information on their trail."[202]

(Continued)

The Amex turned that information over to the SEC, which contacted the U.S. Attorney in March, 1999. The U.S. Attorney then brought in the FBI to find the source of the inside information. Because Goldman Sachs and Credit Suisse First Boston had handled all the deals in question, investigators quickly zeroed in on Freeman as someone who had access to information at both banks.[203] When telephone records revealed calls between Freeman and other suspects, the "Great Chat Room Conspiracy" was finished.

John Freeman was arrested on January 6, 2000. He pleaded guilty to twelve felony counts of insider trading and one count of conspiracy and agreed to help the government pursue the case. James Cooper was arrested on February 20, 2000. He pleaded guilty to seven counts of insider trading and one count of conspiracy and also agreed to cooperate. Remarkably, Freeman and Cooper had never even met in person.[204]

The "Great Chat Room Conspiracy" signaled the emergence of a hospitable new public arena for a crime once largely restricted to the private world of the Wall Street elite. In the 1980s, when the term "insider trading" entered the popular lexicon, it was a crime committed by the Boeskys and Levines of the world, professionals who exchanged secret information in person or via the telephone. But a decade later insider trading clearly had moved well beyond its traditional boundaries and into cyberspace. The U.S. Attorney in charge of the case called it a good example of "insider trading, millennium style."[205]

She said it showed how the nature of insider trading had changed as the public's captivation with the stock markets, and the explosion of financial information on the Internet, had led to a culture in which more people are searching desperately for the latest edge or hot tip. . . . "This is a case of Wall Street meeting Main Street and coming back again—over the Internet."[206]

The "Chat Room" case even had a little touch of Hollywood thrown in. One of the defendants traded in an account he named Blue Horseshoe Investments. In the movie *Wall Street*, Blue Horseshoe is a code name for the ruthless corporate raider Gordon Gekko (played by Michael Douglas). When Gekko says in the film: "Blue Horseshoe loves Anacott Steel," he means that he is buying Anacott stock on the basis of inside information.[207] An investigator for the Amex, who helped break the case did not find this homage to pop culture at all amusing: "A lot of us saw that movie. . . . With Blue Horseshoe it was like they were trying to rub our face in it."[208]

The Internet also played a role, albeit less conspicuously, in one of the most unusual insider trading cases to hit Wall Street. One month after the Chat Room defendants were charged, the trial of James J. McDermott, Jr., began in a New York Federal Court. McDermott, the former chairman of the investment bank Keefe Bruyette & Woods (KBW), stood accused of violating his fiduciary duties when he was chief executive of KBW by passing confidential non-public information to two confederates, who in turn traded on these illicit tips via Internet accounts.[209]

McDermott's accomplices were Anthony Pomponio, a New Jersey businessman and McDermott's mistress, Kathryn B. Gannon. What drew media and public attention to what otherwise might have been just another routine insider trading case was the revelation that Gannon, under her stage name Marilyn Star, was a porno actress and adult-film star. Indeed co-accessory Pomponio was seldom even mentioned by name in the press; he was usually simply dubbed "one other man."[210] Most of the media attention was reserved for Ms. Gannon.

McDermott, a married man with a $4 million annual income, began his relationship with Gannon in 1997. Over a two-year period he supplemented Gannon's $100,000 income with $80,000 in checks[211] *and* secret information about six KBW clients—mainly smaller or regional banks—which were the targets of merger or acquisition efforts.[212] Gannon shared the inside information with Pomponio, with whom she was also having an affair. Together they reaped an illegal profit of $170,000.[213]

James J. McDermott was convicted of six counts of insider trading and one count of conspiracy. On August 3, 2000, he was sentenced to eight months in prison. He was also fined $25,000 and ordered to perform 300 hours of community service. The trial judge, Kimba Wood, who had sentenced so many other white-collar defendants including Michael Milken, commented once again that securities fraud carries a heavy social cost by undermining investor confidence in the economy. Judge Wood, however, displayed some mercy in this case. McDermott's prison term was less than half of what federal sentencing guidelines recommend. Wood believed that McDermott was needed at home to care for a daughter with special needs.[214]

Before his sentence was handed down, McDermott turned toward the spectators inside the courtroom and apologized in a firm voice: "I was called a stud stock picker, a master of the universe. Those things couldn't be further from the truth."[215]

On December 13, 2000, Anthony Pomponio was convicted of insider trading, conspiracy, and perjury and sentenced to 21 months in prison.[216] The X-rated defendant Kathryn Gannon, aka Marilyn Star, fled to her hometown of Vancouver and faced extradition. She returned to the U.S., pled guilty, and began serving a 3-month jail term in late 2002.

More recent insider trading cases include the following:

- In 2007, Eugene Plotkin, a former Goldman Sachs analyst, pleaded guilty to insider trading, admitting he participated in a scheme that helped generate $6.7 million in illegal profits.[217] The 28-year-old Plotkin admitted paying an analyst at Merrill Lynch to leak information on pending mergers and acquisitions and paying two employees of a printing company to reveal the contents of *Business Week* magazine ahead of publication.[218] Among other charges, he and a former co-worker traded on their inside information in several accounts, including those of his partner's girlfriend, an exotic dancer, and his partner's aunt, a retired underwear seamstress in Croatia.[219] After pleading, Plotkin really began *pleading*. He told the court: "Words cannot express how sorry I am for the harm I have caused to others, especially my family."[220] Eugene Plotkin was even more sorry in January 2008, when he was sentenced in federal court to nearly five years in prison.[221]

- Two weeks after Eugene Plotkin was sentenced, a more unusual insider trading case was settled by the SEC. Eugene Tapanes, a Canadian oceanographer, was part of the crew who discovered what may be the richest shipwreck treasure in history. He was aboard the *Ocean Alert* when it was surveying the ocean floor off the coast of Gibraltar. Odyssey Marine, a publicly traded Florida-based corporation that locates and excavates treasure-laden shipwrecks, owned the ship. On March 30, 2007, Tapanes identified an anomaly on the ocean floor that turned out to be the *Black Swan*, a long lost treasure ship. Within weeks, Odyssey Marine had recovered more than 17 tons of gold and silver coins, as well as other historical artifacts. The find is estimated at more than $500 million.[222] Tapanes and the rest of the crew were required to sign non-disclosure and confidentiality agreements prohibiting them from disclosing the find or trading in Odyssey Marine stock because of their nonpublic knowledge of the discovery.[223] In the months prior to the announcement of the recovered treasure, Tapanes, in violation of the agreements, bought 42,000 shares of Odyssey stock. As soon as the announcement was made, Tapanes's stock jumped over 80 percent, netting him a profit of $107,000. When federal regulators uncovered Tapanes's violation of trust, they filed a suit against him. In January, 2008, the case was settled when the treacherous treasure hunter agreed to pay a $216,000 fine.[224]

- Michael Guttenberg, a former institutional client manager in the equity research department of UBS and David Tavdy, a former trader at the Assent brokerage, both pleaded guilty in 2008 to charges of insider trading.[225] Guttenberg sold nonpublic data from UBS stock analysts about potential downgraded and upgrades to Tavdy. Tavdy then used this private information illegally to make at least $15 million for hedge funds and $10 million for his personal account.[226] In November 2008 and February 2008, Guttenberg and Travdy were given sentences of 6 and one-half years and 63 months, respectively.[227]

- A federal jury convicted Hafiz Mohammed Zubair Naseem, a former Credit Suisse investment banker, in 2008, on charges of insider trading. Naseem made $7.5 million by leaking information about pending deals, including the $32 billion private equity buyout of the TXU power company. He would call a friend in his native Pakistan, who would then trade on the unlawful tips. Following the verdict, Naseem was immediately taken into custody and locked up to await sentencing because he was considered a flight risk.[228] A few months later, Naseem was sentenced to 10 years in prison.[229] Prosecutors had argued "a substantial sentence is necessary to send a message to Naseem [and] others on Wall Street and in similar positions where client confidences are absolutely necessary and required for the security of our capital markets."[230] The judge obviously agreed that a harsh sentence was needed to discourage insider trading. In his words: "It happens too much. It's a behavior that has to be deterred."[231] He added, "A lot of people aren't caught and should be caught."[232]

A 1996 SEC report noted—in surprisingly gentle language—that traders regularly share clients' secrets: "Market makers may at times be tempted to overlook their obligations to deal fairly with their customers."[233] Finance professor Nasser Arshadi, an authority on insider trading, is more blunt in his conclusion that "the law has not been effective" in deterring insider trading.[234]

Why has deterrence apparently not been more successful? Perhaps because the risk/reward ratio of white-collar crime remains a bargain in the minds of some market insiders. At first glance, the heavily publicized sentences that culminated in 1990, as well as some of the tough sentences in more recent cases, may appear to qualify as examples of what labeling theorist Harold Garfinkle termed "successful degradation ceremonies."[235] Just how "successful" they actually were, though, is open to interpretation, especially when one considers the post-release lifestyles of the most visibly sanctioned offenders. Dennis Levine became the head of his own firm; Ivan Boesky retired to a European estate; and Michael Milken lectured at a major university while sitting atop a fortune estimated at $500 million—carefully hidden in a maze of partnerships, junk bonds, and hugely valuable stock warrants from the 1980s. One former associate has compared Milken's personal finances to "the lost city of Atlantis."[236] It seems as though degradation ceremonies have been devalued almost as much as Drexel's bonds.

In fact, Milken, though beset by health problems, staged a remarkable business comeback. In 1994, he helped arrange media mogul Rupert Murdoch's $500 million investment in New World Communications Group. In 1995, he reportedly was paid $40 million by Murdoch to arrange a $2 billion deal—the largest fee ever paid to a "consultant." In 1996, Milken was promised $50 million for helping to facilitate the proposed merger between Turner Communications and Time Warner.[237] The consensus on Wall Street is that Milken has nimbly violated the spirit of his 1990 consent agreement with the government, under which he was banned from the securities business. One analyst has declared: "I think what he's doing makes a mockery of the SEC."[238]

A novel insider trading scandal has emerged in recent years, involving doctors at some of nation's foremost research universities, where new drugs are tested for biotech companies.

CASE STUDY
Martha Stewart Living—In a Cell

Dr. Samuel Waksal, the former CEO of the biotech company ImClone Systems, was arrested at his home on June 12, 2002, after, being indicted for conspiracy to commit securities fraud. He was charged with tipping off two people, his father and one of his daughters, to sell ImClone stock the day before federal regulators rejected the company's application for a new cancer drug, Erbitux. In the wake of the disappointing news, ImClone's stock plunged 84 percent. ImClone had reportedly been warned of the rejection two days before it happened. It was further revealed that before the FDA rejection was announced, four of Waksal's relatives sold a total of $400,000 in company stock. Additionally, one of his daughters reportedly netted $2.5 million from her sale.[239] All told, Waksal relatives sold more than $10 million in ImClone stock within a 48-hour period.[240]

Waksal, who had stepped down as ImClone CEO just three weeks earlier, was also charged with perjury for allegedly lying to the SEC about his inside tips. The SEC had already filed a civil lawsuit in federal court against him. The government was seeking a substantial civil penalty from Waksal and a restitution order requiring him to pay back the millions of dollars in losses avoided by his family and friends.[241] The SEC further charged that Waksal had tried to sell nearly 80,000 of his own ImClone shares for about $5 million, but two different brokers would not execute the order.[242]

Sam Waksal pleaded not guilty, turned in his passport, and was released on $10 million bail. His lawyers asserted his innocence; they characterized the case as "entirely circumstantial." "The government misread the evidence,"[243] they insisted. Within a month, however, Waksal was holding plea negotiations with federal prosecutors.[244] In August, ImClone filed a suit against its former CEO, claiming that Waksal ordered the destruction of documents important to the government's case.[245]

Sam Waksal was something of an oddity in the staid pharmaceutical industry. Although considered a first-rate scientist, he was also known for his glitzy parties and celebrity friends, such as Mick Jagger.[246] One of those friends was the ubiquitous maven of American domesticity, Martha Stewart. Like the Waksal family, Stewart had unloaded all 4,000 of her ImClone shares two days before the FDA action.[247] She netted about $200,000 from the sale. She steadfastly denied ever having received any non-public information about the company. Nobody seemed to believe her.

Merrill Lynch announced that it had placed Stewart's broker at Merrill Lynch, Peter Bacanovic, who had sold the shares on her behalf, "on administrative leave pending further investigation."[248] The brokerage firm said it had suspended the man after an in-house investigation had "raised factual issues regarding a client transaction."[249] The "factual issues" are as follows: The same broker reportedly had sold a big chunk of ImClone stock for Waksal's daughter. He then allegedly tried to reach Stewart. A memo from Stewart's secretary filled with notes about "plum puddings and lampshades" contained the broker's message that he "thinks ImClone is going to start trading downward."[250] One member of the House committee investigating ImClone found the memo troubling:

> He didn't say he watched it go down on the market. He said he thinks it's going to, which leads one to believe that was inside information that he had, that he then passed on to Mrs. Stewart.[251]

Stewart, a former stockbroker, had recently been made a member of the New York Stock Exchange's 27-member board of directors. The NYSE Board formulates trading rules and oversees the conduct of exchange members. If Martha Stewart

(Continued)

is ever formally accused, she would be the first board member ever involved in insider trading.[252]

On one of her weekly appearances on the CBS Morning Show, Martha Stewart assured viewers—while chopping cabbage: "I will be exonerated from this ridiculousness."[253] Her version of events differs from almost everyone else's. She insists that she had a stop-loss agreement with her broker to sell ImClone if the price dropped below $60.[254] Ten years have passed and investigators have found no evidence of such an agreement.

Stewart's credibility took another hit when Bakanovic's assistant, Douglas Faneuil, told prosecutors that he had been instructed to tell Stewart that the Waksal family was selling large amounts of stock. According to Faneuil, Bakanovic had blurted: "Oh my God, get Martha on the phone."[255] Faneuil maintained that the stop-loss order explanation had been concocted after the fact on Bakanovic's orders.[256] Phone records indicate that the broker's urgent efforts to reach Stewart had occurred when ImClone was still selling *above* $60.[257]

So much attention was focused on Martha Stewart that the only insider formerly accused of a crime, Sam Waksal, had been largely forgotten. In August 2002, federal prosecutors brought new charges against him, including obstruction of justice and bank fraud.[258] Many believed that these additional charges would expedite a plea bargain agreement under which Waksal would provide evidence against Stewart, whose uncooperative attitude had reportedly angered investigators. Waksal, however, never implicated Stewart.

In 2003, federal judge William Pauley sentenced Sam Waksal to more than seven years in prison and ordered him to pay a $4 million fine.[259] Pauley had received more than 120 letters from friends and family of Dr. Waksal, cancer patients, show business celebrities—even his ex-wife's husband—all extolling Waksal's fundamental decency and asking for leniency.[260] Waksal himself gave an emotional apology to the court, saying: "I am deeply disturbed and so very sorry for my actions."[261] Referring to his attempted cover-up, he called himself a "hysterical fool."[262]

But Judge Pauley was angry and unpersuaded:

The harm you wrought is truly incalculable . . . You abused your position of trust as chief executive officer of a major corporation and undermined the public's confidence in the integrity of the financial markets. Then you tried to lie your way out of it.[263]

In what must surely have been a note of bitter irony to Sam Waksal, ImClone had recently announced that Erbitux, the anti-cancer drug whose impending rejection had propelled Waksal from the boardroom to a prison cell, would be resubmitted for FDA approval. A German pharmaceutical company had released study results supporting the drug's efficacy.[264]

All the while, Martha Stewart's problems continued to mount. As the CEO of Martha Stewart Living Omnimedia, she saw her company's stock lose about 65 percent of its value since the ImClone revelations[265]—nearly a half billion dollars in market value. Disgruntled shareholders, asserting that she had breached her "fiduciary duty" to Omnimedia shareholders, filed a suit against her. The suit claims that her actions had damaged her brand name and reputation.[266] There is some evidence that this claim may not be all that frivolous. A survey of 1,000 consumers reported that while 56 percent had purchased Stewart brand products, about 20 percent said they were less likely to buy the items again.[267]

To make matters worse, about a third of Omnimedia's revenues come from Kmart, the ailing retailer that became yet another once-mighty corporation to fall into bankruptcy amid allegations of questionable accounting.[268] "The Martha Stewart Everyday brand, which covers products such as sheets, towels, paints, and kitchenware, is Kmart's largest volume-producing label, generating about $1.5 billion in sales last year [2001]."[269]

(Continued)

Speculation has been raised about whether Kmart might abandon Stewart.

June 4, 2003, was a day most Americans once could scarcely have imagined. Martha Stewart was arrested and charged with securities fraud, obstruction of justice, conspiracy, and making false statements to investigators and the FBI.[270] Her stockbroker was also arrested and charged with perjury and obstruction of justice.[271] Stewart was arraigned, pleaded not guilty on all counts, and was released without bail. Within hours of her arrest, she stepped down as chairman and CEO of Omnimedia.[272]

The following day, Martha Stewart published an open letter as a full-page ad in *USA Today*. Stewart declared: "I want you to know that I am innocent—and that I will fight to clear my name."[273] She also set up a personal Web site backing her cause. The site received a remarkable 1.7 million hits in its first 17 hours—the vast majority supportive. Even Stewart's critics were impressed.[274]

Conspicuously absent among the charges was one for insider trading. Although investigators may well have believed that Stewart, like a number of others, had benefitted from her friend Sam Waksal's inside information, it was assumed by many legal commentators that the government had opted for the charge of obstruction of justice, because it is generally easier to prove.[275] Securities law experts were hard pressed to recall a successful insider trading prosecution in which an investor—as opposed to a broker—had been prosecuted for piggybacking on someone else's (in this case, Waksal's) sales.[276] Moreover, the relatively insignificant gain realized by Stewart may well have helped discourage a charge of insider trading. She sold her 3,928 shares of ImClone the day before the FDA's rejection of Erbitux was announced. That news sent ImClone stock tumbling 16 percent at the close of trading the next day. By selling when she did, Stewart avoided losses of about $51,000.[277] Clearly, Stewart would argue that such an amount was inconsequential to a woman of her wealth. Whether that

could have persuaded a jury or whether the government could have successfully countered that it was all about ego and winning, rather than money, is anybody's guess.

The charge of securities fraud added an interesting twist to the Stewart indictment.

> Prosecutors say the domestic guru committed securities fraud—that is, she deliberately tried to inflate the stock of her own company—when she stood up in public . . . and denied engaging in insider trading.[278]

It was a high-risk move on the part of the prosecutors. They were, in effect, arguing that Stewart committed fraud by denying guilt of a crime (insider trading) that she had not been formerly accused of. Nevertheless, it would be hard to dispute that—if Stewart had indeed lied about her ImClone trading—thousands of ordinary Omnimedia stockholders were hurt by that alleged attempt to cover up her legal problems.[279]

Some defenders of Martha Stewart have insisted that she was being punished for being a tough, successful woman in the male-dominated milieu of big business. The U.S. Attorney in charge of the case bristles at that allegation:

> "This criminal case is about lying—lying to the FBI, lying to the SEC and lying to investors. . . . That is conduct that will not be tolerated. Miss Stewart is being prosecuted not because of who she is, but what she did."[280]

In the words of one business editor: "It's all ridiculousness, just like Martha says. But here's a tip for the next recipe book: A pinch of greed goes a long way."[281]

Martha Stewart's 2004 trial in Manhattan was an unparalleled media sensation. It was the most closely watched of all the high-profile post-Enron white-collar crime trials up to that time,

(*Continued*)

despite the relatively small amount of money involved. Each day the courthouse was surrounded by hordes of reporters and photographers. Inside the courtroom, celebrity friends of Stewart, such as Bill Cosby and Rosie O'Donnell, lent their support.

The government's star witness was, or course, Douglas Faneuil, who repeated his accusation that he had passed the inside information about Waksal to Stewart on orders from his boss, co-defendant Bakanovic. Prosecutors further contended that Bakanovic had doctored a worksheet of Stewart's after the fact by making the notation "(at) 60."[282] A forensics expert with the Secret Service testified that the mark was made in different ink.[283]

The government trumpeted Stewart's reputation as a ruthless businesswoman. In court, she was portrayed as rude, insulting, demanding, and cheap. According to testimony, she once threatened to take her portfolio elsewhere because she didn't like her brokerage's telephone hold music.[284] Far more damaging was the testimony of Stewart's personal assistant, who claimed that Stewart had altered a computer log of a December 27, 2001, message from Bakanovic. A longtime Stewart friend reluctantly testified that Stewart had confided that she had known the Waksals were dumping their ImClone stock. She said that Stewart had added: "Isn't it nice to have brokers who tell you those things."[285]

Neither Stewart nor Bakanovic testified, and their lawyers called only one witness. The defense's entire case took less than an hour. In closing arguments, the prosecutor termed the story about Stewart's pre-arrangement to sell her ImClone stock at $60 "phony," "silly," and an "after-the-fact cover story."[286] Stewart did receive some good news, however, shortly before the case went to the jury. The judge threw out the controversial securities fraud charge. It was the most serious of all the counts, carrying a maximum sentence of 10 years in prison and a $1 million fine.[287] This would be the last good news Martha Stewart would receive in that courtroom.

On the third day of deliberations, the jury convicted Stewart on all four remaining counts of obstructing justice and lying to investigators. It was considered a sweeping victory for federal prosecutors. Co-defendant Peter Bakanovic, who had largely been ignored by the press coverage, was convicted on four of five criminal counts, including perjury. He was acquitted of one count of altering a work document, presumably because the expert ink analyst from the Secret Service was accused by federal prosecutors of lying repeatedly in his testimony.[288]

An hour after the verdict, Stewart, who had maintained a poker-faced composure throughout the trial, exited the courtroom as a convicted felon. She did not respond to any questions shouted at her by reporters; but on her Web site she posted a statement: "Dear friends, I am obviously distressed by the jury's verdict but I take comfort in knowing that I have done nothing wrong."[289]

The U.S. Attorney for the Southern District of New York did address the media: "The word is—beware—and don't engage in this type of conduct because it will not be tolerated."[290] One of the jurors also spoke to the press and punctuated that sentiment: "Maybe it's a victory for the little guys who lose money in the market because of these kinds of transactions."[291]

At Stewart's sentencing hearing, the judge handed her the maximum punishment recommended under federal guidelines: Five months in prison and five months of electronically monitored house arrest. She was also fined $30,000—less than the amount she had saved by dumping her ImClone stock before it tanked. No longer poker-faced, Stewart fought back tears as she begged the court for leniency. Outside the courtroom, she was less contrite. This time she did address the media. After denouncing her treatment, she smiled and vowed, "I'll be back."[292]

In a pre-recorded television interview with Barbara Walters, which aired that evening, Stewart made what was ridiculed by many as a preposterous comparison: "There are many, many good

(Continued)

people who have gone to prison. . . . Look at Nelson Mandela."[293]

Although her conviction was still under appeal, Stewart opted to serve her sentence sooner rather than later. She explained that she wanted to be home in time for spring gardening. Before dawn on October 8, 2004, she slipped into Alderson federal prison camp, eluding many of the camera crews who had staked out the West Virginia facility.[294]

Martha Stewart returned home in March 2005 after serving her five-month sentence. She was wearing a poncho crocheted by one of her fellow inmates at Alderson. She landed by private jet at a small airport near her 153-acre estate about 40 miles north of midtown Manhattan.[295] Stewart also owned homes in Connecticut, Maine, and Long Island, but had chosen her Katonah, New York mansion as her "prison away from prison" for the next five months.[296]

A month later, Stewart asked the court to end her house arrest early. On her popular Web site, she complained that the electronic monitoring bracelet she was required to wear during her home detention was "somewhat uncomfortable and irritating."[297] "She also told the judge that serving the rest of her sentence would hamper production of her two upcoming television series."[298] In a letter to the judge, Stewart's prosecutor argued: "Minor inconvenience to one's ability to star in a television show is an insufficient ground for resentencing."[299] The judge evidently agreed. She rejected the bid, calling Stewart's sentence "reasonable and appropriate."[300] The judge further wrote:

> "Home detention is imposed as an alternative to imprisonment. It is designed to be confining," "I see no reason to modify the sentence."[301]

When her sentence ended, Martha Stewart returned to television in Fall 2005 with a daytime talk show and a weekly spin-off of Donald Trump's popular *Apprentice* reality show. The talk show was an immediate hit. The *Apprentice* show premiered to lower-than-expected ratings.[302] Those who had hoped to see a female facsimile of Trump's aggressive style and high-handed demeanor were disappointed. Despite Stewart's longstanding reputation as a tyrannical boss, she projected a new vision of a kinder, gentler Martha. Stewart reportedly was softening her image in an effort to revive her company.[303] The new CEO of Martha Stewart Living Omnimedia explained that Stewart could not play the role of demanding diva: "That would not serve the long-term interests of the company or her."[304]

Martha Stewart remains a polarizing figure. Her defenders argue that her prosecution was nothing but an envy-driven—and perhaps even sexist-driven—assault on one of the most successful women in the world. Her detractors insist that she is a criminal, not a role model.[305] During her interview with Barbara Walters, Stewart was steadfast in proclaiming her innocence: "I didn't cheat anybody out of anything."[306] If Martha Stewart truly believes that, it is astonishing that she once sat on the New York Stock Exchange Board of Directors. Her fundamental lack of understanding of the stock market is profound.

> Martha Stewart broke the rules of fair competition. She used her privileged status to gain an illegal advantage over other owners of ImClone's stock. Indeed, her illegal use of inside information is equivalent to theft—she deliberately and unethically salvaged her own investment at the expense of other shareholders.[307]

When Martha Stewart sold her ImClone shares for $60, knowing the stock was about to crash, some person (or persons) bought those shares at that price. The unfortunate buyers were not privy to Stewart's inside information and quickly lost 84 percent of their investment—so that a billionaire could avoid a $50,000 loss. Someone should ask them if they think they were "cheated."

Inevitably, politics was injected into the ImClone scandal. Martha Stewart is a major Democratic contributor and a friend of the Clintons. When she claimed that she was being persecuted by a "right wing conspiracy,"[308] it seemed like she had ripped a page out of Hilary Clinton's playbook. Most observers found her accusation hollow and unconvincing. The ImClone case seems far less about political partisanship than about protecting the integrity of securities markets.

Insider trading is an "equal opportunity" corruptor, Republicans still tread lightly around George W. Bush's years at Harkin Oil and Gas. Harkin bought Bush's failed oil company in 1986, gave him a bunch of stock, and put him on their board. As the son of the sitting vice-president, he was supposed to add some "star power" to the company's image. He sold his stock in 1990 for an $835,000 profit. Eight days later, the board's audit committee disclosed that the company had suffered huge losses, and the value of Harkin stock immediately sank like a rock.[309] "When asked later if he had used insider information to enrich himself while common investors were unaware that they were about to get whacked, George W. said he 'had no idea' that the audit report was going to be awash in red ink."[310] The problem with that denial is that Bush was a *member* of the audit committee.

CASE STUDY

Raj Rajaratnam and his Sinking Galleon

Raj Rajaratnam holds the current record for longest insider trading prison sentence; he will spend the next 11 years of his life in prison.[311] Rajaratnam is Sri Lankan Tamil, born to the South Asia head of the Singer Sewing Machine Co.[312] His family moved to England to escape Sri Lankan ethnic violence and, in 1981, Rajaratnam found his way to the Wharton School at the University of Pensylvania where he earned a master's degree.[313]

Rajaratnam began as a lending officer at Chase Manhattan Bank, joined Needham & Co. as an analyst in 1985, and would become President of that company in 1991.[314] His success at Needham & Co. allowed him to create a hedge fund in 1992 that would eventually become the "Galleon Group." Galleon led Rajaratnam to financial superstardom as the company had a net annualized return of 22.3 percent and, by 2008, the hedge fund was valued at $7 billion.[315]

Rajaratnam's success ended on October 16, 2009, when the Federal Bureau of Investigation arrested him for insider trading.[316] The Southern District U.S. Attorney described the case as the largest in United States history.[317] Rajaratnam was accused of using private information gleaned from Wharton classmates to buy and sell stock.[318] Rajaratnam's "web" of information included executives and insiders at sixteen companies, including Goldman Sachs, Procter & Gamble, Intel, Google, Hilton Hotels, Sun Microsystems, IBM, and Advanced Micro Devices.[319]

Rajaratnam's defense attorney argued that Galleon used the "mosaic theory of investing" where employees would scour the Internet and magazines for all relevant information before making a purchase.[320] The prosecution argued against this theory relying on phone correspondence. In fact, the case against Rajaratnam began with a text message: Don't buy Polycom stock "till I get guidance; want to make sure guidance OK."[321] In 2007, Rajaratnam had provided the Securities and Exchange Commission with documents for a case

(Continued)

against his younger brother and while that case never resulted in charges, the text message from Intel employee Roomy Khan to Rajaratnam served as proof that something illegal may have occurred at Galleon. Khan cooperated with authorities to help convict Rajaratnam.[322]

The stories of Galleon Group relate a "non-traditional" business environment; for the 2007 Super Bowl, the company rented a $250,000 per week mansion replete with a "large shower . . . all-female sex show," and Rajaratnam once gave a female trader $5,000 so he could stun-gun her.[323] Rajaratnam compared himself to a boxer, describ-

ing the 2008 financial crisis by saying, "I'm feeling the pain, but they can't kill me. I'm a warrior."[324]

At trial, Rajaratnam's warrior spirit was tested as tapes of his phone conversations were played: "I heard yesterday from somebody who's on the board of Goldman Sachs that they are going to lose $2 per share."[325] Rajaratnam was found guilty of all 14 counts of conspiracy and securities fraud on May 11, 2011[326] and sentenced to 11 years in prison on October 13, 2011.[327] While this is the longest sentence ever given in an insider-trading case, it's considerably shorter than the possible 24 years and five months originally sought.[328]

STOCK MANIPULATION

Insider trading is an obvious example of illegal stock manipulation; but it is not the only form this crime can take. Sometimes, it is not just the securities markets that are manipulated, but hundreds of thousands of naive *investors* as well.

CASE STUDY
A Piece of WHAT?

In 2003, the Securities and Exchange Commission rocked Wall Street when it announced that it had imposed $1.4 billion in fines and disgorged profits on the country's biggest and most powerful brokerage firms. The settlement, which had been negotiated the previous year, was the largest ever for violations of securities laws. It represented an attempt to win back the trust of investors after years of naked conflicts of interest and deep corruption. One financial reporter wrote at the time:

> Legally, mutual funds belong to their shareholders. In practice, they are often treated as the personal fiefdom of their sponsors. You're a sucker to be a serf.[329]

Most severely punished were Citibank's Salomon Smith Barney ($400 million), Merrill Lynch ($200 million), and Credit Suisse First Boston ($200 million). All three firms were accused of publishing "fraudulent" research reports. Seven other firms, namely, Morgan Stanley, Goldman Sachs, Bear Stearns, Deutsche Bank, JP Morgan Chase, Lehman Brothers, and UBS, published analyst reports described by the SEC as "misleading" and were handed somewhat lesser penalties.[330]

The settlement was built atop the rubble of the once-heralded dot.com boom that drove the stock market indices into the stratosphere in the 1990s before crashing. In the previous two years, the market had lost $8 *trillion* in shareholder value.[331]

"At the heart of the charges were that analysts hoodwinked investors by hyping up the prospects of Internet and other hi-tech companies, while privately dismissing them."[332] Perhaps the
(Continued)

most egregious offender was Henry Blodget, Merrill Lynch's star analyst, who was fined $4 million and barred from the securities industry for life. He routinely ridiculed in private the very stocks he was recommending to Merrill Lynch clients. According to in-house emails, Blodgett once publicly touted a stock he privately described as a *"piece of shit."*

Morgan Stanley's senior analysts beat the drum for a stock named Chemdex, an Internet-based distributor of medical and chemical supplies. Chemdex went public in an initial price offering (IPO) partly underwritten by Morgan Stanley and spiked up 1,620 percent in less than a year. Like so many other Internet stocks, Chemdex burned brightly than crashed ignominiously—dropping from a high of $243.50 to less than $1.00. As Chemdex was sinking into "virtual" oblivion, Morgan Stanley kept its phony "outperform" rating for months. Indeed, over an 8 1/2 month period, during which Morgan Stanley maintained its strong recommendation, Chemdex stock fell *96.2 percent.*[333]

Another damning piece of evidence was a "strong buy" recommendation for AT&T from a senior Salomon Smith Barney analyst, who previously had been bearish on the stock. "Shortly after the analyst's recommendation, AT&T chose Salomon Smith Barney to underwrite financing of its wireless unit for a fee of $45 million."[334] This routine practice by brokerage firms of hyping stocks for companies that are paying them huge fees for their investment banking services was the cornerstone of the government's case.[335] "In just one 12-month period, from mid-1999 to mid-2000, just from IPO activity, Morgan Stanley earned $517 million in fees from bringing IPOs to the public, while investors suffered losses on those IPOs averaging almost 55%."[336] The grotesque imbalance between Wall Street's profits and investors' losses is equally manifest for the other sanctioned firms.

When asked his three most important goals for 2000, a Goldman Sachs analyst wrote in a message: "1. Get more investment bank-

ing revenue. 2. Get more investment banking revenue. 3. Get more investment banking revenue."[337]

The settlement was considered a triumph for New York Attorney General Eliot Spitzer, who had initiated the investigation. Spitzer had released hundreds of documents showing repeatedly that analysts knew their own investment advice was at best biased, at worst bogus.[338] Through 2004, Spitzer racked up an impressive record, charging some of the biggest names in the mutual fund industry with fraud stemming from conflicts of interest that turned ordinary investor into marks. The SEC also did a victory lap, characterizing the settlement as "fair, reasonable and adequate."[339] But was it?

Senator Richard Shelby, chairman of the Senate Banking Committee, didn't think so. He called the fines "relatively small."[340] Other critics agreed with Shelby. It was noted that the $1.4 billion, though immense in absolute terms, was hardly more than a slap on the wrist in terms of the gigantic profits Wall Street firms made in the 1990s by fraudulently pushing overvalued stocks on duped investors.[341] It was further noted that, despite the enormity of the corruption, the case generated only administrative sanctions. No one even got a whiff of prison. There was no mention of incarceration in the settlement[342] (although Credit Suisse First Boston's star investment banker, Frank "Time to Clean Up Those Files" Quattrone, was later indicted, then acquitted, for obstruction of justice[343]). In the words of a Florida journalist: "Had such self-serving actions been the work of shyster stock boiler rooms or mob organizations, people would now be behind bars."[344]

Moreover, the settlement contained no provisions for individual restitution. "None of the money goes back to the investors who suffered the losses"[345]—although massive litigation by betrayed clients against the sanctioned firms is anticipated.

Commentator Dan Rather summed up the whole ugly scandal in one pithy sentence: "For the profit of the few, the many were played for suckers."[346]

During the frenzied bull market of the 1990s, people who never before would have dared buy a common stock were rushing into the market trying to grab their share of the unprecedented boom. If the 1980s were the golden age of insider trading, the '90s became the securities fraud decade. The reason for this is that nothing is more valuable to a swindler than credibility, and never before had phony claims of exploding profits seemed so plausible. At a time when the legitimate markets were rising 30 percent a year (with many blue chip stocks recording gains of 70 percent or more) and some new issues were doubling in value on their first day of trading, promises of instant riches, once the "dead giveaway"[347] of a scam, did not seem so outlandish. In 1998 the chairman of the SEC lamented: "The best markets bring out the worst elements."[348]

From hundreds of boiler rooms nationwide, con artists stalked trusting but inexperienced investors, trying to lure them onto the prosperity bandwagon. A single Long Island operation was making an astonishing one million telephone calls a month.[349] According to a report by the New York State Attorney General: "Regulators close a firm one day, only to find the operation reopen the next day in the same building under a different name."[350]

Like insider trading, securities fraud has moved to the Internet. The mass audience, low costs, and perceived anonymity of cyberspace is obviously attractive to crooks. In fifteen seconds a computer-literate stock hustler can send out an email that can reach a million people. A federal prosecutor has observed: "We're seeing more of the alumni of these notorious boiler rooms migrating to the Internet."[351]

Cyberspace is stuffed with hundreds of exotic investment scams—everything from wireless cable television to ostrich farming.[352] Con artists have masqueraded as financial advisers or licensed brokers on the Internet and solicited investments in fictitious mutual funds. One Michigan scam artist talked a New York investor into sending him $91,000 and cheated a Texas victim out of $10,000. Six months later, the Texan ruefully acknowledged his gullibility: "I was terribly embarrassed. I knew I'd been screwed."[353]

"PUMP AND DUMP"

Internet financial blogs and chat rooms have created a particularly hospitable environment for securities fraud. A Houston day trader was arrested in 2000 for allegedly posting a bogus press release on a Yahoo message board on the Internet stating that the giant communication equipment manufacturer Lucent Technologies expected an earnings shortfall. The day after the phony posting Lucent's stock price fell by 3.6 percent, cutting the company's market value by more than $7 billion.[354] The suspect traded 6,000 shares of Lucent stock the day the false warning was issued.[355]

The most publicized of Internet investment schemes involve microcap fraud. Often called "penny stocks" or "over the counter" stocks, microcap companies, unlike major corporations like Lucent, are often not even required to file periodic reports with the SEC. Thus, public information about these inexpensive, lightly traded, and thinly capitalized enterprises is generally limited. Moreover, they are unlisted on major exchanges, so only a relatively few brokers control the market.

Microcap stock swindlers post messages on "investors" bulletin boards and chat rooms, which abound on the Internet, about supposedly major developments at small companies. The object is to build interest in and increase the buying of the stock so that the price will shoot up. The people behind the fabricated messages then sell their shares on the run-up at an inflated profit and leave other stockholders with near-worthless paper when the stock inevitably plummets. This technique is known as *pump and dump*. For example, an Oklahoma con artist pumped and dumped to drive up the shares of Bagels and Buns, a publicly traded company with no assets, from 38 cents to $7.50 in just four months.[356]

John T. Moran, who ran one of the nation's largest brokerage firms specializing in low-priced securities (J.T. Moran & Co.), with nearly 1,000 brokers in 22 branch offices nationwide and more than 100,000 customer accounts, was convicted of securities fraud in 1991. Using boiler room tactics and high-pressure sales techniques, Moran and his brokers cajoled unwary investors into buying flimsy securities, whose price had been manipulated by the company. Moran was able to buy millions of shares of stocks at low prices, then sell them at fraudulently high prices.[357] More recently, shares of Broadband Wireless International rose a spectacular *10,000 percent* when they were pumped from 12 cents a share in late 1999 to $12 a share in early 2000—and then dumped.[358]

Cole Bartiromo, a 17-year-old California high school student, was sentenced to 33 months in prison in 2002 for using the Internet to swindle investors out of more than $1 million. He had manipulated the stock price of 15 publicly traded companies, in which he had invested. He posted thousands of false and misleading messages about the companies on Internet bulletin boards. When investors bought the stocks based on Bartiromo's postings, he sold the inflated shares, netting $91,000.[359]

Bartiromo's "pump and dump" scam was only the warm-up act for a far more ambitious swindle orchestrated by the young con artist. He raised over $2 million from more than 1,000 investors by offering them "guaranteed" and "risk-free" returns. He used this pool of money to bet on sporting events.[360] It was a pure Ponzi, spending some investors' funds to pay off others.[361]

In 2005, the Securities and Exchange Commission slapped Bartiromo with a $1.3 million fine, a record for Internet-related securities fraud.[362] In an interview from prison, where he was earning 12 cents an hour working in the kitchen, the now 20-year-old ex-millionaire seemed more angry than repentant. He griped that his high school baseball coaches had ruined his chance at a major league career because of the SEC lawsuit.[363] Like so many remorseless victimizers, Cole Bartiromo sees *himself* as the victim. The former teen swindler turned 26 in 2010 and attempted to rebrand himself as the "*Dollar $cholar*" in a bid to win a show on MTV.[364] As of this writing, however, Bartiromo remains jobless and in debt a $2.7 million penalty to the SEC and owes $1.1 million in taxes to the IRS.[365]

Not all "pump and dump" schemes rely on the Internet, however. In June 2010, a former Research and Development executive at Sequenom, Inc., Elizabeth Dragon, pleaded guilty to one count of conspiracy to defraud shareholders. Dragon used insider information about Down's syndrome testing to boost the value of the company's stock.[366] The company issued false claims about the results, misleading investors about the test's "near perfect" success,[367] which resulted in the company's stock jumping dramatically in value from $8 to $25.[368] In April 2009, the stock price dropped sharply on news that test results would be delayed due to mishandling of data.[369] Dragon faced 25 years in prison, but died of natural causes before she could be sentenced.[370]

CASE STUDY
Goldman Sachs and Abacus 2007-AC1

In April of 2010, the SEC claimed that Goldman Sachs committed securities fraud by encouraging foreign investors to invest in a collateralized debt obligation (CDO) without fully disclosing pertinent information about the CDO.[371] This information included the fact that a major hedge fund

(Continued)

had a stake in the operation that would yield it a substantial amount of money, and that it had bet *against* the same CDO it helped Goldman create.[372] After an investigation of Goldman Sachs, the SEC filed a lawsuit against them claiming that they took part in fraudulent deals that caused many European banks to lose billions of dollars.[373] The SEC focused on the collateralized debt obligation deals, known as Abacus 2007-AC1, which intended to entice foreign investors to put their money into the US housing market. One reason these investments were attacked was because the SEC believed that Goldman Sachs executive Fabrice Tourre endorsed the viability and soundness of the markets while he knew that such markets were not truly sound.[374] The Abacus deals allowed Goldman Sachs to avoid a loss in the mortgage market, and when the mortgage market disintegrated, the deals yielded the company a profit.[375]

Robert Khuzami, the lead investigator at the SEC, alleged that Goldman Sachs was allowing John Paulson, the hedge fund manager at Paulson and Co., to influence which mortgage securities were chosen for the investment portfolio which both he and Goldman bet against without disclosing this to buyers.[376] Part of Khuzami's argument is that Goldman Sachs knew this hedge fund manager wielded influence over the choices, yet still told foreign investors that the securities were chosen "by an independent, objective third-party."[377] This third-party was named by Goldman Sachs as ACA Management LLC, which had expertise in handling residential mortgage-backed securities.[378] However, Goldman Sachs did not disclose that a key player in choosing the securities was Paulson and Co., not just ACA Management.[379] John Paulson of Paulson and Co. chose 123 securities to be evaluated for inclusion in the CDO, all of which were selected on the criteria of which would default first.[380] The SEC alleged that ACA and Paulson collaborated to include 90 residential mortgage-backed securities (RMBS), and did not include several Wells Fargo mortgages, which Paulson believed were of higher quality and therefore should not be admitted.[381] None of this information was revealed to investors by Goldman Sachs, and provided the foundation for a civil suit against the company. Fabrice Tourre, one of the Goldman Sachs' executives, helped create and sell the investment, and was the primary person named by the SEC in the lawsuit.[382] While the allegedly deceptive CDO was structured under John Paulson, he was not named in the lawsuit. Tourre knew the impending future of the housing market, yet still relayed to foreign investors that the CDO was sound.[383] In addition to this, it was Tourre who failed to inform foreign investors that the CDO was backed by RMBS selected primarily by Paulson.[384] The most incriminating evidence for Tourre was an email that he addressed to a friend that included proof Tourre knew the housing market was about to fail. The email read: "More and more leverage in the system. The whole building is about to collapse anytime now . . . Only potential survivor, the fabulous Fab[rice Tourre] . . . standing in the middle of all these complex, highly leveraged, exotic trades he created without necessarily understanding all of the implication of those monstruosities [sic]!!!"[385]

The CDO deal closed on April 26, 2007, and by October 24 of that same year, about 83 percent of the RMBS included in the portfolio proposed by Goldman Sachs had downgraded. By January 2008, 99 percent had downgraded, causing investors to lose billions.[386]

The civil fraud charges were filed in April 2010, and Goldman Sachs was supposed to have a response to the suit prepared by June 21.[387] However, on June 18, the SEC granted a request made by Goldman Sachs to extend the response deadline to a later date.[388] On July 15, 2010, the SEC announced that Goldman Sachs would pay $500 million to settle the charges, the largest penalty ever paid by a Wall Street firm. In settling the case, Goldman acknowledged that its marketing materials for the subprime products it sold contained incomplete information.

While there were no criminal charges in the case, Congress had held hearings a few months

(Continued)

earlier to explore whether to provide for more specific criminal statutes for such financial non-disclosures. One of the authors of this book was called to testify as to the potential deterrent effect of such a change in the law.[389] Although Congress later decided not to increase criminal penalties, which was no doubt influenced by the efforts of financial industry lobbyists, in the hearings before a Subcommittee of the Senate Banking Committee, one lawyer offered a pointed analogy as to what had actually transpired in the Abacus case. He argued that it would be equivalent to someone purchasing a new car and not being told by the dealer that a third party would be taking out a life insurance policy on them as soon as they closed the deal.[390] As dangerous and absurd as such a transaction sounds, it's actually much worse. Given the facts of the case, that same third party would also have chosen and designed all of the safety equipment in the car.

CASE STUDY
I Was a Teenage Wheeler-Dealer

In 2000, a New Jersey teenager became the youngest person ever charged with illegal stock dealing. In fact, the 15-year-old high school student became the only minor ever sanctioned by the SEC. Jonathan Lebed was accused of buying large blocks of cheap microcap stocks, then pumping them on the Internet using financial message boards and hundreds of phony names. His investments included an importer of Italian cheese, a computer reseller, and a manufacturer of bendable toy figures based on World Wrestling Federation characters. "Within hours of Lebed's stock purchases, he would use aliases to send false or misleading e-mails, saying the stock was about to 'take off' and would be the 'next stock to gain 1,000%'"[391] and was the "most undervalued stock ever."[392] He would then dump the stock—within 24 hours—and cash in his profits. "In some instances Lebed placed a sell limit order before the market closed on the day he purchased the stock to ensure that he would not miss the price spike while he was in school the next day."[393]

The SEC brought civil fraud charges against the teenage wheeler-dealer for 11 alleged manipulations between August 1999 and February 2000. A settlement was reached in September 2000, under which Lebed neither admitted nor denied the charges and agreed to return $285,000 he had made.[394]

According to the Lebed family's attorney: "The Lebeds feel this is a very fair settlement."[395] That sentiment became even more understandable when an investigation by the television news program *60 Minutes* reported that Lebed's actual profits were about $800,000. The SEC allegedly had ignored 16 other questionable trades Lebed had made, opting to bring charges only on those cases for which the evidence was most abundant.[396] So despite a $285,000 settlement, the precocious trader cleared a profit of about a half million dollars.[397]

While the U.S. attorney's office in New Jersey investigated whether Lebed violated federal securities fraud laws and should be charged with juvenile delinquency, he was not.[398] The Justice Department has *never* prosecuted a minor in a stock fraud case. But Lebed's remarkable escapades underscore how problematic it is becoming to apply traditional criminological theories to a new breed of middle-class, computer-savvy teenagers who are reinventing juvenile delinquency.

On one hand it could be argued that juveniles charged with federal crimes typically are afforded special protection such as sealed charges, closed proceedings, and sealed outcomes; so any deterrent value of bringing a case like Jonathan Lebed's to the courts would be questionable. Moreover, a

(Continued)

former U.S. attorney has characterized any Lebed prosecution as a "grotesque overreaction."[399] He asserts: "It's one thing to pile on to John Gotti. It's another thing to pile on to a kid carried away by his ability to use the Internet."[400]

On the other hand, Lebed's conduct seems a lot more serious than puerile mischief. Every honest, if naive, investor who went down the drain after Lebed dumped his holdings was a victim. The stock market is often a zero-sum game. For every "Abbott" who makes an $800,000 profit a bunch of "Costellos" can suffer an $800,000 loss. The chairman of the SEC characterizes Lebed's scheme as "a wholesale effort at deceiving many investors,"[401] and points out that "[Lebed's] purpose . . . was not to help investors . . . but rather to line his own pockets as soon as he hyped the price of the stock."[402] The district administrator of the Philadelphia office of the SEC that handled the case maintains that Lebed broke securities laws in a number of ways: "He lied, he did anonymous false postings, he purchased cheap stocks knowing that he planned to lie to move the price and then sold in light of the price movement his lies created."[403]

Lebed himself displayed no remorse when interviewed on *60 Minutes*, insisting that he did nothing wrong. He professed: "I'm not aware of one investor that exists that I cheated."[404] In an interview with the *New York Times* his father declared: "I'm proud of my son."[405] He maintains that at least Jonathan "didn't sit behind a garage smoking pot, or stealing wheels off a car."[406] The senior Lebed may have been trying to differentiate between traditional juvenile delinquency and the newer phenomenon of "*white-collar delinquency*." Or perhaps he simply was reminded of garages and wheels and cars by the new Mercedes his son had bought for the family.

Whatever the final outcome of the case, the boy's lawyer predicts: "I think you can expect to see Jonathan Lebed in lots of entrepreneurial activities."[407] Would anyone bet against that?

Michael Saquella, who led a pump and dump spam group, pleaded guilty to fraud in 2007 for orchestrating a scam that bilked naive investors out of more than $20 million.[408] Members of the gang approached 15 small privately-held businesses that needed to raise cash and offered to help raise significant capital through the sale of stock.[409] "Through a series of stock manipulation steps, the conspirators took control of a majority of all of the company's stock—often without the company's knowledge."[410] The fraudsters then bought and sold shares among themselves, making it look like there was investor interest. They also e-mailed spam press releases, creating an artificial demand and pumping up share prices. They would then dump their shares for a huge profit. Saquella received a ten-year federal prison sentence in 2008.[411]

Also in 2008, a new twist on pump and dump was uncovered. Thirugnanam Ramenathan, an Indian native and resident of Malaysia, was sentenced to two years in federal prison for his part in an international fraud ring.[412] Instead of pumping up the price of a dormant penny stock with the customary use of spam messages, Ramenathan cut out the middleman. He hacked into Internet accounts of American brokers, sold the victims' holdings, and bought shares of lightly traded stocks—sending their price way up. The gang then swiftly dumped their own inflated holdings for a big profit.[413] A senior computer security consultant observed: "A heist like this was nothing less than audacious."[414]

THE MOB MOVES IN

With huge amounts of money being invested in securities during the biggest and longest bull market in American history, it was only a matter of time before the sharks of organized crime joined the feeding frenzy. According to a U.S. attorney: "Mobsters go wherever the money is, and obviously the stock market is one of those places."[415] Another federal prosecutor echoes this claim: "Stock manipulation is seen by the mob as an easy way to make money without much effort or risk."[416]

In March 2000, nineteen people were indicted for running a large-scale operation over a nearly three-year period that cheated unsuspecting investors out of nearly $40 million. "In predawn raids 100 federal agents arrested 11 of the 19 people charged in the stock fraud scheme, including the brother-in-law of Salvatore Gravano, the Mafia hitman turned informer better known as Sammy the Bull."[417]

The defendants represented an interesting blend, including the heads of two Manhattan brokerage firms, an alleged capo in the Bonanno crime family, and two members of the Russian Mafia who allegedly laundered the illicit profits through overseas accounts. Thousands of investors were fleeced. "In some cases the stocks these investors held plunged from being worth tens of thousands of dollars to being worthless within seconds."[418]

But cases like the two just described were only the warm-up for the largest securities fraud bust in American history. On June 14, 2000, 600 FBI agents began arresting 120 suspects across the country in the endgame of a one-year undercover investigation code-named "Uptick."[419] Operation Uptick was coordinated by the FBI, the SEC, and the National Association of Securities Dealers (NASD).[420] Uptick used wiretaps and undercover witnesses to penetrate the labyrinthine scam.[421]

Caught in the sting were 57 stockbrokers, 12 stock promoters, 30 officers and directors of companies issuing securities, 5 pension fund officials, 2 accountants, a lawyer, a hedge-fund manager, and a New York City police detective who was also treasurer of the Detective's Endowment Association. The remaining 11 indictees were alleged organized crime figures. "Authorities said the five crime families of New York—the Gambinos, Lucheses, Genoveses, Bonannos, and Columbos—had infiltrated [Wall] Street by taking over a Manhattan investment firm, DMN Capital Investments, using it as a lever to defraud investors."[422] "The charges ranged from racketeering and securities fraud to solicitation of murder, money laundering and extortion."[423]

Investors, many of them elderly, were promised returns of 100% on microcap stocks. "These investors were defrauded of at least $50 million in schemes involving stock manipulation, boiler-room sales and using the Internet to fraudulently hype stocks."[424]

The Mafia has brought in an element of violence to Wall Street seldom seen in the white-collar world of securities fraud. An assistant director of the FBI notes: "From the fish market to the stock market, the methods [the Mob] uses are always the same: violence and the threat of violence."[425] The indictment charged that the DMN used its organized crime ties to terrorize or beat brokers and other market participants who did not agree to cooperate in the scam in return for bribes.[426]

A former member of the New York State Police task force on organized crime offers a pithy postscript: "In the mirror image of Wall Street businessmen who become criminals, now you have criminals becoming Wall Street businessmen."[427]

PONZI SCHEMES: WHAT'S OLD IS NEW

On a hot august day in 2005, Daniel Marino sat down at his keyboard in his Connecticut office to write a letter to investors in Bayou Management, the hedge fund of which he was chief financial officer. The first sentence he typed was: "This is my suicide note and confession."[428] Marino then tapped out six pages detailing a seven-year fraud that cost investors more than $450 million.[429] As Marino's letter revealed, "For the past seven years I have committed a fraud of great magnitude."[430]

Bayou was a group of companies and hedge funds founded by Samuel Israel III in 1996. Investors able to invest at least $200,000 apiece gave Bayou a $300 million start-up and were promised that the fund would grow to $7 billion in ten years. The term "hedge fund" can be misleading. Hedging usually means making an investment for the purpose of reducing risk. It is generally thought of as a conservative, defensive strategy. What makes hedge funds so confusing is that they are anything but conservative. In fact, they involve complex, aggressive, and risky strategies to produce big returns for wealthy investors. Successful hedge funds (as well as those doctored and manipulated look successful) can be very lucrative for their managers. In addition to a one to two percent management fee, hedge funds have "incentive fees," typically 20 percent, on all profits. Traditional investment managers do not receive a piece of the profits.

Eventually, the Bayou fund would attract more than $450 million. But by the end of 1998, the fund had performed badly, and trading losses accumulated quickly. Bayou then created a fake accounting firm, Richmond-Fairfield Associates, to issue sham audits attesting to the fund's phony earnings.[431] Israel and Marino misappropriated money from investors by withdrawing large incentive fees every year, which they were not entitled to since the fund never made a dime of profit. It was all a brazen Ponzi scheme with new money paving over old losses. "Israel, scion of a prominent New Orleans family, and Marino, an accountant from Staten Island, New York, had pulled off one of the biggest scams ever perpetrated in the $1 trillion hedge fund industry."[432]

By 2004, Israel and Marino had stopped trading altogether and looted the rest of Bayou's assets. Nevertheless, they still sent periodic statements to investors, describing profitable trades. They claimed to have made $43 million in 2003, when in fact they had lost $49 million.[433]

Marino may well have succeeded in his suicide attempt if an anxious client had not come to Marino's office to find out why Bayou had suddenly shut down five weeks earlier.

> [I]srael said that there was nothing wrong, other than his messy divorce and the fact that he was suffering from a bad back. Because of these personal problems, he needed to close down the funds, he said, and would hand back the money invested. . . . Few of his clients believed him on either count.[434]

The client found the note and called the police, who located Marino at home in a "disheveled" state. The investor quickly discovered that the rest of Marino's letter was as shocking as its opening line. It bluntly explained that he, Israel, and former partner James Marquez had been defrauding all their investors for six years.[435] Marino's unfulfilled suicide had alerted prosecutors and signaled the end of Bayou Management. Israel and Marino were soon arraigned.

In late September 2005, the two swindlers pleaded guilty to numerous counts of fraud. In a related action, the SEC filed a civil lawsuit against Israel, Marino, and Bayou in an effort to recoup some of the investors' losses.[436]

A year later, James Marquez, Bayou's co-founder, who had left the firm in 2001, pleaded guilty in federal court to conspiracy to defraud.[437] Marquez admitted that he had helped Israel and Marino formulate trading policy and hatch the phony accounting scheme.[438] James Marquez was the first Bayou defendant to be sentenced, in January 2008. He was handed a four and a half year in prison term.[439] The judge said that his creation of a sham accounting firm to mask the scheme was "as reprehensible as anything in the storied history of securities fraud."[440]

A week later, Daniel Marino faced the music. The judge sentenced him to 20 years in prison[441]—a very long white-collar crime sentence that would have been almost unthinkable a decade earlier in the pre-Enron era. The judge was manifestly unforgiving when she said to him:

"You, Daniel Marino, were the linchpin of the fraud. Without your cooperation, they could not have pulled it off."[442] She then added: "I've never met anyone, Mr. Marino, who has stolen this much money."[443] She ordered him to begin serving his prison sentence immediately. Daniel Marino may have been prescient when he wrote in his suicide note: "If there is a hell, I will be there for an eternity."[444]

In April, 2008, it was Samuel Israel's turn. It was not his first brush with the law. In 1996, police stopped him for drunk driving and found crack cocaine in his possession. But now the stakes were so much higher. The same judge who had sternly lectured Marquez and Marino earlier, now excoriated Israel. She called him the "mastermind" of the fraud, adding, "People who commit crimes while wearing a tie do not get a break" but will be "punished severely."[445] Like Marino, Israel was sentenced to 20 years in federal prison. He was also ordered to pay $300 million in restitution and to forfeit a bank account that held more than $100 million.[446]

Samuel Israel was scheduled to report to prison on June 9, 2008—but he failed to show up. Police found his car on the Bear Mountain Bridge north of New York City. The words "Suicide is Painless" were scrawled in the dust and pollen on the hood.[447] A case that had begun with a suicide note now had another one to deal with, provided the next day by Samuel's girlfriend. She claimed Israel had left his home, 40 miles from the bridge, that morning, and told her he was going to jail. Police began dragging the Hudson River, while at the same time launching a fugitive manhunt.[448] Clearly, they were skeptical. First of all, *nobody* ever drives himself to prison. One reporter wondered what Israel had planned to do with his car for the next 20 years. "Is there valet service in the Big House? Do they park it for you until you're sprung?"[449]

Search teams dragging the river soon called it quits. A former investor predicted, "The only place this guy will wash up is a beach in the Bahamas."[450] The focus of the search shifted to area airports and border crossings. It did not take long to figure out how he had pulled off his disappearing act. A few days later, his girlfriend, successful decorator Debra Ryan, was arrested and taken into custody, charged with aiding and abetting his flight. She had helped Israel pack a recreational vehicle with an attached scooter. Early on the morning Samuel was supposed to report to prison, he drove the RV to a rest stop near where he would later abandon his car; she followed him and then drove him home. Federal officials would not reveal who drove Israel's car to the bridge and wrote the "Suicide is Painless" message on the hood or who they believe later drove Israel from the bridge to his RV.[451] Whatever the logistics, Israel made his escape in the waiting RV, headed for parts unknown.[452]

Ryan was released on $75,000 bail. Eleven days later, she received a tearful voice mail.

"Hey, baby, it's me, it's Sam. I love you so much. I'm so sorry, baby. I had no idea you had been arrested."[453]

On June 9, 2009, Judge Kenneth Karas sentenced Debra Ryan to 3 years of probation, a sentence much shorter than the possible 10-year prison sentence for her involvement.[454]

On July 2, 2008, Samuel Israel III, on the run for nearly a month, finally surrendered to police in Massachusetts, 95 miles from the federal prison he had tried unsuccessfully to avoid. His half-baked "suicide" charade was not so painless after all.

Obviously, the Bayou Hedge Fund scam was a major scandal, but six months later the mother of all Ponzis would dwarf it. The financial collapse that shook the U.S. economy so badly in 2008, that it is seriously compared to the economic crisis of the Great Depression, was surely bad enough. But in the final weeks of that year, a shocking story emerged that poured oil on an already raging fire.

CASE STUDY
Madoff Made Off with Billions

On December 11, 2008, the FBI arrested 70-year-old Bernie Madoff, former chairman of the NASDAQ stock exchange and a quiet but highly regarded force on Wall Street for decades. Madoff had confessed to running a massive investment fraud believed to have lost at least $65 billion.[455] According to the FBI, Madoff had informed three senior employees that Bernard L. Madoff Investment Securities, ranked in the top one percent of American securities firms, had been insolvent for years. "Madoff told the employees he was 'finished,' that he had 'absolutely nothing,' that 'it's all just one big lie.'"[456]

When the agents showed up at Madoff's opulent $7 million New York apartment, they told him, "We're here to find out if there's an innocent explanation."[457] According to the agents, Madoff responded, "There is no innocent explanation." He told the agents it was entirely his fault and that he "paid investors with money that wasn't there."[458]

Madoff's sons, who worked for their father, had alerted the FBI. Bernie Madoff had admitted to them on December 10 that his advising business was a "giant Ponzi Scheme."[459] Since 2005, he had been taking money from new investors to pay out cash to earlier ones.[460] Both sons denied any knowledge of their father's scam, and, while rumors persisted that charges were pending, as of late 2011, neither son had been charged.[461] Mark, the elder son, committed suicide on the two-year anniversary of his father's arrest.[462]

The scheme finally came unraveled because some of Madoff's investors needed liquidity in the wake of the ongoing credit crunch and had asked for $7 billion in redemptions—money Madoff did not have.[463] This is how most Ponzi schemes collapse. Too many investors seek to pull out their money at the same time, and the crook atop the pyramid does not have the cash on hand.

A question that many people were asking—and are still asking—is *why* did Bernie Madoff confess? A crisis management expert, Eric Dezenhall, writes that he was "floored" by the confession:

> "My experience with these affairs is that the accused *uber-gonif* [master criminal] tells everyone who will listen, including his legal and damage control team, that the charges against him are 'total bullshit.' Not that some of the allegations are wrong; rather Virtually Every Negative Thing Being Said About Me Is 100% Certified Grade-A Imported Bullshit."

So, again, why did Madoff confess? One possibility is that he bought into two notions floated by the media after almost every scandal. These, according to Dezenhall, are: (1) Confess and the problem will go away; and (2) It's the cover-up that nails you.[464]

In Dezenhall's view, both these canards are nonsense. Confessions are a prelude to conviction, not vindication. As Dezenhall explains: "[A]dmissions don't make your victims and the public want to forgive you. They make them want to *kill* you."[465]

And Dezenhall further argues that the idea that the cover-up is worse than the crime rests on an illusion of visibility.

> "Failed cover-ups may often make the initial crime worse. But the typical model should be built on the many successful cover-ups. When cover-ups work, you don't hear about the initial crime. So the real lesson is: if you are going to do a cover-up, do it well."[466]

Bernie Madoff appeared to reject the reflexive pattern of upperworld denial. But many people suspect that, in fact, he did not; that his confession actually *was* a cover-up of a sort. There was widespread speculation that, by trying to take all the blame himself, Madoff could have been covering

(Continued)

up for accomplices—or even family.[467] Before he was caught, Madoff reportedly was working on a scheme to dole out his firm's remaining $200 million to employees and family members, but his attempt to pay bonuses early drew attention and was not completed before his arrest.[468]

Bernard Madoff had started his brokerage firm five decades earlier with money he had earned as a lifeguard at a New York beach. He was best known for being a pioneer in the business of *market-making*. Market makers act as middlemen between buyers and sellers of stocks.

> It is an essential function for a market like the Nasdaq, which doesn't have an actual trading floor where buyers and sellers can meet face-to-face. Madoff's firm was a major driver behind the growth of the Nasdaq, creating a system that courted brokers who had mostly traded stocks on the larger New York Stock Exchange to do more of their business with the Nasdaq. . . . He brought a lot of business to the Nasdaq.[469]

While many other "boutique" brokerages later sold out to larger firms, Madoff Securities stayed a family business.[470]

In the 1990s, Bernie Madoff used his success as a market maker to help launch an asset management firm. He raised money for his fund by courting investors at county clubs where he was a member. Many of his clients invested in his funds through a network of "feeder funds," which were sold by other firms. These funds carried the brand names of their parent firms, but sent the money to Madoff to be managed. Many of these funds leveraged their investments in Madoff's funds, which amplified the losses they suffered from the implosion of Madoff's company.[471]

Despite the dramatic suddenness of the scandal, there had been warning signs. The Chairman of the Securities and Exchange Commission claimed less than a week after the discovery of the massive Ponzi that "credible and specific allegations" about Madoff had been made to the SEC since at least 1999.[472] Madoff's funds supposedly were low-risk investments. Since 2004, his largest fund had generated consistent returns of 7.3 to 9 percent a year, averaging around 8 percent.[473] Even in 2008, amid a general market collapse, Madoff's fund reported that it was up 5.6 percent through November, while the S&P 500 stock index fell 38 percent.[474] Madoff claimed to follow a *split-strike conversion* strategy, which entails owning stock and buying and selling options to limit downside risk. Many experienced options traders questioned how that strategy could generate those kinds of returns so consistently.[475] "For years there were whispers on Wall Street about Bernard Madoff's hedge funds. The cynics said the returns were too good, too steady and Madoff's operation always looked too slim for the tens of billions of dollars it was managing."[476]

The ripple effect of the Madoff scandal was devastating—and international. Investors lost billions of dollars in the UK, France, Japan, Switzerland, and Spain.[477] In the U.S., some of victims were billionaires, such as New York real estate magnate Mortimer Zuckerman[478] and New York Mets owner Fred Wilpon—who reportedly lost $300 million.[479] However, most victims were not nearly billionaires. Among Madoff's alleged victims were baseball legend Sandy Koufax and actor John Malkovich.[480] An SEC investigator interviewed more than 30 other alleged victims; some had entrusted Madoff with all their savings. He described their pain:

> They were living comfortable lives and serene retirements. . . . These people are panicked. These people are sorrowful. These people are angry. And many are now destitute.[481]

The 69-year-old dean of a Massachusetts law school learned that he and a friend might have lost millions of dollars between them. He said in an interview:

> "This is a major disaster for a lot of people . . . You work all your life, you finally manage
> *(Continued)*

to save up something, and somebody who's entrusted with it, turns out suddenly he's a crook. Lots of people are getting fully or partially wiped out."[482]

Indeed, on the day the story broke, about a dozen angry investors gathered in the lobby of the Lipstick Building in midtown Manhattan, where Madoff Securities is headquartered, and demanded to know the fate of their money. One of them groused, "We're getting screwed left and right."[483] A rival hedge fund manager would later state it in more elegant terms. He said that these victims' nest eggs had gone to "money heaven."[484]

Bernie Madoff's gigantic swindle was both a Ponzi scheme *and* an affinity scam.

The damage appears to be deepest in the world of Jewish philanthropy, where Madoff was a leading figure. The North Shore-Long Island Jewish Health System said it lost $5 million. The Julian J. Levitt Foundation, based in Texas and focused on Jewish causes, lost about $6 million.[485]

Yeshiva University, a New York institution where Madoff served on the board, lost $14.5 million.[486] Also, New Jersey Senator Frank Lautenberg, one of the wealthiest members of Congress, entrusted his family's charitable foundation to Madoff. A charity headed by movie director Steven Spielberg, the Wunderkinder Foundation, was another major victim.[487] The Elie Wiesel Foundation for Humanity, founded by the Nobel Peace Prize laureate, which runs centers in Israel to help Ethiopian Jews and Darfuri refugees, along with other humanitarian work, lost **all** of its assets.[488]

One attorney, who specializes in hedge funds, noted: "It's surprising that the auditors for these various funds didn't identify that the underlying assets were not there."[489] The difference between the Madoff case and other hedge fund fraud cases in which auditors have already been held liable was

that, amazingly (or maybe not), Madoff was not a client of any of the major accounting firms. Madoff's company used a small New York City accounting firm, which reportedly had its office in a strip mall and had only three employees—a secretary, an accountant, and a partner in his 70s who lived in Florida.[490] Why the tiny size of Madoff's accounting firm didn't raise a giant red flag is anybody's guess.

Indeed, red flags were apparent . . . if one was looking for them. Harry Markopolos was the chief investment officer for Rampart Investment Management.[491] One of Ramparts business partners, Access International, had accounts with Madoff's hedge fund. Rene-Thierry Magon de la Villehuchet, the chief executive officer of Access, met with Rampart officials in 1999 and explained the amazing returns he was receiving through Madoff's hedge fund.[492] The Rampart management was intrigued and tasked Markopolos to design a strategy like Madoff's.

Upon inspection, Markopolos noted more than a few problems with Madoff's investment strategy. Markopolos believed the structure was too poorly conceived to make money and, if it did, it would not have made money so consistently as the paperwork claimed.[493] With four hours of work, Markopolos announced the only way to maintain Madoff's numbers was through fraud. Markopolos took his findings to the SEC in 2000, 2001, 2005, 2007, and 2008.[494] The memo he sent in November 2005 was titled "The World's Largest Hedge Fund is a Fraud," and described 30 different warning signs over the course of 21 pages.[495] He had analyzed 14 years of data to write the report. The SEC did not investigate Madoff after any of Markopolos' attempts.[496]

Twelve days after Madoff's arrest, two days before Christmas, Access' CEO Villehuchet was found in his Manhattan office with his wrists slashed and a box-cutter nearby. The 65-year-old founder had lost as much as $1.4 billion to Madoff's Ponzi scheme.[497] A statement issued by his family said that Villehuchet "Could not cope with the

(Continued)

pressure following the outbreak of the scandal. This is a farewell from someone who had done nothing wrong."[498] It is not yet known if Villehuchet was the subject of any planned feeder fund lawsuits. He was eulogized by a friend as an "aristocrat but not a snob." If any proof of that were needed, the friend added that when Villehuchet was sailing his yacht, "he was one of the boys."[499]

Just as unusual as Madoff admitting his crimes, on March 12, 2009, he pleaded guilty to all the charges against him including: mail fraud, making false statements, money laundering, perjury, securities fraud, and wire fraud.[500] While Madoff's two assistants, David Friehling and Frank DiPascali, have plead guilty to various charges[501] none were ever filed against Madoff's sons or wife and some believe that this is due to Madoff's guilty plea and insistence that he alone was responsible for the Ponzi scheme.[502]

After pleading guilty, Madoff explained that he began the scheme in 1991 and maintained it for nearly two decades by depositing money from investors into his personal Chase Manhattan Bank account.[503] He would then simply pay from the same account when investors asked for withdrawals. Continuing the simplicity, to maintain the scheme's records, Madoff used only one server in the "back office" on the 17th floor of the Lipstick

Building in New York City.[504] This computer, an IBM AS/400, was decades old and required data to be entered by hand. To keep security tight, Madoff allowed his legitimate business, on the 18th and 19th floors, to use email, but the 17th floor staffers were barred from electronic communication.[505]

On June 29, 2009, Madoff was sentenced to 150 years in prison, the maximum sentence allowed.[506] For Madoff, at 71, this meant a life sentence. Neither of Madoff's sons spoke to him during his trial, some argue through anger, while others argue to avoid charges of their own.[507] Irving Picard, the court-appointed trustee in charge of returning Madoff's pilfered funds, filed a civil suit against the brothers on October 2, 2009.[508] As mentioned earlier, on the second anniversary of Madoff's arrest, one of the sons committed suicide in his apartment.[509] He was the third person to take his life after Access' Villehuchet in 2008 and a British soldier who had lost his entire family's savings, William Foxton, in 2009.[510] Ruth Madoff, Bernie's wife, gave up $77.5 million of her $80 million as part of Bernie's sentencing and was also sued by Picard for stolen funds.[511]

Picard has been successful at reclaiming $9.1 billion of the $17.3 billion claimed by victims.[512] He has begun mailing out checks; the first batch worth $2.5 total was sent on September 20, 2012.[513]

Unfortunately, it took a national economic crisis and a major recession to uncover Madoff's Ponzi scheme. Financial crashes always seem to reveal crooks and fraudsters. As Warren Buffett puts it: "After all, you only find out who is swimming naked when the tide goes out."

There is an old Wall Street adage that sometimes the bulls win, sometimes the bears—but never the pigs. If it were only so.

Notes

1. Quoted in: Anderson, Dennis. "Mouseketeer Darlene Goes on Trial Today." *Houston Chronicle*. November 30, 1998: p. A3.
2. *Ibid.*
3. *New York Times*. "Former Mouseketeer Guilty in Stock Swindle." December 12, 1998: p. A10.
4. Anderson, *op. cit.*
5. *New York Times*, December 12, 1998, *op. cit.*
6. Anderson, *op. cit.*
7. *New York Times*. "Former Mouseketeer Will Be Jailed for Fraud." March 12, 1999: p. A20.
8. Sheets, Kenneth R. "How the Market Is Rigged Against You." *U.S. News & World Report* 101, December 1, 1986: 44–51.

9. *Ibid.*

10. Durham, Brad. "Party's Over in the U.S.: End of the Greedy '80s." *WORLDPAPER*, January 26, 1992: p. 6.

11. *Wall Street Journal.* "Two Agree to Plead Guilty in the Collapse of Technical Equities." July 5, 1988: p. E26.

12. Lewis, Anthony. "Maintain Laws Against Securities Fraud." *Houston Chronicle*, May 23, 1995: p. 16A. See also: Keenan, William, Jr., "On the Trail of the Serpent." *Sales & Marketing Management* 147, September, 1995: 84–85.

13. Sterngold, James. *Burning Down the House: How Greed, Deceit, and Bitter Revenge Destroyed E. F. Hutton.* New York: Summit Books, 1990.

14. Coleman, James W. *The Criminal Elite* (Third Edition). New York: St. Martin's Press, 1994: p. 89.

15. Thio, Alex. *Deviant Behavior* (Third Edition). New York: Harper & Row, 1988.

16. McCool, Grant and Graybow, Martha. "Madoff Pleads Guilty, is Jailed for $65 Billion Fraud." *Reuters.* March 13, 2009.

17. Cho, Jang Y. and Shaub, Michael K. "The Consequences of Insider Trading and the Role of Academic Research." *Business & Professional Ethics Journal* 10: 83–98.

18. The Economist: "SEC: Next Please." January 24, 1987: p. 74.

19. In our description of the Thayer case, we rely heavily on Mark Stevens' (1987) excellent account.

20. Stevens, *op. cit.*, p. 18.

21. Thio, *op. cit.*

22. Stevens, *op. cit.*, p. 21.

23. Winans, R. Foster. *Trading Secrets: Seduction and Scandal at* The Wall Street Journal. New York: St. Martin's Press, 1986: p. 13.

24. *Ibid.*, p. 12.

25. Francis, Diane. "Business as Usual in the Greed Game." *Maclean's* 101, November 7, 1988: p. 11.

26. Winans, *op. cit.*, p. 303.

27. Frantz, Douglas. *Levine & Co.: Wall Street's Insider Trading Scandal.* New York: Henry Holt, 1987: p. 352.

28. Dentzer, Susan. "Greed on Wall Street: A Spectacular Insider-Trading Case Scandalizes the Investment Community." *Newsweek*, 107 May 26, 1986: p. 46.

29. Brill, Steven. "The Rise and Fall of an Insider." *U.S. News & World Report* 101, December 1, 1986: 52–54.

30. DeMott, John S. "Finger Pointing: Wall Street's Scandal Grows." *Time* 128, July 14, 1986: p. 46.

31. Stewart, James B. *Den of Thieves.* New York: Simon & Schuster, 1991.

32. Frantz, *op. cit.*

33. The numbers are taken from a chart constructed by Dentzer and colleagues (1986): p. 45.

34. Stewart, *op. cit.*

35. Frantz, *op. cit.*

36. *Ibid.*

37. Stewart, *op. cit.*

38. Dentzer, *op. cit.*

39. Welles, Chris. "The Mysterious 'Coincidences' in Insider Trading Cases." *Business Week*, September 8, 1986: 76–77.

40. Quoted in Taylor, John. "The Insiders." *New York* 26, April 19, 1993: p. 183.

41. Levine, Dennis. "The Insider." *New York Magazine*, September 16, 1991: 38–49.

42. Reese, Jennifer. "Boy, Have I Got a Deal for You." *Fortune* 127, March 8, 1993: p. 135.

43. Stewart, *op. cit.*

44. Marks, Peter. "Ethics and the Bottom Line." *Chicago Tribune Magazine*, May 6, 1990: p. 26.

45. Powell, Bill. "The Levine Case: New Names." *Newsweek* 108, July 14, 1986: p. 55.

46. Labich, Kenneth. "The Fast Track Ends for One Baby Boomer." *Fortune* 113, June 9, 1986: p. 101.

47. The confusing and at times contradictory details of Ivan Boesky's youth and early career have been gleaned from a variety of sources, most notably Frantz (1987), Stevens (1987), and Stewart (1991).

48. Frantz, *op. cit.*, p. 146.

49. *Ibid.*

50. *Ibid.*

51. Wyser-Pratte, Guy. *Risk Arbitrage II.* New York: New York University Press, 1982. Wyser-Pratte relates an early example of classic risk arbitrage involving the famous Rothschild bank of London. When Wellington defeated Napoleon at Waterloo, Rothschild received the news first—via carrier pigeon. In a bold strategy, the bank began unloading its British holdings, which unleashed a selling panic on the London Stock Exchange. Rothschild then secretly began buying back the now-undervalued British government bonds. By the time the Waterloo news finally arrived by more conventional (and much slower) means, the bank had made a financial killing.

52. Boesky, Ivan F. *Merger Mania.* New York: Holt, Rinehart & Winston, 1985.

53. Frantz, *op. cit.*, p. 148.

54. *Ibid.*, p. 149.

55. *Ibid.*

56. Stevens, *op. cit.*

57. Frantz, *op. cit.*

58. *Ibid.*

59. Stevens, *op. cit.*, p. 125.

60. *Ibid.*

61. *The Economist.* "Insider Trading." November 22, 1986: 15–16.

62. Tell, Lawrence J. "Inside Information: It Isn't Always Easy to Define." *Barron's* 66, November 24, 1986: 56–57.

63. Stewart, *op. cit.*

64. Quinn, Jane B. "Stocks: The Inside Story." *Newsweek* 109, March 16, 1987: p. 54. See also *New York Times.* "Boesky Payout to Investors." July 12, 1993: p. 5.

65. Edgerton, Jerry. "What the Boesky Scandal Means to You and Your Money." *Money* 16, January, 1987: 64–67.

66. Stein, Benjamin J. "The Reasons Why: What Motivated the Insiders." *Barron's* 67, February, 23, 1987: 16, 22.

67. Tabb, William. "What the Boesky Case Means: The Apple Falls Near the Tree." *The Nation* 243, December 13, 1986: 668–672.

68. Rowan, Hobart. "White Knuckles on Wall Street." *Washington Post*, November 20, 1986: p. A27.

69. Tabb, *op. cit.*

70. Russell, George. "A Raid on Wall Street: Agents Put the Cuffs on Insider Traders." *Time* 129, February 23, 1987: 64–66.

71. Baer, Donald. "Handcuffs on Wall Street." *U.S. News & World Report* 102, February 23, 1987: 38–39.

72. *Ibid.*

73. Kinkead, Gwen. "Ivan Boesky: Crook of the Year." *Fortune* 115, January 5, 1987: 48–49.

74. Dickerson, John F. "Battling Boeskys." *Time* 141, May 3, 1993: p. 57.

75. Stewart, *op. cit.*

76. Stewart, James B. and Hertzberg, Daniel. "Unhappy Ending: The Wall Street Career of Martin Siegel Was a Dream Gone Wrong." *Wall Street Journal*, February 17, 1987: pp. 1, 30.

77. *Ibid.*

78. *Ibid.*

79. Baer, *op. cit.*

80. Frantz, *op. cit.*, p. 161.

81. Stewart, *op. cit.*

82. Henriques, Diana. "Handcuffing the Street?: Effects of the Inside-Trading Scandal Will Be Severe." *Barron's* 67, February 16, 1987: 18–24.

83. Pauly, David. "New Arrests on Wall Street: Who's Next in the Insider-Trading Scandal?" *Newsweek* 109, February 23, 1987: 48–50.

84. Stolley, Richard B. "The End of an Ordeal." *Fortune* 128, October, 1993: 138–146.

85. Quint, Michael. "Repayment and Ban Set in Insider-Trading Case." *New York Times*, July 8, 1993: p. 4. See also, Moses, Jonathan N. "SEC Suit Settled by Ex-Partner of Goldman Sachs." *Wall Street Journal*, June 8, 1993: p. 14.

86. *The Economist.* "Insider Trading Cases: A Bridge Too Far?" April 18, 1987: 76–77.

87. Russell, *op. cit.*

88. Byron, Christopher. "Happily Ever After." *Esquire* 123, April, 1995: p. 60.

89. Bruck, Connie. *The Predator's Ball: The Junk Bond Raiders and the Man Who Staked Them.* New York: Simon and Schuster, 1988.

90. *Ibid.*, p. 29.

91. Alcaley, Roger E. "The Golden Age of Junk." *New York Review of Books* 41, May 26, 1994: p. 32.

92. Bruck, *op. cit.*

93. Stewart, *op. cit.*, p. 43.

94. Norris, Floyd. "The Breakdown of 'Junk': Drexel's Innovations Built Some Fortunes but the Costs May Hurt the Nation Badly." *New York Times*, November 22, 1990: pp. A1, D4.

95. Bruck, *op. cit.*

96. *Ibid.*

97. *Ibid.*, p. 49.

98. Bruck, *op. cit.*

99. *Ibid.*, p. 60.

100. *Ibid.*

101. Schwartz, Steven F. "The Frequent Liars Program: Providing Incentive for Wall Street's Snitches." *Barron's* 68, March 7, 1988: p. 72.

102. *The Economist.* "Ivan Boesky: Ever So Helpful." December 26, 1987: 33–34.

103. Stewart, *op. cit.*

104. *Ibid.*

105. Stewart and Hertzberg, *op. cit.*

106. Bruck, *op. cit.*

107. Stewart, *op. cit.*

108. *Ibid.*, p. 201.

109. Zey, Mary. *Banking on Fraud.* New York: Aldine De Gruyter, 1993.

110. *Ibid.*

111. *Ibid.*

112. Taub, Stephen. "From Rats to Riches." *Financial World* 163, April 26, 1994: 22–26.

113. *Ibid.*, p. 391.

114. *Wall Street Journal.* "Drexel: Prosecution and Fall." February 15, 1990: p. A14.

115. Andrews, Suzanna. "Michael Milken Just Wants to Be Loved." *New York*, June 10, 1996: p. 26.

116. *Ibid.*, p. 28.

117. *Ibid.*, p. 28.

118. Samuelson, Robert J. "The Super Bowl of Scandal." *Newsweek* 108, December 1, 1986: p. 64.

119. *Ibid.*, p. 16.

120. Stevens, *op. cit.*, p. 254.

121. Francis, *op. cit.*, p. 11.

122. Meulbroek, Lisa K. "An Empirical Analysis of Illegal Insider Trading." *Journal of Finance* 47, 1992: 1661–1699. See also, *The Economist.* "Inside Out." May 22, 1993: p. 86.

123. *The Economist.* "Cheating Is Wrong… Isn't It?" May 7, 1988: p. 73. See also, Leland, Hayne E. "Insider Trading: Should It Be Prohibited?" *Journal of Political Economy* 100, August, 1992: 839–857.

124. Fuhrman, Peter. "The Securities Act of 1988?" *Forbes* 139, March 9, 1987: 40–41.

125. Cho and Shaub, *op. cit.*

126. Alpert, William M. "Judgment Day: Ivan Boesky Draws Three-Year Jail Term." *Barron's* 67, December 21, 1987: 24–25.

127. *The New Republic.* "The Other Scandal." May 23, 1987: p. 6.

128. Anders, George and Mitchell, Constance. "Junk King's Legacy." *Wall Street Journal*, November 20, 1990: p. 1.

129. Stewart, *op. cit.*, p. 430.

130. Zey, *op. cit.*, p. 55.

131. *Ibid.*

132. Noer, David M. *Healing the Wounds: Overcoming the Trauma of Layoffs and Revitalizing Downsized Organizations.* San Francisco: Jossey-Bass, 1993.

133. Quoted in Martz, Larry. "True Greed." *Newsweek* 108, December 1, 1986: 48–50.

134. Associated Press. "Downsizing Proving Costly, Strategists Say." *Houston Post*, July 6, 1994: pp. C1, C4.

135. Powell, Bill and Friday, Carolyn. "The Feds Finger the King of Junk." *Newsweek*, September 19, 1988: 42–44.

136. Stewart, *op. cit.*

137. Andrews, *op. cit.*, p. 25.

138. Glassman, *op. cit.*, p. 27A.

139. Stein, Benjamin J. "The Biggest Scam Ever?" *Barron's*, February 19, 1990: 8–9, 30–32.

140. *Ibid.*, p. 8.

141. Bruck, *op. cit.*, 206–207. See also, Hylton, Richard D. "On Wall St., New Stress on Morality." *New York Times*, September 11, 1991: pp. D1, D3.

142. *Ibid.*

143. Anders and Mitchell, *op. cit.*

144. Heins, John. "Tom Spiegel's (Dubious) Claim to Fame." *Forbe's* 142, November 14, 1988: 153–156.

145. Salwen, Kevin G. "Three Ex-Officials of Lincoln Savings State Fraud Charges with the SEC." *Wall Street Journal*, September 25, 1991: p. A5.

146. Salwen, *op. cit.*

147. *New York Times.* "Too Much Milken Moralizing." November 27, 1990: p. A22.

148. *New York Times.* "Stunning Justice in the Milken Case." November 22, 1990: p. A26.

149. Rudolph, *op. cit.*, p. 54.

150. Eichenwald, Kurt. "Milken Gets 10 Years for Wall St. Crimes: Term is Longest of Any Given in Scandal." *New York Times*, November 22, 1990: A1, D5.

151. Lenzner, Robert. "Warren Buffett's Idea of Heaven: 'I Don't Have to Work with People I Don't Like'." *Forbes 400*, October 18, 1993: 40–48.

152. Will, George. "Keep Your Eye on Giuliani: Handcuffs on Wall Street Wrists Stress that Crimes Can Be Committed in Genteel Surroundings." *Newsweek* 109, March 3, 1987: p. 84.

153. Henriques, Diana B. "House Panel Assails Treasury Regulation." *New York Times*, September 5, 1991: pp. D1, D26.

154. *Ibid.*, p. 84.

155. Work, Clemens P. "A 'Chinese Wall' that's Less than Great at Stopping Secrets." *U.S. News & World Report* 105, July 11, 1988: p. 42. See also, Collingwood, Harris. "Was Morgan Stanley Asleep at the Switch?" *Business Week*, July 11, 1988: 26–27; and *Time* 132. "The Littlest Insider." July, 11, 1988: p. 45.

156. Antilla, Susan. "Stock Picks Plauged by Leaks." *New York Times*, January 22, 1993: p. D1.

157. Szockyj, Elizabeth. "Insider Trading: The SEC Meets Carl Karcher." *Annals of the American Academy of Political and Social Science* 525, 1993: 46–58.

158. Mahar, Maggie. "Wheel of Misfortune." *Barron's*, May 6, 1991: p. 18.

159. *New York Times.* "Insider Cases Are Settled." February 13, 1993: p. 11.

160. Fuerbringer, Jonathan. "Salomon Brothers Admits Violations at Treasury Sales." *New York Times*, August 10, 1991: pp. 1, 37.

161. Bartlett, Sarah. "Solomon's Errant Cowboy." *New York Times*, August 25, 1991: pp. 1, 10.

162. Fuerbringer, Jonathan. "Dismissed Salomon Trader Sold Stock Before Scandal." *New York Times*, August 29, 1991: pp. D1, D6.

163. *New York Times.* "Insider Case Is Settled." March 11, 1993: p. D5.

164. Harlan, Christi. "Two Are Convicted of Insider Trading by Houston Jury." *Wall Street Journal*, July 7, 1993: p. 8B.

165. *New York Times.* "An M.B.A. Is Withheld." May 21, 1993: p. D18.

166. France, Mike. "Insider Traitors." *New York* 28, May 1, 1995: 15–16.

167. *New York Times.* "S.E.C. Suit Is Settled." January 14, 1993: p. D16.

168. Moses, Jonathan M. "More Are Named In Probe of Motel 6 Insider Trading." *Wall Street Journal*, March 5, 1993: p. B4. See also, *New York Times.* "Insider Case Is Expanded." March 5, 1993: p. D9.

169. *Wall Street Journal.* "Insider-Trading Ruling." July 1, 1993: p. B5.

170. *US News & World Report.* "Grumman's Suspicious Rise." Vol. 116, March 21, 1994: p. 14.

171. *Ibid.*

172. Pogrebin, Robin. "Aboodi Who?" *New York* 28, February 6, 1995: 23–25.

173. Jensen, Rita H. "Cravath Lawyer Admits to Insider Trading." *ABA Journal 81*, September, 1995: p. 26.

174. *Wall Street Journal.* "Former Trader Sentenced." February 25, 1993: p. B12.

175. Antilla, Susan. "The Murky World of Front-Running." *New York Times*, February 7, 1993: p. 15.

176. Barrett, Amy. "Insider Trading." *Business Week*, December 12, 1994: p. 70.

177. *Houston Post.* "17 Implicated in AT&T Insider Trading." February 10, 1995: pp. C1, C3.

178. Barrett, *op. cit.*, p. 71.

179. *Ibid.*

180. Baldo, Anthony. "Sweeping the Street." *Financial World*, August 16, 1994: 61–63. See also: Kelly, Kate and Craig, Susanne. "NYSE Probe Reaches 5 of 7 Specialist Firms." *Wall Street Journal.* April 18, 2003: C1. Kelly, Kate and Craig, Susanne. "Big Board is Probing Specialists for Possible 'Front-Running'." *Wall Street Journal.* April 17, 2003: A1. Ip, Greg and Craig, Susanne. "Trading Cases: NYSE's 'Specialist' Probe Puts Precious Asset at Risk: Trust." *Wall Street Journal.* April 18, 2003: A1.

181. Vinzant, Carol. "The New Improved Game of Insider Trading." *Fortune* 139, June 1999: p. 115.

182. *Ibid*

183. *Ibid*, p. 116.

184. *Ibid*, p. 116.

185. Drew, Christopher. "THE MARKETS." *New York Times.* March 15, 2000: p. C1. See also: McMorris, Francis A., Smith, Randall, and Schroeder, Michael. "Insider Case Involves a Temp at Two Brokers and Web Ring." *Wall Street Journal.* March 15, 2000: pp. C1, C13; Witheridge, Annette. "Wall Street Hit by Cyber Scam." *The Scotsman.* March 16, 2000: p. 13.

186. Freeman, John. J. and Labate, John. "19 Charged in Dollars 8.4m Insider Trading Case." *Financial Times.* March 15, 2000: p. 23.

187. *Cleveland Plain Dealer.* "Temp Allegedly Leads Insider Trading Ring." March 15, 2000: p. 4C.

188. Walsh, Sharon. "Office Temp Gave Out Merger Secrets Online." *Washington Post.* March 15, 2000: p. A01.

189. O'Donnell, Jayne. "Inside Trading with a Net Connection." *USA Today.* March 27, 2000: p. 1B.

190. *Ibid.*

191. Valdmanis, Thor. "Internet Played Role in Inside-Trading Case." *USA Today.* March 15, 2000: p. 1B.

192. Valdmanis, *op. cit.*

193. Smith, Greg B. "Nab Temp in Stock Scam." *Daily News.* March 15, 2000: p. 7.

194. Tompkins, Wayne. "Six in State Accused of Insider Trading." *Louisville Courier-Journal.* March 15, 2000: p. 1.

195. O'Donnell, *op. cit.*

196. *Ibid.*

197. *Ibid.*

198. *The Guardian.* "Chat Room Trades Result in Charges." March 16, 2000: p. 28.

199. Smith, *op. cit.*

200. *Ibid.*

201. O'Donnell, *op. cit.*, p. 1B.

202. Quoted in: Farrell, Greg. "Net Snags Inside Trading Suspects." *USA Today.* March 16, 2000: p. 3B.

203. O'Donnell, *op. cit.*

204. *Ibid.*

205. Quoted in: Drew, *op. cit.*, p. C1.

206. *Ibid.*, p. C1.

207. O'Donnell, *op. cit.*, p. 1B.

208. Quoted in *Ibid*, p. 1B.

209. Labate, John. "Wall St. Braced for Unusual Insider Trading Case." *Financial Times.* April 10, 2000: p. 8.

210. *Ibid.*

211. Neumeisier, Larry. "'Marilyn Star' a No Show." *abcnews.com.* April 10, 2000.

212. Labate, *op. cit.*

213. Neumeisier, *op. cit.*

214. *Ibid.*

215. Quoted in *Ibid.*

216. *Reuters.* "Businessman Gets Jail for Using Trade Tips from Porn Star." *Yahoo!. Finance.* December 14, 2000.

217. Neumeister, Larry. "Guilty Plea in Insider Trading Case." *securities.stanford.edu.* April 29, 2007.

218. Guehenno, Claire M. "Grad Pleads Guilty to Insider Trading." *thecrimson.com.* April 30, 2007.

219. "Ex-Goldman Associate Is Sentenced in Insider Trading Case." *nytimes.com.* January 3, 2008.

220. Quoted in Sherman, B. "Ex-Goldman Sachs Worker Pleads Guilty to Insider Trading." *oregonlive.com.* August 28, 2007.

221. Douglas, Stewart. "Goldman Sachs Man Sees a 5 Year Sentence." *bankingtimes.co.uk.* January 4, 2008.

222. Duggan, Ed. "Treasure Finder Loses Stock Windfall." *South Florida Business Journal* (online). January 18, 2008.

223. Foggo, Daniel. "Ocean Surveyor Guilty of Insider Trading." *business.timesonline.co.uk.* January 19, 2008.

224. Gordon, Marcy. "SEC Fines Shipwreck Explorer." *Washington Post.* January 18, 2008: p. D8.

225. *nytimes.com.* "2 Plead Guilty For Insider Trading." February 28, 2008.

226. *stockbrokerfraud.com.* "Ex-UBS Executive Pleads Guilty to Insider Trading and Could Spend 90 Years in Prison." March 13, 2008.

227. "Former Broker is Sentenced to 5 Years for Insider Trading." *nytimes.com.* February 24, 2009:B7.

228. Graybow, Martha and Honan, Edith. "Ex-Credit Suisse Banker Found Guilty of Insider Trading." *reuters.com.* February 4, 2008.

229. *dawn.com.* "Convict Gets 10 Years in Prison: Insider Trading Scam." May 31, 2008.

230. Quoted in *nbc.com.* "Ex-Credit Suisse Banker Gets 10 Years Jail Sentence." May 31, 2008.

231. Quoted in *Ibid.*

232. Quoted in Haider, Masood. "Convict Gets 10 Years in Prison: Insider Trading Scam." *dawn.com.* May 31, 2008.

233. Quoted in *Ibid*, p. 116.

234. Quoted in *Ibid*, p. 119.

235. Garfinkle, Harold. "Conditions of Successful Degradation Ceremonies." *American Journal of Sociology* 50: 353–359.

236. Quoted in Andrews, *op. cit.*, p. 29.

237. Andrews, *op. cit.*

238. Quoted in Scott, Walter. "Personality Parade." *Parade*, May 12, 1996: p. 2.

239. *nysscpa.org.* "Former ImClone CEO Arrested in Alleged Securities Fraud Plot." June 9, 2002.

240. *Houston Chronicle.* "Inside Info Is Alleged at ImClone." June 13, 2002: 2.

241. *Ibid.*

242. *money.cnn.com.* "ImClone Ex-CEO Nabbed." June 12, 2002.

243. Quoted in *Ibid.*

244. *money.cnn.com.* "Waksal, Prosecutors in Talks." July 12, 2002.

245. *siliconvalley.com.* "ImClone Files Suit Against Ex-CEO Waksal." August 14, 2002.

246. Agovino, Theresa. "The Party's Over/ImClone Scandal Ends Ex-CEO Waksal's Fun." *Houston Chronicle.* June 30, 2002: C7. *Houston Chronicle.* "Inside Info Is Alleged at ImClone." June 6: C2.

247. *news.bbc.co.uk.* "Ex-ImClone Boss Charged with Fraud." June 12, 2002. *Houston Chronicle.* "ImClone Case May Ensnare Martha Stewart." June 14, 2002: C1.

248. *news.bbc.co.uk.* "Martha Stewart Broker Suspended." June 22, 2002.

249. Quoted in *Ibid.*

250. Blakemore, Bill. "Martha's Sale." *abcnews.com*, June 23, 2002.

251. Quoted in *Ibid.*

252. *Ibid.*

253. Quoted in *Houston Chronicle.* "Inquiry Is 'Ridiculousness'/Stewart Chops ImClone Questions Short on TV Show." June 26, 2002.

254. O'Donnell, Jayne and Farrell, Greg. "Panel Ponders Stewart Subpoena." *usatoday.com.* August 8, 2002.

255. Quoted in *foxnews.com.* "Martha Stewart Convicted on All Four Counts." March 8, 2004.

256. *Houston Chronicle.* "Stockbroker's Assistant Alleges He Was Forced to Tip Off Stewart." August 6, 2002: C5. Gasparino, Charles. "Merrill Lynch Assistant Says He Urged Sale After Waksal, Family Sold Shares." *msnbc.com*, August 6, 2002. Fineberg, Tina. "Martha Stewart Faces More Heat." *usatoday.com.* August 6, 2002.

257. *time.com.* "Martha's Untidy Story." August 11, 2002.

258. *cbsnews.com.* "ImClone Exec in Trouble." August 8, 2002.

259. Usborne, David. "ImClone's Waksal Jailed for Seven Years." *news.independent.co.uk.* June 11, 2003.

260. Hurtado, Patricia. "Waksal's Friends, Family Stand by Their Man." *www.nynewsday.com.* June 10, 2003.

261. Quoted in Hess, Diane. "Sam Waksal Gets Seven Years for ImClone Scandal." *www.thestreet.com.*

262. Quoted in Hurtado, *op. cit.*

263. Quoted in Hays, Constance L. "ImClone's Waksal to Pay Heavy Price." *Houston Chronicle.* June 11, 2003: 1C, 4C.

264. Hess, *op. cit.*

265. Lewis, Al. "Martha: A Dash of Deceit?" *denverpost. com*, August 11, 2002.

266. Madore, James T. "Stewart Gets Sued." *newsday. com*, August 3, 2002.

267. Sindrich, Jackie. "Stewart Mess Repels Some Buyers, Survey Says." *Houston Chronicle*, July 21, 2002: C8.

268. *money.cnn.com*. "Kmart Files Chapter 11." January 22, 2002.

269. Moses, Alexandra R. "Kmart's Image Could Suffer from Martha Stewart's Case." *Houston Chronicle*, June 28, 2002: C3.

270. Scannel, Kara and Cohen, Laurie P. "Martha Stewart, Broker Indicted." *Wall Street Journal*. June 5, 2003: C1, C9. Countryman, Andrew. "Stewart Indicted in Insider-Trading Case." *Houston Chronicle*. June 5, 2003: 1A, 12A. McClam, Erin. "Martha Stewart Pleads Innocent to Charges." *cnnmoney.com*. June 4, 2003.

271. *Ibid.*

272. Farrell, Greg. "Stewart Charged, Steps Down." *USA Today*. June 5, 2003: 1B.

273. McClam, Erin. "Martha Stewart Resigns From Media Company." *cnnmoney.com*. June 6, 2003.

274. Horovitz, Bruce. "Stewart Uploads Her Cause to Web Site." *USA Today*. June 6, 2003: 3B.

275. Masters, Brooke E. "Stewart Pleads Not Guilty to All Charges." *washingtonpost.com*. June 5, 2003.

276. *Ibid.*

277. Eng, Paul. "Martha Stewart Indicted: Pleads Not Guilty." *abcnews.com*. June 5, 2003.

278. McClam, Erin. "Stewart's Denial Now Part of Case." *Houston Chronicle*. June 6, 2003: 1C, 2C.

279. *Ibid.*

280. Quoted in Eng, *op. cit.*

281. Martin, *op. cit.*

282. *Ibid.*

283. *Ibid.*

284. Scheiber, Dave. "His music miffed Martha." *sptimes.com*. February 19, 2004.

285. Quoted in *Ibid.*

286. Quoted in *foxnews.com*, *op. cit.*

287. *money.cnn.com*. "Stewart Convicted on All Charges." March 5, 2004.

288. Mcclam, Erin. "Stewart Sentenced to 5 Months in Prison and Vows: 'I'll Be Back.'" *detnews.com*. July 17, 2004.

289. Quoted in *money.cnn.com*, *op. cit.*

290. Quoted in *Ibid.*

291. Quoted in *foxnews.com*, *op. cit.*

292. Quoted in Mccan, *op. cit.*

293. Quoted in *Ibid.*

294. Masters, Brooke A. "Stewart Begins Prison Term." *Washington Post*. October 9, 2004: E1.

295. Fitzgerald, Jim. "Martha Stewart Arrives Home With Media Horde." *usatoday.com*. March 4, 2005.

296. *foxnews.com*. "Martha Stewart Released From Prison." March 5, 2005.

297. Quoted in *moneycentral.msn.com*. "Judge Nixes Martha Stewart's Bid For New Sentence." April 11, 2005.

298. *Ibid.*

299. Quoted in *Ibid.*

300. Quoted in *Ibid.*

301. Quoted in *Ibid.*

302. *money.cnn.com*. "Get Used to the New, Softer Martha." September 29, 2005.

303. *Ibid.*

304. Quoted in *Ibid.*

305. Starr, Steven. "Martha Stewart Is a Criminal, not a Role Model." *yaledailynews.com*. February 6, 2004.

306. Crawford, Krysten. "Martha: I Cheated No One." *money.cnn.com*. July 20, 2004.

307. Starr, *op. cit.*

308. Stanley, Barbara. "Martha Stewart's Mess: Not a Right Wing Conspiracy." *toogoodreports.com*, August 26, 2002. *Houston Chronicle*. "Democrats Postpone Stewart Event." June 16, 2002: A3.

309. Hightower, Jim. "Just Another Corporate Greedhead." *austinchronicle.com*, July 19, 2002.

310. *Ibid.*

311. Pulliam, Susan and Bray, Chad. "Trader Draws Record Sentence." *wsj.com*. October 13, 2011.

312. Mehta, Suketu. "The Outsider." *thedailybeast.com*. October 23, 2011.

313. *Ibid.*

314. Burton, Katherine and Kishan, Saijel. "Raj Rajaratnam Became Billionaire Demanding Edge." *bloomberg.com*. October 19, 2009.

315. *Ibid.*

316. de la Merced, Michael and Kouwe, Zachery. "Arrest of Hedge Fund Chief Unsettles the Industry." *nytimes.com*. October 18, 2009.

317. *Ibid.*

318. Mehta, *op. cit.*

319. Pulliam, *op. cit.*

320. Lattman, Peter and Ahmed, Azam. "Hedge Fund Billionaire is Guilty of Insider Trading." *nytimes.com*. May 11, 2011.

321. Pulliam, *op. cit.*

322. *Ibid.*

323. *Ibid.*

324. Lattman, *op. cit.*

325. *Ibid.*

326. *Ibid.*

327. Pulliam, *op. cit.*

328. *Ibid.*

329. Middleton, Timothy. "Don't Let Crooks Manage Your Money." *moneycentral.msn.com*. September 9, 2003.

330. Gordon, Marcy. "Wall St. Firms to Pay $1.4B in SEC Deal." *www.yourlawyer.com*. April 29, 2003. English, Simon. "Wall Street Rocked by $1.4bn Fines." *www.telegraph.co.uk*. December 21, 2002.

331. Simon, December 21, 2002, *op. cit.*

332. Tran, Mark. "$1.4bn Wall Street Settlement Finalised." *www.guardian.co.uk*. April 28, 2003.

333. Trigaux, Robert. "$1.4-Billion Settlement Just a Slap on Wall Street's Wrist." *www.sptimes.com*. May 5, 2003.

334. Marder, David E. "Will the $1.4B Settlement Change Wall Street?" *boston.bizjournals.com*. January 20 2003.

335. *Ibid.*

336. Harding, Si. "The Punishment of Wall Street Firms." *www.thebullandbear.com*. May 3, 2003.

337. Gordon, April 29, 2003, *op. cit.*

338. Marder, *op. cit.*

339. McClam, Erin. "SEC Defends $1.4B Wall Street Settlement." *seattlepi.nwsource*. June 16, 2003. On April 12, 2005, the SEC hit 20 former NYSE floor traders and investment specialists with civil charges, accusing them of fraudulent trading between 1999 and 2003 designed to bolster the profits of their firms. That same day, the Department of Justice filed criminal charges against those same individuals, accusing them of abusing their positions in order to reap millions of dollars in profits that should have gone to outside investors. (Farrell, Greg. "20 Former NSYE Floor Traders Charged." *USA Today*. April 13, 2005. 1A.)

340. Quoted in Gordon, Marcy. "Senators Scrutinizing New $1.4 Billion Settlement with Wall Street Firms." *www.montanaforum.com*. May 7, 2003.

341. Harding, *op. cit.*

342. *The Salt Lake Tribune*. "Wall Street Sharps." *www.sltrib.com*. December 28, 2002.

343. Paczkowski, John. "Feds Charge Quattrone with Binge and Purge." *www.siliconvalley.com*. April 2003. *news.bbc.co.uk*. "Corruption Charge for Bank's Fallen Star." March 7, 2003. Quattrone was the head CSFB's Global Technology Group and handled shares in "hot" new listings by high-tech firms. It was alleged that he kept a list of about 300 favored clients—known as the "Friends of Frank"—to whom he allocated shares in these sought after listings, guaranteeing them big profits. This practice—tantamount to giving out cash gifts—is a violation of trading rules. One of the "Friends of Frank" reportedly reaped a 58,000 percent profit. Quattrone was also accused of encouraging his team of analysts to issue overly enthusiastic research reports, thus inflating the value of those stocks. The obstruction of justice charge stemmed from an email Quattrone sent his department during the SEC investigation, allegedly urging employees to purge their files of incriminating documents.

344. Trigaux, *op. cit.*

345. Harding, *op. cit.*

346. Rather, Dan. "Tainted Stock Data Played Investors for Suckers." *Houston Chronicle*. May 4, 2003: 8C.

347. Henry, David. "Bull Market Brings Rush of Con Artists." *USA Today*. February 12, 1998: p. 3B.

348. Quoted in *Ibid*, p. 3B.

349. *Ibid.*

350. Quoted in *Ibid*, p. 3B.

351. Quoted in: Lowry, Tom. "Stock Hustlers Creep Out of Boiler Room and Onto Internet." *USA Today*. August 23, 1999: p. 1B.

352. Consumers' Research. "On-Line Investment Schemes: Fraud in Cyberspace." Vol. 77, August, 1994: 19–22.

353. *Ibid.*, p. 56

354. *Seattle Times*. "Day Trader Charged with Fraud for False Lucent Press Release." March 31, 2000: p. E5. See also: *New York Times*. "Trader Is Arrested in False-Report Case." March 31, 2000: p. C2; *Los Angeles Times*. "Day Trader Held in Profit-Warning Scheme." March 31, 2000: p. C3.

355. *Wall Street Journal*. "Day Trader Is Charged with Posting on Web False Lucent Warning." March 31, 2000: p. C18. See also: *Ottawa Citizen*. "Phony Lucent Scare on Web Leads to Day Trader's Arrest." March 31, 2000: p. D3.

356. Spears, Gregory. "Cops and Robbers on the Net." *Kiplinger's Personal Finance Magazine*, February 1995: 56–59.

357. Hagedorn, Ann. "Ex-Moran Chief Enters Guilty Plea in Stock Fraud Case." *Wall Street Journal*. July 22, 1991: p. A2.

358. Andrejczak, Matt and O'Brien, Stephanie. "SEC Brings Charges in Fraud Sweep." *cbsmarketwatch.com*. September 6, 2000.

359. *billingsgazette.com*. "High School Schemer Hit With Record Fine." May 12, 2005.

360. *cbsnews.com*. "Cyberscamming Teens." February 14, 2002.

361. Reckard, E. Scott. "O.C. Man, Who as Teenager Ran Online Scam, Fined $1.3 Million." *Los Angeles Times*. May 11, 2005: C2.

362. *billingsgazette.com*, *op. cit.*

363. Reckard, *op. cit.*

364. Hardesty, Greg. "Former Teen Swindler Tries to Start Over." *ocregister.com*. December 10, 2010.

365. *Ibid.*

366. Fikes, Bradley. "Sequenom Exec Pleads Guilty to Securities Fraud." *nctimes.com.* June 3, 1999.

367. *Ibid.*

368. Perry, Tony. "Former San Diego Biotech Executive Pleads Guilty to Lying to Pump Up Stock Price." *latimes.com.* June 3, 2010.

369. *Ibid.*

370. Edwards, Jim. "Death of an Insider: R&D Chief Passes Before She Can Testify in Stock Fraud Case." CBS News. March 25, 2011.

371. U.S. Securities and Exchange Commission. "SEC Charges Goldman Sachs With Fraud in Structuring and Marketing of CDO Tied to Subprime Mortgages." *www.sec.gov.* April 16, 2010.

372. *Ibid.*

373. Story, Louise and Morgenson, Gretchen. "S.E.C. Accuses Goldman of Fraud in Housing Deal." *nytimes.com.* April 16, 2010.

374. Quinn, James. "Goldman Sachs, Fabrice Tourre and the Complex Abacus of Toxic Mortgages." *telegraph.co.uk.* April 16, 2010.

375. Story, *op. cit.*

376. U.S. Securities and Exchange Commission, *op. cit.*

377. Quoted in *Ibid.*

378. *Ibid.*

379. *Ibid.*

380. Quinn, *op. cit.*

381. *Ibid.*

382. Story, *op. cit.*

383. Quinn, *op. cit.*

384. *Ibid.*

385. Quoted in *Ibid.*

386. U.S. Securities and Exchange Commission, *op. cit.*

387. Rosenbaum, Eric. "Goldman Gets Extension in Fraud Case: Report." *thestreet.com.* June 18, 2010.

388. *Ibid.*

389. Pontell, Henry N. "Wall St. Fraud and Fiduciary Responsibilities: Can Jail Time Serve as an Adequate Deterrent for Willful Violations?" Testimony before the Subcommittee on Crime and Drugs, Committee on the Judiciary, United States Senate, One Hundred Eleventh Congress, Second Session, May 4, 2010, Serial No. J-111-88. Washington DC: U.S. Government Printing Office, pp. 132–141.

390. *Ibid.*

391. Knox, Noelle. "Teen Settle Stock-Manipulation Case." *usatoday.com.* September 21, 2000.

392. *cnn.com.* "Teen Stock Tout to Pay $285,000 for 'Pump and Dump' Scheme." September 21, 2000.

393. *abcnews.com.* "Precocious 'Pump and Dumper'?" September 21, 2000.

394. *Ibid.*

395. Quoted in Knox, *op. cit.*

396. Associated Press. "Manipulating a Profit." *abcnews.com.* October 20, 2000.

397. Associated Press. "Stock Manipulator's Crime Did Pay." *usatoday.com.* October 20, 2000.

398. Bloomberg. "Teen Stock Manipulator Not Out of Woods." *usatoday.com.* October 5, 2000.

399. Quoted in *Ibid.*

400. Quoted in *Ibid.*

401. Quoted in Associated Press, *abcnews.com. op. cit.*

402. Quoted in *Ibid.*

403. Quoted in *cnn.com. op. cit.*

404. Quoted in Associated Press, *abcnews.com. op. cit.*

405. Quoted in Bloomberg, *op. cit.*

406. Gelsi, Steve. "Teen Defends Stock-Promotion Actions." *cbsmarketwatch.com.* October 19, 2000.

407. Quoted in *abcnews.com.* September 21, 2000, *op. cit.*

408. Keizer, Gregg. "Pump-and-Dump Spam Nets Scammers $20 Million." *computerworld.com,* September 18, 2007.

409. Gaudin, Sharon. "Four Guilty in E-Mail Pump-and-Dump Case That Netted $20 Million." *informationweek.com.* September 7, 2007.

410. Quoted in *Ibid.*

411. U.S. Securities and Exchange Commission (press release). "Stock Promoter Receives 10-Year Sentence For Orchestrating Spam-Fueled Pump-and-Dumps of Unregistered Offerings." March 19, 2008.

412. Mark, Roy. "Pump-and-Dump Hacker Gets 2 Years." *eweek.com,* September 9, 2008.

413. *sophos.com.* "New-Style Pump-and-Dump Hacker Sentenced," September 9, 2008.

414. Quoted in *Ibid.*

415. Quoted in: Mulligan, Thomas S. "120 Charged in FBI Probe of Mafia Securities Scams." *Los Angeles Times.* June 15, 2000: p. 1A.

416. Quoted in: Lowry, Tom. "Mob Linked to Stock Fraud." *USA Today.* February 6, 1998: p. 1B.

417. Feuer, Alan. "19 Charged in Stock Scheme Tied to Mob." *New York Times.* March 3, 2000. p. B3.

418. *Ibid.*

419. Knox, Noelle. "FBI Swoops Down on Wall Street Mob Authorities Arrest 120 in Farthest-Reaching Securities Fraud Yet." *USA Today.* June 15, 2000: p. 1B. See also: McNair, James. "9 in Area Accused of Stock Fraud." *Miami Herald.* June 15, 2000: p. 1A.

420. Anderson, Lisa. "Feds Charge 120 in Stock Fraud Scheme." *Chicago Tribune*. June 15, 2000: p. 1A.

421. Mulligan, *op. cit.*

422. Kaul, Donald. "Seems Like the Mob Got a bit Exuberant, Too." *Houston Chronicle*. June 22, 2000: p. 24A.

423. Walsh, Sharon. "120 Charged in Probe of Mob on Wall St." *Washington Post*. June 15, 2000: p. A1.

424. *Ibid*, p. A1.

425. Quoted in Knox, *op. cit.*, p. 1B.

426. Knox, Noelle. "Mob Linked to Stock Scam." *USA Today*. June 15, 2000: p. 1A.

427. Quoted in: O'Harrow, Robert, Jr. "On Wall Street Families Cooperated." *Washington Post*. June 15, 2000: p. A21.

428. Doran, James. "Suicide Note Rang Alarm Bells Over Hedge Fund Millions." *timesonline.co.uk*. September 5, 2005.

429. Cantrell, Amanda. "Bayou Founder, CFO Plead Guilty to Fraud." *cnnmoney.com*, September 29, 2006.

430. Burton, Katherine and Urban, Rob. "Bayou Fraud Exposes Tale of Lies, Drugs, Violence." *bloomberg.com*, October 27, 2005.

431. Cantrell, *op. cit.*

432. Burton and Urban, *op. cit.*

433. Cantrell, *op. cit.*

434. Doran, *op. cit.*

435. *Ibid*.

436. *msnbc.com*. "Bayou Hedge Fund Founder, CFO Plead Guilty." September 29, 2005.

437. *newyorkpost.com*. "Bayou Big: I'm Guilty," December 15, 2006.

438. *northcountygazette.org*. "Third Broker Pleads Guilty in Bayou Hedge Fund Scam," December 19, 2006.

439. United States Attorney, Southern District of New York. "Bayou Principal Sentenced to 51 Months for Conspiring to Defraud Investors of More Than $10 Million." January 22, 2008.

440. Quoted in *bloomberg.com*. "Bayou Sentencing," January 22, 2008.

441. United States Attorney, Southern District of New York (press release). "Bayou Funds Ex-CFO Sentenced to 20 Years in Federal Prison for Defrauding Investors of More Than $450 Million." January 29, 2008.

442. Graybow, Martha. "Bayou Ex-CFO Sentenced to 20 Years in Prison." January 29, 2008.

443. Quoted in *Ibid*.

444. Siegel, David. "Suicide or Scam? Hedge Fund Faker Vanishes on Way to the Hoosegow." *Washington Post*. June 14, 2008: p. C1.

445. Quoted in Siegel, Aaron. "Bayou 'Mastermind' Gets 20-Year Sentence." *investmentnews.com*, April 15, 2008.

446. *Ibid*.

447. Kronenberg, Jerry. "Scammer Leaves Suicide Note, Disappears." *bostonherald.com*, June 11, 2008.

448. Kennedy, Helen. "Hedge-Fund Swindler Disappears After Leaving 'Suicide Note' at Bridge." *nydailynews.com*, June 11, 2008.

449. Siegel, *op. cit.*

450. *Ibid*.

451. Dolan, Laura. "Missing Hedge Fund Manager's Girlfriend Arrested." *cnn.com*. June 19, 2008.

452. Schwartz, Nelson. "Girlfriend Arrested in Disappearance of Samuel Israel 3rd, Fugitive Bayou Fund Chief." *iht.com*. June 20, 2008.

453. Weinreb, Karen. "Beauty and the Bandit." *marieclaire.com*, December, 2008.

454. United States Attorney. "Debra Ryan, Former Companion of Convicted Swindler Samuel Israel, is Sentenced to 3 Years of Probation for Helping Him Avoid Jail." *justice.gov*. June 9, 2009.

455. McCool, Grant and Graybow, Martha. "Madoff Pleads Guilty, is Jailed for $65 Billion Fraud." *Reuters*. March 13, 2009.

456. Neumeister, Larry. "Former Nasdaq Leader Accused of Operating Massive Fraud Scheme." *Houston Chronicle*, February 12, 2008.

457. Quoted in *Ibid*.

458. Honan, Edith and Wilchins, Dan. "Bernard Madoff Arrested Over Alleged $50 Billion Fraud." *yahoonews.com*, December 12, 2008.

459. Voreacos, David and Glovin, David. "Madoff Turned in by Sons After Confessing $50 Billion Fraud." *bloomberg.com*, December 12, 2008.

460. Goldstein, Matthew. "Credit Crunch Unmasks Madoff." *msnbc.com*. December 12, 2008.

461. Neumeister, Larry and Hays, Tom. "After 3 Years, Chance of More Madoff Charges Fade." *thefiscaltimes.com*. October 3, 2011.

462. Caruso, David and Dobnik, Verena. "Madoff's Eldest Son Hangs Himself in NYC Apartment." *foxnews.com*. December 11, 2010.

463. Krantz, Matt. "Officials: $50B Lost in Fraud." *usatoday.com*, December 12, 2008.

464. *Ibid*.

465. Quoted in *Ibid*.

466. Quoted in *Ibid*.

467. *Ibid*.

468. Lieberman, David; Gogoi, Pallavi; Howard, Teresa; McCoy, Kevin; and Krantz, Matt. "Investors Remain

Amazed Over Madoff's Sudden Downfall." *usatoday. com*. December 15, 2008.

469. Gandel, Stephen. "Wall Street's Latest Downfall: Madoff Charged With Fraud." *time.com*. December 12, 2008.

470. *Ibid.*

471. *Ibid.*

472. Quoted in Krantz, Matt and Gogoi, Palavi. "SEC Looks Into Madoff Red Flags." *USA Today*, December 17, 2008: p. 1B.

473. Honan and Wilchins, *op. cit.*

474. Applebaum, Binyamin, Hilzenrath, David S., and Paley, Amit R. "Investors Reel From 'One Big Lie.'" *Houston Chronicle*, December 14, 2008: p: A34.

475. *Ibid.*

476. Goldstein, *op. cit.*

477. *newsvine.com*. "Alleged Madoff Fraud Has Worldwide Exposure," December 11, 2008. *google.com*. "Top Investors Duped in Madoff's Alleged Fraud," December 13, 2008.

478. *newsvine.com.*, *op. cit.*

479. Honan and Wilchins, *op. cit.*

480. McCoy, Kevin. "More Madoff Victims Named." *USA Today*, February 6, 2009: 1B.

481. Neumeister, Larry. "Former NASDAQ Chairman Madoff Confesses to 'Epic' Fraud." *sun-sentinel.com*, December 12, 2008.

482. Quoted in *Ibid.*

483. Stempel and Plumb, *op. cit.*

484. *Ibid.*

485. Applebaum et al., *op. cit.*

486. "Yeshiva University Revises Madoff Losses to Just $14.5m." *theyeshivaworld.com*. December 30, 2008.

487. *newsvine.com*, *op. cit.*

488. Bone, James. "Elie Wiesel Foundation for Humanity Victim of Alleged Swindle by Bernie Madoff." *timesonline.co.uk*, December 20, 2008.

489. Quoted in *Ibid.*

490. *Ibid.*

491. Kerber, Ross. "Man Who Blew Whistle on Madoff is Wary of Limelight." *boston.com*, January 8, 2009.

492. Markopolos, Harry. "How I Got the Goods on Madoff, and Why No One Would Listen." *businessweek.com*, March 11, 2010.

493. Markopolos, Harry. "How to Spot a Fraud." *businessweek.com*, September 22, 2011.

494. *cbsnews.com*. "The Man Who Figured Out Madoff's Scheme." June 10, 2009.

495. Blodget, Henry. "Busting Bernie Madoff: One Man's 10 Year Crusade." *businessinsider.com*, December 17, 2008.

496. *cbsnews.com*, *op. cit.*

497. Marino, Joe and Schapiro, Rich. "Bernie Madoff Should Rot with Rats, Victim's Pal Says." *nydailynews.com*, December 25, 2008.

498. Quoted in *foxnews.com*. "Report: Hedge Fund Founder Who Lost $1.4B in Madoff Scandal Dead in Apparent Suicide," December 23, 2008.

499. Quoted in Goldman, Adam and Hays, Tom. "NYPD: Madoff Investor Commits Suicide in Office." Associated Press, December 23, 2008.

500. United States Attorney, Southern District of New York (press release). "Bernard L. Madoff Pleads Guilty to Eleven-Count Criminal Information and is Remanded into Custody." March 12, 2009.

501. Pavlo, Walter. "David Friehling, Madoff's Accountant, Sentencing Postponed . . . Again." *forbes.com*, September 16, 2011.

502. Margolick, David. "Did the Sons Know?" *vanityfair.com*, July 2009.

503. *nytimes.com*. "The Text of Madoff's Plea Allocution." March 12, 2009.

504. Bandler, James and Varchaver, Nicholas. "How Bernie Did It." *cnn.com*, April 30, 2009.

505. *Ibid.*

506. Henriques, Diana. "Madoff Sentenced to 150 Years in Prison." *nytimes.com*. June 29, 2009.

507. Margolick, *op. cit.*

508. Lucchetti, Aaron. "Madoff Trustee Sues Swindler's Family." *wsj.com*, October 3, 2009.

509. Henriques, Diana and Baker, Al. "A Madoff Son Hangs Himself on Father's Arrest Anniversary." *nytimes.com*, December 11, 2010.

510. *telegraph.co.uk*. "Bernard Madoff Fraud Victim Committed Suicide to Avoid Bankruptcy Shame." June 11, 2009.

511. Neumeister, Larry. "Ruth Madoff's Fur Coat Taken By The Feds." *huffingtonpost.com*, July 3, 2009.

512. *wsj.com*. "$2.5 Billion Distributed to Madoff Victims." September 20, 2012.

513. *Ibid.*

7

Corporate Fraud

Janice, a 64-year-old office manager for an Enron Corp. subsidiary, retired in 2000. For 16 years she had made numerous sacrifices in order to contribute the maximum-allowed 15 percent of her paycheck each month into her 401k-retirement plan. She had watched her fund mushroom to nearly $700,000 as Enron built its reputation as one of the fastest growing and most profitable corporations in the world. But when Enron stock began to decline in late 2001, Janice said she "begged and pleaded" with the administrators of her 401k plan to let her withdraw her hard-earned money. They refused.[1] When she finally was allowed to sell her stock, it was like alchemy in reverse: gold had turned to lead. Her $700,000 had become $20,000. Today, Janice has been forced to abort her retirement and return to work; she now struggles to make ends meet. In her words: "I haven't had any heat or air conditioning on since October."[2]

> I am a woman of simple means. I couldn't have spent $700,000. But I could have helped my children. Instead, now they have to help me with the groceries. That wasn't the way it was supposed to be. . . . I thought I would have a dignified retirement. Nobody should have to go through this.[3]

All of us who have watched our own retirement funds steadily evaporate, since Enron tipped over the first domino in a shocking fission of corporate failures, have come to know that Janice's story is far from unique. Edward, a 55-year-old sheet metal worker saw his Enron account plummet from $450,000 to $4,500.[4] Charles, a 63-year-old retired pipefitter, who had spent 33 years working for Enron in its various incarnations, accumulated a robust retirement fund of $1.3 million. When he left the company in 2000, he anticipated a comfortable retirement. A year later he watched in helpless horror as his nest egg was wiped out. Today he is dead broke.

These rags-to-riches-back-to-rags tales and thousands more just like them have stunned the country. How could the seventh-largest corporation in the U.S. lose 99 percent of its value so quickly? How could Janice's, Edward's, and Charles' American Dream become a national nightmare?

The Enron story begins in the 1950s, when a pair of Houston pipeline companies working along the Gulf of Mexico merged under the name Houston Natural Gas (HNG). In 1985, a Nebraska-based gas company, InterNorth, which was building a pipeline network between the Texas Panhandle and the Midwest, merged with HNG. The new company took the name Enron. Enron's first CEO, Kenneth Lay, aspired to make his company the foremost natural gas pipeline operator in North America. Within a year, Enron was operating a 64,000 mile pipeline linking the Great Lakes with Texas. By the early 1990s, Enron had become a multi-national corporation, with plants and pipeline sites in Europe, Asia, and Latin America.[5] In the United States, Enron had become the dominant force in marketing both natural gas and electricity. In 1995, Lay's earlier aspiration of pipeline supremacy was already passéd. Lay had a new and grander vision: "To become the world's leading energy company."[6]

When the Federal Energy Regulatory Commission initiated the deregulation of energy markets in 1996, Enron was poised to be *the* major player. The company was soon creating markets for everything from water, to coal, to paper—to Internet bandwidth.[7] Like June, in the Rodgers and Hammerstein song, Enron seemed to be "busting out all over." Even Houston's new state-of-the-art major league baseball stadium bore its now familiar name and crooked E logo. It was Ken Lay who threw out the first ball when the Houston Astros played their inaugural game at Enron Field in 1999.

Enron had constructed a new business model, which could be described only by a new word—*commoditization*. "Control the assets that are needed to control the commodity, create a standard platform or 'hub' for that commodity, and establish a network of trading partners to deal in that commodity."[8] When Enron stock hit its all-time high of $90.56 in August, 2000, few persons may have fully understood Enron's model, peppered with arcane terms like *costless collars*, *multiple triggers*, and *weather derivatives*. But when the company issued its annual report in late 2000 and claimed to have *tripled* its revenues since 1998, that was language anyone could understand. Moreover, the report maintained that Enron had only "scratched the surface" of a $3.9 *trillion* market.[9] Ken Lay's vision expanded in tandem with the Enron revolution. By 2001, it wasn't just about energy anymore. Lay's stated goal was: "To create the world's leading company."[10]

Kenneth Lay, the son of a rural minister and the holder of a doctorate in economics, guided Enron to the highest summit of corporate America. He also amassed a personal fortune. A former associate quotes him as once saying: "I don't want to be rich, I want to be world-class rich."[11] As one of the highest-paid executives in the country, he clearly achieved that goal. He also justly earned a reputation for philanthropy. Charities all over Houston were beneficiaries of his and his company's generosity. When he stepped down as Enron CEO in 2000 and passed the controls to his underboss, Jeffrey Skilling, it was widely believed that he was laying the groundwork for a political career—perhaps a run at the mayor's office in Houston. He had long been attracted to politics. He had donated nearly $1 million to candidates since 1989 (about 90 percent of which went to Republicans). Senator Phil Gramm of Texas was a favorite recipient of Lay's largess. Gramm's wife Wendy was given a lucrative seat on the Enron Board of Directors five months after the Futures Trading Commission, which she had chaired, made a ruling highly favorable to Enron. The Enron Corp. Political Action Committee was an early and major contributor to the George W. Bush presidential bid. Lay personally donated $290,000 to his friend's campaign. Following the election, he was named as an advisor to the presidential transition team. There was even talk about a possible cabinet position.

Meanwhile, back at Enron, Jeff Skilling had assumed day-to-day command. Skilling, holder of a Harvard MBA, had joined Enron in 1990 and had become Lay's closest lieutenant.

An aficionado of dangerous "extreme sports," he has been characterized as a supremely competitive man who loved to take risks. The two men seemed well-suited to make a formidable Mr. Inside-Mr. Outside team.

> Lay . . . would be the faceman on the street, telling investors, analysts, employees, and regulators the story of Enron's future. Lay would publicly preach about markets and mission statements, while Skilling was deep inside the Enron core, masterminding the company's clean and mean culture and its strategy for changing the world. It was a strategy of controlling markets through trading, while being light on assets.[12]

Five days before Jeffrey Skilling became CEO of Enron, an extraordinary discussion was taking place inside the offices of Arthur Andersen, the country's leading accounting firm whose list of high-end clients included mighty Enron. The issue under debate was whether Andersen should retain Enron as a client. Andersen's auditors were concerned over Enron's prolific use of limited partnerships to disguise debt. From an ethical standpoint, Andersen's obligation was clear. At the very least, Enron had been engaging in risky and deceptive accounting practices. Its exuberant annual report was a house of cards. The company's cash flow bore little relationship to reported earnings.[13] And Anderson knew it. Its audit team had ignored the advice of in-house experts more than once to please its demanding client.[14] From a business standpoint, Andersen was caught in a painful dilemma. Enron was a major client, generating revenues of $52 million the previous year in auditing and consulting fees.[15] Decisions needed to be made—decisions that would affect the accounting giant in ways that were scarcely imaginable at the time. Arthur Andersen and Company was a "dead man walking." It had less than two years to live.

Limited partnerships are typically set up as a perfectly legal way to raise venture capital. One or more general partners manage the business, while "limited" partners contribute money. The limited partners incur no liability beyond their capital contributions.[16] Enron's limited partnerships, however, were not simply a way to raise money. Enron used them to hide colossal debt. Ken Lay's expansive vision had required a huge amount of capital, and Enron's debt was growing at a very rapid pace. By shifting debt to a limited partnership, Enron was able to maintain its A-rating, while in fact the company was in serious financial trouble. If Enron's true financial picture were revealed and its investment grade rating reduced, it would have to pay much higher interest rates on borrowed money.[17] To make a mundane analogy, it is akin to an individual, unable to get a bank loan, who must resort to maxing out his high-interest credit cards.

To avoid such costly repercussions, Enron established limited partnerships that enabled it to transfer much of its debt to affiliate companies (which in theory were "independent" but of course were not). Ultimately, it was these partnerships that were doing the borrowing—thus protecting Enron's precious credit rating. According to reports, Enron may have been involved with about *3,000* limited partnerships and shell companies[18]—many with names like Chewco and JEDI, inspired by Star Wars characters.[19] Chewco (named after the hirsute Wookie) reportedly allowed Enron to keep $600 million in debt off its books.[20] In many cases, Enron capitalized the partnerships with notes that were convertible into shares of Enron stock. And if some of these shells failed, so what? "[N]o accountability was required . . . it was all off the books."[21]

The partnerships often took stakes in each other, "creating an interlocking network of ownership."[22] For example, Enron made a $12.5 million loan to Kafus Industries, a Canadian company that makes fiberboard from recycled materials. In 1999 Enron increased the loan to $20 million and received a note convertible into Kafus shares. It then sold the Kafus stake to another partnership, SE Thunderbird. SE Thunderbird was controlled by Blue Heron, which in turn was controlled by Whitewing Associates, a partnership whose sole member was Whitewing Management, which was controlled by Egret I, another Enron affiliate.[23] If these byzantine machinations seem almost incomprehensible to any outsider looking in, that's the whole idea. "Beyond a certain point, complexity *is* fraud."[24]

There was yet a third purpose served by Enron's limited partnerships, in addition to raising capital and hiding debt: Insiders reaped huge profits. And so the Enron saga now turns to the third member of the slick triumvirate (what one financial editor has dubbed "Enron's Axis of Evil"[25])—Chief Financial Officer Andrew Fastow, who earned more than $30 million from the limited partnerships. His total investment had been just a few thousand dollars.

Andrew Fastow, who would one day come to be known as "Fast Andy," earned an MBA at the prestigious University of Chicago. He joined Enron in 1990 and was a vice-president by the age of 31. In 1998 he was promoted to chief financial officer (CFO). The following year, he was received an Excellence Award from CFO Magazine for his skill in managing Enron's capital.[26] The award lauded the "unique financing techniques pioneered by Fastow."[27] Fastow would be the last recipient. CFO Excellence Awards are no longer handed out, because their longtime sponsor—Arthur Andersen and Company—has understandably backed out.[28]

Fastow was widely regarded as Jeff Skilling's protégé. He has been described as a quiet, almost shy, man. In sharp contrast to his high-profile fellow triumvirs, he rarely granted interviews, seldom met with financial analysts, and was largely unknown even to most of Enron's employees. But he was also noted for his quick temper. A former executive has said of Fastow: "He didn't have a lot of patience with people who weren't as smart as him."[29] In his new position, he set up and operated the limited partnerships that were used to fund Enron projects and help Enron maintain its impressive balance sheet and lofty stock price.[30] His two major offshore partnerships were LJM and LJM2. LJM is the initials of Fastow's wife and two sons. As the sole managing partner of the LJM's, Fastow earned his $30 million through assorted fees and profit participation in transactions with Enron.[31] Perhaps "earned" should be put in quotation marks, since the LJM 99 partnerships eventually cost Enron at least $35 million in cash and more than $1 billion in shareholder equity.[32]

And as if Enron didn't have enough problems looming over the horizon, all was *not* quiet on the Western front. California had been one of the first states to deregulate its energy markets, and by May 2001, the price for natural gas had soared. California politicians accused Enron of manipulating market prices. One state senator later declared: "The deregulation, led by Enron, has become perhaps the greatest fraud ever perpetrated on the American consumer."[33] If some of the rhetoric rang hollow, it may have been because Enron was the biggest political contributor in the entire state and had spent millions of dollars on lobbying there since 1998.[34] The state was sinking ever-deeper into a major energy crisis. In just five months, the price of wholesale electricity had jumped 528 percent.[35] Consumers were livid. Enron was blamed for power shortages and rolling blackouts. In July 2001, a protester from a California consumer group threw a cream pie into Jeff Skilling's face. A month later, Skilling abruptly resigned citing "personal reasons." He was replaced by Ken Lay, back at the controls after just five months. In hindsight, this should have raised a "red flag." Relatively young and hugely successful CEOs seldom walk off into the sunset without an explanation. The financial press, mesmerized by Enron's dazzling bottom line, missed a critical wake-up call.

In early October, Lay presided over the Enron energy summit at the Ritz-Carlton in Washington, D.C. He told the assembled policymakers that the key to national prosperity was more energy deregulation.[36] At the same time, back in Houston, Enron executives were working the phones, breaking bad news to the country's leading corporate credit-rating agencies: Enron was about to report major losses for the third quarter.[37] The company's survival was hanging in the balance, but efforts to "spin" its $638 million loss as a consequence of a "one-time" $1 billion write-off tied to a series of complex partnership deals were being received skeptically. "We were questioning and scratching our heads about the type of accounting they were using,"[38] a representative of Moody's Investor's would later recall. By mid-November, Standard and Poor's would downgrade Enron's debt to "junk" status.[39]

Lay himself tried to reassure securities analysts in an October 16 conference call. Although he pledged to provide a full explanation of the $1 billion loss, what he gave the analysts were "vague details and nearly impenetrable jargon."[40] Then, almost casually, he dropped another bombshell. The value of shareholder's equity (Enron's net worth) would be reduced by $1.2 billion because of an "accounting error."[41] Lay quickly assured the group that there would be no further write-offs.

The following day, the *Wall Street Journal* began a series of exposes of the LJM partnerships and the $1.2 billion "accounting error."[42] Lay traveled to Boston to convince analysts that all was fundamentally sound at Enron.

> What the analysts wanted to know about was the $1.2 billion error . . . in that morning's paper. Instead, the Enron chairman attacked the critical press coverage . . . Lay vigorously defended Fastow and assured . . . there were no more losses . . .

A week later, Andrew Fastow was fired.

The following week, Lay entered a Houston hotel to face 1,600 frightened shareholders, with another 5,000 hooked up on the Internet. Most of them worked for Enron. In a prepared statement, he expressed great sympathy for their battered retirement funds. In his words: "I am incredibly sorry. But we are going to get it back."[43] One irate employee asked Lay if he was "on crack."[44]

Whatever Ken Lay was on, it evidently did not affect his instinct for self-preservation. Over the next three days he took a total of $23 million in cash advances from his company. He immediately began repaying the money by transferring some of his Enron stock to the company. Over time, he reportedly borrowed about $70 million, always covering the debt with Enron stock.[45] *It was a slippery way to unload stock while circumventing immediate reporting requirements*. A board member later called this Lay's "ATM approach."[46]

On October 31, The Securities and Exchange Commission (SEC) launched a formal investigation of Enron. Enron quickly revised its financial statements to reduce earnings by an additional $586 million over the previous four years. The company also revealed that it had to pay a debt of $690 million that year and another $6 billion by the following year. Enron was imploding. On that same day, Enron's employee investment accounts were frozen, leaving workers to watch helplessly as their retirement funds plunged. The next day, Dynegy, a much smaller energy company, proposed a $10 billion buyout of Enron. Ten days later, however, the proposal was abandoned. Ironically, Dynegy would soon get snared in its own legal problems, not unlike those of Enron. A year later, the company would pay a $3 million fine to settle a civil fraud case brought by the SEC. Dynegy had artificially inflated revenue, earnings, and cash-flow figures it reported to investors.[47] Three former executives were indicted on securities fraud charges.[48] A senior Dynegy trader would also be indicted on criminal fraud charges relating to the alleged manipulation of gas price indices during the California energy crisis.[49] And *this* was the company that wanted to take over Enron.

When Dynegy pulled the ladder, Enron was finished. On December 4, 2001, it became the largest U.S. corporation up to that time ever to file for bankruptcy. Thousands of employees were laid off. Most of them had lost up to 90 percent of their 401k retirement savings. Those workers who once barely recognized the name Andrew Fastow were now unlikely to ever forget it.

The White House was soon scrambling for higher ground. The president had campaigned aboard the Enron corporate jet. Ken Lay was an old family friend and major contributor who had helped finance the controversial Florida recount. He had also helped President Bush and Vice-President Cheney formulate the administration's pro-deregulation energy policy. The president used to call him affectionately "Kenny Boy." Now, if he was mentioned at all, it was distantly as Mr. Lay. In an effort to demonstrate that he understood the victims' pain, the president announced that his mother-in-law had lost $8,000 on Enron stock. The pathetic story was generally greeted with derision. One columnist wrote of the Bush family: "They'll be able to laugh around the Thanksgiving table for years over this one. The table of course is made of solid mahogany, 14 feet in length and is valued at well over $10,000."[50]

One week before Christmas, the Senate Commerce Committee, which had begun conducting hearings on the demise of Enron (along with nine other congressional committees and subcommittees) heard from shareholders and former workers, who were still trying to figure out what happened to their money. In the words of one senator: "This is not your average business failure. This is a tragedy for many, including workers and investors who appear to have been cheated out of billions.[51] Indeed, the lost shareholder equity was estimated at $63 billion.[52] The president of the International Brotherhood of Electrical Workers, the largest union in the utility industry, shared the outrage:

> It's unconscionable that hard-working, dedicated workers were forced to sacrifice their life savings to prop up a failing company. Those who ran the company into the ground certainly aren't wiped out financially—just the workers who made their success possible.[53]

The reference to the selective nature of the ruination was a resonant one. While rank-and-file employees were locked into plummeting 401k's, prohibited from bailing out, top executives literally made out like bandits. It is alleged that 29 executives and directors of Enron sold $1.1 billion worth of stock while knowing the company was in danger of collapse.[54] Andrew Fastow sold about $23 million in Enron stock before the company went public with its financial troubles. Skilling dumped $67 million of his Enron holdings. And Kenneth Lay earned more than $146 million from options trades—during which time he was still encouraging employees to put *all* their retirement money into Enron stock.[55]

The Chairman of the Senate Commerce Committee compared Enron to the *Titanic*—with one glaring difference: "In the Titanic, the captain went down with the ship. Enron looks to me like the captain gave himself and his friends a bonus, then lowered himself and the top folks down the lifeboat ladder, hollered up and said, 'By the way, everything is going to be just fine'."[56] The doomed passengers could have waved goodbye as the captain and senior crew sailed off to the Land of Ill-Gotten Gains.

Ken Lay asserted his constitutional protection against self-incrimination and chose not to testify before the senate committee because of what he termed the "prosecutorial" nature of the hearing.[57] In a brief prepared statement, a haggard-looking Lay told the committee: "I am deeply troubled about asserting these rights because it may be perceived by some that I have something to hide."[58]

If Ken Lay were "deeply troubled," he was not alone. Enron employees and investors, facing financial ruination, watched his non-testimony angrily. One of them was the executive administrative assistant at Enron's New York office. She had once earned more than $100,000 a year. Back then, she profoundly admired Lay, seeing him as a kind of benevolent father figure. Today she says she detests him. "I trusted him as much as I do my husband and my parents. I feel betrayed."[59] By the time her unemployment benefits were exhausted and her savings were nearly gone, she was on anti-depression medication and anti-anxiety pills. She was training to become a pet groomer. When asked to explain her new career choice, her response was terse: "I trust animals. They are not going to rob you."[60]

As 2002 began, the story took a violent turn. J. Clifford Baxter, vice-chairman of Enron, committed suicide by shooting himself in the head while sitting in his parked car. Baxter, whom Skilling would eulogize before a congressional committee as his "best friend," was reportedly tormented by the company's collapse and his shattered reputation. Ironically, Baxter had been one of the few members of the inner circle to express serious concerns about the LJM partnerships.[61]

When the House Energy and Commerce Subcommittee convened its hearings in February 2002, once again Lay declined to testify, as did Fastow. Fastow told the members: "I would like to answer the committee's questions, but on the advice of my counsel, I respectfully decline."[62] The chairman of the committee dubbed Fastow the "Betty Crocker of cooked books."[63] However, to the surprise of many, Jeffrey Skilling opted to waive his Fifth Amendment right and testify. What followed must have astonished anyone who had ever known him. Jeff Skilling, about whom a former Enron insider once said: "[He] was known to *himself* . . . as the smartest human being ever to walk the face of the earth,"[64] portrayed himself as a near-imbecile who had little idea how the company he had once headed did business. He asserted: "I was not aware of any financing arrangements designed to conceal liabilities or inflate profitability."[65] He failed to persuade a single member of the bipartisan committee, who blasted him from all sides of the political spectrum. He was even blind-sided from a most unlikely direction. His 77-year-old mother didn't seem to believe him either. She said in an interview: "When you are the CEO and you are on the board of directors, you are supposed to know what's going on with the rest of the company . . . He's going to have to beat this the best way he can."[66] One committee member said that Skilling was relying on a "*Hogan's Heroes* defense, in which Sgt. Schultz repeatedly claims, 'I know nothing'."[67]

The most compelling testimony came from Enron's former Vice-President for Corporate Development, Sherron Watkins, who became the first company insider to acknowledge under oath that somebody was actually responsible for the Fall of the House of Enron. Watkins, who holds two accounting degrees and had once worked for Arthur Andersen, had become concerned about the labyrinthine partnership arrangements while working under Fastow. After weeks of mustering up the nerve, she first expressed her concerns in a memo to Lay the previous August—a few days after Skilling resigned.

> She told him she was nervous Enron would implode in a wave of accounting scandals.
>
> She . . . consulted Enron security personnel, concerned that "Mr. Fastow might do something vindictive."[68]

On August 22, Watkins met with Lay. She presented him with a six-page letter. Among other things, she pointed out how Enron was propping up a partnership named Raptor (inspired by Jurassic Park) that had no hard assets in order to conceal heavy losses.[69] According to Watkins, the Raptor partnership had been used to disguise at least $500 million in losses for which Enron would become liable.[70] Perhaps the most memorable passage was her quoting of a manager from Raptor's principal investment group: "I know it would be devastating to all but I wish we would get caught. We're such a crooked company."[71]

Watkins told the committee that Lay seemed genuinely concerned and promised to have a team of corporate attorneys review the controversial partnership deals. But she would later say that she felt like a "lone fish swimming upstream."[72] On October 15, Enron's law firm, Vinson & Elkins, issued a nine-page report asserting that Enron had done nothing wrong. Watkins remained uneasy, however. Since Vinson & Elkins had collected fees for work on Raptor and other limited partnerships, Watkins worried about a conflict of interest.[73] On October 30—a week before Enron would report its huge losses—Watkins warned Lay one more time: "We need to come clean."[74]

In her testimony, Sherron Watkins was mildly critical of Ken Lay for his inattention to the imminent disaster but maintained that Lay did not fully understand the gravity of the crisis. She placed the major blame on Jeffrey Skilling and Andrew Fastow, whom she accused of "duping" Lay.[75] She further accused Skilling and Fastow of intimidating subordinates "into accepting some structures that were not truly acceptable."[76] She directly contradicted Skilling's earlier testimony that he "knew nothing" about the partnerships. She maintained that the fraudulent partnerships were the reason for Skilling's abrupt resignation: "It's my opinion that he [Skilling] could foresee these problems."[77] She described Skilling as "a very intense, hands-on manager"[78] and said that she "would find it hard to believe that he was not fully aware."[79] As for Fastow, "Watkins said there was a common saying around the company's Houston headquarters about the apparent conflict of interest Fastow had as both an Enron executive and the head of the partnerships: 'Heads, Mr. Fastow wins; Tails, Enron loses.'"[80]

On June 22, 2002, the first major league baseball game was played at newly renamed Minute Maid Park—formerly Enron Field. Houston lost 8-0.

By late summer 2002, Congress had passed and the president had signed the Corporate Fraud Bill, providing blue-collar prison time for white-collar criminals. But the case against Enron appeared to be stalled, even though its once sizzling stock was by now worthless and no longer even traded. So, while executives from other disgraced corporations were doing "perp walks" on the network news, the Enron scandal, which had dominated public attention when the year began, seemed to be treading water. Some critics were suggesting that the company was redeeming a ream of political I.O.U.'s from its long list of campaign contribution recipients. Some partisans were even wondering if Kenneth Lay's ties to the Bush administration were providing a shield to the moribund corporation. But on August 21, the first shoe finally dropped.

Michael Kopper, once the managing director of Enron Global Finance and Andy Fastow's right-hand man, became the first former Enron executive to plead guilty to criminal charges. Kopper, a graduate of the London School of Economics, was considered a "brilliant lieutenant."[81] He had worked for Enron since 1994 and had left shortly before the collapse to run one of Fastow's partnerships.[82] Kopper and his domestic companion turned a modest $125,000 investment in Chewco and Chewco Management into $12 million using Enron's network of off-balance-sheet limited partnerships.[83] Kopper was allowed to run some of the partnerships with the understanding that he would kick back money to Fastow.[84]

In a plea bargain arrangement with federal prosecutors, Kopper agreed to plead guilty to one count of conspiracy to commit wire fraud and one count of conspiracy to use stolen property (money laundering).[85] He thus became the first Enron figure convicted of a crime. As part of the deal, Kopper, who had earlier invoked the Fifth Amendment when he was called before Congress to testify, agreed to cooperate with investigators in possible future cases against Fastow and other senior Enron executives.[86] Kopper also agreed to turn the $12 million illicit profit over to the government, to be disbursed to those defrauded by Enron. The Justice Department also asked a federal judge to freeze about $23 million controlled by Fastow and other executives in the hope that the court will later order those funds to be forfeited as well.[87] Kopper's potential value as a friendly witness was considered crucial. One securities lawyer observed: "He could give them [federal prosecutors] a color-enhanced map of Fastow's movements and thoughts."[88] Kopper's attorney said that his client felt "deep regret" for his conduct.[89]

Kopper's "regret" is not difficult to understand. On November 17, 2006, he was sentenced to three years and one month in prison.[90] On the other hand, it could have been much worse. He could have received a 15-year sentence. His agreement to cooperate with the government earned him some leniency.[91] Likewise, Mark Koenig, Enron's former investor relations chief who had testified so effectively against Skilling and Lay, received a reduced 18-month sentence an hour after Kopper was sentenced.[92]

In April, 2007, Christian Rahaim, a former Enron human resources executive, received a sentence of five years and three months in prison. Rahaim was the only former Enron executive to plead guilty to a crime committed after the company failed. He had stolen nearly $3 million from the company after it went bankrupt. Before being sentenced, Rahaim told the judge that his crime was "not my normal behavior."[93] "I made a mistake, and that's something I have to live with."[94] But the judge was unmoved. Citing the sophistication and the greed of Rahaim's crime, his imposed sentence exceeded the advisory federal sentencing guidelines.

In early October 2002, it was finally Andrew Fastow's turn to do the increasingly familiar corporate "perp walk." He surrendered to the FBI and was charged with fraud.[95] On Halloween, he was formally indicted on 78 counts by a federal grand jury. The 32-page indictment was no treat. It included multiple charges of fraud, money laundering, and conspiracy.[96] He stood accused of receiving about $30 million in illegal kickbacks funneled through Michael Kopper or family members and of siphoning money from his web of partnerships. He pleaded not guilty to all charges.[97]

Nowhere in the indictment were the names Lay or Skilling mentioned. Certainly Fastow was a major player—the biggest Enron fish landed by the government to that point—but it seemed inconceivable to some financial journalists that Fastow's illicit $30 million alone could have killed a company that supposedly had assets worth $62 billion with sales of $150 million.[98] It was assumed by many that the government was working its way methodically up the food chain.

But the government wasn't done with Fastow yet. A new wave of Enron indictments came down in May 2003. Included were 31 additional charges, including tax fraud and insider trading, against Fastow, bringing the total to 109 counts. He re-entered a plea of not guilty. His maximum prison sentence had climbed to more than 1,000 years.[99] His attorney deadpanned that, "When it was only 700 years, we weren't taking it seriously."[100]

The new wave of indictments also included six other former executives from Enron Broadband—and Andrew Fastow's wife Lea, a former assistant treasurer at Enron.[101] Mrs. Fast Andy was charged with the usual troika of fraud, conspiracy, and tax evasion for her role in a deal involving California wind farms.[102] Prosecutors accused her of helping her husband create sham partnerships that generated illegal kickbacks. It was further alleged that she had tried to use her father, a prominent Houston businessman, to give the partnerships the appearance of independence.[103] Lea Fastow pleaded not guilty. Many observers believed that the government's hardball strategy would be to use the threat of his wife's potential imprisonment for 37 years as a bargaining chip for Andrew Fastow's cooperation.

The Broadband defendants also pleaded not guilty. Once again, it appeared that the government hoped to use these second- and third-tier indictments as a means to climb to the very top of the Enron Pyramid where Lay and Skilling resided. Echoing that belief, one of the defendant's lawyers observed: "Prosecuting this guy is like prosecuting the piano player in a whorehouse."[104]

Enron, in its voracious hunger for new markets, had pioneered the trading of Internet bandwidth. The concept may have been hard to grasp, but it sure sounded good. *Fortune* magazine lauded Enron's vision in 2000: "If any old-world company could thrive in the Internet era, it's this one."[105] Seven former executives from Enron Broadband Services were indicted on hundreds of charges of securities fraud, insider trading, money laundering, and conspiracy.[106] According to the indictments, Enron Broadband was "pump and dump" played on a grand scale. Accusations include making false representations about the capabilities of broadband business (Enron Broadband was claimed to be worth $41 billion) to analysts and then dumping their own stock at multi-million dollar profits when their exaggerated predictions caused the stock price to inflate.[107] Perhaps this was the "thriving" *Fortune* meant. While Enron Broadband Services executives were indicted, the majority were not punished heavily or, in some cases, at all: Joseph Hirko and Kevin Howard won appeals and had their convictions vacated; both later pled to reduced charges.[108] Michael Krautz had two trials, the first ended in a mistrial and in the second he was acquitted.[109] Rex Shelby's trial resulted in a hung jury, but he later pled to reduced charges. F. Scott Yaeger's case also culminated in a hung jury, but the government chose not to pursue another trial.[110]

There were several notable Enron convictions in 2003: Ben Glisan, a former Enron treasurer, pleaded guilty to conspiracy in exchange for the dropping of 20 other assorted counts of fraud and money laundering.[111] He was handed a five-year sentence. Glisan was immediately taken into custody to begin serving his time, thus becoming the first Enron executive to go to prison.[112] Timothy Belden, former chief trader for Enron Power Marketing in Portland, Oregon, admitted to one count of conspiracy in 2003 for making false statements to federal investigators during their probe of fraudulent market practices. As part of his plea, Belden agreed to cooperate with prosecutors.[113] Three months later, Jeffrey Richter, former head of Enron's California energy trading desk, also pleaded guilty to helping manipulate prices during the California energy crisis.[114] In his plea, Richter admitted to participation in two fraudulent schemes: (1) **Load Shift**, in which Enron traders submitted false energy schedules to the California market to create the appearance of congestion and this would trigger payments to the company for easing the fake congestion, allowing Enron to profit from its own lies;[115] (2) a complex scheme dubbed **Get Shorty**, in which Enron traders sold fictitious emergency backup power the company didn't even possess.[116]

In January 2004, the government's step-by-step strategy was validated when Andrew Fastow changed his plea to guilty and agreed to a 10-year prison sentence *without parole* and the forfeiture of over $20 million.[117] Lea Fastow also pleaded guilty in exchange for a five-month sentence.[118]

As part of his deal, Mr. Fastow agreed to cooperate with authorities in future cases. No names were mentioned specifically, but everyone understood whom those "future cases" likely would involve. It was anticipated that Fastow would help implicate Ken Lay and Jeff Skilling.[119] Sherron Watkins' attorney, a former prosecutor, predicted: "I certainly think that his information will be very key."[120]

Five weeks after Fastow's plea, a handcuffed Jeff Skilling was led into a Houston courtroom, where he was charged with 35 counts of conspiracy, securities fraud, and insider trading.[121] He pleaded not guilty to all counts and posted a $5 million cashier's check as bail.[122]

> The indictment was filed by the Enron Task Force, a joint unit of the Justice Department, the FBI and the Internal Revenue Service in cooperation with the Securities and Exchange Commission. The SEC separately announced civil charges of securities fraud and insider trading against Skilling.[123]

Enron's former chief accounting officer, Richard Causey, was also charged with six counts of fraud.[124]

On July 8, 2004, the Justice Department, after a long and methodical climb, finally planted its flag at the top of Mount Enron. Kenneth Lay, who had become the symbol of corporate malfeasance to many Americans, surrendered to authorities after being indicted on 11 counts of fraud, insider trading, and manipulating financial reports.[125] In a concurrent action, the Securities and Exchange Commission filed a civil complaint against Lay, seeking to recover $90 million in illicit proceeds from stock sales.[126]

> "Kenneth Lay is charged with abusing his powerful position . . . and repeatedly lying in an effort to cover up the financial collapse that caused devastating harm to millions of Americans," said U.S. Assistant Attorney General Christopher Wray during a press briefing at the Justice Department.[127]

Among the charges was the allegation that Lay had continued to sell $26 million in Enron shares even as he assured employees and the public that he was *buying* shares and that the stock was a "bargain."[128]

Lay pleaded not guilty and posted a $500,000 bond. Theoretically, Lay faced up to 175 years in prison, if convicted. In a statement he released, Lay asserted that he had "done nothing wrong:"

> "I continue to grieve as does my family over the loss of the company, my failure to be able to save it. But failure does not equate to a crime."[129]

Lay's attorney blamed Andy Fastow, who would undoubtedly be testifying against his client, for the collapse of Enron. Skilling's lawyer had earlier portrayed Fastow as the real criminal as well. Presumably, Fastow would be a key witness against his client too. Lay and Skilling not only shared a mutual "Blame Andy" defense, but they would be also sharing the same courtroom. In February 2005, a federal judge in Houston ordered the two defendants to stand trial together (along with Richard Causey) in January 2006.[130]

Ken Lay was the 31st Enron-related defendant to face criminal charges[131]—but he wasn't the last. Ongoing investigations continued to yield results, and new cases continued to trickle in, even after Lay's arrest. For example, former Enron executive Dan Boyle was sentenced to nearly four years in prison in mid-2005 for his role in a Nigerian barge scam. The case involved the sham sale of three energy-generating barges to Merrill Lynch's investment banking division. The false profits from the "sale" helped Enron defraud its shareholders by pumping its earnings and bolstering its share price.[132] Two Merrill Lynch bankers, Robert Furst and William Fuhs, each received 37-month sentences for their parts in the scheme.[133]

But these cases were little more than warm-up acts. The true headliners were still Ken Lay and Jeff Skilling. And on January 31, 2006, Lay and Skilling took center stage as their long-awaited federal trial began in Houston. Three weeks earlier, Richard Causey, their co-defendant, agreed to plead guilty and serve a seven-year prison sentence.[134] Most observers believed that by cutting Causey loose from the trial prosecutors could reduce the need for highly technical testimony and streamline the case against Lay and Skilling. "For a company that once seemed so complex that almost no one could understand how it actually made its money, the cases ended up being simpler than most people envisioned. . . . lying—to investors, employees, and government regulators—in an effort to disguise the crumbling fortunes of their energy empire."[135]

The prosecution called 22 witnesses, many of them disgraced former Enron executives—including, of course, "Fast Andy" Fastow. But Fastow, who had been heralded for months as the government's "star witness," proved disappointing. He testified for days in a lifeless monotone that jurors found ineffective. One juror would later call Fastow "repulsive." In the words of another juror: "Fastow was Fastow."[136] According to jurors, the most persuasive insider witnesses were Mark Koenig, former head of investor relations at Enron, who was at the time awaiting sentencing, and Ben Glisan, Enron's former treasurer, who was then the only Enron defendant already behind bars.[137]

The most dramatic witnesses for the defense were the defendants themselves. Skilling was first. For two weeks, he "lectured, reminisced, joked and argued for his innocence . . . trying to turn the government's tale of a company brought down by fraud to one of a business undone by a few bad apples and uncontrollable market forces."[138] But under intense cross-examination he became contentious, evasive, and amnesic—the good CEO with the bad memory.

Skilling's complicated description of Enron's profitability was dismissed as financial gibberish. He tried to commandeer the proceedings, which only seemed to affirm his reputation as a "control freak." At one point, he even raised his own objection, drawing a rebuke from the judge.[139]

In a memorable exchange, the prosecution made a character issue out of Skilling's personal investment in a company run by his former girlfriend. Skilling claimed he had invested $60,000. It was actually $180,000. He contended that her firm had done only $3,000 in business with Enron. It was actually $450,000.[140] Yet Skilling testified that the possibility of a conflict of interest had never occurred to him.[141]

Next, it was Ken Lay's turn. Lay long had cultivated an affable public image, and some Enron-watchers feared that he might be able to charm the jury. But his grandfatherly mask slipped early and often. He turned out to be his own worst enemy. Lay, who outside the courtroom had called the government's witnesses "trained monkey," asserted that *he* was the victim of character assassination. Several times during direct examination, he angrily challenged his own lawyer. "Where are you going with this, Mr. Seacrest?" he asked from the witness stand, as if he were being cross-examined.[142] He evidently could not stop being the chief executive.

He said: "I accept full responsibility for everything that happened at Enron."[143] Then he proceeded to blame everyone else for the collapse. Fastow, he asserted, was the real crook. Short-sellers, he charged, had conspired to sink his company. The *Wall Street Journal*, he claimed, had created a "run on the bank."[144] He cited a down-turning economy, Skilling's sudden resignation, and even the terrorist attacks on the World Trade Center.[145] In short, it was everyone's fault but his own. If there is a hall of fame for historical revisionists, Ken Lay had made a strong case for induction on the first ballot.

> Never mind that the short sellers, and for that matter, the Journal were right. Fastow's thefts amounted to, as Lay's own lawyers put it, "crumbs." Lay's argument essentially is that Enron could not survive the truth.[146]

Lay indignantly declared that he had done nothing illegal or improper when he told employees he was buying stock and they should too—even though he was quietly selling millions of dollars in stock back to the company.[147] When he was cross-examined, he argued his points fiercely. He attacked the prosecutor for being "unfair." He defended his lavish lifestyle as his company was failing: expensive trips to places like the French Riviera; a yacht chartered for $200,000 to celebrate his wife's birthday. (The name of the luxurious boat, ironically, was *Amnesia*.) The jurors watched attentively as Lay explained: "It's the type of lifestyle that's difficult to turn off and on like a spigot."[148] When Lay claimed he was now broke and in debt, some jurors reportedly rolled their eyes.

The remaining testimony came from character witnesses for the two defendants. Jeff Skilling's integrity and managerial practices were vouched for by some local entrepreneurs and some business school professors. None of them was especially compelling. Ken Lay, on the other hand, had assembled an all-star team. Men like former Houston mayor Bob Lanier and Houston Astros owner Drayton McLane praised Lay. A retired admiral described Lay as "straight as a string."[149] Rev. Bill Lawson, pastor emeritus at the Wheeler Avenue Baptist Church and a legend in Houston's African-American community, said that Ken Lay "loved the Lord."[150]

As soon as the four-month trial had adjourned and the jury had withdrawn to deliberate, Ken Lay began a second trial in front of the same judge. He stood accused of bank fraud in his personal finances. These charges had been separated from the main case and were argued at a bench trial (no jury). The bench trial took just four days, but because the Enron jury was still deliberating, the judge withheld announcing his verdict until the jury's verdict was in. Two days later, after six days of deliberations, the jury returned. It convicted Jeff Skilling on 19 of 28 counts, including conspiracy and insider trading. Ken Lay was convicted on all six counts of conspiracy and fraud *and* the four counts of bank fraud from the bench trial.[151] Skilling was stoic; Lay was visibly stunned.

The jurors decided that the two defendants repeatedly had lied to cover up fraudulent accounting practices and business failures. One juror sadly told reporters: "I wanted very, very badly to believe what they were saying."[152] Clearly, she could not.

After more than four years of investigations, prosecutors were exuberant.[153] An assistant U.S. attorney declared the verdicts to be a message to all chief executives. "CEOs cannot hide behind accountants; they can't hide behind lawyers; they can't hide behind claims of ignorance . . . especially when they're paid tens of millions of dollars to be faithful stewards of shareholders and investors."[154]

Given the magnitude of the crimes and the defendants' arrogance and utter lack of contrition, many legal analysts expected the sentences to be very heavy.[155] And, for Jeff Skilling, heavy it was. He was sentenced, in October, 2006, to 24 years and four months in prison,[156] by far the longest term received by any Enron defendant. Victims unleashed five years of anger on Skilling and begged the judge to send him to prison for life.

> "Mr. Skilling has proven to be a liar, a thief, and a drunk, flaunting an attitude above the law," said 22-year Enron employee Dawn Powers Martin. "He has betrayed everyone who has trusted him. Shame on me for believing the management of Enron."[157]

During the first week of 2009, a Federal Appeals Court upheld Skilling's conviction but ordered that he be given a new prison sentence after ruling that the trial judged had erred in his calculations.[158] Not content with this ruling, Skilling appealed. The Supreme Court heard arguments on March 1, 2010,[159] and issued its opinion on June 24, 2010.[160] The Court applied the "Honest Services" clause, which differentiates between crimes for private gain versus crimes for employer interest, and wrote that "The government did not, at any time, allege that Skilling solicited or accepted side payments from a third party for making these misrepresentations. It is therefore clear that, as we read [the law] Skilling did not commit honest-services fraud."[161] The case was handed back down to the 5th Circuit Court of Appeals in an effort to determine which charges needed to be dismissed as a result of the Supreme Court opinion. On April 6, 2011, the 5th Circuit ruled that even without "Honest Services" as part of Skilling's case, there was "overwhelming evidence" that Skilling had intended to commit fraud and re-sentenced him to 24 years in prison.[162] Skilling once again appealed, but the Supreme Court denied hearing the case for a second time.[163]

As for Ken Lay, there would be no sentence. The Enron saga took its final shocking turn. On July 5, 2006, about six weeks after his conviction, Lay suddenly died of heart failure, while on a pre-sentencing vacation in Aspen Colorado. He was 64. [164]

The remaining criminal cases involved Enron's troubled broadband division. That division's former chief operating officer, Kevin Hannon, was sentenced to two years in prison for conspiracy in 2007. Hannon had schemed with other executives to exaggerate Enron's broadband capabilities to impress analysts and inflate the value of company stock. He could have been handed a five-year sentence, but was accorded leniency after testifying against Lay and Skilling at their trial the year before.[165]

About two weeks later, Kenneth Rice, the former CEO of Enron's broadband division, was sentenced to 27 months in prison for securities fraud. Like so many other Enron defendants, his potential eight to ten year sentence was reduced in exchange for having cooperated with the government.[166] Rice was the fifteenth, and likely the last, former Enron executive to go to trial, although three more defendants from the broadband division still had to be re-tried after a mistrial in 2005.[167]

In February, 2008, three former British bankers, Gary Bermingham, Giles Darby, and Gary Mulgrew, were sentenced to 3 years and one month in prison for their part in a scheme with Andrew Fastow to cheat their employer, Greenwich NatWest, out of millions of dollars.[168]

The first of the remaining defendants from the 2005 hung jury in the broadband case, former top executive Joseph Hirko, pleaded guilty in October, 2008, to one count of wire fraud[169] and agreed to pay $8.7 million in restitution.[170] He chose to plead out rather than face a second trial. The agreement called for him to serve 12–16 months in prison.[171]

There is also a substantial civil side to the Enron legal saga. In 2008, Lou Pai, who ran Enron Energy Services, the company's retail energy division, agreed to pay a $31.5 million fine to the SEC. The amount was second only to Jeff Skilling's $45 million criminal fine among the many individual fines that have been levied in the Enron case since 2002. Pai, a colorful high-liver, known to frequent strip clubs, was one of the more elusive figures at Enron and has never been charged with any crimes.[172]

Of far greater consequence was a $40 billion class action suit filed by Enron shareholders (Enron Creditors Recovery Corp.)—mostly against eleven banks and brokerages, who allegedly contributed to the massive accounting fraud. By the end of 2007, more than $7 billion in settlements had been negotiated with such defendants as Citigroup,[173] J.P. Morgan Chase,[174] Canadian Imperial Bank of Commerce (which two years earlier had been fined $80 million by the SEC for helping Enron cook its books),[175] Credit Suisse Group,[176] Merrill Lynch,[177] and Deutsche Bank.[178] As of 2012, the $7.2 billion to be paid is the largest settlement for a shareholder suit ever.[179]

In 2008, a federal judge approved a plan to distribute the settlement money to shareholders and investors. She also approved $688 million in attorneys fees—a record for a securities fraud case.[180] In a separate settlement announced in 2008, Citigroup, which had already settled for $2 billion in the class action, agreed to pay an additional $1.6 billion to Enron creditors.[181]

WHO KILLED ENRON?

Enron has been described retrospectively as everything from an insurance company selling price stability, to a hedge fund selling peace of mind, to a merchant bank selling energy. There is some measure of validity in each of those depictions, but they do Enron far too much credit. For Enron was, at its core, a giant humbug.[182] It combined the worst elements of classic and modern frauds. It was a Ponzi scheme (Chapter 2), in which those at the top of the pyramid became rich at the expense of those at the bottom. Indeed, one might say that Enron was mainly in the business of selling its own *stock*. That seemed to be its only consistently profitable activity. Enron was thus a "pump and dump" scam (Chapter 6) as well, in which shareholder value was grossly inflated through doctored earnings statements and bloated hype, so that a conscienceless elite could cash in their chips for big money while rank-and-file investors were wiped out. Enron was also an insider trading scandal (Chapter 6) of flagrant proportions. And, in the case of the limited partnerships, Enron was nothing but a high-stakes con game.

To understand what happened to Enron, a straightforward question must be asked: How did Enron actually make money? The answer now seems obvious: Almost no one seems to know. Enron's profitability was largely an article of faith. This raises a second fundamental question: "Why were so many people willing to believe in something that so few actually understood?"[183] The answer is that, like Enron's management, investors cared only about the stock price. The fact that the company didn't make much money was lost inside a maze of partnerships within partnerships. Maybe the truth was hard to find; but maybe no one was looking very hard. "If a few analysts thought there might be something fishy about what they called 'subjective accounting,' investors didn't particularly care as long as the profits rolled in."[184] Listeners may not have understood Andy Fastow when he explained the partnerships; but he sure sounded convincing: "We strip out price risk, we strip out interest rate risk, we strip out all the risks. What's left may not be something that we want."[185] So "what's left" becomes a limited partnership. Unanswered (and probably unasked) was another basic question: If Enron doesn't want it, why would anyone else? It just didn't seem to matter. After all, the partnerships were supported by Enron stock, which, according to Jeff Skilling's manic mantra, was way undervalued and could only go up. Apparently, Isaac Newton's 17th century laws of gravity had no place in a 21st century business model.

Every large corporation has its own signature culture. Enron's, created largely by Skilling, was a blend of cutting-edge and "cutting-throat." It has been called a "culture of arrogance." The company's hard-nosed approach toward its customers is reflective of this.

> The old notion of customer service was based on the long haul—you had to nurse and coddle customers to keep them. But Enron had new markets and new ideas—customers had to come to them. Over time, the company stopped referring to its business clients as customers and began calling them "counterparties."[186]

Skilling encouraged creative tension among employees. "Teamwork, never that important in a trading culture, went the way of the eyeshade and the abacus."[187] It has been said that Enron traders were afraid to go to the bathroom for fear that a colleague would steal information from their computer screens.[188] In such a climate of fear it is easy to understand why any negative information was likely to be swept under the rug. "[D]elivering bad news had career-wrecking potential."[189] Thus, Enron became an environment where mistakes were never made; or, rather, never acknowledged. A former employee has described the aggressive Enron culture this way: "They roll you over and slit your throat and watch your eyes while you bleed to death."[190]

Enron post-mortems cannot ignore the abysmal failure of the company's board of directors. Directors of publicly held corporations have one paramount responsibility: to protect the best interests of shareholders. To accomplish this mission, boards are expected to select and oversee competent and ethical management to run the company on a day-to-day basis.[191] Serious doubts have been raised about *whose* interests were being protected at Enron. Some directors had lucrative consulting contracts or other business arrangements with Enron. Others had ties to charities and institutions that received large donations from Enron.[192] These potential conflicts of interest created what one scholar has termed a "lax culture that unfortunately breeds this kind of disaster."[193] In its report, released in July 2002, the Permanent Subcommittee on Investigations of the U.S. Senate harshly condemned the Enron board for its "lack of independence."[194]

There was perhaps another reason Enron's directors went along with the company's high-risk accounting practices. The board was significantly overpaid. The subcommittee report noted that Enron board members received $350,000 in cash and stock for their work in 2000—about double what directors typically earn at comparable publicly traded corporations.[195]

Since the collapse, many board members have condemned Lay, Skilling, Fastow, and all the other miscreants who destroyed Enron. Directors have claimed to be stunned by the fraudulent accounting methods that have been revealed. Some commentators have compared their reaction to what is known as the "*Casablanca* maneuver"[196]: the act of brazenly denying one's participation in a questionable activity, in the face of damning evidence. The term is a reference to a scene in the classic movie when Chief of Police Claude Rains closes down Humphrey Bogart's night-club because he is "shocked" to discover that gambling is going on there. As soon as he says this, a croupier approaches him and hands him his roulette winnings.

Ample evidence exists that the Enron board's hypocrisy is more than a match for Claude Rains'. According to meeting minutes going back to 1997, the board of directors repeatedly approved risky accounting practices, including moving debt off the company books.[197] Perhaps the strongest indication that the board knew the score was its formal decision to waive the conflict of interest provision of Enron's code of ethics in order to permit Andrew Fastow to serve simultaneously as managing partner of the LJM's and other partnerships and as chief financial officer of Enron. One director, the former dean of a major graduate business school, declared after the bankruptcy: "We did our job. . . . [blah blah blah] . . . We are not detectives."[198] His second contention is obviously correct. Detectives are rarely if ever paid $350,000 a year. His first contention is, at the very least, arguable.

In 2000, *Chief Executive* magazine ranked Enron as one of the nation's five best boards.[199] One shudders to imagine the five worst.

So, who killed Enron? Certainly, its top leadership deserves much of the blame. A former Enron employee has dubbed the company "Greed Incorporated."[200] "Compensation plans often seemed oriented toward enriching executives rather than generating profits for shareholders."[201] The same would seem to apply to its overpaid and underattentive board of directors.

Arthur Andersen and Company share in the guilt. Its auditors were neither vigilant nor scrupulous. Its managers put profits above professional integrity. The classic textbook, *The Economic Structure of Corporate Law*, insists that only honest companies can pass the inspection of experienced external auditors, because the reputational cost of false certification to the auditor is greater than any gains to be made.[202] Criminologist William K. Black has called this contention a "myth." Black, a former top government investigator, points out that during the savings and loan crisis, *every* fraudulent S&L got a clean bill-of-health from a reputable accounting firm.[203]

Stock analysts failed to analyze. "Wall Streeters find it hard to admit that they don't understand something."[204] Brokerage houses accepted the Enron propaganda like it was holy script. The day before Enron declared bankruptcy, six major research analysts still had a *strong buy* rating on the company.[205] Moreover, Enron generated enormous fees for investment bankers—a fact hardly conducive to asking tough questions. Indeed, class action lawsuits were filed against some major financial institutions by Enron investors who lost billions of dollars. The lead plaintiff, the

University of California system, reportedly lost $145 million from its pension and endowment funds when Enron collapsed.[206] The litigation charges that the defendants had assisted Enron in defrauding its shareholders by helping the company raise money even as it was imploding. In June 2005, the two biggest defendants agreed to settle: Citigroup for $2 billion[207] and J.P. Morgan for $2.2 billion.[208] The lawsuit was scheduled to go to trial in 2006, but after Citigroup and Morgan withdrew it was expected that the remaining defendants would opt to settle as well.

Some of the corporate attorneys involved in Enron litigation were infected by the contagion. William Lerach, whose high-profile legal victories included a $7 billion judgment against Enron, was sentenced to two years in federal prison in 2008 for his role in a lucrative kickback scheme involving class action suits against some of the country's biggest corporations.[209] Several other lawyers had pled guilty to similar charges.

The financial press, *whose job it is to ask questions*, was more likely to fawn than ferret. Simply put, Enron "had Wall Street beaten into submission."[210]

Certain economists even blame shareholders.[211] That they behaved greedily is undeniable, but without gold fever there probably wouldn't be a stock market. The culpability of amateur investors, many of them blue collar employees, seems less palpable than that of the professionals. If Enron was a great shark at the top of the food chain, investors were the krill resting at the bottom. Everybody from the company itself, to the accountants, to the analysts and brokers, to the financial press were beating the Enron drum. What were the odds that all of them could be wrong? As it turned out: nearly 100 percent. But blaming victimized investors for believing people they thought they could trust is like blaming Watergate (Chapter 9) on everyone who voted for Richard Nixon.

Ultimately, Enron succumbed to its own arrogant culture. Enron's deadly sin was hubris— "an overweening pride, which led people to believe they can handle increasingly exotic risk without danger."[212] The company was the poster child of the so-called New Economy of the 21st century—an economy in which people scrambled to buy clothes exactly like the ones the emperor *wasn't* wearing. The crowned heads of Enron believed they would write a new chapter in the annals of American business. It turned out to be Chapter 11.

If a corporation whose recklessness and dishonesty has devastated thousands of innocent victims and hung a cloud of public distrust over American financial markets even deserves an epitaph, perhaps a fitting one can be paraphrased from *The New York Times*[213]: Enron was not much of a company, but it was one hell of a stock.

CASE STUDY
Arthur Andersen—Accounting and Accountability

guilt/culpability

On October 12, 2001, just four days before Enron publicly disclosed its shocking $600 million third quarter loss, accountants who audited Enron's books for Arthur Andersen received an extraordinary message. An e-mail sent by Nancy Temple, Andersen's Chicago-based lawyer, "reminded" the workers of the company's "document and retention" policy and urged compliance. The memo, in effect, directed workers to destroy all audit material relating to Enron except for the most basic "work papers."[214]

Nine days later, David Duncan, an Andersen partner who ran the Houston office and was chief

(Continued)

outside auditor for Enron, sent out an "urgent" email requesting a meeting of all of Andersen's Houston employees involved with the Enron account. Again, the audit managers were instructed to comply with the document destruction policy. The following day, a less veiled message went out from Kimberly Latham, an Andersen manager in Houston. This memo indicated that the destruction of Enron documents was so important that employees should work overtime to get it done.[215] The "Great Shred-a-thon" had begun.

It was obvious that Andersen was not simply trying to get an early jump on spring cleaning. Although there are no codified regulations on how long accounting firms must retain documents, most are typically held for several years.[216] But both Congress and the SEC were beginning their Enron investigations, and it was likely that Andersen's records would be subpoenaed. Enron's malodorous financial statements had been signed by Andersen auditors. The stock market was going into the tank, and the country was getting angry. The last thing Andersen wanted was a paper trail.

By the time Andersen CEO Joseph Berardino was called before the House Energy and Commerce Committee in February 2002, much of his company's Enron documents were confetti. Berardino attempted to minimize Andersen's role in the convoluted partnership arrangements at the heart of the Enron scandal. He blamed Enron's demise on "bad business decisions,"[217] not on any misconduct on Andersen's part. "At the end of the day, we do not cause companies to fail," Berardino said.[218]

Berardino's testimony was scorned by the committee. The prevailing belief was that Andersen's executives must have known that Enron was hiding massive debt. One member told Berardino: "You're not some innocent."[219] Berardino was very clear in his insistence that his company bore no culpability but was evasive on almost every other matter. At one point he declared: "I don't know what we knew and when we knew it." Another member shot back: "It's not acceptable."[220] Berardino also rejected suggestions

that he was trying to place all the blame on David Duncan, who had been fired. "We're not looking for fall guys," he insisted.[221] Maybe not, but a month later Berardino himself resigned under pressure.[222]

Anyone hearing the tone of the House inquiry didn't require profound insight to realize that Arthur Andersen and Company was in big trouble. On March 14, a federal grand jury indicted the 89-year-old firm on charges of obstruction of justice. The Justice Department alleged that Andersen had conspired to destroy incriminating Enron documents.[223] Andersen again blamed the Houston office under David Duncan, whom it described as a "rogue partner." However, prosecutors charged that the shredding was not confined to Houston. It had spread to other Andersen offices, from Chicago to London.[224]

The case against Andersen took a major turn in April. David Duncan, the former partner who had overseen the shredding in Houston, entered into a plea bargain with federal prosecutors. He agreed to plead guilty to a single count of obstruction of justice and cooperate with the government in its case against Andersen. In exchange, it was believed that he would avoid incarceration.[225] It was a serious blow to the Andersen defense and probably even a bigger threat to Jeff Skilling. Skilling had proclaimed ignorance of Enron's accounting tricks in his congressional testimony. As Andersen's top player on the lucrative Enron account, Duncan was well-positioned to counter Skilling's claims.[226] But that was still down the road. The government's first order of business was to nail Andersen.

When the trial began in May, Duncan was one of the government's first witnesses. He admitted that he knew he had committed a crime when he instructed his colleagues to shred Enron documents. The defense was in the odd position of having to prove that Duncan had done nothing wrong—despite his confession in open court—because under the law an entire partnership can be found criminally liable for the acts of one of its partners.[227]

(Continued)

The most contentious issue in the trial turned out to be whether or not prosecutors would be allowed to introduce evidence of Andersen's previous history of SEC violations. When the judge ruled in the government's favor, it was a major blow to the defense.[228] A year earlier, Andersen had agreed to pay $110 million as part of a settlement in a class action suit brought by shareholders against another Andersen client, the Sunbeam appliance company. Sunbeam had been forced to restate its financial results for six consecutive quarters.[229] It was later revealed that Andersen had also shredded incriminating Sunbeam documents.[230] Less than two months after the Sunbeam settlement, Andersen agreed to pay federal regulators $7 million in connection with charges that it filed misleading audits of yet another client, Waste Management, Inc.[231] Andersen was portrayed as a firm that had "repeatedly caved in to client demands that it approve bogus financial statements."[232]

On June 15, 2002, Arthur Andersen and Company, once one of the world's top accounting firms, was convicted of obstruction of justice after a grueling six-week trial.[233] However, in May 2005, the Supreme Court overturned the Andersen conviction unanimously on the ground that jury instructions did not convey the requisite consciousness of wrongdoing.[234] The decision was considered a major defeat for the Justice Department, though for Arthur Andersen it was little more than a symbolic victory. As of this writing, Andersen is still in business—barely. Clients have deserted in droves. The firm no longer even audits publicly traded corporations. As of this writing, its handful of remaining employees consists mainly of lawyers fending off civil litigation.[235] Unless it is bought out by a competitor, it is considered doomed. The company now acknowledges that it made what it terms "errors in judgment."[236] One could respond that wearing a striped tie with a plaid shirt is an "error in judgment." What Arthur Andersen did is a *crime*.

WORLDCOM

The dubious record for the nation's largest corporate bankruptcy, set by Enron in late 2001, would prove to be short-lived. In the summer of 2002, one of the world's biggest telecommunications companies would choke on its own treachery.

In 1983 four men met in a coffee shop in Hattiesburg, Mississippi, to hammer out the details for starting a new telephone service company. The company would be called LDDS or Long Distance Discount Service. The name was suggested by their waitress.

Within ten years, LDDS had acquired more than a half dozen communications companies and had expanded its reach throughout the U.S. In 1994, LDDS acquired IDB WorldCom, an international company, and soon changed its name to WorldCom, Inc. Bernie Ebbers, one of the four founders, became WorldCom's first CEO. Three years later, Ebbers announced a $37 billion merger with rival MCI. In 1999, WorldCom and rival Sprint proposed a gigantic $115 billion merger, which was later called off. In less than two decades, the company created in a Mississippi coffee shop had accumulated 20 million customers and became one of the great success stories of the New Economy. Or, had it?

By 2000, WorldCom stock, which had peaked in 1997 at $64.50, was sagging badly. Within a year, a crushing $30 billion debt would lead to the sudden resignation of Bernie Ebbers in April, 2002. Shareholders were also raising serious questions about $366 million Ebbers had borrowed from the company.[237] Over about seven years, Ebbers had racked up a mountain of personal debts from a variety of lenders to pay for yachts, timberland, and other extravagant purchases, including the largest ranch Canada.[238] Ebbers reportedly liked to spend his weekends riding around on his tractor and wanted to live a life that was one part feudal baron and one part cowboy—a fast-lane life that was ultimately underwritten by shareholders.

In an attempt to salvage WorldCom, new CEO John Sidgmore laid off 17,000 workers and fired Chief Financial Officer Scott Sullivan.[239] But the horse had not only left the barn, it had already been slaughtered and boiled down into glue. On June 24, WorldCom stock dropped below $1, closing at 91 cents. The next day, WorldCom hit the fan. The company announced that it had inflated its bottom line for more than a year by improperly accounting for $3.9 billion.[240] WorldCom stock closed the day at 20 cents.

WorldCom had cooked its books by classifying ordinary expenses as capital expenditures.[241] What should have been a huge loss was dressed up as a $1.4 billion annual profit.[242] To borrow from the jargon of the advertising industry, WorldCom had "put lipstick on a pig." The company had also boosted its revenues by drawing on reserves it had set aside to cover various losses—a gimmick known as "cookie jar" accounting.[243]

It was later revealed that WorldCom's executives earned $104 million in salaries and bonuses based upon the phony numbers.[244] WorldCom's accountant for the 16 months in question had been none other than Arthur Anderson and Company. If this were a movie, it might have been titled *Son of Enron*.

Within 24 hours, the SEC had filed fraud charges.[245] The SEC said that the financial irregularities were of a magnitude never seen before.[246] WorldCom stock dropped to *9 cents* and trading was halted. Global markets were reeling from what was being called the biggest accounting fraud in American history. A leading telecommunications analyst summed it up: "This is just another nail in the coffin of confidence."[247] President Bush condemned the fraud as "outrageous."[248] He did not indicate, however, whether his mother-in-law was a WorldCom shareholder.

On July 21, 2002, WorldCom made it official. Its ethical bankruptcy had affected financial bankruptcy.[249] By the end of the year, the company had yet another CEO, Michael Capellas, who had assumed the helm without either pay or an employment contract, awaiting approval from federal judges overseeing the WorldCom bankruptcy. When he was finally approved, Capellas tried to break the company away from its opprobrious past. He demanded the resignation of six board members—the last remaining allies of Bernie Ebbers.[250] A few months later, Capellas fired 5,000 more employees.[251]

When Bernie Ebbers and Scott Sullivan were called to testify before the House Financial Services Committee, they "plead the Fifth" and kept silent. The hearings did give Congress another chance to pound on Arthur Andersen's house of accounting horrors, which had approved WorldCom's books. One member declared: "I think the theme has become clear. All the people who are supposed to be checking each other are in fact collaborating with each other."[252]

Bernie Ebbers' attorneys told congressional investigators that Ebbers had been unaware of the illicit transactions. They blamed former CFO Sullivan. However, WorldCom's lawyers insisted that Ebbers had been fully aware of the string of fraudulent earnings reports.[253]

On August 28, 2002, Scott Sullivan, once considered by Wall Street as one of the most respected CFOs, was indicted for securities fraud, conspiracy, and making false filings to the SEC.[254] Eight months later, Sullivan was indicted again for bank fraud. The charges allege that he made false financial statements in order to secure a $4.25 billion line of credit for WorldCom— by this time renamed MCI.[255] He faced potentially more than 100 years in prison. Many analysts expected, however, that some kind of plea-bargain deal would be struck. They believed that Ebbers, not Sullivan, was the primary target of the Justice Department. A voicemail sent by Sullivan to Ebbers in 2001, expressing worry over "accounting fluff," seemed to suggest that Ebbers knew there were two sets of books.[256]

Ebbers was indicted in 2004 on federal charges of securities fraud, conspiracy, and falsely filing with the Securities and Exchange Commission.[257] Much of the information contained in the indictment had been provided by Scott Sullivan, the chief architect of the massive crimes that had cost WorldCom investors billions of dollars. Sullivan, still facing the possibility of growing old in prison, had agreed to help Ebbers' prosecution in exchange for leniency. It was yet another "textbook example of how cooperating with prosecutors can pay."[258] A former high-ranking official in the U.S. Attorney's office in Manhattan noted: "Even a brazen scammer in the soup can help his cause with the government."[259]

At Ebbers' trial the following year, Sullivan testified that he had acted under Ebbers' direction, insisting that Ebbers had intimidated him into committing fraud so that WorldCom could meet Wall Street's expectations.[260] Ebbers' own testimony at the trial revealed an astonishing ignorance about the finances of a corporation he had built. But the prosecutor told the jury that Ebbers was the only person who had the authority to orchestrate the scheme.

> "He was WorldCom and WorldCom was Ebbers. He built this company. He ran it.
> Of course he directed this fraud."[261]

After a six-week trial, the jury made clear what—and whom—it believed. Bernie Ebbers was convicted of all charges.[262] Most legal analysts were predicting a sentence of somewhere between five and ten years.[263] They were so wrong.

On July 13, 2005, Bernard J. Ebbers was sentenced to 25 years in prison.[264] Because there is no parole in the federal system, it was essentially a life sentence for the 63-year-old ex-tycoon, once known as the "Telecom Cowboy."[265] It was the toughest punishment for corporate wrong-doing ever handed down.[266] Ebbers audibly gasped, then sat motionless wiping away tears as the sentence was read. Ebbers had asked for leniency, citing failing health, his history of community service, and his own personal financial losses from WorldCom's collapse.[267] The judge, however, was unswayed, citing the extent of investor losses.

> "Mr. Ebbers' statements deprived investors of their money," the judge said. "They might
> have made different decisions had they known the truth." . . . Moreover, she said, "It
> seems clear to me that Mr. Ebbers was a leader of criminal activity in this case."[268]

Judge Barbara Jones concluded: "I find that a sentence of anything less would not reflect the seriousness of this crime."[269]

The "seriousness of the crime" was iterated during the sentencing hearing in the testimony of financially ruined former WorldCom employees. One of them described how he had rose through the ranks of the company's sales division only to be laid off in 2003 without notice. He said he had lost all his money, his medical benefits, and was still unemployed. "I was one of the hard-working employees at a great company that was destroyed by Bernard Ebbers."[270]

Meanwhile, having fulfilled his end of the deal, Scott Sullivan pleaded guilty to three criminal counts a month later and received a relatively light five-year prison sentence. However, he also settled civil charges against him by agreeing to surrender nearly all his assets—including the $5 million he had hoped to receive from the sale of his uncompleted mansion in Florida.[271]

The accounting fraud at WorldCom/MCI, once estimated at $3.9 billion, is now pegged at $11 billion. In mid-2003, the company agreed to pay a fine of $500 million, by far the largest fine for financial fraud ever imposed by the Securities and Exchange Commission.[272] The WorldCom scandal, following on the heels of Enron, squelched claims by opponents of regulation that Enron was an anomaly.[273] If the wave of corporate scandals has taught us nothing else, it has demonstrated the need for serious vigilance, comprehensive reforms, and aggressive enforcement.

". . . IT WAS A VERY BAD YEAR"

Global Crossing

The crash of WorldCom was both a cause and an effect of a collapsing telecom sector. One of the first casualties of 2002 was Global Crossing, a large voice and data carrier, which declared bankruptcy on January 28.[274] It was the fourth-largest corporate bankruptcy in history. Global Crossing, Bermuda-based but headquartered in Beverly Hills, laid fiber-optic cables beneath the Atlantic and Pacific Oceans. It had once been a Wall Street favorite but was now buried in debt. The following week, the SEC raised questions about the company's accounting practices. The company's former vice-president of finance, Roy Olofson, had raised allegations that Global Crossing and its auditor—*Arthur Andersen*—had inflated revenues. The alleged scheme involved the swapping of long-term contracts with other carriers, then reporting the new contracts as revenue and the outgoing ones as a capital expense.[275] One of the swaps in question was a $17 million deal in 2000 between Global Crossing and *Enron*.[276] Global Crossing vigorously denied the allegation, claiming that Olofson had been fired and was now merely seeking revenge. Olofson insisted he had been fired only because he had asked questions about the company's books.[277]

When the House Energy and Commerce Committee, which was also conducting the Enron investigation, held hearings on the Global Crossing bankruptcy, it asked the company to turn over documents relating to executive pay and bookkeeping.[278] Olofson was also charging that his former employer had been shredding incriminating documents since the SEC launched its probe.[279] Global Crossing confirmed that it had shredded relevant documents at its offices in New Jersey, Minneapolis, Montreal, Toronto, and Rochester (New York) but characterized the shredding as "isolated incidents."[280] Of course, simple semantics decree that if enough "isolated incidents" occur, they are no longer isolated.

Like others before them, Global Crossing executives walked away from the debacle with personal fortunes. Company founder Gary Winnick sold shares worth $734 million before the company went bust.[281] Winnick cultivated a "tough guy" reputation. He reportedly once asked a temporary worker in an elevator at Global if she knew who he was. She didn't, so he fired her.[282]

Global Crossing eventually was sold for $250 million to Asian interests in August 2002. It was a far cry from the company's peak value of $50 billion.[283]

A public corporation became a public-be-damned corporation. Creditors would be lucky to get pennies on the dollar, employees lost significant portions of their retirement funds, and investors were stuck with a $60 stock that had dropped to 7 cents a share.[284] Securities markets are supposed to operate on a risk-reward basis; yet top executives at Global Crossing were not only rewarded for failure, but their multi-million dollar returns also seemingly had come with no risk at all.

On the last business day of 2002, the Justice Department dropped its probe of Global Crossing.[285] Shareholders who had lost billions of dollars would have to go the class action lawsuit route. A settlement was announced in 2004, under which investors who lost money would share $245 million and former workers would receive $80 million.[286]

Although there have been no criminal indictments or "perp walks" resulting from the Global Crossing debacle, the fetor of influence peddling permeates the case. Like Enron, Global Crossing had been a major political contributor; but while Enron mostly funded Republican candidates, Global Crossing was a Democratic cash machine. In fact, it had contributed more to the

Democratic party than Enron had given to *both* parties. Moreover, Terry McAuliffe, Chairman of the Democratic National Committee, had struck the mother lode. He had invested $100,000 in the company, then sold out less than two years later just before the stock crashed, for $18 million—a profit of *18,000 percent.*[287]

Qwest Communications

The SEC investigation of Global Crossing spread to another major telecom company, Qwest Communications, the country's fourth largest long distance carrier. Qwest and WorldCom had engaged in a fierce bidding war in 1999 over the acquisition of U.S. West, a large regional phone company. Qwest ultimately prevailed.[288] Once again, accounting irregularities were at the core of the inquiry.[289] It was alleged that Qwest had artificially pumped up its revenues over a period of several years.[290]

One of the issues raised by investigators involved a trade of fiber optic network capacity and other assets between Qwest and *Enron* in 2001, at a time when each was struggling to meet revenue expectations.[291] The trade was valued at more than $500 million—a figure alleged to have been inflated by both companies.[292]

The SEC also suspected Qwest of collusion with its competitors. According to *The Wall Street Journal,* Qwest had struck secret deals, offering smaller carriers discounts for using Qwest's infrastructure, on the understanding that the carriers would not oppose Qwest's rapid expansion.[293] This and other allegations battered Qwest's once-adored stock. Already staggering under a $26 billion debt load, the company's credit was downgraded to junk status by Standard & Poor's in May.[294] A week later, Qwest dropped its independent auditor—Arthur *You-Know-Who.*[295]

While Qwest investors were taking a beating, top executives were prospering. CEO Joseph Nacchio, who was ousted in June 2002, reportedly had made $227 million unloading company stock during the period when profit numbers were exaggerated.[296] In addition, Nacchio's 2001 compensation had increased a whopping 600 percent over the previous year to $27 million.[297] Other executives similarly sold off their stock at a profit of more than $250 million.[298] Board member Philip Anschutz, Qwest's largest shareholder and one of the Republican Party's biggest campaign donors, reportedly made almost $1.5 *billion* dumping stock before the accounting scandal was exposed.[299] Shareholder-rights advocates have long demanded that executives should be restricted from selling shares until they retire to prevent them from profiting from insider information.[300] Qwest's "Executive Fire Sale" would certainly appear to reinforce that argument.

The Justice Department began a criminal investigation of Qwest in July 2002. The company initially denied reports of the probe but later confirmed that it was indeed under investigation and pledged to cooperate fully.[301] On July 28, Qwest issued a statement acknowledging that it had incorrectly accounted for more than $1.1 billion in transactions from 1999 to 2001. In addition to its questionable fiber-optics capacity deal with Enron and other firms, Qwest said that it *might* have "improperly accounted for services acquired from other telecommunications carriers and for communications equipment that it sold."[302]

On October 22, 2004, Qwest agreed to pay $250 million to settle fraud charges brought by the Securities and Exchange Commission. The money would be distributed to defrauded investors according to a provision of the Sarbanes-Oxley Act, a law passed by Congress in 2002 in response to the wave of corporate accounting scandals.[303]

But the SEC was not finished with Qwest. In 2005, it filed charges against Joseph Nacchio and six other top executives accusing them of orchestrating a "massive financial fraud."[304] The civil suit alleged that Nacchio had created a "culture of fear"[305] and had put "enormous pressure on employees to meet revenue and earnings goals through bogus sales procedures that became an addiction."[306]

Later that same year, Robin Szeliga, the former chief financial officer of Qwest, pleaded guilty to insider trading.[307] Ms. Szeliga admitted to improperly selling 10,000 shares of Qwest stock in 2001 for a net profit of $125,000, based on nonpublic information that Qwest would fail to meet revenue targets.[308] Sentencing was postponed. In keeping with the "food chain" strategy, it was widely believed that Ms. Szeliga ultimately would be able to bargain her possible 10-year prison sentence down to probation if she agreed to cooperate with the government in widely expected future cases.[309] "Szeliga may have been in a position to know what executives knew and when they knew it, including former CEO Joe Nacchio."[310]

The predictions were accurate. Szeliga was given probation and fined $250,000 in return for agreeing to testify against Nacchio[311], which she did at his trial the following year.[312] It was a narrow trial, less about large-scale corporate conspiracies than about Nacchio's personal stock trading. Szeliga told the jury that she repeatedly had warned Nacchio in 2001 that Qwest's public financial projections were vastly overhyped. The government accused Nacchio of ignoring all warnings, failing to inform shareholders of mounting problems, and dumping millions of dollars worth of stock to protect his own wealth.[313] The counts on which Nacchio was convicted represented $52 million in illegal stock sales.[314]

In April, 2007, Joseph Nacchio, who had built Qwest Communications into the fourth largest telecommunications company in the U.S. and then presided over a $100 million drop in market value,[315] was convicted of insider trading.[316] After the trial, a woman who claimed to have lost $100,000 in retirement savings told the press: "It has been a long time coming."[317] The U.S. Attorney for Colorado made no effort to conceal his jubilation. He told the press: "Convicted felon Joe Nacchio has a very nice ring to it."[318]

Joseph Nacchio was sentenced to six years in prison and ordered to repay the $52 million.[319] All the celebrating may have been premature, however. In March, 2008, a federal appeals court voted 2-1 to overturn Nacchio's conviction and ordered a new trial.[320] Prosecutors then asked the entire appeals court to reconsider and it agreed. In July, the court granted a rare second oral argument—this one before a nine-judge panel—to be heard in late 2008.[321] A three-judge panel from the U.S. Court of Appeals for the Tenth Circuit overturned Nacchio's conviction on March 17, 2008,[322] but the full Tenth Circuit reversed the decision on February 25, 2009.[323] Nacchio appealed to the Supreme Court, the Court denied hearing his case, and on April 19, 2009, he began his six-year sentence.[324]

Adelphia

In 2002, the SEC conducted a probe into the accounting practices of Adelphia Communications, the sixth-largest cable provider in the U.S. The main issue involved $2.3 billion in loans Adelphia backed to limited partnerships owned by the family of Chairman John Rigas.[325] Rigas, the 77-year-old son of Greek immigrants, had built Adelphia into a cable powerhouse. (Adelphia is the Greek word for brotherhood.) He had grown up living over his parent's small hot dog joint on the outskirts of Coulersport, Pennsylvania. Adelphia still housed its corporate headquarters in this rural hamlet, despite being five hours away from the nearest airport—in Buffalo. As the cable industry exploded, Rigas acquired a reputation as a defender of traditional morality and family values. Shortly after purchasing Southern California's largest cable provider, he pulled all adult-oriented TV channels off the system.[326] But, like Charles Keating, the notorious S&L operator of the 1980s (Chapter 8) who was also a major leader in a boisterous campaign against pornography,

Rigas' anti-smut fervor was not accompanied by any corresponding business morality. One securities analyst, whose firm owned some of Adelphia's bonds, said of the Rigas family: "They misled shareholders and bondholders about the total value of the company by concealing liabilities."[327]

The company also faced an additional $500 million in liability for bank loans to a spinoff telephone company that was now in bankruptcy.[328] Adelphia itself filed for bankruptcy in June 2002.[329] Its battered stock was trading for 14 cents; it had lost 99 percent of its value. Scores of lawsuits had been filed against it by both shareholders and cable subscribers. It was the target of both a federal probe and two state grand jury investigations.

John Rigas had been ousted a month earlier, and the company soon filed a lawsuit against him, his wife, his three sons, his daughter, his son-in-law, and 20 companies controlled by the family. The suit charged the defendants with violation of the Racketeer Influenced and Corrupt Organizations Act (RICO), breach of fiduciary duties, waste of corporate assets, abuse of control, breach of contract, unjust enrichment, fraudulent conveyance, and conversion of corporate assets.

Adelphia also dismissed its auditors, Deloitte & Touche.[330] The firm denied any complicity, arguing that Adelphia's board had pressured it to rush its audit in order to soothe creditors and help avoid bankruptcy. Its accountants insisted that they had refused to resume the audit after discovering that the Rigas family had used $700 million of funds borrowed from the company to buy Adelphia stock without public disclosure.[331] This blame game will likely be sorted out in court, as Deloitte has also been named in shareholder lawsuits.

The day Adelphia fired Deloitte & Touche, it issued new financial results for the prior two years and acknowledged that earnings, customer numbers, and sales figures had all been overstated by the Rigas family.[332] According to the Justice Department: "Although the financial affairs of Adelphia and the Rigas Family Entities intermingled . . . the financial results of the Rigas Family Entities were not combined with Adelphia's on Adelphia's official financial statements."[333] The extent of the alleged corruption was stupefying in its profligacy. The company admitted that off-balance-book loans totaling more than $4.5 billion had been used by the Rigas "to buy more than $1 billion in Adelphia stocks and bonds, help pay for the Buffalo Sabres pro hockey team, bankroll movies to be produced by a Rigas daughter, and pay for automobiles on behalf of a Rigas-owned dealership."[334] John Rigas was allegedly sucking up so much money from Adelphia that his son Tim had to put him on a $1 million a month "allowance"—on top of his $1.9 million salary. The family also owned lavish vacation homes in Mexico, Colorado, and South Carolina, as well as two luxury apartments on Manhattan's Upper East Side. Rigas' son Tim had a $700,000 membership in an upscale golf club. Three private jets carried Tim and his friends to African safaris and castles in the south of France.[335]

Conspicuous consumption is of course not illegal, *per se*. If Adelphia had been entirely family owned and operated, there are *legal* (or at least semi-legal) creative accounting methods to permit the use of company cash for personal benefit. But Adelphia was a publicly owned corporation. Thus, most of the family's "pricey perks" were being paid for by shareholders. *That's theft.* The *Wall Street Journal* accused the Rigas family of using the company as its own private "piggy bank."[336]

On the morning of July 24, 2000, U.S. Postal Inspectors arrested Rigas and his sons Tim and Michael.[337] They were charged with conspiracy, securities, bank, and wire fraud. Potentially, they faced federal prison time of 100 years each if convicted on all counts.[338] The Bush Administration, stung by accusations that it was dragging out the Enron case because of the president's well-known ties to Ken Lay, reportedly wanted a highly visible corporate fraud arrest.[339] Thus, camera crews had been tipped off by Washington officials and were lined up at New York's main post office, where Rigas would be arraigned. Handcuffed and stripped of his shoelaces and belt, the aging mogul's "perp walk" was captured live on television. When Bush was informed of the arrests, his one-word reply was, "Good!"[340]

Rigas' arrest, which undoubtedly will help all the civil litigation pending, had an extraordinary effect on the securities markets. That same day the Dow Jones Industrial Average shot up *488 points.* Noted journalist Carl Hiaasen wrote that the Bush Administration had successfully played the "Adelphia card."

> Those who have dealt with their local cable company couldn't be shocked to hear that there might be stealing and deceit at high levels. The surprise was that the feds actually had busted somebody for it. . . . Apparently, the mere sight of a CEO in handcuffs was enough to send the stock markets soaring.[341]

The following day, Adelphia, which had been a rotting corpse for months, officially filed for bankruptcy.[342] By August, the investigation had widened to include possible charges of tax violations against the company.[343]

Two former Adelphia executives, James R. Brown (vice president for finance)[344] and Timothy A. Werth (director of accounting)[345] also were arrested. Each pleaded guilty and both agreed to testify against the Rigas family. Rigas' attorney maintains that the family's activities, while complex, were not criminal. He insists: "There's been a major distortion here."[346] That defense may prove to be a "tough sell." It is not by chance that the biggest share of financial misstatement cases, such as Qwest, Global Crossing, WorldCom, and Adelphia seem to be in the telecommunications sector. "Telecoms are notorious for their murky, hard-to-understand accounting practices. Even professional analysts who follow these firms for a living . . . have trouble following some of their book-keeping."[347]

After eight days of deliberations, John Rigas and his son Timothy were convicted in July 2004 of all the charges except wire fraud.[348] Rigas' other son Michael was acquitted of conspiracy, and the jury hung on the remaining counts against him.[349]

The fallen cable magnates were sentenced in 2005. John Rigas was handed a 15-year prison term, while Timothy Rigas, Adelphia's former chief financial officer, received a 20-year sentence.[350] U.S. District Judge Leonard Sand told the elder Rigas: "Were it not for your age and health I would impose a sentence far greater than I do today."[351] Nevertheless, it was still likely a life sentence for the 80-year-old crook. And, just in case it wasn't, a federal grand jury three months later indicted John Rigas for evading $300 million in income tax.[352] If the case ever comes to trial, it would be one of the largest personal income tax evasion cases in U.S. history.[353]

Tyco

It used to be said that the business of America is business. In recent years, it seemed like the business of business was fraud. A new and ugly kind of corporate culture appeared—rooted in greed, selfishness, and a lack of human empathy. People of privilege and power indulged in an orgy of what one penitent white-collar criminal now terms "malignant self-love."[354]

Consider the example of Dennis Kozlowski, whose self-love was not only "malignant" but extravagant beyond reason. The former CEO of Tyco, a conglomerate whose products range from steel fence posts to fiber optic cable,[355] Kozlowski reportedly spent $135 million of his company's money to finance his ultra-lavish lifestyle. Most of these funds came in the form of large loans from Tyco that were later forgiven. These transactions were never even reported to shareholders.[356] Some of his purchases were extravagant beyond belief. For starters, he paid $6,000 for a now-infamous shower curtain.[357] But that was only the beginning. Tyco provided the [SEC] with a list of allegedly unauthorized purchases, including $15,000 for [an] umbrella stand, $6,300 for a sewing basket, $17,000 for a 'traveling toilette box,' a $2,2000 waste basket, $2,900 for coat hangers, $5,900 for a set of sheets, a $1,650 appointment notebook, and a $445 pincushion."[358] The poet Alexander Pope once made an observation that may seem unfairly cynical—until one encounters a Dennis Kozlowski: "If you want to know what God thinks of money, just look at the people He gave it to."

Kozlowski was indicted in New York for tax evasion in June 2002. He had purchased six paintings, including a Renoir and a Monet, for $13.1 million. In order to avoid paying more than $1 million in New York state sales taxes, he allegedly shipped empty crates to Tyco headquarters in Exeter, New Hampshire—a state with no sales tax—then transported the paintings back to his 13-room Manhattan apartment.[359] The day before his indictment, Tyco announced Kozlowski's resignation.[360]

Tyco was also plagued by other serious accounting problems. The company announced restatements of $135 million in pretax income in 2002. Two months later, it acknowledged using accounting tricks to boost earnings and inflate reported "profits" by $382 million. Three months later, it announced another $265 million change due to more accounting problems. And in mid-2003, the company disclosed yet another $1.2 billion accounting irregularity.[361]

Dennis Kozlowski was further indicted on more state charges accusing him of looting Tyco of about $600 million. Charges were also filed against former Tyco CFO Mark Swartz,[362] who would later be charged with federal tax evasion as well.[363] But the "feds" would have to wait their turn. New York wasn't finished with Tyco. The company's former general counsel, Mark Belnick, was charged with grand larceny, involving his acceptance of an unauthorized "special bonus" of $12 million in cash and stock.[364] And Frank Walsh, Jr., a former outside director, pleaded guilty in December, 2002, to felony charges related to his receipt of an undisclosed $20 million payment from the company.[365] The Walsh case is notable on at least two accounts. Outside directors are seldom if ever convicted of crimes. And, as of this writing, Walsh remains the only Tyco indictee to admit his guilt. Manhattan District Attorney Robert Morgenthau described Tyco as a "criminal enterprise" in which executives sought to loot the company from the inside.[366]

Morgenthau tried Dennis Kozlowski and Mark Swartz twice. The first trial in 2004 ended in a mistrial when the jury was deadlocked 11-1 for conviction. The lone holdout for acquittal reportedly had received a menacing telephone call.[367] In the second trial in 2005, both defendants were convicted of stealing hundreds of millions of dollars from Tyco and given 25-year prison sentences. They would have to serve at least eight years and four months to be eligible for parole.[368]

> Assistant District Attorney Owen Heimer asked the judge for the maximum sentence of 30 years, saying Kozlowski had "committed theft and fraud on an unprecedented, staggering scale." He said Kozlowski and Swartz stole so much from the company that "Tyco became a worldwide symbol of kleptocratic management."[369]

The British newspaper *The Guardian* offered a trenchant observation: "[T]he name Kozlowski—once synonymous with deal-making—is likely to become a byword for outrageous corporate greed."[370]

Rite Aid

In June, 2002, three former top executives of Rite Aid—including former chairman and CEO Martin Grass—were indicted for what regulators called a securities and accounting fraud that led to a $1.6 billion restatement of earnings, one of the biggest ever. Rite Aid is the third-largest pharmacy chain in the U.S. The company had been reeling since 1999, when accounting problems dropped the stock from more than $50 a share to less than $3.

Rite Aid had earlier reached a civil settlement with the SEC. The new criminal charges included securities fraud, conspiracy, making false statements to the SEC, obstruction of justice, and tampering with witnesses.[371] "The indictment alleges that the former executives misled board members, vastly inflated profits, defrauded vendors, deceived lenders and auditors, and fabricated documents—even creating notes from a fictitious meeting to gain access to an $800 million emergency loan."[372]

When Grass, the son of the company's founder, became CEO in 1995, he almost immediately embarked on a path of what the SEC termed "dishonesty and misconduct."[373] His crimes were two-pronged: He manipulated earnings and defrauded investors; and at the same time orchestrated a series of moves designed to enrich himself through illegal compensation agreements.[374] For example, Grass and his co-defendants claimed over $50 million in bogus credits for damaged and outdated merchandise, which pumped up the company's books. The problem was that the goods were *not* damaged. Grass and his cronies exploited an agreement with vendors that allowed them to take big deductions for such merchandise. Rite Aid sold off an array of products at a discount, then billed the vendors for the lost income, falsely claiming the damaged/outdated deductions. They also fabricated a summary of a non-existent compensation meeting, then backdated letters in which shares were to be awarded to them. They ended up with double the number of shares they were entitled to under their incentive contracts.[375] Grass also made secret real estate deals with the company for his own benefit and promised hush money to a potential whistle-blower.[376]

In a scene all-too reminiscent of the Enron/Andersen nexus, Rite Aid's auditors, KPMG—the third largest accounting firm in the country—agreed the following year to pay a $125 million settlement to its embattled client's shareholders. The SEC called the accounting fraud at Rite Aid "one of the most egregious ever" and filed a civil suit against three former KPMG officers.[377] Martin Grass also agreed to pay $1.45 million to shareholders.[378]

A week before his trial was scheduled to begin, Grass struck a deal with prosecutors and pleaded guilty to two counts of conspiracy. The deal called for an eight-year prison sentence. If he had been convicted of all 37 charges against him, it could have resulted effectively in a life sentence.[379] He also agreed to penalties totaling more than $3.5 million.[380] Martin Grass thus joined Sam Waksall (Chapter 6) as the second former high-profile CEO in a single week to land in prison. The fact that high-profile corporate criminals are agreeing to relatively harsh deals rather than defending themselves at trial suggests that the federal courts are out for blood. A noted professor of securities law observes: "The potential defendants in these cases are getting the message right now—this is not a time to go before an angry jury and an angry judge."[381]

HealthSouth

HealthSouth Corporation, based in Birmingham, Alabama, is one of the nation's largest health-care services providers. At its height, it dominated the rehabilitation services market, generating reported revenue of nearly $4.4 billion. HealthSouth first landed on the SEC's radar screen in late 2002, when CEO and founder Richard Scrushy sold $75 million of his stock only days before the company posted a big loss. After the SEC announced an investigation, HealthSouth hired an outside law firm to determine whether or not Scrushy had engaged in insider trading. The law firm concluded that Scrushy had not. But the government was not convinced.

Former chief financial officer Weston Smith, realizing that accounting fraud inevitably would be detected and fearful of the newly enacted Sarbanes-Oxley Act, which mandated tough sentences for executives participating in falsified earnings reports, went to authorities. He was followed soon after by CFO William Owens and a mob of other HealthSouth employees.[382] Owens agreed to wear a wire in a failed attempt to get Scrushy to incriminate himself. In March, 2003, the FBI executed a search warrant at HealthSouth's headquarters.

The following day, HealthSouth and Scrushy were accused by the SEC of falsifying the company's earnings. Since 1996, Scrushy allegedly had instructed the company's senior officers and accountants to overstate earnings reports in order to meet investor expectations and inflate the price of HealthSouth stock. The company put Scrushy on administrative leave.

On March 31, 2003, HealthSouth fired Richard Scrushy. Although he had founded the company and was the force behind its impressive rise, he would receive no "golden parachute." The company also fired its auditing firm, Ernst & Young.[383] From then on, the skies seemed to open up, as indictment and guilty pleas rained down for much of 2003. The same day Scrushy was pushed out the door, vice president for finance Emery Harris became the first HealthSouth executive to plead guilty. A few weeks later, five more officers of HealthSouth pleaded guilty to fraud and filing false records. They admitted conspiring to falsify HealthSouth's earnings by at least $1.4 billion. Those pleading guilty were Kenneth Livesay, chief information officer; Rebecca Kay Morgan, group vice president; Cathy Edwards, vice president for asset management; Angela Ayers, vice president for finance and accounting; and Virginia Valentine, assistant vice president for finance and accounting.[384] The U.S. Attorney in charge of the case announced that he expected additional charges would be filed against other HealthSouth executives who were currently cooperating with investigators and had not yet been charged. In an interview, he said: "It's moving at warp speed."[385]

The six defendants were sentenced in December, 2003. Emery Harris was given a term of five months in prison with three years of supervised release with five months of unsupervised home detention. The U.S. Court of Appeals later ruled that the trial judge had erred in computing the amount of money Harris had cost investors and ordered a second sentencing. The government declined, however, to seek more prison time for Harris, who by then had already completed his five months of incarceration.[386] Livesay was given five years probation. Livesay also had his sentence overturned by the appeals court—twice—on the same grounds as Harris. But, once again, the government declined to increase his sentence, citing Livesay's "invaluable contribution" to the HealthSouth (i.e., Scrushy) investigation.[387]

The four women were also spared prison terms. Ayers, Edwards, Morgan, and Valentine were each sentenced to four years probation, including six months of unsupervised home detention.[388] Each defendant was also fined. Ms. Morgan was the big loser. She was ordered to pay $235,000 in forfeiture.[389]

A few days after the first wave of guilty pleas, another former CFO, Michael Martin, agreed to plead guilty to fraud and falsifying financial information. Like the others, he stuck a plea deal and agreed to cooperate with investigators.[390] He was originally sentenced to what had become the familiar five months of probation. But this time, the government balked. It appealed what it regarded as an overly light sentence. Martin later was sentenced to seven days in jail, but the government appealed again. Finally, in 2006, he was sentenced to three years in prison.[391]

A week after Martin's guilty plea, HealthSouth's just-fired treasurer, Malcolm McVay, pleaded guilty to charges of fraud, conspiracy, and cooking the company's books.[392] Once again, the sentence was five years probation.[393] At the time, McVay's financial expertise was considered critical to the government's eventual case against Scrushy. Like with Livesay, an appeals court later opened the door for a tougher sentence but the lower court declined.[394]

The day after McVay's plea, it was former CFO Aaron Beam's turn. Beam, an original founder of HealthSouth, pleaded guilty to bank fraud. He had provided false reports of the company's financial condition to banks and other lenders when applying for extensions of credit.[395] Beam agreed to cooperate with investigators in their case against Scrushy. Indeed, when he was sentenced in 2005, the government acknowledged his "substantial assistance" in helping forensic auditors piece together details of the fraud. For that reason, he was handed only a three month prison sentence. He could have received a maximum of 30 years.[396]

Next came former CFO Weston Smith, the worried "whistle-blower," who had been the first to come forward months earlier. Smith pleaded guilty to fraud and conspiracy and admitted that he had knowingly certified HealthSouth's phony earnings statements, in violation of the Sarbanes-Oxley Act.[397] A week later, then-current CFO William Owens, who had worn a wire to help the government build its case against Scrushy, pleaded guilty to similar charges.[398]

In September, 2005, Weston Smith was sentenced to 27 months in prison and ordered to forfeit $1.5 million.[399] William Owens received the longest sentence by far of any HealthSouth executive up to then when he was handed a five-year prison term in December. The conventional wisdom regarding his sentence was that, since his tenure as CFO had coincided with the height of the accounting fraud, he was more culpable than the other plea bargaining defendants.[400] A no-nonsense judge told Owens: "Corporate offenders are nothing more than common thieves wearing suits and wielding pens."[401]

In July, 2003, Richard Botts, senior vice president for tax and Will Hicks, vice president of investments, pleaded guilty to conspiracy and fraud.[402] Botts was later sentenced to five years of probation and ordered to forfeit $265,000 in illicit gains.[403] Hicks received two months probation and was ordered to pay $50,000 in restitution.[404]

In all, the government won 17 guilty pleas from HealthSouth executives, including all five chief financial officers since the company was founded.[405] It may seem curious that most of these co-conspirators and accessories to an alleged $7.2 billion corporate fraud received such light sentences. However, the government's strategy was clear. It was willing to swap wrist-slapping in exchange for help in nailing the big target—Richard Scrushy. But the old adage about best laid plans was once more validated, as the HealthSouth case was about to take a shocking turn.

In November, 2003, the government finally moved in on Richard Scrushy, charging him with 85 counts of conspiracy, fraud, and falsely certifying financial statements. He was the first CEO charged under the Sarbanes-Oxley Act of 2002, which heightened financial reporting requirements for public corporations and enhanced penalties for violations. The indictment was 38 pages long. There would be no plea bargain here. Scrushy faced up to 650 years in prison if convicted on all counts. The indictment claimed that between 1996 and 2002 Scrushy received $267 million in compensation from HealthSouth, including "more than $53 million in bonuses and stock options valued at more than $206 million" when he exercised them.[406] Federal prosecutors contended that his bonuses and options "were tied directly or indirectly to the performance of HealthSouth" and that the compensation was inflated as a result of fraud and conspiracy.[407] The government was demanding that Scrushy forfeit assets totaling more than $278 million that he derived from his alleged crimes. "The assets include real estate he owns in Alabama and Florida, a 92-foot yacht, several other boats, two Cessna airplanes, diamond jewelry, luxury vehicles and 11 paintings, including works by Pablo Picasso, Marc Chagall, and Joan Miró."[408]

Scrushy's 2005 trial was very much a media event. The government paraded one convicted former CFO after another and each of them laid the blame on Scrushy. However, there was no direct paper trail. Although Scrushy did not testify, his lawyers continually argued that it was these disgraced executives who had committed the fraud without Scrushy's knowledge. It was the familiar

"Sergeant Schultz" ("I know nothing") defense, which had been used by other CEOs like Ken Lay and Bernie Ebbers—both of whom were convicted. But not Richard Scrushy. After a four-month trial and an incredible seven weeks of deliberation, the jury acquitted him of all counts.[409]

It was a stunning defeat for the government. Its "up the food chain" strategy, so successful in earlier cases, had exploded in its face. A former U.S. Attorney noted: "This may be the first time that the Sergeant Schultz defense has worked."[410] The prosecutors, who listened to the verdict in stone-faced silence, had proved to be no match for Scrushy's skill at public grandstanding. Speaking to reporters outside the courtroom, Scrushy lashed out at prosecutors for what he called "two years of torture."[411]

An Internet Website devoted to the HealthSouth case offers an unsettling postscript:

> If Scrushy masterminded the fraud, as all the press material suggests, then he escaped justice. If, on the other hand, the real conspirators duped him and are now blaming him, then they escaped with extremely lenient sentences. One way or another, the real criminal or criminals escaped, and the penalties paid for a massive crime were trivial.[412]

Three additional postscripts from 2006 are worth noting. Hannibal "Sonny" Crumpler, a former vice president and division controller, was the only HealthSouth executive—other than Scrushy—to plead not guilty. His outcome, however, was very different. Sonny was convicted and sentenced to eight years in prison. That was the longest term imposed in the huge accounting scam.[413]

HealthSouth announced that it had agreed to pay $445 million to settle investor lawsuits filed in the wake of the fraud. It also filed a suit against its former accountants, Ernst & Young, who, in turn, filed a countersuit against HealthSouth. A lot of lawyers would be running up a lot of billable hours.

And, finally, those who were convinced that Richard Scrushy had wriggled off the hook must have felt some measure of "I told you so" satisfaction when he was convicted of paying $500,000 in bribes to Alabama governor Don Siegelman in exchange for a seat on the state healthcare board.[414] Scrushy was later sentenced to six years and 10 months in prison.[415] This case will be described in more detail in Chapter 10, when we examine political corruption.

Halliburton

Yet another company that has been the target of accusations of "creative accounting" is Halliburton, a multi-billion dollar energy exploration company. Starting in 1998, Halliburton began counting as revenue money it had not yet collected from clients, because those charges (cost overruns on construction projects) were in dispute.[416] By assuming it would be able to collect these speculative funds, the company allegedly was able to inflate its profits by $234 million over a four-year period.[417]

Halliburton failed to disclose its questionable bookkeeping techniques to investors (or the SEC) until 18 months later, when it was "revealed" in a footnote buried deep inside the company's annual report.[418] Since then, more than a dozen lawsuits have been filed against Halliburton, alleging fraud. Some experts concur that the company played fast and loose with accounting laws. Others maintain that what Halliburton practiced was just good, aggressive accounting; that the company may have tip-toed right up to the fraud line but never crossed it.[419]

Two facts about Halliburton stand out. First, its CEO during most of the time in question was Dick Cheney, who sold his Halliburton stock options for $35 million when he resigned to run successfully for vice president in 2000. Second, Halliburton's accounting firm during Cheney's tenure was the ubiquitous Arthur Andersen and Company. In fact, Cheney actually appeared in a testimonial video for Andersen, thanking it for going "over and above the just-sort-of-normal, by-the-books audit arrangement."[420] If Cheney wanted an "audit arrangement" that was something other than "normal," he certainly picked the right accountant.

After taking office in 2001, the vice president was conspicuously inconspicuous—rarely appearing in public, often stashed away in some secret location. The official explanation cited concerns over post-9/11 national security; but with so much litigation pending against Halliburton, more than a few die-hard skeptics suggested that Dick Cheney might have been ducking subpoenas.

At the end of 2003, Halliburton re-surfaced in the news. A Pentagon audit found that the company had overcharged for fuel it brought into Iraq from Kuwait. Kellogg Brown and Root, a unit of Halliburton, had received a no-bid U.S. government contract to supply oil-rich Iraq with gasoline. By 2003, the company had rung up $2 billion in business from that contract.[421] According to the report, Halliburton allegedly overcharged the Army by $1.09 per gallon for nearly 57 million gallons of gasoline delivered to citizens in Iraq—a potential $61 million discrepancy.[422] In its response to the accusation, Halliburton claimed its pricing was justified because of the high cost of security and a shortage of fuel trucks.[423] A 2004 report by the Pentagon's Defense Contract Audit Agency (DCAA) later alleged that Halliburton had charged $27.5 million to deliver $82,000 worth of gasoline. The DCAA report called the price "illogical."[424] Pentagon officials said they also were concerned with Halliburton's contracts for rebuilding Iraq's oil infrastructure and assisting U.S. troops there. The contracts were awarded without competitive bidding and totaled $15.6 billion.[425] Senator Frank Lautenberg called for Senate hearings on the Pentagon's findings. In a letter to the Senate Government Affairs Committee, Lautenberg noted: "I have long been troubled by the continued growth of the Pentagon's no-bid contracts with Halliburton."[426]

Vice President Cheney may have been out of town at the time, but the outraged public's loud demand for corporate accountability was heard in Washington, even above the orchestral ringing of campaign cash registers. Congress was surely listening when it passed the Sarbanes-Oxley Act of 2002—the toughest piece of corporate governance legislation ever enacted. The law imposes new duties on public corporations and their executives, directors, auditors, and attorneys, as well as securities analysts. The act provides significantly expanded rulemaking by the Securities and Exchange Commission and the creation of the Public Company Accounting Oversight Board (PCAOB). Among the act's 11 major provisions is the requirement that corporate CEOs assume personal responsibility for the honesty of their company's financial statements. Misrepresentations could mean prison time.[427]

President Bush initially opposed the central provisions of Sarbanes-Oxley; but, with public outrage at a fever pitch in the wake of the high-profile corporate accounting scandals, he reversed his position and "cast himself as the 'protector of the small business and the rank-and-file worker' when he signed the bill into law."[428] Nevertheless, the Bush Administration has tried to gut Sarbanes-Oxley, at least since Bush's second term began in 2005.[429] Bush's Treasury Secretary Henry Paulson was critical of the act almost from the moment he assumed his position in 2006.[430] By early 2007, the SEC, led by Bush appointee Christopher Cox, a former congressman who had always championed a pro-business, anti-regulation philosophy, was actively seeking to curtail investor lawsuits.[431] In his 2007 State of the Economy speech, President Bush—while stopping short of arguing for repeal—said of Sarbanes-Oxley: "We need to change the way the law is implemented."[432] In 2008, some free market advocates, such as Steve Forbes and

Donald Trump, were arguing for a weaker Sarbanes-Oxley.[433] Others, like former Speaker Newt Gingrich[434] and former presidential candidate Representative Ron Paul[435], were less diffident. They wanted Sarbanes-Oxley repealed altogether. The country's leading business lobby, the U.S. Chamber of Commerce, placed the loosening of Sarbanes-Oxley requirements high on its published 2008 agenda.[436]

On the other hand, the Association of Certified Fraud Examiners strongly supports Sarbanes-Oxley[437] and a member of the Public Company Accounting Oversight Board, created by Sarbanes-Oxley, has called the act a huge success for the average investor. In response to complaints that the law has increased accounting costs for public companies, that board member counters: "I'm still trying to find investors who are worried about the costs of audit fees."[438]

While its first major test in the aforementioned HealthSouth case may have been a disappointment to many, Sarbanes-Oxley most likely has had a significant deterrent effect on financial reporting fraud since its passage in the wake of the accounting meltdown of 2002. Nevertheless, serious cases still do surface.

For example, in June 2005, Roys Poyiadjis, the former CEO of AremisSoft, a now-defunct software company, was fined $200 million by the Securities and Exchange Commission for the illegal profits he reaped by selling shares of AremisSoft stock while making fraudulent public statements about the company's finances.[439] A week later, Bristol-Myers-Squibb, the giant drugmaker, agreed to pay $300 million to defer federal prosecution on a charge of conspiring to commit securities fraud relating to alleged accounting irregularities.[440]

Other recent fraudulent reporting scandals include the following:

Computer Associates

In 2006, Sanjay Kumar, the former CEO of Computer Associates (CA), pleaded guilty to securities fraud, obstruction of justice, and perjury for his role in a $2.2 billion accounting scheme at the giant software company. It was a Horatio Alger story turned sour. Sanjay Kumar and his family had emigrated to the U.S. in 1976 to escape the civil unrest in his native Sri Lanka and had worked his way up the ladder of success—then down the road to perdition. Kumar improperly booked software license revenues in order to meet Wall Street analysts' quarterly earnings expectations, then lied to investigators.[441] Among its "creative accounting" methods, CA had used "35-day months" to extend financial reporting periods and inflate revenues.[442] Kumar also made a $3.7 million payoff to a customer who threatened to tell the government about a bogus software deal while the investigation was pending.[443] He also tampered with a computer in order to conceal incriminating evidence.[444] The scandal eventually cost CA shareholders more than $400 million.[445]

Sanjay Kumar was sentenced to 12 years in prison. Though it was by no means a light sentence, he could have received a life term.[446] He was also hit with an $8 million fine and was ordered to pay $800 million back to victims of the fraud. Kumar agreed to a $52 million down payment he would raise by liquidating assets, including trusts, luxury cars, and a yacht.[447] He further agreed to pay an ongoing 20 percent of his annual income once he gets out of prison.[448] Clearly, Kumar will have to earn an extraordinary salary or live an incredibly long life to ever pay all the money back.

Refco

Refco was a financial services company, best known as a commodities and futures broker. At its zenith, the firm held over $4 billion in about 200,000 customer accounts. It also had an uproarious and checkered history.

Ray E. Friedman, the son of a Jewish grocer, grew up poor on the Protestant plains of Iowa. His parents bought chickens and eggs in the countryside and re-sold them in Sioux City. Young Friedman had found his future calling. As an adult, he bought a used egg truck and started American Produce, a farm products wholesaler. In 1952, Friedman was indicted for selling substandard chickens to Army troops during the Korean war. He pled guilty, expecting to pay a modest fine, but an irate judge accused him of falsifying time stamps on slaughtered chickens and sentenced him to prison. He was paroled after two years and returned home jobless and broke.[449]

In the early 1960s, Friedman began trading agricultural commodities at the livestock exchange in Sioux City, while sitting on an old orange crate. In 1964, the new Chicago Mercantile Exchange began trading cattle futures, and Friedman became a fixture there. As his success and reputation grew, he was granted a presidential pardon in 1966, thanks to the intervention of his stepson Thomas Dittmer, an Army officer who worked in the Johnson White House. Three years later, Friedman and Dittmer formed a partnership in a commodities trading company they named Ray E. Friedman & Company, known as Refco. The two men prospered, and, in 1974, Friedman sold his share to Dittmer and "retired" after buying a hotel/casino in Las Vegas.[450]

Since its founding, Refco generated nearly 300 Commodity Futures Trading Commission (CFTC) enforcement actions, arbitration cases, and customer reparations complaints. The firm had long been accused of according some customers preferential treatment. One beneficiary was future senator, presidential candidate, and Secretary of State Hillary Clinton, the wife of then-Governor Bill Clinton of Arkansas.

Dittmer also benefitted by trading for himself. In 1983, the CFTC fined Refco and Dittmer $525,000 and suspended Dittmer from trading for four months for allegedly trying to corner some commodity markets. In 1992, Ray Friedman, still "retired" and living in Florida, was fined $590,000 by the CFTC, which also suspended the 78-year-old from trading for two months for allegedly trying to corner the frozen pork-bellies market.[451]

That same year, Ray Friedman's grandson, star trader Bradley Reifler, was the subject of a customer reparations complaint filed with the CFTC. A Texas businessman lost $2.3 million by following a trading strategy that Reifler had allegedly boasted using. The complaint was settled privately.

In 1994, Dittmer moved Refco from Chicago to Wall Street; but the firm's longstanding problems with the CFTC followed him to New York. Under pressure, Dittmer resigned.

The new CEO of Refko was British citizen Philip Bennett. Dittmer earlier had hired Bennett as CFO. His promotion to CEO was meant to inject professional management into a firm that was run largely on traders' instincts. After assuming the reins, Bennett negotiated the acquisition of 16 smaller competitors and watched Refco's revenues grow by an annual average of nearly 24 percent through 2004.[452] Refco grew into a global empire with operations in 14 countries.[453] The end result was catastrophic.

Bennett pushed the company toward institutional customers and away from its traditional base of buying and selling agricultural commodities for individuals. When he decided to take Refco public in 2005, troubling cracks began to appear.[454] The prospectus disclosed that Bennett and a private equity firm he'd invited to buy into Refco had pushed Refco's debt above $1 billion, in part to fund a special dividend to himself and his new partners.[455] The document indicated that Refco did not meet SEC standards for public stock offerings. Nevertheless, Refco went public in August, 2005.

Within a week, it was revealed that Bennett hid a huge personal debt to the firm. Beginning in the 1990s, Bennett extended credit to customers so they could trade in Refco accounts. When some customers failed to repay the loans, Bennett concealed hundreds of millions of dollars in losses from securities regulators and company auditors by shifting the losses to a third-party company he controlled. He then disguised the losses as receivables owed to Refco by Bennett's company.[456] In October, 2005, Refco declared bankruptcy, and Bennett stepped down. By November, Refco stock, which had an Initial Price Offering (IPO) of $27.48 two months earlier, was selling for 65 cents a share. That month, Bennett was indicted for orchestrating a criminal conspiracy for years to disguise up to $720 million in personal debts to Refco by shifting unpaid trading obligations off the firm's financial statements each quarter.[457]

On February 15, 2008, Bennett pleaded guilty to 20 counts of fraud, taking full responsibility for his actions.[458] It was not a customary plea bargain for leniency, and there was no deal. He faced up to 315 years in prison and the forfeiture of $2.4 billion. The judge herself warned that in the "post-Enron era" of corporate crime prosecutions, defendants had to face "the possibility that their residence in the Bureau of Prisons is the last residence they're going to have."[459] Bennett burst into tears.[460]

Four and a half months later, Phillip Bennett was sentenced to 16 years in federal prison. Prosecutors called his crimes "historic" and accused him of "deep ethical depravity."[461] In their court filing, they wrote:

> The defendant's criminal conduct was motivated by greed that drove him to lie and scheme in ways previously unimaginable, brought him wealth that has scarcely been seen before in a criminal fraud case, launching Bennett into the rarefied air of a billionaire. . . . In terms of scope, length, sophistication, harm and criminal benefits, Bennett stands on a plateau of criminality that frankly makes comparisons difficult.[462]

In a plea for mercy, Bennett argued that he was motivated by concern for Refco employees. It seemed more likely he was motivated by concern for his stable of high-end sports cars, including seven Ferraris, his $20 million airplane, his luxury homes, and more than $29 million in artwork.[463] Bennett was 59 years old when he reported to prison, so it remains to be seen whether the judge's grim warning that he could be outlived by his sentence will prove prophetic.

Fannie Mae

The Federal National Mortgage Association (FNMA), commonly known as Fannie Mae, is a stockholder-owned corporation, chartered by Congress. Its purpose is to purchase and securitize mortgages in order to ensure that funds are consistently available to the institutions that lend money to home buyers. Its business model is at once both simple and complex:

> Fannie Mae buys mortgages, then either holds onto them or packages them into sale as bonds to investors. It also buys and sells the mortgage-backed securities it produces . . .

By 2004, Fannie Mae was the fourth-largest company in the United States, in terms of assets. In September of that year, The Office of Federal Housing Enterprises Oversight (OFHEO) released a report alleging widespread accounting irregularities. The OFHEO raised serious questions about the validity of Fannie Mae's financial statements. The report cited one instance when the company inappropriately deferred $200 million of estimated expenses, which enabled management to receive full annual bonuses. Had the expenses been recorded properly, there would have been no bonuses.[464] The report also detailed numerous transactions over a period of several years, in which Fannie Mae management deliberately smoothed out its earnings to show investors that it was a low-risk company.[465] By the end of the year, Fannie Mae's CEO and CFO were forced out by the board of directors. KPMG, the large auditing firm that approved the company's accounting, was also fired.[466]

The OFHEO findings closely matched those it had reported the previous year regarding its investigation of the Federal Home Loan Mortgage Corporation (FHLMC), Fannie Mae's younger sibling, known as Freddie Mac. It is another government sponsored enterprise created to provide competition for Fannie Mae and to increase the availability of funds to finance home ownership. Freddie Mac's charter essentially is the same as Fannie Mae's. In 2003, Freddie Mac revealed that it had understated earnings by almost $5 billion, one of the largest corporate restatements in American history. As a result, it was fined $125 million. The fine was then a record; but *Forbes* called the amount "peanuts."[467]

In 2006, OFHEO and the SEC announced a $400 million fine against Fannie Mae. The SEC would get $350 million of that amount, one of the largest penalties ever in an accounting fraud case. The money would be used to compensate investors victimized by the alleged violations.[468] Regulators charged that Fannie Mae had engaged in "extensive financial fraud" over six years by misstating its earnings by $10.6 billion so its executives could collect hundreds of millions of dollars in bonuses.[469]

> The aim, OFHEO said, was always the same: To shape the company's books, not in response to accepted accounting rules but in a way that made it appear that the company had reached earnings targets, thus triggering the maximum possible payout for executives.[470]

The blistering report cited instance after instance of doctored earnings and questionable accounting maneuvers. For example, Fannie Mae had engaged in two transactions with investment banker Goldman Sachs that improperly pushed $107 million of earnings into future years.[471] A picture was painted of a kleptocratic corporate culture fostered by corrupt management, a weak board of directors, and ineffective internal controls. According to congressional testimony by the former head of OFHEO, Fannie Mae employees had even falsified signatures on accounting transactions to help the company meet its 1998 earnings targets.[472]

Freddie Mac jumped back into the spotlight in 2007 after it agreed to pay a $50 million fine to settle charges by the SEC that it had perpetrated a multibillion-dollar accounting fraud.[473] In addition, four former executives agreed to pay a total of $515,000 in fines and $275,000 in restitution.[474] The SEC announced that the $50 million Freddie Mac agreed to pay would be distributed to injured shareholders.[475] At least two class-action lawsuits have been filed against Fannie Mae, covering different time periods.[476]

In 2008, OFHEO announced that former Fannie Mae CEO Franklin D. Raines, who had also once served as President Clinton's budget director, agreed to pay a $24.7 million fine for allegedly manipulating earnings over a six-year period. Two other executives agreed to pay fines of $6.4 million and $275,000 for their role in the accounting scandal.[477]

Senator Richard Shelby of the Senate Banking Committee noted, after a 2008 briefing by U.S. Treasury officials, that about half the regulatory capital of Fannie Mae and Freddie Mac was made up of deferred tax credits, which could be deducted from taxes on profits. But these tax credits were worthless unless the troubled lenders generated profits—which they hadn't done in the four previous quarters. "'That's not even real money,' said Senator Shelby. 'They found out they had a house of cards.'"[478]

Fannie Mae's business model, which benefitted mortgage brokers, politicians, homeowners—and, above all, its own arrogant executives—was a fragile illusion.

Mortgage lending is inherently risky and volatile. People who make (or buy) mortgages assume the risk that people won't pay them back.[479]

Fannie Mae had convinced itself and others that massive exposure to interest rate volatility can be a low-risk business, able to generate smooth, safe, and predictable earnings. The overriding economic lesson gleaned from the alleged fraud is the danger of believing one's own lies. Mark Twain said it best: "It ain't what you don't know that gets you into trouble. It's what you know for sure that just ain't so."

AIG

American International Group (AIG) is a major insurance corporation based in New York City. In 2008, the Forbes Global 2000 List ranked AIG as the world's 18th largest corporation. Because of a recent liquidity crisis tied to the collapse of the subprime mortgage market (discussed in Chapter 8), which required a massive government bail-out, that may no longer be true; but in 2000, AIG was seemingly prospering as the country's biggest insurance company. It was also participating in a serious ongoing accounting fraud.

In May, 2005, AIG announced that an internal review had uncovered accounting irregularities allegedly orchestrated by its two top executives. According to the company's statement, false accounting entries had inflated AIG's value by $100 million between 2000 and 2004.[480] AIG said that its restated financial report would lead to a reduction of $2.7 billion—3.3 percent of the net worth or the company.[481] One of the alleged conspirators (and AIG's biggest shareholder), former longtime CEO, Maurice "Hank" Grenberg, had already resigned in March, amid regulatory scrutiny by then-New York Attorney General Eliot Spitzer.

A second accounting scandal surfaced in 2006. It involved the common industry practice of reinsurance, whereby insurers transfer parts of their risk portfolios to other parties. It is roughly akin to bookmakers "laying off" large bets. Christian Milton, AIG's former vice-president of reinsurance, was indicted, along with four former executives of General Reinsurance (General Re) for their participation in a 2000–2001 fraud.[482] Hank Greenberg was an unindicted co-conspirator.[483] General Re, owned by Warren Buffett's company Berkshire Hathaway, had helped AIG inflate its loss reserves illegally by $500 million to assure analysts that its loss reserves—a crucial indicator—were not too low.[484] A sham transaction was concocted, under which AIG would refund General Re's $10 million premium and pay General Re a $5 million fee for the phony deal.[485] After the inflated loss reserves were first revealed, AIG shares plunged. Shareholders lost an estimated $1.4 billion to the fraud.[486]

In February, 2008, Christian Milton and the four General Re executives, including former CEO Ronald Ferguson, were convicted of fraud and conspiracy.[487] Although Buffett was on the witness list, he never testified. In his closing arguments, the U.S. Attorney boiled the case down to one sentence: "This case is about truth, a choice to lie and deception to cover it up."[488] The judge was equally pithy in September when he sentenced Ronald Ferguson to two years in prison: "This transaction was designed to cook the books of AIG."[489]

Ironically, that same month, the Federal Reserve was rescuing AIG with an $85 billion infusion of credit. Under the terms of the bailout, the U.S. government assumed an 80 percent ownership stake in AIG.[490] It should be noted that just days after the bailout, AIG spent

$440,000 on a retreat for its executives at a posh California resort[491]—complete with banquets, golf outings, and $23,400 worth of spa treatments.[492]

On August 1, 2011, the United States Court of Appeals for the Second Circuit threw out the convictions for General Re executives Ronald Ferguson, Elizabeth Monrad, Robert Graham, and Christopher Garand, as well as AIG executive Christian Milton.[493] The three-judge panel was unanimous, and Chief Judge Dennis Jacobs explained the decision citing improper evidence used during trial. The jury was shown that AIG's stock price fell after the General Re reinsurance deal, though the deal did not cause the decline and this had "prejudiced the defendants."[494]

"Chainsaw Al"

Before Wall Street fell in love with Ken Lay and the Enron gang, it was celebrating the career of Albert Dunlap. He was known as "Chainsaw Al," a nickname he reportedly relished. A West Point graduate, born in 1937, Dunlap was the CEO of cup maker Lily Tulip in the 1980s. It was there that his "slash and burn" style of management was honed. He closed the company's headquarters and two factories, fired most senior managers and half the headquarters staff, and laid off a large number of workers. In his two-and-a-half year tenure, Lily Tulip's stock price soared from $1.77 to $18.55.[495] After several other CEO stints, Dunlap ended up at struggling Scott Paper in 1994.[496] He fired 11,000 employees—including half the managers and 20 percent of the hourly workers—closed factories, slashed R&D spending, and eliminated the company's $3 million charity budget. Scott's value stood at $3 billion when Dunlap arrived. In late 1995, he sold Scott to Kimberly-Clark for $9.4 billion, pocketing $100 million for himself.[497]

Al Dunlap's biographer considered him the personification of profit at any price.[498] But, unlike many of his peers, he didn't try to paint over his ruthlessness with any sort of "tough but compassionate" public relations veneer. He was what he was—and was perfectly comfortable with that—even when he later landed in trouble. In contrast to the Michael Milkens of the world (Chapter 6), Chainsaw Al was never "photo op'ed" taking poor kids (or unemployed workers, for that matter) to a ballgame.

> What distinguishes Dunlap from his colleagues is that he takes pride in his toughness, expressing only cursory regret for having cashiered thousands of his workers. When *Newsweek* ran a cover story about corporate layoffs, Dunlap contributed a gleeful column about how wonderful such firings are for stockholders. . . . He posed as Rambo on the cover of *USA Today*.[499]

In mid-1996, Chainsaw Al took his act to Sunbeam, a well known appliance company that had become stagnant. The day his hiring was announced, Sunbeam's stock rose nearly 60 percent—the largest single day jump in the history of the New York Stock Exchange. Dunlap himself boasted: "People are banking on me."[500] He fired 25 percent of the workforce, sold off subsidiaries employing another 3,000 workers, eliminated corporate charity, and shut down 18 of 26 factories.[501]

Dunlap's callous brand of capitalism has been dubbed "Dunlapism." "Dunlapism begins and ends at Wall Street. Its *sole* credo is: "How can we make our stock worth more?"[502] It is the antithesis of the "stakeholder capitalism"[503] now touted by business ethics professors. Stakeholder capitalism values loyalty to workers, responsibility to communities, and corporate philanthropy.[504] Dunlapism sneers at those things. It was the perfect corporate religion for its time—housed in the Church of the Bottom Line.

Dunlapism may have repulsed many people—especially those left jobless in its wake. But Al Dunlap's turnaround results made him a legend. Business writer David Plotz assesses Chainsaw Al from two different perspectives. Neither is very flattering. First the case for the "defense":

> It's easy to hate Dunlap for the wrong reason, which is that he is a brutal, heart-less, arrogant bastard. According to *Business Week*, Dunlap skipped the funerals of both his parents, failed to support (or even pay attention to) the child from his first marriage, and refused to help pay for his niece's cancer treatments. But to criticize Dunlap for his cruelty is akin to scolding a lion for killing an antelope. Dunlap lacks conscience? Well, so does the market. If Wall Street were a CEO, it would skip its parents' funerals too.[505]

Plotz's point about the reality of corporate culture can be persuasive, if filtered through sufficient moral detachment. Regrettably, struggling companies sometimes *do* need to shed workers in order to recover. Indeed, Dunlap was part of an era when the market routinely rewarded lay-offs with rising stock prices. As mobster Meyer Lansky used to say, business is business.

Plotz's second assessment of Chainsaw Al is far less forgiving. Here is his case for the "prosecution":

> But there is a right reason to hate Dunlap, which is this: He's not as good as he looks. Dunlap does not know how to build a company. If capitalism is "creative destruc-tion," Dunlapism is simply destruction. He prettifies struggling companies for Wall Street, but undermines them in the long term. Both *Barron's* and *Business Week* have chronicled how Dunlap has built his "turnarounds" on cosmetic measures designed to pump up stock prices.[506]

At Sunbeam, Dunlap's methods backfired dramatically. After two years on the job, the company's stock had plummeted from $53 to $11.75. Sunbeam, a $1 billion firm before Dunlap arrived, fell into bankruptcy.[507] Subsequently, Dunlap was accused of complicity in massive accounting irregularities that inflated Sunbeam's earnings during his brief tenure. Six company insiders revealed that Sunbeam's revenues had been padded. Six quarters of earnings had to be restated.[508] As noted earlier, Sunbeam's auditor at that time was none other than Arthur Andersen & Company, an all-too familiar name to followers of accounting scandals. In the summer of 1998, Chainsaw Al, who had turned firing into a spectator sport, was *fired*.

Dunlap was sued by shareholders and by the SEC. In 2002, he agreed to pay $15 million to settle. He also was barred from ever again working as an executive at a public company.[509]

A year after he was fired, "Unemployed Al" Dunlap was paid $500,000 for a series of five lectures in Australia. Each lecture contained his signature misanthropic line: "If you want a friend, buy a dog."[510]

An especially devious example of questionable accounting involved Coca-Cola. In mid-2003, an internal auditing committee reported that the company's fountain division had improperly overvalued $9 million in equipment.[511] By the standards of this chapter, that's an insignificant amount of money. What makes the story noteworthy is that the auditing committee also acknowledged that the fountain division had rigged a marketing test of Frozen Coke at the Burger King Chain, one of Coca-Cola's largest customers.[512] The company hired people to spend up to $10,000 to buy "value meals" in the test market site of Richmond, Virginia, thus fraudu-lently boosting the demand for Frozen Coke. The skewed sales resulted in a $65 million Frozen

Coke investment by Burger King.[513] It was a scheme that seemed more likely to be hatched by Pinky and the Brain than the upper management of one of America's most iconic corporations. That Coca-Cola would stoop to such a sleazy tactic is a sad commentary on the business ethics of the New Millennium.

Indeed, the New Millennium has not exactly showcased corporate morality at its finest thus far. Phony earnings, inflated revenues, doctored financial statements, and an assortment of other crimes, old and new, have assaulted the slumping U.S. economy.

As we have seen, a cadre of elite executives looted their failing companies and became astonishingly wealthy by cashing in billions of dollars worth of overvalued stock on an unsuspecting market. In many cases, this was stock that they never even bought in the customary way. It had been "handed to them via risk-free options."[514] When the dust settled, shareholders had lost most or all of their investments. And employees had watched their retirement funds circle the drain, along with their jobs.

But money wasn't even the most important thing these gluttonous predators stole. They robbed the public of their faith in the U.S. economy. In 2002, investor confidence fell to levels not seen since the Great Depression[515]—levels that would not be approached again until the economic meltdown of 2008. Even pillars of the economic mainstream have decried what one of them, Federal Reserve Chairman Alan Greenspan, called "infectious greed."[516] Such greed left unchecked threatens our very way of life. There is nothing upon which capitalism depends more than the trust of the citizenry. White-collar crime can no longer be dismissed as the "other" crime problem. The stakes are too high.

Notes

1. *Inside Enron.* "The Victims." Vol. iii, 2002. 34–45.
2. Quoted in *Ibid.*, p. 44.
3. Quoted in *Ibid.*, p. 44.
4. *Ibid.*
5. Cruver, Bruce. *Anatomy of Greed: The Unshredded Truth from an Enron Insider.* NY: Carroll & Graf, 2002.
6. Quoted in *Ibid.*, p. 21.
7. *Ibid.*
8. *Ibid.*, p. 21.
9. *Ibid.*
10. Quoted in *Ibid.*, p. 22.
11. Quoted in *Ibid.*, p. 23.
12. *Ibid.*, p. 24.
13. McLean, Bethany. "Why Enron Went Bust." *Fortune.com.* December 24, 2001.
14. Witt, April and Behr, Peter. "Losses, Conflicts Threaten Survival." *Washington Post.* July 31, 2002, p. A1.
15. *usatoday.com.* "Andersen, Justice Make Closing Cases in Trial." June, 5, 2002.
16. *buyandhold.com.* "Educate Yourself—Under the Oak." August 26, 2002.
17. Hobson, Melody. "Enron's Red Flags." *abcnews.com*, February 1, 2001.
18. *buyandhold.com, op. cit.*

19. Kadlec, Daniel. "Enron: Who's Accountable?" *time.com*, January 13, 2002.
20. *buyandhold.com, op. cit.*
21. *Ibid.*
22. Steffy, Loren. Andrew Fastow, Mystery CFO." *Bloomberg Markets*, January 2002: 39–42.
23. *Ibid.*
24. O'Rourke, P. J. "How to Stuff a Wild Enron." *theatlantic.com.* April 2002.
25. Szala, Ginger. "Enron's Axis of Evil." *Futures*, March 2002: p. 8.
26. Altman, Daniel. "The Taming of the Finance Officers." New York Times. April 14, 2002.
27. Banham, Russ. "Andrew S. Fastow—Enron Corp." *CFO*, October 1999.
28. Altman, *op. cit.*
29. Quoted in Barboza, David and Schwartz, John. "The Financial Wizard Tied to Enron's Fall." *New York Times*, February 6, 2002; A1.
30. Dart, Bob. "Former CFO Fastow Was Complex Character in Enron Drama." *coxnews.com*, February 7, 2002.
31. Cruver, *op. cit.*
32. Steffy, *op. cit.*

33. Kasindorf, Martin. "Calif. Officials: Enron Is Key in Energy 'Fraud'." *usatoday.com*, April 12, 2002.
34. Britt, Russ. "Enron's Long Shadow in Golden State." *cbs.market/watch.com*. March 5, 2002.
35. *Ibid.*
36. Witt and Behr, *op.cit.*
37. *Ibid.*
38. Quoted in *Ibid.*, p. 2.
39. *Online NewsHour*. "The Rise and Fall of Enron." January 2002.
40. *Ibid.*, p. 2.
41. *Ibid.*
42. Emshwiller, John and Smith, Rebecca. "Enron Jolt: Investments, Assets Generate Big Losses." October 17, 2001: C1, C17.
43. Quoted in *Ibid.*, p. 9.
44. Forest, Stephanie A. and Zellner, Wendy. "The Enron Debacle." *BusinessWeek online*. November 12, 2001.
45. Goldberg, Laura. "Lay Borrowed Millions, Repaid Enron with Stock." *Houston Chronicle*, February 16, 2002: A1.
46. Quoted in Witt and Behr, *op. cit.*, p. 10.
47. Well, Jonathan and Sapsford, Jathon. "Dynegy to Pay $3 Million Fine to Settle SEC Civil-Fraud Case." *Wall Street Journal*. September 25, 2002: A3.
48. Goldberg, Laura. "Trio Indicted in Deal at Dynegy." *Houston Chronicle*. June 13, 2003: 1C, 9C.
49. Smith, Rebecca and Barrionuevo, Alexei. "Dynegy Ex-Trader is Indicted on Criminal-Fraud Charges." *Wall Street Journal*. January 29, 2003: A6.
50. Hendricks, Anthony G. "Mother-In-Law Loses on Enron." *democraticunderground.com*. January, 28, 2002.
51. Quoted in *click2houston.com*, *op. cit.*
52. *Ibid.*
53. Quoted in *Ibid.*
54. Dunbar, John, Moore, Robert, and Sylwester, Mary-Jo. "Enron Executives Who Dumped Stock Were Heavy Donors to Bush." *Center for Public Integrity*. January 10, 2002, 1–8.
55. Schulman, Miriam. Enron: "What Ever Happened to Going Down With the Ship?" *Makula Center for Applied Ethics, Santa Clara University*. March 2002.
56. Quoted in *Ibid.*
57. O'Donnell, Jayne. "Former Enron CEO Decides not to Testify." *USA Today*, February 4, 2002: 1B.
58. Quoted in Mason, Julie. "Lawmakers Roast Lay for Firm's Fall." *Houston Chronicle*, February 13, 2002: 1A, 19A.
59. Quoted in Rice, Harvey and Murphy, Bill. "Employees Lives Transformed in Aftermath of Enron Collapse." *Houston Chronicle*. October 23, 2002: p. 10A.
60. Quoted in *Ibid*, p. 10A.
61. Murphy, Bill. "Debacle Tormented Former Executive." *Houston Chronicle*, February 9, 2002: 21A.
62. Quoted in Mason, Julie. "Skilling Says He Did no Wrong." *Houston Chronicle*, February 8, 2002: 1A.
63. *politicalamazon.com*. "Quote of the Day." February 14, 2002.
64. Quoted in Cruver, *op. cit.*, p. 24.
65. Quoted in Mason, February 8, 2002, *op. cit.*, 1A.
66. Quoted in Taub, Stephen. "Hollings Disses Pitt." *cfo .com*. February 12, 2002: 1.
67. Quoted in Mason, February 8, 2002, *op. cit.*, 1A.
68. *rense.com*. "Enron's Lay Duped by Top Execs, Whistleblower Says." February 14, 1001: 2.
69. *fortune.com*. "Text of the Letter from Enron Executive Sherron Watkins to Chairman Kenneth Lay as Released by the House Energy and Commerce Committee." January 16, 2001.
70. Bracaccio, David. "Marketplace: News Archives." *marketplace.org*, February 14, 2002.
71. *fortune.com.*, *op. cit.* 5.
72. Quoted in Hebert, H. Josef. "Enron Whistleblower Says Lay Was Duped." *nctimes.net*, February 15, 2002: 1.
73. Duffy, Michael, *et al.* "What Did They Know and . . . When Did They Know It?" *Time Atlantic* 159: 1–8.
74. Quoted in Hebert, H. Josef. "'We Need to Come Clean,' Enron Executive Told Lay." *suntimes.com*, February 14, 2002: 1.
75. Povich, Elaine S. "Whistle-Blower Says Managers Kept Enron CEO Lay in Dark." *Newsday* 4, February 15, 2002.
76. Clift, Eleanor and Thomas, Rich. "No Accounting for It." *Newsweek* 139, February 25, 2002: 34–35.
77. Quoted in *rense.com.*, *op. cit.*, 3.
78. Quoted in Hebert, February 15, 2002, *op. cit.*, 1.
79. Quoted in *Ibid*, p. 1.
80. Quoted in Douglass and Yesner, *op. cit.*, p. 2.
81. Murphy, Bill. "Profile: Michael Kopper." *houston-chronicle.com*, August 22, 2002.
82. Hays, Kristen. "Enron's Insider's Revelations Point to Greed Helping Drive Company." *cbc.ca*, August 24, 2002.
83. *pressdemocrat.com*. "Ex-Enron Exec Tells of Kickbacks to Boss." August 22, 2002.
84. *cbc.ca*. "Michael Kopper Becomes First Ex-Enron Exec to Plead Guilty." August 21, 2002. Pizzo, Stephen. "Enron Exec Kopper Cops a Plea." *corpwatch.org*, August 22, 2002.
85. Radigan, Joseph. "For Kopper, a Different Kind of Roll-Over." *cfo.com*, August 22, 2002.

86. *pressdemocrat.com*, *op. cit.*

87. *usatoday.com*. "Former Enron Exec Pleads Guilty." August 21, 2002.

88. Quoted in *usatoday*, August 21, 2002, *op. cit.*, pp. 2–3.

89. *indolink.com*. "Former Enron Executive Pleads Guilty of Fraud." August 22, 2002.

90. *MSNBC.com*. "Two Ex-Enron Execs Get Reduced Sentences," November 17, 2006.

91. Taub, Stephen. "Enron's Kopper Reports to Prison." *CFO.com*, January 31, 2007."

92. *MSNBC.com*, November 17, 2006, *op. cit.*

93. Hays, Kristen. "Enron Thief Learns Fate." *Houston Chronicle*, April 20, 2007: D1, D4.

94. Quoted in *Ibid*.

95. *cnnmoney.com*. "Ex-Enron Exec Charged." October 2, 2002.

96. *click2houston.com*. "Former Enron Exec Fastow Indicted." October 31, 2002; *cnnmoney.com*. "Enron Ex-CFO Indicted." November 1, 2002.

97. Babinek, Mark. "Former Enron Exec Fastow Pleads Not Guilty." *newsday.com*. November 6, 2002; Flood, Mary. "Fastow Pleads Not Guilty to 78-Count Indictment." *Houston Chronicle*. November 7, 2002: C1, C2.

98. Ackman, Dan. "Andrew Fastow, Fall Guy." *forbes.com*. October 3, 2002.

99. Hays, Kristen. "Former Enron Chief Pleads Innocent." *amarillonet.com*. May 20, 2003.

100. Quoted in *msnbc.com*. "Ex-Enron CFO Re-Enters Plea." May 19, 2003.

101. *news.bbc.co.uk*. "New Charges in Enron Case." May 1, 2003; Anderson, Curt. "Fresh Charges Over Enron." *heraldsun.news.com.au*. May 1, 2003; *cbsnews.com*. "New Slew of Enron Indictments." May 1, 2003.

102. Flood, Mary and Fowler, Tom. "Charges Grow for Ex-Enron Execs." *Houston Chronicle*. May 2, 2003: 1A, 16A.

103. *newstribune.com*. "Federal Indictments Expand Against Ex-Enron Executives." May 2, 2003.

104. Quoted in Hull, C. Bryan. "Former Enron Execs Charged in New Indictments." *news.yahoo.com*. May 2, 2003.

105. Kirkpatrick, David. "Enron Takes Its Pipeline to the Net." *Fortune* 141. January 24, 2000: 1C–3C.

106. Flood, Mary and Fowler, Tom. "Ex-Enron Executive Pleads Not Guilty." *Houston Chronicle*. May 8, 2003: C2. Flood, Mary and Fowler, Tom. "Broadband Pair Indicted on Numerous Fraud Charges." *Houston Chronicle*. March 27, 2003: C1. Fowler, Tom and Flood, Mary. "5 Former Enron Workers Indicted." *Houston Chronicle*. April 30, 2003: 1A, 8A.

107. Flood, Mary and Fowler, Tom. "5 More Could Be Charged." *Houston Chronicle*. April 26, 2003: 1A, 16A. Murphy, Bill. "Fast Living, Quick Riches Filled Enron Exec's Days." *Houston Chronicle*. May 18, 2003: 1A, 21A.

108. Thomsen, Linda. "Enron: Ten Years Later." *davispolk.com*. December 1, 2011.

109. *Ibid*.

110. *Ibid*.

111. *cbc.ca*. "First Enron Executive Goes to Prison." December 4, 2003.

112. *Ibid*.

113. Flood, Mary. "Ex-Trader Pleads Guilty to Schemes." *Houston Chronicle*. February 5, 2003: C1, C6.

114. *Ibid*.

115. *Ibid*.

116. *Ibid*.

117. *talkleft.com*. "Andrew Fastow Pleads Guilty, Cooperates." January 14, 2004.

118. *Ibid*.

119. *money.cnn.com*. "Fastow and His Wife Plead Guilty." January 14, 2004.

120. Quoted in *Ibid*.

121. Hundley, Kris. "Cuffed and on Display, Skilling Pleads Innocent." *St. Petersburg Times* (online). February 20, 2004.

122. *pbs.org*. "Former Enron Chief Executive Indicted, Pleads Not Guilty." February 19, 2004.

123. Kay, Joseph. "Former Enron CEO Jeffrey Skilling Indicted." *wsws.org*. February 24, 2004.

124. *Ibid*.

125. Said, Carolyn. "Ex-Enron Chief Ken Lay Enters Not Guilty Plea." *San Francisco Chronicle* (online). July 8, 2005.

126. *news.bbc.co.uk*. "Enron Ex-Boss Pleads 'Not Guilty'." July 8, 2004.

127. *Ibid*.

128. Ackman, Dan. "Ken Lay Indicted, and Fights Back." *forbes.com*. July 8, 2004.

129. Quoted in *Ibid*, p. 1A.

130. Johnson, Carrie. "Lay, Skilling Go on Trial in January." *Washington Post*. February 25, 2005: p. E3.

131. Iwata, Edward. "Enron's Ken Lay: Cuffed but Confident." *usatoday.com*. July 15, 2004.

132. Flood, Mary. "Ex-Enron, Merrill Execs Sentenced." *Houston Chronicle* (online). May 15, 2005.

133. *Ibid*.

134. Fowler, Tom and Roper, John C. "Causey Pleads Guilty, Leaving Just Skilling, Lay." *Houston Chronicle* (online), January 9, 2006.

135. Barrionuevo, Alexei. "Enron Chiefs Guilty of Fraud and Conspiracy." *New York Times* (online), May 25, 2006.

136. Quoted in Pasha, Shaheen and Seid, Jessica. "Lay and Skilling's Day of Reckoning." *money.cnn.com*, May 25, 2006.

137. *Ibid.*

138. Fowler, Tom. "Enron: Skilling's Preparation Showed." *Houston Chronicle*, April 22, 2006: A1, A22.

139. Steffy, Loren. "Prosecution Scores Direct hits on Skilling." *Houston Chronicle*, April 21, 2006: D1, D4.

140. Fowler, *op. cit.*

141. Steffy, *op. cit.*

142. Goodwyn, Wade. "On the Stand, Enron's Lay and Skilling Reverse Type." *npr.org*, May 5, 2006.

143. Flood, Mary. "Lay Proclaims His Innocence." *Houston Chronicle*, April 25, 2006: A1, A6.

144. Steffy, Loren. "A Return to Lay's World." *Houston Chronicle*, April 25, 2006: D1, D6.

145. Flood, *op. cit.*

146. Steffy, *op. cit.*

147. Flood, Mary. "Another Testy Day for Lay." *Houston Chronicle*, April 28, 2006: A1, A14.

148. Quoted in Flood, Mary. "Lay Defends Lavish Habits and Bit Cash Withdrawals." *Houston Chronicle*, May 2, 2006: A6.

149. Quoted in Wice, Brian W. "Straight as a Sting." *click2houston.com*, May 2, 2006.

150. *Ibid.*

151. *foxnews.com*. "Enron's Lay, Skilling Found Guilty of Conspiracy and Fraud," May 25, 2006. *npr.org*. "Jury Declares Lay and Skilling Guilty of Fraud," May 25, 2006.

152. Quoted in *msnbc.msn.com*. "The Enron Trial," May 25, 2006.

153. Ivanovich, David. "The Lessons of Victory." *Houston Chronicle*, May 28, 2006: D1, D5.

154. Quoted in Goodwyn, Wade. "Jury Declares Lay and Skilling guilty of Fraud." *npr.org*, May 27, 2006.

155. *Ibid.*

156. *msnbc.com*. "Enron's Skilling Gets 24 Years," October 23, 2008.

157. Quoted in *Ibid.*

158. Hays, Kristen. "Skilling May Receive Less Prison Time." *Houston Chronicle*, January 7, 2009: A1, A9. Jones, Ashby. "Enron CEO Jeffrey Skilling to Get New Jail Sentence." *theaustraliannews.com*, January 7, 2009.

159. *baltimoresun.com*. "High Court Hears Ex-Enron CEO Skilling's Appeal." March 2, 2010.

160. Liptak, Adam. "Justices Limit Use of 'Honest Services' Law Against Fraud." *nytimes.com*, June 24, 2010.

161. Quoted in *Ibid.*

162. Levine, Dan. "U.S. Appeals Court Upholds Jeff Skilling Conviction." *reuters.com*, April 6, 2011.

163. Cohn, Scott. "Skilling Presses on Despite Supreme Court Defeat." *cnbc.com*, April 16, 2012.

164. *cbsnews.com*. "Enron's Ken Lay Dies at 64," July 5, 2006. *msnbc.com*. "Enron's Ken Lay Dies of Heart Disease," July 5, 2006.

165. Lozano, Juan A. "Ex-Enron Exec Sentenced to 2 Years." *msnbc.com*, June 4, 2007.

166. Hays, Kristen. "Company Insider Gets 27 Months." *Houston Chronicle*, June 19, 2007: A1, A6.

167. *usatoday.com*. "Former Enron Broadband Executive Pleads Guilty," June 19, 2007.

168. Hays, Kirsten. "British Trio Sentenced to 3 Years in Prison." *Houston Chronicle*, February 23, 2008: D1, D5.

169. *networkworld.com*. "Ex-Enron Broadband Exec Pleads Guilty to Wire Fraud," October 15, 2008.

170. *USAToday*. "Former Enron Broadband Executive Pleads Guilty," October 14, 2008.

171. Hays, Kristen. "Guilty Plea Likely in Enron Case." *Houston Chronicle*, October 14, 2008: D1, D4.

172. Hays, Kristen. "Enron Civil Settlement: $31.5 Million." *Houston Chronicle*, July 30, 2008: A1, A8.

173. Goldstein, Matthew. "Enron Class Getting $2.4 Billion From CIBC." *thestreet.com*, August 2, 2005.

174. *Ibid.*

175. *Ibid.*

176. *Los Angeles Times*. "Credit Suisse to Pay Enron Settlement of $90 Million," May 10, 2006: C6.

177. *nytimes.com*. "Merrill Lynch Settles an Enron Lawsuit," July 7, 2006.

178. *iht.com*. "Enron Settles 'MegaClaims' Litigation With Deutsche Bank," December 18, 2007.

179. Goldstein, August 2, 2005, *op. cit.*

180. *chicagotribune.com*. "Shareholders, Others to Split $7.2 Billion in Enron Lawsuits," September 10, 2008.

181. Read, Madlen. "Citi Settlement Ends Enron Creditors' 'Mega Claims' Suit." *Washington Post*, March 27, 2008: D4.

182. *Platt's Energy Economist*. January 30, 2002.

183. McClean, Bethany. "Why Enron Went Bust." *fortune.com*. December 24, 2001.

184. Swartz, Mimi. "How Enron Blew It." *Texas Monthly*. November 2001: 138–139, 174–178.

185. Quoted in *Ibid*,

186. Swartz, *op. cit.*

187. *Ibid.*

188. McLean, *op. cit.*

189. *Ibid.*

190. Quoted in Swartz, *op. cit.*, 175.

191. Statement of the Business Roundtable on Corporate Governance Principles Relating to the Enron Bankruptcy.

192. Abelson, Reed. "Concerns Surface About Enron Board's Independence." *kcstar.com.* December 2, 2001.

193. Quoted in *Ibid,*

194. Permanent Subcommittee on Investigations of the Committee on Governmental Affairs, United States Senate. "The Role of the Board of Directors in Enron's Collapse." July 8, 2002.

195. Johnson, Carrie. "Enron Board Aided Collapse, Senate Panel Says." *Washington Post*, July 7, 2002: A10.

196. *politicalamazon.com.* "Enron Does a Casablanca." August 26, 2002.

197. Day, Kathleen and Behr, Peter. "Enron Directors Backed Moving Debt Off Books." *Washington Post.* January 31, 2002: A1.

198. Quoted in *Houston Chronicle.* "Board Told About Deals, Records Indicate." February 14, 2002: 15A.

199. *Director's Monthly.* "The Rise and Fall of Enron: Principles for Director Focus." January 31, 2002.

200. Cruver, *op. cit.*

201. McLean, *op. cit.*

202. Easterbrook, Frank H. and Fischel, Daniel R. *The Economic Structure of Corporate Law.* Cambridge, MA: Harvard University Press: 1996.

203. Black, William K. "Repeating the Past." *newsday. com*, July 7, 2002.

204. *Ibid.*

205. Wee, Heesun. "Enron in Perfect Hindsight." *businessweek.com.* December 19, 2001.

206. Roper, John C. "Citigroup Agrees to $2 Billion Settlement." *Houston Chronicle*, June 11, 2005: A1, A12.

207. *Ibid.*

208. Flood, Mary. "Another Bank Reaches Deal in Enron Case." *Houston Chronicle*, June 15, 2005: D1, D2.

209. Adelman, Jacob. "Scheme Nets Lawyer 2-Year Term." *Houston Chronicle*, February 12, 2008.

210. McLean, *op. cit.*

211. Winig, Eric. "No Pity for Greedy Enron Workers." *washingtonbizjournal.* January 21, 2002.

212. *Ibid.*

213. Morgenson, Gretchen. "A Bubble No One Wanted to Pop." *New York Times*, January 14, 2002. A1.

214. Weisskopf, Michael *et al.* "Enron: Who's Accountable?" *time.com*, January 13, 2002.

215. Povich, Elaine S. "Memo Ordered Overtime to Shred Enron Documents." *newsday.com,* January 25, 2002.

216. Weisskopf, *op. cit.*

217. Ivanovich, David. "Auditor Tries to Downplay Enron Role." *Houston Chronicle*, February 6, 2002: 1.

218. Quoted in *Ibid.*

219. Quoted in *Ibid.*

220. Quoted in *Ibid.*

221. Quoted in *Ibid.*

222. *Online NewsHour Update.* "Arthur Andersen CEO Resigns." March 27, 2002.

223. Farrell, Greg. "Indictment Could Shred Andersen." *usatoday.com,* March 15, 2002.

224. *Ibid.*

225. Farrell, Greg. "Central Andersen Figure Pleads Guilty." *usatoday.com,* April 9, 2002.

226. *Ibid.*

227. Johnson, Carrie. "Enron Auditor Admits Crime." *Washington Post*, May 14, 2002: A1.

228. Farrell, Greg. "Jury Will Hear of Andersen's Past Scandals." *usatoday.com*, May 7, 2002.

229. Taub, Stephen. "Andersen Pays $110 Million in Sunbeam Settlement." *cfo.com*, May 2, 2001.

230. Farrell, Greg. "Andersen papers lost in Sunbeam case." *USA Today.* January 30, 2002.

231. Moreno, Jenalia. "Andersen Settles Charges Over Audits." *chron.com*, June 20, 2001. *cbsnews.com.* "Prosecutor: Andersen Feared the Law." May 7, 2002.

232. Farrell, Greg. "Neither Side Blinked, So Judgment Day Has Arrived." *usatoday.com,* May 6, 2002.

233. Beltran, Luisa *et al.* "Andersen Guilty." *cnnmoney. com,* June 16, 2002.

234. Mears, Bill. "Arthur Andersen Conviction Overturned." *cnn.com*, May 31, 2005.

235. Roper, John C. "Government Won't Retry Andersen Criminal Case." *Houston Chronicle.* November 23, 2005.

236. Sloan, Allan. "How Arthur Andersen Begs for Business." *Newsweek*, March 18, 2002: 6.

237. *money.cnn.com.* "Ebbers Out at WorldCom." April 30, 2002.

238. Pulliam, Deborah S. and Mollenkamp, Carrick. "Easy Money: Former WorldCom CEO Built an Empire on Mountain of Debt." *Wall Street Journal*, December 31, 2002: A1.

239. Maney, Kevin *et al.* "Prosecutors Target WorldCom's Ex-CFO." *usatoday.com*, August 29, 2002. *siliconvalley.com.* "Prosecutors Target WorldCom's Ex-CFO." June 27, 2002. Garcia, Beatrice E. "A Fast Rise, Faster Fall." *siliconvalley.com.* June 27, 2002.

240. Kaplan, Karen and Granelli, James S. "WorldCom Says It Inflated Books by $3.9 Billion." *Los Angeles Times*, June 26, 2002: A1, A17.

241. *usatoday.com*. "WorldCom Reports Massive Accounting Change." June 26, 2002.

242. *Ibid.*

243. Cohen, Laurie P., Pulliam, Susan, and Solomon, Deborah. "World Com Report Suggests Ebbers Knew of Accounting Irregularities." *Wall Street Journal*, March 12, 2003: A3.

244. Larsen, Peter *et al.* "WorldCom Heads Earned $104m as Fraud Occurred." *biz.yahoo.com*, August 12, 2002.

245. *bbc.co.uk*. "Disgraced WorldCom Faces Fraud Charge." June 27, 2002.

246. *msnbc.com*. "SEC Files Fraud Charges Against WorldCom." June 26, 2002.

247. Quoted in *foxnews.com*. "WorldCom Discloses $3.8 Billion Accounting Scandal, Global Markets Reel." June 28, 2002: 1.

248. *bbc.co.uk*, June 27, 2002, *op. cit.*

249. Backover, Andrew. "WorldCom Files for Chapter 11 Protection." *USA Today*. July 22, 2002: 1A. Sweet, Laurel J. "Phone Giant Files Ch. 11: WorldCom Bankruptcy Largest in U.S. History." *businesstoday.com*, July 22, 2002.

250. Sandberg, Jared. "Six Directors Quit as WorldCom Breaks With Past." *Wall Street Journal*, December 18, 2002: A6.

251. *Wall Street Journal*. "WorldCom, Inc.: New Job Cuts to Total 5,000 in Struggle to Exit Chapter 11." February 4, 2003: B8; Young, Shawn. "WorldCom Plans '03 Chapter 11 Exit." *Wall Street Journal*, March 27, 2003: B7.

252. Quoted in Krim, Jonathan and Stern, Christopher. "2 Key WorldCom Witnesses Silent." *Washington Post*, July 9, 2002: A1.

253. *ananova.com*. "Former WorldCom CEO Was 'Aware of Fraud.'"

254. *washingtonpost.com*. "Ex-WorldCom CFO Scott Sullivan Indicted." August 28, 2002. *asia.news.yahoo.com*. "Former Top WorldCom Executive Indicted." August 29, 2002.

255. Scannell, Kara. "WorldCom Ex-Chief of Finance Faces New Bank-Fraud Charges." *Wall Street Journal*, April 17, 2003: B2. Scannell, Kara. "More Charges in WorldCom Case—Ex-Finance Chief Pleads Not Guilty to New Counts of Filing False Statements." *Wall Street Journal*, April 23, 2003: B4.

256. Cohen, *et al.* A3.

257. *xchangemag.com*. "Ebbers Indicted." April 1, 2004.

258. Farrell, Greg. "Sullivan Gets 5-Year Prison Sentence." *USA Today*, August 12, 2005: 1B.

259. Quoted in *Ibid*, 3B.

260. Ackman, Dan. "Bernie Ebbers Guilty." *forbes.com*, March 15, 2005.

261. *cbc.ca*. "Ebbers Convicted of Massive WorldCom Fraud." March 15, 2005.

262. *Ibid*.

263. Ackman, Dan, *op. cit.*

264. Cowley, Stacy. "Ebbers Sentenced to 25 Years for WorldCom Fraud." *networkworld.com*, July 13, 2005.

265. *msnbc.com*. "Ebbers Sentenced to 25 Years in Prison." July 13, 2005.

266. Bayot, Jennifer. "Ebbers Sentenced to 25 Years in Prison for $11 Billion Fraud." *corpwatch.org*, July 13, 2005.

267. Crawford, Krysten. "Ebbers Gets 25 Years." *money.cnn.com*, July 13, 2005.

268. Bayot, *op. cit.*

269. Quoted in *msnbc.msn.com*, *op. cit.*

270. Quoted in Crawford, *op. cit.*

271. Farrell, *op. cit.*

272. *Houston Chronicle*. "WorldCom to Pay Record Fine." May 20, 2003: 1B, 4B.

273. *usatoday.com*. "After WorldCom, When will Regulators Wake Up?" August 28, 2002.

274. *thedigest.com*. "Global Crossing Bankrupt." January 28, 2002.

275. Olavsrud, Thor. "Global Crossing Denies Accounting Improprieties." *internetnews.com*. February 4, 2002. Berman, Dennis K. "Global Crossing's Accounting for 'Swap' Trades to be Amended." *Wall Street Journal*, October 22, 2002: A 10. Berman, Dennis K. "Global Crossing Board Report Rebukes Counsel." *Wall Street Journal*, March 11, 2003: B9.

276. *Houston Chronicle*. "Enron, Global Crossing Said to Craft Deceitful Deal." May 21, 2002, C13.

277. *money.cnn.com*. "FBI, SEC Investigating Global." February 8, 2002.

278. Ackman, Dan. "House Committee to Investigate Global Crossing." March 13, 2002.

279. Garretson, Cara. "U.S. House Probes Global Crossing on Shredding." *infoworld.com*. July 23, 2002.

280. Meyerson, Bruce. "Global Crossing Confirms 'Isolated' Shredding of Documents." *cincinnatienquirer.com*. June 25, 2002.

281. Fabrikant, Geraldine and Romero, Simon. "How Executives Prospered as Global Crossing Collapsed." *newyorktimesonline*. February 11, 2002.

282. Hopkins, Jim. "Global's Warning Signs Were There, Wall St. Was Unaware." *usatoday.com*, February 26, 2002.

283. Meyerson, Bruce. "Bankrupt Global Crossing Being Sold for $250 Million." *cnn.com*. August 9, 2002.

284. *Ibid.*

285. *accounting.smartpros.com.* "Justice Ends Scrutiny of Global Crossing." December 30, 2002.

286. Morgenson, Gretchen. "Global Crossing Settles for $325 Million." *nytimes.com*, March 20, 2004.

287. Barrett, Tom. "The Real Scandal Is Global Crossing Not Enron." *conservativetruth.org*, March 10, 2002. King, Michael. "Enron and Global Crossing: A Double-Standard? Paper published by the National Center for Public Policy Research, March 2002.

288. Olavsurd, Thor. "SEC's Global Crossing Probe Spreads to Qwest." *opticallynetworked.com*, February 11, 2002.

289. Kawamoto, Wayne. "Qwest Receives SEC Inquiry." *isp-planet.com*, March 12, 2002.

290. *dcinternet.com.* "Qwest Scrambles." February 15, 2002.

291. Hedges, Michael. "Qwest Trade With Enron Questioned." *Houston Chronicle*, July 11, 2002; C1.

292. *Ibid.*

293. Solomon, Deborah. "States Probe Qwest's Secret Deals to Expand Long-Distance Service." *The Wall Street Journal*, April 20. 2002: A1, A10. Legard, David. "Qwest Faces New Probe on Collusion." *nwfusion.com.* April 29, 2002.

294. *ca.news.yahoo.com.* "Jumped by S&P, Qwest Communications Joins Host of Fallen Telecom Angels." May 22, 2002. *internetnews.com.* "Trouble Mounts at Qwest." May 23, 2002.

295. *phoenix.bizjournals.com.* "Qwest Drops Andersen." May 31, 2002.

296. Leonhardt, David. "Qwest Leader Unloaded Stock as Books Cooked." *Houston Chronicle*, July 30, 2002; C1.

297. *news.com.com.* "Qwest Chairman Paid $27 million." April 9, 2002.

298. Leonhardt, *op. cit.*

299. *money.cnn.com.* "Qwest Insiders Made Millions." July 30, 2002.

300. Leonhardt, *op. cit.*

301. Henderson, Khali. "Qwest Faces Criminal Investigation." *phoneplusmag.com*, July 10, 2002. Vittore, Vince. "Justice Department Investigating Qwest." *telephonyonline.com*, July 10, 2002.

302. Romero, Simon. "Accounts Misstated at Qwest." *iht.com*, July 30, 2002.

303. Haley, Colin C. "Qwest Settles Fraud Charges." *internetnews.com*, October 22, 2004.

304. *kvoa.com.* "SEC Charges Former Qwest CEO, 6 Others With 'Massive Financial Fraud'." March 16, 2005.

305. *Ibid.*

306. *Ibid.*

307. Taub, Stephen. "Ex-CFO of Qwest Enters Guilty Plea." *cfo.com*, July 14, 2005.

308. Shore, Sandy. "Ex-Qwest CFO Pleads Guilty to Charge." *channels.netscape.com*, July 14, 2005.

309. Taub, *op. cit.*

310. Shore, *op. cit.*

311. Shore, Sandy. "Former Qwest Finance Chief Sentenced." *boston.com.* July 28, 2006.

312. Vuong, Andy. "Defense Requests Nacchio Mistrial." *denverpost.com.* March 26, 2007.

313. Johnson, Carrie. "Nacchio Guilty of Insider Trading." *Washington Post.* April 20, 2007: D1.

314. Frosch, Dan. "Ex-Chief at Qwest Found Guilty of Insider Trading." *New York Times.* April 20, 2007.

315. Voreacos, David and Rosenblatt, Joel. "Ex-Qwest Chief Nacchio's Conviction Turnedon Call." *bloomberg.com.* April 20, 2007.

316. *northcountrygazette.org.* "Qwest CEO Nacchio Guilty of Insider Trading," April 20, 2007.

317. Quoted in *denverpost.com.* "Nacchio Conviction 'A Long Time Coming'," April 19, 2007.

318. Quoted in Frosch, *op. cit.*

319. Harden, Mark. "Judge Sentences Nacchio." *Denver Business Journal* (online). July 27, 2007.

320. Banda, P. Solomon. "Appeals Court Orders New Trial for Nacchio." *cbs4denver.com.* March 17, 2008.

321. Avery, Greg. "Nine-Judge Panel Will Hear Nacchio Appeal." *denverbizjournals.com.* July 30, 2008.

322. United States Court of Appeals, Tenth Circuit. "UNITED STATES v. NACCHIO UNITED STATES of America, Plaintiff-Appellee, v. Joseph P. NACCHIO, Defendant-Appellant. No. 07-1311." March 17, 2008.

323. *nytimes.com.* "Appeals Court Restores Qwest Insider Trading Conviction." February 25, 2009.

324. *coloradodaily.com.* "Supreme Court Refuses to Hear Joseph Nacchio Appeal." October 5, 2009.

325. Make, Jonathan and Sanders, Holly M. "Adelphia Says SEC Probing Its Books." *Pittsburgh Post-Gazette*, April 18, 2002: E1.

326. Hofmeister, Sallie. "Adelphia Submits Bankruptcy Filing." *Los Angeles Times*, June 26, 2002: C1, C11.

327. Quoted in *Ibid.*, E1.

328. *nytimes.com.* "Adelphia May Be Liable for Millions in Loans." March 20, 2002.

329. Hoffmeister, Sallie. "Adelphia Submits Bankruptcy Filing." *Los Angeles Times*, June 26, 2002: C1, C11.

330. Bergstrom, Bill. "Adelphia Calls Auditor Deloitte Unreasonable." *Los Angeles Times*, July 9, 2002: C4.

331. *businessweek.com*. "Adelphia vs. Deloitte in a Game of Blame." June 27, 2002.

332. Hofmeister, Sallie. "Adelphia Says Results Were Overstated." *Los Angeles Time.* June 11, 2002: C1, C13.

333. Quoted in Hofmeister, Sallie. "Spendthrift Adelphia Mogul Only Tip of Iceberg." *Los Angeles Time.* July 28, 2002: 8D.

334. *businessweekonline.com, op. cit.*

335. Hofmeister, July 28, 2002, *op. cit.*

336. *Wall Street Journal.* "CEOs in Handcuffs." July 26, 2002: A10.

337. *New York Times.* "Key Adelphia Figures Arrested." June 25, 2002: 1B, 4B.

338. Berkowitz, Harry. "Scandal Bad News for Cable Industry." *newday.com*, July 25, 2002. Fink, James, and Hartley, Tom. "Arrests Speed Rigases' Demise." *buffalo.bizjournals.com*, July 29, 2002.

339. Carney, James and Dickerson, John F. "Inside the Mind of the CEO President." *time.com*, July 28, 2002. *biz.yahoo.com.* "Rigas Attorney Offered Low-Key Surrender of Former Adelphia CEO, But Feds Ignored Request." July 28, 2002.

340. Quoted in *Ibid.*

341. Hiaasen, Carl. "Arrest CEO, Buy Stocks, Watch Dow Jones Go Up." *Miami Herald*, July 28, 2002: B1.

342. Hofmeister, Sallie. "Adelphia Submits Bankruptcy Filing." *Los Angeles Times*, July 26, 2002: C1, C11.

343. *nytimes.com.* "Adelphia Probe Widens to Tax Violations." August 7, 2002.

344. Markon, Jerry. "Former Executive of Adelphia Plans to Plead Guilty." *Wall Street Journal*, November 14, 2002: A6.

345. *Wall Street Journal.* Ex-Aide at Adelphia Pleads Guilty to Role in Accounting Scandal." January 13, 2003: C6.

346. Quoted in *www.nytimes.com.* "Adelphia Investigators Allege Abuse." July 28, 2002.

347. *internetnews.com.* "Legitimate Business Tool Creates Scrutiny." February 14, 2002.

348. Masters, Brooke A. and White, Ben. "Adelphia Founder, Son Convicted of Fraud." *Washington Post* (online). July 9, 2004; *money.cnn.com.* "John Rigas Guilty of Conspiracy." July 8, 2004.

349. *msnbc.msn.com.* "Adelphia Founder John Rigas Found Guilty." July 8, 2004.

350. Lieberman, David. "Adelphia's Founder Gets 15 Years; Son Gets 20 Years." *USA Today.* June 21, 2005: 1A; *money.cnn.com.* "Adelphia Founder Sentenced to 15 Years." June 20, 2005.

351. Quoted in *mindfully.org.* John Rigas: Adelphia Founder Is Sentenced to 15 Years." June 20, 2005.

352. Kirchgaessner, Stephie. "Adelphia Founder Indicted on Tax Evasion." *msnbc.msn.com*, October 7, 2005.

353. *cnn.com.* "Adelphia Founder Indicted in Tax Scheme." October 7, 2005.

354. Vaknin, Samuel. "Malignant Self-Love." Skopje, Macedonia: Narcissus Publications, 1999.

355. Weber, Harry R. "Sweeping Up at Tyco." *Houston Chronicle*, July 28, 2002: 2D.

356. *nytimes.com.* "Tyco Ex-CEO Spent Lavishly." August 7, 2002.

357. Wilson, Craig. "$5,000 for a Shower Curtain? That's Really Cleaning Up." *usatoday.com*, September 10, 2002.

358. *cnnmoney.com.* "Tyco Wants Its Money Back," September 17, 2002.

359. Berenson, Alex and Vogel, Carol. "Ex-Tyco Chief Is Indicted in Tax Case." *nytimes.com*, June 5, 2002.

360. *contractormag.com.* "Tyco in Turmoil." June 3, 2002.

361. Maremont, Mark. "Tyco Is Likely to Report New Woes." *Wall Street Journal*, April 30, 2003: C1, C11.

362. Cohen, Laurie P. and Maremont, Mark. "Tyco Ex-Director Pleads Guilty." *Wall Street Journal*, December 18, 2002: C1.

363. Armstrong, David. "Former Executive at Tyco is Charged with Tax Evasion." *Wall Street Journal*, February 20, 2003: B2.

364. Scannell, Kara and Cohen Laurie P. "Charges Against Tyco Ex-Counsel Expand to Include Grand Larceny." *Wall Street Journal*, February 4, 2003: A3.

365. Cohen, Laurie P. and Maremont, Mark. "Tyco Ex-Director Pleads Guilty." December 18, 2002: C1.

366. *Wall Street Journal.* "The Tyco Mystery." March 25, 2003: A 16.

367. *cbsnews.com.* "Tyco Execs Sentenced." September 19, 2005.

368. Maull, Samuel. "Ex-Tyco Execs Get Up to 25 Years in Prison." *boston.com*, September 19, 2005.

369. *Ibid.*

370. *buzzle.com.* "How Tyco Spent Millions to Keep Kozlowski in the Monet." August 7, 2002.

371. *cnnmoney.com.* "Ex-Rite Aid Execs Indicted." June 21, 2002.

372. Atkinson, Bill. "Indictment: A Federal Investigation Reveals How Desperate Rite Aid's Executives Became as They Struggled to Keep the Company from Bankruptcy." *advocate611.com*, June 22, 2002.

373. Jackson, Peter. "Ex-Rite Aid Executives Accused of $1.6 Billion Fraud." *enquirer.com*, June 22, 2002.

374. Atkinson, *op. cit.*

375. *Ibid.*

376. *www.newsday.com*. "Three Rite Aid Executives Charged in Fraud." June 24, 2002.

377. Voreacos, *op. cit.* Caruso, *op. cit.*

378. *www.timesleader.com*. "Former Rite Aid Chairman Settles Shareholders' Suit." April 9, 2003.

379. *thebostonchannel.com*. "Former Rite Aid CEO Pleads Guilty to Conspiracy." June 17, 2003.

380. Scolforo, Mark. "Rite Aid Ex-CEO Pleads Guilty." *southbendtribune.com*, June 18, 2003. *cnnmoney.com*. "Ex-Rite Aid Chief Pleads Guilty." June 17, 2003.

381. Quoted in Covert, James. "Ex-Rite Aid CEO's Guilty Plea Highlights Harsher Courts." *cnnmoney.com*, June 17, 2003.

382. *uow.edu.au*. "HealthSouth Staff and the Fraud." October, 2007.

383. Abelson, Reed. "HealthSouth Fires Chief Executive and Audit Firm." *nytimes.com*, April 1, 2003.

384. *nytimes.com*. "5 HealthSouth Officers Plead Guilty to Conspiracy." April 4, 2003.

385. Quoted in *Ibid*.

386. *latimes.com*. "HeathSouth Executive's Sentence Stands." September 29, 2004.

387. Walton, Val. "Ken Livesay Gets Five-Year Probation Sentence For Third Time For HealthSouth Crime." *The Birmingham News* (online), July 17, 2008.

388. Abelson, Reed. "4 of 5 HealthSouth Executives Spared Prison Terms." *nytimes.com*, December 11, 2003.

389. Department of Justice (press release). "Five Defendants Sentenced in HealthSouth Fraud Case." December 10, 2003.

390. *latimes.com*. "Ex-CFO at HealthSouth to Plead Guilty." April 9, 2003.

391. Taub, Stephen. "Former HealthSouth CFO Gets Three Years." *cfo.com*, September 12, 2006.

392. Schneider, Craig. "Top Ten? HealthSouth Ex-Treasurer Pleads Guilty." *cfo.com*, April 23, 2003.

393. Taub, Stephen. "Former HealthSouth CFO Gets Three Years." September 12, 2006.

394. Cook, Dave. "HealthSouth CFO Avoids Prison, Again." *cfo.com*, February 23, 2007.

395. United States Department of Justice (press release). "Former HealthSouth Chief Financial Officer Aaron Beam Charged With Bank Frraud." April 24, 2003.

396. Carrns, Ann. "HealthSouth Ex-Finance Chief Gets Three-Month Prison Term." *Wall Street Journal*, April 26, 2005: C3.

397. *accounting.smartpros.com*. "Sarbanes-Oxley Claims First CFO." March 28, 2003.

398. Mackay, Steven. "HealthSouth CFO Pleads Guilty in Federal Court." *birminghambizjournals.com*, March 26, 2003. U.S. Department of Justice (press release).

"HealthSouth Executive William Owens Charged in Corporate Fraud Conspiracy." March 26, 2003.

399. Gargis, Peggy. "Ex-HealthSouth CFO Gets 27 Months in Jail." *redorbit.com*, September 22, 2005. Taub, Stephen. "Former HealthSouth CFO Gets 27 Months." *cfo.com*, September 22, 2005. Reeves, Jay. "HealthSouth Whistle-Blower Gets 27 Months." *USAToday*. September 22, 2005.

400. *lawprofessors.typepad.com*. "Former HealthSouth CFO Receives Five Year Sentence—Did He Tell the Truth?" December 10, 2005.

401. Quoted in Johnson, Carrie. "5 Years for HealthSouth Fraud." *Washington Post*, December 10, 2005: D1.

402. United States Departmentof Justice (press release). "HealthSouth Executives Richard Botts and Will Hicks Agree to Plead Guilty to Conspiracy to Commit Securities, Mail Fraud." July 31, 2003.

403. *nytimes.com*. "HealthSouth Sentence." June 3, 2004.

404. Taub, Stephen. "Former HealthSouth CFO Gets 27 Months." *cfo.com*, September 22, 2005.

405. Schneider, Craig. "At HealthSouth, No More CFOs Left to Prosecute." *cfo.com*, April 28, 2003.

406. Bassing, Tom. "HealthSouth's Scrushy Indicted on 85 Counts." *birminghambizjournals.com*, November 4, 2003.

407. *Ibid*.

408. *Ibid*.

409. Crawford, Krysten. "Ex-HealthSouth CEO Scrushy Walks." *CNN Money*. June 28, 2005.

410. Quoted in *Ibid*.

411. Quoted in *Ibid*.

412. "HealthSouth Staff and the Fraud," *op. cit.*

413. *latimes.com*. "HealthSouth Executive Sentenced to Eight Years." June 16, 2006.

414. Johnson, Carrie. "Jury Convicts HealthSouth Founder in Bribery Trial." *Washington Post*, June 30, 2006: D1.

415. Davidson, Laurence Viele. "HealthSouth Founder Scrushy Sentenced in Bribery Scheme." *seattletimes. nwsource.com*, June 29, 2007.

416. Douglass, Linda. "Cheney's Corporate Liability." *abcnews.com*, July 19, 2002.

417. Scheer, Robert. "Cheney's Grimy Trail in Business." *www.commondreams.org*. June 16, 2002.

418. Douglass, *op. cit.*

419. *Ibid*.

420. Scheer, *op. cit.*

421. Pleming, Sue. "Pentagon Audit Finds Halliburton Guilty of Price Gouging." *independent-media.tv,* December 11, 2003.

422. *cbsnews.com*. "Halliburton: $61M Overcharge?" December 12, 2003.

423. Pleming, *op. cit.*

424. Miller, T. Christian and Mazzetti, Mark. "Pentagon Audit Calls Halliburton's Price 'Illogical'." *Los Angeles Times* (online), March 15, 2005.

425. *cbsnew.com*, *op. cit.*

426. Quoted in *Ibid.*

427. Musoff, Jay K. and Newman, Brian H. "Criminal Provisions of Sarbanes Have Yet to Make an Impact." *New York Law Journal*, July 19, 2004.

428. *mediamatters.org.* "Blitzer: Bush 'Usually Gets His Way' Despite Opposition; History Shows Otherwise." February 24, 2006.

429. Labaton, Stephen. "Corporate America Moving to Defand Recent Regulations." *Houston Chronicle*, October 29, 2006: A5.

430. Schmidt, Robert. "Treasury Secretary Paulson Aims to Protect Corporate Criminals." *truthout.org*, October 9, 2006.

431. Labaton, Stephen. "S.E.C. Seeks to Curtail Investor Suits." *nytimes.com*, February 12, 2007.

432. Sahadi, Jeanne. "Bush: Mind CEO Pay, Change How Sarbanes-Oxley Works." *cnnmoney.com*, January 31, 2007.

433. Jenks, Edmund. "It's Time to Gore Sarbanes-Oxley Now." *nowpublic.com*, September 30, 2008.

434. Gingrich, Newt. "Repeal Sarbanes-Oxley." *sfgate. com*, November 5, 2008.

435. Paul, Ron. "The Current Economic Situation— Necessity of Change." *forbes.com*, March 4, 2008.

436. *uschambermagazine.com.* "Chamber Pushes Bold 2008 Policy Agenda." January, 2008.

437. *insurancejournal.com.* "ACFE Says 2004 Fraud Statistics Report Shows Need for Sarbanes-Oxley Requirements." July 9, 2004.

438. Farrell, Greg. "Sarbanes-Oxley Law Has Been a Pretty Clean Sweep." *usatoday.com*, July 29, 2007.

439. *channels.netscape.com.* "Ex-AremisSoft CEO to Pay $200 Million." June 9, 2005.

440. Schmit, Julie. "Drugmaker to Pay $300M to Defer Case." *USAToday.* June 16, 2005: 1B.

441. *cnnmoney.com.* "Ex-CA Chief Kuman Pleads Guilty," April 25, 2006.

442. Taub, Stephen. "Kumar Pleads Guilty in CA Fraud." *cfo.com*, April 24, 2006.

443. *cnnmoney.com*, April 25, 2006, *op. cit.*

444. Lombardi, Candace. "Former CA Exec Kumar Sentenced to 12 Years." *news.zdnet.com*, November 2, 2006.

445. Weiss, Todd H. "Former CA CEO Kumar Gets 12 Years in Prison." *computerworld.com*, March 11, 2006.

446. de la Merced, Michael J. "Ex-Leader of Computer Associates Gets 12-Year Sentence and Fine." *nytimes.com*, November 3, 2006.

447. *nytimes.com.* "Ex-Software Executive Begins Prison Term," August 15, 2007.

448. Fay, Joe. "Ex-CA Boss Kumar Checks in for 12 Year Sentence." *theregister.co.uk*, August 15, 2007.

449. Smith, Eliot Blair. "Refco's Flameout Ends History of Ups and Downs." *USAToday*, November 9, 2005.

450. *Ibid.*

451. *Ibid.*

452. *Ibid.*

453. Bansol, Paritosh. "Refco's Ex-Ceo Pleads Guilty to Fraud." *reuters.com*, February 15, 2008.

454. *Ibid.*

455. *Ibid.*

456. Nasaw, Daniel. "Refco Chief Sentenced to 16 Years." *guardian.co.uk.* July 3, 2008.

457. Smith, Elliot Blair. "Ex-Refco CEO Faces 8-Count Indictment." *USAToday.* November 11, 2008.

458. Quinn, James. "Refco Chief Phillip Bennett Pleads Guilty to Fraud." *telegraph.co.uk.* February 20, 2008.

459. Quoted in Glovin, David and Hurtado, Patricia. "Ex-Refco Chief Bennett's Plea May Help Former Deputies." February 16, 2008.

460. *tipreport.com.* "Phil Bennett Faces 315 Years in Prison over Refco." February 15, 2008.

461. Nasaw, *op. cit.*

462. *Ibid.*

463. *Ibid.*

464. Hilzenrath, David S. "Report Slams Fannie Mae." *Washington Post.* September 23, 2004: A1.

465. *Ibid.*

466. *mortgagenewdaily.com.* "Fannie Mae Scandal Topples Two Execs." December 22, 2004.

467. Weinberg, Ari. "Shaking Steady Freddie." *forbes. com.* December 11, 2003.

468. *msnbc.com.* "Report: Fannie Mae Manipulated Accounting," May 23, 2006.

469. Day, Kathleen. "Study Finds 'Extensive Fraud' at Fannie Mae." *Washington Post.* May 24, 2006: A1.

470. *Ibid.*

471. *Ibid.*

472. Gordon, Marcy. "Report: Fannie Mae Manipulated Accounting." *cnn.com.* May 23, 2006.

473. Taub, Stephen. "SEC Settle Accounting Charges With Freddie Mac." *cfo.com*, September 27, 2007.

474. *msnbc.com.* "Freddie Mac Settles Accounting-Fraud Charges." September 28, 2007.

475. *Ibid.*

476. Tyson, James. "Judge Limts Fannie Mae Class Action to Holders from 2001–2004." *securities.stanford.edu*, January 7, 2008. *aboutlawsuits.com*. "Fannie Mae Class Action Lawsuit Filed for Investors." September 10, 2008.

477. *nytimes.com*. "Scandal to Cost Ex-Fannie Mae Officers Millions." April 19, 2008.

478. Quoted in Jetuah, David. "Fannie Mae and Freddie Mac's Accounting Branded a 'House of Cards.'" *financialdirector.co.uk*, September 10, 2008.

479. Gross, Daniel. "The Truth About Fannie." *slate.com*, October 7, 2004.

480. Jenson, Julia. "AIG Accounting Tricks Directed by Greenberg and Smith." *financegates.com*, May 4, 2005.

481. *Ibid.*

482. Barr, Alistair. "Ex-AIG, GenRe Execs Charged: WSJ." *marketwatch.com*, February 1, 2006.

483. *cfo.com*. "Five Guilty in General Re/AIG Scheme, February 25, 2008.

484. Browning, Lynnley. "Prosecutors Say Ex-A.I.G. Executives Created a Fraud." *nytimes.com*, February 12, 2008.

485. Jagger, Suzy. "Five Guilty of Fraud That Led to AIG Chief's FAll." *timesonline.co.uk*, February 26, 2008.

486. Voreacos, David and Mills, Jane. "General Re, AIG Fraud Cost $1.4 Billion." *bloomberg.com*, September 26, 2008.

487. *news.bbc.co.uk*. "Ex-Bosses Convicted of AIG Fraud," February 26, 2008.

488. Quoted in Voreacos, David and Mills, Jane. "Former AIG, General Re Officials Convicted of Fraud." *washingtonpost.com*, February 26, 2008.

489. Quoted in Lorson, Ted. "Ex-General Re Chief Gets 2-Year Sentence for Fraud." *forbes.com*, December 16, 2008.

490. Trumbull, Mark. "AIG Bailout: Where Does Financial Crisis Lead Next?" *csmonitor.com*, September 18, 2008.

491. *msnbc.com*. "White House Calls AIG Spa Trip 'Despicable'." October 8, 2008.

492. *chigagotribune.com*. "AIG, Spa," October 8, 2008.

493. Lattman, Peter. "Court Overturns 5 Gen Re and A.I.G. Fraud Convictions." *nytimes.com*, August 1, 2011.

494. *Ibid.*

495. Plotz, David. "Al Dunlap: The Chainsaw Capitalist." *slate.com*. August 31, 1997.

496. *cnnmoney.com*. "Sunbeam Directors Say They 'Lost Confidence' in CEO Albert Dunlap." June 15, 1998.

497. Plotz, *op. cit.*

498. Byrne, John A. *Chainsaw: The Notorious Career of Al Dunlap in the Era of Profit-at-Any-Price.* NY: Collins, 2003.

499. *Ibid.*

500. Walker, Rob. "Ken Lay, Al Dunlap, and the 'Genius of Capitalism.'" *slate.com*. January 15, 2002.

501. Plotz, *op. cit.*

502. *Ibid.*

503. See Franklin, Allen, Carletti, Elena, and Marquez, Robert. "Stakeholder Capitalism, Corporate Governance and Firm Value." *knowledte@wharton.com*. August 4, 2007.

504. Plotz, *op. cit.*

505. *Ibid.*

506. *Ibid.*

507. Walker, *op. cit.*

508. *Ibid.*

509. Roland, Neil and Mathewson, Judy. "Sunbeam Ex-CEO 'Chainsaw Al' Dunlap Settles SEC Case." *securities.stanford.edu*. September 4, 2002.

510. Quoted in *businessweek.com*. "Chainsaw Al," October 18, 1999.

511. *www.chron.com*. "Coca-Cola Says It Cheated in Burger King Tests." June 17, 2003.

512. *Ibid.*

513. Weber, Harry. "Coca-Cola Admits Manipulating Promotion that Misled Burger King." *www.cbc.ca*, June 20, 2003.

514. Gimein, Mark. "The Greedy Bunch." *fortune.com*. September 2, 2002.

515. Nocera, Joseph. "System Failure." *fortune.com*. June 24, 2002.

516. Quoted in Maloy, T. K. "Greenspan Blasts 'Infectious Greed'." *washtimes.com*. July 16, 2002.

Fiduciary Fraud

In the classic 1946 movie, *It's a Wonderful Life*[1], a young man named George Bailey (portrayed by James Stewart) inherits the leadership of a small savings and loan institution from his father. Honest and selfless, George barely makes a living from the family business; indeed, he seems to be the lowest-paid bank president in the country. The Bailey Bros. Building & Loan Association is conspicuously unobsessed with extravagant salaries and escalating profits. Its funds are reserved to help the working-class families of Bedford Falls obtain mortgages for the modest little homes of their dreams. But through an unfortunate set of circumstances, culminating in the theft of a large deposit by a villainous slumlord, the Building & Loan becomes insolvent—just as a state bank examiner unexpectedly arrives to audit its books. Believing that his business and personal reputation are about to crumble and that he will probably go to prison, Bailey jumps off an icy bridge on Christmas Eve in a desperate suicide attempt and is rescued by a guardian angel dispatched from heaven to restore his shattered idealism. Ultimately, the Building & Loan is saved by the loyalty of its depositors, and George Bailey lives to lend another day.

In the aftermath of the calamitous savings and loan crisis, it seems natural to speculate about how George Bailey might have reacted if *It's a Wonderful Life* had been set in the 1980s instead of the 1940s. Would he be renamed George Bailout? Suppose his unworldly "guardian" had come from a less celestial and more sulfuric venue. Might he have tried to keep his bank afloat by making risky, unlawful investments in the hope of striking it rich? Might he have juggled the books, then bribed the auditor? Might he simply have looted the remaining funds and sailed off to Bora Bora, leaving his depositors holding an empty bag? Would the film's familiar penultimate line—"Every time a bell rings, an angel gets his wings"—be replaced by a more up-to-date piece of doggerel?: "Every time a bell peals, a banker lies and steals!"

Luckily for Bedford Falls, George Bailey was not Charles Keating but the product of a more virtuous era; for the most expensive white-collar crime epidemic in history occurred as the result of fraud in financial institutions during the 1980s. The savings and loan debacle of that decade resulted in almost $200 billion in short-term losses to taxpayers, with the eventual cost predicted to be five times more, as it accumulates—with interest—over the next several decades. A significant portion of this cost is believed to be the result of criminal fraud on the part of savings and loan operators, borrowers, and other entrepreneurs.

Financial institutions (banks, savings and loans or "thrifts," financial service companies, pension funds, and insurance companies) handle "other people's money." They are entrusted to properly invest and oversee large amounts of funds which are deposited with them.

The traditional crime of embezzlement by lower level employees has become overshadowed by concerns with upper-level management—sometimes with the help of outsiders—mismanaging and looting their own companies. As this chapter will examine, these crimes result in massive losses to investors, shareholders, beneficiaries, consumers, and taxpayers. Consider the following "whirlwind tour" of financial crimes.

- In a Southern California case, Douglas P. Blankenship was convicted of masterminding a $25 million fraud against financial institutions, companies, and private investors in 17 states. Blankenship posed as a wealthy real estate developer and was able to secure funds through phony loan applications. He and 13 accomplices pleaded guilty to defrauding Puget Sound National Bank of $4.5 million, and stealing millions more from other institutions and investors. The federal judge who sentenced him to the maximum term of 9 years for his crimes characterized Blankenship as a "danger to the public."[2]

- In 1992, a federal judge in Los Angeles sentenced Westley Scher to almost 6 years in prison and ordered him to pay $26.7 million to defrauded investors. Scher was a principal of FSG Financial Services, Inc., of Beverly Hills and other related companies that marketed phony municipal bonds. Investors thought they were buying tax-free securities that were issued and backed by local government. Prosecutors found that there were in fact no bonds, and hundreds of investors were defrauded over a six-year period.[3]

- In a New Jersey case, Louis Angelo, former president of an airplane charter service, was found guilty and sentenced to 18 months in federal prison, three years supervised release, and 200 hours of community service for participating in a scheme to defraud banks in Georgia, Indiana, New Jersey, and Massachusetts of more than $6 million. Angelo and his associates had financed executive aircraft purchases for more than their actual prices, skimming the excess money for themselves. He reportedly received more than $700,000 from his serial frauds.[4]

- In Miami, a former financial planner, Henry Gherman, was convicted on federal embezzlement and mail fraud charges. In the early 1980s, Gherman embezzled close to $10 million from clients of Financial and Investment Planning, Inc., of North Miami Beach and later fled to Asia. In 1988, he was arrested in Tokyo and extradited to Florida to face criminal charges.[5]

- In 1988, a federal judge in Austin, Texas, sentenced the former president of National Bank of Texas to the maximum term of 12 years in prison for engaging in fraud that contributed to the bank's failure. Richard Homer Taylor had pleaded guilty to charges related to a scheme in which designated individuals obtained so-called "nominee loans" under his approval and then transferred the funds to him.[6]

- In Boston, William J. Lilly, who was convicted of defrauding two failed banks of more than $9 million, was sentenced to 5 years imprisonment and ordered to pay $5.7 million in restitution. Lilly had directed buyers of condominiums in Massachusetts to sign purchase agreements on which he had misstated their assets and down payments. He used those meretricious documents to obtain a $7 million loan from First Mutual Bank for Savings in Boston. He then sold the fraudulent mortgages for $9 million to a thrift in Florida. Government regulators subsequently seized both financial institutions, and many of the mortgages went into default.[7]

- In 1994, a federal judge in Baltimore sentenced Tom Billman to 40 years in prison and ordered him to pay $25 million in restitution for looting his failed savings and loan institution years earlier.[8] After his thrift collapsed in the mid 1980s, Billman fled the country and led investigators on a four-year international manhunt. After using his two yachts to sail the Mediterranean and traveling the world under false passports, the posse finally caught up with Billman in Paris in 1993 and returned him to Baltimore to stand trial.[9] The captive fugitive was convicted on 11 counts related to his stealing at least $28 million from his depositors. At Billman's sentencing, the judge commented: "Society is finally saying that this conduct is intolerable and unacceptable."[10]

- In Little Rock, Arkansas, the former chairman of failed FirstSouth F.A., at one time the largest savings and loan in the state, was sentenced to four years in prison and fined $75,000 for looting his financial institution. Howard Weichern, Jr., was convicted in 1990 of loan fraud for concealing from both regulators and shareholders an agreement that two borrowers would not be liable for paying back their loans.[11]

- In Los Angeles, the former head of Family Savings and Loan was convicted on charges related to his illegal purchase of that financial institution. Oliver Trigg, Jr., was sentenced to more than 7 years in prison for perpetrating "an elaborate scheme" to buy the thrift with its own funds.[12] While serving on the thrift's board, Trigg had utilized a dummy company he controlled to sell land in Whittier, California, to Family Savings at an inflated price. Trigg then used some of the profit from the sale (about $1.7 million out of the total $2.7 million he had "earned") to buy a controlling interest in the thrift. A jury decided that he had illegally exploited his position on the board of directors to arrange the transaction. He was found guilty of conspiracy, bank fraud, money laundering, and tax fraud.[13]

These cases represent just a small sample of the financial frauds perpetrated in the recent past. Their vast monetary cost is incontrovertible, and their effects resonate broadly throughout all segments of the economy and society as a whole. This chapter considers some of the major forms of fiduciary frauds in various financial institutions, including the savings and loan industry, pension funds, insurance companies, financial service companies, and mortgage companies.

THE S&L IMPLOSION

The devastation of the savings and loan (or "thrift") industry in the 1980s will cost the American taxpayer hundreds of billions of dollars. Estimates range from a "mere" $200 billion to a mind-boggling $1.4 trillion by the year 2021.[14] This latter figure translates into about $5,500 for every man, woman, and child in America.[15] A private investigator hired by the federal government to uncover swindled thrifts put the projected cost in perspective: "Every family in America is going to make the equivalent of car payments for the savings and loan fiasco. The only question is whether it's going to be a Chevrolet or a Cadillac."[16]

One industry consultant claims that only 3 percent of the total bailout costs are directly due to crime.[17] Likewise, a number of economists have downplayed the role of crime in the savings and loan crisis.[18] However, there is extensive evidence that white-collar crime *was* a key ingredient in the debacle. The National Commission on Financial Institution Reform, Recovery and Enforcement speculates that losses due directly to criminal fraud "probably amount[ed] to 10 to 15 percent of total net losses."[19] Long-time thrift regulator, William Black, former Senior Deputy Chief Counsel of the Office of Thrift Supervision and chief legal officer for the western region, maintains, "fraud and insider abuse caused on a *lower* bound estimate, 25 percent of total S&L

failure losses."[20] A Resolution Trust Corporation (RTC) report estimates that about 51 percent of insolvent thrifts had suspected criminal misconduct referred to the FBI.[21] Finally, a General Accounting Office (GAO) study of 26 of the most costly thrift failures found that *every one* of these institutions was a victim of major insider fraud and abuse.[22] The GAO further suggests that criminal activity was a central factor in as many as 70–80 percent of thrift failures.[23] Thus, there appears to be ample support for the contention that material fraud played a significant role in the S&L debacle, despite the claims of detractors—most of whom have produced no empirical data to support their position that fraud was minimal. So while there may be little consensus as to the exact amount of fraud and deliberate insider abuse involved, there is substantial agreement that these swindles constitute the most costly series of white-collar crimes in American history.[24]

ORIGINS OF A FINANCIAL DISASTER

Economic conditions of the late 1970s substantially undermined the health of the savings and loan industry and ultimately contributed to the dismantling of the traditional boundaries within which they operated. Perhaps most importantly, high interest rates and slow growth squeezed the industry at both ends. Locked into low-interest mortgages from previous eras and precluded from offering adjustable rate mortgages (ARMS), and prohibited by Regulation Q from paying more than 5.5 percent interest on new deposits despite inflation reaching 13.3 percent by 1979, the industry suffered steep losses. Compounding the problem (so to speak) was the development of money market Mutual Funds by Wall Street, which allowed middle-income investors to buy shares in large denomination securities at high money-market rates, which triggered "disintermediation"—that is, mass withdrawals of deposits from savings and loans.

Confronted with rising defaults and foreclosures as the recession deepened and increasing competition from new high-yield investments, savings and loans seemed doomed to extinction. The industry's net worth fell from $16.7 billion in 1972 to a *negative* net worth of $17.5 billion in 1980 with 85 percent of the country's S&Ls losing money.[25]

While policy makers had gradually loosened the restraints on S&Ls since the early 1970s, it was not until the *laissez-faire* fervor of the early Reagan Administration that this approach gained widespread political acceptance as a solution to the rapidly escalating savings and loan crisis. In a few strokes, Washington dismantled most of the regulatory infrastructure that had kept the thrift industry together for four decades.[26] These deregulators were convinced that the free enterprise system works best if left alone, unhampered by perhaps well-meaning but ultimately counterproductive government controls. Many knowledgeable onlookers disagreed passionately and pointed the finger of blame for the subsequent gush of S&L abuses directly at deregulation. One critic said of deregulation: "[It] allowed the real estate developers, with a borrower's mentality, to own banks, replacing the sober, conservative bankers. It's like giving the fattest kid on the block the keys to the candy store."[27]

Two major laws were passed in the early 1980s which opened the doors to the impending disaster. In 1980, the Depository Institutions Deregulation and Monetary Control Act was signed into law,[28] followed in 1982 by the Garn-St. Germain Act.[29] These laws provided for a loosening of government control over the industry, which both dramatically expanded their investment powers and moved them farther away from their traditional role as providers of home mortgages for the working class—a role idealized so memorably in *It's a Wonderful Life*. Deregulatory changes included: a phasing out of limits on deposit interest rates; permitting thrifts to make commercial real estate loans, business and consumer loans, and direct investments in their own properties; authorization to issue credit cards; and increasing federal deposit insurance from

$40,000 to $100,000 per savings account. Moreover, the Garn-St Germain Act allowed thrifts to provide 100 percent financing, requiring no down payment from the borrower, in an effort to attract new business to the desperate industry.

Industry regulators quickly jumped on the *laissez-faire* bandwagon. The elimination of the 5 percent limit on brokered deposits in 1980 gave thrifts access to unprecedented amounts of cash. "Brokered deposits" were placed by middlemen who aggregated individual investments as "jumbo" certificates of deposit (CDs). Since the maximum insured deposit was $100,000, these brokered deposits were packaged as $100,000 CDs commanding high interest rates. So attractive was this system to all concerned—brokers who made hefty commissions, individual investors who received high interest for their money, and thrift operators who now had almost unlimited access to these funds—that between 1982 and 1984, brokered deposits as a percentage of total thrift assets increased 400 percent.[30]

By 1984, federally insured thrifts had access to $34 billion in brokered deposits.[31] The National Commission on Financial Institution Reform, Recovery, and Enforcement points out that, even without brokered deposits, thrifts would have been able to grow rapidly through the combination of insured deposits and risky capital ventures. Nonetheless, as they observe: "Brokered deposits proved to be a convenient and low cost means of raising vast sums."[32]

Regulators also abandoned the requirement established in 1974 that thrifts have at least 400 stockholders, with no one individual owning more than 25 percent of the stock. This effectively allowed a single entrepreneur to operate a federally insured savings and loan. Furthermore, single investors could now start thrifts backed up by noncash assets, such as land or real estate. Presumably hoping that this move would attract innovative entrepreneurs who would rescue the industry, the regulators seemed oblivious to the disastrous potential of virtually unlimited charters in a vulnerable industry.

Following deregulation, losses continued to escalate. In 1982, the Federal Savings and Loan Insurance Corporation (FSLIC) spent over $2.4 billion to close or merge insolvent savings and loans, and by 1986 the federal insurance agency was itself declared insolvent.[33] With the number of insolvent thrifts climbing steadily, FSLIC, knowing that it had insufficient funds to cope with the disaster, slowed the pace of closures, allowing technically insolvent institutions to stay open. Not surprisingly, the "Zombie" thrifts,[34] as they came to be known, continued to hemorrhage. In the first half of 1988, the thrift industry reported that it had lost an unprecedented $7.5 billion.[35] It is now known, of course, that the actual losses were much higher.

Unfortunately, the effect of deregulation (or "unregulation" as some call it) was to attract an unsavory breed of entrepreneur to an industry already troubled. These hustlers did not see an opportunity to help rebuild the industry but a chance to plunder it through various get-rich-quick schemes. Savings and loans became "money machines" or mere shell organizations by which unscrupulous individuals could enrich themselves. After the thrift had served its purpose and was insolvent—that is, bankrupt—it could be left for dead. Government regulators then had to act as undertakers, "cleaning up" the remains by reimbursing depositors whose funds had been squandered and stolen, and attempting to sell off the remaining assets of the thrift for whatever price they could get.

"INSIDER" THRIFT FRAUDS

While the list of potential frauds open to thrift operators and related outsiders is a long one, researchers have classified them into three distinct categories of white-collar crime: (1) "desperation dealing," (2) "collective embezzlement," and (3) "covering up."[36] The categories often overlap in actual cases, both because one individual may commit several types of fraud and because the same business transaction may involve more than one type. Each type of offense is considered in turn.

Desperation Dealing

After lengthy hearings and testimony, the House Committee on Government Operations concluded:

> [N]ormally honest bankers (including thrift insiders) . . . resorted to fraud or unsafe practices in efforts to save a battered institution. In those cases an incentive existed to turn an unhealthy financial institution around by garnering more deposits and then making even more speculative investments, hoping to "make it big."[37]

In his testimony, former Federal Home Loan Bank Board (FHLBB) Chair M. Danny Wall described the bind of thrift operators: "[They were] on a slippery slope of a failing institution trying to save probably their institution first and trying to save themselves and their career."[38] It is this "slippery slope" of fraud that constitutes "desperation dealing."

The factors that triggered this effect in the thrift industry are similar in some ways to those described in other white-collar crime studies. In an overview and synthesis of white-collar crime theory, Coleman points out that the "demand for profit is one of the most important economic influences on the opportunity structure for organizational crime."[39] Geis' famous study of the electrical equipment price-fixing conspiracy (Chapter 2) reveals the central role played by the corporate emphasis on profit maximization and the consequent corporate subculture conducive to, or at least tolerant of, illegal behavior.[40] Similarly, Farberman argues that the necessity to maximize profits within the context of intense competition produced a "criminogenic market structure" in the automobile industry.[41]

Desperation dealing by thrift operators is akin to these other white-collar crimes in that it too is motivated by the profit imperative. In the case of an insolvent S&L, the profit imperative takes on special urgency as managers struggle to turn the failing institution around. But desperation dealing is also distinct in a number of ways from these traditional white-collar crimes. While the corporate crime described above resulted in increased profits and long-term liquidity for the company, desperation dealing in the thrift industry was a gamble with very bad odds. Unlike corporate crimes in the industrial sector, these financial crimes usually contribute further to the *bankruptcy* of the institution.

Examples include violations of loans-to-one-borrower limits, inadequate underwriting, and other unsafe practices. While the specific type of violation may vary, what they have in common is that they are motivated by a desperate effort to save a failing enterprise. Like the gambler with dwindling funds, desperation dealers "go for broke." More often than not, they end up "broke."

Collective Embezzlement

While much attention has been paid in congressional testimony and elsewhere to the desperation dealing just described,[42] research has shown that self-interested fraud was the more frequent and costly form of misconduct.[43] Most S&L crimes were not committed by desperate entrepreneurs trapped by economic forces. "They were perpetrated by crooks who funneled investors' money into dummy corporations, hid assets in their wives' maiden names and performed other acts of larcenous legerdemain."[44] Such premeditated fraud for personal gain on the part of thrift management has been referred to as "collective embezzlement."[45]

The Commissioner of the California Department of Savings and Loans stated in 1987: "*The best way to rob a bank is to own one.*"[46] Collective embezzlement, or "looting," entails the siphoning off funds from a savings and loan institution for personal gain, at the expense of the institution itself and with the implicit or explicit sanction of its management. This "robbing of one's own bank" has been estimated to be the single most costly category of crime in the S&L debacle, having precipitated a significant number of the largest insolvencies to date.[47] The GAO concludes that, of the S&Ls it studied, "almost all of the 26 failed thrifts made transactions that were not in the thrift's best interest. Rather, the transactions often personally benefitted directors, officers, and other related parties."[48]

Embezzlement is by no means an isolated or uncommon form of white-collar crime. The advent of computers and their proliferation in business makes access to "other people's money" easier than ever (Chapter 9). Not surprisingly, the toll from such crime is considerable. Conklin noted that between 1950 and 1971, at least 100 banks were made insolvent as a result of embezzlement.[49] Moreover, in the mid-1970s commercial banks lost almost five times as much money to embezzlers as they did to armed robbers.[50]

The traditional embezzler is usually seen as a lower-level employee working alone to steal from a large organization. Sutherland noted: "[T]he ordinary case of embezzlement is a crime by a single individual in a subordinate position against a strong corporation."[51] Similarly, Cressey, in his landmark study, *Other People's Money*, examined the motivations of the lone embezzler (discussed in Chapter 12).[52] The *collective* embezzlement, however, differs in important ways from this traditional model.[53]

Collective embezzlement constitutes not only deviance *in* an organization,[54] but deviance *by* the organization. Not only are the perpetrators themselves in management positions, but the very goals of the institution are to provide a money machine for owners and other insiders. The formal goals of the organization thus comprise a "front" for the real goals of management, who not infrequently purchased the institution in order to loot it, then discard it after it serves its purpose. It is a prime example of what Wheeler and Rothman have called "the organization as weapon": "[T]he organization . . . is for white-collar criminals what the gun or knife is for the common criminal—a tool to obtain money from victims."[55] The principal difference between Wheeler and Rothman's profile of the organization as weapon and the case of collective embezzlement in the S&L industry is that the latter is an organizational crime *against* the organization's own best interests. That is, the organization is both weapon *and* victim. This form of financial crime is referred to repeatedly in government documents[56] and was highlighted by informants in a major research study as the most egregious form of thrift fraud.[57]

Covering Up

A considerable proportion of the criminal charges leveled against savings and loan institutions involved attempts to cover up or hide both the thrift's insolvency and the fraud that contributed to that insolvency.[58] "Covering up" is usually accomplished through a manipulation of S&L books and records. This form of fraud may have been the most pervasive criminal activity of thrift operators. Of the alleged 179 violations of criminal law reported in the 26 failed thrifts studied by the GAO, 42 were for covering up, constituting the single largest category.[59] The same study found that *every one* of those thrifts had been cited by regulatory examiners for "deficiencies in accounting."[60]

Covering up has been employed to a variety of ends by S&L operators. First, it is used to produce a misleading picture of the institution's state of health, or more specifically, to misrepresent the thrift's amount of capital reserves, as well as its capital-to-assets ratio. Second, deals may be arranged which include covering up as part of the scheme itself. For example, in cases of risky insider loans, a reserve account may be created to pay off the first few months (or years) of a development loan to make it look current, whether or not the project has failed or was phony in the first place. Third, covering up may be used after the fact to disguise illegal investment activity. Previously honest bankers, responding to the competitive pressures of the 1980s and the deregulated thrift environment, may have stepped over the line into unlawful risk-taking or other illicit attempts to save their ailing institutions and their own reputations. In such cases, covering up became an essential part of the fraud.[61]

One of the most devious ways to disguise unlawful income is through money laundering. Money laundering refers to taking the proceeds from illicit operations and running them through banks and other institutions, which in turn, issue them back in the form of "clean" paper that can be accounted for as legitimate income.[62] The practice is most often associated with the illegal drug trade, but it also became an element of the S&L scandal. For example, a former executive of Community Savings of Maryland was indicted on charges of looting $28 million from that thrift and laundering those funds in Swiss banks.[63]

While savings and loan frauds occurred nationwide, California and Texas accounted for a preponderance of the worst thrift failures and frauds. Southern California, which federal authorities have long dubbed the "fraud capital of the United States," was home to numerous insolvencies in which financial crimes played a significant role. The notorious case of Charles Keating's Lincoln Savings and Loan of Irvine, which will be analyzed later in this chapter, is perhaps the best known illustration.

Another major Southern California case involved North America Savings and Loan of Santa Ana. A federal grand jury returned a 40-count indictment against former executive consultant, Janet F. McKinzie, and five business associates. The indictment charged that the failed financial institution had operated as a fraudulent enterprise almost since its inception in 1983. The North America Savings case was the first on the West Coast to use racketeering laws (the Racketeer-Influenced and Corrupt Organization Act, or RICO statute) to bring charges against thrift executives. The defendants were accused of looting more than $16 million from depositors in a systematic attempt to use the institution as a front for bogus real-estate transactions, then utilizing part of the fraudulent earnings to make the thrift appear to have adequate capital long after it was insolvent. The remainder of the looted funds was siphoned off to purchase expensive Newport Beach homes, Rolls Royces, and other luxury items. A 15-month FBI investigation concluded that the failed thrift represented the worst case of insider fraud uncovered at a California S&L at that time and could be directly traced to the fraudulent activities of the institution's management.

One scheme used by the looters of North America Savings involved the creation of a series of phony real-estate escrows into which $11 million in thrift funds were deposited and then diverted back to the thrift's operators. Another $5.6 million was stolen through the creation of false billings for fictitious construction costs related to two real estate projects, payments for which were diverted to a company owned by Janet McKinzie.[64]

McKinzie's co-conspirator, Dr. Duayne Christensen, a Westminster, California dentist, had invested $6 million to open North America Savings in 1983. He was killed in a single-car freeway crash just hours before state regulators seized the thrift.[65] On March 29, 1990, Janet McKinzie was convicted of looting the S&L. After an eight-week trial, a jury found her guilty of 22 of 26 counts, including racketeering, conspiracy, bank fraud, and interstate transportation of stolen property. Her creative defense had centered around her self-portrayal as a "helpless victim" duped into carrying out the fraud because she was being pumped full of prescription drugs by the thrift's chairman, Dr. Christensen.[66] But prosecutors painted a dramatically different picture of the pair. They charged that the couple was a "modern day Bonnie and Clyde, stealing millions of dollars to enrich themselves."[67] McKinzie was sentenced to 20 years in prison and ordered to pay $13 million in fines. Numerous thrift outsiders were also convicted in related schemes.[68] The collapse of North America Savings and Loan cost taxpayers more than $120 million.[69]

In another infamous Southern California case of S&L fraud, two former owners of Ramona Savings and Loan, Donald Mangano (who ran a construction company) and John Molinaro (a rug salesman), were handed sentences of 15 years and 12 years respectively as a result of looting their thrift between 1984 and 1986. The pair had used the thrift as a money machine for pumping up their other businesses, making loans to projects being built by Mangano and Sons Construction Company and carpeting the projects' floors with rugs purchased from Molinaro. The collapse of Ramona cost taxpayers approximately $70 million.[70] To their presumable relief, at least no one compared Mangano and Molinaro to Bonnie and Clyde.

"OUTSIDER" THRIFT FRAUDS

Savings and loan fraud was not confined to insiders. "Outsiders" from various occupations and professional groups often joined thrift officers in the largest scams. Industry regulators and FBI investigators have reported that appraisers, lawyers, and accountants were among the most frequent co-conspirators; indeed, their compromised services made many of the S&L scams possible. Perhaps foremost in this regard were accountants, whose audits allowed many fraudulent transactions to go unnoticed. Professional accounting firms were highly paid for their services, and thus could easily turn a blind eye when evidence of wrongdoing surfaced. One study conducted by the General Accounting Office reports that, of eleven failed thrifts in Texas, six involved such laxity on the part of auditors that investigators referred them to professional and regulatory agencies for formal action.[71]

Appraisers were central players in the epidemic of fraud as well. As assessors of property values, appraisers are essential to the real estate and banking systems. In some states where the thrift industry was particularly hard hit, such as Texas, the appraisal business is entirely unregulated. Like many other professionals involved in the thrift crisis, appraisers were susceptible to designing their results to meet clients' wishes, as they are particularly dependent on repeat business and referrals. Thrift regulators have reported that inaccurate and inflated appraisals were found in the wreckage of failed thrifts throughout the country.[72]

Accountants, lawyers, and appraisers interested in retaining lucrative contracts with S&Ls in the 1980s were confronted with the tension between safe banking procedures, legal statutes and fiduciary regulations, and professional standards on one hand, and the demands of their clients on the other. Periodically the line was crossed, or even erased, as these "outsiders" violated not only professional codes of conduct but, in some cases, the law. Much as the criminogenic environment of the S&Ls triggered insider abuse and fraud, the very structure of the relationship between insiders and professionals on the outside assured that some segment of those outsiders would become accomplices to fraud.

Criminal Networks

Another consistent theme in the S&L debacle is the degree to which the financial resources of the thrift industry and individual thrift executives enabled troubled savings and loans to secure the support of influential policymakers.[73] Regarding the collapse of thrifts in Texas, a staff member of the Senate Banking Committee predicted: "What you're going to find in these thrifts is a sort of mafia behind them. I don't mean Italians, but I'm using it in a generic sense: a fraudulent mutual support."[74]

The nature of many of the crimes permeating the thrift industry depended on this "mutual support." A Senate Banking Committee memo delineates the four most common forms of fraudulent transactions: land flips, nominee loans, reciprocal lending arrangements, and linked financing.

LAND FLIPS In a land flip, a piece of property, usually commercial real estate, is sold back and forth between two or more partners, inflating the sales price each time and refinancing the property with each sale until the value had increased several times over. In one of the most infamous cases, a Dallas developer and his partner purchased a parcel of land outside of Dallas. They then sold it to each other inflating the price from $5 million to $47 million in less than a month.[75] The final loan was defaulted on, leaving the partners with hefty profits and the lending institutions with short-term points and fees. A flip scam requires an organized network of participants—at a minimum, two corrupt borrowers (who are often affiliated with the lending thrift) and a corrupt appraiser.

NOMINEE LOANS Nominee loan schemes involve loans to a "straw borrower" outside the thrift who is indirectly connected to the thrift. Nominee loans are used to circumvent regulations limiting the permissible level of unsecured commercial loans made to thrift insiders. Don Dixon, the owner and operator of the infamous Vernon Savings and Loan in Texas, provides an extreme example of how nominee loans can be used in a fraudulent manner. Dixon established a network of over thirty subsidiary companies for the sole purpose of making loans to himself and other insiders.

RECIPROCAL LENDING Reciprocal lending arrangements are similarly designed to evade restrictions on insider loans. These arrangements were used extensively in the mid-1980s by thrift officers and directors, who, instead of making loans directly to themselves—which would have sounded an alarm among regulators—agreed to make loans to *each other*, with each loan contingent on receiving a comparable loan in return. One investigation in Wyoming in 1987 revealed a "daisy chain" of reciprocal loans among four thrifts which resulted in a $26 million loss to taxpayers.[76]

LINKED FINANCING Finally, linked financing is "the practice of depositing money into a financial institution with the understanding that the financial institution will make a loan conditioned upon receipt of the deposits."[77] These transactions usually involved brokered deposits in packages of $100,000, the limit on FSLIC insurance. Deposit brokers often received a generous nonrecourse loan, which was frequently defaulted on, in return for these deposits.

Investigators and regulators report finding variations of these four basic "mutual support" scams over and over in their autopsies of insolvent savings and loans. In each of these schemes a network of participants is absolutely essential. Arthur Leiser, an examiner with the Texas Savings and Loan Department for 35 years, kept a diary and noted the relationships among savings and loan operators, developers, brokers, and a variety of borrowers. One network recorded by Leiser included 74 participants. According to Leiser's calculations, practically all the insolvent thrifts in Texas were involved in such networks.[78]

The conspiratorial quality of thrift frauds was not confined to Texas or the southwest. In a speech to the American Bar Association in 1987, William Weld, Assistant Attorney General and Chief of the Criminal Division at the Justice Department (later Governor of Massachusetts), declared: "We now have evidence to suggest a nationwide scheme linking numerous failures of banks and savings and loan institutions throughout the country."[79] That same year, the GAO reported that 85 criminal referrals had been made to the Department of Justice relating to the 26 insolvent thrifts in its study, involving 182 suspects and 179 violations of criminal law.[80]

These crimes were sometimes facilitated by connections between perpetrators and those in a position to shield them from prosecution. At the lowest level of field inspectors and examiners, evidence has surfaced of collusion with fraudulent thrift operators. One strategy of thrift executives was to woo examiners and regulators with job offers at salaries several times higher than their modest government wages. When "Erv" Hansen, owner of Centennial Savings and Loan in Santa Rosa, California, was questioned by examiners about his extravagant parties, excessive compensation schemes, and frequent land flips, he hired the Deputy Commissioner of the California Department of Savings and Loans, making him an executive vice-president and doubling his $40,000 a year state salary. According to an interview with Hansen's partner, the new employee's chief assignment was to "calm the regulators down."[81] Similarly, Don Dixon at Vernon Savings hired two senior officials from the Texas Savings and Loan Department, and according to one official, "provided prostitutes along the way."[82]

Even more important than these relatively infrequent forms of explicit collusion, were connections between thrift industry executives and elected officials. Not only was the powerful U.S. League of Savings and Loans, with its generous campaign contributions and lobbying efforts, a significant force behind the deregulation that provided the opportunities for fraud in the first place, but financial pressure was brought to bear by the operators of fraudulent institutions in order to avoid regulatory scrutiny. While the "Keating Five" case is by far the most well-publicized instance of political influence-peddling to stave off official actions in response to thrift violations, it was only one square in a sinister quilt. The repercussions of bribery and political corruption in the S&L tragedy go far beyond one or two institutions. The connections between former House Speaker Jim Wright, Congressman Tony Coelho, and thrift executives illustrate this pattern.[83] Such ties were replicated throughout the country, most notably in California, Texas, Arkansas, and Florida, where failures proliferated and losses soared. One senior official in Florida reported that to his knowledge, *all* the Florida thrifts that managed to stay open after insolvency did so with the help of their owners' and operators' well-placed political connections.[84]

REFLECTING ON FRAUD

Representative Henry Gonzalez, Chair of the House Committee on Banking, warned FBI Director William Sessions of the urgency of dealing with thrift crime:

> The issue is very, very serious. We cannot allow . . . a loss of faith in the deposit insurance system . . . Confidence is at the root of everything because if we lose the confidence of the people, no system will stand up to that.[85]

GAO Director Harold Valentine called thrift fraud and the financial collapse to which it contributed, "perhaps the most significant financial crisis in this nation's history."[86] The Department of Justice referred to it as "the unconscionable plundering of America's financial institutions."[87] A senior staff member of the Senate Banking Committee explained the attention being given to thrift fraud:

> This industry is very close to the heart of the American economy! We teetered on the edge of a major, major problem here. Well . . . we got a major problem, but we teetered on the edge of a major collapse. . . . You know, all these [financial] industries could bring down the whole economy.[88]

In summary, the major federally funded study on S&L fraud and the response of the government to the ensuing debacle concluded the following:[89]

- Crime and deliberate fraud were extensive in the thrift industry during the 1980s, contributing to the collapse of hundreds of institutions and increasing the cost of the taxpayer bailout.
- Deregulation of the thrift industry in the early 1980s, combined with continued deposit insurance, were key elements of a criminogenic industry environment. In particular, these policy changes increased the opportunities for fraud while decreasing the risks associated with fraud.
- While there were numerous variations of fraudulent thrift deals, four basic types of transactions provided the vehicle for the most egregious frauds. These are land flips, nominee loan schemes, linked financing, and reciprocal lending. Further, frauds consisted generally of three types of misconduct: "desperation dealing," "collective embezzlement," and "covering-up."
- Thrift crimes typically involved networks of insiders, often in association with affiliated outsiders.
- Fraud was correlated with specific organizational characteristics at failed S&Ls. Institutions that were stock-owned, were less involved in the home mortgage market, and undertook strategies that led to dramatic growth in assets, were the sites and vehicles for the most frequent, most costly, and most complex white-collar crime.
- The government response to thrift fraud focused on containing the financial crisis, rather than punishing wrongdoing *per se*.
- Despite the urgency of this response and its unprecedented scale, its effectiveness is limited by the complex nature of these frauds, resource constraints, inter-agency coordination difficulties, and inherent structural dilemmas related to financial regulation.
- A relatively high proportion of those formally charged in major thrift cases were convicted (91 percent), and of those, a significant proportion (78 percent) received prison sentences.
- Thrift offenders received relatively short prison sentences compared to those convicted of other federal offenses.
- Significant amounts of fraud will go undetected, and a large proportion of individuals suspected of major thrift offenses will never be prosecuted.

One high official put the S&L crisis in particularly graphic terms when he compared the damage to a major environmental disaster, too enormous to be cleaned up effectively:

> I feel like it's the Alaskan oil spill. I feel like I'm out there with a roll of paper towels. The task is so huge, and what I'm worrying about is where can I get some more paper towels? I stand out there with my roll and I look at the sea of oil coming at me, and it's so colossal![90]

Given the best available evidence, at least one thing is certain from this sad chapter in American history—which makes it all the sadder: The incredible financial losses directly attributable to white-collar crimes that were discovered and recorded in official statistics on the savings and loan crisis represent only "the tip of the iceberg."[91]

CASE STUDY
Charles Keating—"A Not-So-Wonderful Life"

The collapse of Lincoln Savings and Loan of Irvine, California, the most expensive thrift failure (a more than $3 billion cost to taxpayers), is notorious not only because of its massive losses, but because it serves as a prime example of all the excesses and corruption which plagued the industry. Congressman Gonzalez characterized the case of Lincoln Savings and its flamboyant owner, Charles H. Keating, Jr., as nothing less than a "mini-Watergate."[92] Keating, a Phoenix real estate developer, had an eclectic past. Once a national champion swimmer, Keating became a major anti-pornography crusader who traveled the country battling smut for Republican administrations. In 1980, he served as campaign manager for John Connally's ill-fated run for the Republican presidential nomination.[93] There was another side to Keating, however, which was conveniently forgotten when he was allowed to purchase Lincoln with junk bonds sold by Michael Milken and the now-defunct firm of Drexel Burnham Lambert. In 1979, Keating had settled charges brought by the Securities and Exchange Commission which alleged illegal and fraudulent transactions regarding his loans from a bank in his home state of Ohio.[94]

Keating bought Lincoln Savings and Loan in 1984 and quickly transformed it from a traditional small thrift which made home mortgage loans into his own (and his family's) personal money machine. Lincoln traded in junk bonds, huge tracts of undeveloped real estate, and Keating's "masterpiece"—the Phoenician Hotel in Scottsdale, Arizona. The resort was financially doomed from the start because of Keating's lavish spending on all aspects of the project; Keating embarked on a $260

million spending spree made that much easier because it involved other people's money. Given it's staggering cost, government regulators estimated that to turn a profit, the Phoenician would need to have a 70 percent occupancy rate with an average room cost of $500 per night.[95]

The preposterous Phoenician Hotel was not Keating's only questionable business practice, however. He used Lincoln to provide a steady source of funding to his real estate company, American Continental Corporation. The thrift became involved in a series of fraudulent real estate deals designed to pump money into American Continental. He named his son, a 28-year-old college drop-out and former busboy, chairman of the board of Lincoln and paid him nearly one million dollars. Keating took nearly two million. In total, nearly $34 million was paid to the Keating family from the thrift and parent company.[96]

As government regulators discovered what was happening at Lincoln and other thrifts that were "flying high" (and blind) with reckless investments, Keating fought back using his political clout. Keating's lawyer, Lee Henkel, was appointed to the Federal Bank Board and was soon embroiled in scandal after proposing a rule that directly favored Lincoln and only one other S&L. He resigned soon thereafter.[97]

Keating hired a slew of prestigious law firms, as well as an accountant from one of the country's largest firms, which for years had attested to the soundness of Lincoln's books, and paid him over $900,000 per year. He paid Alan Greenspan, who was to become the Chairman of the Federal Reserve Board, to prepare an economic report declaring

(Continued)

that Lincoln was on sound financial footing. As writer Michael Waldman notes: "Greenspan's letter said that Lincoln was as sound as seventeen other 'thriving' thrifts. Within three years, sixteen of them would be bankrupt."[98] Keating also offered lucrative employment to his nemesis, Ed Gray, who was then chief S&L regulator, leading the charge against direct investments such as those that Lincoln recklessly had made. Gray refused Keating's offer.

Finally, and most ignominiously, Keating contributed $1.4 million to the campaigns and causes of five U.S. Senators who would later become known as the "Keating Five." They were: Alan Cranston, Democrat from California; Dennis DeConcini, Democrat from Arizona; Don Riegle, Democrat from Michigan and Chair of the Senate Banking Committee; John McCain, Republican from Arizona; and John Glenn, Democrat from Ohio and former astronaut. In 1987, Gray was called to a meeting in DeConcini's office, where he found Senators DeConcini, McCain, Cranston, and Glenn. In arguing for their "friend," DeConcini offered a deal which consisted of Lincoln making more traditional home loans if Gray would ease up on the direct investment rule and leave Lincoln alone.

Another meeting took place a week later with the full Keating Five, which also included the San Francisco regulators who were putting together the case against Lincoln. One of the regulators, Bill Black, took meticulous notes at the meeting which clearly indicate that the senators were attempting to thwart the government agency's actions regarding Lincoln. The regulators informed the senators that they were going to file a criminal referral with the Justice Department. Gray later stated that the Keating Five meetings "were exercises in naked political power on behalf of a major political contributor."[99]

When Ed Gray's term as Bank Board Chairman expired, M. Danny Wall, a self-described "child of the Senate," was appointed as his replacement. Wall had reportedly met with Keating several times and later took the San Francisco regulators off the Lincoln case. This was a curious

move given the evidence they had amassed against the thrift. Lincoln remained in operation for two more years, during which time it continued to hemorrhage big losses.[100] In testimony before the House Banking Committee in 1989, before which Keating had refused to testify by invoking the Fifth Amendment, Wall admitted that he had bungled the Lincoln case: "We have all learned some tough lessons from this case. We made some mistakes."[101] This weak concession seemed to take the matter rather lightly. In testimony given by the two chief regulators in San Francisco whom Wall had removed from the Lincoln case, Wall and other top officials were accused of undercutting regulatory actions against Lincoln, despite strong evidence of wrongdoing.

William Black, who was one of the San Francisco regulators, was unequivocal about the stench of influence peddling hanging over the Lincoln investigation: "Chairman Wall's instructions . . . to achieve a 'peaceful' resolution with Lincoln assured the outcome. All that remained was to negotiate the terms of the bank board's surrender."[102] Black further maintained that Lincoln was given effective veto power over which government officials would negotiate the case, which accountants would audit its books, and which officials would supervise it's day-to-day activities.[103]

In April 1989, Keating's wild ride on the backs of taxpayers came to an end. The government seized Lincoln Savings and uncovered what was described as "a web of fraud and deceit with few parallels in the history of finance."[104] New accountants, after careful review, concluded that Lincoln, through a series of phony real estate transactions, had been showing "profits" by giving its money away.[105] In 1989, the government filed a $1.1 billion racketeering lawsuit against Lincoln.

The Senate Ethics Committee held lengthy hearings on the actions of the Keating Five but found no impeachable offenses, although Cranston received the strongest reprimand. At the hearings, Gray responded indignantly to Cranston's accusations that he, Gray, had mischaracterized the

(Continued)

nature of the meetings: "Your continuing efforts to, yes, intervene with regulators in behalf of Lincoln has occurred at the expense of taxpayers and perhaps even thousands of debt holders. I would hope that in the future, the taxpayers' interests—rather than political contributors—would be given the priority."[106] DeConcini boldly told the committee that his intervention on behalf of contributor Keating "was not only a right but an obligation."[107] Moreover, he accused the committee's counsel of "manufacturing" a case against the Keating Five.[108] In a deposition given to investigators, Cranston, a liberal Democrat, stated that Keating, a conservative Republican, had donated nearly $1 million to his political activities because Keating was a "patriot who believes in democracy."[109] In 1991, the Senate Ethics Committee found Cranston to have violated Senate rules by intervening on Keating's behalf while soliciting large campaign contributions from him.[110] M. Danny Wall was later forced to resign as a result of the Lincoln mess. Calling for Wall's removal as chief S&L regulator, Congressman Gonzalez blamed Wall and other federal regulators for not stopping the looting of Lincoln by officials of American Continental and for allowing Lincoln to become Charles Keating's personal "cash machine."[111] Just days before Lincoln was seized by the government, Wall was still expressing confidence in Keating and arguing for alternatives to a federal takeover.[112]

In that same year, another more disturbing scam perpetrated by Keating came to light. It involved the illegal sale of junk bonds in Lincoln's parent real estate company, American Continental Corporation, also controlled by Keating. Over 20,000 customers, mostly elderly or poor, were tricked into buying the bonds at Lincoln branch offices through high pressure sales tactics, which had led them to believe that the bonds were government-insured. One company sales memo sounded like it had been cribbed from the sleaziest boiler room operation: "[T]he weak, meek and ignorant are always good targets."[113] Some of the victims had invested their life savings, thinking that

the soon-to-be-worthless bonds were a safe haven for their retirement funds. One elderly man, who was distraught over losing his $200,000 life savings in the Lincoln collapse, killed himself.[114]

In the meantime, Keating not only offered no apologies, but also went on the offensive, campaigning against the "injustice" which government regulators had perpetrated against him. Claiming that overzealous regulators had left him impoverished, Keating denied claims that he had hidden funds in foreign bank accounts.[115] Regarding his namesake senators, he said that they "had done darn well and should be congratulated."[116] Despite his cry of indigence, a few months later regulators filed a $40.9 million claim for restitution against Keating, charging him and associates with using phony tax shelters and shady land deals to plunder Lincoln Savings.[117]

Keating legally challenged the government's takeover of his thrift. In denying Keating's claims, U.S. District Judge Stanley Sporkin ruled that the government was "fully justified" in seizing Lincoln, and noted that the thrift was "in an unsafe and unsound condition to transact business."[118] Judge Sporkin added that Keating and his accomplices had "abused their positions through actions that amounted to a looting of Lincoln."[119]

Finally, in September 1990, Keating and three others were indicted by a grand jury in Los Angeles on charges of securities fraud regarding the sale of almost $200 million in American Continental bonds at Lincoln branches.[120] A superior court judge refused to reduce Keating's $5 million bail, arguing that given his pursuit by regulators, creditors and prosecutors, "he has significant reasons not to stay around."[121] Bail was reduced, however, for Keating's co-conspirators, Judy J. Wischer, former American Continental president, and Robin S. Symes and Ray C. Fidel, both former Lincoln presidents.[122] After a month-long stay at the L.A. County Jail, Keating finally was released when a federal judge lowered his bail to $300,000.[123] Keating was convicted on December 4, 1991, his 68th birthday. Still strongly proclaiming that the

(Continued)

regulators were to blame for the demise of his financial empire, Keating was found guilty on 17 of 18 counts related to the sale of junk bonds at Lincoln Savings branches.[124]

Just eight days after his conviction on state charges, Keating again pleaded innocent after a federal grand jury indicted him and four associates on 77 counts of racketeering, bank fraud, and other charges, culminating a 2 1/2-year investigation into the failure of Lincoln Savings and Loan.[125] Facing numerous investor and government lawsuits, Keating, the champion swimmer, was in way over his head and sinking fast. His insurance carrier refused to pay any additional legal bills, claiming that he had reached the $5 million limit on his policy.[126]

On April 10, 1992, Charles Keating remained emotionless in court as Judge Lance Ito sentenced him to the maximum term of 10 years in prison[127] for duping Lincoln depositors into buying his uninsured bonds.[128] Keating's children and grandchildren wept as he was hauled off to jail after Ito denied his lawyer's request that he be set free on bail pending his appeal.[129]

In the biggest fraud trial ever, federal prosecutors rested their case against Keating in December 1992,[130] and in January, he and his son were found guilty of racketeering, conspiracy, and fraud.[131] Keating was convicted on 73 counts, while his son was found guilty on 64. The verdict exposed Keating, who was already incarcerated at the time on his state conviction, to a maximum of 525 years in prison.[132] The younger Keating was slightly less vulnerable—facing only 475 years.

While the prospect of having the Keatings locked up for the rest of their lives no doubt gratified some of their defrauded investors, Keating's victims, who lost much or all of their life savings, had more immediate concerns. As one investor in Lincoln's worthless bonds put it" "The thing is now, where do we find his money?"[133] Government efforts to recoup Keating's loot were largely fruitless, however. Keating's 20,000-acre dream community, Estrella, the single largest real estate venture of Lincoln, was valued at less than ten cents on the dollar.[134]

Before his sentencing on the federal charges, prosecutors had asked for a relatively stiff term of 25-30 years in prison, claiming that Keating had shown no remorse, despite convictions in two trials, and that he had perjured himself repeatedly and thus deserved extra punishment for obstructing justice.[135] As one Assistant U.S. Attorney explained: "Despite the findings of two criminal juries that he is guilty of fraud beyond a reasonable doubt, defendant Keating still refuses to shoulder any of the blame for the devastation his conduct caused . . . Instead, he continues to blame everyone but himself."[136] In calling Keating's fraud "staggering in its proportion," a U.S. district judge sentenced him to 12 years and 7 months in prison for looting Lincoln Savings and Loan and defrauding investors in American Continental of more than $250 million.[137]

The state and federal convictions have done little to make Charles Keating repentant. In fact he has remained steadfast in his refusal to deliver the standard *mea culpa* declaration. That defiance set Keating apart from most of his upperworld criminal counterparts. Not only was he not sorry, he would not even pretend that he was. He again asserted that Lincoln's failure and his own legal and financial demise were due to vindictive regulators who were out to get him.

In late 1993, the cost of liquidating the remaining assets of Lincoln Savings was raised to over $3.4 billion,[138] and subsequent estimates have gone even higher. In 1996, Keating won his appeal on the state securities fraud conviction, which means that he "only" had to serve his 12-year federal sentence.[139] In overturning the state conviction, a federal appeals judge ruled that Keating's constitutional due process rights were denied because his state conviction was based on "nonexistent legal theory" and erroneous jury instructions from Judge Ito.[140]

Three years later, Charles Keating received more good news. On December 2, 1996, an

(Continued)

appellate court overturned his federal convictions, finding that jurors in the case had improperly learned about his prior state court conviction. On November 9, 2000, the decade-long criminal case against Keating finally ended quietly as prosecutors formally withdrew fraud charges, representing the final act among state and federal cases and civil and government lawsuits against him. Still unrepentant, he said he had learned his lesson: "Stay . . . out of the government's way . . . Don't mess with the regulators."[141] It was reported that prosecutors dropped the case for practical reasons, including the deaths and old age of witnesses, the 4 1/2 years Keating had

already served in federal prison, and his guilty plea in federal court.[142]

Whether a bank or thrift failure and investor loss of the magnitude of Lincoln Savings and Loan could happen again is doubtful. Observers were stunned at the scale of the losses. One thing is certain, however. As Michael Manning, a lawyer involved in unraveling Keating's "deals" noted: "[N]o thrift operator rivaled Keating's combination of risky investments, political influence, multimillion-dollar payments to family and friends and sheer, bold arrogance."[143] Charles Keating indeed earned the title of "poster boy" of the savings and loan debacle.

PENSION FUND FRAUD

One of the most callous forms of white-collar predation entails the looting of money from retirees and workers who have deposited their savings in pension funds. For example, Alan Bond, former CEO of Albriond Capital Management, was sentenced to 12 years in prison in 2002 for cheating pension funds out of millions of dollars.[144] Bond was convicted of defrauding clients by sending unprofitable securities trades to their accounts while directing most of the profitable ones to himself. In investment fraud parlance this scheme is known as "cherry picking."[145] Bond took more than $6 million dollars in kickbacks from brokerage firms while his clients lost more than $56 million.[146] Alan Bond was a highly regarded bond manager well known as a frequent guest on television's *Wall Street Week with Louis Rukeyser* as well as his participation in *Black Enterprise's* Investment Roundtable.[147]

Pension funds are loosely regulated in the United States and can take many forms, but their mission is inviolate: to provide sound and profitable investments for individuals and companies. Many persons rely on such institutions to manage their money for retirement. As the following case further illustrates, that trust can easily be broken—with devastating results.

CASE STUDY
First Pension = "Worst" Pension

One of the largest pension fund scams occurred in California. First Pension Corporation of Irvine was charged in 1994 with stealing or misappropriating up to $124 million from its investors. The company was set up as a pension fund administrator to help clients create various retirement accounts,

including IRAs, and Keoughs. It was also alleged that the corporation, through its "direct participation program," enticed investors into buying trust deeds offered by other companies owned by the same individuals who owned First Pension. As much as $100 million was never invested at all, but

(Continued)

utilized in a Ponzi scheme, whereby new investor money was used to pay dividends and interest on older investments, until the pyramid collapsed and First Pension declared bankruptcy.[148]

First Pension, which was run by business-man, William E. Cooper, had purportedly invested $350 million for about 8,000 individuals, mostly from the Southern California region. The company filed for bankruptcy in 1994, after another company, Summit Trust Company, which was also controlled by Cooper, was seized by regulators. Summit Trust Company served as the custodian for First Pension investors' money. The president of Summit told regulators that $10 million in funds had been transferred without his authority. Summit was soon taken over by the government.[149] By May 1994, the FBI and the Securities and SEC were engaged in ongoing investigations of First Pension, Cooper, and two other owners, Robert Lindley and Valerie Jensen.[150] The government estimated that as much as $124 million could have been lost to fraud, forgery, and outright theft, through an "elaborate pyramid scheme that misled clients into thinking they were investing in mortgages that did not in fact exist."[151]

Despite their lawyers' proclamations that their clients were cooperating with authorities, none of the three principals appeared at a hearing in June 1994 where they were to be questioned under oath as to the whereabouts of the missing investor funds. Their absence certainly did little to ease the fears of investors, one of whom, an unemployed man who had given Cooper's firm $120,000 from a pension and inheritance, all the money he had scrimped and saved.

The U.S. Attorney's office in Los Angeles filed formal charges against Cooper, Lindley, and Jensen in July, 1994. The defendants had earlier signed agreements to plead guilty and cooperate with the investigation.

One example of the extraordinary level of deceit at First Pension involved Cooper's hiring of an actress to portray a state auditor after he was confronted by an employee about the fact that no trust deeds existed in the mortgage pools.[152]

The actress, who was given a forged California Corporations Department business card, sat in the offices of Vestcorp Securities, a First Pension-related firm, and pretended to review files for three weeks. Later, a letter was drafted on phony official stationery stating that the business records were in order.[153]

Although Cooper and his associates pleaded guilty to mail fraud, their explanations provided scant relief to the investors they had swindled. After First Pension's first year of operation, Cooper claimed he knew that he was breaking the law but continued in an attempt to recoup substantial losses. Lindley's excuse for his behavior was similarly flimsy. Jensen claimed that she did not initially understand that what she was doing was illegal. Cooper was sentenced to a 10-year prison term, while Lindley and Jensen were sentenced to 9 years and 4 years respectively.

In 1995, investors filed a class action lawsuit against the California Corporations Department which regulates businesses in that state, charging negligence in handling First Pension. The suit alleges that the Department and its Commissioner knew about the illegal pension administration but refused to conduct an examination or warn investors.[154] The state had never investigated First Pension, even though it admittedly had received a written complaint regarding the bogus audit conducted by Cooper's "actress."[155] In 2000, the California Corporations Department agreed to a nonmonetary settlement, under which it pledged to improve its vigilance and to better help investors detect and report fraud.[156] That same year, about 350 investors, mostly elderly retirees, who had lost about $136 million in First Pension settled with former accounting giant Coopers & Lybrand (now PricewaterhouseCoopers). About a month earlier, Coopers had been found liable by a California jury of misrepresenting First Pension's financial condition, concealing materials, and abetting the company's managers in the fraud. The terms of the settlement were not announced.[157]

INVESTMENT AND FINANCIAL SERVICES FRAUD

Southern California was the headquarters of another extremely large Ponzi scheme, involving the Irvine-based investment firm, Institutional Treasury Management, headed by Steven Wymer. In 1992, Wymer pleaded guilty to numerous federal fraud charges and was ordered to refund $209 million to clients, although authorities doubted that they would be able to recoup even half of that sum. Wymer had lured clients to his investment firm by promising spectacular returns and then used the money for illegal securities speculation and exorbitant personal spending. His investors were mostly municipalities and government agencies which lost about $174 million.[158] The fraud was uncovered when SEC examiners noticed "irregularities" in the account of the city of Marshalltown, Iowa.

Wymer began diverting clients' funds in 1986. He later claimed to have done so because he was "embarrassed to admit" that the firm that preceded Institutional Treasury Management—Denman & Co.—had incurred huge losses on accounts.[159] Wymer told a federal judge: "Convinced that I could recover these lost funds, I concealed the losses by sending out false account statements . . . I began taking money from other clients to make up the losses and sending false statements, audit confirmations, and other documents to those clients to cover up the diversion of their funds."[160]

Wymer's justification for his behavior is virtually identical to the "official" explanation of how huge financial losses occurred during the S&L crisis. Proponents of this purely economics-based view discount the role of cupidity in financial institution fraud. They typically claim that owners, pushed to the brink of insolvency by various market conditions, "gambled for resurrection" by making risky investments that could produce a high return. In reality, this "desperation" excuse falls apart when one examines the actual portfolios of the worst thrift failures, which reveal that their investments were not only unsafe and illegal, but usually involved substantial fraud as well.[161]

Moreover, Wymer's "altruistic" alibi might appear more reasonable had he not squandered his clients' remaining funds on expensive personal luxury items. If he had been *making* money for clients, such symbols of success could be more readily justified. But by *losing* other peoples' money, while amassing real and personal property totaling $10-15 million, including houses in Newport Beach, New York City, Sun Valley, Idaho, and Palm Beach, Florida, along with 13 cars, Wymer was just another greedy crook caught looting the cash drawer.

Standing before the court, his voice cracking, Wymer recited the customary white-collar pledge of contrition: "I am deeply sorry for and ashamed of what I have done. Unfortunately, my illegal activities have greatly hurt some of my clients, my wife, my daughter and my family."[162] One of his prosecutors resolved that Wymer would spend considerable time behind bars: "He was robbing Peter to pay Paul. He acted out of greed and he certainly lived a very lavish lifestyle as a result."[163] Wymer was sentenced to serve nearly 15 years in prison and to forfeit $9 million in assets. Prosecutors noted, however, that Wymer had spent more than $29 million on himself—"far more than he says he earned and far more than he has agreed to forfeit."[164]

Wymer's crimes, as destructive as they were, told only part of the story of the extent of illegal activities in the financial services industry. Before his sentencing, Wymer appeared before a congressional committee and told the members that broker-dealers had helped him defraud investors. While Wymer did not name these other firms, his certainty could be taken as an attempt to diffuse his own culpability in the matter, an SEC investigatory official concurred that Wymer had in fact escaped attention through the complicity of broker-dealer employees who falsified documents and allowed him access to clients' money. Wymer also commented that investment fraud is "common," that regulatory ineptitude aided his crimes, and that federal reform measures were necessary to curb abuses.[165]

The Institutional Treasury Management case illustrates a number of important points about financial crime, its extent, and the need for better control mechanisms. As a postscript to this massive swindle, it should be emphasized that the biggest losers were taxpayers. Most of the money stolen and squandered by Wymer belonged to municipalities and government agencies, which were enticed into investing because of the lure of high returns. If there is a moral to the story, it is simply this: In times of fiscal constraint in government, officials must be extremely wary of lavish entrepreneurial claims. The Orange County bankruptcy (detailed in Chapter 13) has demonstrated the folly of gambling away public funds on high-risk, high-return investments in the hope of increasing revenues without raising taxes. Getting something for nothing may be a universal aspiration, but it is seldom a realistic one.

INSURANCE COMPANY FRAUDS

Insurance is one of the most pervasive businesses in America; almost everyone comes into contact with this industry at some point in their lives. Insurance companies sell over $400 billion of new policies every year to businesses and individuals.[166] Although the major insurers are generally conservative and reputable, a smaller number of rogue companies have the potential to wreak havoc on the entire industry. Insolvencies have increased dramatically since the early 1980s. Between 1982 and 1992, approximately 100 life insurers were declared insolvent, 73 of them between 1990 and 1992.[167] Officials note that fraud has played a major role in 30–50 percent of those failures.[168]

Federal oversight is woefully deficient in the largely unregulated insurance industry, which comprises more than 5,000 companies and controls more than $2 trillion in assets.[169] States do regulate insurers operating within their jurisdiction and require that many of them contribute to a "guaranty fund" which is supposed to pay claims against a failed company. In practice, however, it has been reported that many claimants in such circumstances receive no benefits. Moreover, increases in guaranty fund assessments resulting from claims are passed along to consumers in the form of higher premiums.[170]

When the mass media and, for that matter, the general public, discuss insurance fraud, they generally refer to beneficiary frauds perpetrated by customers who send in false claims to their carriers for payment. This emphasis is understandable, since beneficiary fraud is a significant problem for the industry and incurs great financial loss. It is nevertheless arguable whether beneficiary frauds—as draining and annoying as they are—really contribute the bulk of losses within the industry. The fact is that insurers themselves are in a much better position to reap immense illicit profits than beneficiaries, however dishonest. Let us consider some of the frauds committed by unscrupulous insurance companies.

One common form of fraud is known as "premium diversion," whereby funds intended to cover claims are diverted for other purposes. Small "fly-by-night" companies have been known to do this, then simply disappear after collecting premiums or after complaints about claims begin to pour in. More sophisticated schemes rely on creating a network of service and affiliate companies which fraudulently bill larger companies for ambiguous items such as "operating costs."[171] William Shackelford, the former head of an automobile insurance company in North Carolina was once known as a very generous man. The problem was, as a federal prosecutor put it, "his generosity was with other people's money."[172] Shackelford, an auto-racing fan, gave away almost $16 million in premiums to friends, family, and stock-car drivers before he was convicted and imprisoned for fraud.

Another way that insurers can cheat customers is by creating phony assets. Insurers must show that they have sufficient assets to meet capitalization requirements to pay potential claims. Given lax regulation, spurious insurers can often pretend to have more assets than they actually do—and get away with it. Regulators, who are vastly understaffed for serious financial examinations, jokingly refer to their annual audits of companies as "one second solvency tests."[173] Some companies temporarily "rent" assets for the requisite "one second" to place them on their books as genuine corporate holdings when regulators examine them. One company, for example claimed it owned $20 million in Texas real estate. The property had been condemned by the city of San Antonio, and had a value nowhere near $20 million.[174] Another company claimed $72 million in Indonesian war bonds. Since these dubious bonds are not traded anywhere, it is impossible to determine what they are worth, if anything.[175] While these may be unusually creative examples, companies can also simply lie about, borrow, or rent more reasonable-sounding assets as well.

Yet another form of insurance fraud, involving small business scams, has also been quite common.[176] Since it can be difficult for employees in small companies to obtain low-cost health insurance, a new organizational form has emerged to meet their needs—and sometimes clean out their wallets. The Multiple Employer Welfare Arrangement (MEWA) was created by Congress to help small businesses obtain reasonably priced health care coverage for their employees. A MEWA is usually organized through industry associations and consists of several small companies who pool their funds to provide health coverage for all employees. Once cited as a "godsend," the Insurance Commissioner of Massachusetts now complains that MEWAs "have turned out to be a major-league disaster."[177] Investigators have found that some firms that administer MEWAs are fraudulent enterprises—"virtual money machines for the unscrupulous."[178]

Crooks have had a field day with MEWAs because of even looser regulatory oversight than exists for the insurance industry as a whole. A federal law exempts MEWAs from state regulation, including requirements, which licensed insurers must meet, regarding minimum assets and contributions to state guaranty funds.[179] Thus, unlike traditional health insurers, practically anyone can start a MEWA with virtually no capital, paying off tomorrow's claims with today's premiums, making them "ticking time bombs for consumers."[180] Government reports indicate that, between January 1988 and June 1989 alone, MEWAs did not pay at least $123 million in claims to almost 400,000 covered workers and their beneficiaries.[181]

The failure of Transit Casualty Company, which has been called the "Titanic" of insurance company failures, with a cost of over $3 billion, illustrates yet another major and very expensive mechanism for fraud in the insurance industry. According to a congressional committee, the causes of Transit's insolvency were "management incompetence, excessive reinsurance, and reckless expansion."[182] Reinsurance is a legitimate practice in the industry, which allows companies to sell their policies to other companies ("reinsurers") so that they can write additional policies and are not "wiped out" in the event of a disaster precipitating a deluge of expensive claims. It is crudely analogous to one bookmaker "laying off" sizable bets with another to protect himself from potentially unaffordable losses. In the insurance industry this practice generally is beneficial to all concerned, unless the reinsurer is undercapitalized, or, worse yet, fraudulent.

Reinsurance companies function outside of the formal regulatory system because they do not directly affect consumers. In the recent past many have operated offshore, where bank secrecy laws of other countries can protect them. Firms looking to expand quickly (as in Transit's case) frequently turn to reinsurance companies.

As is the case with other types of financial institutions, the reinsurance system is flawed by avarice. While technically reducing their liabilities through the sale of their policies, insurers remain liable for claims that the reinsurer cannot pay. In other words, if the reinsurer is insolvent, undercapitalized, or simply fraudulent, the insurer (and the state guaranty fund) is left holding the bag. This explains why reinsurance has been called the "'black hole' of solvency regulation."[183]

But the villain is not always the reinsurer. Mendacious primary insurers can use reinsurers to inflate their net worth artificially by reducing their required reserves by the amount of risk supposedly transferred to the reinsurer. The federal government's General Accounting Office (GAO) found that four large insurance company failures were attributable to questionable reinsurance transactions.[184]

OFFSHORE INSURANCE SCAMS

One of the strangest aspects of offshore insurance company scams is their preposterous ties to fictitious countries. At first glance, it seems hard to believe that swindlers could ever get away with registering their fraudulent companies in make-believe nations, complete with phony currency and bogus passports. One would like to think that investors, customers—and especially regulators—would catch on quickly. But perhaps in a "geography challenged" age when a large percentage of American high school students reportedly can't find the Pacific Ocean on a map, it really isn't too surprising.

CASE STUDY
Fantasy Islands[185]

In the mid-1970s when Herbert Williams, alias Little Bird on the Shoulder, created the Sovereign Cherokee Nation Tejas out of a sandbar in the middle of the Rio Grande River, he was ahead of his time in the evolution of white-collar crime. Not only did his newly formed country issue bonds and passports (with an "official" seal that proclaimed that the country had been "Created By An Act of God"), but he also envisioned the Cherokee Nation Tejas as an offshore tax haven for insurance companies, banks, and other businesses. Williams' concept of creating a country out of nearly thin air was greatly advanced with the advent of the Internet, which allowed him to hoist his flag in cyberspace with very little physical effort.

Many of the techniques for creating a "cyber-country" were pioneered by an ex-con named Branch Vinedresser, alias Mark Logan Pedley, who was the founder of the Dominion of Melchizedek, a self-proclaimed "ecclesiastical and constitutional

sovereignty." When Melchizedek was created in 1990, Vinedresser claimed that the country was located on an island (actually two rocks that jut out of the Atlantic ocean) called Malpelo, lying 400 miles off the coast of Columbia. This pair of rocks is already recognized as Columbian territory—and is underwater most of the year. Vinedresser later asserted "jurisdiction" over a 14 million square mile section of Antarctica.

Whatever the true political and geographical status of these land areas, the real heart of Melchizedek is on its Web site, *www.melchizedek.com*. On that Web site one can find information about: Dominion University, where one can become a "Doctor of Law" or a "Doctor of Philosophy"; The Dominion of Melchizedek World Wide Stock Exchange; the Melchizedek Bible; and the Dominion Bar Association. Instructions are also provided on: how to become a citizen of Melchizedek; how to obtain a passport and drivers

(Continued)

license issued by Melchizedek; how to form a corporation under the laws of Melchizedek; and how to start a bank or insurance company with a charter issued by the virtual country.

Over the years, the Dominion of Melchizedek has been involved in a wide array of scams: providing licenses to fraudulent banks and insurance companies; charging Filipinos, desperate to leave their country in search of work, $3,500 for phony Melchizedek passports; and conning Australians out of $10 million invested in Melchizedek-licensed companies. This self-proclaimed "postmodern state" even negotiated to be formally recognized by several actual countries and at one point *declared war against France* for conducting nuclear tests too close to its claimed territory in the South Pacific.

The Dominion of Melchizedek broke new ground (figuratively of course, since it has no real ground) for white-collar criminals around the world by refining a new strategy for fraud. The success of the strategy is evidenced by all the numerous Melchizedek "wannabes" that have sprung up literally out of nowhere.

One of those imitators was the Kingdom of EnenKio, a "country" that consisted of three small, largely uninhabited islands with a total area of 6.6 square miles, located about halfway between Hawaii and Guam. The problem with this scheme was that the U.S. government claimed that the land was actually part of Wake Island, an atoll administered by the Department of the Interior. EnenKio's government-in-exile was led from Hawaii by its self-proclaimed "Minister Plenipotentiary" (otherwise known as Robert Moore) who held court on the country's website where the many financial opportunities offered by EnenKio were described enthusiastically. Among those dubious investments were bonds issued by the government of EnenKio that purportedly were to be used to build a 200-room floating hotel. The hotel was to be "moored in the lagoon of the atoll where the King (King Hermios) resides." In October 2000 the SEC ordered Moore and his kingdom to stop selling the bonds. Another of EnenKio's entrepreneurial ventures involved the sale of "economic passports" for fees ranging from $500 to $10,000. The potential value of these passports was illustrated in early 2000 when EnenKio's "foreign minister" announced that the country had signed a deal with Kuwait to provide passports to the roughly 112,000 stateless Arabs who lived in that country. When it learned that EnenKio was a make-believe nation, the Kuwaiti government quickly scuttled the deal.

An innovative solution to the problem of finding unoccupied *terra firma* for one's new country was proposed by a Tulsa, Oklahoma, native whose given name was Howard Turney, but who used the title Prince Lazarus Long (a character in one of science fiction writer Robert Heinlein's books). In the late 1990s, the Prince announced on his elaborate website that he planned to establish a sovereign domain—the Principality of Utopia—to be located on a series of platforms that would resemble large offshore drilling rigs and would be enough to support "1,200 apartments, a 350,000 square foot shopping mall, five hotels, a bank, a 50,000 square foot medical center," a casino, and a university. In order to fund the venture, the Prince offered $350 million in bonds that claimed to return 9.5 percent annually. He described New Utopia as "a tax haven designed to 'out Cayman' the Cayman Islands. With no taxes of any kind, its citizens will be able to live anywhere in the world, tax free, so long as their assets are located or titled in New Utopia." The SEC saw the venture a bit differently and in 1999 obtained a court order prohibiting the sale of the bonds.

It is easy to laugh at such ridiculous schemes. But there is a more serious point to be made about these "virtual nations." Many of their established features are already in place in actual countries. By 1999, for example, economic citizenships were not only offered by the ersatz Kingdom of EnenKio, but were also sold by a number of recognized Caribbean countries—including Belize, Dominica, and Grenada. At a time when political boundaries are constantly being redrawn and nations come and go, the gap between the Dominion of Melchizedek and the real world seems to be shrinking by the hour.

Sometimes, official reactions to insurance scams are pitifully slow. California Pacific Bankers and Insurance Ltd., which was purportedly based in the aforementioned (and *non-existent*) "Dominion of Melchizedek," openly operated in the state for months before regulators closed its doors.[186] In Maryland, the case of fugitive Martin Bramson's International Bahamian Insurance Company brought an even slower response, despite an insider's tip to regulators *ten years* before authorities moved on the case.[187] Bramson and some family members used a complex and sophisticated web of offshore companies to sell fake malpractice insurance to thousands of doctors and health care professionals at below-market rates. The Bramsons operated 53 companies, some of which were registered in Micronesia, the British Virgin Islands, and the Bahamas.[188]

There are a number of reasons for such foot-dragging which allows this kind of criminal activity to flourish. For one, regulators and investigators are outgunned by their small numbers relative to the mammoth size of the insurance industry. For another, state insurance commissioners are known for their coziness with the industry, which sometimes results in official corruption or appointees to the job who are inept or unmotivated to confront their friends or benefactors. In Wyoming and Louisiana, for example, insurance commissioners have been convicted of taking bribes from those under their watch.[189] The good news is that things appear to be changing in this area, albeit slowly. Commissioners in some states have beefed up regulations, and the FBI has increased investigations. On the other hand, needed federal legislation has met with substantial opposition—from certain state commissioners and from much of the insurance industry itself.[190]

CASE STUDY
Teale—as in "Steale"

Congressional investigators looking into insurance company fraud have concluded:

> There is strong evidence to suggest that the insurance fraud that we have identified is global in nature. We have merely exposed the tip of a number of international white-collar criminal syndicates.[191]

On the roster of criminal insurance syndicates, one name is legendary: Alan Teale. In a few short years starting in the early 1980s, Teale and his associates were able to create a farflung empire of insurance companies both within and outside U.S. borders that bilked thousands of unsuspecting individuals out of millions of dollars they thought was going to provide them with insurance coverage. Teale's story reveals just how easy it is

for clever con men (and women) to stay one step ahead of regulators, who are hamstrung by a crazy quilt of insurance laws and regulations that limit their ability to pursue these financial pirates.

Teale, a native of England, got his start working for the legendary Lloyds of London where he learned the insurance trade. In the early 1980s he emigrated to south Florida where he eventually became director of the Miami-based Insurance Exchange of the Americas (IEA), an ambitious company that sold reinsurance plans worldwide and whose founders saw it as the new Lloyds. The Exchange attracted an interesting group of investors that included Michael Milken and his brother. IEA was known for its flashy investments and underwriting. In one case, the syndicate underwrote 50 percent of a New Jersey racetrack's offer to pay $2 million to the owners of a Kentucky Derby winner

(Continued)

if their horse continued its winning streak in New Jersey. When the horse crossed the finish line ahead of the field, IEA lost a million dollars.[192] After the Exchange, regulators were left to settle $200 million in claims ended for about 5 cents on the dollar.[193]

In the mid-1980s, Teale moved to Georgia where he established the new headquarters for his fraudulent insurance empire. Teale's flagship was the Victoria Insurance Company, a property and casualty insurer based in Atlanta. Victoria was in operation only 18 months before it was shut down by regulators; but in that short period it collected $16 million in premiums and, when it was closed, left $20 million in unpaid claims. One of the specialty lines offered by Victoria was disability coverage to professional athletes, particularly football players. Such well-known NFL stars as Jim Kelly, Bo Jackson, and Joe Montana paid as much as $115,000 for policies that would pay off in the event of a career-ending injury, only to find out later that their policies were bogus. In one case, a former running back for the Atlanta Falcons testified that after a knee injury put an end to his career, he thought he would receive the $320,000 provided for by his policy. Instead, he found that Victoria was bankrupt and he would receive nothing. He eventually went to work as a hospital aide earning $6.35 an hour.[194]

In a variation on this scheme, another Teale-backed company sold liability policies to high school athletic programs. When the company went under in 1992, it left 60 catastrophically injured teenagers without any financial support. Some were quadriplegics; others were in nursing homes.[195]

Teale and his associates were able to fool regulators into thinking that their companies were financially sound by ceding much of their insurance business to Teale-owned reinsurers operating offshore where it was difficult for regulators to verify their assets. The principal assets for one of these offshore companies was $25 million in "treasury notes" issued by an entity that called itself the Sovereign Cherokee Nation Tejas. This "sovereign nation" turned out to be a sandbar in the middle of the Rio Grande river whose "chief" did business out of an office, building in Dallas. When investigators called the office, they spoke to a representative who referred to himself as Wise Otter, but who "spoke with a very distinct British Accent."[196] Inquiries into the financial holdings of the Nation revealed that among them was a plaster-of-paris facemask of Marlon Brando, valued (by the owners) at $1.5 million.[197]

Teale's spectacular career in insurance fraud came to an end in 1993 when federal authorities arrested him. He died in prison while serving a 17-year sentence. Wise Otter, alias Dallas Bessant, was sentenced to six months in prison for his role in one of Teale's schemes.

MORTGAGE FRAUD AND THE 2008 FINANCIAL MELTDOWN

In 2008, Rabbi Leib Pinter, co-principal of the defunct Olympia Mortgage Company of Brooklyn, pleaded guilty to engineering a $44 million mortgage scam.[198] The money Pinter misappropriated had been dispersed by the Federal National Mortgage Association ("Fannie Mae"), the government sponsored pool of home mortgages, to refinance 257 home mortgages. When Olympia refinanced a Fannie Mae mortgage loan, Fannie Mae wired the money to an Olympia account. Olympia was then required to pay off the underlying mortgage loan by remitting the outstanding balance to Fannie Mae.[199] Instead of using the funds to pay off the original loans, Pinter stole the money, leaving $44 million in unpaid mortgages that had been refinanced through Olympia.[200] Olympia gave up its mortgage lender license in 2004 after an FBI investigation of mortgage fraud. As part of his plea, Pinter agreed to a 10-year prison sentence.[201] Rabbi Pinter had a criminal record going back to 1978, when he was sentenced to two years in prison for bribing Congressman

Daniel Flood (see Chapter 10) to obtain favorable treatment for some social services programs he was operating.[202]

In 2009, Nicole Lyder was sentenced to two years in a Boston jail after pleading guilty to forgery, larceny, and other criminal charges. She had provided false financial information about clients to Brea, California-based Fremont Investment & Loan, then collected thousands of dollars in commissions. She worked with low-income clients to qualify them for subprime mortgage loans they unknowingly could not afford. When her clients later realized that they could not afford the monthly payments, they lost their homes through foreclosure.[203] Before it sold all its assets in 2008, Fremont Investments had a Better Business Bureau rating of D.[204] A 2007 investigation by the Federal Deposit Insurance Corporation (FDIC) reported that the firm was operating without effective risk-management policies and procedures in its subprime mortgage operations. Fremont was making subprime mortgage loans without assessing borrowers' ability to repay "in a way that substantially increased the likelihood of borrower default."[205]

In the cosmic scheme of things, the few thousand dollars in commissions Nicole Lyder scavenged from a predatory lender hardly qualifies as the crime of the century. But subprime mortgage fraud is one of the main reasons for the current national surge in foreclosures—and worse.

The recent collapse of the subprime mortgage market set in motion an economic chain reaction that created depression-like conditions in the housing market and pushed the U.S. economy into recession. The problems originated with the Community Reinvestment Act (CRA) of 1977, which required banks to offer credit for "underserved" populations. The CRA provided incentives to help low-income borrowers buy homes. In 1995, the Clinton administration authorized subprime loans under the CRA. Congress then imposed penalties for noncompliant banks and added provisions for the securitization of subprime loans. As a result, mortgage lenders relaxed the financial qualifications for buying a house and offered mortgage loans to credit-impaired households, albeit at higher interest rates to compensate for the greater risk. These mortgages were designated "subprime" because of the borrowers' weak credit histories.

It would be hard to argue against the good intentions of the CRA and its subsequent expansion. Indeed, the home ownership rate in the U.S. had soared to 69 percent by 2004, an all-time high.[206] But it also would be difficult to deny the unintended and disastrous consequences. Despite the inherent risks associated with subprime mortgages, many lenders further lowered their underwriting standards, which only elevated the risks.

In October 2000, Fannie Mae jumped in and purchased $2 billion worth of subprime securities. By 2004, it was buying 44 percent of all subprime securities and selling them to banks and investors. That's how Fannie Mae is supposed to make money—selling mortgages. The more they sell, the more money they make. In its own interest, Fannie Mae wanted to increase the number of mortgages sold. This was accomplished by offering "affordable mortgages" to low-income borrowers.[207] "Affordable" often meant no money down, no income verification, and low variable rates. Bad credit? No credit? It didn't seem to matter all that much.

But it should have mattered. In 2005, more than 90 percent of the loans issued by Fannie Mae were variable rate. Relaxed underwriting standards introduced even more risk into the system, "some of it motivated by fraud and misrepresentation."[208] Beginning in 2006, there was an escalating number of defaults and foreclosures. By the end of 2007, more than 17 percent of subprime borrowers had fallen behind on their mortgage payments.[209] And, as borrowers stopped paying, some banks stopped lending. The subprime market caved in.

The first to suffer was the housing market when new construction and sales of new and existing homes plunged. This was soon followed by a decline in home values, which worsened the mortgage market's financial problems by reducing the value of the collateral securing these loans. As many subprime borrowers found themselves owning houses worth less than the debt owed on them, their incentive to default increased.[210]

Because so many of these loans had been re-packaged by Fannie Mae and others into mortgage-backed securities, the growing default problem soon spread to Wall Street and international financial markets.

The global economic crisis ignited by the subprime market collapse can easily be blamed on the bad judgment of many borrowers and the shortsighted avarice of many lenders. But the dysfunctional mortgage industry of recent years has also generated a lot of alleged fraud and abuses.

Bear Stearns

Bear Stearns was founded in 1923 and grew to become a major global investment bank and securities broker. In 1985, it became a publicly traded corporation and by 2007 it was the seventh largest securities firm, with $66 billion in capital and over $350 billion in total assets. Between 2005 and 2007 it placed first in *Fortune's* "America's Most Admired Company" survey. Today, it is not admired at all. In fact, it no longer even exists.

Bear Stearns was the first company to securitize CRA loans in 1997. It may have seemed like a profitable move at the time, but 10 years later, everything started falling apart. In June 2007, the company had to pledge a collateralized loan of up to $3.2 billion to bail out one its subprime hedge funds, the Bear Stearns High-Grade Structured Credit Fund.[211] In addition, the company had to negotiate with other banks to make collateralized loans to bail out another subprime fund, the Bear Stearns High-Grade Structured Credit Strategies Enhanced Leverage Fund.[212] The latter fund in particular is a good example of the danger of funds that use borrowed money to make investments. The Enhanced Leveraged Fund, true to its name, was leveraged 3 to 1, "meaning for every dollar invested in a risky bond, the fund would borrow another three."[213] That strategy works well only in good times. Declining value can crush a hedge fund. A month later, these funds were worth less than a corner lemonade stand, losing nearly all of their value as the market for subprime mortgages rapidly declined. Within weeks, investors took legal action against Bear Stearns. The co-president of the firm was forced to resign. Faced with a wildfire of rumors about its losses in the mortgage industry and a report of major liquidity problems, investors began pulling out. Bear Stearns, suffering its first annual loss in 83-years, was running out of cash and was on the verge of bankruptcy.[214]

On a weekend in mid-March, 2008, the Federal Reserve took a dramatic measure. It negotiated a bargain-basement sale of Bear Stearns to JP Morgan Chase. The price was a rock-bottom $236 million—about $2 dollars a share. The low price was stunning, especially considering that Bear Stearns shares had been trading at $30 the previous Friday. The company's headquarters building in New York is valued at $1 billion by itself.[215]

In June, a pair of Bear Stearns executives were arrested and charged with fraud in the collapse of the two hedge funds. The government charged that the duo had concocted a web of lies to persuade investors to stay in the two mortgage-heavy funds that had evaporated the previous year. According to the federal prosecutor: "They lied in the futile hope that the funds would turn around and that their income and reputations would remain intact."[216]

On November 10, 2009, the two executives, Ralph Cioffi and Matthew Tannin, we found not guilty of all charges including conspiracy, securities fraud, and wire fraud.[217] They were alleged to have cost 300 investors approximately $1.6 billion, but jurors felt as if "They were scapegoats for Wall Street" and, in reference to the monetary damage, asked, "How much can two men do?"[218]

Merrill Lynch

Merrill Lynch was a global financial services firm and the world's largest brokerage house, with client assets exceeding $1.8 trillion. The firm was founded in 1914 and went public in 1971.

Merrill Lynch became one of the largest players in the subprime game. It bought subprime loans from nonbank institutions, securitized them into Asset Backed Securities (ABSs), then sliced them up according to risk. It created Collateralized Debt Obligations (CDOs) out of the riskier portions of the ABSs and then sold them to investors around the world, who often purchased these CDOs with money borrowed from Merrill Lynch. In other words, Merrill Lynch greatly increased its exposure to the subprime industry by financing both ends of the transaction. Of course, like the other big Wall Street players, Merrill Lynch was generating commissions on every step of the process.[219]

The only component to the subprime module Merrill Lynch lacked was its own mortgage origination company. So in February 2007, it purchased subprime lender First Franklin.[220] Since, by that time, defaults were already accelerating in the subprime market generally, and in First Franklin specifically, it was a bad deal. In late October, Merrill Lynch reported a net third-quarter loss of $2.4 billion and acknowledged writing off $8.4 billion from failed investments in mortgage-linked securities. "The massive write-off exceeded the [firm's] net earnings for all of 2006. It equals about one-eighth of the investment bank's total market capitalization."[221]

In March 2008, Merrill Lynch closed First Franklin, just a year after purchasing it. By this time, Merrill Lynch began to see the writing on the subprime wall. The Bear Stearns hedge funds that had collapsed the previous year had borrowed $850 million from Merrill Lynch, which had to take control of $850 million in questionable bonds when the two hedge funds went belly-up.[222]

In August, Merrill Lynch announced an agreement with the Commonwealth of Massachusetts, under which it would reimburse the city of Springfield $13.9 million in a dispute over bad investments.[223] The state's top securities regulator accused Merrill Lynch of fraud and misrepresentation. Merrill Lynch had invested the money in risky CDOs tied to the subprime market without the Western Massachusetts city's permission. The $13.9 million dwindled to $1.2 million as the subprime mortgage market deteriorated.[224]

In September, it was reported that Merrill Lynch had lost $51.8 billion in mortgage-backed securities.[225] The losses, were, of course, attributed to its large mortgage portfolio in the form of CDOs. When investors lost confidence in Merrill Lynch's solvency, the show was over. That month, Merrill Lynch was sold to Bank of America thanks largely to a $25 billion injection of federal money from the government's newly enacted $700 billion Troubled Assets Relief Program (TARP).[226] All things considered, it was a pretty good deal for Merrill Lynch stockholders (maybe not so good for BA stockholders). The price was .8595 shares of BA stock for one share of Merrill Lynch stock—about $50 billion or $29 a share. This price represented a premium of 70 percent over the most recent closing price and a 38 percent premium over Merrill's book value of $21. On the other hand, it also represented a discount of 61 percent from Merrill's stock price a year earlier.[227] But good deal or bad, in contrast to its rival Lehman Brothers (which collapsed hours after the Bank of America deal was first announced), Merrill Lynch had survived—barely. Merrill Lynch had become a ward of Bank of America, and Bank of America had become a ward of the state.

Merrill Lynch was back in the news in early 2009, when it was reported that CEO John Thain, a former head of the New York Stock Exchange, had demanded a $10 million bonus from the Merrill board for "saving" the company.[228] As recently as 2007, Merrill Lynch had paid Thain more than $83 million, making him the highest paid CEO on Wall Street.[229] Amid a public outcry, Thain soon agreed to waive his bonus.[230]

Thain had also rushed out billions of dollars in bonuses to Merrill Lynch employees before the Bank of America deal became final on January 1. As just one small example, his chauffeur received $230,000 for one year's work.[231] What was perhaps most outrageous to the public, whose taxes had funded TARP, were reports that Thain had spent $1.2 million to redecorate his office when he assumed command there in 2007. In a profligate shopping spree all-too reminiscent of former Tyco chairman (and convicted felon) Dennis Kozlowski's conspicuous consumption, including his notorious $6,000 shower curtains (see Chapter 7), Thain personally signed off on $87,000 for an area rug, another $87,000 for two chairs, over $14,000 for a wastebasket, and many other high-end accoutrements.[232] Included in the bill was an $800,000 fee to celebrity decorator Michael Smith, who redesigned the Obama White House for just $100,000.[233]

One financial columnist has noted: "Now, $1.22 million is not a material amount of money given the scope of Merrill's problems, but it is indicative of how out of touch and arrogant John Thain was and presumably is."[234]

On January 23, 2009, John Thain, who had become the new poster boy for Wall Street greed, resigned from Merrill Lynch. He had become a financial and personal embarrassment to Bank of America. Yet its embarrassment was remarkably short-lived, because four days later BA received an additional $20 billion TARP bailout.[235]

Lehman Brothers

Lehman Brothers was founded in 1850 in Birmingham, Alabama, by three immigrant siblings from Bavaria. After the Civil War, the firm moved to New York City and, over time, grew into a major global financial services company, becoming the primary dealer in U.S. Treasury securities. Lehman brothers went public in 1994, and, by 2007, it had more than $275 billion in assets under management. Then the wind began to shift. In August 2007, Lehman closed its subprime lender, BNC Mortgage. The company said that poor conditions in the mortgage market "necessitated a substantial reduction in its resources and capacity in the subprime space."[236]

In 2008, Lehman faced unprecedented losses in the continuing subprime mortgage crisis. Lehman held a large position in this sinking market and was unable to escape. In the second fiscal quarter it reported losses of $2.8 billion and was forced to sell off $6 billion in assets to raise cash.[237] The firm announced that it intended to lay off 1,500 employees—6 percent of its workforce—just ahead of its third quarter reporting deadline in September.[238] Investors' confidence continued to erode, and on September 9, Lehman stock lost nearly half its value when it plunged 45 percent to $7.79.[239] The next day, the company announced a loss of $3.9 billion.[240] On September 11, the stock dropped another 40 percent, as Lehman was looking for a buyer.[241]

Just days before Lehman Brothers imploded, executives at Neuberger Berman (a Lehman subsidiary) sent out an electronic memo urging Lehman's top managers to do away with their seven-figure-plus bonuses in order to "send a strong message to both employees and investors that management is not shirking accountability for recent performance."[242] Lehman Brothers Investment Management Director George Herbert Walker IV (a cousin of President Bush) dismissed this proposal and actually apologized to other members of the executive committee that the very idea of bonus reduction had even been suggested: "I'm not sure what's in the water at

Neuberger Berman. I'm embarrassed and I apologize."[243] A year earlier, Lehman Brothers also hired the President's brother, former Florida governor Jeb Bush, as a private equity adviser.[244]

On September 15, 2008—the same day Merrill Lynch was bought out by Bank of America—Lehman Brothers announced it was filing for Chapter 11 bankruptcy protection.[245] It was the largest failure of an investment bank since Michael Milken's firm, Drexel Burnham Lambert, went under during the junk bond collapse 18 years earlier (see Chapter 6). Lehman stock tumbled over 90 percent that day.[246]

It is especially sad for a company, whose founders and patriarchs had built it upon a reputation for integrity and philanthropy, to fall so far so fast. But, perhaps even more so than Bear Stearns or Merrill Lynch, Lehman Brothers reaped what it had sown. Years before its demise, the company had established working relationships with some of the sleaziest firms in the mortgage business. For example, in 2000 *The New York Times* revealed how Lehman Brothers had helped bundle and securitize millions of dollars worth of subprime mortgages arranged by Irvine, California-based First Alliance Financial.[247]

During the 1990s, First Alliance was one of the nation's largest subprime mortgage lenders, specializing in loans for home buyers with poor credit ratings and low incomes.[248] First Alliance marketed its loans through slick telemarketing and direct-mail solicitations. Customers who visited First Alliance's loan offices in response to the solicitations were subjected to a lengthy sales presentation that misled them about the existence and amount of loan origination fees (commonly called "points") and other fees that First Alliance charged—which typically amounted to 10 to 25 percent of the loan.[249] In 2003, the Federal Trade Commission and six states settled a "predatory lending" suit against First Alliance for about $75 million. The money would be distributed to an estimated 18,000 homeowners who had been charged excessive fees and interest rates.[250] Officials called it the largest case of its kind in history—at least up to then.

A few months later, a federal jury ruled that Lehman Brothers had aided and abetted First Financial's fraud scheme.[251] The total award was $51 million, with Lehman held responsible for 10 percent of that amount. Since First Financial had already settled with the FTC, it did not have to pay any additional penalty. Lehman Brothers, however, was left with a $5.1 million judgment to pay.[252] Lehman was also closely involved with the mortgage insurance company Conseco, which was fined $27 million in 2002 for violating consumer protection laws.[253]

In addition, Lehman owned Aurora Loan Services, a Colorado-based mortgage payment collector notorious for speedy and ruthless foreclosures.[254] When one Brooklyn homeowner, currently suing Aurora, fell a few weeks behind on his payments, he received a foreclosure notice from Aurora. He had already mailed in the payments that would have brought him up to date.

> He contacted Aurora to plead his case, but, incredibly, the company refused to accept the payments. Instead, company officials moved ahead with the foreclosure. No matter what he did, Aurora would not work with him to resolve the debt. . . . "I had the money, and I sent them the money, but they didn't want it," he says. "It's like they would rather have had the house back."[255]

The man went before a judge, who immediately tossed the case out because Aurora did not hold title to the house. But Aurora quickly purchased the title from its parent company, Lehman Brothers, for $10 and initiated another foreclosure action. The man lost his home and millions of dollars in future real estate appreciation.[256] If one truly is judged by the company one keeps (or the company one owns), then Lehman Brothers must be judged harshly.

The New York Stock Exchange delisted Lehman Brothers after it went bankrupt in late 2008. As of this writing, the firm still exists—barely. Lehman Brothers became a penny stocks investment company trading on the largely unregulated Pink Sheets—for about a nickel a share.

As of 2012, there have been no criminal cases brought against any executives at Merrill Lynch, Countrywide Financial, Lehman Brothers, or Bear Stearns.[257] There have been some major civil cases, although these are relatively few and far between. While some judgments are sizeable, they pale in comparison to the dollar amounts lost in the crisis. Most notably, Goldman Sachs agreed to pay a $550 million settlement as the result of a civil case brought by the SEC, the largest single penalty ever received by the agency from a Wall Street firm. The SEC charged that the company had misled investors regarding the sale of subprime mortgage products. Goldman acknowledged that its marketing materials did not disclose all information. No executives were named in the suit.[258]

Four years after its collapse, Lehman Brothers, facing pressure from institutional creditors for money owed, paid $22.5 billion to settle its debts in April 2011.[259]

In the largest class-action lawsuit of its kind to date, Bank of America agreed to a $2.43 billion settlement related to its acquisition of Merrill Lynch right before the latter company collapsed as the financial crisis became known. The lawsuit alleged that Bank of America and some of its officers made false or misleading statements about both companies' financial health.

The deal—struck on the same weekend in 2008 when Lehman Brothers collapsed—came into question later after Bank of America disclosed that Merrill would post $27.6 billion in losses that year. That added significantly to Bank of America's financial problems, causing it to ask for an additional $20 billion on top of the $25 billion bailout it had already received from the government. It has since repaid all $45 billion.

After reaching the settlement, Bank of America continued to deny shareholders' allegations that it had hid crucial information, and said that it agreed to the terms to get rid of the uncertainties, burden and costs related to the lawsuit.[260]

CASE STUDY
LIBOR—Money from Nowhere

The London Interbank Offered Rate (LIBOR) is the daily average of estimated interest rates top London banks expect to be charged by other banks.[261] This number is used as a benchmark for interest rates worldwide. It is calculated for fifteen borrowing periods and ten different currencies.[262] As a result, credit card agencies and mortgage lenders worldwide use LIBOR to set their own interest rates. Since mortgages, student loans, and other derivatives are tied to this number, any manipulation would affect many borrowers. In 2008, $300 trillion in derivatives were tied to LIBOR.[263]

In 2008, the *Wall Street Journal* revealed that underperforming banks might have manipulated the LIBOR during the 2008 financial crisis.[264] Banks report a low interest rate when they are confident in the market and a higher interest rate when there is less confidence. Thus, dishonest banks may report numbers lower than they actually expect to falsely demonstrate confidence. The *WSJ* article was controversial and the British Bankers' Association (BBA) maintained LIBOR was reliable throughout the 2008 financial crisis, but new evidence paints another picture.[265]

(Continued)

LIBOR manipulation can net large profits for banks. For example, in 2009 Citigroup announced that it would make $936 million during the first quarter if net interest rates fell .25 percent that quarter and $1.9 billion if they fell by 1 percent immediately.[266] A trader commenting on the scandal said for every 0.01 percent LIBOR changed, banks could gain "about a couple of million dollars."[267]

Reuters announced on February 28, 2012, that the U.S. Department of Justice had begun a criminal investigation on LIBOR manipulation.[268] On June 27, 2012, Barclays was fined $360 million by the U.S. government (Commodity Futures Trading Commission and Department of Justice) along with £59.5 million by the British government (Financial Services Authority) for manipulating the LIBOR from 2005 until 2012 to both gain illegal profit and make the bank appear healthy.[269] The legal action led to the resignations of Barklays chairman of the board of directors, Marcus Agius,[270] and chief executive officer, Bob Diamond.[271]

On July 27, 2012, the *Financial Times* revealed that LIBOR manipulation had not only occurred in 2008, but also may have been common practice as far back as 1991.[272] The New York Federal Reserve released documents showing that the Bank of England knew the LIBOR rate was being manipulated in 2007, while in 2008, then-New York Fed President (and now U.S. Secretary of the Treasury), Timothy Geithner had written a memo to Bank of England chief Mervyn King urging him to fix problems within LIBOR.[273] The British Serious Fraud Office has begun a criminal investigation to determine both the depth and pervasiveness of the rate manipulation, and the individuals responsible for it.[274]

Financial institution fraud is, unfortunately, a very real and very costly part of American life. It takes many forms and exacts a gigantic social toll. Its victims are from all segments of society: corporations and employees, governments and taxpayers, young and old, rich and poor, professionals and blue-collar workers.

In a competitive marketplace, individuals and businesses are always hungry for higher returns on their investments. This can have a positive effect on financial services, keeping such companies efficient and opening new investment opportunities, as well as benefitting the entire economy. The same conditions, however, with too little regulation or enforcement oversight, can invite scam artists whose phantom organizations are designed only to bilk investors. The number of such fake institutions has risen dramatically, according to federal banking authorities.[275] Swindlers play on human greed—the eternal quest for the "quick buck"—and lure their prey with promises of guaranteed high returns, typically much higher than more legitimate enterprises offer. The best advice to investors is also the oldest: if a deal sounds too good to be true, it probably is.

Shortly before Christmas in 1990, the *Wall Street Journal* held a private screening of *It's a Wonderful Life* for a panel of savings & loan experts. During the movie's stirring finale, as George Bailey's depositors bring him their hats and bowls and cookie jars filled with enough hard-earned cash to save his S&L, one of the panelists declared: "It's just what the taxpayers will do."[276]

Notes

1. See: Fretts, Bruce. "Everybody's Favorite S&L Movie." *American Heritage*, February/March 1991: 62–63.
2. *Los Angeles Times*. "Blankenship Sentenced to Prison." September 28, 1991: p. D2.
3. *Wall Street Journal*. "Former High Official With FSG Financial Sentenced to Fraud." May 27, 1992: p. B2.
4. *Wall Street Journal*. "Ex-Air-Charter Official in New Jersey Gets 18-Month Sentence." June 13, 1995: p. B4.
5. *New York Times*. "Ex-Financial Planner Pleads Guilty." February 9, 1995: p. D16.
6. *Wall Street Journal*. "Ex-Texas Bank Aide Gets 12-Year Sentence for Committing Fraud." June 14, 1990: p. B8.

7. *Wall Street Journal.* "Massachusetts Man Gets Prison Sentence in Bank-Fraud Case." November 5, 1991: p. C22.

8. *New York Times.* "Prison Term in S&L Case." June 22, 1994: p. D8.

9. *Ibid.*

10. *Ibid.*

11. *Wall Street Journal.* "Arkansas S&L, Head Sentenced to Prison and Fined $75,000." March 18, 1991: p. A9G.

12. White, George. "Former Family S&L Chief Gets 7-Year Sentence." *Los Angeles Times*, April 23, 1991: p. D2.

13. *Ibid.*

14. United States Congress. House Committee on Ways and Means. 1989. *Budget Implications and Current Tax Rules Relating to Troubled Savings and Loan Institutions: Hearings Before the Committee.* 101st Cong., 1st sess. Washington, DC: Government Printing Office, 22 February, 2 and 15 March, p. 2; United States Congress. Senate Committee on Banking, Housing, and Urban Affairs. 1989. *Problems of the Federal Savings and Loan Insurance Corporation (FSLIC): Hearings before the Committee, Part 3. S. Hrg. 101–127, no.* 101st Cong., 1st sess. Washington, DC: Government Printing Office, 3, 7–10 March, p. 9; Hill, G. Christian. 1990. The Never Ending Story: An Introduction to the S&L Symposium. *Stanford Law & Policy Review* 2 (Spring): 21–24.

15. Meigs, A. James and Goodman, John C. "What's Wrong with Our Banking System?" *Consumers' Research*, March 1991: 11–17.

16. Quoted in Sheehy, Sandy. "Super Sleuth—White-Collar Criminals Beware: Ed Pankau Is Looking for You." *Profiles*, July, 1992: p. 38.

17. Ely, Bert. 1990. Crime Accounts for Only 3% of the Cost of the S&L Mess. Alexandria, Virginia: Ely & Company, Inc. Unpublished report, 19 July.

18. See for example, Ely, 1990; White, Lawrence J. 1991. *The S&L Debacle.* New York: Oxford University Press; Litan, Robert E. 1993. "Deposit Insurance, Gas on S&L Fire." *Wall Street Journal,* July 29, 1993, p. A10.

19. National Commission on Financial Institution Reform, Recovery and Enforcement. *Origins and Causes of the S&L Debacle: A Blueprint for Reform. A Report for the President and Congress of the United States.* Washington, D.C.: Government Printing Office, July, 1993.

20. Black, William. "The Incidence and Cost of Fraud and Insider Abuse." Staff Report No. 13, National Commission on Financial Institution Reform, Recovery and Enforcement, 1993, p. 75 (emphasis in the original).

21. Resolution Trust Corporation. *Report on Investigations to Date. Office of Investigations, Resolutions, and Operations Division.* December 31, 1990.

22. U.S. General Accounting Office. *Thrift Failures: Costly Failures Resulted From Regulatory Violations and Unsafe Practices: Report to Congress.* GAO/AFMD-89-62. Washington, DC: Government Printing Office, June, 1989.

23. U. S. General Accounting Office. *Failed Thrifts. Internal Control Weaknesses Create an Environment Conducive to Fraud, Insider Abuse and Related Unsafe Practices.* Statement of Frederick D. Wolf, Assistant Comptroller General, Before the Subcommittee on Criminal Justice, Committee on the Judiciary, House of Representatives. GAO/T-AFMD-89-4. Washington, DC: Government Printing Office, March 22, 1989; United States Congress. House Committee on Government Operations. *Combatting Fraud, Abuse, and Misconduct in the Nation's Financial Institutions: Current Federal Reports are Inadequate: 72d Report by the Committee on Government Operations.* H.Rpt No. 100-1088. 100d Cong., 2d sess. Washington, DC: Government Printing Office, 13 October 13, 1988.

24. United States General Accounting Office. *Bank and Thrift Fraud: Statement of Harold Valentine, Associate Director, Administration of Justice Issues. Testimony Before the Subcommittee on Consumer and Regulatory Affairs.* Committee on Banking, Housing, and Urban Affairs. U. S. Senate. Washington, DC: Government Printing Office, 6 February, 1992, p. 1.

25. Pizzo, Stephen, Fricker, Mary, and Muolo, Paul. *Inside Job: The Looting of America's Savings and Loans.* New York: McGraw-Hill, 1989.

26. Mayer, Martin. *The Greatest Bank Robbery Ever: The Collapse of the Savings and Loan Industry.* New York: Charles Scribner's Sons, 1990.

27. Quoted in Sheehy, *op. cit.,* p. 39.

28. DIDMCA; P.L. 92–221.

29. P.L. 97–320.

30. U.S. General Accounting Office. *Thrift Industry Restructuring and the Net Worth Certificate Program: Report to Congress.* GAO/GGD-85-79. Washington, DC: Government Printing Office, 1985. p. 7.

31. Pizzo, et al., *op. cit.*

32. National Commission on Financial Institution Reform, Recovery and Enforcement, *op. cit.*, p. 47.

33. United States Congress. House. Subcommittee on Financial Institutions Supervision, Regulation and Insurance, Committee on Banking, Finance, and Urban Affairs. Financial Institutions Reform, Recovery, and Enforcement Act of 1989 (H.R.1278): Hearings before the Subcommittee, Part 1. Serial No. 101–12. 101st Cong., 1st sess. Washington DC: Government Printing Office, March 8, 9, 14, 1989, p. 286.

34. Meigs and Goodman, *op. cit.*

35. Eichler, Ned. *The Thrift Debacle.* Berkeley: University of California Press, 1989.

36. Calavita, Kitty and Pontell, Henry N. "'Heads I Win, Tails You Lose': Deregulation, Crime and Crisis in the Savings and Loan Industry." *Crime & Delinquency* 36, 1990: 309–341.

37. House Committee on Government Operations, 1988, *op. cit.*, p. 34.

38. *Ibid.*, p. 46.

39. Coleman, James. "Towards an Integrated Theory of White Collar Crime." *American Journal of Sociology* 93, 1987: p. 427.

40. Geis, Gilbert. "White Collar Crime: The Heavy Electrical Equipment Antitrust Cases of 1961." In Marshall Clinard and Quinney Richard (Eds.). *Criminal Behavior Systems: A Typology.* New York: Holt, Rinehart & Winston, 1967.

41. Farberman, Harvey A. "A Criminogenic Market Structure: The Automobile Industry." *Sociological Quarterly* 16, 1975: 438–457.

42. Lowy, Martin. *High Rollers: Inside the Savings and Loan Debacle.* New York: Praeger, 1991; Pilzer, Paul Z. and Dietz, Robert. *Other People's Money: The Inside Story of the S&L Mess.* New York: Simon and Schuster, 1989; O'Shea, James. *The Daisy Chain: How Borrowed Billions Sank a Texas S&L.* New York: Pocket Books, 1991.

43. Pontell, Henry, Calavita, Kitty, and Tillman, Robert. "Fraud in the Savings and Loan Industry: White-Collar Crime and Government Response." Final Report of Grant #90-IJ-CX-0059 submitted to the National Institute of Justice, Office of Justice Programs, U.S. Department of Justice, October, 1994.

44. Sheehy, *op. cit.*, p. 39.

45. Calavita and Pontell, 1990, *op. cit.*

46. Quoted in U.S. Congress. House Committee on Government Operations 1988, *op. cit.*, p. 34 (emphasis in the original).

47. U.S. Congress. House Committee on Government Operations 1988, *op. cit.*, p. 41; U.S. General Accounting Office. *Thrift Failures: Costly Failures Resulted From Regulatory Violations and Unsafe Practices: Report to Congress.* 1989, *op. cit.*, p. 19.

48. U.S. General Accounting Office. *Thrift Failures: Costly Failures Resulted From Regulatory Violations and Unsafe Practices: Report to Congress.* 1989, *op. cit.*, p. 19.

49. Conklin, John E. *Illegal, But Not Criminal: Business Crime in America.* New York: Spectrum Books, 1977.

50. *Ibid*, p. 7

51. Sutherland, Edwin. *White Collar Crime: The Uncut Version.* New Haven: Yale University Press, 1983; p. 231.

52. Cressey, Donald R. *Other People's Money: A Study of the Social Psychology of Embezzlement.* Glencoe, IL: Free Press, 1953.

53. Calavita and Pontell, 1990, *op. cit.*

54. Sherman, Lawrence. *Scandal and Reform.* Berkeley: University of California Press, 1978.

55. Wheeler, Stanton, and Rothman, Mitchell L. "The Organization as Weapon in White Collar Crime." *Michigan Law Review* 80, 1982: p. 1406.

56. U.S. Congress. House Committee on Government Operations 1988, *op. cit.*; U.S. General Accounting Office. *Thrift Failures: Costly Failures Resulted From Regulatory Violations and Unsafe Practices: Report to Congress.* 1989, *op. cit.*

57. Pontell, et al., 1994, *op. cit.*

58. *Ibid.*

59. U.S. General Accounting Office. *Thrift Failures: Costly Failures Resulted From Regulatory Violations and Unsafe Practices: Report to Congress.* 1989, *op. cit.*

60. *Ibid.*, p. 40.

61. Pontell et al., 1994, *op. cit.*

62. Kerry, John. "Where Is the S&L Money?" *USA Today Magazine,* September, 1991: 20–21.

63. *Ibid.*

64. Murphy, Kim. "Racketeering Charged by U.S. in S&L Failure," *Los Angeles Times,* April 12, 1989: p. 1.

65. It may be worth noting that research by David Phillips speculates that many fatal single-vehicle "accidents" might be disguised suicides (Phillips, David P. "Suicide, Motor Vehicle Fatalities, and the Mass Media: Evidence Toward a Theory of Suggestion." *American Journal of Sociology* 84, 1979: 1150–1174).

66. Crouch, Gregory. "McKinzie Found Guilty in North America S&L Case," *Los Angeles Times,* March 30, 1990: p. D1.

67. *Ibid.*, p. D1

68. Crouch, Gregory. "Santa Ana Thrift Figure Gets 20 Years," *Los Angeles Times,* July 21, 1990: p. A1.

69. *Ibid.*

70. Pizzo, et al., *op. cit.*

71. U.S. General Accounting Office. *CPA Audit Quality: Failures of CPA Audits to Identify and Report Significant Savings and Loan Problems: Report to the Chairman, Committee on Banking, Finance and Urban Affairs, House of Representatives.* GAO/AFMD-89-45. Washington DC: Government Printing Office, February, 1989.

72. Pontell, et al., 1994, *op. cit.*

73. Pizzo, et al., *op cit.*; Adams, James R. *The Big Fix: Inside the Savings and Loan Scandal.* New York: John Wiley and Sons, Inc., 1990; United States Congress. House Committee on Standards of Official Conduct. *Report of the Special Outside Counsel in the Matter of Speaker James C. Wright, Jr., Richard J. Phelan, Special Outside Counsel.* 101st Cong., 1st sess. Washington, DC: Government Printing Office, February 21, 1989.

74. Quoted in Calavita, Kitty, and Pontell, Henry N. "Savings and Loan Fraud as Organized Crime: Toward A Conceptual Typology of Corporate Illegality." *Criminology* 31, 1993: p. 534.

75. *New York Times.* "4 Convicted of Defrauding Texas Savings And Loan." November 7, 1991, p. C16; Pizzo, et al., *op. cit.*

76. United States Congress. House Subcommittee on Commerce, Consumer, and Monetary Affairs. Committee on Government Operations. *Adequacy of Federal Efforts to Combat Fraud, Abuse, and Misconduct in Federally Insured Financial Institutions: Hearing Before the Subcommittee.* 100st Cong., 1st sess. Washington DC: Government Printing Office, November 19, 1987: pp. 79–80, 129–130.

77. U.S. Congress. House Committee on Government Operations 1988, *op cit.*, p. 42.

78. United States Congress. House Committee on Banking, Finance, and Urban Affairs. *Effectiveness of Law Enforcement Against Financial Crime (Part I): Field Hearing before the Committee, Dallas, Texas.* Serial No. 101–111. 101st Cong., 2d sess. Washington, DC: Government Printing Office, April 11, 1990: pp. 804–872.

79. Quoted in Pizzo, et al., *op. cit.*, p. 279.

80. U.S. General Accounting Office, 1989, Thrift Failures, *op. cit.*

81. Quoted in Pizzo, et al., *op. cit.*, p. 47.

82. Personal interview with Henry Pontell, Kitty Calavita and Robert Tillman.

83. Jackson, Brooks. *Honest Graft: Big Money and the American Political Process.* New York: Alfred A. Knopf, 1988; United States Congress. House Committee on Standards of Official Conduct, 1989, *op cit.*

84. Pontell, et al., 1994, *op. cit.*

85. U.S. Congress. House Committee on Banking, Finance and Urban Affairs, 1990, *op. cit.*, p. 15.

86. U.S. General Accounting Office, 1992, *op. cit.*, p. 19.

87. United States Department of Justice. *Attacking Savings and Loan Institution Fraud: Department of Justice Report to the President.* Washington, DC: Government Printing Office, 1990.

88. Personal interview with Henry Pontell, Kitty Calavita and Robert Tillman.

89. Pontell, Henry N., Calavita, Kitty and Tillman, Robert. "Fraud in the Savings and Loan Industry: White-Collar Crime and Government Response." Executive Summary of Grant #90-IJ-CX-0059, National Institute of Justice, Office of Justice Programs, U.S. Department of Justice, October, 1994: pp. 42–45.

90. Quoted in Pontell, Henry N., Calavita, Kitty, and Tillman, Robert. "Corporate Crime and Criminal Justice System Capacity: Government Response to Financial Institution Fraud." *Justice Quarterly* 11, September, 1994: p. 400.

91. *Ibid,* p. 395.

92. Waldman, Michael. *Who Robbed America?: A Citizen's Guide to the Savings & Loan Scandal.* New York: Random House, 1990; p. 92.

93. *Ibid.*

94. *Ibid.*

95. *Ibid*

96. *Ibid.*

97. *Ibid.*

98. *Ibid.*, pp. 94–95.

99. *Ibid.*, p. 97.

100. *Ibid.*

101. Quoted in Weir, Jeff. "Keating Takes the Fifth." *Orange County Register,* November 22, 1989, p. 1.

102. Quoted in Eaton, William J. "Top Regulator Blocked S&L Seizure, Panel Told." *Los Angeles Times,* October 27, 1989, p. A1.

103. *Ibid.*

104. Waldman, *op. cit.*, p. 97.

105. *Ibid.*

106. Quoted in Granelli, James S. "Senators, Ex-Regulator Waging War of Letters." *Los Angeles Times,* November 8, 1989: p. A15.

107. Quoted in Berke, Richard L. "DeConcini is Adamant on his Help for Keating." *New York Times,* January 10, 1991: p. A16.

108. Rosenblatt, Robert A. "DeConcini Lashes Out at Ethics Panel Counsel." *Los Angeles Times,* November 20, 1990: p. A1.

109. Quoted in Fritz, Sara and Rosenblatt, Robert A. "Keating Contributed as 'Patriot' Cranston Says." *Los Angeles Times,* November 30, 1990: p. A4.

110. Fritz, Sara. "Ethics Panel Says Cranston Broker Rules in Keating Ties." *Los Angeles Times,* February 28, 1991: p. A1.

111. Quoted in Fritz, Sara. "House Panel Assails Wall's Policy to 'Trust Keating.'" *Los Angeles Times,* November 22, 1989: p. A1.

112. *Ibid.*

113. Quoted in Waldman, *op. cit.,* p. 98.

114. Connelly, Michael. "Elderly Victim of Lincoln S&L Loss Takes Own Life." *Los Angeles Times,* November 29, 1990: p. A1.

115. Rosenblatt, Robert A. "Keating Vows to Keep Fighting to Regain S&L." *Los Angeles Times,* May 10, 1990: p. D3.

116. Quoted in *Ibid.,* p. D3.

117. Rosenblatt, Robert A. and Granelli, James S. "Keating, 5 Others Ordered to Pay $40.9 million." *Los Angeles Times,* August 10, 1990: p. D1.

118. Quoted in Jackson, Robert L. "U.S. Judge Denies Keating Challenge to Seizure of S&L." *Los Angeles Times,* August 24, 1990: p. D1.

119. Quoted in *Ibid.,* p. D1.

120. Granelli, James S. "Sealed Indictments Reportedly Name Keating, 3 Others." *Los Angeles Times,* September 18, 1990: p. D1.

121. Quoted in Granelli, James S. "Judge Refuses to Lower $5-Million Bail for Keating." *Los Angeles Times,* September 22, 1990: p. D1.

122. *Ibid.*

123. White, George. "Keating Got Star Treatment During Stay in County Jail." *Los Angeles Times,* October 20, 1990: p. D1.

124. Granelli, James S. and Bates, James. "Keating Guilty of Fraud; Faces 10-Year Term." *Los Angeles Times,* December 5, 1991: p. A1.

125. Granelli, James S. "Keating Indicted on New Charges of Bank Fraud." *Los Angeles Times,* December 13, 1991: p. A1.

126. Granelli, James S. "Keating Insurer Stops Paying His Legal Bills." *Los Angeles Times,* February 26, 1992. p. D1.

127. Ito, of course, would become the most famous judge in America three years later when he presided at the sensational O. J. Simpson murder trial.

128. *New York Times,* "Keating is Sentenced to 10 Years for Defrauding S.&L Customers." April 11, 1992: p. A1.

129. *Ibid.*

130. Granelli, James S. "Prosecutors Rest Case Against Keating." *Los Angeles Times,* December 2, 1992: p. D2.

131. Granelli, James S. "Keating, Son Guilty of U.S. Fraud Charges." *Los Angeles Times,* January 7, 1993: p. A1.

132. *Ibid.*

133. Quoted in *Ibid.,* p. A1.

134. Granelli, James S. "Keating's Dream is Devalued." *Los Angeles Times,* June 2, 1993: p. D1.

135. Granelli, James S. "U.S. Atty. Seeks 25- to 30-Year Keating Term." *Los Angeles Times,* July 3, 1993: p. D1.

136. Quoted in *Ibid.,* p. D2.

137. Quoted in Granelli, James S. "Keating Gets 12 Years in Federal Fraud Case." *Los Angeles Times,* July 9, 1993: p. A1.

138. Granelli, James S. "Forecast is Now $3.4 Billion to Liquidate Lincoln Savings." *Los Angeles Times,* October 31, 1993: p. D1.

139. Granelli, James S. "Keating's U.S. Appeal Takes on New Import." *Los Angeles Times,* April 5, 1996: p. D1.

140. *Ibid.,* p. D5.

141. Recard, Scott E. "Prosecutors Withdraw Charges Against Keating." *Los Angeles Times,* April 5, 1996: D1.

142. *Ibid.,* C2.

143. Quoted in *Ibid.,* C2.

144. *New York Times* (online). "Prominent Wall Street Figure Convicted of Fraud." June 10, 2002.

145. *Ibid.*

146. Lewis, Latif. "Alan Bond Sentenced." *blackenterprise. com,* June 10, 2002.

147. *Ibid.*

148. Myers, David W. "First Pension Allegations Spark 'Direct Participation' Concern." *Los Angeles Times,* May 18, 1994: p. D1.

149. Gomez, James M. "SEC Joins Hunt for $10 Million Missing From Investment Firm." *Los Angeles Times,* April 29, 1994:p. D2.

150. Hiltzik, Michael A. "Millions May Be Missing From First Pension Corp." *Los Angeles Times,* May 11, 1994: p. A1.

151. Hiltzik, Michael A. "SEC Says First Pension Ran Pyramid Scam." *Los Angeles Times,* May 14, 1994: p. D1.

152. *Ibid.*

153. *Ibid.*

154. Granelli, James S. "First Pension Investors Sue State for $17 Million." *Los Angeles Times*, October 27, 1995: p. D6.

155. *Ibid.*

156. *latimes.com.* "First Pension Settlement Reached," October 10, 2000.

157. Ballon, Marc. "First Pension Investors Settle With Accountants." *Los Angeles Times*, August 20, 2000: C1.

158. Stevens, Amy. "Wymer Pleads Guilty to Charges of Fraud Scheme." *Wall Street Journal*, September 30, 1992: p. B10.

159. *Ibid.*, p. B10.

160. Quoted in *Ibid.*, p. B10.

161. Black, William K., Kitty Calavita, and Henry N. Pontell. "The Savings and Loan Debacle of the 1980s: White Collar Crime or Risky Business?" *Law and Policy* 17, 1995: 23–55.

162. Gomez, James M. "Wymer is Guilty in Huge Fraud." *Los Angeles Times*. September 30, 1992: p. D1.

163. Quoted in *Ibid.*, p. D5.

164. *New York Times.* "Money Manager Sentenced to 15-Year Term for Fraud." May 13, 1993: p. D6.

165. *Ibid.*

166. Headden, Susan, Witkin, Gordon, and Lord, Mary. "Preying on the Helpless." *U.S. World and News Report*, May 24, 1993: 48–52.

167. Hoge, Nettie. "Cracks in the Rock." *Dollars & Sense*, June, 1992: 6–8.

168. Headden, et al., *op. cit.*

169. *Ibid.*

170. *Ibid.*

171. *Ibid.*

172. *Ibid.*, p. 48.

173. *Ibid.*, p. 50.

174. *Ibid.*

175. *Ibid.*

176. *Ibid.*

177. *Ibid.*, p. 50.

178. *Ibid.*, p. 51.

179. Employment Retirement Security Act of 1974. P.L. 93–406. http://www.ssa.gov/OP_Home/comp2/F093-406.html

180. U.S. Congress, Senate, Permanent Subcommittee on Investigations, Committee on Governmental Affairs, "Fraud and Abuse in Employer Sponsored Health Benefit Plans." 100 Congress, 2nd Session, May 15, 1990: p. 122. In the early 1990s, a number of states began to change their laws, with federal approval, so that MEWAs could be more closely regulated by state insurance commissions.

181. *Ibid.*, p. 51.

182. U.S. Congress. House. Committee on Energy and Commerce. Subcommittee on Oversight and Investigations. "Failed Promises: Insurance Company Insolvencies," February, 1990. Washington, DC: Government Printing Office; p. 31.

183. *Ibid.*, p. 60.

184. Headden, Witkin, and Lord, *op. cit.*

185. Source: Tillman, Robert. Global Pirates: *Fraud in the Offshore Insurance Industry.* Boston: Northeastern University Press, 2002.

186. *Ibid.*, p. 52.

187. *Ibid.*

188. *Ibid.*

189. *Ibid.*

190. *Ibid.*

191. *Ibid.*, p. 112.

192. Dannen, Frederic. "Miami vice." *Institutional Investor* 20, 1986: pp. 170–174.

193. U.S. Congress, Senate, Permanent Subcommittee on Investigations, Committee on Governmental Affairs, "Efforts to Combat Fraud and Abuse in the Insurance Industry: Part II." 102nd Congress, First Session, June 26, 1991; p. 33.

194. U.S. Congress, Senate, Permanent Subcommittee on Investigations, Committee on Governmental Affairs, "Efforts to Combat Fraud and Abuse in the Insurance Industry: Part I." 102nd Congress, First Session, April 24, 1991: pp. 22–53.

195. Ridenhour, Ron. "Plundered Lives." *Penthouse*, December, 1993: p. 58.

196. U.S. Congress, Senate, Permanent Subcommittee on Investigations, Committee on Governmental Affairs, "Efforts to Combat Fraud and Abuse in the Insurance Industry: Part III." 102nd Congress, 1st Session, July 19, 1991: p. 79.

197. *Ibid.*, p. 90.

198. Cohen, Stefanie. "$44 Mil Fannie Fleecer." *nypost.com*, September 12, 2008.

199. *mortgagefraudblog.com.* "Olympia Mortgage Principals Indicted." May 14, 2008.

200. DeStefano, Anthony M. "2 charged With Looting Millions in Mortgage Scams." *newsday.com*, May 8, 2008.

201. McCool, Grant. "New York Lender Admits to Fraud of Fannie Mae." Reuters. September 11, 2008.

202. Lubasch, Arnold. "Rabbi Who Said He Bribed Flood Gets Two Years and $17,000 Fine." *New York Times*, June 23, 1978: A1.

203. McKim, Jennifer B. "Broker Says She's Guilty in Subprime Loan Case." *boston.com*, January 14, 2009.

204. Blake, Rob K. "Fremong Investment & Loan Review." *themortgageinsider.net,* October 29, 2008.

205. *Ibid.*

206. Utt, Ronald D. "The Subprime Mortgage Market Collapse: A Primer on the Causes and Possible Solutions." *heritage.org,* April 22, 2008.

207. *Ibid.*

208. *Ibid.*

209. *Ibid.*

210. *Ibid.*

211. Cresswell, Julie and Bajaj, Vikas. "$3.2 Billion Move by Bear Stearns to Rescue Fund." *nytimes.com,* June 23, 2007.

212. Goldstein, Matthew. "Bear Stearns' Subprime Bath." *businessweek.com,* June 12, 2007.

213. *Ibid.*

214. Godoy, Maria. "Fed's Moves Highlight Fragile State of Market." *npr.org,* March 21, 2008.

215. *Ibid.*

216. Quoted in Clark, Andrew. "Feds Charge Bear Pair With Fraud Over $1.4bn Sub-Prime Collapse." *guardian.co.uk,* June 20, 2008.

217. Hays, Tom. "Ralph Cioffi, Matthew Tannin Verdict: Ex-Bear Stearns Hedge Fund Managers Not Guilty on All Fraud Charges." *Huffingtonpost.com.* November 10, 2009.

218. *Ibid.*

219. Adama, Nick. "Merrill Lynch and the Subprime Mortgage Market." *ezinearticles.com,* October 20, 2008.

220. Gray, Barry. "Merrill Lynch *Reports* Billions in Losses Amidst Growing Signs of US Recession." *wsws.org,* October 26, 2007.

221. *Ibid.*

222. Adama, *op. cit.*

223. Quaratiello, Frank. "Merrill Lynch Settles Up." *bostonherald.com,* August 22, 2008.

224. *latimes.com.* "Merrill Lynch Accused of Fraud For Risky Sub-Prime Investments," February 2, 2008.

225. Miller, Brett and Ho, Chua Kong. "Merrill Lynch Cut to 'Sell' at Goldman on Writedowns." *bloomberg.com,* September 5, 2008.

226. Drawbaugh, Kevin. "Bank of America in Talks for More Bailout Funds." *newsdaily.com,* January 15, 2009.

227. Karnitschnig, Matthew, Mollenkamp, Carrick, and Fitzpatrick, Dan. "Bank of America Reaches Deal for Merrill." *wjs.com,* September 14, 2008.

228. marketwatch.com. "Cash for Trash?" January 18, 2009.

229. Read, Madlen. "Thain Out at BOA After Losses at Merrill Lynch." *knoxnews.com,* January 24. 2009.

230. Quinn, James. "Merrill Lynch's John Thain Waives Bonus After Outcry." *telegraph.co.uk,* December 8, 2008.

231. *msnbc.com.* "Former Merrill CEO Thain Resigns from BofA." January 23, 2009.

232. *nytimes.com.* "Thain's Office Overhaul Said to Cost $1.2 Million." January 22, 2009.

233. *Ibid.*

234. Bissonette, Zac. "Merrill Lynch Spent $1.22 Million Redecorating for John Thain." *bloggingstocks.com,* January 22, 2009.

235. Fein, Alan. "Bank of America Gets 2nd Bailout." *axcessnews.com,* January 27, 2009.

236. Kulikowski, Laura. "Lehman Brothers Amputates Mortgage Arm." *thestreet.com,* August 22, 2007.

237. Anderson, Jenny and Dash, Eric. "Struggling Lehman Plans to Lay Off 1,500." *nytimes.com,* August 29, 2008.

238. *Ibid.*

239. *afp.google.com.* "Lehman Brothers in Freefall as Hopes Fade For New Capital," September 10, 2008.

240. White, Ben. "Lehman Sees $3.9 Billion Loss and Plans to Shed Assets." *nytimes.com,* September 11, 2008.

241. Anderson, Jenny. "As Pressure Builds, Lehman Said to Be Looking For a Buyer." *nytimes.com,* September 11, 2008.

242. Palij, Philip. "Architects of Destruction." *ourfuture.org,* December 2, 2008.

243. Quoted in *Ibid.*

244. *reuters.com.* "Lehman Hires Jeb Bush as Private Equity Adviser." August 30, 2007.

245. Wearden, Graeme, Teather, David, and Treanor, Jill. "Banking Crisis: Lehman Brothers Files For Bankruptcy Protection." The Guardian. September 15, 2008.

246. cnn.com. "Lehman Brothers Collapse Stuns Global Markets." September 15, 2008.

247. Ross, Brian. "Lehman Had Long Relationship With Suspect Mortgage Brokers." *abcnews.com,* September 15, 2008.

248. Harney, Kenneth R. "First Alliance Mortgage Settles 'Predatory Lending' Charges For Up to $60 Million." *realtytimes.com,* March 22, 2002.

249. *ftc.gov.* "Home Mortgage Lender Settles 'Predatory Lending' Charges." March 21, 2002.

250. Harney, *op. cit.*

251. Reckard, E. Scott. "Lehman Bros. Held Liable in Fraud Case." *Los Angeles Times,* June 17, 2003: C1.

252. *mortgagegrapevine.com.* "Lehman Brothers Gets Hit For $5.1 Million Judgment For Aiding First Alliance in Predatory Loans." June 24, 2003.

253. Rayman, Graham. "Wall Streetwalkers: The Sleazy Lehman Brothers Subsidiary." *villagevoice.com*, November 5, 2008.

254. *Ibid.*

255. *Ibid.*

256. *Ibid.*

257. Morgenson, Gretchen and Story, Louise. "In Financial Crisis, No Prosecutions of Top Figures." *nytimes.com.* April 14, 2011.

258. *Ibid.*

259. Sandler, Linda. "Lehman Brokerage Payout Call Gets Louder After Four Years." *businessweek.com*, September 15, 2012.

260. Graybow, Martha and Rothacker, Rick. "BofA Pays $2.4 Billion to Settle Claims Over Merrill." *reuters.com*, September 28, 2012.

261. Zibel, Alan. "What is LIBOR, and How Does it Affect You?" *seattletimes.com*, September 30, 2008.

262. *Ibid.*

263. *Ibid.*

264. Mollenkamp, Carrick and Whitehouse, Mark. "Study Casts Doubt on Key Rate." *wsj.com.* May 29, 2008.

265. Gyntelberg, Jacob and Wooldridge, Philip. "Interbank Rate Fixings During Recent Turmoil." *Bank of International Settlements Quarterly Review,* March 2008.

266. Snider, Connan and Youle, Thomas. "Does the LIBOR Reflect Banks' Borrowing Costs?" *ssrn.com*, April 2, 2010.

267. *economist.com.* "Eagle Fried." June 30, 2012.

268. Mollenkamp, Carrick. "U.S. Conducting Criminal LIBOR Probe." *reuters.com.* February 28, 2012.

269. Treanor, Jill. "Barclays fined £290m as Bid to Manipulate Interest Rates is Exposed." *Guardian.co.uk,* June 27, 2012.

270. *reuters.com.* "Barclays Chairman Resigns Over Interest Rate Rigging Scandal." July 2, 2012.

271. *bbc.co.uk.* "Barclays Boss Bob Diamond Resigns Amid LIBOR Scandal." July 3, 2012.

272. Keenan, Douglas. "My Thwarted Attempt to Tell of LIBOR Shenanigans." *ft.com,* July 27, 2012.

273. Treanor, Jill and Rushe, Dominic. "Timothy Geithner and Mervyn King Discussed LIBOR Worries in 2008." *guardian.co.uk.* July 17, 2012.

274. Treanor, Jill. "Serious Fraud Office to Investigate LIBOR Manipulation." *guardian.co.uk,* July 6, 2012.

275. *Los Angeles Times.* "Phantom Banks Bilk Investors Out of Millions." September 12, 1994: p. D6.

276. Quoted in Suskind, Ron. "Help Me, Clarence! The Building & Loan Has Lost Billions!" *Wall Street Journal,* December 14, 1990: pp. A1, A11.

9

Crimes by the Government

No area of white-collar crime is more infectious than crimes by the government. A government that breaks the law encourages emulation by other elite institutions. In 1928, Justice Louis Brandeis wrote a famous dissent in an early case involving the domestic surveillance of citizens, in which he warned that governmental lawlessness was "contagious." Brandeis further noted that persons in power who disregard or violate the Constitutional tenets upon which the United States was built place our political contract in jeopardy: "In a government of laws, the existence of the government will be imperiled if it fails to observe the law scrupulously."[1]

In this chapter, we will examine how some officials of the American government have discarded fundamental principles of democracy, civil liberty, and morality in the name of expedience. Three illustrative topics will be considered: (1) the use of human "guinea pigs;" (2) violation of sovereignty; and (3) abuse of power.

USE OF HUMAN GUINEA PIGS

Officially condoned abuses of unknowing or unwilling human subjects immediately suggest the crimes of the Third Reich, where military doctors performed hideous medical experiments on concentration camp prisoners. Without a doubt, no society ever carried human experimentation to such a monstrous extreme; but the United States does have a shameful history of its own.

At the core of the Nazi atrocities was the concept of eugenics—the "improvement" of the human race through such practices as selective breeding and compulsory sterilization. Even before this perverted synthesis of social Darwinism and Mendelian biology was tried in Germany, the eugenics movement thrived in the U.S. In fact, the United States and Germany remain the only "civilized" Western nations in which sterilization laws were enforced. By the time the infamous Nuremberg Laws were enacted in Germany in 1935, providing for sterilization of those who were considered genetically unfit to propagate the species, an estimated 20,000 Americans deemed feeble-minded or morally degenerate already had been sterilized—12,000 in California alone.[2]

In 1933, the *Journal of the American Medical Association* published a report entitled "Sterilization to Improve the Race." Although the subject of the report was Germany's new sterilization laws, the uncritical language helped provide American eugenics statutes with a veneer of scientific respectability:

> Countless individuals of inferior type and possessing serious hereditary defects are propagating unchecked with the result that their diseased progeny becomes a burden to society and is threatening within three generations to overwhelm completely the valuable strata. . . [S]terilization is the only sure means of preventing the further hereditary transmission of mental disease and serious defects.[3]

Between 1924 and 1972, the state of Virginia sterilized over 8,300 mentally retarded citizens.[4] This practice, rooted in what has been called the "biology of stupidity,"[5] was upheld by the U.S. Supreme Court in a landmark 1927 ruling in *Buck v. Bell.*[6] This case involved the first victim of Virginia's Compulsory Sterilization Law—a teenage girl named Carrie Buck, who had been committed to the notorious Lynchburg Colony for Epileptics and the Feebleminded and subsequently was sterilized without her agreement or understanding.[7] Writing for the Court, Justice Oliver Wendell Holmes declared: "Three generations of imbeciles is enough."[8]

Lamentably, the fate of Carrie Buck was no aberration. The total number of Americans sterilized under eugenics statutes has been estimated at 63,000.[9] Although many of these laws have been repealed, sterilization without a subject's consent still was permitted in 14 states as recently as 1985.[10] In a more modern variation on this theme, a mother, charged in 1991 with beating her children after she caught them smoking, was sentenced by a California court to a year in prison. A condition of her release on probation at the end of that period was that she be given the contraceptive drug Norplant, which must be implanted *surgically* in a woman's forearm.[11] Civil libertarians have expressed concern that such compulsory contraception violates medical ethics by involving doctors in operations that have nothing to do with medicine, *per se*, and abrogates women's rights to control their procreative capacity. As one observer has noted: "Far from being part of a new trend, these cases hark back to old-fashioned eugenics plans to 'improve' society by ensuring that 'undesirables' do not reproduce."[12]

While most states ended their forced sterilization programs by the early 1970s, we are still living with the legacies of these horrific policies today. In 1933, North Carolina established the Eugenics Board of North Carolina whose stated mission was to "protect children of future generations and the community at large."[13] Between 1933 and 1974, when the practice was ended, more than 7,600 individuals, over 2,000 of them under the age of 18, underwent forced sterilization. While North Carolina law allowed sterilization for three categories of conditions—epilepsy, sickness, and feeblemindedness—the procedure was imposed on a much broader range of victims whose perceived deficiencies included things like homosexuality and sexual promiscuity.[14] The effort emerged in the midst of the broader eugenics movement referred to above. The North Carolina program received significant support from wealthy local backers, like hosiery king James Hanes, who joined forces with national eugenics leaders like Dr. Clarence Gamble, the heir to the Proctor & Gamble fortune. The local elites formed the Human Betterment League and embarked on an extensive public relations campaign to promote the Eugenics Board and its practices. These rich supporters of the program claimed that their motivations were humane, but in fact their primary concerns were more self-serving.

> The rich helped bankroll the program's expansion, and part of the motivation was financial. Awash with inherited money, Hanes and Gamble were concerned about how much welfare mothers and the mentally ill were costing taxpayers.[15]

In April 2012, the Governor of North Carolina announced she was putting $10.3 million in the state's budget to compensate the victims of the program with $50,000 each for their suffering.[16] However, in June, when the state's legislature approved a budget, no money was allocated for compensation. One state senator summed up the feelings of many of those opposed to compensation when he said: "A great wrong was done, but we didn't do it."[17]

It also is worth noting that one of the most widely discussed books in recent years is *The Bell Curve*,[18] published in 1994, a pseudo-scientific affirmation of racially based theories of intellectual inferiority. Some critics have attacked this book as a harbinger of a potential revival of the eugenics movement in the 21st Century.

The Tuskegee Syphilis Experiment

The best-documented human guinea pig case in American history is the Tuskegee Study of Untreated Syphilis in the Negro Male.[19] For forty years, between 1932 and 1972, the United States Public Health Service, in cooperation with local health officials, withheld all treatment from more than 400 syphilitic men in an economically depressed, predominantly black county in rural Alabama. The purpose of the Tuskegee study was to compare the incidence of death and debilitation among untreated subjects with a treated sample of syphilitic men, as well as a healthy control group. "[S]yphilis is a highly contagious infection spread by sexual contact, and . . . if untreated, it can lead to blindness; deafness; deterioration of the bones, teeth, and the central nervous system; heart disease; insanity; and even death."[20] An infected mother may transmit syphilis to a fetus.[21]

All the untreated subjects were uneducated black sharecroppers and laborers. The Tuskegee study thus has to be viewed within the context of the ingrained racist beliefs permeating the American medical establishment of the time. The social Darwinism that had spurred the eugenics movement had generated a fallacious agreement "that the health of blacks had to be considered separately from the health of whites."[22] Many doctors thought that Africans were genetically pre-disposed toward sexual promiscuity. "In this atmosphere it was not surprising that physicians depicted syphilis as the quintessential black disease."[23]

The Tuskegee study emerged from a syphilis control survey that had been carried out by Alabama health officials in 1930 at the instigation of a local white plantation owner who had noticed a decline in the live birth rate among his 700 black tenants and had attributed it to syphilis. A curious feature of the program was its avoidance of the word "syphilis." Instead, the health officials told subjects that they had come to test people for "bad blood"—a catchall phrase from the rural black argot, used for everything from indigestion to pellagra.[24]

The survey revealed even a higher incidence of syphilis than had been expected, so, when the program was terminated in 1932, some doctors from the U.S. Public Health Service (PHS) perceived what one termed a "ready-made opportunity"[25] to study untreated syphilis in a living outside the world of modern medicine.

The afflicted men identified by the survey were sent an imposing letter, which invoked the authority of the Macon County Health Department, the Alabama State Board of Health, the U.S. Public Health Service, and even Tuskegee Institute, the eminent college known as the "black Harvard."[26] The opening paragraph read:

> Some time ago you were given a thorough examination and since that time we hope you have gotten a great deal of treatment for bad blood. You will now be given your last chance to get a second examination. This examination is a very special one and

after it is finished you will be given a special treatment if it is believed you are in a condition to stand it.[27]

The letter closed with an ominous exhortation, written in capital letters that jumped off the page: "REMEMBER THIS IS YOUR LAST CHANCE FOR SPECIAL TREATMENT."[28] In its skillful exploitation of the subjects' ignorance and desire for medical care, the letter was a "masterpiece of guileful deceit."[29] Among the "special treatments" in store were spinal taps performed without anesthesia.[30]

Participants were not told about the true nature of the experiment. The idea of the study was to observe the subjects over the course of their lives and eventually bring them to autopsy. Burial stipends would be provided to the families of the deceased. Over the next four decades, 161 autopsies were performed.

No therapeutic intervention ever was provided for the subjects, neither for their wives who invariably contracted the disease, nor for their children who subsequently were born with congenital syphilis. Even when antibiotics became available in 1946, and penicillin emerged as an effective drug for syphilis, treatment still was denied.[31] This is particularly troubling, because the advent of penicillin seemingly obviated any rational purpose to the experiment. As one PHS officer finally would acknowledge, 38 years too late: "Nothing learned will prevent, find, or cure a single case of infectious syphilis or bring us closer to our basic mission of controlling venereal disease in the United States."[32] Indeed, the only contribution the Tuskegee study ever made to medical science was keeping laboratories supplied with syphilitic blood samples for testing purposes. "The benefit seems small when one remembers that some of the blood donors later died from syphilis."[33]

In 1965, a young venereal disease investigator employed by the PHS first heard about the ongoing Tuskegee Study from co-workers. "He had difficulty believing the stories."[34] After reviewing all the articles and official documents on the experiment, he was horrified and began warning his superiors that the ethical and racial aspects of the study were potentially explosive: "The excuses and justifications that might have been offered for starting the study in 1932 were no longer relevant. . . . [Subjects] were nothing more than dupes and were being used as human substitutes for guinea pigs."[35]

Two years after joining the PHS, the investigator resigned. The following year he wrote a letter to the director of the Division of Venereal Diseases, re-expressing grave moral concerns about the experiment. In 1972, he finally told the "bad blood" story to the press. The outrage was predictable. Senator Abraham Ribicoff labeled the Tuskegee study a "frightening instance of bureaucratic arrogance and insensitivity."[36]

Seventy surviving subjects sued the government, and in 1974 an Alabama court awarded each $37,500. When divided by 40 years, that sum worked out to $2.50 a day.[37]

The "bad blood" study was by no means the government's only 40-year excursion into human experimentation. From 1938 to at least 1978, "there was an effort made by the agencies of the U.S. government to develop sophisticated techniques of psycho-politics and mind control."[38] This dangerous research involved tens of thousands of subjects—many of them involuntary.[39] These unwitting human guinea pigs were victimized by an amoral cadre of psychiatrists, psychologists, and chemists under contract to various government agencies, most notably the CIA.[40]

Among the areas under study were: (1) the use of hypnosis to induce amnesia or elicit false confessions;[41] and (2) the refinement of powerful conditioning techniques, such as sensory deprivation, desensitization, and aversion therapy, to control human behavior;[42] In the words of one journalist, these and other methods "were eventually developed and used to reduce some of our own citizens to a zombie state in which they would blindly serve the government."[43] In 1958, the CIA even prepared a report which suggested that the intelligence agencies might control people through drug addiction. "The report went so far as to recommend that wounded GIs who had become addicts to pain-killing drugs be recruited from hospitals."[44]

One of the most chilling examples of mind control research was that of Dr. David Cameron at the Allen Memorial Institute in Montreal, Canada. The CIA funded the "brainwashing" experiments Cameron conducted between 1957 and 1963. A Canadian facility was utilized because Cameron's work was so repulsive in nature that, for once, the CIA was apparently unwilling to violate the proscription against the conducting of domestic operations by the agency.

Cameron specialized in two mind control techniques: *depatterning* and *psychic driving*. The objective of depatterning is the disintegration of a subject's personality. This was accomplished through: (1) repeated electroconvulsive shock treatment—at levels up to forty times the intensity considered safe; (2) massive doses of hallucinogenic drugs—including LSD; and (3) lengthy periods of drug-induced sleep—lasting as long as ninety days.[45] Psychic driving is aimed at breaking down a subject's free will. Individuals were locked in a darkened cell and bombarded incessantly with selected messages. These unfortunate subjects were the hospitalized mental patients at Allen Memorial. Cameron's work destroyed the minds, bodies, and lives of his victims.[46] That it was financed and supported by the American government compounds the outrage.

The CIA, in fact, has a long history of complicity in medical abuse. Its immediate predecessor, the Office of Strategic Services (OSS), once tested the effects of concentrated marijuana on suspected Communists.[47] When the CIA began experimenting with LSD in the early 1950s, it determined that members of the borderline underworld would make the best subjects, because even if they realized that they had been drugged, they would not go to the police. LSD was administered covertly to prostitutes, addicts, and petty criminals. One agent even slipped some LSD to a lieutenant of mob boss Lucky Luciano.[48] "[The CIA] reasoned that if they had to violate the civil rights of anyone, they might as well choose marginal people."[49]

In 1953, the agency decided to test LSD on a group of unsuspecting scientists from the Army Chemical Corps. The drug was mixed into their after-dinner drinks. "The dose pushed one of its victims—Frank Olson—into a psychotic confusion; several days later . . . Olson [apparently] leapt to his death from a New York hotel window."[50] For 26 years, the cause of Olson's death had been concealed from his family, who had been led to believe that he had committed suicide because of an unexplained mental breakdown.[51] When Olson's family was finally told the circumstances of his death, they questioned that he had jumped. On June 2, 1994, more than forty years after Frank Olson's purported leap, his body was exhumed. Forensic remains revealed that "[s]kull injuries and the lack of cuts on the body were inconsistent with the CIA's description of events surrounding his death."[52] Whatever really happened to Frank Olson seems destined to remain a mystery.

The first Director of the CIA, Allen Dulles, had approved another early method of testing mind-altering drugs on unwitting subjects. "[A]n arrangement had been made with the Bureau of Narcotics whereby the CIA financed and established 'safe houses' in which federal narcotics agents could dispense the drugs and record the reactions of those who took them."[53] The San Francisco "safe house" even employed prostitutes,[54] who would drug their customers—whose behavior then would be observed by agents through two-way mirrors.[55] The victims were chosen randomly in bars and off the street. Many of these unwary "johns" subsequently required hospitalization.[56]

During the Cold War the CIA also tested knockout drugs and incapacitating substances at Georgetown University. These experiments were disguised as legitimate "anticancer" research.

"[T]he pool of subjects consisted of terminal cancer patients who had no idea they were being used as guinea pigs in a CIA drug project."[57]

The CIA, however, is not the only branch of the government with a record of questionable involvement in human experimentation. The military had engaged in unethical medical practices at least since 1900, when Dr. Walter Reed used Army volunteers to test his theory that deadly yellow fever was transmitted by mosquitoes. Reed's soldiers permitted themselves to be bitten by infected insects. Medical historians now wonder how much the Army had pressured these "volunteers" to risk contracting a disease for which there was no known treatment.[58] Researchers funded by the United States Army once fed hepatitis viruses to retarded infants at New York's Willowbrook State School.[59] Moreover, the Army itself conducted covert germ warfare tests over a 20-year period. In 1950, the Army blanketed the San Francisco region with a microorganism called *Serratia marcescens.* "Worried about the effects of lethal germs that might be sprayed by the Soviet Union on an unsuspecting American public, the Pentagon had decided to unleash its own, supposedly harmless, bacteria into the air and trace the germs along their windblown journeys until they settled into the lungs of American citizens."[60] Although the Army still maintains that *Serratia marcescens* is harmless, there is considerable evidence that it can be lethal. "In the late 1970s, doctors in the San Francisco area reported a surge of infections and death caused by *Serratia marcescens.*"[61]

One of the Army's most brazen experiments took place over a four-day period in 1966. Another micro-organism, this one called *Bacillus subtilis,* was dumped into the heart of the New York City subway system. A report on this test, released later under the Freedom of Information Act, described the scene:

"When the cloud engulfed people," the report says, "they brushed their clothing, looked up at the grating apron and walked on.". . . The experiment was a huge success. Everyone was breathing the bacteria and no one was ever aware of it.[62]

Bacillus subtilis is nearly indestructible, and most of the bacteria dropped in 1966 may remain throughout the 21st Century.[63]

[H]ow dangerous is *Bacillus subtilis*? It is dangerous indeed if one happens to be allergic to it, or is very old, very young, very ill or very anything that classifies a person as a compromised host. Might such people have been riding the subways? Of course. But beyond that, the exposed commuters became carriers, and took the bacteria with them as they traveled to their homes, to their offices or to hospitals to visit elderly relatives."[64]

A spokesperson for the Army's scientific division defended its simulated biological warfare tests by characterizing them as less hazardous than an urban bus ride:

"[W]hen you get on the bus in Philadelphia or New York, you're going to be riding with a bunch of people—the Chinese, the Vietnamese, the blacks, the lower-class Irish and all these people—that may have tuberculosis and never know it, and be coughing in your face, and end up exposing you to a far more serious type of organism than what was being sprayed into the air."[65]

The bigotry and contempt for humanity that oozes out of every crack in the preceding statement goes a long way toward answering the inevitable "How could they do that?" questions.

The use of unknowing human guinea pigs is not unique to the Army, however. In the late 1950s, doctors working for the Air Force fed about 100 Alaskan Eskimos radioactive drugs to test nuclear survival in Arctic climates.[66] As recently as 1972, the Air Force was supporting LSD research at the Universities of Missouri and Minnesota. One misled subject, an 18-year-old girl, went into a catatonic state for three days.[67]

The U.S. Navy has the distinction of overseeing perhaps the most sickening of all the military experiments. The Navy earned this dubious honor between 1943 and 1945 because the research in question was so gruesome that even the Army was reluctant to participate. At a time when the horrors of Auschwitz were still hidden from the world, the Navy was building its own gas chambers—not in Eastern Europe but in Washington, D.C., and Maryland.

As always, military secrecy provided a permissive environment for cruelty and abuse. Wartime documents reveal that the sailors were ordered into the chambers and threatened with court-martial if they refused.[68]

Some of the experiments were termed—meaning the exposure to mustard gas continued until the subject was "broken."[69] One of those "broken" was a 17-year-old sailor, who had just completed his basic training in mid-winter. He was asked to volunteer to test clothing under tropical conditions. Thinking he would be sent to a warmer climate, he put his name on the list. In fact, he traveled only 25 miles, and the "tropical clothing" consisted of a gas mask.

Today, 50 years later, he is totally disabled.

Unfortunately, philosopher George Santayana's familiar warning about the consequences of failing to learn from the past[70] was punctuated during the Persian Gulf War in 1990. An unapproved pretreatment drug for nerve gas attacks, that had never been clinically tested, was administered to American soldiers without their consent.

Radiation Experiments

In November 1993, a newspaper in Albuquerque, New Mexico, uncovered documents revealing that the government had injected 18 civilians with highly radioactive plutonium in the 1940s in an effort to determine what doses workers could be exposed to safely. Rumors of widespread secret radiation testing, which had been circulating for decades, could no longer be dismissed officially. A week after the Albuquerque story broke, the government acknowledged that it had conducted 800 radiation tests on humans, some of whom were unaware of the risks. As the scandal unfolded over the next year, it became apparent that there was plenty of blame to go around.

The now-defunct Atomic Energy Commission (AEC), for example, sanctioned research at the University of Chicago in the 1950s involving the cremation of 44 newly deceased infants and the chemical analysis of residual radioactive material in their ashes.[71] This designated "Chicago Baby Project" was meant to determine the fallout effects from the nuclear weapons tests of that period. Official reports indicated that parents probably were not notified or asked permission for the use of their children's corpses in the experiments.[72] In another AEC-sponsored study, at the Massachusetts General Hospital, researchers injected pregnant women with radioactive iodine 24 hours before scheduled therapeutic abortions. A day later, the doctors then removed the fetuses intact to measure how much radiation was absorbed in the patients' thyroid glands.[73]

The AEC also practiced human experimentation on live subjects at least through the late 1960s, when 14 workers at the Hanford nuclear weapons plant in Washington State purposefully were exposed to promethium—a substance used in the manufacture of atomic bombs.[74]

Mentally retarded teenage boys at the Fernald State School in Massachusetts were used as guinea pigs in radiation studies sponsored by the AEC and conducted by Harvard University and the Massachusetts Institute of Technology between 1946 and 1956. The boys were fed radioactive milk and breakfast cereal in order to study the body's digestive ability.[75] These innocent "volunteers" were told that they were joining a "science club."[76]

In late 1997, MIT and Quaker Oats agreed to pay $1.85 million to 15 former residents of the Fernald School who were fed radiation-spiked breakfast cereal in nutrition experiments conducted in the 1940s and 1950s. This research, conducted to give Quaker Oats a competitive advantage in the cereal market, was conducted without the informed consent of the children's parents.[77]

Researchers from Harvard and Boston University fed radioactive iodine to 60 mentally retarded children at the Wrentham State School, also in Massachusetts, in the early 1960s, in order to test a possible antidote to fallout from nuclear blasts.[78] In 1994, a state panel condemned this research in unmistakable terms: "For government researchers concerned about radioactive fallout to use institutionalized children is an insult to the children, their families and to everyone concerned with individual rights and dignities."[79]

The Defense Department, too, has engaged in questionable radiation experiments on humans. During the 1950s, substantial amounts of radiation were released into the environment as a part of a secret military program aimed at developing a weapon that would kill enemy soldiers with radioactive fallout. In at least twelve underground tests, at the Los Alamos Laboratory in New Mexico, the Army detonated conventional bombs containing large concentrations of nuclear materials. In some cases, the ensuing radioactive cloud of particles was detectible in communities 70 miles away.[80]

To medical researchers, more interested in obtaining federal funds and winning academic honors than in maintaining ethical standards, the poor were an especially appealing target for human experimentation. One scientist has defended the use of "charity" patients as an economically fair exchange of services: "We were taking care of them, and felt we had a right to get some return from them."[81] For example, a team of researchers from Tulane University conducted a series of radiation experiments at New Orleans' Charity Hospital in 1946, under a grant from the U.S. War Department (the forerunner of the Defense Department). These experiments involved at least 300 patients.

> For more than a decade, mostly black female patients swallowed or were injected with the radiation equivalent of up to 100 chest X-rays in one experiment . . . The research could be unpleasant, sometimes requiring test subjects to endure 118-degree heat, intestinal blisters or diarrhea.[82]

At the time, Charity Hospital was a manifestation of an overtly racist society. The facility was woefully overcrowded and underfunded, 25 patients might share a single toilet, "and the bedridden could suffer malnutrition if family members did not feed them."[83] In a 1994 interview, a former member of the Tulane research team portrayed the radiation experiments as a blessing to the "lucky" subjects:

> The patients that we used for research really loved us. They really did. . . . They got the most attention. We saw them several times a day. We cared about their diets.[84]

However, the Vice-Chancellor for Research at Tulane Medical Center provided a less philanthropic retrospective:

> "The whole population of the hospital was used for guinea pigs."[85]

Between 1942 and 1946, the U.S. Army conducted research in which dying patients were exposed to powerful X-rays in order to examine the effect of radiation on the body. One subject was a California house painter believed to be suffering from terminal stomach cancer. He was injected with plutonium at a level "many times the so-called lethal textbook dose."[86] He was never told the nature of the experiment, and, in a gruesome good news/bad news scenario, a biopsy performed the next day revealed that he had an ulcer, not cancer.

Another experimental subject abused by the Army was a 17-year-old soldier who, in 1957, was ordered to stand up a few thousand yards from ground zero and watch the detonation of a hydrogen bomb.[87] "In 1988, at the age of 49, he had already suffered two strokes, deterioration of the spine and muscle weakness so severe he was confined to a wheelchair."[88]

Between 1960 and 1972, the Defense Department sponsored research at the University of Cincinnati Medical School in order to discover how much radiation a soldier could endure before becoming disoriented.[89] Eighty-six cancer patients, ranging in age from 9 to 84, were exposed to intense doses of radiation at levels "that were known to make people acutely ill."[90] Most of these hapless patients were indigent; 60 percent were black.[91] Nine of the first 40 subjects died within 38 days.[92]

When the Cincinnati researchers first published their findings in 1969, in the *Archives of General Psychiatry*, they insisted that informed consent had been obtained from each subject.[93] According to the Nuremberg Code of 1947—a statement of internationally recognized bioethical principles composed by the War Crimes Tribunal—informed consent is an absolutely inviolable requirement for human experimentation.[94] However, the Cincinnati researchers also reported that their 16 initial subjects had a mean educational level of 4.2 years, a low functioning mean IQ, and strong evidence of cerebral organic deficit.[95] It is highly questionable if the notion of "informed consent" can be applied to such subjects in any meaningful way. Moreover, the very title of the article, "Total and Half Body Irradiation: *Effect on Cognitive and Emotional Processes* [italics added], suggests that "cancer therapy was *not* the true purpose of the research."[96]

In 1994, Dr. David Egilman of Brown University analyzed the Cincinnati study and came to a disturbing conclusion: the "terminal" subjects were not even terminally ill. Egilman contends that most of the subjects were in relatively good health prior to irradiation, and that at least 8 and probably more than 20 of them died as a result of the experiment.[97]

Following an exhaustive two-year archival study of classified documents undertaken by the Department of Energy at the request of President Clinton, the federal government admitted in 1995 that 4,000 radiation experiments had been conducted between 1945 and 1974.[98] Most of the subjects were infants, pregnant women, terminally ill patients, poor people, or other vulnerable targets.[99] As one professor of medicine has observed: "That's the history of human experimentation. It's always using the poor or women, never white middle-class men."[100] Among the more exploitative examples of such studies are the following:

- Washington University researchers injected about 140 children, most of them healthy newborns or premature infants, with radioactive sodium. Likewise, researchers at the Beth Israel Hospital in Boston injected tracer doses of radioactive sodium into terminally ill patients.[101]

- Columbia University researchers also gave 880 pregnant women tracer doses of radioactive sodium. Today, of course, doctors "strongly urge pregnant women to avoid radiation exposure."[102]

- Researchers at Vanderbilt University gave 819 pregnant women radioactive iron to determine its effect on fetal development.[103] "A follow-up study of children born to the women found a higher-than-normal cancer rate."[104]

- A research team from the Massachusetts General Hospital injected or fed radium to 20 elderly residents of a nursing home to measure the passage of that substance through their bodies. This same hospital also injected 12 terminal brain tumor patients with uranium to determine the dose at which kidney damage begins to occur.[105]
- Researchers at Boston's Brigham and Women's Hospital injected subjects with radioactive sodium, then removed a section of rib to see how much had been absorbed into the bones.
- Doctors from Harvard Medical School gave kidney transplant patients the equivalent of 65 chest X-rays to see how the exposure would affect the risk of organ rejection. The study ended abruptly when the radiation killed one patient in 28 days.[106]

The principal objectives of these studies was "to determine how quickly the radioactivity was digested or absorbed by the human body and how much damage it caused."[107] In 1994, the Chair of the congressional subcommittee that had investigated the propriety of the radiation experiments stated: "The appalling truth is that in some cases American citizens were used as nuclear calibration instruments."[108]

Finally, it is worth pondering that, in the United States, *no one* has ever been convicted of a crime involving the violation of the right to informed consent in a medical experiment that has caused harm.[109]

Prison Experiments: Who Gives a Damn?

Another controversial form of human experimentation is the use of American prisoners as subjects for medical research. In a 1950 memorandum to the Atomic Energy Commission, Dr. Joseph Hamilton of Livermore National Laboratory in California expressed his concern that "tests aimed at discovering at what level radiation would injure soldiers would conjure up images of Nazi concentration camp experiments if performed on humans."[110] Indeed, after World War II, the issue of experimentation on prisoners was stressed at the Nuremberg War Crimes trials.

Obviously, informed consent had no relevance to the Nazis, but in the United States participation usually is "voluntary," in the technical sense that prisoners must sign consent forms and waivers. However, the psychological defenselessness of a captive role makes genuine consent illusory. "[B]ecause a prisoner has limited choices, his consent to such experimentation cannot be obtained without at least the appearance of coercion."[111] The American Civil Liberties Union has estimated that approximately 10 percent of the American prison population participates in medical and drug experiments.[112]

In 1961, some Harvard University scientists gave a group of inmates at the Concord State Prison in Massachusetts between two and five doses of pellocybin, a dangerous hallucinogenic drug. The flamboyant psychopharmacologist, Timothy Leary, directed this research.

> He once used Harvard students in some of his drug experiments, and Harvard fired him two years after the Concord experiment when his own drug usage became public. . . . Later on, he was imprisoned for smuggling hashish from Afghanistan. President Nixon once described him as "the most dangerous man in America."[113]

The purpose of the Concord prison study was to test whether pellocybin could reduce the high recidivism rate among parolees. All of the participating inmates were chosen because they were scheduled for parole within three months. By 1965, four years after receiving the drug, 59 percent of the subjects were back behind bars.[114]

Between 1963 and 1971, 131 inmates in Washington and Oregon agreed to have their testicles exposed to very high levels of X-rays. This experiment was designed by the government to determine the minimum dose that would cause healthy men to become sterile. While consent forms did indicate some of the risks, no mention was made that radiation could cause testicular cancer. Furthermore, no follow-up studies ever were conducted on the prisoners after the conclusion of the study.[115] A 23-year-old convict, for example, had his testicles bombarded with a dose of radiation equivalent to twenty X-rays in 1965. He had received a stipend of $5 for his participation. Thirty years later, he complained of lumps on his body, along with testicular pain and chronic rashes. Other ex-convicts from similar studies have voiced the same complaints.[116]

At some prisons, pharmaceutical corporations have competed vigorously to purchase exclusive rights to conduct drug toxicity tests on inmates.[117] In 1975, some prisoners testified at a U.S. Senate hearing concerned with human experimentation. One was James Downey, who had been a state prisoner in Oklahoma:

> He told of having participated in a planned thirty-day program to test a potent new drug intended to cure liver ailments. Downey said he was told it was a new "wonder" drug, and was assured it would have no adverse effects.[118]

After 11 days on the "wonder" drug, Downey became very sick. He was denied any medical attention for several days and then was told he had measles. He was assured that his illness was unrelated to the drug; but Downey later learned that he was suffering from drug-induced hepatitis.[119] From the experimenters' point of view, there are two reasons why prisoners make convenient human subjects. First, because the studies take place in an outcast environment, if prisoners such as James Downey become seriously ill—or even if they happen to die—it is unlikely to generate much public concern.[120] Second, prison studies are economical. Downey told the Senate that he had volunteered in order to earn money for cigarettes. One doctor has remarked that prisoners are ideal for medical experimentation because they are "cheaper than chimpanzees."[121]

VIOLATION OF SOVEREIGNTY

In Chapters 3 and 4, we examined how American corporations have exported environmental crime and crimes against employees. There is, unfortunately, nothing unique about this pattern; most domestic varieties of white-collar crime also have been committed abroad, either by American companies or by the United States government itself. These offenses range from bribery and covert manipulation to outright interference in the affairs of other nations.

Bribery of government officials commonly is used to obtain business contracts in many foreign countries. This practice is often concealed in company books under such euphemistic entries as "facilitating payments."[122] Although bribery violates both American and international law, it has continued for many decades, because the penalties seldom exceed the gains.[123] During the 1970s, nearly 400 American corporations admitted making payments totaling $750 million to foreign officials.[124] Among the more notorious examples were the following:

- Mobil Oil contributed nearly $2 million to Italian political parties, concealing this information from its own stockholders. Exxon later admitted to a Senate subcommittee that it had given over $50 million to Italian politicians, including some Communists.[125]
- The Northrup Corporation passed on cash "gifts" of $450,000 to two Saudi Air Force generals, who in turn helped Northrup close a massive arms deal with the Saudi Arabian government.[126]

- Lockheed admitted that it had spent more than $22 million on payments to foreign officials and political organizations, in such places as Indonesia, Iran, and the Philippines. Lockheed also had paid Prince Bernhard of the Netherlands $1 million to arrange sales of its planes to the Dutch government. Moreover, Lockheed's bribery of Japanese government officials led to the worst political scandal in that nation's postwar history.[127]

- Two units of Litton industries pleaded guilty in 1999 to fraud and conspiracy involving illegal payments the company made to obtain defense business in Greece and Taiwan. The company agreed to a fine of $16.5 million and an additional $2 million to reimburse the Justice Department for the cost of its investigation.[128]

American corporations long have insisted that political bribery is a traditional and necessary cost of doing business overseas.[129] This self-serving argument ignores the considerable damage that corporate bribery inflicts on our national image abroad. It also disrespects the principle of national sovereignty, which is the cornerstone of global order. For example, a single corporation—Lockheed—effectively toppled a government in Japan, nearly destroyed the Dutch monarchy, corrupted national elections in Germany, Portugal, and Brazil, and caused the arrest of a former Italian prime minister.[130]

Agencies of the American government have disregarded the sovereignty of other nations even more recklessly than corporations. It is ironic that the United States, which was founded upon the sanctity of self-determination, has such a sorry record of denying that right to others. For example, when the Iranian government attempted to nationalize the properties of American oil companies in the early 1950s, the CIA engineered a coup that restored the dictatorial Shah to the throne.[131] In the 1960s, the CIA financed the overthrow of the left-wing government of Ecuador[132] and played a pivotal role in an Indonesian revolution in which at least 500,000 people were killed.[133]

In fact, it is now acknowledged that the CIA participated in the overthrow or attempted overthrow of numerous regimes around the world, including ones in Syria, Somalia, the Sudan, Angola, Ghana, Guatemala, and Guyana.[134] In each of these countries, "CIA intrusion has left a trail of poverty, social chaos, and political repression."[135]

During the Vietnam War, Congress had by law forbidden the hiring of mercenaries from neighboring countries or the deployment of American troops in those countries. Nevertheless, the CIA organized unlawful secret armies composed of ethnic minorities from Laos and Thailand to fight along the borders of North and South Vietnam.[136] Even more dismaying, when American troops illegally invaded Cambodia, soldiers' death certificates were falsified to read that they had died elsewhere.[137]

One of the best-known case of illegal foreign intervention occurred in Chile in the 1970s. This case represented an unsavory alliance between the governmental and corporate establishments. Since the 1920s, a giant conglomerate, International Telephone and Telegraph (ITT), had built or purchased telephone companies throughout Latin America. Over time, however, the rise of nationalization policies in that region had left ITT with only one remaining South American telephone company—in Chile, a nation conspicuously lacking a strong nationalist movement. This enterprise was worth $150 million, and ITT was determined to hold on to it.

The CIA, too, had an interest in Chile. In the 1966 Chilean election, the agency had contributed $20 million in American taxpayers' money to a victorious pro-American presidential candidate. When Chile expanded its telephone service shortly after the election, ITT received the contract, despite a lower bid from a Swedish company.[138]

During the next election, in 1970, the CIA and ITT worked in tandem against the popular socialist candidate, Salvador Allende. An estimated $13 million was spent to thwart Allende's candidacy, including the bribery of Chilean legislators to cast electoral votes against Allende.[139] Despite these concerted efforts, Allende was elected. ITT then began an intensive lobbying campaign in Congress and the State Department aimed at preventing the expropriation of American holdings in Chile. As a result, the White House stopped all loans and foreign aid to Chile, which fomented discontent in the Chilean army and provoked disruptive labor strikes.[140] Furthermore, the CIA spent millions of dollars—much of it contributed by ITT—to destabilize the Allende government. Allende was assassinated in 1973 and replaced by an oppressive military junta, friendly to American corporate and political interests.[141]

While there is only circumstantial evidence that the CIA was actively involved in the Allende assassination, that ubiquitous agency has been implicated more clearly in the murders of several other foreign leaders—such as Dominican dictator Rafael Trujillo and South Vietnamese president Ngo Din Diem.[142] The Senate Select Subcommittee on Intelligence uncovered evidence that the CIA had planned the assassination of Congolese leader Patrice Lumumba, under orders from President Eisenhower.[143] The Committee also has reported at least eight separate death plots against Cuban president Fidel Castro, ranging from lacing a box of Castro's cigars with lethal botulinium toxin to attempting to give him a poisoned wet suit for scuba diving.[144]

In 1997, a newly declassified memorandum revealed that in 1960 the CIA approached Chicago crime boss Sam Giancana and offered him $150,000 to arrange a Mafia "hit" on Castro. Giancana, who would later himself be a victim of a mob hit, turned the offer down.[145]

Recently, it was also revealed that a Salvadoran "death squad" had been trained in the United States in 1981, with the knowledge of the Reagan Administration. Those troops later massacred dozens of peasants in El Salvador.[146]

In 1984, a book entitled *Psychological Operations in Guerrilla Warfare*, attributed to the CIA, was distributed widely in Nicaragua.

> While not concerned with killing for direct military purposes, the book takes a generous attitude to killings that may be done for propaganda effect. There is a lot about "armed propaganda," and page 32 has useful hints on what to tell the population if, while proselytizing a village, you find it necessary to shoot a citizen who is trying to leave.[147]

The book also contains a primer on the selection of appropriate targets for "neutralization" (i.e., assassination), such as judges or police officers.[148] It is not by caprice that the CIA's Clandestine Services division has been labeled "the President's personal 'Saturday Night Special.'"[149]

The Iran-Contra Affair

The Iran-Contra Affair is a tale of an "invisible government"[150] sustained through deceit and contempt for the rule of law. The roots of this maze of crimes and cover-ups may be traced back to the foreign policy agenda of the new Reagan Administration in 1981. It was President Reagan's announced intention to encourage the removal of the Marxist Sandinista government in Nicaragua. Initially, there was nothing furtive about this policy; the President publicly had supported aid to the Contras, a pro-American rebel army engaged in a guerrilla war against the Sandinistas.

Congress, though, was less willing to authorize funding for an interventionist policy and passed a series of amendments between 1982 and 1986 (known as the Boland Amendments—

after their principal author, a Massachusetts congressman), severely limiting or prohibiting the appropriation of funds on behalf of the Contras. By that time, however, the White House had committed itself to backing the Contras at all costs.

> This policy could not be carried out without defying Congress. Open defiance was politically unfeasible. The only other way was to do it covertly.[151]

The Administration formulated two types of schemes for circumventing the legally imposed restraints. The first method was to give the task of arming the Contras to the National Security Council (NSC). Congress explicitly had proscribed the use of funds by the Defense Department and the CIA or any other intelligence agency on behalf of the Contras. The NSC was not technically an intelligence agency, so its utilization provided the administration with a way of evading the spirit of the law, if not the letter. The second method was to employ "private" or "third-party" funds, on the assumption that only official United States funds had been prohibited.[152] The NSC also would implement this plan. The NSC was headed by national security adviser Robert McFarlane, who had been instructed by President Reagan to keep the Contras together "body and soul."[153] McFarlane assigned this task to his chief "action officer," Marine Lieutenant Colonel Oliver North.

North, a decorated Vietnam veteran, who reportedly once had suffered a two-year emotional breakdown after the war, became the designated "contact" between the NSC and the Contras. He was appointed Deputy Director for Political Military Affairs, a vague title that removed him from the NSC chain-of-command and made him answerable only to McFarlane. In effect, an obscure soldier became a one-man operation. His job was to recruit others to help fund the Contras.

Foremost among the "others" to whom North turned were a pair of international arms dealers, retired Air Force Major General Richard Secord and his business partner, an Iranian-born American citizen named Albert Hakim. Ultimately, Secord and Hakim sold about $11 million worth of weapons to the Contras.[154] Much of their proceeds were stashed away in Swiss bank accounts. Secord later told Congress that he had been motivated solely by patriotism and would gladly give his share of the profits to the Contras.[155] He never did.

Obviously, the Contras required a large influx of cash in order to pay for weapons and equipment. In order to deceive Congress, millions of dollars had to be raised privately. This was accomplished in part through nonprofit conservative foundations. While private citizens were entitled to raise money for the Contras on their own, official cooperation by the administration entailed a criminal conspiracy—especially when donations were disguised as humanitarian assistance.

The "third-country" strategy began in 1983 when overtures were made to Israel and South Africa regarding aid to the Contras. In 1984, Saudi Arabia agreed to contribute $1 million a month, ostensibly from private funds, to help the Contras survive. The following year, the Saudis' monthly contribution was raised to $2 million. The total Saudi contribution eventually exceeded $30 million.[156] The administration realized that Nicaragua was of no real interest to Saudi Arabia (the two countries did not even have diplomatic relations); thus, the money was solicited as an opportunity for the Saudis to curry personal favor with President Reagan.

The government of Taiwan also contributed $2 million after North promised that Nicaragua would recognize the Taiwanese regime once the Sandanistas were ousted. In addition, President Reagan vetoed a bill which would have placed restrictions on imported Taiwanese textiles.[157]

The "private" and "third-country" contributions enabled the Contras to survive well into 1985. That year, the American ambassador to Costa Rica, Lewis Tambs, was instructed by North to obtain permission from the Costa Rican government for the construction of a "private" airstrip to be used to supply the Contras. When he subsequently was asked if he thought that building a secret pro-Contra military installation in a neutral country violated the Boland Amendments, Tambs replied that he had never read those amendments, since, in his words: "I have difficulty reading a contract for a refrigerator."[158]

The governments of Guatemala, El Salvador, and Honduras also were pressured into coop-eration. Honduras was particularly important, because the main Contra force was based there; all supplies had to be brought there for distribution.[159] For example, another arms dealer, retired Major General John Singlaub, purchased weapons from Eastern Europe for $4.8 million, shipped them to Honduras, and sold them to the Contras for $5.3 million.[160]

Concurrent, though seemingly unrelated, events on the other side of the globe were to further complicate an already Byzantine enterprise. Another item on the Reagan foreign policy agenda was the punishment of the Iranian regime led by the ferociously anti-American Ayotollah Khomeini. Khomeini had overthrown the despised Shah in early 1979. The following November, a group of Iranian students had stormed the United States embassy in Tehran on Khomeini's behalf and kidnapped a group of innocent Americans, holding them hostage for 444 days. In 1982, the White House accused Iran of supporting international terrorism and launched a vigor-ous campaign to block the sale of arms to that nation.

By 1984, however, another group of hostages was being held in Lebanon by Islamic extrem-ists under Khomeini's control. Ronald Reagan looked the American people in the eye and stated his position in resolute terms: "The United States gives terrorists no rewards... We make no deals."[161] These words later would come back to haunt the President like Marley's ghost.

On August 6, 1985, McFarlane met with Reagan to discuss a proposal to use Israel for the sale of 100 TOWs (an acronym for Tube-launched Optically-tracked Wire-guided missiles) to Iran, with the deal to be followed by the release of the American hostages. The President later acknowledged that he had authorized the sale, then said that he had *not* authorized the sale, and finally claimed that he had no recollection one way or the other.[162] In any case, two weeks later 96 TOWs were transferred by Israel to Iran. No hostages were released.[163]

Israeli and Iranian negotiators met again in September. The Iranians indicated that one hostage would be released in exchange for an additional 400 TOWs. On September 15, 408 missiles arrived in Tehran, and the first hostage—Presbyterian minister Benjamin Weir—was released.[164] In November, 19 Hawk missiles were delivered from Israel to Iran aboard a CIA plane. No hostages were released.

As 1985 drew to a close, an emotionally exhausted Bud McFarlane resigned as National Security Adviser and was replaced by his deputy, Vice-Admiral John Poindexter.[165] In one of his first acts, Poindexter presented a "finding" to President Reagan. A finding is a written document describing the need for and nature of covert operations and requires the President's signature.[166] Reagan signed that finding, which retroactively authorized the Hawk shipment.[167] A year later, Poindexter destroyed the finding on the ground that it would be politically embarrassing if it ever were revealed publicly. "He could not have realized what a good prophet he was going to be."[168]

Of all the documents written during this period, however, the most notorious was undoubt-edly the so-called "diversion memorandum." Drafted by North in April 1986 and forwarded to Reagan and Poindexter, it summarized the Iranian operations and indicated the use of arms sale profits for the Contras in Nicaragua.[169] "Those few lines created more future trouble for North than anything else he ever said or wrote."[170]

On July 26, a second hostage—Father Lawrence Jenko, director of Catholic Relief Services in Beirut—was released. Two weeks later, 240 Hawk missile parts were shipped to Iran.[171]

By the middle of 1986, however, reports were beginning to appear in the press connecting North to fund-raising activities on behalf of the Contras. When a supply plane linked to a CIA "front" was shot down over Nicaragua in October, that incident provided an unmistakable disclosure of an illegal, covert American policy. "As might have been expected, a denial reflex took over in official circles."[172] CIA Director William Casey nervously advised North to shut down the operations. North began shredding incriminating documents and destroying ledgers and address books. The spool was starting to unravel. "North was now a man in a hurry."[173]

The news of North's secret role in the arms-for-hostages deals with Iran burst onto the front pages on November 6. When the story broke, North reportedly sat at a computer terminal in his office at the National Security Council and tapped out a weirdly-coded confidential computer memo to a colleague:

> Oh, Lord. I lost the slip and broke one of the high heels. Forgive please. Will return the wig on Monday.[174]

As of this writing, nearly 25 years later, it is still not clear to anybody what this cryptic— and rather kinky—message means.

On November 13, in a speech drafted by North and polished by White House writers, President Reagan addressed the nation and stated: "We did not—repeat—did not trade weapons or anything else for hostages nor will we."[175] A poll in the *Los Angeles Times* reported that only 14 percent of the public believed the President.[176] Even Republican icon Barry Goldwater was skeptical. In his words: "I think President Reagan has gotten his butt in a crack on this Iran thing."[177]

Reagan, unaccustomed to harsh rejection, was shaken.[178] He held a press conference on November 19, which would be remembered as the worst public performance of his presidency. He conceded that a small amount of arms had been sold to Iran, but that he was terminating all such sales. He claimed that he had the legal right not to have informed Congress. When he described the TOW missile as a "shoulder-mounted" weapon, a reporter, who explained to the Commander-in-Chief that TOWs were ground-to-ground weapons fired from tripods, corrected him.[179]

Reagan's worst blunder occurred when he categorically denied any "third country" involvement. Secretary of State George Schultz already had disclosed to the press that the United States *had* condoned the Israeli shipment of arms to Iran the previous year. Schultz had to meet with Reagan and correct him the day after the press conference. Schultz later testified: "[I]t was not the kind of discussion I ever thought I would have with the President of the United States."[180]

For Reagan, the time had come for damage control. He decided to fire Poindexter and transfer North out of the NSC. But damage control is a two-way street: On November 21, North instructed his young secretary, former fashion model Fawn Hall, to alter a series of NSC documents from his files. She and North also shredded documents until 4:15 a.m.[181] When she later testified before Congress, the intensely loyal Hall was asked whether she had realized that altering these documents was wrong. "Sometimes," she said, "you have to go above the written law."[182]

The next Presidential press conference must have been a painful experience for a politician whose brilliantly successful career had been built upon superb communicative talent. After a few brief remarks, in which he claimed that he had not been fully informed of the Iranian activities, Reagan turned the microphone over to Attorney General Edwin Meese. "After his fiasco on November 19, he could not be trusted—or could not trust himself—to go on the stage and face a disbelieving, tumultuous press conference alone."[183]

Meese acknowledged the diversion of funds from Iranian arms sales to the Contras. He implied that North may have been guilty of violating the law—without presidential authorization.

North reportedly was stunned by what he perceived as abandonment by his superiors. He realized that he was in real danger of being convicted of criminal acts. When his office was sealed by NSC security, Fawn Hall smuggled documents out inside her clothing. But surreptitiously removing a few documents, as well as shredding or altering a handful of others, was not going to save Oliver North. "Like many other things North did, this effort to hide the traces of his activity was marked as much by ineptitude as by anything else."[184] A paper trail connecting three continents could not be erased one page at a time.

> So many hundreds of incriminating documents and memoranda were left or recovered that it was possible to reconstruct the course of the Iran and contra affairs in extraordinary detail. Even the diversion, "the deepest, darkest secret of the whole activity," as [North] called it, came to light.[185]

The Iran-Contra Affair effectively was finished. North was not the only figure to be racing ahead of the posse, however. Reagan's friends were urging him to hire a criminal lawyer to defend his position. "[S]ome of those close to Reagan expected him to be one of the prime victims of the scandal."[186] The President immediately appointed a Special Review Board, headed by former Senator John Tower, to study the conduct of the NSC staff. Both houses of Congress created select committees to investigate Iran-Contra. An Independent Counsel also was appointed to prosecute any criminal offenses.[187]

In May 1987, the House and Senate began rare joint hearings on the Iran-Contra Affair. All the major figures testified—with the exception of the President and CIA Director Casey, who died on the second day of the hearings. America heard the feisty Secord explain the logistics of the operation, the contrite McFarlane, three months after a failed suicide attempt, implicate the President in a robotic monotone, and the unrepentant Poindexter blame Congress and the press for distorting the importance of Iran-Contra. Witnesses—from the unscrupulous Hakim, to the glamorous Hall, to the pugnacious leader of the Contras, Adolfo Calero, to a roll call of supporting players—appeared on millions of American television screens.[188] This cast, however, had to settle for roles in the chorus; center-stage belonged to Oliver North.

North strode into the hearing room in full Marine uniform, complete with six rows of medals. Although he had not worn his uniform in five years at the NSC, it was an effective strategy. North's lawyers had packaged him for the American public as a persecuted patriot. By the time the hearings had concluded, the press had coined the term, "Olliemania."

> There were Ollie T-shirts, Ollie bumper stickers, Ollie dolls, Ollie haircuts, Ollieburgers (shredded beef topped with shredded American cheese and shredded lettuce), Ollie recipes, and even Ollie-for-President boomlets.[189]

North presented himself as a defiant hero, an obedient soldier, a blameless scapegoat whose conduct had been dictated or approved by his superiors. He defended the need for covertness and deception, and made clear his low opinion of Congress. With moist eyes, he even spoke of his widowed mother who scrubbed floors to feed her children. It was bathos of Nixonian proportions, executed with far more skill.

> In an astonishing role reversal, North succeeded in transforming the pre-hearings public perception of him as mysterious cowboy run amok—a lone ranger whose horse jumped the fence for a romp through Indian Country without authorization—

to persecuted patriotic victim, just following orders. . . He was the Marlboro Man without the Marlboro. The Rebel With a Cause.[190]

The television critic in *The Washington Post* compared North's performance to James Stewart's in the classic movie *Mr. Smith Goes to Washington*. The critic offered a piquant metaphor: "[L]ike they say in pro wrestling, Ollie North is the 'television champion.'"[191] Unlike the wrestling arena, however, it was not left to vociferous fans to designate the villains. That responsibility belongs to the courts.

On March 11, 1987, Robert McFarlane pleaded guilty to four misdemeanor counts of withholding information from Congress. He was placed on 2 years probation and fined $20,000. He had avoided a prison sentence by agreeing to cooperate with the government in its prosecution of the other Iran-Contra cases.[192]

On March 16, a federal grand jury returned criminal indictments against Oliver North, John Poindexter, Richard Secord, and Albert Hakim.[193] Secord made an agreement with the prosecutor in November, under which he pleaded guilty to one felony count and agreed to testify against North and Poindexter in exchange for the dropping of 11 other charges.[194] Like McFarlane, Secord was sentenced to 2 years probation.[195] Hakim also received 2 years probation (and a $5,000 fine). In an unusual agreement, however, Hakim was allowed to keep a share of the $1.7 million surplus from the arms sales, which was still sitting in Swiss banks.[196] Poindexter became the only Iran-Contra figure to receive a prison term, when he was given a 6-month sentence in 1990 for lying to Congress. Poindexter was the highest White House official since Watergate to be incarcerated for illegal acts committed in office.[197]

As for Oliver North, he worked out an agreement under which he pleaded guilty to three of twelve felony counts, thus avoiding the ignominy of a prison sentence. He was, however, fined $178,785 and ordered to perform 1,200 hours of community service.[198] Many observers considered this a surprisingly light sentence. Not only had North participated in the Iran-Contra cover-up by lying to Congress and shredding key documents, he also had acknowledged using $13,000 of Iran-Contra proceeds to purchase a security system for his home.[199] Moreover, North was accused of cashing $2,000 worth of traveler's checks, part of a $90,000 donation by Contra leader Adolfo Calero meant to help retrieve the hostages from Lebanon. This represented something of a "reverse diversion," with funds going from the Contras to Iran. North's alleged embezzlement was akin, then, to a "diversion of a diversion." North used the siphoned funds to purchase everything from dry-cleaning, to groceries, to hosiery, to snow tires. When Calero was shown a chart during the congressional hearings, documenting the dozens of traveler's checks cashed by North, he staunchly defended North's integrity. "He conceded to Senator Rudman that it did not snow in Nicaragua, but he was sure that North could explain the expenditures."[200] On September 16, 1991, a divided appeals court overturned North's conviction on technical grounds regarding the immunity which had been granted to his congressional testimony. A few weeks later, Poindexter's conviction was reversed on the same grounds.[201] North pronounced himself "totally exonerated."[202] Most journalists rejected this claim as a "wild overstatement,"[203] noting that the reversal had nothing to do with the facts of the case.[204] Ironically, North had wriggled off the hook using the very sort of legal loophole which his hardline supporters habitually berate in their "law and order" and "soft on crime" rhetoric.

Oliver North became a luminary on the lecture circuit, commanding $30,000 for an appearance. He was the Republican nominee for a U.S. Senate seat in Virginia in 1994, but was defeated in a very costly and bitterly fought election—the most conspicuous exception to a national Republican landslide. A short time later, he became the host of a nationally syndicated daily radio program.

ABUSE OF POWER

More than 150 years ago, political philosopher John Stuart Mill wrote: "A governing class not accountable to the people are sure, in the main, to sacrifice the people to the pursuit of separate interests and inclinations of their own."[205] Mill's message about the need for accountability has lost none of its timeliness. Even the government of the United States, democratically elected and Constitutionally restrained, has at times been willing to "sacrifice" the rights of its citizens on behalf of some extralegal "higher" purpose. Most of these abuses of power have occurred under the guise of national security.[206]

Consider the ignominious example of the internment of Japanese-American citizens during the Second World War. In 1942, President Roosevelt issued an Executive Order evacuating over 100,000 Japanese-American residents of California, Oregon, and Washington and herding them into barbed wire enclosures under military guard.[207] Victims of racial prejudice and war hysteria, they were branded as traitors and robbed of their businesses and farms. Virtually every one of them, as far as we know, were loyal citizens; most of them were too young or too old to pose any plausible threat.[208]

Moreover, citizens of Japanese ancestry in Central and South American countries were rounded up, handed over to American authorities, transported to the United States, and thrown into concentration camps as well.[209] It is difficult to characterize that abuse of power in any terms other than kidnapping.

In this section, we will analyze the most resonant example in American history of government divorced from accountability—the crimes of Watergate.

Watergate

The cluster of crimes known collectively as "Watergate" has come to symbolize the abuse of political power in America. Richard Nixon, who had won re-election by a huge majority, had to jettison the core of his administrative staff; then, facing certain impeachment, conviction, and removal from office, he himself was forced to resign.[210]

Watergate lies on the cusp between the two types of political crime differentiated by political scientist Theodore Lowi: "Little Corruption," the bribery and individual malfeasance examined in Chapter 8; and "Big Corruption," in which governmental deviance is normalized through political authority.[211] Clearly, Watergate abounded with "Little Corruption." Consider the following examples:

- The Committee to Re-elect the President (known as derisively as CREEP) was indicted for campaign spending violations, following an investigation by the General Accounting Office.[212] It was later revealed that CREEP also had failed to report a secret fund of millions of dollars in campaign contributions.[213]

- The House Banking and Currency Committee reported that CREEP had channeled money through a Luxembourg bank in order to circumvent campaign-spending laws.[214]

- John Mitchell and Maurice Stans, former cabinet members, solicited an illegal $200,000 cash contribution to CREEP from Robert Vesco, a financier accused by the Security and Exchange Commission (SEC) of a $244 million stock fraud. Mitchell later arranged a meeting between Vesco and SEC Chairman William Casey after the $200,000 was delivered.[215]

- Illegal campaign contributions were solicited from some of the biggest corporations in America, such as Chrysler, American Airlines, and Ashland Oil. One company, American

Motors, was asked for an illegal contribution of $100,000, but rejected the request. It later was given a second chance, at the "bargain" rate of only $50,000.[216] Some corporate executives testified that they were blackmailed by CREEP into giving large donations. For example, the vice-president of Gulf Oil maintained that he had been led to believe that a refusal to contribute would have placed his company on a "blacklist" with respect to government contracts.[217]

- "The *Wall Street Journal* [published] documents revealing that President Nixon had been told of the dairy industry's huge campaign contributions, had expressed his gratitude, and two days later had given them highly profitable price-support increases."[218]

- Republican officials donated $50,000 from campaign funds to pay for a 1972 dinner honoring Vice-President Spiro Agnew, who would later resign in disgrace (Chapter 8).[219]

- The brother-in-law of White House Chief of Staff H. R. Haldeman received $50,000 in diverted campaign contributions for helping to arrange the purchase of President Nixon's California home.[220]

- Nixon's close friend, banker "Bebe" Rebozo, channeled $50,000 from laundered campaign funds for Nixon's private use. The money had paid for a swimming pool, putting green, and pool table at Nixon's Florida home. "Another $4,562 had gone into the purchase of diamond earrings for the President's wife."[221]

- "[T]he Joint Committee on Internal Revenue Taxation . . . disclosed that [Nixon] used every tax dodge and loophole to escape paying $432,787 in income taxes."[222] The report revealed that the President had grossly underestimated his income and had deducted nearly a half million dollars for donating some of his presidential papers, a vastly inflated figure. Nixon also had charged the government for nearly $100,000 in personal expenses—including $5,000 to throw a lavish party for his daughter.[223]

Outrageous as these offenses were, a review of American history makes clear (and as Chapter 10 will underscore) that corrupt politicians have never been in short supply. Why, then, has the stain of Watergate been so indelible? The naked dishonesty it revealed at the highest level of government is not easily forgotten: campaign contributions illegally donated or extorted, the "skimming" of these funds for gifts to the President's friends and relatives, the purchase of political favors, the sale of ambassadorships, the President's own questionable tax returns.

Beyond all this, however, Watergate was "Big Corruption," a Constitutional crisis of the first magnitude, perhaps America's closest brush with despotism. It revealed the creation of a "shadow government, a secret 'state within a state.'"[224] It signified an attempt to replace a traditional "rule of law" morality with a kind of "new Machiavellianism,"[225] layered with psychopathy and marbled with paranoia.

In the midst of the Senate hearings in 1973, a national poll reported that a majority of the public rated Watergate as the *worst* scandal in American history.[226] Decades later, Watergate remains our transcendent political crime. In perpetual motion, it glides on tightropes of our consciousness; often drifting away, but always coming back.

The scandal began inauspiciously with what President Nixon's Press Secretary dismissed as a "third rate burglary."[227] Early on the morning of June 17, 1972, five men were arrested in national headquarters of the Democratic Party on sixth floor of the swank Watergate Complex in Washington, D.C. The burglars were carrying electronic surveillance equipment.

"Incredulity, sometimes accompanied by cynical laughter, typified the initial public reaction to the bungled break-in."[228] After all, President Nixon's re-election was a virtual certainty;

polls put him far ahead of any Democratic rival. Nixon was already on his way to the most smashing presidential landslide in American political history.[229] "One had to suspend logic and belief to link the president or the president's men with the transgressions of Watergate."[230]

Even when it was revealed that the burglars worked for a special "plumber's unit" of CREEP, the press and public paid scant attention to the incipient scandal. However, from the summer of 1972 through the spring of 1973, a federal grand jury heard testimony in connection with the Watergate burglary. Before too long, the public was not laughing anymore. Stories began to surface about great sums of money allegedly funnelled into Republican intelligence operations. "Bit by bit, the stone wall erected by the White House began to crumble, and the American people learned, not just about the Watergate break-in itself, but about a whole series of related crimes."[231]

On August 1, 1972, journalists Carl Bernstein and Bob Woodward reported in the *Washington Post* that a $25,000 check intended for Nixon's campaign had been deposited in the bank account of one of the Watergate burglars.[232] Later, CREEP admitted that a $30,000 campaign contribution from the Philippine sugar industry, solicited on behalf of an "urgent White House project,"[233] also had helped pay for the Watergate cover-up.

CREEP officials reportedly thwarted the FBI during its Watergate investigation. Acting FBI Director L. Patrick Gray III turned over the bureau's Watergate file to White House Counsel John Dean. On April 27, 1973, the *New York Daily News* further revealed that Gray had destroyed documents belonging to Watergate conspirator E. Howard Hunt. Gray reportedly had been acting under orders from Nixon's chief of domestic affairs, John Ehrlichman.[234] Gray resigned that same day.

A month later, a memorandum was disclosed in which the Deputy Director of the CIA said that H. R. Haldeman, the powerful White House Chief of Staff, told him, "It is the President's wish that the CIA help block an FBI investigation of Nixon campaign money."[235] The money in question had been "laundered" in a Mexican bank. When former CIA Director Richard Helms appeared before the Senate Foreign Relations Committee, he was asked why he had never informed the President of White House efforts to enlist the CIA in a Watergate cover-up. Helms replied: "Frankly, I wanted to stay as head of the agency."[236]

During this same time, all charges were dismissed in the "Pentagon Papers" trial of former Defense Department analyst, Daniel Ellsberg, who had been accused of leaking to the press classified documents that concerned efforts by the Pentagon to deceive Congress into supporting the corrupt regime in South Vietnam. The judge in the Ellsberg case declared that the government had "incurably infected the prosecution."[237] Specifically, it had been revealed that Watergate conspirators E. Howard Hunt and G. Gordon Liddy had carried out a burglary of the office of Ellsberg's former psychiatrist in an effort to uncover discrediting information. In addition, Helms' successor as CIA Director, James Schlessinger, conceded that the CIA had cooperated in the burglary at the instigation of John Ehrlichman.[238] Later testifying before the Watergate Committee, Ehrlichman defended the practice of political espionage and argued that the President had the power to break the law if he believed national security was endangered.[239]

Incredibly, it was also revealed that the judge in the Ellsberg case had been invited to President Nixon's California home where he was asked if he would be interested in becoming the new Director of the FBI. This brazen overture later would be characterized by members of the Senate Watergate Committee as attempted bribery.[240]

CREEP used a secret fund to finance intelligence-gathering operations against the Democrats. Democratic presidential contenders and their families were followed, and dossiers were assembled on their personal lives. For example, probes were ordered on close associates of Senator Edward Kennedy, including his mother, Rose.[241] False and defamatory stories about

Democratic candidates were leaked to the press, and letters were forged in the name of prominent Democrats. In addition, Republican saboteurs stole Democratic campaign files and hired provocateurs to disrupt the Democratic National convention.[242] When H. R. Haldeman, who controlled the espionage fund, later appeared before the Senate Watergate Committee, he set a new standard for evasive testimony. He responded "I can't remember" or "I don't know" to more than 150 questions.[243]

One of the ringleaders of the Republican political sabotage conspiracy was the President's appointments secretary, Dwight Chapin. He employed a former Treasury Department attorney, Donald Segretti, to engage in a series of "dirty tricks" against the Democrats. In 1972, Segretti distributed a phony letter on the stationery of then-Democratic presidential front-runner, Senator Edmund Muskie, accusing rival presidential aspirants, Senators Henry Jackson and Hubert Humphrey, of sexual misconduct.[244] Segretti later testified before the Senate Committee concerning "all the acts of forgery, libel, burglary, and character assassination he performed to get Nixon re-elected."[245] Patrick Buchanan, Nixon's caustic speech writer, also testified before the Committee and admitted participating in the sabotage of the Muskie presidential campaign. Buchanan further admitted to having urged the White House "to use the IRS against . . . Nixon's enemies list."[246]

Richard Nixon, however, did not limit the use of illegal surveillance to his enemies. He once had ordered the Secret Service to wiretap the phone of his brother Donald, out of fear that Donald Nixon's financial dealings might embarrass the re-election campaign.[247] Likewise, on the same day the Senate Watergate Committee began its televised hearings in May of 1973, the *New York Times* reported that the National Security Adviser, Henry Kissinger, had ordered the wiretapping of some of his own aides between 1969 and 1971.[248]

In June, 1973, the *Washington Post* printed a summary that Woodward and Bernstein had obtained of John Dean's testimony at a closed meeting of the Senate Watergate Committee. According to this report, Dean said that Nixon had requested the IRS to stop tax audits of his friends. Dean reportedly also testified that Nixon had ordered him to keep a list of troublesome reporters, so that they could be punished after the 1972 election.[249] In his public testimony, Dean revealed that Nixon's "enemies list" contained hundreds of names singled out for persecution.[250] For example, Daniel Schorr, the CBS White House correspondent and one of the most respected journalists in Washington, had been subjected to an intense FBI investigation.[251]

Dean also maintained that President Nixon had been aware of the Watergate cover-up from the beginning. Nixon denied this and suggested that the unscrupulous Dean had misled him. At a televised question and answer session before an audience of newspaper editors on November 17, 1973, Richard Nixon delivered the most memorable line of his long political career: "I am not a crook."[252]

During the Watergate hearings, Alexander Butterfield, head of the Federal Aviation Administration and a former Nixon aide, stunned the Committee when he revealed that Nixon secretly had tape-recorded all White House conversations, including those relating to Watergate.[253] For the first time in 166 years, a President of the United States was subpoenaed.[254] Nixon refused to cooperate. For months thereafter, the President disobeyed a court order to surrender eight Watergate tapes. Instead, he offered special Watergate prosecutor Archibald Cox sanitized written "summaries" of the subpoenaed conversations. When Cox rejected that deal, Nixon ordered Attorney General Elliot Richardson to fire Cox. When Richardson refused, Nixon fired him. When Deputy Attorney General William Ruckelshaus also refused, Nixon fired him, too. Finally, Solicitor General Robert Bork agreed to dismiss Cox. An indignant press quickly labeled this remarkable sequence of events the "Saturday Night Massacre."[255] The "third-rate burglary" had become what John Dean would call a "cancer on the Presidency."[256]

While the tapes were being transcribed, Nixon's attorney informed the Watergate court about an unexplainable 18 1/2 minute buzz that "blots out a crucial discussion about Watergate between Nixon and Haldeman on a key tape."[257] The angry judge, John Sirica, demanded an explanation. Rose Mary Woods, the President's longtime secretary, testified that she had been transcribing the tape for the President and accidentally had erased it while answering the telephone. According to her story, while "reaching for [the phone] with one hand, with the other she mistakenly pushed the 'record' instead of the 'stop' button on her recorder, while keeping her foot on the operating treadle."[258] When Woods attempted to demonstrate what allegedly had happened, she resembled a sideshow contortionist as she twisted her body into a grotesque posture. Her ludicrous explanation was met with almost universal scorn. In fact, months later a panel of technical experts reported that someone had "made at least five separate, deliberate *hand* erasures on the tape."[259]

On July 24, 1974, the American people discovered incontrovertibly that their President was indeed a crook. In its decision in *United States v. Richard M. Nixon*, the Supreme Court unanimously ordered that the President surrender the subpoenaed tapes. The most damaging one turned out to be a conversation between Nixon and Haldeman recorded less than a week after the Watergate break-in. On that tape, Haldeman informs Nixon that the burglars had been financed by CREEP campaign funds, and Nixon orders Haldeman to use the CIA to impede the FBI investigation. This tape has become known as the "smoking gun;"[260] it effectively ended the Nixon Presidency. Three days after the tapes were released, the House Judiciary Committee approved a Bill of Impeachment against the President of the United States. Twelve days later, Nixon resigned.

Watergate proved to be a mucilaginous trap; the harder Nixon had tried to extricate himself, the more entangled he had become in crimes, cover-ups, and cover-ups of cover-ups. And like some prehistoric tar pit, Watergate has left a legacy of remains that begs for explanation. Although it obviously was a seminal event, the fundamental meaning of Watergate can be understood in various ways. Interpretation, of course, depends on the perspective of the interpreter.

To many journalists, for example, Watergate was about money. The investigative reports of Bernstein and Woodward, which first revealed the dimensions of the scandal, focused on the illegal contributions, the secret funds, the payoffs and influence peddling. Watergate, however—as we already have observed—transcended "Little Corruption." It must be examined more broadly to grasp its full significance.

To many social psychologists, Watergate was about destructive obedience to a malevolent authority figure, Richard Nixon. Indeed, any retrospective consideration of Watergate must begin with Nixon. Three generations of armchair psychoanalysts have feasted upon the Nixon psyche and its web of contradictions. He has been characterized as a man admired by millions of citizens, who chose to obsess over a relative handful of enemies, real and imagined; a man renowned for his political cunning, yet capable of committing acts of almost unfathomable stupidity; a man seized by a grandiose need for praise, yet filled with petty spite and primal hatred. Columnist Stewart Alsop once said of Nixon: "He behaved as if he were waging war, not politics."[261]

One of Richard Nixon's most striking contradictions was that he could inspire such fierce loyalty in his staff. Given the history of his career, that loyalty could not have been based on any reasonable expectation of reciprocity. His instinct for survival had always been intensely selfish. It was vintage Nixon that he tried to make a scapegoat of the young sycophant, John Dean; or that he retired to opulent exile, pardoned by President Ford for any crimes he might have committed while in office, while some of his closest associates and oldest friends, such as Haldeman, Ehrlichman, and Mitchell, went to prison for crimes committed on his behalf. Nixon's character flaws were nearly as familiar a part of the American landscape as McDonald's arches, so Watergate seems more likely to have been inspired by Nixon the authority figure than by Nixon the inspirational leader.

Whether Nixon personally ordered the burglaries or the extortion of campaign contributions is largely irrelevant. Those acts "were consistent with an operating style that the President himself had followed in the past and was clearly sanctioning, even if he was not familiar with all of the details."[262] It is characteristic of an authoritarian environment that the moral principles which generally govern human relationships cease to apply.

[W]hen immoral, criminal, or corrupt acts are explicitly ordered, implicitly encouraged, tacitly approved, or at least permitted by legitimate authorities, people's readiness to commit or condone them is considerably enhanced. The fact that such acts are authorized seems to carry automatic justification for them.[263]

"[S]ituational pressures to 'win at all costs' were particularly appealing to the . . . persons who comprised the leadership of the Nixon administration."[264] One merely has to scrutinize the testimony and demeanor of most of the witnesses before the Senate Watergate Committee to discern "an orientation to authority based on unquestioning obedience to superior orders."[265] When one Senator asked John Ehrlichman, for example, whether the President's power to protect national security extended to the commission of murder, Ehrlichman coolly replied: "I do not know where the line is."[266]

To many political sociologists, Watergate was about power.

Watergate was a scandal motivated by the quest for political power. Although Richard Nixon left the office of the President a far wealthier man than when he entered it, Watergate is not a tale of personal aggrandizement. For the most part, money was simply a means to an end.[267]

Max Weber's early concept of *legitimacy* seems particularly germane to Watergate. A "legitimate" political system is "generally accepted by the populace as ruling in accord with consensual values and norms."[268] In Weber's view, a regime forfeits its legitimacy when it no longer enjoys that acceptance. In other words, "political authorities are [only] legitimate to the extent that the citizens perceive them as holding their positions by right."[269]

When it subverted the 1972 presidential election, the Nixon Administration lost its legitimacy. "Voters who had voted for President Nixon considered their vote to have been fraudulently claimed and felt betrayed."[270] Nixon's "power disease"[271] and its symptomatic intolerance for opposition pulled an unwary nation ever closer to a police state: "The illegal wiretaps [and] political espionage represented, in large part, an attempt to weed out government officials who could not be relied upon to be absolutely loyal to the President."[272]

Also, in the inevitable manner of a police state, the pretext of national security was used to justify every illegal act. Nixon always had both the capacity and the inclination to relegate his opponents to a "less-than-human category, outside of the bounds of human sympathy, and fair game for whatever forms of suppression might be required."[273] Dissenters were persecuted; those citizens consigned to Nixon's "enemies list"—that is, those who opposed the President—were harassed by federal agencies from the IRS to the FBI to the Secret Service to the Post Office.

There were the "Harvards," the Kennedys, the "upper intellectual types," the "establishment," the Jews, the Italians. The famous "enemies list" . . . included such dangerous folk as Carol Channing, Steve McQueen, Barbara Streisand, Gregory Peck, Bill Cosby, Tony Randall, and Joe Namath.[274]

Logic decrees that the hypocrisy of an amoral president carried to power upon the shoulders of "law and order" rhetoric would generate profound effects upon a deceived electorate. A president's responsibility, after all, reaches far beyond his role as Commander-in-Chief of the armed forces or administrator of the Executive Branch. The White House is first and foremost a place of moral leadership. Richard Nixon poisoned the well of political rectitude. His abdication of moral leadership, through his routinization of "Big Corruption," was the ultimate crime of Watergate.

Applying classical sociological theories to Watergate yields some disturbing predictions. For example, the loss of political legitimacy engendered by the scandal might be expected to have produced a general state of normlessness (what Durkheim termed "anomie") or a weakening of the social bonds that tie citizens to critical institutions (what Marx called "alienation"). Did this actually occur? The answer appears to be yes. As one analysis concluded at the time: "Watergate may affect the maintenance of supportive attitudes toward the political system."[275]

A 1976 study reported: "There was a clear and general loss of confidence . . . in the executive branch of the federal government concomitant with the unfolding of the Watergate scandal, and this loss was dispersed or extended to political leaders in general."[276] A 1979 survey revealed that those voters who had misplaced their trust in Richard Nixon, and thus felt most betrayed, became significantly more cynical about people in general than those who had not voted for Nixon.[277]

It is not difficult to understand why Watergate exacerbated public cynicism. For instance, of the twenty-one business executives sanctioned for illegal presidential campaign contributions uncovered by the Watergate Special Prosecutor, just five were convicted of "willful violations" (a felony). Of these, only three officials of the Associated Milk Producers Cooperative were handed short prison terms. The remaining two, Thomas Jones, CEO of the Northrup Corporation, and shipbuilder/sports mogul George Steinbrenner, were slapped with financially inconsequential fines.[278] Moreover, "with the one exception of campaign financing, no major reforms have been enacted as a direct response to Watergate."[279]

Perhaps most disturbing of all is the effect of Watergate on young Americans of that period. Research on political socialization suggests that "instead of being uninterested in and insulated from political events, children may be one of the more affected segments of the population."[280] Comparative studies of grade-school children's political attitudes in the pre- and post-Watergate era report that children of the post-Watergate era were much more cynical about politics[281] and less respectful of the presidency.[282]

Among college undergraduates, evidence has been presented that Watergate reduced political interest.[283] Moreover, a 1976 study of young voters revealed a negative correlation between support for Richard Nixon and subsequent scores on a moral judgment scale. One implication of this finding is that the cognitive dissonance produced by having voted for a disgraced president may have depressed moral judgment among some young voters.[284] Indeed, CREEP regularly hired undergraduate interns to infiltrate Democratic campaigns and spy for Republicans in exchange for college credits.[285]

Ironically, 1972 was the first presidential election in which 18- to 20-year-old voters were allowed to participate. Instead of those new voters making the electoral process more idealistic, the electoral process may have made those new voters less idealistic. One researcher reports that, in the wake of the Watergate scandal, political attitudes of first-time voters became almost indistinguishable from those of their parents.[286] The young subjects of the post-Watergate studies now comprise the dominant demographic segment in the United States. If they are less idealistic, less trusting, and more cynical than they might otherwise have turned out to be, this is indeed a sad legacy of Watergate.

Finally, it is chilling to ponder the "what ifs" of Watergate. What if a night watchman had not stumbled accidentally upon the burglars? What if an obscure White House aide had not off handedly revealed the existence of the White House tapes? Such questions can be answered only-subjunctively, but the crisis of legitimacy created by Nixon's imperious assault on the Constitution may not have occurred without these turns of fate. Democracy often rests at the top and tyranny at the bottom of a slippery slope. Could a second-term Nixon, unable to run again, have shucked any lingering pretense of moral restraint? It is surely fortunate that we will never know.

Our consideration of abuses of power now continues with an examination of the records of several federal agencies in the areas of unlawful surveillance and persecution. We will conclude by analyzing the most vile of all government abuses—that of torture.

The FBI: Of all government agencies, the FBI has conducted the most vindictive domestic intelligence campaigns.[287] The Bureau of Investigation (forerunner of the FBI) began intelligence-gathering operations just prior to World War I. Its General Intelligence Division (GID), headed by an ambitious young former cataloguer for the Library of Congress, named J. Edgar Hoover, "spied on citizens who criticized the war, opposed the draft, or participated in militant labor organizing efforts."[288] By the end of the war, the energetic Hoover already had created a substantial index and file system covering suspected political radicals, including such prominent liberals as Fiorello LaGuardia, who later would be mayor of New York City. When Hoover was put in command of the renamed Federal Bureau of Investigation in 1924, he was ordered to abolish the GID; the mission of the new FBI was to investigate crimes, not engage in political activities. For over a decade, the bureau observed this restriction.[289] During this period, Hoover, a master publicist, cultivated the FBI's "gangbuster" image in a series of sensational cases.

However, as World War II approached, Hoover was called upon to supervise domestic intelligence operations. President Franklin Roosevelt issued a series of secret instructions to Hoover, authorizing the bureau to conduct broad surveillance programs aimed at American citizens. Hoover was empowered to engage in warrantless searches, wiretapping, and bugging against persons suspected of Communist or fascist sympathies.[290]

A few days after the war began in Europe in 1939, Roosevelt issued a proclamation officially placing the FBI in charge of all investigations of espionage, sabotage, and subversive activities.[291] This document has come to be known as the "Magna Carta" of the bureau's intelligence mission.[292] Hoover seized on the statement as an authorization for virtually unlimited investigative powers. Espionage and sabotage were clearly defined statutory offenses; subversion was not. Congress had never said what specific kinds of "subversive activities" were crimes, so Hoover took this task upon himself.[293]

Hoover personally supervised the surveillance of such "dangerous" radicals as blind and deaf author Helen Keller, who must have been the easiest target in the history of surveillance, and Justice Felix Frankfurter, one of the more conservative jurists ever to sit on the modern Supreme Court. Such excesses underscored the danger of police power limited only through self-regulation. At what point does a permissible law enforcement technique like surveillance begin to encroach upon the Constitutional rights of citizens regarding free speech, free assembly, or security against unreasonable search and seizure? To Hoover, such a question was better suited to high school civics classes; it had no relevance to the real world of national security.

The vagueness of domestic intelligence laws gave the FBI such latitude that abuses by agents were inevitable. "And once they had moved into the gray area—say, by tailing someone they mistrusted but had no evidence against—it was a short step into the black area of clear illegality."[294] When a powerful agency turns its resources against persons who have committed no crimes, prosecution becomes persecution.

> [N]o federal judge would give permission to the F.B.I. to install a wiretap or search an office when there was no probable cause to believe that the target had done anything wrong. Stymied by the law and yet firm in the belief that subversives were out to bring down the Republic, the F.B.I. began pursuing them in the only way left to it; by breaking the law.[295]

The sedition provisions of the Alien Registration Act of 1940, known as the Smith Act,[296] as well as postwar measures such as the Loyalty Program of 1947,[297] the Internal Security Act of 1950,[298] and the Communist Control Act of 1954,[299] expanded the FBI's authority to spy on American citizens. Hoover even had a 300-page file on Richard J. Daley, who would become the scourge of the New Left in the 1960s. The dossier spans Daley's political career from state senator in the 1940s to his election as mayor of Chicago in the 1950s up to his death in 1976. A writer who has chronicled the FBI explains: "It was typical of Hoover to try to just gather any information he could about powerful politicians as a way of making sure he maintained his own seat of power."[300]

Two programs, COMINFIL and COINTELPRO, were directed at Communist infiltration. In addition to the Communist Party, however, agents also penetrated liberal organizations like the American Civil Liberties Union, civil rights groups like the NAACP, peace organizations like SANE, and professional coalitions like the National Lawyers Guild. "Any group or organization that advocated social change or reform was fair game for the bureau."[301]

During the "Red Scare" decade, the American Communist Party, by the FBI's own estimate, never exceeded 80,000 members, but the FBI opened about 500,000 files on "subversive" organizations.[302] A favorite target was the tiny and completely legal Socialist Workers Party (SWP), whose membership was estimated at 1,000.[303] As even the bureau admitted, the SWP was not under the control or influence of any foreign power and was "in active opposition to the Communist party."[304] Yet, the FBI kept the SWP under surveillance for 34 years, burglarized the party's offices on 94 different occasions in just one six-week period,[305] and sent anonymous letters to members' employers.[306] The FBI expended tens of thousands of man-hours to generate an 8-million-page dossier on a "small, peaceable, and wholly ineffectual political party."[307]

The FBI also conducted checks on over 6 million government employees for possible disloyalty. Thousands of individuals were subjected to adversarial hearings on vague charges of membership, or even "sympathetic association" with allegedly subversive organizations.[308] According to the Center for National Security Studies, not a single case of espionage was uncovered by those investigations.[309]

The FBI likewise engaged in "smear" campaigns against selected citizens by leaking derogatory information to friendly media contacts.

> FBI agents conducted anonymous-letter operations to have subversives fired from their jobs. The bureau also recruited other organizations, such as the American Legion, to launch similar actions. The bureau brought pressure on universities and schools to have professors and teachers fired. Many of these initiatives were successful.[310]

Apparently, no occupational position was beyond the bureau's reach. Documents obtained under the Freedom of Information Act[311] revealed over 2,000 pages of FBI files on members of the Supreme Court,[312] who it deemed politically suspect during the Cold War years. Chief Justice Earl

Warren and Associate Justices Hugo Black and Abe Fortas were among those listed.[313] Partic
attention was paid to liberal Justice William O. Douglas, whose file stretched from 1937 to 197£
In 1969, President Nixon, who despised Douglas,[315] arranged for some FBI material to be pa:
to then-Representative Gerald Ford, who was requested to move to impeach Douglas. Ford c(
plied, but when he bitterly denounced Douglas on the floor of the House in 1970, his speech
so riddled with errors that even a Nixon ally in the Department of Justice observed: "Ford really
blew it. . . You don't start down that road without having the facts."[316] In the end the Douglas
impeachment attempt vaporized.

A new kind of political activism emerged in the 1960s. A nonviolent civil rights movement,
along with a more aggressive "black power" movement, converged with an anti-Vietnam War
movement, a student protest movement, and a woman's liberation movement to ignite one of
the most turbulent periods in modern American history. Hoover, predictably, viewed the new
politics of dissent as subversive. Over the course of the decade, the FBI files expanded to encompass over one million Americans. "The FBI went after the whole spectrum of political dissent:"[317]
from the American Nazi Party to the Jewish Defense League; from the Ku Klux Klan to the Black
Panther Party; from the Southern Christian Leadership Conference to the Nation of Islam; from
the John Birch Society to Vietnam Veterans Against the War; from the idealistic militancy of the
Students for a Democratic Society to the anarchic rage of the Weathermen; from Malcolm X to
Jane Fonda. The sixties, it is said, brought roses to the cheeks"[318] of political intelligence units.

In 1968, the FBI began an operation dubbed "New Left"—a program of covert persecu-
tions under the pretext of counterintelligence. For example, an attack was orchestrated against
Antioch College, a small school in Ohio noted for its involvement in social causes. The bureau
traced the postgraduate careers of a number of former student leaders, hoping to uncover a
consistent record of low achievement. The plan was to publicize that information and discredit
Antioch as an educational institution. To the FBI's regret, it discovered that the Antioch graduates were leading successful lives.[319]

Many other examples of the New Left program related to the alleged sexual licentiousness
of young political radicals. The "eroticizing of the New Left"[320] reflected the institutionalized
prudery of the FBI, fueled by the Director's well-known puritanical attitudes about sex. In one
case, a white woman who belonged to ACTION, a biracial St. Louis civil rights organization,
married a man who did not share her political agenda. The FBI sent an anonymous letter to the
husband, hoping to foment marital discord and distract the wife from her activism:

> Look man, I guess your old lady doesn't get enough at home or she wouldn't be shuck-
> ing and jiving with our black men in ACTION, you dig? Like all she wants to integrate
> is the bedroom and we black sisters ain't gonna take no second best from our men.[321]

To the bureau's delight, the couple's marriage did indeed break up.[322]

Movie actress Jean Seberg was another victim of New Left. Seberg was a financial supporter
of the Black Panther Party. In a sordid ploy to embarrass her publicly, the FBI sent a letter to
Hollywood gossip columnists, alleging that the father of Seberg's unborn child was a prominent
Black Panther leader:

> I was in Paris last week and ran into Jean Seberg who was heavy with baby. I thought
> she and Romain had gotten together again but she confided the child belonged to
> [name deleted] of the Black Panthers. The dear girl is getting around. Anyway, I
> thought you might get a scoop on the others.[323]

The *Los Angeles Times* printed this "blind" item—which was completely untrue—and it subsequently was reported throughout the print media. When *Newsweek* published the story, Seberg and her husband, author Romain Gary, successfully sued for libel. Seberg, however, suffered a miscarriage and a psychotic breakdown, and eventually committed suicide.[324]

It is well documented that the American civil rights movement has been subjected to intense FBI scrutiny for more than fifty years. When President Roosevelt empowered the bureau to gather information on the activities of subversive groups and organizations in the late 1930s, Hoover used that mandate to link the struggle for racial equality with Communist infiltration. Hoover had no personal sympathy for the egalitarian goals of the civil rights movement. "At worst he was a 'primitive racist' and, at best, someone with the racist instincts of a white man who had grown up in Washington when it was still a southern city."[325]

Hoover warned that a Communist-inspired "messiah" one day would attempt to indoctrinate Afro-Americans. After the Supreme Court rejected the "separate but equal" doctrine in 1954, a number of civil rights leaders and organizations found new prominence: Roy Wilkens and the National Association for the Advancement of Colored People; James Farmer and the Congress of Racial Equality; John Lewis and the Voter Education Project. "But it was the Reverend Martin Luther King, Jr. and the Southern Christian Leadership Conference that came to symbolize the nonviolent movement."[326] Hoover saw King as the sinister black messiah he had long feared.

Hoover's view of King filtered through the entire bureau. Following King's memorable "I Have a Dream" speech in Washington, the FBI's Intelligence Division denounced King in a memo to the Director: "We must mark him now as the most dangerous Negro of the future in this nation from the standpoint of Communism, the Negro, and national security."[327]

The vendetta against Martin Luther King has been characterized as the "most ignoble chapter in the history of FBI spying and manipulation."[328]

> All of the arbitrary power and lawless tactics were marshaled to destroy King's reputation and the movement he led. The FBI relied on its vague authority to investigate "subversives" to spy on King and SCLC; its vague authority to conduct warrantless wiretapping and microphonic surveillance to tap and bug him. The campaign began with his rise to leadership and grew more vicious as he reached the height of his power; it continued even after his assassination.[329]

The investigation of King began in earnest in 1962 with the knowledge and tacit approval of President John Kennedy who publicly claimed to be a King supporter. In 1963, Attorney General Robert Kennedy, another self-professed King ally, approved Hoover's request for wiretaps on King.

Less than two weeks after the Kennedy assassination, while the country still mourned, the FBI held an all-day conference to plan the destruction of King and the civil rights movement. Among the proposals discussed were "using ministers, 'disgruntled' acquaintances, 'aggressive' newsmen, 'colored' agents, Dr. King's housekeeper, and even Dr. King's wife or 'placing a good looking female plant in King's office' to develop discrediting information and to take action that would lead to his disgrace."[330]

Early in 1964, an electronic "bug" placed in King's Washington hotel room apparently picked up information about King's extramarital sexual activities. Throughout that year, the FBI offered this and other King tapes to journalists around the country.[331] This vicious "smear" campaign was known to President Johnson and many of his closest advisers, such as Special Presidential Assistant Bill Moyers, yet another King "admirer"; but not one official, including the President, was willing to risk a confrontation with Hoover.[332]

The most infamous episode occurred in 1968, 34 days before Martin Luther King was to be awarded the Nobel Peace Prize. King received a tape, allegedly made while he was in a hotel room with a woman. Accompanying the tape was an astonishing unsigned note from the FBI, which seemingly urged King to commit suicide:

> King, there is only one thing left for you to do. You know what it is. You have just 34 days in which to do it. (This exact number has been selected for a specific reason.) It has definite practical significance. You are done. There is but one way out for you. You better take it before your filthy fraudulent self is bared to the nation.[333]

Although a subsequent meeting between Hoover and King averted a public scandal, the FBI's war on King took a toll, both on the civil rights leader personally and on the movement he had come to represent.

> [T]he smear campaign caused donors to turn away from SCLC and created faction- alism in the civil rights movement over whether King should continue to lead. The FBI did "expose" and "disrupt" the movement. And the anguish this caused for King is incalculable.[334]

In 1988—20 years after King's death and 16 years after Hoover's—the Southern Christian Leadership Conference still was protesting harassment by the FBI.[335]

As a further illustration that the bureau's disdain for civil liberties and intolerance of politi- cal dissent have survived Hoover, declassified documents reveal that Ronald Reagan used the FBI in the 1980s to conduct covert surveillance and infiltration of groups of Americans opposed to the President's policies in Central America, including Amnesty International and the American Federation of Teachers. Despite an intensive intelligence campaign, no evidence of criminal wrongdoing ever was produced.

In his classic *Olmstead* dissent, discussed at the outset of this chapter, Justice Brandeis fur- ther observed: "The right to be left alone is the most comprehensive of rights and the right most valued by civilized men."[336] Regrettably, the FBI has never fully grasped this fundamental truth. The inexorable expansion of electronic eavesdropping, that so troubled Justice Brandeis in 1928, approached critical mass in 1995, when the Bureau proposed a national wiretapping system to monitor simultaneously 1 out of every 100 telephone lines in some parts of the country.[337]

The IRS: "No agency of the U.S. federal government retains more information on American citizens than the Internal Revenue Service."[338] Its files contain financial records of all working Americans, corporations, and organizations, which make agency records a formidable tool in campaigns by the government against political targets. "Most likely under pressure from the FBI, the IRS focused its selective enforcement capabilities throughout the 1950s on dissident organi- zations and individuals."[339] During the 1960s, the IRS served as the Kennedy Administration's "hired gun" against chosen targets—mainly right-wing extremist groups. In 1963, President Kennedy used the IRS to develop an aggressive plan, called the Ideological Organizations Project, to examine the tax-exempt status of 10,000 political organizations.[340] That project was aban- doned after Kennedy's assassination.

Between 1966 and 1974, the IRS and the FBI engaged in a persecutive alliance, which even a high-ranking IRS official termed "probably illegal."[341] Tax records were used to "disrupt and neu- tralize the political threat of the New Left."[342] The idea was that prosecutions and convictions of any kind, such as for tax evasion, could remove the leaders of dissident movements—by putting them in prison. For example, of the 90 individuals designated as "Key Black Extremists" by the FBI, the tax files on 72 were passed to the bureau by the IRS. The FBI also used IRS-released contribution lists of political organizations, including the SCLC led by Martin Luther King. It was hoped that a publicized tax investigation would raise doubts about King and his group among donors and thereby reduce contributions.[343]

In 1969, the IRS created a Special Service Staff (SSS) to examine what it termed "ideological organizations." "Its purpose was to gather information on political groups and individuals . . . and to stimulate audits by local and district IRS offices based upon this information."[344] Like J. Edgar Hoover, Paul Wright, who headed the SSS, justified any improprieties on the ground "that he was participating in an effort to save the country from dissidents and extremists."[345] The SSS did not even pick its own targets; they were provided by outside agencies, mainly the FBI. By 1973, the SSS possessed surveillance files on over 8,500 Americans, including Mayor John Lindsay of New York City and Nobel Prize winning scientist Linus Pauling, and over 2,800 organizations, such as the Americans for Democratic Action and the California Migrant Ministry.[346]

No President ever used the IRS as a punitive weapon more than Richard Nixon. Nixon pressured the IRS to audit selected persons on his notorious "enemies list." Nowhere in American political history did John Stuart Mill's warning of unaccountability, abuse of power, and the sacrifice of Constitutionality to some dubious higher purpose (in this case, Nixon's re-election) ever ring truer than in Watergate.

The Defense Department: During the social upheaval of the late 1960s, military intelligence agencies collected vast amounts of information about the activities, financial affairs, sex lives, and psychiatric histories of persons engaged in "domestic unrest"—a term the Army applied to anyone seeking to change government policy. By 1971, the Army possessed over 80,000 biographical dossiers and over 211,000 "subversive files" on organizations. None of those targeted individuals was affiliated with the armed forces, nor were any of the targeted organizations, such as Americans for Democratic Action and the Urban League.[347]

> Army agents infiltrated Resurrection City during the 1968 Poor People's March on Washington. Agents also posed as students to monitor classes in Black Studies at New York University. The army infiltrated the October and November 1969 moratorium marches around the country. Military personnel even posed as newspaper reporters and television newsmen during the 1968 Democratic National Convention in Chicago to tape interviews with demonstration leaders.[348]

The NSA: Between 1952 and 1974, the National Security Agency, the most secretive of all American intelligence agencies,[349] compiled files on 75,000 American citizens. The first NSA surveillance program was called SHAMROCK and involved the interception of all private cables leaving the United States. Eventually, "the NSA was intercepting some 150,000 messages per month . . . dwarfing the CIA's mail-opening program."[350]

The second NSA domestic intelligence program was called MINARET and involved the monitoring of international telephone communications of individuals and organizations on a designated "watch list," ranging from political groups, to celebrities, to ordinary citizens. "[T]he names on the list included the peaceful, nonviolent, and totally legal."[351]

After the *New York Times* ran a sensational story in 1974 documenting the CIA's history of domestic surveillance against American citizens[352] and the 1976 revelations of the United States Senate Committee to Study Governmental Operations With Respect to Intelligence Activities, chaired by Senator Frank Church, Congress passed the Foreign Intelligence Surveillance Act

(FISA). FISA restricted any surveillance of U.S. citizens to those suspected of having contact with "foreign powers" and terrorist organizations. The act required that the administration submit evidence for warrantless surveillance within 24 hours of the onset of the surveillance to the Foreign Intelligence Surveillance Court (FISC). The FISC is made up of seven Federal District Court judges appointed by the Chief Justice of the Supreme Court and meets in a secret, sealed room in the Department of Justice Building.[353]

The NSA is perhaps best known for its ECHELON operation, an automated global interception and relay system.[354] ECHELON goes back to the late 1940s and, of course, as technology has advanced, its capabilities—and its priorities—have expanded enormously. Huge ground-based radio antennae around the world intercept satellite transmissions and tap surface traffic, gathering all these transmissions indiscriminately and distilling the desired information through artificial intelligence programs. ECHELON monitors everything from communications satellites to radio transmissions to undersea telephone cables. It also intercepts Internet and e-mail transmissions through so-called "sniffer" devices and uses search software to scan for Web sites that might be "of interest."[355] Computers sort out whatever they have been programmed to sort out—for example, words and phrases (such as "bomb," "terrorist," and "blow up"), particular telephone numbers, or particular persons' names. ECHELON reportedly may intercept as many as three billion communications every day. "It's been estimated 'E' sifts through 99.9999 percent of all global communications to get at the 0.0001 percent that is of interest to it."[356]

ECHELON has eavesdropped on numerous public officials, including the late Senator Strom Thurmond (when he was 86-years-old),[357] Princess Diana (the NSA admits having over 1,000 pages on Diana, reportedly because of her work promoting the banning of land mines—a position opposed by the Pentagon),[358] Mark Thatcher, the son of former British Prime Minister Margaret Thatcher (because of his involvement in a large arms contract between Britain and Saudi Arabia),[359] and even Mother Theresa[360] and the Pope.[361] In addition, charities operating overseas are monitored, including Amnesty International and Christian Aid,[362] because they sometimes have access to controversial regimes. A former NSA employee, who spent 20 years in intelligence has said: "Anybody who is politically active will eventually end up on the NSA's radar screen."[363]

ECHELON has also been used for commercial espionage. For example, according to the German news magazine *Der Spiegel*, the NSA intercepted messages in 1990 about a pending $200 million telecommunications deal between Indonesia and a Japanese satellite manufacturer. President George H.W. Bush intervened on the basis of the intercepted intelligence and convinced the Indonesian government to split the contract between the Japanese company and AT&T.[364] For years the NSA denied any participation in industrial espionage, but, in 2000, former CIA director James Woolsey wrote a confirming article in the *Wall Street Journal*, titled "Why We Spy on Our Allies."[365] Woolsey's argument was that spying was the only way for the U.S. to level the commercial playing field because of what he alleged was widespread corporate bribery in Europe.

Since ECHELON is a highly classified operation, it is conducted with little or no external oversight. Indeed, it is so top-secret that even its successes are not publicly acknowledged. For example, it is believed (but never verified) that ECHELON was instrumental in the capture of international terrorist "Carlos the Jackal" and was used to help identify two Libyans accused of planting a bomb on PanAm Flight 103 that exploded over Scotland in 1988, killing 271 people. But, however successful ECHELON may be in capturing terrorists, international drug dealers, and other criminals, it has also been used for indiscriminate "data mining" and other purposes well outside its original mission. Serious privacy concerns have been raised about its ability to monitor ordinary citizens for their political affiliations or for no probable cause at all—in violation of the First, Fourth, and Fifth Amendments of the U.S. Constitution.

A week after the 9/11 terrorist attacks, Congress overwhelmingly passed a two joint resolutions, each known as AUMF. One was Authorization for Use of Military Force Against Terrorists (the other was Authorization for Use of Military Force Against Iraq). The AUMF regarding terrorists said in part:

> [T]he President is authorized to use all necessary and appropriate force against those nations, organizations, or persons he determines planned, authorized, committed, or aided the terrorist attacks that occurred on September 11, 2001.

The Bush Administration interpreted AUMF as an authorization to override FISA, though there is no evidence that Congress intended this. In fact, former Senator Tom Daschle, majority leader at the time, would later write in a *Washington Post* editorial:

> "I can state categorically that the subject of warrantless wiretaps of American citizens never came up. I did not and never would have supported giving authority to the president for such wiretaps. I am also confident that the 98 senators who voted in favor of authorization of force against al Qaeda did not believe that they were also voting for warrantless domestic surveillance."[366]

According to Ronald Kessler's book *The Terrorist Watch* (a staunch defense of the AUMF), the NSA began escalating its domestic surveillance program two weeks after 9/11, following an Oval Office meeting between President Bush and NSA director Michael Hayden.[367] Actually, the escalation probably began seven months before 9/11 with Operation Groundbreaker, in which domestic call monitoring and the eavesdropping on U.S. citizens was contracted to AT&T.[368] It was the largest outsourcing in the history of American intelligence, worth an estimated $2 to $5 billion.[369] Shortly thereafter, the NSA began awarding research contracts to other large telecommunications companies for a data-mining program called Novel Intelligence from Massive Data (NIMD).[370] FISA requires that warrantless domestic surveillance must have a probable cause that the target is a terrorist. NIMD has no such limitation. The program collects information on American citizens not suspected of any crime or any terrorist connections.[371] NIMD represents the largest data base ever assembled, containing detailed phone records of tens of millions of citizens.[372]

In early 2002, President Bush signed a secret executive order allowing the NSA to eavesdrop on Americans within the country without the court-approved warrants ordinarily required for domestic spying.[373] A former senior official noted: "This is really a sea change. . . . It's almost a mainstay of this country that the N.S.A. only does foreign searches."[374] The executive order would not be revealed in the media until the end of 2005, when it was reported in the *New York Times*.[375] In response, Vice President Dick Cheney insisted that President Bush had the authority to order warrantless eavesdropping. He defended the NIMB program as "good, sound policy" and "the right thing to do," insisting that the program had "saved thousands of lives."[376]

In late 2002, AT&T built a secret, highly secured room in its network operations center in Bridgeton, Missouri, used to conduct secret government wiretapping operations. Moreover, according to retired AT&T technician turned whistle-blower Mark Klein, AT&T's central office in San Francisco contains a secret data-mining center used to monitor phone and Internet traffic. According to Klein: "I simply do not believe [the administration's] claims that the NSA's spying program is really limited to foreign communications or is otherwise consistent with the NSA's charter or with FISA."[377]

The American Civil Liberties Union and other advocacy groups filed a lawsuit against the government, claiming that the NSA's warrantless wiretapping was unconstitutional. In 2006, a federal judge in Detroit agreed and ordered a halt to the program.[378] The ACLU hailed the decision, saying "It's another nail in the coffin of executive unilateralism."[379] Officials of the Bush administration decried the ruling, insisting that the NSA surveillance was both lawful and a vital tool to protect the country. One veteran official declared: "It is guaranteed to be overturned."[380] That turned out to be an accurate prediction, as the 6th U.S. Circuit Court of Appeals overturned that decision in 2007, ruling that the plaintiffs had not been shown to be directly affected by any Fourth Amendment violations, and therefore lacked standing to sue.[381] On February 18, 2008, the U.S. Supreme Court declined to hear the ACLU's appeal, allowing the 6th Circuit's ruling to stand. The decision was rendered on procedural grounds and said nothing about the merits of the case. The ACLU expressed its disappointment with the Court's refusal:

> Congress enacted the Foreign Intelligence Surveillance Act intending to protect the rights of U.S. citizens and residents, and the president systematically broke that law over a period of more than five years. It's very disturbing that the president's actions will not be reviewed by the Supreme Court. It shouldn't be left to executive branch officials alone to determine what limits apply to their own surveillance activities and whether those limits are being honored. Allowing the executive branch to police itself flies in the face of the constitutional system of checks and balances.[382]

The legal director of the ACLU added: "The Court's unwillingness to act makes it even more important that Congress insist on legislative safeguards that will protect civil liberties without jeopardizing national security."[383]

When he was a candidate, President Obama pledged that there would be no warrantless wiretapping in his administration;[384] so, at this writing, the future of the NSA's domestic surveillance program is unsettled. It continues, however, to generate fierce controversy. Many people argue that we are in a state of war and that national security trumps civil liberties.[385] Some concede that even if warrantless searches *are* illegal, Congress should make them legal.[386] Many others passionately disagree and see the specter of Big Brother looming. One of them is the distinguished legal scholar Lawrence Tribe of Harvard University. In a 2006 letter to Congressman John Conyers, Tribe argued that the AUMF cannot be a license to violate the Fourth Amendment's "right of the people to be secure . . . against unreasonable searches and seizures." The letter concluded: "It follows that the presidential program of surveillance at issue here is a violation of the separation of powers—as grave an abuse of executive authority as I can recall ever having studied."[387]

The CIA: From 1953 to 1973, the Central Intelligence Agency intercepted, opened, and photographed 250,000 personal letters, generating an index of 1.5 million names.[388] It also collected arrest reports from state and local police forces—including "the names of 300,000 persons arrested for homosexual acts."[389]

Beginning in the 1960s, the agency regularly monitored the overseas activities of so-called "domestic dissidents." Purportedly interested only in Americans believed to be foreign agents, the CIA spied on a vast range of traveling citizens with no apparent foreign intelligence value.[390] For example, singer Eartha Kitt was put under surveillance for at least 10 years while living and working in Paris.[391] Under this program, known as Operation CHAOS, the CIA reported on many anti-war activists, as well as expatriates like Kitt. Agents "burglarized their hotel rooms and their homes, eavesdropped on their conversations, and bugged their phones."[392]

As part of the CHAOS project, the CIA also spied on political radicals *inside* the United States, in violation of its 1947 charter. It created detailed files on 7,000 American citizens and 1,000 groups, including peace and civil rights organizations.[393] Operation CHAOS ended officially in 1974, but by then the ban on domestic CIA activity had become effectively inoperative. In 1981, President Reagan issued an Executive Order formally rescinding that prohibition, thus enabling the CIA to conduct covert domestic operations.[394]

TORTURE AMERICAN-STYLE

The use of torture by governments has a long, ignominious history. For over 2,000 years, from the red-hot irons of ancient Rome to the rack and thumbscrews of the Middle Ages, anyone interrogated by officials of the state could expect to suffer unspeakable cruelty. In the past 200 years or so, from the Age of Enlightenment, when social philosophers like Bentham and Beccaria spoke out against the horrors of torture, to the present time, when organizations like Amnesty International and Human Rights Watch lead sustained anti-torture campaigns, the practice of state-sponsored torture has declined among civilized nations and persons. Nevertheless, it remains a popular method of repression and punishment in totalitarian regimes and terrorist organizations. Philosopher Hannah Arendt regards torture as an indispensible tool of totalitarianism.[395] Moreover, as recent history has revealed, democratic governments still sometimes use it as well.

Most formalized definitions of torture are fundamentally similar, though they may differ in the amount of specificity each contains. Some are quite broad:

> "Torture" means the intentional infliction of severe pain or suffering, whether physical or mental, upon a person in the custody or under the control of the accused.

> Rome Statute of the International Criminal Court

Others are more detailed:

> Any act by which severe pain or suffering, whether physical or mental, is intentionally inflicted on a person for such purposes as obtaining from him or a third person information or a confession, punishing him for an act he or a third person has committed or is suspected of having committed, or intimidating or coercing him or a third person . . . when such pain or suffering is inflicted by or at the instigation of or with the consent or acquiescence of a public official or other person acting in an official capacity.

> United Nations Convention Against Torture

The Bush administration created a newer and narrower definition:

> Physical pain amounting to torture must be equivalent in intensity to the pain accompanying serious physical injury, such as organ failure, impairment of bodily function, or even death.

> Justice Department Memorandum, August 1, 2002

The Bush position notwithstanding, official U.S. tolerance of torture has diminished significantly in modern times. Once, the so-called "third degree" was the norm for police interrogation. Consider the opinion rendered by a New York City magistrate in a 1922 investigation of the beating of suspects with wet blackjacks and rubber hoses:

> "It is almost impossible to secure evidence in many cases that will result in the conviction of the guilty without obtaining either a confession from the defendant or information from sources hostile to the ends of justice. Hence, when a crime is committed, the custom is to take into custody the suspect and others who are supposed to have knowledge of the occurrence and obtain from them whatever information is possible. It is obvious that, if they are reluctant to speak, they can be induced to do so only by the use of force."[396]

In stark contrast, a New York City judge sentenced an NYPD officer to 30 years in prison for a 1997 interrogation, during which the officer jammed the handle of a plunger into a suspect's rectum. The judge was not the least bit tolerant, condemning the officer's brutality as an "unusually heinous" crime.[397]

While American law enforcement agencies may now eschew torture, the same cannot be said for American intelligence agencies and the U.S. military. Indeed, the use or encouragement of torture by the CIA has a documented history going back nearly 50 years. A now-declassified 1963 CIA training manual, titled *Counterintelligence Interrogation* describes the torture methods used against prisoners during the Vietnam War.[398] Another declassified document, *Human Resource Exploitation Training Manual—1983*, details techniques of torture used by the CIA against suspected subversives in Central America during the 1980s.[399] Like its 1963 progenitor, the 1983 manual describes stripping suspects naked and keeping them blindfolded. "These interrogation rooms should be windowless, dark and soundproof, with no toilets."[400] According to the manual:

> "The 'questioning' room is the battlefield upon which the 'questioner' and the subject meet. . . . However, the 'questioner' has the advantage in that he has total control over the subject and his environment."[401]

Solitary confinement and sensory deprivation are recommended as ways to induce stress and anxiety. "The more complete the deprivation, the more rapidly and deeply the subject is affected."[402] "[P]sychological coercion has been considered effective for most of the life of the agency, and its slippery definition might allow it to squeeze through loopholes in a law that seeks to ban prisoner abuse."[403] The manual cites the results of experiments conducted on volunteers who allowed themselves to be suspended in water while wearing blacked out goggles and ear muffs. "The stress and anxiety became almost unbearable for most subjects."[404]

The manual discourages physical torture, "advising interrogators to use more subtle methods to threaten and frighten the suspect."[405] However, in the shameless manner of O.J. Simpson's notorious "If I Did It" book, the CIA explains—"hypothetically" of course—how to conduct physical torture. The document's introduction states: "While we do not stress the use of coercive techniques, we do want to make you aware of them and the proper way to use them."[406]

Moreover, the manual actually says that such methods are justified when subjects have been trained to resist noncoercive measures.[407]

> "The pain which is being inflicted upon him from outside himself may actually intensify his will to resist. On the other hand, pain which he feels he is inflicting

upon himself is more likely to sap his resistance. . . . For example, if he is required to maintain rigid positions such as standing at attention or sitting on a stool for long periods of time, the immediate source of pain is not the 'questioner' but the subject himself. . . . After a period of time the subject is likely to exhaust his internal motivational strength."[408]

A Honduran unit known as Battalion 316 was trained by CIA instructors in the early 1980s, at the height of the Reagan administration's war against communism in Central America. A CIA spokesman later told the Senate Intelligence Committee: "The course consisted of three weeks of classroom instruction, followed by two weeks of practical exercises, which included the questioning of actual prisoners by the students."[409] It was for that purpose the 1983 manual was written.

The manual advises interrogators to "manipulate the subject's environment, to create unpleasant or intolerable situations."[410] In a 1997 interview, a former member of Battalion 316 said that CIA instructors had taught him to discover what his prisoners loved and what they hated: "If a person did not like cockroaches, then that person might be more cooperative if there were cockroaches running around the room."[411]

The manual also suggests that interrogators show their prisoners letters from home to convey the impression that the prisoners' relatives are suffering or are in danger.[412] Another former member of Battalion 316 recalled using this technique:

"The first thing we would say is that we know your mother, your younger brother. And better you cooperate, because if you don't, we're going to bring them in and rape them and torture them and kill them."[413]

ABC News has reported that the CIA has a list of six "Enhanced Interrogation Techniques," instituted in 2002.[414] One of them is called "Cold Treatment," in which the prisoner is left to stand naked in a cell kept at 50 degrees and constantly doused with cold water.[415] One detainee reportedly died of hypothermia after he was left to stand naked and wet throughout the harsh Afghanistan night.[416]

According to the *Washington Post*, a CIA detention center in Afghanistan used psychological interrogation techniques known as "stress and duress" tactics, sometimes called "torture lite."[417] Two prisoners died there in 2002. It was initially announced that autopsies had attributed one death to a heart attack and the other to a pulmonary embolism.[418] After a criminal investigation, military pathologists re-classed the modes of death as "homicide," attributing both deaths to "blunt force injuries."[419]

The former section chief of the FBI's International Terrorism Operations has called psychological torture a "voodoo science."[420] The American Medical Association and the American Psychiatric Association have banned their members from participating in interrogations, but the issue has divided the American Psychological Association (APA), which has not forbidden such participation by members. The Army maintains that military psychologists help to make interrogations "safe, legal and effective."[421] In fact, a specially convened APA task force ruled in 2006 that psychologists *could* assist in military interrogations. Critics within the organization believed that the task force had been rigged. Six of the 10 members had ties to the armed services, which ignited conflict of interest charges.[422]

One theory was that the A.P.A. had given its stamp of approval to military interrogations as part of a quid pro quo. In exchange, they suspected the Pentagon was working to allow psychologists—who, unlike psychiatrists, are not medical doctors—to prescribe medication, dramatically increasing their income. (The military has championed modern-day psychology since World War II, and continues to be one of the largest single employers of psychologists through its network of veterans' hospitals. It also funded a prescription-drug training program for military psychologists in the early 90s.)[423]

In 2007, dozens of angry psychologists wrote a joint letter to the APA's president arguing that abusive interrogations violate the ethics of that organization:

"We write you as psychologists concerned about the participation of our profession in abusive interrogations of national security detainees. . . . It is now indisputable that psychologists and psychology were directly and officially responsible for the development and migration of abusive interrogation techniques, techniques which the International Committee of the Red Cross has labeled 'tantamount to torture.'"[424]

A few months later, the APA rejected a proposed measure that would have flatly prohibited members from taking any part in interrogations at U.S. military detention centers.[425] The APA did, however, did vote to reaffirm its opposition to torture and restricted members from taking part in interrogations involving any of more than a dozen specific practices, including stress positions or sleep deprivation, forced nakedness, hooding, mock executions, simulated drowning (waterboarding), sexual and religious humiliation, the exploitation of phobias, the use of mind-altering drugs, the use of dogs to frighten detainees, exposing prisoners to extreme heat and cold, physical assault, and threats against a prisoner's family.[426] As is now known, most, if not all, of these techniques were utilized in an exotic-sounding place destined to become the symbol of American torture.

During the brutal regime of Iraqi dictator Saddam Hussein, Abu Ghraib, 20 miles outside of Bagdad, was one of the world's most infamous prisons, complete with repulsive living conditions, weekly executions, and routine torture.[427] After U.S. and coalition military forces overthrew Saddam in 2003, Abu Ghraib was cleaned up, repaired, and turned into the Bagdad Correctional facility, a U.S. military prison. While many of the inmates held there were common criminals, some were suspected of being "high value" war criminals and terrorists.[428]

After the Iraqi government fell, Brigadier General Janis Karpinski, an Army reservist, was named commander of the 800th Military Police Brigade and was put in charge of military prisons in Iraq. Karpinski was an experienced intelligence officer, who had served in the Special Forces and in the 1991 Gulf War; but, like most of the 3,400 reservists under her command, she had no training in handling prisoners.[429] In December, 2003, Karpinski described the daily lives of Abu Ghraib prisoners in an interview with the *St. Petersburg Times*: "[L]iving conditions now are better in prison than at home. At one point we were concerned they wouldn't want to leave."[430] But almost right from the start, stories of mistreatment and abuse at Abu Ghraib began quietly circulating. A major investigation of the Army's prison system was undertaken. A month after her rosy interview, Gen. Karpinski was formally admonished and suspended. She would later be demoted to colonel.

In February 2004, a report written by Major General Antonio M. Taguba, not meant for public release, was completed. "Its conclusions about the institutional failures of the Army prison system were devastating."[431] The report described numerous instances of "sadistic, blatant, and wanton criminal abuses" at Abu Ghraib:[432]

Breaking chemical lights and pouring the phosforic [sic] liquid on detainees; pouring cold water on naked detainees; beating detainees with a broom handle and a chair; threatening male detainees with rape; allowing a military police guard to stitch the wound of a detainee who was injured after being slammed against the wall of his cell; sodomizing a detainee with a chemical light and perhaps a broom stick, and using military work dogs to frighten and intimidate detainees with threats of attack, and in one instance actually biting a detainee.[433]

Taguba had also collected extremely graphic photographs and videotapes taken by American soldiers as the abuses were occurring—although he did not include this stunning evidence in his report because of their sensitive nature.

> The photographs tell it all. In one, Private England, a cigarette dangling from her mouth, is giving a jaunty thumbs up sign and pointing to the genitals of a young Iraqi, who is naked except for a sandbag over his head, as he masturbates. . . . In another, England stands arm in arm with Specialist Graner; both are grinning and giving the thumbs-up behind a cluster of perhaps seven naked Iraqis, knees bent, piled clumsily in a pyramid. . . . Then there is another cluster of hooded bodies, with a female soldier standing in front, taking photographs. Yet another photograph shows a kneeling, naked unhooded male prisoner, head momentarily turned away from the camera, posed to make it appear that he is performing oral sex on another male prisoner, who is naked and hooded.[434]

Taguba would later tell reporter Seymour Hersh that a video showing a male American soldier sodomizing a female detainee was too inflammatory to make public. "It's bad enough that there were photographs of Arab men wearing women's panties," Taguba said.[435]

The photos, however, did find their way into the press. In April, 2004, the American public was shocked by televised photographs from Abu Ghraib showing hooded Iraqis stripped naked, posed in contorted positions, and suffering humiliating abuse while American soldiers stood by smiling.[436]

The Taguba report contained quotes from prisoners that added to the horror. Detainee No. 151362 stated:

> "They said we will make you wish to die and it will not happen . . . They stripped me naked. One of them told me he would rape me. He drew a picture of a woman to my back and made me stand in a shameful position holding my buttocks.". . . 'Do you pray to Allah?' one asked. I said yes. They said '[expletive] you. And [expletive] him.' One of them said, 'You are not getting out of here health[y], you are getting out of here handicapped.' And he said to me, 'Are you married?' I said, 'Yes.' They said, 'If your wife saw you like this, she will be disappointed.' One of them said, 'But if I saw her now she would not be disappointed now because I would rape her.' . . . They ordered me to thank Jesus that I'm alive. . . . I said to him, 'I believe in Allah.' So he said, 'But I believe in torture and I will torture you.'"[437]

By early 2005, seven members of the 372nd Military Police Company had been charged with various counts of assault, conspiracy, indecent acts, maltreatment, and dereliction of duty.[438] In all, military courts martial convicted 12 persons. Most of the sentences were relatively minor, involving a few months of incarceration or, at least in one case, merely a reduction in rank. Three of the sentences, however, were more substantial.

Private First Class Lynndie England, one of the "stars" of the leaked photographs was sentenced to three years behind bars. She blamed her boyfriend, Specialist Charles Graner, the other notable figure in the original photos, claiming she had been "lured in" by Graner.[439]

Staff Sergeant Ivan Frederick received an eight-year sentence.[440] In a letter to his family, Frederick related a chilling story about an Iraqi prisoner, under the control of what the Abu Ghraib guards called OGA—"Other Government Agencies"—a euphemism for the CIA. The prisoner had been brought to Frederick's unit for questioning. Frederick wrote:

> "They stressed him out so bad that the man passed away. They put his body in a body bag and packed him in ice for approximately 24 hours in the shower. . . . The next day the medics came and put his body on a stretcher, placed a fake IV in his arm and took him away."[441]

The prisoner described by Frederick was one of eight so-called "ghost" detainees investigated by the military. They allegedly were incarcerated at Abu Ghraib but kept off the prison's roster at the request of the CIA. According to the investigation, the prisoner observed by Frederick had been detained by Navy Seals, who had hit him in the head with a rifle butt during his arrest, which apparently led to his death. "But the investigation suggested that the detainee might have survived if he had been screened by doctors, as would have been required had he been properly registered with the military."[442]

Army Reserve Specialist Charles Graner, noted earlier, received the harshest of all the Abu Ghraib sentences—10 years in prison. "Led from the courtroom in handcuffs and leg chains, Graner twice answered 'No Ma'am' when asked whether he had any regrets or apologies."[443] He insisted that he had not enjoyed participating in what he called "irregular treatment"[444]—an assertion seemingly belied by his grinning visage in the photos. He also steadfastly claimed that he had been obeying his superiors, following orders from higher-ranking interrogators when he and the other guards abused their prisoners.[445]

Graner's "Nuremberg" defense was self-serving no doubt, but it did raise disturbing questions about a possible cover-up along the chain of command. There were no officers convicted of any crimes related to Abu Ghraib. Indeed, Sergeant Frederick was the highest-ranking soldier found guilty. The only officer to be charged, Lieutenant Colonel Steven Jordan, was acquitted in 2007 and received a simple reprimand.[446] Colonel Thomas Pappas, the top military intelligence officer stationed at Abu Ghraib, received only a nonjudicial reprimand for two counts of dereliction, including allowing the use of dogs during interrogation.[447]

The most ironic casualty of Abu Ghraib was General Antonio Taguba, whose frank report was the catalyst of the scandal. In 2007, civilian Pentagon officials forced him into retirement because he had been too "zealous."[448] Taguba's assignment to investigate Abu Ghraib was a classic no-win predicament. In his words: "If I lie, I lose. And if I tell the truth, I lose."[449]

Indeed, so unpopular was the Taguba report in Pentagon circles that the Army undertook a second investigation of military detention operations in Iraq. This second report reached very different conclusions. Although acknowledging that the soldiers assigned to Abu Ghraib were poorly trained and ineffectively organized, none of these flaws were blamed directly for the abusive treatment. Instead, the report attributed the abuse to the "unauthorized action taken by a few individuals."[450] The report echoed the Pentagon's longstanding argument that a handful of rogue soldiers were responsible for the misconduct at Abu Ghraib.[451]

Likewise, after the shocking photos were revealed on television, Secretary of Defense Donald Rumsfeld quickly assured Congress that the abuses were "perpetrated by a small number of U.S. military."[452] He referred to them as "a few bad apples."[453] But Congress was unconvinced. A report issued by the Senate Armed Services Committee concluded that Rumsfeld and other high-ranking Bush administration officials were responsible for the harsh interrogations that took place at Abu Ghraib. The committee chairman, Sen. Carl Levin, stated: "Attempts by senior officials to pass the buck to low ranking soldiers while avoiding any responsibility for abuses are unconscionable."[454]

According to the senate report, the prisoner abuses at Abu Ghraib were "not simply the result of a few soldiers acting on their own. . . . [Rumsfeld's] authorization of aggressive interrogation techniques and subsequent interrogation policies and plans approved by senior military and civilian officials conveyed the message that physical pressures and degradation were appropriate treatment for detainees in U.S. military custody."[455]

In 2006, former General Janis Karpinski, who had been in charge of Abu Ghraib until being relieved of her command soon after the scandal broke, told a Spanish newspaper that she had seen a letter signed by Rumsfeld authorizing the mistreatment of detainees and the use of harsh interrogation techniques. According to Karpinski: "The methods consisted of making prisoners stand for long periods, sleep deprivation . . . playing music at full volume, having to sit in uncomfortably [sic] . . . Rumsfeld authorized these things."[456] Karpinski added that a notation in the margin of the letter, in the same handwriting as Rumsfeld's apparent signature, said, "Make sure this is accomplished."[457]

Karpinski's extraordinary allegation was met with understandable skepticism in some quarters, since she had already lied earlier when she described the reluctance of some Iraqi detainees to leave the supposedly comfortable conditions at Abu Ghraib. On the other hand, her story did not conflict with Rumsfeld's hard line image. Indeed, a month before Karpinski's interview with *El Pais*, the increasingly unpopular Rumsfeld had already resigned as Secretary of Defense, largely due to public criticism over the Iraq War.

Historian Alfred W. McCoy, who has written extensively on the practice of torture worldwide, writes that the Abu Ghraib photographs "are snapshots not of simple brutality or even a breakdown in 'military discipline.' What they record are CIA torture techniques that have metastasized like an undetected cancer inside the U.S. intelligence community over the past half century."[458]

> That iconic photo of a hooded Iraqi with fake electrical wires hanging from his arms shows, not the sadism of a few "creeps," but the telltale signs of sophisticated torture. The prisoner is hooded for sensory deprivation. His arms are extended for self-inflicted pain.[459]

McCoy has called the CIA's discovery of psychological torture "The first real revolution in this cruel science since the 17th century."[460]

The Geneva Convention clearly states: "Prisoners of war who refuse to answer may not be threatened, insulted, or exposed to any unpleasant or disadvantageous treatment of any kind."[461] At Abu Ghraib, prisoners were subjected to "unpleasant" treatment of almost *every* kind. Abu Ghraib was the culmination of secret CIA policy begun during the Cold War and formalized in those two infamous torture manuals. Because, even though Abu Ghraib was a military facility, the fingerprints of the CIA cover its walls. "The CIA was the lead agency at Abu Ghraib, enlisting Army intelligence to support its mission."[462]

In 2005, yet another military investigation report was released. This one involved a detention camp, half a world away from Iraq, in Cuba. The Guantanamo Bay Naval Base, on the southeastern end of the island, was established in 1898 in the aftermath of the Spanish-American War. Under the 1903 Cuban-American Treaty, the United States was granted a perpetual lease of the area—a lease the Cuban government has long considered illegal. Since 2002, the base has contained a detainment camp for military combatants from Afghanistan and for other suspected terrorists from around the world. Unlike Abu Ghraib, however, Guantanamo does not house Iraqi captives, since they are considered POWs.

The Guantanamo report detailed how Saudi national Mohamed Qahtani, the alleged "20th hijacker" in the 9/11 terrorist attacks, was interrogated in 2002 while being confronted by snarling military dogs. Qahtani also had a leash attached to his chains and was forced to parade around with women's underwear on his head while wearing a bra.[463]

"The military has long contended that abuses at Guantanamo were aberrations for which soldiers have been disciplined."[464] But the 2005 findings presented strong evidence that the abusive practices seen in the photographs from Abu Ghraib were not the invention of a small group of thrill-seeking military police officers. "The report shows that they were used on Qahtani several months before the United States invaded Iraq."[465]

Defense Secretary Rumsfeld approved the techniques used on Qahtani as part of a special interrogation plan aimed at breaking down the stubborn detainee. Rumsfeld had approved a list of 16 harsh techniques for use at Guantanamo. Most of these techniques, involving intimidation and humiliation, were described in general terms and were subject to broad interpretation by interrogators.[466] Qahtani endured sleep deprivation and many of the harshest of the approved techniques. The report found that the cumulative effect of those tactics "resulted in degrading and abusive treatment" but stopped short of torture. Moreover, the techniques reportedly forced the silent Qahtani to talk, achieving what were described as "solid intelligence gains."[467] Given the reprehensible nature of Qahtani's alleged complicity in the 9/11 attacks, this can be a tempting neutralization. However, it ignores a fundamental moral truth: "Torture is defined by what is done to the victim, not by the usefulness of the information obtained."[468]

Furthermore, whether Qahtani's mistreatment reflected a "special plan" for him alone or was standard operating procedure at Guantanamo is, at the very least, debatable. Documents released in 2004 reveal that over a two-year period detainees held at Guantanamo were shackled to the floor in fetal positions for more than 24 hours, left without food and water, and allowed to urinate and defecate on themselves.[469]

According to FBI memos, never meant to be disclosed publicly but leaked to the press in late 2004, FBI agents said that they had witnessed detainees subjected to extreme heat and extreme cold, and the routine use of snarling dogs—contrary to previous statements by senior Defense Department officials[470]—and that one detainee was bombarded with ear-splitting rap music and flashing strobe lights while he was wrapped in an Israeli flag. One of the agents alleged that the "softening up" techniques had been approved by then-Deputy Defense Secretary Paul Wolfowitz.[471] Another agent described a detainee, who was almost unconscious on the floor of an interview room, with a pile of hair next to him. "He had apparently been literally pulling his own hair out throughout the night."[472] One of the memorandums described female interrogators forcibly squeezing male prisoners' genitals and smearing prisoners with red fluid said to be menstrual blood.[473]

When Donald Rumsfeld was asked in 2005 about the force-feeding of hunger-striking detainees at Guantanamo—a practice that involved inserting tubes as wide as fingers directly through stomachs and nostrils without anesthesia, as prisoners convulsed and vomited blood—Rumsfeld replied: "I'm not a doctor."[474] It was an interesting comment by Rumsfeld, since actual doctors were among his harshest critics. A report released in 2005 by a Massachusetts-based group of health professionals, Physicians for Human Rights, states that "since at least 2002, the United States has been engaged in systematic psychological torture" of Guantanamo detainees.[475] The group concluded that the interrogation practices at Guantanamo had "led to devastating health consequences for the individuals subjected to them."[476] This was confirmed by a senior Bush administration official in early 2009, when he revealed that the interrogation of Mohammed al-Qahtani was so intense that he had to be hospitalized twice at Guantanamo with bradycardia, a life-threatening condition in which the heart rates drops below 60 beats a minute. "At one point, Qahtani's heart rate dropped to 35 beats a minute, the record shows."[477]

The United States is a signee of the 1984 United Nations Convention against Torture and Other Cruel, Inhuman or Degrading Treatment or Punishment, under which the U.S. agreed to submit to U.N. scrutiny of its compliance with the convention.[478] That agreement was put to the test in 2006, when the United Nations Committee Against Torture released its report on Guantanamo.[479] The report happened to be issued one day after two Guantanamo detainees tried to kill themselves by overdosing on antidepressants. Their attempts brought to 41 the number of inmates who had tried to commit suicide there since 2002.[480] The U.N. panel, comprised of nine international experts, called on the United States to close the detention center at Guantanamo Bay.[481] The report also called for the prosecution of officers and politicians "up to the highest level" who are responsible for the torture of detainees. The Bush administration denounced the report as a "hatchet job."[482]

The State Department's top lawyer told reporters:

> "We acknowledge that there were serious incidents of abuse. We've all seen Abu Ghraib. . . . [But] clearly our record has improved over the last few years."[483]

The United Nations report was especially critical of the worst of the CIA's six "Enhanced Interrogation Techniques" practiced at Guantanamo, that of waterboarding—the simulation of the sensation of drowning.[484] After visiting Guantanamo in 2007, a Finnish law professor serving as a U.N. investigator said that he "strongly suspected" the CIA of using torture on terrorism suspects and suggested that many prisoners were not being prosecuted to keep the abuse from emerging at trial. He also accused the CIA of destroying videotapes in 2005 that recorded al-Qaeda suspects undergoing waterboarding.[485]

Waterboarding consists of strapping the person being interrogated on to a board as pints of water are forced into his lungs through a cloth covering on his face. The victim's mouth is forced open in a process of slow-motion suffocation.[486] Dating back to the Spanish Inquisition, the practice was reportedly perfected by Dutch traders in the 17th century for use against their British rivals in the East Indies.[487] It was banned in Western Europe during the Age of Enlightenment in the early 19th century, when people found it "morally repugnant."[488]

But waterboarding did not disappear by any means and experienced something of a revival in the 20th century. The British used it against both Jews and Arabs in Palestine in the 1930s; the Japanese used it in World War II; The French used it in Algeria in the 1950s; and the Khmer Rouge used it on its own people in Cambodia in the 1970s.[489] Waterboarding also was a favored tool of Latin American dictators in the 1970s and 1980s, particularly in Chile and Argentina, where it was known as *submarino*.[490]

Waterboarding was condemned by the United States in 1901 during the Spanish-American War, when an Army major was sentenced to 10 years of hard labor for waterboarding an insurgent in the Philippines.[491] At the Tokyo War Crimes Trials in the 1940s, several Japanese soldiers were convicted by American-dominated tribunals for waterboarding.[492] It was designated as illegal by American generals in Vietnam in 1965, after a photograph of a U.S. soldier waterboarding a North Vietnamese prisoner appeared in *The Washington Post*. Within a month, the soldier was court-martialed and drummed out of the Army.[493] When the Khmer Rouge employed it, the United States again condemned waterboarding as torture. Cases have even been uncovered on U.S. soil. In 1983, Texas Sheriff James Parker was convicted of waterboarding prisoners in order to obtain confessions. He was sentenced to 10 years in prison.[494]

Malcolm Nance, an advisor on terrorism to the U.S. Department of Homeland Security, has publicly denounced the practice. He claims to have witnessed "hundreds" of waterboarding training exercises and has concluded that "waterboarding is a torture technique—period."[495] Nance actually allowed himself to experience the waterboarding ordeal when he was chief of training at the U.S. Navy Survival, Evasion, Resistance, and Escape School (SERE) in San Diego, where trainees were taught to endure torture.

> "Unless you have been strapped down to the board, have endured the agonizing feeling of water overpowering your gag reflex, and then feel your throat open and allow pint after pint of water to involuntarily fill your lungs, you will not know the meaning of the word. . . . In the media, waterboarding is called 'simulated drowning,' but that's a misnomer. It does not simulate drowning, as the lungs are actually filling with water. There is no way to simulate that. The victim *is* drowning. . . . Call it 'Chinese Water torture,' 'the barrel,' or 'the waterfall,' it is all the same."[496]

According to Nance, waterboarding victims typically go into hysterics as water fills their lungs. "How much the victim is to drown depends on the desired result and the obstinacy of the subject."[497] Moreover, in Nance's words, "The lack of physical scarring allows the victim to recover and be threatened with its use again and again."[498]

In 2006, more than 100 American law professors sent a highly critical open letter to Attorney General Alberto Gonzalez. It read in part:

> We are particularly concerned about your continuing failure to issue clear statements about illegal interrogation techniques, and especially your failure to state that "waterboarding"—a technique that induces the effects of being killed by drowning—constitutes torture, and thus is illegal. We urge you to make such a statement now.[499]

In a 2007 op-ed piece in *Jurist*, one of the signees, Professor Benjamin Davis, went even further. He called for the criminal prosecution of the leaders who put the torture policy in place. He closed with the following:

> "In the military they talk about different spanks for different ranks. It is time for the spanks to be much more severe at the higher level than they have been in the past. Or, in Latin, *refluat stercus*[500] [making "manure" roll uphill]

In another, more surprising, attack from the legal profession, four retired Judge Advocate Generals (JAGs)—two admirals and two generals—wrote to Senate Judiciary Committee Chairman Patrick Leahy in 2007 during the confirmation hearings of Michael Mukassey for the position of Attorney General to replace the departing Alberto Gonzalez:

> In the course of the Senate Judiciary Committee's consideration of President Bush's nominee for the post of Attorney General, there has been much discussion, but little

clarity about the legality of "waterboarding" under United States and International law. We write because this issue above all demands clarity: **Waterboarding is inhumane, it is torture, and it is illegal.**[501] [emphasis added]

Mukassey was confirmed but not before his nomination sparked a heated debate over the legality of waterboarding[502]—especially after Mukassey refused to define it as torture.[503] Three months later, in 2008, Mukassey appeared before the Senate Judiciary Committee and may have set a new administration standard for hypocrisy. He testified that he could not say that waterboarding was always illegal but would consider it torture *if it were done to him*.[504]

A few days later, CIA Director Michael Hayden acknowledged to the Senate Intelligence Committee that three "high value" al-Qaeda suspects had been waterboarded at Guantanamo.[505] It was the first public admission by the CIA that it was using waterboarding on detainees.[506] Hayden also cast doubt on the legality of waterboarding: "[I]n my own view, the view of my lawyers and the Department of Justice, it is not certain that technique would be considered legal under current statutes."[507] That same day, Stephen Bradbury, head of the Justice Department Office of Legal Counsel, told a House Judiciary Committee panel that waterboarding *is* currently illegal. It was the first such outright acknowledgement by a senior Bush administration official.[508]

Congress tried to make it official in March 2008, when it voted to outlaw waterboarding. President Bush blasted the move, suggesting that those who supported the measure did not "understand the nature of killers."[509] Bush vetoed the legislation, saying in his weekly radio address: "[I]t would take away one of the most valuable tools in the war on terror. . . . This is no time for Congress to abandon practices that have a proven record of keeping America safe."[510] An irate Amnesty International attacked the president's decision: "No-one, not even a President, can authorize torture. Anyone who orders, condones or carries out torture exposes themselves to criminal liability under international law."[511]

In the final weeks of the lame-duck Bush administration, Vice-President Dick Cheney, long considered the architect of America's war on terror, admitted in an interview that he had personally authorized the waterboarding of the three "high value" suspects at Guantanamo and had also approved the "enhanced interrogation" of 33 other detainees there.[512] Cheney specifically took issue with the notion that waterboarding is torture: "Was it torture? I don't believe it was torture."[513] In another interview, Cheney added: "We don't do torture. We never have."[514] Cheney's "tortured" definition of torture seemed to echo Humpty Dumpty's encounter with Alice in *Through the Looking Glass*: "When I use a word, it means what I choose it to mean."[515]

Cheney's defense of waterboarding was no surprise. Two years earlier he had defended the waterboarding of terrorism suspects as a "no brainer."[516] To this, Amnesty International responded:

> "What's really a no-brainer is that no U.S. official, much less a Vice President, should champion torture. Vice President Cheney's advocacy of water-boarding sets a new human rights low at a time when human rights is already scraping the bottom of the Bush administration barrel."[517]

Senator John McCain weighed in on the waterboarding controversy. McCain, a former POW who had endured torture at the hands of his Vietnamese captors, was able to lend a personal insight to the debate that no other major American political figure could provide. In 2005, he wrote:

[I]f you gave people who have suffered abuse as prisoners a choice between a beating and a mock execution, many, including me, would choose a beating. The effects of most beatings heal. The memory of an execution will haunt someone for a very long time and damage his or her psyche in ways that may never heal. In my view, to make someone believe that you are killing him by drowning is no different than holding a pistol to his head and firing a blank. I believe that it is torture, very exquisite torture.[518]

McCain called on President Bush to ban the torture of detainees in U.S. custody. After months of opposition and attempts to weaken the measure by exempting the CIA, the White House finally agreed in late 2005.[519] McCains's proposal drew overwhelming support from senators and representatives of both parties.[520] McCain said: "We've sent a message to the world that the United States is not like the terrorists. We have no grief for them, but what we are is a nation that upholds values and standards of behavior and treatment of all people, no matter how evil or bad they are."[521]

When President Bush signed the bill outlawing torture, however, he quietly reserved the right to bypass the law under his powers as commander-in-chief. After approving the bill, Bush issued a "signing statement"—an official document in which a president lays out his interpretation of a new law. Bush declared that he would view the interrogation limits in the context of his broader powers to protect national security. In other words, Bush believed he could waive the torture restrictions at will.[522] Lost in the shuffle was the unassailable fact that totalitarian regimes around the world—including many governments the United States opposes—almost always sanction torture on the grounds of national security.[523]

Bush's threat to discard the anti-torture law was not empty rhetoric. In 2008, he vetoed the annual intelligence authorization bill, which would have required the CIA to follow the Army Field Manual rules on interrogations, which specifically prohibit torture of suspects, most notably waterboarding. The President said he vetoed the bill because the CIA interrogation program has already prevented a number of terrorist attacks and is vital to making sure that continues.[524] Bush called the CIA's interrogation techniques "safe and lawful."[525] By ignoring inconvenient facts, the President seemed to employ a perverse *Wizard of Oz* strategy—telling the American public to pay no attention to the torture behind the curtain.

Also in 2008, it was revealed that the Bush administration had issued a pair of secret memos to the CIA in 2003 and 2004 that explicitly endorsed the agency's use of waterboarding.[526] In one of the memos, the Justice Department told the CIA that its interrogators would be safe from prosecution for torture if they believed "in good faith" that harsh techniques used to break down prisoners would not cause "prolonged mental harm."[527] The memos were the first—and, for years, the only—actual documentation of the administration's consent for the CIA's use of "Enhanced Interrogation Techniques," such as waterboarding, to extract information from captured al-Qaeda members.[528] The ACLU, which had obtained the heavily censored memos, released the following statement:

These documents supply further evidence, if any were needed, that the Justice Department authorized the CIA to torture prisoners in its custody. The Justice Department twisted the law, and in some cases ignored it altogether, in order to permit interrogators to use barbaric methods that the U.S. once prosecuted as war crimes.[529]

A few days before assuming office in 2009, President-elect Barack Obama pledged that his administration would not engage in torture. "We will abide by the Geneva Convention. We will uphold our highest ideals."[530] A week later, Obama's Attorney General-nominee, Eric Holder, faced the Senate Judiciary Committee and made an unambiguous statement: "Waterboarding is torture."[531] Holder also asserted that the U.S. detention facility at Guantanamo Bay would be closed as quickly as possible.[532] And the following week Dennis Blair, Obama's National Intelligence Director-nominee, likewise pledged that there would be no torture on his watch. However, to the disappointment of many, he refused to say whether he believes waterboarding is torture.[533]

In February 2009, Senator Patrick Leahy, chairman of the Senate Judiciary Committee, called for an independent "truth commission" to investigate Bush administration abuses, including its use of torture.[534] President Obama did not embrace Leahy's proposal, saying that backward-looking investigations would be a diversion.[535] In addition, CIA Director-nominee, Leon Panetta, announced that CIA officers who participated in harsh interrogations will not be prosecuted if they had acted on legal orders from the Bush administration.[536] Left unaddressed is the basic question of whether orders to torture can be "legal."

The practice of torture by a government, like that of slavery or genocide, falls under a special legal category known as *jus cogens*—Latin for "higher law." "This means that no country can ever pass a law that allows torture. There can be no immunity from criminal liability for violation of a *jus cogens* prohibition."[537] Under the Eighth Amendment to the U.S. Constitution, which expressly forbids "cruel and unusual punishments," torture is *always* illegal. Moreover, torture is criminalized under several federal statutes, including the Anti-Torture Act, the War Crimes Act (which bans waterboarding), the McCain Amendment to the Detainee Treatment Act, as well as the more generic federal assault laws.[538] The prohibition of torture is also universally accepted under international law; and, for over 100 years, the Supreme Court has held that customary international law is part of U.S. law.[539]

In addition, when the United States ratifies a treaty, that treaty becomes part of the Law of the Land under the Supremacy Clause of the Constitution.[540] Such would be the case with the Senate-ratified Geneva Convention and the Senate-ratified Convention Against Torture.[541] In a 2006 public debate, former Deputy Assistant Attorney General John Yoo, who had authored the Bush administration's shamefully narrow "organ failure or death" definition of torture (noted earlier), claimed that commander-in-chief powers mean that no law can restrict the President's actions in pursuit of war. As an example, Yoo further argued (hypothetically, one hopes) that no treaty can stop the President from torturing someone by crushing the testicles of that person's child.[542]

At the core of the torture debate that has erupted since 9/11 is the basic question of effectiveness. Moral considerations aside, does torture even work? A military intelligence specialist who was sent by the Pentagon to assess interrogations in Iraq—more than a year before the Abu Ghraib scandal—concluded that torture is simply "not a good way to get information."[543] "The intelligence community, including professional interrogators, is virtually unanimous on the point that, as a means of interrogation, torture is effective at one thing—extracting false confessions."[544] Senator John McCain has written: "In my experience, abuse of prisoners often produces bad intelligence because under torture a person will say anything he thinks his captors want to hear—whether it is true or false."[545] According to McCain, when he was a POW he was once physically coerced to provide the names of the members of his flight squadron. He gave them the names of the Green Bay Packers offensive line—and the abuse was suspended.[546]

On the other hand, Bush, Cheney, Rumsfeld, and other masterminds of the war on terror continue to insist that valuable intelligence and life-saving information has been derived from interrogation tactics that most Americans would consider torture. Pulitzer Prize-winning journalist Dianne McWhorter writes that torture represents absolute power when it is imposed without regard to the guilt of its victims.[547] But when some of the victims are actual criminals or undeniable terrorists, this provides the torturers with moral cover. Moments after Attorney General-nominee Eric Holder told the Senate that the use of waterboarding is torture, then-CIA Director Michael Hayden declared: "These techniques worked."[548] Hayden credited waterboarding for the 2007 confession of Guantanamo prisoner Khalid Sheik Mohammed, who admitted to beheading *Wall Street Journal* reporter Daniel Pearl[549]—a gruesome crime that was widely disseminated on the Internet in 2002.[550] In the turbulent post-9/11 era, tales of "fruitful" torture are seductive and have found a receptive audience in some unexpected quarters. For example, Harvard Law Professor Alan Dershowitz, a stalwart civil libertarian, has proposed the use of "torture warrants" in emergency situations.[551] Dershowitz argues that placing torture under strict judicial guidelines would help keep it from sliding down a slippery slope into non-emergency usage.[552]

Even some who doubt its value in the acquisition of good intelligence has raised arguments supporting the torture of suspected terrorists. They assert that torture is not just about extracting information. It is also designed to break the victim's will and deter others in his social surroundings. "As an interrogation tool, torture is a bust. But when it comes to social control, nothing works quite like torture."[553]

Of course, torture cannot be analyzed in a morally detached vacuum, so removing moral considerations from the debate is impossible. Susan J. Crawford is a staunch Republican, a retired judge who served as general counsel for the Army during the Reagan administration and as Pentagon inspector general when Dick Cheney was Secretary of Defense. In 2007, she was named convening authority of military commissions by the Defense Department. Just days before President Bush left office in 2009, she became the first senior administration official responsible for reviewing the practices at Guantanamo to state publicly that Mohamed Qahtani was tortured:

> "I sympathize with the intelligence gatherers in those days after 9/11, not knowing what was coming next and trying to gain information to keep us safe. . . . But there still has to be a line that we should not cross. And unfortunately what this has done, I think, has tainted everything going forward."[554]

The line Susan Crawford warns of crossing is also the *bottom line* of the torture issue. It is indisputable that the worst American excesses pale in comparison to the bestial crimes committed by 21st century jihadists, who seem determined to drench the world in blood. However, as Crawford appears to recognize, if the United States aspires to lead the war against terrorism, it must do so not only through its military might but through the example set by its principles and ideals. Otherwise, a war between good and evil becomes a war between bad and worse.

Despite the Bush administration's efforts to minimize it and rename it, almost everyone understands that prisoners at Abu Ghraib and Guantanamo were tortured. What is far more polarizing is whether such exigent practices may be justified in the post-9/11 era. Many Americans insist that the war against terrorism is a literal battle for survival and not an abstract law school debate. In their view, if laws banning torture need to be bent a little—or even a lot—that is an unfortunate but necessary cost of victory. But many other Americans—no less patriotic—cannot accept torture as a defensible policy. Their arguments have little to do with terrorists, who have forfeited any decent claim to sympathy. It is not about them; it is about *us*. If we allow ourselves to sink to the level of our enemies, they win.

Notes

1. *Olmstead v. United States*, 277 U.S. 438 (1928).
2. Allen, Garland E. "The Misuse of Biological Hierarchies: The American Eugenics Movement, 1900-1940." *History and Philosophy of the Life Sciences* 5, 1983: 105–128.
3. *Journal of the American Medical Association.* "Sterilization to Improve the Race." September 9, 1933: p. 866.
4. Reinhold, Robert. "Some Unfortunate Verdicts on Writing Science into the Law." *New York Times*, March 9, 1980: p. 8E. For a historical review of the American eugenics movement, see also: Rafter, Nicole H. "Claims-Making and Socio-Cultural Context in the First U.S. Eugenics Campaign." *Social Problems* 39, 1992: 17-35.
5. Barker, David. "The Biology of Stupidity: Genetics, Eugenics and Mental Deficiency in the Inter-War Years." *British Journal of Health Science* 22, 1989: 347-375.
6. Leonard, Arthur S. *Sexuality and the Law: An Encyclopedia of Major Legal Cases.* New York: Garland Publishing, 1993.
7. Smith, J. David and Nelson, K. Ray. *The Sterilization of Carrie Buck.* Far Hills, NJ: New Horizon Press, 1989.
8. *Buck v. Bell*, 274 U.S. 200 (1927).
9. Reinhold, Robert. "Virginia Hospital's Chief Traces 50 Years of Sterilizing the 'Retarded'." *New York Times*, February 23, 1980: p. 6.
10. Stroman, Duane F. *Mental Retardation in Social Context.* Lanham, MD: University Press of America, 1989.
11. Platt, Steve. "Fertility Control." *New Statesman and Society* 4; 1991: 11.
12. *Ibid.* p. 7.
13. Zucchino, David. "In N.C., Compensation for Forced Sterilization Will Have to Wait." *latimes.com*, June, 20, 2012.
14. Begos, Kevin. "Lifting the Curtain on a Shameful Era." *http://againsttheirwill.journalnow.com/*, 2002.
15. *Ibid.*
16. Begos, *op cit.*
17. PBS Newshour. "North Carolina Drops Payment to Forced Sterilization Victims." *http://www.pbs.org/newshour/bb/law/jan-june12/sterilization_06-21.html,* June 21, 2012.
18. Herrnstein, Richard J. and Murray, Charles. *The Bell Curve.* New York: Free Press, 1994.
19. Jones, James H. *Bad Blood: The Tuskegee Syphilis Experiment—A Tragedy of Race and Medicine.* New York: The Free Press, 1981; p. 91.
20. Mintz, Morton and Cohen, Jerry. *Power, Inc.: Public and Private Rulers and How to Make Them Accountable.* New York: Viking, 1976; p. 477.
21. Jones, *op. cit.*
22. *Ibid.*, p. 16.
23. *Ibid.*, p. 24.
24. *Ibid.*
25. *Ibid.*, p. 44.
26. *Ibid.*
27. *Ibid.*, p. 127.
28. *Ibid.*, p. 127.
29. *Ibid.*, p. 126.
30. Stolberg, *op. cit.*
31. Mintz and Cohen, *op. cit.*
32. Jones, *op. cit.*, p. 202.
33. *Ibid.*, p. 202.
34. *Ibid.*, p. 191.
35. *Ibid.*, pp. 192, 193.
36. Quoted in Mintz and Cohen, *op. cit.*, p. 478.
37. Cohn, Victor. "Experiment Settlement is Faulted." *Washington Post*, December 16, 1974: p. A24.
38. Bowart, Walter. *Operation Mind Control.* New York: Dell, 1978; p. 23.
39. Eitzen, D. Stanley and Timmer, Doug A. *Criminology: Crime and Criminal Justice.* New York: John Wiley & Sons, 1985.
40. Bowart, *op. cit.*
41. *Ibid.*
42. *Ibid.*
43. *Ibid.*, p. 73.
44. *Ibid.*, p. 81.
45. Thomas, Gordon. *Journey into Madness: The True Story of Secret CIA Mind Control and Medical Abuse.* New York: Bantam Books, 1989.
46. *Ibid.*
47. Marks, John. "Sex, Drugs, and the CIA: The Shocking Search for an 'Ultimate Weapon'." *Saturday Review*, February, 3, 1970: 12–16.
48. *Ibid.*
49. *Ibid.*, p. 14.
50. *Ibid.*, p. 13.
51. Bowart, *op. cit.*
52. *Houston Post.* "LSD Death Inquiry." July 13, 1994: p. A16.
53. Bowart, *op. cit.*, p. 107.

54. Marks, *op. cit.*

55. Eitzen and Timmer, *op. cit.*

56. Halperin, Morton H., Berman, Jerry J., Borosage, Robert L., and Marwick, Christine M. *The Lawless State: The Crimes of the U.S. Intelligence Agencies.* New York: Penguin Books, 1977. Reprinted by permission of Penguin Books USA.

57. Lee, Martin A. "C.I.A.: Carcinogen." *The Nation*, June 5, 1982: p. 675

58. Stolberg, *op. cit.*

59. Rothman, David J. "Government Guinea Pigs." *New York Times*, January 9, 1994: p. 21.

60. Cole, Leonard A. "Americans as Guinea Pigs: The Army's Secret Germ-War Testing." *The Nation*, October 23, 1982: p. 397. Reprinted by permission of *The Nation*.

61. *Ibid.*, p. 399.

62. *Ibid.*, p. 398.

63. *Ibid.*

64. *Ibid.*, pp. 398–399

65. Quoted in *Ibid.*, p. 399.

66. Jones, October 18, 1993, *op. cit.*

67. Budiansky, Stephen. "The Cold War Experiments." *U.S. News and World Report*, January 24, 1994: p. 34.

68. Jones, October 18, 1993, *op. cit.*

69. *Ibid.*, p. 1A.

70. "Those who cannot remember the past are condemned to repeat it." (Santayana, George. *Reason in Common Sense*, Volume One in "The Life of Reason." NY: Dover, 1980. This work was first published in 1905.)

71. Schneider, Keith. "Stillborns' Ashes Used in Studies of Radiation, Documents Show." *New York Times*, May 5, 1994: p. B12.

72. Lee, Gary. "Stillborn Babies Used in '50s Radiation Test: Energy Dept. Widens Disclosure of Experiments.'" *Washington Post*, May 3, 1995: p. A3.

73. Allen, Scott. "43 Given Radiation in Mass. Research." *Boston Globe*, August 18, 1995: pp. 27, 31.

74. Schneider, Keith. "A Spreading Light on Radiation Tests." *New York Times*, January 14, 1994: p. A14.

75. *New York Times.* "Paper Says Experiment Exposed 19 Retarded Youths to Radiation." December 27, 1993: p. A17.

76. *New York Times.* "2 Recall 1949 Radiation Tests on Them." January 14, 1994: p. A14.

77. Yemma, John. "Ex-Fernald Residents Awarded $1.85m." *Boston Globe*. December 31, 1997: pp. B1, B7.

78. Allen, Scott. "Radiation Test Used Retarded Children at Wrentham." *Boston Globe*, February 9, 1994: p. 20.

79. Quoted in *Ibid.*, p. 20.

80. Schneider, Keith. "Trying to Build Secret Weapons, U.S. Spread Radiation in 1950s." *New York Times*, December 16, 1993: p. A1.

81. MacPherson, Karen. "40's Ethics Policies Ignored in Human Radiation Testing." *Houston Chronicle*, January 23, 1995: p. 2A.

82. Allen, Scott. "Free Care Came with a Price." *Boston Globe*, February 28, 1994: 25-26.

83. *Ibid.*, p. 25.

84. *Ibid.*, p. 25.

85. *Ibid.*, p. 26.

86. Herken, Gregg and David, James. "Doctors of Death." *New York Times*, January 13, 1994: p. 21.

87. Gallagher, Carole. *American Ground Zero: The Secret Nuclear War.* Cambridge, MA: M.I.T. Press, 1993.

88. Watkins, T. H. "Under the Mushroom Cloud." *Washington Post*, May 2, 1993: p. 7.

89. Schneider, Keith. "Cold War Radiation Test on Humans to Undergo a Congressional Review." *New York Times*, April 11, 1994: p. D9.

90. Schneider, Keith. "Energy Official Seeks to Assist Victims of Tests." *New York Times*, December 29, 1993: p. 1.

91. Schneider, April 11, 1994, *op. cit.*

92. Schneider, December 29, 1993, *op. cit.*

93. Gottschalk, Louis A., Kunkel, Robert, Wohl, Theodore, Saenger, Eugene L., and Winget, Carolyn N. "Total and Half Body Irradiation: Effect on Cognitive and Emotional Processes." *Archives of General Psychiatry* 21, 1989: 574-580.

94. Howard-Jones, Norman. "Human Experimentation in Historical and Ethical Perspectives." *Social Science & Medicine* 16, 1982: 1429-1448.

95. Gottschalk *et al.*, *op cit.*

96. Egilman, David S. and Reinert, Alexander. "What Is Informed Consent?" *Washington Post*, January 14, 1994: p. 23.

97. *Ibid.*

98. Hoversten, Paul. "Clinton Apologizes for Radiation Tests." *USA Today*, October 4, 1995: p. 10A.

99. Kong, Dolores. "1800 Tested in Radiation Experiments." *Boston Globe*, February 20, 1994: pp. 1, 22.

100. *Ibid.*, p. 22.

101. *Ibid.*, p. 22.

102. Allen, Scott. "MIT Records Show Wider Radioactive Testing at Fernald." *Boston Globe*, December 31, 1993: p. 1.

103. Schneider, Keith. "Scientists Share in Pain of Experiment Debates." *New York Times,* March 3, 1994: p. A12.

104. Schneider, Keith. "Secret Nuclear Research on People Comes to Light." *New York Times*, December 17, 1993: p. A1.

105. Markey, Edward J. "Compensating America's Nuclear Guinea Pigs." *Boston Globe*, January 13, 1994: p. 15.

106. Allen, August 18, 1995, *op. cit.*

107. Markey, *op. cit.*, p. 15.

108. Markey, *op. cit.*, p. 15.

109. Jones, October 17, 1993, *op. cit.*

110. Allen, Scott and Kong, Dolores. "'50 Memo Warned Radiation Tests Would Suggest Nazism." *Boston Globe*, December 28, 1993: p. 1.

111. Mintz and Cohen, *op. cit.*, p. 480.

112. Mitford, Jessica. *Kind and Usual Punishment: The Prison Business*. New York: Knopf, 1973.

113. McGrory, Brian and Murphy, Sean. "Inmates Used in '60s Drug Tests." *Boston Globe*, January 1, 1994: p. 16.

114. *Ibid.*

115. Schneider, December 17, 1993, *op. cit.*

116. Hoversten, *op. cit.*, p. 10A.

117. Mitford, *op. cit.*

118. Mintz and Cohen, *op. cit.*, p. 479.

119. *Ibid.*

120. Mitford, *op. cit,*

121. *Ibid.*, pp. 139–140.

122. Rakstis, Ted J. "The Business Challenge: Confronting the Ethics Issue." *Kiwanis Magazine,* September 1990: p. 30.

123. Beck, Paul J. and Maher, Michael W. "Competition, Regulation and Bribery." *Managerial and Decision Economics* 10, 1989: 1–12.

124. Roebuck, Julian, and Weeber, Stanley C. *Political Crime in the U.S.: Analyzing Crime By and Against Government*. New York: Praeger, 1978.

125. *Ibid.*

126. *Ibid.*

127. *Ibid.*

128. *Houston Chronicle*. "Litton Units to Pay $18.5 Million in Fraud Case." July 1, 1999: p. 3C.

129. Hershey, Robert D. "Payoffs: Are They Stopped or Just Better Hidden?" *New York Times,* January 29, 1978: p. 23.

130. Sampson, Anthony T. *The Arms Bazaar*. New York: Viking Press, 1977.

131. Eitzen and Timmer, *op. cit.*

132. Roebuck and Weeber, *op. cit.*

133. Agee, Phillip. *Inside the Company: CIA Diary*. New York: Stonehill Publishing, 1975.

134. Roebuck and Weeber, *op. cit.*

135. *Ibid.*

136. Halperin, *op. cit.*

137. Wise, David. *The Politics of Lying*. New York: Vantage, 1973.

138. Sampson, Anthony T. *The Sovereign State of ITT*. New York: Stein and Day, 1973.

139. Eitzen and Timmer, *op. cit.*

140. Roebuck and Weber, *op cit.*

141. Agee, *op. cit.*

142. Eitzen and Timmer, *op. cit.*

143. *U.S. News & World Report*. "CIA Murder Plots—Weighing the Damage to U.S." December 1, 1975: 13–15.

144. Powers, Thomas. "Inside the Department of Dirty Tricks." *The Atlantic* 244, 1979: 33-64.

145. Myers, Laura. "CIA Asked Mafia to Kill Castro, Newly Declassified Memo Reveals." *Houston Chronicle*. July 2, 1997: p. 9A.

146. Krauss, Clifford. "How U.S. Actions Helped Hide Salvador Human Rights Abuses." *New York Times,* March 21, 1993: pp. 1, 10,

147. *The Economist*. "America and Nicaragua: Read (Almost) All About It." October 27, 1984: p. 25.

148. *Ibid.*

149. Borosage, Robert L. "What to Do with Intelligence Agencies." *Working Papers* 4, 1977: p. 41.

150. Bradlee, Jr., Ben. Guts and Glory: The Rise and Fall of Oliver North. New York: Donald Fine, 1988.

151. Draper, Theodore. *A Very Thin Line: The Iran-Contra Affairs*. New York: Hill and Wang, 1991; p. 27.

152. *Ibid.*

153. Bradlee, *op. cit.*

154. Draper, *op. cit.*

155. Magnuson, Ed. "Patriots Pursuing Profits." *Time,* June 8, 1987: 24–25.

156. Draper, *op. cit.*

157. Bradlee, *op. cit.*

158. Quoted by Draper, *op. cit.*, p. 98.

159. Draper, *op. cit.*

160. *Ibid.*

161. *New York Times*. "Transcript of Reagan's Remarks on the Hostages." July 1, 1985: p. A17.

162. Cohen, William S. and Mitchell, George J. *Men of Zeal: A Candid Inside Story of the Iran-Contra Hearings*. New York: Viking, 1988.

163. *Ibid.*

164. *Ibid.*

165. Bradlee, *op. cit.*

166. Draper, *op. cit.*

167. Cohen and Mitchell, *op. cit.*

168. Draper, *op. cit.*, p. 216

169. Cohen and Mitchell, *op. cit.*

170. Draper, *op. cit.*, p. 302

171. Cohen and Mitchell, *op. cit.*

172. Draper, *op. cit.*, p. 355.

173. *Ibid.*, p. 417

174. Quoted in: Wine, Michael. "White House E-Mail Gives Peek at Hi-Jinks During Iran-Contra." *Houston Chronicle,* November 26, 1995: p. 2A.

175. *New York Times.* "Transcript of Remarks by Reagan About Iran." November 14, 1986: p. A8.

176. Reagan, Ronald. *An American Life.* New York: Simon and Schuster, 1990.

177. Draper, *op. cit.*, p. 475.

178. Reagan, R. (2011). *An American life.* New York: Simon & Schuster.

179. Draper, *op. cit.*

180. Cohen and Mitchell, *op. cit.*, p. 28.

181. *Ibid.*

182. Bradlee, *op. cit.*, p. 491.

183. Draper, *op. cit.*, pp. 541–542.

184. *Ibid.*, p. 551.

185. *Ibid.*, p. 551.

186. *Ibid.*, p. 552.

187. Morganthau, Tom. "Ollie North's Secret Network." *Newsweek,* March 9, 1987: 32–37.

188. Bradlee, *op. cit.*

189. *Ibid.*, p. 538.

190. *Ibid.*, p. 538.

191. Shales, Tom. "On the Air: The High Drama of a Duel." *Washington Post,* July 8, 1987: p. B2.

192. Kaplan, Fred. "Judge Gives McFarlane $20K Fine." *Boston Globe,* March 4, 1989: pp. 1, 4.

193. Dellinger, Walter. "Case Closed." *The New Republic,* January 9 & 16, 1989: 15–16.

194. Kaplan, Fred. "Secord Guilty Plea Avoids Trial." *Boston Globe,* November 5, 1989: p. 3.

195. Yost, Peter. "Secord, Iran-Contra Figure, Gets 2 Years' Probation." *Boston Globe,* January 26, 1990: p. 5.

196. Wines, Michael. "Hakim on Probation in Iran-Contra Deal but Shares Proceeds." *New York Times,* February 2, 1990: pp. A1, A18.

197. Johnston, David. "Iran-Contra Role Brings Pondexter 6 Months in Prison." *New York Times,* June 12, 1990: pp. A1, A19.

198. Lowther, William. "A Forgiving Sentence." *Maclean's* July 17, 1989: p. 23.

199. Lamar, *op. cit.*

200. Cohen and Mitchell, *op. cit.*, p. 97.

201. Johnston, September 17, 1991, *op. cit.*

202. Johnston, David. "Judge in Iran-Contra Trial Drops Case Against North After Prosecutor Gives Up." *New York Times,* September 17, 1991: pp. A1, A19.

203. *New York Times.* "Oliver North Beats the Rap."[Editorial], September 17, 1991: p. A20.

204. Gartner, Michael. "Oliver North's Disloyalty." *USA Today,* October 18, 1994: p. 11A.

205. Mill, John Stuart. *Dissertations and Discussions: Political, Philosophical, and Historical.* New York: Haskell House, 1975.

206. Eitzen and Timmer, *op. cit.*

207. Daniels, Roger. *Concentration Camps USA: Japanese-Americans and World War II.* New York: Holt, Rinehart, and Winston, 1972.

208. Girdner, Audrie and Loftis, Anne. *The Great Betrayal: The Evacuation of the Japanese-Americans During World War II.* London: MacMillan, 1969.

209. Weglyn, Micki. *Years of Infamy: The Untold Story of American Concentration Camps.* New York: William Morrow and Company, 1976.

210. Archer, Jules. *Watergate: America in Crisis.* New York: Thomas Y. Crowell, 1975: p. 270.

211. Lowi, Theodore. "The Intelligent Person's Guide to Political Corruption." *Public Affairs* 82; 1981: 1–8.

212. Congressional Quarterly. *Watergate: Chronology of a Crisis.* Washington, D.C.: Congressional Quarterly, Inc., 1974.

213. *Ibid.*

214. *Ibid.*

215. *Ibid.*

216. *Ibid.*

217. Cook, Fred J. *The Crimes of Watergate.* New York: Franklin Watts, 1981.

218. *Ibid.*, p. 112.

219. *Congressional Quarterly, op. cit.*

220. Archer, Jules. *Watergate: America in Crisis.* New York: Thomas Y. Crowell, 1975.

221. *Ibid.*, p. 236.

222. *Ibid.*, p. 224.

223. *Ibid.*

224. Wrong, Dennis H. "Watergate: Symptom of What Sickness?" *Dissent* 23, 1974: p. 502.

225. Brown, Bruce. "Watergate: Business as Usual." *Liberation* July/August 1974, p. 22.

226. Erskine, Hazel. "The Polls: Corruption in Government." *Public Opinion Quarterly* 37, 1973: 628–644.

227. Quoted in Silverstein, Mark. "Watergate and the American Political System." In Markovits, Andrei S. and Silverstein, Mark (Eds.), *The Politics of Scandal: Power and Process in Liberal Democracies.* New York: Holmes & Meier, 1988; 15-37.

228. Cook, *op. cit.*, p. 2.

229. *Ibid.*

230. Silverstein, *op. cit.*, p. 15.

231. Cook, *op. cit.*, p. 2.

232. Bernstein, Carl and Woodward, Bob. *All the President's Men*. New York: Simon and Schuster, 1974.

233. *Congressional Quarterly*, *op. cit.*, p. 139.

234. Wieghart, James. "FBI Chief to Tell of Burning Hunt File." *New York Daily News*, April 27, 1973: pp. 1, 81.

235. *Congressional Quarterly*, *op. cit.*, p. 149.

236. *Ibid.*, p.150.

237. Bernstein and Woodward, *op. cit.*, p. 313.

238. *Congressional Quarterly*, *op. cit.*

239. Ehrlichman, John. *Witness to Power*. New York: Simon and Schuster, 1982.

240. *Ibid.*

241. *Congressional Quarterly*, *op. cit.*

242. Bernstein and Woodward, *op. cit.*

243. Archer, *op. cit.*

244. *Congressional Quarterly*, *op. cit.*

245. Archer, *op. cit.*, p. 200.

246. *Ibid.*, p. 200.

247. Archer, *op. cit.*

248. Hersh, Seymour M. "Kissinger Said to Have Asked F.B.I. to Wiretap a Number of His Aides." *New York Times*, May 17, 1973: pp. 1, 35.

249. Woodward, Bob and Bernstein, Carl. "Dean: Nixon Asked IRS to Stop Audits." *Washington Post*, June 20, 1973: pp. A1, A7.

250. Dean, John. *Blind Ambition: The White House Years*. New York: Simon and Schuster, 1976.

251. Cook, *op. cit.*

252. Feinberg, Barbara S. *Watergate: Scandal in the White House*. New York: Franklin Watts, 1990.

253. *Congressional Quarterly*, *op. cit.*

254. Barker, Karlyn and Pincus, Walter. "Watergate Revisited." *Washington Post*, June 14, 1992: p. A1.

255. Cook, *op. cit.*

256. *Ibid.*, p. 112.

257. Feinberg, *op. cit.*, p. 216.

258. Archer, *op. cit.*, p. 216.

259. *Ibid.*, p. 216.

260. Archer, *op. cit.*

261. Quoted in *Ibid.*, p. 271.

262. Kelman, *op. cit.*, p. 307.

263. Kelman, Herbert C. "Some Reflections on Authority, Corruption, and Punishment: The Social-Psychological Context of Watergate." *Psychiatry* 39, 1976: 303–317.

264. Candee, Dan. "The Moral Psychology of Watergate." *Journal of Social Issues* 21, 1975: p. 183.

265. Kelman, *op. cit.*, p. 307.

266. Cook, *op. cit.*, p. 139.

267. Silverstein, *op. cit.*, p. 33.

268. Dunham, Roger G. and Mauss, Armand L. "Waves from Watergate: Evidence Concerning the Impact of the Watergate Scandal upon Political Legitimacy and Social Control." *Pacific Sociological Review* 19, 1976: p. 470.

269. Kelman, *op. cit.*, p. 304.

270. Vidich, A. J. (1975). *Political Legitimacy in Bureaucratic Society: An Analysis of Watergate*. Retrieved from http://books.google.com/books?id=VxGypwAACAAJ

271. Barber, James D. "The Nixon Brush with Tyranny." *Political Science Quarterly* 92, 1977: p. 594.

272. Archer, *op. cit.*, p. 274.

273. Kelman, *op. cit.*, p. 311.

274. *Ibid.*, p. 603.

275. Hershey, Marjorie R. and Hill, David B. "Watergate and Preadults' Attitudes Toward the President." *American Journal of Political Science* 19, 1975: 703–726.

276. Dunham and Mauss, *op. cit.*, p. 485.

277. Zimmer, Troy. "The Impact of Watergate on the Public's Trust in People and Confidence in the Mass Media." *Social Science Quarterly* 59, 1979: 743–751.

278. Jensen, Michael C. "Watergate Donors Still Riding High." *New York Times*, August 24, 1978: pp. 1, 7.

279. Hedlo, Hugh, Brown, Fred R., and Dillon, Conley. "Watergate in Retrospect: The Forgotten Agenda." *Public Administration Review* 36, 1976: p. 306.

280. Hawkins, Robert P., Pingree, Suzanne, and Roberts, Donald F. "Watergate and Political Socialization: The Inescapable Event." *American Politics Quarterly* 3, 1975: p. 406.

281. Arterton, F. Christopher. "The Impact of Watergate on Children's Attitudes toward Political Authority." *Political Science Quarterly* 89, 1974: 269–288.

282. Dennis, Jack and Webster, Carol. "Children's Images of the President and of Government in 1962 and 1974." *American Politics Quarterly* 3, 1974: 386–405.

283. Fowlkes, Diane L. "Realpolitik and Play Politics: The Effects of Watergate and Political Gaming on Undergraduate Students' Political Interest and Political Trust." *Simulation & Games* 8, 1977: 419–438.

284. Garrett, James B. and Wallace, Benjamin. "Cognitive Consistency, Repression-Sensitization, and Level of Moral Judgment: Reactions of College Students to the Watergate Scandals." *Journal of Social Psychology* 98, 1976: 69–76.

285. *Congressional Quarterly*, *op. cit.*

286. Chaffee, Steven H. and Becker, Lee B. "Young Voters' Reactions to Early Watergate Issues." *American Politics Quarterly* 3, 1975: 360–386.

287. Roebuck and Weeber, *op. cit.*

288. Halperin, et al., *op cit.*, p. 94.

289. Donner, *op. cit.*

290. Halperin, et al., *op. cit.*

291. Harris, Richard. "Reflections: Crime in the F.B.I." *The New Yorker,* August 8, 1977: 30–42.

292. Donner, *op. cit.*

293. Harris, *op. cit.*

294. Harris, *op. cit.*, p. 39.

295. *Ibid.*, p. 39.

296. Donner, *op. cit.*

297. Halperin, et al., *op. cit.*

298. Donner, *op. cit.*

299. Halperin, et al., *op. cit.*

300. Quoted in: *Houston Chronicle.* "Hoover's FBI Targeted Chicago's Daley." August 31, 1997: p. 11A.

301. Halperin, et al., *op. cit.*, p. 107.

302. *Ibid.*

303. Donner, *op. cit.*

304. Halperin, et al., *op. cit.*, p. 117.

305. Harris, *op. cit.*

306. Eitzen and Timmer, *op. cit.*

307. Harris, *op. cit.*, p. 40.

308. Donner, *op. cit.*

309. Halperin, et al., *op. cit.*

310. *Ibid.*, p. 113.

311. Mauro, Tony. "Striking Gold with the FOIA: How FBI's Court Files Came to Light." *Legal Times,* September 12, 1988: p. 22.

312. Charas, Alexander. "How the FBI Spied on the High Court." *Washington Post,* December 3, 1989: pp. C1, C4.

313. Charns, Alexander. *Cloak and Gavel: FBI Wiretaps, Bugs, Informers, and the Supreme Court.* Urbana, IL: University of Chicago Press, 1992.

314. *New York Times.* "F.B.I. Kept Close Watch on Douglas." July 22, 1984: p. 42.

315. Ehrlichman, J. (1982). *Witness to power: the Nixon years.* New York: Simon and Schuster.

316. Charns, 1992, *op. cit.*, p. 113.

317. Halperin, et al., *op. cit.*, p. 117.

318. Donner, *op. cit.*, p. 28.

319. *Ibid.*

320. *Ibid.*, p. 235.

321. Eitzen and Timmer, *op. cit.*, p. 346.

322. Harris, *op. cit.*

323. Rawls, Wendell, Jr. "F.B.I. Admits Planting a Rumor to Discredit Jean Seberg in 1970." *New York Times,* September 15, 1979: pp. 1, 6.

324. Eitzen and Timmer, *op. cit.*

325. O'Reilly, Kenneth. "The FBI and the Civil Rights Movement During the Kennedy Years—From the Freedom Rides to Albany." *Journal of Southern History* 54, 1988: p. 202.

326. Halperin, et al., *op. cit.*, p. 62.

327. *Ibid.*, p. 78.

328. *Ibid.*, p. 63.

329. *Ibid.*, p. 64.

330. *Ibid.*, p. 80.

331. Navasky, Victor. *Kennedy Justice.* New York: Athenium, 1971.

332. *Ibid.*

333. Harris, *op. cit.*, p. 40.

334. *Ibid.*, p. 89.

335. *Jet.* "Lowery Blasts FBI for Spying on SCLC, Others." February 15, 1988: p. 4.

336. *Olmstead v. United States, op. cit.*

337. Markoff, John. "FBI Seeks Massive Wiretap Capabilities." *Houston Chronicle,* November 2, 1995: p. 11A.

338. Halperin et al., *op cit.*, p. 187.

339. *Ibid.*, p. 190.

340. *Ibid.*

341. *Ibid.*, p. 194.

342. *Ibid.*, p. 195.

343. *Ibid.*

344. *Ibid.*, p. 199.

345. *Ibid.*, p. 299.

346. *Ibid.*

347. Halperin et al., *op. cit.*

348. *Ibid.*, 165. Since 1968, political conventions have been frequent targets of abusive practices and violations of civil liberties. At the 2004 Republican National Convention in New York City, for example, the NYPD arrested more than 1,800 people, mostly for minor violations. Many of them were herded into pens at a Hudson River pier and fingerprinted—instead of being released on summonses or desk appearance tickets, "which are more customary for charges that amount to little more than a traffic ticket." Some of them were detained for up to two days to keep protestors off the streets during the convention. (McFadden, Robert D. "City is Rebuffed on the Release of '04 Records." *nytimes.com,* August 7, 2007.)

349. Donner, Frank J. *The Age of Surveillance: The Aims and Methods of America's Political Intelligence System.* New York: Knopf, 1980.

350. Halperin et al., *op. cit.*, p. 175.

351. *Ibid.*, p. 176.

352. Hersh, Seymour. "Huge CIA Operation Reported in US against Antiwar Forces, Other Dissidents During Nixon Years." *newyorktimes.com,* December 22, 1974.

353. Poole, Patrick S. "Echelon: Part Two: The NSA's Global Spying Network." *Nexus Magazine (online),* October/November 1999.

354. *strange-loops.com.* "The Echelon System," June 19, 2003. Echelon is operated by the intelligence agencies in five nations: the United States (NSA), the United Kingdom, Canada, Australia, and New Zealand. However, the NSA clearly takes the lead in the operation of Echelon.

355. Campbell, Duncan. "Inside Echelon: The History, Structure and Function of the Global Surveillance System Known as Echelon." *echelononline.com,* July 25, 2000.

356. Ross, Sherwood. "NSA May Be Reading Windows Software in Your Computer." *opednews.com,* October 16, 2007.

357. Poole, Patrick S. "Echelon: Part I: The NSA's Global Spying Network." *Nexus Magazine (online),* August/September 1999.

358. Fielding, Nick and Campbell, Duncan. "Spy Agencies Listened in on Diana." *Sunday Times UK (online),* February 27, 2000.

359. Canizares, Alex. "Europeans Irked Over Orbital Snooping." *fas.org,* February 28, 2000.

360. Blair, Mike. "Satellite Spy System." *libertylobby.org,* January 22, 2006.

361. *Ibid.*

362. *Ibid.*

363. Quoted in Fielding and Campbell, *op cit.*

364. *strange-loops.com, op. cit.*

365. Woolsey, S. James. "Why We Spy on Our Allies." *Wall Street Journal (online),* March 17, 2000.

366. Quoted in *ombwatch.org.* "Concern Grows Over Unauthorized Domestic Spying," January 11, 2006.

367. Kessler, Ronald. *The Terrorist Watch: Inside the Desperate Race to Stop the Next Attack.* New York: Three Rivers Press, 2008.

368. Harris, Andrew. "Spy Agency Sought U.S. Call Records Before 9/11, Lawyers Say." *bloomberg.com,* June 30, 2006.

369. Lever, Rob. "Breaking the Code." *globalsecurity.org,* September 1, 2001.

370. O'Harrow, Robert. *No Place to Hide.* New York: Free Press, 2006.

371. Lichtblau, Eric. "Spy Agency Mined Vast Data Trove, Officials Report." *nytimes.com,* December 24, 2005.

372. Cauley, Lesley. "NSA Has Massive Database of Americans' Phone Calls." *usatoday.com,* May 11, 2006.

373. Ramasastry, Anita. "Why the Foreign Intelligence Surveillance Act Court Was Right to Rebuke the Justice Department." *news.findlaw.com,* September 4, 2002.

374. Quoted in Risen, James and Lichtblau, Eric. "Bush Lets U.S. Spy on Callers Without Courts." *nytimes.com,* December 16, 2005.

375. Risen, James and Lichtblau, Eric. "Bush Secretly Lifted Some Limits on Spying in U.S. After 9/11, Officials Say." *nytimes.com,* December 15, 2005.

376. *cnn.com.* "Cheney: Bush Has Right to Authorize Secret Surveillance," December 20, 2005.

377. Quoted in Singel, Ryan. "Whistle-Blower Outs NSA Spy Room." *wired.com,* April 7, 2006.

378. Eggen, Dan and Linzer, Dafna. "Judge Rules Against Wiretaps." *Washington Post,* August 18, 2006: A1.

379. Quoted in Liptak, Adam and Lichtblau, Eric. "Judge Finds Wiretap Actions Violate the Law." *nytimes.com,* August 18, 2006.

380. Quoted in *Ibid.*

381. Head, Tom. "ACLU v. NSA—What Happens Next in the ACLU v. NSA Wiretapping Case?" *civilliberty.about.com,* 2009.

382. Quoted in ACLU (press release). "Supreme Court Refuses to Review Warrantless Wiretapping Case." February 19, 2008.

383. Quoted in *Ibid.*

384. *news.cnet.com.* "Obama: No Warrantless Wiretaps if You Elect Me," January 8, 2008.

385. Blanchard, Ken. "Bush Right on Warrantless Searches." *sdpolitics.com,* January 16, 2009.

386. Kondracke, Mort. "Bush, Congress Should Legalize NSA Surveillance." *realclearpolitics.com,* February 17, 2006.

387. Tribe, Lawrence. Letter to Congressman John Conyers, Jr., January 6, 2006.

388. Borosage, Robert L. "What to Do with the Intelligence Agencies." *Working Papers* 4, 1977: 38–45.

389. Halperin, et al., *op. cit.,* p. 148.

390. *Ibid.*

391. Hersh, Seymour M. "CIA Keeps Eartha Kitt File." *Washington Star News,* January 3, 1975: p. 7.

392. Halperin et al., p. 149.

393. *Ibid.*

394. Cannon, Terence. "The CIA under Reagan." *World Marxist Review,* August 1983: 69–72.

395. Arendt, Hannah. *The Origins of Totalitarianism.* NY: Schocken Books, 2004 (originally published in 1951).

396. *New York Times* (online). "Says Usual Police Practice Is to Club," January 29, 1922.

397. Fried, Joseph R. "Volpe Sentenced to a 30-Year Term in Louima Torture." *nytimes.com,* December 14, 1999.

398. Central Intelligence Agency. *KUBARK: Counterintelligence Interrogation,* July 1963. KUBARK is a code name for the CIA.

399. Central Intelligence Agency, *Human Resources Exploitation Training Manual*—1983.

400. Cohn, Gary, Thompson, Ginger, and Matthews Mark. "Torture Was Taught by CIA; Declassified Manual Details the Methods Used in Honduras; Agency Denials Refuted." *Baltimore Sun* (online), January 27, 1997.

401. Quoted in CIA, 1983, *op. cit.*

402. *Ibid.*

403. Benjamin, Mark. "The CIA's Favorite Form of Torture." *salon.com,* June 7, 2007.

404. Cohn et al., *op. cit.*

405. Cohn et al., *op. cit.*

406. CIA, 1983, *op. cit.*

407. Cohn et al., *op. cit.*

408. CIA, 1983, *op. cit.*

409. Quoted in Cohn et al., *op. cit.*

410. CIA, 1983, *op. cit.*

411. Quoted in *Ibid.*

412. *Ibid.*

413. Quoted in *Ibid.*

414. Ross, Brian and Esposito, Richard. "CIA's Harsh Interrogation Techniques Described." *abcnews.com,* November 28, 2005.

415. Whitaker, Raymond. "The Torture Files." *presidentbush.com,* December 4, 2005.

416. Ross and Esposito, *op. cit.*

417. Ladisch, Virginie. "'Stress and Duress:' Drawing the Line Between Interrogation and Torture." *crimesofwar.com,* April 24, 2003.

418. Priest, Dana and Gellman, Barton. "'Stress and Duress' Tactics Used on Terrorism Suspects Held in Secret Overseas Facilities." *Washington Post* (online), December 26, 2002.

419. Ladisch, *op. cit.*

420. Eban, Katherine. "The Psychology-Torture Connection." *vanityfair.com,* June 18, 2008.

421. Eban, Katherine. "Rorschach and Awe." *vanityfair.com,* July 17, 2007.

422. *Ibid.*

423. *Ibid.*

424. Benjamin, Mark. "The CIA's Torture Teachers." *salon.com,* June 21, 2007.

425. Thanawala, Sudhin. "US Psychologists Scrap Interrogation Ban." *washingtonpost.com,* August 20, 2007.

426. Vedantam, Shankar. "APA Rules on Interrogation Abuse." *Washington Post,* August 20, 2007: A3.

427. Hersh, Seymour M. "Torture at Abu Ghraib." *newyorker.com,* May 10, 2004.

428. *Ibid.*

429. *Ibid.*

430. Martin, Susan Taylor. "Her Job: Lock Up Iraq's Bad Guys." *sptimes.com,* December 14, 2003.

431. Hersh, 2004, *op. cit.*

432. ARTICLE 15-6 INVESTIGATION OF THE 800TH MILITARY POLICE BRIGADE.

433. *Ibid.*

434. Hersh, 2004, *op. cit.*

435. Quoted in Hersh, Seymour M. "The General's Report." *newyorker.com,* June 25, 2007.

436. McCoy, Alfred W. "The Hidden History of CIA Torture: America's Road to Abu Ghraib." *commondreams.org,* September 9, 2004.

437. ARTICLE 15-6 INVESTIGATION OF THE 800TH MILITARY POLICE BRIGADE, *op. cit.*

438. Zernike, Kate. "Detainees Describe Abuses by Guard in Iraq Prison." *nytimes.com,* January 13, 2005.

439. *msnbc.com.* "England Gets 3 Years For Prison Abuse," September 28, 2005.

440. Wong, Edward. "Trial Date Set For Another Reservist in Prison Abuse Case." *nytimes.com,* October 22, 2004.

441. Quoted in Hersh, 2004, *op. cit.*

442. Jehl, Douglas and Johnston, David. "C.I.A. Expands Its Inquiry Into Interrogation Tactics." *nytimes.com,* August 29, 2004.

443. *cnn.com.* "Graner Sentenced to 10 Years For Abuses," January 15, 2005.

444. *Ibid.*

445. *msnbc.com.* "Graner to Testify at Lynndie England's Sentencing," May 4, 2005.

446. Dishneau, David. "Abu Ghraib Officer's Sentence: Reprimand." *usatoday.com,* August 28, 2007.

447. Smith, R. Jeffrey. "Abu Ghraib Officer Gets Reprimand." *Washington Post,* May 12, 2005: A 16.

448. Cloud, David S. "General Says Prison Inquiry Led to His Forced Retirement." *nytimes.com,* June 17, 2007.

449. Quoted in Hersh, 2007, *op. cit.*

450. Schmitt, Eric. "Army Report Says Flaws in Detention Didn't Cause Abuse." *nytimes.com,* July 23, 2004.

451. *Ibid.*

452. Quoted in McCoy, *op. cit.*

453. Quoted in Fisher, William. "Rumsfeld's 'Bad Apples' Didn't Fall Far From the Tree." *commondreams.org,* December 20, 2008.

454. Quoted in *Ibid.*

455. *Ibid.*

456. Quoted in *commondreams.org.* "Rumsfeld Okayed Abuses Says Former U.S. General," August 25, 2006.

457. *Ibid.*

458. McCoy, 2004, *op. cit.*

459. *Ibid.*

460. *Ibid.*

461. *Ibid.*

462. Quoted in McCoy, Alfred W. "Torture at Abu Ghraib Followed CIA's Manual." *commonsdreams. org,* May 14, 2004.

463. White, Josh. "Abu Ghraib Tactics Were Frist Used at Guantanamo." *Washington Post,* July 14, 2005: A1.

464. Lewis, Neil A. and Schmitt, Eric. "Inquiry Finds Abuses at Guantanamo Bay." *nytimes.com,* May 1, 2005.

465. *Ibid.*

466. *Ibid.*

467. *Ibid.*

468. *Los Angeles Times.* "It's Torture; It's Illegal," February 2, 2008: A20.

469. Eggen, Dan and Smith, R. Jeffrey. "FBI Agents Allege Abuse of Detainees at Guantanamo Bay." *Washington Post,* December 21, 2004: A1.

470. *washingtonpost.com.* "The Truth About Abu Ghraib," July 29, 2005.

471. Eggen and Smith, *op. cit.*

472. Quoted in *Ibid.*

473. Lewis and Schmitt, *op. cit.*

474. Quoted in Watson, Paul Joseph. "Rumsfeld Openly Admits Guantanamo Torture." *infowars.com,* November 3, 2005.

475. *Ibid.*

476. *Ibid.*

477. Woodward, Bob. "Detainee Tortured Says U.S. Official." *Washington Post,* January 14, 2009: A1.

478. *forbes.com.* "US Acknowledges Torture at Guantanamo; in Iraq, Afghanistan—UN," June 24, 2005.

479. United Nations Committee Against Torture. "Consideration of Reports Submitted by States Parties Under Article 19 of the Convention." May 18, 2006.

480. Lynch, Colum. "Military Prison's Closure Is Urged." *Washington Post.* May 20, 2006: A1.

481. Wright, Tom. "Close Guantanamo, UN Panel Urges." *iht.com,* May 19, 2006.

482. Coughlin, Con. "UN Inquiry Demands Immediate Closure of Guantanamo." *telegraph.co.uk,* February 13, 2006.

483. Quoted in Lynch, *op. cit.*

484. Lynch, *op. cit.*

485. Nebehay, Stephanie. "U.N. Rights Envoy Suspects CIA of Guantanamo Torture." *reuters.com,* December 13, 2007.

486. Doyle, Leonard. "Waterboarding Is Torture—I Did It Myself, Says US Advisor." *The Independent* (online), November 1, 2007.

487. Weiner, Eric. "Waterboarding: A Tortured History." *npr.com,* February 4, 2007.

488. *Ibid.*

489. *Ibid.*

490. *hrw.org.* "CIA Whitewashing Torture," November 20, 2005.

491. *abcnews.com.* "History of an Interrogation Technique: Water Boarding," November 29, 2005.

492. Weiner, *op. cit.*

493. *Ibid.*

494. Wallach, Evan. "Waterboarding Used to Be a Crime." *Washington Post,* November 4, 2007: B1.

495. Quoted in *abcnews.com,* November 29, 2005, *op. cit.*

496. Nance, Malcolm. "I Know Waterboarding Is Torture—Because I Did It Myself." *nydailynews. com,* October 31, 2007.

497. Quoted in Doyle, *op. cit.*

498. Nance, *op. cit.*

499. Human Rights Watch. "Open Letter to Attorney General Alberto Gonzalez." *hrw.org,* April 5, 2006.

500. Davis, Benjamin. "Endgame on Torture: Time to Call the Bluff." *Jurist* (online), October, 2007.

501. Quoted in Belle, Nicole. "Retired JAGs Send Letter to Leahy: "Waterboarding Is Inhumane, It Is Torture, and It Is Illegal." *crooksandliars.com,* November 2, 2007.

502. Shane, Scott. "A Firsthand Experience Before Decision to Torture." *nytimes.com,* November 7, 2007.

503. *democracynow.org.* "Despite Waterboarding Stance, Senate Committee Approves Mukassey's Attorney General Nomination," November 7, 2008.

504. *Los Angeles Times,* February 2, 2008, *op. cit.*

505. Tran, Mark. "CIA Admit 'Waterboarding' al-Qaida Suspects." *guardian.co.uk,* February 9, 2008.

506. *bbc.co.uk.* "CIA Admits Waterboarding Inmates," February 5, 2008.

507. Quoted in *military.com.* "Hayden: Waterboarding May Be Illegal," February 8, 2008.

508. Schor, Elana. "US Official Admits Waterboarding Presently Illegal." *guardian.co.uk,* February 14, 2008. Another administration heavyweight, Secretary of State Condoleezza Rice, admitted for the first time in late 2008 that, as early as 2002, when she was national security advisor, she had led high-level discussions about subjecting suspected al-Qaeda terrorists detained at military installations to waterboarding. (Fisher, William. "Rumsfeld's Bad Apples Didn't Fall Far From the Tree." *commondreams.org,* December 20, 2008.)

509. Quoted in *newser.com.* "Bush Rips Congress on Waterboarding Ban," February 15, 2008.

510. Quoted in Eggen, Dan. "Bush Announces Veto of Waterboarding Ban." *washingtonpost.com,* March 8, 2008.

511. Amnesty International (press release). "USA: Water Torture is Always Illegal." February 15, 2008.

512. Leopold, Jason. "Cheney Admits He 'Signed Off' on Waterboarding of Three Guantanamo Prisoners." *onlinejournal.com,* December 29, 2008.

513. *Ibid.*

514. Quoted in Duss, Matthew. "Cheney the Failed Architect." *guardian.co.uk,* December 17, 2008.

515. Carroll, Lewis. *Alice's Adventures in Wonderland and Through the Looking Glass.* New York: Signet Classics, 2000. [Originally published in 1899.]

516. Quoted in Eggen, Dan. "Chaney's Remarks Fuel Torture Debate." *Washington Post,* October 27, 2006.

517. Amnesty International (press release). "Amnesty International's Response to Cheney's 'No-Brainer' Comment." October 26, 2006.

518. McCain, John. "Torture's Terrible Toll." *newsweek. com,* November 21, 2005.

519. White, Josh. "President Relents, Backs Torture Ban." *Washington Post,* December 16, 2005: A1.

520. Miller, Greg and Reynolds, Maura. "McCain Wins Agreement From Bush on Torture Ban." *Los Angeles Times,* December 16, 2005: A1.

521. *cnn.com.* "McCain, Bush Agree on Torture Ban," December 15, 2005.

522. Savage, Charlie. "Bush Could Bypass New Torture Ban." *boston.com,* January 4, 2006.

523. *Washington Post.* "Legalizing Torture," June 9, 2004: A20.

524. Landers, Ken. "Bush Veto Allows CIA Torture to Continue." *abc.net.au,* March 10, 2008.

525. Quoted in *Ibid.*

526. Warrick, Joby. "CIA Tactics Endorsed in Secret Memos." *Washington Post,* October 15, 2008: A1.

527. Hess, Pamela and Jordan, Lara Jakes. "CIA Torture Memo: Harsh Interrogation Legal If It's in 'Good Faith.'" *huffingtonpost.com,* July 25, 2008.

528. Warrick, *op. cit.*

529. American Civil Liberties Union (press release). "ACLU Obtains Key Memos Authorizing CIA Torture Methods," July 24, 2008.

530. Quoted in *msnbc.com.* "Obama: U.S. Will Not Torture," January 9, 2009.

531. Quoted in Margasak, Larry. "Holder: Waterboarding Is Torture." *usnews.com,* January 15, 2009.

532. Bresnahan, John. "'Waterboarding Is Torture,' Says Holder." *politico.com,* January 16, 2009.

533. Hess, Pamela. "Obama Intel Nominee Says No Torture on His Watch." Associated Press (online), January 22, 2009.

534. Phillips, Kate. "Judiciary Chairman Calls For Commission to Delve into Bush Practices." *nytimes. com,* February 9, 2009.

535. Leopold, Jason. "Obama Signals He Doesn't Back Leahy's Plan to Probe Bush Abuses." *onlinejournal. com,* February 10, 2009.

536. Hess, Pamela. "No Punishment Planned for CIA Interrogators." *Houston Chronicle,* February 7, 2009: A10.

537. Cohn, Marjorie. "Under U.S. Law Torture Is Always Illegal." *counterpunch.org,* May 6, 2008.

538. American Civil Liberties Union (press release). "Is Torture Illegal? Let Us Count the Ways." November 8, 2007.

539. The Paquete Habana, 175 U.S. 677 (1900).

540. This principle was established by the United States Supreme Court in one of its earliest landmark decisions in *Martin v. Hunter's Lessee,* 14 U.S. 304 (1816).

541. American Civil Liberties Union, May 8, 2007, *op. cit.*

542. Watts, Philip. "Bush Advisor Says President Has Legal Power to Torture Children." *informationclearinghouse. info,* January 8, 2006.

543. Quoted in Applebaum, Anne. "The Torture Myth." *Washington Post,* January 12, 2003: A21.

544. Duss, *op. cit.*

545. McCain, *op. cit.*

546. *Ibid.*

547. McWhoter, Dianne. "Don't Punt on Torture' *USA Today,* February 11, 2009: 11A.

548. *cbsnews.com.* "CIA Director: Harsh Interrogations Were Effective," January 15, 2009.

549. Murdock, Deroy. "Waterboarding Has Its Benefits." *nationalreview.com,* November 5, 2007. *abcnews.com.*

"CIA Director's Strong Defense of Interrogation Techniques," January 15, 2009.

550. Burger, Timothy J. and Zagrin, Adam. "Fingering Danny Pearl's Killer." *time.com,* October 12, 2006.

551. Dershowitz, Alan M. *Shouting Fire: Civil Liberties in a Turbulent Age.* NY: Little, Brown, 2002.

552. Dershowitz, Alan M. "Want to Torture? Get a Warrant." *sfgate.com,* January 22, 2002.

553. Klein, Naomi. "Torture's Dirty Secret: It Works." *thenation.com,* May 12, 2005.

554. Quoted in Woodward, *op. cit.*

10

Corruption of Public Officials

At the beginning of the 18th Century, the governor-general of colonial New York was Edward Hyde (Lord Cornbury), a first cousin of the Queen of England. Among other things, Governor Hyde was a drunkard and an unabashed transvestite, with a penchant for addressing the New York Assembly while wearing one of his wife's hooped gowns. Hyde was also a crook.[1] He was as thoroughly dishonest in his public role as he was outlandish in his private life. He routinely accepted kickbacks and bribes, and gave large, illegal land grants to his friends in exchange for cash.[2] In 1707, he claimed to have received secret information that the French were preparing to invade New York by sea. He taxed the citizenry 1,500 pounds, ostensibly for the construction of protective batteries around the harbor. The French invasion was, of course, a fabrication, and Hyde used the funds to build a lavish new home for himself.

Hyde's behavior prompted so many complaints from the Assembly that he was removed from office and briefly imprisoned.[3] This may have been the first major political corruption scandal in American history. It would not be the last.

Indeed, the misuse of public authority for private gain has been a persistent phenomenon throughout American history. If the abuses of power described in the previous chapter conform to Lowi's notion of "Big Corruption," bribery and misappropriation represent "Little Corruption." In this context, the "Little" sobriquet does not mean trivial or uncostly; it merely distinguishes the crimes of renegade individuals from organizational deviance.

In the first section of this chapter, we will examine how officials within various branches of the government have violated the public trust and breached the public interest. In the second section, we will focus on police corruption as a distinct but closely related form of white-collar crime.

POLITICAL CORRUPTION

The simplest explanation of political corruption is that it reflects the frailty of human nature.[4] Political scientist James Q. Wilson has offered a pithy rule-of-thumb: "[M]en steal when there is a lot of money lying around loose and no one is watching."[5] More complex (though not necessarily more valid) explanations of corruption generally are rooted in the interaction between the individual and the social structure. Thus, corruption has been attributed variously to ambivalence toward behavioral norms,[6] the existence of wealthy elites denied direct formal influence on political policy,[7] as well the intrinsic flaws in organizational arrangements and bureaucratic procedures.[8]

Most basically, official behavior can be considered corrupt when it "deviates from the formal duties of a public role" for personal gain.[9] This is a useful little definition, because "all illegal acts are not necessarily corrupt and all corrupt acts are not necessarily illegal."[10] For example, former Congressman Allan Howe was plainly guilty of an unlawful act when he was convicted in 1976 of soliciting two undercover policewomen posing as prostitutes.[11] However, his behavior might not be construed as truly corrupt, since he did not betray his official position. But when former Congressman Wayne Hays put his mistress on the federal payroll as a secretary that same year—despite her admitted inability to type, file, or even answer the telephone[12]—that would meet the corruption criterion, since Hays' conduct involved a misuse of public office. Conversely, the craterous loopholes in campaign finance laws may encourage conduct that is technically legal yet inevitably corrupting.

In earlier generations, some functionalists suggested that corruption might not be inherently evil because it serves as a "lubricant which eases the rigid wheels of a bureaucracy."[13] It was argued that government cannot be carried on efficiently without corruption.[14] "Corruption may be ethically unsavory, but, according to some economists, it may also be economically beneficial. In a country where elaborate bureaucracies make it hard to start companies, import or export goods, or simply get a passport, bribes can cut through red tape, serving as what's called 'speed money.'"[15] Most modern scholars, however, perceive the overall social effects of political corruption as unmistakably dysfunctional.[16]

The Executive Branch

In the United States, access to power and resources permits incumbents to buy political support by selling political favors. Corruption is further perpetuated because elected officials "can often engage in illegal activities without being reprimanded at the polls."[17] Of course, there are only two elected officials in the entire executive branch of the federal government, a president and a vice-president. So, despite occasional anomalies like Spiro Agnew, known instances of "Little" corruption at this highest level of elective office have been relatively rare. More typically, when presidential (or vice-presidential) malfeasance has occurred, it has taken the form of "Big" corruption aimed at promoting an administration's organizational goals, as was the case with Watergate, the Iran-Contra affair, and other such abuses of executive power.

An exception to this thesis would be some of the well-documented fund-raising excesses of the Clinton Administration. From dispensing overnight stays in the White House's fabled Lincoln Bedroom in exchange for hefty campaign contributions,[18] to the illegal Democratic National Committee (DNC) fund-raiser at the Hsi Lai Buddhist monastery in California,[19] to the suspicious contributions made by South Korean and Chinese companies,[20] Clinton and the DNC appeared to engage in a level of influence peddling not seen since Watergate.

Year by year, scandal by scandal, the corruption of American politics seems only to get worse. Writing in 1999, the veteran political reporter Elizabeth Drew ruefully observed:

> Indisputably, the greatest change in Washington over the past twenty-five years . . . has been the preoccupation with money. . . . The culture of money dominates Washington as never before; money now rivals or even exceeds power as the preeminent goal.[21]

"Little" corruption, however, has never been a stranger to the myriad federal agencies which comprise the executive branch. Unelected administrators and government agents often have the same value to the buyers of influence and special favors as do elected officials.[22] Bureaucrats cannot make laws, but they can determine the way laws are carried out through their administrative authority and regulatory powers. "The mere structural availability of the opportunity for illicit gain is sufficient motivation for some corrupt employees."[23]

Structural facilitation of corruption can be illustrated by the experiences of three large federal agencies—the Department of Agriculture, the Department of Defense, and the Department of Homeland Security.

The Department of Agriculture

The USDA was rocked in the 1970s by revelations that government grain inspectors were being bribed to misgrade substandard or adulterated grain and to overlook the short-weighting of grain shipments.[24] The Bunge Corporation, one of the world's largest grain exporters, admitted that it had bribed an inspector to ignore a shipment infested with insects. "In a case brought against the Archer-Daniels-Midland Company and the Garnac Grain Company, a government investigator indicated that the two companies saved about $450,000 worth of grain annually through short-weighting, and that misgrading added another $1.2 million to company coffers."[25]

While corrupt USDA inspectors have allowed adulterated grain to leave the country, inspectors from the Food and Drug Administration have been convicted of accepting bribes to allow adulterated food *into* the country. Four such officials knowingly approved more than 20 tons of contaminated seafood in 1988.[26]

More recently, the head of the USDA's Cooperative State Research Service was removed from his job in 1995 after investigators found that he had lobbied Congress illegally in order to steer $1.8 million in research contracts to friends.[27]

The Department of Defense

"One of the most common forms of government corruption involves the purchasing agents who decide which firms are to supply the government with various products and services."[28] In 1776, the Continental Congress granted a gunpowder contract to the firm of Willing, Morris & Company.[29] Both Willing and Morris were members of the Congressional committee that had issued the contract. They cleared a profit of 12,000 pounds.[30]

Today, since government purchases total hundreds of billions of dollars annually and make up nearly one-quarter of our gross national product,[31] the incentives for corruption are obvious. Pentagon bid-rigging scandals involving $700 toilet seats[32] and platinum-coated hammers[33] have underscored the great potential for abuse within the military-industrial complex. This was never more evident than in the case of Melvyn Paisley.

Paisley served as Assistant Secretary of the Navy for Research and Development between 1981 and 1987 and was largely responsible for procurement. "[W]hile in office, he corrupted the bidding process on hundreds of millions of dollars of weapons systems in order to divert contracts to those who secretly bought his services."[34] Consider just two examples of Paisley's gross misconduct.

In 1985, Paisley and his partner, defense consultant William Galvin, conspired to induce the Navy to select the big industrial firm Martin Marietta as the prime contractor on a classified government research program. The complicated scheme involved Paisley and Galvin forming a company named Sapphire Systems, which would become a subcontractor on the program in collusion with Martin Marietta. Paisley's financial interest in Sapphire was, of course, carefully concealed. Seven months later, Paisley awarded a $900,000 contract to Martin Marietta and $300,000 to Sapphire Systems—his own company.[35]

That same year, Paisley also conspired with the Sperry Corporation (now Unisys) to rig the bidding to supply the Navy with a sophisticated airport surveillance system. "He went to extraordinary lengths to persuade his Pentagon colleagues to alter the terms of the competition in ways that would favor Sperry."[36] Paisley also passed secret information to Sperry concerning rival bids, which allowed Sperry to come in as the low bidder and win the $45 million contract.[37]

Even after Paisley left the Pentagon in 1987, he continued to collect large deferred "consulting" fees from companies with whom he earlier had conspired. Over just a 15-month period, he was paid more than $500,000.[38]

Melvyn Paisley was arrested as part of Operation Ill Wind, the biggest federal investigation of defense procurement fraud ever conducted. In addition to Paisley, this operation led to the convictions of 8 other government employees, 42 corporate executives and defense consultants, and 7 major corporations.[39] As the highest-ranking official uncovered by Ill Wind, Paisley received the stiffest sentence—4 years in prison. Ironically, a Congressional committee once had asked him what should be done about corrupt defense contractors. Paisley's prophetic reply: "[Y]ou have to hang them from a tree where everyone can see them."[40]

In January, 2008, Michael Cantrell, an engineer with the United States Army Space and Missile Defense Command in Huntsville, Alabama, along with his deputy Doug Ennis, pleaded guilty to taking $1.6 million in bribes from government contractor Maurice Subilia.[41] Subilia also pleaded guilty to bribing a public official a year later.[42] Cantrell and Ennis had effectively plotted "to turn America's missile defense program into a personal cash machine."[43] Cantrell offered up a stale "everybody else was doing it" defense:

> "The contractors are making a killing. The lobbyists are getting their fees and the contractors and lobbyists are writing out campaign checks to the politicians. Everybody is making money here—except us."[44]

Evidently, Cantrell's mother was one of those rare ones who had never asked her children: "If everybody jumped off a cliff, would you?"

The Department of Homeland Security

The United States Department of Homeland Security (DHS) is responsible for protecting American territory from terrorist attacks, securing the U.S. borders, and responding to natural disasters. In 2003, the DHS absorbed the former Immigration and Naturalization Service (INS) and assumed its duties. It divided the enforcement and services functions of the INS into two separate and new agencies: U.S. Customs and Border Protection and U.S. Citizenship and Immigration Services (ICE). Both of these agencies have been plagued by major corruption scandals.

U.S. CUSTOMS AND BORDER PROTECTION   Bribery of federal officials by Mexican drug smugglers and human traffickers has risen sharply along the 2,000-mile border from San Diego, California to Brownsville, Texas. Since 2004, hundreds of public employees have been charged with helping to move narcotics or illegal immigrants across the U.S.-Mexican border. *Thousands* more are reportedly under investigation.[45]

Among the recent cases are the following:

- Jorge Reyeros, a naturalized American citizen born in Colombia, spent more than 20 years with U.S. Customs, working his way up to supervisor with duties at the Newark, New Jersey, airport and seaport. From that position, he helped smuggle **tens of thousands of kilos of cocaine** into the United States. Reyeros's crimes actually pre-dated the formation of the Department of Homeland Security by nearly four years. "In brief remarks to the judge before he was sentenced, Jorge Reyeros declared flatly, "I'm innocent." The judge rejected that declaration as "nonsense" and handed Reyeros a 24-year prison sentence."[46]

- A Mexican drug trafficking ring paid Border Patrol agent Juan Alfredo Alvarez $1.5 million to wave trucks loaded with a ton or more of marijuana through checkpoints outside of Hebbronville, Texas.[47] Alvarez was sentenced to 20 years in prison.[48]

- Customs Service inspector Michael Taylor collected thousands of dollars in bribes each week for allowing marijuana and illegal aliens to be smuggled through lanes he was staffing at the world's busiest border crossing in San Ysidro, California, outside of San Diego.[49] Taylor was sentenced to 4 1/2 years in prison.[50]

- Two border patrol agents, Oscar Ortiz and Eric Balderas, were each convicted of smuggling illegal immigrants from Tecate, a remote area east of San Diego. Balderas and Ortiz received $300 per person from a smuggling organization for looking the other way.[51] A wiretap recorded Balderas boasting: "We don't do anything, just clear the way, and we get $300 per head."[52] The two agents also drove illegal immigrants across the border for $1,800 to $2,000 per person—sometimes in government vehicles. Ortiz received a 5-year sentence, and Balderas was sentenced to 2 years. Ortiz's sentence was longer because of additional charges. It was revealed that he himself was an illegal alien.[53]

- Border Patrol agent David Duque, Jr., sold identification documents, including passports, birth certificates, green cards, and social security cards at his checkpoint in Falfurrias, Texas.[54] Duque also received a $5,000 bribe from a government informant for permitting cocaine to pass through the checkpoint, after advising the informant how to package the cocaine in order to get it past drug-sniffing dogs.[55] Duque was sentenced to 14 years in prison.[56]

- Customs officer Fernando Arango, stationed in Nogales, Arizona, took a $50,000 bribe from a government informant to allow an RV Arango believed was packed with 440 pounds of cocaine to pass through a border crossing. Arango had instructed the man to buy an RV and provided details about how to construct a hidden compartment to stow the drugs. He further instructed his supposed accomplice to hire an elderly couple to drive across the border, saying that he "controlled" the crossing and that "for $3,000 per kilogram, he would assure safe passage of the cocaine."[57] In another testimonial to DHS screening, it was later revealed that Arango had a felony arrest record for marijuana trafficking in 1989.[58] He jumped bail, then fled to Colombia but re-surfaced 10 years later, working as a police informant in Florida. His law enforcement contacts in Florida had helped him obtain a job with Customs and Border inspection.[59] Arango was sentenced to 9 years in prison.[60]

- Michael Gilliland, an ex-marine and 16-year border agent, took between $70,000 and $120,000 in bribes at his assigned station at the Otay Mesa Port of Entry on the California-Mexican border.[61] Gilliland conspired with two female smugglers to permit caravans of cars, each sometimes packed with 10 or more migrants, to cross the border unimpeded.[62] Gilliland received a 5-year sentence.[63]

- Two Border Patrol agents, Samuel McClaren and Mario Alvarez, took more than $300,000 in payoffs from a smuggling organization. The two El Centro, California-based agents used their government-issued Chevrolet Tahoe to smuggle illegal aliens. Each of them received prison sentences of more than 6 years.[64]

- Texas-based Border Patrol agent Reynaldo Zuniga helped two Mexican criminals smuggle 11 bricks of cocaine into the U.S. He used his government vehicle to pick up one of the men along the Rio Grande river and drive him to a fast-food restaurant across the border.[65] Zuniga made at least five trips before his arrest. He received a prison sentence of more than 7 years.[66]

- Four Border Patrol agents, who all worked at the Sierra Blanca, Texas checkpoint, accepted bribes to allow cocaine and 750 illegal immigrants into the U.S. Agent Aldo Erives enlisted fellow agents Robert Espino, David Garcia, and Jesus Delgado, and coordinated safe passage by calling them and telling them what vehicles to wave through at what time. Erives, Espino, Garcia, and Delgado received prison sentences of 10 1/2, 8, 2, and 1 year respectively.[67]

- An Arizona Border Patrol agent, Michael Gonzalez, was caught on videotape stealing a 23-pound bundle of marijuana while on duty. A state police officer stopped a pickup truck with drugs concealed in the bed. The driver fled, abandoning the truck, and the officer gave chase on foot. Gonzalez then arrived on the scene. Patrol mounted video from the officer's car showed Gonzalez, in his Border Patrol uniform, walking to the tailgate, removing a bale of marijuana, putting the drugs in his trunk, and driving away.[68] Gonzalez received a 7 1/2 year prison sentence.[69]

- U.S. Customs and Border Protection agent Salomon Ruiz pleaded guilty in February 2009, for accepting bribes to help smuggle cocaine.[70] He was sentenced to 14 years in federal prison and was fined $14,000.[71] Ruiz guided more than 11 pounds of cocaine across the Rio Grande.[72]

- Until May of 2008, Luis Alarid would have been classified as a modern success story who beat the odds of impoverished youth.[73] He grew up with very little money, living in often-abusive foster homes. Alarid, however, managed to turn his fate around and become a highly decorated officer in both the Army and the Marines.[74] After serving two tours in Iraq, Alarid had the necessary qualifications to become a Customs and Border Protections officer in Southern California. His sterling reputation was short-lived, however.

  Just a few months after joining the Customs and Border Protection staff, Luis Alarid was arrested for allegedly smuggling illegal aliens into the United States along with more than 100 kilograms of marijuana. One vehicle he waved through allegedly contained 18 illegal aliens and more than 170 pounds of marijuana, and was driven by his uncle. Evidence suggests that Alarid was working for a Mexican smuggling crew that included many members of his family. Prosecutors believe that Alarid had planned to work for this crew all along. Alarid allegedly made at least $200,000 from illegal aliens for their entry into the United States, which he used to buy expensive products such as flat-screen televisions and a motorcycle. Luis Alarid was fined $200,000 for his crimes and sentenced to 7 years in prison.[75]

- In May of 2010, Jeffrey Daft, a former US Customs and Border Protection officer, was indicted on charges of lying to obtain federal compensation and four counts of mail fraud. In his application for compensation with the Federal Employees Compensation Action, he falsely denied self-employment. After an investigation, however, federal investigators found that Daft did not report ownership of two companies: RC Bods and Herzog Racing. Because of his omission, Daft was able to receive employment compensation totaling $315,000.

- In June 2010, Eric Macias was sentenced to prison for aiding drug traffickers smuggle marijuana and cocaine across the United States border. Macias had worked for U.S. Customs and Border Protection since 2005, and aided traffickers in smuggling illicit drugs from March 2006 to February 2008. He was arrested in January 2009, but was not sentenced until June 2010. Shortly before his arrest, he had taught smugglers how to avoid detection when smuggling marijuana, and had escorted two shipments of cocaine. During his tenure as a border patrol agent, Macias accepted $14,000 in bribes. Macias also admitted to distracting other border patrol officers while smugglers passed by. He would later catch up and continue his escort service. Macias will spend 6 years in prison for his crimes.[76]

- Richard Cramer was once a highly respected Immigration and Customs Enforcement (ICE) officer. He had a 26-year history on the job, was regarded as a high-ranking officer, and was a front-runner in the war against drugs.[77] Government officials were shocked to discover that Cramer had been working for the other side during the drug war. Cramer secretly worked for high profile drugs lords and aided in the trafficking of hundreds of pounds of cocaine.[78] His position as an officer within ICE allowed him access to secret documents, which he allegedly sold to numerous smugglers for as low as $2,000 per document while working in Guadalajara.[79] In addition, Cramer allegedly provided drug dealers with inside information on U.S. government warrant and investigation procedure.[80] Cramer was arrested in Arizona on September 4, 2009.[81] In exchange for aiding the government with its prosecutions of other cases, all but one of Cramer's charges were dropped.[82] Prosecutors recommended a 2-year prison term for Cramer, but he has yet to be sentenced.[83]

As drug dealers have become more brazen and the volume and value of drugs have skyrocketed, many federal officials are openly concerned about corruption along the U.S.-Mexican border[84]—as well they should be. A number of factors have been cited as contributors to the corruption epidemic. First are sloppy hiring and screening processes. The massive buildup of Border Patrol agents since 9/11 suggests that hiring standards have been lowered.[85] The DHS may insist that the vast majority of Border Patrol agents are law-abiding—and this is no doubt true—but the aforementioned Ortiz and Arango cases, involving agents hired with criminal records and fake American citizenship, indicates that something is seriously wrong with the screening process.

Second is inadequate training. According to the head of the Border Patrol agents union, morale at the agency is "pathetic," stemming in part from career-ending allegations made against agents by illegal immigrants.[86]

Third, and perhaps most important, are weak internal controls. Some critics have argued that there has been no effective internal oversight of border agents since the creation of the Department of Homeland Security.

And finally, there is the ever-present greed factor. To maintain their profit structure, the Mexican drug cartels have to import in large quantities, and this places a premium on paying off border patrol agents.[87] In the words of one investigator: "If you have a corrupt inspector, he can make $35,000 to $40,000 with a flick of the hand."[88]

Weak internal controls may also be at the core of the corruption surrounding the other big criminal enterprise taking place at the border—human trafficking. "[A]s smugglers demand higher and higher fees to bring illegal immigrants into the United States, their efforts to bribe those guarding the border have intensified.[89] "The division of the DHS into multiple agencies with overlapping responsibilities has meant no coordinated approach to investigation."[90] "While corruption is growing, the number of internal investigators overseeing a vastly expanding work-force is stagnant or even shrinking."[91]

U.S. CITIZENSHIP AND IMMIGRATION SERVICES: Selling green cards and approving visas with-out background checks was a nagging problem when the INS was part of the Justice Department. Now, in the post-9/11 era, corruption at the U.S. Citizenship and Immigration Services ("ICE") is an even more serious cause for concern.[92] An ICE employee has warned: "Terrorists need immi-gration documents to embed in our society and work here without raising alarm bells. . . . They are always looking for that documentation to live among us."[93] The former head of internal affairs at ICE echoes that warning in a more ominous tone: "After the next attack when they find out that an employee was bribed by a terrorist or bribed by a spy, it's going to be too late."[94]

Most of the bribery cases at ICE do not involve suspected terrorists or spies; but no one can say for sure that none of them deny with certainty that more dangerous crimes may yet be uncovered. Among the recent corruption cases are the following:

- Robert Schofield, a 30-year federal employee who was an ICE district office supervisor in Fairfax County, Virginia, pocketed more than $600,000 in bribes for falsifying documents to help unqualified Asian immigrants obtain American citizenship. Schofield "earned" up to $10,000 per immigrant.[95] U.S. Attorney Chuck Rosenberg said: "The breadth and scope of Mr. Schofield's fraud and corruption are truly stunning."[96] Schofield was sentenced to 15 years in prison for bribery and naturalization fraud.[97]

- Santiago Efrain Valle, an ICE agent in El Paso, Texas, tried to extort $20,000 from an immigrant detainee in exchange for dismissing pending immigration charges and chang-ing the detainee's risk classification.[98] Valle later accepted the money from undercover federal agents. He received a 44-month prison sentence.[99]

- Phillip Browne, a Manhattan district adjudication officer for ICE, conspired with his sister and others to provide hundreds of fraudulent green cards in a scheme that netted more than $1 million.[100] Browne's sister, Beverly Mozer-Browne, owned Help Preparers, a Queens, New York business that purportedly provided financial and legal services but was, in reality, a front for the procurement of illegal permanent residence documents— sometimes by arranging sham marriages between illegal immigrants and American citi-zens.[101] Phillip Browne was sentenced to 2 1/2 years in prison for his part in the scam.[102]

- Rafael Pacheco, Jr., an ICE agent in Tampa, Florida, took almost $18,000 in bribes from a Mexican narcotics trafficker. In return, Pacheco accessed government databases to obtain restricted information about the drug dealer and passed it on to him.[103] Pacheco also wrote a letter to a U.S. consulate in Mexico falsely claiming that the drug dealer was assisting law enforcement. The letter was used to facilitate the entry of his criminal benefactor's family into the United States.[104] Pacheco received a 7-year prison sentence.

- Jimmie Ortega, a Manhattan district adjudication supervisor for ICE, took tens of thou-sands of dollars in bribes for granting United States citizenship to ineligible aliens. Ortega solicited and received bribes of between $1,500 and $4,000 from at least 20 aliens in con-nection with the scheme.[105] He was sentenced to 3 1/2 years in prison.[106]

- Robert Walton, an immigration employee for 20 years, accepted bribes in the form of valu-able jewelry and $5,000 in cash for approving citizenship and residency for immigrants who did not meet requirements. Walton claimed the money was a loan and the jewelry pieces were "thank you" gifts. He was handed a 1-year prison sentence,[107] without saying, "You're welcome."

As with U.S. Customs and Border Protection, there is reason to question the effectiveness of screening and internal controls at U.S. Immigration and Customs Enforcement. For example, in the aforementioned Schofield case, Robert Schofield had a checkered on-the-job history, to say the least. He had been the target of numerous allegations of bribery dating back more than 10 years prior to his arrest.[108] He once granted resident status to an unqualified Filipino woman, who then became a live-in nanny for his stepchild for a year.[109] In 1991, while working for the INS, he reportedly wrecked an investigation of an Asian brothel in Washington, D.C., after having an affair with an informant.[110] He was demoted over this incident for "conduct unbecoming a government employee." Schofield soon fled to East Asia, where he made $36,000 worth of unauthorized purchases on his government-issued credit card. He later returned to the U.S., and when the Department of Homeland Security took over the INS in 2003, he, incredibly, became a supervisor.[111] How a crook like Schofield managed to salvage his career has never publicly been explained.

The former head of internal affairs at U.S. Immigration and Customs Enforcement, quoted earlier, has called the corruption at ICE "absolutely outrageous" and again warns of the ramifications on national security: "Remember, one officer can grant citizenship at the time of his choosing at the place of his choosing to a person of his choosing—with impunity. So if he wants to give Osama bin Laden U.S. citizenship, he can."[112]

The Legislative Branch

For the first half-century of American independence, members of Congress commonly sold their influence to private interests, as if that practice were part of their job description. In an 1833 letter to the president of the National Bank, Senator Daniel Webster complained indignantly that his retainer had not been "*refreshed* as usual."[113] Webster threatened to discontinue his legislative services to the bank if it failed to send him his customary payment. Understandably, public resentment over such corruption of their legislators grew, and, in 1853, Congress passed its first "conflict of interest" statute.

Most critics contend that at the heart of Congressional corruption is the manner by which American political campaigns are funded. "The overwhelming majority of voters believe the current system for financing campaigns is basically unsound."[114] Such a national consensus is not hard to explain. The cost of running for office has increased exponentially since the days of Daniel Webster. (In fact, senators were not even popularly elected in Webster's time.) After the Supreme Court ruled in 1976[115] that statutory limits upon Congressional election expenditures were unconstitutional, members of Congress (and would-be members) came to depend increasingly upon special interest groups for campaign contributions.[116] The result has been "a parasitic symbiosis between the public and private sectors."[117] In 1986, the Deputy Solicitor of the Department of Labor articulated this disheartening conclusion:

> Virtually every member of Congress has been compelled to become a crook. Most of them, we can hope, regret the necessity of having had to accept a life of crime as the price of holding office, but crooks they certainly are.[118]

Political action committees (PACs) are one very convenient source of campaign money. Although federal law limits direct PAC contributions to $5,000, the law can be circumvented easily through the use of so-called "soft money"—legally unrestricted donations to political parties, as opposed to restricted donations to individual candidates. During the 1992 presidential election, for example, the Republican National Committee collected $70 million in "soft money." A Republican group known as "Team 100" consisted of 270 donors of $100,000 or more. The Democrats also had an elite group of their own, called "The Managing Trustees," for donors of over $200,000.[119] A 1995 study by the nonpartisan Center for Public Integrity, titled "The Buying of the President," concluded that the American political system resembles "a giant auction."[120]

The proliferation of "soft money" in the 1996 presidential campaign dwarfed the 1992 figures. The Republican and Democratic parties amassed a record-breaking $170 million in unregulated contributions.[121] It was a short-lived record, however. In 2000 the two major parties received over $226 million in "soft" money.[122]

The 2004 presidential campaign was the first to follow the enactment of the Bipartisan Campaign Reform Act of 2002 (known as the McCain-Feingold Bill after its chief senate sponsors). The new law banned "soft money" contributions from corporations and labor unions, but also raised the limit of individual donations to national committees of political parties.[123] This trade-off actually made the 2004 presidential election the most expensive up to that time. Candidates George W. Bush and John Kerry raised a combined total of nearly $700 million.[124] In 2008, candidates Barack Obama and John McCain shattered that record after raising a combined *$999 million*.[125] Political money has been compared to water. "If you try to block it, it will simply divert itself into another stream."[126]

An analysis of the spending for the 1986 Congressional elections proclaimed that "[t]he statistical evidence staggers the mind."[127] PACs contributed $132.2 million to Congressional candidates—28 percent of total receipts. Incumbents in the Senate and the House received $89.5 million, challengers received $19.2 million, and the balance went to open-seat candidates.[128] It has been quipped that the United States produces "the best politicians money can buy."[129]

While the explicit quid pro quo arrangements of the Webster era may now be relatively rare, PACs unquestionably extract an implicit price for their financial support. One lobbyist openly acknowledges that PAC funds represent "a civilized approach to vote-buying."[130] Another lobbyist admits: "We're skirting the edge of felonious conduct."[131] Lobbying and political fund raising have fundamentally distorted our democratic system.[132] In 1996, a retiring congressman described a system of institutionalized corruption in remarkably blunt terms:

> No lobbyist ever made a contribution without expecting something in return . . . The only reason it's not bribery is that Congress gets to say what's bribery.[133]

The power of PAC money was made apparent, for example, in 1982, when Congress was debating a Federal Trade Commission regulation requiring the disclosure of known defects in used cars. One unnamed Congressman was quoted as declaring: "I got a $10,000 check from the National Auto Dealers Association. I can't change my vote now."[134] Apparently, he was not alone; Congress overturned the regulation, even though it clearly served the public interest.

An illustration of a well-heeled lobbying blitzkrieg was provided when baby food was not included in a 1993 bill authorizing an aid package for the former Soviet Union. Immediately, the Gerber Company pulled out its checkbook.

> For Gerber, the stakes were high. Someday the republics would buy their own baby food; they would probably choose the brand they had come to know through U.S.

aid. So the company started spending big bucks in Washington. It hired a lobbying firm to press its case, and a Gerber executive traveled to Washington weekly. The result: a second aid bill . . . paving the way for U.S. taxpayers to send Gerber products to Russia.[135]

Some lawmakers argue that lobbyists perform a valuable service by providing them with important information on critical issues. In 1995, the House Majority Whip, Representative Tom DeLay of Texas, attacked a proposal to limit lobbyists' gifts to members of Congress as a "leftist plot."[136] Defenders of the current system also contend that campaign contributions do not dictate Congressional votes. This position espouses an "investment theory" of politics.[137] From this perspective, campaign contributions are viewed not as covert bribes, but as investments in candidates who are likely to share a donor's point of view. As one critic has noted: "Congressmen don't have to chase money with their votes; there's so much around they can cop all they want no matter what their stance on a specific issue."[138] In 2008, even in the midst of a severe economic slump, lobbying in Washington surged to $3.3 billion—up from $2.9 billion in 2007 and more than double the total four years earlier.[139]

We have thus far looked at Congressional corruption as an institutional phenomenon. We now turn our attention to an individual level of analysis.

In recent times, most of the offenses involved in most of the successful prosecutions of corrupt federal legislators have fallen into three general categories: (1) violations of election laws; (2) payroll fraud; and (3) bribery. Each of these areas reflects the sort of betrayal that moved one federal judge to ponder aloud, while passing sentence on a convicted Congressman: "If people who make the laws can't obey them, who can we expect to?"[140]

Violation of Election Laws

In 1975, The Securities and Exchange Commission revealed that the Gulf Oil Corporation had maintained a multi-million dollar secret fund from which it had made illegal corporate campaign contributions, clumsily disguised as personal donations.[141] The money had been funneled into Gulf's Bahamian subsidiary and then dispersed to selected political candidates, mostly influential incumbents. Gulf's gift list read like a "Who's Who" of the U.S. Senate, containing such prominent names as Hubert Humphrey, Henry Jackson, Howard Baker, and Russell Long.[142] The biggest contribution, $100,000, reportedly was given to Minority Leader Hugh Scott, who announced his retirement shortly after the Gulf story was reported by the media.[143] When the scandal was uncovered, Gulf acted as if *it* were the victim; its chairman called it a "tragic chapter in the history of Gulf Oil."[144] Gulf even sent letters to its powerful beneficiaries, requesting that they return the illegal gifts.[145] It seemed as though Gulf believed that the Senate could be purchased with a money-back guarantee.

In 1997, freshman Representative Richard Tonry of Louisiana went to prison for receiving and conspiring to receive illegal campaign contributions. However, Tonry resigned from office. In his farewell message to the House, he vowed to return and urged his fellow legislators to "Keep my seat warm."[146] Except perhaps on C-SPAN, Tonry never saw that seat again.

In 1994, 9-term Representative Carroll Hubbard, Jr., of Kentucky was sentenced to 3 years in prison after pleading guilty to conspiracy to file false campaign finance reports. The presiding judge called the case a "sad and sorry tale" of official misconduct.[147] The judge further noted the he had received a deluge of letters from Hubbard's embittered constituents urging *against* leniency.[148]

Congressman Jay Kim of California, the nation's first Korean-born congressman, pleaded guilty in 1997 to federal charges of accepting and hiding more than $200,000 in illegal contributions.[149] He later received a sentence of 2 months house arrest and 1 year probation, along with a $5,000 fine.[150] Despite pleas from his own party, Kim refused to resign his House seat, but was easily defeated in the 1998 Republican primary.[151]

Payroll Fraud

In addition to campaign funds, another tempting source of ready cash which some unscrupulous members of Congress have tapped illegally is their generous budget allowance. A number of legislators have been convicted of diverting money from their payrolls to their pockets. Representative J. Irving Walley of Pennsylvania received a suspended prison term and 3 years probation after admitting that he had forced kickbacks from his staff and used the funds for his own expenses.[152] Less fortunate was Representative James Hastings of New York, who received a 2 to 5 year sentence for the same type of offense. Hastings had extorted kickbacks from two of his Congressional employees and used the money to buy cars and snowmobiles.[153]

Representative Charles Diggs of Michigan was handed a 3-year prison term for carrying out a fraudulent scheme in which he increased the pay of employees in his Washington and Detroit offices and kept the surplus to help pay mounting alimony costs and to inject needed cash into a struggling Detroit funeral parlor he owned.[154] Representative Frank Clark of Pennsylvania utilized a somewhat different strategy. Instead of diverting employees' paychecks to help pay his household expenses, Clark put his entire household staff on the Congressional payroll.[155] After pleading guilty, Clark was sentenced to 2 years in prison.[156]

CASE STUDY
James Traficant

On April 4, 2002, a federal grand jury in Cleveland indicted James Traficant, Jr., a 59-year-old 9-term Democratic congressman from Ohio, on 10 counts ranging from soliciting bribes, to evading taxes, to extorting money from his own staff.[157] Among other things, he was accused of forcing staff members to kick back part of their salary to him. One staffer allegedly was required to turn over $2,500 from his monthly paycheck.[158] Three other staffers from his office were made to bale hay, repair barn walls, and build a corral for his horse farm.[159]

Traficant was one of the most flamboyant and controversial members of the House. He was known for his loud, out-of-fashion clothes, spiky gray toupee, and bizarre arm-waving speeches peppered with his signature phrase, "Beam me up, Scotty." A Conservative Democrat who usually voted with the Republicans, he was so estranged from his own party that he was the only member of Congress without a committee assignment. Although not a lawyer, he chose to represent himself. He pleaded not guilty at his arraignment and then added, "By reason of *sanity* [emphasis added]."[160]

At his trial, which began in March 2002, Traficant continually roared at witnesses and prosecutors, displaying the same blustery theatrics that he often exhibited on the House floor. The proceedings have been described as "part 'Sopranos' and part 'Three Stooges.'"[161] He accused every single government witness of lying. At one point he started throwing boxes around the courtroom.[162]

On April 11, Rep. James Traficant was convicted on all 10 counts. Three days later, he announced his candidacy for re-election, running

(*Continued*)

as an Independent.[163] Within minutes of the verdict, the House of Representatives began ethics proceedings against him.[164] In July, the House voted 420 to 1 to expel him.[165] The only vote against expulsion came from the most notorious member in all of congress—lame-duck Rep. Gary Condit, who had been defeated in a primary for re-election after being linked romantically to a murdered congressional intern.[166]

Ex-Rep James Traficant was sentenced to 8 years in prison on July 29, 2002. The sentence was actually longer than the one prosecutors had requested.[167] The judge, who had endured Traficant's histrionics throughout the trial, was in no mood for mercy. She told him emphatically that he is not above the law. Defiant to the bitter end, Traficant accused the judge of aiding the prosecution. She ordered him to sit down.[168]

Bribery

Bribery is the offense most likely to lead to the criminal prosecution of legislative officeholders. Congressional influence peddling can range from overt acts, such as the buying of a member's vote on a particular piece of legislation or the introduction of a bill aimed at benefitting some generous special interest group, to more subtle behaviors, such as providing help in securing government contracts or intervening in the federal bureaucracy on a benefactor's behalf.[169]

For instance, when Representative John Dowdy of Texas walked into an Atlanta airport in 1971, he was handed a bag containing $25,000. The money was to buy his influence in halting a federal probe of a Maryland construction company.[170] Upon conviction, Dowdy received an 18-month prison sentence. Special prosecutor Stephen Sachs had argued that it was important that Dowdy serve time, both as a deterrent to other public officials and an affirmation that the war on crime must transcend social and occupational boundaries. As Sachs noted: "There are an awful lot of people in jail and in prisons who have done far less than Mr. Dowdy and have had far less opportunity."[171]

Another typical case is that of Representative Bertram Podell of New York, who was jailed for selling favors to a Florida air taxi company trying to obtain a Caribbean route from the government.[172] A more insidious example is Representative Frank Brasco, also of New York, who was bribed to obtain lucrative post office hauling contracts for a trucking firm headed by a reputed mobster.[173] Brasco received a 3-month sentence for what the prosecutor termed an "extraordinary sequence of corruption."[174]

Representative Richard Hanna of California became a key figure in the notorious "Koreagate" scandal of the late 1970s.[175] A prominent Korean businessman named Tongsun Park, who represented the Korean rice industry in America, testified that he had given a total of $850,000 to 31 members of Congress in order to advance his business interests and the interests of the South Korean government. Hanna was one of Park's biggest beneficiaries, collecting $246,000.[176] In 1978, Hanna pleaded guilty to conspiring with Park to defraud the United States.[177] Park, however, denied any wrongdoing. In his words: "I thought I was taking part in the American political process. So far as I was concerned, I was helping Congressional friends who were loyal to me."[178] Missing from this defense, of course, is any recognition that members of the United States Congress are not supposed to be "loyal" to foreign lobbyists.

If one had to choose a single model of the corrupting effects of entrenched legislative power, one could hardly do better than Representative Daniel Flood of Pennsylvania. A former Shakespearean actor, known for his mellifluous oratory and distinctive waxed mustache, Flood parlayed his seniority and great popularity with voters into one of the most influential power bases in Congress. True to his name, he "flooded" his home district with federal funds. "His constituents could be born at the Daniel J. Flood Rural Health Center, be educated at the Daniel J. Flood Elementary School, be employed in the Daniel J. Flood Industrial Park, and retire in the Daniel J. Flood Elderly Center."[179]

But Flood's agenda was not limited to the life-spans of his constituents; he also used his considerable influence and well-honed political skills for personal profit. He took so many bribes it was hard to keep track of them all. He pocketed $5,000 from a businessman trying to sell disaster housing to the government for victims of Hurricane Agnes. He was paid $50,000 to obtain new certification for a chain of California trade schools about to lose its accreditation.[180] Flood collected regular payoffs, totaling $89,000, from a Washington conference center in exchange for channeling funds from the government's family planning program.[181] A banker gave him $4,000 worth of stock for using his influence to persuade the Treasury Department to approve a merger.[182] A New York rabbi paid Flood $5,000 to help his religious school receive millions of dollars in federal grants.[183] Flood once joked: "Little birdies fly by and drop these goodies on my desk."[184]

After his indictment, Flood struck a very generous plea bargain with the government, under which he agreed to plead guilty to one misdemeanor charge in exchange for the dropping of 11 felony counts.[185] Because of his advanced age, he received no prison time and was placed on short-term probation.[186] He died 15 years later at the age of 90.

Finally, it should be noted that the tripartite division of Congressional misconduct employed here is merely a convenient device for expositive purposes. The three categories are by no means mutually exclusive. Consider, for example, the sordid case of Representative Frederick Richmond of New York, who managed to blend all three varieties of corruption—in addition to a drug charge,[187] a securities violation,[188] and the solicitation of a male prostitute.[189] Richmond once even obtained a clerical job in the House of Representatives for an escaped convict.[190]

Richmond hid illegal corporate campaign contributions by converting them to traveler's checks or by swapping equivalent amounts of cash for unaddressed personal checks from district residents, who were then listed as individual contributors. Most of them did not even know the destination of their checks.[191]

Richmond's payroll practices also raised serious ethical questions. His Congressional aides received paychecks from private companies owned or controlled by Richmond, in violation of federal statutes. The assistant treasurer of Richmond's campaign committee testified that she made regular deposits into the account of the Richmond Corporation, but had no idea what that company did.[192]

Worst of all, Richmond reportedly accepted large bribes from a Brooklyn shipbuilding firm for his help in securing $310 million in Navy repair contracts.[193] In 1982, Richmond pleaded guilty to federal charges and resigned from Congress.[194] He was sentenced to a year and a day in prison.[195]

CASE STUDY
Operation ABSCAM

In 1978, Melvin Weinberg, international con artist and convicted swindler, was facing a prison sentence for fraud after pleading guilty in a Pittsburgh federal court. The FBI's New York office, which had been looking for informants involved in white-collar crimes to help the bureau make some

(Continued)

criminal cases, decided to conscript Weinberg in exchange for probation. Operation ABSCAM, the most depraved scandal in Congressional history, was born.[196]

With the bureau's cooperation, Weinberg set up a phony company known as Abdul Enterprises, purportedly owned by a fictitious Arab sheik. The cover story claimed that "Abdul" was a multi-millionaire who wanted to pull his money out of Moslem banks (which paid no interest in accordance with Islamic proscriptions against usury) and invest it in profitable American business ventures.

Among the first notable figures snared in the ABSCAM net was Angelo Errichetti, the colorful mayor of Camden, New Jersey, and one of the most influential politicians in that state. Errichetti accepted payoffs from Abdul's representative (Mel Weinberg) in exchange for helping the sheik obtain an Atlantic City casino license. "Abdul" was so grateful for the mayor's assistance that he even presented him with an impressive gift—a "priceless" tribal dagger that Weinberg had bought for $2.75 at a Greek flea market.[197] Erichetti was delighted.

In his Runyonesque style, Melvin Weinberg would later say: "I never met a straight politician the whole time I was in New Jersey. They must hafta screw 'em in the ground when they die."[198] As if to prove Weinberg's point, Mayor Errichetti introduced him to New Jersey's best-known political figure, Senior U.S. Senator Harrison Arlington Williams, Jr., who turned out to be incredibly greedy—even by ABSCAM standards. Williams and three partners (including a close associate of aged mob boss Meyer Lansky) proposed a lucrative investment opportunity for the sheik's money. The Williams group would borrow $100 million from Abdul and purchase the country's largest titanium mine in Virginia.

This deal, they claimed, would give them a virtual monopoly on titanium in the U.S.

Williams, as one of the highest-ranking Democrats in the Senate, could channel govern-ment and defense contracts to his partners.[199] Obviously, he knew his participation in the deal had to be as subterranean as the mine, since using his office to help secure titanium contracts would be a blatant federal crime. What he did not know was that his meetings with Weinberg were being tape-recorded. In another of Weinberg's inimitable phrases, Senator Williams "had been left standing bare-assed in Macy's window."[200]

In July 1979, Errichetti was told that "Abdul" and an ersatz emir named "Yassir" were concerned about political unrest in their homeland and would like to remain in the United States.

Within days, the mayor had arranged meetings between the Abdul organization and two Congressmen from Philadelphia, Michael ("Ozzie") Myers and Raymond Lederer, with additional meetings in the works. Errichetti told Weinberg that the Congressmen would pledge the use of their offices to help Abdul and Yassir obtain asylum. The price would be $100,000 per Congressmen (later "marked down" to $50,000). The FBI rented a three-room suite in a hotel at New York's Kennedy Airport and set up hidden cameras and microphones. It recalled the old tale of the spider and the fly.

On August 22, 1979, Mel Weinberg welcomed Erichetti and Myers into the web. Myers, a hard drinking former longshoreman with a ninth-grade education, who once had been arrested for punching a waitress in the mouth hours before his swearing-in ceremony, was steered to the couch in direct view of the camera.

The scene would become familiar to tens of millions of television viewers. When Myers was asked directly if he could guarantee that the Arabs would have no problems getting asylum in the United States, he boasted of his Congressional power.

Myers was given a briefcase containing the $50,000 payoff. He left the meeting alone through the hotel's rear exit—reportedly at a dead run.

Congressman Lederer's performance mirrored that of Myers. He promised to push a bill

(*Continued*)

on behalf of Abdul and Yassir. The man who had once headed Philadelphia's Criminal Probation Department calmly took a $50,000 bribe. One of the highlights of the Lederer tape was his memorable understatement: "I'm no Boy Scout."[201]

In addition to Erichetti, another key middleman in Operation ABSCAM was Philadelphia attorney and veteran influence peddler Howard Criden. Criden had assured Weinberg that bribable Congressmen were in plentiful supply. He bragged: "I can get you about anyone you want."[202]

True to his boast, Criden produced Representative Frank Thompson of New Jersey, chairman of the powerful promised House Administration Committee. Thompson accepted the usual $50,000 and to recruit more Congressmen, particularly his friend John Murphy of New York. ABSCAM was becoming a rogues' parade.

When Murphy arrived 11 days later for his session before the ABSCAM camera, he was asked if he could help with Abdul's immigration difficulties. He replied, "I don't think that there will be any problem."[203] Murphy was given the now-customary suitcase full of cash, most of which reportedly went to Thompson and Criden as "finders fees." It seemed that Murphy's greed transcended a five-figure payoff; he had a far more ambitious, nine-figure scheme in mind. He made a pitch for a $100 million loan so that he secretly could buy a Puerto Rican shipping line. Murphy chaired the House Merchant Marine and Fisheries Committee, a position from which he said he could guarantee passage of legislation to make his shipping enterprise highly profitable.[204]

The next Congressman to snap at the bait was John Jenrette, Jr., of South Carolina. Jenrette was a member of the important House Appropriations Committee—and a heavy alcoholic. He was deeply involved in a failing real estate venture that was under federal investigation, and he needed money. When he was asked by an undercover agent if he would accept the sheik's bribe, he declared: "I've got larceny in my blood. I'd take it in a goddamn minute."[205]

The final ABSCAM catch was Representative Richard Kelly, a former judge who recently had gained national attention when he urged Congress to let New York City go broke and "sink" into the ocean after a financial crisis. Kelly was delivered by three more intermediaries: attorney William Rosenberg, who reportedly was[206] wealthy Long Island accountant Stanley Weisz, who claimed he also could get Abdul forged gold certificates;[207] and convicted gangster and former Mafia bodyguard Gino Ciuzio, who bragged that he "owned" Kelly.[208]

Kelly provided the most visually compelling moment captured in the ABSCAM tapes when, in order to double-cross Rosenberg, Weisz, and Ciuzio, he refused the suitcase and feverishly stuffed 250 hundred-dollar bills into all his pockets.[209]

The unprecedented sting operation ended a short time later. In an interview conducted the following year, Mel Weinberg expressed his disappointment: "I think we coulda got at least a third of the whole Congress."[210]

When the ABSCAM tapes were shown publicly, seven members of Congress—"distinguished gentlemen," as they like to call each other—had disgraced themselves in full view of a disgusted nation. One by one, they would pay a heavy price for their cupidity.

Ozzie Myers offered a curious "I may be greedy but I'm not corrupt" brand of defense, in which he claimed that the money was not a bribe because he had no real intention of lifting a finger on behalf of the expatriate Arabs. "[I] saw it as a way to pick up some easy money for doing absolutely nothing."[211]

Myers also testified that he had spent all the money in just two weeks "to pay tuition at his children's private schools, buy appliances at Sears, and finance construction at his hunting club in upstate Pennsylvania."[212] He further claimed that he was drunk at the meeting. At one point during the trial, his lawyer rewound the tape and gave the jury an "instant replay" of Myers "dribbling bourbon

(*Continued*)

down his chin."[213] The former Congressman pre-sumably was quite sober when a federal jury convicted him of bribery. He was sentenced to three concurrent 3-year prison terms.

Raymond Lederer was the only one of the six indicted House members who was re-elected in 1980. In fact, his jury was being selected while he was being sworn in.[214] Lederer was convicted of bribery and, like Myers, received three 3-year sentences. He resigned his seat after the House Ethics Committee recommended his expulsion.[215] While appealing his conviction (which would not be overturned[216]), he reportedly worked at various times as a bartender, doorman, and carpet cutter.[217]

Harrrison Williams, the would-be titanium magnate, stood trial in 1981. He combatively dismissed his recorded statements to Mel Weinberg as what he called meaningless "baloney," meant only to impress Abdul's organization into giving his friends a $100 million loan.[218] He denied any financial stake in the mining venture. He asserted that the one interest he had to make it the safest mine in the country.[219] Williams' claims were ridiculed by the prosecutor,[220] who denounced him as "a corrupt public official."[221] Williams was found guilty—the first incumbent senator to be convicted of a crime since 1905.[222] In February 1982, he received a 3-year prison term.[223] A month later, facing certain expulsion, he resigned from the Senate.[224]

Frank Thompson, who had bragged to Abdul's bagmen (bribe collectors) that he was the most important Democrat in New Jersey,[225] was convicted of conspiracy.[226] The fleet of ships that John Murphy had dreamed of owning sunk into the sea of oblivion when he, too, was handed a 3-year prison term.[227]

Like so many politicians caught up in scandal, when John Jenrette stood trial he claimed that excessive drinking had clouded his judgment.[228] This defense proved no more successful for Jenrette than it had been for Ozzie Myers. A federal jury convicted him after only 4 1/2 hours of deliberation.[229] He later was handed a 2-year prison sentence.[230] In an odd postscript, a few months after the trial Jenrette's estranged wife announced that she had found $25,000 stashed in a brown suede shoe in her husband's closet.[231] Some of the hundred-dollar bills were traced to ABSCAM.[232]

Of all the dubious defenses employed by the ABSCAM defendants, none was greeted with more journalistic scorn and public hilarity than that of pocket-stuffing Richard Kelly—the last to stand trial. At a pre-trial news conference, Kelly self-righteously maintained that he had only *pretended* to take the $25,000 bribe as part of a one-man investigation of corruption that he was conducting. He blamed the FBI for "blowing his cover."[233] One sardonic reporter asked Kelly if he was planning to plead insanity.[234] Despite all the ridicule, Kelly still managed to earn the lightest of the Congressional sentences—6- to 18-months confinement at Elgin Air Force Base in his home state of Florida.

Despite its success, ABSCAM remains one of the most controversial law enforcement operations in recent American history. At least two problematic issues deserve consideration. First, the central role of Melvin Weinberg, a career criminal, represented a troubling strategy on the part of the FBI. According to Weinberg: "There's only one difference between me and the Congressmen I met on this case. The public pays them a salary for stealing."[235] But the public also paid Weinberg's salary, and, according to at least one witness, he was stealing too. In a sworn statement made in 1982, Weinberg's wife alleged that he had perjured himself and had siphoned some of the ABSCAM bribe money into his own pocket.[236] If proven, Marie Weinberg's charges might have compelled the courts to throw out all the ABSCAM convictions. In a dramatic and mysterious turn, however, she committed suicide two weeks later, hanging herself in a vacant condominium near her Florida home.[237]

The second and more fundamental issue is whether enticed bribery is an appropriate law enforcement technique for apprehending white-collar criminals[238] or whether it constitutes unlawful entrapment, that is, "the covert facilitation of crime by or on behalf of government agents,"[239] In the past, when entrapment usually was reserved

(*Continued*)

for prostitutes, homosexuals, or drug dealers, it generated little critical attention, except
among a handful of scholars and civil libertarians.[240] ABSCAM, however, changed the dynamics of entrapment; the targets were not denizens
of the social fringe, but high elected officials—
"distinguished gentlemen" of Congress. Suddenly,
the fairness of undercover tactics and the moral
acceptability of enticed bribery had become fod-
der for mass debate. Was it justifiable to solicit
crimes which otherwise might not have been committed? Is vulnerability to theatrically contrived
temptation equivalent to true corruption?[241]

Many persons argued—including, of course, the
defendants—that the mission of the FBI is to catch
criminals, not create them.

Yet, however much the ABSCAM defendants were tricked or beguiled, the conduct they
exhibited is wholly indefensible. These were men
to whom we had entrusted the integrity of our government, and they behaved like pigs at a trough. A
treatise on political ethics written two years before
ABSCAM asked rhetorically: When can a gift
become a bribe?[242] Maybe a warning was etched
in the ashes of seven incinerated careers that, for
Congress, the safest answer is "always."

Among the more recent cases of congressional bribery, the most flagrant (and unfragrant)
has to be that of Representative Randy Cunningham.

CASE STUDY
"Duke" Cunningham

Randy "Duke" Cunningham was an eight-term
Republican congressman from San Diego. A former
fighter pilot and decorated Vietnam War hero, he
was one of the most blustery and belligerent lawmakers, who once challenged a Democratic member to a
fist fight on the House floor.[243] He was also known
for occasional racial slurs and nasty homophobic
remarks.[244] And when it came to corruption, Duke
was in a class by himself. In exchange for lucrative
defense contracts, Cunningham received a mansion
in Rancho Santa Fe, California, one of America's
wealthiest communities,[245] a Rolls Royce,[246] a
$140,000 luxury yacht[247] (named the *Duke-Stir*),
museum quality antiques,[248] $40,000 Persian rugs,[249]
and heaps of cash. Between 2000 and 2005, the total
of Cunningham's bribes was set at a stunning $2.4
million.[250] In terms of dollar amount, that made
Duke Cunningham **the most corrupt member of
Congress ever uncovered in U.S. history.**

Authorities first became suspicious of
Cunningham in 2005 when he sold his Del Mar,
California, home to defense contractor Mitchell
Wade for $700,000 above the market price.[251]
Wade admitted to investigators that he had also
given Cunningham over $1 million in "gifts."
Wade's company had received over $150 million
in government contracts since 2002. Wade later
pleaded guilty to bribery.[252] Duke initially denied
all allegations of corruption, but on November 29,
2005, he threw in the crying towel and tearfully
acknowledged his culpability. He pleaded guilty to
charges of bribery, conspiracy, and tax evasion. He
resigned from office the same day.[253]

The most startling revelation to emerge from
the government's case was that Cunningham actually had a "bribery menu" hand written on one of
his congressional note cards, bearing the seal of the
United States Congress. The card shoed an escalating

(Continued)

price scale for bribes, depending on the size of the desired defense contract.[254]

There is an old maxim that warns: Be careful what you wish for; you may get it. On March 3, 2006, Duke Cunningham, the brazen arch-conservative legislator, who had once sponsored the "No Frills" Prison Bill and had long argued for tougher sentences, received the toughest sentence ever meted out to a former congressman indicted while still in office—8 years, 4 months,[255] surpassing the 8-year sentenced handed to James Trafficant in 2002. The federal prosecutor wrote: "The length, breadth and depth of Cunningham's crimes against the people of the United States are unprecedented for a sitting member of Congress. So, too, should be his sentence."[256]

The judge hammered Cunningham, questioning aloud how Duke could have betrayed his constituents for a bunch of frivolous luxuries. "You weren't wet. You weren't cold. You weren't hungry and yet you did these things."[257] A former Republican House colleague of Cunningham was even more brutal, declaring that Duke's naked greed rose to the level of treason.[258]

Before the sentence was handed down, Duke Cunningham told the judge:

"[A]fter years of service, I made a very wrong turn, Your Honor. . . . I did it to myself. I could have said no and I didn't. It was me."[259]

It sure was.

CASE STUDY
Bob Ney

Representative Robert "Bob" Ney, a six-term Republican congressman from Ohio, was known as the "Mayor of Capitol Hill" because the House Administration Committee he chaired oversaw operations in the Capitol complex. From that position, he grabbed 15 minutes of publicity (as well as ridicule) when he mandated a culinary rebuke of France's lack of support for the 2003 Iraq invasion by ordering the House food services menus to change "french fries" to "freedom fries."[260] In 2006, Ney received even more publicity, albeit unwanted, when he pleaded guilty to taking bribes in the Jack Abramoff influence-peddling scandal.[261]

Abramoff, a former "superlobbyist" and Republican fundraiser, was the central figure in a series of sensational political scandals. He pleaded guilty in 2006 to fraud, conspiracy, and tax evasion, agreeing to help prosecutors probe congressional corruption.[262] Abramoff had been a member of the Bush administration's 2001 Transition Advisory Team and he and his lobbying team used his con-

tacts there to log almost 200 contracts with the Bush administration in the first 10 months of 2001.[263] His lobbying was especially focused on Native-American tribes seeking to open gambling casinos—from the Choctaws of Mississippi to the Coushattas of Louisiana to the Kickapoos of Texas. When Abramoff realized the size of one Indian tribe's contributions to Democrats, he e-mailed an ally: "I'd love to get our mitts on that moolah."[264] Abramoff and his business partner Michael Scanlon—aide to then-Speaker of the House Tom Delay—conspired to bilk Indian casino gambling interests out of an estimated $85 million.

One of the bribery cases described by Abramoff in his plea agreement involved a person identified as "Representative #1. "It was later confirmed that "Representative #1 was Bob Ney."[265] Rep. Ney agreed to introduce and seek passage of legislation that would lift a federal ban on gaming for two Texas Indian tribes. He also agreed to assist legislation financially benefitting a California

(*Continued*)

tribe.[266] In addition, Ney introduced legislation that would have allowed the Tiguas Indians of Texas to re-open their casino. Abramoff instructed tribe officials to contribute $32,000 to Ney's campaign.[267] When the proposal never got off the ground, the impoverished tribe would later claim that Abramoff, Scanlon, and Ney, who had promised that the measure would win Senate support, had defrauded it.

Ney had also helped Abramoff and a partner purchase SanCruz Casinos, a Florida-based fleet of yachts offering gambling "cruises to nowhere." Ney entered comments in the Congressional Record reprimanding SanCruz for "not paying customers properly" and accused its owner, Gus Boulis, of "taking illegal bets."[268] In a second entry, Ney praised Abramoff's partner as a "respected member of his community."[269] Ney also suggested that the Attorney General of Florida was taking steps "to prevent Santa Cruz from conducting operations all together."[270] Ney's statements were intended to pressure Boulis to sell to Abramoff on favorable terms. In return, a PAC named SunCruz for Ney donated $10,000 to the Republican National Congressional Committee. After the sale, Abramoff used part of his new $500,000 SanCruz salary to purchase luxury skyboxes at three professional sports venues. Ney later held a fundraiser at one of those skyboxes.[271] As a violent postscript, Gus Boulis, whom Ney had called a "bad apple" in the Congressional Record was gunned down Mafia-style in 2001.[272]

In 2002, Ney, in his capacity of House Administration Committee Chair, approved a license for Foxcom Wireless, an Israeli telecommunications company, to install wireless antennas for the U.S. House. "His decision bypassed the usual bidding processes."[273] Ney refused to make public copies of any documents relating to the agreement, on the grounds that the Freedom of Information Act does not apply to Congress. Foxcom subsequently paid Abramoff $330,000 for lobbying.[274]

Ney had taught English in Iran in the 1970's and had a long-standing interest in that country. He was, in fact, the only member of Congress fluent in Farsi. In 2003, he traveled to London on a trip paid for by Nigel Winfield, a three-time ex-felon, whose convictions included tax evasion and attempting to defraud Elvis Presley.[275] Winfield owned Cyprus-based FN Aviation and wanted to sell U.S.-made airplane parts in Iran, for which he would need special permits. "The London trip included a meeting at a casino where, in an earlier trip, Ney had won $34,000 on an initial bet of $100."[276] Upon his return, Ney personally lobbied then-Secretary of State Colin Powell to relax U.S. sanctions on Iran.[277]

Bob Ney confessed to his crimes as part of his guilty plea in October, 2006, admitting that he had performed official acts for Abramoff's lobbying clients, receiving in exchange luxury vacation trips, campaign contributions, and other things of value.[278] In a statement distributed to reporters after the court session, Ney said: "I accept responsibility for my actions and I am prepared to face the consequences of what I have done."[279] He also said: "I will be resigning from Congress."[280] It must have been a painful moment for a congressman who had become a champion of election reform following the Bush-Gore debacle of 2000. Ney also announced that he had entered an alcohol rehabilitation program.

In January, 2007, Bob Ney was sentenced to 30 months in prison.[281] He offered the customary apology, to which the judge responded: "You have a long way to go to make amends for what's happened."[282]

In separate 2006 trials, Jack Abramoff was handed two federal prison sentences: 6 years for defrauding the Native-American tribes and 70 months for his fraudulent dealings with SunCruz Casinos. The latter sentence was reduced in 2008 to 45 months to be served concurrently with the remainder of his other sentence.[283] The reduction reflected Abramoff's cooperation with federal prosecutors. At his sentence reduction hearing, a weeping Jack Abramoff described himself as a "broken man."[284] On June 8, 2010, Abramoff was released from prison to a halfway house[285] and by the end of the month was working at a pizzeria.[286] His sentence was complete on December 3, 2010, when he both left the halfway house and his job at the pizzeria.[287] Abramoff claims to be completely reformed and released a book, *Capitol Punishment: The Hard Truth About Corruption From America's Most Notorious Lobbyist,*" in which he details his exploits and offers suggestions for reform.[288] At the time of this writing, Abramoff hosts a show on XM Satellite Radio where he discusses political reform.[289]

As of 2012, the most recent member of Congress to be convicted of corruption is Senator Ted Stevens of Alaska, that state's dominant political figure for more than four decades and the longest-serving Republican in U.S. Senate history. In October, 2008, the then-84-year-old Stevens was convicted by a Washington, D.C., jury of violating federal ethics laws for failing to report some $250,000 in gifts and services from friends that he used to renovate his home.[290]

Following the verdict, a visibly shaken Ted Stevens declared: "I am innocent."[291] A few weeks later, the voters of Alaska effectively responded: "No, you're not." Stevens, who had seldom faced serious opposition in previous election races, was defeated in his run for a seventh term—although the vote was surprisingly close.[292]

Ted Stevens was the first senator to be convicted of criminal charges since Republican David Durenberger of Minnesota pleaded guilty to five misdemeanor counts involving outside income and the misuse of public funds in 1995.[293]

The Judicial Branch

Judicial corruption may occur less frequently than legislative corruption, but it is hardly unknown. A number of state and local jurists have been convicted of official corruption. Consider the following examples:

- In 1985, New York State Judge William C. Brennan was found guilty of federal racketeering charges.[294] Brennan accepted nearly $50,000 in bribes to fix criminal cases involving gambling, narcotics, organized crime, and attempted murder.[295] He received a 5-year prison term and a $209,000 fine. In pronouncing sentence, the trial judge declared that "[n]o crime is more corrosive of our institutions than bribery of our judges."[296]

- A New York Civil Court Judge, Samuel Weinberg, pleaded guilty in 1987 to racketeering charges. Judge Weinberg owned several rent-controlled buildings in Brooklyn and Queens and had harassed elderly, low-paying residents with fraudulent eviction notices. He had also hired arsonists to torch his property.[297] Weinberg, whose callous treatment of his aged tenants brought new definition to the word "heartless," begged for mercy on the grounds that he was too old to go to prison.

- Roy Gelber, a judge in Dade County Florida, pleaded guilty in 1991 to racketeering charges related to the taking of bribes from drug-trafficking defendants.[298] Gelber implicated several of his judicial colleagues, two of whom later were convicted of accepting a total of $266,000 in payoffs.[299]

- In 1993, Judge Jose Luis Guevara of Zapata County, Texas, was convicted of six drug counts. A videotape played at his trial showed Guevara at a local airstrip rushing to welcome the pilot of a plane loaded with cocaine. Guevara was arrested as part of Operation Prickly Pear, a federal narcotics sting that decimated local government in Zapata County. In addition to the judge, the sheriff and county clerk were sent to prison.[300]

Between 1984 and 1989, 15 judges from Chicago's Cook County courts were convicted of assorted bribery, extortion, racketeering, and conspiracy charges. Two other implicated jurists committed suicide before facing certain indictments.[301] They all had been targets of Operation Greylord,[302] an aggressive FBI crackdown on flagrant corruption inside the country's largest municipal court system, where more than 6 million cases are filed each year.[303] For 3 1/2 years, FBI agents, carrying concealed recorders, worked undercover posing as defendants, defense attorneys, prosecutors, and crime victims. They created phony cases and participated in numerous bribery schemes.[304] A Chicago lawyer, when asked later how many judges he had bribed over a 10-year period, offered this memorable reply:

> I didn't count them. I just bribed them. It was kind of like brushing your teeth. I did it every day.[305]

One of the convicted judges, Thomas Maloney, had accepted payoffs to fix murder cases.[306] Perhaps equally troubling, it has been alleged that Maloney, who was handed a 16-year prison sentence, was unduly harsh in non-bribed cases to deflect attention from his leniency in the bribed cases.[307]

The centerpiece of the Greylord probe was Senior Cook County Judge Richard LeFevour, who, according to a federal prosecutor, had "peddled justice like it was apples."[308] LeFevour was found guilty on all 59 counts lodged against him[309]—including the acceptance of eight automobiles and $400,000 in cash payoffs in return for dismissing countless drunken driving cases over more than a decade.[310] He received a 12-year prison sentence.[311]

Many state and local judges must run for office and are thus as dependent as any other politicians on campaign contributions. Consequently, even the caretakers of American justice are not immune to conflicts of interest. For example, the Houston-based conglomerate Tenneco has admitted that it made illegal cash contributions to a state district judge in Louisiana who was running for an appellate court seat. That judge later rendered a decision involving a labor dispute injunction that was highly favorable to Tenneco.[312]

An Illinois Supreme Court Justice and his opponent raised about $9 million for their 2004 contest—one of the costliest judicial elections ever. The victorious incumbent later lamented: "Basically, that's obscene for a judicial race . . . How can people have faith in the system?"[313] As if to prove his point, that same justice later refused to recuse himself in a high-stakes case involving one of his main benefactors.[314] After a 2006 election, an Ohio Supreme Court Justice complained about the price of campaign money:

> "I never felt so much like a hooker down by the bus station. . . . Everyone interested in contributing has very specific interests. They mean to be buying a vote."[315]

A statewide race for the Texas Supreme Court costs hundreds of thousands of dollars, and "contributions of $10,000 and up from lawyers who practice before the court are not uncommon."[316] The danger of placing judges on the auction block was demonstrated in 1984 in the largest civil suit in American history. The Texas-based Pennzoil Company had agreed orally to buy a 40 percent interest in the Getty Oil Company for $110 a share. Subsequently, New York-based Texaco tendered a written offer to buy 100 percent of Getty stock at $128 a share, an agreement quickly accepted by Getty. Pennzoil sued, accusing Texaco of unlawful interference with a binding contract.[317]

One of the half-dozen lawyers representing Pennzoil was Houston attorney Joe Jamail, a star litigator known as the "king of torts." Jamail donated $10,000 to the campaign fund of the judge assigned to the case and solicited thousands of dollars in additional contributions from members of the Houston bar—even though that judge was facing no real opposition. As things turned out, it was probably one of the best $10,000 investments ever made.

> When Texaco attorneys suggested [the judge] disqualify himself from the case, he claimed that "mere bias or prejudice" was no ground for disqualification. On nearly every motion, he ruled against Texaco.[318]

The jury awarded Pennzoil $10.53 *billion*, forcing Texaco, then the fifth-largest corporation in the United States, into bankruptcy. Texaco appealed to the Texas Supreme Court—whose nine justices had already received $238,000 in contributions from Jamail and $117,000 more from other Pennzoil attorneys. "The justices refused even to allow Texaco to present oral arguments."[319] Pennzoil and Texaco eventually agreed to settle for $3 billion. "Jamail made at least $200 million out of the case."[320]

In a blistering editorial, the *New York Times* declared: "The behavior of the Texas courts has been reminiscent of what passes for justice in small countries run by colonels in mirrored sunglasses."[321] A San Antonio newspaper was even more colorful in its denunciation: "The Texas Supreme Court resembles a dead fish that has been in the refrigerator far too long. People as far away as New York can smell it."[322]

In contrast to Texas judges, federal jurists are appointed for life. Campaign contributions are, thus, not a consideration to members of the federal bench, but a few have nonetheless managed to disgrace themselves in other ways. Since the Constitution was written, only seven federal officials have been impeached and removed from office. All of them were judges.

In 1986, Federal District Judge Harry Claiborne of Nevada became the first such case in 50 years when the U.S. Senate convicted him of the requisite "high crimes and misdemeanors" and stripped him of his judicial position.[323] A federal jury earlier had found Claiborne guilty of tax evasion for his failure to report more than $100,000 in personal income.[324] He was handed a 2-year prison sentence.[325]

Although both the Senate and the courts convicted Claiborne, it should be noted that these were independent events. This separation of criminal and political sanctions was underscored in 1989, when District Judge Alcee Hastings of Florida became the only federal official ever to be impeached and removed from office despite a jury *acquittal*.[326] Hastings had been found not guilty in 1983 of conspiracy to commit bribery—even though his alleged co-conspirator, a disbarred Washington lawyer, was convicted of the same crimes in a separate trial.[327] "A panel of federal judges, following their own three-year investigation, concluded that Hastings was guilty of the crimes and recommended impeachment."[328] The Senate found that Hastings had solicited a $100,000 bribe from an undercover FBI agent posing as a defendant in a racketeering case before him.[329]

Also in 1989, the familiar words of "Impeach" and "Nixon" were paired in headlines for the first time since Watergate. The Nixon in question, however, was not the former president, but Federal District Judge Walter Nixon of Mississippi, who had been convicted of perjury in 1986. Nixon had lied to a federal grand jury investigating drug smuggling.[330] The case involved the son of a business associate who had given Nixon a "sweetheart deal" on oil and gas royalties. "The businessman was trying to win leniency for his son, who had been indicted on drug charges."[331] Nixon began serving a 5-year prison sentence in 1988 and was removed from office by the Senate the following year.[332]

In a similar case, Federal District Judge Robert Collins of Louisiana was convicted in 1991 of bribery, conspiracy, and obstruction of justice. Collins was paid $16,500 by a convicted drug dealer to obtain a lighter sentence in a case that was pending in Federal Court. Collins later sentenced that defendant to 3 1/2 years in prison—considerably less than the 8 years recommended by the government. Collins may have been a competent jurist, but he was a bungling crook. Two days after the trial, FBI agents found most of the bribe money in a cabinet in Collins' courthouse chambers; the balance was found in the judge's wallet.[333] Collins received a prison term of 6 years and 10 months[334]—nearly twice as long as the sentence he had "sold." Mercifully, he resigned from the bench, sparing a weary Senate from yet another judicial impeachment trial.

From the ceremonial robes they wear to the solemnity of the rituals they command, everything about judges reflects the exalted station to which the public has elevated them.

> When a judge enters a courtroom, men rise. Rarely is another civil officer addressed as "Your Honor," in the ordinary course of his functions. This is not in specific tribute to the man but to acknowledge what the man, as judge, symbolizes. Regardless of the level at which a judge serves—from magistrate's court to the Supreme Court—the office is customarily, legally, and almost instinctively regarded as sacrosanct.[335]

It is difficult, then, to overstate the social cost of judicial corruption. To citizens, judges are the trustees of due process, the guardians of equal protection. Therefore, no profession demands more unswerving honesty. Judges who descend into the iniquitous realm of white-collar crime do more than shame themselves; they skew the scales of justice. A judge who is suborned by one side in a legal confrontation renders the other side unequal under the law; the rule of law then becomes the rule of fraud.[336]

State and Local Government

In 1986, Attorney General Edwin Meese announced a Justice Department crackdown on state and local political corruption: "We've got a full court press on this stuff . . . We intend to go on knocking such corrupt heads—that's our business, that's our job."[337] Meese's crusade may seem a bit sanctimonious in retrospect, given that at least 225 Reagan appointees,[338] including Meese himself, have faced allegations of ethical or criminal wrongdoing[339]—an unprecedented number. Nevertheless, the Attorney General was quite correct in his assertion of widespread corruption at the nonfederal levels of our political system. "Political corruption in state and local governments is an old and abiding phenomenon."[340] In fact, the same year Meese articulated the government's "get-tough" policy, a survey of the 93 U.S. attorneys reported that over 100 state and local officials had been indicted for corruption, with many more under investigation by federal grand juries.[341]

Between 1970 and 1985, criminal indictments were brought against 7 governors or former governors,[342] more than 60 state legislators,[343] nearly 50 mayors,[344] as well as a considerable assortment of county officials. A striking aspect of most of these cases is how correspondent they are to the various forms of federal corruption described previously in this chapter.

- When prosecutors charged New York legislators with padding the state payroll with "no show" jobs doled out to friends, relatives, and campaign workers in 1987,[345] it was reminiscent of the Congressman Hays scandal.

- The corrupt USDA meat inspectors of the 1970s could have been the prototypes for the 11 building inspectors in Boston who were convicted in 1986 of accepting payoffs in exchange for overlooking code violations.[346]

- Melvyn Paisley's crimes within the Defense Department had their counterpart in those of Atlanta aviation commissioner Ira Jackson, who received a 3-year prison sentence in 1994 for using his influence to win favorable contracts for airport businesses in which he held secret interests.[347]

- The dark side of presidential and congressional campaign funding was mirrored when the New York City Investigations Department reported in 1993 that the City Comptroller, Elizabeth Holtzman, was "grossly negligent"[348] in receiving a $450,000 campaign loan from a bank she had selected to underwrite millions of dollars in city bonds.[349]

- Even Senator Williams' naked conflict of interest, uncovered in Operation ABSCAM, was echoed (albeit on a much less grand scale) when John Harwood, Speaker of the Rhode Island House of Representatives, was fined in 1994 for introducing numerous pieces of legislation designed to enrich himself and his clients.[350]

- And finally, the most treacherous Congressional bribery cases are more than matched in shock voltage by the 1974 conviction of Spiro T. Agnew, who had resigned as vice-president when it was revealed that he had taken large kickbacks from contractors in exchange for construction projects during his terms as Baltimore County executive and governor of Maryland.[351]

State Corruption

Agnew was not the first former governor to be sanctioned for corruption. He was not even the first one that year. Federal Judge Otto Kerner became federal prisoner Number 00037-123 in 1974,[352] following his conviction for bribery, fraud, conspiracy, and tax evasion. During Kerner's term as governor of Illinois a few years earlier, he had accepted stock in a local racetrack in exchange for the assignment of lucrative racing dates. The tax charges stemmed from Kerner's declaration of his illicit racetrack profits as capital gains. According to the IRS, *bribes must be treated as regular income.*[353]

Spiro Agnew's successor as governor of Maryland, Marvin Mandell, apparently was undeterred by Number 00037-123's fall from grace. Mandell was convicted of fraud and racketeering charges in 1977. Like Otto Kerner, he took bribes from racetrack owners in exchange for special favors.[354] He was handed a 4-year prison sentence[355]—one year more than Kerner had received. Afterward, an unremorseful Mandel stood on the steps of the federal courthouse and told the public that he did not regret his actions.

> He said it calmly, almost proudly . . . He admitted to a feeling of "satisfaction" with his 25-year career in politics. He said he started with nothing and was back to nothing. Then he shrugged.[356]

In 1978, a Tennessee Chancery Court, citing evidence collected by the FBI, accused Governor Ray Blanton of participation in a scheme to sell paroles and sentence commutations to state prisoners.[357] In one instance, investigators alleged that relatives of a convict who was serving a 60-year term for armed robbery and murder paid $85,000 in bribes to aides of the governor so that the man could be released on parole.[358]

A week before his term expired, Governor Blanton held what might be described as a "Going Out of Business Sale" when he granted executive clemency to 52 inmates—nearly half of whom were convicted murderers. Blanton claimed that his actions were meant solely to help relieve prison overcrowding in the state. Among those whose sentences were commuted was

Roger Humphreys, the son of one of Blanton's political allies, who was serving a lengthy term for the murders of his ex-wife and her lover. Humphreys had shot the couple eighteen times, stopping to reload frequently. The treatment Humphreys had received while locked up had already generated cries of cronyism. Within only 2 months of entering prison, Humphreys had been made a trustee and had been assigned employment as a photographer for the state tourist department. He had been given the use of a state car and had been sent on photographic assignments throughout Tennessee.[359]

Blanton's successor was sworn in 3 days early, after federal prosecutors warned that the lame duck governor might free all potential witnesses in the parole-selling investigation.[360] Even after he was summarily ousted from office, Blanton continued trying to pardon 30 additional convicts, insisting unsuccessfully that he was still the rightful governor.[361]

"As an outgrowth of the pardons and paroles investigation, Governor Ray Blanton was indicted and convicted of conspiring to take kickbacks for liquor-store licenses."[362] Because it was a federal case, Blanton would miss the opportunity to serve in one of the state prisons he had made less crowded. His conviction later was reversed "reluctantly" by a U.S. Appeals Court—not on the merits of the evidence, but on the technical grounds that the trial judge had not questioned jurors sufficiently about their biases.[363]

Then came Governor Jim Guy Tucker of Arkansas, who in 1996 was convicted of fraud and conspiracy by a federal jury.[364] Tucker was involved in a deal with co-defendants James and Susan McDougal, operators of the failed Madison Guaranty Savings and Loan, to arrange a $3 million loan backed by fraudulently overvalued real estate appraisals. In addition, Tucker had received a $150,000 loan from Madison Guaranty used as a down payment for a $1.2 million water and sewer utility. This transaction was also overvalued, producing a bogus profit for Madison's books at a time when it was under heavy scrutiny by examiners.[365] Following the verdict, Tucker announced his resignation from office to work on his appeals. Arkansas Lieutenant Governor Mike Huckabee replaced Tucker, calling the conviction "a sad day for the state."[366]

What separated this case from the dozens of sleazy S&L scams that have proliferated since the 1980s (Chapter 8) is that the McDougals were former business partners of President Clinton and First Lady Hilary Rodham Clinton in an unsuccessful land development venture known as Whitewater. Clinton was Tucker's predecessor as governor of Arkansas. Although he was not formally implicated in any of the criminal charges, the President had a visible role in the trial, when he was subpoenaed by the defense to testify via videotape.[367]

Arizona long has had the reputation as one of the most hard nosed states when it comes to law enforcement and punishment. In the early 1990s, Governor Fife Symington was the embodiment of tough talking law and order rhetoric. He once declared: "Crime is not traced through the lack of material things. It happens through loss of values."[368] In 1997 Symington proved how right he was when he was convicted in federal court of seven counts of fraud.

The Symington administration was "tainted almost from the start."[369] Soon after taking office he was sued by the Resolution Trust Corporation for his role in directing a failed Phoenix savings & loan institution. Despite his troubles he won re-election in 1994; but the scandals just kept coming. A year into his second term a court ruled that Symington was personally liable for a $10 million loan from six pension funds to his defunct real estate company. He declared personal bankruptcy.[370]

When he was indicted on 23 felony counts, Symington insisted he had never tried to defraud creditors. He blamed it all on "sloppy accountants."[371]

But 40 prosecution witnesses and 1,400 documents were enough for the jury to find him guilty. Assistant U.S. Attorney David Schindler called Symington a classic con man, who falsely inflated his net worth when he wanted to borrow and pleaded poverty when he wanted to refinance a loan on more favorable terms. Between 1989 and 1991, for instance, his declared net worth swung between $12 million and minus $23 million.[372]

The disgraced governor was sentenced to 2 1/2 years in prison and resigned from office. Although that conviction was later overturned on appeal, prosecutors continued to pursue the case and were preparing to retry him. In 2001 it was reported that Symington was within days of striking a bargain with prosecutors under which he would agree to plead guilty to one felony count in exchange for avoiding any prison time. During the negotiations, however, Symington received a presidential pardon from Bill Clinton in the waning days of his administration and walked away.[373]

When Fife Symington resigned from office in 1997, he became the second Arizona governor in a decade to step down as a result of a corruption scandal. Governor Evan Meacham was impeached and removed from office in 1998 on charges of obstructing justice and misusing state money—although he was acquitted of those charges in a criminal trial.[374]

Next in the docket was former Rhode Island governor Edward DiPrete, who pleaded guilty in 1998 to charges of bribery, extortion, and racketeering, admitting that he had accepted $250,000 in exchange for state contracts while in office. As part of his plea bargain agreement, DiPrete was sentenced to one year in a prison work release program in exchange for having the remaining charges dropped. DiPrete had accepted numerous kickbacks from architects, engineers, and others in search of state business in exchange for construction contracts during his years as governor between 1985 and 1991.[375]

CASE STUDY
Edwin Edwards

Edwin Edwards, the boisterous, flamboyant former four-term Democratic governor of Louisiana, was no stranger to the criminal justice system. His on-again off-again gubernatorial career spanned three decades, during which he had been the subject of 22 grand jury investigations.[376] These earlier probes included such issues as cattle sales to state prisons and an attempt to relocate the Minnesota Timberwolves of the National Basketball Association to New Orleans.[377] Edwards had been tried twice before, in 1985 and 1986, on racketeering charges related to questionable hospital and nursing home deals, from which he had made $2 million. The first jury deadlocked and the second acquitted him.[378] An admitted high-stakes gambler who once won $220,000 on one of his frequent trips to Atlantic City, he had earned a colorful reputa-

tion for legal invincibility. He always seemed able to wisecrack his way out of one scrape after another.

But Edwards' fabled luck ran out in 2000, when a federal jury in Baton Rouge convicted him on 17 counts of extortion and racketeering. Both while in office and later, he had extorted hundreds of thousands of dollars from wealthy businessmen seeking licenses to operate riverboat casinos.

The case came to light in 1997 when FBI agents raided Edwards' home and office, seizing records and more than $400,000 in cash. Unlike Edwards' previous trials, however, much of the evidence was electronic. This time jurors would see and hear Edwards in action. Prosecutors built their case on 24,000 hours of secretly recorded telephone conversations and videotapes made by a camera that agents had hidden inside the

(Continued)

office Edwin Edwards shared with his son and co-defendant, Stephen Edwards.[379]

The government's star witness was businessman Edward DeBartolo, Jr., owner of the San Francisco 49ers—one of the crown jewels of the National Football League. In 1998 he pleaded guilty to concealing Edwards' extortion plot. In exchange for two years probation, DeBartolo agreed to testify against Edwards. DeBartolo had won a license in 1997 for a floating casino along Shreveport's Red River. Edwards, out of office at this time but still politically influential, had demanded and received $400,000.[380] DeBartolo handed Edwards his payoff in a briefcase stuffed with cash at the San Francisco airport.[381] According to DeBartolo, Edwards had also wanted a $50,000 a month consulting fee, a per-head commission on every customer entering the casino, and 1 percent of the gross revenues.[382] Flanked by his 50-year-old daughter and 33-year-old wife, Edwards denounced his longtime friend DeBartolo to reporters as "the Linda Tripp of Louisiana."[383] Edwards added: "I hope the 49ers lose this Sunday."[384]

Prosecutors also paraded in contractors and designers who testified Edwards paid in cash when he was building a home. In all, Edwards paid $733,567 in cash for his $1.4 million house. A delivery man said Candy Edwards [the defendant's wife] paid him $4,500 in $100 bills. When he stepped inside to collect the money, he said he saw $100 bills lying on the floor.[385]

In his closing argument, a federal prosecutor pointed to Edwards and told jurors: "Look him straight in the eye and tell him he's guilty."[386] Three weeks later, those jurors did exactly that.

On January 8, 2001, 73-year-old Edwin Edwards, who had been the most dominant Louisiana politician since the legendary Huey Long, was handed a stiff 10-year prison sentence. His son was also convicted and sentenced to 7 years. Colorful and unrepentant to the end, Edwards has compared his fate to a Chinese proverb: "If you sit by a river long enough, the dead bodies of your enemies will float by you. I suppose the feds sat by the river long enough, and here comes my dead body."[387]

The next former governor to fall from grace was John G. Rowland of Connecticut. Rowland was once considered a rising young star of the Republican Party. That perception changed forever on June 21, 2004, when he announced his resignation in order to pre-empt certain impeachment. Rowland's career and reputation began to unravel the previous December when he admitted accepting renovations for his home—a hot tub and a new heating system—paid for by state contractors and state employees. Other clumsy bribes soon came to light. Prosecutors charged that Rowland also had accepted $107,000 in airplane flights and vacations.[388] The FBI even accused Rowland of skimming money from a low-stakes poker game he hosted.[389]

Six months after his resignation, under a plea agreement with federal prosecutors, the ex-governor pleaded guilty to one count of conspiracy to steal honest service. At his sentencing hearing in March 2005, John G. Rowland was contrite. He said he was "ashamed" and accepted full responsibility for his betrayal of the public trust.[390] He was sentenced to 1 year and 1 day in prison plus three years probation. It was a lighter punishment than the government had sought. The lead prosecutor had argued before the sentence was handed down:

"Honest government matters. It has to matter. Send that message, send it loud and clear. Without the rule of law, we are all lost."[391]

Former Alabama governor Don Siegelman was convicted in 2006 of a bribery scheme in which he traded official favors for campaign contributions. Richard Scrushy, former CEO of HealthSouth, arranged $500,000 in donations to Siegelman's campaign for a state lottery in exchange for giving Scrushy a seat on a state hospital regulatory board.[392] In 2007, both Siegelman and Scrushy were given prison sentences of nearly 7 years.[393]

A tearful Siegelman pleaded for leniency, but the prosecutor, citing Siegelman's history of pushing for tough anti-crime legislation while he was the attorney general and later governor of Alabama, declared: "To say that when someone takes a harsh stance and then turns around and commits a crime they should be given lenient punishment, that's the height of hypocrisy."[394]

Unlike most of the corruption cases described in this chapter, the Siegelman conviction has generated a great deal of controversy.

> The frame-up of Siegelman and businessman Richard Scrushy is so crystal clear and blatant that 52 former state attorney generals from across America, both Republicans and Democrats, have urged the US Congress to investigate the Bush administration's use of the US Department of Justice to rid themselves of a Democratic governor who "they could not beat fair and square," according to Grant Woods, former Republican Attorney General of Arizona and co-chair of the McCain for President leadership committee. Woods says that he has never seen a case with so "many red flags pointing to injustice."[395]

In 2008, the CBS television program *60 Minutes* aired a damning indictment of the railroading of Siegelman. "Extremely coincidental 'technical difficulties' caused WHNT, the CBS station covering the populous northern third of Alabama, to go black during the broadcast."[396]

The argument goes that Siegelman had been framed for being a popular Democratic governor in a Republican state. The finger was pointed at President Bush's Machiavellian political advisor Karl Rove. One could also offer an alternate theory under which Scrushy was the true target, and Siegelman was merely collateral damage. As detailed in Chapter 7, the huge HealthSouth scandal had deeply embarrassed the government. After a host of HealthSouth executives—including all five chief financial officers in the company's history—had agreed to plead guilty and testify against Scrushy in exchange for relatively light sentences, Scrushy was *acquitted* in a 2005 trial leaving lots of egg on the face of the Justice Department. Perhaps the bribery case was payback.

However, sometimes the best course is to rely on Occam's Razor, a venerable principle which states that when multiple competing hypotheses are equal in other respects, choose the one requiring the fewest assumptions. Maybe Siegelman and Scrushy were simply guilty as charged.

Corruption by state officials is of course by no means confined to governors' mansions. In 2003, former Texas Attorney General Dan Morales pleaded guilty to mail fraud and tax evasion charges. Morales, who had served two terms between 1991 and 1998 and had once been the rising star of Texas's ailing Democratic Party, agreed to serve 4 years in prison.[397] The charges against Morales painted an outrageous picture of official misconduct and ethical bankruptcy. Morales had tried to funnel millions of dollar in legal fees from the $17.3 billion settlement in the state's tobacco lawsuit.[398] He also diverted more than 80 percent of his campaign funds during his unsuccessful run for governor in 2000 and used the money to pay his criminal defense attorneys.[399] A month before his trial, Morales's bail had been revoked when he was accused of lying on loan applications to buy two luxury cars—after he had earlier told the judge that he was indigent and in need of a court-appointed lawyer.[400] The former politics editor of the *Houston*

Chronicle characterized Dan Morales's misdeeds as "astonishing" and concluded: "I guess he has four years to think about these things."[401]

More recently, former New Jersey state senator Wayne R. Bryant was convicted in 2008 of using his position as one of the state's most influential lawmakers to help a local medical school acquire $10.5 million in state grants. Bryant had solicited a $38,000 a year "low-work" job at New Jersey's University of Medicine and Dentistry in exchange for his services in order to pad his state pension.[402] And what a pension it was. Bryant had been dubbed in the press the "king of double dipping" because he collected salaries from four public jobs. In addition to his legislative salary of $49,000 and his $38,000 no show position with the medical school, Bryant was also an adjunct professor at the Camden campus of Rutgers University for $35,000 per year and collected $75,000 in 2005 as the municipal attorney of Lawnside, New Jersey—where his brother was the mayor.[403]

The U.S. Attorney who prosecuted Bryant said that the case had been the most significant of the 132 public corruption cases he had won:

> "The brazen arrogance of Wayne Bryant—to believe that he was completely beyond the reach of the law, to extort state institutions for personal profit in return for the funding of good and worthwhile programs that serve the poor, the disadvantaged and the need of our state—is simply the most disgusting conduct I've seen by a public official in my seven years as U.S. Attorney."[404]

In July 2009, Wayne Bryant (along with the dean of the medical school) received a sentence of 4 years in prison.[405] If Bryant ends up working there, it would become his fifth public job.

CASE STUDY
George Ryan

George Ryan served as Republican governor of Illinois from 1999 to 2003. The 72-year-old Ryan was convicted of racketeering and fraud in April 2006 after a lengthy trial.[406] Most of the charges involved a "licenses for bribes" conspiracy that had infected a number of state agencies during Ryan's tenure as Illinois secretary of state, an office he held prior to his election as governor.

The scandal broke in 1994 with a fiery van crash that killed six children. The fatal wreck exposed a scheme inside Ryan's office, in which unqualified truck drivers obtained licenses in exchange for cash payoffs.

The accident was caused when the metal undercarriage fell from a truck driven by Ricardo Guzman, who had obtained his license by paying off state officials, according to testimony. Guzman, who did not speak English, did not understand warnings from fellow truckers about the undercarriage as he was starting up the vehicle. After it fell from the truck, the undercarriage hit a van . . . setting it on fire.[407]

A state investigator testified that a top Ryan aide and a key Ryan fundraiser had blocked him from investigating the crash.[408]

An Operation Safe Roads probe led to other types of graft linked to Ryan. Indeed, by the time Ryan went to trial, 74 former state officials, lobbyists, truck drivers, and others had already been convicted.[409] Now it was George Ryan's turn. His jury concluded that Ryan had steered state business

(Continued)

to his associates in exchange for cash and gifts for himself and his family, including Caribbean vacations.[410] "Jurors said they had found no single 'smoking gun,' just layer upon layer of evidence, all of which, one juror said, added up to a painful education about what had happened at the highest levels of Illinois government."[411]

During his term as governor, George Ryan had drawn international praise when he commuted the sentences of every prisoner on Illinois's death row. His condemnation of capi-

tal punishment had garnered him a Nobel Peace Prize nomination.[412] If that had been the zenith of his political career, his conviction three years later was surely the nadir. The federal prosecutor called Ryan's quashing of the driver's licenses bribery tragedy "a low-water mark for public service."[413]

In September 2006, George Ryan was sentenced to 6 1/2 years in prison. When he addressed the court, he apologized in plain words: "People of this state expected better, and I let them down."[414]

County Corruption

Numerous county officials also have been indicted for corruption. In the 1980s, more than 150 county commissioners in Oklahoma were convicted of defrauding taxpayers in an intricate kickback scheme. One Oklahoma County purchased enough lumber to rebuild every one of its bridges four times, yet not a single bridge was repaired.[415] New Jersey's Bergen County Utilities Authority awarded bond underwriting contracts on a no-bid basis to the investment banking firms that had made large campaign contributions to county politicians. The county ended up $600 million in debt.[416]

An FBI sting, code-named Operation Pretense, led to the convictions of a number of county supervisors in Mississippi. Those counties not only had overpaid far for heavy equipment, but, in some cases, investigators could not even find the equipment.[417] This variety of white-collar crime is virtually as old as recorded history. Officials who oversaw the building of the ancient pyramids reportedly engaged in "creative accounting" and "cooked" the Pharaohs' ledgers regarding the costs and amounts of equipment and materials they used.[418]

A pair of cases resulting in criminal convictions can exemplify corruption at the county level. The first case is that of Ronald Benoit, the Justice of the Peace in Jefferson County, Texas. One of Benoit's responsibilities was to collect fines for traffic tickets from motorists. The fact that voters kept Benoit in office for 11 years suggests that he performed this task efficiently. The problem was that he often collected the fines, dismissed the charges, then kept the money for himself. After pleading guilty to theft, he was given 2 years probation, ordered to make restitution for the thousands of dollars he stole, and required to sign an agreement never to seek elected office again.[419]

The second case is that of Andrew Hinshaw, the former tax assessor of Orange County, California. Hinshaw accepted "gifts" of expensive stereo equipment from the Tandy Corporation, parent company of the Radio Shack chain, after he had denied Tandy a favorable tax exemption. When he later changed his mind and granted the exemption, it earned him a criminal indictment. Hinshaw was convicted of bribery and sentenced to 1 to 14 years in prison.[420] A party leader demonstrated no special acumen when he assessed the damage to Hinshaw's career: "I think the conviction puts a serious crimp in his political future."[421]

Municipal Corruption

The mindset of Middle America long has harbored a "deep strain of anti-urbanism."[422] So, while graft (or, as it was once called, "boodle"[423]) can refer to bribery and payoffs at any level of government, the term usually is associated with big-city corruption. Historically—from Boss Tweed and his Tammany Hall dynasty in New York,[424] to Mayor "Big Bill" Thompson and his gangster-friendly administration in Chicago,[425] to Tom Prendergast and his powerful Kansas City machine[426]—graft has always been the "common cold" of American politics.[427]

To cite just one flagrant example, a number of local officials have been accused in recent years of soliciting bribes from investment bankers in return for helping the bankers grab a piece of the lucrative ($1 billion a year) municipal bond underwriting market—a practice that has been dubbed "pay to play."[428] In 2007, two executives from the Dallas office of Bear Stearns, the scandal-ridden investment banking and securities company discussed in Chapter 8, pleaded guilty to bribing elected officials in El Paso, Texas, in order to secure government contracts to underwrite more than *$1.5 billion* in local bond deals since 1999.[429]

Local corruption is an especially incendiary betrayal because the city represents the layer of government closest to the people.

> Local government is the testing ground for self-government. Rascals might be expected in the Sacramento capitol or in the U.S. Congress, but dishonesty in local government comes terribly close to violating the institutions that most directly concern the people.[430]

Although the urban "machine" (at least in its formerly omnipotent incarnation) may now be virtually extinct in the United States, "boodle" is definitely alive and kicking. It is estimated that, between 1970 and 1990, criminal convictions of local officials increased by *900 percent*.[431] Graft cases have been prosecuted in most major American cities (e.g., Chicago,[432] Philadelphia,[433] Atlanta,[434] Cleveland,[435] San Diego,[436] and Miami[437]), as well as a great many smaller municipalities. The mayors of Syracuse, New York,[438] and Pawtucket, Rhode Island,[439] for example, each extorted about $1 million from city contractors. In 1995, Congressman Walter Tucker III, an ordained minister, was convicted of extorting $30,000 in bribes while he was mayor of Compton, California, earlier in the decade.[440]

But if one wishes to find truly voracious corruption in its natural habitat, little Compton is not the place to look. One must travel about 3,000 miles east and cross the Hudson River.

New York has a tradition of corruption, almost mythic in magnitude. In a city as big and as rich as New York, containing such an immense municipal bureaucracy, "bribery and kickbacks have been going on since the Tweed era."[441] Tweed and his urban pirates may be long gone, but a series of sensational cases in the late 1980s illustrates the extent to which corrupt officials can still pillage a city. More than 100 individuals—including Democratic Party leaders as well as elected and appointed officials—were ensnared by state and federal investigations.[442] Graft was uncovered in at least 9 city agencies, including the Housing Authority, the Taxi and Limousine Commission, and the city's Health and Hospitals Corporation.[443] The administration of Mayor Edward Koch fell into shambles.[444] Koch ceased shouting out his signature slogan—"How'm I doin'?" The answer had become painfully obvious.

The worst scandal occurred in the Parking Violations Bureau (PVB) of the New York Transportation Department.[445] In January 1986, the mayor's close friend Donald Manes, the borough president of Queens and a major force in city government, was found by police in a car near LaGuardia Airport, bleeding from both wrists. Manes claimed two men had kidnapped him.

Within days, Manes' protégé, Geoffrey Lindenauer, deputy director of the PVB, was arrested for extorting $5,000 from a company hired to collect delinquent parking fines.[446] Lindenauer eventually would be charged with taking $410,000 in payoffs from collection agencies contracted by the PVB.[447] In the previous two years, the city had paid private firms $31 million to collect just $85 million in overdue parking fines,[448] so the stakes were more than ample to sustain a system of institutionalized plunder.

From his hospital bed, Donald Manes soon admitted that his purported abduction had been a botched suicide attempt, spurred by overwhelming depression. The source of that depression became much clearer when Geoffrey Lindenauer entered into an agreement with prosecutors, under which most of the charges against him would be swapped for his testimony against several of his superiors—including Manes. Two days after Lindenauer's plea bargain was struck, Donald Manes, facing certain indictment and likely imprisonment, successfully committed suicide by stabbing himself in the heart.[449]

Lindenauer's testimony was instrumental in the government's case against one of the most powerful politicians in the city—Stanley Friedman, Democratic leader of the Bronx.[450] Friedman was a part owner of a company the city was paying $22 million to supply hand-held computers to the PVB. Lindenauer had manipulated the bidding process on Friedman's behalf, so that the company, Citisource, Inc., would encounter no significant competition for the lucrative contract. On top of that, Citisource had fraudulently misrepresented itself. For starters, Friedman's company claimed to have 30 employees—in reality, it had only one.

> And while the company said it had a prototype computer, it actually had nothing. Koch canceled the contract. Friedman went to City Hall and protested with amazing sangfroid. "We are virtually on target with a fine product," he explained.[451]

Stanley Friedman was convicted of federal racketeering and conspiracy charges in November, 1986. The following March, he was given a 12-year prison sentence.[452] His trial painted such a vulgar picture of New York politics that when Lindenauer responded to a question during his lengthy testimony by replying, "I can't give you an honest answer on that one," the courtroom erupted in laughter.[453]

Joseph Ganim, the former mayor of Bridgeport, Connecticut—that state's largest city— was convicted of bribery, racketeering, and other charges in 2003 in one of the biggest corruption cases in Connecticut history.[454] Ganim had awarded city contracts to favored friends and also had extorted suppliers to kick back some of their proceeds to him in cash and favors.[455] He was sentenced to 9 years in prison for systematically using his office to enrich himself. The judge called Joseph Ganim's crimes "the stuff that cynicism is made of."[456]

In 2008, several U.S. mayors were convicted of corruption. Among those cases were the following:

- Jim Hayes, the former mayor of Fairbanks, Alaska, was found guilty of working with his wife to steal money from social-service grants between 2001 and 2005. Hayes altered checks to divert hundreds of thousands of dollars from nearly $3 million in grants issued to his wife's LOVE tutoring and mentoring center. He used some of the laundered money to help build a new church for his congregation, but also spent some on personal items, such as a big-screen plasma television for the couple's home.[457] Hayes was sentenced to 5 1/2 years in prison; his wife was given 3 years.[458]

- Sharpe James, the former five-term mayor of Newark, New Jersey, was convicted of corruption connected to a cut-rate land flip scheme.[459] James had conspired to arrange the heavily discounted sale of nine city properties to his mistress, who in turn quickly resold them for more than $600,000 in profit.[460] U.S. Attorney Christopher J. Christie, who prosecuted the case, said after the verdict: "For 36 years, Sharpe James reigned over this city. Today he is taught a lesson: that for those who disgrace their public office, for those who betray the public trust, there is only one place for you, and that is federal prison."[461] And federal prison was exactly where 72-year-old Sharpe James was put, after he was handed a 27-month sentence.[462] That sentence was far less than the 20 years the government had asked for. The lenient judge noted that James had not taken any bribes. The disappointed prosecutor disagreed with that reasoning: "I don't think it makes a difference if you get bribed with money or get bribed with sex."[463] But lenient or not, the sentence did leave some observers hopeful that it might end Newark's awful reputation as a "trough for opportunistic public officials."[464] Regrettably, that corrupt reputation has been well-earned. James's predecessor as mayor had pleaded guilty to tax fraud in 2002, and *his* predecessor had served 5 years in federal prison for taking $1.4 million in kickbacks from city contractors.[465] Sharpe James was also convicted on charges that he used city-issued credit cards to pay for $58,000 of personal expenses while he was mayor—including trips with several women (other than his wife) to Martha's Vineyard, Puerto Rico, the Dominican Republic, and Rio de Janeiro.[466]

• Mims Hackett, Jr., former mayor of Orange, New Jersey (three miles from Newark), was convicted *twice* in 2008. First, he pleaded guilty to federal charges of attempted extortion, after admitting to taking a $5,000 bribe from an undercover FBI agent, who was part of a statewide sting probing municipal insurance contracts.[467] A few hours later, the 66-year-old politician pleaded guilty in a state court to a separate charge of official misconduct, after admitting to improperly billing his city more than $5,700 for meals and other expenses that he had simply made up.[468] Hackett received a 9-month prison sentence on the federal charge[469] and in 2009, he was sentenced to 5 years in prison on the state charges.[470]

One common thread running through these cases is that the convicted mayors were not "rookies." They had all been elected and then re-elected by their constituents. Apparently, they grew so comfortable in their positions that they came to believe they could break the law with impunity.[471]

POLICE CORRUPTION

As we have seen throughout this chapter, some public officials, both elected and appointed, have bartered their influence and have used their positions to solicit or extort bribes. Police corruption shares important structural similarities with political corruption. However, there is also a fundamental difference, related to the status of the corrupters, which makes police misconduct deserving of separate consideration. Many elected officials and appointed regulators have the power to sell favors, such as lucrative government contracts, to other white-collar criminals. Law enforcers, too, have something valuable to sell—immunity from the law—but their buyers more typically are "common" (i.e., blue-collar) criminals.[472]

Like political corruption, police corruption is an illegal use of official authority for personal gain. "Personal gain" distinguishes police corruption from certain other forms of police misconduct, such as brutality or violations of constitutional rights, committed by law enforcers in pursuit of organizational goals. "Official authority" distinguishes police corruption from simple police criminality and thus excludes street crimes like rape or burglary, even though such offenses may be (and have been) committed by police officers.[473]

Periodic corruption scandals have plagued virtually every major urban police department in the United States—New York City,[474] Chicago,[475] Houston,[476] Philadelphia,[477] Detroit,[478]

Cleveland,[479] Washington, D.C.,[480] Dallas,[481] Miami,[482] Atlanta,[483] and New Orleans,[484] to cite just a recent sampling. A 1999 investigation of the Rampart Division of the Los Angeles Police Department uncovered a list of crimes allegedly committed by officers ranging from perjury, to drug dealing, to robbery, to shooting unarmed suspects and then framing them for assault.[485]

Moreover, police corruption exists in smaller cities and towns as well. The chief of police in Rochester, New York, for example, was convicted on drug trafficking charges in 1991.[486] The chief of the Newark, New Jersey, police department pleaded guilty in 1996 of stealing $30,000 from a police fund.[487] Four West New York, New Jersey, police officers, including the chief, pleaded guilty in 1998 to taking part in a $600,000 bribery and kickback scheme. They had coerced local merchants to install video gambling machines.[488] Fifteen officers in Inglewood, California, were sanctioned in 1994 for running a local bookmaking operation—from department telephones.[489]

The sheriff of Bristol, Virginia, a mountain town on the Tennessee border, killed himself the day after a grand jury began investigating charges against him of embezzling $377,000. The sheriff allegedly had stolen money paid to the town for housing surplus prisoners from Washington, D.C., in the Bristol jail. He had used these funds to buy a new house, several vehicles, and certificates of deposit for his children. More than $60,000 in cash was found in a desk drawer in his office.[490]

Furthermore, police corruption is not limited to municipal departments. County and state forces also have experienced their share of misappropriation. For three years, the chief of the Niagara County jail in upstate New York charged all his personal groceries to taxpayers through jail accounts. The former county sheriff was also sentenced for stocking his refrigerator with thousands of dollars worth of jailhouse food.[491] In 1998, the sheriff of Star County Texas resigned after pleading guilty to conspiracy charges. He had been referring prisoners to a local bail bondsman in exchange for kickbacks. The payments often were delivered directly to his office.[492] The biggest county law enforcement scandal involved 26 deputy sheriffs from Los Angeles County, who were convicted of skimming millions of dollars from drug money seized in their investigations.[493] Dozens of other deputies were forced to retire. In all, more than a third of the entire elite L.A. County narcotics unit was implicated.[494]

Barker and Roebuck have devised a useful typology of police corruption.[495] They identify a number of categories, of which we will examine six:

Corruption of Authority

Corruption of authority encompasses a wide variety of unauthorized material inducements, anything from discounted underwear to free commercial sex. According to one survey, 31 percent of all wholesale or retail businesspersons in three major cities acknowledged that they give free or discounted merchandise, food, or services to police officers.[496] While this practice may seem trivial compared to those uncovered in ABSCAM or Greylord, there are hidden costs. First of all, the image of law enforcement is demeaned by such behavior. As a former police officer once observed: "[T]he public generally concedes that policemen are the world's greatest moochers."[497] For a profession which depends so heavily on the respect and cooperation of the citizenry,[498] such an image cannot help. More importantly, acceptance of gifts or discounts—even from reputable merchants—initiates a conditioning process that can normalize other, more reprehensible, types of police corruption.[499]

Kickbacks

"In many communities, police officers receive goods, services, or money for referring business to towing companies, ambulances, garages, lawyers, doctors, [bail] bondsmen, undertakers, taxi cab drivers, service stations, [and] moving companies."[500] Some departments reputedly condone these arrangements, provided the corrupter is a legitimate businessperson,[501] while others consider such conduct to be a gross violation of professional ethics and apply strict sanctions.

Shakedowns

A shakedown occurs when a law enforcement officer receives a payoff in exchange for not making an arrest. Shakedowns can range in seriousness from accepting a gratuity from a "respectable" citizen trying to avoid a traffic charge to taking a bribe from an apprehended criminal bargaining for release.[502] In New York City motorists once commonly kept ten-dollar bills clipped to their driver's licenses. When stopped for a traffic violation, they would hand the license to the officer, who would pocket the bill and wave the driver on.[503] At the more sinister end of the continuum, New York drug pushers reportedly always carry a hefty wad of emergency cash to try to buy their way out of arrests. Occasionally they succeed.[504]

The Fix

The most familiar violation in this category involves officers who agree to dispose of traffic tickets in exchange for a fee. A far more serious type of "fix," however, entails the quashing of criminal prosecutions—in effect, a delayed shakedown. The fixer is often a detective who conducts or controls the investigation upon which the prosecution is based.

"The investigating officer usually agrees to 'sell the case,' that is, withdraw prosecution in return for some material reward; he either fails to request prosecution, tampers with the existing evidence, or gives perjured testimony."[505] According to reports, it is even possible in some police departments to fix murder cases.[506]

Opportunistic Theft

Opportunistic theft includes practices such as stealing money from arrestees or unconscious accident victims. One writer tells of a former Miami policeman who routinely stole any cash he could find from every dead body he encountered.[507] More significantly, this category also includes keeping all or part of money, property, or drugs seized as evidence in raids.[508] As the Los Angeles skimming case mentioned earlier illustrates, this crime potentially can involve enormous amounts of money.

Protection of Illegal Activities

Persons engaging in illegal activities and seeking to operate without police interference sometimes pay individual officers (or even entire precincts) protection money. This is especially the case with so-called "victimless crimes,"—e.g., drugs, gambling, prostitution. Attempts to legislate morality appear to have contributed substantially to police corruption because bribes generated by victimless crimes are more easily rationalized. This enhanced capacity for neutralization was demonstrated by one officer when he discussed his attitude toward gambling payoffs: "Hell, everybody likes to place a bet once in a while . . . Sure there are honest cops on the force . . . [b]ut most of us are realistic."[509] An analysis of drug payoffs describes how corrupted officers would commonly remark that "it's just drug money," implying that there is a different standard for theft of illegally generated revenues compared to theft of lawful profits.[510] Not all protection money, however, emanates from victimless crime—even assuming there is such a thing. "Officers in some departments also receive protection payoffs from robbers, burglars, jewel thieves, confidence men, fences and forgers."[511]

How might police corruption be explained? Since complicated questions seldom inspire simple answers, numerous hypotheses have been generated. Some have rested upon structural aspects of law enforcement. Three factors in particular have been suggested most frequently: (1) structural opportunity; (2) an institutionalized code of silence; and (3) inadequate organizational controls.

Structural Opportunity

By definition, police work places officers in close proximity to a wide array of illegal activities and an abundance of illicit profits. Such continuous exposure inevitably yields opportunities for bribes and payoffs. "Not only can police officers offer valuable services merely by being a little less vigilant, but they also are in constant contact with people who desire those services and have no compunctions about breaking the law to purchase them."[512]

Patrol officers generally work alone or with a single partner. "Despite the quasi-military chain of command and such innovations as two-way radio, the fact is that most police supervisors most of the time cannot know what their officers are doing."[513] Law abiding citizens are even less cognizant of police activities. Crime and vice are photosensitive, so many law enforcers must work in a murky, subterranean milieu, far removed from public view. We often watch them cruise by in their patrol cars, we occasionally receive traffic citations from them, but seldom do we personally witness the police in their most serious professional role—investigating crimes and arresting criminals. Low managerial and civic visibility affords officers such wide behavioral discretion that the opportunities for corruption are unavoidable.[514]

The Code of Silence

Enhancing structural opportunity is the so-called "Blue Wall of Silence"[515]—a cultural norm that proscribes officers from informing on corrupt colleagues. Intense group cohesiveness greatly reduces the risk of exposure and thus helps tenuate the line between observer and participant. In 1997, the nation was horrified by a vicious attack on a suspect inside a New York City police station. The victim, a Haitian immigrant, was beaten, tortured, and sodomized by the wooden handle of a toilet plunger. At least 20 officers were in the vicinity when the gruesome incident transpired. "Yet only four officers eventually came forward and testified; no one came forward immediately and none of these officers demanded immediate medical attention."[516] The victim was left bleeding in a holding cell for three hours until paramedics were finally summoned. During this period, the officer who had forced the plumbing tool into the victim's anus had brandished his weapon around the station house for all to see and bragged about what he had done. He was confident that his fellow officers would cover for him.[517] A New York borough commander has compared the Blue Wall of Silence to omerta—the Mafia's code of secrecy.[518] "[I]t is a fact of life that telling on an officer is viewed as a betrayal worse than corruption itself."[519]

Consider the experience of New York Detective Bob Leucci. After Leucci testified against his former partners regarding skimming, shakedowns, and fixes in the Narcotics Bureau, he was transferred to internal affairs and assigned to teach routine training courses. The topic of his first lecture was surveillance techniques, but the real lesson was about the sanctity of the silence code.

In the middle of the classroom a hand shot up.

"What did you say your name was?"

"Detective Leucci."

"Are you *the* Detective Leucci?"

"I'm Detective Leucci."

"I don't think I have anything to learn from you," said the student. He got up and walked out of the classroom and did not come back.[520]

As Leucci discovered, violation of the perverse "loyalty over integrity" credo can carry severe group sanctions. The penalty can be a professional life sentence because the "informer" label hangs around a police officer's neck for his or her whole career.

One rookie officer in Brooklyn saw fellow officers turn against her when she reported her partner for theft. They harassed her for years, leaving notes on her locker calling her a rat. She transferred, but abuse followed her to the next precinct.[521]

Moreover, the physical risk of accusing corrupt colleagues can be far more costly than peer ostracism. "Police officers can hold the power of life and death over one another. They have to be certain that when they radio for help, it will come."[522] A former New York City Police Commissioner has acknowledged that "fear of being abandoned under fire is one reason corruption persists."[523] Perhaps no single moment underscores this contention more than one which occurred in a California courtroom in 1997. A San Francisco police officer, the victim of a vicious sexual assault, was cited for contempt when she refused to testify against her alleged assailant, her ex-husband—a fellow officer. "She feared that if she spoke out against another cop, the word would be out and other officers might refuse to back her up in a dangerous situation."[524]

The Blue Wall of Silence places honest police officers, pressured to obey the code, in a Catch-22 predicament; for working alongside corrupt colleagues can sometimes be as perilous as abandonment by them. One officer has vividly described the hazardous dilemma faced by good cops who protect bad cops:

Suppose, she said, she confronts a drug dealer on a corner who is secretly paying off her partner. She and the dealer both draw their guns. Her partner is standing behind her. Whom does he help?[525]

Organizational Controls

Structural opportunity is further reinforced by inadequate internal controls. "Police departments simply have not provided sufficiently rigorous supervision and training on matters related to the dynamics of corruption."[526] Furthermore, many police administrators have been unwilling to confront corruption as a systemic problem, subscribing instead to the notion of a "few bad apples." The Pennsylvania Crime Commission's investigation of the Philadelphia Police Department, for example, "found that although the top administrators were not corrupt, they repeatedly ignored the pervasive nature of the problem, insisting that it existed only in isolated individual cases."[527] By reducing the level of analysis from the whole organization to the deviant member, the "bad apple" theory provides yet another layer of protection to corrupt officers. It is obviously very difficult for police leadership to fight corruption and deny its existence simultaneously.

Rather than concentrating on structural flaws, however, some explanations of corruption have stressed personality features indigenous to police officers. New recruits may bring their own constellation of traits to the job, but police work also fosters the development of certain superordinate attitudes. One survey of the research in this area concludes that there *is* a "police personality."[528] For example, "[p]olice officers tend to be somewhat more impulsive, aggressive, and willing to take risks than people in other occupational groups."[529] Each of these traits could be a desirable quality in law *enforcers*, but, in the wrong mix, the same traits are also characteristic of law*breakers*.

Other studies reveal that police officers tend to feel more isolated than most people. They typically are suspicious of and defensive toward outsiders, and so choose to separate themselves from the public.[530] "Sensing the uneasiness so many of the rest of us feel in the presence of even an off-duty officer, those in police work tend to avoid social contacts with the general public and to retreat into the company of other officers."[531] Law enforcement can be a uniquely stressful and demoralizing job; the high rates of alcoholism, suicide, divorce, and domestic violence among police officers attest to this fact.[532] The hours, the uniform, the inherent danger, the acquired world-weary cynicism, along with other factors, likely encourage withdrawal from the societal mainstream. The resulting "us-versus-them" mentality could be very receptive to the transmission of a deviant tradition within a department.

Another trait which researchers have linked to the police personality is a false perception of invulnerability, stemming from the power and authority vested in the badge.[533] Many who wear the badge—even those who tarnish it—may feel safely insulated from allegations of corruption. As one officer has stated: "Who's going to take the word of a junkie over a cop?"[534] But, as the following analysis of the New York Police Department illustrates, such reckless self-assurance has created an expanding class of convicted felons consisting of "ex-cops."

CASE STUDY
The NYPD

"As long as New York City has had police, it has had police corruption."[535] In 1894, Captain Max Schmittberger, the force's preeminent bagman, made a lengthy confession before the Lexow Committee of the State Senate. According to Schmittberger, a $300 payment was required to join the force, and every subsequent promotion entailed an escalating fee demanded by the ruling Tammany Hall political machine. A lucrative precinct could cost a prospective captain $15,000—an enormous price tag in those days. Another witness, Inspector "Clubber" Williams,[536] reluctantly acknowledged possessing a large personal fortune, a luxurious estate, and a steam-powered yacht. "Williams claimed to have accumulated his wealth through real-estate speculation in Japan—an explanation so fantastic that no one could disprove it."[537]

The Lexow Committee revealed police corruption "on a scale that remains astonishing."[538] A department-wide protection racket flourished with the full knowledge of the police chief. Yearly kickbacks from whorehouses and saloons approached $10 million[539]—at a time when the average wage for skilled labor in the U.S. was $5.95 a week.[540] Shortly after Theodore Roosevelt became Police Commissioner of New York City in 1895, he began firing officers who were receiving regular payoffs from the city's many brothels.[541] In 1931, Governor Franklin D. Roosevelt commissioned a special investigation, which reported widespread corruption among New York City's vice squad.[542] Both Roosevelts, products of a sheltered upper class, discovered in their adulthood what most average New Yorkers probably knew as young-

(Continued)

sters: The NYPD has a considerable presence of corruption.

This is not to imply that most New York cops are crooked. In fact, according to former Deputy Mayor Milton Mollen, whose commission carefully studied the problem and released a detailed report in 1994: "[T]he vast majority of police officers throughout the city do not engage in corruption."[543] But even if the percentage of corrupt officers is quite small—say 3 percent—when a force contains 30,000 members[544] spread across 76 precincts in five boroughs, corruption that may be modest in relative terms can be considerable in absolute terms. After all, if "only" 3 percent of New Yorkers had the measles, it rightly would be called an epidemic.

Indeed, it must have seemed like an epidemic in 1951 when 35 New York policemen were indicted for criminal conspiracy. They were all beneficiaries of bookie Harry Gross, who reputedly spent $1 million a year on police payoffs to protect his $20 million a year gambling empire.[545]

In keeping with an approximate 20-year scandal cycle, the Knapp Commission of the 1970s (named for its chairman, New York attorney Whitman Knapp) revealed an entrenched system of corruption inside the NYPD. Large networks of officers collected bribes from bookies and prostitutes, often passing their payoff money up the chain of command.[546]

Undercover agents, in the employ of the commission, recorded misconduct so normalized that one almost expected Social Security taxes to be withheld from payoffs. For example, patrolman William Phillips was taped negotiating a monthly protection price with an undercover investigator he believed was an agent of an elegant New York brothel:

> "Now define the deal," says Teddy . . . "We're going to get protection from the precinct?"
>
> "Division," reiterates Phillips. "Division, borough, and precinct. Listen, you give me the money, you're not going to have any problems, I'm telling you that right now."[547]

Confronted with such bald evidence of his guilt, Phillips (who would later go to prison for murdering a pimp) was co-opted by the Knapp Commission and became a friendly witness at its hearings. He described payoffs from every construction site in the city to ignore dust violations, from every double-parked delivery truck to look the other way, from every seedy bar to move arrests of brawlers and dope pushers out to the street so as not to jeopardize precious liquor licenses. According to Phillips, corruption had become so out of control in the NYPD, that some cops were bribing other cops.[548]

> From rookies prying $2 a week out of impoverished Puerto Rican bodegas, to division commanders exacting $1,500 a month tithes from district gamblers, Phillips testified, hardly a cranny of the whole department is free of some kind of graft.

The real money, however, was where it had always been—in vice. In the words of Officer Phillips: "I never knew a plain-clothes man yet . . . that wasn't on the 'pad.'"[549] In its final report, the Knapp Commission found that plain-clothes detectives received regular payoffs, amounting to as much as $3,500 a month, from each of the protected illicit operations under their jurisdiction.[550] Again, the extent to which this deviance could be normalized was striking. Newly assigned detectives had to serve a 60-day "apprenticeship" before they were entitled to a share of the bribe money. When supervisors were involved, they got a share-and-a-half. When a detective was transferred out of a precinct, his partners in crime gave him two months "severance pay."[551]

In its time, the Knapp Commission was perceived largely as a success. Courageous departmental "whistle-blowers" like Bob Leucci, David Durk,[552] and the legendary Frank Serpico[553] became heroic figures to the public (though not, of course, to their peers behind the Blue Wall). A new police commissioner embraced the panel's

(*Continued*)

recommendation of a comprehensive shake-up within the NYPD.[554] Corruption was said to have decreased.

By the 1980s, however, rampant misconduct was back, and the stakes had escalated. The bookie and the pimp, long the symbols of urban vice, were displaced in primacy by the crack cocaine dealer. "[T]he crack trade and its gusher of illicit cash [were] testing the integrity of American law enforcement as never before."[555] Police corruption, which once had consisted mainly of "grasseaters"—as the Knapp Commission labeled officers who took graft from prostitutes and gamblers[556]—now was dominated by a new breed of "meat eaters"—cops so aggressively corrupt that they were indistinguishable from the most predatory street criminals. A former Bronx patrolman, Bernie Cawley, explained to the Mollen Commission why his comrades knew him as the "Mechanic:"

> "Because I used to 'tune people up,'" he placidly explained. "It's a police word for beating people." Suspects? he was asked. "No, I was just beating people up in general."[557]

In four years on the job, Cawley claimed to have "tuned up" more than 400 persons. "Who's going to catch us?" he said, shrugging. "We're the police."[558]

For the NYPD, still recovering from its pommeling at the hands of the Knapp Commission, the worst was yet to come. The first domino tipped over in Brooklyn in 1992, when Officer Michael Dowd and five other policemen were arrested for drug-trafficking. Dowd's corruption had been the worst-kept secret in the NYPD. Over a period of 6 years, 16 complaints had been filed against him, alleging that he had been taking bribes, robbing drug dealers, and selling cocaine. Dowd came to work in a $35,000 Corvette, owned four suburban homes,[559] and was sometimes picked up by limousine at the station house for Atlantic City gambling trips—all on a salary of $400 a week.[560] Witnesses had even observed Dowd snorting cocaine off the

dashboard of his patrol car.[561] "[Yet], senior officials repeatedly ignored allegations against Officer Dowd or blocked efforts to check them out."[562] When he finally was apprehended, it was by local police in Long Island, outside NYPD jurisdiction.

It was soon evident that the arrest of Dowd and his five-man "crew" was just the initial spasm of an impending avalanche. Dowd had formed a criminal organization in Brooklyn of 15 to 20 fellow officers. "Politicians and the media started asking what had happened to the system for rooting out police corruption established 21 years ago at the urging of the Knapp Commission."[563]

Michael Dowd lived up to his billing as the most crooked cop in New York by continuing his illegal activities even after his arrest, reportedly corresponding with drug dealers from his jail cell about a planned "Butch Cassidy" escape to Central America.[564] Dowd was convicted in 1994 and received a long prison sentence. The full weight of the criminal justice system fell on him like Dorothy's house; he would not even be eligible for parole for at least 11 years. He had apologized to the court for disgracing his badge and had begged for leniency, but Federal Judge Kimba Wood, who had once sent Michael Milken to prison (Chapter 6), was unimpressed with Dowd's sudden contrition. Judge Wood told Dowd that his crimes "betray an immorality so deep that it is rarely encountered."[565]

A month after Dowd's arrest, the Mollen Commission was created to assess the extent of corruption in the NYPD[566] and to determine why Michael Dowd's superiors seemingly had shut down their eyes, ears, and brains. As a result of the commission's public hearings, three more Brooklyn officers—known as the "Morgue Boys," because they divided up their loot in an abandoned coffin factory[567]—were arrested for staging a series of illegal raids on local crack houses for the purpose of stealing cash and drugs.

The corruption exposed in the Brooklyn precincts was numbing in its profligacy, but it proved to be only the warm-up act for Harlem's 30th

(Continued)

Precinct—which the acerbic New York media soon would dub the "Dirty Thirty."[568] Persistent suspicions that the 30th Precinct was a center for rapacious brutality were confirmed in the summer of 1993, when internal affairs investigators watched through binoculars as a uniformed officer stole a kilo of cocaine from a Harlem drug dealer.

> [W]ord immediately spread on the street that the police officer, patrolman George Nova, was holding an auction. Drug runners flagged down his patrol car to put in their bids. Within hours he had three separate offers, and by early dawn he had a deal: one kilo, sold for $16,000 cash.[569]

Their surveillance of Nova had led internal affairs into a world where "police officers ran through Harlem like a gang of thugs."[570] The following March, a sting operation videotaped three of Nova's colleagues from the 30th Precinct "breaking into an apartment, beating up an occupant, searching for drugs, and stealing cash."[571] Within weeks, 11 more of the 30th's "finest" were led away in handcuffs.[572] There was nothing petty about the charges. One officer was accused of shooting a drug dealer while stealing his cocaine; another was alleged to have pocketed $100,000 while illegally searching an apartment.[573] The police commissioner walked into the 30th Precinct station house a month later and personally stripped the badges off two drug-dealing officers.[574] By the end of the year, 29 officers, one-quarter of the precinct's entire roster, had been arrested[575]—including only the second female officer ever formally charged in a major NYPD corruption case.[576]

In contrast to the mess in Brooklyn, which had been depicted as a rank-and-file crime spree, two supervisors from the "Dirty Thirty" were among those arrested.[577] One of them, Sergeant Kevin Nannery, was accused of leading a squad called "Nannery's Raiders,"[578] that would tear down apartment doors and rob drug dealers,"[579] using faked 911 calls as a pretext.[580] The supervisors' arrests

highlighted the issue of accountability, which had always been so discomfiting to police administrators during corruption scandals. Deputy Inspector Thomas Sweeney, who had taken command of the 30th Precinct in April, after the first wave of arrests, was unusually candid in his condemnation of senior officers: "Superior officers should have known if there were violations of the law . . . Of course they should have known."[581]

The Mollen Commission shared Sweeney's conclusion, when it issued its final report. That report assailed a "willful blindness" to corruption throughout the ranks of the NYPD.[582] It even suggested that perhaps as many as 40 corruption cases involving senior officers had been "buried" by the Internal Affairs Bureau.[583] According to the commission, "The principle of command accountability, which holds commanders responsible for fighting corruption, completely collapsed."[584] The report took several previous police commissioners to task, implying that they had been more interested in containing corruption scandals than containing corruption.[585]

Heightened *internal* controls were one of the two main recommendations urged by the Mollen Commission. Evidence that this advice was heeded may be inferred from the resolute response of the NYPD leadership in 1995 to another precinct out of control—this one in the Bronx. Thirteen patrol officers and three sergeants from the 48th Precinct were indicted on various counts of thievery, perjury, and brutality. One of those charged was accused of stealing $400 from a man preparing to buy a Christmas present for his mother. Another of the indictees allegedly stole a victim's dog. The police commissioner offered no cover-up; instead he quickly apologized to the people of New York. Mayor Rudolph Giuliani noted that there was no "willful blindness" on the part of the police this time; they had acted expeditiously to prevent another "Dirty Thirty" from ripening on the vine. "This is precisely what you want the Police Department to do," he said. "It is exactly what didn't happen a few years ago."[586]

(*Continued*)

The other major recommendation from the Mollen panel was a proposal to increase *external* controls,[587] through the creation of a small police commission, independent of the NYPD. That body would be empowered to perform continuous assessments of the department's systems for preventing, detecting, and investigating corruption and to conduct, whenever necessary, its own corruption investigations.[588] If the historical two-decade scandal cycle runs true to form, such a commission could be quite busy around the year 2020.

NOTES

1. Hyde's wife, Lady Cornbury, reportedly was quite a thief herself. She was notorious for going on shopping sprees—in other people's homes. If she saw something she liked, such as a piece of furniture or jewelry, she would send for it the following day, claiming it in the name of the Crown. Before long, whenever local aristocrats heard her carriage wheels turn toward their houses, they would quickly hide their valuables. (Ross, Shelley. *Fall from Grace: Sex, Scandal, and Corruption in American Politics from 1702 to the Present.* New York: Ballantine Books, 1988.)

2. One of Hyde's illegally deeded tracts was renamed Hyde Park as part of the deal. Ironically, two centuries later it would become the family home of another New York governor, Franklin Delano Roosevelt. (Ross, *op. cit.*)

3. Ross, *op. cit.*

4. Rogow, Arnold and Lasswell, Harold. *Power, Corruption, and Rectitude.* Englewood Cliffs, New Jersey: Prentice-Hall, 1963.

5. Wilson, James Q. "Corruption: The Shame of the States." *The Public Interest 2*, 1966: p. 31.

6. Gillespie, Kate and Okruhlik, Gwenn. "The Political Dimensions of Corruption Cleanups: A Framework for Analysis." *Comparative Politics,* October 1991: 77–95.

7. Scott, James C. "Corruption, Machine Politics, and Political Change." *American Political Science Review* 63, 1969: 1142–1157.

8. Bunker, Stephen G. and Cohen, Lawrence E. "Collaboration and Competition in Two Colonization Projects: Toward a General Theory of Official Corruption." *Human Organization* 42, 1983: 106–114.

9. Nye, Joseph S. "Corruption and Political Development: A Cost-Benefit Analysis." *American Political Science Review* 61, 1967: p. 417.

10. Peters, John G. and Welch, Susan. "Political Corruption in America: A Search for Definitions and a Theory." *American Political Science Review* 72, 1978: 974–984.

11. Dean, Suzanne. "Jury Convicts Rep. Howe in Sex Solicitation Case." *Washington Post,* July 24, 1976: pp. A1, A6.

12. *New York Times.* "Paper Says an Aide to House Unit Calls Its Head Her Lover." May 23, 1976: p. 33.

13. Gillespie and Okruhlik, *op. cit.*, p. 79.

14. Ford, Henry J. "Municipal Corruption." *Political Science Quarterly* 19, 1904: 673–686.

15. Surowiecki, James. "The Payola Game." *The New Yorker* (online), April 24, 2006.

16. McMullen, M. "A Theory of Corruption." *Sociological Review* 9, 1961: 82–86. See also, Werner, Simcha B. "New Directions in the Study of Administrative Corruption." *Public Administration Review,* March/April 1983: 146–154.

17. Rundquist, Barry S., Strom, Gerald S., and Peters, John G. "Corrupt Politicians and Their Electoral Support: Some Experimental Observations." *American Political Science Review* 71, 1977: p. 955.

18. Freund, Charles P. "What Lincoln Bedroom?" *msn.com.* January 24, 1997.

19. *www.reagan.com.* "Fund-Raising Scandal Timeline." May 13, 1998.

20. *Ibid.*

21. Drew, Elizabeth. *The Corruption of American Politics.* Seadaucus, NJ: Birch Lane Press, 1999; p. 61.

22. Coleman, James W. *The Criminal Elite: The Sociology of White-Collar Crime* (Second Edition). New York: St. Martin's Press, 1989.

23. *Ibid.*, p. 87.

24. Sobel, Lester A. *Corruption in Business.* New York: Facts on File, 1977.

25. Coleman, 1989, *op. cit.*, p. 90.

26. DeWaal, Caroline S. and Obester, Tricia. "Seafood Safety: Consumers and Manufacturers at Risk." *USA Today Magazine,* July 1994: 24–26.

27. *Houston Post.* "USDA Official Removed." February 9, 1995: p. A22.

28. Coleman, 1989, *op. cit.,* p. 90.

29. Amick, George. *The American Way of Graft.* Princeton, NJ: Center for Analysis of Public Issues, 1976.

30. Coleman, 1989, *op. cit.*

31. Amick, *op. cit.*

32. *Business Week.* "Let's Throw the Book at Defense Bid-Riggers." July 4, 1988: p. 128.

33. *The Economist.* "Defence Spending: Pop Goes the Weasel." June 25, 1988: 26–27.

34. Ross, Irwin. "Inside the Biggest Pentagon Scandal." *Fortune,* January 11, 1993: p. 88.

35. *Ibid.*

36. *Ibid.,* p. 90.

37. *Ibid.*

38. *Ibid.*

39. *Ibid.*

40. Quoted in *Ibid.,* p. 92.

41. United States Department of Defense (press release). "Maine Man Charged With Bribery Scheme Involving U.S. Army Space and Missile Command in Huntsville." December 16, 2008.

42. *wmtw.com.* "Defense Contractor Accused of Skimming Military Money, January 24, 2009.

43. Lipton, *op. cit.*

44. Lipton, Eric. "Midlevel Insider Drains Millions from Defense." *Houston Chronicle,* October 12, 2008: A4.

45. Vartabedian, Ralph, Serrano, Richard A. and Marosi, Richard. "Rise in Bribery Tests Integrity of US Border." *latimes.com,* October 23, 2006.

46. Marsico, Ron. "Ex-Customs Boss Gets 24 Years." *nj.com,* January 27, 2006.

47. Pinkerton, James. "Corruption Crosses the Border With Agent Bribes—U.S. Officers Have Been Charged With Taking Money to Let Traffickers Cross Checkpoints." *houstonchronicle.com,* May 29, 2005.

48. Reddick, Clay. "Border Patrol Agent, Brother Going to Jail." *Laredo Morning Times,* February 28, 2006: 1, 14.

49. *nctimes.com.* "Ex-San Diego Customs Official Sentenced to Probation," January 14, 2006.

50. *signonsandiego.com.* "INS Official Gets 3 Years Probation," January 14, 2006.

51. Spagat, Elliot. "Border Agent Gets 5-Year Sentence in Smuggling Case." *seattletimes.com,* July 29, 2006.

52. Quoted in *usatoday.com.* "How Can Country Be Secured If Some of Those Guarding Gates Have Turned?" September 24, 2006.

53. Spagat, *op. cit.*

54. *osdir.com.* "Cash, Cars, Jewelry: Some Corruption Cases Involving Immigration Officers," September 24, 2006.

55. Vartabedian, et al., *op. cit.* See also: *nytimes.com.* "Texas Border Agent Pleads Guilty," September 6, 2006.

56. *johnfloyd.com.* "Former Border Patrol Agent Sentenced to Prison For Bribery and Unlawful Transfer of ID Documents," December 7, 2006.

57. *osdir.com, op. cit.*

58. Marizco, Michael. "U.S. Agent Had Prior Arrest on Pot Charge." *dailystar.com,* October 13, 2005.

59. *tusconcitizen.com.* "Customs Agent Pleads Guilty in Bribery Case," October 28, 2006.

60. Office of the United States Attorney, District of Arizona (press release). "Border Official Sentenced to 9 Years in Prison," February 13, 2007.

61. *kpbs.org.* "Former Border Inspector Sentenced," February 15, 2007.

62. *osdir.com, op. cit.*

63. *kpbs.org, op. cit.*

64. Soto, Onell R. "Ex-Border Patrol Agents Sentenced For Accepting Bribes." *signonsandiego.com,* October 31, 2006.

65. *judicialwatch.org.* "Another U.S. Border Agent Helps Mexican Smugglers," June 10, 2008.

66. *freerepublic.com.* "Ex-Border Patrol Agent Sentenced to Seven Years For Smuggling," December 23, 2008.

67. *osdir.com, op. cit.*

68. *usatoday.com,* "Cash, Cars, Jewelry: Some Corruption Cases Involving Immigration Officers," September 24, 2006.

69. *azstar.net.* "7.5 Years For Pot-Stealing Border Patrol Agent," June 21, 2007.

70. *krgv.com.* "Border Patrol Agent Pleads Guilty," February 2, 2009.

71. Greenblatt, Mark. "FBI: Corrupt US Border Agents a 'Serious' Threat." *khou.com.* May 24, 2011.

72. Roebuck, Jeremy. "Feds: Border Patrol Agent Guided Drugs For Bribe." *nbpc.net,* December 4, 2008.

73. U.S. Federal Bureau of Investigation. "Border Officer who Allowed Illegal Aliens, Marijuana to be Smuggled Into U.S. Sentenced to Seven Years in Prison." *fbi.gov.* February 20, 2009.

74. *Ibid.*

75. *Ibid.*

76. Hernandez, Daniel. "U.S. Border Officer Gets 20 Years for Corruption, Smuggling Drugs." *latimes. com.* September 1, 2010.

77. Rotella, Sebastian. "Former U.S. Anti-drug Official's Arrest 'A Complete Shock.'" *latimes.com.* September 17, 2009.

78. Marizco, Michel. "Obstruction Charges Now Set for Cramer." *nogalesinternational.com.* December 7, 2009.

79. *Ibid.*

80. Rotella, *op. cit.*

81. *Ibid.*

82. Marizco, *op. cit.*

83. *Ibid.*

84. Johnston, David and Verhovek, Sam Howe. "Drug Trade Feeds on Payoffs at Mexico Line." *nytimes.com,* March 24, 1997.

85. Pomfret, John. "Briber at Border Worries Officials." *washingtonpost.com,* July 15, 2006.

86. Vartabedian, et al, *op. cit.*

87. Johnston and Verhovek, *op. cit.*

88. Quoted in *Ibid.*

89. Pomfret, *op. cit.*

90. *lawenforcementcorruption.com.* "Corrupt U.S. Agents Aid Human Smuggling at Border," February 6, 2009.

91. *Ibid.*

92. *dojgov.net.* "U.S. Citizenship and Immigration Services—Homeland Security Employees Aiding Islamic Extremists For Cash," September 11, 2007.

93. *Ibid.*

94. *usatoday.com,* September 24, 2006, *op. cit.*

95. Makon, Jerry. "Immigration Official Pleads Guilty to Falsifying Documents." *Washington Post,* December 1, 2006: A16.

96. Quoted in *cnn.com.* "DHS Official Admits Taking Bribes to Fake Documents," December 1, 2006.

97. United States Attorney's Office, Eastern District of Virginia (press release). "Citizenship and Immigration Services Supervisor Sentenced for Bribery and Naturalization Fraud." April 20, 2007.

98. *usatoday.com,* September 24, 2006, *op. cit.*

99. Caldwell, Alicia A. "ICE Agent Sentenced to 44 Months For Seeking Bribes." *Laredo Morning Times,* July 13, 2007: 6A.

100. *usatoday.com,* September 24, 2006, *op. cit.* Feuer, Alan. "2 Plead Guilty to Falsifying Green Cards." *nytimes.com,* September 8, 2007.

101. Cornell, Kati. "Scammer Jail Break." *nypost.com,* February 21, 2008. *northcountrygazette.org.* "Woman Sentenced For Immigration Fraud Scheme," February 21, 2008.

102. United States Attorney, Southern District of New York (press release). "Former Immigration Official Sentenced to Two and a Half Years in Prison For Participating in Massive Immigration Fraud Scheme." December 19, 2007.

103. *Ibid.*

104. Kouri, Jim. "Crime Story: Corrupt Cop Aided Mexican Drug Trafficker." *renewamerica.us,* April 2, 2006.

105. *northcountrygazette.org.* "Immigration Officer Guilty of Taking Bribes," January 11, 2008.

106. United States Attorney, Southern District of New York (press release). "Former Immigration Official Sentenced to 3 and a Half Years in Prison For Taking Bribes in Exchange For Granting Citizenship to Aliens." January 10, 2008.

107. *usatoday.com,* September 24, 2006, *op. cit.*

108. *osdir.com, op. cit.*

109. *Ibid.*

110. *DOGgov.net, op. cit.*

111. Markon, *op. cit.*

112. Quoted in *usatoday.com,* September 24, 2006, *op. cit.*

113. McGrane, Reginald C. (Ed.). *The Correspondence of Nicholas Biddle Dealing with National Affairs 1807–1844.* Boston: Houghton Mifflin, 1919; p. 218.

114. Radelat, Ana. "Congress in Crisis." *Public Citizen,* May/June, 1990: p. 15.

115. *Buckley v. Valeo,* 429 U.S. 1, 28 (1976).

116. Welch, William M. II. "The Federal Bribery Statute and Special Interest Campaign Contributions." *Journal of Criminal Law & Criminology* 79, 1989: 1347–1373.

117. Gillespie and Okruhlik, *op. cit.,* p. 79.

118. Weeks, Joseph R. "Bribes, Gratuities and the Congress: The Institutionalized Corruption of the Political Process, the Impotence of Criminal Law to Reach It, and a Proposal Change." *Journal of Legislation* 13, 1986: p. 123.

119. Barnes, Fred and Wildavsky, Rachel F. "Is Washington for Sale?" *Reader's Digest,* February 1993: 46–51.

120. Quoted in *Boston Globe.* "Report Ties Cash, Politics." January 12, 1996: p. 10.

121. Lawrence, Jill and Hasson, Judi. "Donations to Both Parties Skirt Limits Set by Reform." *USA Today,* October 28, 1996: pp. 1A, 2A.

122. Miller, Alan C. and Miller, T. Christian. "Election Was Decisive in Arena of Spending: Ever Higher Sums." *Los Angeles Times.* December 8, 2000: pp. 1A, 8A.

123. Suellentrop, Chris. "Follow the Money." *Boston Globe* (online), June 26, 2005.

124. *opensecrets.org.* "2004 Presidential Election," April 9, 2005.

125. Zibreg, Christian. "The 2009 Presidential Election in Numbers." *tgdaily.com,* November 6, 2008.

126. Suellentrop, *op. cit.*

127. Welch, *op. cit.*, p. 1349.

128. *Ibid.*

129. Kramer, Michael. "The Best Pols Money Can Buy." *Time* 140, December 14, 1992: p. 49.

130. Quoted in Welch, *op. cit.*, p. 1350.

131. *Ibid.*, p. 1350.

132. Drew, Elizabeth. *Politics and Money: The New Road to Corruption.* New York: MacMillan, 1983.

133. Quoted in *Ibid.*, p. 2A.

134. Welch, *op. cit.*, pp. 1350–1351.

135. Barnes and Wildavsky, *op. cit.*, p. 45.

136. Bernstein, Alan. "DeLay Sees Limit to Lobbyists' Gifts as Attack on Free Speech." *Houston Chronicle,* April 15, 1995: p. 29A.

137. Ferguson, Thomas and Rogers, Joel. *Right Turn.* New York: Hill and Wang, 1986.

138. Kramer, *op. cit.*, p. 49.

139. Schouten, Fredreka. "Lobbying Spending Tops $3B in '08." *USA Today,* January 27, 2009: 5A.

140. Smith, J. Y. "Hanson Is Ordered to Prison." *Washington Post,* April 19, 1975: p. A7.

141. *New York Times.* "S.E.C. Finds $4.2-Million in Gulf Bribes." May 3, 1975: pp. 15, 25.

142. Smith, Robert M. "'Illegality' Cited in Gulf Payments." *New York Times,* December 31, 1975: pp. 1, 35.

143. Sobel, *op. cit.*

144. Quoted in Robert M. Smith, *op. cit.*, p. 1.

145. *New York Times.* "Gulf Asks Return of Illegal Gifts." March 1, 1976: pp. 1, 46.

146. *Washington Post.* "Tonry Sentenced to Prison, Fined in Election Fraud." July 29, 1977: p. A8.

147. Quoted in Locy, Toni. "'Sad and Sorry Tale' of Misdeeds: 3 Years Given Ex-Lawmaker." *Houston Chronicle,* November 10, 1994: p. 6A.

148. *Ibid.*

149. Eljera, Bert. "Kim Pleads Guilty to Illegal Donations." *asianweek.com,* August 8–14, 1997. MacArthur, Mac. "Congressman Jay Kim: Just the Tip of the Iceberg." *americanpolitics.com,* December 1997.

150. Associated Press. "Republican House Seat in Jeopardy." *freerepublic.com,* April 30, 1998.

151. *abcnews.com.* "Miller Takes Over for Kim." January 19, 1999.

152. Robinson, Thomas S. "Ex-Rep. Whalley Put on Probation." *Washington Post,* October 16, 1973: p. A2.

153. Robinson, Timothy S. "Ex-Congressman Faces Prison." *Washington Post,* February 1, 1977: p. A7.

154. Meyer, Lawrence. "Diggs Sentenced to Three Years; Could Keep Seat." *Washington Post,* November 21, 1978: pp. A1, A10.

155. *New York Times.* Supplementary Material. September 6, 1978: p. 11.

156. *Washington Post.* "Ex-Rep. Clark Is Sentenced." June 13, 1979: p. A2.

157. Kropko, M. R. "Ohio Congressman Is Indicted on Racketeering, Other Charges." *Houston Chronicle,* May 5, 2001: A3.

158. Pierre, Robert E. and Eilperin, Juliet. "Traficant Is Found Guilty on All 10 Counts." *Houston Chronicle,* April 12, 2002: A2.

159. Kropko, *op. cit.*

160. Quoted in Sheeran, Thomas J. "Congressman to Face Trial Without Attorney." *Houston Chronicle,* May 12, 2001: A26.

161. Dart, Bob. "'Political Goliath' Fights Court With Offbeat Style." *Houston Chronicle,* March 24, 2002: A11.

162. Snow, Kate. "Traficant Jury Still Deliberating in Trial of Ohio Congressman." *cnn.law.com,* April 10, 2002.

163. *usgovinfo.about.com.* "Convicted Traficant Vows to Run Again." April 15, 2002.

164. Pierre, Robert E. and Eilperin, Juliet. "Traficant Is Found Guilty." *Washington Post,* April 12, 2002: A1.

165. Eilperin, Juliet. "House Votes 420 to 1 to Expel Traficant." *Washington Post,* April 25, 2002: A1.

166. *Houston Chronicle.* "House Kicks Out Traficant." July 25, 2002: A4.

167. *cnn.com.* "Ex-Rep Traficant Sentenced to 8 Years." July 30, 2002.

168. *usatoday.com.* "Traficant Gets 8 Years on Corruption Charges." July 30, 2002.

169. Coleman, 1994, *op. cit.*

170. *Houston Post.* "Former Rep. John Dowdy Dies at 83," April 15, 1995. pp. A23, A24.

171. Meyer, Lawrence. "Judge Fines Dowdy $25,000, Gives Him 18 Months in Prison." *Washington Post,* February 24, 1971: p. A5.

172. *Washington Post.* "Ex-Rep. Podell Sentenced." January 10, 1975: p. A10.

173. *Washington Post.* "Rep. Brasco Sentenced in Bribe Scheme." October 23, 1974: p. A7.

174. *Ibid.*, p. A7.

175. For a comprehensive analysis of Koreagate, see: Moore, Robin and Perdue, Lew. *The Washington Connection.* New York: Condor, 1977.

176. Halloran, Richard. "The Korea Probe Clearly Is Sinking in the West." *New York Times,* March 26, 1978: p. E5.

177. Halloran, Richard. "Ex-Rep. Hanna Concedes Guilt in Korea Case." *New York Times,* March 18, 1978: pp. 1, 11.

178. Quoted in Coleman, 1994, *op. cit.*, p. 52.

179. Coleman, 1994, *op. cit.*, p. 51.

180. *Ibid.*

181. *New York Times.* "F.B.I. Studies Flood and Passman Ties to Contracts." February 23, 1978: p. A18.

182. Coleman, 1994, *op. cit.*

183. Lyons, Richard D. "Daniel Flood, 90, Who Quit Congress in Disgrace, Is Dead." *New York Times,* May 29, 1994: p. 34.

184. Quoted in *Ibid.*, p. 34.

185. *Ibid.*

186. Flood's former administrative aide was the government's key witness against him. The aide also would be instrumental in the subsequent conviction of another Pennsylvania Congressman, Joshua Eilberg, who accepted bribes from a Philadelphia hospital in exchange for helping the hospital win a $14.5 million grant from a federal anti-poverty agency. (Schaffer, Jan. "Guilty Plea Ends Trial of Eilberg." *Washington Post,* February 25, 1979: pp. A1, A11.)

187. Blumenthal, Ralph. "Clashes Said to Have Marked U.S. Discussions on Richmond." *New York Times,* August 30, 1982: pp. A1, B4.

188. Noble, Kenneth B. "Richmond to Pay Walco $425,000 in S.E.C. Case." *New York Times,* February 10, 1982: pp. D1, D16.

189. Carroll, Maurice. "Richmond, a Wealthy Businessman, First Entered Politics as a 'Reformer'." *New York Times,* August 26, 1982: p. B2.

190. Blumenthal, Ralph. "Rep. Richmond Helped Fugitive Get Job on Payroll of House Doorkeeper." *New York Times,* February 22, 1982: p. B3.

191. Blumenthal, Ralph. "Lawmaker's Funds Clouded by Flaws." *New York Times,* January 18, 1982: pp. A1, B4.

192. Blumenthal, Ralph. "Rep. Richmond Payroll Raises Ethics Questions." *New York Times,* January 19, 1982: p. B3.

193. Blumenthal, Ralph. "Richmond Admits Guilt in U.S. Case and Quits House." *New York Times,* August 26, 1982: pp. A1, B2.

194. *Ibid.*

195. Fried, Joseph P. "Richmond Sentenced to a Year and a Day and Fined $20,000." *New York Times,* February 11, 1982: pp. A1, B9.

196. Greene, Robert W. *The Sting Man: Inside ABSCAM.* New York: E. P. Dutton, 1981.

197. *Ibid.*

198. Quoted in *Ibid.*, p. 158.

199. Babcock, Charles R. "Williams Shown Boasting He Could Aid Mine Venture." *Washington Post,* April 2, 1981: pp. A1, A11.

200. Quoted in Greene, *op. cit.*, p. 184.

201. Quoted in *Washington Post.* "U.S. Says Rep. Lederer Promised 'Me' for $." January 7, 1981: p. A7.

202. Quoted in Greene, *op. cit.*, p. 207.

203. Quoted in Anderson, Jack. "Thompson and Murphy on FBI Tapes." *Washington Post,* November 10, 1980: p. D15.

204. Greene, *op. cit.*

205. Kiernan, Laura. "Jenrette and Stowe Guilty on 3 Counts in Abscam Trial." *Washington Post,* October 8, 1989: pp. A1, A8,

206. Greene, *op. cit.*, p. 242.

207. *Ibid.*

208. *Ibid.*

209. Kamen, Al. "Ex-Rep. Kelly Sentenced in Abscam Case." *Washington Post,* January 13, 1984: p. A5.

210. *Ibid.*, p. 249.

211. Quoted in Babcock, Charles. "Rep. Myers: Never Meant to Help 'Sheik'." *Washington Post,* August 26, 1980: pp. A1, A4.

212. Quoted in Babcock, Charles R. "Myers Testifies He Spent 'Sheik' Cash in 2 Weeks." *Washington Post,* August 27, 1980: p. A10.

213. Babcock, August 26, 1980, *op. cit.*, p. A4.

214. *Washington Post.* "Lederer on Hill as Abscam Trial Jury Is Selected." January 6, 1981: p. A6.

215. *Washington Post.* "Rep. Lederer Resigns Seat over Abscam Conviction." April 30, 1981: p. A8.

216. Barbash, Fred. "Justices Refuse to Review 4 Abscam Convictions." *Washington Post,* June 1, 1983: p. A4.

217. *Washington Post.* "Ex-Congressman Lederer Loses Philadelphia Steamfitter Job." June 22, 1981: p. A26.

218. Babcock, Charles R. "Sen. Williams Dismisses His Statements on Influence as 'Just Plain Hot Air'." *Washington Post,* April 28, 1981: p. A9.

219. *Ibid.*

220. Babcock, Charles R. "Senator's Claims Are Ridiculed by Abscam Prosecutor." *Washington Post,* April 28, 1981: p. A9.

221. Babcock, Charles R. "Prosecution Calls Williams 'a Corrupt Public Official'." *Washington Post,* April 1, 1981: p. A9.

222. Babcock, Charles R. "Williams Convicted in Abscam." *Washington Post,* May 2, 1981: pp. A1, A2.

223. Babcock, Charles R. "Williams Sentenced to 3 Years." *Washington Post,* February 17, 1982: pp. A1, A8.

224. Peterson, Bill. "Williams, Facing Expulsion, Resigns from U.S. Senate." *Washington Post,* March 12, 1982: pp. A1, A6.

225. Anderson, Jack. "Thompson and Murphy on FBI Tapes." *Washington Post,* November 10, 1980: p. D15.

226. *New York Times.* "Thompson Given 3-year Sentence." October 26, 1983: p. B2.

227. Anderson, Jack. "New Evidence Could Clear Abscam Figure." *Washington Post,* December 15, 1982: p. B21.

228. *Washington Post.* "Drink Flawed Jenrette's Judgment, Trial Is Told." September 25, 1980: p. A13.

229. Kiernan, *op. cit.*

230. Kamen, Al. "Jenrette Sentenced to 2 Years in Prison on Abscam Charges." *Washington Post,* December 10, 1983: p. A2.

231. Maxa, Rudy. "Jenrette Split: Episode II." *Washington Post,* January 13, 1981: pp. B1, B4.

232. Babcock, Charles R. "Some Jenrette Cash Traced." *Washington Post,* January 14, 1981: pp. A1, A5.

233. Anderson, Jack. "Kelly Spins a Spooky Abscam Yarn." *Washington Post,* March 31, 1980: p. C23.

234. Sinclair, Ward. "Kelly: Wanted to Expose 'Arabs'." *Washington Post,* February 8, 1980: p. A8.

235. Greene, *op. cit.*, p. 232.

236. Anderson, Jack. "'Sting Man' May Have Kept Abscam Money." *Washington Post,* January 18, 1982: p. B23,

237. Babcock, Charles R. "Wife of Key Abscam Witness Is Found Hanged in Florida." *Washington Post,* January 27, 1982: pp. A1, A12.

238. Marx, Gary T. "Who Really Gets Stung? Some Issues Raised by the New Police Undercover Work." *Crime & Delinquency* 28, 1982: 165–193.

239. Braithwaite, John, Fisse, Brent, and Geis, Gilbert. "Covert Facilitation and Crime: Restoring Balance to the Entrapment Debate." *Journal of Social Issues* 43, 1987: p. 5.

240. *Ibid.*

241. The entrapment debate would be reignited a few years later in the aftermath of Operation Greylord (discussed later in the chapter), another fruitful FBI sting—this one involving Chicago judges. The American Civil Liberties Union complained vigorously that Greylord's indiscriminate use of electronic surveillance techniques seriously abridged privacy rights and due process. Defenders of Greylord countered that corrupt judges, by virtue of their power and position, are so insulated against criminal liability that extraordinary measures are required in order to achieve even minimal success in policing the judiciary. (See Shipp, E.R. "What's Proper in Policing the Judiciary?" *New York Times,* January 1, 1984: p. 28.)

242. Small, Joseph. "Political Ethics." *American Behavioral Scientist* 19, 1976: 543–566.

243. Blood, Michael H. "Cunningham Loses Battle—With Himself." *San Jose Mercury News* (online), March 4, 2006.

244. Archibold, Randall C. "Former Congressman Sentenced to 8 Years in Prison." *nytimes.com,* March 3, 2006.

245. Blood, *op. cit.*

246. Archibold, *op. cit.*

247. Blood, *op. cit.*

248. *Ibid.*

249. Hettana, Seth. "Former Congressman Gets Eight-Plus Years." *Santa Maria Times* (online), March 3, 2006.

250. *kgmb9.com.* "Former GOP Rep. Gets 8 Years in Prison," March 3, 2006.

251. Calbreath, Dean. "Anatomy of a Bribe: Ex-Lawmaker's Web of Cash, Contracts." *San Diego Union-Tribune* (online), March 4, 2006.

252. Perry, Tony. "Defense Contractor Pleads Guilty to Bribing Lawmaker." *Houston Chronicle,* February 25, 2006: A17.

253. Kucher, Karen, Gross, Greg, Martinez, Angelica, and Baker, Debbi Farr. "'Duke' Gets 8 years, 4 months in Prison." *signonsandiego.com,* March 3, 2006.

254. Ross, Brian. "From Cash to Yachts: Congressman's Bribe Menu." *abcnews.com,* February 27, 2006.

255. Kamen, Al. "Cunningham's Hard Cell." *washingtonpost.com,* November 30, 2005.

256. Quoted in Kucher et al., *op. cit.*

257. Quoted in Hettena, *op. cit.*

258. Eckert, Toby. "Cunningham's List Appalling, They Say." *San Diego Union Tribune* (online), February 22, 2006.

259. Quoted in Kucher et al., *op. cit.*

260. *bbc.co.uk.* "US Congress Opts for 'Freedom Fries'", March 12, 2003. Ney's idea was hardly original. During WWI, frankfurters became "hot dogs" as a protest against Germany, and the name stuck. On the other hand, sauerkraut was renamed "liberty cabbage," and, like "freedom fries," that name never got off the ground.

261. Cochran, John. "Rep. Bob Ney Pleads Guilty to Bribery Charges." *abcnews.com,* October 13, 2006.

262. Drinkard, Jim and Johnson, Kevin. "Former Lobbyist Pleads Guilty." *usatoday.com,* January 3, 2006.

263. *usatoday.com.* "Controversial Lobbyist Had Close Contact With Bush," May 5, 2005.

264. Drinkard and Johnson, *op. cit.*

265. Weisman, Jonathan. "GOP Leaders Seek Distance From Abramoff." *washingtonpost.com,* January 3, 2006.

266. *thesmokinggun.com.* "Ex-Delay Aide in Corruption Pie," November 21, 2005.

267. *tpmmuckraker.com.* "Bob Ney."

268. Chiachiere, Ryan. "Rep. Bob Ney Tied to Abramaoff Indictment?" *tpmcafe.com,* August 12, 2005.

269. *Ibid.*

270. *Ibid.*

271. *Ibid.*

272. *cleanupwashington.org.* "Hall of Shame/Rep. Bob Ney (R-Ohio)."

273. *derechos.org.* "The Abramoff Affair: Snapshots From an Empire of Corruption," November 29, 2005.

274. Grimaldi, James. "Lawmaker's Abramoff Ties Investigated." *washingtonpost.com,* November 17, 2005.

275. *tpmmuckraker.com, op. cit.*

276. *Ibid.*

277. Bailey, Holly, Hosenball, Mark, and Isikoff, Michael. "Ney's Gambles." *Newsweek,* September 21, 2006.

278. Schmidt, Susan and Grimaldi, James V. "Ney Sentenced to 30 Months in Prison For Abramoff Deals." *Washington Post,* January 20, 2007: A3.

279. Yost, Pete. "Rep. Bob Ney Pleads Guilty in Congressional Bribery Scandal." *seattletimes.com,* October 13, 2006.

280. *msnbc.com.* "Rep. Ney Pleads Guilty in Lobbying Scandal," October 13, 2006.

281. Department of Justice (press release). "Former Congressman Robert W. Ney Sentenced to 30 Months in Prison For Corruption Crimes." January 19, 2007.

282. Yost, *op. cit.*

283. Anderson, Curt. "Judge Reduces Abramoff Sentence." *boston.com,* September 11, 2008.

284. Quoted in *Ibid.*

285. *cnn.com.* "Abramoff Transferred From Prison to Halfway House." June 8, 2010.

286. Leibovich, Mark. "Abramoff, From Prison to Pizzeria Job." *nytimes.com,* June 23, 2010.

287. *cbslocal.com.* "Abramoff Concludes Stint at Kosher Pizzeria." December 13, 2010.

288. Smith, Jeffrey. "In Jack Abramoff's Memoir, 'Capitol Punishment,' an Unrepentant Reformer?" *washingtonpost.com.* December 9, 2011.

289. Grove, Lloyd. "Jack Abramoff on His New Talk Radio Show, Lobbying Reform and More." *thedailybeast.com,* July 16, 2012.

290. Lewis, Neil A. "Alaska Senator Is Guilty Over His Failure to Disclose Gifts." *nytimes.com,* October 28, 2008.

291. Quoted in Apuzzo, Matt and Holland, Jesse J. "Stevens Convicted on All Counts." *huffingtonpost.com,* October 27, 2008.

292. Kane, Paul. "Ted Steven Loses Battle For Alaska Senate Seat." *Washington Post,* November 19, 2008: 1A.

293. *nytimes.com.* "Ex-Senator Is Guilty of Expense Abuses," August 23, 1995.

294. Rangel, Jesus. "Judge in Queens Is Found Guilty in Bribery Trial." *New York Times,* December 13, 1985: p. A1.

295. *New York Times.* "Brennan Case Goes to Jurors." December 12, 1985: p. B10.

296. Buder, Leonard. "Brennan Given a 5-year Sentence and Fined $209,000 for Bribery." *New York Times,* February 4, 1986: p. B3.

297. Buder, Leonard. "A Suspended Judge Pleads Guilty to Racketeering in Realty Work." *New York Times,* April 2, 1987: p. B3.

298. *New York Times.* "4 Florida Judges Are Indicted in Federal Corruption Inquiry." September 25, 1991: p. 16.

299. *New York Times.* "2 Judges Guilty in Florida Corruption Inquiry." April 28, 1993: p. A18.

300. Bentayou, Frank. "Busting Public Corruption." *American Legion Magazine* 138, April, 1995: 34–35.

301. Patterson, Bill. "Operation Greylord's Scorecard Nearly Complete." *Washington Post,* August 25, 1989: p. A5.

302. The name Greylord was taken from a term for British judges, who wear distinctive grey wigs while presiding.

303. Kose, Kevin. "9 Are Indicted in U.S. Probe of Chicago Court Corruption." *Washington Post,* December 15, 1983: pp. A1, A2.

304. Patterson, *op. cit.*

305. Quoted in Witt, Elder. "Is Government Full of Crooks, or Are We Just Better at Finding Them?" *Governing,* September 1989: p. 33.

306. Greenhouse, Linda. "Justices Consider How the Taint of a Corrupt Judge Should Be Measured and Remedied." *New York Times.* April 15, 1997: p. A18.

307. *Ibid.*

308. Quoted in Klose, 1985, *op. cit.* p. A3.

309. Klose, Kevin. "Senior Judge Guilty in 'Greylord' Case." *Washington Post,* July 14, 1985: p. A3.

310. Lacaya, Richard. "Passing Judgment on the Judges." *Time* 127, January 20, 1986: p. 66.

311. *Time.* "Corruption: A Club for Bribery." June 11, 1984: p. 33.

312. Smith, Robert M. "Tenneco Reports 'Sensitive' Gifts in U.S. and Abroad." *New York Times,* February 15, 1976: pp. 1, 34.

313. Quoted in Mauro, Tony. "Can Money Obstruct Justice?" *USA Today,* February 26, 2009: 9A.

314. *Ibid.*

315. Quoted in *Ibid.*

316. *The Economist.* "Texas: Politics in Court." July 25, 1987: 21–22.

317. Shannon, James. *Texaco and the $10 Billion Jury.* Englewood Cliffs, NJ: Prentice Hall, 1988.

318. Methvin, Eugene H. "Justice for Sale." *Readers Digest* 134, May 1989: p. 133.

319. *Ibid.,* p. 134

320. *Ibid.,* p. 135

321. *New York Times.* "Bankrupt: Texaco and Texas Justice." April 14, 1987. p. A30.

322. Quoted in Methvin, *op. cit.,* p. 134

323. Thornton, Mary. "Senate Convicts Claiborne, Strips Him of Judgeship." *Washington Post,* October 10, 1986: pp. A1, A18.

324. Turner, Wallace. "U.S. Judge in Nevada Convicted of Filing False Income Tax Forms." *New York Times,* October 11, 1984: pp. 1, 13.

325. Thornton, *op. cit.*

326. McAllister, Bill. "Hastings Backers Accuse Senate of Racism in Vote." *Washington Post,* October 21, 1989: p. A4.

327. Marcus, Ruth. "Senate Deliberates Judge Hastings's Fate." *Washington Post,* October 20, 1989: p. A14.

328. Marcus, Ruth. "Senate Urged to Remove Hastings." *Washington Post,* October 19, 1989: p. A4.

329. Marcus, Ruth. "Senate Removes Hastings." *Washington Post,* October 21, 1989: pp. A1, A4.

330. Seligman, Daniel. "The Case of the Crooked Bench." *Fortune* 123, March 25, 1991: 139–140.

331. Biskupic, Joan. "Familiar Words—Nixon, Impeach—But Unusual Test of Power." *Washington Post,* October 11, 1992: p. A3.

332. *Washington Post.* "U.S. Judge Enters Prison." March 24, 1988: p. A1.

333. Marcus, Frances F. "U.S. Judge is Convicted in New Orleans Bribe Case." *New York Times,* June 30, 1991: p. 13.

334. *New York Times.* "U.S. Judge Is Given Prison Sentence." September 7, 1991: p. 12.

335. Borkin, Joseph. *The Corrupt Judge: An Inquiry into Bribery and Other High Crimes and Misdemeanors in the Federal Courts.* New York: Clarkson N. Potter, 1962.

336. *Ibid.*

337. Maas, Arthur. "U.S. Prosecution of State and Local Officials for Political Corruption: Is the Bureaucracy Out of Control in a High-Stakes Operation Involving the Constitutional System?" *Publius: The Journal of Federalism* 17, 1987: p. 199.

338. Ross, *op. cit.* As of this writing, the most recent Reagan appointee to be convicted of criminal charges was former Secretary of the Interior James Watt, who was sentenced to 5 years probation, fined $5,000, and ordered to perform 500 hours of community service in 1996 for attempting to mislead a grand jury investigation of influence peddling in the Reagan administration's Department of Housing and Urban Development. Watt originally was charged with 18 felony counts but entered an agreement with the government to plead guilty to a single misdemeanor charge (Locy, Tony. "Watt Given Probation on Grand Jury Charge." *Houston Chronicle,* March 13, 1996: p. 8A. Also: *USA Today.* "Washington." March 13, 1996: p. 5A).

339. When New York Congressman Mario Biaggi was convicted in 1988 of accepting a $4 million bribe from the Wedtech Corporation in exchange for no-bid government contracts, he contended that Wedtech's true partner in corruption was Ed Meese, who had helped the company secure a $32 million Army engine contract. After the Biaggi verdict, U.S. Attorney Rudolph Giuliani (later elected Mayor of New York City) characterized Meese as "a sleaze." (Quoted in Lardner, George Jr. and Yen, Marianne. "Twice-Convicted Biaggi Surrenders House Seat." *Washington Post,* August 6, 1988: p. A12.)

340. Maas, *op. cit.,* p. 199.

341. *Ibid.*

342. *Ibid.*

343. *Ibid.* For a brief description of some typical cases against legislators in four states (Arizona, South Carolina, California, and Texas), see *Washington Post.* "7 Lawmakers Charged in Bribe Sting." February 7, 1991: p. A7.

344. Blakey, Robert. "The RICO Civil Fraud Action in Context." *Notre Dame Law Review* 58, 1982: 237–349.

345. Kolbert, Elizabeth. "Payroll-Abuse Investigation Seen as Watershed in Albany." *New York Times,* April 6, 1987: pp. A1, B4.

346. Maas, *op. cit.*

347. *New York Times.* "2 Sentenced in Atlanta Airport Scheme." April 16, 1994: p. A8.

348. Wayne, Leslie. "Investing; for Municipal Bonds, Scandals Spur Change." *New York Times,* September 18, 1993: p. 31.

349. *New York Times.* "Ms. Holtzman's Duty." September 11, 1993: p. 20.

350. Thomas, Frank and Morgan, Thomas J. "Speaker Harwood Pays $5,000 to Settle Ethics Matter, Denies He Erred." *Providence Journal-Bulletin,* September 3, 1994: pp. A1, A5.

351. Cohen, Richard M. and Witcover, Jules. *A Heartbeat Away: The Investigation & Resignation of Vice President Spiro T. Agnew.* New York: Viking Press, 1974.

352. *New York Times.* "Kerner arrives in Ky. to Begin 3-Year Term." July 30, 1974: p. A11.

353. Weissman, Joel. "Kerner Gets 3-Year Jail Term." *New York Times,* April 20, 1973: p. A3.

354. Baker, Donald P. "Mandel Trial Judge Spurns Sentence Recommendations." *Washington Post,* October 4, 1977: p. C1.

355. Becker, Elizabeth and Baker, Donald. "Mandel Given Sentence of Four Years in Prison: Fine not Imposed." *Washington Post,* October 8, 1977: pp. A1, A8.

356. Maraniss, David A. "Mandel Given Sentence of Four Years in Prison: Has no Regrets." *Washington Post,* October 8, 1977: pp. A1, A8.

357. Raines, Howell. "Judge Says Tennessee Governor Illegally Used His Parole Powers." *New York Times,* December 21, 1978: p. 21.

358. *New York Times.* "Tennessee Governor Questioned by Grand Jury on Alleged Bribes." December 23, 1978: p. 9.

359. *New York Times.* "Blanton Grants Clemency to 52 Tennessee Convicts." January 17, 1979: p. 14.

360. Raines, Howell. "Gov. Blanton of Tennessee Is Replaced 3 Days Early in Pardons Dispute." *New York Times,* January 18, 1979: p. 16.

361. Raines, Howell. "Even After Blanton Was Ousted, He Tried to Aid 30 More Convicts." *New York Times,* January 19, 1979: p. A12.

362. Maas, Peter. *Marie: A True Story.* New York: Random House, 1983; p. 415.

363. Shabecoff, Phillip. "Blanton Verdict in Tennessee Upset." *New York Times,* April 12, 1983: p. L9.

364. Jefferson, James. "Tucker Gets Probation in Whitewater." *Boston Herald,* August 20, 1996: p. 3.

365. Hasson, Judi. "Whitewater Verdicts: Guilty." *USA Today,* May 29, 1996: p. 1A; Pressley, Sue Ann. "Arkansans Rally to Defense of Their Indicted Governor." *Houston Chronicle,* June 23, 1995: p. 6A.

366. Quoted in Page, Susan. "Arkansas Gov Will Resign, Then Appeal." *USA Today,* May 29, 1996: p. 3A.

367. Mathis, Nancy. "Clinton's Former Partners Convicted of Fraud." *Houston Chronicle,* May 29, 1996: pp. 1A, 8A; Nichols, Bill. "For Clinton, Ripples of Concern." *USA Today,* May 29, 1996: p. 3A.

368. Quoted in: Serrill, Michael. "Bad Debts, Bad Judgments." *Time,* v. 150. September 15, 1997: p. 92.

369. *Ibid.*, p. 92.

370. *Ibid.*

371. *Ibid.*, p. 92.

372. *Ibid.*, p. 92.

373. *Houston Chronicle.* "Man Was to Plead Guilty Until Pardon." January 25, 2001: p. 10A.

374. *Ibid.*

375. *Houston Chronicle.* "Rhode Island Ex-Governor Pleads Guilty for Bribery, Racketeering." December 12, 1998: p. 11A.

376. Tedford, Deborah. "Edwards Guilty of Extortion." *Houston Chronicle.* May 10, 2000: pp. 1A, 16A.

377. Zganjar, Leslie. "Casino-Licensing Graft Evidence Stacks up Against Ex-La. Governor." *Houston Chronicle.* October 1, 1998: p. 17A.

378. Deslatte, Melinda. "Ex-Louisiana Gov. Faces Sentencing." *yahoo!news.com,* January 7, 2001.

379. Gott, Natalie. "Former La. Governor on Trial." *abcnews.com,* January 10, 2000.

380. Zganjar, *op. cit.*

381. Gott, Natalie. "Trails of Money, Stacks of Cash May Cost Edwards in Latest Trial." *Houston Chronicle.* April 24, 2000: p. 4A.

382. Zganjar, *op. cit.*

383. Edwards' odd reference was to Monica Lewinsky's "friend" Linda Tripp, who secretly recorded phone conversations they had shared regarding Lewinsky's alleged sexual relations with President Bill Clinton.

384. Quoted in Sack, Kevin. "49ers Co-Owner Pleads Guilty to Concealing Extortion Plot." *Houston Chronicle.* October 7, 1998: pp. 1A, 10A.

385. Quoted in Gott, *Houston Chronicle, op. cit.*, p. 4A.

386. Quoted in Gott, *Houston Chronicle, op. cit.*, p. 4A.

387. Quoted in Tedford, *op. cit.*, p. 1A.

388. *cbsnews.com.* "Guilty Plea for Ex-Conn. Governor," December 23, 2004.

389. Christofferson, John. "Former Connecticut Gov. Rowland to Plead Guilty in Corruption Case, He Tells Judge." *sfgate.com,* December 23, 2004.

390. Kurtzenberg, Brad. "Ex-Connecticut Governor Rowland Gets 1 Year Prison Sentence." *elitestv.com,* March, 2005.

391. Quoted in *Ibid.*

392. *usatoday.com.* "Ex-Governor of Ala. Convicted of Bribery," June 30, 2006: 3A.

393. Mandaro, Laura. "Ex-HealthSouth CEO Gets Jail Sentence." *marketwatch.com,* June 28, 2007.

394. Quoted in *foxnews.com.* "Ex-Alabama Governor, Don Siegelman, HealthSouth CEO Get 7 Years in Prison," June 28, 2007.

395. Roberts, Paul Craig. "Going to Jail For Being a Democrat: How Alabama Gov. Don Siegelman Got Roved." *counterpunch.com,* March 3, 2008.

396. *Ibid.*

397. Elliott, Janet. "Morales Guilty of Fraud, Tax Charges." *Houston Chronicle.* July 18, 2003: 1A, 14A.

398. *Ibid.*

399. Herman, Ken and Hafetz, David. "Morales Pleads Guilty to Mail Fraud, Tax Evasion." *statesman.com,* July 17, 2003.

400. King, Michael. "Naked City." *austinchronicle.com,* August 16, 2003.

401. *Ibid.*

402. Benson, Josh. "IN PERSON: Smiling Through the Storm." *nytimes.com,* February 27, 2005.

403. Landfield, Steven. "Little Hope For Change With the Foxes Still in Charge." *njjewishnews.com,* April 6, 2006.

404. Quoted in Rothma, C.J. "Former Sen. Wayne Bryant Is Found Guilty in Corruption Case." *nj.com,* November 19, 2008.

405. Graber, Trish. "Former Sen. Wayne Bryant Gets Four Years in Prison for Bribery, Fraud." *nj.com,* July 25, 2009.

406. *cnn.com.* "Ex-Governor Guilty of Racketeering," April 18, 2006.

407. Edsall, Thomas B. and Lydersen, Kari. "Ryan Guilty of Corruption." *washingtonpost.com,* April 19, 2006.

408. *Ibid.*

409. Robinson, Mike. "Former Illinois Governor Guilty in Corruption Case." *seattletimes.com,* April 16, 2006.

410. Robinson, Mike. "Ex-Governor of Illinois Given 6 1/2 Year Term." *Houston Chronicle,* September 7, 2006: A3.

411. Davey, Monica and Ruethling, Gretchen. "Former Illinois Governor Is Convicted in Graft Case." *nytimes.com,* April 17, 2006.

412. *counterpunch.org.* "Governor Ryan Nominated for Nobel Prize," January 17, 2003.

413. Quoted in O'Connor, Matt and Bush, Rudolph. "Ryan Convicted in Corruption Trial." *Chicago Tribune* (online), April 17, 2006.

414. Quoted in Robinson, *op. cit.*

415. Witt, Elder. "Is Government Full of Crooks, or Are We Just Better at Finding Them?" *Governing,* September 1989: 33–38.

416. *Ibid.*

417. *Ibid.*

418. Marvin, Mary Jo. "Swindles of the 1990s: Con Artists Are Thriving." *USA Today Magazine,* September 1994: 80–84.

419. *Houston Chronicle.* "Former JP Sentenced." December 6, 1995: p. 19A.

420. *Washington Post.* "Rep. Hinshaw Gets 1–14 Years in Jail." February 25, 1976: p. A12.

421. Quoted in *Ibid.*, p. A 12.

422. Callow, Alexander. *The City Boss in America.* New York: Oxford University Press, 1976.

423. "Boodle" came from boedel, the Dutch word for property. Sometime after Nieuw Amsterdam became New York City, "boodle" was applied specifically to property misappropriated by politicians—particularly New York politicians. (Logan, Andy. "Around City Hall: Upstairs, Downstairs." *The New Yorker,* August 21, 1989: 80–86.)

424. Callow, Alexander B. *The Tweed Ring.* New York: Oxford University Press, 1966.

425. Enright, Richard T. *Capone's Chicago.* Lakeville, MN: Northstar Mascher Books, 1987.

426. Miller, Richard L. *Truman: The Rise to Power.* New York: McGraw-Hill, 1986.

427. Callow, 1976, *op. cit.*, p. 33.

428. Pare, Terence P. "The Big Sleaze in Muni Bonds." *Fortune* 132, August 7, 1995: 113–120.

429. Fonce-Olivas, Tammy. "Ex-Bankers' Bribery Led to $1.5 Billion of Work in EP." *elpasotimes.com,* December 31, 2007.

430. *Ibid.*, p. 141.

431. Witt, Elder. "Is Government Full of Crooks, or Are We Just Better at Finding Them?" *Governing* 2, 1989: 32–38.

432. Witt, *op. cit.*

433. Groson, Lindsey. "Corruption Is Brotherly in Philadelphia." *New York Times,* November 11, 1986: p. E4.

434. Applebome, Peter. "Scandal Casts Shadow Over Atlanta Mayoral Race." *New York Times,* November 18, 1993: p. A16.

435. Hicks, Jonathan. "Subpoena Jolts Black Mayors Meeting." *New York Times,* April 27, 1991: p. 8.

436. *New York Times.* "After 5 Years, Case Against Former Mayor of San Diego is Resolved." January 2, 1991: p. A14.

437. *USA Today.* "Miami City Official Pleads Guilty." October 10, 1996: p. 3A. Bacon, John. "Miami Bribe." *USA Today,* October 30, 1996: p. 3A.

438. Witt, *op. cit.*

439. *New York Times.* "Former Mayor Gets 5 1/2 Years for Extortion." February 2, 1992: p. B10.

440. *Houston Chronicle.* "Congressman from California Convicted of Extortion, Resigns." December 13, 1995: p. 14A.

441. *The Economist.* "New York: Unhappy Days Are Here Again." February 1, 1986: p. 21.

442. O'Connor, Colleen and McKillop, Peter. "The Big Apple Is Beset by Rotten Apples." *Newsweek* 109, March 30, 1987: p. 30.

443. Hornblower, Margot. "Scandals Unfold in New York." *Washington Post,* March 10, 1986: p. A6.

444. Newfield, Jack and Barrett, Wayne. *City for Sale: Ed Koch and the Betrayal of New York.* New York: Harper & Row, 1988.

445. Barrett, Wayne. "The Scandal that Won't Go Away." *Village Voice,* April 13, 1993: pp. 10–12, 31–37.

446. Hornblower, Margot. "Manes Protégé Indicted in Bribery Case." *Washington Post,* February 25, 1986: p. A3.

447. Hornblower, March 10, 1986, *op. cit.*

448. Weiss, Phillip. "Koch and the Bosses." *The New Republic* 194, March 10, 1986: 12–15.

449. McFadden, Robert D. "Manes Is a Suicide, Stabbing Himself at Home in Queens." *New York Times,* March 14, 1986: A1, B20.

450. *New York Times.* "Corruption Trial: A Clash of Tactics." November 23, 1986: p. 42.

451. Weiss, *op. cit.*, p. 14

452. Lynn, Frank. "Bronx Chief Quits and Friedman Gets 12-Year Sentence." *New York Times,* March 12, 1987: pp. A1, B14.

453. Meislin, Richard J. "A Not Very Pretty Picture of the City." *New York Times,* November 9, 1986: p. E4.

454. *latimes.com.* "Bridgeport Mayor Guilty of Corruption Charges," May 20, 2003.

455. Cowan, Alison Leigh. "Federal Judge Sentences Former Mayor of Bridgeport to 9 Years in Corruption Case." *nytimes.com,* July 2, 2003.

456. Quoted in *Ibid.*

457. Eshelman, Christopher. "Former Mayor Jim Hayes Found Guilty on 16 Counts." *newsminer.com,* February 14, 2008. United States Attorney, District of Alaska. "Former Fairbanks Mayor Found Guilty of Conspiracy, Misapplication of Government Grant Funds, Money Laundering and Filing False Tax Returns." February 14, 2008.

458. Eshelman, Christopher. "Former Fairbanks Mayor Jim Hayes, Wife Report to Prison in Texas." *newsminer.com,* June 16, 2008. *Houston Chronicle.* "Ex-Mayor and Wife to Serve Time," May 3, 2008: A16. United States Attorney, District of Alaska. "Former Fairbanks Mayor and Wife Sentenced to Federal Prison For Conspiracy, Misapplication of Governmental Grant Funds, Money Laundering and Filing False Tax Returns." May 2, 2008.

459. *foxnews.com.* "Jury Convicts Ex-New Jersey Mayor of Corruption," April 16, 2008.

460. *wcbstv.com.* "Ex-Newark Mayor Sharpe James Guilty of Corruption," April 16, 2008.

461. Quoted in Jones, Richard G. "Former Mayor Guilty of Fraud in Newark Sales." *nytimes.com,* April 17, 2008.

462. Feuer, Alan and Schweber, Nate. "Former Newark Mayor Is Sentenced to 27 Months." *nytimes.com,* July 30, 2008.

463. Quoted in *foxnews.com.* "Former Newark, N.J. Mayor Sharpe James Sentenced to 2 Years, 3 Months in Federal Prison." July 29, 2008.

464. Jones, *op. cit.*

465. *Ibid.*

466. Rao, Mythili. "Ex-mayor Convicted in Land-for-Love Case." *cnn.com,* April 16, 2008.

467. *nj.com.* "Orange Mayor Mims Hackett Pleads Guilty to Corruption Charge," May 27, 2008. *Houston Chronicle.* "Corruption Probe Snares Mayor," May 28, 2008: A7.

468. Chen, David. "Caught in Sting, Mayor and Ex-Lawmaker Pleads Guilty in 2 Courts." *nytimes.com,* May 28, 2008. Office of the Attorney General (press release). "Orange Mayor Mims Hackett, Jr. Pleads Guilty to State Charge of Official Misconduct & Federal Charge of Attempted Extortion." May 27, 2008.

469. Dilworth, Kevin. "Mims Hackett Sentenced to 9 Months in Federal Prison." *nj.com,* October 21, 2008.

470. Office of the Attorney General (press release). "Former Orange Mayor Mims Hackett Jr. Sentenced to Five Years in Prison for Official Misconduct in Case Filed by Attorney General." January 23, 2009.

471. Levine, Rhonda. "Newark's Former Mayor, Sharpe James, Convicted of Fraud." *associatedcontent.com,* April 16, 2008.

472. Coleman, 1994, *op. cit.*

473. Sherman, Lawrence W. *Scandal and Reform: Controlling Police Corruption.* Berkeley: University of California Press, 1978.

474. Nelson, Jill. "Blue Plague." *New York Times.* May 20, 1994: p. 27.

475. *New York Times.* "Chicago Police Officer Guilty." August 11, 1994: p. 13A.

476. Graves, Rachel. "5 HPD Officers Charged in Bribery Racket." *Houston Chronicle,* July 12, 2003: 1A, 17A.

477. *New York Times.* "Police Union Officials Guilty in Philadelphia." February 19, 1995: p. 39. *Houston Chronicle.* "Philadelphia Police Scandal Keeps Growing." March 21, 1996: p. 12A. Smith, Jim. "Judge Sends Message: Corrupt Officers Get Long Prison Sentences." April 17, 1996: p. 14A.

478. *Newsweek.* "A Detroit Police Corruption Probe." Vol. 114, December 18, 1989: p. 30. See also: *The Economist.* "Secret Self-Service?" February 16, 1991: p. 23.

479. Gladwell, Malcolm. "In Drug War, Crime Sometimes Wears a Badge." *Washington Post,* May 19, 1994: pp. A1, A16.

480. Locy, Toni. "Ex-Officer Says Greed Guided Him into Net of Drug Sting." *Washington Post,* October 20, 1994: pp. C1, C8. See also: Duggan, Paul. "D.C. Officers Plead Guilty in Drug Case." *Washington Post.* April 17, 1994: p. B3; Locy, Toni. "3 D.C. Officers Found Guilty in Corruption Case." *Washington Post.* November 19, 1994: p. B1; Harmon, John, Taylor, Troy, and Washington, Dwayne. "Stiff Sentences for Crooked Cops." *Washington Post.* May 29, 1995: p. A 14.

481. Hollandsworth, Skip. "The Seduction of Cruiser and Bruiser." *Texas Monthly,* September 1993: 128–141.

482. Sechrest, Dale and Burns, Pamela. "Police Corruption: The Miami Case." *Criminal Justice and Behavior* 19: 294–313.

483. *Jet.* "First Black Woman to Run a Big City Police Force Cracks Down on Corruption." Vol. 88, October 2, 1995: 8–13.

484. *New York Times.* "9 New Orleans Officers Are Indicted in U.S. Drug Case." December 8, 1994: p. 18; Sewell, Dan. "New Orleans Police Officers Find Themselves Being Policed." *Houston Chronicle,* April 21, 1996: p. 25A.

485. *Houston Chronicle.* "Investigation to Zero In on L.A. Police." September 22, 1999: p. 10A. Lelyveld, Nita. "Latest LAPD Scandal Taints City's Criminal-Justice System." *Houston Chronicle.* September 26, 1999: p. 21A. *USA Today.* "Poor Supervision, LAPD Culture Faulted in Scandal." March 2, 2000: p. 3A.

486. Gladwell, *op. cit.*

487. Haygood, Wil. "Billy Celester's Hard Rise, Swift, Fall." *Boston Globe,* August 11, 1996: pp. A1, A24.

488. Johnson, Kevin. "New Breed of Bad Cop Sells Badge, Public Trust." *USA Today.* April 16, 1998: p. 8A.

489. Dillow, Gordon. "15 Officers Disciplined in Inglewood." *Los Angeles Times,* May 25, 1994: p. B1.

490. O'Harrow, Robert, Jr. "Va. Sheriff Target of Probe Commits Suicide." *Washington Post,* January 23, 1992: pp. B1, B6.

491. Bentayou, *op. cit.*

492. Johnson, *op. cit.*

493. Reich, Kenneth. "3 More Former Deputies Guilty in Skimming." *Los Angeles Times,* August 30, 1994: pp. B1, B4.

494. Morganthau, Tom. "Why Good Cops Go Bad." *Newsweek* 124, December 19, 1994: 30–34.

495. Barker, Thomas and Roebuck, Julian. *An Empirical Typology of Police Corruption: A Study in Organizational Deviance.* Springfield, IL: Charles C. Thomas, 1973.

496. Reiss, Albert J., Jr. *The Police and the Public.* New Haven: Yale University Press, 1972.

497. Quoted in Deutsch, Albert. *The Trouble with Cops.* Boston: Crown, 1955; 47–48.

498. Cooksey, Otis E. "Corruption: A Continuing Challenge for Law Enforcement." *FBI Law Enforcement Bulletin,* September 1991: 5–9.

499. Stern, Mort. "What Makes a Policeman Go Wrong?" *Journal of Criminal Law, Criminology and Police Science* 63, 1992: 98–101.

500. Roebuck, Julian and Barker, Thomas. "A Typology of Police Corruption." *Social Problems* 21, 1974: p. 429.

501. Barker and Roebuck, *op. cit.*

502. *Ibid.*

503. Burnham, David. "How Corruption Is Built into the System—and a Few Ideas for what to Do about It." *New York* 119, September 21, 1970: 1–18.

504. Cook, Fred J. "The Pusher Cop: The Institutionalizing of Police Corruption." *New York,* August 16, 1971: 22–30.

505. Barker and Roebuck, *op. cit.*, p. 34.

506. Roebuck and Barker, *op. cit.*

507. Messick, Hank. *Syndicate in the Sun.* New York: MacMillan, 1968.

508. Roebuck and Barker, *op. cit.*

509. Skolnick, Jerome H. *Justice Without Trial: Law Enforcement in Democratic Society.* New York: John Wiley, 1966: p. 208.

510. Carter, David L. "Drug-Related Corruption of Police Officers: A Contemporary Typology." *Journal of Criminal Justice* 18, 1990: p. 93.

511. Barker and Roebuck, *op. cit.*, p. 28.

512. Coleman, 1994, *op. cit.*, p. 45.

513. Johnston, Michael. Political *Corruption and Public Policy in America*. Monterey, CA: Brooks/Cole, 1982; p. 85.

514. *Ibid.*

515. Bragg, Rick. "Blue Wall of Silence: Graft Shielded Behind Old Code." *New York Times,* April 26, 1994: pp. B1, B2.

516. Collins, Allyson. "Justice Won't Prevail Until Blue Wall of Police Silence Comes Down." *Houston Chronicle.* June 13, 1999: p. 4C.

517. *Ibid.*

518. *Ibid.*

519. *Ibid.*, p. B1.

520. Daly, Robert. *Prince of the City: The True Story of a Cop Who Knew Too Much.* Boston: Houghton Mifflin, 1978; p. 311.

521. Bragg, *op. cit.*, p. B2.

522. *Ibid.*, p. B2.

523. *Ibid.*, p. B2.

524. Hoover, Ken. "S.F. Cop Refuses to Testify in Sex Assault Case." *San Francisco Chronicle.* April 2, 1997: p. A15.

525. *Ibid.*, p. B2.

526. Carter, *op. cit.*, p. 95.

527. Coleman, 1987, p. 95.

528. Lefkowitz, Joel. "Psychological Attributes of Policemen: A Review of Research and Opinion." *Journal of Social Issues* 31, 1975: 7–20.

529. Johnston, *op. cit.*, p. 83.

530. Westley, William A. *Violence and the Police.* Cambridge, MA: M.I.T. Press, 1970.

531. Coleman, 1994, *op. cit.*, p. 45.

532. Krauss, Clifford. "Police Problems' Scale Eludes Senior Officials." *New York Times,* May 9, 1994: p. B3.

533. Carter, *op. cit.*

534. Quoted in Carter, *op. cit.*, p. 93.

535. Lardner, James. "The Whistle-Blower—Part I." *The New Yorker* 69, July 5, 1993: 52–56.

536. Williams' unusual nickname came from his feisty declaration that there was more law at the end of his nightstick than in all the statute books.

537. *Ibid.*, p. 58.

538. Hirschorn, Michael. "Good Cop, Bad Cop." *New York* 27, July 11, 1994: p. 15,

539. *Ibid.*

540. *New York Times.* "What the Census Reveals." May 2, 1894: p. 7.

541. Jeffers, H. Paul. *Commissioner Roosevelt: The Story of Theodore Roosevelt and the New York City Police, 1895–1897.* New York: Wiley, 1994.

542. Davis, Kenneth S. *FDR: The New York Years 1928–1933.* New York: Random House, 1985.

543. Krauss, Clifford. "Police Corruption in New York: As Expected, a Blight Returns." *New York Times,* March 21, 1994: p. B3.

544. The NYPD is by far the largest police department in the United States—more than 2 1/2 times bigger than the second largest force, Chicago's.

545. Conklin, William R. "Gross Gets 12-Year Term: Police Graft Story Bared." *New York Times,* September 28, 1951: pp. 1, 22.

546. Krauss, March 7, 1994, *op. cit.*

547. *Newsweek.* "Cops on the Take." November 1, 1971: p. 43.

548. Krauss, March 7, 1994, *op. cit.*

549. *Newsweek,* November 1, 1971, *op. cit.*, p. 43.

550. Commission to Investigate Allegations of Police Corruption in New York City. "Police Corruption in New York: The Knapp Commission." In M. David Ermann and Richard J. Lundman (Eds.), *Corporate and Governmental Deviance: Problems of Organizational Behavior in Contemporary Society* (Second Edition). New York: Oxford University Press, 1982: 155–166.

551. *Newsweek,* November 1, 1971, *op. cit.*

552. Lardner, James. "The Whistle-Blower—Part II." *The New Yorker* 69, July 12, 1993: 39–59.

553. Maas, Peter. *Serpico: The Cop Who Defied the System. New York:* Viking Press, 1973. See also: *New York.* "Serpico Testifies." Vol. 26, April 19, 1993: p. 130.

554. Buckley, Tom. "Murphy Among the 'Meat Eaters'." *New York Times Magazine,* December 19, 1971: pp. 11, 42, 44–49.

555. Morganthau, *op. cit.*, p. 30.

556. Buckley, *op. cit.*

557. Lacayo, Richard. "Cops and Robbers." *Time* 142, October 11, 1993: p. 43.

558. *Ibid.*, p. 43.

559. Bonfante, Jordan. "Cops and Robbers." *Time* 142, October 11, 1993: 42–43.

560. Treaster, Joseph B. "Corruption in Uniform: The Dowd Case; Officer Flaunted Corruption and His Superiors Ignored It." *New York Times,* July 7, 1994: p. 1.

561. Armao, Jospeh and Cornfeld, Leslie U. "How to Police the Police." *Newsweek* 124, December 19, 1994: p. 34.

562. Treaster, *op. cit.*, p. 1.

563. Lacayo, *op. cit.*, p. 43.

564. Treaster, Joseph B. "Convicted Police Officer Receives a Sentence of at Least 11 Years." *New York Times,* July 12, 1994: p. 1.

565. Quoted in *Ibid.*, p. 1.

566. Wolff, Craig. "Corruption in Uniform: Chronology; Tracking Police Corruption over the Years." *New York Times,* July 7, 1994: p. B3.

567. *New York Times.* "3 Officers Will Face Shakedown Charges." March 8, 1994: p. B3.

568. *The Economist.* "The Police: NYPD Blues." April 30, 1994: 29–30.

569. Gladwell, *op. cit.*, p. A1.

570. *Ibid.*, p. A1.

571. Krauss, Clifford. "Officers Held in Police Sting after Robbery Is Videotaped." *New York Times,* March 19, 1994: pp. 1, 27.

572. Krauss, Clifford. "11 More Officers Taken off Duties in 30th Precinct." *New York Times,* May 5, 1994: pp. A1, B4.

573. *The Economist,* April 30, 1994, *op. cit.*

574. Pooley, Eric. "Has Bill Bratton Gone Soft?" *New York* 27, July 11, 1994: 24–26.

575. *New York Times.* "Former 39th Precinct Officer Pleads Guilty." December 20, 1994: p. 6.

576. Holloway, Lynette. "Equality on Police Force: Women Arrested Too." *New York Times,* October 2, 1994: p. 35.

577. Krauss, Clifford. "14 More Officers Arrested at a Shaken 30th Precinct." *New York Times,* September 29, 1994: pp. A1, B3.

578. Sullivan, John. "Ex-Sergeant Is Sentenced In Police Corruption Case." *New York Times.* June 17, 1997: p. B3.

579. Krauss, Clifford. "At 30th Precinct, 2 Supervisors' Rise and Fall." *New York Times,* September 30, 1994: pp. B1, B3.

580. Armao, Joseph and Cornfeld, Leslie U. "When Cops Betray Their Communities." *Newsweek* 124, December 19, 1994: p. 32.

581. Quoted in Krauss, Clifford. "On Their Watch: 30th Precinct Scandal Raises Issues on the Accountability of Supervisors." *New York Times,* October 3, 1994: p. B8.

582. Krauss, Clifford. "Corruption in Uniform: The Overview; 2-Year Corruption Inquiry Finds a 'Willful Blindness' in New York's Police Dept." *New York Times,* July 7, 1994: p. 1.

583. *The Economist,* April 30, 1994, *op. cit.*

584. *Ibid.*, p. 30.

585. Treaster, Joseph B. "Mollen Panel Says Buck Stops with Top Officers." *New York Times,* July 10, 1994: p. 21.

586. Krauss, Clifford. "16 Officers Indicted in Brutality in Bronx." *New York Times,* May 4, 1995: p. A4.

587. It has been argued for years that civilian review boards are one of the most effective ways to eliminate police misconduct. See, for example: Glazer, Sarah. "Police Corruption: Can Brutality and Other Misconduct Be Rooted Out?" *CQ Researcher* 5, November 24, 1995: pp. 1041, 1043.

588. Mollen Commission. "Excerpts." *New York Times,* July 7, 1994: p. B2.

11

Medical Crime

There can be little doubt that the U.S. health care system is vulnerable to fraud, waste, and abuse. Given the wide array of private and public services, insurance plans, medical corporations, and treatment facilities, it is very difficult to pinpoint losses due to crime in the gargantuan, trillion-dollar-a-year health care industry—an industry that consumes 15.2 percent of our gross national product, making it the *largest business in the country*.[1] But even in the absence of a precise estimate, the sheer cost of medical care in America assures that even relatively small amounts of crime add up to illicit profits of sizable magnitude. The FBI estimates that between 3 and 10 percent of all health care expenditures are lost to fraud. Currently, those expenditures total $2.4 trillion annually. Using the upper bound, this means that the FBI estimates a staggering $240 billion a year[2] is stolen from taxpayers and insurers as a result of health care fraud[3] on the part of physicians and, to a lesser extent, other providers such as dentists,[4] pharmacists,[5] psychologists,[6] chiropractors,[7] and podiatrists.[8] Another estimate provided by the Institute of Medicine places U.S. healthcare fraud at a much higher level: *$750 billion a year*.[9] This is *over a half-trillion dollars* more than the FBI estimate. Regardless of the actual cost, it seems clear that health care fraud alone accounts for a large proportion of the total cost of white-collar crime in the United States each year. Moreover, the dollars drained have serious physical consequences as well—especially for the most needy among us, who depend on government benefit programs such as Medicaid and Medicare.

A notorious Southern California case, one of the largest health fraud operations in history, uncovered a gang of unscrupulous doctors and medical entrepreneurs. Mobile laboratories offered "free" tests, and clinics provided misrepresented services and bogus diagnoses in a potential billion-dollar false billing scheme to defraud health insurance companies. Masterminded by Michael and David Smushkevich, two Russian immigrant brothers, the conspiracy reached its peak between 1986 and 1988 when investigators found that it encompassed 1,000 separate companies and 400 bank accounts around the world.[10] The ring included a dozen people who set up hundreds of phony corporations and fake businesses to bill insurance companies and launder the money received from them.

Patients were solicited from "boiler rooms," where slick telemarketers "pitched" full physical examinations with state-of-the-art diagnostics at little or no fee. The exams were conducted in "rolling labs" at such places as health clubs, shopping malls, and retirement homes. Medical charts were falsified to make it appear that each test was essential. In one case, a two-hour examination of an Irvine, California, woman resulted in $7,500 in billings—despite the fact that she was not feeling ill and had no physical symptoms.[11] Since most insurance policies do not cover preventive procedures, patients were required to fill out medical history forms that were later "doctored" to show that the tests were medically necessary, and thus eligible for payment. Sometimes diagnostic tests were performed *before* the patient had even been examined.

About $50 million was paid by government and private insurers before the scam was detected. It unraveled, ironically, when a physician working for Pacific Mutual Insurance received a telephone solicitation from one of the boiler rooms. When he went for his "free" examination, he filled out a medical history form without being asked anything about his current health. Soon thereafter, his insurance company (and employer) received a bill for $7,500, with diagnoses showing high blood pressure, diabetes, heart disease, and cancer. The doctor had none of those conditions. Authorities raided the Smushkevichs' offices and clinics eight months later, after they received other similar complaints of fraudulent diagnoses.

One of the physicians involved in the conspiracy, Dr. William O. Kuperschmidt, was convicted on charges of mail fraud, money laundering, and racketeering, slapped with a huge $50 million fine, and ordered to forfeit two properties and all assets of a medical enterprise that included three clinics operating in southern California. Michael Smushkevich, the alleged ringleader, denied any criminal wrongdoing, arguing that the case should be handled in civil court "and focus on who determines what tests were 'medically necessary.'"[12] David Smushkevich fled to Amsterdam, while his attorney claimed that his fugitive client was "absolutely" innocent.[13] In 1993, however, both brothers were found "absolutely" guilty of multiple fraud charges.[14]

Insurers were not the only victims of the Smushkevich scam, however. There was a ripple effect that unjustly penalized innocent patients as well. One California chiropractor, who was in excellent health and an active athlete, had his application for a life insurance policy rejected months after his medical record had been smeared with unfounded diagnoses, including heart defects and obstructive pulmonary emphysema. It took him two years to clear his record.

In 2005, federal and state law enforcement officials alleged that California clinics paid thousands of patients to undergo unnecessary surgical procedures, then billed insurers and employers for as much as $1.3 billion for fraudulent medical services.[15] The FBI estimates that $350 million in bogus claims had already been paid by insurance companies to surgical clinics in Southern California.[16] Investigators believe that a complex fraud network had been set up, involving dozens of doctors, about 100 clinics, and thousands of patients willing to endure unnecessary surgery in exchange for payment.[17]

According to the chief of the FBI's health care fraud unit, clinics initially focused on Vietnamese patients, whom they recruited through newspaper ads and in nail salons. Later, participating clinics used networks of recruiters traveling the country in search of patients, who were paid between $200 and $2,000 to have totally unneeded colonoscopies or surgeries. Doctors were accused of creating false diagnoses and in some cases coaching patients on how to lie about their supposed illnesses if ever questioned by investigators.[18] "Thousands of patients were flown to California from 44 states, Puerto Rico, and the District of Columbia over three years, and many were given free or discounted cosmetic surgeries instead of cash payments."[19] Officials have dubbed the alleged fraud operation "Rent-a-Patient."[20]

Health care rip-offs have substantial secondary effects on consumers and businesses in terms of higher costs for government health programs and increases in insurance premiums. The traditional medical insurance reimbursement fraud, involving a single perpetrator, has changed, according to authorities, and more sophisticated and costly crimes involving "cartel-type frauds" are becoming more commonplace. Criminal organizations of that type have been found all across the country.[21]

In this chapter we will examine some of the major forms of medical crimes, relate a sample of illustrative case histories, and discuss enforcement problems as well as emerging areas for future concern.

EQUIPMENT SALES

Some of the most devious operators in the health care field have treated government programs such as Medicare, the government health program for the elderly, like open checkbooks. Senior citizens, the inveterate targets of so many forms of consumer fraud, are particularly susceptible to scams involving the marketing of "durable medical products" such as seat lift chairs, oxygen concentrators, home dialysis systems, and other sometimes unnecessary equipment at inflated costs. Medicare can be an easy mark. It often fails to account for the legitimacy of suppliers, since no documentation is required.[22] A 2007 report from the Government Accounting Office said that Medicare improperly paid about $700 million for medical equipment and supplies from 2005 to 2006. While some of the questionable payments were the result of mistakes made by legitimate companies, many stemmed from fraud and abuse.[23] Medicare scammers actually prefer equipment to drugs because drugs are more closely monitored.[24]

One case in Philadelphia, involving over 2,200 fraudulent claims filed in 1988 and 1989, bilked Medicare out of millions of dollars. The companies filing the false claims, Federal Home Care and Home Health Products, were owned by Mark Mickman, the former proprietor of a television rental business. While issuing a court injunction in 1989, a federal judge labeled Mickman's operation "an out and out scam."[25] Mickman employed teenage girls in a telemarketing scheme operated out of shopping centers in the Philadelphia area. The girls called Medicare beneficiaries who had responded to an ad offering a "free Medicare covered package." The telemarketers would then obtain Medicare numbers and ask if they had any physical conditions or problems. If they did, Mickman's firm "could help." Although Medicare requires a 20 percent co-payment, they were told that Medicare would cover 100 percent of the cost. In a bench opinion, Judge Donald Van Artsdalen said: "Teenagers who had no medical training were making medical diagnoses upon which sophisticated, expensive equipment was being purchased for patients that neither needed nor wanted the equipment."[26]

The scam worked because doctors, whose authorization is needed for such claims, signed precompleted forms, allowing Mickman to bill Medicare successfully. Rip-off artists sometimes fake the signatures or pay off corrupt doctors to sign forms. In other instances, doctors may sign the forms mistakenly or succumb to pressure from patients to do so.

In some frauds the equipment is not only nonessential, but outrageously overpriced as well. A chunk of flimsy foam that cost a supplier about $28 was charged to Medicare as a $900 "dry floatation mattress" for bedsores. Another profit-gouging item is a transcutaneous electronic nerve stimulator which generates electrical impulses that can control pain. The components could be bought at Radio Shack for about $50, but Medicare is sometimes billed as much as $500 per unit.[27] Prices for equipment also vary by region, allowing suppliers to set up "branch offices" that are little more than mail drops in the more profitable states.[28]

Besides the outright crooks who have intentionally conducted business in a fraudulent manner, there are firms which aggressively market their products to unsuspecting patients, while keeping barely within the technical boundaries of current law. In a variation of the classic "bait and switch" technique, medical equipment companies compile lists of beneficiaries—usually those enrolled in Medicare—by placing ads which offer free gifts or services. High-pressure salespersons call on the beneficiaries, find out their health conditions and needs, then sell them equipment and supplies. Obviously, rules which allow such deceptive practices invite fraud and abuse. As an official in the California Medical Association put it, "There's no limit to what an American entrepreneur can conjure up to sell products."[29]

A more recent medical equipment case involved CG Nutritionals, a subsidiary of Abbott Laboratories. The company pleaded guilty in federal court to obstructing a criminal health care investigation. It agreed to pay $600 million in fines.[30] "The settlement stems from Operation Headwaters, a broad federal inquiry into fraudulent sales of tube-feeding gear and other medical equipment."[31] Prosecutors set up a phony store in Illinois, and agents posing as retailers of medical devices videotaped Abbott salespeople urging them to overcharge Medicare.[32]

In mid-2003, federal authorities began handing down fraud indictments involving motorized wheelchairs and scooters. According to investigators, medical equipment companies had been combing senior centers across Texas and Louisiana for more than a year, bringing people to Houston by the busload for wheelchairs they often did not need.[33] "'Recruiters' get a fee for bringing people in . . . In some cases, doctors get a kickback for signing a 'certificate of medical necessity' after a brief checkup."[34] Motorized wheelchairs are among the most expensive medical equipment, and the revenue they generate has led to an explosion of illegality. In 2000, Medicare paid $49 million for motorized wheelchairs and scooters. By 2002, that figure had more than tripled to $168 million.[35] A 2005 report from the Government Accounting Office revealed that Medicare was overcharged for durable medical equipment, including motorized wheelchairs and scooters, by $900 million—about 10 percent of the total payments, much if not all due to fraud.[36]

Medicare is supposed to pay for a motorized chair only for patients who would otherwise be bedridden and who cannot operate a manual chair. However, the FBI has interviewed scores of elderly people who could walk without canes or walkers, yet received offers of free wheelchairs or scooters. One elderly man reportedly took his to a pawn shop and hocked it for $300.[37]

Prosecutors also alleged that the companies under investigation routinely overcharge Medicare by sending patients cheaper chairs than those billed for. As the investigation moves through other states, the total cost of this fraud is expected to be immense. According to the U.S. Attorney for Texas: "The harder we look, the more we see."[38]

One of the biggest of the Texas cases involved Dr. Anant Mauskar of Houston, who was convicted in federal court of prescribing expensive motorized wheelchairs for patients who didn't need them—in return for kickbacks of $200 each. Marketers recruited patients for Mauskar, then billed Medicare up to $7,000 for the prescribed wheelchairs. The crooked companies gave patients cheaper motorized scooters and pocketed the difference—sometimes as much as $5,000.[39] Some of the patients who were transported to Dr. Mauskar's clinic were not even examined. As a result of this and other schemes, Mauskar collected $1.4 million from Medicare.[40] In 2006, 73-year-old Anant Mauskar was sentenced to more than 11 years in prison.[41]

In 2007, the Center for Medicare & Medicaid Services (CMS), the HHS agency that pays the bills, announced a two-year effort to crack down on fraudulent medical suppliers. The initiative focused on the "high risk" areas of South Florida and Southern California, identified as "hotbeds" of durable medical equipment scammers. The Department of Health and Human Services and the Department of Justice formed a Medicare Fraud Strike Force. A similar initiative the previous year resulted in 770 suppliers having their billing privileges revoked. In the first three months of the new initiative, 56 individuals in South Florida were charged with fraudulently billing Medicare for more than $258 million.[42]

In 2008, the CMS expanded its initiative to more than 70 metropolitan areas.[43] In late December, the agency further announced that suppliers must obtain surety bonds. "[T]hat means these companies will have to pay around $1,500 each in return for a performance bond that guarantees Medicare up to $50,000 if the supplier doesn't ultimately meet its obligations to the agency."[44]

One way scammers have squeezed money out of Medicare is by using the provider ID numbers of dead doctors. The findings of a congressional investigation released in 2008 reported that equipment suppliers, between 2000 and 2007, used the ID numbers of 1,500 deceased physicians to submit bills for such devices as wheelchairs and oxygen equipment. Some of these doctors had been dead for as long as 15 years before the suppliers' claims were filed.[45] "One doctor's number was used 484 times from 2003 to 2006, even though the physician died in 1999 . . . netting suppliers $544,789."[46] One member of the Senate Homeland Security and Governmental Affairs Committee declared: "Using the ID numbers of dead doctors, these scam artists have treated Medicare like an ATM machine."[47]

Also in 2008, a federal jury convicted Gustavo Smith for operating multiple Medicare fraud schemes. Smith owned Medstar, a Miami pharmacy that in one year had billed $3 million for durable medical equipment, including negative pressure wound pumps and wound care supplies. At Smith's trial, the jury heard testimony from patients, whose names were used by Medstar to submit bills to Medicare. "The patients testified that they never received any equipment from Medstar and did not have a medical need for the equipment."[48] Several doctors, who supposedly wrote prescriptions for the equipment, also testified that they had never written those prescriptions and had never prescribed the types of equipment billed by Medstar.[49] Another Smith-owned company, Orthotics Filters, billed approximately $2.9 million in fraudulent claims to Medicare for the same wound pumps and wound supplies equipment being billed by Medstar. This equipment, likewise, was never actually provided to any Medicare beneficiaries.[50] Gustavo Smith was later sentenced to 10 years and 10 months in prison.[51]

Despite the increased enforcement efforts, however, the problem of durable medical equipment scams persists. In another 2008 case, cited by the GAO, "a fraudulent company billed Medicare for $4.4 million in supplies and services that were never delivered, ultimately receiving $2.2 million in payments."[52] A spokesman for the American Association for Homecare, which represents the medical supplies industry, said in 2008: "Medicare has done a terrible job of keeping criminals out of the system."[53] The executive director of the California Association of Medical Product Suppliers recently offered a gloomy assessment of the problem: "It's one of the most frustrating things in the industry. The fraud never seems to end."[54]

HOME CARE FRAUD

Home care services constitute a relatively new area for fraud by unscrupulous providers. The trend toward outpatient treatment, shorter hospital stays, and new technologies have led to a burgeoning home care industry. In fact, home health care is now considered the nation's fastest growing industry. "That growth has been driven by the large numbers of disabled and low-income people who want to spend their final years at home, as well as by government policies intended to encourage home health care as an alternative to more costly hospitals and nursing home care."[55] Like all thieves who follow the scent of money, rip-off artists have zeroed in on this lucrative market. The home care business, as one law enforcement official in New York put it, is "attracting the sharks."[56]

Medicare and Medicaid, the government insurance programs for the elderly and the poor, reportedly lose over $2 billion a year to home care fraud.[57] Private insurers undoubtedly lose many millions of dollars more. Home care fraud is particularly difficult to investigate, since it entails a plethoric menu of services provided in thousands of private residences. More than 12,500 companies provide such services, mostly to the aged.

One of the largest home care fraud cases was settled in New York in 1990 against Professional Care, Inc. An inside informant verified that the company had systematically over-billed the state Medicaid system. Medicaid is the federally mandated, but state-run, program that provides medical care for the indigent. During a four-year period, Professional Care was reimbursed for home care services performed by untrained workers, or in some instances, no workers at all. It was also found that many more hours were charged than were actually provided.[58] The firm pleaded guilty to grand larceny and falsification of business records, and its two highest officers were convicted of conspiracy. A total of $5.2 million in fines and restitution were levied.

In 1996, Jack and Margie Mills, owners of ABC Home Health Services—one of the giants of the industry, operating in 22 states—were convicted and imprisoned for bilking Medicare out of more than $14 million. The couple had lived a lavish lifestyle, replete with private jets, luxurious mansions, magnificent jewelry, exclusive country club membership, and world travel. The problem was that all of this opulence (and more) was paid for by taxpayers. The couple were adding extravagant personal expenses to the nearly $50 million a month that ABC was billing the government. Included in the fraudulent claims were their son's BMW. Prosecutors would later say that Jack Mills had used Medicare as his own private trust fund.[59]

There is also concern over the growing "home infusion services" market, in which companies provide for intravenous drugs and nutrients in the patient's residence. A 1991 New York study showed that home infusion companies sold drugs for between 157 percent and 1,066 percent more than retail pharmacies.[60] One New York company charged $9.84 for sterile water that costs $2 at a pharmacy.[61] In Washington, D.C., home infusion charges double annually—due in large part to drug markups as high as 2,000 percent.[62] A young Massachusetts cancer patient arranged to have his final round of chemotherapy administered at home by a private provider, so he would not miss his first day of college. His family received a bill for $6,450—more than ten times what a major Boston hospital had charged for each previous infusion.[63]

AIDS treatments account for one-quarter or more of total revenues at some infusion firms.[64] The New York City Department of Consumer Affairs has charged that price gouging is particularly blatant for victims of AIDS. For example, a nutritional supplement used by AIDS patients, which wholesales for about $1,300 a month, was billed as high as $10,000.[65] In Seattle, one AIDS patient's bill for 45 days of in-home intravenous medication to ward off blindness and infection came to $47,000.[66]

As one would expect, the bigger the state, the bigger the problem; and the two largest states have uncovered many cases of home care fraud:

NEW YORK   In 1995, Rony Flores, owner of Casa Care Services in New York, was convicted of defrauding Medicaid out of $1.25 million. Flores routinely billed Medicaid for bogus "care" provided by untrained, unqualified employees, many of them illegal immigrants.[67]

In 2007, New York Attorney General Andrew Cuomo announced an industry-wide investigation of home health care agencies, named Operation Home Alone. Home care services had accounted for $1.3 billion of the $35.7 billion spent on Medicaid in New York the previous year. Cuomo called the system "ripe for abuse."[68] New York's "confusing hodgepodge" of regulations and multiple enforcement agencies had resulted in "uneven levels of oversight."[69] In a statement,

Cuomo said: "The evidence we've obtained to date suggests endemic, persistent fraud and malfeasance at all levels of the home health care industry."[70]

In the preceding six months, Cuomo's Medicaid Fraud Control Unit had already implicated several home care aides, including a nurse, who was convicted of falsely billing Medicaid for $150,000 in services.[71] Another aide claimed to be working 24 hours a day while she was out of the state singing "Be My Love" to the judges of *American Idol*. One aide submitted bills for 36 hours a day; and yet another held a full-time job at a grocery store while claiming he was caring for his ailing father.[72]

In a scam known as a "50-50 split," companies conscript patients to hire improperly certified aides, and the companies bill Medicaid for help they never provided. The company and the patients then split the payments.[73]

One of Operation Home Alone's major successes was the case of two Brooklyn men, Nachem Singer and Ervin Rubenstein, who pleaded guilty in 2007 for their role in a scheme that defrauded Medicaid of over $12 million. Singer and Rubenstein operated Immediate Home Care, Inc., a company that employed unqualified, uncertified health aides.

"Medicaid requires home health care aides who primarily care for elderly patients, administer medication and provide services such as catheter care, colostomy care and wound care—to successfully complete a training program licensed by the Department of Health or the State Education Department. All aides must received a minimum of 75 hours of training, including sixteen hours of supervised practical training conducted by a registered nurse and complete a written test conducted in English."[74]

Some of the Immediate Home Care aides provided little or no actual care to patients but would bill for their time—sometimes 24 hours in a single day—and split the proceeds with Singer, Rubenstein, and their patients.[75]

CALIFORNIA   One scam in California, perpetrated against that state's Medicaid program (Medi-Cal), bilked the government out of $9.1 million. A three-year investigation led to charges against American Home Health Care Products, an Oakland-based company, as a result of false claims submitted to Medi-Cal between 1987 and 1988. The company had enticed patients to swap their five monthly Medi-Cal stickers, which are used for obtaining services, in exchange for "free" incontinence supplies. The company would later overcharge Medi-Cal for supplies delivered or make up fictitious orders. The firm also double-billed nursing homes for supplies, which Medi-Cal then paid for.[76]

Another major case occurred in 1995, when John Watts, Jr., owner of United Home Care Services in California, pleaded guilty of defrauding Medicare out of $1.5 million. Watts was a convicted cocaine dealer, who started United Home Care a year after his release from prison. It is indicative of the almost complete lack of regulation in the home care industry that his background was never checked when he applied for and received a California license to run a home care agency. His scam was to submit bills for services never provided to patients never seen. Most of his "patients," in fact, were already dead. Watts would later tell a Senate committee investigating health care fraud: "We didn't start out to do this. But it was just too easy."[77]

In late 2008, a grand jury found that fraud was rampant and "scam artists" were "embedded" in Los Angeles County's home health care program. The head of the District Attorney's Office Welfare Fraud Division conceded: "I think the extent of the fraud is greater than anyone ever realized."[78]

HOSPITAL FRAUDS

Hospital costs constitute the largest portion of the nation's health care expenditures. Anyone who has been hospitalized knows of the unbelievable costs of such familiar items as over-the-counter pain relievers or ordinary bandages. The usual answer given by administrators when they are questioned about what appears to be conspicuous price gouging can be summed up in one word: overhead. And, indeed, when hospital accounting departments must determine the amounts charged for services and items, they take into account the costs of the building, staff, equipment, insurance, and even the unpaid bills of former patients. So, what seems like highway robbery to patients and their families may sometimes be defensible hospital billings.

On the other hand, things that certain hospitals do inarguably constitute mendacious, or even outright criminal, behavior. Hospitals have been known to bill patients for "ghost services"—that is, nonexistent services. And if tests are done incorrectly, the patient can end up footing the bill for the hospital's mistakes. Multiple billings may also occur, where patients are charged more than once for the same service, sometimes from different departments. Hospitals have also been known to "upcode," a practice in which facts of the actual treatment are intentionally altered so that insurance companies will pay the maximum amount for the procedure performed. Other billing tricks known as "fragmentation" or "unbundling" occur as well, whereby a number of charges can be made from what is usually one single less expensive charge for services or procedures.

"Cost shifting" is a technique which hospitals use to attract patients by offering reasonable room rates but then charging sky-high prices for ancillary items. Congressional hearings on the pricing policies of 77 Humana hospitals nationwide revealed that the chain routinely charged $9 for Tylenol tablets, $455 for nursing bras, $104 for $8 sets of crutches, $45 for saline solution which costs the hospital 81 cents, and $1,206 for esophagus tubes which wholesale for $152.[79]

As rapacious as these practices are, hospitals have also been known to engage in even more organized and avaricious schemes which add greatly to the nation's health care costs. For example, federal investigations have revealed that hospitals may routinely demand kickbacks from doctors, a practice under which physicians are required to make payments to the hospitals for patient referrals. Moreover it was found that physicians who refuse to make such payments may lose the right to practice at the hospital altogether. The illegal payments are disguised in hospital records as reimbursements by the doctors for billing, marketing, or other fabricated services.[80] In one case, "radiologists had to pay half of their gross receipts to a hospital's endowment fund."[81] In another, doctors were forced to pay 25 percent of their profits exceeding a set amount as a condition of operating the radiology department.[82] Because such practices obviously drive up government costs, they are illegal under the regulations of Medicare and Medicaid—programs which account for almost 40 percent of hospital spending nationwide.[83] They are also proscribed by both civil and criminal laws. Kickbacks can increase the utilization of services, unnecessary tests and procedures, higher prices, and may lead to unethical and criminal behaviors by doctors in an effort to make back what they have lost through institutionalized extortion.

Tenet Healthcare, the nation's second-largest hospital chain, with more than 100 hospitals in 16 states, settled two large class action lawsuits in 2005. The first, settled in March, involved the systematic overcharging of uninsured patients for services and medications. Tenet agreed to set aside a fund to reimburse patients for the difference between what they were charged and what managed-care companies pay for those same services. The lead attorney for the plaintiffs estimated that the excessive charges totaled more than $200 million.[84]

The second settlement, in November, was even more disturbing. Federal prosecutors settled claims against a Tenet-owned California hospital accused of performing unnecessary heart surgeries to defraud Medicare. The prosecutors alleged that two physicians at the hospital had participated in a "scheme to cause patients to undergo unnecessary, invasive coronary procedures,"[85] such artery bypass surgery and heart valve replacement.[86] In addition to the $54 million settlement, the company agreed to establish a $395 million fund for 675 surviving cardiac patients and 94 families of deceased patients to settle civil litigation.[87] The lawsuit alleged that "some of the deaths have been attributed to the unnecessary surgery."[88]

Rehabilitation centers have also been caught feeding at the trough. A 1995 study by the General Accounting Office uncovered widespread overcharging to Medicare for therapy services.[89] The cost of these services has increased enormously (over 100 percent) between 1990 ($4.8 billion) and 1993 ($10.4 billion), raising concern that some of this growth was the result of fraud and abuse. The GAO found huge markups on therapy services by rehabilitation companies, who supply therapists to the nursing homes, and by the nursing homes themselves. For example, Medicare has been charged $600 per hour or more for therapy, whereas the average salaries for occupational, physical, and speech therapists range from $12 to $25 per hour.[90]

Complaints by beneficiaries and their families, which usually relate to overcharging, have been confirmed by numerous investigations around the country. In Georgia, a Department of Justice investigation of the owner of four rehabilitation companies resulted in an indictment for submitting false claims, mail fraud, wire fraud, and money laundering. In North Carolina, rehabilitation companies have also been found to bill Medicare for overpriced services as well as services never rendered at all. One extensive investigation involved abuses by one company linked to over 130 providers spread over 21 states. The company systematically charged grossly inflated amounts for services. In one instance, Medicare was billed for $8,415, of which a $4,580 fee was included by the billing service just for processing the claim.[91]

In another large health care fraud settlement, National Medical Enterprises, Inc. (NME), a Santa Monica, California-based corporation which manages more than 60 substance abuse and psychiatric hospitals nationwide, paid $379 million in criminal fines, civil damages, and penalties. Previously, the company had settled numerous lawsuits, including one involving six insurers for $125 million.[92] NME had been accused of a host of illegal marketing and billing practices, including instructing hospital administrators to adopt "intake goals" designed to bring patients into the hospitals for lengthy stays and unnecessary treatments.[93] NME also settled other claims including "billing insurance programs multiple times for the same service, billing insurance programs when no service was actually provided, and billing Medicare for payments made to doctors and others that were solely intended to induce referrals of patients to the facilities."[94] According to one lawsuit, a patient entered an NME facility for a two-week evaluation and was not allowed to leave for 11 months.[95]

A closer look at psychiatric hospital frauds will show how such scams are perpetrated.

Psychiatric Hospitals

For many decades, American psychiatric hospitals were predominantly public institutions where mentally ill citizens were warehoused and forgotten. In the 1950s and 1960s, many patients were rendered docile through lobotomies and crude psychosurgery in which an instrument known as an "icepickalon" was inserted into the brain through an eye socket and used to dig out prefrontal tissue. "[A] good deal of the patient's personality often ended up in the operating room wastebasket."[96] Even today, some state mental hospitals are still described as "filthy, backward institutions where patients are frequently tied down, locked up, and sometimes left lying in their own excrement."[97] When inpatient insurance coverage for mental health and substance abuse problems grew in the 1970s, however, *private* for-profit psychiatric hospitals became "cash cows."

In the 1980s, as insurance companies were hit by exceedingly high costs in this area of coverage and began scrutinizing payments, lengths of hospital stays were shortened. Consequently, many psychiatric hospitals became increasingly desperate for patients. The need to fill beds has resulted in a veritable catalogue of fraudulent and abusive practices designed to maximize revenue: patients abducted by "bounty hunters"; patients hospitalized against their will until their insurance ran out; false diagnoses; overbilling; unnecessary treatments; and kickbacks paid for the recruitment of patients.[98]

One profoundly disturbing case occurred in Texas in 1991, where 14-year-old Jeremy H. was taken from his home by two uniformed men, after his younger brother lied about Jeremy's purported drug use. Jeremy was brought to Colonial Hills Hospital, a psychiatric institution in San Antonio owned by the Psychiatric Institutes of America (PIA). His family had thought the two abductors were law enforcement officers; his grandmother later told a Texas State Senate committee investigating health care fraud that they had acted like the "Gestapo."[99] Jeremy was detained for six days with no contact with his family and was released only after a state senator intervened on his behalf. It was later discovered that the "officers" who took him away were security guards employed by a private firm hired by Colonial Hills for the delivery of patients. It was also revealed that the "doctor" who had admitted Jeremy was using false credentials.

The attorney representing Jeremy's family claimed that the boy had been dragged away because he was covered for a wide range of mental health benefits under CHAMPUS (Civilian Health and Medical Program for the Uniformed Services), the federal health plan for the families of military personnel. After six days of "treatment," Jeremy's family received a bill for $11,000—which CHAMPUS paid. However, CHAMPUS asked the Department of Defense to investigate the case. Jeremy's abduction also spurred state legislative hearings which produced allegations of fraud and abuse at 12 other PIA facilities in Texas and a number of other national hospital chains operating in that state.[100]

Texas appears to have become a breeding ground for all sorts of shamelessly aggressive recruitment practices because of the dramatic proliferation of psychiatric hospitals there since the mid-1980s and the resulting intensity of cutthroat competition for insurance dollars. Texas may also be particularly susceptible to aggressive fraud because, according to the Texas Commission on Alcohol and Drug Abuse, about one-fifth of its adult population experiences at least one alcohol-related problem during any given year.[101] The state is saturated by formidable marketing campaigns, "with hotlines and slick billboards, television, magazine, newspaper and radio advertisements promoting the benefits of treatment for depression or alcohol and drug abuse."[102] Patient referral firms, known as "headhunters," even infiltrate local Alcoholics Anonymous groups in order to deliver prospective patients to contracted hospitals. One such firm had a quota to deliver 60 patients each month to a Fort Worth hospital.[103]

Houston-area school counselors have reportedly been offered reward money to refer troubled students to psychiatric treatment centers. "Public service" counselors, telephone hot lines, and other "help groups" have allegedly been established by private hospitals to learn covertly about prospective patients' insurance rather than their medical needs. Those who are insured are then duped into hospital programs.[104]

Some former hospital admissions officers have contended that they were fired on the basis of their "conversion rates"—the ratio of telephone inquiries converted to hospital admissions. In the words of one discharged employee: "There was tremendous pressure to get people into the hospital. I felt like a used-car salesman."[105]

Other deplorable practices include "[i]nsurance 'cash-ectomies' in which corporate psychiatric hospitals overcharge for doctor visits that last two to three minutes if they occur at all."[106] One Texas hospital reportedly charged $150 per day for the use of an ordinary television as a therapeutic device. Another scam utilizes "golden handcuff" contracts between hospitals and psychiatrists. This practice, under which psychiatrists may earn "salaries" of up to $300,000 for recruitment, has been described as the "outright buying and selling of patients."[107]

Perhaps the most despicable fraud of all involves the looting of the Texas Crime Victim's Compensation Fund, which provides for counseling and mental health treatment for crime victims and their families. According to an investigative report in the *Houston Chronicle*, hospitals may have falsified diagnoses in order to qualify for coverage under this fund. In 1991, Texas withheld payment on $3.1 million of claims to the 12 PIA (Psychiatric Institutes of America) facilities in the state. Over just a 2 1/2 month period, PIA had billed that amount for the questionable treatment of crime victims.[108]

Fraud charges have been brought against hospitals in many other states as well, including New Jersey, Florida, Alabama, and Louisiana. One California hospital created an employee incentive contest in which "staffers could win prizes—from a color television to a Caribbean cruise—for bringing in new patients."[109] Like Texas, California has been swamped by sleazy recruitment schemes generated by private psychiatric hospitals. A veteran administrator for one such facility has been quoted anonymously:

> I never had anybody from the corporate office ask me about the needs of a patient. All they want to know is the [hospital] census and the profits . . . It's a whore's market.[110]

In 1992, federal investigations were launched in more than a dozen states. Not all the resulting allegations concerned illegal patient recruitment schemes. Patients who *voluntarily* sought help have claimed that they were virtually "imprisoned" in psychiatric hospitals. One such case involved a woman whose doctor referred her to a hospital in Texas after she had suffered a psychotic reaction to a pain medication. This patient thought she would be there for a day or two. Instead, her stay lasted three months, during which time the hospital tried to change her status from "psychiatric" to "medical," which would have increased her insurance coverage from $50,000 to $1,000,000. She was also heavily sedated and kept isolated from family and visitors. Her doctor warned her that she would be kept "in a mental hospital the rest of her life"[111] if she fought for release. After her insurance was exhausted, she was finally sent home with a bill for over $48,000.[112]

A few indignant doctors have come forward, relating astonishing stories of greed, ethical violations, and corruption at psychiatric hospitals. In response, hospitals have claimed that generalizing from isolated patient complaints "is extremely dangerous to people who need care."[113] Although diagnoses may change during a patient's stay, hospital officials argue that this does not mean that patients are detained for insurance purposes. But even if isolated cases may not prove that wrongdoing and fraud are the norm, they certainly offer compelling evidence that some psychiatric hospitals do take advantage of patients through predatory recruitment, kickback schemes, and false diagnoses. How many hidden cases exist remains a matter of speculation, however, because of a shrinking investigative capacity.

Insurance companies themselves have also been blamed for the skyrocketing growth of private psychiatric hospitals by offering more generous benefits for inpatient care than outpatient care.[114] A spokesperson for the American Psychological Association has described this bias toward institutionalization as "a perverse incentive where people wind up in the hospital because they can't afford outpatient care."[115]

While the policies of some private psychiatric hospitals can be justly termed "reprehensible," it is difficult to find an adjective sufficient to describe patient abuses at certain *public* mental hospitals. For example, a federal judge has ruled that the state of Tennessee had violated the constitutional rights of mentally retarded residents of the Arlington Developmental Center (ADC), a state-operated institution. Among other things, the judge ruled: "[P]sychiatric and psychological services were virtually nonexistent. Medical care was below any minimum standard and well below the medical malpractice standard."[116] The Justice Department estimated that at least 25 patients at ADC had died of aspiration pneumonia, an infection caused by food entering the lungs when patients are fed while lying down instead of sitting up.[117] It was further revealed that the causes of these preventable deaths had been officially recorded as heart failure or respiratory arrest. A Justice Department witness characterized this policy as a shabby subterfuge: "Everybody who dies has stopped breathing or their heart has stopped. . . . What we have here are quiet little murders."[118]

America's most malignant public repository for the mentally retarded was Forest Haven in Washington, D.C. During just a two-year period, at least ten Forest Haven residents died of aspiration pneumonia. The exact death toll can never be known, but the problem was believed to date back at least 20 years.[119] The total number of victims of Forest Haven's routine negligence could easily exceed one hundred. A former assistant attorney general for civil rights has declared that Forest Haven constituted "the deadliest known example of institutional abuse in recent American history."[120] In 1994, Forest Haven, battered by litigation, was closed forever.

SELF-REFERRALS

A major reason for the ballooning cost of medical care in the United States rests in the practice of self-referral, through which a physician sends patients for ancillary services to a company in which he or she has a financial interest. Such a custom may not be illegal, *per se*, but can create abundant opportunities for ethical violations in the name of extra profits. Doctors who invest in laboratories, pharmacies, surgical centers, and physical therapy facilities can earn enormous sums of money through needless referrals of patients. "As early as 1989, a government study revealed that physicians who owned diagnostic labs ordered up to 45 percent more tests than those who did not."[121] The U.S. Department of Health and Human Services estimates that one quarter of the labs in this country are owned by doctors who refer their patients there.[122] There is also a serious matter of price-gouging. One study conducted in Florida reported that doctor-owned labs charge on the average 40 percent more than other labs in the state.[123]

In California, where legislation has been introduced to ban self-referrals, Congressman Pete Stark has commented:

> "Physician ownership/referral arrangements represent an exploding virus which ultimately will erode the trust patients have traditionally placed in their physicians. The sad thing is that we are quickly getting to the point where each of us is going to have to wonder if we are getting referred for a health service because we need it or because it would fatten our physician's dividend check."[124]

Self-referrals pose a transparent conflict of interest for physicians. The practice can easily open the door to fraud through the intentional provision of unnecessary but profitable services. Arnold

Relman, a former editor of the distinguished *New England Journal of Medicine* has observed: "Basically, we're talking about a kickback or a bribe that has so far avoided existing regulations."[125] Relman estimates, based on a survey of doctors by the American Medical Association (AMA), that between 50,000 and 75,000 physicians have a financial interest in ancillary medical services.[126] The AMA opposes legislation to ban doctors from investing in such services, claiming (as always) that doctors know best and that self-referrals help ensure better treatment. On the other hand, it seems virtually impossible to imagine that self-referrals could be divorced entirely from the profit motive. Patients have every right to expect that their doctors will direct them to high-quality and fairly priced services for purely medical reasons and not entrepreneurial ones.

MEDICARE FRAUD

When President Lyndon Johnson signed the legislation creating Medicare and Medicaid in 1965 to provide senior citizens and the poor with government funded health care, the ink was hardly dry before critics warned that "scam artists, crooked providers, and criminal rings would rob the healthcare programs blind."[127] Sadly, the critics were right. As we have already noted, the federal Medicare program has been rife with fraud and abuse for decades. For example, Medicare spent more than $6 billion in 1995—roughly $30,000 per patient—on kidney dialysis treatment. This sum represented 80 percent of the total dialysis billing in the United States.[128] An investigative report by the *New York Times* that year alleged that National Medical Care,[129] the largest chain of kidney centers in the country, cut costs and raised profits by using obsolete and potentially dangerous dialysis machines. Moreover, this callous policy has been emulated by other private kidney treatment facilities. As a consequence, American dialysis patients are more than twice as likely to die in a given year as patients in Western Europe or Japan.[130]

A 1997 report by the Department of Health and Human Services revealed that Medicare was wasting hundreds of millions of dollars a year on unnecessary ambulance services provided to elderly patients. About 10 percent of Medicare beneficiaries use ambulances each year. According to the report, in 26 states Medicare was paying more for routine nonemergency transportation than for advanced life support emergency transportation.[131] The Inspector General of HHS said that more than 100 ambulance services had been cited for civil and criminal violations in the previous five years. She noted that Medicare's system of paying for ambulance services is so complex that it "encourages fraud and abuse."[132]

The report concluded that, "Medicare payments for ambulance services appear to lack common sense." The report provided some dramatic examples. A woman, who had earlier been convicted of Medicaid fraud, used "front men" to form an ambulance company. She then billed Medicare for transporting multiple patients in unlicensed personal vehicles.[133] An Illinois ambulance company falsified and back-dated trip records to justify ambulance services provided to nursing home residents who did not need them.[134] An Indiana ambulance operator improperly billed Medicare when he took patients from nursing homes to medical appointments at doctors' offices and clinics. The ambulances also billed Medicare for oxygen that was never provided.[135] The owner of an Ohio ambulance company altered trip tickets to show that patients were bedridden, when, in fact, the patients were in wheelchairs or, in some instances, were able to walk from the ambulance to the hospital. He also billed for ambulance service when patients were transported in a company station wagon.[136]

The Government Accounting Office (GAO) estimates that at least 10 percent of total expenditures is lost to fraudulent Medicare practices.[137] The list of scams that have been uncovered seems almost endless. In California, for example, a nursing home operator bilked Medicare out of almost $4 million and probably would have gotten away with it had he not sloppily misaddressed forged invoices from fictitious firms in "New Hamshire,"[sic] or "Lubbock, Mississippi [Texas]."[138] In Florida, senior citizens were solicited door-to-door for their Medicare numbers, supposedly to be used in a "free milk program." Instead, their IDs were utilized by crooks to defraud Medicare of $14 million.[139] In an effort to drum up business at the government's expense, a home health care service, operating in 22 states, billed Medicare for $85,000 for "gourmet popcorn" which was sent to doctors as an inducement for them to use the company's services.[140]

Nursing homes, like the afore-mentioned, are prone to financial ripoffs tied to the Medicare program. A joint investigation by the Justice Department and the Office of the Inspector General for the Department of Health and Human Services resulted in the largest settlement to date in a nursing home fraud case. In 2000, Beverly Healthcare, the nation's largest nursing home chain, agreed to pay a civil fine of $170 million and a criminal fine of $5 million for falsely inflating the number of hours nurses spent caring for Medicare patients. "[T]he chain had submitted false nurse sign-in sheets and other fabricated documents to support the bills."[141]

A 2008 report released by America Watchdog and its Corporate Whistleblower Center concluded that the government is being over-billed and defrauded by nursing homes that do not provide the minimum hours per day per patient required by Medicare. According to the report, less than 50 percent of Medicare patients in nursing homes are getting the required amount of hours. "[S]enior citizens are dying in US nursing homes, because they are in many cases, not getting anything near the mandatory time/hours per day in care."[142]

In 1995, the University of Pennsylvania agreed to pay $30 million to settle allegations that it had submitted an estimated $10 million dollars in false Medicare claims over a six-year period. At the time, this was the largest Medicare settlement ever paid by a single health care provider.[143] In another major case, involving two of the nation's biggest clinical laboratories, the government received $39.8 million to settle fraud charges involving the submission of unnecessary lab tests.[144] The firms, Metwest (a subsidiary of Unilab) and Metpath (a unit of Corning, Inc.) were accused of including an HDL test in their basic blood chemistry screening exam, but were billing the government separately for it without the knowledge of the physicians who ordered the exam. In statements issued by the two companies, they were careful to note that the settlement "does not constitute an admission by [either company] with respect to any issue of law."[145]

The alleged violations in the Metwest/Metpath case were similar to those in a previous settlement with National Health Laboratories, Inc., which paid the government $111.4 million— at that time the largest health care provider settlement in history. After a two-year investigation initiated by a whistleblower,[146] the company pleaded guilty to two charges of submitting false claims. The president and CEO Robert E. Draper forfeited $500,000 and spent 3 months in prison.[147] Investigators found that the company had charged the government $18 each for three tests which were supposed to be part of a single basic blood series test. Private insurers, in contrast, were charged only about 65 cents for the same tests.[148]

Project Jump Start, initiated in 1993, was one of the most ambitious Medicare investigations and scrutinized 132 hospitals. The findings revealed that some of the hospitals routinely submitted phony claims to obtain Medicare payments for unapproved procedures.[149]

> [M]any of the hospitals changed billing codes for noncovered experimental devices to fool Medicare examiners into thinking they were paying for approved procedures. Atherectomies—performed to drill out plaque in clogged arteries—were commonly billed as angioplasties.[150]

A Sacramento hospital obtained Medicare reimbursement for experimental defibrillators and pacemakers by deleting the word "experimental" from forms.[151] One whistle-blower has even charged that doctors actually hold seminars on how to dupe Medicare.[152]

Individual physicians can cheat the Medicare system by billing patients excessively. Three common means are overcharges, retainers, and waivers.

Overcharges

Some doctors make patients sign "contracts" for services such as surgery. These can be at rates much higher than Medicare's covered amounts, requiring patients to pay much more than required by law. In New York, for instance, a doctor can charge no more than 15 percent above Medicare's approved rate. Yet in one example, a 70-year-old retired truck driver illegally paid over $1,100 more than required by law for hand surgery costing a total of $2,601.[153] It is estimated that in 1993 alone almost 1.5 million Medicare beneficiaries were illegally overcharged, with costs totaling about $101 million.[154]

Retainers

Some doctors cheat the system by requiring new patients to pay up-front "retainers" for a package of services purportedly not covered by Medicare in order to receive comprehensive treatment. Such packages are illegal if they are knowingly sold to patients who already have such coverage in their Medicare-supplement policies.

Waivers

Doctors may ask patients to waive their right to have the physician bill Medicare directly, leaving the patient to pay for such services as telephone calls, medical conferences, and prescription refills—services which Medicare considers part of the fees it pays to doctors. Physicians can also use what is called a "global waiver," under which a number of vague services are listed that Medicare "may not" pay for. The patient is asked to pay these costs directly. The only type of waiver which is legal is one where a specific *uncovered* procedure is listed, such as cosmetic surgery.[155]

Doctors can also bleed the Medicare system by prescribing the most expensive drugs, rather than generics. According to the 2008 report by America's Watchdog, this practice accounts for up to 15 percent of all Medicare/Medicaid overcharges.[156] Doctors can get rewards from drug makers for prescribing the more expensive versions. For example, physicians can earn phony consulting fees, either in cash or in the form of free trips to vacation spots where they are treated to first-class accommodations. "All they have to do is give a talk (to a possibly empty room) for an hour."[157] This ill-disguised bribery costs taxpayers billions of dollars.

In recent years, a number of states have intensified their battles against Medicare fraud. These more aggressive efforts have reaped some dividends. For example, in 2008, the federal government announced a $60 million fraud settlement with Lester E. Cox Medical Systems, a Missouri hospital chain. The government had accused Cox of violating the False Claims Act, the nation's primary tool for combating fraud against taxpayer funds.[158] Dating back to 1995, Cox committed various unlawful acts, including submitting fraudulent cost reports to obtain Medicare funds and entering into illegal arrangements with doctors that violated the Anti-Kickback Statute, and other misconduct.[159] Although the settlement was by no means small, the government acknowledged that it was far less than the true amount of the alleged fraud and took into account Cox's "ability to pay."[160]

CASE STUDY
Lying and Outlying in New Jersey

In 2006, St. Barnabas Health System, the largest health care network in New Jersey, agreed to pay a $265 million settlement, to resolve fraud charges brought by federal prosecutors. St. Barnabas, which employs 5,000 doctors and operates 10 hospitals and a network of clinics and nursing homes, is also New Jersey's largest Medicare provider[161] and the second largest employer in the entire state.[162]

Medicare pays extra money to hospitals caring for the very ill (and very expensive) patients known as **outliers**,[163] because their needs stretch beyond the typical parameters of the program. The supplemental payment system is meant to serve as an incentive for hospitals to handle such cases.[164] According to prosecutors, the executives of St. Barnabas inflated their bills for their outliers and, by doing so, systematically bilked the government out of at least $630 million between 1995 and 2003.[165]

The roots of this particular type of fraud go back to the 1990s, when administrators at hospitals around the country—including St. Barnabas—turned to unscrupulous accounting firms that promised to help them maximize their financing from Medicare. "By exploiting loopholes in the complex formula that Medicare uses to reimburse providers for their most expensive cases . . . many

hospitals' federal aid doubled, quadrupled or increased 10 times."[166] Indeed, St. Barnabas received more Medicare money than some national chains 10 times its size.[167] It is especially interesting to note that St. Barnabas is designated as a *non-profit* hospital.[168]

A year later, another New Jersey hospital, the Warren Hospital, paid the government $7.5 million to settle allegations that it inflated Medicare claims between 1998 and 2003. Like St. Barnabas, the Warren Hospital's bogus claims involved outliers. Treatments for such patients are considered easier to manipulate than ordinary claims because they tend to be complicated and often subjective.[169]

In 2008, the words Medicare fraud and New Jersey were linked again after the Cooper University Hospital of Camden agreed to pay the government $3.85 million, plus interest, to settle yet another Medicare fraud case.[170] Between 2001 and 2003, Cooper University Hospital improperly increased its charges to outliers to obtain enhanced reimbursement from Medicare.[171]

An analyst at Taxpayers Against Fraud, a leading watchdog organization, recently stated: "The way the system has operated, it's almost irresponsible corporate governance for Hospitals not to cheat Medicare."[172]

Enforcement in the Medicare program is problematic. One of the ways that fraud could be ferreted out of the system is through the vigilance of patients who report phony billings. Complaints are handled by "carriers," that is firms (usually insurance companies) which are paid to process Medicare claims and investigate billings that are suspicious or out of line. As budgets shrink, however, carriers are strained merely to provide the basic service of processing and paying legitimate claims without scrutinizing potentially phony ones. Because of this, the GAO has found that even when carriers are *called by patients* with information relating to possible fraud and wrongdoing, few follow-ups will occur since there is little or no incentive for the companies to do so.[173] Examples of ignored abuses include the incredible case of an elderly man who complained that he was charged for a pregnancy test.[174]

A government investigator captured the frustration of elderly whistleblowers when he commented, "We went looking for a paper trail and couldn't find one."[175] If carriers do not follow up on obvious and provable scams that are virtually handed to them by patients, it is difficult to believe that they can effectively police the Medicare system. This ends up costing taxpayers tens of billions of dollars a year—money that could be used to improve health care for the elderly or help reduce the federal deficit.

The words of former FBI Director Louis J. Freeh before a Senate committee in 1995 summed up the failure of government efforts to deal with fraud in public health care spending: "The problem is so big and so diverse that we are making only a small dent in addressing the fraud."[176] Given the immense costs of such crimes, then and even more so now, Freeh's assessment underscores the importance of reform in the health care arena. But dismantling Medicare—a piece at a time—is not the same as reforming it. Members of Congress (who enjoy perhaps the best group health insurance plan in the world) seem to find it all too easy to cut others' health care benefits to save money.

As more control over government health care passes to the states, reflecting the renascent federalism that emerged in the 1990s and the economic crisis that began in 2008, it is doubtful if fraud control will be funded in the future even at the already inadequate levels decried by Louis Freeh. Under pressure to reduce costs, Medicare is likely to evolve into a new system of managed care, utilizing the HMO (Health Maintenance Organization) model to regulate medical decisions.[177] HMOs, with their flat-fee structure, may very well reduce the incentive for overtreatment, but a whole new laundry list of potential offenses may fill that void—such as negligence *under* treatment to reduce overhead and drive up profits.[178] Indeed, Medicare fraud has already found a home in the emerging HMO system. International Medical Centers (IMC), the largest Medicare HMO in the country at the time, declared bankruptcy in 1986 *after* receiving $360 million from the government. The company's failure was attributed to exorbitant salaries and illegal practices. After he was indicted by a federal grand jury, the founder of IMC fled the country to avoid prosecution.[179]

Yet, as inadequate as Medicare fraud enforcement has been, it has still managed to achieve some notable successes. The Department of Health and Human Services and the Justice Department have channeled $10.4 billion into the Medicare trust fund since 1997. The money was recouped by prosecuting companies and individuals who have cheated the program.[180]

MEDICAID FRAUD

As with Medicare, Medicaid violations constitute a threat to the health of Americans and to the financial resources of the nation. The program has been hammered by fraud almost since its inception. The first major scandal surfaced in 1973, when *New York Daily News* reporter William Sherman wrote a twelve-part Pulitzer Prize-winning series documenting his personal experiences posing as a patient in New York City's Medicaid clinics—known pejoratively as "Medicaid mills." A few years later, Senator Frank Moss of Utah followed suit, presenting himself as an indigent patient at several New York City clinics complaining that he had a cold. His visits led to blood and urine tests, follow-up appointments, and prescriptions to be filled at pharmacies adjacent to the clinics.[181] Moss's Congressional subcommittee concluded that Medicaid was "not only inefficient, but riddled with fraud and abuse."[182] The committee recommended that the federal government allocate funds for enforcement.

In response, Congress enacted the Medicare and Medicaid Anti-Fraud and Abuse Amendments of 1977. Among its provisions, the Amendments upgraded violations from misdemeanors to felonies and required more disclosure as to ownership of health care facilities.[183] Congress also passed legislation enabling states to establish Medicaid Fraud Control Units (MFCU).[184] Despite these and other attempts to crack down, however, Medicaid fraud has continued to flourish, and, if anything, has grown more sophisticated. Typically, fraudulent practices involve billing for services never rendered and/or intentional overutilization of unnecessary services. The fee-for-service structure of Medicaid, wherein providers are paid according to the bills they submit, leaves the program open to looting. Indeed, some providers seem to treat Medicaid as a virtual license to print money. An inspector general for the Department of Health and Human Services has concluded: "A welfare queen would have to work mighty hard to steal $100,000. Somebody in the practitioner or provider community can burp and steal $100,000."[185]

It has been argued that abuses in Medicaid are even more extensive than in Medicare because of the negative feelings of some health professionals toward welfare patients, whose behavior and personal habits (and perhaps their poverty itself) are a source of contempt.[186] Indicative of this disdain is the feeble excuse offered by a dentist, whose license was suspended in 1995 because of complaints that he had physically abused patients. He was one of the largest individual Medicaid providers of any type in Texas, collecting over $600,000 from the program in the previous year alone. At his hearing before the Texas Board of Health, his defense was that he never turns away Medicaid patients—even though many of them are "dirty" and "smell bad."[187]

As a social problem, Medicaid fraud has never garnered enough official attention to be rectified. In 1995, for example, a California psychiatrist was allowed to remain in a $102,000 administrative position at a Los Angeles county mental health center for months after being convicted of defrauding the state Medi-Cal system of more than $150,000.[188] This figure was the product of a plea bargain; the actual amount of the fraud is believed to be $1.3 million. Typical of the many charges against the doctor was his submission of 37 claims for a patient he saw only one time.[189]

Official laxity was further illustrated when a New York City journalist used two "rented" Medicaid cards to obtain thousands of dollars of unnecessary medical exams, tests, and prescriptions in a short period of time. In "playing the doctors" (a term widely used by junkies and hustlers throughout the city) the reporter visited over 15 clinics and saw more than two dozen physicians, therapists, and lab technicians. While he was piling up prescriptions and bills, the reporter also observed dozens of others who were doing the same thing—most likely to re-sell the drugs on the black market. In New York State alone, it is estimated that "playing the doctors" costs taxpayers hundreds of millions of dollars a year.[190]

Uncovered Medicaid violations merely scratch the surface of the true extent of the problem. One investigator acknowledges that the only crooks who are caught are the reckless or stupid ones—"the fish who jump into the boat."[191] Some of the blatant offenses reflect such gross arrogance that they cross the border into absurdity. Investigations have documented cases in which daily psychotherapy sessions have totaled more than 24 hours, X-rays have been taken without film, and bills have been submitted for circumcisions done on female infants and hysterectomies performed on male patients.[192]

There is nothing farcical, however, about a truly monstrous example of Medicaid fraud, described as "shocking" by the presiding judge. This case concerned a Los Angeles ophthalmologist, Dr. Jose Manaya, who was convicted in 1984 on charges related to unnecessary eye surgeries. Unnecessary surgery, intentionally performed, is legally equivalent to assault. It can involve not only theft, but maiming and death as well.[193] Dr. Manaya had subjected poor, mostly Hispanic patients to needless cataract surgery in order to collect Medi-Cal fees of $584 per eye. Manaya went through myopic Medi-Cal patients like Sherman through Georgia; he collected about a million dollars over a period of five years. In one instance, a 57-year-old woman was totally blinded after he operated on her one sighted eye. Investigators discovered that when Manaya's patients had private medical insurance or were well off financially, the operations were done with skill and success. If the patients were on Medicaid, however, the surgery was performed in a quick and careless manner.[194]

Remarkably, Dr. Manaya received fervent support from many members of the medical community, who urged leniency. The response of the judge, who handed down a 4-year sentence, made his feelings clear: "It's astounding how they could write these letters. They seem to think the whole trial was a contrivance by the attorney general's office."[195] What had particularly upset him was how the letter writers, in their zeal to portray Manaya as a "victim," virtually ignored the criminally abused patients. The judge noted: "In not one of these letters has there been one word of sympathy for the true victims in this case, the uneducated, Spanish-speaking people, some of whom will never see a sunrise or a sunset again."[196]

It would be a mistake to conclude from the Manaya case that the most virulent forms of Medicaid fraud and abuse are limited to physicians only. Investigators have begun scrutinizing the practices of pediatric dentists who participate in Medicaid. Many of these specialists are believed to opt routinely for expensive and potentially dangerous procedures, including stainless steel crowns, hospitalization, and general anesthesia, in lieu of more conservative alternatives such as in-office fillings and local anesthesia.[197] Regulators who have sought out second opinions have found that very young patients from needy families often require little or no work, despite the expensive treatments proposed by their Medicaid providers. One expert has concluded: "Some of these things that are being done are just money down the drain, because these kids are going to be losing their [baby] teeth shortly."[198] As with the Manaya case, however, there is more at risk than money when greed turns reckless. The overuse of anesthesia by pediatric dentists trying to perform as much work as possible at one sitting "endangers children and could be considered child abuse."[199] In 1991, a three-year-old Medicaid patient in Texas died of respiratory arrest "after her dentist gave her a 'cocktail' of three sedatives and injected her gums with a local anesthetic."[200] The dentist received a 30-day suspension. In a 1994 Texas case, a *13-month-old* Medicaid patient died while under general anesthesia in a hospital where she had been put by her dentist, who planned to put crowns on four of her eight teeth.[201]

While outrageous Medicaid violations may make headlines, a public outcry demanding a change in enforcement policies has thus far not materialized. One reason for this may be that the victims—low-income persons—do not command much respect or sympathy from an increasingly anti-poor public. Indeed, providers themselves often hold the victims responsible for the fraud.[202] Another problem is that the issue of fraud is often seen as peripheral to the major tasks of containing overall costs and improving our health care delivery system. In this context, overutilization of services, the core of fraud and abuse, can be seen as no more than a distraction from the major concern: "The underavailability of health care in the United States."[203]

Medicaid Murder?

One of the nation's most bizarre Medicaid fraud cases involved Dr. Olga Romani, who arrived in the United States from Cuba in 1960. Claiming to have graduated from the University of Havana medical school (where official transcripts are unobtainable in the United States), she began practicing in Miami in 1967 while she completed her state licensing requirements. In 1974, she pleaded guilty to charges related to the unlawful practice of medicine, and received a sentence of five years probation.[204] The case was prosecuted after two women whom she had treated for acne complained that they were left disfigured as a result.[205] Between 1976 and

1981, Olga Romani became the second largest Medicaid provider in Florida and operated two clinics. By 1980, she had received $184,000 in reimbursement for medical services from the state.[206] In March, 1981, she was arrested on racketeering charges alleging that she had stolen more than $97,000 from Medicaid by billing for services never performed.[207] For example, Romani had billed Medicaid after purportedly treating one of her patients for diaper rash. During the trial, the patient was asked by the prosecutor whether he was in fact receiving such treatment. The jurors and spectators chuckled as Eddie James King, a 19-year-old, 220-pound Florida A&M football player, answered "No." After King had visited her twice for a "cold," Romani billed Medicaid for 51 visits, claiming payments of $1,885.[208] Another witness, whose Medicaid recipient number was used by the defendant to bill the state for 165 visits, testified that she had never even met Romani. After a parade of other witnesses offered similar testimony, the jury took only one hour to convict Romani on 24 counts of filing false claims and 24 counts of receiving payments to which she was not entitled.[209] One attorney estimated that the money stolen by Romani could have been used to treat more than 10,000 needy patients.[210] Olga Romani received a 20-year sentence in prison for Medicaid fraud, showing little emotion as the judge passed sentence.

If the Romani case had ended there, it would be a modestly interesting example of occupational crime. But there was much more to come. Soon after her sentencing, Romani became the central suspect in the murder of her partner, Dr. Gerardo DeMola, who was shot to death in his car at a hospital parking lot a few weeks before Romani's indictment on the fraud charges in 1981.[211] Romani was believed to have paid $10,000 for a contract killing because she feared that her former associate might testify against her in the fraud case.[212] Later, after she was indicted on murder charges, prosecutors produced a "hit list" which included Demola's name as well as others involved with the investigation. Romani attempted to explain away the list by claiming that it was to be delivered to a Santerian priest who had asked for the names of persons with whom she might be involved in future legal disputes.[213] Santeria, an arcane mixture Christianity and voodoo, is a Caribbean religion, which stresses the casting of spells and curses. She did not believe in Santeria, Romani contended, but wrote out the list of her "enemies" on the advice of her accountant, who said it might ease her mind.[214]

During her murder trial Romani was evasive, sometimes incoherent, and did not make a credible witness. Convicted in 1983, she was sentenced to life imprisonment with a 25-year mandatory sentence on the murder charge and received another 30 years for conspiracy.[215] The murder conviction was later overturned on procedural grounds, but Olga Romani continues to serve time on her fraud and conspiracy convictions.

Investigators and prosecutors continue trying to fight the good fight and do snatch a meaningful victory here and there. But Medicaid fraud remains an expensive—and sometimes tragic—crime that seems destined only to get worse in the wake of the 2008 economic collapse that will undoubtedly swell the ranks of the newly poor. "Doctors [like Olga Romani] who lie about their credentials, clinics that don't do necessary medical screenings and health care companies that sweep their low-income recipients under the rug are all part of the increasing problem of Medicaid fraud."[216]

An example of successful investigations and prosecutions can be found in North Carolina, where, according to a 2009 report from that state's Attorney General's office, 17 criminal convictions and 15 civil settlements for Medicaid abuse were obtained in 2008. The various cases involved doctors, nurses, hospitals, nursing homes, pharmacies, and other health care providers. More than $52 million was recovered.[217]

Locking up a handful of crooked doctors, nurses, and pharmacists affirms the "justice" part of the criminal justice system, and may have a deterrent effect as well. But, in the battle against Medicaid fraud, the "criminal" part of the criminal justice system is often hidden away in the executive suites of corporate America. In 2008, pharmaceutical giant Merck & Co. was the target of one of the biggest U.S. health care frauds ever. Merck agreed to pay $671 million to settle claims that it had overcharged the government for four popular drugs and bribed doctors to prescribe its drugs.[218]

Another large pharmaceutical company, Cephalon, perpetrated a much more serious type of Medicaid fraud. In 2008, Cephalon agreed to pay a fraud settlement of $375 million and a criminal penalty of $50 million for marketing three of its drugs on an off-label (i.e., unapproved) basis for years in order to widen their potential market and boost sales.[219] The FDA approves drugs for specific purposes, which are noted in the drugs' labeling. The law prohibits drug companies from promoting drugs beyond those found to be safe and effective by the FDA.[220]

The three off-label drugs were: (1) **Provigil**, approved to help keep patients suffering from narcolepsy, sleep anpnea, or shift-work sleeping disorder. Cephalon was promoting the drug to treat the fatigue accompanying mental illnesses, such as schizophrenia, migraine headaches, and even children with attention deficit hyperactivity disorder.[221] (2) **Gabitril**, was approved for the treatment of partial seizures in epileptic patients. Cephalon was pushing doctors to prescribe it for insomnia and anxiety.[222] And, most dangerous of all (3) **Actiq**, a "medicated lozenge on a handle" approved only for cancer patients when their usual pain medicine is unable to control extreme pain. The potential side effects of Actiq include respiratory depression, which can be life-threatening. Actiq has been linked to about 100 deaths, yet Cephalon was marketing it almost as if it were "actual lollipops instead of a potent pain medication intended for a specific class of patients."[223] Medicaid and other federally funded health care programs sometimes will pay for off-label uses of drugs if such use is supported by credible medical research. But that was not at all the case with Cephalon. A Washington, D.C., attorney, who represents the company "whistle-blower" who revealed the illegal practices of his employer, has said: "Not only were these uses marketed by Cephalon not approved by the FDA, there was absolutely no literature published in any medical compendia that supported them."[224] The U.S. Attorney in charge of the case declared: "[Cephalon] subverted the very process put in place to protect the public from harm, and put patients' health at risk for nothing more than boosting its bottom line."[225] Cephalon's bottom line was, in fact, boosted substantially. The government's investigation reported that more than 80 percent of the sales of Provigil, Gabritil, and Actiq were for off-label usage.[226]

These were large corporate fraud cases, involving millions of victims, billions of dollars in profits and hundreds of millions of dollars in fines and settlements. But they were eclipsed by a more recent case involving the pharmaceutical giant, GlaxoSmithKline (GSK). In the summer of 2012, the company pleaded guilty to criminal charges and agreed to pay *$3 billion*—to date, the largest health care fraud settlement in history—to settle charges that, among other violations, it had marketed its top-selling drugs for purposes not approved by the FDA.[227] One of those drugs, Wellbutrin, had been approved only for the treatment of depression, but GlaxoSmithKline promoted it as an effective treatment for weight loss, sexual dysfunction, substance addictions and Attention Deficit Hyperactivity Disorder. To persuade doctors to prescribe the drug for these purposes the company engaged in an expensive marketing campaign (part of which was aptly named "Operation Hustle") that included paying physicians to attend promotional meetings held at lavish resorts in places like Jamaica where they listened to speeches by other physicians (paid by Glaxo) about the wonders of WellButrin.[228]

GlaxoSmithKline was also charged with promoting Advair, an asthma treatment drug, for unapproved uses, exposing some patients who took it to unnecessary health risks. But GSK executives saw huge profits in the drug. In 2001, the company held a product launch meeting in Las Vegas, attended by thousands of sales representatives, at which Advair's product manager was very explicit about the potential riches to be had in selling the drug.

> There are people in this room who are going to make an ungodly sum of money selling Advair . . . That's the way it should be. When GSK makes money you make money. The more you sell the more you make. God Bless America.[229]

Statements like this give one a clue about how hugely profitable the pharmaceutical industry is and how large the incentives are to cut corners and break the law in efforts to persuade physicians to prescribe certain medications. While the $3 billion GlaxoSmithKline paid in penalties may sound like a lot of money, one has to keep in mind that over the periods in question, the sales of three of the drugs it marketed for unapproved uses brought in over $27 billion to the company.[230] One implication is that the deterrent effect of the penalties may not be as great as they might first appear. As one commentator put it: "a $3 billion settlement for half a dozen drugs over 10 years can be rationalized as the cost of doing business."[231] The single case against GlaxoSmithKline more than doubled the amount obtained through fraud claim settlements with drug companies in 2011. The figure rose from $2.5 billion in 2011 to $6.6 billion as of September, 2012.[232]

An especially callous Medicaid scam was also uncovered in 2008. Rudra Sabaratnam, the owner of the City of Angels Hospital in southern California, defrauded Medi-Cal by recruiting homeless people to receive unnecessary health services.[233] Subaratnam and his accomplice Estill Mitts, the operator of an "assessment center" in the Skid Row area of Los Angeles, enticed homeless people with the promise of payments in return for acting as hospital patients.[234] Mitts hired "stringers" to recruit the homeless Medi-Cal beneficiaries, including drug addicts and the mentally ill, who were then given fake medical diagnoses and transported to Sabaratnam's hospital.[235] Prospects received a small sum of money, typically $20 to $30—although sometimes a pack of cigarettes was sufficient.[236] Local police first became suspicious when they began to notice ambulances returning homeless people to Skid Row, five at a time.[237]

At least two other hospitals and numerous other executives were later implicated. The depraved scheme shuffled thousands of indigents through hospitals over a four-year period and billed Medi-Cal (or, in some cases, Medicare) for costly and unjustified medical procedures. Certain of the treatments were potentially harmful.[238] Authorities said the hospitals used the homeless as "human pawns."[239]

Estill Mitts pleaded guilty in September, 2008, and Rudra Subaratnam followed suit two months later.[240] The U.S. Attorney in charge of the case warned: "There is too much money being stripped from public healthcare programs and the potential impact to those with legitimate needs is too great to let those orchestrating such frauds escape prosecution."[241]

PSYCHIATRISTS—"LAST AMONG EQUALS?"

While there are numerous examples of Medicaid fraud which have been documented in the popular media and the criminological literature,[242] psychiatrists stand out as the most frequently accused and sanctioned group among medical specialties.[243] Psychiatrists represent about 8 percent of all physicians but about 20 percent of all doctors suspended from Medicaid for fraudulent practices.[244] Some enforcement officials feel that such a finding validates their view that psychiatrists are more prone to violating the laws regulating Medicaid. This conforms to the generally low popular esteem in which psychiatrists are held relative to other medical specialists.[245]

The explanation for the overrepresentation of psychiatrists in Medicaid fraud cases, however, may be more oblique than the attribution of a greater propensity to cheat the program. Almost all doctors bill Medicaid (or any other insurance program, for that matter) for specific services rendered, such as examinations, tests, X-rays, surgeries and the like. The issue of fraud usually centers on whether these services were actually provided to patients. The practice of psychiatry provides an exception to this pattern, which is probably responsible for their higher rate of violations found in official statistics. Psychiatrists submit bills for *time*—that is, their payments are based upon the time they spend with patients (typically 50-minute "hours") and not upon complex procedures or medical interventions. This distinction makes apprehension much less complicated in the case of psychiatrists, since investigators can more readily determine (sometimes using nothing but a wristwatch) if the time periods that have been billed conform to those actually spent with patients. As especially easy enforcement targets, psychiatrists as a group may thus be labeled as more "criminal" than other doctors, even though they are no more or less prone to dishonesty.

Nonetheless, documented cases of occupational crimes by psychiatrists reveal an ugly side to their specialty. Most notably, the sexual abuse of emotionally vulnerable patients by sleazy psychotherapists is a recurring infraction of both legal and professional codes. Although white-collar crime usually connotes fraud, theft, or some other form of financial misappropriation, the extortion of sexual favors in exchange for medical services clearly meets Sutherland's definitional criteria: offenses committed by relatively respectable persons within their occupational roles.[246] The number of doctors disciplined for sexual misconduct reportedly doubled between 1990 and 1994.[247] Again, psychiatrists appear to be overrepresented. In a 1986 survey, 7 percent of male psychiatrists and 3 percent of female psychiatrists reported sexual contact with a patient. In addition, about two-thirds of the respondents said they had seen at least one patient who reported having sex with another therapist, of whom only 8 percent had reported the incident to authorities.[248]

FERTILITY FRAUD

One of the most obnoxious types of medical malfeasance is perpetrated against women and couples who are having problems trying to conceive. Given their oftentimes heightened emotional states and willingness to try almost anything, they are particularly vulnerable to fraud and other misdeeds. "Fertility fraud" has begun to surface as a new form of crime in the medical profession, as rapid advances in knowledge and technology—sometimes outpacing ethical and legal considerations—allow for a range of offenses which simply were not possible earlier. At least two chilling cases have come to light in recent years.

The first case involved a Virginia-based fertility doctor, Cecil Jacobson. Renowned as a brilliant geneticist, Jacobson, who had helped develop the amniocentesis procedure in the United States, referred to himself as "the babymaker." He told patients desperate to conceive: "God doesn't give you babies . . . I do."[249] With patients giving him their trust—and money—Jacobson deceived them in return by telling a number of women they were pregnant when in fact they were not and by secretly inseminating others with his own sperm.

Jacobson fathered children for numerous couples who believed they were receiving other donor sperm. Some of these mothers-to-be became suspicious, however, after receiving a tip and ordered genetic tests which showed that the doctor himself had fathered their babies. Jacobson originally denied, then later admitted, these charges. His attorney argued that "if the doctor had used his own sperm" it was done in the interest of providing the patient with a "clean and good" sample for their own protection from AIDS.[250]

Jacobson had also administered hormone treatments to some patients, which simulated the effects of early pregnancy. Women testified before the Virginia Medical Board that he had even shown them sonograms of what he said was "their fetus," including such details as heartbeats, thumb-sucking, and various movements. He even gave them snapshots of the purported fetus to keep with them. A few weeks later he would tell them that their babies had died. The U.S. Attorney who prosecuted the case declared: "It's basic fraud of the cruelest sort."[251]

On March 4, 1992, Dr. Cecil Jacobson was convicted on 52 felony counts of fraud and perjury related to his impregnating patients with his own sperm, and lying to others that they had become pregnant. Prosecutors produced DNA evidence showing that Jacobson had fathered at least 15 children through patients who were tested and alleged that he could have fathered up to 75 more through patients who had not come forward for testing.

Because no fraud statutes then existing covered artificial insemination, the government was forced to rely on wire and mail fraud charges; Jacobson had used the Postal Service and the telephone to communicate with patients for billings and appointments. On the witness stand, the doctor admitted using his own sperm to impregnate patients, but could not recall exactly how many. His lawyer argued that it did not really matter since such an act is not illegal. Jacobson stated that he had never intended to mislead patients and that he had "dedicated his life to couples who were desperate to have children."[252] Jacobson actually seemed surprised by the reaction to his behavior. Whether he truly was or not may not be that important. More telling was the insensitivity to his patients he acknowledged at his trial: "I was totally unaware of the anger, anguish and hate I have caused—until these proceedings."[253]

Jacobson received a 5-year prison sentence in 1992. At his sentencing, a former patient had this to say about the doctor's conduct: "He took away the most important thing in the world from all of us. He told us we were going to have a baby, and then it was gone."[254]

While Dr. Jacobson was deceiving patients in Virginia, the second fertility scandal was developing at the University of California, Irvine (UCI). The school's Center for Reproductive Health has become the focus of very serious allegations of widespread wrongdoing. The director of the Center, one of the foremost fertility experts in the world and creator of a revolutionary fertility technique known as "GIFT" (gamete intrafallopian transfer) has been accused, along with his two partners, of numerous violations. All three doctors are currently under investigation by local, state, and federal authorities and apparently have fled the country.

The scandal was first reported by staff members in 1994 and came to public attention a year later. The university has since closed the Center and filed suit against the doctors, claiming that they have violated university policies, prescribed an unapproved fertility drug, performed research on patients without their consent, and "stole" eggs or embryos from patients in order to impregnate others.[255] One couple learned from medical records that three of their embryos had been implanted in another patient. They later discovered that they were the biological parents of twins born to that patient.[256] The victimized couple has declared: "What happened to us was nothing less than theft by doctors who acted for their own profit and prestige."[257]

After the scandal erupted, UCI began an internal investigation which suggested "irregularities" at the Center. The university, however, has been accused by some observers of dragging its feet in an attempt to control the damage to its reputation. Other critics have been even more damning, accusing the university of turning a blind eye in order to keep the prestigious—and very profitable—Center alive.[258]

There are now hundreds of fertility centers around the country, and "clinics have found that touting their success rates is their best marketing tool."[259] False promises and exaggerated claims may well have motivated the fraudulent practices at UCI. The scandal has resulted in

California Senate hearings, the resignation of the UCI Medical Center's director and accusations that the university punished at least one whistleblower by demoting her.[260]

If all the imputed ethical lapses at the Center for Reproductive Health were not enough, major financial wrongdoing has also been alleged. There is a great deal of money to be made in assisted reproduction. Most procedures reportedly average about $8,000.[261] An audit concluded that the three UCI doctors had failed to report nearly $1 million in income at the expense of patients, insurance companies, and the university. Auditors further charged that the doctors had kept more than $167,000 in cash disbursements and had failed to disclose more than $800,000 under a contract which required them to share some of their fees with the university.[262] During one period of time, two of the doctors reportedly were given envelopes of cash to take home with them each day. The auditors concluded that "each month the physicians split the cash amongst themselves."[263]

Efforts by the university to investigate the case were stymied by the doctors' lack of cooperation in turning over patient records. More stonewalling was revealed in 1995, when a former patient complained that the director had attempted to persuade her to sign a retroactive consent form, granting permission to donate eggs he had already removed from her two years earlier. When UCI officials tried to obtain these records, the director denied their requests.

After formal charges were brought against the three doctors, there were public demonstrations by patients and medical students who rallied in support of the physicians, claiming that they were dedicated and skilled practitioners. One patient who bore a healthy child through the director's GIFT technique stated in an interview: "I believe he works for God."[264]

All three doctors have since been dismissed from the university. One of them, Dr. Sergio Stone, was convicted on fraud charges. Dr. Ricardo Asch, former director of the center, at this writing is practicing medicine in Tijuana, Mexico, where he continues to help make babies and has avoided extradition to the United States to face criminal charges. Dr. Jose Balmaceda also fled the country and at this writing remains at large in Chile.

Some bioethicists argue that competition to succeed in the growing area of fertility technology could cause doctors to cut moral corners. This is all the more likely because there is little regulation in the fertility field. One expert in medical ethics at the University of Pennsylvania maintains: "There is less regulation here than there would be in the animal-breeding industry."[265]

There is so much money to be made by "fertility" doctors, that some criminals have even skipped the part about going to medical school. In 2007, Dolores Rodas, an illegal immigrant from Ecuador, set up a phony family practice in The Bronx, New York. Among her patients were three couples that she treated for infertility. Two of the couples were charged more than $3,000 for worthless quackery, including painful injections in the genitals.[266] She bilked a middle-aged couple, desperate for a baby, out of more than $50,000. She performed numerous "medical" procedures on them in her apartment. At one point, she told the 44-year-old woman that she was pregnant with twins but had miscarried. The woman later had to seek help at a hospital after she began bleeding. Rodas also injected the 40-year-old man at least 13 times with a substance that made his genitals swell.[267] In 2008, Dolores Rodas was sentenced to one year in prison for grand larceny and practicing medicine without a license. After serving her sentence, she will be deported back to Ecuador.[268]

RESEARCH FRAUD

Fraudulent medical research appears to be relatively rare; but it does occur. In 1974, Dr. William Summerlin, a senior researcher at the renowned Sloan-Kettering Cancer Institute in New York, used a Magic Marker to make black patches of fur on white mice in an attempt to prove that his experimental skin graft technique was working.[269] Summerlin's stunning subterfuge prompted Al Gore, then a young congressman, to hold the first congressional hearings on research fraud.[270]

In 1989, Dr. Stephen Breuning, a psychologist at the University of Pittsburgh, pleaded guilty to falsifying his research findings. According to the National Institute of Mental Health (NIMH), Breuning alone was responsible for about one-third of all the scholarly literature on the controversial use of the drug Ritalin as a therapy for hyperactive children. An NIMH investigation revealed that Breuning had "knowingly, willfully and repeatedly engaged in misleading and deceptive practices in reporting results of research."[271] Breuning's research was never performed as described in his NIMH grant applications, and his claimed results were never attained. Breuning was sentenced to 60 days in prison—the first federal conviction for research fraud.[272]

In March 2005, the worst case of medical research fraud since Breuning's was reported:

CASE STUDY
Funded Fakery

Dr. Eric Poehlman, an award-winning researcher at the University of Vermont, admitted fabricating data on a purported link between menopause and obesity. His fraudulent research had made his grant proposals more appealing and his articles more publishable, which would in turn keep his laboratory going. Poehlman had used his falsified data to secure nearly $3 million in federal grants. Between 1992 and 2002, Poehlman's faked research was published in numerous medical journals.[273]

Poehlman's misconduct was first detected by an undergraduate student serving as his lab technician. When he was asked to analyze some preliminary test results from 150 post-menopausal women, who were subjects in a project called the Vermont Longitudinal Study of Aging, the technician observed that Poehlman's expectation that the women's health would broadly decline after menopause was not supported by the data. Indeed, some of the subjects actually showed improvement in their cholesterol levels and blood pressure.[274] Poehlman took the computer disk from his assistant, ostensibly to look for clerical errors and statistical anomalies. After he returned it, "the data painted a much darker picture of post-menopausal health."[275] When the young man compared the original data to the revised data, it was clear that

Poehlman had reversed the order of test findings, making it appear that the women's health had gotten worse, not better. He reported Poehlman to the university. The technician later said: "I could not escape the fact that a powerful, respected scientist was . . . layering lie upon lie.[276]

While the University of Vermont was investigating the accusation, Poehlman resigned his tenured professorship and accepted an endowed chair—a high honor reserved for senior scholars—at Université de Montreal, which apparently knew nothing about the allegations. He would later resign this position as well.[277]

In 2005, after five years of denials and with the threat of prison looming, Eric Poehlman finally confessed. He pleaded guilty to falsifying information on a federal grant application. "The plea came with an especially devastating admission; he acknowledged that his most noted research, the longitudinal study on menopause, was almost entirely fabricated. Poehlman had tested only 2 women, not 35."[278]

The U.S. Attorney for Vermont said:

"Dr. Poehlman fraudulently diverted millions of dollars. . . . This in turn siphoned millions of dollars from the pool of resources

(Continued)

available for valid scientific research proposals. As this prosecution proves, such conduct will not be tolerated."[279]

The following year, Eric Poehlman became the first scientist ever sent to prison in the U.S. for fabricating data. He was sentenced to a year behind bars followed by two years probation. The judge, to whom he had lied four years earlier, declared: "When scientists use their skill and their intelligence and their sophistication and their position of trust to do something which puts people at risk, that is extraordinarily serious."[280]

Poehlman also became the first person ever to be barred for life from any federal research funding.[281] But the damage was already done.

Poehlman's fraud had likely diminished the public's trust in science and research.

The scientific process is meant to be self-correcting. Peer review of scientific journals and the ability of scientists to replicate one another's results are supposed to weed out erroneous conclusions and preserve the integrity of the scientific record over time. But the Poehlman case shows how a committed cheater can elude detection for years.[282]

Like many academicians, Eric Poehlman had succumbed to the austere "publish or perish canon." In his case, however, he both published *and* perished.

NURSING HOME ABUSES

With people living longer and families spread farther apart, more and more Americans are forced to rely on nursing homes and other residential institutions for long-term care.[283] "Nursing homes now consume eight cents of every dollar spent on health care."[284] In 2007, there were 1.7 million elderly and disabled Americans in nursing homes. The industry owes its spectacular growth to the federal government, which began dispensing Medicare and Medicaid funds in the 1960s on behalf of the elderly poor.[285] Since the nursing home industry is dominated by enterprises run for profit, and its personnel are among the lowest-paid health workers, quality of care may not be an overriding consideration in many facilities.

Congress passed the Nursing Home Reform Act in 1987, which requires the nursing home industry to comply with federal regulations related to the quality of care of the elderly residents of nursing homes. The act requires that "a nursing home facility must care for its residents in such a manner and in such an environment as will promote maintenance or enhancement of the quality of life of each resident."[286] But there seems little doubt that profit trumps patients at many nursing homes.

For example, the Habana Health Care Center, a 150-bed nursing home in Tampa, Florida, was purchased by a group of large private investment companies in 2002. The new managers quickly cut costs. Within months, the number of registered nurses at the facility was half what it had been a year earlier. The investors were soon earning millions of dollars in profits from Habana and the 48 other nursing homes they had purchased.[287] But at what cost to the patients? Over the following three years, 15 Habana residents died from what their families contend was negligent care.[288]

Thousands of nursing homes have been bought by Wall Street investment companies in recent years, including such private equity firms as Carlyle Group—better known for buying companies like Dunkin Donuts.[289] "As such investors have acquired nursing homes, they have often reduced costs, increased profits and quickly re-sold facilities for significant gains."[290] This is a business model that may work very well for donuts, but government data reveals that residents at those nursing homes have suffered. They are worse off, on average, than they were under previous owners. According to the Centers for Medicare and Medicaid Services, these residents "have fared more poorly than occupants of other homes in common problems such as depression, loss of mobility and loss of ability to dress and bathe themselves."[291]

Because nursing home patients are not fully able to care for themselves—let alone confront unprincipled owners or unresponsive staff—a good deal of mistreatment has been known to occur. Elderly residents are frequently preyed upon by greedy nursing home operators and related medical and health personnel. As an Alabama county official has warned: "There are vultures out there watching for vulnerable elderly."[292] In one case reported in Houston, for example, an aged woman was so neglected that her death was not even discovered until *rigor mortis* had set in. Another woman at the same facility had to be hospitalized for rat bites.[293] Nursing home residents are among the most vulnerable and helpless citizens in the U.S. This can be illustrated by a 2009 Maryland identity fraud case, in which a nursing assistant stole information from her patients, used it to apply for credit cards, and charged more than $8,600 in their names. She was later sentenced to five years in prison.[294] The nursing home industry also provides an environment that too often is conducive to woeful abuses against the elderly. A sad history of inhumane conditions and overcharging for services—if they are provided at all—has made nursing homes the target of numerous state and federal investigations. For example, a nursing home for veterans, run by the State University of New York at Stony Brook, came under investigation by state officials less than 5 months after it opened for reportedly abusing and neglecting patients, several of whom died under questionable circumstances.[295]

Other similar scandals include the following cases:

- In Florida, state officials removed 6 elderly people from a nursing home after they found one of them suffering from deformities caused by neglect and others strapped into urine-soaked chairs or in beds covered with feces.[296] In another Florida case, an 88-year-old man, suffering from Alzheimer's disease and cancer, was restrained in bed for so many hours he developed such severe bedsores that they "ate through his skin, muscles, and bones." There is no delicate way to put it: over a four-month period, the patient actually rotted to death.[297]

- In 1990, a federal judge upheld a jury's $250,000 damage award to the family of a nursing home resident in Mississippi who was physically abused and allowed to remain in her own excrement for extended periods of time.[298]

- An 81-year-old man, suffering from Alzheimer's disease, was reluctantly placed in an Alabama nursing home by his family. Three months later, the patient broke his hip and became permanently bedridden when he slipped on his own urine. Aides began keeping him tied up and heavily sedated. He developed bedsores and bruises, including an unexplained black eye. He had entered the home at a robust 182 pounds. When he died two years later—his body curled into a fetal position—he weighed 94 pounds.[299]

Some of the worst nursing home horror stories have been reported in North Carolina, where more than 50,000 patients reside in long-term care facilities. Operators of these facilities regularly contribute substantial sums of money to the campaign coffers of state and local politicians and have profited in return by slack regulation and an ineffectual sanctioning system of paltry fines.[300] Conditions are not necessarily any worse in North Carolina than in other states, but local investigative journalists there have taken an acute interest in this topic, and so there seems to be greater documentation of pervasive negligence—as the following vignettes sorrowfully recount:

- In 1991, an elderly nursing home resident wandered out of the building unattended, fell into a drainage ditch and drowned. The state fined the home $250.[301]

- In 1992, social workers found a bedsore on a nursing home patient's foot that was so infected that gangrene had developed and it had become infested with maggots. It required amputation.[302]

- For a period of at least 16 days, an 89-year-old nursing home patient's hands, face, and vagina swelled abnormally. The staff failed to notify a physician as her condition deteriorated. One morning, a nurse found her with "frothy mucous" around her mouth and "puffy breathing," but did not even check her vital signs or assess her condition. The patient died 25 minutes later.[303]

- A 65-year-old retired mill worker, crippled by arthritis and suffering from diabetes, was placed in a nursing home after he became unable to administer his insulin shots himself. For 7 days, he received the wrong dose of insulin from the staff. In addition, he was not fed until hours after his injections, which lowered his blood sugar to a dangerous level. When he eventually became unresponsive, a nurse stuck a tube down his nose and pumped orange juice into his stomach in order to raise his blood sugar. Another nurse soon reinserted the tube for more orange juice; then the first nurse returned and pumped in still more juice. None of this had been done with a doctor's approval. Finally, paramedics were called to rush the patient to a hospital. When he coughed up orange foam in the ambulance, the paramedics found the feeding tube coiled in his mouth. It had not been taped into place, contrary to standard procedure. The liquid had emptied into his lungs instead of his stomach. Within hours, he was dead. The man had literally *drowned in orange juice*.[304]

- North Carolina also contains 450 rest homes. Because this type of long-term residential facility is not legally required to provide 24-hour care, rest homes are even less regulated than nursing homes.[305] In 1991, an Alzheimer's patient disappeared from one of these places and was never found.[306] In 1992, staff members at another rest home "punished an unruly resident by slapping her, pinching her breasts, swinging her by her arms and legs, and forcing a bar of soap into her mouth."[307] The owner, the largest rest home operator in the state, was fined $500. Three weeks after checking into a rest home, another Alzheimer's patient was found hanging from her bed, "asphyxiated by a restraining device designed to keep her from getting up."[308] This time the fine was $3,000—high by North Carolina standards, despite the fact that the state contributes nearly $100 million a year to its rest home industry.

But North Carolina is hardly unique when it comes to nursing home horror stories. Every state has had its share of scandals. In 2008, two Massachusetts brothers, Joel and Todd Logan, pleaded guilty to stealing funds and neglecting patients at five nursing homes they formerly owned. Between 2001 and 2003, the Logans used state Medicaid funds for their personal use, "failing to provide nursing home patients with food, medicine, bed linens, and sanitary conditions."[309] Instead, they spent the money at race tracks and on personal luxuries such as boats.

An even more chilling case occurred in Missouri:

The 88-year-old woman at Claywest House nursing home near St. Louis was totally reliant on staff for her care. There was nothing she could do about the ants crawling all over her. Or the waste she helplessly waited in during the weeks leading up to her death.

The problem at Claywest was poor staffing. "And as investigators would later learn, the shortage wasn't an oversight. It was built into the system—a decision that led to horrific conditions."[310]

Federal charges were brought against Claywest and its top administrators accusing them of "padding their balance sheets on the backs of helpless residents in their care."[311] The FBI, which investigated the case, concluded that the criminal conditions at Claywest were all the result of its management company's decision to cut costs. One FBI agent said: "They were trying to make a buck."[312] In the words of another agent: "Service was so bad and so neglectful that patients were essentially being charged for worthless services."[313]

The Claywest House nursing home was later fined $180,000. The CEO of the management company was convicted of conspiracy and sentenced to 18 months in prison, and the company president received two months behind bars for his role.[314]

In 2002, a minority report prepared for Democratic members of the U.S. House Government Reform Committee described a rising tide of abuse and mistreatment in American nursing homes. According to the report: "Common problems include untreated bedsores, inadequate medical care, malnutrition, dehydration, preventable accidents, and inadequate sanitation and hygiene."[315] Rep. Henry Waxman of California, the ranking minority member on the committee, added in a briefing: The report found that *30 percent* of the nursing homes in the United States were cited for abuse between 1999 and 2000.[316] Among the violations described in the report were the following:

> "Numerous instances of physical abuse, such as the case where a nursing home attendant walked into a female resident's room, shouted "I'm tired of your ass, hit the resident in the face and broke her nose."[317]
>
> "In another case, attendants bribed a brain-damaged patient with cigarettes to attack another resident, then watched the two fight."[318]

The report also documents instances of residents being punched, slapped, choked, or kicked by staff members, causing injuries such as fractured skulls or lacerations. In one such instance, a male attendant sexually assaulted an elderly female resident while bathing her.[319]

A month after the House released the minority report, the Senate Select Committee on Aging watched a videotaped deposition given in 1998 by a 75-year-old nursing home resident. The woman, wearing a metal neck brace, looked into the camera and described how she had been severely beaten by a nursing home attendant who discovered she had soiled herself. "He choked me and he went and broke my neck. . . . He broke my wrist bones, in my hand. He put his hand over my mouth."[320] Two days later, the woman died.

An 18-month study by the Government Accounting Office, released in 2002, reported that 50 percent of abuse reports from nursing homes came two or more days after caregivers first heard the allegations. The delay hampered evidence gathering and made prosecuting the cases more difficult.[321] The director of the National Center on Elder Abuse (NCEA) suggested another reason for attacks going unnoticed: "The biggest problem is that these people are hidden. There is very little traffic going into these [nursing] homes from relatives of the victims or people who could observe what's going on."[322] According to the NCEA, unreported cases of elder abuse outnumber reported cases by a ratio of 5-to-1.

According to a report titled "Is Grandma Drowsy or Is She Drugged?" many nursing homes have resorted to giving patients powerful sedatives and psychotropic drugs to keep them docile, thus increasing profits by minimizing care.[323] A major study released in 1988 by Harvard Medical School found that 58 percent of residents in 12 Massachusetts nursing homes were prescribed sedatives, tranquilizers or mind altering drugs, often in excessive doses, and more than one drug at a time.[324] While in some cases the need for such drugs could be justified, continued understaffing and lack of mental health care in nursing homes was also related to their use. Staff doctors can give nurses "blank checks" for prescriptions for residents, and oftentimes families and the residents themselves are unaware of which drugs are being given.[325]

Two other studies, conducted by researchers at Yale and the University of Minnesota, showed that large numbers of nursing home residents "are tethered to their beds or wheelchairs or given powerful tranquilizing drugs without documentation that they are needed."[326] In 1991, an article in the *Journal of the American Medical Association* reported that the prescription of antipsychotic drugs without an appropriate diagnosis is an established practice in nursing homes.[327]

POLICING DOCTORS: PHYSICIAN HEAL THYSELF?

While it should be stressed that the vast majority of physicians and other health providers are honest and dedicated to quality care, it does not take a large contingent of deviant practitioners to steal enormous sums of money or cause extensive physical harm. Control of these miscreants has been a thorny public policy issue for some time. Doctors reflexively argue that their profession is capable of policing itself. After all, who knows more about medical procedures and potential errors and mistakes than them? There is, however, at least one glaring flaw in this linear assumption. Physicians are seldom willing to report colleagues who practice medicine below generally accepted standards. Often, even in egregious cases, doctors will not come forward to identify fellow professionals who are putting patients at great risk.

A case involving an 8-year-old Colorado boy, who died during minor surgery after his anesthesiologist *fell asleep* during the operation, dramatically illustrates the fatal consequences of the medical profession's traditional code of silence. This doctor had been reported to the hospital by colleagues on at least *six* prior occasions for appearing to doze during surgery. In each instance, the hospital had handled the accusations internally, through its confidential peer review process.[328]

The victim's parents buried their son believing that he had died from natural causes and not at the hands of a snoozing specialist. Only after receiving an anonymous telephone call did they press for a formal investigation. The state medical board finally stripped the doctor of his license, condemning his professional conduct as "abhorrent."[329] One may well ask why it took six episodes of sleeping at the switch and the needless death of an innocent child to remove this menacing misfit.

Much like the "Blue Wall of Silence" described in Chapter 8, which inhibits honest law enforcement officers from weeding out corrupt ones, the preceding case underscores the folly of a cultural norm that encourages the many ethical practitioners to "circle the wagons" around the few disreputable ones. Other doctors must take responsibility for dangerously deviant medical practitioners and seriously police their profession, if they do not want government regulators and prosecutors to do it for them. Until physicians repudiate their self-serving "Us" versus "Them" mentality, their calls for less outside intervention seem more than a little hypocritical.

If anything, it would appear that *increased* intervention is needed. In 1994, the number of disciplinary actions taken against physicians by state medical boards reached an all-time high—topping 4,000 for the first time.[330] Yet, according to a report by the Public Citizen Health Research Group, titled *13,012 Questionable Doctors*, two-thirds of doctors disciplined in 1995 for substandard, incompetent, or negligent care were allowed to continue practicing with little or no restriction.[331] The report declares: "If airline pilots were so poorly regulated as physicians, we would have [a] plane crashing every day."[332]

Not surprisingly, among the biggest sources of disciplinary laxity are Medicare and Medicaid defrauders.[333] Reportedly, 30 percent of doctors barred from the Medicare program are not even penalized by state medical boards.[334]

Since the mid 1980s, as evidence of the cost and extent of medical fraud has grown, private insurance companies have also become more actively engaged in fraud detection and prevention. Yet many experts still criticize the health insurance industry for not doing enough in this area. A 1990 survey conducted by the Health Insurance Association of America found that only half of the companies questioned had formed fraud prevention units.[335] With great sums of money at risk, some skeptics believe that the industry has not moved fast enough or far enough. Part of the reason for this sluggishness is that, like with so many white-collar crimes, the costs of insurance fraud are merely passed along to consumers—in this case, in the form of higher premiums. Anti-fraud enforcement in government programs, where the pressure to turn a profit is absent, is even more deficient. The Health Care Financing Administration (HCFA), for example, which runs the Medicare program, has continually come under attack for being too lax and for providing loopholes for fraud to occur. HCFA has also been criticized for taking too long to implement new laws designed to control fraud and for reducing payments to private contractors for fraud prevention.[336]

The bottom line may be, however, that there is simply too big a system to police, given the government's limited resources and halfhearted commitment. As things stand now in the world of medical crime, the "cops" are catching only a handful of the "robbers."

Notes

1. World Health Organization. "World Health Statistics 2011." who.int. 2011.

2. Federal Bureau of Investigation. "Financial Crimes Report to the Public, *Fiscal Years*, 2010–2011." fbi.gov. 2012.

3. Witkin, Gordon, Friedman, Doran, and Guttman, Monika. "Health Care Fraud." *U.S. News & World Report*, February 24, 1992: 34–43.

4. *Houston Chronicle*. "Easy Prey." November 20, 1995: p. 20A.

5. U.S. Department of Justice. "Government Fraud." 1989: 4–10.

6. Geis, Gilbert, Pontell, Henry N., Keenan, Constance, Rosoff, Stephen M., O'Brien, Mary Jane, and Jesilow, Paul. "Peculating Psychologist: Fraud and Abuse Against Medicaid." *Professional Psychology: Research and Practice* 16, 1985: 823–832.

7. Makeig, John. "Chiropractor Receives 8 Years in Fraud Case." *Houston Chronicle*, November 16, 1995: p. 37A.

8. Ropp, Kevin L. "Wisconsin Foot Doctor Jailed for Selling Drug Samples." *FDA Consumer* 29, 1995: p. 36.

9. Institute of Medicine. "Best Care at Lower Cost: The Path to Continuously Learning Health Care in America." iom.edu. September 6, 2012.

10. *Ibid.*

11. *Ibid.*

12. Witkin et al., *op cit.*, p. 36.

13. *Ibid.*, p. 36.

14. Moffat, Susan, "Brothers Enter Guilty Pleas in Massive Insurance Fraud." *Los Angeles Times*, March 17, 1993, p. 12.

15. Zwillich, Todd. "FBI Cites Massive Medical Fraud Investigation." foxnews.com, March 14, 2005.

16. *Ibid.*

17. *Ibid.*

18. *Ibid.*

19. *Ibid.*

20. *Ibid.*

21. Witkin et al., *op cit.*

22. Feldstein, Dan. "Wheelchair Scam Drains Millions From Medicare." *Houston Chronicle*, August 17, 2003" 1A. 21A.

23. Appleby, Julie. "Medicare Bilked of $77M Like 'an ATM.'" *USA Today*, July 9, 2008: 1A.

24. Feldstein, *op. cit.*

25. *Ibid.*

26. *Ibid.*

27. *Ibid.*

28. *Ibid.*

29. Miller, Rena. "Reimbursement Schemes Costly for Medicare." *Los Angeles Times*, June 17, 1991: p. A16.

30. *Houston Chronicle.* "Abbott Labs Fines Total $600 Million," July 24, 2003: 1B, 4B.

31. *Ibid.*, 1B.

32. *Ibid.*

33. *Ibid.*

34. *Ibid,* 1A.

35. *Ibid.*

36. *crossbennett.com.* "Medical Equipment Fraud: Almost 1 Billion in Medicare Overpayments For Wheelchairs, Oxygen Supplies, etc.?"

37. *Ibid.*

38. Quoted in *Ibid.*, A21.

39. *frauddigest.com.* "Health Care Fraud," November 17, 2005.

40. Yembrick, John. "Texas Conviction of Physical Therapist." *mathiasconsulting.com,* November 17, 2005.

41. *asipp.org.* "Doc Sentenced in Medicare/Medicaid Fraud," June 26, 2006.

42. U.S. Department of Health and Human Services (press release). "HHS Fights Durable Medical Equipment Fraud." July 2, 2007.

43. Colliver, Victoria. "Medicare Moves to Reduce Fraud Over Medical Equipment." *sfgate.com,* January 9, 2008.

44. Rubenstein, Sarah. "Fighting Equipment Fraud, Medicare Amps Up Rules For Suppliers." *wsj.com,* December 29, 2008.

45. Appleby, *op. cit.*

46. *Ibid.*

47. Quoted in *Ibid.*

48. Department of Justice (press release). "Miami Jury Convicts Pharmacy Owner of Medicare Fraud." April 24, 2008.

49. *Ibid.*

50. *Ibid.*

51. Federal Bureau of Investigation (press release). "Owner of Medical Equipment Company Sentenced to 130 Months in Prison For Health Care Fraud." July 2, 2008.

52. *Ibid.*

53. Quoted in Appleby, *op. cit.*

54. Quoted in Hines, Lora. "Agency Fighting Medical-Equipment Fraud." *pe.com,* November 8, 2008.

55. Confessore, Nicholas and Kershaw, Sarah. "As Home Health Care Industry Booms, Little Oversight to Counter Fraud." *nytimes.com,* September 2, 2007.

56. Witkin et al., *op cit.,* p. 38.

57. Eisler, Peter. "Home Health Care Fraud on the Rise." *USA Today,* November 12, 1996: pp. 1A, 2A.

58. *Ibid.*

59. Eisler, Peter. "Ga. Couple's Fall a Jolt to the Industry." *USA Today,* November 12, 1996: p. 7A.

60. *Ibid.*

61. Lord, Mary. "A High-Priced Hookup." *US News & World Report* 116, May 9, 1994: 63–69.

62. *Ibid.*

63. *Ibid.*

64. *Ibid.*

65. *Ibid.*

66. Lord, *op. cit.*

67. *Ibid.*

68. New York State Office of the Attorney General. Press Release, "Operation 'Home Alone' Nets Convictions of Leaders of $12 Million Home Care Fraud" by Eric T. Schneiderman, Attorney General, August 27, 2007. Reprinted by permission of New York State Office of the Attorney General.

69. Confessore and Kershaw, *op. cit.*

70. Quoted in Solomont, Elizabeth. "Endemic Fraud Seen in Home Health Care." *nysun.com,* August 21, 2007.

71. *Ibid.*

72. *Ibid.*

73. *Ibid.*

74. New York State Office of the Attorney General, *op. cit.*

75. Confessore, Nicholas. "2 in Brooklyn Plead Guilty to Fraud in Home Care." *nytimes.com,* August 28, 2007.

76. Fellner, Jonathan, "AG Sting Uncovers Medi-Cal Fraud," *Los Angeles Daily Journal,* November 17, 1989, p. 4.

77. Quoted in Eisler, *op. cit.*

78. Quoted in Anderson, Troy. "In-Home Care Fraud Is Rampant." *dailybreeze.com,* December 26, 2008.

79. Frantz, Douglas, "Humana Under Fire for High Markups." *Los Angeles Times,* October 18, 1991: p. D3.

80. Pear, Robert, "U.S. Says Hospitals Demand Physicians Pay for Referrals." *New York Times,* September 27, 1992, p. A1.

81. *Ibid.*, p. A1.

82. *Ibid.*

83. *Ibid.*

84. Colliver, Victoria. "Tenet Healthcare Settles Lawsuit." *sfgate.com,* March 11, 2005.

85. Quoted in *medicalnewstoday.com.* "Tenet Physicians Settle Case Over Unnecessary Heart Procedures at Redding Medical Center, USA," November 17, 2005.

86. Chorney, Jeff. "Tenet Settles Bogus Heart Surgery Claims." *ect.org,* December 22, 2004.

87. *medicalnewstoday.com, op. cit.*

88. Charatan, Fred. "Dozens of Patients Allege Unnecessary Heart Surgery." *pubmedcentral.nih.gov,* May 17, 2003.

89. United States General Accounting Office. "Medicare: Tighter Rules Needed to Curtail Overcharges for

Therapy in Nursing Homes," Washington, D.C.: GAO/HEHS-95–23, 1995.

90. *Ibid.*
91. *Ibid.*
92. *New York Times.* "National Medical Settlement." March 9, 1994: p. C18.
93. Schine, Eric, and Yang, Catherine. "Migraines for National Medical." *Business Week,* September 13, 1993: 74–75.
94. *Corporate Crime Reporter.* "National Medical Enterprises Hit With Record Fine in Health Care Fraud Case." July 4, 1994: p.4.
95. Yang, Catherine and Schine, Eric. "Put the Head in the Bed and Keep It There." *Business Week* (Industrial/Technology Edition) 3341, October 18, 1993: 68–70.
96. Washington, Harriet A. "Human Guinea Pigs." *Emerge,* October 1994: p. 29.
97. *Houston Chronicle.* "Mental Hospitals Blasted." December 21, 1995: p. 23 A.
98. Witkin et al., *op cit.*
99. *Ibid.*
100. *Ibid.*, p. 41.
101. Smith, Mark. "Law Targets Psychiatric Care System Abuses." *Houston Chronicle,* September 8, 1991: pp. 1A, 20A.
102. Smith, Mark. "Marketing Blitz Straddles Line of Medical Ethics." *Houston Chronicle,* September 8, 1991: p. 20A.
103. Smith, Mark. "Profitable Addictions: Claims of 'Bounty Hunting' for Patients Probed." *Houston Chronicle,* September 8, 1991: p. 20A.
104. *Ibid.*
105. Smith, "Law Targets . . . ," *op. cit.*, p. 20A.
106. *Ibid.*, p. 20A.
107. *Ibid.*, p. 20A. A less formal "golden handcuff" agreement guaranteed one San Antonio psychiatrist tickets to University of Texas football games in exchange for recruitment services.
108. *Ibid.*
109. Smith, "Marketing Blitz . . . ," *op. cit*, p. 20A
110. Quoted in Smith, "Law Targets . . . ," p. 20A.
111. Witkin, *op. cit.*, p. 41.
112. *Ibid.*
113. *Ibid.*, p. 42.
114. Smith, "Marketing Blitz . . . ," *op. cit.*
115. Quoted in *Ibid.*, p. 20A.
116. Waas, Murray. "Bleak House." *Los Angeles Times,* April 3, 1994: p. 10.
117. *Ibid.*
118. Quoted in *Ibid.*, p. 10.

119. *Ibid.*
120. Quoted in *Ibid.*, p. 10.
121. Lord, *op. cit.*, p. 65.
122. Sternberg, Stephen. "Double Dipping Doctors." *Mother Jones* 18, May-June, 1993: p. 29.
123. *Ibid.*
124. Quoted in *Ibid.*, p. 29.
125. Quoted in Spiegel, Claire. "Doctor's Use of Own Labs: Good Ethics?" *Los Angeles Times,* Feb. 17, 1989: p. 1.
126. *Ibid.*
127. Streur, Russell. "Doctoring the Books." *imakenews. com,* August 14, 2006
128. Eichenwald, Kurt. "Trouble in Dialysis-Care Industry Puts Lives on the Line." *Houston Chronicle,* December 4, 1995: p. 3A.
129. National Medical Care is a division of W.R. Grace Corporation, one of the main defendants in the Woburn children's leukemia cluster examined in Chapter 3.
130. *Ibid.*
131. Pear, Robert. "Medicare Pays Millions in Ambulance Overbilling, Report Says." *nytimes.com,* November 9, 1997.
132. Quoted in *Ibid.*
133. *Ibid.*
134. *Ibid.*
135. *Ibid.*
136. *Ibid.*
137. Shogren, Elizabeth. "Rampant Fraud Complicates Medicare Cures." *Los Angeles Times,* October 8, 1995: p.1.
138. *Ibid.*
139. *Ibid.*
140. *Ibid.*
141. Rubin, Allan. "Nursing Homes and Medicare Fraud." *therubins.com,* February 6, 2000.
142. *nyinjuries.com.* "Report on Medicare/Medicaid Overbilling and Fraud in 2007 Focuses on Nursing Homes/Rehab Centers, Pharmaceuticals, Boutique Hospitals," January 14, 2008.
143. *Houston Chronicle.* "Medicare Settlement Set." December 13, 1995: p.17A.
144. Rundle, Rhonda. "Corning Unit, Unilab Pay $39.8 million to Settle Allegations of Medicare Fraud." *Wall Street Journal,* September 14, 1993: p. A6.
145. *Ibid.*, p. 1.
146. Epstein, Aaron. "Blowing the Whistle." *Wichita Eagle,* March 6, 1994: p. 1D.
147. Sims, Calvin. "Company to Pay $111 million in Health-Claims Fraud Suit." *New York Times,* December 19, 1992: p.1.

148. *Ibid.*

149. Found, Edward T. and Headden, Susan. "The Hospital Fraud Inquiry that Fizzled." *US News & World Report* 119, December 18, 1995: p. 42.

150. *Ibid.*, p. 42.

151. *Ibid.*

152. *Ibid.*

153. *Consumer Reports.* "How Medicare Patients are Bilked: *Overcharges,* Retainers and Waivers." August, 1994: p. 527.

154. *Ibid.*

155. *Ibid.*

156. *newyorkinjuries.com.* "Report on Medicare/Medicaid Overbilling and Fraud in 2007 Focuses on Nursing homes/Rehab Centers, Pharmaceuticals, Boutique Hospitals," January 14, 2008.

157. *Ibid.*

158. Finch McCranie L.L.P. (press release). "Hospital System Settles Medicare False Claims Act Allegations for $60 Million." July 26, 2008.

159. *Ibid.*

160. *Ibid.*

161. *fiercehealthcare.com.* "St. Barnabas to Pay $265M For Medicare Fraud," June 15, 2006.

162. *redorbit.com.* "N.J. Firm Settles $265M Medicare Fraud Case," June 15, 2006.

163. *healthcare-economist.com.* "Medicare Fraud: $630 Million." August 21, 2006.

164. *bizjournals.com.* "Cooper University Hospital Settles Medicare Fraud Case," September 24, 2008.

165. Kochieniewski, David. "Hospitals Grew With Medicare Paying the Way." *nytimes.com,* August 20, 2006.

166. *Ibid.*

167. *Ibid.*

168. *healthcare-economist.com, op. cit.*

169. *nj.com.* "Warren Hospital to Pay $7.5M to Settle Medicare Fraud Case." December 10, 2007.

170. *nj.com.* "Camden Hospital Will Pay $3,85M to Settle a Medicare Fraud Case." September 25, 2008.

171. *bizjournals.com, op. cit.*

172. Quoted in Kocieniewski, *op. cit.*

173. Anderson, Jack and Van Atta, Dale. "Medicare: Whistle-Blowing in the Wind." *Washington Post,* August 21, 1991: p. E7.

174. *Ibid.*

175. *Ibid.*, p. E7.

176. Shogren, *op cit.*, p. 1.

177. Gottlieb, Martin. "Medicare's Overhaul Will Place Billions into Coffers of HMO's." *Houston Chronicle,* December 10, 1995: p. 16A. See also: Estrich, Susan. "Politics as Usual with All the Investigations." *USA Today,* December 21, 1995: p. 11A.

178. Jesilow, Paul, Geis, Gilbert, and Harris, John. "Doomed to Repeat Our Errors: Fraud in Emerging Health-Care Systems." *Social Justice* 22, 1995: 125–138.

179. Abramowitz, Michael. "Collapse of a Health Plan: How Did Such a Good Idea Turn Out So Bad?" *Washington Post,* June 23, 1987: p. A1.

180. Young, Jeffrey. "Federal Investigators Recoup $2.2B in Healthcare-Fraud Prosecutions." *thehill.com,* February 14, 2008.

181. United States Senate, Subcommittee on Long-Term Care, Special Committee on Aging. Fraud and Abuse Among Practitioners Participating in the Medicaid Program. Washington, D.C.: Government Printing Office, 1976.

182. *Ibid.*

183. Hogue, Elizabeth, Teplitsky, Sanford V., and Sollins, Howard L. *Preventing Fraud and Abuse: A Guide for Medicare and Medicaid Providers.* Owings Mills, MD: National Health Publishing, 1988.

184. Jesilow et al.

185. Quoted in Witkin, *op. cit.*, p. 34.

186. Geis, Gilbert, Henry N. Pontell and Paul D. Jesilow, "Medicaid Fraud. In Scott, Joseph E. and Hirschi, Travis (Eds.), *Controversial Issues in Crime and Justice.* Newbury Park, CA: Sage Publications, 1988: 17–39.

187. Morris, Jim. "Dentist Accused of Abuse Taken off Advisory Panel." *Houston Chronicle,* December 2, 1995: pp. 1A, 18A.

188. Meyer, Josh. "Convicted Doctor Kept on Public Payroll." *Los Angeles Times,* November 30, 1995: pp. A3, A28.

189. *Ibid.*

190. Kennedy, Douglas. "Healthy Spoils From Very Sick System." *New York Post,* April, 18, 1995: Part III, p. 5.

191. *Ibid.*, p.18.

192. Pontell, Henry N., Rosoff, Stephen M., and Goode, Erich. "White Collar Crime." In Goode, Erich (Ed.), *Deviant Behavior* (Fourth Edition). Englewood Cliffs, NJ: Prentice Hall, 1994: 345–371.

193. Lanza-Kaduce, Lonn, "Deviance Among Professional: The Case of Unnecessary Surgery." *Deviant Behavior* 1, 1980: 333–359. Lanza-Kaduce reports that as much as 15 percent of all the elective surgery performed in the United States—that is, operations not involving emergencies or life-threatening circumstances—are unnecessary. For example, it is claimed that 90 percent of all tonsillectomies are unneeded, and 15 percent of all hysterectomies (surgical removal of

the uterus) are said to be performed in the absence of pathology.

194. Welkos, Robert. "Doctor in Blindings Gets 4-Year Prison Term, Fine." *Los Angeles Times,* April 25, 1984: pp. 1, 6.

195. *Ibid.,* p. 6.

196. *Ibid.,* p. 6.

197. Morris, Jim. "Cavities in the State's Dental Fraud Effort." *Houston Chronicle,* December 17, 1995: pp. 1A, 20A.

198. *Ibid.,* p. 20A.

199. *Ibid.,* p. 20A.

200. *Ibid.,* p. 20.

201. *Ibid.*

202. *mlive.com.* "Medicaid Fraud Victimizes Public, State, Experts Say," March 21, 2008.

203. Jesilow, Paul, Henry N. Pontell, and Gilbert Geis. *Prescription for Profit: How Doctors Defraud Medicaid.* Berkeley: University of California Press, 1993, p. 35.

204. Eady, Brenda. "MD Claims Innocence in Medicaid Scheme." *Miami Herald,* March 29, 1981: p. 4B.

205. *Ibid.*

206. Messerschmidt, Al. "Witnesses Dispute Doctor's Claims." *Miami Herald,* January, 16, 1982: p. 2B.

207. Eady, Brenda. "Medicaid M.D. Accused of Fraud," *Miami Herald,* March 14, 1981: p. 1B.

208. Messerschmidt, *op. cit.*

209. Markowitz, Arnold. "Jury Takes 1 Hour to Convict Doctor of Medicaid Fraud." *Miami Herald,* January 23, 1982: p. 1B.

210. Personal Interview.

211. Katzenbach, John. "MD Charged in Contract Killing," *Miami Herald,* September 4, 1982: p. B1.

212. *Ibid.*

213. Grimm, Fred. "Alleged Hit List was for 'Voodoo Man' Doctor Says," *Miami Herald,* February 2, 1983: p. 1B.

214. *Ibid.*

215. Grimm, Fred. "Woman Doctor Convicted in Plot to Kill Partner, Sentenced to Life," *Miami Herald,* February 4, 1983: p. 1D.

216. *mlive.com, op. cit.*

217. Perlmutt, David. "Busts Recover Millions in 2008 Medicaid Fraud." *charlotteobserver.com,* January 9, 2009.

218. Johnson, Linda A. "Merck Settlement Has $671 Million Price Tag." *Houston Chronicle,* February 8, 2008: D2.

219. Silverman, Ed. "Cephalon Pays $435 Million For Medicaid Fraud." *pharmalot.com,* September 29, 2008.

220. *phillipsandcohen.com.* "Cephalon Pays $425 Million to Settle Unique Off-Label Marketing Case Brought by Whistleblower," September 29, 2008.

221. *Ibid.*

222. *Ibid.*

223. *pharmalot.com, op. cit.*

224. Quoted in *phillipsandcohen.com, op. cit.*

225. Quoted in *pharmalot.com, op. cit.*

226. *phillipsandcohen.com, op. cit.*

227. Thomas, Katie and Schmidt, Michael. "Glaxo Agrees to Pay $3 Billion in Fraud Settlement." *nytimes.com,* July 2, 2012.

228. *United States v. GlaxoSmithKline PLC and Glaxo-smithKline LLC.* Case No. 11-10398-RWZ (D.Ma. 2011) ("Complaint").

229. *Ibid.* p. 47.

230. Thomas and Schmidt. *op. cit.*

231. *Ibid.*

232. *Los Angeles Times.* "Fraud Claim Settlements Rise." September 28, 2012: p. B2.

233. *northcountrygazette.* "Homeless Recruited by Hospital in Fraud Scheme," August 7, 2008.

234. *cnn.com.* "Hospital Chief, Shelter Director Used Homeless For Fraud," August 7, 2008.

235. *northcountrygazette, op. cit.*

236. Connell, Rich, Dimassa, Cara Mia, and Winton, Richard. "3 Hospitals Accused of Using Homeless For Fraud." *latimes.com,* August 7, 2008.

237. *Ibid.*

238. *Ibid.*

239. *USA Today.* "FBI: L.A. Hospital CEO Arrested in Probe of Homeless Scheme," August 6, 2008.

240. United States Attorney's Office (press release). "Former Hospital C.E.O. Pleads Guilty to Paying Kickbacks in 'Skid Row' Healthcare Fraud Scheme." December 12, 2008.

241. Quoted in Mojaher, Shaya Tayefe. "FBI Arrests Hospital Executives For Medicare Fraud." *nysun.com,* August 6, 2008.

242. Jesilow, Pontell and Geis, *op. cit.*

243. Geis, Gilbert, Jesilow, Paul, Pontell, Henry, and O'Brien, Mary Jane. "Fraud and Abuse by Psychiatrists Against Government Medical Benefit Programs." *American Journal of Psychiatry* 142: 231–234.

244. *Ibid.*

245. Rosoff, Stephen M. and Leone, Matthew C. "The Public Prestige of Medical Specialties: Overviews and Undercurrents." *Social Science & Medicine* 32, 1991: 321–326.

246. Sutherland, Edwin H. *White-Collar Crime.* NY: Holt, Rinehart and Winston, 1949.

247. Hilts, Philip J. "Punished Doctors Keep on Practicing." *Houston Chronicle,* March 29, 1996: p. 9A.

248. Gartrell, Nanette, Herman, Judith, Olarte, Sylvia, Feldstein, Michael, and Localio, Russell. "Psychiatrist-Patient Sexual Contact: Results of a National Survey, I: Prevalence." *American Journal* of *Psychiatry* 143, 1986: 1126–1131.

249. Elmer-Dewitt, Phillip. "The Cruelest Kind of Fraud." *Time,* 138, December 2, 1991: p. 27.

250. *Ibid.*, p. 27.

251. *Ibid.*, p. 27.

252. *Ibid.*, p. 27.

253. Quoted in Howe, Robert F. "Citing Cruel Lies by Jacobson, Judge Gives Him 5 Years, Fine." *Washington Post,* May 9, 1992: p. D1.

254. Quoted in *New York Times.* "Fertility Doctor Gets Five Years." May 9: 1992, p. 8.

255. Cowley, Geoffrey, Murr, Andrew, and Springen, Karen. "Ethics and Embryos." *Newsweek,* June 12, 1995: p. 66.

256. Challender, Debbie. "Fertility Fraud: Why One Mother May Never Know Her Babies." *Redbook,* December 1995: pp. 84–87, 116–118. The UCI case is not the only recent scandal involving fertility centers. In 1995, a clinic at the University Hospital in Utrecht, the Netherlands botched an in vitro procedure by fertilizing a woman's eggs with sperm from both her husband and another man. As a result, the woman gave birth to twin boys—one white and one black.

257. *Ibid.*, p. 84.

258. Marquis, Julie. "Legislators Blast UCI's Fertility Center Role." *Los Angeles Times,* June 7, 1995: p. B1.

259. Challender, *op. cit.*, p. 86

260. Kelleher, Susan and Nicolsi, Michelle. "UCI Report: Clinic Doctors Punished Whistleblower." *Orange County Register,* June 4, 1995: p. 1.

261. Challender, *op. cit.*

262. Wagner, Michael G. "Audit Ascribes Undue Profits to Fertility Doctors." *Los Angeles Times,* June, 5, 1995: p. 1.

263. *Ibid.*

264. *Ibid.*, p. 1.

265. Quoted in Weber, Tracy and Marquis, Julie. "In Quest for Miracles, Did Fertility Clinic Go Too Far?" *Los Angeles Times,* June 4, 1995, p. 1.

266. Office of The Bronx District Attorney (press release). "Grand Jury Files Additional charges Against Woman Who Treated at Least Ten Patients While Pretending to Be a Doctor." April 3, 2007.

267. Buffa, Denise. "Fertility 'Faker.'" *nypost.com,* March 30, 2007.

268. Buffa, Denise. "Fertility Quack Jailed." *nypost.com,* January 31, 2008.

269. Mendoze, Martha. "Allegations of Fake Research Reach New Heights." *The Burlington Free Press.* October 7, 2005: 8.

270. *Ibid.*

271. Quoted in corporate *wellness.4u.com.* October 13, 2005.

272. *Ibid.*

273. Goldberg, Carey and Allen, Scott. "Ex-Vermont Scientist Won Nearly $3M From US." *Boston Globe* (online). March 18, 2005.

274. *Ibid.*

275. *Ibid.*

276. Quoted in *Ibid.*

277. *Ibid.*

278. Interlandi, Jeneen. "An Unwelcome Discovery." *nytimes.com,* October 22, 2006.

279. Quoted in Goldberg, *op. cit.*

280. Quoted in Interlandi, *op. cit.*

281. Goldberg, *op. cit.*

282. Interlandi, *op. cit.*

283. Bates, Eric. "No Place Like Home." *Southern Exposure,* Fall 1992: 17–21.

284. *Ibid.*, p. 19.

285. Wilkes, James L. "Nursing Home Nightmares." *USA Today,* August 20, 1996: p. 11A.

286. Pringle, Evelyn. "Nursing Home Fraud Neglect & Abuse Much Too Common." *onlinejournal.com,* September 29, 2006.

287. Duhigg, Charles. "Study Finds Profits Trump Patients at Some Nursing Homes." *Houston Chronicle,* September 23, 2007: A3.

288. *Ibid.*

289. *Ibid.*

290. *Ibid.*

291. *Ibid.*

292. Quoted in Calvert, Scott. "The Vulnerable Elderly." *Birmingham News,* August 15, 1993: p. 13A.

293. Trafford, Abigail. "The Tragedy of Care for America's Elderly." *U.S. World & News Report,* April 24, 1978: p. 56.

294. Holland, Earl. "Ex-Nursing Home Worker Sentenced in Identity Theft." *delmarvanow.com,* January 23, 2009.

295. McQuiston, John T. "Health Dept. Studies Reports of Abuse at Nursing Home." *New York Times,* February 29, 1992: p. 28.

296. *New York Times.* "6 Found in Nursing Home Filth, Florida Says." November 26, 1987: p. A28.

297. Wilkes, *op. cit.*, p. 11A.

298. Lewin, Tamar. "Nursing Home Damages Upheld." *New York Times,* September 5, 1990: p. A20.
299. Bates, *op. cit.*
300. Ready, Tinker. "Resting Uneasy." *Southern Exposure,* Fall 1992: 22–25.
301. *Ibid.*
302. *Ibid.*
303. Williams, Paige and Garloch, Karen. "Pain and Profit." *Charlotte Observer,* September 27, 1992: p. A1.
304. *Ibid.*
305. Ready, *op. cit.*
306. *Ibid.*
307. *Ibid.,* p. 24.
308. *Ibid.,* p. 22.
309. Nuss, Jeannie M. "Ex-Nursing Home Owners Admit Fraud, Neglect." *boston.com,* July 24, 2008.
310. *Ibid.*
311. *Ibid.*
312. Quoted in Federal Bureau of Investigation (press release). "Nursing Home Horror." April 20, 2007.
313. Quoted in *Ibid.*
314. *Ibid.*
315. Quoted in Ruppe, David. "Elderly Abused in 1 in 3 Nursing Homes: Report." *abcnews.com,* July 30, 2002.
316. Ruppe, *op. cit.*
317. Sherer, *op. cit.*
318. Ruppe, *op. cit.*
319. *Ibid.*
320. Quoted in Robinson, Bryan. "'He Choked Me:' Why Some Elderly Attacks Go Unnoticed." *abcnews.com,* March 7, 2002.
321. *Ibid.*
322. Quoted in *Ibid.*
323. Findlay, Steven. "Is Grandma Drowsy, or is She Drugged?" *U.S. World & News Report,* June 12, 1989, p. 68.
324. *Ibid.*
325. *Ibid.*
326. Kolata, Gina. "Nursing Homes are Criticized on How They Tie and Drug Some Patients." *New York Times,* January 23, 1991: p. A16.
327. Jencks, Stephen F. and Clauser, Steven B. "Managing Behavior Problems in Nursing Homes." *JAMA* 265, 1991: 506–507.
328. Siegal, Barry. "Medicine's Fatal Code of Silence." *Los Angeles Times,* August 24, 1995: A16–A17.
329. Siegal, Barry. "A Death Cracks the Shell of Privacy." *Los Angeles Times,* August 25, 1995: A1, A22–A23. Criminal charges of reckless manslaughter have also been filed by the District Attorney's office in Denver. At this writing, the case has yet to be adjudicated.
330. *People's Medical Society Newsletter.* "Disciplining the Docs." Volume 14, 1995: p. 6.
331. Levy, Doug. "Many 'Bad' Doctors Evade Censure." *USA Today,* March 29, 1996: p. 2D.
332. Quoted in *Ibid.,* p. 2D.
333. *People's Medical Society Newsletter, op. cit.*
334. *Ibid.*
335. U.S. General Accounting Office, *op. cit.*
336. *Ibid.*

12

Computer Crime

In the late 19th century, the French social theorist Gabriel Tarde constructed his *law of insertion*, which noted how newer criminal modes are superimposed on older ones through imitative learning and technological innovation.[1] Thus, for example, the European highwayman of the 18th century prepared the way for the American stagecoach bandit of the 19th century. Likewise, the train robber of the 19th century was the progenitor of the 20th Century truck hijacker. Now, as the 21st century unfolds, Tarde's insight is being validated again—this time in ways Tarde himself scarcely could have imagined.

Today, corrupted software programs are replacing the falsified ledger, long the traditional instrument of the embezzler. The classic weapons of the bank robber as well can now be drawn from a far more sophisticated arsenal containing such modern tools as automatic teller machines and electronic fund transfers. In short, white-collar crime has entered the computer age.

Computer crime has been defined broadly as "the destruction, theft, or unauthorized or illegal use, modification, or copying of information, programs, services, equipment, or communication networks."[2] Donn B. Parker, one of the country's leading computer crime researchers, offers a less formal definition of computer crime as any intentional act associated with computers where a victim suffers a loss and a perpetrator makes a gain.[3] Under these definitional guidelines, the following offenses all could be classified as computer crimes: (1) electronic embezzlement and financial theft; (2) computer hacking; (3) malicious sabotage, including the creation, installation, or dissemination of computer viruses; (4) Internet scams; and (5) utilization of computers and computer networks for purposes of personal, commercial, or international espionage. Each of these offenses will be examined in this chapter; however, it would be instructive to consider first the history of this problem and how fast it has grown.

For obvious reasons, computer crime has a relatively short history. Its most immediate precursor was the invention of the so-called blue box in the early 1960s. The blue box was an illegal electronic device capable of duplicating the multifrequency dialing system developed by AT&T. The telephone company had described its new direct-dialing technology in its technical journals, apparently confident that no one in the general public would ever read or at least understand such esoteric information. How wrong they were. "Ma Bell" became the first casualty of the first law of electronic crime: *if it can be done, someone will do it*. Motivated by a curious blend of mischievousness and greed, a cadre of young wizards tape-recorded piccolos and other high-pitched sounds, and thus created the blue box, which gave them unauthorized access to the entire Bell network. They called themselves "phone phreaks." One ingenious phreak even discovered that a give-away whistle packaged in Cap'n Crunch cereal produced a perfect 2600-cycle tone that allowed him to place overseas telephone calls without paying charges.

Although occasional arrests were made, phone phreaking was more or less hidden from the public—both by the phreaks themselves who feared exposure *and* by the telephone company which feared an epidemic. But in 1971, a popular magazine "blew the whistle" (appropriately enough!) with the publication of an explosive article entitled "Secrets of the Little Blue Box."[4]

Among the first generation of phone phreaks, some achieved legendary status: Jerry Schneider, the shameless self-promoter who appeared on the *60 Minutes* television program in 1976 and used his telephone to raise the overdraw limit on Dan Rather's personal checking account from $500 to $10,000, as millions of viewers looked on—including a stunned Rather;[5] Joe the Whistler, blind since birth but possessing perfect musical pitch and an uncanny ability to call anywhere in the world by whistling into a receiver;[6] the six-member gang—dubbed the "Gay Phone Phreaks" by the tabloid press—who placed an untraceable $19,000 twelve-hour call to Indonesia;[7] and rising above them all was the king of the phreakers—Captain Crunch.

Captain Crunch (John Draper) took his "nom-de-phreak," of course, from the breakfast cereal with the direct-dialing whistle. At the time of the famous *Esquire* article,[8] Crunch was a 28-year-old walking encyclopedia of telephony. Despite three convictions, he has never considered himself a criminal and utilizes the same neutralization techniques as his hacker brethren, claiming he performs a valuable public service by exposing weaknesses in communication systems. Captain Crunch's early ambition was to phreak legally in the employ of the phone company. Reportedly, he was quite dismayed when AT&T hired his old friend Joe the Whistler, but not him.[9]

As a devoted member of the '60s counterculture, Captain Crunch's favorite activity was spying electronically on the government. While he was serving a 4-month prison sentence in 1977, "He tweaked the coil of an FM radio with a nail file to listen in on guards' [telephone] conversations."[10]

It is not difficult to find a perverse charm in the exploits of Captain Crunch—or those of his co-legends. Even the austere Donn Parker acknowledges personal affection for the Captain.[11] But the blend of social immaturity and grand egotism that gave the pioneer phone phreaks their "Robin Hood" images also gives them the potential to teach their extraordinary skills (intentionally or otherwise) to career criminals. Thus, Parker argues, despite their individual charms, Captain Crunch and his crew are "dangerous."[12]

Furthermore, there arose a second generation of phone phreaks, more dangerous—and less charming—than the first. A 1993 survey by TAI (Telecommunications Advisors, Inc.) reveals that 70 percent of respondents report that they have been victims of telephone toll fraud.[13] TAI interprets this finding as an indication that toll fraud may be a greater risk than previously believed. As the report observes: "[I]n 1990, 70 percent of respondents probably did not even know what toll fraud was, but it is now a thriving underground business."[14]

A 1992 published interview with a young phone phreak reveals once more that the familiar litany of neutralization techniques continues to be recited by members of the hacker subculture. This phreak insists that fraudulent calls are of no consequence to multi-million dollar corporations[15] (denial of victim again). He further asserts that his actions express his anti-capitalist political beliefs. This latter claim seems to flirt with hypocrisy, since he admittedly is making a considerable profit from his crimes.

And how much money can an ambitious anti-capitalist make? A 1992 Congressional committee estimated that toll fraud costs $2.3 billion annually.[16] In 1993, the International Communications Association complained to the FCC that over a five-year period 550 incidents of toll fraud had cost its members alone $73.5 million.[17] Long-distance carriers are reluctant to reveal how much they lose each year to computer fraud, but one expert has estimated that losses now approach $4 billion, which is of course passed on to consumers as a covert "fraud tax."[18] In 1994, an MCI employee was arrested and charged with stealing more than 100,000 calling card numbers that were used to make $50 million worth of long-distance calls. Fifty million dollars was roughly 9 percent of MCI's net profits for the entire year.[19]

The rapidly-growing cellular telephone industry has been hit particularly hard by illegally accessed calls; losses industry-wide are now at $300 million a year and climbing.[20] The drawback to cellular phones is that they can be scanned easily using an inexpensive Radio Shack scanner.[21] The numbers can then be programmed into another cellular phone, making it a "clone" of the original phone.[22] Bills in the hundreds of thousands of dollars can be run up on unsuspecting victims.[23] Cordless telephones are also considered easy prey.[24]

Here are a few examples of notable toll fraud cases:

- NASA (a perennial target of hackers and phreakers), reportedly lost $12 million in unauthorized calls over a two-year period as a result of computer tampering at its Johnson Space Center in Houston.[25]

- The chief of police of St. Croix in the U.S. Virgin Islands was convicted in 1992 of long-distance telephone fraud. He stole and used access codes from Caribbean Automated Long-Line Services (CALLS). CALLS claimed its losses may have been as high as $185,000.[26]

- Also in 1992, the Christian Broadcast Network lost $40,000 to a phone phreak who had hacked into its system and regularly placed calls to Pakistan.[27]

- In 1995, the Pacific Mutual Insurance company lost $250,000 to toll fraud in four days, and Avnet, a computer service company, lost $500,000 over one long weekend.[28]

One of the most contentious aspects of toll fraud is the assessment of responsibility for illegally accessed codes. In a battle of titans worthy of Greek mythology, Japan's Mitsubishi Corporation and AT&T counter-sued in 1991 over AT&T's alleged failure to warn its customers of the potential for unauthorized use of phone systems and Mitsubishi's failure to pay a $430,000 bill accumulated by 30,000 unauthorized calls allegedly placed by phreaks who had cracked their system.[29] The two companies eventually settled out of court in 1992.

In response to the issue of liability, American insurance firms and long-distance carriers now are providing coverage against toll fraud.[30] In 1992, for example, The Travelers Corporation offered $1 million in protection for $49,000 with a $100,000 deductible. At the lowest end, a $50,000 policy was available for $2500 with a $5,000 deductible.[31] These steep premiums exemplify some of the substantial indirect costs of phone phreaking.

Another cause for concern is the movement of phone phreaks into the area of industrial espionage. The proliferation of fax machines has created one of the easiest ways to steal corporate information. Computer criminals can now break into a phone line and produce a "shadow" version of the faxes received.[32] According to security experts, most corporations currently are vulnerable to data leaks resulting from telephone espionage.[33]

Finally, a common toll fraud scheme involves sidewalk "call-sell operators," who buy stolen outdialing access codes and use them to make or sell long-distance calls, often overseas. The charges for these calls, which can run into huge amounts of money, later show up on the victimized party's telephone bill.[34] Some of the stolen codes are purchased from "shoulder surfers"—persons who hang out at airports using their eyes and ears to steal access numbers from careless business travelers making long-distance calls.[35] Most of the access codes, however, are peddled by hackers who simply program their computers to "war dial"—that is, to dial "800" numbers randomly and rapidly.[36] They are able to call tens of thousands of "800" numbers in a single night and record all those answered by the "unique carrier tone of computers."[37] "Call-sell operators" then offer customers long-distance calls via the victim's phone system. These customers are often recent immigrants, too poor to afford telephones of their own, who wish to speak to relatives and friends in their native countries. In New York City, throngs of homesick foreigners reportedly line up in front of designated phone booths where well-dressed "call-sell operators" charge them $30 to talk for 10 minutes.[38]

By the time the phone phreak subculture had established itself, the fledgling computer industry had graduated from the self-contained mainframe to interactive linkage and primitive networks. Once again, the first law of electronic crime was activated, as computer buffs now could use terminals to explore powerful mainframes previously off limits. A new term entered the public lexicon—hacker. In the 1970s, the early hackers began using school computers for a variety of misdeeds—most notably the alteration of grades. However, since few schools even had computers then, hacking was still a relatively minor nuisance.

Today, of course, that is no longer the case. Virtually all schools in the United States have computers—*and hackers*. In 2003, for example, the University of Michigan expelled a graduate student, a 24-year-old Chinese citizen, for hacking a computer system and using information to get copies of final exams.[39] In 2007, a Colorado high school student pleaded guilty to hacking into his school's computers and changing his grades.[40] These were not rare offenses. In a recent, more or less typical, case, 13 students aged 14 to 17 at Klutztown High School in Pennsylvania bypassed security with school-issued laptops and downloaded games, music—and pornography. They also spied on district administrators and teachers.[41] One-third of the entire student body allegedly had the "secret" password. One administrator said: "The kids basically stumbled through an open rabbit hole and found Wonderland."[42]

By the end of the 1970s, modems and computerized bulletin board services (BBSs) appeared, and, by the early 1980s, the home PC had become increasingly common. To the hackers this was the missing ingredient—a high-tech skeleton key that could open a myriad of locked doors. For example, in 1985 twenty-three teenagers broke into a Chase Manhattan Bank computer by telephone, destroying accounting records and changing passwords. No money was stolen, but customers effectively were denied access to their own files.[43]

Predictably, the first generation of hackers, for all their mischief, were only setting the stage for far more insidious types of computer crime; for what may have begun as a questionable hobby shared by a network of adolescent misfits has been co-opted by a more malevolent class of white-collar criminal. Some individuals began employing the basic hacker methodology to break into systems, not as a vandalic prank or simply to do it, but to steal. "Computers have created opportunities for career criminals, an increasing number of whom are becoming computer literate."[44] An early (and ongoing) example involves the planting of an unauthorized program—known as a Trojan Horse. A Trojan Horse program can transfer money automatically to an illegal account whenever a legal transaction is made.[45] To many skilled thieves and embezzlers, this was akin to striking the mother lode.

How common and how costly has computer crime become? It is now believed to be the fastest-growing category of crime in America.[46] A 1986 survey asked respondents if they believed that their companies were being victimized by computer crime. Only 7 percent said yes.[47] A

1993 survey reported that *70 percent* of the more than 400 companies responding admitted to at least one security infringement in the previous 12 months; 24 percent put the loss per incident at more than $100,000.[48] The head of the organization which conducted the latter survey noted: "The problem is much more serious than expected."[49] Of the 150 large companies surveyed by Michigan State University in 1995, 148 said they had suffered from computer crime; 43 percent said they had been victimized 25 times or more.[50]

Computer crime is no longer just an American problem. It has been uncovered in both Canada[51] and Mexico,[52] as well as Western European nations, such as the United Kingdom,[53] Sweden,[54] The Netherlands,[55] Germany,[56] Switzerland,[57] and Italy.[58] Viruses have been created in such distant places as Bulgaria and South Africa.[59] Hackers reportedly have proliferated in France and Israel,[60] India and Singapore,[61] and Russia (where they are called *chackers*).[62] China has moved to the forefront of hacking with successful cyber attacks against U.S. government agencies and officials[63] and Fortune 500 companies.[64] State secrets and intellectual property have undoubtedly been compromised or stolen. Likewise, computer security has become a major concern in Japan,[65] Hong Kong,[66] Australia,[67] India,[68] Ukraine,[69] Estonia,[70] and New Zealand.[71] In fact, a New Zealand teenager, Owen Thor Walker, was the leader of an international ring of illegal hackers. Using viruses, worms, and Trojan Horse programs, Walker and his gang took control of 1.3 million computers around the world without their owners' knowledge. Walker pleaded guilty in 2008. And in one especially malignant use of computer technology, an Argentine kidnapping ring illegally accessed financial records to determine how much ransom victims could pay.[72]

Estimates in 2012 place the worldwide loss from cyber crime between $250 billion and $1 trillion per year, but these numbers are hard to establish and come from computer security manufacturers who have a vested interest in selling security software when they publish their research.[73] This remarkably wide range of estimates no doubt reflects the substantial variation that exists in defining what qualifies as computer crime. Thieves can steal anything from entire systems[74] to transportable laptop and notebook computers[75] to integrated circuits, semiconductors, or memory chips[76]—all of which can be resold for their illicit "street value." Is hardware theft computer crime? Tens of millions of federal tax returns are now filed electronically. In 1989, IRS agents arrested a Boston bookkeeper for electronically filing $325,000 worth of phony tax refund claims.[77] A 1993 report by the General Accounting Office warns the IRS of its potential vulnerability to a number of new electronic schemes.[78] Should this be classified as tax fraud or computer crime? The Internet offers sociopathic young malcontents an opportunity to download "The School Stopper's Textbook," which instructs students on how to blow up toilets and how to "break into your school at night and burn it down."[79] Is this criminal incitement or free speech? Dealers in child pornography utilize the Internet and computer bulletin board services to advertise materials and exchange information.[80] Pedophiles also use the Internet to "troll" for potential adolescent victims.[81] This is obviously felonious conduct of the most offensive sort, but can it really be considered computer crime? Computer systems have assisted the daily operations of prostitution rings.[82] Illegal gambling records are now routinely computerized.[83] Organized crime uses computers in many of its operations, from bribery to hijacking,[84] and illegal drug cartels employ computers to describe clients and distribution networks.[85] The computer has also become an indispensable tool for "laundering" drug money[86] and other organized crime revenues. Money laundering is now a $100 billion a year industry in the United States.[87] Should all those billions of dollars be considered part of the cost of computer crime? The truth is that there is little consensus in these matters. In fact, some experts have adopted an "agnostic" position that the true cost is unknowable. To further complicate estimation, it has been suggested that within a short time, virtually *all* business crime will conform to what now is considered computer crime.[88]

Another gray area in estimating the losses from computer crime is software piracy. No one knows the actual cost of this offense, but a study conducted by the Software Publishers Association (SPA) claims that $7.4 billion worth of business application software was counterfeited in 1993—a figure nearly equal to the total legitimate revenues for the entire industry in that same year.[89] In addition to business applications, piracy also entails the illegal copying of software for personal use—known as "softlifting."[90] A Massachusetts bulletin board service raided by the FBI had subscribers from 36 states and 11 countries, who paid $99 a year to download illegally copied personal software.[91]

Foreign piracy of American software is an extremely costly problem. Some countries provide no copyright protection at all for software, and many that do have copyright laws choose not to enforce them.[92] Computer software is predominantly an American asset (American companies control about 80 percent of the world market); so other nations "tend to be slow to provide protection for goods they don't produce themselves."[93] In 1993, just seven countries—South Korea, Spain, France, Germany, Taiwan, Thailand, and Poland—reportedly cost American software companies more than $2 billion. In each of these countries pirated American software was said to account for between 75 and 90 percent of the total software in use.[94] The former chairman of the International Trade Subcommittee of the U.S. Senate has stated that the elimination of piracy would significantly shrink the American trade deficit.[95] An overseas dealer, for example, was selling pirated copies of the popular *Lotus 1-2-3* spreadsheet software (which usually retails for around $200) for $1.50![96] To put it in perspective, this means that for every $100 in pirated Lotus sales generated by this dealer, MicroPro, the manufacturer of Lotus, lost nearly $15,000 in legitimate sales. Similarly, in China a pirated CD-ROM containing 70 popular software programs is available for just $100. The legitimate price is $10,000 in the United States, where millions of dollars were spent to develop it.[97]

When one considers as well the vast amount of undetected software piracy certain to exist, guessing the bottom line jolts the imagination. Indeed, based on their survey of 45,000 American households, McGraw-Hill Information Systems conservatively estimates that there is one pirated copy of software for every authorized copy.[98] The Software Publishers Association places the ratio at *seven to one*.[99] The Business Software Alliance reports that for every two dollars of software purchased legitimately in 2006, one dollar was obtained illegally. The BSA places the annual losses at $40 Billion worldwide[100] Although the United States has the lowest PC software piracy rate in the world, 20 percent of its software reportedly is unlicensed,[101] costing local governments $1.7 billion a year in lost taxes.[102] The Federation Against Software Theft (FAST) believes that figure will increase in the wake of the current economic downturn. FAST predicts that, as hard-pressed businesses look for ways to save money, more companies may be willing to risk breaking the law in the name of cost-cutting.[103]

To cite just one recent prosecution, brothers Maurice and Thomas Robberson were sentenced in federal court in 2008 after pleading guilty to felony copyright infringement. Thomas Robberson made more than $150,000 selling pirated software with a retail value of nearly $1 million through *BestValueshoppe.com* and *TheDealDepot.net*.[104] Maurice Robberson grossed more than $855,000 selling pirated software with a retail value of nearly $5.6 million through *CDsalesUSA.com* and *AmericanSoftwareSales.com*.[105] Assistant Attorney General Alice Fisher said in a statement: "People who steal the intellectual property of others for their personal financial gain, while defrauding consumers who think they are buying legitimate products, will be punished for their crimes, as today's sentences prove."[106]

A newer form of piracy involves Internet sites known as Warez. Warez sites are subterranean—though often "conspicuously subterranean"—Web sites which provide copyrighted programs for downloading. With a little bit of expertise and a couple of quick clicks of a mouse one can download thousands of dollars worth of commercial software, copyrighted computer games, even the latest movies. Most computer games are available illegally on Warez sites before they're even available for public release. Some movies, such as *Star Wars: The Phantom Menace* and *Austin Powers: The Spy Who Shagged Me*, were on the Internet before they were released to theaters.[107] HBO's popular show *Game of Thrones* has more illegal digital viewers each week than paid television viewers.[108]

People who create Warez sites are known as "crackers" because they "crack" copy protection codes. Most of them are teenage boys, who trade Warez like baseball cards. They use a program called a machine code monitor, which allows them to read protected disks one byte at a time—an operation known as "boot tracing." At critical points in the sequence they insert new instructions and "liberate" the disk. Groups such as the Inner Circle, Addiction, and the Phrozen Crew pass gigabytes of pirated software through cyberspace. Warez groups have even created their own brazenly illegal, "in your face" Web sites.[109]

One of the most notorious Warez trading networks was the underground group DrinkOrDie (DoD). It was founded in 1993 in Moscow by two Russian hackers calling themselves "deviator" and CyberAngel. By 1995, DoD was global. By late 2001 it was out of business. DrinkOrDie was shut down in a law enforcement raid known as Operation Buccaneer. The American co-leader of DrinkOrDie, John Sankus, known by his screen name "eriFlleH" (HellFire spelled backwards), pleaded guilty in early 2002 and was sentenced to 46 months in prison.[110] His sentence was later reduced to 18 months after he agreed to help the government capture other members of the group. As a result, 16 other members were convicted. DoD's Australian co-leader, Raymond Griffiths, known as Bandido, fought extradition for three years until he finally became the first Australian extradited to the U.S. for copyright infringement.[111] In 2007, Griffiths was sentenced to 51 months in prison. U.S. Attorney Chuck Rosenberg underscored the government's resolve to stamp out Warez: "Whether committed with a gun or a keyboard, theft is theft."[112]

From 2007 to 2009, there was a spate of Warez-related criminal prosecutions, including the following cases:

- Christopher Eaves, a member of the pioneering Warez group Apocalypse Crew, was convicted of illegally sharing music, movies, video games, and computer software. His was the fiftieth felony conviction resulting from the Operation Fastlink crackdown on the so-called "warez scene," involving the FBI, the Justice Department, and Interpol. Apocalypse Crew was responsible for providing copyrighted music online before its official release.[113]

- Paul Emch was sentenced to 12 months in prison in another Operation Fastlink conviction. Emch was a leader of the Warez group MaGE, which had a huge collection of pirated material.[114]

- Kevin Fuchs and Kifah Maswadi of Florida were convicted of supplying cracking and testing software in the so-called "Warez scene." Fuchs was sentenced to eight months in prison, and Maswadi received 15 months. Maswadi had earned a reported $390,000 selling pirated video games.[115]

- Barry Gitarts, known as "Dextro," was sentenced to 18 months in jail for copyright infringement. Gitarts was another member of Apocalypse Crew, who operated a Warez site used to store thousands of music files, movies, software, and games.[116]

- Eli El was sentenced to 30 months in prison for his part in an organized online software distribution conspiracy involving 20,000 copyrighted works, including video games, DVDs and music CDs before they were commercially available to the public.[117]

- Daniel Jaeger pleaded guilty to conspiracy to commit copyright infringement. His arrest stemmed from another multinational software piracy investigation known as "Operation Higher Education." Jaeger built and maintained a Warez server called "DataStream" (DS), which stored and distributed pirated software and other digital media.[118]

- David Fish was given a 30-month prison sentence for criminal copyright conspiracy. Fish served as a Warez site operator, as well as a scriptor, equipment supplier, broker, and encoder. His work involved cracking copyright controls and uploading pirated content.[119]

- And in February 2009, Greg Hurley, the final defendant from Operation Higher Education, pleaded guilty of participating in a Warez ring responsible for tens of thousands of copies of pirated media.[120]

- Jammie Thomas-Rasset may be the most famous file-sharing defendant, and she merely was a consumer, not provider, of pirated music. In 2007, Thomas-Rasset declined a settlement offer of $4,000 for the infringement of 24 songs by the Recording Industry Association of America (RIAA), a group representing the major record labels in the U.S.[121] Thomas-Rasset was subsequently the first defendant in the U.S. to be brought to trial under charges of copyright infringement for digital music piracy. The jury found her liable and awarded the record companies statutory damages of $222,000.[122] Thomas-Rasset appealed and was granted a new trial. Again, Thomas-Rasset declined a new $25,000 settlement and went to trial.[123] In 2009, she lost again and was ordered to pay $1,920,000, a figure later ruled by the presiding judge to be "monstrous."[124] The judge reduced the judgment to $54,000, but the record labels declined this reduced amount and a third trial began.[125] In 2011, this newest jury upheld the $54,000 award and the labels again appealed.[126] In 2012, the Eight Circuit Court of Appeals replaced the $54,000 award with the original $222,000 amount.[127] As of this writing, Thomas-Rasset plans to take her case to the Supreme Court. In doing so, she will become the second file-sharer to attempt to have the Supreme Court hear her case after the Court denied another file-sharer, Joel Tenenbaum, in May 2012.[128]

Warez is now more problematic than ever given the proliferation of high-speed Internet connections in U.S. households and new technologies such as BitTorrent.[129] In the past, Warez sites hosted the cracked software themselves, but this method of distributing Warez was slow and was susceptible to official surveillance and subsequent criminal charges, such as those in the examples above. High-speed Internet connections and BitTorrent allow Warez to be hosted in a distributed manner that is not only more convenient for the pirate consumer, but also the Warez provider. Large files that traditionally took hours to download can now be acquired in minutes, and those who provide access to the illegal content, such as the popular BitTorrent site *The Pirate Bay,* have been extremely resilient to lawsuits.[130]

As with traditional software piracy, it is difficult to put a price tag on Warez piracy because no one can determine how many people are downloading illegal Warez and how many of them would otherwise buy legal versions. But the figure is certainly high and growing rapidly.

The ultimate cost of computer crime is further clouded because there is a huge "dark figure" of unreported cases. "Because of public humiliation, liability issues, and security inadequacies, many corporations do not report computer crime losses, especially large ones."[131] Businesses often hire so-called "cyber-posses," private security firms that monitor for intrusions and identify system flaws that gave unauthorized entry, instead of reporting hacker assaults to law enforcement authorities.[132] The reason for bypassing the law is that many victims believe they stand to lose more by revealing their vulnerabilities to customers and clients than from the crimes themselves.[133] The fear of "copycat" incidents also probably discourages the reporting of security breaches.[134] Furthermore, when it is information that is stolen, rather than money, the loss may be incalculable in terms of dollars. A survey of major corporations conducted by Computer Security Institute, released in 1996, found that only 17 percent of those suffering electronic intrusions notified authorities.[135]

Finally, the estimation of computer crime losses perhaps is most complicated by the clandestine nature of the crimes themselves. The most proficient electronic thieves are able to cover up all traces that a crime has been committed.[136] As the president of a major computer security consulting firm has noted: "We only read about the failed computer criminals. The really successful ones are never detected in the first place."[137]

However, even if the actual computer crime loss figure can only be guessed, no one questions that the losses are enormous. A survey by ComSec, an organization of computer security professionals, reports that 36 of 300 companies responding (12 percent) acknowledged losses of $100,000 or more in just the first three months of 1993, with another 42 (14 percent) losing between $10,000 and $100,000. For the preceding year, 69 percent of respondents admitted security problems, with 53 percent of those problems resulting in losses of at least $10,000.[138] Once more, the findings far exceeded the predictions of the startled investigators.

But survey data and raw numbers, however robust, are an undramatic way to tell a dramatic story. To understand the dimensions and the dangers of computer crime, we must examine the crimes themselves. So let us now consider in more detail the categories of computer crime suggested earlier.

EMBEZZLEMENT AND FINANCIAL THEFT

According to recent FBI statistics, the average armed bank robbery nets $3,177.[139] The Data Processing Management Association reports that the average computer crime loss may be as high as $500,000.[140] This great disparity reveals that while there are physical limitations to the potential payoff available to the blue-collar robber—large amounts of money have weight and take up space—the white-collar thief who can access the appropriate computer can steal a fortune without moving anything heavier than some decimal points. As if to demonstrate this lack of physical limitations, millions of gallons of heating oil from Exxon's Bayview refinery were misappropriated by altering computer files.[141] A gang of rogue employees in a major railroad's computerized inventory center once "stole" 200 30-ton boxcars.[142] Without a doubt, the modern thief can steal more with a computer than with a gun.[143] In addition, bank robbers must face the prospect of getting shot at; not so the computer criminal. Dillinger never had it so good.

One of the most famous bank-related computer crimes, however, did involve the physical movement of hard cash. For three years, beginning in 1970, the chief teller at the Park Avenue branch of New York's Union Dime Savings Bank embezzled over $1.5 million from hundreds of accounts. Despite having no formal computer training, he was able to shift non-existent money around from account to account, falsifying quarterly interest payments and satisfying visiting auditors with remarkable ease. So slick were his manipulations that, reportedly, he had difficulty explaining the intricacies of his crime to the bank's executives after his arrest.[144] He eventually served 15 months of a 20-month sentence. At last report, he was driving a taxicab in New Jersey. None of his pilfered funds has ever been recovered.

His eventual downfall happened almost by accident—as a by-product of an entirely different case. A routine police raid on a "bookie joint" revealed that he had been betting as much as $30,000 a day on sporting events. "If his indiscreet bookmakers had not kept his name in their files, he might well have kept up his embezzlement for quite a while longer than he did."[145]

It is interesting to note that the Union Dime Savings case serves as a perfect model of criminologist Donald Cressey's earlier research on the social psychology of embezzlement. According to Cressey, embezzlers typically go through a three-stage process. In stage 1, they are faced with what they perceive to be an unshareable financial problem—that is, a need for money which they cannot share with spouses, relatives, or friends. A $30,000 a day gambling habit on an $11,000 a year salary[146] would certainly seem to qualify in this regard. In stage 2, they recognize an opportunity to solve their problem secretly. This opportunity rests in the positions of trust which they hold. A position of chief teller, of course, would provide just such an opportunity. Finally, in stage 3, they manage to avoid internalizing a criminal identity by rationalizing their acts as borrowing rather than stealing.[147] It is the curse of compulsive gamblers like the Union Dime teller to continue expecting a financial recovery, even as the debts keep mounting. As we shall see, such labored rationalization is a recurring theme among computer criminals.

Embezzlement is a traditional crime, but computers have done for it what the microwave did for popcorn. It is no coincidence that between 1983 and 1992—the pubescent years of the computer revolution—arrests for embezzlement rose 56 percent.[148] As one state official has observed: "All scams are old, it's merely the technology that's changing."[149] In 1991, someone, believed to be an employee, used the computer in the payroll department of a prestigious New York bank to steal $25 million without leaving a trace. As of this writing, the case remains unsolved—not because there are no suspects, but because there are too many. "[H]undreds of employees had access to the same data that appear to have made at least one of them very rich."[150] This case underscores the findings of numerous major studies which report that most computerized theft is committed by authorized users, trusted insiders, and skilled employees.[151] "The easiest way into a computer is usually the front door."[152]

Not all electronic embezzlers work for banks. An employee in the computer center of a big-city welfare department stole $2.75 million, over a nine-month period, by entering fraudulent data into the computerized payroll system and thereby creating a phantom work force complete with fake social security numbers. He would intercept the weekly paychecks "earned" by the fictitious crew, endorse and cash them, and dream of early retirement. He was uncovered only when a police officer found a fistful of phony checks in his illegally parked rental car.[153]

As we have already noted, some embezzlers have employed a Trojan Horse—the "bad" program concealed inside the "good" program—as a means of diverting cash into fraudulent accounts. This is the most common method used in computer fraud.[154] Dishonest programmers have also planted "trap doors" or "sleepers" into the instructions which allow them to bypass security safeguards and siphon off cash using an imposter terminal.[155] A common variation on this method involves a practice known as "*salami slicing.*" This type of fraud has been around for many years and was known in the pre-byte era as "rounding down."[156] Salami techniques divert (or, in keeping with the metaphor, "slice off") very small amounts of assets from very large numbers of private accounts. The stolen assets are so small, sometimes a few cents or even just a fraction of a cent per transaction, that they do not make a noticeable dent in any single account.[157]

How many people, after all, will bother to stoop down to retrieve a dropped penny? But when multiplied over a million or so bank transactions at computer speed, these "dropped pennies" can turn into tens or hundreds of thousands of dollars—well worth stooping for. For example, in the 1980s an employee at an investment firm used a computer to set up false accounts and filled them by diverting three-tenths of a cent interest from actual accounts.[158] In 1992, a hacker bragged to *Forbes* magazine that he had broken into Citibank's computers and for three months had quietly skimmed a penny or so from each account. He boasted that when he had accumulated $200,000, he quit.

One of the more spectacular salami attacks took place in California at around the same time as the Union Dime Savings case. Over a six-year period, the chief accountant for a large produce company siphoned more than $1.5 million from his employers. While studying computer technology, he developed a program able to add small sums to disbursement accounts in payment of phony produce orders.[159] He later claimed that his motivation was simply to receive a promised annual bonus he felt he had been cheated of.[160] He decided he was entitled to three-quarters of one percent of the company's gross, and he began looting the company at exactly that rate. "He did this by devising a special algorithm—a set of rules for making calculations—which he used as a master program to alter the company's accounting data in the computer."[161] Because this firm grossed $30 million a year, pennies became dollars and dollars became a fortune.

When he eventually was arrested and tried, he pleaded *nolo contendere* (no contest), perhaps expecting the same sort of typically light sentence his counterpart at Union Dime Savings was to receive. Instead he was sentenced to ten years in San Quentin and served just over five. Upon release, he became—what else?—a computer consultant.

The stark difference in the punitive sanctions meted out in these two roughly equivalent embezzlement cases underscores how confused the general public often is about computer crime. Depending upon how a prosecutor chooses to present a case, a jury is apt to perceive a computer criminal as anything from a pathetic "nerd" gone bad to an electronic terrorist threatening the very foundation of the American way of life.

Sometimes embezzlers are not low- or mid-level employees of a company, but those at the very top.[162] This certainly would apply to the notorious Equity Funding scandal. This case well illustrates the lack of definitional consensus regarding computer crime. Because the Equity Funding case is considered by some to be mainly one of securities fraud, rather than true computer fraud, many analyses of computer crime never mention Equity Funding—although it is arguably one of the most costly white-collar crimes ever perpetrated.

In the early 1970s, the Los Angeles based insurance firm and mutual fund company programmed its computer to issue insurance policies on people who did not exist and then sell those fake policies to other companies, through a system of reinsurance customarily employed in that business to spread actuarial risk and increase cash flow.[163] This was done to inflate the price of Equity Funding stock which had begun to fall after a spectacular run-up in the early 1960s. The scheme grew over time to epic proportions. By 1972, 65 percent of Equity Funding's policies were fraudulent.[164] Fictitious policyholders, or persons already dead, were carrying $3.2 billion in life insurance. Some of the conspirators were skimming from the resale proceeds, and other conspirators were skimming from the skimmers.

It has been observed that, as computer crimes go, the Equity Funding fraud was not a particularly sophisticated one and would have been uncovered sooner or later, if only because there were just too many people involved.[165] The most effective computer crimes probably are the work of a single individual or at most a small gang. Moreover, because management itself conducted the fraud, there was little incentive to conceal the misuse of the computer from company officials. In the final analysis, Equity Funding was simply a gigantic Ponzi scheme run amok.[166]

When someone from outside the victimized organization commits the computer fraud, embezzlement becomes theft. Here again, banks are a frequent target. In 1980, for example, the Wells Fargo bank of San Francisco lost $21 million allegedly to two boxing promoters who used a computer for illegal EFTs (electronic fund transfers).[167] In 1988, seven men were convicted of stealing $70 million from the First National Bank in Chicago through fraudulent EFTs.[168] In absolute terms, this is a great deal of money; but, in relative terms, it hardly makes a ripple in the more than $1 trillion that is transferred electronically by American banks each day.[169]

Probably the best-known EFT case is that of Stanley Mark Rifkin, who stole $10.2 million from California's Security National Bank in less than an hour.[170] Rifkin was a computer programmer who was creating a back-up system for Security National's wire room—the bank's communication center from where between two and four billion dollars are transferred every day. The purpose of the back-up system was to allow the bank to continue making EFTs even if the primary system crashed.[171] Rifkin, of course, had to learn the system intimately, and, as his education continued, he began to think about robbing the bank. On October 25, 1978, he stole an employee access code from the wall of the wire room, walked to a nearby telephone booth, and transferred the $10.2 million to a New York bank and then to Switzerland. The next day, the cash was converted into diamonds.[172]

Rifkin may have been a brilliant computer programmer, but he turned out to be an inept criminal. He was arrested ten days later after attempting to sell some diamonds in Beverly Hills. He was convicted in March 1979 and received a sentence of 8 years in federal prison.

Beginning in the mid-1980s, officials in several states began uncovering a simple but alarmingly effective form of electronic bank robbery. An individual would open an account and eventually receive computer-coded deposit slips. Near the beginning of a month, he or she then would place some of those deposit slips on the counter where blank deposit slips normally would be. When customers unknowingly used them, the money would be deposited in the criminal's account. By the time the irate customers questioned their monthly bank statements, the thieves had emptied their accounts and were nowhere to be found.[173]

Another form of electronic larceny came to light in 1987, when nine Pittsburgh teenagers were arrested for computer fraud. They had made thousands of dollars in purchases using stolen credit card numbers. They had obtained these numbers by using their PCs to break into the files of a West Coast credit card authorization service, which provided them with a lengthy list of valid credit card numbers and expiration dates.[174]

More recently, Western Union discovered that hackers had made electronic copies of the credit and debit card information from over 15,000 consumers who transferred money on the company's Web site.[175] And online retailer Egghead.com had to notify its 3.5 million customers (including one of the authors of this book) that a hacker had accessed their financial information.[176] Other victims include the Internet search service RealNames, whose computer containing 20,000 credit card numbers was infiltrated.[177] Hackers also put thousands of stolen credit card numbers from creditcards.com on the Web after the company ignored a $100,000 extortion demand.[178] America Online, once the world's largest Internet service provider, fell prey to hackers who utilized a "Trojan Horse" to gain access to member accounts.[179] And even mighty Microsoft, maybe the most alluring of all targets, was hacked in 2000. Intruders, using a program called QAZ Trojan, were able to view highly confidential source codes for future software products.[180] Microsoft CEO Bill Gates has himself been a victim. A hacker altered three stories on the Web site of the *Orange County Register* (a large Southern California newspaper), making one read that Gates had been arrested for breaking into NASA computers.[181]

In 1993, one of the most brazen computer crimes in memory occurred in Connecticut. Two ex-convicts built a homemade automatic teller machine, wheeled it into a shopping mall, and planted it there for 16 days. The bogus machine even contained money for some users, thus enhancing its legitimate veneer. But despite its clever masquerade, it was just a subspecies of

Trojan Horse, designed to copy secret access codes from customers' ATM cards. This allowed the criminals to withdraw more than $100,000 from banks in six states.[182] They were arrested two months later on a variety of fraud, theft, and conspiracy charges.

HACKING

In its original sense, the word "hacker," coined at MIT in the 1960s, simply connoted a computer virtuoso. "However, beginning in the 1970s, hackers also came to describe people who hungered to know off-limits details about big computer systems—and who were willing to use devious and even illegal means to satisfy this curiosity."[183] The pioneer hackers of the 1960s and 1970s probably exemplified sociologist Edwin Lemert's classic concept of primary deviance[184]—that is, their conduct would have been described by observers as norm violating. Of course, computers were so new then, there may have been few clear norms to violate. If their intent was not to destroy private files, could they be considered vandals? If their intent was not to steal data, could they be considered thieves? Perhaps the least ambiguous way to characterize them was as trespassers.

On the other hand, there was likely little, if any, of Lemert's notion of secondary deviance[185]—that is, no deviant self-identify on the parts of the hackers themselves. Indeed, their mastery of skills that may have seemed more magic than science to the general public endowed them with a sense of intellectual elitism. "[A]mong these young computer outlaws was a sense of superiority to the bureaucrats whose systems they could so easily infiltrate."[186] As one author, commenting on the first generation of hackers, has observed: "[T]o be a computer hacker was to wear a badge of honor."[187]

Most hackers display what Jay "Buck" Bloombecker, director of the National Center for Computer Crime Data, terms a "playpen mentality."[188] They see breaking into a system as a goal, not a means to some larcenous end.

> Sipping cola and munching pizza, they work through the night, often alone, their computers linked to the outside world by modems. They share their successes with confidants whom they often know only through voice or electronic messages. Many are teenagers whose parents don't know a modem from a keyboard.[189]

At least two categories of "playpen" hackers have been identified: creative "showoffs," who break into data bases for fun, rather than profit; and "cookbook hackers," the most common category, defined as computer buffs who coast along the global Internet computer network without any specific target, twisting electronic door knobs to see what systems fly open.[190] The "recipes" used by the "cookbook" hackers generally are those that have been developed by the more knowledgeable "showoffs." Many of these recipes apparently are of gourmet quality. A security analyst for AT&T has estimated that less than 5 percent of intrusions into computer systems by outsiders are even detected, let alone traced.[191]

Hackers might be thought of as a deviant subculture. They ascribe to a set of norms, which apparently they take very seriously, but which often conflicts with the norms of the dominant society. They have their own peculiar code of ethics, known as the "cyberpunk imperatives."[192] For instance, they believe computerized data are public property and that passwords and other security features are only hurdles to be jumped in pursuit of these communal data.[193] A famous hacker known as The Knightmare has summed up this haughty creed: "Whatever one mind can hide, another can discover."[194] There is even an ultimate proscription: "Hackers will do just about anything to break into a computer except crashing a system. That's the only taboo."[195]

Another way of looking at young hackers is from the perspective of Sykes and Matza's well-known "drift" theory of juvenile delinquency.[196] Hackers might be viewed in this manner as fundamentally conforming youths who drift into occasionally deviant behavior through the use of such "neutralizations" as the claim that they are only trying to expose lax security systems[197] or merely learn more about computers.[198] These may seem like lame rationalizations, but more than one young hacker has justified his misconduct on those very grounds.

Furthermore, even the most sophomoric intentions can go terribly awry. A group of seven Milwaukee high school students, devoted electronic joyriders who called themselves the "414" gang, learned this lesson in 1983. They were from all accounts nice young men—loving sons, Eagle Scouts, exemplary students. But, in the name of "fun-and-games," they managed to break into a file at the Los Alamos, New Mexico, nuclear weapons facility and also erase a confidential file at New York's Memorial Sloan-Kettering Cancer Center.[199] When they were apprehended, they denied any criminality in their actions. Their public statements seemed to be drawn directly from Sykes and Matza's inventory of neutralization techniques: "[I]t's not our fault" [denial of responsibility]; "We didn't intend harm" [denial of injury]; "There was no security" [denial of victim].[200]

Like the fabled sorcerer's apprentice, the 414s became intoxicated with their inordinate power and failed to contemplate maturely the consequences of their actions. This sort of irresponsibility has been the hackers' bane from the very beginning. If there is such a construct as *white-collar delinquency*, teenage hackers are its embodiment.

Beyond the "playpen mentality," however, there is a dark side to hacking, personified by a very different species of "stunt hacker" whose motivations are undeniably malicious. One such individual revealed this dark side in an article he wrote under the ominous pen name Mr. X:

> I can turn off your electricity or phone, destroy your credit rating—even take money out of your bank account—without ever leaving the keyboard of my home computer. And you would never know I was the one ruining your life![201]

If one doubts the plausibility of Mr. X's frightening boast, consider that in 1985 seven New Jersey teenagers were arrested for stealing $30,000 worth of computer equipment, which they had billed to total strangers on "hacked" credit card numbers.[202] Hackers have also invaded credit files[203]—including those at TRW, the nation's largest credit information storage system.[204] In 1985, a Houston loan officer utilized the bank's credit-checking computer terminal to steal the records of a Fort Worth couple. He used that information to open 21 bogus accounts in their name and ran up bills of $50,000.[205] Anyone who has ever been victimized in this manner has experienced the living hell of the credit pariah. If one's credit rating is sabotaged, one can no longer apply for a mortgage or loans of any kind. Even renting an apartment may become impossible.[206] As one victim has lamented: "There's only one problem with having good credit. Someone may steal it."[207]

Consider as well the career of "Dr. Demonicus." A bright young man with awesome computer skills, his lack of interest in academics landed him behind the counter of a fast-food restaurant after graduating from high school. His ambition, however, soon transformed him from a classic underachiever to a wealthy alleged felon. According to the charges in a federal indictment, he would scan telephone directories for the names of presumably well-heeled doctors and lawyers, then hack the local credit bureau for their credit card numbers. He was further accused of using those numbers to buy $200,000 worth of merchandise, which he would have delivered to vacant houses held by the Department of Housing and Urban Development. Later, like a postman in reverse, he would allegedly drive his daily route and collect his packages. As of this writing, Dr. Demonicus has not yet gone to trial. If convicted, he faces up to 50 years in prison.[208]

Computers have become the principal tool in sophisticated identity theft scams. For example, in 2001 a hacker utilized library computers, Web-enabled cell phones, and virtual voice mail to dupe credit bureaus into providing detailed reports on victims chosen from the *Forbes* list of the richest people in America. These data were used to gain access to credit cards and brokerage accounts. The list of targets included such notable figures as Steven Spielberg, Oprah Winfrey, Martha Stewart, Ted Turner, Ross Perot, George Lucas, and Warren Buffet.[209] Police called this crime "one of the most ambitious identity-theft schemes they had ever seen."[210] A detective with the New York Police Department's computer investigations unit said of the hacker: "He's the best I've ever found."[211]

A journalist has offered a first-person account of his own brush with identity theft—also called "true-name" computer because the criminal adopts a real identity.[212] A hacker, 1,000 miles away, had pulled the writer's file from a credit-reporting agency.

> In minutes . . . he had a virtual summary of my life. And he did it as fast as kids unwrap birthday presents.[213]

Using the pilfered credit, the thief went on a $100,000 shopping spree.

An elusive network of young Middle Eastern hackers reportedly stole thousands of credit card numbers from commercial Internet sites and used them to buy computers, stereos, and satellite dishes.[214] The group, known as the Q8 Hackers and led by someone calling himself y2y, maintained a Web site where hackers freely exchanged credit card numbers and "how-to" advice on computer crime. The group frequently changed its Web address to frustrate investigators. Although there is no evidence of any links between the Q8 network and organized terrorism, one of Q8's sites contained a threatening message: "May God send all the damnations in the world to who backstabbed us [sic]."[215]

Identity theft, such as that committed by Q8, is currently exploding.[216] The Federal Trade Commission reports that it receives about 1,700 calls per week to its hotline: 1-877-ID-THEFT.[217] The FTC estimates that 4.7 percent of the American population—about 10 million people—were victims of identity theft in 2002, with total losses of $53 billion.[218] In 2003, identity theft in the U.S. reportedly grew by more than 40 percent.[219] That figure had increased by more than 50 percent in 2005, when more than 15 million Americans were victimized.[220] In 2006, the average loss on new account fraud more than doubled, and the percentage of funds consumers managed to recover dropped significantly.[221] One researcher, involved in collecting those data stated: "Hackers are exploiting Internet auctions, non-regulated money transmittal systems, the ability to impersonate lottery and sweepstake contests, and other types of imaginative scams."[222]

One of those "other types of imaginative scams" was uncovered in 2005, targeting citizens who allegedly failed to report for jury duty. Actually, the victims had never even been summoned for jury duty. The person receives a phone call from someone claiming to be an official court "jury coordinator," who threatens that an arrest warrant has been issued for not showing up. When the victim protests that he or she had never been summoned, the scammer asks for a Social Security number and a date of birth so he can verify the information and "cancel the arrest warrant." This intimidation tactic results in the acquisition of personal information by identity thieves.[223]

As the preceding scam illustrates, the entry point for many identity thieves are Social Security numbers, the obtainment of which is like batting practice to skilled hackers. Social Security numbers have become a *de facto* national ID card—a purpose for which they were never intended. In the 1930s, revulsion at the Nazi's "Show us your papers" regimentation led

Americans to insist that the new cards be clearly marked "Not for Identification."[224] But, thanks to businesses seeking quick credit checks and bureaucrats seeking blind efficiency, Social Security numbers today have become a kind of electronic currency. And "[with] the onset of e-commerce, pressure on people to reveal their private Social Security Numbers has increased tenfold."[225] In late 2002, federal authorities announced the breakup of what was then alleged to be the largest identity theft ring in U.S. history. A desk worker at a Long Island company was arrested and charged with stealing credit reports from more than 30,000 persons over a three-year period.[226] The suspect's employer provided software and hardware to clients, such as car dealerships and rental offices, needing to perform routine credit checks. The suspect allegedly used clients' passwords and subscriber codes to download victims' financial information, including credit card numbers and bank accounts. He then allegedly sold the data to a gang of Nigerian nationals in New York City for $30 per victim.[227] According to the FBI:

> "The potential windfall was probably greater than the content of a bank vault, and they didn't even need a getaway car. All they needed was a phone and a computer."[228]

Even after he resigned from his employer, the suspect allegedly supplied one of his co-conspirators with a laptop computer equipped to download credit reports at will.[229] The U.S. Attorney in charge of prosecuting the case stated: "With a few keystrokes, these men essentially picked the pockets of tens of thousands of Americans and, in the process, took their identities, stole their money and swiped their security."[230]

More recent identity theft prosecutions include the following cases:

- A husband-and-wife team, Vijay and Supriti Soni, pleaded guilty to identity theft. They used their Irvine-California-based companies, First Countryside Realty and Fastrak Funding, to misappropriate clients' personal information and steal their credit. Local police began investigating the couple after a client, who had bought a house through them, received a bill for $6,000 worth of furniture she did not buy. She noticed the Soni's business phone number on the receipt.[231] Vijay Soni was later sentenced to one year in jail. Supriti Soni, convicted on 19 counts, was sentenced to three years in prison.[232]

- Fernando Ferrer, Jr., owner of Advanced Medical Claims in Naples, Florida, was convicted of stealing the identities of 1,130 patients and using the pilfered data to commit Medicare fraud. He was sentenced to 87 months in prison and ordered to pay $2.5 million in restitution.[233]

- Justin Perras was convicted in federal court of conspiring to commit computer fraud and identity theft. He broke into the Accurint database (owned by Lexis Nexis) and obtained user login identifications and passwords. Perras was sentenced to one year in prison and $105,000 in restitution.[234]

- Mario Bonilla, a Colombian national, was convicted in federal court of aggravated identity theft. His scheme accumulated more than 600 victims worldwide, including employees of the U.S. Department of Defense. Bonilla had installed keylogging software on hotel business-center computers and Internet lounges in order to steal passwords and other personal data. He then used complex computer intrusion methods to steal money from accounts. The court put the losses from his scheme at $1.4 million. Bonilla was sentenced to nine years in prison.[235]

- John Schiefer, a California computer security consultant known in botnet circles as "Acidstorm," was convicted in federal court for using armies of compromised "zombie" computers to steal the identities of victims throughout the country by extracting information from their personal computers through the Paypal Web site and other financial institutions.[236] Shiefer used the stolen information to access victims' bank accounts.[237] He admitted to infecting at least 250,000 computers.[238] John Schiefer was sentenced to four years in prison and was ordered to pay $19,000 in restitution.[239]

- In late 2008, Daman Toey became the first person to plead guilty for his part in the world's biggest criminal computer hack,[240] the theft of information on about 46 million credit and debit card accounts from nine major retail chains, including TJX, the company which operates the T.J. Maxx and Marshall's discount department stores.[241] Prosecutors were hopeful that Toey, who claimed to have only an eighth grade education, would agree to testify against the alleged ringleader and other members of the gang.[242]

One especially outrageous development has been the emergence of child identity theft. Their clean credit record makes children ideal victims.[243] And, because such a crime is not usually uncovered until the victims try to establish credit later in life, it can go undetected for 10 or 15 years.[244] About five percent of the complaints the Federal Trade Commission received in 2005 regarding identity theft were from individuals younger than 18.[245] That year, an estimated 500,000 identities were stolen from children.[246] By 2007, that figure had increased by two percent.[247] Computer crooks steal children's Social Security numbers and use them to obtain credit cards and open accounts.[248] A 2008 study reported that child identity theft victims had an average of $12,779 in fraudulent debt.[249] An example of how much debt an innocent child can accrue would be a 10-year-old Dallas girl, who had 17 credit cards and had been approved for a $42,000 loan.[250] Although the culprit later turned out to be her own mother—not a cybercrook—the girl will likely face a lifetime of blemished credit. She was deep in debt and didn't even know it.

Currently, identity theft continues to skyrocket, due in large measure to the explosion of "phishing" scams, described later in this chapter.

As more and more personal records are stored electronically, the danger mushrooms. "For a few hundred dollars anyone can buy someone's complete medical history."[251] A Maryland bank was caught using stolen records to cancel loans of customers with cancer.[252] A Federal Trade Commissioner has declared: "It is now possible to capture and use information in ways that were unimaginable a few years ago. It's an incredible risk to personal privacy."[253] For example, a 13-year-old girl copied the names and telephone numbers of former emergency room patients from the computer at the University of Florida Medical Center. As a prank, she telephoned seven of these individuals and falsely told them that they had tested positively for the AIDS virus. One young woman thought the joke was so funny that she attempted suicide after receiving the call.[254]

Many hackers seem to be petulant egomaniacs. One, who calls himself Garbage Heap, for example, has bitterly complained to *ComputerWorld* magazine that his talent deserves more appreciation.[255] If respect is really his goal, Garbage Heap might want to think about picking a new pseudonym.

CASE STUDY
America's Most Wanted "Nerd"

The infamous case of Kevin Mitnick is a vivid example of how a hacker can degenerate from prankster to public enemy. Like many renegade hackers, he began his deviant career in high school by breaking into the school's main computer system. Later, he managed to hack into the central computer of

(Continued)

the entire Los Angeles Unified School District. After dropping out of school in 1981, at the age of 17, he was arrested as part of a hacker ring that had stolen key manuals from Pacific Telephone. Mitnick was prosecuted as a juvenile and placed on probation. The following year, he was in trouble again. This time he used publicly available computers at the University of Southern California to break into numerous systems—including some at the U.S. Department of Defense. His probation was revoked, and he spent 6 months in a California Youth Authority facility.[256]

Up to this point, Mitnick arguably was still more brat than criminal. He had not yet stolen money or damaged data; but a manifest pattern of escalating havoc already was emerging. Exploring private off-ramps along the information superhighway may be a challenging recreation but it does not pay the rent, and as many hackers get older they become more profit-oriented.[257] In 1988, Mitnick, now 25, was arrested for repeatedly breaking into a computer software system at the Digital Equipment Corporation in Massachusetts. He copied the software, which had cost DEC more than $1 million to develop. He further cost DEC more than $4 million in downtime. And if this were not enough, Mitnick had also broken into the computer system at Leeds University in England by telephone, using the sixteen unauthorized MCI long-distance telephone account numbers in his possession.[258]

A notable aspect to this case is the way Mitnick was portrayed both by the government and the media. He became the symbol of computer crime and the future shock paranoia it generates in society. Mitnick has been labeled "the Willie Horton of computer crime"[259]—a reference to the notorious rapist who was made the symbol of violent crime during the 1988 presidential election. Even a former hacking cohort of Mitnick, known as

Susie Thunder, once declared: "He's really crazy. . . He's dangerous."[260] He was denied bail and spent 7-1/2 months in jail awaiting trial—a very unusual fate for a white-collar criminal. So frightened were the authorities of Mitnick's skills and potential for electronic vengeance that all his telephone calls had to be dialed by others. Finally, Mitnick entered into a plea bargain and, in 1989, received a 1-year sentence to be followed by entry into a rehabilitation program for computer addiction.

By 1993, however, Mitnick was the subject of an intense FBI manhunt.[261] He was suspected of stealing software and data from a number of leading cellular phone manufacturers. It is further alleged that, in an ironic role reversal, Mitnick, while a fugitive, "managed to gain control of a phone system in California that allowed him to wiretap FBI agents who were searching for him."[262] One frustrated agent said of Mitnick, "He should have been locked up long ago."[263] In a 1994 telephone interview with a freelance journalist, the fugitive Mitnick discussed why he was unable to resist the temptation of technology: "People who use computers are very trusting, very easy to manipulate."[264]

On February 15, 1995, Kevin Mitnick was arrested in North Carolina and accused of violating the terms of his probation by stealing an almost inestimable number of data files and at least 20,000 credit card numbers from computers.[265] He was indicted again in 1996 on charges of stealing millions of dollars in software.[266] Kevin Mitnick was convicted and served five years in federal prison.[267] Released in 2000, he announced plans to start up a computer security firm—presumably to help companies protect themselves from people like him. Eternally unrepentant, Kevin Mitnick has summed up his baleful career in four words: "I love the game."[268]

Kevin Mitnick's placement on the FBI's Ten Most Wanted list underscores how seriously hacking is now treated by the criminal justice system. Between 1986 and 1992, only 9 of 129 computer criminals convicted in California courts were sent to prison.[269] Today, those same courts were handing out serious time. Hacker Kevin Poulsen, for example, was sentenced to nearly 5 years in prison for using his computer to block all telephone calls to California radio contests—

except his own calls. Poulsen's manipulations enabled him to win two Porsches, two Hawaiian vacations and $22,000 dollars in cash.[270]

In 1992, a group of young hackers, ranging in age from 18 to 22, and calling themselves by such exotic names as Phiber Optik, Acid Phreak, Outlaw, and Scorpion,[271] were arrested for corrupting the databases of some of the largest corporations in America. The MOD, alternately known as the Masters of Destruction[272] or the Masters of Deception,[273] allegedly stole passwords and technical data from Pacific Bell, Nynex, and other telephone companies; Martin Marietta, ITT, and other Fortune 500 companies; several big credit agencies; two major universities; and the Educational Broadcasting Network.[274] The damage caused by these hackers was extensive. One company alone, Southwestern Bell, suffered losses of $370,000.[275]

In what resembles a high-tech parody of urban gang warfare, the MOD apparently were motivated by a fierce competition with a rival "gang," the Legion of Doom.[276] Donn B. Parker, who has interviewed Phiber Optik,[277] has noted the importance of one-upmanship in the hacker subculture: "Computer hacking is a meritocracy. You rise in the culture depending on the information you can supply to other hackers."[278] Phiber Optik (John Lee) has also gleefully boasted that he could commit a crime with just five strokes on a keyboard. He claimed, for example, that he could get free limousines, airplane flights, hotel rooms, and meals "without anyone being billed." Young Mr. Optik acknowledged, however, that his time in prison had been "no fun."[279]

One of the most disturbing aspects of malicious hacking involves the area of national security. A 24-year-old hacker known as Captain Zap was arrested in 1981 for breaking into the White House's computers. In 1983, a 19-year-old UCLA student used his PC to enter the Defense Department's international communications system.[280] In 1991, a gang of Dutch hackers managed to crack Pacific Fleet computers during the Persian Gulf War.[281] Two young hackers broke into computers at the Boeing Corporation—a major defense contractor[282]—and later used their home computers to examine confidential government agency files.[283] An 18-year-old Israeli hacker was accused of the most organized attack ever on the Pentagon's computer system.[284] A report from the American military's inspector-general found "serious deficiencies in the integrity and security" of a Pentagon computer used to make $67 billion a year in payments.[285]

Even more alarming is a report released by the General Accounting Office (GAO) in 1996, which determined that hackers had attacked Pentagon computer systems as many as 250,000 times the previous year and had gained entry in two of every three attempts.[286] The GAO concluded: "At a minimum, these attacks are a multimillion dollar nuisance to defense. At worst, they are a serious threat to national security."[287] Members of Congress have expressed great concern over such stories, calling for tougher sanctions and the federalization of all computer crime.

In early 1998, the Pentagon's computer networks were hit by what was described as the "most organized and systematic assault"[288] ever launched against them. Although no classified documents appeared to have been tampered with, a deputy defense secretary called the matter "a very serious long-term problem."[289] A few weeks later, two California teenagers, ages 16 and 17, were arrested by the FBI and accused of the cyber-attacks. The boys, who went by the code names Makaveli and TooShort, had used "sniffer" programs to intercept Pentagon passwords. They also had placed "back-door" programs in the military computers in order to re-enter at will.[290] They had leapfrogged from their local Internet Service Provider (ISP) into the Pentagon systems, as well as systems at the University of California at Berkeley, MIT, and two sites in Mexico.[291]

Makaveli and TooShort pleaded guilty to charges of juvenile delinquency and were put on three years probation—and deprived of any unsupervised computer access. They were also ordered to perform 100 hours of community service and pay $5,525 in restitution.[292] This case strongly underscores the gaping moral schism between hackers and victims. The government stressed that the boys' activities "had the potential to disrupt military communications throughout the world."[293] TooShort's lawyer argued that the hackers had no malicious intentions and were simply trying to explore advanced computer systems. He added: "I call it the Mount Everest effect. They did it to prove they could."[294]

Cyber-attacks on the government are an escalating problem. It is now believed that at least six or seven government computers are hacked successfully every day. Moreover, many government systems are invaded for months before the violation is even noticed. For example, a group called GlobalHell defaced Web sites operated by the White House and the Senate.[295] In 1997, a hacker interfered with the transmission of medical data from astronauts orbiting the earth.[296] And, in 1998, a hacker gang, called Noid, broke into military computers and were able to download software that controls the positioning of satellites.[297]

Also in 1998, the leader of still another cyber-gang, called #conflict, was arrested on charges of illegally breaking into two computers at NASA's Jet Propulsion Laboratory (JPL) in California. One of the sites was an internal e-mail server; the other involved satellite design and mission analysis of future space flights. According to federal agents, the suspect, 20-year-old Raymond Toricelli (code name Rolex), had gained access to more than 800 computers, including many at major universities, and possessed 76,000 passwords. In an act of arrogant defiance, Rolex actually used one NASA computer to host an Internet chat room devoted to hacking techniques.[298] Toricelli received a four-month prison sentence in 2001.[299]

The break-ins at JPL were so serious that "one of the computers had to be taken off-line and other permanently decommissioned."[300] In addition to Rolex, #conflict's membership included Blood, Endless, Zerox, and Bomb. Among their activities was a planned attempt to rig the online voting for the annual MTV Movie Awards.

Rolex was 20 years old when he was arrested. So, unlike Makaveli and TooShort in the NASA break-in discussed earlier, if he is convicted it will not be for juvenile delinquency; and he will not be spanked and sent to his room without his supper—or his modem. He faces up to 16 years in prison and a fine of $375,000.[301]

Indeed, the courts appear to be increasingly inclined to treat even teenage hacking as something much more serious than puerile mischief. In 2001, a teenage hacker, with the code-name Coolio, was sentenced to 9 months to 1 year in jail for breaking into a Los Angeles Police Department Web site. Coolio defaced the LAPD site with pro-drug slogans and images, including one depicting Donald Duck with a syringe in his arm.[302] According to the U.S. Attorney prosecuting a Massachusetts teenager, who had caused a system crash at a local airport and knocked out tower-to-planes communication for six hours: "These are not pranks. This is not like throwing spitballs at your teacher."[303]

Raymond Steigerwalt, a former member of the international hacking group Thr34t Krew (TK), was sentenced to 21 months in federal prison in 2005 for his part in the creation of a Trojan Horse that infected and damaged at least two computers belonging to the Department of Defense.[304] And a 16-year-old Miami hacker was sentenced to six months at a juvenile detention center for invading NASA, as well as Pentagon computers that monitor potential for nuclear, chemical, and biological attacks.[305] The young man told the court: "Never Again. It's not worth it. Because all of it was for fun and games, and they're putting me in jail for it."[306]

In 2005, a former University of Texas student was convicted of breaking into the school's computer system, gathering 37,000 names and Social Security numbers.[307] He was sentenced to five years probation and 500 hours of community service. He was also ordered to pay the university $170,000 in restitution. The terms of his probation forbid him to use the Internet for those five years, except for work or school and only with the pre-approval of his probation officer.[308] He could have received up to six years behind bars.[309] Although the government had asked for prison time, the federal prosecutor praised the sentence: "Computer hacking is not some funny game that shows how smart you are. It's a crime that can hurt people."[310]

That same year, hundreds of MBA applicants failed their first test of business ethics. They were caught hacking into software to check on the status of their applications to several top-tier business schools. The problem was first discovered at Harvard University. The school said that 119 prospective students hacked into the files of ApplyYourself, an outsourcing company that handles admissions applications for Harvard and many other universities. Break-ins were also uncovered at Stanford, MIT, Duke, Carnegie Mellon, Dartmouth, and possibly other schools. Using instructions posted by anonymous sources on a number of business school bulletin boards, the hackers were able to discover their acceptance status weeks before decision letters were sent out.[311]

Harvard and most other affected schools decided to summarily reject the hackers' applications.

> Harvard decided these potential students are not tomorrow's leaders. In a statement, Harvard Dean Kim B. Clark called the hacking "unethical," saying Harvard wants to educate principled leaders with "a strong moral compass and intuitive sense of what is right and wrong." Says Clark: "Those who have hacked into this Web site have failed to pass that test."[312]

The most disheartening aspect of this hacking scandal is that, despite Dean Clark's assessment, many of the elite students involved probably *are* tomorrow's leaders.

In 2007 and 2008, a number of criminal convictions resulted from an FBI investigation named "Operation Bot Roast."[313] Twenty-four year-old Jason Downey was sentenced in federal court to one year in prison for operating a network of 6,000 compromised PCs[314] to launch a denial of service attack that impaired various computer systems on the Internet and caused more than $20,000 in damage.[315] The following year, 21-year-old Gregory King pleaded guilty in a California federal court to transmitting code to cause damage to a protected computer and was sentenced to two years in prison. Like Downey, King admitted to using a "botnet" (short for robot network) to conduct denial of service attacks on two different Web sites.[316] A botnet is a network of infected zombie computers that can infect other computers and thus propagate itself. The owners of the infected computers do not know that their computers have been infected, but their computers can be secretly directed by the person in control of the botnet—the so-called "bot herder." In a denial of service attack, a bot herder directs the botnet to flood a victim computer with information and thereby disable it.[317] Botnets have been called the all-purpose "Swiss Army Knives" of cybercrooks.[318]

Several other "Operation Bot Roast" cases are worth noting. A juvenile hacker, known as "Dshocker" pleaded guilty in a Massachusetts federal court to creating a botnet of infected computers and directing them to perform cyberattacks. He was sentenced to 11 months in a juvenile detention facility.[319] Robert Matthew Bentley was sentenced in a Florida federal court to 41 months in jail for hijacking hundreds of PCs to create a botnet that infected a company's network of computers in Europe with pop-up advertisements (adware) that cost a reported $65,000 to detect and repair.[320] And Adam Sweaney, a Tacoma, Washington, computer technician, pleaded guilty in federal court to infecting PCs with Trojan Horses that built a "proxy" botnet that he later rented out to spammers. For $500, Sweaney could send *50 million* spams out to e-mail addresses.[321]

In 2007, hackers swiped sensitive data from at least 1.3 million job seekers at the popular Monster Worldwide employment Web site. Using the stolen contact information, scammers sent out Trojan Horse e-mails. The infected computers were incorporated into a "zombie" network to spread spam, deliver more infections, and collect and store more stolen data.[322]

When the House Financial Services Committee held hearings on computer hacking in 2003, one of its star witnesses was none other than convicted hacker Kevin Mitnick. Now a security consultant, he warned of newly discovered security flaws in consumer information systems: "The bad guys are going to look for the weakest link in the security chain."[323] He ought to know.

An especially costly form of hacking are *denial of service attacks*, which involve the deliberate bombardment of commercial Web sites causing them to crash. In late 2005, Anthony Scott Clark pleaded guilty to using a computer worm to launch attacks against eBay, the Internet auction house. Two years earlier, Clark, who was then 18 years old, and some accomplices infected about 20,000 computers with a malicious program that allowed them to direct the machines at eBay, overwhelming the popular Web site. The U.S. Attorney's office said that the cost of the attack may have run into millions of dollars.[324]

CASE STUDY
The Amazing Adventures of Mafiaboy

On February 7, 2000, a coordinated cyber-attack was launched against the world's busiest e-commerce sites. The attacks began on a Monday, with a three-hour assault on Yahoo.com, one of the world's most popular Web sites. They continued on Tuesday, temporarily crippling many other major sites, including Amazon.com, eBay, Buy.com,[325] ZDNet,[326] and E-trade.[327] By Tuesday night it had spread to a leading media site, CNN.com.[328] The magnitude of the damage was estimated to exceed $1.2 billion.[329] Security experts and the companies themselves believed that the nature of the attacks seemed too similar to be coincidental.[330] The basic mechanisms for denial of service attacks are relatively simple:

The attacker hits a site so frequently that legitimate surfers can't get in. In distributed attacks the hackers take over a large number of computers connected to the Internet and force those computers to pound the site simultaneously. The subverted computers called 'zombies,' respond to a single command from the attacker, who conveniently hides in anonymity while the zombies do the dirty work.[331]

When the FBI launched an international manhunt for the culprit or culprits, the chief investigator joked, "computer systems were so vulnerable that any technologically savvy 15-year-old could have been behind the sabotage."[332] He was exactly right. By the following week, the FBI had zeroed in on a suspect—a 15-year-old Canadian hacker, who calls himself Mafiaboy. The ninth-grader had left a careless digital trail along with boastful dialogue in Internet chat rooms.[333] He was known to Canadian cybercrime authorities but was generally not regarded as especially sophisticated or dangerous. "Mafiaboy is known in the hacker underground as a 'script kiddie,' a beginning hacker who simply downloads attack software ("scripts") offered by Web sites, rather than creating or modifying his own software tools."[334] Scripts are available on the Internet—if one knows where to find them—and require "only that a user identify a target and decide when to commence and when to quit the attack."[335] The rest is mainly automated.

Mafiaboy, a juvenile of course under Canadian law, was arrested in June on two counts of *mischief*.[336]

(Continued)

In a curious, though unrelated, sidelight to the case, Mafiaboy's father (Mafiaman?) was also arrested and charged with conspiracy to commit assault. Canadian police, who had tapped the telephones at Mafiaboy's house, heard conversations between his father and another man about plans to assault a business associate.[337]

Like so many adult criminals, Mafiaboy's downfall was largely the result of his own need to feel important. "[He] left a trail of electronic bread crumbs, using Internet chat rooms to discuss his plans for attacking Web sites and then boast about having carried out the attacks."[338] He bragged that he had hacked big computers at major American universities, including Harvard and Yale,[339] and utilized them to bombard the Web sites. Some of the hackers who heard Mafiaboy's loose lips (or, in this instance, "loose fingers") called the FBI.

In January 2001, nearly a year after the massive cyber-attack, the now 16-year-old Mafiaboy pleaded guilty to what had been raised to 55 counts of mischief.[340] The young Montrealer was sentenced to eight months in a youth detention center.[341]

Mafiaboy's "mischief" serves as an unsettling reminder of how much harm can be inflicted suddenly on the "new economy" by a reckless teenager. A former federal prosecutor, now head of an Internet security firm, observed: "If a 15-year-old in Montreal can do that much damage, imagine what a concerted effort by real professionals, industrial competitors or foreign governments can do."[342]

As for Mafiaboy himself: he has been called "your smarter-than-average computer geek with one foot in the doghouse and the other foot in the computer hall of fame."[343] A 17-year-old friend marvels: "He shut down all those companies. He's got my respect."[344] A neighbor, whose daughter plays in the same basketball league as Mafiaboy, articulates an ambivalent reaction: "You wouldn't want your kids to emulate him. On the other hand, he'll probably get a great job with an Internet company and make lots of money some day."[345]

In the preceding case and elsewhere, this chapter describes vividly the life and times of stereotypical teenage hackers. It needs to be stressed, however, that in recent years, grown-up hackers have begun to take center stage. International crime rings utilize hacking in large-scale identity theft operations and extortion plots involving denial of service attacks.[346] And if the criminal justice system still is not quite sure what to do with youthful cyber-criminals, it is now dealing with adult offenders with increasing harshness.

After the defense department suffered a rash of computer intrusions in 1998,[347] federal authorities began investigating Max Ray Butler, a well-known computer security expert known in cyberspace as Max Vision. Butler, who operated his own Silicon Valley "intrusion detection" firm, specialized in running penetration tests—attempting to break into corporate networks to demonstrate vulnerable security.[348] Butler's arrest in 2000 shocked the tight-knit computer security industry.[349] He had been considered a "white hat" hacker—one who used his skills ethically to understand and secure systems. He always had been highly critical of the malicious "black hat" hackers—those who break into systems for profit and glory.[350] Infact, Butler was an FBI informant, who had infiltrated the electronic underground to aid the bureau. Agents called him "the equalizer."[351] He was accused of hacking into computers belonging to the Department of Energy's Argonne National Laboratories in Illinois, the Brookhaven National Laboratory in New York, NASA's Marshall Flight Center in Alabama, the offices of the Secretary of Transportation and the Secretary of Defense in Washington, DC, and other unspecified government facilities.[352] He was indicted on 15 counts of breaking into and damaging hundreds of computers.[353] In a plea agreement, Max Ray Butler admitted to one felony charge of unauthorized access to protected computers, recklessly causing damage.

In May, 2001, "Max Vision" began serving an 18-month prison term."[354] In a telephone interview with the reformed ex-hacker Kevin Poulson, he admitted his guilt but argued that incarceration was not the appropriate punishment for a hacker. "I really feel out of place."[355]

Actually, Max was not out of place at all. Two months earlier, another hacker, Jesus Oquendo (known as Sil) was sentenced to 27 months in prison. Sil had worked for a company called Collegeboardwalk.com, which had shared office space with one of its investors, Manhattan venture capital firm Five Partners Asset Management. When his employer went bust, Oquendo hacked into Five Partners' system. Using a "sniffer" program that intercepted and recorded electronic traffic on the Five Partners network—including unencrypted passwords—he was able to obtain the password of a Five Partners employee who had an account on another system belonging to New York City computer wholesaler RCS Computer Experience. Oquendo sought to install a similar "sniffer" program on the RCS system. In the process, he deleted the entire RCS database, costing the company about $60,000 to repair. To add insult to injury—literally—Oquendo left the victim a taunting message on its network: "I have just hacked into your system. Have a nice day."[356]

Unlike most apprehended hackers, Oquendo refused a plea bargain, opting to face a jury. Perhaps the guilty verdict was the jury's way of saying: "We have just convicted you. Have a nice day."

Two recent malicious hacking cases involved disgruntled employees. Abedelkader Smires, who worked for Internet Trading Technologies Corporation in New York, was sentenced to eight months in prison for launching a denial-of-service attack against the company. The firm's software system, which allows securities dealers to trade stocks online, was disrupted for three days, resulting in the potential loss of several hundred thousand dollars. Smires had threatened to quit unless the company increased his compensation. He had demanded an immediate payment of $70,000 plus $50,000 in stock options. A tentative agreement was reached, but Smires backed out and raised his demands. When no new offer was forthcoming, Internet Trading Technologies' computer system came under an attack from a PC located at a Kinko's copy shop in Manhattan.[357] The attacks continued for four days. The United States Secret Service's Electronic Crime Task Force eventually tracked Smires down to a computer located at the Queens College campus in Flushing, New York, where he taught night classes.[358]

The other sabotage case was that of Claude Carpenter. He worked as a systems administrator for Network Resources, a subcontractor to the Internal Revenue Service. Carpenter was not well-regarded by his employer and had been admonished several times for tardiness and inefficiency. Following a dispute between Carpenter and a co-worker, Carpenter's supervisor prepared a draft letter of dismissal and sent it to the project manager. That same day, Carpenter logged into three servers to which he had no right to possess root access and inserted several lines of destructive computer code. Once executed, the code wiped out all of the data on the servers. The next day, Carpenter was fired. "During the following two weeks Carpenter called the system administrator room several time to ask if 'everything was ok,' 'if the machines were running ok,' or 'if anything was wrong with the servers.'"[359] After his activities were discovered, the IRS shut down the three servers in order to remove the destructive code. Carpenter later pleaded guilty to intentionally causing the damage and deleting the data. He was sentenced to 15 month in prison.[360]

Another computer criminal who hacked his way into a prison cell was Oleg Zezev. He was the chief information technology officer at Kazkommerts Securities, located in the former Soviet republic of Kazakhastan. In the spring of 1999, Bloomberg LP, the financial media service owned by Michael Bloomberg (who would later be elected mayor of New York City) provided database services to Kazkommerts. As a result, Kazkommerts was provided with the software needed to gain access to Bloomberg's services over the Internet. Those services were canceled a few months later because Kazkommerts did not pay its bill.[361] In March 2000, Zezev manipulated

Bloomberg's software and bypassed the firm's security system in order to gain unauthorized access to the system. He sent a number of e-mails to Michael Bloomberg demanding $200,000 in exchange for revealing how he had infiltrated the company's state-of-the-art computer.[362] Michael Bloomberg, acting in conjunction with the FBI, agreed to meet with Zezev in London. The meeting was recorded by an undercover videotape. Zezev was arrested in a London hotel room and subsequently extradited to the United States. He was convicted in 2003 of attempted extortion and computer hacking.[363] He was handed a 51-month prison term. In sentencing Oleg Zezev, Federal Judge Kimba Wood stated: "Your crime was a very serious one because of its threat to international commerce and the integrity of data that the financial community relies upon to do its business."[364] Zezev replied: "Thank you very much."[365]

CASE STUDY
The "Hack Back" Sting

In 2000, two hackers in Chelyabinsk, Russia, gained unauthorized access into a San Diego-based Internet service provider (ISP) by opening an account with a stolen credit card number. Once inside, they hacked the system to take control of the firm's computer.[366]

Alexy Ivanov and Vasly Gorshkov then launched a series of cyber-attacks against e-commerce companies and credit card processors. They pilfered thousands of credit card numbers, converting some of them into cash via the PayPal online payment company in order to purchase computer parts from eBay auctions.[367] They also stole financial information from a number of other American banking and technology companies and attempted to extort large sums of money for so-called "security services."[368] This pair of crooks cost their victims an estimated $25 million.[369]

In a novel "sting" operation, the FBI set up a fake company named Invita Computer Security and lured Ivanov and Gorshkov to Seattle for high-paying job interviews. Upon arrival, the two men were asked to demonstrate their skills by scanning the Invita computer network for

vulnerabilities. After showing off their prowess, the stung Slavs were quickly arrested. The FBI had equipped the Invita computer with a "digital wiretap"[370] that logged every keystroke. Agents were later able to retrieve the men's passwords and download evidence off their computer networks in Russia.[371]

Vasily Gorshkov was convicted in 2002 of multiple counts of conspiracy, hacking, and fraud. He was handed a three-year prison sentence.[372] A year later, Alexy Ivanov was also convicted and sentenced to four years in prison.[373] The cases represented the first time the FBI successfully had enticed cyber-criminals to the United States and the first time the Bureau had seized extra-territorial digital evidence.[374]

In an audacious claim, both defendants unsuccessfully argued that when the FBI had downloaded evidence from their Russian networks, it had violated *their* right to privacy. Hackers invoking the sanctity of computer privacy might be the cybercrime version of the old joke about the boy who murdered his parents, then asked the court for mercy because he was an orphan.

In 2002, Congress left no doubt about how serious an issue computer crime has become. By a wide margin, the House and Senate passed the Cyber Security Enhancement Act. The legislation established within the Department of Justice an Office of Science and Technology. It also eases police restrictions for conducting Internet wire taps without a court order. And the bill provides for tougher punishment—including life sentences for certain types of computer hackers.[375]

CASE STUDY
We Are Legion—Anonymous

Most cyber criminals hack for fun or monetary gain, but another form of computer crime has emerged in the past twenty years: "hacktivism."[376] This form of hacking is motivated by political, rather than recreational or economic drives. While most traditional hacking has negative consequences for the general populace, "hacktivists" see themselves as friends of the people attempting to right apparent wrongs. *Anonymous* is one group that has repeatedly taken down or otherwise disrupted the normal online operations of large corporations and governments.[377] Below are some of the attacks the group claims credit for.

- Anonymous hacked The Church of Scientology via a denial-of-service attack in January 2008.[378] The group declared this as the beginning of "Project Chanology" an effort to bring attention to what Anonymous believed were illegal activities of the Church of Scientology. The initial attack was spurned in response to a video by Tom Cruise speaking about the virtues of Scientology. The video was posted to YouTube, but the site removed the clip under the threat of litigation from the Church.[379] Seeing this as censorship, Anonymous began a two-year campaign of attacks as a form of protest.
- In 2011, *WikiLeaks*, a Web site devoted to freeing classified information, lost its primary revenue stream when MasterCard and Visa stopped allowing the site to use their services to process payments.[380] Anonymous, claiming defense of the whistle-blowing Web site launched a denial-of-service attack on the credit card companies. The attacks made the news, but did not succeed in interrupting the public's ability to use their credit cards.
- Anonymous has also been active in the Middle East, leading attacks on the Iranian government during the country's 2009 elections, as well as orchestrating hacks against the Tunisian government in 2009 and 2010, and the Egyptian government in 2011.[381] The group's efforts also include providing Internet access to the people of these countries when their governments censored or otherwise initiated Internet "black outs" during mass protests.
- Most recently, in January 2012, the Web sites of the Department of Justice and the Federal Bureau of Investigation were hit with a denial-of-service attack from Anonymous in response to the shuttering of Megaupload, a popular file-sharing Web site accused of copyright infringement.[382]

While hacktivism is not limited to Anonymous, the group has found continued success through its decentralized structure and large membership. Traditional hacker collectives consist of a handful of members and operate within a structured hierarchy. Anonymous is a loosely formed group that chooses its targets collectively. To execute its denial-of-service attacks, the group relies on a "volunteer botnet."[383] Though similar to the botnets used by spammers, there is a major difference: the botnets utilized by Anonymous are *not* created through Trojan Horse programs on the computers of unwitting users, but instead are created willingly by volunteers through its "Low-Orbiting Ion Cannon," a piece of software designed to stress-test networks. To launch an attack, Anonymous simply announces their target, provides a link for LOIC use, and legions of followers provide the computational force to bring down large sites such as those of MasterCard and Visa in 2011.[384] Those particular attacks were done under a branch of Anonymous known as "LulzSec." In the months that followed the attack the FBI captured one of the members of LulzSec, 28-year-old U.S. resident Hector "Sabu" Monsegur, and turned him into an informant.[385]

(Continued)

With Monsegur's cooperation, the FBI was able to capture two other hackers in the group: 19-year-old U.K. resident Ryan Cleary[386] and 18-year-old U.K. resident Jake "Topiary" Davis.[387] After the Visa and MasterCard attacks, but before the arrest of Monsegur, Cleary, and Davis, LulzSec announced it would end its "50 days of lulz" hack-spree and fold back in with the rest of Anonymous.[388] The continued presence of Anonymous online and its repeated attacks, despite the FBI's capture of three notable members, shows the resilience of the group's non-traditional structure and the size of the pool of members willing to forge ahead despite law enforcement's attempts to end the "lulz."

VIRUSES AND WORMS

One reason for so much congressional anxiety is the threat of pernicious computer viruses—once a rare phenomenon, now, some claim, approaching epidemic proportions.[389] A virus is an instructional code lodged in a computer's disk operating system that is designed to copy itself over and over. A virus may have four different phases: (1) *dormancy*, in which the virus does not destroy files, thus establishing a false sense of trust and complacency on the user's part; (2) *propagation*, in which the virus begins to replicate; (3) *triggering*, in which the virus is launched by some occurrence, such as a particular date; (4) *damaging*, in which the virus carries out the actual harm intended by its author.[390]

A computer can be infected with a virus for months or even years without the user's knowledge.[391] When an infected computer comes in contact with an uninfected piece of software, the virus is transmitted. Computerized bulletin boards are major targets for infection.[392] Viruses can also be hidden on USB thumbdrives.[393] "[T]he potential for widespread contagion is enormous."[394]

Some viruses are relatively innocuous, such as the so-called Peace virus. Designed by a 23-year-old Arizona programmer, it showed up on the screens of thousands of Macintosh computers in 1987, flashed a single peace message, then erased itself and disappeared.[395] The Peace virus, like most American computer viruses, is derived from the first-generation Stoned virus, which announces its presence by printing the message "Your PC is now stoned," followed by a demand to legalize marijuana.[396]

Like Stoned, certain viruses might be described as playful:

> A rogue program . . . featured a creature inspired by *Sesame Street* called the Cookie Monster. Students trying to do useful work would be interrupted by . . . messages saying: "I want a cookie." . . . The message would be repeated with greater . . . frequency until users typed the letters C-O-O-K-I-E on their terminal keyboards.[397]

Far less playful, however, is the Rock Video virus that entertains unsuspecting users with an animated image of Madonna—then erases all their files and displays the ignominious taunt, YOU'RE STUPID.[398]

A raunchier variation on the celebrity theme appeared in 2001 with the Jennifer Lopez virus. It was actually a third-generation copycat of two similar viruses from earlier in that year. All were versions of the destructive Chernobyl virus.[399] First came the fast-spreading Anna Kournikova virus (VBS/SST virus), an e-mail-based worm, which masqueraded as a provocative picture of the beautiful tennis player. The e-mail came with the subject line "Here you have :o)" and an attachment called *AnnaKournikova.jpg.vbs*.[400] A month later it was back in a new form known as the "naked wife" virus (W32/Naked). The naked wife worm arrived as an e-mail attachment disguised as a flash movie,[401] even plagiarizing the logo of JibJab, a reputable flash developer.[402] The subject line read, "FWD: Naked Wife," and the message text said, "My wife never look [sic] like that;-) Best Regards."[403] While the flash movie was "loading," the virus deleted several vital system files and also sent itself to everyone in the user's Microsoft Outlook address book.[404] Those who clicked on the file not only suffered damage to their computers but never even saw a naked wife. What they saw was a short cartoon followed by a vulgar message, signed by "BGK" (Bill Gates Killer).[405] "Naked Wife" reportedly infected at least 18 major American corporations.[406] The Jennifer Lopez virus appeared a few months later as another provocative e-mail. Its subject line reads, "Where are you" and the attachment was titled *JENNIFERLOPEZ_NAKED.JPG.vbs*.[407] Like its predecessors, this worm was designed to trick the unwary user by promising visual gifts appealing to baser instincts.[408] Unlike the early Madonna Rock Video virus, these newer worms wreaked havoc without even offering actual glimpses of glamorous celebrities as compensation.

Virus writers can be motivated by any number of factors, including a desire for recognition, the furtherance of a socio-political cause, or a craving for personal revenge.[409] Probably the first major criminal prosecution involving a computer virus was that of Donald Burleson in Texas. He worked in the computer room of a Fort Worth securities-trading firm and was responsible for assuring that the company's password system operated properly. Burleson, a man of unconventional political beliefs, was a member of a fanatical tax protest movement. He argued frequently with his employers over the issue of federal withholding tax, which he insisted not be deducted from his paycheck. In 1985, when his employers learned he was planning to sue them to force them to stop withholding his taxes, he was fired. Before turning in his keys, the enraged Burleson planted a "worm." A worm is similar to a virus, except it is not contagious and only infects its host computer.[410]

A few days later, the director of accounting discovered to his horror that "168,000 commission records no longer existed on the computer—they had been deleted from the system!"[411] This, of course, would make the month's payroll impossible to calculate. Burleson was arrested and became the first person every tried for sabotage by virus.[412] He was convicted in 1988, fined $12,000, and placed on seven years probation.[413]

In 1988, Robert Morris, a Cornell University graduate student, planted the infamous Internet virus which infected a vast network of 6,000 computers stretching from Berkeley to Princeton to MIT and caused at least a quarter of a million dollars in damage.[414] Morris became the first person convicted under the Computer Fraud and Abuse Act of 1986.[415] He was sentenced to three years probation, fined $10,000, and ordered to perform 400 hours of community service.[416] Some members of both the computer community and the general public received this comparatively light sentence with hostility.[417] Sanctioning hackers remains a controversial topic, since they are characteristically so far removed from any popular criminal stereotype. Virus authors are often adolescents—"kids who are a little bit short on social ethics."[418]

On the other hand, Morris was not a kid, and his offense was hardly trivial. It has been reported that when his virus entered the computers at the Army's Ballistic Research laboratory in Maryland, system managers feared the United States had been invaded.[419]

Some viruses appear deceptively benign. In December 1987, a seemingly harmless "Christmas Tree" virus, designed by a German student, was loosed on the worldwide IBM network. Instructions to type the word "Christmas" would flash on a terminal screen. Users who complied with this innocent-sounding request tripped a virus that ultimately infected 350,000 terminals in 130 countries. IBM had to shut down its entire electronic mail system for two days to contain the spread.[420]

Viruses are sometimes placed in so-called "logic bombs." In other words, the virus program contains delayed instructions to trigger at some future date or when certain pre-set conditions are met, such as a specific number of program executions.[421] An early example was the Jerusalem virus, so named because it was discovered at Hebrew University. This virus, which had the potential to cause a computer to lose all its files instantly, was set to go off on the 40th anniversary of the State of Israel. Fortunately, the virus was eradicated well before that date.[422] Additional examples are the Joshi virus, which instructed the user to type "Happy Birthday Joshi" and was set to activate on January 5, 1993, and the Casino virus, set to activate on January 15, April 15, and August 15, 1993. Casino was a particularly mischievous virus that challenges the user to a slot-machine game and damages files if the user loses.[423]

Newer "stealth" viruses are much more complex than the earlier generations just described, hiding inside the computer memory whenever an antivirus scanning program searches the hard drive.[424] One of the worst of this new breed is the Mutating Engine virus. Unleashed by a Bulgarian known as the Dark Avenger, Mutating Engine can change form every time it replicates.[425]

According to the U.S. Department of Energy, so-called "macro" viruses now pose a significant threat to computers. An early macro strain, Concept, became the world's number one virus in just six months: "Faster than any in history,"[426] according to the head of the National Computer Security Association. Concept does not destroy data—it repeatedly flashes an annoying numeral onscreen—but it is very expensive to eradicate. "Other strains overseas, notably one called Hot, are more sinister, says William Orvis of CIAC (Computer Incident Advisory Capability). 'How much do you want to bet that they'll come here?'"[427]

Macro viruses are actually "worms." They spread so fast because they can be transmitted through e-mail and because they infect documents, rather than programs. The Melissa virus has shut down thousands of e-mail servers. It is sent in the form of a Microsoft Word e-mail attachment. It copies itself, then sends out a list of Internet porn sites to the first 50 names in the victim's e-mail address book. The original virus has been traced to a posting in the Internet news group alt.sex. Melissa's victims include Merrill Lynch, Paine Webber, Intel, Compaq, Lockheed Martin, Indiana University, the state government of North Dakota, the U.S. Department of Energy, the daily show-business newspaper *Variety*, and even *Security* magazine.[428] Melissa spread faster than any previous virus and reportedly infected more than 100,000 computers.[429] The government placed the cost of the damage at $80 million.[430]

David L. Smith, the creator of the Melissa virus, was arrested in New Jersey in 1999. He revealed, among other things, that he had named Melissa after a Florida stripper.[431] Two years later, he was handed a 20-month prison sentence. Under federal sentencing guidelines, he could have received up to five years but was afforded some leniency because of his ongoing cooperation with the government.[432]

On May 4, 2000, the notorious Love Letter virus (also dubbed the "Love Bug") began attacking an estimated 45 million computers, in the form of an e-mail attachment with the subject line "ILOVEYOU." Other mutations were disguised as a joke or a Mother's Day gift order. When victims open the attachment, "it begins a destructive process that overwrites system and data files and downloads a password-thieving program from the Internet."[433] While Melissa only sends itself to the first 50 names in the victim's e-mail address book, the Love Bug is far more damaging. It sends itself to all the names in all the victim's address books and it destroys files too.[434] Estimates of the damage to e-commerce were as high as $10 billion, surpassing even the infamous Melissa.[435] At least four classified systems in three separate defense agencies were contaminated. One of them was the top-secret National Security Agency.[436]

Almost immediately, electronic evidence convinced U.S. investigators that the Love Bug had originated in the Philippines. They soon identified a prime suspect, code-named Spyder.[437] Because Philippine law does not cover his alleged crime, Spyder was not charged. He was 15 years old.

In early 2003, "Storm Worm" was one of the larger Trojan Horse attacks to date. It was unusually timely, as it was launched during a major storm in Central Europe and was contained in an e-mail carrying the subject line "230 dead as storm batters Europe." "Cybercriminals took advantage of social engineering, using the news of the European storm to get people to open the attached malicious file, which promises more news on the weather emergency."[438] The recipient must open the file for the Trojan Horse to execute. The file then creates a back door to a computer that can be exploited later to steal data or post spam.[439] Storm Worm, believed to be created by Russians, came "storming" back in 2007, when it started generating Christmas- and New Years-related e-mail spam which offered links to infected Web sites that tried to install malware on victims' computers.[440]

CASE STUDY
The Worms of August

Those who study computer crime may very well remember 2003 as the "Year of the Worm." In January, the SQL Slammer worm, also known as the Sapphire worm, caused numerous denial of service attacks and dramatically slowed down Internet traffic. At the time, Slammer was the fastest worm in history, doubling in size every 8.5 seconds and infecting more than 90 percent of vulnerable computers within 10 minutes.[441] True to its name, Slammer slammed Ohio's Davis-Besse nuclear power plant and disabled a safety monitoring system there for nearly five hours.[442]

Slammer, however, was only setting the stage for a memorable summer. In the space of two weeks in August, three destructive viruses were loosed on the world's computers. The first one was the Blaster worm, also known as MSBlaster or LoveSAN. It exploited a flaw in Microsoft operating systems. Since it did not arrive as an e-mail attachment, users were slow to recognize any infection. As a result, Blaster spread very rapidly— at a reported rate of 30,000 PCs per hour.[443] The infection caused computers to reboot frequently and disrupted users' Internet browsing.[444] Blaster appeared to be a vendetta against Microsoft. In addition to crashing systems, it carried a message to the company's founder and chairman: "Billy Gates why do you make this possible? Stop making money and fix your software."[445]

While Blaster was still causing havoc, a second worm appeared. It was a bizarre twist. The Nachi worm, also called the Welchia worm, was dubbed a "vigilante" worm or a "Good Samaritan" worm or a "friendly" worm. It was designed to delete Blaster and install the proper security patch on vulnerable computers.[446] Contained inside Nachi's code was the text: "I love my wife & baby."[447] After infecting a computer, Nachi sought out and destroyed any copies of the Blaster worm. A senior technology consultant observed: "The writer of the Nachi worm may want to be seen as the Dirty Harry of the Internet world."[448]

But, as they say, no good deed goes unpunished; and the problem with "good" worms is that, even if well-intended, they're not all that good. An anti-virus is still a virus. Nachi was programmed to uninstall itself, but not until 2004. Moreover, it opens up a port that reportedly renders the system vulnerable to remote commands.[449] Nachi may have caused even more problems than Blaster because of the propagation technique it used. It swamped network systems with traffic and caused denial-of-service to critical servers.[450] For example, it affected computers within the U.S. Navy

(Continued)

Marine Corps Intranet, reducing capacity by 75 percent.[451] "So much for the notion of a benevolent worm—there's no such thing."[452] An anti-virus software executive clearly agreed when he warned: "I wouldn't trust a virus author to fix my PC."[453]

The Blaster and Nachi worms were continuing to bombard corporate and government networks and slow down the Internet when the third "Worm of August" struck. The Sobig worm began attacking e-mail systems globally on August 19 and by the next day it had already been declared the fastest-spreading virus of all time.[454] Sobig spread through Windows on PCs via e-mail. It overwhelmed e-mail servers. Some users were getting up to 100–200 infected e-mails a day, and as many as one out of every four e-mails had Sobig attachments.[455] One veteran computer service technician declared: "It's a wildfire spread. . . . Some programmer is in love with it."[456] The Sobig virus deposited a Trojan Horse (hacker back door) that turned victims' PCs into spam machines.[457] Spam is the computer term for ubiquitous junk e-mail. Some experts believed that Sobig had been designed to subvert PCs for commercial spammers. One Internet executive concluded:

> "Sobig appears to have been written by people who are trying to find ways to relay spam. . . . Up to now, the worms have been written by people who are trying to be cool. This looks like a money worm."[458]

In 2004, the worst of the virus outbreaks was the attack of Netsky-P. It was not only disseminated by e-mail, it was spread by file-sharing systems offering downloadable pictures of celebrities like Brittany Spears and Arnold Schwarzenegger.[459] Another major outbreak was Zafi-B, which had the ability to speak in multiple languages. "Zafi replicated itself in Hungarian, German, Dutch, English, Italian, Swedish, and Russian."[460] One European e-security director described Zafi-B as "smart."[461]

Sven Jaschan, an 18-year-old German high school student, created the Netsky worm.[462] Jaschan is also the self-confessed author of the Sasser worm.[463] Unlike many viruses, the Sasser worm does not travel by e-mail. It makes its way around the Internet unaided[464] by exploiting security holes in Microsoft's Windows software.[465] During a single week in May 2004, Sasser hit hundreds of thousands of computers, continually shutting them down and rebooting them.[466] Sasser infected at least seven large companies.[467] Jaschan attributed the shutting down of infected computers to poor programming.[468] German police arrested Sven Jaschan in 2005 with the help of the FBI and Microsoft.[469] He was convicted and received a 21-month suspended sentence. Under German law he could have been given a 5-year prison term, but the prosecutors opted for leniency because Jaschan was a minor at the time of his offenses.[470]

The Netsky worm staged a comeback in 2007, riding the coattails of fictional wizard Harry Potter.[471] It was timed for the release of the latest Harry Potter movie and novel. The new Netsky P version, dubbed W32/Hairy-A, automatically infected PCs when users attached USB drives.[472] If users allowed their USB drives to "auto-run," they saw a file named *HarryPotter-TheDeathlyHallows.doc*. Inside the word file was the simple phrase, "Harry Potter is dead."

> After infecting Windows computers, the worm creates a number of new users, namely the book's main characters—Harry Potter, Hermione Granger and Ron Weasley. After logging in, users are shown the following message via a batch file: "read and repent; the end is near; repent from your evil ways O Ye folks; lest you burn in hell . . . JK Rowling especially."[473]

A number of variants of the infamous Blaster worm (described earlier) have also been created. One of these was Blaster-B, which attacked nearly 500,000 computers, causing more than $1 million in damage.[474] In 2004, a young Minnesota man pleaded guilty to downloading the original Blaster worm, modifying it to Blaster-B, and releasing it on the Internet a year earlier when he was 18 years old.[475] Jeffrey Lee Parson was sentenced in 2005. Unlike his far more destructive German counterpart, Sven Jacschan, Parson's young age did not shield him from incarceration. He was given 18 months in prison.[476] Prosecutors had asked for 37 months, but the judge chose a lighter sentence because of the 320-pound Parsons' history of mental health problems and grim home environment.[477]

Some of the fastest-spreading viruses were variants of the Sober worm. Sober-M is a mass e-mailing virus that affects systems running Microsoft Windows. The e-mail containing Sober-M is deliberately written in bad English in an apparent attempt to convince recipients that it is not a virus.[478] Sober-P is spread by using German messages for German Windows users. Recipients are told they have won tickets to the World Cup soccer matches.[479]

Computer viruses and worms remain perennial and very costly nuisances. In 2007, Richard Honour pleaded guilty in federal court to releasing malicious computer viruses (malware) that damaged systems across the country.[480] Honour's programs infected users of Internet Relay Chat (IRC) with a program called WindowMedia.exe, which installed a back door that gave him access to compromised computers.[481]

While some worms are released to cause mischief, such as Blaster, Welchia, and Sasser, others are released to make money. These worms rely on creating a "botnet," sold to spammers for a profit. One such worm was "Koobface," which spread through Facebook, MySpace, and Twitter in mid-2008.[482] Once infected, the worm would scour the host machine for passwords to social networking sites and send fake messages to the user's friends in an effort to get them to click an infected link and further expand the spread of the worm. It was estimated that between 2009 and 2010, the worm made its author $2 million in revenue.[483] In 2012, Facebook revealed the results of a three-year investigation into the matter and fingered the Russian men responsible: Stanislav Avdeyko (leDed), Alexander Koltyshev (Floppy), Anton Korotchenko (KrotReal), Roman P. Koturbach (PoMuc), and Svyatoslav E. Polichuck (PsViat and PsycoMan).[484]

In 2009, the Conficker worm, also known as the Downadup worm and the Kido worm, sprang to life.[485] Conficker is considered the worst worm infection since Slammer, infecting an estimated nine million personal computers around the world.[486] It was spread by a newly discovered Microsoft Windows flaw[487] and, like the Harry Potter worm, by USB thumb drives.[488] Conficker burrows deep into the operating system and "tricks" the computer into running the infected program[489] by modifying the way "autorun" works when a user plugs in a drive or a memory stick.[490] As we have seen, worms like Conficker not only ricochet around the Internet at lightning speed, they also harness infected computers into unified botnet systems controlled by clandestine masters, who can send out remote commands to perform illegal activities.[491] Microsoft has put up a $250,000 bounty for information on the Conficker worm's "bot herders."[492]

In 2010 and 2012, two highly sophisticated worms named Stuxnet and Flame were found spreading through Middle Eastern computer networks. Stuxnet, the first to appear, had two phases. First, it spread harmlessly, but indiscriminately through Iranian networks.[493] Second, once it found Siemens Industrial software and equipment, the worm subverted and crippled the "supervisory control and data acquisition" infrastructure of the equipment.[494] Siemens equipment is what Iran uses to enrich uranium and, while the worm was harmless for other Iranian computer users, it damaged the ability of the Iranian government to produce nuclear material. Of all the infections worldwide, 60 percent were in Iran.[495]

The second worm, Flame, was again found in Iran, but also throughout the rest of the Middle East. The worm had the ability to spread both via local area networks and USB thumb-drives. It was able to monitor, record, and retransmit audio, screenshots, keyboard activity, and network traffic.[496] Furthermore, it turned each Bluetooth-enabled computer it infected into a "beacon" that would download the contact information of nearby cellphones.[497] The worm contained a "kill" command that could be triggered remotely and would instantly wipe the worm from any infected machine.[498]

The extremely sophisticated nature of both worms and their specific targets lead many security experts to believe that no individual or group could have authored such a program without nation-state support.[499] Indeed, in early summer 2012, *The New York Times* reported that both worms were part of joint U.S.—Israeli covert program called "Operation Olympic Games."[500] The newspaper reported that the program had begun under President George W. Bush and expanded under President Barack Obama.

For whatever reason, computer viruses have captured the public's imagination. Perhaps the term itself, with its mad scientist imagery and plague-like connotation, has generated a perverse blend of fright and titillation. In any event, the media seldom underplay a virus story. Studies reveal that the level of public interest in viruses is a direct function of increasing or decreasing media attention.[501] Critics of the media have argued that the virus "epidemic" has been over-blown, that there are more problematic computer crime issues worthier of public concern. They cite as evidence the "media hype" over the Michelangelo virus, which was supposed to infect millions of computers worldwide on March 6, 1992, (Michelangelo's birthday) and erase everything it touched. "In the end, scattered copies of Michelangelo were found—but nowhere near the millions predicted."[502] On the other hand, futurists predict that computer extortion, using the mere threat of a "stealth" virus, will be one of the major crimes of the 21st Century.[503]

INTERNET SCAMS

"The Internet has accelerated almost every aspect of modern life"[504]—including white-collar crime. For years, the FBI has been warning citizens that "thousands of con artists, grifters, fraud-sters, and other denizens of the dark are trolling for victims online"[505] Some varieties of telemarketing fraud described in Chapter 2 have spread to the Internet. A state securities commissioner has warned: "Don't believe that just because it's on a computer, that it's true. Computers don't lie, but the people who put messages on computers lie."[506] In 2012, a mother and son team made over $909,000 selling stolen Lego toys on the international bidding Web site eBay.[507] The two stole expensive Lego sets from local Florida Toys 'R' Us stores and resold the ill-gotten goods online for pure profit. The use of online resellers such as eBay has given traditional thieves one more way to scam buyers, and this time, from the relative safety of their own home.

Cyberspace is stuffed with hundreds of "exotic" offers—everything from ostrich farming[508] to Russian mail-order brides.[509] A popular e-mail scam involves offers to sell "cable descrambler kits," allowing buyers to receive cable television without paying the subscription fee. According to the FTC's Bureau of Consumer Protection, there are two small problems with this scheme. The kits don't work, and stealing cable service is a crime.[510]

Other crooks have masqueraded as financial advisers or licensed brokers on the Internet and solicited investments in fictitious mutual funds. One Michigan scam artist talked a New York investor into sending him $91,000 and cheated a Texas victim out of $10,000. Six months later, the Texan ruefully acknowledged his gullibility: "I was terribly embarrassed. I knew I'd been screwed."[511]

In the years since, the ranks of the "screwed" have only grown bigger. The reported losses from Internet fraud topped $485.3 million in 2011.[512] This was an all-time high, easily eclipsing the reported figure of $198.44 million in 2006[513] and $239 million in 2007.[514]

Although Ponzis, investment scams, and other con games seemingly have been around forever, the Computer Age has added a new element: the Internet's ability to spread these frauds at the speed of light. As a result, "fraud burns through the Internet in a matter of days."[515] Mass e-mailings—"spam"—circulate word of new get-rich-quick schemes to thousands upon thousands of potential marks with a single click.[516] While mass e-mailings might not sound particularly injurious, engineers at Microsoft and Google estimate spam costs society $20 *billion* per year.[517] Adding insult to injury, the same engineers believe that all of the spammers in the world make only $200 million in revenue. This high cost to return ratio comes from that fact that sending massive amounts of e-mails costs money and bandwidth, plus wastes the time of non-buying readers. In fact, the companies claim only one per 25,000 people buy something through spam.[518]

In a recent case, two members of an international spam gang, James Schaffer of Arizona and Jeffrey Kilbride of California, were convicted of bombarding Internet users with unsolicited pornography and using sophisticated technology to conceal their identities.[519] The so-called "dirty duo" reportedly took in over two million dollars from their porno-spam operation.[520]

Jeremy Jaynes was one of the most prolific "spammers" in the world. It has been estimated that he would send out as many as **500,000** mass e-mailings a month, hawking everything from pornography, to software that promises to clean computers of private information, to a service for choosing penny stocks to invest in, to a "FedEx refund processor" that promised $75-an-hour work but did little more than give buyers access to a Web site of delinquent FedEx accounts.[521]

Jaynes procured millions of e-mail addresses from a stolen database of America Online customers. He also obtained e-mail addresses of users of the online auction house eBay.[522] Relatively few people responded to Jayne's pitches. His "hit" rate was "only" about one credit card order for every 30,000 e-mails he sent out. That may not sound like a successful business model, but at $40 per order with a base of a half million e-mails, Jaynes was raking in as much as $750,000 a month.[523] He ran his business from a nondescript house in North Carolina. But Jeremy Jaynes' actual home was a mansion in another part of the state that was dubbed the "House that Spam Built."

Jaynes was convicted in Virginia in 2005 for using false Internet addresses and aliases to send spam. Under Virginia law, sending unsolicited bulk e-mail is not itself a crime, unless the sender masks his identity.[524] The volume of Jayne's e-mails elevated his offense to a felony. It was the nation's first felony spam conviction.[525] Jeremy Jaynes received a 9-year prison sentence.[526] The headline almost writes itself: "Spammer to Slammer."

The next "Spam King" to fall was Christopher "Rizler" Smith, who made millions of dollars selling medications online. In 2005, federal authorities raided Smith's home, seizing his passport and $4.2 million in assets. At the same time, the FBI closed down his 95-employee company, Xpress Pharmacy. Smith had sent out more than *one billion* e-mails selling "penis pills" and other questionable products. In his final year of operation alone, Rizler Smith reportedly made more than $18 million.[527] Smith was charged with selling prescription drugs without a license, but he fled to the Dominican Republic using a phony passport.

When he returned to the U.S. a few months later, Rizler Smith was arrested at the airport in Minneapolis-St. Paul. Two years later, he was handed a 30-year federal prison sentence.[528] That very tough sentence reflected the perceived seriousness of Smith's crimes. As one senior technology consultant has observed: "Pharmacy spammers are amongst the lowest of the low when it comes to Internet crime, not only deluging people with millions of unwanted e-mails but also potentially putting them at risk through dangerous medications."[529]

Next to stand trial was Robert Soloway, the man authorities dubbed "the King of Spam." Soloway pleaded guilty of fraud in 2008.[530] He used compromised "zombie" computers to send out many millions of junk e-mails. The case was the first in which federal identity theft statutes were used to prosecute a spammer.[531] Soloway used a program called Dark Mailer to pump out bulk advertisements for his company, Newport Internet Marketing, which sold software—*for spamming*.[532] He reportedly made over $700,000 between 2005 and 2007 selling his spamming software.[533] Robert Soloway was sentenced to 47 months in federal prison.[534]

The Jaynes, Smith, and Soloway cases suggest that "Spam world" has more "kings" than professional wrestling. The mass media seem to stick a crown on every big-time spammer. Indeed, another media-dubbed "King of Spam," Sanford "Spamford" Wallace, lost an unprecedented civil award of $230 million in 2008. The popular MySpace Web site successfully sued Wallace for bombarding MySpace users with unsolicited advertisements for pornography and gambling. Wallace had lured MySpace users to reveal their login information through phishing techniques. "Spamford" Wallace failed to show up in court for the civil trial.[535] As a result, he was ordered to pay $230 million by the court.[536] In 2009, Wallace filed for bankruptcy[537] and was ordered to pay Facebook $711 million in damages for additional crimes against that company, as well.[538] Given the bankruptcy, it is unlikely either company will ever be paid.

"Spam King" Alan Ralsky was indicted in 2008 for running an international spamming and stock fraud scheme.[539] Before the FBI shut down his Detroit-based operation, he allegedly sent out more than *100 million* e-mails every day. In June 2009, Ralsky pleaded guilty to wire fraud, mail fraud, and money laundering charges.[540] He also admitted guilt under the CAN-SPAMM Act and, by helping convict other spammers, was given a reduced sentence of four years, three months in prison and a fine of $250,000.[541]

Of all the dethroned "Spam Kings," the one with the most dramatic story is Edward "Eddie" Davidson of Denver, who ran an international spam empire. Davidson used sub-contractors to flood cyberspace with spam, pitching a wide variety of products from penny stocks to watches and perfume.[542] He was sentenced to 21 months in prison but escaped from the minimum-security federal prison camp after a few months of incarceration.[543] Just four days later, Eddie Davidson fatally shot his wife and young daughter, and then turned the gun on himself in an apparent murder-suicide.[544] The U.S. Attorney, who had prosecuted Davidson, said: "What a nightmare, and such a coward. Davidson imposed the 'death penalty' on family members for his own crime."[545]

To put spam attacks into numerical perspective, consider that there are more than a billion electronic mailboxes in the world. Annual e-mail traffic exceeds 50 billion messages. And the estimated cost of sending bulk e-mails is .01 cents per message—that is a million e-mails cost a sender about $100.[546] Virginia's assistant attorney general, who prosecuted Jeremy Jaynes, has done the math: "When you're marketing the world, there are enough idiots out there."[547]

Early in 2006, in the first case of its kind, a 20-year-old Los Angeles man pleaded guilty to using hundreds of thousands of "zombie" computers to damage systems and send out massive waves of spam. Jeanson Ancheta was a member of the "Botmaster Underground," a secret network of hackers skilled in "bot" attacks.[548] As noted earlier, a bot is a program that surreptitiously installs itself on a computer, allowing the computer to be controlled by the hacker ("bot herder").[549] The "botnet" created by zombie computers can harness their collective power to send out huge amounts of spam. Botnets can also inflict considerable damage to computers.

Among the computers Ancheta attacked were some at the Weapons Division of the U.S. Naval Air Warfare Center in China Lakes, California.[550]

The following are two other prolific and costly categories of Internet fraud:

PHISHING

The word "phishing" comes from a metaphor describing how early computer criminals used e-mail lures to *fish* for passwords and financial data from a sea of Internet users. Spelling it with a "ph" was probably some sort of tribute to the original hackers, the phone phreaks. The term was coined in the 1990s by hackers who were stealing America Online accounts by scamming passwords from unsuspecting AOL subscribers. By 1996, hacked accounts were called "phish" and were traded routinely by hackers as a form of electronic currency: for example, 10 working AOL phish for a piece of hacking software or some cracked Warez code.[551] Over the years, the definition of what constitutes a phishing attack has expanded. The term now covers not only obtaining user account details but also includes accessing all personal and financial data.[552]

Phishing is a blend of technical deceit and what hackers call "social engineering" (manipulation and deception of designated victims). It is a scam in which the attacker sends an e-mail purporting to be from a valid financial or e-commerce provider—a technique known as "spoofing." The e-mail often uses fear tactics in an effort to prod the intended victim into visiting a fraudulent website (e.g., "We've lost your password," "Your account has been suspended"). Phishing e-mails normally utilize copied images and text styles used on the legitimate Web site in order to portray the e-mail as genuine. Many consumers are fooled into thinking an e-mail is authentic simply because it contains, for example, a bank's logo. To enhance authenticity, "some phishing e-mails also have genuine links to the company's privacy policy and other pages on the legitimate web site."[553] Once at the bogus site, which generally looks and feels like the valid site, victims are instructed to log in to their accounts and enter sensitive financial information, such as their bank PIN numbers or their Social Security numbers. That information is then surreptitiously sent to the attacker, who uses it to engage in credit card and bank fraud—or outright identity theft.[554]

Phishing attacks by e-mail employ many of the same tools and techniques used by spammers. While the delivery medium may vary, the targets increasingly have become home PCs that previously have been compromised by a Trojan Horse program. This allows phishers (along with spammers and Warez pirates) to use the host PC as a message propagator. Consequently, tracking back a phishing attack to its initiating criminal can be extremely difficult. Phishers can deliver specially crafted e-mails to millions of e-mail addresses within a few hours—or minutes using a Trojan Horse network.

Phishing e-mails typically have subject lines that appear to be related to the purported sender—for example "Important Notice For All Internet Banking Users."[555] Sometimes, a key word is deliberately misspelled in order to bypass spam filters; something many people would not recognize at a quick glance.[556] For example, the popular search engine Google has been written as Googkle. It is also quite easy to forge a sender's address, since most people would not know a real commercial e-mail address from a realistic-sounding fake one. Links within a phishing e-mail can be deliberately disguised in a further attempt to deceive the recipient. This can be done a number of ways, but one especially insidious technique is to display a link to a genuine Web site, then add to it in white text against a white background, making the alteration invisible to the naked eye. For example, a recipient may see a link that appears to be displayed as *http:// www.real-site.com* but may actually read *http://www.real-site.com@**fraud-site.com***. Clicking on the "real-site" link would, of course, take the unwary victim to the "fraud-site."

Fraud-sites supporting phishing e-mails are designed to mirror real sites in order to trick consumers into thinking they are at a trusted company's genuine Web site, where they would feel secure giving out personal information. Even the URL can sound like the real thing. One phishing scam targeted customers of Barclays Bank using the URL *http://www.barclays.validation.com.* It seemed like it *could* have been Barclays URL, but it wasn't.[557] Likewise, phishers have created Web pages that appear to be the site of the Internal Revenue Service—the URL even includes *www.irs.gov.* Victims are lured there by fake IRS e-mails claiming that the individual is either due a refund or has tax problems. The unreal site serves only one real purpose: to harvest private financial information.[558]

In recent years, phishing has spread like a plague. According to a study by MessageLabs, a New York e-mail security firm, the number of phishing e-mails increased *1,200 percent* in 2004.[559] The chief information analyst at MessageLabs called it "a very dangerous trend."[560] That figure reportedly increased another 28 percent in 2005,[561] as 57 million Internet users in the U.S. received e-mails linked to phishing scams, and about 1.7 million of them were tricked into divulging personal information.[562] Senator Patrick Leahy, who introduced the Anti-Phishing Act of 2005, warned that the billions of dollars in short-term losses were just the tip of the iceberg: "In the long-term, phishing undermines the public's trust in the Internet. By making consumers uncertain about the integrity of the Internet's complex addressing system, phishing threatens to make us all less likely to use the Internet for secure transactions."[563] In 2007, a survey by Gartner, Inc., one of the world's leading information technology research and advisory companies, reported that the cost of phishing attacks in the United States soared to $3.2 billion, and 3.6 million citizens lost money.[564] The security division of technology giant EMC reported that phishing scams rose another 66 percent in 2008 and that 68 percent of U.S. bank brands were attacked.[565]

Much of the recent success of phishers lies in the use of "flax flux" attacks, a technique with which botnets hide phishing delivery sites behind an ever-changing network of compromised hosts ("zombie" computers) acting as proxies.[566]

The popular Google e-mail service (Gmail) became a prime phishing target in 2008. Customers received the following personalized e-mails:

> Dear [Customer's First Name],
>
> We are having congestions [sic] due to the anonymous registration of Gmail accounts, so we are shutting down some Gmail accounts, and your account was among those to be deleted. We are sending you this e-mail so that you can verify and let us know if you still want to use this account.
>
> Customer Care
>
> GMail Team[567]

But rather than coming from Gmail's "Customer Verification" [sic] Department, the bogus e-mails come from cybercrooks looking to extract login information.[568] Fortunately, the e-mail is riddled with bad grammar and spelling mistakes, which tipped off many Google customers. Unfortunately, many others took the bait.

So what happens to the personal data collected by phishing scams? If the victim provided bank account information, cyber-crooks are likely to hijack the victim's bank account. Passwords can be changed, locking victims out of their own accounts. "The fraudsters may empty the victim's bank account by electronically transferring funds to a temporary account they have fraudulently set up using someone else's personal information."[569] The cash is then withdrawn before either victim is aware of what has occurred. Crooks may also write and cash counterfeit checks on the victim's account.[570] Time is on the side of the phisher. He can store the information, waiting until there is the desired amount of money in the account. "The victim has no idea, until it's too late."[571]

If the victim provided credit card information, his or her card can be used to make unauthorized purchases. The credit card number can also be sold to organized fraud rings.[572] If the phishing scam has "socially engineered" the victim's ATM card and ATM PIN numbers, fraudsters can create duplicate cards and clean out the victim's account through ATM withdrawals.[573]

The most serious consequence of phishing scams is identity theft. The pilfered personal information can be used to apply for new credit cards, using the victim's name, credit history, and billing address. Victims are then left to explain a mountain of bills and try to repair their fractured credit ratings and clear their spoiled reputations long after the cyber-crook has disappeared.[574] Once, identity thieves were "dumpster divers," who would trowel through rubbish bins looking for documents containing personal financial data. Now they simply "go phishing" and ask their victims for the information.

In one recent case, for example, Jeffrey Goodin of California was convicted in federal court of operating a sophisticated phishing scheme designed to dupe AOL users so he could steal their personal and credit card information.[575] He was later sentenced to 70 months in prison—a fraction of the maximum 101 years he could have received.[576] Goodin posed as an AOL billing department representative and steered thousands of customers to a number of bogus Web sites he maintained.[577] Victims were then instructed to submit their personal data under threat that if they failed to do so their Internet services accounts would be suspended.[578] Goodin, or people he sold the data to, used the information to make fraudulent purchases. At his trial, it was unclear how much money Goodin had made as a result of his phishing expedition, but the Assistant U.S. Attorney, who represented the government, said: "You could spend years figuring out how many individuals were in fact scammed."[579]

In another recent case, Michael Dolan of Connecticut also took aim at AOL customers. Dolan was convicted in federal court of aggravated identity theft.[580] Dolan was the alleged mastermind of an elaborate scam in which he and five confederates used malicious software to harvest names and e-mail addresses from AOL chat rooms. The targets were then spammed with electronic greeting cards, purportedly from *Hallmark.com*, but which actually installed a Trojan Horse that prevented them from logging into their accounts without entering their credit card number, bank account numbers, and other personal information.[581] The data were used to create fake debit cards, which were used to make online purchases. According to prosecutors, the gang raked in $400,000 from more than 250 victims.[582] Michael Dolan was sentenced to seven years in prison.[583] To pun AOL's familiar catch-phrase: "You've got *jail*."

THE NIGERIAN SCAM

There is a district in Lagos, Nigeria, named Festac Town. It is here on these teeming, grimy streets that a growing community of young men live and scheme. "By day they flaunt their smart clothes and cars and hang around the Internet cafes, trading stories about successful cons and near misses, hatching new plots."[584] At night, in those same Internet Cafes, they hunker down at computers and bait traps for unwary marks. The tens of thousands of bogus e-mails each of them may send out have become known collectively overseas as the Nigerian scam, or sometimes 4-1-9 fraud. They themselves simply call it 419—a reference to Section 419 of the Nigerian penal code which pertains to fraud.[585]

The Nigerian scam has been around since the early 1980s, when it began as postal fraud. As cyber-technology developed over the years, many different Nigerian scams have evolved—from crooked real estate pitches, to commodities fraud, to currency conversion schemes, to phony lottery swindles.[586] The most common form, however, is an electronic variation of a classic con game known as the "pigeon drop." "The way the pigeon drop works is that the scam artists convince you that they have "found" money—money that has unclear ownership, and you can gain a share of it if you just do a few things to show good faith."[587] Naturally, the way you show good faith is to give them some money for "safe-keeping" until the "found" money clears some sort of hurdle. Usually the victim is required to pay "advance fees"—sometimes $5,000 or more—to cover things like attorney charges or bribes of officials. Once they have your cash, however, they quickly disappear, and you discover too late that you have been ripped off.[588]

The Nigerian version of the "pigeon drop" starts with bulk e-mails. A potential victim typically will receive an unsolicited communication from a Nigerian claiming to be a senior government official, or the widow of a senior government official, or a corrupt barrister or bank officer, who is seeking an individual into whose account he can deposit millions of dollars in funds in order to get that money out of the country. A tale is told, usually involving a someone who has died and left a lot of money behind of questionable provenance, sitting dormant waiting to be "liberated."

Here are a pair of tales that have been e-mailed to one of the authors of this book:

Mr. Johnson Emeka, a Branch Manager for the United Bank of Africa had a customer, a foreign resident, who died three years ago leaving $7.5 million in an unclaimed account. If you are willing to pose as the deceased's next of kin, Mr. Johnson and his associates will obtain the necessary legal documentation to support your claim, so that the money can be transferred to your account. "The whole procedures will last only five working days to get the fund retrieved successfully without a trace even now or in future. Your response is only what we are waiting for as we have arranged all necessary things. . . . For your assistance we have agreed to give you twenty-five percent (25%) of the Total sum."

Hajia Mariam Abacha, the widow of former Nigerian dictator, General Sani Abacha, has shipped a metal trunk to a security company in Amsterdam. The trunk contains a $15 million bribe that her late husband was paid by a Russian firm as part of a deal for a steel plant. Because she is not free to leave Nigeria, Mrs. Abacha and her family need your help. "Please if you can assist us claim this consignment, kindly contact me on my e-mail so that the Air-way bill will be prepared in your name and sent to enable you to claim the consignment as the beneficiary. . . . Conclusively, we have jointly agreed to give you 30% of the total sum."

Perhaps because the very word "Nigeria" has become a red flag through reputation and repetition, some of the scammers now prefer to set their tales elsewhere. A few of the letters, purportedly from other African countries, may be the work of local copycats, but most are believed still to originate in Nigeria.[589] Mrs. Suzana Vaye, the widow of the murdered Liberian Deputy Minister of Public Works, needs you to help her transfer $21.5 million. Dr. John Ballas, the Auditor General of a major bank in Mauritius, is looking for an "honest" person to help him launder $32 million. In a letter soaked in bathos, Mrs. Melissa Pointer, grieving widow of a Chevron/Texaco executive in Kenya, informs you that she is dying of esophageal cancer and has only a few weeks to live. Because she is a devout born-again Christian, Mrs. Pointer begs you to let her transfer her $3.5 million estate to your account in order to keep it out of the hands of her late husband's heathen relatives. All she asks is that you promise to distribute the money to orphanages.

The Nigerian e-mail scammers prefer targeting Americans, whom they see as rich and easy to fool—an irresistible combination to any electronic predator. They also rationalize their crimes by denying there are any real victims. They share a mistaken belief that their prey will be reimbursed by the U.S. government.[590] Some of their outlandish tales even feature Americans in lead roles. A U.S. Army Special Forces commando found $36 million in drug money while conducting a secret search-and-destroy mission against the Taliban in Afghanistan. He stashed the money in luggage but wants to hide it in your bank account. A man was delivering a large sum of cash to the World Trade Center on 9/11. Although he miraculously escaped from the collapsed building, his colleagues believe that he is dead. He has kept the cash and now needs to quietly deposit the money in your account.[591] In one of the newest renditions, the unclaimed money belonged to a U.S. soldier killed in Iraq. An official with the U.S. Immigration and Customs Enforcement agency said of this latter tale: "This really is one of the worst e-mail scams we've ever seen. . . . This is really despicable."[592]

A barely coherent e-mail received by this author in 2005, sets a new standard for layering one fraudulent tale over another:

> Dear Sir:
>
> Good day to you. I may have to trouble your sense of personal achievement and reward for an opportunity properly taken advantage of.
>
> I am Mr. David Jones, a representative and attorney to Kenneth Lay, the former Chairman & CEO, Enron Corp. Industry: Energy & Natural Resources Home, presently in jail and facing trial on charges of corruption and embezzlement of funds while in Power. He deposited fifteen million united states dollars ($15,000,000.00) with me when he was in power as the chairman.
>
> I am contacting you because I want you to deal with the Finance House and claim the money on my behalf since I have declared that the funds belong to my foreign business partner. . . . I hope to trust you as a God fearing person who will not sit on this money when you claim it but rather assist me properly to share in this ratio, 60% to me and 40% to you. When I receive your positive response I will give you viable information relating to this project i.e. the Finance institution where the money was deposited and the required documentation that will enable you to lay claim to the funds, which is very important. What I need is for you to indicate your interest that you will assist us by receiving the money as the beneficiary.
>
> Once I have your details, the finance institution will contact you for Release of funds to your account. As soon as the payment is effected, and the amount mentioned above is successfully transferred into your account . . . you will be paid based on a certain percentage agreed on by both parties. I guarantee you that this transaction will be executed under a legitimate arrangement that will protect you from any breach of the law. Please get in touch with me urgently by E-mail.

Even more recently, in 2008, three defendants, two from Nigeria and one from Senegal, pleaded guilty in federal court to using spam e-mails that promised victims millions of dollars that the defendants falsely claimed to control. American citizens reportedly lost $1.2 million by giving these crooks advance fees.[593] In one scenario, the defendants sent e-mails purporting to be from an individual suffering from terminal throat cancer who needed assistance distributing approximately $55 million to charity.[594] One of the defendants obtained victims' trust by telephoning them and disguising his voice to sound like he was suffering from throat cancer.[595]

The Nigerian scam provokes two fundamental questions. First, "Why Nigeria?" There are a number of explanations. Nigeria is the most populous and well-educated country in Africa. English, the *lingua franca* of computer fraud, is its official language. But, despite being oil-rich, it is also a nation in economic shambles. A quarter of urban college graduates are unemployed; so crime offers tempting career opportunities.[596] The 419 scam is reportedly the **third largest industry** in Nigeria.[597] Also, Nigeria is politically unstable, shifting back and forth between shaky democracy and brutal military rule. In such an environment, regulation and enforcement have been lax or non-existent. Arrests have been rare.[598] Monies stolen are almost never recovered.[599] Indeed, some victims, who have traveled to Nigeria seeking their money, have been murdered.[600]

Those who argue that Nigeria is now cracking down on scammers point to the recent 16-year sentence given to Mike Amadi, who had set up a Web site offering "juicy but phony procurement contracts."[601] But the Amadi case seems more of an aberration. He signed his letter as Nuhu Ribadu, who happens to be the head of Nigeria's Economic and Financial Crimes Commission.[602] Amadi was probably punished more for his effrontery than his fraud.

The second question is, "Who would ever fall for these awkwardly phrased e-mails with their implausible tales?" The answer is: more people than you might think. Although the "hit" rate may be only one percent or less, the sheer size of their nets all but assures an ample catch. According to one former scammer, "When you get a reply, it's 70 percent sure that you'll get the money."[603] Between 1989 and 2003, the Nigerian scam had raked in an estimated $5 billion.[604] That figure is, of course, even higher now. The U.S. Secret Service says that the fraud costs victims hundreds of millions of dollars each year.[605] Its Financial Crimes Division "receives approximately 100 telephone calls from victims and potential victims and 300–500 pieces of related correspondence per day."[606]

The special agent in charge of an FBI cybercrime squad has been dealing with Nigerian Internet scams for years. He has come to two basic conclusions: "[Nigerians] are just great at social engineering. . . . And Americans are very gullible."[607]

How gullible? In 2007, Richard Dompier of Oregon lost $200,000 in funds from the New Millennium Group investment company he ran to a Nigerian Internet scam. What made this case especially interesting was that Dompier himself was a swindler. The New Millennium Group was an international Ponzi scheme, involving silver ingots, that bilked investors out of more than $2.5 million.[608] Dompier was later sentenced to 10 years in federal prison.[609] His Nigerian tormentor remains long gone and hard to find. The case conjures up memories of the old doggerel about big fleas being bitten by little fleas.

Most victims of 419 are a good deal more sympathetic than Richard Dompier, however. Dr. Louis Gottschalk, a renowned psychiatrist, who worked at the University of California, Irvine medical plaza that still bears his name, lost a reported $3 million over a ten-year period to a Nigerian Internet scam.[610] Gottschalk had gained national prominence in 1987 when he revealed the results of his own studies suggesting, for the first time, that President Reagan had begun losing his mental faculties as early as 1980.[611] Ironically, when the swindle was discovered in 2006, Gottschalk, then 89-years-old, was himself confronted with allegations of mental incompetence by his family.[612] He died in 2008.

The grammatically challenged young scammers in Festac Town have an anthem, a popular song in Nigeria titled *I Go Chop Your Dollars*:

> 419 is just a game, you are the losers, we are the winners.
>
> White people are greedy . . .
>
> White men, I will eat your dollars . . . and disappear.
>
> We are the masters, you are the losers.[613]

ESPIONAGE

The misuse of computers as tools for industrial, political, and international espionage is another cause for major concern. A major FBI sting operation in 1982, for instance, targeted more than twenty employees of the Hitachi and Mitsubishi corporations of Japan, who were suspected of stealing data from IBM.[614] Since then, industrial espionage by means of computer has exploded, increasing by a reported 260 percent between 1985 and 1993.[615]

In 1992, American companies suffered losses from computer-related industrial espionage exceeding $1 billion. It is estimated that more than 85 percent of these crimes were committed or aided by employees. Sometimes the motive is to settle a grudge. An NBC employee embarrassed *Today* show host Bryant Gumbel by breaking into confidential computer files and publicly releasing a nasty memo Gumbel had written about his jovial colleague, weatherman Willard Scott.[616] Sometimes the motive is simply to make some money.[617] For example, employees with access to equipment and passwords can download strategic data or client lists and sell them to unscrupulous competitors. Because of the number of company insiders with such access, as well as the number of mercenary outsiders capable of breaking through passwords and cracking data encryption, many computer networks have proven vulnerable to spying and data theft.[618]

A Canadian-based computer company filed a $5 million lawsuit in 1992 against a former employee, alleging that he copied the firm's entire customer database and used it to establish his own competing business.[619] At about that same time, computerized trade-secret data were stolen from a California technology company.[620] Six months later, the head of a rival firm and a former employee of the victimized firm were indicted on charges of conspiracy and data theft.[621] These criminal indictments were considered precedent-setting because electronic industrial espionage cases traditionally had been fought in the civil court arena.[622]

Occasionally, industrial espionage and virus infection are melded into a single computer crime. Consider the plight of the head of a British technology company whose latest product was sabotaged with a software virus by a rival exhibitor during a 1993 trade show for potential customers. In an open letter to an industry journal, this embittered executive writes in a tone more suggestive of a street crime victim:

> There is a fair chance that whoever planted the virus is reading this . . . I understand why your bosses told you to do it. I'm going to pursue this with the full weight of the law, and if I ever find out who you are, may God help you.[623]

Computers have also been used illegally to obtain confidential information "that can help or hinder political candidates at all levels of government."[624] A dramatic example of political espionage occurred in New York in 1992. The medical records of a Congressional candidate were hacked from a hospital computer by an unknown party and sent to a newspaper. Those records revealed that the candidate once had attempted suicide, and this information soon was published in a front-page story. The candidate won the election, despite the publicity regarding her medical history, but the personal aftermath of this electronic invasion of her privacy serves as a reminder of why this book is as much about victims as villains. "It caused me a lot of pain," she would later say, "Especially since my parents didn't know."[625]

Computer crime in the area of international espionage is more difficult to assess. The covert nature of spying makes it hard to determine the actual number of incidents.[626] Moreover, since by definition this brand of white-collar crime often involves material classified as secret by the government, details of certain cases probably have been concealed from public scrutiny. The media, however, has reported a few stories. An arrest warrant was issued in 1996 for a 22-year-old former Harvard student who allegedly used stolen university passwords to break into American military computers from his home in Argentina.[627] When a young Washington-area hacker was arrested for breaking into a Pentagon computer system, he demonstrated his proficiency to investigators by cracking an Air Force system as they looked on. It took him 15 seconds.[628]

In 1994, two hackers broke into the computers at Griffiss Air Base in New York. "By the time authorities became aware of their presence five days later, the pair had penetrated seven computer systems, gained access to all information in the systems, copied files—including sensitive battlefield simulations—and installed devices to read the passwords of everyone entering the systems."[629] The two hackers were able to use the pilfered passwords to launch more than 150 intrusions through the Griffiss system into other military, government, and commercial systems. In one case, they accessed a Korean computer facility. For several anxious hours, investigators did not know if the installation in question was in North or South Korea. The concern was that the North Koreans would interpret an intrusion from an American military base as act of war. To the relief of authorities, the target turned out to be the South Korean Atomic Research Institute.[630] Eventually, one of the hackers was identified as a British 16-year-old, calling himself "Datastream Cowboy." He was quickly arrested. His accomplice and mentor, still at large and known only as "Kuji," is believed to be a foreign agent.[631]

The most widely chronicled computer espionage case is that of the so-called "Hanover Hackers" in 1989. This incredible case could not have had a more mundane origin. Clifford Stoll, a systems manager at a University of California laboratory, was asked by his supervisor to help resolve a *75-cent* discrepancy in billing for computer time. Stoll traced the error to an unauthorized user and, over the next 10 months, painstakingly tracked the hacker to Hanover, Germany. The culprit was identified as 24-year-old Markus Hess, and it was later learned that Hess led a group of young West German men who were selling American military data to the Soviet KGB in exchange for cash and cocaine. This spy ring consisted of five members of West Germany's notorious Chaos Computer Club, which had achieved European hacking stardom in 1987 by breaking into two NASA computers.[632] The Hanover Hackers had used the California computer as a launch pad to illegally access U.S. military computers at sites such as the Pentagon, the White Sands Missile Range, and the Redstone Missile Base.[633]

Of the five original Hanover Hackers, the youngest one was not charged in exchange for testifying against his friends; another was burned to death in what was either a hideous suicide or a brutal murder. The remaining three who stood trial were convicted in 1990. Germany was reuniting, the Cold War was winding down, and no one seemed particularly anxious to lock the defendants up and throw away the keys. That they sold classified computer data to the Russians was undeniable; but just how valuable those data were was not at all clear. For one thing, the relatively small payments they received did not seem commensurate with a major espionage success.

When the U.S. National Security Agency assessed the damage, one of their scientists observed in a memo: "Looks like the Russians got crooked."[634] In one of those truth-is-stranger-than-fiction twists, that scientist was Robert Morris, Sr., whose son had released a notorious Internet virus eighteen months earlier.

The sentences handed down ranged from 1 year and 8 months to 2 months. All the defendants were put on probation, because their drug problems had, in the opinion of the judges, clouded their judgment and mitigated their responsibility.[635]

International online espionage has not gone away. In 2011, suspected Chinese hackers used simple phishing techniques to gain access to high-ranking U.S. government officials' computers.[636] The attack was easy and effective: Chinese hackers sent targeted e-mails to various officials in U.S. government agencies with titles such as "Fw: Draft US-China Joint Statement." The e-mail contained a fake, yet authentic-looking, Gmail link that prompted the recipient to re-enter his or her login and password, which were consequently captured by the Chinese hackers. Later, the hackers would log in to the now compromised account and set all incoming and outgoing e-mail to also blind-carbon-copy the hacker.[637] Both the targeted nature of the attack and the source of the initial phishing e-mail lead Google to believe the attack was commissioned by the People's Liberation Army.[638]

While not in direct response to the Chinese hack, the National Security Agency held a classified briefing for the U.S. Senate in early 2012 due to the growing threat of digital foreign attacks.[639] Generals Keith Alexander and Martin Dempsey pushed the Senate to enact legislation that would regulate privately owned infrastructure. The goal was to harden targets such as electric utilities, chemical plants, and waters systems to defend against crippling cyber attacks. The Chamber of Commerce and the business lobby opposed such legislation, however, arguing that it would result in too much government interference with the free market system. The Republicans in the Senate filibustered and the measure fell short of the 60 votes needed to break it.[640] To date there are no major cyber-security laws in the U.S.

International computer espionage in the United States appears to be taken more seriously than in Europe. Indeed, it has been called the single most important security issue of the 1990s.[641] This concern may have originated in the early 1980s, when the Reagan administration withdrew funding for an international research center in Vienna, because its computers were tied to other research centers in both the United States and the Soviet Union. A fear was expressed that this connection might have allowed the Russians to log in to American computers and scan for classified data.[642]

Under the Computer Fraud and Abuse Act of 1986, it is illegal to tamper with any computer system used by the federal government or by government contractors. The act empowers the FBI to investigate the damage, destruction, or alteration of any data stored in such systems.[643] A representative case occurred in 1990 when personal computers at NASA and the EPA were infected with the SCORES virus—although the FBI ultimately turned this case over to local police because of difficulty in proving the suspect's intent to contaminate government computers.[644]

The first indictment of an American hacker on espionage charges occurred in 1992. The accused spy was a computer programmer from California. He allegedly stole secret Air Force flight orders for a military exercise at Fort Bragg, North Carolina.[645] Although the value of this material to the international intelligence community is dubious, the illegal possession of classified computer data is considered espionage—"even if no attempt is made to pass it to a foreign government."[646]

As equipment becomes increasingly sophisticated, the threat of computer espionage gets more serious. Compression technology has already reached a level where a common USB thumbdrive, purchased at Wal-Mart for under $10, can hold about 10,000 books in digital form. In fact, in 2011, a bank executive was caught doing just that. The employee stole 1,500 confidential documents from his employer, Boston Private Bank & Trust with nothing more than a simple drag-and-drop.[647]

Like viruses and worms, **spyware** has become another scourge of free enterprise. As a tool for corporate espionage, spyware presents a serious security threat to companies. This was demonstrated dramatically in 2005 when an Israeli author came upon parts of his unfinished book on the Internet. Since he had not shared his work with anyone, he notified the police. It was later discovered that the book had been stolen from his computer by his former son-in-law, who had used a Trojan Horse program to swipe it.[648]

The ensuing investigation of the son-in-law's computer revealed dozens of affected companies, including Israel's top telecommunications corporations and the local division of Hewlett-Packard.[649]

> Dubbed "Trojangate," the incident resulted in nearly 20 arrests, with some reports indicating that there were hundreds—perhaps thousands—of documents stolen from multiple Israeli firms.[650]

Among those arrested were nine private investigators working in Israel, who were accused of planting Trojan Horses on computers to steal corporate secrets. The men were indicted on numerous charges, including industrial espionage, hacking, fraud, and invasion of privacy.[651] Also arrested were two persons in the UK, who were accused of creating a custom piece of spyware. They allegedly had been hired by the private investigators. The investigators allegedly had been retained by several companies, who ordered the espionage to gather confidential information about rival companies' customers and such things as upcoming bids.[652]

The Israeli spyware case raises the serious question of whether an American "Trojangate" is possible. The signs indicate that the answer is yes. A recent research project placed a computer with fake critical business documents on the Internet. It was a "honeypot"—a tempting lure designed to entice hackers and study their techniques. The project produced some troubling revelations.

> [V]irus writers are now authoring programs designed specifically to look for documents flagged as "confidential" or "critical."[653]

The "honeypot" warning was validated on September 28, 2005, when William F. McMenamin pleaded guilty in federal court to conspiracy to misappropriate trade secrets. He was the executive vice-president of Business Engine Software Corp., a privately owned manufacturer of enterprise application software products. BES's chief competitor was Niku Corp., a publicly traded company headquartered in California. Under his plea agreement with prosecutors, McMenamin admitted that he had conspired with other BES executives to access illegally Niku's computer network repeatedly over a 10-month period.[654] BES had misappropriated and copied Niku's trade secrets in order to gain a competitive advantage.[655]

Also troubling are growing concerns about Chinese industrial espionage. At least one Trojan Horse program—Myfip—used to steal files from infected computers has been traced to servers in China. A computer security researcher has traced all the e-mails containing the Myfip attachment to a single address in China. He stated that it is "'highly likely' that the program was used for espionage against American high-tech and manufacturing firms."[656]

It is believed that Myfip was developed originally as a way to steal student exam papers and then expanded so that it can now copy many types of documents, including Microsoft Word Files.[657] Some analysts are even warning that similar spyware may be targeting government agencies in a bid to steal state secrets.[658]

Anti-fraud systems, such as voice-recognition spectrographs, now are appearing on the market.[659] Similarly, unauthorized computer access can be obstructed through biometric technology, including retina scanners, hand print readers,[660] and DNA identification devices,[661] as well as by the development of highly sophisticated "firewall" software that shields private information from hackers, thieves, and spies.[662] But computer criminals, as Gabriel Tarde might well have predicted, respond consistently to improved security technology with improved criminal technology,[663] and they will no doubt in time find a way to keep apace. This, in turn, will encourage still more advances in security and continue a neverending cycle of thrust and parry.

Notes

1. Tarde, Gabriel. *The Laws of Imitation*. Gloucester, Massachusetts: Peter Smith, 1962. This book was published originally in 1903.

2. Perry, Robert L. *Computer Crime*. New York: Franklin Watts, 1986.

3. Parker, Donn B. *Fighting Computer Crime*. New York: Scribners, 1983.

4. Rosenbaum, Ron. "Secrets of the Little Blue Box." *Esquire* 76, October, 1979: 222–226.

5. Bloombecker, *op. cit.*

6. Parker, 1983, *op. cit.*

7. *Ibid.*

8. Rosenbaum, *op. cit.*

9. Parker, 1983, *op. cit.*

10. *Ibid.*

11. *Ibid.*

12. *Ibid.*, p. 180.

13. Daly, James. "Toll Fraud Growing." *Computerworld* 27, 1993: 47–48.

14. *Ibid.*, p. 47.

15. Herman, Barbara. "Yacking with a Hack: Phone Phreaking for Fun, Profit, & Politics." *Teleconnect* 10, 1992: 60–62.

16. Quinn, Brian. "$2.3 Billion: That's About How Much Toll Fraud is Costing Us a Year (Maybe More)." *Teleconnect* 10, 1992: 47–49. See also Taff, Anita. "Users Call for Toll Fraud Laws to Distribute Losses." *Network World* 9, 1992: 27–28.

17. Dodd, Annabel. "When Going the Extra Mile Is Not Enough." *Network World* 10, 1993: 49–50.

18. Titch, Steven. "Get Real About Fraud." *Telephony* 227, October 17, 1994: p. 5.

19. *Ibid.*

20. McMenamin, Brigid. "Why Cybercrooks Love Cellular." *Forbes* 150, 1993: p. 189.

21. Panettieri, Joseph C. "Weak Links: For Corporate Spies, Low-Tech Communications Are Easy Marks." *Information Week*, August 10, 1992: 26–29.

22. Flaum, *op. cit.*

23. Kapor, Mitchell. "A Little Perspective, Please." *Forbes* 15, June 21, 1993: p. 106.

24. *Ibid.*

25. Rill, Derick. "Hackers Reach Out and Touch NASA." *Houston Post*, December 6, 1990: p. A22.

26. Luxner, Larry. "V.I. Official Convicted in Fraud Case." *Telephony* 222, 1992: 20–22.

27. Lewyn, Mark. "Phone Sleuths Are Cutting Off the Hackers: Corporations and Phone Companies Join to End Long-Distance Fraud." *Business Week*, July 13, 1992: p. 134.

28. Falconer, Tim. "Cyber Crooks." *CA Magazine* 128, December, 1995: 12–17.

29. *Washington Post*. "AT&T, Mitsubishi Settle Phone Suit." October 13, 1992: p. c3.

30. Daly, James. "Get Thee Some Security." *Computerworld* 27, 1993: 31–32. See also Daly, James. "Out to Get You." *Computerworld* 27, 1993: 77–79.

31. Brown, Bob. "Insurer Adds Phone Fraud Protection." *Network World* 9, 1992: 1–2.

32. Panettieri, *op. cit.*

33. *Ibid.*

34. Urbois, Jeff. "Saving Your Company From Telephone Fraud." *MacWEEK* 6, 1992: p. 22.

35. Marvin, Mary Jo. "Swindles in the 1990s: Con Artists Are Thriving." *USA Today Magazine*, September 1994: 80–84.

36. Colby, Richard. "Anatomy of a Toll Fraud." *Portland Oregonian,* July 5, 1992: p. 1.

37. Jahnke, Art. "The Cops Come to Cyberspace." *Boston Magazine,* November 1990: p. 90.

38. *Ibid.*

39. *cnn.com.* "Univ. of Mich. Expels Accused Hacker," August 13, 2003.

40. *thedenverchannel.com.* "Golden High Student Pleads Guilty to Changing Grades," May 7, 2007.

41. Trask, Mike. "Klutztown Hackers: It Was Just So Easy." *readingeaglearchives.com,* June 25, 2005.

42. Quoted in Rubinkam, Michael. "Students Charged With Computer Tresspass." *cnn.com,* August 10, 2005.

43. Francis, Dorothy B. *Computer Crime.* New York: Dutton, 1987.

44. Parker, Donn B. "Computer Crimes, Viruses, and Other Criminoids." *Executive Speeches* 3, 1989: 15–19.

45. Perry, *op. cit.*

46. Meyer, Michael. "Stop! Cyberthief!" *Newsweek,* February 6, 1995: 36–38.

47. McEwen, J. Thomas. "The Growing Threat of Computer Crime." *Detective,* Summer 1990: 6–11.

48. *PC User.* "Security Survey Reveals Huge Financial Losses," April 21, 1993: p. 20. As testimony to how fast computer crime had grown, surveys conducted just five years earlier had reported the cost of most computer crimes to be less than $10,000 (Gilbert, Jerome. "Computer Crime: Detection and Prevention." *Property Management* 54, March/April 1989: 64–66).

49. *Ibid.*

50. Anthes, Gary H. "Security Plans Lag Computer Crime Rate." *Computerworld* 29, November 6, 1995: p. 20.

51. Wood, Chris. "Crime in the Computer Age," *Maclean's 101,* January 25, 1988: 28–30.

52. Sherizen, Sanford. "The Globalization of Computer Crime and Information Security." *Computer Security Journal* 8, 1992: 13–19.

53. Sykes, John. "Computer Crime: A Spanner in the Works." *Management Accounting* 70, 1992: p. 55. This article notes the exploits of England's "Mad Hacker." See also: Hearnden, Keith. "Computer Crime: Multi-Million Pound Problem?" *Long Range Planning* 19, 1986: 18–26; and Evans, Paul. "Computer Fraud—The Situation, Detection and Training." *Computers & Security* 10, 1991: 325–327.

54. Saari, Juhani. "Computer Crime—Numbers Lie." *Computers & Security* 6, 1987: 111–117.

55. Norman, Adrian R. D. *Computer Insecurity.* London: Chapman and Hall, 1989.

56. Hafner, Katie and Markoff, John. *Cyberpunk.* New York: Touchstone, 1991.

57. Bird, Jane. "Hunting Down the Hackers." *Management Today,* July, 1994: 64–66.

58. Rockwell, Robin. "The Advent of Computer Related Crimes." *Secured Lender* 46, 1990: pp. 40, 42.

59. Sherizen, *op. cit.*

60. Major, Michael J. "Taking the Byte out of Crime: Computer Crime Statistics Vary as Much as the Types of Offenses Committed." *Midrange Systems* 6, 1993:; 25–28.

61. Gold, Steve. "Two Hackers Get Six Months Jail in UK." *Newsbytes,* May 24, 1993: 1–2.

62. Sherizen, *op. cit.* See also: McHugh, David. "Hackers, Pirates Thrive in Russia's Tech Underworld." *USA Today.* June 1, 2000: p. 17A.

63. Thomas, Pierre. "Chinese Hack Into US Chamber of Commerce, Authorities Say." *abcnewsgo.com.* December 21, 2011.

64. Nakashima, Ellen. "Chinese Leaders Ordered Google Hack, U.S. Was Told." *washingtonpost.com.* December 5, 2010.

65. *Ibid.*

66. McGrath, Neal. "A Cleft in the Armour." *Asian Business* 31, 1995: p. 26.

67. Hooper, Narelle. "Tackling the Techno-Crims." *Rydge's,* September, 1987: 112–119.

68. *crime-research.org.* "Top Computer Crime in 2007," May 17, 2007.

69. Moscaritolo, Angela. "TJX Hacker Gets 30-Year Prison Sentence." *scmagazineus.com,* January 8, 2009.

70. *Ibid.*

71. Ceramalus, Nobilangelo. "Software Security." *Management-Aukland* 41, 1994: 26–27.

72. Sherizen, *op. cit.*

73. Rajagopalan, Megha and Maass, Peter. "Does Cybercrime Really Cost $1 Trillion?" *nationof-change.org.* August 1, 2012.

74. McLeod, Ken. "Combatting Computer Crime." *Information Age 9,* January, 1987: 32–35.

75. Daly, James. "Out to Get You." *Computerworld* 27, March 22, 1993: 77–79.

76. Bloombecker, J. J. "Computer Ethics: An Antidote to Despair." *Mid-Atlantic Journal of Business* 27, 1991: 33–34.

77. Flanagan, William G. and McMenamin, Brigid. "The Playground Bullies Are Learning How to Type." *Forbes* 150, December 21, 1992: 184–189.

78. Quindlen, Terry H. "IRS Computer Systems Are Catching More Fishy Tax Returns: GAO Praises Agency for Reeling in Electronic Cheaters But Urges

Tighter Controls." *Government Computer News* 12, 1993: p. 67.

79. Diamond, Edwin and Bates, Stephen. "Law and Order Comes to Cyberspace." *Technology Review* 98, October, 1995: p. 29.

80. Torres, Vicki. "New Puzzle: High-Tech Pedophilia." *Los Angeles Times,* March 5, 1993: p. B3. Also: Snider, Mike. "On-Line Users Cheer Arrests for Child Porn." *USA Today,* September 15, 1995: p. 1D.

81. Wickham, Shawne K. "Crimes in Cyberspace Posing New Challenges for Law Enforcement." *New Hampshire* News, March 6, 1994: p. 1A. See also: *Bay Area Advertiser* (Clear Lake, Texas). "Cyberspace Porn Figures in Assault Case of Two Teens." December 6, 1995: 1–2. Villafranca, Armando. "Ex-Guard Jailed in Computer Porn Case." *Houston Chronicle.* December 6, 1995: pp. 25A, 33A. *aol.com.* "Disgrace Follows Child Porn Bust." November 7, 1998. Rather, Dan. "Cybercrime: Oh, What a Wicked Web We Weave." *Houston Chronicle.* January 28, 2001: p. 6C.

82. McEwen, *op. cit.*

83. McEwen, J. Thomas. "Computer Ethics." *National Institute of Justice Reports* (U.S. Department of Justice), January/February 1991: 8–11.

84. Chester, Jeffrey A. "The Mob Breaks into the Information Age." *Infosystems* 33, March, 1986: 40–44.

85. *Ibid.*

86. Moore, Richter H., Jr. "Wiseguys: Smarter Criminals and Smarter Crime in the 21st Century." *Futurist,* September/October 1994: 33–37.

87. Kerry, John. "Where Is the S&L Money?" *USA Today Magazine,* September, 1991: 20–21.

88. Major, *op. cit.*

89. *Houston Post.* " 'Pirates' Cheat Computer Software Industry out of Billions by Illegal Copying, Study Says," July 5, 1994: p. C9.

90. Simpson, Penny M., Banerjee, Debasish, and Simpson, Claude L. Jr. "Softlifting: A Model of Motivating Factors." *Business Ethics* 13, 1994: 431–438,

91. Marshall, Patrick G. "Software Piracy." *CQ Researcher,* May 21, 1993: 435–448.

92. Taft, Darryl K. "Software Piracy Rates Tied to Cultural Factors." *Computer Reseller News* 585, July 4, 1994d: pp. 69, 72.

93. *Ibid.,* p. 437. Copyright protection is one of the most complicated areas of international law. Some nations take a very territorial approach, usually providing protection only for works first published in that country (Forscht, Karen A. and Pierson, Joan. "New Technologies and Future Trends in Computer

Security." *Industrial Management & Data Systems* 94, 1994: 30–36).

94. *Ibid.*

95. *Ibid.*

96. Elmer-DeWitt, Phillip. "Invasion of the Data Snatchers." *Time* 132, September 26, 1988: 62–67.

97. *USA Today.* "Punishment for Pirates." February 6, 1995: p. 10A.

98. Francis, *op. cit.*

99. Marshall, *op. cit.*

100. Blau, John. "Software Piracy Hits $40B Worldwide, Says Study." *infoworld.com,* May 16, 2007.

101. Fiveash, Kelly. "BSA: Software Piracy's 'Tragic' Impact on US Society." *channelregister.co.uk,* July 18, 2008. According to NationMaster.com, which ranks software piracy rates by country Armenia has the highest rate of 93 percent.

102. *Ibid.*

103. Savvas, Antony. "Economic Downturn May Lead to More Software Piracy." *computerweekly.com,* July 14, 2008.

104. Gross, Grant. "Brothers Sentenced For Software Piracy." *infoworld.com,* March 7, 2008.

105. *Ibid.*

106. Quoted in *Ibid.*

107. Rosoff, Stephen M. "Who Carez About WAREZ?: The 'Other' Software Piracy." Paper presented to the Western Society of Criminology. Hawaii, May 2000. Presumably, the cracker subculture contains moles at game producers and within the technical side of the movie industry.

108. Kain, Erik. "HBO Has Only Itself to Blame for Record 'Game of Thrones' Piracy." *forbes.com.* May 9, 2012.

109. Rosoff, *op. cit.*

110. United States Attorney, Eastern District of Virginia (press release). "Warez Leader Sentenced to 46 Months." May 16, 2002. *out-law.com.* "Leader of DrinkOrDie Warez Group Pleads Guilty," February 28, 2002.

111. *torrentfreak.com.* "Extradited Warez Leader Pleads Guilty, Faces 10 Years in Prison," April 21, 2007.

112. Quoted in Cullen, Drew. "DrinkorDie Warez Leader Jailed for 51 Months." *channelregister.co.uk,* June 23, 2007.

113. *betanews.com.* "US DOJ Gets 50th Warez Conviction," May 14, 2007.

114. *torrentfreak.com.* "Warez Bust: Leader Sentenced to Prison," November 4, 2007.

115. *gaygamer.net.* "ESA Pleased With Piracy Prison Sentences," August 22, 2008.

116. *torrentfreak.com.* "Warez Scene Member Sentenced to 18 Months Jail," September 20, 2008.

117. Modine, Austin. "Warez Land Man 30 Months in Prison." *channelregister.co.uk,* September 5, 2007.

118. *northcountrygazette.com.* "Guilty Plea in Software Piracy Scheme," March 31, 2008.

119. Leyden, John. "US Warez Sitemaster Jailed For 30 Months." *theregister.co.uk,* May 1, 2008. p2pon.com. "Court Sentences Warez Site Operator to 30 Months," May 5, 2008.

120. Kravets, David. "Final Guilty Plea Wraps Up Federal 'Warez' Crackdown." *voices.allthingsd.com,* February 3, 2009.

121. Leeds, Jeff. "Labels Win Suit Against Song Sharer." *nytimes.com.* October 5, 2007.

122. *Ibid.*

123. Anderson, Nate. "Thomas-Rasset Voys to Pay Nothing, So Third Trial Inevitable." *arstechnica.com.* January 28, 2010.

124. *Ibid.*

125. Healy, Jon. "The RIAA's Latest Victory Over Jammie Thomas-Rasset." *latimes.com.* November 5, 2010.

126. Johnson, Casey. "It's Not Over Yet, Jammie Thomas: RIAA Appeals Damage Reduction." *arstechnica.com.* August 22, 2011.

127. Sandoval, Greg. "Appeals Court Sides with RIAA, Jammie Thomas owes $222,000. *cnet.com.* September 11, 2012.

128. Anderson, Nate. "File-Sharer Will Take RIAA Case to Supreme Court." *arstechnica.com.* September 11, 2012.

129. *bittorrent.com.* "Delivering the World's Content." Accessed July 29, 2013.

130. Boxall, Andy. "BitTorrent Traffic Returns to Normal in UK, Despite Pirate Bay ISP Block." *digitaltrends. com.* July 16, 2012.

131. *Ibid.*, p. 25.

132. Zuckerman, M. J. "Businesses Bypass Law to Fend off Hackers." *USA Today,* June 6, 1996: p. 3A.

133. Parker, Donn. "Computer Crime." *Financial Executive* 2, December, 1986: 31–33. Fields, Gary. "Reno Seeks Increased Cybercrime Reporting." *USA Today.* June 19, 2000: p. 3A.

134. Didio, Laura. "Security Deteriorates as LAN Usage Grows." *LAN Times* 7, 1993: 1–2.

135. Zuckerman, *op. cit.*

136. Roufaiel, Nazik S. "White-Collar Computer Crimes: A Threat to Auditors and Organization." *Managerial Auditing* 9, 1994: 3–12.

137. Quoted in Schuyten, Peter J. "Computers and Criminals." *New York Times,* September 27, 1979: p. D2.

138. Didio, *op. cit.*

139. U.S. Department of Justice. "FBI Uniform Crime Reports 1991" in *Crime in the United States* 1991, 1992: p. 13.

140. Nawrocki, Jay. "There Are too Many Loopholes: Current Computer Crime Laws Require Clearer Definition." *Data Management* 25, 1987: 14–15.

141. Prasad, Jyoti N., Kathawala, Yunus, Bocker, Hans J., and Sprague, David. "The Global Problem of Computer Crimes and the Need for Security." *Industrial Management* 33, July/August 1991: 24–28.

142. Brandt, Allen. "Embezzler's Guide to the Computer." *Harvard Business Review* 53, 1975: 79–89.

143. For a detailed consideration of electronic bank robbery, see: Radigan, Joseph. "The Growing Problem of Electronic Theft." *United States Banker* 103, June, 1993: 37–38; Radigan, Joseph. "Info Highway Robbers Try Cracking the Vault." *United States Banker* 105, May, 1995: 66–69; Sherizen, Sanford. "Criminologist Looks into Mind of High-Tech Thief." *Bank Systems & Equipment* 25, November, 1988: 80–81; Sherizen, Sanford. "Future Bank Crimes." *Bank Systems & Technology* 26, October, 1989: pp. 60, 62; Sherizen, Sanford. "Warning: Computer Crime Is Hazardous to Corporate Health." *Corporate Controller* 4, 1991: 21–24; Sobol, Michael I. "Computer Crime Trends: A Brief Guide for Banks." *Bank Administration* 63, June, 1987: p. 52.

144. Whiteside, Thomas. *Computer Capers: Tales of Electronic Thievery, Embezzlement, and Fraud.* New York: Thomas Y. Crowell, 1978.

145. *Ibid.*

146. Conklin, John E. *"Illegal But Not Criminal": Business Crime in America.* Englewood Cliffs, New Jersey: Prentice-Hall, 1977.

147. Cressey, Donald R. *Other People's Money: A Study in the Social Psychology of Embezzlement.* Belmont, California: Wadsworth, 1971.

148. Touby, Laurel. "In the Company of Thieves." *Journal of Business Strategy* 15, 1994: 24–35.

149. Quoted in Flaum, David. "Scams Remain the Same Except Cons Now Use Newest Toys in Thievery." *Memphis Commercial Appeal,* August 14, 1994: p. C3.

150. Violino, Bob. "Are Your Networks Secure?" *Information Week,* April 12, 1993: p. 30.

151. Alexander, Michael. "The Real Security Threat: The Enemy Within." *Datamation* 41, July 15, 1995: 30–33. See also: Alexander, Michael. "Computer Crime: Ugly Secret for Business" (Part I). *Computerworld* 24, March 12, 1990: pp. 1, 104; Ubois, Jeff. "Risky Business." *Midrange Systems* 8, July 14, 1995: 21–22;

Stuller, Jay. "Computer Cops and Robbers." *Across the Board* 26, June, 1989: 13–19; Carter, Roy. "The Psychology of Computer Crime." *Accountancy 101,* April, 1988: 150–151; Clemons, Keith. "Computer Security: A Growing Concern." *Computerdata* 12, January, 1987: p. 7; Lewis, Mike. "Computer Crimes: Theft in Bits and Bytes." *Nations Business* 73, February, 1985: 57–58.

152. Cheswick, William R. and Bellovin, Steven M. "Secure Your Network: Keep the Riffraff Out." *Computer Reseller News* 609, December 12, 1994: p. 161.

153. Brandt, *op. cit.*

154. Hancock, Wayland. "Understanding Computer Viruses" (Part II). *American Agent & Broker* 65, December, 1993: 61–63.

155. Prasad et al., *op. cit.*

156. Francis, *op. cit.*

157. *Ibid.*

158. *Ibid.*

159. Whiteside, *op.cit.*

160. Disgruntled employees are believed to be responsible for as much as 25% of all computer abuse (Harper, Doug. "Computer Crime May Be Close to Home." *Industrial Distribution* 83, February, 1994: p. 41). A potentially serious threat may have emerged as a result of the severe staff cutbacks caused by the downsizing movement in corporate America, which has produced a growing number of angry and bitter workers (Daly, *op. cit.*). See also: Crino, Michael D. and Leap, Terry L. "What HR Managers Must Know About Employee Sabotage." *Personnel,* May, 1989: 31–38,

161. *Ibid.*, p. 93

162. Kabay, Mich. "Is Your Boss Tampering with Data?" *Computing Canada* 18, April 27, 1992: p. 29.

163. Seidler, Lee. *The Equity Funding Papers: The Anatomy of a Fraud.* New York: Wiley, 1977.

164. Kabay, *op. cit.*

165. Whiteside, *op. cit.*

166. *Ibid.*

167. Thornton, Mary. "Age of Electronic Convenience Spawning Inventive Thieves." *Washington Post,* May 20, 1984: A1, A8–A9.

168. Flanagan and McMenamin, *op. cit.*

169. Adam, John A. "Data Security." *IEEE Spectrum* 29, 1992: 18–20. See also Sherizen, Sanford. "Future Bank Crimes." *Bank Systems & Technology* 26: 60, 62.

170. Schuyten, *op. cit.*

171. Bloombecker, Buck. *Spectacular Computer Crimes.* Homewood, Illinois: Dow Jones-Irwin, 1990.

172. *Ibid.*

173. Thornton, *op. cit.*

174. Roberts, Ralph and Kane, Pamela. *Computer Security.* Greensboro, North Carolina: Compute! Books, 1989.

175. *cbs.marketwatch.com.* "Hackers Hit Western Union Web Site." September 10, 2000.

176. Harris, Ron. "Online Retailer Egghead.com Hacked." *schwab-news.excite.com.* December 22, 2000.

177. *Ibid.*

178. *Ibid.*

179. *Houston Chronicle.* "Vandals Hack into AOL With 'Trojan Horse' Virus." June 17, 2000: pp. 1C, 3C. In its heyday, AOL was always a favorite target of hackers. In 1997, Nicholas Ryan, a hacker known as "Happy Hardcore," pleaded guilty to violating the Computer Fraud and Abuse Act after invading the AOL network. (*timewarner.com.* "Hacker Sentenced For Felony Conviction Under Federal Computer Fraud and Abuse Act," March 28, 1997.)

180. *Houston Chronicle.* "Hackers Pry into Microsoft source Code." October 28, 2000: pp. 1C, 3C.

181. *Houston Chronicle.* "Gates a Victim of Newspaper Hacker." October 12, 2000: p. 2A.

182. *Houston Chronicle.* "Duo Arrested in Phony Teller Machine Scheme." June 30, 1993: p. 6A. See also: *Wilmington News Journal.* "Automated Teller Machine Fraud Grows, and Information Is the Key." June 13, 1993: p. G1.

183. Roush, Wade. "Hackers Taking a Byte out of Computer Crime." *Technology Review* 98, April, 1995: p. 34.

184. Lemert, Edwin M. *Human Deviance, Social Problems, and Social Control.* Englewood Cliffs, New Jersey: Prentice-Hall, 1967.

185. *Ibid.*

186. Roush, *op. cit.*, p. 34.

187. Hafner and Markoff, *op. cit.*, p. 11.

188. Quoted in Beyers, Becky. "Are You Vulnerable to Cybercrime: Hackers Tap in for Fun, Profit." *USA Today,* February 20, 1995: p. 3B.

189. Carr, O. Casey. "Their Call Is to Steal Over the Phone, So Beware of Hackers." *Seattle Times-Post Intelligence,* September 8, 1991: p. E1.

190. *Houston Post.* " 'Billy the Kid' Hacker Was not a Threat to Networks." February 17, 1995: p. 15.

191. *Ibid.*

192. Stephens, Gene. "Crime in Cyberspace." *Futurist* 29, September, 1995: p. 25.

193. McEwen, J. Thomas. "Computer Ethics." National Institute of Justice Reports, January/February 1991: 8–11.

194. Quoted in Cizmadia, Robert A. "Secrets of a Super Hacker" (Book Review). *Security Management* 38, September, 1994: p. 197.

195. *Ibid.*, p. 9.

196. Sykes, Gresham M. and Matza, David. "Techniques of Neutralization: A Theory of Delinquency." *American Sociological Review* 22, 1957: 664–666.

197. Kabay, Mich. "Computer Hackers Are No Vigilantes." *Computing Canada* 18, 1992: p. 36. The claim of helping to expose lax security is not limited to juvenile hackers. Recently, a 41-year-old man, using a so-called "John the Ripper" Internet password-cracking tool, broke into computers at NASA's Sonny Carter Training Facility in Houston. His lawyer argued that he had performed a service for his country by calling attention to security deficiencies. The prosecutor scoffed at this claim: "Patriots don't use 'John the Ripper' to hack into government computers." (Brewer, Steve. "Man Pleads No Contest to Computer Hacking." *Houston Chronicle.* October 9, 1999: p. 36A.)

198. Keefe, Patricia. "Portraits of Hackers as Young Adventurers Not Convincing." *Computerworld* 26, 1992: p. 33.

199. O'Driscoll, Patrick. "At 17, a Pro at Testifying on Computers." *USA Today*, September 26, 1983: p. 2A.

200. quoted in Francis, *op. cit.*, p.28.

201. quoted in Francis, *op. cit.*, p. 35.

202. *Ibid.*

203. Van Brussel, Carolyn. "Arrest of N.Y.C. Hackers Hailed as 'Breakthrough'." *Computing Canada* 18, 1992: p. 1.

204. Benedetto, Richard. "Computer Crooks Spy on Our Credit." *USA Today*, July 22–24, 1984: p. 1A.

205. Boyd, Robert S. "In Cyberspace, Private Files Are Becoming an Open Book." *Houston Chronicle,* December 8, 1995: p. 3G.

206. Kirvan, Paul. "Is a Hacker Hovering in Your Horoscope?" *Communications News* 29, 1992: p. 48.

207. Shaw, Stephen J. "Credit Crime." *St. Petersburg Times,* August 23, 1992: p. 1D.

208. Meyer, *op. cit.*

209. *Houston Chronicle.* "Identity-Theft Scam Targeted Celebrities," March 21, 2001: 5A.

210. *Ibid.*

211. Quoted in *Ibid.*

212. Perry, Nancy J. "How to Protect Yourself From the Credit Fraud Epidemic." *Money* 24, August, 1995: 38–42.

213. *Ibid.*, p. 1D. For a similarly harrowing first-person account, see also: Sullivan, Stacy. "Ensnared in the Nightmare of a Missing Identity." *Houston Chronicle.* May 30, 2000: p. A15.

214. *Houston Chronicle.* "Hacker Web Site a Hub for Fraud." November 17, 2002: 4A.

215. *Ibid.*, 4A.

216. Henderson, Robert B. "Cyber Crimes Increase in County." *Houston Chronicle.* December 20, 2000: This Week, p. 2.

217. *Houston Chronicle.* "Feds Cracking Down on Fake IDs." January 13, 2000: p. A3.

218. *fraudwatchinternational.com.* "Fraudulent Phishing Scams." October 12, 2005.

219. *Ibid.*

220. *gartner.com.* "Gartner Says Number of Identity Theft Victims Has Increased," March 6, 2007.

221. *Ibid.*

222. Quoted in McCarthy, Caroline. "Study: Identity Theft Keeps Climbing." *cnet.com*, February 22, 2007.

223. *netscape.com.* "Beware! A Cunning New ID Theft Scam," December 18, 2005.

224. Safire, William. "'Identity Theft' Demands Legislation." *Houston Chronicle.* May 12, 2000: p. A42.

225. *Ibid.*

226. Roberts, Paul. "Identity Theft Highlights Serious Security Flaws." *pcworld.com.* November 27, 2002. *cnn.com.* "Feds Charge 3 in Massive Credit Fraud Scheme." November 26, 2002.

227. Sullivan, Bob. "Huge Identity Theft Ring Busted." *www.msnbc.com.* November 25, 2002.

228. Quoted in Neumeister, Larry. "Huge Identity Theft Ring Broken Up; 3 Arrested." *Houston Chronicle.* November 26, 2002: 10A.

229. Rosencrance, Linda. "Identity Theft Case Seen as Largest in U.S. History." *www.computerworld.com.* November 26, 2002. *www.itworld.com.* "Identity Theft Raises Questions About Security." November 27, 2002.

230. Joyce, Erin. "Identity Theft Case Called largest Ever." *www.nternetnews.com.* November 25, 2002.

231. Bonilla, Denise. "O.C. Couple Found Guilty of Clients' Identity Theft." *Los Angeles Times,* August 21, 2003: B6.

232. Gittelsohn, John. "WaMu Loaned Millions to O.C. Home Flippers With Fraud History." *ocregister.com,* September 19, 2008.

233. Freeman, Liz. "Medicare Fraud: Collier Man Sent to Prison For 87 Months." *naplesnews.com,* May 4, 2007.

234. U.S. Department of Justice (press release). "Defendant Sentenced For Conspiracy to Commit Computer Fraud and Identity Theft." March 5, 2007.

235. Lawson, Stephen. "Colombian Man Sentenced For Computer Fraud." *infoworld.com,* April 14, 2008.

236. United States Attorney, Central District of California (press release). "Information Security Consultant Pleads Guilty to Federal Wiretapping and Identity Theft Charges." April 16, 2008. *outlookseries.com.* "IT Security Consultant John Schiefer aka Acid, Acidstorm Guilty of Botnet ID Theft," April 1, 2008.

237. *iht.com.* "Los Angeles Hacker to Plead Guilty to Infecting 250,000 Computers to Steal Identities," November 10, 2007.

238. Tung, Liam. "U.S. 'Botmaster' Faces Up to 60 Years Prison." *zdnetasia.com,* December 11, 2007.

239. Hruska, Joel. "Security Admin, Botmaster Sentenced to Four Years in Prison." *arstechnica.com.* March 5, 2009.

240. Grant, Ian. "TJX Hacker Pleads Guilty." *computerweekly.com,* September 16, 2008.

241. Lifsher, Mark. "Victims, Retailers Collide on ID Theft Bill." *Los Angeles Times,* October 2, 2007: C1, C12.

242. Kerber, Ross. "Hacker Pleads Guilty in Breach." *boston.com,* September 12, 2008.

243. Alexander, Max. "Child Identity Theft." *Readers Digest,* March 5, 2006: 84–85.

244. Yip, Pamela. "Children Are Appealing Targets for ID Theft." *dallasnews.com,* August 18, 2008.

245. *Ibid.*

246. *whostolemyidentity.com.* "Child Identity Theft," April 27, 2007.

247. Yuille, Brigette. "Stolen Innocence: Child Identity Theft." *bankrate.com,* January 3, 2007.

248. Yip, *op. cit.*

249. *reuters.com.* "Recent Javelin Study Shows Children Are at Risk For Identity Theft," October 28, 2009.

250. Shamilian, Janet. "NBC: ID Theft Hits Children Close to Home." *msnbc.com,* March 3, 2005.

251. Rather, Dan. "What They Know About You Certainly Can Hurt You." *Houston Chronicle.* November 21, 1999: p. 6C.

252. *Ibid.*

253. Quoted in Boyd, *op. cit.,* p. 3G.

254. *Ibid.*

255. Hyatt, *op. cit.*

256. Rebello, Kathy. "'Sensitive Kid' Faces Trial." *USA Today,* February 28, 1989: 1B–2B.

257. Anthes, Gary H. "Taking a Byte out of Computer Crime." *Computerworld* 29, May 22, 1995: p. 56.

258. *Ibid.*

259. Bloombecker, *op. cit.,* p. iv.

260. *Ibid.,* p. 142.

261. The FBI has jurisdiction to investigate computer crime cases under the federal Computer Fraud and Abuse Act of 1986 (Betts, Mitch. "Recovering from Hacker Invasion." *Computerworld* 27, January 25, 1993: pp. 43, 45). Federal authority to prosecute computer crimes was later expanded under the omnibus crime bill of 1994 (Betts, Mitch. "Statute Outlaws Viruses." *Computerworld* 28, October 10, 1994: p. 65).

262. Markoff, John. "Computer Pirate Still Eluding the Law." *Houston Chronicle,* July 4, 1994: p. 13A.

263. *Ibid.*

264. Quoted in Littman, Jonathan. "In the Mind of 'Most Wanted' Hacker, Kevin Mitnick." *Computerworld* 30, January 15, 1996: p. 87.

265. *Houston Post,* February 17, 1995, *op. cit.*

266. Tamaki, Julie. "Computer Hacker Faces New Federal Charges." *Los Angeles Times,* September 27, 1996: p. A22.

267. Ho, David. "Ex-Computer Hacker Granted Radio License." *Houston Chronicle.* December 27, 2002: 5A.

268. Quoted in Littman, *op. cit.,* p. 88.

269. Bloombecker, Jay J. "My Three Computer Criminological Sins." Communications of the ACM 37, November, 1994: 15–16.

270. *USA Today.* "Hacker Case." April 12, 1995: p. 3A.

271. Brown, Bob. "Indictment Handed Down on 'Masters of Disaster'." *Network World* 29, 1992: p. 34.

272. Moses, Jonathan M. "Wiretap Inquiry Spurs Computer Hacker Charges." *Wall Street Journal,* July 9, 1992: p. B8.

273. Thyfault, Mary E. "Feds Tap into Major Hacker Ring." *Information Week,* July 13, 1992: p.15.

274. Schwartau, Winn. "Hackers Indicted for Infiltrating Corporate Networks." *Infoworld* 14, 1992: p. 56. See also: Daly, James. "Frustrated Hackers May Have Helped Feds in MOD Sting." *Computerworld* 26, 1992: p. 6.

275. Schwartau, *op. cit.* See also: Daly, James. "Wiretap Snares Alleged Hackers." *Computerworld* 26, July 13, 1992: pp. 1, 14; *Wall Street Journal.* "Hackers Plead Guilty." March 22, 1993: p. B2; *Wall Street Journal.* "Hacker is Sentenced." June 7, 1993: p. B2.

276. Tabor, Mary B. W. "Urban Hackers Charged in High-Tech Crime." *New York Times,* July 23, 1992: p.A1. For a detailed account of the rivalry between the Masters of Destruction and the Legion of Doom see Sterling, Bruce. *The Hacker Crackdown.* New York: Bantam Books, 1992.

277. Littman, Jonathan. "Cyberpunk Meets Mr. Security." *PC-Computing* 5, 1992: 288–293.

278. Quoted in Francis, *op. cit.*, p. 25.

279. Quoted in *Ibid.*, p. 25.

280. Meddis, Sam. "Lawmakers: Pull Plug on Hackers." *USA Today,* November 4, 1983: p. 3A.

281. *USA Today.* "Blabbermouth Computers." July 27, 1993: p. 8A. During the Gulf War, hackers reportedly invaded VAX systems using computer commands to search for key phrases such as "Desert Storm" and "Patriot Missile" (Forscht and Pierson, *op. cit.*).

282. *New York Times.* "US Charges Young Hackers." November 15, 1992: p. 40.

283. *Government Computer News.* "Feds Charge 2 in Computer Break-in." November 23, 1992: p. 8.

284. *Houston Chronicle.* "Netanyahu Lauds Teen-Age Hacker Who Broke into Pentagon Site." March 20, 1998: p. 21A.

285. Collins, Chris. "Hackers' Paradise." *USA Today,* July 6, 1993: p. 5A.

286. Zuckerman, M. J. "Hackers Crack Pentagon." *USA Today,* May 23, 1996: p. 1A.

287. Quoted in *Ibid.*, p. 1A

288. *Houston Chronicle.* "Pentagon Battling 'Systematic Assault' by Hackers." February 26, 1998: p. 15A.

289. Quoted in *Ibid*, p. 15A.

290. *Houston Chronicle.* "Pentagon Teen Hackers Ordered to Stay Off Line." November 6, 1998: p. 2A.

291. *Ibid.*

292. *Ibid.*

293. Quoted in *Ibid,* p. 2A.

294. Quoted in *Ibid,* p. 2A.

295. Goldman, John. J. and McFarlane, Usha L. "Man Accused of Hacking into NASA Computers." *Los Angeles Times.* July 14, 2000: p. A15.

296. *Ibid.*

297. *Ibid.*

298. *Ibid.*

299. Leyden, John. "NASA Hacker 'Rolex' Jailed For Four Months." *theregister.co.uk,* September 6, 2001.

300. *Ibid.*

301. *Ibid.*

302. Frothingham, Stephen. "Teen Hacker 'Coolio' Pleads Guilty." *schwab-news.excite.com.* January 2, 2001.

303. Quoted in: *USA Today.* "Hacker Case." March 19, 1998: p. 3A.

304. *lawprofessors.com.* "21 Month Sentence For Computer Hacker," May 9, 2005.

305. *USA Today.* "Teenage NASA Hacker Facing Jail, Says It Wasn't Worth It." September 25, 2000: p. 3A.

306. Quoted in *Ibid,* p. 3A.

307. *Houston Chronicle.* "UT Hacker Faces Up to 6 Years in Prison." June 13, 2005: B3.

308. Kreytak, Steven. *statesman.com.* September 7, 2005.

309. *Houston Chronicle,* June 13, 2006, *op. cit.*

310. Quoted in Kreytak, *op. cit.*

311. Gloeckler, Geoff and Merritt, Jennifer. "An Ethics Lesson for MBA Wannabes." Business Week. March 9, 2005.

312. Quoted in *Ibid.*

313. Krebs, Brian. "Feds Put More Botmasters, Phishers Behind Bars." *washingtonpost.com,* November 27, 2007.

314. Claburn, Thomas. "'Bot Master' Gets 12 Months in Federal Prison." *informationweek.com,* October 26, 2007.

315. *scmagazineus.com.* "Kentucky Botmaster Gets Year in Prison," October 29, 2007.

316. United States Attorney, Eastern District of California (press release). "Computer Hacker Pleads Guilty and Agrees to Two Years in Federal Prison." June 10, 2008.

317. *Ibid.*

318. Goodin, Dan. "FBI Crackdown on Botnets Gets Resuts, but Damage Continues." *theregister.co.uk,* November 29, 2007.

319. United States Attorney, District of Massachusetts (press release). "Juvenile Computer Hacker Pleads Guilty." November 18, 2008.

320. Grant, Ian. "Florida Court Jails Hacker Robert Bentley For Adware Attack." *computerweekly. com,* June 12, 2008. *bbc.co.uk.* "Jail Sentence For Botnet Creator," June 12, 2008. Burch, Jamie. "International Computer Hacker Sentenced." *wkrg. com,* June 11, 2008.

321. *mircscripts.us.* "True Crime: The Botnet Barons," September 24, 2007.

322. Acohido, Byron. "Cyberthieves Stole 1.3 Million Names." *USA Today,* August 24, 2007: 1B.

323. Ho, David. "Ex-Convict Tells Lawmakers Hackers seek 'Weakest Link'." *Houston Chronicle.* April 4, 2003: 8A.

324. *Houston Chronicle.* "Hacker Admits '03 eBay Attack," December 29, 2005: A10.

325. Richtel, Matt and Robinson, Sara. "Hacking Wave Hits High-Profile Sites on Internet." New York Times. February 9, 2000: pp. 1C, 12C.

326. Leonhard, Woody. "The New Internet Security Threat." *Smart Business.* July 2000: pp. 102–118.

327. Iwata, Ed. "Digital Trail, Chat Room Boasts Led to Teen Hacker." *USA Today.* February 16, 2000: p. 3B.

328. Richtel and Robinson, *op. cit.*

329. Leonhard, *op. cit.*

330. Richtel and Robinson, *op. cit.*

331. Leonhard, *op.cit.*, p. 105.

332. Johnson, Kevin, Zuckerman, M.J., and Solomon, Deborah. "Online Boasting Leaves Trail." *usatoday. com.* June 7, 2000.

333. Iwata, *op.cit.*

334. *Ibid,* p. 3B.

335. Anwar, Yasmin. "Hacker Known as Mischievous Kid." *usatoday.com.* June 7, 2000.

336. Johnson, Kevin and Zuckerman, M.J. "Teen Arrested in E-Commerce Hacks." *usatoday.com.* June 7, 2000.

337. *usatoday.com.* "Hacker's Father Nabbed for Assault Plans." June 7, 2000.

338. Johnson et al.

339. *usatoday.com.* "Hacker 'Mafiaboy' Pleads Guilty." January 18, 2001.

340. *Ibid.*

341. *wired.com.* "'Mafiaboy' Sentenced to 8 Months," September 13, 2001.

342. Quoted in Johnson et al.

343. Anwar, *op. cit.*

344. Quoted in *Ibid.*

345. Quoted in *Ibid.*

346. *theage.com.au.* "International Crime Rings, Not Hackers, True Internet Villains," August 6, 2006.

347. Poulson, Kevin. "Max Vision Pleads Guilty." *securityfocus.com.* September 26, 2000.

348. Delio, Michelle. "A 'White Hat' Goes to Jail." *wired. com.* May 22, 2001.

349. *abcnews.go.com.* "Computer Informant Arrested." September 26, 2000.

350. Delio, *op. cit.*

351. Poulson, Kevin. "Max Vision: FBI Pawn?" *securityfocus.com.* May 8, 2001.

352. *abcnews.go.com, op. cit.*

353. *Ibid.*

354. Krebs, Brian. "Defense Department Hacker Gets 18 Months in Prison." *computeruser.com.* May 24, 2001.

355. Quoted in Poulson, Kevin. "Max Vision Begins 18-Month Term." *theregister.co.uk.* May 7, 2001.

356. *cipherwars.com.* "New York City Computer Security Expert Convicted by Jury of Computer Hacking and Electronic Eavesdropping." March 13, 2001.

357. Harrison, Ann. "Programmer Rejects $70K Bonus, Is Charged With Online Attack." *computerworld. com.* March 20, 2000.

358. Radcliffe, Deborah. "The Cyber-Mod Squad Sets Out After Crackers." *computerworld.com.* June 19, 2000.

359. *usdoj.gov.* "Lusby, Maryland Man Pleads Guilty to Sabotaging IRS Computers." July 24, 2001.

360. Vasishtha, P. "Contract Employee Jailed for Sabotage." *gen.com.* November 18, 2001.

361. *theage.com.au.* "Hacker Who Threatened Bloomberg Gets Prison." July 2, 2003.

362. *Ibid.*

363. *usdoj.gov.* "Kazahastan Hacker Sentenced to Four Years Prison for Breaking into Bloomberg Systems and Attempted Extortion." July 1, 2003.

364. Quoted in *Ibid.*

365. Quoted in Miller, Adam and Geller, Andy. "Bloomburglar." *nypost.com.* July 2, 2003.

366. U.S. Department of Justice. "Russian Computer Hacker Indicted in California for Breaking into Computer Systems and Extorting Victim Companies." Press Release. 2001.

367. U.S. Department of Justice. "Russian Computer Hacker Convicted by Jury." Press Release. June 20, 2001.

368. U.S. Department of Justice, *op. cit.*

369. *securityfocus.com.* "Russian Computer Hacker Gets 4-Year Term." July 25, 2003.

370. Delio, Michelle. "'Stung' Russian Hacker Guilty." *wired.com.* October 17, 2001.

371. *in.tech.yahoo.com, op. cit.*

372. U.S. department of Justice. "Russian Computer Hacker Sentenced to Three Years in Prison." Press Release. October 4, 2002.

373. U.S. Department of Justice. "Russian Hacker Sentenced to Four years in Prison for Supervising Criminal Enterprise Dedicated to Computer Hacking, Fraud, and Extortion." Press Release. July 25, 2003.

374. *in.tech.yahoo.com, op. cit.*

375. Mark, Roy. "House Votes Life for Malicious Hackers." *dc.internet.com.* July 16, 2002.

376. Mills, Elinor. "Old-time Hacktivists: Anonymous, You've Crossed the Line." *news.cnet.com.* March 30, 2012.

377. *Ibid.*

378. Landers, Chris. "The Internets Are Going to War." *citypaper.com.* January 25, 2008.

379. Denton, Nick. "The Cruise Indoctrination Video Scientology Tried to Suppress." *gawker.com.* January 15, 2008.

380. Fullerton, Elizabeth. "UK Police Arrest WikiLeaks Backers for Cyber Attacks." *Uk.reuters.com.* January 27, 2011.

381. Tynan, Dan. "A Conversation with Commander X." *itworld.com.* February 18, 2011.

382. Rattay, Wolfgang. "Internet Strikes Back: Anonymous' Operation Megaulpoad Explained." *rt.com.* January 20, 2012.

383. BBC News. "Pro-Wikileaks Activists Abandon Amazon Cyber Attack." December 9, 2010.

384. Warren, Christina. "How Operation Payback Executes Its Attacks." *mashable.com.* December 9, 2010.

385. Roberts, Paul. "LulzSec Informant Sabu Rewarded with Six Months Freedom for Helping Feds." *sophos.com.* August 23, 2012.

386. Cluley, Graham. "Ryan Cleary Charged with LulzSec DDoS Attack on SOCA and Other Websites." *sophos.com.* June 22, 2011.

387. Cluley, Graham. "Jake Davis Named as Suspected Hacker Topiary by UK Police." *sophos.com.* July 31, 2011.

388. Weisenthal, Joe. "Notorious Hacker Group LulzSec Just Announced That It's Finished." *businessinsider.com.* June 25, 2011.

389. Powell, Douglas. "Mopping Up After Michelangelo." *Toronto Globe and Mail,* March 7, 1992: p. D8.

390. Greenberg, Ross M. "Know Thy Viral Enemy." *Byte,* June, 1989: 175–180.

391. Hancock, op, cit.

392. *Credit Union Management.* "Operations: A Viral Epidemic." Vol. 12, May, 1989: p. 28.

393. Mills, Elinor. "USB devices spreading viruses." *cnet.com.* November 20, 2008.

394. Elmer-DeWitt, Phillip. "Invasion of the Data Snatchers." *Time* 132, September 26, 1988: p. 63.

395. *Ibid.*

396. Powell, *op. cit.*

397. *Ibid.*, p. 66.

398. *Ibid.*

399. Sandoval, Greg. "Virus Poses as Nude Jennifer Lopez Photos." *InfoSec News* (online), May 42, 2001.

400. Leyden, John. "Anna Kournikova Virus Spreading Like Wildfire." *theregulator.co.uk,* February 12, 2001.

401. Lynch, Ian. "Naked Wife Virus Exposes Unwary Users." *vnunet.com,* March 7, 2001.

402. Landesman, Mary. "Naked Wife." *antivirus.about.com,* March 6, 2001.

403. DiSabatino, Jennifer. "'Naked Wife' Virus Carries Malicious Payload." *computerworld.com,* March 7, 2001.

404. *news.bbc.co.uk.* "New Virus Strikes Computers," March 6, 2001.

405. *Ibid.*

406. Stenger, Richard. "'Naked Wife' Virus Wreaks Havoc on Internet." *cnn.com,* March 7, 2001.

407. Olavsrud, Thor. "Promises of Jennifer Lopez Nude Deliver Destructive Virus." *internetnews.com,* June 1, 2001.

408. *zdnet.co.uk.* "Virus Dresses Up as a Naked Jennifer Lopez," June 1, 2001.

409. *USA Today.* "Hot on the Trail of Virus Writers," May 7, 2001: 3D.

410. Garfinkel, Simon L. "Lax Security Lets Hackers Attack." *Christian Science Monitor,* October 13, 1989: 12–13.

411. Bloombecker, *op. cit.*

412. Lewyn, Mark. "First 'Computer Virus' Trial Starts Today." *USA Today,* September 6, 1988: p. 3B.

413. Lewyn, Mark. "Computer Verdict Sets 'Precedent'." USA Today, September 27, 1988: p.1A.

414. Bloombecker, *op. cit.*

415. Alexander, Michael. "Supreme Court Refuses Morris Appeal." *Computerworld* 25, October 14, 1991: p. 14.

416. Hafner and Markoff, *op. cit.*

417. Daly, James. "Virus Vagaries Foil Feds." *Computerworld* 27, July 12, 1993: pp. 1. 15.

418. Powell, *op. cit.*, p. D8

419. *Ibid.*

420. Bloombecker, *op. cit.*

421. Adams, Tony. "Of Viruses and Logic Bombs" (Part I). *Australian Accountant* 58, May, 1988: 83–85.

422. Elmer-DeWitt, *op. cit.*

423. Daly, James. "Viruses Ringing in the New Year." *Computerworld* 27, 1992: p. 79.

424. Hyatt, Josh. "Computer Killers." *Boston Globe,* March 3, 1992: p. 35.

425. Powell, *op. cit.*

426. Kim, James. "Virus Strain New 'Hazard' to Computers." *USA Today,* March 1–3, 1996: p, 1A.

427. Quoted in *Ibid.*, p. 1A.

428. Kornblum, Janet. "Widespread Melissa Virus Snarls E-Mail Servers." USA Today. March 30, 1999: p. 1B.

429. Markoff, John. "Guilty Plea Is Expected in Virus Case." *nytimes.com,* December 9, 1999.

430. United States Attorney, District of New Jersey. "Creator of 'Melissa' Computer Virus Pleads Guilty to State and Federal Charges." December 9, 1999.

431. Delio, Michelle. "A Virus Writer Heads to Prison." *wired.com,* May 3, 2002.

432. U.S. Attorney's Office, District of New Jersey. "Creator of Melissa Computer Virus Sentenced to 20 Months in Federal Prison." May 1, 2002.

433. Silverman, Dwight. "PC Users Left Lovestruck by Vicious Virus." *Houston Chronicle.* May 5, 2000: pp. 1A, 18A.

434. *Ibid.*

435. *Ibid.*

436. *www.msnbc.com.* "FBI Says It Has ID'd Virus Suspect." May 5, 2000.

437. *Ibid.*

438. *cnet.com.* "Damage Control," February 6, 2003.

439. *Ibid.*

440. Gage, Deborah. "Computer Worm Spreads Holiday Infection." *sfgate.com,* December 29, 2007.

441. Moore, David, Paxson, Vern, Savage, Stefan, Shannon, Colleen, Staniford, Stuart, and Weaver, Nicholas. "The Spread of the Sapphire/Slammer Worm." *caida.org,* January 26, 2003.

442. Poulsen, Kevin. "Slammer Worm Crashed Ohio Nuke Plant Net." *theregister.co.uk,* August 20, 2003.

443. Jacques, Robert. "Blaster Infects 30,000 PCs per Hour." *vnunet.com.* August 18, 2003. Messmer, Ellen. "Blaster Worm Causes Havoc." *nwfusion.com.* August 13, 2003.

444. Jung, Helen. "Microsoft Outwits Blaster Worm." *eweek.com.* August 17, 2003.

445. *news.com.au.* "Blaster Worm Causes Havoc." August 13, 2003.

446. *msnbc.com.* "Good Version of Worm Circulates." August 18, 2003.

447. *sophos.com.* "Nachi Worm Tries to Undo Blaster Damage—but no Virus Is a Good Virus, Says Sophos." August 19, 2003.

448. Quoted in *Ibid.*

449. de la Cruz, Albert Pangilnan. "Malware on the Loose." *itmatters.com.* August 20, 2003.

450. Naraine, Ryan. "'Friendly' Welchia Worm Wreaking Havoc." *enterpriseitplanet.com.* August 20, 2003.

451. *washingtontimes.com.* Welchia Worm Hits U.S. Navy Marine Corps." August 20, 2003.

452. *wininformant.com.* "Welchia/Nachia Worm: Vigilante or Poor Disguise?" August 19, 2003.

453. Quoted in Thomson, Iain. "Anti-Blaster Worm Spreads—and Patches." *vnunet.com.* August 18, 2003.

454. Richmond, Riva. "Sobig Virus Spread Is Fastest Ever." *biz.yahoo.com.* August 20, 2003. Dennis, Margaret. "So Big is So Big." *net4nowt.com.* August 20, 2003. Harris, Shane. "So, So Big." August 26, 2003.

455. Ford, C. Benjamin. "So Big Virus Proves So Annoying for Computer Users." *gazette.net.* August 22, 2003.

456. Quoted in *Ibid.*

457. Richmond, *op. cit.*

458. Quoted in Dolinar, Lou. "'Sobig Computer Worm Attack Eases." *newsday.com.* August 22, 2003.

459. *itvibe.com.* "Netsky-P Virus Still Causing Problems." June 4, 2004.

460. *Ibid.*

461. Quoted in *Ibid.*

462. Kawamoto, *op. cit.*

463. *news.bbc.co.uk.* "Teen 'Confesses' to Sasser Worm." May 8, 2004.

464. *news.bbc.co.uk.* "Sasser Net Worm Disruption Grows." May 4, 2004.

465. *sophos.com.* "The Latest News on the Sasser Internet Worm Outbreak." May 1, 2004.

466. *bbc.news.co.uk,* May 8, 2004, *op. cit.*

467. *bbc.news.co.uk,* May 4, 2004, *op. cit.*

468. *Ibid.*

469. *Ibid.*

470. *wired.com.* "Sasser Worm Creator Avoids Lockup." July 9, 2005.

471. *cnet.com.* "Harry Potter and the Worm of Doom," June 22, 2007.

472. *networkworld.com.* "Harry Potter Worm Says he Is Dead," June 29, 2007.

473. Gaudin, Sharon. "Harry Potter Worm Claims Wizard Hero Is Dead." *informationweek.com,* July 6, 2007.

474. *infoworld.com.* "Blaster Worm Author Gets Jail Time." January 28, 2005.

475. *technewsworld.com.* "Jeffrey Lee Parsons Pleads Guilty to Blaster Worm Crime." August 12, 2004.

476. Levy, Paul. "Prosecutors Ask 37-Month Sentence for Hopkins Teen in Internet Worm Case." Minneapolis *Star Tribune* (online). January 26, 2005.

477. *virusbtn.com.* "Minimum sentence for Blaster Author." January 31, 2005.

478. Llet, Dan. "Sober Worm Makes a Comeback." *cnetnews.com.* April 19, 2005.

479. Kawamoto, Dawn. "Sober Worm Variant Makes the Rounds." *cnetnews.com.* May 2, 2005.

480. *usdog.gov.* "Washington State Man Pleads Guilty to Charges of Transmitting Internet Virus," February 15, 2007.

481. Goodwin, Dan. "Man Pleads Guilty to Spreading Trojan via IRC." *theregister.co.uk,* February 22, 2007.

482. Whitney, Lance. "Koobface Malware Makes a Comeback." *news.cnet.com.* April 9, 2010.

483. Villeneuve, Nart. "Koobface: Inside a Crimewave Network." *infowar-monitor.net/koobface.* November 12, 2010.

484. Protalinski, Emil. "Facebook Exposes Hackers Behind Koobface Worm." *zdnet.com.* January 17, 2012.

485. Maxcer, Chris. "Kido Worm Keeps on Truckin' vis USB Thumb." *technewsworld.com,* January 16, 2009.

486. Markoff, John. "Worm Infects Millions of Computers Worldwide." *nytimes.com,* January 23, 2009.

487. Lemos, Robert. "Downadup Worm Infects More Than 3.5 Million." *securityfocus.com,* January 14, 2009.

488. *guardian.co.uk.* "Has the Downadup/Conflickr Worm Peaked?" January 25, 2009.

489. *skynews.com.* "Computer Worm Goes Out of Control," January 19, 2009.

490. *tech.yahoo.com.* "Downadup/Conflicker Worm Infects 9 Million PCs," January 21, 2009.

491. Markoff, *op. cit.*

492. Acohido, Byron. "Conflicker Worm Infects More Than 9 Million PCs." *usatoday.com,* February 16, 2009.

493. *nytimes.com.* "Iran's Nuclear Agency Trying to Stop Computer Worm." September 25, 2010.

494. Falliere, Nicolas. "Stuxnet Introduces the First Known Rootkit for Industrial Control Systems." *symantec.com.* August 19, 2010.

495. *reuters.com.* "Cyber Attack Appears to target Iran-Tech Firms." September 24, 2010.

496. *securelist.com.* "The Flame: Questions and Answers." May 28, 2012.

497. Zetter, Kim. "Meet 'Flame,' The Massive Spy Malware Infiltrating Iranian Computers." *wired.com.* May 28, 2012.

498. *bbc.com.* "Flame Malware Makers Send 'Suicide' Code." June 8, 2012.

499. *Ibid.*

500. Sanger, David. "Obama Order Sped Up Wave of Cyberattacks Against Iran." *nytimes.com.* June 1, 2012.

501. Zalud, Bill. "Doing the Virus Hustle." *Security* 27, 1990: 42–44.

502. Burgess, John. "Viruses: An Overblown Epidemic?" *Washington Post,* December 30, 1992; F1, F3.

503. Moore, *op. cit.*

504. *npros.com.* "Net Fraud Is Tangled Web for Victims, Police." June 3, 2002.

505. *pcworld.com.* "Top Five Online Scams." May 16, 2995.

506. Flaum, *op. cit.*

507. Dusto, Amy. "Mother and Son arrested in Alleged eBay Scam." *internetretailer.com.* August 24, 2012.

508. *Consumers' Research.* "On-Line Investment Schemes: Fraud in Cyberspace." Vol. 77, August, 1994: 19–22.

509. Kabay, M.E. "Mail-Order Bride Scams." *networkworld.com,* September 11, 2007.

510. *fraudguides.com.* "FTC's Dirty Dozen Email Scams," July 14, 1998.

511. *Ibid.*, p. 56

512. Hoover, J. Nicholas. "ID Theft, Online Fraud Rose Slightly in 2011." *informationweek.com.* May 14, 2012.

513. Vilches, Jose. "US Citizens Lost $239 Million From Internet Fraud in 2007." *techspot.com,* April 8, 2008.

514. Claburn, Thomas. "Internet Fraud Loss for 2007 Tops $239 Million." *informationweek.com.* April 4, 2008.

515. *npros.com, op. cit.*

516. Hiltzik, Michael A. and Piller, Charles. "Internet Snares Scam Victims." *Los Angeles Times* (online). November 10, 2002.

517. Madrigal, Alexis. "All the Spammers in the World May Only Make $200 Million a Year." *theatlantic. com.* August 7, 2012.

518. *Ibid.*

519. Raisbeck, Fiona. "Duo Found Guilty of International Spam Campaign." *scmagazineuk.com,* June 20, 2007.

520. Scott, Gina M. "First Prosecution Under CAN-SPAM Act Returns Guilty Verdict." *govtech.com,* June 26, 2007.

521. Hunter, Chris. "How Jeremy Jaynes Earned $750K per Month for Spamming." *spamfo.co.uk.* November 15, 2004.

522. *Ibid.*

523. *Ibid.*

524. Barakat, Matthew. "9-Year Sentence for Junk E-Mails." *Houston Chronicle.* April 9, 2005: D1.

525. Swartz, Jon. "Spammers Convicted; First Felony Case." *USA Today,* November 4, 2004: 1B.

526. *techdirt.com.* "Crackdown on Spam Continues With Tough Sentence in Virginia," April 8, 2005.

527. Leyden, John. "Penis Pill Purveyor Faces Prison." *theregister.co.uk,* July 6, 2005.

528. Modine, Austin. "Spammer Gets 30 Years in the Slammer." *theregister.co.uk,* August 2, 2007.

529. Quoted in Carr, Jim. "Pharmacy Spam King Given 30-Year Jail Sentence." *scmagazineus.com,* August 7, 2007.

530. *washingtonpost.com.* "'Spam King' Pleads Guilty," March 15, 2008.

531. *Houston Chronicle.* "Suspected Spammer Could Go to Slammer," May 31, 2007: A12.

532. Goodin, Dan. "Seattle Dark Mailer Faces 47-Month Sentence." *theregister.co.uk,* July 23, 2008.

533. Carter, Mike. "'King of Spam' Dethroned With 47-Month Sentence in Seattle Court." *seattletimes.com,* July 23, 2008.

534. *Atlanta Business Chronicle* (online). "'Spam King' Soloway Given 47-Month Prison Sentence," July 23, 2008.

535. *domainb.com.* "MySpace Wins Record $230 Million Award Against 'Spam King' Sanford Wallace," May 14, 2008.

536. Albanesius, Chloe. "Facebook Sues Spammer for Deceptive Wall Posts." *pcmag.com,* March 4, 2009.

537. Smith, Justin. "'Spam King' Sanford Wallace Files for Bankruptcy as Judge Rules Facebook's Lawsuit Can Proceed." *insidefacebook.com.* June 12, 2009.

538. Cutler, Kim-Mai. "Facebook Wins $711 Million in Damages Against 'Spam King' Wallace." *venturebeat. com.* October 29, 2009.

539. Hoffman, Stefanie. "Ralsky Indictment Won't Reduce Spam." *crn.com,* January 7, 2008.

540. Federal Bureau of Investigation. "Detroit Spammer and Four Co-Conspirators Plead Guilty to Multi-Million-Dollar E-Mail Stock Fraud Scheme." *fbi.gov.* June 22, 2009.

541. *upi.com.* "'Spam King' Pleads Guilty in Detroit." June 23, 2009.

542. Nicholson, Kieren. "Prison For Colorado Spam King." *denverpost.com,* April 29, 2008.

543. Federal Bureau of Investigation (press release). "Internet Spammer Walks Away From Florence Prison Camp." July 22, 2008.

544. *denverpost.com.* "Missing 'Spam King' Kills Self, Family," July 24, 2008.

545. Quoted in *kdka.com,* "Colo. Cops: 'Spam King' Kills Wife, Daughter, Self," July 25, 2008.

546. *spacedaily.com.* "Spam: Some Pretty Amazing Measures." April 20, 2004.

547. Quoted in Barakat, *op. cit.*

548. *zeenews.com.* "'Botmaster' Pleads Guilty to Computer Crimes," January 24, 2006.

549. Acohido, Byron and Swartz, Jon. "Techie Pleads Guilty to Hijacking Computers." *USAToday,* January 24, 2006: 3B.

550. *zeenews.com, op. cit.*

551. *ngssoftware.com.* "The Phishing Guide." October 14, 2005.

552. *Ibid.*

553. *fraudwatchinternational.com,* op.cit.

554. Landesman, Mary. "Phishing Scams." *antivirus. about.com.* April 10, 2005.

555. *fraudwatchinternational.com, op. cit.*

556. *Ibid.*

557. *Ibid.*

558. Alexander, *op. cit.,* pp. 86–87.

559. Gaudin, Sharon. "Phishing Scams Increase 1,200% in 6 months." *esecurityplanet.com,* April 23, 2004.

560. Quoted in *Ibid.*

561. Moore, Cathleen. "Phishing Attacks, and Cures, Grow More Sophisticated." *infoworld.com,* September 23, 2005.

562. *ngssoftware.com, op. cit.*

563. Quoted in U.S. Senator Patrick Leahy. Speech on the Senate Floor. February 28, 2005.

564. *gartner.com.* "Gartner Survey Shows Phishing Attacks Escalated in 2007," December 17, 2007.

565. Siciliano, Robert. "Phishing Attacks Rise Dramatically in 2008." *finextra.com,* February 20, 2009.

566. *Ibid.*

567. *topclickmedia.co.uk.* "Year of Phishing—2008," December 9, 2008.

568. Leyden, John. "Google Calendar Phishing Scam Surfaces." *theregister.co.uk,* December 30, 2008.

569. *fraudwatchinternational.com, op. cit.*

570. *Ibid.*

571. *Ibid.*

572. *Ibid.*

573. *Ibid.*

574. *Ibid.*

575. Prince, Brian. "Man Found Guilty of Targeting AOL Customers in Phishing Scam." *channelinsider.com,* January 12, 2007.

576. *virusbtn.com.* "Phisher Gets Six Years," June 14, 2007.

577. Leyden, John. "AOL Phisher Nets Six Years' Imprisonment." *theregister.co.uk,* June 13, 2007.

578. Leyden, John. "AOL Phishing Fraudster Found Guilty." *channelregister.co.uk,* January 17, 2007.

579. Quoted in Gaudin, Sharon. "California Man Gets 6-Year Sentence For Phishing." *informationweek. com,* June 12, 2007.

580. United States Attorney's Office, District of Connecticut (press release). "Man Pleads Guilty to Participating in Elaborate Internet "Phishing" Scheme." August 22, 2007.

581. McMillan, Robert. "AOL Phisher Gets Seven Year Sentence." *pcworld.com,* August 13, 2007. *sophos. com.* "AOL Identity Thief Faces Seven Year Jail Sentence," Agust 23, 2007.

582. Leyden, John. "AOL Phisher Jailed For Seven Years." *theregister.co.uk,* August 14, 2007.

583. Hruska, Joel. "You've Got Jail! AOL Spammer Sentenced to Seven Years." *arstechnica.com,* August 14, 2007.

584. *cnn.com.* "Nigeria Cracking Down on E-Scams." August 8, 2005.

585. *fraudwatchinternational.com.* "Major Internet Frauds—Nigerian 419 Scams." October 14, 2005.

586. Sullivan, Bob. "'Nigerian Scams' Keep Evolving." *msnbc.msn.com.* June 10, 2005.

587. *utdallas.edu.* "The '4-1-9' Nigerian Scam." January 10, 2002.

588. *Ibid.*

589. Glasner, Joanna. "Nigeria Hoax Spawns Copycats." *wired.com.* June 18, 2002.

590. Dixon, *op. cit.*

591. *Ibid.*

592. Quoted in Sullivan, *op. cit.*

593. Gross, Grant. "Three Plead Guilty in Nigerian Spam Scheme." *nytimes.com,* January 30, 2008.

594. *Ibid.*

595. *Ibid.*

596. *cnn.com, op. cit.*

597. *Ibid.*

598. Sullivan, *op. cit.*

599. *home.rica.net.* "The Nigerian Scam Defined." July 3, 2005.

600. *utdallas.edu, op. cit.*

601. *Ibid.*

602. *Ibid.*

603. Quoted in Dixon, *op. cit.*

604. Wong, Chin. "Beware the Nigerians." *info.com.ph.* October 28, 2003.

605. Glasner, *op. cit.*

606. *fraudwatchinternational.com, op. cit.*

607. Quoted in Sullivan, *op. cit.*

608. *crimes-of-persuasion.com.* "Pyramid Investment Scammer Falls Victim to Nigerian Money Scam," January 7, 2007.

609. Internal Revenue Service (press release). "Promoter of International Pyramid Scheme Sentenced to 10 Years in Prison." September 12, 2007.

610. *Houston Chronicle.* "Millions Lost to Internet Scam, Suit Claims," March 3, 2006: A5.

611. Usborne, David. "Reagan Psychologist 'Lost Up to $3M in Internet Scam.'" *The Independent* (online), March 3, 2006.

612. Lobdell, William. "UCI Psychiatrist Bilked By Nigerian E-Mails, Suit Says." *Los Angeles Times,* March 2, 2006: B1.

613. Dixon, *op. cit.*

614. Parker, 1983, *op. cit.*

615. Lee, Moon. "The Rise of the Company Spy." *Christian Science Monitor,* January 12, 1993: p. 7.

616. Lopez, Ed. "Can Your Computer Keep Secrets?" *Miami Herald,* March 13, 1989: Business Section, p. 1.

617. Rothfeder, Jeffrey. "Holes in the Net." *Corporate Computing* 2, 1993: 114–118.

618. Violino, *op. cit.*

619. Buchok, James. "$5M Suit Filed Over Database Copying Claim." *Computing Canada* 18, 1992: 1–2.

620. O'Connor, Rory J. "High-Tech Cops Wade Through Digital Dump of Information." *San Jose Mercury News,* October 24, 1992: 10D–11D.

621. Groves, Martha. "2 Indicted on Trade-Secret Theft Charges." *Los Angeles Times,* March 5, 1993: p. D1.

622. Ratcliffe, Mitch. "Symantec Execs Face Felony Rap in Borland Case." *MacWEEK 7,* 1993: 1–2.

623. "Jules." "On the Use of Weapons." EXE 10, 1993: 52–53.

624. Forcht and Pierson, *op, cit.*, p. 32.

625. Hasson, Judi. "Access to Medical Files Reform Issue." *USA Today,* July 27, 1993: 1A–2A. In 1995, legislation was introduced in the United States Senate aimed at protecting the privacy of patients' health records. The senator who sponsored the bill argued: "Doctors and nurses and pharmacists may know things about us we don't even tell our spouses or friends" (Quoted in Boyd, *op. cit.*, p. 3G).

626. Lee, *op. cit.*

627. Rosenberg, Carol. "Argentine Unmasked as Computer Hacker." *Houston Chronicle,* March 30, 1996: p. 8A.

628. Roush, *op. cit.*

629. Zuckerman, M. J. "Hacker Pair Illustrate Pentagon's Vulnerability." *USA Today,* May 23, 1996: p. 3A.

630. *Ibid.*

631. *Ibid.*

632. Hafner and Markoff, *op. cit.*

633. Stoll, Clifford. *The Cuckoo's Egg.* New York: Doubleday, 1989.

634. Hafner and Markoff, *op. cit.*

635. Stoll, *op. cit.*

636. Wee, Sui-Lee and Oreskovic, Alexei. "Google Reveals Gmail Hacking, Says Likely from China." *reuters.com.* June 2, 2011.

637. Arthur, Charles. "Google Phishing: Chinese Gmail Attack Raises Cyberwar Tensions." *guardian.co.uk.* June 1, 2011.

638. Wee and Oreskovic, *op. cit.*

639. Dilanian, Ken. "U.S. Chamber of Commerce Leads Defeat of Cyber-Security Bill." *latimes.com.* August 3, 2012.

640. *Ibid.*

641. *Ibid.*

642. Hafner and Markoff, *op. cit.*

643. Belts, Mitch. "Recovering From Hacker Invasion." *Computerworld* 27, 1993: p. 45.

644. *Houston Post.* "Dallas Police Investigate Suspect in Spreading of Computer Virus." December 29, 1990: p. 19.

645. Markoff, John. "Hacker Indicted on Spy Charges." *New York Times,* December 8, 1992: p. 13.

646. *Ibid.*, p. 13.

647. Grillo, Thomas. "Boston Bank Accuses Former Executive of Stealing Secrets." *bostonherald.com.* May 17, 2011.

648. Millard, Elizabeth. "Spyware as Corporate Espionage Threat." *newsfactor.com.* July 19, 2005.

649. *Ibid.*

650. *Ibid.*

651. *techweb.com.* "Nine Indicted in Israeli Spyware Espionage Case." June 8, 2005.

652. *Ibid.*

653. *msnbc.msn.com.* "Israeli Espionage Case Points to New Net Threat." October 16, 2005.

654. *cybercrime.gov.* "Software Executive Admits to Conspiring to Misappropriate Chief Competitor's Trade Secrets" (Press Release). September 29, 2005.

655. Camuso, Pat. "Software Exec Admits to Conspiring to Misappropriate Competitor's Secrets." *tristate-news.com.* October 6, 2005.

656. Lever, Rob. "Security Experts Warn of Chinese Cyberattacks for Industrial Secrets." *forbes.com.* July 24, 2005.

657. *Ibid.*

658. *Ibid.*

659. Quinn, *op. cit.*

660. Falconer, *op. cit.*

661. Stephens, *op. cit.*

662. Cheswick, William R. and Bellovin, Steven M. *Firewalls and Internet Security: Repelling the Wily Hacker.* Reading, MA: Addison-Wesley, 1994.

663. For example, criminologist Gene Stephens has warned that the development of virtual-reality technology portends fantastic new varieties of computer fraud: "In the future, a virtual-reality expert could create a hologram in the form of a respected stockbroker or real estate broker, then advise clients in cyberspace to buy certain stocks, bonds, or real estate. Unsuspecting victims acting on the advice might later find that they had enlarged the coffers of the virtual-reality expert, while buying worthless or nonexistent properties" (Stephens, *op. cit.*, p. 27).

13

Conclusions

Crime committed within a privileged class was a favorite dramatic theme of Shakespeare. Yet even the sapient Bard seemed at times perplexed by the enigma of elite corruption:

> O, that deceit should dwell
>
> In such a gorgeous palace!
>
> *Romeo and Juliet.* Act III, Scene 2.[1]

In the preceding chapters, we have explored a lot of corrupt "palaces"—from the lavish offices of predaceous swindlers, to the ornate cathedrals of religious hucksters, to the stately chambers of porcine legislators. By now it may seem that the authors have endeavored to document a simple fact: people are basically greedy and dishonest and, given half a chance, will steal anything that's not nailed down. Such an interpretation, however, would be far from accurate. Most people, most of the time, do *not* engage in fraud, embezzlement, bribery, and cover-ups. Rather, these acts involve persons occupying certain societal roles and transpire only under certain conditions. In this final chapter, we will consider some of the factors that give rise to white-collar criminality, along with some changes that need to be made in order to control it.

We will also re-examine both official and public responses to white-collar crime. Many commentators have suggested that white-collar crime flourishes because of a generally tepid reaction by law enforcement and other government agencies. Why does it seem that so many upperworld criminals are never brought to justice? Why do those few who are sanctioned seem to receive punishments so remarkably lenient? Moreover, why do convicted white-collar offenders suffer so little of the stigma and opprobrium that the citizenry attaches to "common" criminals? These are important questions that need to be addressed.

We will investigate, too, the consequences of white-collar crime. Chapter 1 briefly noted some of the injuries inflicted by these offenses. Here that discussion will expand, focusing on the human and environmental destruction, the economic costs, and the social damage wrought.

CAUSES OF WHITE-COLLAR CRIME

Today, just as Sutherland observed more than a half-century ago, scholarly theories of crime still overwhelmingly emphasize street crimes and the characteristics of those who commit them. Much effort has gone into searching for the peculiar physiological or psychological traits that differentiate the criminal from the noncriminal—from Lombroso's early notion of the "born" criminal,[2] to Freud's concept of the underdeveloped conscience,[3] to more recent attempts to locate violent lawbreakers at the low end of the IQ distribution curve.[4] A review of such literature reveals that white-collar offenders are generally left out of the theoretical picture.

Conventional theories of crime, moreover, often have a tautological quality in that they define criminality in terms of the same factors they posit as causes. If crime is defined as acts committed by young, poor males who score low in IQ tests, explaining those acts through theories that stress age, poverty, and cognitive capacity is not very illuminating. Furthermore, the fact that upperworld criminals are typically older, more affluent, and superior in measured intelligence raises questions that cannot be answered by such circular reasoning. The elucidation of elite criminality requires a revised definition of crime and a higher level of analysis.[5]

Such an approach is not concerned with explanations that focus on "types" of people. It is assumed, in other words, that white-collar criminals are not significantly different, in terms of their personalities or psychological makeups, than other people. Therefore, one need not attempt to create a profile of the "typical" white-collar criminal. Indeed, one of the striking things about white-collar offenders is how similar they are to "respectable" members of society.

As we have seen, the epidemic of financial scandals that scarred the 1980s spread its infection across Washington, Wall Street, and even the once-staid Savings and Loan (S&L) industry. Was this, as Chapter 6 suggests in its examination of insider trading, the inevitable outgrowth of a "greed culture" that dominated American society during that decade? Culture, from the sociological viewpoint, is certainly important; but many sociologists are uncomfortable with purely cultural explanations of behavior, preferring instead to look for underlying social structural causes. They study the structural relationships that exist among individuals within the context of societies, institutions, and organizations.

So, in attempting to identify the causes of white-collar crime, we will focus on three basic levels of sociological analysis. We will see how *societies, institutions,* and *organizations* generate the opportunity, motives, and means for white-collar criminality.

Societal Causes

This is the level of analysis in which cultural explanations of white-collar crime are rooted. Of course, all criminal acts are committed by individuals. But as sociologists emphasize, individual decisions are always made in larger societal contexts that present and provide support for particular options, making behavior that might otherwise seem unethical or unlawful appear as reasonable and legitimate. Ironically, when individuals engage in white-collar crime, though they are breaking the law, they are often *conforming* to cultural values—such as the accumulation of wealth.

In 1938, the esteemed American sociologist Robert Merton published an article that was to become famous (entitled "Social Structure and Anomie") in which he wrote: "[C]ontemporary American culture continues to be characterized by a heavy emphasis on wealth as a basic symbol of success, without a corresponding emphasis on the legitimate avenues on which to mark towards this goal."[6] At the same time, in Merton's view, American culture places negative sanctions on those who fail to achieve material success, attributing their failure to personal deficiencies and character flaws such as laziness. Merton observed that one response to this pressure is for certain individuals to turn to more "innovative" means to succeed, including, in some cases, criminal activities.[7] It is very significant that, in Merton's formulation, the standard of material success is not an objective one but exists on a sliding scale—so that even the relatively well-off may feel their aspirations are blocked and may thus resort to crime to achieve culturally defined goals.

In a similar vein, criminologist James W. Coleman has written more recently that the ultimate sources of white-collar criminality lie in the "culture of competition" that pervades American society. Coleman describes our industrial economy as one that includes a market structure which produces not only profits and losses but winners and losers.[8] The result is a "win at any cost" morality that encourages even the scrupulous entrepreneur or executive to bend the rules—or to engage in outright fraud and deception—in order to stay ahead of the competition. And while these pressures may be found in any society that produces "surplus wealth,"—that is, wealth beyond what is required for subsistence—they are felt most acutely in advanced capitalist societies like ours, where upward mobility is regarded as a right.

These cultural views on the virtue of materialism also find support in economic theories, most notably in the writings of the 18th century philosopher Adam Smith. In his classic *The Wealth of Nations,* published in 1776, Smith wrote:

> It is not from the benevolence of the butcher, the brewer, or the baker, that we expect our dinner, but from their regard to their own interest. We address ourselves, not to their humanity but to their self-love, and never talk to them of our own necessities but of their advantages.[9]

To Smith, it was this natural pursuit of self-interest that created, in his famous phrase, "the invisible hand of the marketplace" and ensured social order and prosperity. More than 200 years later, Ivan Boesky, whose criminal exploits are chronicled in Chapter 6, echoed the same sentiments in his commencement speech to the graduating class of the University of California business school: "You can be greedy and still feel good about yourself."[10]

Adam Smith's extolment of the individual accumulation of wealth has been refined further in contemporary economics, most prominently by Milton Friedman. From the perspective of Friedman and his apostles, people are "utility maximizers" guided by the rational pursuit of self-interest in free markets. In Friedman's opinion, concepts like "the social responsibility of business" are oxymorons, since corporations should have but one goal—to make a profit.[11]

Far from being an esoteric abstraction, known only to a select group of academics, this acquisitive creed is transmitted to the real world of commerce via business schools, where future executives are indoctrinated with its self-justifying precepts. Studies of MBA students have found that they often internalize the values implicit in Friedman's economic vision. One survey of graduate business students reported that "many students were willing to do whatever was necessary to further their own interests, with little or no regard for fundamental moral principles."[12]

Neoclassical economics provides individuals with ready-made rationalizations for their behavior. This is what sociologist C. Wright Mills referred to as "vocabularies of motives"—the verbal means by which people can justify and account for their behavior.[13] These accounts can be used to explain away criminal acts of all sorts. White-collar offenders frequently employ what theorists Gresham Sykes and David Matza call "techniques of neutralization,"[14] mechanisms that allow them to annul any potential guilt or internal conflict stemming from conduct on their part that breaks laws to which they claim ostensible allegiance. A 1987 marketing study concluded that neutralization plays a major role in unethical business practices.[15]

The five commonly recognized neutralization techniques are:[16]

1. ***Denial of responsibility:*** Offenders argue that they are not personally accountable for their actions because of overriding factors beyond their control. For example, ghetto price gougers typically justify usurious interest rates on the grounds that low-income consumers are "deadbeats."

2. ***Denial of injury:*** Offenders contend that their misconduct causes no direct suffering. For example, producers of the rigged television quiz shows insisted that they merely had enhanced the dramatic appeal of innocuous programs designed only to entertain.

3. ***Denial of victim:*** Offenders claim that violated parties deserved whatever happened. For example, many computer hackers maintain that anyone leaving confidential data files unprotected is really at fault for any subsequent break-ins.

4. ***Appeal to higher loyalties:*** Offenders depict their conduct as the by-product of an attempt to actualize a higher value. For example, Richard Nixon and Oliver North portrayed their respective crimes as acts of patriotism—as did the CIA torturers at Abu Ghraib and Guantanamo.

5. ***Condemning the condemners:*** Offenders seek to turn the tables on their accusers by claiming to be the true victims. For example, S&L crook Charles Keating repeatedly blamed regulators, prosecutors, politicians, journalists, and just about everyone else—everyone, that is, except himself.

In their avowals of innocence, corporate criminals also draw on what has been termed the "folklore of capitalism"[17] to recast themselves as misunderstood visionaries or persecuted dissidents. At the zenith of his career, when he was moving billions of dollars through the economy, junk bond impresario Michael Milken was fond of portraying himself as an agent of social change, a "social engineer" whose activities were restructuring society.[18]

In a similar manner, some white-collar criminals try to evoke images of the frontier. They liken themselves to pathfinders, blazing new trails through unchartered business terrain. This theme was sounded by a pair of notorious environmental criminals in an interview they gave from federal prison. Prior to their incarceration, the Colbert brothers ran a successful company which purchased toxic chemical wastes from American manufacturers and then illegally dumped them in Third World countries. In their interview, the Colberts steadfastly denied any guilt:

> We were, in a sense, innovators ahead of the times . . . We're basically pioneers in the surplus chemical business, which is something that's a necessary business for society.[19]

Psychologist/philosopher Julian Edney, who has written extensively on selfishness and social inequality, has argued that greed should be listed as a mental pathology in the American Psychiatric Association's *Diagnostic and Statistical Manual* (*DSM IV*)—the standard compendium of mental disorders used by all psychotherapists.[20] A perfect example is provided by David Novak, a successful "sentencing consultant" for convicted white-collar criminals. One of his clients was convicted of running a boiler room stock scam that swindled investors out of $296 million, financially destroying many of them. This client saw absolutely nothing wrong with what he had done. "People who bought Krispy Kreme lost a lot of money too," he rationalized to Novak.[21]

> After one exceptionally long day, leaving the lawyer's office, Novak took [the client] to task. "If this was such a good deal, why didn't you get your parents into it?" he asked. The client, who was quite close with his parents, didn't appreciate Novak's repartee. In fact, "I thought he was going to punch me," Novak remembers.[22]

Novak, who almost never speaks ill of his clients, later said of this one: "This guy was probably as close to sociopathic as I've ever seen."[23] Novak's use of the sociopath/psychopath terminology hit the bull's-eye.

Psychopathic Wealth

When the authors of this book were growing up in the 1950s, there was a generation entering the corporate arena far different than today's crop. Their personalities were shaped by the Great Depression and their experiences in World War II. They entered that arena with relatively modest expectations, especially when compared with their current counterparts. They wanted to participate in a burgeoning postwar economy. They wanted good jobs and economic security. They wanted to help build successful companies. Few of them likely expected to live like feudal lords, for there was far less wealth in American society then than there is now. They believed that if they paid their dues, worked hard, developed good products and services, were creative and took prudent risks, they would be rewarded—as many of them surely were.

The corporate culture of the 1950s was very conformist. The "overnight" success stories, such as Xerox or Polaroid, were far more the exception than the rule. Indeed, the mid-20th century was not a time when great fortunes were being made overnight. Entrepreneurialism was not really a big part of the American business milieu at that time, for there was little venture capital available. With the Depression still gliding on the tightropes of their collective memories, Americans didn't feel comfortable taking big gambles; and it wasn't encouraged.

The hallmark of that generation of young executives was what has been termed *patient wealth*. It was a time when almost nobody got rich quickly. Going public and making a billion dollars weeks later was not in their mentality or imagination.

Today's business leaders grew up in a very different America—an America that showcased enormous amounts of wealth. It now appears clear that many of them internalized a profound sense of entitlement. They expected things sooner, rather than later. They were the product of a much more materialistic society. "In your face" opulence that once would have been embarrassing had become the norm in their world. Not only do today's corporate elite seem to believe they should make fortunes quickly, but there are also far fewer restrictions on conspicuous consumption. One need only think of former Tyco CEO Dennis Koslowski's (Chapter 7) $15,000 umbrella stand and $6,000 shower curtains, paid for by hapless shareholders. Greed thy name is Koslowski.

This dramatic transition has been fueled by a greed so out of control that even *Fortune* magazine—which once voted Enron the best company in the United States six years in a row—featured a cover in 2003 displaying pigs in Armani suits.[24] Former Treasury Secretary Robert Reich notes that the very rich now live in a "parallel universe" with its own separate rules.[25] This small elite class increasingly has become disconnected from the social mainstream and the responsibilities of good citizenship. A generation of executives who *make* things has been replaced by a generation who *take* things. The wealth they possess or aspire to possess is not a patient wealth. But to call it merely "impatient" wealth is to understate what has happened in corporate America. A more resonant term can be borrowed from the psychiatric lexicon, a term used to describe persons intensely selfish, conspicuously lacking in human empathy, and dispositionally unable to delay gratification. We seem to have entered an Age of **Psychopathic Wealth**.

The earnings gap between the CEOs of major corporations and their rank and file employees has widened steadily and dramatically. It is currently more than 500 to 1. While the average American is now working harder for less money, major CEOs not only enjoy huge salaries and incredibly lucrative stock option deals, but they also receive golden parachutes, forgivable loans, and a plethora of other financial benefits. The result is that the richest 1 percent of Americans now own more wealth than the bottom 95 percent—an unprecedented disparity. Historians Will and Ariel Durant concluded four decades ago that the gap between the wealthiest and poorest Americans has become greater than at any time since Imperial Rome.[26]

One of the more startling economic trends in recent decades has been the accelerated growth in the divide that separates those at the top and those at the bottom of American society. Between 1979 and 2007, the average income for all households grew by 62 percent. But that figure varied considerably depending on where you were on the income pyramid. Those in the top 1 percent of the pyramid saw their household incomes increase by 275 percent. The 20 percent of the population with the lowest incomes saw their incomes rise by a meager 18 percent.[27] These differences are even more dramatic in certain parts of the country. In 2009 in New York City, home to both Wall Street "masters of the universe" as well as struggling immigrant cab drivers, the top 1 percent of individual tax filers earned 32.5 percent of all income in the city; the comparable figure for the top 1 percent in the entire United States was 16.9 percent.[28] Statistics like these led Nobel prize-winning economist Joseph Stiglitz to recently write that we now live in a society "Of the 1 percent, by the 1 percent, and for the 1 percent."[29]

But evidently, all the aforementioned "legal" benefits aren't enough. As the recent corporate scandals reveal all too clearly, some greedy CEOs—along with other top executives—have illegally inflated the value of their firms' assets. This not only raises the value of the company's stock, but in particular also increases the value of their own stock options, which have become the currency of senior management. Overstating earnings also makes exorbitant salaries, bonuses, and perquisites appear more justifiable.

It would be comforting to conclude that the problem is confined to a few highly publicized "bad apples"—the Enrons, WorldComs, Adelphia, Qwests, Global Crossings, and others. But no one can say this with any real confidence. Indeed, the evidence suggests otherwise. It suggests the emergence of a *kleptocratic* corporate culture—that is, a culture ruled by thieves. In the words of a former Securities and Exchange Commission (SEC) enforcement chief: "There is always greed and misconduct in the business world. But in today's society, more people tend to believe they can get away with it."[30]

Nearly 1,000 public corporations were forced to correct their financial statements between 1998 and 2003. The Enrons may be only the visible part of the financial reporting iceberg. As the economic collapse of 2008 revealed, what lay below the surface is so large that it is almost too scary to look.

The contemporary "Age of Excess" has spawned a number of real-life characters who seem to have walked off the pages of Tom Wolfe's novel *The Bonfire of the Vanities*. One of those is former Long Island entrepreneur David H. Brooks.

CASE STUDY
America's Most Ostentatious War Profiteer

On November 25, 2005, David H. Brooks, CEO of a Long Island company that manufactured bulletproof vests for the military, threw a bat mitzvah party for his daughter in Manhattan. Unlike the vast majority of similar events, this party attracted considerable media attention because of its lavish extravagance.

(Continued)

Sparing no expense, Brooks rented out two floors of the famed Rainbow Room and invited over 300 guests. For musical entertainment he hired the legendary rock band Aerosmith, rock stars Tom Petty and Don Henley, and rapper 50-Cent to perform at the fete. Brooks himself appeared in a magenta suede biker outfit and handed out $122,000 worth of iPods and digital cameras to the guests. Total costs for the party were estimated to exceed $10 million.[31]

This would have been just another story of corporate excess and bad taste, were it not for the fact that at the time Brooks was under investigation by the Securities and Exchange Commission and the FBI. In the fall of 2007 he was accused by federal prosecutors of insider trading, accounting fraud and tax evasion in a case that came down to individuals who were consumed by "naked greed" and "the lies and the fraud that they used to satisfy that greed."[32] According to the U.S. Attorney's office, Brooks and his co-defendant lied to investors about the company's profitability and sold off their shares of the company's stock in a scheme that netted them $190 million. Brooks used his share of the ill-gotten gains to fund a lavish lifestyle that included, not only his daughter's bat mitzvah, but also: a $194,000 Bentley automobile and an armored vehicle for his personal use, a facelift for his wife, grooming fees and vitamins for his stable of 100 horses, a "family vacation" to Europe that cost $75,000, and a $100,000 diamond-studded belt buckle in the shape of an American flag.[33] Brooks was eventually convicted and as of this writing is awaiting sentencing.

This was not the first time Brooks had run afoul of the law. In 1992, the SEC banned him from the securities industry for five years because of his connection to an insider-trading scheme. In 1995 he bought a company that specialized in protective body armor. By 2004 the company's fortunes were soaring as it won contracts to supply most of the military vests used by U.S. troops in Iraq and Afghanistan. However, in 2005 the Marines and the Army recalled 23,000 of the vests after reports surfaced that the vests had "critical, life-threatening flaws." [34] Brooks would be described in the media as "America's most ostentatious war profiteer."[35]

Congresswoman Louise Slaughter, writing at the height of the Iraq War, expressed her disgust with the Brooks case in the following way.

> The downfall of David H. Brooks is, at its heart, a story that combines the worst elements that have come to define the Bush administration; combining corruption reminiscent of Enron, questionable sole-source contracts awarded to companies unable to produce the lifesaving equipment needed for war, and greed and excess on an unconscionable scale. The consequence of these dealings has been disastrous for our troops in harm's way, too many of whom, without enough or properly manufactured body armor, ended up paying the ultimate price.[36]

This is a very different perspective on Brooks and his enterprises than the one found on his Web site which describes the convicted felon as: "the man, the myth, the legendary humanitarian."[37]

On the other hand, there is reason for some optimism. The mass media have finally discovered psychopathic wealth, and the issue appears to have caught the public's attention. In 2003, a story broke that CEO Donald J. Carty of American Airlines, in an effort to avert bankruptcy, had successfully negotiated a $1.8 billion savings package with the company's three labor unions. He had convinced his pilots, mechanics, flight attendants, and baggage handlers that they must accept major pay cuts of between 15 and 25 percent or parent company AMR would collapse, taking their jobs and pensions down with it.

What Carty neglected to make clear at the time was that his plea for shared sacrifice did not include himself. When AMR filed a required report with the SEC, only then was it revealed that—at the same time Carty was negotiating the labor pay cuts—he was secretly crafting hefty retention bonuses for himself and a handful of top executives that would reward them for staying at their posts until 2005. Carty's bonus would total $1.6 million, twice his annual salary. The press wanted to know how this could have happened. And why a CEO whose company had lost over $5 billion in the previous two years deserved a seven-figure bonus just for showing up?

This was the type of story that once easily could have gone unnoticed—especially at a time when the drums of war in Iraq were drowning out competing noises. But, in journalistic parlance, this tale of naked greed had "legs." It *was* noticed by an incensed public, and as a result the bonuses were rescinded and Carty was forced to resign.

Since the stock market imploded in 2008, maybe the Age of Psychopathic Wealth is drawing to a close. Or maybe not. It often appears that executive compensation in corporate America has become almost totally divorced from performance.[38] Recent stories reveal executives of insolvent corporations indulging in orgies of self-indulgence with taxpayer money that they had gone begging for. Examples would include the opulent AIG retreat of 2008 (Chapter 7). Northern Trust Corp. sponsored a professional golf tournament in 2009, during which it hosted a series of lavish dinners and concerts.[39] The company flew in hundreds of clients and employees for a week of excesses, putting them up at fancy hotels.[40] A few months earlier, Northern Trust had received $1.6 billion in government bailout loans.

Harvard philosopher Michael Sandel has recently written an insightful critique of the broader conditions that give rise to what we have called "psychopathic wealth." Sandel argues that the financial crisis that began in 2008 led to the end of an era of "market triumphalism," an era that began in the early 1980s when Ronald Reagan and Margaret Thatcher "proclaimed their conviction that markets, not government, held the key to prosperity and freedom."[41] According to Sandel, "the financial crisis did more than cast doubt on the ability of markets to allocate risk efficiently. It also prompted a widespread sense that markets have become detached from morals . . ."[42] On a more pessimistic note, Sandel observes that we are still living in a "market society," in which "market values seep into every aspect of human endeavor."[43] Ours is a society in which virtually "everything is for sale"; a society in which we pay children to read books, jail inmates can pay for upgrades to better cells, insurance companies pay people to lose weight and individuals in a variety of situations can pay people to stand in lines for them.

So what's wrong with this? According to Sandel, markets have a corrupting and corrosive effect on social relations and promote a tendency to commodify things whose value is difficult to express in economic terms. One of these is human life. To illustrate this point Sandel discusses "dead peasants insurance," in which companies are able to take out life insurance policies on their employees, without the employees' knowledge, which, in the event of the employee's death, *pay the company*, not the employee's survivors. As we pointed out in Chapter 2, WalMart took out "dead peasants" policies on more than 350,000 of its lower-level employees and reportedly used the proceeds from them to fund its executive retirement plan. While these policies may make financial sense, they violate fundamental moral principles as they create conditions "where the workers are worth more dead than alive . . . [and] treats them as commodity futures rather than employees . . ."[44] Under current tax laws the death benefits from these policies are tax-exempt, a fact which leads Sandel to state: "It is hard to see why the tax system should encourage companies to invest billions in the mortality of their workers rather than in the production of goods and services."[45]

Whether America's corporate elite will continue to believe they are entitled to all the benefits of the free market with none of the risks or will be deterred by the sobering image of fallen executives working in prison laundries remains to be seen. Change may be in the air, but so always is the heady scent of big money. In the eternal battle between greed and accountability, most of us would probably bet on greed. It usually wins.

Institutional Causes

While culture may provide the rationalizations for white-collar crime, it is specific institutions that provide the means and opportunities. Not all industries are contaminated by fraud. For instance, higher education, an institution with which the authors are intimately familiar, experiences very little fraud (with the exception of rare cases of falsified research noted in Chapter 11) simply because there is very little to be gained through deception. On the other hand, industries like the popular music business (Chapter 5), where sales for a single album may reach many millions of dollars, afford considerable incentive for bribery and corruption. At the same time, the unregulated character of the record industry and the individualistic basis of decision making by music broadcasters also provide ample opportunity for illegal conduct. Thus, certain industries are structured in ways that provide both the incentives and the opportunities for white-collar crime, and, therefore, one must examine that structure to discover root causes.

The concept of "criminogenic industries" is used to describe the factors that facilitate fraud in industries like the music business. Needleman and Needleman state that the defining feature of criminogenic industries is that "their internal structures—economic, legal, organizational and normative—play a role in generating criminal activity within the system, independent at least to some degree from the criminal's personal motives."[46] The automobile industry, for example, has been described as "criminogenic" because it has a market structure characterized by a high concentration of manufacturers who exert control over the distribution process[47] and because excessive pressures from manufacturers on dealers to increase sales[48] create the conditions that give rise to extensive fraud and abuse at the retail level. Likewise, the largely unregulated and decentralized nature of automotive repair makes it another prime site for deceptive practices. As we saw in Chapter 2, numerous investigations have found that overcharging, billing for unnecessary work, and the sale of phantom parts are common practices at auto repair shops around the country—findings that may come as no surprise to any car owner who has ever left a mechanic's shop feeling more beat-up than the car.

And then there is the used car business. Fairly or otherwise, perhaps no figure has come to embody the fast-talking flim-flam artist more than the used car dealer. One of the oldest and best known used car scams is odometer rollback, known as "clocking." This occurs when illegal changes are made to the mileage shown on a used vehicle's title and odometer in order to mask high mileage on a late-model car.[49] When the new car market struggles (as in the Recession of 2009), used car sales typically accelerate and more vehicles get clocked.[50] With the proliferation of leased and rental cars in recent years, odometer tampering has become a very lucrative criminal activity and is now recognized as a serious form of white-collar crime.[51] Clocking can add four or five thousand dollars to the price of a late-model used car.[52] In 2008, the National Highway Traffic Safety Administration estimated that more than 450,000 car buyers fell victim to odometer fraud.[53] The total cost to consumers has been estimated to be as high $10 billion per year.[54] To cite one example, Robert "Bobby Cars" Fiorello, owner of several used car dealerships in New Jersey, pleaded guilty in 2008 to altering hundreds of odometers on late-model, high-mileage automobiles. Some odometers were rolled back as much as 100,000 miles.[55]

A more recent type of used car fraud is the illicit—and dangerous—sale of so-called "flood cars." In the aftermath of the three devastating 2005 Gulf Hurricanes—Katrina, Rita, and

Wilma—more than 500,000 vehicles were submerged under water.[56] When the waters receded, what remained were extremely hazardous vehicles. Obviously, modern vehicles with their computer chips and sophisticated electrical systems suffer permanent damage when submerged for any length of time. For those reasons, insurers usually "totaled" these cars—that is, took them from their owners and paid off insurance claims. One would assume this was the end of the road for the "Katrina cars," but that was not the case at all. Flood cars soon appeared in used car lots far from the Gulf Coast.[57]

California, with its huge, lucrative market, was notorious as a favorite dumping ground for hurricane cars, thanks to a criminogenic chain of fraud. Insurers ship them to so-called "salvage pools," where they are auctioned off to the highest bidder. "[U]nlicensed rebuilders buy them, give them a power wash and replace the upholstery, and sell them to unscrupulous auto dealers, who in turn foist them off on unsuspecting used car buyers—often teenagers buying their first cars."[58] The insurers get a cut of the proceeds from the auction, reducing their losses by millions of dollars.[59]

CASE STUDY
High-Stakes Cheating

A far less obvious example of a criminogenic "industry" is public school education. This was not always the case, but the advent of so-called "high-stakes" testing has created a pressurized environment under which "cheating has spread from the examinees to the examiners."[60] Since the 1990s, standardized tests have been used widely to assess the performance of not just students but also teachers, principals, schools, and entire districts.[61] Following the passage of the No Child Left Behind Act of 2001, high-stakes testing was mandated, and tests meant to evaluate students' progress are now utilized as much to both reward and punish schools and individual educators.

The kinds of incentives that fuel a criminogenic industry are built into the testing system. Jobs, bonuses, and school accreditation are all tied to test scores.[62] In California, for example, teachers in schools with large increases in test scores may be eligible for merit raises as big as $25,000.[63] In Pennsylvania, schools that improve their students' performance on that state's test can receive performance incentive rewards of hundreds of thousands of dollars.[64]

On the other side of the coin, schools face negative sanctions under the No Child Left Behind Act if they fail to meet specified annual gains in state tests.[65] The states themselves also punish failure. In Kentucky, for example, schools are censured if their scores go down.[66] In some states, abysmal test scores have resulted in entire staffs being fired and required to reapply for their own jobs.[67] A researcher who conducted a major study of this problem, titled *Rotten Apples: An Investigation of the Prevalence and Predictors of Teacher Cheating,* drew a harsh conclusion: "Once the outcome of these tests started to matter, was it any surprise that teachers began to cheat?"[68]

There are numerous ways for educators to manipulate test scores. Cheating can occur before a test even is administered. Tests received from a state usually are stored at schools prior to test dates and are not always inventoried.[69] For example, children at a Lawrence, Massachusetts, school performed nearly perfectly after their teacher got a copy of the exam ahead of time and used it to practice.[70] Pretest manipulation can also occur when teachers suggest to students likely to attain low scores that

(Continued)

they should stay home on test day.[71] Still another exclusionary practice is to divert students likely to score low into special education classes, which are exempted from many state assessment tests. In Texas, the percentage of special education students jumped by one-third the year that test scores began to count toward school ratings.[72]

Cheating during a test is even more common. Examples include the following:

- A poll of North Carolina teachers reported that 35 percent admitted that they personally had cheated while administering standardized tests or knew of colleagues who had done so. Such practices ranged from the relatively subtle, such as giving extra time on timed tests or suggesting possible answers, to more flagrant actions, like giving students dictionaries and thesauruses for use on a state-mandated writing exam.[73]
- A study of the Memphis, Tennessee, school system revealed extensive cheating, "including a teacher who displayed correctly filled-in answer sheets on the walls of her classrooms."[74]
- In Indiana, a third-grade teacher was suspended after being accused of tapping students on the shoulder when they marked wrong answers.[75]
- An Ohio teacher was accused of physically moving students' pencil-holding hands to correct answers on multiple choice questions.[76]

Other cheating scandals involving public school teachers have been reported in Rhode Island,[77] Connecticut,[78] New York,[79] Wisconsin,[80] Washington State,[81] Florida,[82] Louisiana,[83] Virginia,[84] Mississippi,[85] and California.[86] Systematic alteration of scores after tests have been handed in is more intricate and more likely to be undertaken by school administrators than teachers. A Maryland principal had to resign after being accused of cheating on the statewide achievement test. She allegedly had gone through students' test booklets, then called underper-

forming students to her office and suggested that they change their answers. Unlike many of the schools tarnished by cheating scandals, hers was a top-ranked school in an affluent community.[87] In Michigan, another principal allegedly changed test answers on the state exam. Her teachers had been told to take erasers off students' pencils so that a "magic eraser" could be used to make corrections for them.[88] School administrators in Austin, Texas, entered incorrect student-identification numbers on the answer sheets of low-scoring students, which invalidated their scores, thus raising their schools' average performance.[89] There are also cases in which administrators simply failed to submit some students' test forms.[90] One Texas educator observes critically: "In no other arena are those who stand to benefit or suffer according to test results in charge of testing. Law schools do not give bar exams, nor do driving schools give drivers' license exams."[91]

The *Rotten Apples* study used test scores from third- to seventh-grade students in the Chicago public schools in order to develop and test a statistical technique for identifying likely cases of cheating by teachers and administrators. A substantial number of classrooms, flagged by the researchers' "cheating algorithm," were retested under closely monitored conditions. Scores declined by more than a full grade equivalent.[92]

Some schools may have legitimate explanations for improbable test patterns, but in many cases, "the gaps are so wide that experts say it's difficult to imagine a cause other than cheating."[93] In 2004, a Houston elementary school in an economically depressed neighborhood finished in the bottom 2 percent of the state in the fourth grade math test but had the highest scores in Texas in the fifth grade math test.[94] No other school in the state was even close. "In scale-score points, the distance between [it] and the No. 2 school was as large as the gap between No. 2 and No. 116."[95] Not one of the school's fourth graders got a perfect or near-perfect score; but 92 percent of the fifth graders did.[96] A statistician who investigates cheating compared that to a weekend duffer beating Tiger Woods by 10 strokes.[97] Yet in 2005, less than a year later, the superintendent of the Houston Independent School District unveiled a $14.5 million incentive-pay proposal designed to award cash bonuses to teachers who boost test scores of low-income students.[98]

A 2003 report on testing fraud issued by Harvard University's Kennedy School of Government concluded: "If there are incentives in place, people will find a way to game the system."[99] Many years ago, W.C. Fields suggested an even simpler explanation: "Anything worth winning is worth cheating for."[100]

One of the clearest illustrations of institutional criminogenesis was the corruption of Wall Street in the 1980s (Chapter 6). The "merger mania" of the era was orchestrated by investment banks and law firms, whose members were privy to valuable information about impending deals. The restricted nature of that information and the tremendous profits it could yield created both opportunities and incentives for insider trading.

Organizational Causes

In many white-collar crimes the motivation is straightforward—individual material gain. This would be the case, for example, when a Sheraton Corporation food buyer was sentenced to 15 months in prison for taking "hundreds of thousands of dollars" in kickbacks from produce wholesalers.[101] It would also certainly be the case with many of the notorious criminals portrayed in these pages, such as Charles Ponzi, Ivan Boesky, or Jim Bakker.

However, in many of the other cases discussed in this book, individuals carried out the criminal schemes, but the ultimate benefit went to a larger organization, typically a corporation. A basic distinction in the analysis of white-collar crime is between what is known as "occupational crime" and what is labeled "corporate crime."

Clinard and Quinney defined occupational crime as "offenses committed by individuals in the course of their occupations and the offenses of employees against their employers" and corporate crime as "offenses committed by corporate officials for their corporation and the offenses of the corporation itself."[102] Occupational crime would include bank employees who embezzle, physicians who defraud health benefit programs, mechanics who overcharge or bill for needless services, and politicians who accept bribes and kickbacks.

Corporate crimes, on the other hand, usually are more complex and involve individuals who violate the law to advance the interests of the organization. One example would be James Donnell, former vice president at Affiliated Computer Services, who was convicted in 2004 of cheating the company's clients out of $3.8 million by inflating customer invoices.[103] Corporate crime already has been designated the "crime of choice" for the 21st century.[104] One author has characterized the modern corporation as a "pathological institution."[105]

In preceding chapters we have looked at numerous instances of corporate crime. The illegal dumping of hazardous waste by companies well aware of the serious consequences, the knowing exposure of workers to unsafe conditions, and the deliberate sale of dangerous products are all examples of corporate crime, where the offenses frequently were carried out by supervisors and managers who claimed to be "just following orders."

More recently, the idea of corporate crime has been extended into more traditional categories of criminal law, such as homicide. In Chapter 3, we considered the infamous Pinto case, in which the Ford Motor Company was charged with "reckless homicide" after three teenagers died when their Pinto burst into flames after being struck from the rear by another vehicle. Although Ford eventually was acquitted—largely because of a procedural technicality—a significant legal precedent was set in the area of corporate criminal liability.

Some criminologists have sought to extend the concept of corporate liability to encompass organizations of all types, including government agencies and even nonprofit organizations. Schrager and Short distinguished "organizational crime" from individual offenses by defining it as illegal acts committed by "an individual or a group of individuals in a legitimate formal organization in accordance with the operative goals of the organization."[106] Other theorists have used similar terms, such as "organizational deviance"[107] and "elite deviance."[108]

Whatever the terminology, organizational crime also includes acts of governmental deviance described in Chapter 9, such as the FBI's unlawful surveillance and persecution of American citizens, the burglaries, dirty tricks, and cover-ups overseen by the White House in the Watergate scandal, and the abuses of power precipitated by the Iran-Contra Affair. To this list one could add the well-documented involvement of the CIA in drug trafficking around the world—particularly in Southeast Asia and Latin America.[109] These were all illegal activities undertaken by individuals on behalf of the covert agenda (but not the mandated goals) of official agencies and political administrations.

Why do some organizations promote "deviance" while others do not? Sometimes it is simply a matter of the greed of the individuals leading the organization. For example, Mickey Monus, cofounder and president of the 300-unit Phar-Mor drugstore chain, was convicted in 1995 of a mammoth fraud and embezzlement scheme that drove his own company into bankruptcy.[110]

CASE STUDY
The Mickey Monus Club

The flamboyant Monus was well-known for his extravagant lifestyle. His palatial home even featured a full-size indoor basketball court.[111] In fact, Monus was such a rabid basketball fan that he launched his own professional league—for short players—in 1987.[112] The World Basketball League (WBL) was a financial fiasco from the start and folded in 1992. The only reason it lasted that long was that Monus siphoned off $10 million from Phar-Mor to keep the league afloat.[113]

But embezzling $10 million to save a minor-league sports operation was only a moderately interesting sidebar to the real story; for Mickey Monus was a major-league crook. By keeping two sets of books—one actual, one "doctored"—Monus, assisted by several other Phar-Mor insiders, was able to misstate the company's sales and earnings, and defraud investors and creditors out of more than $1 billion.[114]

Newsweek called it the biggest corporate fraud of the 20th century.[115]

Monus was convicted in federal court on 48 separate counts and handed a whopping 20-year prison sentence. He would have to wait at least 17 years for parole.[116] In a statement to the presiding judge, Mickey declaimed his farewell address to the troops:

> The important thing is not the numbers to me . . . but the employees—all those dedicated, loyal and highly motivated people. I want them to know the sorrow and regret that I have. The sorrow and regret will live with me for the rest of my life.[117]

Those 20,000 "dedicated, loyal" employees—many put out of work—doubtless shared Mickey's "sorrow and regret" when Phar-Mor fell under bankruptcy protection and began closing stores.

Not all organizational deviance conforms to the "greedy leader" model exemplified by Mickey Monus, however. In many cases, it has more to do with the environment in which the organization operates. Some sociologists have carried Merton's notion of blocked aspirations to a higher level of analysis, suggesting that a particularly significant aspect of a criminogenic corporate environment is the "strain" placed on organizations. A case study of organizational misconduct by another drug store chain concluded that organizations, like individuals, may seek illegal means to achieve economic success when legitimate avenues are blocked and when opportunities are available to attain material goals unlawfully.

Executives of the chain reportedly ordered employees to falsify Medicaid claims after state officials had rejected earlier claims for administrative reasons. Those executives believed that reimbursement for the false claims was "owed" to the company.[118] A survey of retired middle managers from Fortune 500 companies reported that the most important cause of unlawful or unethical practices in their corporations, according to respondents, was the pressures applied by top management to show profits and reduce costs.[119]

Organizational Culture

Finally, a number of scholars have pointed to the internal norms and values that guide behavior within organizations as key determinants of whether organizational members will engage in white-collar crime. These norms and values are subsumed under the larger category of *organizational culture*, which has been defined as "the amalgam of beliefs, ideology, language, ritual and myth"[120] found within organizational settings. In her classic analysis of the events that led up to the tragic *Challenger* space shuttle disaster in which seven crew members died shortly after take-off, Diane Vaughan developed the concept of the "normalization of deviance" to explain how the managers, engineers, and others at NASA were able to proceed "as if nothing were wrong when they continually faced evidence that something *was* wrong."[121] (emphasis in original) The "definition of the situation" of acceptable and unacceptable risk became part of the specific culture surrounding the subgroup within NASA responsible for making the decision to launch or not, and it was this definition, rather than the technical information available to them, that ultimately led to the fateful decision to launch the *Challenger*.[122] Vaughan's theoretical framework had a substantial impact on subsequent analyses of environmental and worker safety disasters as well as research on organizational deviance.

One of the puzzling aspects of much corporate crime is the fact that few of those involved display any particular propensity for crime prior to joining the organization. Their willingness to engage in crime on behalf of their employers seems to emerge within the particular context of their work environment. The explanation for this fact may be found in the way that certain organizations promote what Ashforth and Anand call the "normalization of corruption."[123] With this concept they seek to explain how corrupt acts "become embedded in organizational structures and processes, internalized by organizational members as permissible and even desirable behavior, and passed on to successive generations of members . . ."[124] This embedding of corruption works along three dimensions: (1) *institutionalization*, the process by which corrupt practices are enacted as a matter of routine, often without conscious thought about their propriety; (2) *rationalization*, the process by which individuals who engage in corrupt acts use socially constructed accounts to legitimate the acts in their own eyes; and (3) *socialization*, the process by which newcomers are taught to perform and accept corrupt practices."[125] Numerous accounts of the Enron Corporation show how all of these factors combined to create the "culture of arrogance" that was "a blend of cutting-edge and 'cutting throat,'" that we noted in Chapter 7. This culture was revealed in a transcript of a conversation between Enron energy traders about how they were ripping off consumers at the height of the California electricity crisis: "It's kinda hard to say we shouldn't do this even though it's allowed because . . . you know, I mean, that's what we do."[126] Even for those traders who knew what they were doing was wrong, few ever acted upon their concerns for fear of rocking a comfortable boat. As one former Enron trader put it: "I was never comfortable on the trading floor at Enron, and if I had questions, I didn't ask them. You know. I didn't want confirmed what I suspected to be true, that what I was doing was, in fact, unseemly or was at least unethical, if not worse."[127]

CASE STUDY
Olde Whine in New Bottles

A prime example of a deviant corporate culture was revealed at the Olde Discount Corp., a leading discount brokerage chain. The company and three of its senior officials—including its founder and chairman—was fined more than $5 million by the SEC for fraudulent sales practices. The Commission found that Olde "willfully violated the antifraud provisions of the federal securities laws."[128] The Commission determined that "Olde's compensation, production, hiring, and training policies *created an environment* that enabled the firm's brokers to engage in abusive sales practices, such as churning, unauthorized and unsuitable trading, and lying to customers [emphasis added]."[129] The SEC further ruled that the Olde environment was one "where the pressure to sell overshadowed customer suitability determinations."[130]

Under its compensation policies, Olde gave substantially higher payouts to its brokers for selling special venture stocks—that is, stocks recommended by Olde—than for other stocks. "Olde's compensation system induced its brokers to sell those stocks in which they had the greatest financial interest without considering the suitability of such stocks for their customers."[131]

Olde's production policies created overt pressure to sell. In order to maintain their commission privileges, Olde brokers were required to sell an average of two new special venture stock positions—worth at least $20,000—every day.[132] By requiring brokers to push special venture stocks or run the risk of termination or lower commissions, Olde insured that its brokers would aggressively sell special venture stocks. In addition, Olde brokers needed to convince each of their customers to buy at least one Olde-recommended stock every six months. Customers not meeting this criterion would be reassigned.[133]

Olde's hiring and training practices encouraged its brokers to use high-pressure sales techniques. Brokers were taught to "cross-sell"—that is, "to convince customers who wanted to buy non-Olde recommended stocks, on which brokers received little compensation, to buy special venture stocks instead."[134]

Brokers were told, "Why let someone buy a stock you're not going to get paid on?" Brokers were taught to create "a sense of urgency" and to tell customers that if they did not buy immediately, they would not be able to get the stock tomorrow.

Brokers were to continue to "pitch" a stock to their customers until they agreed to buy. Brokers were also taught to use sales scripts that contained false statements, such as "the price of the stock is going up" and that the broker had been "watching the stock for two years." In addition, brokers were told

(*Continued*)

to make misleading statements to customers concerning the financial interest of Olde.[135]

Working in such a criminogenic environment, it is easy to see why Olde brokers at various branch offices throughout the country engaged in what the chairman of SEC termed "egregious" abuses and practices that "put the firm and its brokers in conflict with the interests of its clients."[136]

Organizations like Olde Discount provide not only the context for white-collar crimes but often the means to commit them. In practice, then, it may be very difficult to distinguish between acts that promote the goals of an organization from those that primarily benefit individuals, since, in many cases, "individuals and their organizations often reap mutual advantage from criminal conduct."[137] In fact, organizations can be used by members as "weapons" in the commission of crimes. As one study observed: "[O]ccupation and organization are to the world of white-collar crime what the knife and the gun are to street crimes."[138] Thus, elements like size, ownership form, and administrative structure can be used by organizational members to commit and later hide their crimes. This notion was applied to a study of fraud among insolvent S&Ls which found that "those institutions that were stock-owned . . . were the sites and vehicles for the most frequent, the most costly and the most complex (as measured by the number of individuals involved) amounts of white collar crime."[139]

RESPONSES TO WHITE-COLLAR CRIME

Given the abundant opportunities that many persons have to engage in white-collar crime, it is interesting that more people do not. The most obvious reason for this is the fear of punishment. Despite the fact that relatively few individuals who cheat on their taxes are ever actually prosecuted, the knowledge that some have been (including the treasurer of the United States, as described in Chapter 1) is enough to keep most of us reasonably honest when we turn in our 1040s in April. In other words, many citizens do not cheat on their taxes simply because of strong moral compunctions but because the law *deters* them—especially when their personal reputations are at stake. For example, some experts have suggested "shaming" tax delinquents by publishing their names and pictures in local newspapers.[140] When the IRS reported $300 million in unpaid 2007 taxes, that amount included sizable bills owed by such celebrity tax delinquents as singer Dionne Warwick ($3.7 million), comedian Sinbad ($2.1 million), and former Clinton aide and current Fox News analyst Dick Morris ($1.5 million).[141] The argument goes that fear of embarrassment would deter tax evaders in general, but especially high-profile figures. Indeed, several persons nominated by President Obama in early 2009 to fill key positions in his administration were "shamed" into withdrawing their names because of revelations of unpaid back taxes.

Classical criminological notions of deterrence rest on the fundamental utilitarian premise that people will seek pleasure and avoid pain. So, when the potential risks associated with a behavior—such as a crime—outweigh the potential gains, an individual will decide rationally against the behavior. Much of our criminal law is based on this assumption about human nature.

A central concern about white-collar crime is that the risk-reward ratio is out of balance—that is, the potential rewards greatly outweigh the risks. Given the low probability of apprehension and the likelihood of light punishment, white-collar crime appears to be a "rational" course of action in many cases. The sometimes indifferent response to white-collar criminals stands in sharp contrast to the harsh punitive treatment customarily accorded to street criminals—a contrast summed up in Jeffrey Reiman's pithy observation that "the rich get richer and the poor get prison."[142] The comparative leniency shown white-collar offenders has been attributed to several factors related to their status and resources, as well as to the peculiar characteristics of their offenses. First, the relatively high educational level and occupational prestige of many white-collar offenders are seen as creating a "status shield" that protects them from the harsh penalties applied with greater frequency to "common" criminals. Many judges identify with defendants whose background and standing in the community are similar to their own. When three former executives of C.R. Bard Corporation, one of the world's largest medical equipment manufacturers, were convicted in 1996 of conspiring to test unapproved heart surgery catheters in human patients, the sympathetic judge reluctantly sentenced them to 18 months in federal prison. He almost seemed to be scolding the jury when he said: "I don't regard the defendants as being evil people or typical criminal types."[143] The U.S. attorney who prosecuted the case could not have disagreed more. He characterized the callous executives as "evil people doing evil things . . . for money."[144]

A second leniency factor punctuates one of the world's worst-kept secrets—that life is seldom fair. White-collar defendants' high incomes enable them to secure expensive legal counsel, whose level of skill and access to defensive resources are generally unavailable to lower-class defendants. In addition, the emerging field of "sentence consulting" of "post-conviction mitigation" has emerged, providing convicted white-collar offenders with assistance in sentence reduction, such as demonstrations of charitable generosity or evidence of ailing health. Despite the "country club" mythology, there are no pleasant prisons; so these advisors also "pad the landing" when white-collar crooks fall from grace and land in a cell. One consultant, David Novak (mentioned earlier), says of his privileged clients: "They have absolutely no idea what it is they're facing. . . . Unfortunately, they've heard a lot about 'Club Fed' and at the same time they have seen movies like 'The Shawshank Redemption,' so they are not quite sure whether to bring their golf clubs or they are just in fear for their lives."[145]

Finally, white-collar crimes frequently involve complicated financial transactions in which the victims are either aggregated classes of unrelated persons, such as stockholders, or large government agencies, such as the IRS—neither of which engender the kind of commiseration that individual victims of street crimes can elicit from judges and juries.

Anecdotal evidence from a number of cases seems to support the proposition that white-collar criminals can receive lighter sanctions. Michael Milken's initially tough 10-year sentence was later cut to 3 years, and he was released after serving only 24 months in a minimum-security facility. Likewise, two of the most notorious S&L crooks in Texas—Don Dixon and "Fast Eddie" McBirney—whose corrupt savings and loans eventually cost the taxpayers $3 billion, had their original sentences substantially reduced.[146]

Evidence of a more empirical nature also supports the leniency hypothesis. A study of persons suspected by federal regulators in Texas and California to be involved in serious savings and loan crimes revealed that only between 14 and 25 percent were ever indicted. The study also examined the sentences imposed in S&L cases involving mean losses of a half-million dollars and found that the average sentence was three years—significantly less than the average prison terms handed to convicted burglars and first-time drug offenders in federal court.[147] It would appear that burglars and first-time drug offenders are considered by the courts to be more serious threats to public security than are thrift looters who can destabilize the entire economy.

A study of California Medicaid providers convicted of defrauding that state's health care system produced similar findings (Chapter 11). It reported that, when compared to a control group of "blue-collar" offenders charged with grand theft (the same charge leveled at the Medicaid fraud offenders), the Medicaid fraud defendants—many of whom were physicians—were less than half as likely to be incarcerated. This disparity is made even more conspicuous by the fact that the median financial losses from the Medicaid offenses were more than 10 times the median losses from the control group's crimes.[148]

On the other hand, it should be noted that, although the findings from these kinds of focused studies may seem clear, the results yielded by broader analyses of class-based sentencing differentials are less consistent. While many studies have supported the leniency hypothesis,[149] others have reported no evidence that higher-status defendants are punished any less severely than lower-status ones.[150] Some have even produced the contrary finding that higher-status defendants receive longer, not shorter, sentences.[151] So, the issue of social status and punitive leniency remains unresolved[152]—especially in the post-Enron era.

The lengthy sentences imposed on some high-profile white-collar offenders in the few short years since the Enron meltdown suggest that the rules of the game are changing dramatically. Indeed, a serious legal debate is now going on over whether the sentences imposed on corporate criminals have become *too long*. This is an argument that Sutherland probably never heard in his lifetime nor may even have imagined.

CASE STUDY
Tough Math—From Zero to Life

On March 25, 2004, Jamie Olis, a former senior director for Dynegy, the Houston-based energy company that had once tried to buy its mortally wounded neighbor Enron, was sentenced in federal court to 24 years and 4 months for fraud and conspiracy.[153] The Korean-born Olis had been convicted a year earlier of participating in a 2001 scheme, code-named Project Alpha, to disguise a $300 million loan as cash flow in order to help the company meet Wall Street expectations.[154] Dynegy's cash flow had been lagging its earnings, causing consternation among analysts and lowering share price.[155] The scheme also had helped Dynegy claim an improper $79 million tax benefit.[156] After Project Alpha was uncovered, Jamie Olis' illegal actions eventually cost Dynegy investors more than $500 million, and the company soon unraveled.[157]

Olis' co-defendant and former boss, Gene Shannon Foster, had earlier cut a deal with prosecutors that guaranteed him no more than five years in prison and probably less. Shannon also agreed to testify against his former subordinate.[158] This time, the government would be moving *down* the food chain. Witnesses at the trial named about a dozen higher-ranking Dynegy executives as co-conspirators, but at this writing none have been indicted for any wrongdoing. Unless Olis agrees to testify against them—something he has thus far refused to do—they may never be formally charged.[159] One interested observer, the attorney representing Enron whistle-blower Sherron Watkins, notes: "To get the guys at the top, you need to get the guys in the middle."[160]

Olis had been offered the same plea bargain as Shannon, but, against the advice of counsel, he had refused to settle. He reportedly had been argumentative in meetings with federal prosecutors, offering explanations for each incriminating document.[161] He was convinced that a jury would acquit him. He believed that everything he had done was legal. He never testified; in fact, he rested his case without calling a single witness. In his opening statement, his lawyer characterized Olis as "just

(Continued)

a tax guy doing his job."[162] But the government's case was strong. Olis' own e-mails had warned colleagues to "never, never, never" share details of Project Alpha. Another of his e-mails even joked about his fear of a good prosecutor making him "cry" on the witness stand.[163] The jury found him guilty in less than two hours.[164]

The judge told Olis: "I take no pleasure in sentencing you to 292 months."[165] But the judge also declared that the punishment "reflects Congress' intent that white-collar corporate fraud defendants receive harsh sentences."[166]

And therein lies the tale. Was the judge's contention correct? Did Congress intend that Jamie Olis, a mid-level manager in a corrupt corporation, be sent to prison for so long that his infant daughter would likely be in college by the time he was released?

The debate centers on the federal sentencing guidelines for financial crimes, adopted in 2001 and updated in 2003, in response to public outrage over the corporate scandals. The guidelines call for adjusting sentences based on the severity of the fraud. For a defendant with no criminal history, for example, the "base level" guideline for a fraud conviction is zero to six months in prison. Judges then have to consider approximately 20 possible adjustments to this sentence, including:

- The amount of the "loss" attributable to the fraud;
- The number of victims of the fraud;
- Whether the fraud involved "special skills" or "sophisticated" means;
- Whether the defendant worked in the investment business or as an officer or director of a public company.[167]

The most influential of the factors is the *estimated loss*. If the fraud is estimated to cause losses of less than $5,000 (the lowest category), there is no increase in the sentence. Above $5,000, there are 15 escalating categories up to "more than $400 million" (the highest category) with corresponding increases in sentences.

All else being equal, for example, if the loss estimate is $1 million to $2.5 million, the guideline sentence jumps to 64 to 78 months, or five to seven years. If the loss is more than $400 million, the guideline is 292 [Olis' sentence] to 365 months, or 24 to 30 years. If a $400 million fraud also affected more than 250 victims, moreover, the guideline calls for a life sentence.[168]

The judge in the Olis case settled on a loss estimate of $105 million. This was the amount the University of California retirement fund had lost on Dynegy stock, a loss the university attributed to Project Alpha.[169] Adding in the other factors from the guidelines, he recommended the 24-year sentence. Prosecutors and other retributionists defend the guidelines, arguing that if you steal more money or cause more losses it is reasonable that you serve more time.

On the other hand, critics of the guidelines argue that they have a chilling effect on productivity. Financial writer James K. Glassman labels the reaction of politicians to the corporate scandals as "hysterical." He argues that "The penalty for failure today is not merely lower earnings; it is lawsuits, prosecution, huge fines, and long prison terms."[170] Glassman may be correct about failure causing lawsuits and even fines; but he is mistaken about prosecution. Long prison terms are not caused by mere failure; they are caused by serious criminal behavior.

Another financial author, Henry Blodget, echoes Glassman's sentiments. Blodget writes that the tough sentencing guidelines have made it "shockingly risky" to work at a major corporation.[171] This is an unpersuasive argument built upon a persuasive premise. Certainly, the risk-reward ratio is central to capitalism. Economist John Maynard Keynes was a proponent of risk-taking, which he called "animal spirits."[172] Historian Walter A. McDougall maintains that the U.S. economy was built by "scramblers, gamblers, scofflaws, and speculators."[173] But there are many ways to define acceptable risk-taking, and Blodget's definition seems overly broad. He is a former dot-com analyst, who was once a major star on Wall Street—until he was barred from the securities industry for phony and self-serving research ratings.[174] It might just as easily be argued that Blodget and his ilk have made it "shockingly risky" to buy dot-com stocks.

Nevertheless, Blodget and Glassman's side appears to have prevailed. On November 1, 2005, the 5th U.S. Circuit Court of Appeals overturned Jamie Olis' 24-year sentence,[175] though it let his conviction stand. The court explicitly challenged the careful calculations set forth in the federal sentencing guidelines. Accordingly, Jamie Olis' sentence was reduced to six years.

The appellate court's ruling about Olis' sentence led to a 5- to 10-year reduction of former Enron president Jeff Skilling's 24-year sentence (Chapter 7). Nevertheless, the effective "life sentences" being served by Bernie Ebbers (WorldCom) and John Rigas (Adelphia) seem to belie the traditional notions of white-collar criminals getting "slapped on the wrist." But even if some high-status defendants still do receive preferential treatment, is that necessarily a bad thing? The presumption that differential sentencing has a deleterious effect on our system of justice and on society in general has been challenged by certain scholars. In a provocative article entitled, "Do We Punish High Income Criminals Too Heavily?" John Lott answers his own question with an emphatic "Yes." Lott argues that, because wealthy defendants experience a proportionately greater decline in income following a criminal conviction than do poorer defendants, their punishment will be unduly harsh if they receive the same sentences as their low-income counterparts who are convicted of the same crimes.[176] The solution he recommends is to allow upperworld criminals to "buy justice"—that is, to use their lighter sentences to offset the more serious extralegal sanctions they face.[177] Thus, for example, suppose that a bank president and a bank teller are each convicted of embezzlement and sentenced to two years in prison. Suppose further that, upon release, the bank president's income declines 90 percent—from $1 million a year to $100,000—and the teller's declines "only" 50 percent—from $20,000 a year to $10,000. According to Lott's extraordinarily curious notion of justice, the bank president should have been "compensated" for his or her greater loss of income by a shorter sentence.

Critics of Lott's "wealth maximization" approach contend that using money as the unit of measure "violates the principle of the equality of individuals before the law."[178] Furthermore, "wealth maximization arguments seem to assume that wealthy offenders suffer from 'collateral penalties'"—that is, society punishes white-collar criminals in ways that go far beyond the courtroom, such as a dramatic alteration of their standing in the community and their ability to earn a living. One of the flaws in such reasoning is that its underlying premise may be false, at least in many cases. After interviewing several dozen convicted white-collar criminals who had completed their sentences about their post-release lifestyles, *Forbes* magazine concluded that: "U.S. society is forgiving and often forgetting about white-collar convictions."[179] One of those interviewed was David Begelman, who was convicted of embezzlement in 1978 when he ran Columbia Pictures.[180] Within months of his conviction, he was back in the movie business, running MGM Studios and he later went on to become a successful independent film producer.[181]

Further evidence of the forgiving attitude of business toward professionals who cheat and defraud clients is found in an SEC study of "rogue brokers," persons who had been the subject of official investigations for violating securities laws. The SEC found that many of the brokers had little difficulty securing jobs after their brushes with the law; in fact, two-thirds were still employed in the securities industry.[182] Likewise, the Medicaid fraud study cited earlier reported that only 12 percent of the convicted doctors had their licenses to practice medicine revoked.[183]

Moreover, in some states the laws actually protect the wealth of convicted white-collar criminals. Just before Martin Siegel was indicted in New York for insider trading (Chapter 6), he moved his family to Florida, where he purchased a $3.25 million beachfront home. It might just be that Siegel preferred mild Florida winters to those in New York. But it seems more likely that he was trying to safeguard his assets from the onslaught of impending litigation by taking advantage of a Florida law that prohibits the seizure of a person's legal residence. This archaic statute, originally enacted as a populist measure to prevent banks from displacing homesteaders, has resulted in Florida becoming a haven for white-collar criminals seeking to shelter their loot from the government by "investing" in expensive mansions.[184]

EFFECTS OF WHITE-COLLAR CRIME

The opening chapter noted that people often fail to express the kind of outrage over corporate crime that they do over street crimes because it is usually more difficult to visualize the damage wrought by white-collar offenses. Television often ignores or downplays corporate crime as well because those crimes lack the dramatic elements that fit the needs of the electronic media: clearly defined victims and villains; illegal actions that are easily understood and can be described in quick sound bytes; motivations like jealousy and rage that can be vividly portrayed; and heroes in the form of police or prosecutors, who apprehend and then punish those responsible. In contrast, white-collar crimes are frequently confusing; the perpetrators, because of their social status, are not easy to cast as lawbreakers; the injury caused by these crimes (as in the case of toxic dumping, for example) may take years to develop; and the resolution of the cases often occurs outside of criminal courts and away from television cameras in private negotiations between offenders and anonymous government officials. For these reasons, television often shows little interest in cases of corporate criminality, while at the same time deluging us with sensational stories of murder, mayhem, and madness.

Nonetheless, as this book has stressed repeatedly, the effects of white-collar crimes are in many ways more serious than those of "common" crime. These harmful consequences fall into three categories: environmental and human costs; economic costs; and social costs. Let us consider each of these effects in more detail.

Environmental and Human Costs

Most Americans usually shrug off the kinds of dire prophecies of environmental destruction issued by ecologists as alarmist hyperbole—until disasters like the Exxon Valdez or Love Canal occur. Only then does the public recognize the terrible threat posed by industrial irresponsibility. Corporate apologists often depict these events as tragic but unpredictable "accidents" that no amount of legislation could prevent. After the Union Carbide catastrophe at Bhopal, India, in 1984 (Chapter 4), when a storage tank containing deadly gas burst and killed at least 2,500 people, some American magazines actually portrayed Union Carbide as the "victim"—expressing concern over the impact of the disaster on the company's reputation and future profitability. In contrast, Indian publications all focused on the true victims and consistently referred to the event as a "crime."[185] Indeed, on July 31, 2009, an Indian court issued an arrest warrant for the former CEO of Union Carbide (now owned by Dow Chemical) for his role in the Bhopal disaster 25 years earlier. At this writing, there is no indication that the U.S. will extradite the now-89-year-old man.[186]

The American media's unwillingness to see such disasters as manifestations of corporate crime was also evident in their response to the tragic 1991 fire at the Imperial chicken processing plant in North Carolina (Chapter 4) that killed 26 workers, who were trapped inside because management had chained the emergency exits shut to prevent employee pilferage. Despite the eventual manslaughter conviction of the plant's owner, the media tended not to focus on criminal culpability but on an alleged breakdown in government safety regulations, particularly the failure of OSHA to inspect the plant adequately.[187]

Economic Costs

One of the more immediate effects of corporate criminality is the drag it places on the economy. Chapter 1 pointed out that the annual costs to Americans from all white-collar crimes runs into hundreds of billions of dollars; the total from personal fraud alone is more than $40 billion. In certain industries, the costs are especially high. For instance, the General Accounting Office has estimated that at least $100 billion (10 percent of the nearly $1 trillion spent by Americans on health care every year) is lost to fraud and abuse.[188]

Who pays these costs? Are they equally shared by all members of society? Should some groups—particularly those who may have profited from the crimes—absorb a larger share of the cost? The evidence indicates that the burden is *not* shared equally across society but is shifted to the middle- and lower-income segments of the population. Because these costs are typically passed on to taxpayers, they represent a "regressive tax" imposed on those individuals least able to pay. At the same time, companies victimized by white-collar crime or slapped with punitive fines for their own offenses pass the costs on to consumers.

Chapter 8 noted that the multibillion cost of bailing out failed S&L was paid for mainly through the issuance of government bonds, which eventually must be redeemed by taxpayers. In theory, the progressive nature of the American tax structure means that wealthy citizens would pay a higher proportion of their incomes to cover the bill. In reality, however, the loopholes and tax shelters enjoyed by high-income individuals mean that the bulk of the burden will fall on the middle class. The S&L bailout also forced reductions of government spending in other areas, notably the social services frequently needed by low-income persons—none of whom had benefitted from the extraordinarily high interest rates that corrupt thrifts paid to depositors during the I-got-mine years of the "greed decade." In contrast, the government chose to cover all lost deposits of the bankrupt S&Ls (not just those under $100,000, as the law required). This meant, for example, that many wealthy depositors were able to reap the benefits of the high interest rates offered by the S&L—without assuming any of the risks when they failed.[189] The economic elite, who never miss an opportunity to rail contemptuously against welfare payments to the poor, thus became the shameless beneficiaries of the biggest "entitlement" program ever implemented by the American government.

An illustration of how the economic costs of white-collar crime can generate a "ripple effect" is provided by the bankruptcy of Orange County, California. Because of fraud and gross mismanagement in one self-indulgent venue, every city, town, and school district in the United States will have to pay more to borrow money from now on.[190]

CASE STUDY
The Orange County Bankruptcy

On December 6, 1994, officials of Orange County, California, one of the most affluent areas in the country, made an announcement that shocked the nation. The archconservative Board of Supervisors had declared the county bankrupt, with financial losses amounting to between $1.5 and $2 billion. It was the largest municipal failure in history. Known for its upscale lifestyle, mediterranean climate, and attractive beaches, Orange County also has a less savory reputation. On frequent occasions federal authorities have referred to it as the "fraud capital of the United States." As a hotbed of investor frauds (Chapter 2), S&L failures and mortgage fraud (Chapter 8), medical fraud (Chapter 11), and other assorted economic crimes, the bankruptcy merely underscored what many people already knew about Orange County. Simply put, white-collar crime is a way of life there.

The county's collapse, dramatic enough because of its sheer size, was that much more injurious because of the numerous municipalities, school districts, public agencies, and private citizens who had invested in the once fabled County Investment Pool. The pool had produced spectacular returns for years before taking a nosedive in value. Run by former county treasurer Robert Citron, the pool had outperformed all other government investments in the state and the nation by such a large margin that Citron became known as a "financial guru." Citron, a college dropout and the lone Democrat in a staunchly Republican administration, played the role of master money manager in a government simultaneously hungry for revenues yet fiercely anti-taxation. As former county supervisor Thomas Riley put it: "This is a person who has gotten us millions of dollars. I don't know how the hell he does it, but it makes us all look good."[191] Little did Riley know that these words, spoken only months before the county declared

bankruptcy, would soon ring hollow to investors in the failed fund.

Despite numerous warnings from public and private sources, Riley and his colleagues on the board of supervisors refused to acknowledge what should have been obvious to even those untrained in high finance: The way Citron performed his "magic" was by taking enormous risks with public funds. Instead, local politicians ignored recommendations for increased oversight of the treasurer's office. As long as Citron "did whatever he did," elected officials could rest comfortably knowing that they would not have to ask constituents to cough up additional taxes to pay for public services. In a place where tax hikes occur about as often as Viva Castro rallies, politicians had plenty of incentive to shut their eyes.

Admittedly, this head-in-the-sand strategy worked very well for a while. Citron's portfolio generated about $500 million above what would have been earned using the state's more conservative investment approach.[192]

Citron's purported financial acumen, however, was later exposed as an unquestioning dependence on the advice of investment brokers, most notably the giant firm of Merrill Lynch. In testimony before a state senate committee investigating the bankruptcy, Citron said he was there "simply to tell the truth."[193] He expressed apologies to the people of Orange County for following the wrong course and for his over-reliance on the advice of others. The "financial guru" now claimed that he was a vestal investor debauched by the wolves of Wall Street:

> I had never, nor have I ever, owned a share of stock. My primary training was on-the-job. Due to my inexperience, I placed a great deal of reliance on the advice of market professionals. This reliance increased as the

(*Continued*)

number and types of investments permitted by the Government Code were liberalized, and as financial instruments became more complex . . . [I]n retrospect, I wish I had more education and training in complex government securities.[194]

In a further twist that could only be considered weird, it was later learned that among those "others" consulted by Citron were a 900-number psychic and a mail-order astrologer, who gave him interest-rate predictions.[195]

Betting that interest rates would remain low, Citron invested heavily through the use of derivatives, which would pay high returns as long as interest rates remained depressed. Derivatives are complex financial instruments whose value is tied to something extrinsic, such as interest rates or stock indices. The chairman of the American stock exchange has called derivatives "the 11-letter four-letter word."[196] According to *Fortune* magazine: "[T]he nightmare of Orange County . . . brought to life the dread of many Wall Streeters, a major loss of public money linked to derivatives. Many of these derivatives bear the fingerprints of Merrill Lynch."[197]

Merrill Lynch officials, however, noted that they had warned Citron about his portfolio on numerous occasions and were not willing to shoulder the blame for the pool's collapse. Nevertheless, Merrill Lynch profited mightily by selling derivatives and other securities to the county and underwriting bond transactions. On two different occasions the investment house sold the county an additional $277 million[198] and $855 million[199] of the very derivatives that they later claimed they had warned him about.

Orange County acted like a compulsive gambler, while Merrill Lynch and other brokerage houses behaved like croupiers offering an acquisitive community new chances to spin the wheel.[200] Once the county was "hooked" on its source of revenue, brokers could divert blame from themselves by providing written documentation that they had warned of the risks involved and thus were in compliance with vague securities laws. When asked why they continued to sell these shaky investments to Citron after their own analysis showed potential danger, a Merrill Lynch spokesman would only say: "Well, that's a legitimate question."[201]

Unfortunately, the legitimate answer has yet to be ascertained. Huge lawsuits filed against the brokerage resulted in a settlement of $400 million with the county as the Wall Street giant continued to deny culpability. The company also settled its criminal case for an additional $30 million.[202] In what at the very least appears as an ironic twist, the Board of Supervisors, with the support of the new county treasurer who claimed that the county could save $800,000 a year, approved a new policy in August 2002 that would *again* allow Merrill Lynch to do business with Orange County.[203]

To compound the disaster, the county leveraged (i.e., "borrowed") $12 billion in public money in order to maximize the profits on its investments. After all, "the more you invest, the more you can earn."[204] . . . Or lose.

And what was the public purpose of those borrowings? It was to give county agencies, cities and school and water districts a little extra in their budgets. That way, government officials and county residents could get around the realities of life in a time of stern voter resistance to taxes and vocal protests about the size of government.[205]

By pleading guilty to six counts, including misappropriation of public funds and making false material statements in connection with the sale of securities, Robert Citron reluctantly accepted some responsibility for the debacle. He did not, however, cause the debacle by himself, nor was he the only person involved who broke the law. County supervisors were charged by the SEC with "official wrongdoing," the highest civil sanction short of criminal indictment. Assistant County Treasurer Matthew Raabe was convicted on charges related

(Continued)

to his crafting of a scheme to help conceal Citron's failed investments. He was sentenced to three years in prison.[206] The conviction was later overturned on appeal, with the appellate court agreeing that Raabe did not receive a fair trial based upon "overwhelming conflicts of interest" on the part of the county prosecutor's office, which had suffered financially as a result of the bankruptcy.[207]

After reprimanding him for "gambling with public money," and failing his office and obligations, Judge J. Stephen Czuleger sentenced Robert Citron to a year in jail and fined him $100,000. He first imposed, then suspended, a six-year prison term recommended by the prosecution, because of Citron's cooperation, contrition, and failing health. The disgraced treasurer ended up serving his time on work furlough.[208]

It is becoming clearer, however, that Citron was merely the hapless technician in a triangle of power that linked Wall Street with Orange County's visible and invisible governments.[209]

The incredible lack of oversight and the bungling greed that was exposed in the bankruptcy provide important lessons for municipal finance. Remarkably, many economists, just as in the case of the S&L scandal, prefer not to label such activities as "real" crimes. For example, in characterizing the bankruptcy, the dean of the business school at a local university described the county as "a living laboratory of financial mismanagement and gov-

ernment ineptitude—if not outright irresponsibility."[210] This is certainly not a flattering depiction, but mismanagement, ineptitude, and irresponsibility are not crimes. Fraud, however, is a crime; and fraud is what Robert Citron pleaded guilty to.

Similarly, as if to completely deny the role of white-collar crime in the worst government bankruptcy ever, the first academic book on the collapse, which focuses on Citron and his ill-fated derivatives, *does not even mention the terms "crime" or "fraud"* nor acknowledge their significance in the bankruptcy.[211] Such lenient analysis tends to characterize financial wrongdoings as a consequence of the "risky business" present in everyday financial transactions. Given the strong evidence to the contrary, that point of view is at best incomplete and potentially misleading; at worst it can form the basis of misguided and highly destructive public policy.

One does not need Citron's psychic reader to recognize that a criminogenic environment conducive to fraud existed in Orange County, which allowed for the ensuing financial disaster. To ignore the role of white-collar crime in the bankruptcy and instead assign the explanation to "risky business" is to disregard the existence of the *real* political, economic, and social contexts within which such events take place. Presciently capturing the "real" Orange County, a fitting epitaph was coined years ago by a wise comic-strip possum named Pogo: "We have met the enemy, and he is us."

Other municipalities, most of them far less prosperous and guilty of no wrongdoing, have to share the bill for the Orange County debacle because municipal investors must now consider bankruptcy and default a feasible alternative to debt. In other words, Orange County has raised the level of risk for lenders, who will accordingly demand higher interest from *all* municipal bond issuers. This may be an affront to distributive justice, but it is no surprise. The diffusion of accountability is a common by-product of fiscal recklessness. Consider, for example, all the commercial banks that failed in the 1980s due to fraud and abuse. Federal regulators were able to cover the costs of those failures, while avoiding a direct S&L-type bailout, by raising the premiums paid to federal deposit insurance funds by member institutions. Banks then passed on the increased expenditure to customers in the form of higher interest rates on credit card balances—without any corresponding increase in the interest paid to depositors on their savings accounts. In effect, this transfer of debt represented a silent bailout of the banking industry funded by consumers.[212]

The same sort of buck-passing is also seen in a wide variety of other businesses, where the costs of white-collar crime are absorbed by consumers in the form of higher prices for goods and services. While malfeasant corporations always try to portray themselves somehow as "victims"—of unfair regulations, political persecution, or whatever—it is ultimately ordinary citizens who pay the tab. In this way, white-collar crime contributes to the widening economic gap between the "haves" and the "have nots" of American society.

Social Costs

In addition to the environmental damage, the human destruction, and the economic losses, there are less tangible but other very serious social consequences of white-collar crime. The impact of upperworld criminality tends to radiate, influencing people's attitudes toward society and each other. Chapter 1 observed how persistent, unpunished corporate and governmental corruption can produce feelings of cynicism among the public, remove an essential element of trust from everyday social interaction, delegitimate political institutions, and weaken respect for the law. One could identify many specific effects—as previous chapters have done—but a negative consequence still remaining for consideration is the relationship between white-collar offenses and other forms of crime. There is a connection, both direct and indirect, between "crime in the suites" and "crime in the streets."

White-collar criminality surely encourages and facilitates other types of crime. Indirectly, the existence of elite lawbreaking promotes disrespect for the law among ordinary citizens and provides ready rationalizations for potential street criminals seeking to justify their misconduct. Underclass youths who see or hear about local politicians taking bribes, police officers stealing drugs, or merchants cheating customers are able to minimize the harms caused by their own crimes by arguing that "everybody's doing it," or "we're no worse than anybody else," or "that's the way the system works." For many poor, young urbanites, crime among the rich and powerful affirms the futility of legitimate work and demonstrates the monetary and status rewards that accompany illegal activities. A member of a Puerto Rican street gang in Chicago vividly articulated this cynical worldview:

> We grew up at a time when people were making money and making it quick. You know, we saw on television people getting rich overnight. Then we saw, you know, you had the white-collar criminals—you know the guys who are just like us but never get caught, except that everybody knows that they are crooks. You had all these guys becoming filthy rich. And what do you think that's going to tell us? Shit, it didn't tell me to go and get a job at McDonalds and save my nickels and dimes.[213]

For such young offenders from the underclass, it seems, a life of hustling on the streets represents a "rational" alternative to the limited opportunities offered to them by legitimate society—just as Merton had proposed seven decades ago.

White-collar criminality also promotes other forms of crime in more direct ways. One of the allegations from the Iran-Contra hearings (Chapter 9), for example, was that a number of small banks with ties to organized crime were used by American officials to channel funds illegally to the Nicaraguan Contras.[214]

Organized crime, in fact, has long depended on corruption for its existence. In 1895, the Lexow Commission, investigating the New York Police Department, reported that "money and promise of service to be rendered are paid to public officials by the keepers or proprietors of gaming houses, disorderly houses or liquor saloons . . . in exchange for promises of immunity from punishment or police interference."[215] Nearly 75 years later, the President's Commission on Law Enforcement and Administration of Justice reached the same conclusion: "All available data indicate that organized crime flourishes only where it has corrupted local officials."[216] From organized crime's point of view, this relationship is functional—bribery of cops and politicians enables it to conduct its illicit business free of official interference.[217] From the perspective of society and the victims of organized crime, however, this depraved symbiosis is wholly dysfunctional.

White-collar criminal activities support the illegal drug industry as well. Corrupt banks are central to the operations of the international cartels that import billions of dollars in cocaine and other drugs into the United States each year. Given the cash-heavy nature of drug sales, distributors and retailers are faced with the inevitable problem of converting huge amounts of cash into forms that can be more easily invested or transported overseas. Federal law requires that financial institutions must report all transactions of $10,000 or more. This creates a dilemma for drug dealers who may accumulate millions of dollars in cash. But for a price, unscrupulous bankers can "launder" that money, converting it into more legitimate forms without reporting it to the authorities. At a time when banks are coming under increased scrutiny, drug dealers are turning to other financial institutions, like insurance companies, to launder their cash.[218] Money laundering, of course, is not limited to drug dealers but can be found anywhere that a group has a need to disguise its sources of income—most notably with the operators of gambling casinos in the United States, who launder cash skimmed from profits in order to evade taxes.[219]

CONTROLLING WHITE-COLLAR CRIME

When the Republican majority won control of Congress in 1994, it quite naturally sought to impose its self-reliant philosophy—enunciated in its "Contract with America"—on the public. Many citizens, unhappy with the *status quo,* embraced this pact; but others managed to control their enthusiasm. Critics contend that beneath the Contract's seductive rhetoric, one finds the same vision espoused by Adam Smith and his disciples: a society dominated by the marketplace, a society in which the government has limited power to protect consumers, a society in which citizens have few legal recourses to challenge the ascendancy of corporations, and a society in which the people essentially must place their trust in the "good will" of bankers, manufacturers, brokers, and the other conductors of the free market.

The Contract was a blueprint for a *laissez-faire* economy. One of its clauses proposed a moratorium on new governmental regulations and would subject all existing regulations—including such areas as environmental pollution, employee safety, and consumer protection—to a cost-benefit analysis to determine if they impede commerce in any way. Those rules determined to be too "costly" would be eradicated.[220]

Securities regulation was a major target of the Contract. Legislation has already been proposed (unsuccessfully) to downgrade the SEC's original watchdog function. Such an action would effectively have enfeebled much of the investor protection law that has underpinned U.S. capital markets for decades.[221] Another clause, approved by Congress in 1995 under the guise of "tort reform," made the recovery of money lost to securities fraud extremely difficult in federal court. The bill included a much higher burden of proof of intent and penalties for persons who sue and do not win.[222]

The Contract also called for the capping of product liability awards by juries. Vocal critics of America's tort system, such as former vice president Dan Quayle, contend that the willingness of juries to make excessive multimillion-dollar awards to plaintiffs strangles the economy by discouraging companies from introducing new products. A common example used to support this argument is that of Monsanto, which has developed a patented phosphate fiber substitute for asbestos but has kept if off the market because it fears potential lawsuits. In fact, the Environmental Protection Agency (EPA) believes this asbestos substitute to be as carcinogenic as asbestos, so Monsanto's decision not to sell it may be based on sound corporate policy and not intimidation.[223] Nevertheless, Quayle and his cohorts seem intent on bestowing blanket immunity on manufacturers by exploiting the universal unpopularity of ambulance-chasing lawyers.

There was another notable aspect to the Contract with America. It called for the implementation of much harsher punishment for "street" criminals but said virtually nothing about the punishment of white-collar offenders.

Deregulation represents a movement in exactly the wrong direction in the fight against white-collar crime. When the corporate establishment—through its congressional surrogates—tells the American people, "We want to get government off *your* backs," they almost always mean, "We want to get government off *our* backs"—a very different proposition. It is impossible to imagine how the absence of an SEC could have prevented the insider trading epidemic, or how the elimination of banking restrictions would thwart another savings and loan crisis, or how doing away with the EPA would render future Love Canals less likely. Advocates of *laissez-faire* solutions do point out, with some justification, that government regulations have already failed to prevent the aforementioned calamities. Yet, calling for their abolishment because they have been less than entirely successful seems dangerous and absurd. If budget slashing forces regulatory agencies to cut back on enforcement, prosecutors "may well find that the cuffs are on them."[224]

But if deregulation moves us in the wrong direction, then what might the right direction be? A number of suggestions to curb white-collar criminality can be offered, requiring changes of three types: legal, institutional, and social.

Legal Changes

It has been proposed that new laws that impose tougher penalties on white-collar criminals might well deter some potential offenders. More punitive federal sentencing guidelines have resulted in more white-collar crime convictions.[225] Adhering to the new guidelines would also serve to redress the sentencing imbalance between white-collar and traditional "common" criminals.[226] A federal prosecutor has declared: "You deal with white-collar crime the same way as street crime. You try to raise the likelihood they will be caught and punished."[227]

But whether this new toughness serves as a general deterrent is not at all clear. Current laws likely fail to deter because white-collar offenders are aware of the frequent lack of vigorous enforcement and the relatively low probability that their crimes will be detected or punished severely.

For example, in 2008 movie star Wesley Snipes was convicted on three misdemeanor counts of failing to file tax returns.[228] He was probably the highest-profile tax evasion defendant since hotel empress Leona Helmsley, the so-called Queen of Mean, was convicted in 1989 of evading $1.2 million in federal income taxes.[229] Although Snipes did receive a three-year sentence, he had faced up to 16 years in prison but was acquitted on the more serious felony charges—despite never even filing a tax return between 1999 and 2004.[230] The government was clearly disappointed with the relative leniency shown to Snipes. The prosecuting attorney had told the court in a sentencing memorandum: "In the defendant Wesley Snipes, the court is presented with a wealthy, famous and inveterate tax scofflaw. If ever a tax offender was deserving of being held accountable to the maximum extent for his criminal wrongdoing—Snipes is that defendant."[231]

The system of regulatory codes and administrative agencies that monitor corporate conduct and respond to criminal violations is another important part of the legal apparatus. Some scholars believe that we do not need more regulation; rather, we need "smarter" regulation. Simply applying harsher laws to corporations and individuals, they argue, will only produce a subculture of resistance within the corporate community "wherein methods of legal resistance and counterattack are incorporated into industry socialization."[232] Regulation works best when it is a "benign big gun"—that is, when regulators can speak softly but carry big sticks in the form of substantial legal penalties.[233]

Joseph T. Wells, the founder and chairman of the Association of Certified Fraud Examiners, has offered a newer strategy: *executive transparency*. Wells argues for a law requiring corporate executives to open up their own personal bank accounts for scrutiny by auditors and regulators.[234] The rationale is that in many of the high-profile corporate fraud cases, the fraud is not discovered until after the money has been frittered away. Wells cites the huge "loans" Bernie Ebbers gave to himself so that he could buy hundreds of thousands of acres of timberland and the biggest cattle ranch in Canada; the profligate spending by the Rigas family, including the construction of their own private golf course; the millions of dollars embezzled by Mickey Monus to finance his personal basketball league; and the grotesque self-indulgence of Dennis Kozlowski. As Wells notes, major corporate fraud cases almost always begin at the top.[235]

> To head off the financial rape of public corporations, I would suggest a law that requires selected company insiders to furnish their individual financial statements and tax returns to independent auditors. They should also sign an agreement allowing access to their private banking information. The data should be available in cases where suspicions arise.[236]

Executives of public corporations have a fiduciary duty to act in the best interests of shareholders,[237] and Wells' call for "transparency" seems consistent with that duty.

A hierarchical structure of corporate sanctions also has been proposed, in which the first response to misconduct consists of advice, warnings, and persuasion; then escalates to harsher responses culminating in what is termed "corporate capital punishment" or the dissolution of the offending company.[238] The goal of this model is compliance: "Compliance is thus understood within a dynamic enforcement game where enforcers try to get commitment from corporations to comply with the law and can back up their negotiations with credible threats about the dangers faced by defendants if they choose to go down the path of non-compliance."[239] The strength of such a system is that it works at multiple levels and holds all the actors involved—"executive directors, accountants, brokers, legal advisers, and sloppy regulators"[240]—accountable for criminal misconduct.

Institutional Changes

Preceding chapters have highlighted numerous examples of "criminogenic industries"—industries whose structure and traditional practices seem to encourage, or even embrace, criminal behavior. Any successful preventive strategy must therefore seek to "deinstitutionalize" white-collar crime, that is, remove its institutional sources. This is by no means an easy task. About 20 percent of the 1,000 largest American corporations already have "ethics officers," who help formulate codes of proper conduct.[241] A *Wall Street Journal* reporter, however, has written that these codes "are little more than high-sounding words on paper."[242]

Sociologist Amitai Etzioni has suggested that a better way to encourage ethical business conduct is to "foster associations and enforce moral codes somewhat like those of lawyers and physicians" in the business community.[243] Such associations would lack legal authority, but they could discipline violators through public censure and other informal control mechanisms.

Another way to change the environment in which corporate organizations do business is to create internationally agreed upon standards of conduct. This would be particularly important in the case of American companies that operate in—and often export white-collar crimes to—foreign countries. The most significant step in this direction has been the United Nations' attempt to draw up a Code of Conduct for multinational corporations. That document sets standards of acceptable behavior for global firms. Among other things, the Code calls upon multinationals to abstain from corrupt practices, such as political bribery, and to carry out their operations in an environmentally sound manner.[244] With these same goals in mind, the Clinton administration proposed a code of ethics for American firms operating overseas. Known as the Model Business Principles, this code encourages companies to adopt more scrupulous behavior abroad by "providing a safe and healthy workplace . . . pursuing safe environmental practices . . . and complying with U.S. laws prohibiting bribery."[245]

Neither of these proposed codes establishes any authority to sanction violators; they are merely guidelines. Enforcement is left up to individual nations. This could be a significant weakness. Some Third World countries (as we have seen) have shown a willingness to tolerate egregious abuses by American corporations—either because of official corruption or out of desperation for economic growth. Nevertheless, these efforts represent a first step toward battling white-collar crime in a global economy.

SOCIAL CHANGES

Earlier in this chapter it was suggested that Americans tend to have very strong feelings about crime and criminals but are often ambivalent in their responses to those convicted of white-collar offenses. As noted, many corporate lawbreakers have received the support of their colleagues and other prominent members of their community. Even after their convictions, they were quickly accepted back into legitimate society, suffering few of the stigmas and resentments that other types of convicted felons routinely experience. Indeed, it almost seems that we extend a begrudging respect to those who are clever and bold enough to fleece us out of millions. But if we are ever to gain control over white-collar crime, these attitudes must change.

Criminologist John Braithwaite argues that the broader corporate milieu needs to be transformed. Braithwaite calls for the creation of a "communitarian corporate culture" in which organizations draw "everyone's attention to the failings of those who fall short of corporate social responsibility standards [shaming], while continuing to offer them advice and encouragement to improve [reintegration]."[246] A simple, yet very effective form of "shaming" that can be employed when corporations violate the law is adverse publicity—spreading information about misconduct to consumers, who could then express their disapproval by refusing to patronize the offending company.[247] Braithwaite's ideal corporation, "well integrated into the community and therefore amenable to the pressures of social control,"[248] stands in dramatic contrast to Friedman's model of an amoral corporation, divorced from obligations to the community and inevitably producing a criminogenic environment.

Occupy Wall Street: A Movement Toward Change?

The first glimmers of a changed attitude began to emerge on September 17, 2011, when a few dozen protestors unrolled their sleeping bags in Zuccotti Park in downtown Manhattan in what would eventually become the Occupy Wall Street (OWS) movement.[249] In the weeks and months that followed, the movement grew larger and more vocal, spreading to cities across the nation and around the world and garnering enormous media attention. The protestors were often criticized for not having clear-cut policy demands, but their intent was to focus on broader issues, including the growing inequality that was polarizing America, which they encapsulated with the rallying cry: "We are the 99 percent." By focusing on the 99 percent this clever slogan drew attention to the other 1 percent of the income distribution, those who owned and controlled much of the country's wealth and who, in the protestors' and in the eyes of many others, were responsible for many of the nation's social ills.

Much of the Occupy protestors' rage was trained specifically on the financiers, hedge fund managers, investment bankers, stock traders, equity fund executives and all the other cogs of the financial services machine, whom they lumped together under the category, Wall Street (or in London, The City). Protestors carried signs with messages like: "Banks got bailed out, we got sold out" and "I hate corporate greed" and "Wall St. = War St." A related theme equated the actions of these powerful financial players with criminal behavior. Messages like "Prosecute Corporate Criminals" and "Wall St. Where Crime Really Pay$" and "Jail the Banksters" began to appear on signs, tee shirts and bumper stickers distributed by members of the OWS movement. A YouTube video captured protestors at Zuccotti Park singing "All We Are Saying, Is End Corporate Crime," sung to the tune of John Lennon's "Give Peace a Chance."[250]

As the movement gained momentum, a number of mainstream organizations joined in their protests, notably labor unions and community organizations. One of the more improbable instances of collaboration occurred on September 27, 2011, when, not far from Zuccotti Park, 700 uniformed airline pilots marched on Wall St. demanding progress on their union's negotiations with the airlines industry.[251] While not all Americans agreed with the tactics of the OWS protestors, a significant number expressed sympathy with their broader concerns. A nationwide survey of adults conducted in October, 2011, found that 39 percent stated that they strongly or somewhat supported the OWS movement, as compared with 35 percent who said they strongly or somewhat opposed the movement.[252] Another poll conducted at about the same time found that 66 percent of respondents agreed with the statement that money and wealth "should be more evenly distributed" while only 26 percent believed that the "distribution is fair."[253] The Occupy Wall Street movement and the discussions it has spawned signal a growing intolerance of corporate misconduct, specifically, and white-collar crime in general. How long these changed attitudes stay in place, if they will have any effect in elections or on social policy, and whether or not Occupy Wall Street remains a viable social movement—both in the U.S. and globally—remain open questions.

Another way to change the culture of tolerance for white-collar crime is to alter the socialization of future captains of industry. One logical place to look is to the elite MBA programs where many American business leaders are trained. A few years ago, a class at the Columbia

Business School was divided into groups for a simulated negotiation game. Each team was given time to plan its bargaining strategy in private. One group actually planted a "bug" in the room where another group was holding its strategy meeting.[254] A survey of students at the University of Virginia's Darden Graduate School of Business Administration reported that "71 percent believed that being ethical can be personally damaging."[255]

A number of reformers have called for the integration of rigorous ethical analyses into the curricula of business schools.[256] The sad reality, however, is that by that point it may already be too late. Some MBA programs have begun to offer business ethics courses, either as electives or in some cases as requirements;[257] but whether such reform will have any measurable future impact on corporate morality seems a long shot at best. At one leading business school, an elective called Managing in the Socially Responsible Corporation is reportedly ridiculed by students as a useless "touchy-feely" course.[258] A former chairman of IBM has declared: "If an MBA candidate doesn't know the difference between honesty and crime, between lying and telling the truth, then business school, in all probability, will not produce a convert."[259]

Accordingly, pedagogic indoctrination needs to be expanded beyond MBA programs. Critical analyses of commercial and governmental practices should be incorporated into classrooms at all levels of the educational system.[260] As teachers, the attitude that the authors find most common among our students is one of apathy and cynicism—captured in statements like, "What's the difference? The system's rigged anyway." or "What can you do? All politicians are corrupt." This kind of resignation is self-fulfilling and ultimately self-defeating; it allows upperworld criminality to continue without resistance and with the tacit acceptance of its victims. Students and the public at large have to understand that, while business and political corruption are pervasive, they are not unstoppable. Ordinary citizens do possess the means to counter these practices, even if it is only through collective acts like voting against crooked politicians or shunning products from manufacturers that poison the environment.

Pension funds representing the interests of thousands of employees have begun to flex their muscles as large stockholders. When Salomon Brothers was uncovered rigging the treasury bond market in 1991 (Chapter 1), the California Public Employees Retirement System suspended its investment activities with that firm.[261] Similarly, the New York City Employees Retirement System used its influence as a major shareholder in the Reebok Corporation to force a reduction of the extravagant $33 million salary paid to the company's chairman.[262] Both these illustrations suggest the substantial power that citizens can wield over corporations when they pool their economic clout.

Like death, taxes, and *I Love Lucy*, white-collar crime may always be with us. Measures such as those just outlined will not entirely extirpate the problem, but they can help to make it less commonplace and to minimize its fallout. If nothing else, raising the public's consciousness of the depth, dynamics, and disaster of white-collar crime—as this book has tried to do—hopefully can reshape people's view of events like the insider trading scandal and S&L crisis, the recent corporate collapses, the tragedy of carcinogenic pollution, and other licensed assaults on the quality of life in the United States.

Larry the Liquidator, a fictional character in the movie, *Other People's Money*, when considering whether or not his actions are socially responsible, cynically replies, "Who cares?" Larry and the real-life villains he symbolizes deserve an answer. Every law-abiding citizen, every innocent victim, every one of us who has looked on while neo-Vandals in custom-tailored suits have sacked America need to join voices in multimillion-part harmony and assert that *we* care.

Notes

1. Shakespeare, William. *Romeo and Juliet*. New York: Bantam Books, 1980: 69.

2. Lombroso, Cesare. *Crime, Its Causes and Remedies*. Translation by Henry P. Horton. Boston, MA: Little, Brown, 1911.

3. Freud, Sigmund. *A General Introduction to Psycho-Analysis*. Translation by Joan Riviere. New York: Liveright, 1935.

4. Herrnstein, Richard and Murray, Charles. *The Bell Curve: Intelligence, and Class Structure in America*. New York: Free Press, 1994.

5. In sharp contrast to this contention, two well-known criminologists, Michael Gottfredson and Travis Hirschi, have argued provocatively, albeit unpersuasively, that white-collar crime is no different in its essential nature than street crime and that a distinct theory is therefore unnecessary. All crime, they maintain, is essentially the result of individual traits—most notably low self-control. (Gottfredson, Michael and Hirschi, Travis. *A General Theory of Crime*. Stanford, CA: Stanford University Press, 1990).

6. Merton, Robert K. "Social Structure and Anomie." In Robert Merton, *Social Theory and Social Structure*. Glencoe, IL: The Free Press, 1957; 131–160.

7. *Ibid*.

8. Coleman, James W. *The Criminal Elite* (Third Edition). New York: St. Martin's, 1994.

9. Smith, Adam. *The Wealth of Nations*, Vol. 1, New York: P.F. Collier, 1902: 56–57.

10. Barol, Bill. "The Eighties Are Over." *Newsweek* 110, January 4, 1988: 40–48.

11. Friedman, Milton. "The Social Responsibility of Business Is to Increase Its Profit." *New York Times Magazine*, September 13, 1990: 32.

12. Wood, John, Lonenecker, Joseph M., and Moore, Carlos. "Ethical Attitudes of Students and Business Professionals: A Study of Moral Reasoning." *Journal of Business Ethics* 7, 1988: 249–257. See also Walker, Janet. "'Greed Is Good' . . . or Is It? Economic Ideology and Moral Tension in a Graduate School of Business." *Journal of Business Ethics* 11, 1992: 273–283.

13. Mills, C. Wright. "Situated Actions and Vocabularies of Motive." *American Sociological Review* 33, 1968: 46–62.

14. Sykes, Gresham and Matza, David. "Techniques of Neutralization." *American Sociological Review* 22, 1957: 664–670. For empirical applications of this concept to white-collar crime, see Rothman, Mitchell and Gandossy, Robert. "Sad Tales: The Accounts of White-Collar Defendants and the Decision to Sanction." *Pacific Sociological Review* 25, 1982: 449–473; Benson, Michael. "Denying the Guilty Mind: Accounting for Involvement in White-Collar Crime." *Criminology* 27, 1989: 769–794.

15. Vitell, Scott J. and Grove, Stephen J. "Marketing Ethics and the Techniques of Neutralization." *Journal of Business Ethics* 6, 1987: 433–438.

16. From Sykes and Matza, *op. cit.*

17. Thurmon, Arnold. *The Folklore of Capitalism*. New Haven, CT: Yale University Press, 1937.

18. Bailey, Fenton. *The Junk Bond Revolution*. London: Fourth Estate, 1991.

19. Center for Investigative Reporting. *Global Dumping Ground*. Washington, D.C.: Seven Locks Press, 1990; 37.

20. Edney, Julian. "Greed." *g-r-e-e-d.com,* May 17, 2006.

21. Quoted in Johnson, Shane. "When Whitey Goes to Prison." *slweekly.com,* July 1, 2004.

22. *Ibid*.

23. Quoted in *ibid*.

24. Useem, Jerry. "Oink! CEO Pay Is Still Out of Control." *Fortune* 147, April 28, 2003: 56–64.

25. Reich, Robert B. "Secession of the Successful." *New York Times* Magazine, January 20, 1991: 16.

26. Durant, Will and Durant, Ariel. *The Lessons of History*. New York: MJF Books, 1968.

27. Congressional Budget Office. "Trends in the Distribution of Household Income Between 1979 and 2007 Summary." Washington, D.C.: U.S.G.P.O. 2011.

28. New York City Comptroller. "Income Inequality in New York City." New York. 2012.

29. Stiglitz, Joseph. "Of the 1 percent, by the 1 percent, and for the 1 percent." *vanityfair.com*. May, 2005.

30. Strauss, Gary. "How Did Business Get So Darn Dirty?" *usatoday.com*, June 12, 2002.

31. Alger, Selim. "'Bullet-Proof' CEO in $10M 'Scam' Trial." *nypost.com*. Jan. 27, 2010. Alger, Selim and Geller, Andy. "Daddy's 10M 'Bad' Mitzvah." *nypost.com*. October 27, 2007.

32. U.S. Attorney, Eastern District of New York (Press Release). "David H. Broo004ks, Founder and Former Chief Executive Officer of DHB Industries, Inc., and Sandra Hatfield, Former Chief Operating Officer, Indicted for Insider Trading, Fraud, Obstruction of Justice, and Tax Evasion." October 27, 2007.

33. *U.S. v. David Brooks and Sandra Hatfield*. "Indictment" Cr. No. 06-550 (E.D.N.Y.).

34. O'Brien, Timothy. "All's Not Quiet on the Western Front." *nytimes.com*. January 22, 2006.

35. Anderson, Sarah. "The Rise and Fall of a War Profiteer." *alternet.org*. July 13, 2006.

36. Rep. Louise Slaughter. "A Story Ignored: Body Armor Executive Indicted for Massive Fraud." *huffingtonpost.com*. November 7, 2007.

37. *http://davidhbrooks.net/5201.html*. Accessed: 7/24/2012.

38. Farrell, Greg. "Pension Funds Pin Target on CEO Pay." *USA Today,* December 15, 2005. Lerach, William S. "Why Are Bad CEOs Rewarded?" *Houston Chronicle,* November 18, 2007: E5. Swartz, Jon. "Stocks May Fall, But Pay Doesn't." *USA Today,* April 10, 2008: 1B, 2B.

39. Shenoy, Rupa. "Northern Trust Seeks to Repay Bailout Money." *huffingtonpost.com,* February 27, 2009.

40. Bernard, Stephen. "Northern Trust Bank Threw Lavish Parties, Sponsored Tournament After Getting Bailout Funds." *huffingtonpost.com,* February 24, 2009.

41. Sandel, Michael. *What Money Can't Buy*. New York: Farrar, Straus and Giroux, 2012, 6

42. *Ibid.*

43. *Ibid.*, p. 10.

44. *Ibid.*, p. 136.

45. *Ibid.*

46. Needleman, Martin and Needleman, Carolyn. "Organizational Crime: Two Models of Criminogenesis." *Sociological Quarterly* 20, 1979: 517.

47. Leonard, William and Weber, Marvin. "Automakers and Dealers: A Study of Criminogenic Market Forces." *Law and Society Review* 4, 1970: 407–424.

48. Farberman, Harvey. "A Criminogenic Market Structure: The Automobile Industry." *Sociological Quarterly* 16, 1975: 438–457.

49. *washoelegalservices.org*. "Consumer Law: Odometer Fraud," December 29, 2002.

50. *businessweek.com*. "TCC Tip: Odometer Fraud," December 30, 2005.

51. Scripture, James E. "Odometer Rollback Schemes." *totse.com,* January 12, 2009.

52. *businessweek.com, op. cit.*

53. *autopi.com*. "Odometer Fraud," December 29, 2008.

54. *businessweek.com, op. cit.*

55. *nj.com*. "Used Car Dealer Admits to Odometer Scam," August 30, 2008.

56. Redding, Robert L., Jr. "Congress Assesses Flood Vehicle Problem." *asashop.org,* February 29, 2006.

57. Benton, Joe. "Congress Treads Water on 'Flood Car' Bill." *consumeraffairs.com,* December 4, 2006.

58. *Ibid.*

59. *Ibid.*

60. Cizek, Gregory J. "Cheating the Test." *education_next.org*, October 10, 2001.

61. *Ibid.*

62. Magnuson, Peter. "High Stakes Cheating." *naesp.org*, February 2000.

63. Gorman, Linda. "Do Incentives Cause Teachers to Cheat?" *nber.org*, October 10, 2005.

64. Helton, Ajuah. "Allegations of Test Improprieties Cropping Up Across Country." *thenotebook.org*, Spring 2003.

65. *Ibid.*

66. Clowes, George A. "Teachers Cheat in Kentucky." *heartland.org*, November 1, 1997.

67. *nber.org, op. cit.*

68. Quoted in Axtman, Kris. "When Tests' Cheaters Are the Teachers." *Christian Science Monitor* (online), January 11, 2005.

69. *thenotebook.org, op. cit.*

70. Rodriguez, Nancy C. "Cheating Teacher Skews Schools' Test Scores." *Lawrence Eagle Tribune* (online), July 22, 1999.

71. Cizek, *op. cit.*

72. Helton, *op. cit.*

73. Cizek, *op. cit.*

74. *Ibid.*

75. Axtman, *op. cit.*

76. Cizek, *op. cit.*

77. Magnuson, *op. cit.*

78. *Ibid.*

79. Winerip, Michael. "In Bronx, a Possible Case of High School Cheating, but Not by Students." *nytimes.com,* February 8, 2006.

80. *businessweek.com*. "A Spate of Cheating by Teachers." July 5, 2004.

81. *Ibid.*

82. Million, *op. cit.*

83. *Ibid.*

84. Jacob, Brian A. and Levitt, Steven D. "To Catch a Cheat." *ecucationnext.org*, January 6, 2004.

85. Axtman, *op. cit.*

86. Jacob and Levitt, *op. cit.*

87. Million, June. "When a Principal Cheats." *naesp.org*, September 2000.

88. Helton, *op. cit.*

89. Cizek, *op. cit.*

90. Helton, *op. cit.*

91. Quoted in Helton, *op. cit.*

92. Gorman, *op. cit.*

93. Benton, Joshua A. "Tools May Stem Cheating on Tests." *Dallas Morning News* (online), November 19, 2004.

94. *Ibid.*

95. Benton, Joshua and Hacker, Holly K. "Poor Schools' TAKS Surges Raise Cheating Questions." *Dallas Morning News* (online), December 19, 2004.

96. Benton, *op. cit.*

97. Benton and Hacker, *op. cit.*

98. Spencer, Jason. "Trustees Split over Teacher Bonus Plan." *Houston Chronicle*, October 28, 2005: B1, B3.

99. Quoted in Gavel, Doug. "Teachers Caught Cheating on High-Stakes Exams." *ksg.harvard.edu*, November 17, 2003.

100. Fields' memorably ascerbic dictum is a line from his classic 1939 movie *You Can't Cheat an Honest Man.*

101. Foderaro, Lisa W. "Former Sheraton Food Buyer Is Sentenced for Kickbacks." *New York Times*, July 12, 1997: B25.

102. Clinard, Marshall and Quinney, Richard. *Criminal Behavior Systems* (Second Edition). Cincinnati, OH: Anderson, 1986: 189.

103. *bizjournals.com.* "Ex-VP of ACS Convicted of Fraud." January 20, 2004.

104. Johnston, Jeffrey L. "Following the Trail of Financial Statement Fraud." *Business Credit* 97, October 1995: 48.

105. Bakan, Joel. *The Corporation: The Pathological Pursuit of Profit and Power.* New York: Free Press, 2004.

106. Schrager, Laura and Short, James F., Jr. "Toward a Sociology of Organizational Crime." *Social Problems* 25, 1978: 411–412.

107. Ermann, David and Lundman, Richard. "Deviant Acts by Complex Organizations: Deviance and Social Control at the Organizational Level of Analysis." *Sociological Quarterly* 19, 1978: 55–67.

108. Simon, David and Eitzen, Stanley. *Elite Deviance.* Boston: Allyn and Bacon, 1982.

109. McCoy, Alfred. *The Politics of Heroin: CIA Complicity in the Global Drug Trade.* Brooklyn, NY: Lawrence Hill Books, 1991.

110. Collins, Glenn. "Ousted Phar-Mor President Found Guilty in $1 Billion Fraud." *New York Times,* May 26, 1995: D3.

111. Schroeder, Michael and Schiller, Zachary. "A Scandal Waiting to Happen." *Business Week* 3280, June 24, 1992: 32–36.

112. Monus was also one of the original owners of the Colorado Rockies Major League Baseball team. He was forced to sell his stake in the franchise when the Phar-Mor scandal erupted.

113. Brookman, Faye. "Deep Discounter Phar-Mor Declares Bankruptcy." *Drug Topics* 136, September 7, 1992: 84–85; Star, Marlene G. "Phar-More Ills Hurt Strategy." *Pension & Investments* 20, August 17, 1992: 3, 31.

114. Fallon, Geoffrey D. "Yes, Virginia, Some Companies Do Commit Fraud." *Across the Board* 32, 1994: 33; Vachon, Michael. "Phar-Mor Disaster Shakes Private Market Investors." *Investment Dealer's Digest* 58, August 10, 1992: 15–16; Freudenheim, Milt. "Phar-Mor Says Profit Was Faked." *New York Times,* August 5, 1992: D1.

115. Solomon, Jolie. "Mickey's Secret Life." *Newsweek* 120, August 31, 1992: 70–72.

116. *Wall Street Journal.* "Monus, Co-Founder of Phar-Mor, Gets a 20-Year Sentence." December 4, 1995: B5.

117. Quoted in *ibid.*, B5.

118. Vaughan, Dianne. *Controlling Unlawful Organizational Behavior.* Chicago, IL: University of Chicago Press, 1983.

119. Clinard, Marshall. *Corporate Ethics and Crime.* Beverly Hills, CA: Sage, 1983.

120. Pettigrew, Andrew. "On Studying Organizational Cultures." *Administrative Science Quarterly* 24, 1979: 572.

121. Vaughan, Diane. "Rational Choice, Situated Action, and the Social Control of Organizations." *Law & Society Review* 32, 1998: 36.

122. *Ibid.*, p. 36–39.

123. Ashforth, Blake and Anand, Vikas. "The Normalization of Corruption in Organizations." *Research in Organizational Behavior* 25, 2003: 1–52.

124. *Ibid.*, p. 3.

125. *Ibid.*

126. Gibney, Alex [Director]. *Smartest Guys in the Room.* [DVD] 2005. Magnolia.

127. *Ibid.*

128. *sec.gov.* "Olde Discount Settle Sales Practice Abuses Suit." September 10, 1998.

129. *Ibid.*

130. *Ibid.*

131. *Ibid.*

132. *Ibid.*

133. *Ibid.*

134. *Ibid.*

135. *Ibid.*

136. Quoted in *ibid.*

137. Wheeler, Stanton and Rothman, Mitchell. "The Organization as Weapon in White-Collar Crime." *Michigan Law Review* 80, 1982: 1405.

138. *Ibid.*, p. 1426.

139. Tillman, Robert and Pontell, Henry. "Organizations and Fraud in the Savings and Loan Industry." *Social Forces* 4, 1995: 1458.

140. Soled, Jay A. and Ventry, Dennis J. Jr. "A Little Shame Just Might Deter Tax Cheaters." *USA Today,* April 10, 2008: 11A.

141. Cauchon, Dennis. "Tax Delinquents: Who Owes—and How Much—May Be a Surprise." *USA Today,* April 14, 2008: 1A, 4A.

142. Reiman, Jeffrey. *The Rich Get Richer and the Poor Get Prison: Ideology, Crime and Criminal Justice* (Fourth Edition). Boston, MA: Allyn and Bacon, 1995.

143. Quoted in Ranalli, Ralph. "Execs Get 18 Months in Med-Testing Flap." *Boston Herald,* August 9, 1996: 20.

144. Quoted in *ibid.,* 20.

145. Robertson, Tatsha and Krasner, Jeffrey. "Seeking Not-So-Hard Time." *boston.com,* April 9, 2004.

146. Hightower, Susan. "S&L Swindlers Get Early Withdrawal from Prison." *San Diego Union-Tribune,* July 31, 1994: I1.

147. Pontell, Calavita, and Tillman, *op. cit.*

148. Tillman, Robert and Pontell, Henry. "Is Justice 'Collar-Blind'?: Punishing Medicaid Provider Fraud." *Criminology* 53, 1988: 294–302.

149. For example: Hagan, John and Nagel, Ilene. "White-Collar Crime, White-Collar Time." *American Criminal Law Review* 20, 1982: 259–289; Hagan, John, Nagel, Ilene, and Albonetti, Celesta. "Differential Sentencing of White-Collar Offenders." *American Sociological Review* 45, 1980: 802–820.

150. Benson, Michael and Walker, Esteban. "Sentencing the White-Collar Offender." *American Sociological Review* 53, 1988: 294–302.

151. For example: Wheeler, Stanton, Weisburd, David, and Bode, Nancy. "Sentencing the White-Collar Offender: Rhetoric and Reality." *American Sociological Review* 50, 1982: 641–659; Weisburd, David, Waring, Elin, and Wheeler, Stanton. "Class, Status, and the Punishment of White-Collar Criminals." *Law and Social Inquiry* 15, 1990: 222–243.

152. Using criminal defendants who are physicians as a model, Rosoff has argued that the customary "status shield" can be transformed into a target, under certain circumstances—particularly when the offense is a "common" crime rather than a white-collar crime.

153. Hays, Kristen. "Dynegy Executive Gets 24 Years in Prison for Accounting Fraud." *sfgate.com,* March 26, 2004.

154. *bizjournals.com.* "Olis Begins Prison Sentence." May 20, 2004.

155. Hull, C. Bryson. "Ex-Dynegy Exec Gets 24 Years for Fraud." *hostit1.connectria.com,* March 25, 2004.

156. *Ibid.*

157. Hays, *sfgate.com, op. cit.*

158. Hays, Kristen. "24-Year Sentence Looms for Former Dynegy Executive." *thebatt.com,* May 16, 2004.

159. Warren, Susan. "Corporate Crime Martyr Begins His Sentence." *Wall Street Journal* (online), June 14, 2004.

160. Quoted in *ibid.*

161. *Ibid.*

162. Quoted in *ibid.*

163. *Ibid.*

164. *Ibid.*

165. Quoted in Cook, Dave. "Former Dynegy Executive Gets 24 Years." *cfo.com,* March 26, 2004.

166. Quoted in Hays, *sfgate.com, op. cit.*

167. Blodget, Henry. "Zero to Life." *slate.msn.com,* May 6, 2004. Reprinted by permission.

168. *Ibid.*

169. Warren, *op. cit.*

170. Glassman, James K. "Jamie Olis's Tragedy, and Ours." *capmag.com,* April 12, 2004.

171. Blodget, *op. cit.*

172. *forbes.com.* "In Praise of Animal Spirits." February 8, 1999.

173. McDougall, Walter A. *Freedom Just Around the Corner: A New American History: 1585–1828.* New York: HarperCollins, 2004.

174. Gasparino, Charles. *Blood on the Street.* New York: Free Press, 2005.

175. Fowler, Tom. "Court Tosses Lengthy White-Collar Sentence." *Houston Chronicle,* November 2, 2005: A1, A8.

176. Lott, John. "Do We Punish High Income Criminals Too Heavily?" *Economic Inquiry* 30, 1992: 583–608. See also Baum, Sandy and Kamas, Linda. "Time, Money, and Optimal Criminal Penalties." *Contemporary Economic Policy* 13, October 1995: 72–79.

177. Lott, John. "Should the Wealthy Be Able to 'Buy Justice'?" *Journal of Political Economy* 95, 1987: 1307–1316.

178. Baum, Sandy and Kamas, Linda. "Time, Money, and Optimal Criminal Penalties." *Contemporary Economic Policy* 13, October 1995: 74.

179. Machan, Dyan and Button, Graham. "Beyond the Slammer." *Forbes,* November 26, 1990: 284–288.

180. McClintick, David. *Indecent Exposure: A True Story of Hollywood and Wall Street.* New York: Morrow, 1982.

181. *Ibid.*

182. U.S. Securities and Exchange Commission, Division of Market Regulation. "The Large Firm Project." 1995.

183. Tillman and Pontell, *op. cit.*

184. *New York Times.* "Rich Debtors Finding Shelter Under a Populist Florida Law." July 25, 1993: A1.

185. Lynch, Michael, Nalla, Makesh, and Miller, Keith. "Cross-Cultural Perceptions of Deviance: The Case of Bhopal." *Journal of Research in Crime and Delinquency* 26, 1989: 7–35.

186. Eltman, Frank. "Man Wanted in Deadly Gas Leak 'Haunted,' Wife Says." *Houston Chronicle*, August 2, 2009: A25.

187. Wright, John, Cullen, Francis, and Blankenship, Michael. "The Social Construction of Corporate Violence: Media Coverage of the Imperial Food Products Fire." *Crime & Delinquency* 41, 1995: 20–36.

188. Witkin, Gordon, Friedman, Doran, and Guttman, Monika. "Health Care Fraud." *U.S. News & World Report,* February 24, 1993: 34–43.

189. *New York Times.* "Who Should Pay for the S&L Bailout?" September 21, 1990: A31.

190. Petruno, Tom and Flanigan, James. "Orange County in Bankruptcy." *Los Angeles Times,* December 7, 1994: D1.

191. Jorion, Philippe. *Big Bets Gone Bad: Derivatives and Bankruptcy in Orange County.* San Diego, CA: Academic Press, 1995: 7.

192. Brazil, Jeff, Wilogren, Jodi, and Lait, Matt. "O.C. Bankruptcy: Study Casts Doubt on Citron's Financial Record," *Los Angeles Times,* January 8, 1995; A1.

193. Quoted in *Los Angeles Times.* "Orange County Bankruptcy: Key Excerpts from Testimony by Citron, Stamenson." January 16, 1995: A2.

194. *Ibid.,* 22.

195. Nyhan, David. "'95 Offers Many Lessons for What Not to Do in '96." *Boston Globe,* December 31, 1995: 82.

196. Quoted in Loomis, Carol J. "Untangling the Derivatives Mess." *Fortune* 131, May 20, 1995: 50. Another example of the peril of derivatives occurred in 1994–1995, when the financial press began excoriating Bankers Trust New York for allegedly deceiving corporate derivatives clients about the extent of their losses. Three companies, Procter & Gamble, Gibson Greetings, and Mead, Corp., reportedly suffered combined losses of $172 million (*Institutional Investor.* "The Tangled Tale of the Tape." Vol. 29, April 1995: 42–43; Baldo, Anthony. "Sweeping the Street." *Financial World* (Special Issue), August 16, 1994: 61–63.

197. *Ibid.,* 51.

198. Brazil, Jeff. "Merrill's Responsibilities Key to Orange County Suit; Crisis." *Los Angeles Times,* January 15, 1995: A1.

199. Henderson, Nell and Fromson, Brett D. "Merrill Lynch: The Broker Behind Orange County." *Washington Post,* December 10, 1994: F1.

200. In an unrelated 1996 case, investment banker Mark Ferber was convicted of 58 charges relating to illegal kickbacks he had received from Merrill Lynch. A federal jury in Boston ruled that Ferber, who had made millions advising public agencies on municipal finance, had misrepresented himself to clients as unbiased at the same time he was selling his influence to Merrill Lynch for hundreds of thousands of dollars (Nealon, Patricia. "Ferber Is Guilty of Selling Influence." *Boston Globe,* August 10, 1996: A1, A6).

201. Brazil, *op. cit.*

202. Reckard, Scott and Wagner, Michael G. "Merrill Lynch to Pay $400 Million to Orange County." *Los Angeles Times,* June 3, 1998: A1.

203. Reyes, David. "Orange County Renews Its Ties to Merrill Lynch." *Los Angeles Times,* August 14, 2001: B1.

204. Petruno and Flanigan, *op. cit.,* D1.

205. *Ibid.,* D1.

206. Maharaj, Davan *et al.* "Ex-Aide to O.C. Treasurer Gets 3 Years in Prison." *Los Angeles Times,* October 4, 1997: B1.

207. Marosi, Richard and Pasco, Jean O. "O.C. Bankruptcy Conviction Voided." *Los Angeles Times,* November 2, 2000: B1.

208. Wagner, Michael G. *et al.* "Citron Sentenced to a Year in Jail for Role in County Bankruptcy." *Los Angeles Times,* November 20, 1966: A1.

209. Davis, Mike. "Bankruptcy on the Backs of the Poor: Rotten Orange County," *Nation* 260 (4), January 30, 1995: 121.

210. Aigner, Dennis. *UCI Journal* 4, 1995: 2.

211. Jorion, *op. cit.*

212. U.S. Congress, House Committee on Banking, Finance, and Urban Affairs, Subcommittee on Consumer Affairs and Coinage. "H.R. 2440, Credit and Charge Card Disclosure Amendments of 1991." 102nd Congress, Second Session, October 9, 1991.

213. Quoted in Padilla, Felix. *The Gang as an American Enterprise.* New Brunswick, NJ: Rutgers University Press, 1992: 103.

214. Brewton, Pete. *The Mafia, CIA & George Bush.* New York: Time Books, 1994.

215. New York Senate. *Report and Proceedings of the Senate Committee Appointed to Investigate the Police Department of the City of New York.* Albany, NY: 1895: 6.

216. U.S. President's Commission on Law Enforcement and Administration of Justice. Task Force Report: Organized Crime. Washington, D.C.: U.S. Government Printing Office, 1967; 6.

217. Merton, Robert K. *Social Theory and Social Structure.* Glencoe, IL: The Free Press, 1957.

218. U.S. Congress, House Committee on Banking, Finance, and Urban Affairs. "Federal Government's Response to Money Laundering." May 25, 1993.

219. Block, Alan and Scarpitti, Frank. "Casinos and Banking: Organized Crime in the Bahamas." *Deviant Behavior* 7, 1986: 301–312.

220. Gillespie, Ed and Schellhas, Bob (Eds.). *Contract With America.* New York: Time Books, 1994.

221. Cooke, Stephanie. "SEC Under Attack." *Euromoney* 317, September 1995: 84–88.

222. Stein, Ben. "Insecurities Trading." *Los Angeles* Magazine 41, January 1996: 31–33.

223. *Economist.* "Business: Not Guilty." Vol. 326. February 13, 1996: 63–64.

224. Lee, Charles S. "Bit Crime, Big Time." *Newsweek* 126, December 11, 1995: 59.

225. *Ibid.*

226. U.S. Code Congressional and Administrative News. 98th Congress, Second Session, 1984, Vol. 4. St. Paul, MN: West.

227. Quoted in Langberg, Mike. "White Collar Crime Erodes Faith in Business." *San Jose Mercury News,* February 12, 1989: 1E.

228. nytimes.com. "Wesley Snipes Gets 3 Years for Not Filing Tax Returns," April 25, 2008.

229. Fried, Joseph. "U.S. Jury Finds Helmsley Guilty of Tax Evasion but Not Extortion." *nytimes.com,* August 31, 1989.

230. *msnbc.com.* "Wesley Snipes Acquitted of Federal Tax Fraud," February 1, 2008.

231. Quoted in Goddard, Jacqui. "Wesley Snipes Given Three Years for Tax Evasion." *timesonline.co.uk,* April 25, 2008.

232. Ayres, Ian and Braithwaite, John. *Responsive Regulation.* Oxford: Oxford University Press, 1992; 20.

233. *Ibid.*

234. Wells, Joseph T. "Never a Better Time for 'Executive Transparency'." *USA Today,* August 1, 2005: 11A.

235. *Ibid.*

236. *Ibid.*

237. *Ibid.*

238. Fisse, Brent and Braithwaite, John. *Corporations, Crime and Accountability.* Cambridge: Cambridge University Press, 1993.

239. *Ibid.*, 143.

240. *Ibid.*, 230.

241. Yenkin, Jonathan. "Ethics Officers Manage Companies' Morals." *Orange County Register,* August 29, 1993: Business Section, 1.

242. Rakstis, Ted J. "The Business Challenge: Confronting the Ethics Issue." *Kiwanis Magazine,* September 1990: 30.

243. Etzioni, Amitai. *Public Policy in a New Key.* New Brunswick, NJ: Transaction, 1993; 103.

244. U.S. Congress, Senate Committee on Foreign Relations, Subcommittee on International Economic Policy, Trade, Oceans and Environment. "U.N. Code of Conduct on Transnational Corporations." 101st Congress, Second Session, October 11, 1990.

245. *Los Angeles Times.* "White House Unveils Its Overseas Code of Corporate Conduct." March 28, 1995: D1.

246. Braithwaite, John. *Crime, Shame and Reintegration.* New York: Cambridge University Press, 1989.

247. Coffee, John. "No Sound to Damn, No Body to Kick: An Unscandalized Inquiry into the Problem of Corporate Punishment." *Michigan Law Review 79,* 1981: 424–429.

248. Braithwaite, 1989, *op. cit.*, 144.

249. Gitlin, Todd. *Occupy Nation: The Roots, The Spirit and The Promise of Occupy.* New York: HarperCollins, 2012.

250. YouTube. "All We Are Saying Is End Corporate Crime," http://www.youtube.com/watch?v=PBcRxhci39M.

251. Kain, Erik. "Union Airline Pilots Occupy Wall Street." *forbes.com.* September 29, 2011.

252. Pew Research Center/Washington Post. Oct. 20-23, 2011. Survey of 1,009 adults nationwide. *PollingReport.com/politics.htm.*

253. CBS News/*New York Times* Poll. Oct. 19-24, 2011. N= 1,650 adults nationwide. *PollingReport.com/politics.htm.*

254. Marks, Peter. "Ethics and the Bottom Line." *Chicago Tribune Magazine,* May 6, 1990: 26.

255. Rakstis, *op. cit.*, 30.

256. See, for example: Etzioni, *op. cit.*

257. Fraedrich, John P. "Do the Right Thing: Ethics and Marketing in a World Gone Wrong." *Journal of Marketing* 60, January 1996: 122–123.

258. Marks, *op. cit.*

259. Quoted in Mulligan, Hugh A. "Ethics in America." *Richmond Times-Dispatch,* April 6, 1989: F1.

260. For example: Denise A. Monroe has designed a creative social science lesson for elementary school teachers, from which young students can learn about defective consumer products and false advertising (Monroe, Denise A. "Let the Manufacturer Beware." *Journal of School Health* 64, February 1994: 83–84).

261. *Wall Street Journal.* "California Resumes Business Activities with Salomon Unit." November 11, 1992: B5.

262. *New York Times.* "Reebok Vote on Pay Issue." May 6, 1992: 2.

INDEX

A

A. H. Robins Company, 111–112
Abacus 2007-AC1, 260–262
Abbott Laboratories, 488
ABC Home Health Services, 490
ABC News, 77–78, 406
Abdul Enterprises, 443
Aboodi, Oded, 245
Abramoff, Jack, 447–449
Abu Ghraib, 407–410, 411
abuse of power, 388–404
    by Central Intelligence Agency (CIA), 403–404
    by Defense Department, 400
    by Federal Bureau Investigation (FBI), 395–399
    by Internal Revenue Service (IRS), 399–400
    by National Security Agency (NSA), 400–403
    Watergate, 388–395
ACA Management LLC, 261
ACTION, 397
Action for Children's Television (ACT), 56
Actiq, 505
Addeo, Dorothy, 33
Addiction Breaking System, 54
Adelphia Communications, 304–306, 588, 602
adulterated food, 102–104
Advanced Medical Claims, 538
Advanced Micro Devices, 256
adverse decisions, 19
advertisement
    deceptive, 52
    false, 52–57
    informative, 52
    puffing, 52
Advertising Age, 56
Affiliated Computer Services, 594
affinity scams, 212–215
affordable mortgages, 356
Afghanistan, CIA detention center in, 406
Agape, Inc., 6
Age of Excess, 588
Age of Psychopathic Wealth, 590
Agius, Marcus, 362
Agnew, Spiro T., 9, 389, 430, 453
Agriculture, U.S. Department of (USDA), in political corruption, 431
Aguiar-Faria & Sons dairy, 174

airline industry, antitrust legislation against, 73
air pollution, 138–140
Alamo, Tony, 216
Alarid, Luis, 434
Albriond Capital Management, 347
Alexander, Keith, 566
Alien Registration Act of 1940, 396
Allen, A. A., 204–205
Allen, Gracie, 120
Allen, Paul, 60
Allende, Salvador, 382
Allen-MacGregor, Jacquelyn, 218
Allen, Woody, 40
Allied Applicators, 151
Allied Chemical Corporation, 152, 153, 229, 230
Allied Crude Vegetable Oil Refining Corporation, 8–9
Allis-Chalmers, 75
Alsop, Stewart, 392
Alvarez, Juan Alfredo, 433
Alvarez, Mario, 434
Amadi, Mike, 563
Amatex, 170
American Airlines, 73, 388, 589
American Association for Homecare, 489
American Association of Retired Persons (AARP), 41, 46, 78
American Civil Liberties Union (ACLU), 379, 396, 403, 415
American Continental Corporation, 343, 345, 346
American Cyanamid, 246
American Electronics Association, 14
American Family Publishers, 35, 36
American Federation of Teachers, 399
American Home Health Care Products, 491
American Home Products, 105, 246
American International Group (AIG), 58, 76, 317–318, 590
American Lung Association, 138
American Medical Association (AMA), 94, 406, 497
American Motors, 388–389
American Natural Resources (ANR), 231
American Nazi Party, 397
American Produce, 314
American Psychiatric Association, 586
American Psychological Association (APA), 406–407

Americans for Democratic Action, 400
American Sociological Society, 3
American Stores, 231
American Tobacco, 57
American Veterans' Council, 218
America Online, 534
America Online (AOL), 58, 61, 63, 247
America's Watchdog, 498, 499
Amerindo Investment Advisors, 17
Ameritech, 58
Amnesty International, 399, 401, 404, 414
Amoco, Corp., 162
Ancheta, Jeanson, 557–558
Anderson, Annie, 135–136
Anderson v. Pacific Gas and Electric, 136
Andreesen, Marc, 62
Angel at the Fence (Rosenblat), 199
Angelo, Louis, 332
Anheuser-Busch, 229
Anna Kournikova virus, 549
anomie, 394
Anonymous, 548–549
Anschutz, Philip, 303
antiaging drugs, 118
Anti-Defamation League of B'nai Brith, 202
anti-fraud systems, 568
Anti-Phishing Act of 2005, 559
Anti-Torture Act, 416
antitrust laws, 57, 58
Apocalypse Crew, 529
appeal to higher loyalties, 586
Apple Computer, 53, 61, 62, 63
Aquinas, Thomas, 39
Aramony, William, 217–219
Arango, Fernando, 433
arbitrage, 5
arbitragers, defined, 233
Archer Daniels Midland (ADM), 59, 431
Archives of General Psychiatry, 378
ARCO, 73, 149
AremisSoft, 313
Arendt, Hannah, 404
Arlington Developmental Center (ADC), 496
Arnstein, Nicky, 5
arsenic air pollution, 138
Arshadi, Nasser, 250
Arthur Andersen and Company, 283, 284, 296, 297–299, 300, 302, 312, 319
Asarco lead smelting plant, 138